OPERATIONS MANAGEMENT

Goods, Services and Value Chains

OPERATIONS MANAGEMENT

Goods, Services and Value Chains

Second Edition

David A. Collier
The Ohio State University

James R. Evans
University of Cincinnati

THOMSON

SOUTH-WESTERN

Australia · Brazil · Canada · Mexico · Singapore · Spain · United Kingdom · United States

THOMSON
™
SOUTH-WESTERN

Operations Management: Goods, Services and Value Chains, Second Edition
David A Collier and James R. Evans

VP/Editorial Director:
Jack W. Calhoun

Editor-in-Chief:
Alex von Rosenberg

Sr. Acquisitions Editor:
Charles McCormick

Sr. Developmental Editor:
Alice Denny

Sr. Marketing Manager:
Larry Qualls

Content Project Manager:
Brian Courter

Manager of Technology, Editorial:
Vicky True

Technology Project Manager:
Kelly Reid

Sr. Manufacturing Coordinator:
Diane Lohman

Production House:
GGS Book Services

Printer:
Quebecor World Dubuque
Dubuque, Iowa

Art Director:
Stacy Shirley

Internal Designer:
Craig LaGesse Ramsdell

Cover Designer:
Craig LaGesse Ramsdell

Cover Images:
© Getty Imagesme

Photography Manager:
John Hill

Photo Researcher:
Darren Wright

Library of Congress Control Number:
2006903205

For more information about our
products, contact us at:

Thomson Learning Academic
Resource Center

1-800-423-0563

Thomson Higher Education
5191 Natorp Boulevard
Mason, OH 45040
USA

BRIEF CONTENTS

**Supplementary Chapters
(available on the Student CD)**
A. Work Measurement, Learning Curves, and Standards
B. Queuing Analysis
C. Modeling Using Linear Programming
D. Simulation
E. Decision Analysis

CONTENTS

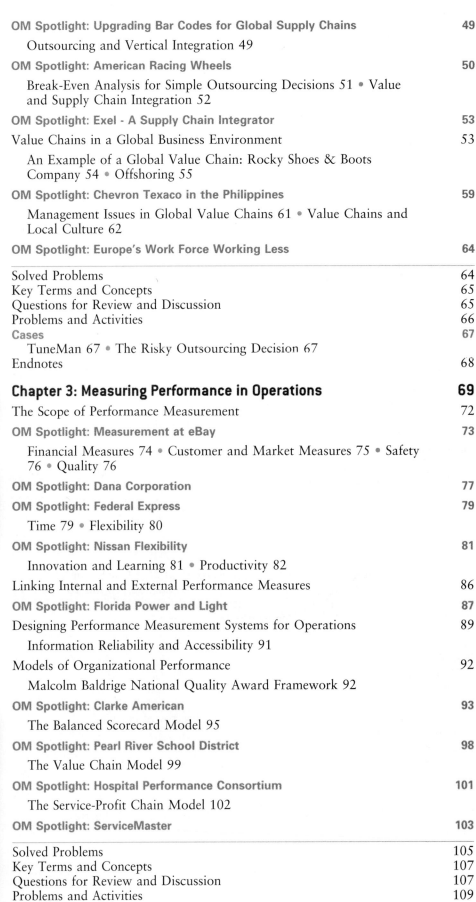

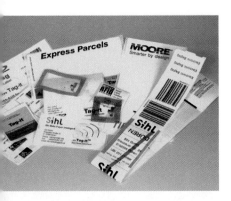

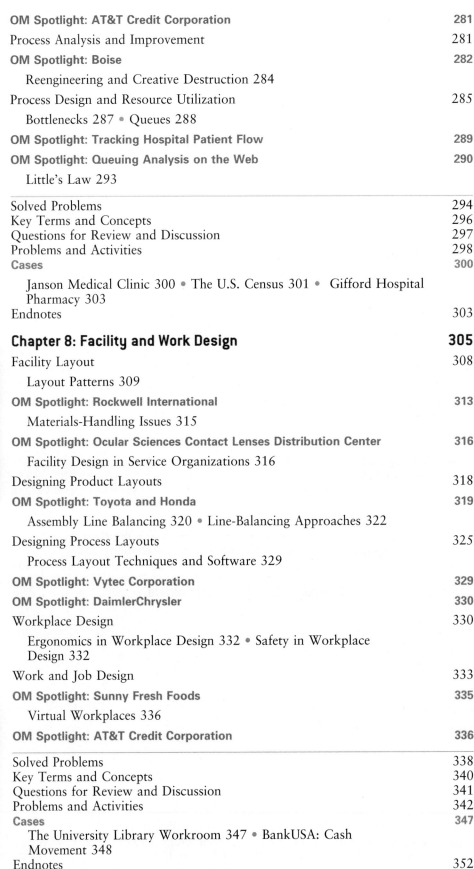

Chapter 11: Forecasting and Demand Planning   **437**

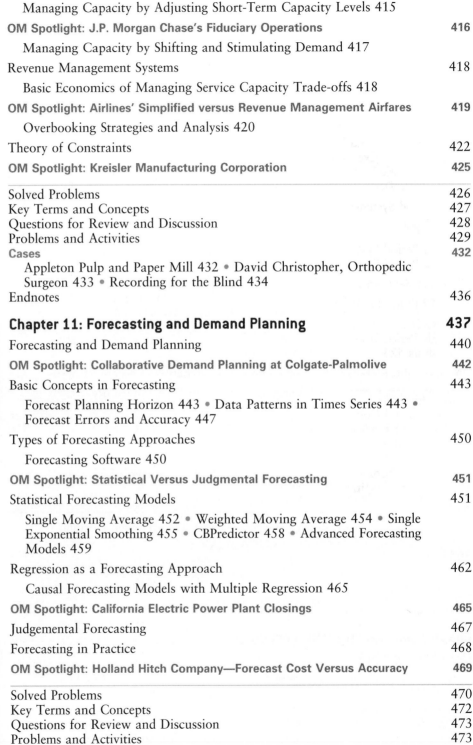

Chapter 17: Lean Operating Systems — 729

Supplementary Chapters
(available on the Student CD)

PREFACE

Operations management (OM) has evolved into one of the most important business disciplines over the last several decades. The roots of OM stem from industrial engineering, strategic management, quality control, and management science. Although OM began with a strong focus in production and manufacturing, one cannot deny the fact that about 80 percent of U.S. jobs are now in the service sector. Goods-producing industries (manufacturing, construction, fishing, forestry, mining, and agriculture) account for the remaining 20 percent but half of those jobs involve service processes. Therefore, 90 percent of the jobs in the U.S. economy involve designing and managing service-, information-, or entertainment-intensive processes. Consequently, most business graduates will work in the service sector, or in service-related aspects of manufacturing firms. The efficiency and effectiveness of goods and service creating processes are vital to our welfare as individuals and the global economy. In today's highly competitive business environment, the need for continual improvement of operations has never been greater.

Several textbooks have been written specifically for service operations management and every introductory OM text has a service component. However, none have truly integrated goods and services from the perspective of the value chain that cuts across the broad scope of business. This book is intended to accomplish this goal. The purpose of *Operations Management: Goods, Services, and Value Chains* is to provide students of business a sound understanding of the concepts, techniques, and applications of contemporary OM, with a strong emphasis on services. The book combines important managerial issues of OM with technical tools and quantitative applications, emphasizing the relevance to students' work and personal lives, and exposing them to state-of-the-art practices in business.

ORGANIZATION OF TOPICS

The book is divided into three major parts. *Part I, Understanding Operations*, focuses on the fundamentals of OM and its role in the business environment.

- Chapter 1 introduces the nature of OM; the differences between goods and services; the concept of a customer benefit package, process, and value chain; the role of quantitative methods in OM; and the history of OM and its current and future challenges.
- Chapter 2 provides an in-depth discussion of value chains and the way in which they support operations from a strategic perspective. This chapter also focuses on value chains in the global business environment and the challenges that organizations face in today's global society.
- Chapter 3 focuses on the importance of good performance measurement as a basis for good decisions, both at the strategic and operational levels of an organization. The principal measures used in operations and the design of

measurement systems are introduced, along with broad models of organizational performance—specifically, the Malcolm Baldrige framework, balanced scorecard, value chain model, and service-profit chain.

- Chapter 4 describes the role of operations strategy in supporting the overall business strategy of an organization. The notions of a customer-driven organization, segmenting markets, and competitive priorities are introduced, and approaches for strategic planning and operations strategy design are described. Special emphasis is given to operations design choice and making key infrastructure decisions to support chosen strategies.

Part II, Designing Operating Systems, addresses the design of operations.

- Chapter 5 builds students' understanding of technology in manufacturing and service operations and in value chains, and introduces several types of important integrated operating systems that students will undoubtedly encounter in the future careers.
- Chapter 6 focuses on the design of goods and services, their role in support the strategic mission of an organization, and specific practices generic to manufacturing product and process design and service delivery system and service encounter design. An integrative case study of Lenscrafters provides a broad view of how these ideas are implemented in practice.
- Chapter 7 focuses on process choice and selection. Both the classic product-process matrix and service positioning matrix are introduced; and tools and approaches used for process design, analysis, and improvement, including the analysis of bottlenecks and queues, and value stream mapping are also described.
- Chapter 8 deals with facility layout and work design issues. This chapter includes discussions of broad facility design issues, assembly line balancing, and human issues associated with workplace and job design.
- Chapter 9 focuses on key issues of supply chain design, including performance measurement, strategic choice, location decisions, and operational management issues. Several quantitative models are introduced for assisting in supply chain design.

Part III, Managing Operations, addresses topics that anyone involved in operations faces on a daily basis.

- Chapter 10 focuses on understanding, measuring, and making both long- and short-term capacity decisions. We also include introductions to revenue management systems and the theory of constraints.
- Chapter 11 describes the important role that forecasting plays in managing capacity and demand, and introduces the common types of quantitative and qualitative forecasting approaches used in practice.
- Chapter 12 addresses inventory management systems and common tools used to manage inventories. The principal emphasis is on fixed quantity and fixed period systems for both deterministic and stochastic demand scenarios. Other special models used in inventory analysis are also introduced.
- Chapter 13 addresses resource management from an overall planning framework, focusing on aggregate planning decisions and strategies, and disaggregation of aggregate plans in both manufacturing and service systems.
- Chapter 14 provides an introductory treatment of operations scheduling and sequencing, with a variety of applications in both manufacturing and services, and discussions of practical tools and approaches for making good scheduling and sequencing decisions.
- Material in Chapters 15 and 16 deal with issues of quality. In Chapter 15, the basic concepts of quality management are introduced along with the philosophies of Deming, Juran, and Crosby, ISO 9000, and Six Sigma. The principal

tools used in quality management are also illustrated. Chapter 16 deals with technical issues in quality control systems, primarily statistical process control.

- Chapter 17 introduces the concept of lean operating systems in goods-producing and service-providing organizations. The philosophy of lean thinking is described and numerous tools and approaches for incorporating lean thinking into an organization are discussed. The chapter includes lean "tours" of manufacturing and service organizations and an overview of Just-In-Time.
- Chapter 18 addresses project management from both an organizational and technical viewpoint. Tools and techniques for planning, scheduling, and controlling projects are illustrated.

The CD-ROM accompanying this book contains supplementary chapters for quantitative methods: work measurement, queuing, linear optimization, simulation, and decision analysis. These topics are referred to in various chapters, and the supplements provide introductions to these techniques. In addition, Microsoft Excel spreadsheets used for examples in this book are included for student use.

PEDAGOGICAL FEATURES

This book is written with the student in mind. Each chapter begins with a summary of key learning objectives and opens with three real or fictitious *customer episodes* that are intended to illustrate practical issues associated with the chapter that students can easily understand and appreciate. Several discussion questions are posed to help students think about the key issues and relate them to their own experiences. *OM Spotlights* describe real organizations using the concepts and methods of the respective chapter to manage the company and peak student interest. Each chapter also has a summary of key terms and concepts, and a set of Review and Discussion Questions intended to provide a study guide for checking comprehension of the material or helping students stretch their thinking about important issues. Excel spreadsheets are used to illustrate quantitative applications throughout the book. Solved Problems are also included to provide additional practice and insight to help students tackle problems in each chapter. Finally, each chapter contains several original cases designed to provide opportunities for applying the principles learned through in-depth case discussions and analyses.

INNOVATIVE TOPICAL COVERAGE

Significant coverage of important contemporary issues in operations management will make the material interesting and accessible. Unique coverage includes:

- Defining value chains in terms of the traditional OM input-process-output model and a pre- and post-service production model.
- In-depth discussions of customer value creation through bundles of goods and services—called customer benefit packages—that require effective OM processes.
- Early focus on OM decisions and issues surrounding global value and supply chains.
- Early emphasis on performance measurement metrics, examples, frameworks, and issues.
- The importance of tying customer wants and needs to operations strategy and building the right infrastructure to gain and maintain competitive advantage.

- Overviews of integrated operating systems (IOS) such as supply chain management (SCM), customer relationship management (CRM), enterprise resource planning (ERP), and revenue management systems (RMS).
- An integrated framework for goods and service design focused on manufacturing and service encounter design.
- Process design and analysis emphasizing value stream mapping, Little's Law, and bottlenecks in goods-producing and service-providing processes.
- The role of the servicescape in service process design.
- Understanding and computing the cash-to-cash conversion cycle for supply chains.
- The GAP model of service quality with its application in an automobile service case study.
- Principles of lean operating systems applied to "lean services."
- Practical case studies focused on services such as assembly line balancing in banking, value chains in the music industry, service guarantees, quality management in a hospital's dietary food service, job workload analysis for an orthopedic surgeon, customer demand forecasting for a bank's help desk GAP analysis in automobile service, and hospital inventory management.

ANCILLARIES FOR STUDENTS

- A student CD is packaged free with each new text. It contains the five supplementary chapters shown in the Table of Contents. The CD also provides Microsoft® Excel data files and templates for use with the end-of-chapter problems. A time-limited version of the Crystal Ball® Professional Edition and Premium Solver for Education Excel add-ins are also included.
- Thomson™NOW! If your instructor has chosen to use ThomsonNOW, a ThomsonNOW slimpack will be bundled with your textbook. You may also purchase access online at www.thomsonedu.com. ThomsonNOW provides the innovative tool you need to learn faster and succeed. ThomsonNOW is a reliable, easy-to-use online suite of resources that will give you the help you need to grasp difficult concepts. For every chapter, personalized learning plans allow students to focus on what they still need to learn. Students can also choose how they read the textbook—via integrated digital ebook or by reading the print version.

ACKNOWLEDGEMENTS

Starting and completing a project as large as this one is takes the support and input of many people. Professor Ruth Seiple, of the University of Cincinnati, and her students Amy Ingram and Bogdan Bichescu provided initial insight into the presentation of challenging material. Other important contributors are those colleagues who reviewed the manuscript and provided valuable suggestions as well as support and guidance. Colleagues at Thomson Business and Economics also deserve special thanks for their contributions to development and production of the book. Our regards go to senior acquisitions editor Charles McCormick, Jr., senior marketing manager Larry Qualls, senior developmental editor Alice Denny, production editor Brian Courter, art director Stacy Shirley and photo researcher Darren Wright.

Many lonely evenings and weekends were spent writing and improving this text and we are especially grateful to our families for putting up with our efforts.

We hope you enjoy this book about an important body of knowledge that we both sincerely care about. As one unknown source once said (and we quote), "Do not follow where the path may lead. Go instead where there is no path and leave a trail." We worked hard at trying to integrate and balance our focus on goods and services, and provide new ways of thinking about bundles of goods and services, and the processes that create and deliver them to customers. If you have any suggestions for improvement, please contact one of us.

David A. Collier   James R. Evans
The Ohio State University University of Cincinnati

ABOUT THE AUTHORS

DAVID A. COLLIER

David A. Collier is a member of the Faculty of Management Science, Fisher College of Business, The Ohio State University. He holds a Bachelor of Science in Mechanical Engineering, a Master's of Business Administration from the University of Kentucky, and a Ph.D. in Production and Operations Management from The Ohio State University. Prior to his academic career, he worked in materials management for Babcock and Wilcox Company.

Dr. Collier is the author of three previous books on service management and quality management: *Service Management: The Automation of Services*, *Service Management: Operating Decisions*, and *The Service/Quality Solution: Using Service Management to Gain Competitive Advantage*. He has published in such journals as *Management Sciences*, *Decision Sciences*, *Journal of Operations Management*, *Production & Operations Management*, *International Journal of Operations and Production Management*, and *International Journal of Service Industry Management*. He is the recipient of five awards for outstanding journal articles and has written and published eight invited book chapters. In addition, seven of his cases have been reprinted in major marketing and operations management textbooks and he has over seventy refereed publications. A 2004 citation review found that over 200 journal articles have referenced his research.

Professor Collier was nominated and selected to the 1991 and 1992 Board of Examiners for the Malcolm Baldrige National Quality Award. He has worked with many organizations such as AT&T, J.P. Morgan Chase Bank, Child Health Corporation of America, Emery Worldwide, Motorola, John Glenn Institute at Ohio State University, and the United States Postal Service. He served as faculty leader for a Six Sigma Black Belt Blended (Clicks and Bricks) Executive Program at the Fisher College of Business. Professor Collier has taught in the Executive MBA program at the University of Warwick in England and in several other international programs.

JAMES R. EVANS

James R. Evans is Professor of Quantitative Analysis and Operations Management and Director of the Total Quality Management Center in the College of Business Administration at the University of Cincinnati. He teaches courses in decision sciences and quality management. He holds bachelor's and master's degrees in industrial engineering from Purdue and a Ph.D. in industrial and systems engineering from Georgia Tech. Dr. Evans is author or co-author of numerous refereed papers and textbooks in decision sciences, simulation, quality management, and operations management. He received the ASQ Philip Crosby Medal for 2003 for *The Management and Control of Quality, 5e.*

Professor Evans has a wide range of professional experience and has served on the Board of Examiners for the Malcolm Baldrige National Quality Award from 1994–2001. He was appointed a Judge for a three-year term beginning in 2005. He also held numerous roles in the Decision Sciences Institute, including Past President in 1997–98, and received the Dennis E. Graowig Distinguished Service Award in 2000. During his 30-year professional career he has been active in the Institute of Industrial Engineers, INFORMS, and POMS, and has served on editorial boards for *IEEE Transactions on Engineering Management, Computers and Operations Research, Decision Sciences, Production and Operations Management, Journal of Operations Management, Quality Management Journal, Production and Inventory Management, INFORMS Transactions on Education,* and *International Journal of Services and Operations Management.*

His consulting experience includes work for Procter & Gamble, AT&T, The Kroger Co., American League of Professional Baseball Clubs, Cincinnati 2012 (Olympic Bid Committee), and various other organizations. The P&G project, of which he was a member of the analytical design team, was a finalist for the INFORMS Franz Edelman Award for Achievement in OR/MS in 1996.

OPERATIONS MANAGEMENT

Goods, Services and Value Chains

Part 1

Understanding Operations

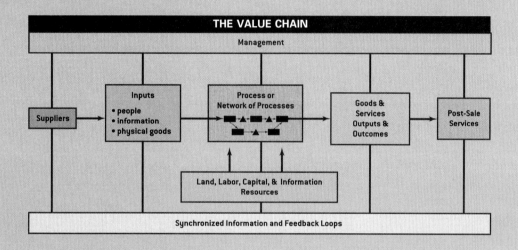

THE VALUE CHAIN

Management

Suppliers

Inputs
- people
- information
- physical goods

Process or Network of Processes

Goods & Services Outputs & Outcomes

Post-Sale Services

Land, Labor, Capital, & Information Resources

Synchronized Information and Feedback Loops

In this section of the book we introduce you to the discipline of operations management and its role in value chains and creating goods and services. You will learn about:

- The nature of OM; the differences between goods and services; the concepts of a customer benefit package, process, and value chain; the role of quantitative methods in OM; and the history of OM and its current and future challenges.
- Value chains and the way in which they support operations from a strategic perspective, their role in the global business environment, and the challenges that organizations face in today's global society.
- The importance of good performance measurement as a basis for good decisions, both at the strategic and operational levels of an organization; the principal measures used in operations and the design of measurement systems; and models of organizational performance—the Malcolm Baldrige framework, balanced scorecard, value chain model, and service-profit chain.
- The role of operations strategy in supporting the overall business strategy of an organization; the importance of taking a customer perspective, how organizations select competitive priorities, designing and selecting the operations infrastructure, and how they implement strategic planning and operations strategy.

Chapter Outline

CHAPTER 1

Goods, Services, and Operations Management

Learning Objectives

1. To understand the nature of OM activities, what operations managers do, and how everyone uses OM principles in their work in all functional areas of business.

2. To understand goods and services and the customer benefit package and why they are important for managing operations.

3. To understand processes and value chains and how they are used to support the creation of goods and services.

4. To understand the role of quantitative methods in operations management and how models can be used to assist in making OM decisions.

5. To be able to identify the key themes in OM that have evolved over the last half-century and understand their impact on goods, services, and operations.

- "Are you ready for college?" Paul asked Andrea as he helped her pack up the car. "Sure! I'm really glad I chose State University. Summer orientation was fantastic! The tour guide gave us so much information I felt like I had been there a year already; we even had a free lunch. When we got to the Admissions Center, I met with a counselor who walked me through everything—class registration, bill payment, financial aid, getting my ID, and purchasing a parking pass. He even printed out my schedule with a map that shows where each class will be. I was through in about an hour. He was able to answer every question I had and told me that he'd be able to help me with career planning, personal financial planning, and health and wellness programs. He even gave me some ideas about campus organizations to join to meet more people in my college. How about you?" "Yeah, I can't wait," Paul replied. But he was really thinking "Why didn't I select State U? During my orientation, I had to wait in a long line to get my classes scheduled, then go across campus to wait in another line for financial aid, to another office to pay my tuition bill, and then to another building for my parking pass—and my parking lot is at least a mile from my dorm. When I had a question, they simply told me they couldn't answer it and I had to go see somebody else. I hope I don't have to go through this every semester."

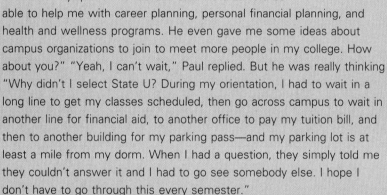

- Andrea was excited to get the new computer her parents bought her as a high school graduation gift. She was especially excited because the package included a new printer and a scanner, which she knew would be useful for projects in industrial design. When she set it up, however, she began to get error messages about some type of "hardware conflict" and could not get the scanner to work. Andrea called the technical support number and immediately reached the support desk. The technician seemed friendly and competent. He was extremely patient, asked numerous questions, and walked her through various reboots and system changes, but still

had no luck in getting the scanner to work. After about an hour, he concluded that the problem was in the computer itself, that she would have to return it, and that they would promptly send a replacement. The new machine came by express delivery in two days. This time, however, the printer did not work! After talking with several different representatives and supervisors, Andrea was able to get a full refund and return the equipment. She finally decided to buy a different brand that worked perfectly and vowed never to deal with this company again.

- McKesson, a giant distributor of pharmaceuticals to drugstores and hospitals has been studying every step it takes to get something done. The company figures out when a machine can do the job or the exact way it is most efficiently accomplished by the human hand. In 2003, the company sold $7 billion more product than in the previous year and used only 500 more workers. In a similar fashion, Eclipse Aviation in Albuquerque found that productivity gains will let the company sell new corporate jets for $1 million, less than half of the old price. This mindset now dominates U.S. industry. "No matter how good it is, it can be done better," stated an executive from Lockheed Martin, whose implementation of such modern approaches as Six Sigma and Lean Manufacturing has helped it find ways to do thousands of things more efficiently, from uploading software in space to assembling aircraft.[1]

Discussion Questions: What experiences similar to Paul's and Andrea's—either good or bad—have you had in dealing with your school, credit card company, phone company, automobile dealer, retail store, or other organization? What does an organization have to excel at to create and deliver a positive customer experience?

These stories of customer experiences illustrate a key theme of this book—*the importance of the design and management of operations for creating goods and services that are valued by customers and society.* The way in which goods and services, and the processes that create and support them, are designed and managed can make the difference between a delightful or unhappy customer experience. In the long run, they can determine how successful an organization is and whether it can compete in today's sophisticated business world. For example, in contrast to Paul's experience of having to wait in lines at different locations, Andrea's satisfying experience in her college orientation resulted from the way in which the university organized and consolidated its services. However, Andrea's experience with the computer company showed that even good service and competent people cannot make up for poorly designed or manufactured products. The economic prosperity of any nation depends on the ability of its people to create and satisfy customer wants and needs.

To compete in today's complex business world, organizations need well-designed and executed operations. The third episode suggests the importance of being productive and continuously improving. Economic growth requires productivity growth.

But productivity does not come from just getting people to work faster. It comes from smarter designs and more efficient processes that lower costs and ultimately raise profits. For example, part of Ford Motor Company's strategy to become more competitive is to improve its mix of vehicle models, strengthen quality, and continue to cut costs.[2] One executive noted that "consumers don't buy cars based on which company is more productive, but . . . the companies who do well can better afford to build higher-quality and more attractive vehicles."[3] Not surprisingly, Nissan, Mitsubishi, and Toyota take the top three spots in surveys of most efficient vehicle assembly plants, but U.S. firms are catching up. Technological change, capital investment, improved labor quality, and other factors are the drivers of productivity growth. Creating an organization that can be productive, improve, and exploit technology requires strong attention to operations management.

Operations management *(OM) is the science and art of ensuring that goods and services are created and delivered successfully to customers.* Applying the principles of OM entails a solid understanding of people, processes, and technology and how they are integrated within business systems to create value. Managing in today's global business environment—which changes continually—is difficult. OM provides both the principles and tools for helping today's managers meet the challenge.

Just how important is OM? Early in 2005, the board of directors for Hewlett-Packard asked CEO Carly Fiorina to step down. Although she was an extremely passionate and high-profile CEO who pushed through a controversial merger with Compaq several years earlier that exceeded expectations, business experts noted that HP needed a hands-on operations person to run the company rather than someone who excelled in strategy and marketing.

Managers in today's complex business world must understand three principal ideas, which form the key themes in this book:

1. the complementary nature of goods and services, and the need to understand and integrate them to compete in today's world and to make key operations decisions;
2. the importance of the value chain and how operations management plays a vital role in helping organizations to achieve long-term competitive advantage; and
3. the importance of understanding that we live in a shrinking world, and that operations decisions must take into account a variety of global and international issues.

The purpose of this chapter is to introduce you to OM, its role in business, and how it supports the creation and delivery of goods and services.

> **Operations management** *(OM) is the science and art of ensuring that goods and services are created and delivered successfully to customers.*

THE NATURE OF OPERATIONS MANAGEMENT

The traditional management paradigm revolves around four basic functions—planning, organizing, directing, and controlling. **Planning** *provides the basis for future activities by developing strategies, goals, and objectives and establishing guidelines, actions, and schedules for meeting them.* A significant amount of planning is involved in selecting the goods and services that an organization offers and designing these goods and services to meet the needs of potential customers. **Organizing** *is the process of bringing together the resources—people, materials, equipment, technology, information, and capital—necessary to perform planned activities.* This includes designing the processes and systems to create and deliver goods and services. **Directing** *is the process of turning plans into realities by assigning specific tasks and responsibilities to employees, motivating them, and coordinating their efforts.* This is

> **Learning Objective**
> To understand the nature of typical OM activities, what operations managers do, and how everyone uses OM principles in their work in all functional areas of business.
>
> **Planning** *provides the basis for future activities by developing strategies, goals, and objectives and establishing guidelines, actions, and schedules for meeting them.*

Organizing *is the process of bringing together the resources—people, materials, equipment, technology, information, and capital—necessary to perform planned activities.*

Directing *is the process of turning plans into realities by assigning specific tasks and responsibilities to employees, motivating them, and coordinating their efforts.*

Controlling—*evaluating performance and applying corrective measures—is necessary to ensure that plans are achieved.*

what operations managers "do" on a daily basis. Finally, **controlling**—*evaluating performance and applying corrective measures—is necessary to ensure that plans are achieved.* This also includes learning from mistakes and best practices and improving operations in the long run. The principles of OM help one to view a business enterprise as a *total system*, in which all of these activities are coordinated not only vertically throughout the organization but also horizontally across multiple functions.

Operations management is the only means by which managers can directly affect the value provided to all stakeholders—customers, employees, investors, and society. Effective operations management is essential to providing high-quality goods and services that customers demand, motivating and developing the skills of the people who actually do the work, maintaining efficient operations to ensure an adequate return on investment, and protecting the environment. Some of the key activities that comprise the discipline of operations management include

- understanding the needs of customers, measuring customer satisfaction, and using that information to develop new and improved goods and services, thereby supporting the long-term strategy of the organization;
- using information about customers, goods and services, operations, suppliers, employees, and costs and finances to make better decisions;
- exploiting technology to design goods, services, manufacturing, and service delivery processes that respond rapidly and flexibly to customer requirements and to improve productivity;
- building quality into goods, services, and processes and continually improving them to reduce errors, defects, and waste and to improve responsiveness and business performance;
- ensuring that material flows and associated operational activities are coordinated across hierarchical, organizational, and functional boundaries, from suppliers to customers;
- creating a high-performance workplace by developing the skills of employees and motivating them through education, training, rewards, recognition, teamwork, empowerment, and other effective human resource practices;
- continually learning from co-workers, competitors, and customers, and adapting the organization to global and environmental changes.

OM principles are not complicated. On the contrary, they are quite simple, but they do require vision and discipline to implement. Len Schlesinger, COO of Limited Brands, noted that "the basics of everyday operating management should never be supplanted by any other big idea" and that the application of basic practices—such as a respect for the importance of the customer experience, a focus on the dynamics of demand, the recognition that an experience is delivered by people, and that profit depends on meaningful differentiation of the product, the experience, and people—are timeless operational initiatives.[4] Quality guru W. Edwards Deming stated simply that people work *in* the system, and managers work *on* the system to improve it continuously with their help. Thus, *the fundamental purpose of operations management is to deliver ever-improving value to customers through the continuous improvement of overall company performance and capabilities.* In the OM Spotlight description of a DuPont plant's experience, we see that application of simple OM principles—seeking the causes of problems, making only what you can sell, modifying the design and operation of the system, measurement, and education and training—can lead to dramatic results.

OM in the Workplace

Many students typically ask, "What do operations managers do?" For an example in manufacturing, see the OM Spotlight on Ferguson Metals.

OM SPOTLIGHT

DuPont[5]

DuPont's May Plant in Camden, South Carolina, employs approximately 125 people and produces roughly 69 million pounds of textile fiber each year. The textile area includes production, shipping, inspection, and testing. Textile fibers are produced in a continuous spinning operation. After fiber is wound on a spool, it is placed on a special buggy that holds many spools. The buggies are wheeled to a test-and-inspection station. Finally, the product is grouped, packaged, and shipped.

Spinning machines cannot be shut down without incurring tremendous startup costs. Even slowing production will adversely affect product consistency and quality. Those facts complicated the job of the plant managers, who faced many problematic issues. The quality of work life for operators, supervisors, and area managers was poor, with many safety problems. Customers' orders were not being met in a timely way. There were constant telephone calls from customers about failing to meet delivery schedules, calls that were often unpleasant and at times confrontational. Other problems were finished goods shortages, excessive backlogs, high inventories, and lost or misplaced yarn. Product-quality variation and production yields were unacceptable. There was ongoing pressure from the marketing group, as well as from plant executives, to stem the flow of customer complaints.

Employees, supervisors, and managers were eager for change. One manager had been exposed to world-class operations management principles and started the journey toward successfully and permanently resolving many of the problems. One critical step was to lock up many of the buggies except when needed for an emergency. With fewer buggies in operation, bottlenecks became acutely visible, and the sources of problems were more quickly identified and corrected. The result was a smoother flow of product through the facility.

Jobs were simplified, and a visual control system was adopted. In the new system, a limited number of buggies were placed only in small marked-off spaces, which limited the amount of inventory and flagged problems. Even forklifts had specific parking places to enable easy identification of the ones that were leaking fluid and posed a safety problem. Employees measured the time it took products to move through the facility and backlogs at each work station, plotting the results so that deviations could be identified quickly and corrected. Extensive on-the-job education and training, supplemented by meetings and individual coaching and counseling, helped to involve all employees in the improvement efforts. Operations management principles and methods were at the core of this improvement effort.

As a result of those initiatives, work-in-process inventory at DuPont's plant was reduced an astounding 96 percent, working capital declined by $2 million, employee suggestions increased 300 percent, and product quality improved 10 percent. Most of the results were achieved within the first three months after implementation of the changes!

Operations managers like Vogel must draw upon skills developed in management, finance, information systems, marketing, and accounting courses. These might include hiring, training, evaluating, and motivating people; justifying the purchase of new technology and resources; consolidating and analyzing data and information to make informed decisions; understanding the needs of customers and markets; and understanding how accounting allocates revenues and costs. In addition, they must also learn a new set of skills such as designing manufacturing and service

OM SPOTLIGHT

Ferguson Metals

Ferguson Metals, located in Hamilton, Ohio, is a supplier of stainless steel and high temperature alloys for the specialty metal market. Ferguson's primary production operations include slitting coil stock and cutting sheet steel to customer specifications with rapid turnaround times from order to delivery (see Exhibit 1.1). Bob Vogel is the Director of Operations and Quality at Ferguson. With only 75 employees, about half of whom are in operations, Bob is involved in a variety of daily activities that draw upon knowledge of not only OM and engineering, but also finance, accounting, organizational behavior, and other subjects. He typically spends about 50 percent of his time working with customers, foremen, supervisors, salespeople, and other staff through email and various meetings, discussing such issues as whether or not the company has the capability to accomplish a specific customer request, as well as routine production, quality, and shipping issues. While he makes recommendations to his direct reports, his interaction is more of a consultant than a manager; his people are fully empowered to make key decisions. The remainder of his time is spent investigating such issues as the technical feasibility and cost implications of new capital equipment or changes to existing processes, trying to reduce costs, seeking and facilitating design improvements on the shop floor, and motivating the work force. For example, one project involves working with the Information Technology group to reduce the amount of paperwork required to process orders. In addition, Vogel is a Metallurgical Engineer who interfaces often with customers regarding materials applications. While understanding specialty metals is certainly a vital part of his job, the ability to understand customer needs, apply approaches to continuous improvement, understand and motivate people, work cross-functionally across the business, and integrate processes and technology within the value chain define Vogel's job as an operations and quality manager.

Exhibit 1.1
Operations Management at Ferguson Metals

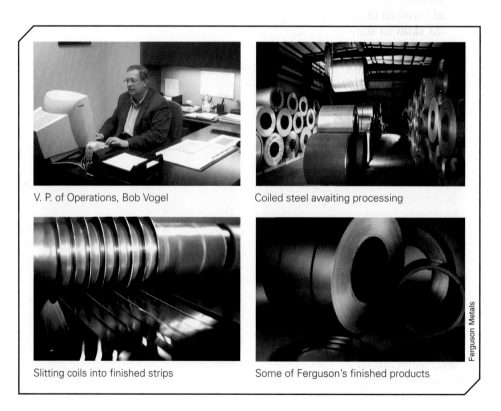

V. P. of Operations, Bob Vogel

Coiled steel awaiting processing

Slitting coils into finished strips

Some of Ferguson's finished products

processes to coordinate the delivery and use of labor, information, materials and supplies; and to develop schedules to execute plans, manage projects, and improve the operating systems to ensure survival of the organization.

However, you need not have the title of "Operations Manager" to "do operations management." Every job entails some aspects of operations management. The ideas and methods of operations management will help you get things done successfully regardless of your functional area of business. As you manage accounting, human resources, or legal, financial, operations, supply chain, environment, service, or marketing processes, you create value for your internal customers (within the organization) and for your external customers (outside the organization). Everyone who manages a process or some business activity should possess a set of basic OM skills. Following are some examples of how our former students are using OM in their jobs, both in manufacturing and in services.

Patrick Kindt studied industrial management in college and is a quality engineer for Johnson Controls Interiors. His primary job responsibility is ensuring the quality of the product (automotive headliners). This includes extensive customer service activities with both suppliers and customers. Some of the OM-related tasks that he performs on a regular basis include analyzing data to make decisions on all purchases and equipment upgrades; optimizing the way machines are run on each process line based on bottleneck cycle times; using statistics, measurement systems analysis, gage calibration studies, and control charting to ensure that processes are under control and capable; working on improvement projects such as scrap reduction and bill-of-material optimization with cross-functional continuous improvement teams; and managing projects involving cycle time reduction, supplier lamination scrap reduction, hydraulic press upgrades, and new gage development.

Teresa Louis was an accounting major in college and works at Chiquita Brands in a division that produces and sells fruit ingredients such as banana puree, frozen sliced bananas, and other types of fruit products. Although primarily an accountant and involved in monthly accounting closings and other accounting tasks, Louis uses OM skills to support her work. These include:

- Quality and customer service issues: If there is a quality issue with a product either at the plant level or the customer level, the accounting group has to account for it in the Inventory Reserve account, which is reconciled during the closing process.
- Performance measurement and evaluation: Part of her responsibility is to look at the monthly profit versus cost analysis by product to calculate a net contribution. She examines the product costs at the plant level to find more efficient and cost-effective methods of production, for example, reducing plant downtimes, which increase the price per pound of the product, or constantly looking for better/cheaper fruit suppliers.
- Managing inventory: Part of the closing process is to reconcile the Inventory Movement because inventory is what drives the fruit commodity business. It is very important to make sure inventory balances and levels are accurate, as this is what the percentage of sales is based on. She is also involved in ensuring inventory accuracy at the company's distribution centers.

Tom James is a senior software developer for a small software development company that creates sales proposal automation software. James uses OM skills in dealing with quality and customer service issues related to the software. He is also extensively involved in project management activities related to the development process, including identifying tasks, assigning developers to tasks, estimating the time and cost to complete projects, and studying the variance between the estimated and actual time it took to complete projects. He is also involved in continuous improvement projects, for example, seeking to reduce development time and increase the efficiency of the development team. Tom was an information technology and management major in college.

Brooke Wilson is a process manager for J. P. Morgan Chase in the Credit Card Division. After several years working as an operations analyst, he was promoted to a production supervisor position overseeing "plastic card production." Among his OM-related activities are

- Planning and budgeting: representing the plastic card production area in all meetings, developing annual budgets and staffing plans, and watching technology that might affect the production of plastic credit cards;
- Inventory management: overseeing the management of inventory for items such as plastic blank cards, inserts such as advertisements, envelopes, postage, and credit card rules and disclosure inserts;
- Scheduling and capacity: daily to annual scheduling of all resources (equipment, people, inventory) necessary to issue new credit cards and reissue cards that are up for renewal and replace old or damaged cards and ones that are stolen;
- Quality: embossing the card with accurate customer information and quickly getting the card in the hands of the customer.

Brooke was an accounting major in college.

Jennifer Snow, a business account manager (outside sales representative) for Cincinnati Bell, focuses on all the communication services, including data, Internet, voice, wireless, security systems, phone systems, long distance, and more. Snow was an information technology and management major in college. Among her OM-related activities are matching her daily/weekly agenda with the strategic focus of the management team; measuring her performance using such indicators as number of appointments/day, number of phone calls/day, number of decision makers contacted, sales closing ratios, number of proposals presented daily, number of recurring dollars sold as percentage of quota, as well as quota attainment on one-time or equipment sales; receiving continuous training on new developments, new products, and new technologies; forecasting her sales in 30-, 60-, and 90-day windows, by individual customer, across product groups, recurring versus nonrecurring revenues, and as a percentage of quota; scheduling daily activities like phone calls, appointments, visits; and working on various types of improvement projects, such as how to provide more selling time for the reps, effective geographic territory management, removing obstacles such as service/billing issues, and increasing activity levels.

Brenda Carr, a marketing major, works as an operations and financial analyst II in the Help Desk area for J. P. Morgan Chase. Among her OM-related activities are forecasting demand and scheduling telephone customer service representatives (CSRs) to answer calls from Chase retail and branch bank offices located throughout the United States; establishing service standards and measuring and evaluating service quality of the customer contact center; preparing Help Desk performance reports using financial, employee, service quality, and customer satisfaction measures; and presenting the Help Desk performance results at weekly and monthly management meetings. This requires good writing and presentation skills and the ability to handle and answer tough questions in front of the management team. Carr notes, "You must be able to take a situation and evaluate it quickly. The calls continuously come in and the internal and external customers need answers now." She also states, "You must be able to sell what you do internally—that is, make people realize you are the knowledge and resolution center for the bank. You make things happen! What we do adds value!"

Learning Objective
To understand goods and services and the customer benefit package and why they are important for managing operations.

A **good** *is a physical product that you can see, touch, or possibly consume.*

A **durable good** *is a product that typically lasts at least three years.*

UNDERSTANDING GOODS AND SERVICES

Understanding goods and services is important in order to design the most appropriate system and manage it effectively. *A* **good** *is a physical product that you can see, touch, or possibly consume.* Examples of goods include oranges, flowers, televisions, soap, airplanes, fish, furniture, coal, lumber, personal computers, paper, and industrial machines. *A* **durable good** *is a product that typically lasts at least three years.*

Vehicles, dishwashers, and furniture are some examples of durable goods. *A nondurable good is perishable and generally lasts for less than three years.* Examples are toothpaste, software, shoes, and fruit. *A service is any primary or complementary activity that does not directly produce a physical product.* Services represent the nongoods part of a transaction between a buyer (customer) and seller (supplier).[6] Common examples of service businesses are hotels, legal and financial firms, airlines, health care organizations, museums, and consulting firms.

Similarities and Differences Between Goods and Services

Goods and services share many similarities. They provide value and satisfaction to customers who purchase and use them. They can be standardized for the mass market or customized to individual needs. They are created and provided to customers by some type of process involving people and technology. Services that do not involve significant interaction with customers (for example, "back office" credit card processing) can be managed much the same way as goods in a factory, using proven principles of OM that have been refined over the years. Nevertheless, some very significant differences exist between goods and services that make the management of service-providing organizations different from managing goods-producing organizations and create different demands on the operations function.[7]

1. Goods are tangible whereas services are intangible. Goods are consumed, but services are experienced. Goods-producing industries rely on machines and "hard technology" to perform work. Goods can be moved, stored, and repaired and generally require physical skills and expertise during production. Customers can often try them before buying. Services, on the other hand, make more use of information systems and other "soft technology," require strong behavioral skills, and are often difficult to describe and demonstrate. As Joseph F. Fredrick, Jr., a senior executive of the Hilton Corporation notes, "We sell time. You can't put a hotel room on the shelf."[8]

2. Customers participate in many service processes, activities, and transactions. Many services require that the customer be present either physically, on a telephone, or online for service to commence. In addition, the customer and service provider often coproduce a service, meaning that they work together to create and simultaneously consume the service, as would be the case with a bank teller and a customer to complete a financial transaction. This means that many services must be performed in the presence of the customer and, hence, operations must respond appropriately. This is not the case for goods producers. Customers are not involved in manufacturing, and operations can be performed at the convenience of the producer.

This characteristic has interesting implications for operations. For example, it might be possible to offload some work to the customer by encouraging self-service (supermarkets, cafeterias, libraries) and self-cleanup (fast-food restaurants, campgrounds, vacation home rentals). The higher the customer participation, the more uncertainty the firm has with respect to service time, capacity, scheduling, quality performance, and operating cost. Many key operations issues, such as facility location and layout, job design, process design, and human behavior, are highly interdependent with service-system design; this will be addressed in later chapters.

A service encounter is an interaction between the customer and the service provider. Service encounters consist of one or more moments of truth—*any episodes, transactions, or experiences in which a customer comes into contact with any*

A nondurable good is perishable and generally lasts for less than three years.

A service is any primary or complementary activity that does not directly produce a physical product.

A service encounter is an interaction between the customer and the service provider.

Moments of truth—any episodes, transactions, or experiences in which a customer comes into contact with any aspect of the delivery system, however remote, and thereby has an opportunity to form an impression.

aspect of the delivery system, however remote, and thereby has an opportunity to form an impression.[9] Employees who interact directly with customers, such as airline flight attendants, nurses, lawyers, fast-food counter employees, telephone customer service representatives, dentists, and bank tellers, need to understand the importance of service encounters to their customers. However, human interaction, either face-to-face or through a contact technology such as a telephone line, is not required to establish a service encounter. A service encounter also includes the interaction the customer has with buildings, equipment, advertisements, brochures, and so on. For example, while driving an automobile, a customer might see a large sign for a store (one moment of truth) but then observe a poorly lit store parking lot (a second moment of truth), believe that the area is not safe, and decide to keep driving and not stop at the store. Customers judge the value of a service and form perceptions through service encounters.

3. The demand for services is more difficult to predict than the demand for goods. Customer arrival rates and demand patterns for such service delivery systems as banks, airlines, supermarkets, telephone service centers, and courts are very difficult to forecast. The demand for services is time-dependent, especially over the short term (by hour or day). For example, the ratio of high to low demand (that is, calls for service) during a given period is as high as 20 to 1 for emergency fire and ambulance services. This places many pressures on service firm managers to adequately plan staffing levels and capacity.

4. Services cannot be stored as physical inventory. In goods-producing firms, inventory can be used to decouple customer demand from the production process or between stages of the production process to ensure constant availability despite fluctuations in demand. Service firms do not have physical inventory to absorb such fluctuations in demand. For service delivery systems, availability depends on the system's capacity. For example, a hospital must have an adequate supply of beds for the purpose of meeting unanticipated patient demand and a float pool of nurses when things get very busy. The combination of nonstorable output and time-dependent demand causes most services to be perishable commodities. Once an airline seat, a hotel room, or an hour of a lawyer's day are gone there is no way to recapture the lost revenue.

5. Service management skills are paramount to a successful service encounter. Service providers have a significant effect on the perceived value of the service as viewed by the customer. Service encounters not only require good operations but also require strong human behavior and marketing skills. Service management *integrates marketing, human resource, and operations functions to plan, create, and deliver goods and services and their associated service encounters.* Service providers require such service management skills as knowledge and technical expertise (operations), cross-selling other products and services (marketing), and good human interaction skills (human resource). For example, a golf course turf service technician who interacts with the golf course superintendent and groundskeeper must have operations knowledge about turf management, fertilization techniques, weed control, and proper use of the application equipment. Second, the technician must have marketing skills to cross-sell other golf course services such as greens repair and restoration and tree removal. Third, the technician must be capable of creating good relationships with customers through effective service encounters. OM principles are useful in designing service encounters and supporting marketing objectives. In goods-producing industries, human interaction skills and marketing are of lesser importance.

6. Service facilities typically need to be in close proximity to the customer. When customers must physically interact with a service facility, for example, post offices, hotels, and branch banks, it must be conveniently located. A manufacturing facility, on the other hand, can be located on the other side of the globe, as long as goods are delivered to customers in a timely fashion. In today's Internet age with

Service management *integrates marketing, human resource, and operations functions to plan, create, and deliver goods and services and their associated service encounters.*

its evolving service technologies, "proximity" need not be the same as location; many services are only a few mouse clicks away.

7. Patents do not protect services. A patent on a physical good or software code can provide protection from competitors. The intangible nature of a service makes it more difficult to keep a competitor from copying a business concept, facility layout, or service encounter design. For example, restaurant chains are quick to copy new menu items or drive-through concepts. At Sleep Inns, nightstands with no legs are bolted to the wall so room cleaners don't have to move furniture to vacuum around the legs. Several economy hotels copied this idea to reduce the number of room cleaners per hotel. However, services can be protected to some extent by copyrights and trademarks and by establishing a standard facility design and product line. For example, in the legal case of *Amstar Corp. vs. Domino's Pizza*, the central question was whether the use by the defendant of a mark or logo to identify its services was apt to confuse the ordinary customer to the detriment of the plaintiff. The first factor the court cited in evaluating the claim of actual or likely confusion was the public's recognition of its products and facility design.

These differences between goods and services have important implications for all areas of an organization, especially for operations. They are summarized in Exhibit 1.2. Some are obvious, others are more subtle. By understanding them, organizations can better select the appropriate mix of goods and services to meet customer needs and create the most effective operating systems to produce and deliver those goods and services. We will elaborate on these ideas throughout this book.

Exhibit 1.2

How Goods and Services Affect Operations Management Activities

OM Activity	Goods	Services
Forecasting	Forecasts involve longer-term time horizons. Manufacturers can use physical inventory as a buffer to mitigate forecast errors. Forecasts can be aggregated over larger time frames (e.g., months or weeks).	Forecast horizons generally are shorter, and forecasts are more variable and time-dependent. Forecasting must often be done on a daily or hourly basis, or sometimes even more frequently.
Facility Location	Manufacturing facilities can be located close to raw materials, suppliers, labor, or customers/markets.	Service facilities must be located close to customers/markets for convenience and speed of service.
Facility Layout and Design	Factories and warehouses can be designed for efficiency because few, if any, customers are present.	The facility must be designed for customer interaction.
Technology	Manufacturing facilities use various types of automation to produce goods.	Service facilities tend to rely more on information-based hardware and software.
Quality	Manufacturers can define clear, physical, and measurable quality standards and capture measurements using various physical devices.	Quality measurements must account for customer's perception of service quality and often must be gathered through surveys or personal contact.
Inventory/Capacity	Manufacturers use physical inventory as a buffer for fluctuations in demand.	Service capacity is the substitute for inventory.
Process Design	Because customers have no participation or involvement in manufacturing processes, the processes can be more mechanistic.	Customers usually participate extensively in service creation and delivery, requiring more flexibility and adaptation to special circumstances.
Job/Service Encounter Design	Manufacturing employees require strong technical skills.	Service employees need more behavioral and service management skills.
Scheduling	Scheduling revolves around movement and location of materials, parts, and subassemblies and can be accomplished at the discretion and for the benefit of the manufacturer.	Scheduling revolves around capacity, availability, and customer needs, often leaving little discretion for the service provider.

A similar classification of OM activities in terms of high/low customer contact was first proposed in the classic article: Chase, R. B., "Where does the customer fit in a service operation?" *Harvard Business Review*, November–December 1978, p. 139.

Customer Benefit Packages

The key objective of an organization and its operations function is to provide some combination of goods and services that customers value. Many commodity items, such as basic raw materials (coal, coffee, chemicals, orange juice, and so on), are pure goods. Entertainment and telecommunication services are pure services. In most cases, however, many "goods" and "services" that we normally think of are a mixture of *both* goods and services. Exhibit 1.3 illustrates a continuum of goods and service content with several examples. Toothpaste, for instance, is high in goods content, but when you purchase it, you are also purchasing some services, such as a telephone call center to field customer questions and complaints. Similarly, a bicycle might seem like a pure good, but it often includes services such as safety instruction and maintenance. At the other extreme in Exhibit 1.3 are psychiatric services, which are much higher in service content but might include goods such as a bill, books, and medical brochures that support the service. A symphony, play, or movie performance is essentially a pure service but may include program brochures and ticket stubs that offer discounts at local restaurants as peripheral goods.

Goods and services are usually bundled together as a deliberate marketing and operations strategy. Mercedes automobiles, for example, bundle a premium good, the automobile, with many premium services. Such services include customized leasing, insurance, and warranty programs that focus on the "financial productivity" of owning a Mercedes vehicle. Other customized services bundled with the vehicle include personalized invitations to drive new cars on a test track, a 24/7 telephone hot line, and invitations to private owner parties. Such bundling is described by the customer benefit package framework.[10]

A **customer benefit package (CBP)** *is a clearly defined set of tangible (goods-content) and intangible (service-content) features that the customer recognizes, pays for, uses, or experiences.* In simple terms, it is some combination of goods and services configured in a certain way to provide value to customers and to fulfill customer wants and needs. A CBP consists of a primary good or service, coupled with peripheral goods and/or services, and sometimes a variant. One example is shown in Exhibit 1.4.

A **primary good or service** *is the "core" offering that attracts customers and responds to their primary wants and needs.* For example, in Exhibit 1.4, an automobile or SUV is the primary good. A checking account would be an example of a primary service

*A **customer benefit package (CBP)** is a clearly defined set of tangible (goods-content) and intangible (service-content) features that the customer recognizes, pays for, uses, or experiences.*

*A **primary good or service** is the "core" offering that attracts customers and responds to their basic needs.*

Exhibit 1.3
Examples of Goods and Service Content

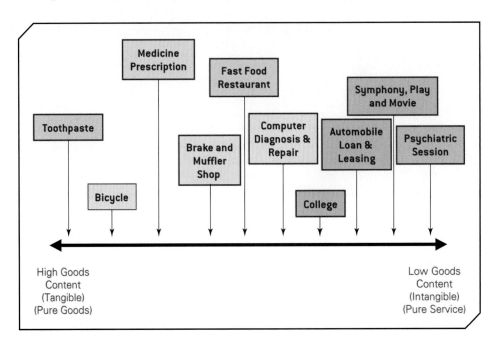

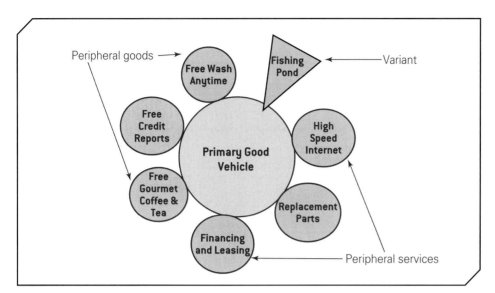

Exhibit 1.4
A CBP Example for Purchasing a Vehicle

for a bank customer. **Peripheral goods or services** *are those that are not essential to the primary good or service, but enhance it.* (The terms *accessory, auxiliary, complementary, facilitating, satellite,* and *supporting* also refer to a good or service feature that is bundled with the primary good or service.) The vehicle might be supported by peripheral goods such as a colorful brochure by model type, printouts of competitor prices and discount service coupons, replacement and repair parts, and free gourmet coffee and tea for customers. Peripheral services might include repair and maintenance service, free WIFI access while waiting, free baby sitting service, warranties, leasing or financing, and free on-line credit reports. Peripheral goods and services for a checking account might include on-line bill payment and designer checks.

A **variant** *is a CBP attribute that departs from the standard CBP and is normally location or firm-specific.* A variant might be a fishing pond where kids can fish while parents shop for vehicles. (See Exhibit 1.4.) Once a variant is incorporated and standardized into all CBP delivery sites it becomes a permanent peripheral good or service. Adding information and entertainment content to the CBP also shifts the CBP configuration from selling just physical goods or services to developing closer and more personal relationships with the customer. The final CBP transformation can be a completely new business model where the CBP and related processes are totally redefined.

In some cases, goods and services content in a CBP framework are approximately equal. For example, McDonald's (food and fast service) and IBM (computers and customer solutions) might argue that their primary goods and services are of equal importance, so a graphical representation would show two equal-sized and overlapping circles as the center of the dual CBP. For some business-to-business CBPs such as custom machining, one could think of the primary business as a professional service—providing customized engineering design assistance and specifications—with the actual physical good (machined part) as a peripheral good.

Finally, we may bundle a group of CBPs together to create a more aggregate or "super CBP." One example would be a combined land-cruise vacation to Alaska, which might consist of a bundle of CBPs such as a travel agency that books the package and optional land excursions from the ship, the land-tour operator that handles hotels, transportation and baggage, and the cruise line that provides air travel, meals and entertainment. Super CBPs raise some interesting issues about pricing strategies and partnerships among firms. For example, a firm might actually be able to charge a premium price for the bundled CBPs than if they were purchased separately.

A major purpose of a CBP is to provide differentiation from competitors' goods and services. One auto mall bundles entertainment with the CBP as a variant that includes a fishing pond and car performance test track. The co-owner of the auto mall views entertainment as a big part of its CBP definition. If customers are having fun,

Peripheral goods or services are those that are not essential to the primary good or service, but enhance it.

*A **variant** is a CBP attribute that departs from the standard CBP and is normally location or firm-specific.*

Exhibit 1.5
Operations Management and
the Customer Benefit Package

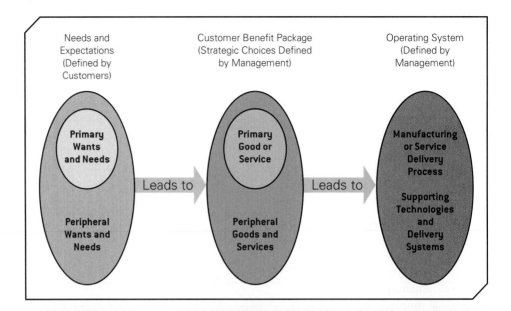

Exhibit 1.6
Customer Wants and Needs,
CBP Definition, and Process
Design Automobile Example

Defined by customers—example wants and needs	CBP features defined by management to fulfill customers wants and needs	Defined by management—processes to create/deliver
Primary want—physical transportation from point A to B	Vehicle	Engineering design processes with customer, dealer, and supplier input
Primary want—low cost/price	Efficient vehicle design and manufacturing processes	Just-in-time value chain designs and all associated processes
Primary want—good vehicle sales experience	Sales process	Hiring, training, recognition and reward dealer processes
Primary want—good vehicle repair service and experience	Vehicle repair service	Hiring, training, recognition and reward dealer repair processes
Peripheral want—good financing options	Finance and lease packages and options	Fast, accurate, customized, and fair financing, lease and credit report processes
Peripheral want—good gourmet coffee and tea in customer areas	Clean high quality coffee and tea service at dealership	Purchasing, coffee replenishment schedule, and cleaning processes
Peripheral want—need place for kids to go and be safe and have fun while parents shop	Free childcare service on high demand days	Check in and out procedures, trained caregiver on duty, and emergency processes
Peripheral want—fun family time	Fishing pond, carousel ride, vehicle test track, and on-site games at this dealership	Entertainment director and associated processes for this auto mall

they will more likely buy cars! Adding entertainment, fun and excitement to a CBP design is one way to differentiate a CBP from competitors' offerings. Exhibits 1.5 and 1.6 illustrate the relationship between customer wants and needs, CBP attributes (features), and the processes that create and deliver each CBP good or service.

The CBP framework is a way to think broadly about how goods and services are bundled and configured together. This framework and terminology fits the realities of today's marketplace, where information, entertainment and service play significant and integrated roles in gaining competitive advantage. To support CPBs, processes must be designed to meet or exceed customer wants and needs. Goods and service process design must begin with understanding customer wants and needs as we will illustrate throughout this textbook. All aspects of "process design and management" require OM expertise and skills—a truly universal and interdisciplinary skill set.

PROCESSES AND VALUE CHAINS

Processes are the building blocks for the creation of goods and services and are vital to many activities in operations management. *A process is a sequence of activities that is intended to create a certain result,* such as a physical good, a service, or information. A practical definition, according to AT&T, of a process is how work creates value for customers.[11] Key processes in business typically include

1. **value creation processes**, focused on primary goods or services, such as assembling dishwashers or providing a home mortgage;
2. **support processes**, such as purchasing materials and supplies, managing inventory, installation, customer support, technology acquisition, and research and development; and
3. **general management processes**, including accounting and information systems, human resource management, and marketing.

Exhibit 1.7 depicts how these different types of process are interrelated. For example, the objective of general management processes is to coordinate key value creation and support processes to achieve organization goals and objectives.

Process thinking differs from the traditional way of viewing an organization by function. Work gets done (or fails to get done) horizontally or cross-functionally, not hierarchically by function. Nearly every major activity within an organization involves a process that crosses traditional organizational boundaries. For example, an order fulfillment process might involve a salesperson placing the order; a marketing representative entering it on the company's computer system; a credit check by finance; picking, packaging, and shipping by distribution and logistics employees; invoicing by finance; and installation by field service engineers. This is illustrated in Exhibit 1.8.

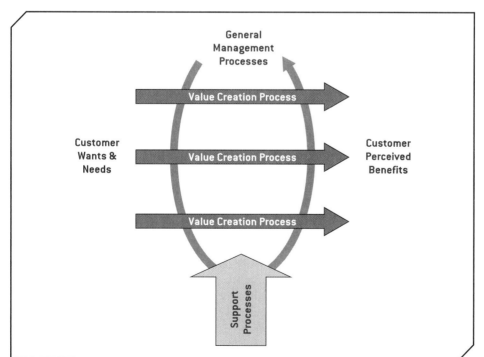

Exhibit 1.7
How Primary, Support, Supplier, and Management Processes Are Related

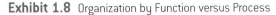

Exhibit 1.8 Organization by Function versus Process

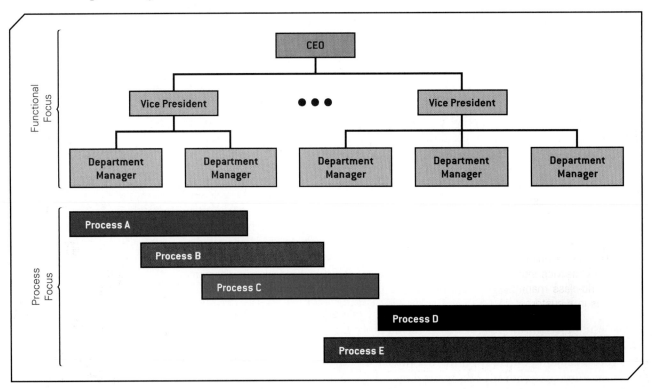

For example, Process A crosses departments but not functional areas, whereas Process C crosses functional areas. Rather than focusing on only a small part, a process perspective links all necessary activities together and increases one's understanding of the entire system. Many of the greatest opportunities for improving organizational performance lie in the functional interfaces—those spaces between the functional boxes on an organization chart where the opportunities for error are great.

A transformation process involves the creation of value in terms of time, place, information, entertainment, exchange, or form utility. The objective of a transformation process is to create an output for a particular customer or market segment that the customer values, thus building a competitive advantage for the firm. Obvious transformation processes are fabrication and assembly, whereby raw materials are transformed into physical goods. Other examples are the transformation of data into reports and statements documenting the financial health of an organization by people in accounting and finance departments. A poor process that results in delays, errors, and unnecessary costs can damage the credibility of the organization, and perhaps even the stock price. Selecting and configuring the right types of transformation processes to create and deliver goods and services is one of the most fundamental decisions in operations management and will be addressed further in later chapters.

The variety of processes within an organization can be illustrated by Pal's Sudden Service (see the OM Spotlight for background about the company). Pal's has three key suppliers who provide the majority of raw materials. A limited supply base reduces product variability and improves consistency and allows Pal's to design in quality, value, and a unique flavor profile. Raw materials enter through a delivery door and are worked forward through the store. Primary processes are order taking, cooking, food assembly, cash collection, and order delivery. One process serves the next in the processing-assembly-packaging line until a finished good is handed to a customer.

Transformation processes, while vital to creating goods and services, cannot be viewed in isolation; they must be viewed from a perspective that integrates all aspects of operations in creating goods and delivering customer experiences. *A value chain is a network of processes that create value for customers.* For example, as

A transformation process involves the creation of value in terms of time, place, information, entertainment, exchange, or form utility.

A value chain is a network of processes that create value for customers.

OM SPOTLIGHT

Pal's Sudden Service

Pal's Sudden Service is a small chain of mostly drive-through quick-service restaurants located in Northeast Tennessee and Southwest Virginia. Pal's competes against major national chains and outperforms all of them by focusing on important customer requirements such as speed, accuracy, friendly service, correct ingredients and amounts, proper food temperature, and safety. Pal's uses extensive market research to fully understand customer requirements: convenience; ease of driving in and out; easy-to-read menu; simple, accurate order system; fast service; wholesome food; and reasonable price. To create value, Pal's has developed a unique ability to effectively integrate production and service into its operations. Pal's has learned to apply world-class management principles and best-in-class processes in a customer-driven approach to business excel-

lence that causes other companies to emulate its systems. Every process is flowcharted and analyzed for opportunities for error, and then mistake-proofed if at all possible. Entry-level employees—mostly high school students in their first job—receive 120 hours of training on precise work procedures and process standards in unique self-teaching, classroom, and on-the-job settings, which is reinforced by a "Caught Doing Good" program that provides recognition for meeting quality standards and high performance expectations. In such performance measures as complaints, profitability, employee turnover, safety, and productivity, Pal's has a significant advantage over its competition.

"Pal's Sudden Service," Reprinted with permission from Pal's, Kingsport, TN. www.PalsWeb.com.

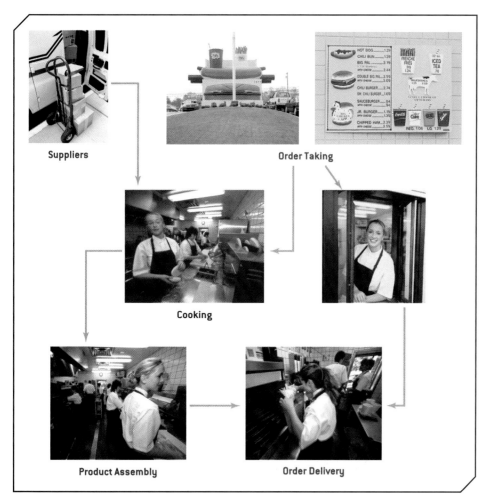

Exhibit 1.9
Pal's Sudden Service Value Chain (*Source:* Pal's Sudden Service)

shown in Exhibit 1.9. Pal's Sudden Service begins with raw materials and suppliers providing items such as meat, lettuce, tomatoes, buns, and packaging; it uses intermediate processes for order taking, cooking, and final assembly; and it ends with order delivery and, it hopes, happy customers. The value chain might even be extended beyond Pal's immediate focus. For instance, there is a process behind planting, growing, harvesting, packing, and distributing lettuce to retail stores. In the next chapter, we will discuss value chains in more detail.

QUANTITATIVE METHODS IN OPERATIONS MANAGEMENT

Learning Objective
To understand the role of quantitative methods in operations management and how models can be used to assist in making OM decisions.

Quantitative methods can facilitate many decisions in OM, for example, forecasting customer demand, allocating capacity, planning production, scheduling work on machines, determining locations for plants and warehouses, transporting finished goods to customers, and staffing and scheduling customer service representatives. Quantitative tools fall into two categories: Some are *problem-specific techniques*, such as methods for finding the best location for a central facility, balancing an assembly line, or sequencing jobs in a process; others are *general tools* useful in solving a variety of problems whose objectives and structures are similar. They include statistical methods and techniques of management science such as linear programming, simulation, and waiting-line theory. These tools have broad applicability. For instance, simulation can be used to analyze proposed designs for a service facility and can also be used to evaluate scheduling policies in a manufacturing plant. These tools are described in the Supplementary Chapters on the CD-ROM accompanying this book. Many of them can be implemented on a spreadsheet, and we use spreadsheets throughout this book when appropriate.

Most quantitative applications are based on a mathematical model—an abstraction of a real scenario. *A* model *is basically a set of assumptions that characterize a decision situation and allow us to draw conclusions about the real situation through some type of analysis.* For example, an airplane designer might test a model of a new airplane wing design in a wind tunnel to learn about its aerodynamic characteristics before attempting to build a real airplane. Similarly, a manager might use a mathematical model to determine what the break-even volume for a production run should be, to predict how long customers will have to wait for a service representative at different times of the day or week, or find the best way to ship finished goods from plants to warehouses at minimum cost.

A model *is basically a set of assumptions that characterize a decision situation and allow us to draw conclusions about the real situation through some type of analysis.*

To illustrate the use of models and quantitative methods in OM, we discuss some simple applications.

A Customer Satisfaction Model

In studying the telephone operations of its customer service call center, a major utility collected sample data on the time that customers stayed on hold and their response to a short satisfaction survey (on a 1–5 scale, 1 being best) at the end of the call. The data are shown in Exhibit 1.10 along with a scatterplot created as an Excel chart. Using the *Add Trendline* option in Excel,* we may develop a linear trendline model for the relationship between Time on Hold and Satisfaction. In this example, the model is

Satisfaction = 0.007(Time on Hold) + 0.9305

---

*After creating an *x-y* scatter plot in Excel, click on the chart to select it, and then select *Add Trendline* from the *Chart* menu. Choose a linear trend line in the *Type* tab, and check the box for *Display equation on chart* in the *Options* tab of the dialog.

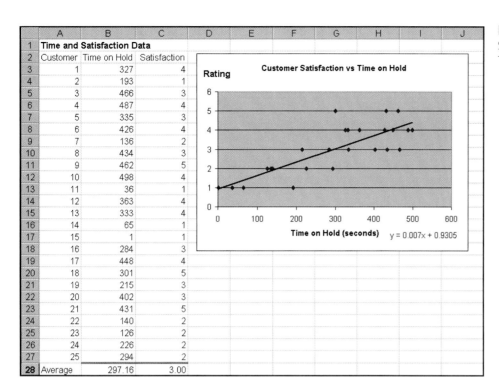

	A	B	C	D	E	F	G	H	I	J
1	Time and Satisfaction Data									
2	Customer	Time on Hold	Satisfaction							
3	1	327	4							
4	2	193	1							
5	3	466	3							
6	4	487	4							
7	5	335	3							
8	6	426	4							
9	7	136	2							
10	8	434	3							
11	9	462	5							
12	10	498	4							
13	11	36	1							
14	12	363	4							
15	13	333	4							
16	14	65	1							
17	15	1	1							
18	16	284	3							
19	17	448	4							
20	18	301	5							
21	19	215	3							
22	20	402	3							
23	21	431	5							
24	22	140	2							
25	23	126	2							
26	24	226	2							
27	25	294	2							
28	Average	297.16	3.00							

Exhibit 1.10

Satisfaction Data and Linear Trend Chart

Although other factors, such as the competence of the phone representatives, influence satisfaction, the model clearly suggests that satisfaction decreases the longer a customer remains on hold. The average time on hold is approximately 300 seconds, and the average satisfaction rating is 3.0. The model suggests that a reduction in the time on hold by 100 seconds will improve the satisfaction rating by 0.7.

To improve customer satisfaction, the manager of the call center operation might change staffing policies to increase the number of customer service representatives during peak call times or exploit technology that informs customers of the anticipated wait time and allows them to hold or defer the call to a later time. In fact, research has shown that customers are willing to wait longer on hold without being dissatisfied if they know the length of the wait in advance.

A Break-Even Model

An industrial electronics manufacturer is considering expanding its production facility to manufacture an electrical component. To assess the value of the expansion, the plant manager has been asked to determine how many units would have to be produced and sold in order to break even. The cost for new equipment and installation is $100,000. Each unit produced would have a variable cost of $12 per unit and sell for $20.

The equation for total cost is

Total cost = Fixed cost + Variable cost

The fixed cost is that portion of total cost that does not vary with the amount produced. If 10,000 units were produced and sold, the total cost would be

Total cost = $100,000 + $12(10,000) = $220,000

The revenue received from selling 10,000 units would be $20(10,000) = $200,000, so at this production level, the firm would incur a loss of $220,000 − $200,000 =

$20,000. However, if 13,000 units were produced and sold, the projected profit would be $20(13,000) − $100,000 − $12(13,000) = $4,000.

The amount of sales at which the net profit is zero—or equivalently, the point where total cost equals total revenue—is called the **break-even point.** We can find the break-even point by developing a simple mathematical model. Let x be the sales volume at the break-even point. Then,

Total cost = 100,000 + 12x
Total revenue = 20x

Setting the total revenue equal to total cost we have

20x = 100,000 + 12x

and hence

x = 12,500

If sales are less than 12,500 units, the firm will incur a loss; if sales are more than 12,500, it will realize a profit. Such information, when combined with sales forecasts, can assist the manager in deciding whether or not to pursue the expansion.

Exhibit 1.11 shows a spreadsheet model for this situation. An Excel data table, shown in columns D and E, provides a simple way of identifying the break-even point. We can also conduct simple sensitivity analyses to investigate the impact of changes in the model data inputs on the result. For example, Exhibit 1.12 shows another Excel data table in which the variable cost is changed at the break-even level of 12,500 units. If the plant manager can lower the variable cost through some type of operations improvements, we can easily see the effect on profitability. However, if costs rise, then the firm will incur a loss.

Using Models in OM

Using powerful software like Microsoft Excel, you can develop and use a variety of models to assist you in making key OM decisions. Of course, many realistic models in operations management are much more complex than these examples. Although you may not always be developing such complex models yourself, it is important to understand how they can be used, how to interpret the results, and the value they provide in making good decisions.

Exhibit 1.12
Sensitivity Analysis of Variable Cost for the Break-Even Model

	G	H
1	Sensitivity Analysis	
2	Variable Cost	$ -
3	$ 10.00	$ 25,000.00
4	$ 10.25	$ 21,875.00
5	$ 10.50	$ 18,750.00
6	$ 10.75	$ 15,625.00
7	$ 11.00	$ 12,500.00
8	$ 11.25	$ 9,375.00
9	$ 11.50	$ 6,250.00
10	$ 11.75	$ 3,125.00
11	$ 12.00	$ -
12	$ 12.25	$ (3,125.00)
13	$ 12.50	$ (6,250.00)
14	$ 12.75	$ (9,375.00)
15	$ 13.00	$(12,500.00)
16	$ 13.25	$(15,625.00)
17	$ 13.50	$(18,750.00)
18	$ 13.75	$(21,875.00)
19	$ 14.00	$(25,000.00)

Exhibit 1.11
Spreadsheet Model for Break-Even Analysis (Break Even Model.xls)

	A	B	C	D	E
1	Break Even Model				Profit
2				Sales Volume	$ -
3	Fixed cost	$ 100,000		10000	$(20,000.00)
4	Variable cost	$ 12		10500	$(16,000.00)
5	Selling price	$ 20		11000	$(12,000.00)
6	Sales Volume	12,500		11500	$ (8,000.00)
7				12000	$ (4,000.00)
8	Total Cost	$ 250,000		12500	$ -
9	Total Revenue	$ 250,000		13000	$ 4,000.00
10	Total Profit	$ -		13500	$ 8,000.00
11				14000	$ 12,000.00
12				14500	$ 16,000.00
13				15000	$ 20,000.00

From a practical standpoint, most models have a number of implicit assumptions, and it is important to understand them when using a model. For example, an assumption in break-even analysis is that time is not a critical variable. At the very least, revenues and costs are assumed to occur simultaneously. In reality, costs are incurred well in advance of their associated revenues. Not having sufficient working capital to maintain a firm until it earns a steady flow of revenues is a very common cause of failure for new businesses. The model also assumes that costs and prices are constant over time. That is rarely true. Not only may the costs of inputs and the price of the product change over time but they may change by disproportionate amounts so that the cost/price relationships are altered.

Another assumption is that neither unit variable costs nor unit prices vary with the quantity produced or sold. Quantity discounts are common in all industries, and the price may be adjusted for many other buyer concessions, such as rapid payment or delayed delivery. Likewise, fixed costs may not be truly fixed over the entire range of output. If the output is low, the firm will trim as many of its fixed charges as possible.

The model also assumes that facilities and equipment have infinite capacity. Actually, as the output increases, the production system's capacity is reached and additional facilities are needed. They produce sudden increases in fixed costs. Finally, the assumption of constant variable and fixed costs per unit implies that a single technology is used over the entire range of output. As output increases or decreases, the typical firm may be forced to change to a different technology. In such cases, both fixed and variable costs are changed.

We see that even in a very simple model such as break-even analysis, a decision maker must draw upon considerable experience and judgment in interpreting the answers and incorporating factors that cannot be quantified. Thus, caution must be exercised in using quantitative decision tools. Simple models are often easier to gain insights from, and such insights are much easier to explain to senior management. Models can be extremely useful when they are properly applied, as we shall see throughout this book.

OPERATIONS MANAGEMENT: A HISTORY OF CHANGE AND CHALLENGE

Learning Objective
To be able to identify the key themes in OM that have evolved over the last half-century and understand their impact on goods, services, and operations.

In the last century, operations management has changed more than any other functional area of business and has become the most important factor in competitiveness. That is one of the reasons why every business student needs a basic understanding of the field. Exhibit 1.13 is a chronology of major themes that have changed the scope and direction of operations management over the last half century. To better understand the challenges facing modern business and the role of OM in meeting them, let us briefly trace the history and evolution of these themes.

A Focus on Efficiency

Contemporary OM has its roots in the Industrial Revolution that occurred during the late eighteenth and early nineteenth centuries in England. Until that time, goods had been produced in small shops by artisans and their apprentices without the aid of mechanical equipment. The "production system" was not complex. Workers were autonomous and self-employed, with deep knowledge of their work and broad skills enabling them to do a job from start to finish. During the Industrial Revolution, however, many new inventions came into being that allowed goods to be manufactured with greater ease and speed. The inventions reduced the need for individual artisans and led to the development of modern factories.

Exhibit 1.13

Five Eras of Operations
Management

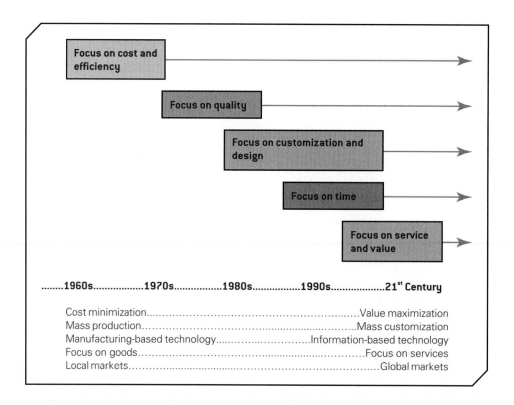

Focus on cost and efficiency

Focus on quality

Focus on customization and design

Focus on time

Focus on service and value

........1960s...............1970s................1980s...............1990s..................21ˢᵗ Century

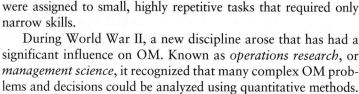

Cost minimization..Value maximization
Mass production...Mass customization
Manufacturing-based technology...........................Information-based technology
Focus on goods..Focus on services
Local markets...Global markets

The concept of interchangeable parts, introduced by Eli Whitney in 1798, paved the way for modern manufacturing. Factories developed into complex systems of interrelated processes that required different methods of managing. Henry Ford put British economist Adam Smith's concept of the division of labor—different workers performing different tasks rather than one worker acquiring the skills necessary to perform the entire job—into practice by introducing the modern assembly line in the early 1900s. That development greatly reduced the costs of manufacturing, paving the way for mass production and making a wide variety of products affordable to the average consumer. Managers drew upon other philosophies, such as Frederick W. Taylor's "science of management," which was based on observation, measurement and analysis of work, improvement in work methods, and economic incentives. His philosophy changed the nature of work dramatically, as workers were assigned to small, highly repetitive tasks that required only narrow skills.

During World War II, a new discipline arose that has had a significant influence on OM. Known as *operations research*, or *management science*, it recognized that many complex OM problems and decisions could be analyzed using quantitative methods. As computing technology evolved at the same time, management science evolved into a powerful set of tools.

During the years following World War II, the United States was in a dominant position in manufacturing. The focus at the time was on goods production, goods-production technology, local markets, and building the country's infrastructure. Televisions, automobiles, appliances, houses, food, highways, and water treatment plants were examples of the mass production industries of the day. Operations managers, grounded in the principles of Taylor, concentrated primarily on efficiency and quantity of production, which led to a higher level of specialization and refinement in job tasks.

As international trade grew in the 1960s, the emphasis on operations efficiency and cost reduction increased. Many companies moved their factories to low-wage countries. Managers became enamored of computers, robots, and other forms of technology. Advanced technology continues to revolutionize and improve production, but in the 1960s and 1970s technology was viewed primarily as a method of reducing costs and distracted managers from the important goal of improving the quality of goods and services and the processes that create them. American business was soon to face a rude awakening.

The Quality Revolution

As Japan was rebuilding from the devastation of World War II, Japanese industry leaned heavily on two U.S. consultants, W. Edwards Deming and Joseph Juran. Deming and Juran told Japanese executives that continual improvement of quality would open world markets, free up capacity, and improve their economy. The Japanese eagerly embraced that message. They embarked on a massive effort to train the work force, using statistical tools developed at Western Electric and other innovative management tools, to identify causes of quality problems and fix them. They made steady progress in reducing defects and paid careful attention to what consumers wanted. Those efforts continued at a relentless pace until, by the mid-1970s, the world discovered that Japanese goods had fewer defects, were more reliable, and better met consumer needs than American goods. As a result, Japanese firms captured major shares of world markets in many different industries such as automobiles and electronics.

Facing a crisis, U.S. business began to take notice. The "quality revolution" began in the United States in 1980 when NBC televised a program entitled "If Japan Can . . . Why Can't We?" featuring W. Edwards Deming and his role in transforming Japanese industry. As a result of that program, Ford Motor Company, and then many other companies, sought to understand Deming's message and transform their management by emphasizing quality. Quality became an obsession with top managers of nearly every major company and the impact continues to this day. In 1987, the U.S. government established the Malcolm Baldrige National Quality Award to focus national attention on quality. The Baldrige program has been instrumental in bringing quality to the attention of top management.

Competing Through Customization and Design

As the goals of low cost and high product quality became "givens," companies began to emphasize innovative designs and product features to gain a competitive edge. Quality meant much more than simply defect reduction—quality meant offering consumers new and innovative products that not only met their expectations but also surprised and delighted them.

Inflexible mass-production methods that produced high volumes of standardized goods and services using unskilled or semiskilled workers and expensive single-purpose equipment, though very efficient and cost-effective, were inadequate for the new goals of increased good and service variety and continual product improvement. The operating system had to change. New types of manufacturing systems—called *lean production systems*—emerged in Japan that enabled companies to manufacture products better, cheaper, and faster than their competitors while facilitating innovation and increased product variety. Today's lean production systems employ multiskilled workers, cross-functional teams, integrated communications, supplier partnerships, and highly flexible, increasingly automated machines to produce wide varieties of products. They focus on effective use of resources, elimination of waste, and continuous improvement, thereby reducing costs and defects. Such systems combine the best features of old-style craft shops and early twentieth-century mass production: the ability to produce a wide variety of customized products delivered with short lead times. Incorporating product innovation with price, quality, and flexibility requires a coordinated effort among all facets of an organization, particularly marketing, finance, and operations.

In recent years, information technology has driven manufacturing capability to new heights. "Agile manufacturing" blends automation and computing technology, allowing companies to customize and produce single quantities of products at mass-production speeds using complex, highly automated, computer-controlled systems that produce a large variety of parts without human intervention.

Time-Based Competition

Quick response is one outcome of lean production. Companies that do not respond quickly to changing customer needs will lose out to competitors that do. An example of quick response is the production of the custom-designed Motorola pager, which is completed within 80 minutes and often can be delivered to the customer the same day. As information technology matured, time became an important source of competitive advantage. Quick response is achieved by continually improving and reengineering processes, that is, fundamentally rethinking and redesigning processes to achieve dramatic improvements in cost, quality, speed, and service. That task includes developing products faster than competitors, speeding ordering and delivery processes, rapidly responding to changes in customers' needs, and improving the flow of paperwork.

The Service Revolution

While the goods-producing industries were getting all the attention in the business community, the popular press, and in business school curricula, service industries were quietly growing and creating many new jobs in the U.S. economy. In 1955, about 50 percent of the U.S. work force was employed in goods-producing industries and 50 percent in service-providing industries. Today, about four of every five jobs are in services.

Exhibit 1.14 documents the structure of the U.S. economy and where people work. This aggregate mix between goods-producing and service-providing industries is forecast to change from 79.8 percent service and 20.2 percent goods in 2001 to 81.8 percent service and 18.2 percent goods in 2008. There are many interesting industry comparisons in Exhibit 1.14, but let's point out just a few. Manufacturing, for example, is expected to account for 11.6 percent of total U.S. employment by 2008, or about 1 in 10 jobs. In 2008, state and local government jobs are expected to be 11.9 percent of total jobs, that is, about the same percent as manufacturing. Business and health services are forecast to grow substantially from 2001 to 2008. Many other countries, such as France and the United Kingdom, also have a high percentage of total jobs in the service sector.

In addition, estimates are that at least 50 percent of the jobs in goods-producing industries are service and information related, such as human resource management, accounting, financial, legal, advertising, purchasing, engineering, and so on. Thus, in 2001, about 90 percent of the jobs in the U.S. economy were service-providing industries [$79.8 + .5 \times 20.2\% = 89.9\%$]. This means that if you are employed in the United States, you will most likely work in a service- or information-related field. Because of these statistics, a principal emphasis in this book is on services—either on service-providing industries such as health care and banking or on how services complement the sale of goods in goods-producing industries such as machine tools and computers, and provide higher value to customers.

Exhibit 1.14
U.S. 2001 Employment and
Projected Change by Major
Industry

U.S. Industry	Percent of Total Employment in 2001	Estimated Percent of Total Employment in 2008
Goods-Producing Sector		
Construction	4.1%	4.1%
Agriculture	2.4	2.2
Mining	0.4	0.3
Fishing, Forestry, Hunting, and Misc.	0.1	0.1
Manufacturing	13.1	11.6
Durable Goods*	7.9	7.0
Nondurable Goods**	5.3	4.6
Total	20.2%	18.2%
Service-Providing Sector		
Transportation	3.2%	3.0%
Communication and Public Utilities	1.8	1.7
Wholesale Trade	5.0	4.5
Finance, Insurance, and Real Estate	5.3	5.2
Agricultural Services	0.6	0.7
Hotels and Lodging	1.3	1.5
Personal Services	0.9	1.0
Business Services	6.9	8.0
Auto Repair and Parking	0.9	1.1
Motion Pictures	0.4	0.5
Amusement and Recreation Services	1.2	1.4
Health Services	7.4	8.6
Legal Services	0.7	0.8
Education Services	1.9	2.2
Child Care and Other Services	2.2	2.6
Membership Organizations	1.8	2.1
Museums and Zoological Gardens	0.1	0.1
Engineering, Architectural, and Management Services	2.6	3.1
Retail Trade and Services	15.9	15.7
Federal Government Services	1.9	1.6
State and Local Government Services	12.2	11.9
Miscellaneous Services	5.5	4.6
Total	79.8%	81.8%
Grand Total	100.0%	100.0%

*Durable goods are items such as instruments, vehicles, aircraft, computer and office equipment, machinery, furniture, glass, metals, and appliances.
**Nondurable goods are items such as textiles, apparel, paper, food, coal, oil, leather, plastics, chemicals, and books.
Source: United States Bureau of Labor Statistics, October 2001, http://www.bls.gov/EMP

However, manufacturing is by no means dead.[12] According to 1998 figures from the United Nations Industrial Development Organization, the value of goods manufactured annually in America is more than 50 percent greater than in Japan and a third larger than the combined output of France, Germany, and Britain. Since the early 1990s, no major industrial nation's output has grown faster. Although manufacturing employs a declining share of the U.S. working population, productivity is up. Output per hour worked in American companies is higher than that of other nations. About 70 percent of Hondas and Toyotas sold in the United States are made by American workers, and the BMW Z-4 sports car is produced in South Carolina. And a strong manufacturing sector is essential for national defense.

The Impacts of Technology and Globalization

Without a doubt, technology has been one of the most important influences on the growth and development of OM during the second half of the twentieth century. Microprocessors have become ubiquitous in most consumer products and industrial processes. Advances in design and fabrication of goods as well as advances in information technology to enhance services have provided the ability to develop products that one could only dream of a few decades ago. They also enable managers to more effectively manage and control extremely complex operations. We will discuss the impact of technology further in Chapter 5.

Also, globalization has changed the way companies do business and must manage their operations. With advances in communications and transportation, we have passed from the era of huge regional factories with large labor forces and tight community ties to an era of the "borderless marketplace." No longer are "American" or "Japanese" products manufactured exclusively in America or Japan. The Mazda Miata, for example, was designed in California, financed in Tokyo and New York, tested in England, assembled in Michigan and Mexico, and built with components designed in New Jersey and produced in Japan. Meshing different cultures and norms, customer interests and values, government regulations, and the like simply makes OM an increasingly challenging discipline.

Modern Challenges

Consumers' expectations have risen dramatically. They demand an increasing variety of products with new and improved features that meet their changing needs. They expect products that are defect-free, have high performance, are reliable and durable, and are easy to repair. They also expect rapid and excellent service for the products they buy. For the services they buy, customers expect short waiting and processing times, availability when needed, courteous treatment from employees, consistency, accessibility and convenience, accuracy, and responsiveness to unexpected problems. Companies must now compete on all these dimensions.

In addition to increased customer expectations, today's workers are different; they demand increasing levels of empowerment and more meaningful work. Technology is different; computers and automation have dramatically changed the nature of work, requiring constant learning and more abstract thinking and on-the-spot decision-making skills. Service plays a much greater role within organizations as well as for the consumer. Finally, the environment is different; we live in a global business environment without boundaries.

One example that clearly shows the importance of good operations management and the challenges that still remain is the automobile industry. The automotive-producing value chain is a complex organization of goods, services, and processes that has a significant impact on the U.S. and world economies. When former General Motors CEO Jack Smith visited Japan in the early 1980s to study Toyota's stamping and assembly operations, he discovered that GM needed twice as many people to build the same number of cars.[13] The company's executive committee, however, dismissed his findings and the company continued doing things as it had in the past, eventually losing its market leadership. Smith and his successor worked at reshaping GM to "run common and lean" through such actions as reducing inefficiencies caused by unique parts and processes—it took five months to change a dealership franchise—simplifying purchasing operations, modernizing factories, installing common computer systems, and eliminating internally competitive marketing processes. However, as *Fortune* magazine noted, "GM still needs to move faster and smarter. One lesson it hasn't learned from Toyota is how to consistently develop successful new models that share common components." Every organization faces similar challenges, and a solid understanding of operations management is vital to every successful manager in the future.

SOLVED PROBLEMS

SOLVED PROBLEM #1

a. Draw a customer benefit package (CBP) for being a member of a "fitness and health club."

b. Make a list of example processes that create and deliver each good or service in the CBP you selected, and briefly describe process procedures and issues.

Solution:

a. One example might be

b. • Food ordering and supply, preparation, delivery, and clean-up processes define the *food service value chain*. For example, how does the food service in the health club ensure accurate and timely ordering of all raw materials necessary to make the food served to customers? How does it make

the chicken salad? Does it throw away all food at the end of the day to ensure fresh food the next day? What are the goods and service quality standards?

• The *child care process* includes rigorous procedures for checking your kid(s) in and out of the child care area. Should the child care process administer medicines to the children? What activities are planned for the kids throughout the day? What should be the qualifications of the caregivers?

• The *swimming lesson process* includes a sign-up phase, potential participant medical examination phase, and a series of classes taught by certified swimming instructors who are trained in emergency services such as CPR. How should we segment the swimming class age groups (target markets)? Should we offer a swimming aerobics class for senior citizens? How does the health club keep people safe yet teach them to swim? What is the lesson plan for each day?

These are a few examples of the processes necessary to design, manage, and operate a successful fitness and health club. Location (customer convenience), super-clean facilities, and a friendly professional staff are probably the top three attributes of a successful health club.

SOLVED PROBLEM #2

An insurance company did an audit of ten customer accounts that were experiencing billing errors. The insurance process to create an accurate bill had several problems, such as the poor quality of its input information and computer keying errors. Management called these customers and asked them to answer a few survey questions over the telephone. The customer satisfaction ratings and number of billing errors during the past year are as follows:

Customer Satisfaction Rating	Average Number of Billing Errors
78	3.2
90	2.1
95	1.4
88	1.3
80	2.7
86	1.9
92	2.3
94	1.1
97	1.6
89	2.9

Is there a performance relationship between customer satisfaction and billing errors? If so, explain it. What do these data suggest that this company should think about?

The data plot shows a significant negative trend, that is, as billing errors decrease customer satisfaction increases. Using the correlation function in Microsoft Excel, we

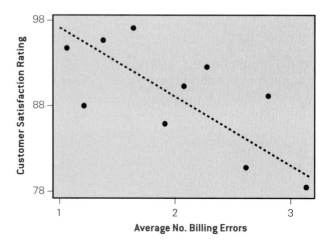

can compute the correlation between customer satis-faction rating and billing errors as $-.716$ to more for-mally quantify this relationship.

Because customer loyalty and retention are adversely affected by the billing process, a support service, it needs to be improved and errors driven to zero. Failure to do so could affect revenue from the primary service—insurance premiums. The company should investigate why the errors are occurring and redesign the process, improve employee training, or introduce better tech-nology as necessary.

SOLVED PROBLEM #3

A not-for-profit organization receives a subsidy of $100,000 per year from the city. The unit revenue for the services it provides is $0.75. The unit variable cost is $1.00, and the annual fixed costs are $50,000.

a. Up to what level will the operations be economical?

b. If the city is willing to increase its subsidy by 25 per-cent, how much additional service can the organi-zation provide if unit revenue is lowered to $0.65?

Solution:

a. Let x be number of units of service provided: Total revenue = $100,000 + $0.75x$; Total cost = $50,000 + $1x$. Setting total revenue equal to total cost, we have $100,000 + $0.75x = $50,000 + $1x$. Solving for x yields $50,000 = $.25x$, or $x = 200,000$ units.

b. In this case, the total revenue would be $125,000 + $0.65x$. Again setting total revenue equal to total cost, we have $125,000 + $0.65x = $50,000 + $1x$. Solving for x yields $x = 214,286$ (rounded), which is about a 7 percent increase in the services the organization can provide.

KEY TERMS AND CONCEPTS

Break-even analysis
Break-even point
Cost minimization/value maximization
Customer benefit package (CBP)
   Peripheral good or service
   Primary good or service
Durable good
Eras of OM
   Cost and efficiency
   Customization and design
   Quality
   Service
   Time
Four functions of management
   Controlling
   Directing
   Organizing
   Planning
General management processes
Good

Local/global markets
Make-or-buy decision
Manufacturing/information-based technology
Mass production/mass customization
Model
Moment of truth
Nondurable good
Operations management
Process
Service
Service encounter
Service management
Structure of U.S. economy—service jobs
Supply chains
Support processes
Transformation process
Trend lines
Value chains
Value creation processes

QUESTIONS FOR REVIEW AND DISCUSSION

1. Explain how operations management activities affect the customer experiences described in the anecdotes at the beginning of this chapter. What "moments of truth" did the customers encounter? In the second situation, what might have been done differently?

2. Describe a customer experience you have personally encountered where the good or service or both were unsatisfactory (for example, defective product, errors, mistakes, poor service, service upsets, and so on). How might the organization have handled it better?

3. Summarize the key activities that comprise the discipline of operations management.

4. Describe how you apply the management functions of planning, organizing, directing, and controlling in your daily life. What types of activities do you perform that are similar to OM activities performed in a business?

5. Why are operations management principles and methods important to managers of activities in such traditional functional areas as accounting, marketing, and finance (for instance, an audit supervisor, sales manager, or loan officer)?

6. Describe how you have used OM, either directly or indirectly, in any recent work experience or student organization activity.

7. What value can good practice of operations management principles provide to an organization? How can it help the personal development of every manager?

8. Define a good and a service. What is the difference between a durable and nondurable good?

9. Explain the key differences between goods and services. What implications do these differences have for organizations trying to provide both goods and services to customers in a balanced CBP? Do you see any conflicts in a goods-producing versus service-providing way of thinking?

10. What do we mean by a *service encounter*? How does this differ from the concept of *moment of truth*?

11. Explain why a bank teller, nurse, or flight attendant must have service management skills. How do the required skills differ for someone working in a factory? What are the implications for hiring criteria and training?

12. What is a *customer benefit package*? Explain its major components, and provide some examples of a CBP with a primary good and a primary service different from those given in this chapter.

13. Give some examples similar to those in Exhibit 1.3, and explain the degree of goods and services content for these examples.

14. What is a process? Explain the difference between value creation, support, and general management processes. Why are processes important in OM?

15. Explain why process thinking is fundamentally different from viewing an organization by functions (as in an organizational chart). What challenges does process thinking pose for managers of traditional functional departments?

16. What is a transformation process? Explain how a college curriculum might be regarded as a transformation process.

17. One of our students, who had worked for Taco Bell, related a story of how his particular store developed a "60-second, 10-pack club" as an improvement initiative and training tool. The goal was to make a 10-pack of tacos in a minute or less, each made and wrapped correctly, and the total within 1 ounce of the correct weight. Employees received recognition and free meals for a day. Employees strove to become a part of this club, and more importantly, service times dropped dramatically. Techniques similar to those used to improve the taco-making process were used to improve other products. Explain how this anecdote relates to process thinking. What would the employees have to do to become a part of the club?

18. What is a value chain and why is it important to understand and study it?

19. What is the role of models and quantitative methods in OM? How can they help operations managers make better decisions?

20. Briefly review the evolution of operations management. What key changes have occurred over the years, and what factors led to these changes?

21. Given the discussion surrounding Exhibit 1.13 on the Five Eras of Operations Management, do you think it is possible to simultaneously minimize costs and time and maximize quality, service, and customization? Explain.

22. Do a quick survey to find out what percentage of your classmates think they will work or do work in the goods-producing versus service-providing sectors of their country's economy. What did you learn? What are the implications for your education and training?

PROBLEMS AND ACTIVITIES

1. Define and draw the bundle of goods and services for the State University customer episode at the beginning of this chapter. List the processes that create each good or service. How many processes on the list provide outstanding goods or services at your school?

2. Draw the customer benefit package (CBP) for one of the items listed here, and explain how your CBP provides value to the customer. Make a list of the processes that you think would be necessary to create and deliver each good or service in the CBP you selected, and briefly describe issues that must be considered in designing these processes.
   - a mid-priced automobile such as a Ford Taurus, Toyota Camry, or Honda Accord
   - playing golf at a public course
   - a bar of soap
   - an airline flight from San Diego to Baltimore
   - a digital camera with personal computer software
   - a new personal computer
   - a credit card
   - a meal at a fast-food restaurant
   - a lawn mower
   - your last will and testament
   - a nursing home for the elderly
   - heart bypass surgery
   - a wireless mobile telephone
   - a one-night stay in a low-budget hotel room
   - a one-night stay in a luxury five-star hotel and conference center

3. Investigate the web sites of some major companies like Xerox, Procter & Gamble, Dell, and so on. List the goods and services they offer. How would you define their customer benefit packages?

4. Review the OM Spotlight for Pal's Sudden Service and find Pal's web site. Based on this information, describe all the OM activities that occur in a typical day at Pal's.

5. Search the web for "plant tours." Write a paper describing the operations in one of the companies you found.

6. Write a brief report on the structure of the agriculture, manufacturing, and service economics in two or three countries of interest to you and compare to the structure of the U.S. economy as described in Exhibit 1.14.

7. The physics laboratory is trying to decide whether it should rent or purchase a copier machine. The cost of renting a machine would be $200 per year including all service calls plus $0.04 (4 cents) per page copied. The cost of purchasing a machine would be $600 plus $50 per year for a service contract in case the machine breaks down. There is no variable cost associated with purchasing the machine. The laboratory will have to purchase its own paper regardless of whether it rents or purchases the copier machine. For what quantities of copies will it be advantageous to rent the machine instead of purchasing it? Explain.

8. A manager of a firm that produces computer hard drives is planning to lease a new automated inspection system. The manager believes the new system will be more accurate than the current inspection process. The relevant information is provided here.

   Current System
   Annual fixed cost = $40,000
   Inspection variable cost per unit = $10 per unit

   New System
   Annual fixed cost = $200,000
   Inspection variable cost per unit = $2 per unit

   a. Suppose annual demand is 17,000 units. Should the firm lease the new inspection system?
   b. Assume the preceding cost factors have not changed. A marketing representative of NEW-SPEC, a firm that specializes in providing inspection processes for other firms, approached the hard drive manufacturer and offered to inspect parts for $12 each with no fixed cost. Demand for the upcoming year is forecast to be 16,000 units. Should the manufacturer accept the offer? If *yes*, how much will it save by hiring NEW-SPEC instead of doing in-house inspection? If *no*, what is the maximum price per unit it should be willing to pay?

CASES

STONER CREEK SHOWCASE

David Paris, the vice president of manufacturing, always thought that Mondays were wonderful and a fresh start to the week. However, he had a strange phone call that morning from Cindy Cave, the vice president of marketing.

"Hi David, this is Cindy."

"Hi Cindy, it sure is a beautiful day," replied David.

"Yes, you're right but that's not why I'm calling. Do you know, David, that customers are calling me because they can't install our showcases at the job sites," responded Cave. "The local contractors are not familiar with our cases and refrigeration equipment and they say we often ship the cases with missing parts. We are going to lose customers!"

"O.K., I'll get right on it and send someone to the job site," Paris said and hung up the telephone.

Once the conversation was over, Paris contacted a regional representative and asked him to visit the job site and report back to Cave. David thought he should review some of his production processes and the quality performance reports. Nevertheless, Cave felt that her responsibility as V.P. of marketing was limited compared to the problem facing the firm.

Company Background

The Cave family founded Stoner Creek Showcase in 1940. Cindy Cave's dad, Bill Cave, was the president of the company. In the mid-1990s, the family-led company had grown to become one of the leading manufacturers of showcases, wall systems, and food merchandising units in the United States. The company operated two plants, one in Ohio and one in Kentucky, to manufacture its array of products. The company's stated mission was "to be a highly respected, family owned, professionally managed, ethical enterprise engaged in marketing and manufacturing quality store fixtures." Stoner Creek showcases were the premier store fixtures in the industry and its showcase quality, on-time delivery to the customer's job site, and innovative designs were typical of the company.

In order to accomplish its goal of excellence, Stoner Creek Showcase arranged its work crew in customer-oriented teams. Each customer first team consisted of five associates: an account executive, who would investigate the customer's needs, determine the most cost-efficient solution, and arrange payment or financing of the customer's order; a sales representative, who would provide all the information required

to effectively administer the order and serve as a single company contact point for the customer; an engineer, who would translate the customer's needs into a customized case and equipment design and manufacturing plan; a product inventory control associate, who would ensure the availability of proper materials to fill the order to the customer's specification; and a shop worker, who would follow the order through the factory and point out critical details of the customer's order to the plant.

The Market

Currently, Stoner Creek Showcase was segmenting the market into product categories instead of using a customer's location or revenue or order size to segment the market. The three target market segments were: supermarket display cases, supermarket accessibles, and glass showcases. Usually, a showcase was defined with a "model #," which corresponded to the model series, the interior color, the temperature application, the type of case, the length, and the height. Each model # represented a corresponding fixed price, and extra features and their associated costs were added to the base price. The firm's catalogue covered a basic set of showcases, but about one-half of sales were customized by features such as length, height, width, glass viewing areas, and type of refrigeration equipment required.

In order to match up with those target market categories, Stoner Creek identified three trade channels: food stores, mass merchandisers, and specialty stores. Food stores accounted for 38 percent of total revenue and included firms like American Stores, A&P, Big Bear, Kroger, Marsh, and Weiss Markets. Mass merchandisers accounted for 34 percent of total revenue and included firms like Kmart, Meijer, Montgomery Ward, Sears, Target, and Wal-Mart. Specialty stores accounted for 25 percent of total revenues and included stores such as Edison Brothers, The Gap, Hallmark, Limited, Schottensteins, TJ Maxx/Marshall's, and United Retail. The remaining 3 percent of total revenue represented many diverse and small Mom and Pop groceries and specialty stores.

Installation Service

Stoner Creek Showcase prided itself on offering customer-friendly service from point of first contact with the company until the finished product was shipped to the job site. However, it debated whether this vision of its business was complete. According to the opinion of company executives, for example, installation at the customer's site had not been an issue until recently because installation of the showcases was considered relatively straightforward, and certainly within the realm of expertise of the local installers. It had been assumed that the region's salesperson could handle the oversight of installing the showcases in the customer's stores. Furthermore, some customers such as Wal-Mart often had their own store display experts and installation crews and did not need, nor welcome, additional service from Stoner Creek Showcase.

Small showcases were shipped as complete units but the larger showcases had to be shipped as separate units. A typical large showcase consisted of about ten major parts that were shipped out individually. There were no detailed installation directions included causing installation to be unduly long and complicated. Sometimes cases would not work correctly simply because packaged elements had been switched with other similar elements prior to shipping. Stoner Creek often had to reship parts free of charge.

Because the company does not track customer complaints by type, Paris had to ask Cave to get the salespersons to collect these data. However, there was no central unit in the company where customer complaints could be accumulated, analyzed, and reported. Although Stoner Creek was prompt to provide substitute parts whenever they were needed and installation directions over the telephone, its usual response to installation problems was to contact directly the local crew that had been responsible for the installation of the showcases. These local crews were not affiliated with Stoner Creek Showcase in any way.

Case Questions

As a consultant to Stoner Creek Showcase, please answer the following questions as best you can given the case information.

1. What are the problems facing Stoner Creek Showcase?

2. How would you define Stoner Creek's current mission and strategy? What if they add installation service?

3. Draw the value chain using three stages and briefly describe each stage.

4. Define customer wants and needs, customer benefit package features, and associated processes for the firm's business (see Exhibits 1.5 and 1.6).

5. Should the company offer installation services? If not, why? If so, how would you justify it? What does a company have to excel at operationally to offer outstanding installation services?

BONNIE BLAINE, DIRECTOR OF HOSPITAL OPERATIONS

"The kid almost died! He's a diabetic! How did that patient get the wrong food tray?" said Bonnie Blaine, director of hospital operations, to Drew Owensboro, the director of dietary services. Bonnie Blaine, a woman in her early fifties, had worked in almost every area of the hospital. By going to school in the evenings for three years, she had earned a Master's in business administration. Owensboro had worked in the hospital for 19 years and had a high school education.

"Bonnie, I don't know! I'll try to find out but it may be impossible. The dietary department is really a very complex operation and it's very difficult to audit or trace anything," Owensboro said in frustration. "Drew, I've got enough problems trying to contain hospital costs without having to worry about patient lawsuits due to poor quality control on our part," Blaine continued. "The kid's family and family doctor are furious! Your employees are all blaming one another, but no one is really doing anything about it. Now fix it or maybe I'll have to get someone else in here to do the job," Blaine said as she turned to answer the telephone.

The Hospital's Dietary Department

The dietary department provides food services to three basic groups: patients, employees, and visitors. The greatest demand for food services comes from the patients, and because of the many different diet requirements which must be fulfilled, this can be rather complex. Each day the patient fills out their required dietetic menu for all three meals for the following day and chooses from several different food items in each food group (entree, vegetable, fruit, dessert, beverage). Since the average patient stay is five days, the dietary department offers different daily menus for two weeks and then repeats the menu selection.

The dietary department, as shown in Exhibit 1.15, is a large department with a total of 124 full-time equivalent (FTE) employees, assuming two part-time employees equals one full-time position. The department has 10 managers (that is, directors, supervisors), 8 clinical dieticians, 9 administrative dieticians (7 of which are also managers), 89 full-time employees, and 30 part-time employees. The 89 direct full-time employees have an average education level of 10.8 years. The annual average salary for a part-time employee is $15,000, full-time food service employees excluding cooks earn $28,000, and clerk employees earn $31,000. Benefits for full-time employees average an additional 20 percent of their annual salary.

Clerical Support in Patient Services

Eight full-time employees in the patient services area fill out diets for each patient, menus for tomorrow's meals, and last-minute changes for today's diets and menus. Central control is necessary due to the myriad of changes, which take place each day because of surgery, discharges, new admittances, or doctor-prescribed diet changes.

The clerks assemble the diets by room and floor and check to see that all menus are properly filled out. When patients are discharged, the clerks pull the patient's diet history from the room number of the floor and file it with the medical records. The prescribed diets of new admittances are to be checked by the clinical nutritionist in charge of the floor, but in the case of emergencies, the clerk calls the floor and speaks to the head nurse about what type of diet is to be presented. Besides the obvious patient health issues with regard to the accuracy of the prescribed diets, the patient and doctor expect the dietary department to "provide timely, neat meals with no errors."

Before each meal, the clerk's office gives the shift supervisor of tray assembly and production the updated list of menus for each patient's room. The clerks sequence the room numbers by floor for easy tray production and delivery. The clerks remain in the office during the day answering phones and messages about diet and menu changes. After each meal, the clerk's office distributes a patient census in terms of trays actually served. Then the process begins all over again for the next meal. Due to the short time between meals, some clerks are working on, say, the breakfast meal while others are working on the lunch meal.

Food Production

The kitchen and patient tray assembly lines are located in the basement of the hospital. The kitchen is a beehive of activity for about 18 hours a day. The regular cooks, special diet cooks, kitchen workers, dieticians, and clerks from patient services are constantly visiting or calling the kitchen concerning patient meals. Meanwhile, food constantly arrives at the loading docks that had been ordered from the hospital's purchasing department or the hospital's food service manager.

Employees are assigned to one of three basic shifts—a breakfast shift that begins at 4 A.M., a lunch shift that arrives at staggered times from 6 A.M. until noon, and a dinner shift that begins at 3:30 P.M. Part-time employees help out during peak demand periods and when full-time employees are absent.

Purchasing

The dietary department obtains its food and supplies from several sources. Bulk items are stored in the hospital's central warehouse and are delivered once a week. Many frozen items are delivered weekly from the state contracts warehouse. The remaining supplies, whether refrigerated, nonrefrigerated, or frozen, are delivered by private vendors at various frequencies during the week.

The hospital food service manager has five employees plus himself (see Exhibit 1.15) to coordinate the incoming food and supply orders. Dietary personnel are not responsible for the transportation of goods. However, they are responsible for receiving and accepting high-quality goods and maintaining that quality through the internal storage of food at the hospital.

Patient Tray Assembly

The food is assembled on each patient tray on a large rotating oval track. Twelve employees staff the tray assembly line. The first position on the tray assembly line is the "caller," who places the patient's menu on a tray and puts the tray on a carrier with the necessary condiments. The second position puts the salad (tossed fruit, macaroni, cottage cheese, tuna, potato, chicken, bean, and chef's salad) and the ordered salad dressing on each tray. The third position puts the breads (white, wheat, rye) and butter on the tray along with jelly. The fourth position is responsible for the ordered cold beverage (soft drink, milk, buttermilk, orange juice, and so on).

Position five places the dessert (pie, fruit jello, and so on) on the tray. The sixth position serves the entrees and starch for each tray. The seventh position serves the ordered vegetables and soups. The special diet cook, who both prepares and serves special foods, handles the eighth position. The ninth position is reserved for the supervisor, who checks each menu to determine if the ordered food is on the proper patient tray. The tenth position, the "loader," covers the tray and loads the tray onto the proper cart, now ready for delivery. Two other workers are also considered to work on the line—the coffee pourer, who works just off the line, and the "runner," who gets special items as needed to keep the tray assembly line moving.

Patient Tray Delivery

Once the clerks in patient services have sequenced the patient menu orders by floor and room numbers and a completed cart of patient trays is assembled in the basement, the tray delivery teams are responsible for the timely delivery and pickup of all patient meals. This particular hospital has 20 floors spread over three wings of the hospital.

Exhibit 1.15   Dietary Department Organizational Chart

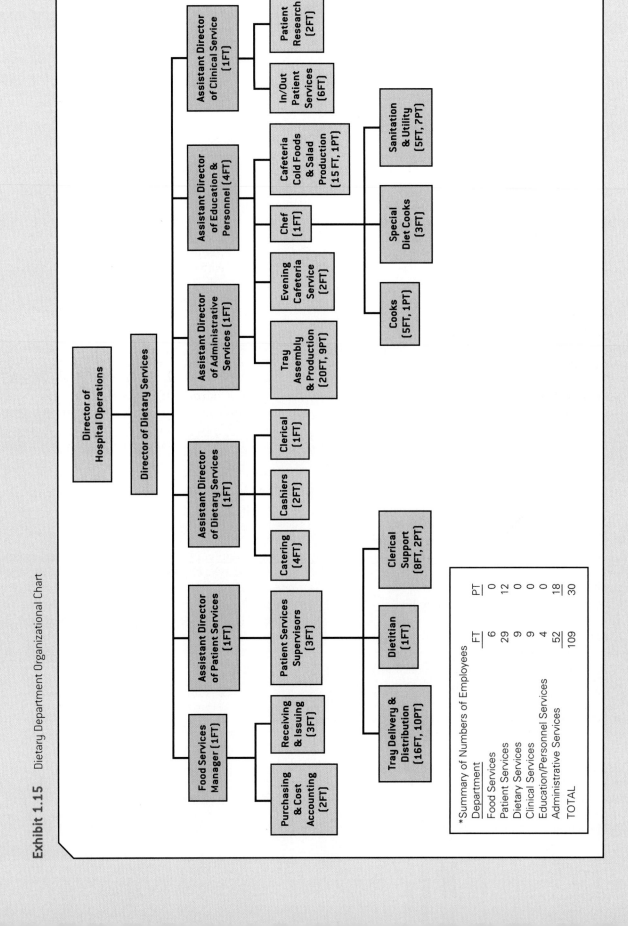

Director of Hospital Operations

Director of Dietary Services

Assistant Director of Patient Services (1FT)
Assistant Director of Dietary Services (1FT)
Assistant Director of Administrative Services (1FT)
Assistant Director of Education & Personnel (4FT)
Assistant Director of Clinical Service (1FT)

Food Services Manager (1FT)

Patient Services Supervisors (3FT)

Catering (4FT)
Cashiers (2FT)
Clerical (1FT)

Tray Assembly & Production (20FT, 9PT)
Evening Cafeteria Service (2FT)

Chef (1FT)
Cafeteria Cold Foods & Salad Production (15 FT, 1PT)

In/Out Patient Services (6FT)
Patient Research (2FT)

Purchasing & Cost Accounting (2FT)
Receiving & Issuing (3FT)

Tray Delivery & Distribution (16FT, 10PT)
Dietitian (1FT)
Clerical Support (8FT, 2PT)

Cooks (5FT, 1PT)
Special Diet Cooks (3FT)
Sanitation & Utility (5FT, 7PT)

*Summary of Numbers of Employees

Department	FT	PT
Food Services	6	0
Patient Services	29	12
Dietary Services	9	0
Clinical Services	9	0
Education/Personnel Services	4	0
Administrative Services	52	18
TOTAL	109	30

Three teams of four delivery aides each deliver trays for each meal. Once the cart is loaded, the delivery team takes the cart and the appropriate hot beverage to the correct floor. After the cart is on the correct floor, the trays are "set up" by the team captain. A "setup" includes putting the correct hot beverage on the tray, checking the patient's name with the room number, and covering the tray. This procedure expedites service, as the other three delivery aides simply deliver trays from room to room. When eight trays are left, the team captain directs one of the aides to go back to the kitchen, get the next cart, and take it to the next floor for which the team is responsible. After delivering all trays to their assigned floors, the team goes back to the initial floor and begins picking up empty trays, putting them on carts, and returning the carts to the kitchen.

The Medical Staff

The doctors and nurses are usually the first to hear complaints about the accuracy of menu orders, the timely delivery and pickup of trays, whether the delivery aides were polite and respectful of the patient's privacy, and the quality of the food. The medical staff is most concerned about the accuracy of prescribed diets for obvious patient health reasons. Occasionally, a doctor would ask a dietician to check or test the content of the

food served the patient. At a few hospitals, the nurses deliver the tray to the patient.

Blaine's Decision

After completing her telephone conversation, Blaine slowly got up from her desk, told her secretary she was not to be disturbed, shut the door, and began to write down a few notes. Some key questions that need to be answered are listed below.

Case Questions

1. What are the problems facing the hospital's dietary food service?
2. What is the cost to the hospital of a minor versus major service upset or failure?
3. What does the value chain look like? Describe features of each area. Provide examples of opportunities for errors at each stage of the value chain.
4. Who is responsible for quality?
5. Define the patient's wants and needs, CBP features, and associated processes.
6. Select a process and discuss how to mistake proof it and improve process performance.
7. How do we turn this dietary food service around? What are your recommendations?

ENDNOTES

[1] Jones, Del, and Hansen, Barbara, "Productivity Gains Roll at Their Fastest Clip in 31 Years," *USA Today*, June 14, 2004, pp. 1B, 2B.
[2] "Ford: Will Slow and Steady Win the Race?" *BusinessWeek*, May 10, 2004, p. 43.
[3] Kiley, David, "U.S. Automakers Increasing Efficiency, Report Says," *USA Today*, June 19, 2003, p. 3B.
[4] *Fast Company*, January 2003, p. 101.
[5] Adapted from Billesbach, Thomas J., "Applying Lean Production Principles to a Process Facility," *Production and Inventory Management Journal* 35, no. 3 (third quarter 1994), pp. 40–44.
[6] Collier, D. A., *The Service/Quality Solution: Using Service Management to Gain Competitive Advantage*, Burr Ridge, Illinois: Jointly published by ASQC Quality Press, Milwaukee, Wisconsin and Irwin Professional Publishing, 1994, pp. 16, 63–64, 167.
[7] These differences between goods and services were first defined by Sasser, W. E., Olsen, R. P., and Wyckoff, D. D., *Management of Service Operations*, Boston: Allyn and Bacon, 1978, pp. 8–21, and later improved and expanded by Fitzsimmons, J. A., and Sullivan, R. S., *Service Operations Management*, New York: McGraw-Hill, 1982, and Collier, D. A. "Managing A Service Firm: A Different Management Game" *National Productivity Review*, Winter 1983–84, pp. 36–45.
[8] Collier, D. A. "New Orleans Hilton & Hilton Towers," *Service Management: Operating Decisions*, Englewood Cliffs, New Jersey: Prentice-Hall, Inc., 1987, p. 120.
[9] Carlzon, Jan, CEO of Scandinavian Airlines Systems first defined a moment of trust or truth. See Peters, T. J., and Austin, N., *A Passion for Excellence: The Leadership Difference*, New York: Warner Books, 1985, pp. 58 and 78.
[10] Collier, D. A., *The Service/Quality Solution: Using Service Management to Gain Competitive Advantage*, Burr Ridge, Illinois: Jointly published by ASQC Quality Press, Milwaukee, Wisconsin and Irwin Professional Publishing, Chapter 4, pp. 63–96.
[11] *AT&T's Total Quality Approach*, AT&T Corporate Quality Office, 1992, p. 6.
[12] Siekman, Philip, "The Big Myth About U.S. Manufacturing," *Fortune*, October 2, 2000, 244[C]–244[E].
[13] Taylor, III, Alex, "GM Gets Its Act Together. Finally," *Fortune*, April 5, 2004, pp. 136–146.

Chapter Outline

CHAPTER 2

Value Chains

Learning Objectives

1. To define value and three ways to increase it, to describe a value chain using input-output or pre- and postservice paradigms, and to distinguish between a value chain and supply chain.

2. To describe the role of operations, vertical integration, and outsourcing in designing and managing value chains, and to apply break-even analysis to simple outsourcing decisions.

3. To describe the nature of a multinational enterprise and value chains in a global environment, to explain the advantages and disadvantages of offshoring decisions, to identify difficulties associated with managing global value chains, and to recognize the role of local culture in managing nondomestic operations.

- Bulky appliances like dishwashers, refrigerators, and washing machines were thought to be insulated from global competition and imports because of their size. "Big boxes of air are expensive to ship across the ocean," says Maytag Corporation's Jim Starkweather.[1] Nevertheless, China's Haier Inc. and South Korea's LG Electronics, which started out small with microwaves and mini-refrigerators, are now moving to bigger appliances and are creating intense global competition. LG Electronics, along with several other Asian appliance makers, is opening factories in Mexico to save on shipping. Although Maytag sources dishwasher components and subassemblies from around the world, such as General Electric motors from China and wiring harnesses from Mexico, it still assembles them in a sprawling factory in Jackson, Tennessee. The pressure is on Maytag to move its appliance assembly out of the United States.

- "What happened to U.S. steel jobs is going to happen to white collar jobs," declared a Lucent Technologies worker in Columbus, Ohio. Computer programming, call centers, engineering, accounting, payroll, billing, architecture, art design, and office support are just a few of the information-intensive jobs that can be done overseas at a much lower cost. The average annual salary, for example, of computer programmers in 2003 was $63,331 in the United States, $8,952 in China, and $5,880 in India. The Internet makes it possible to move these jobs anywhere on the planet. A 2002 study by Massachusetts-based Forrester Research predicts that by 2015, 3.3 million U.S. jobs and $136 billion in wages will move offshore.[2]

- At a time when more than 98 percent of all shoes sold in the United States are made in other countries, Allen-Edmonds Shoe Corp. is a lonely holdout against offshoring. Allen-Edmonds invested more than $1 million to completely overhaul its manufacturing process into a leaner and more efficient system that could reduce 5 percent from the cost of each pair of shoes. However, moving to China could save as much as 60 percent. But John Stollenwerk, chief executive, will not compromise on quality and believes that Allen-Edmonds can make better shoes, and serve customers faster, in the United States. An experiment in producing one model in Portugal resulted in lining that wasn't quite right and stitching that wasn't as fine. Stollenwerk noted, "We could take out a few stitches and you'd never notice it—and then we could take out a few more. Pretty soon you've cheapened the product, and you don't stand for what you're about."[3]

> **Discussion Questions:** What is your opinion of companies that move operations to other countries with cheaper labor rates? In the long run, do you think that such decisions help or hurt business competitiveness and national economies? Should governments influence or legislate such decisions?

The advances in transportation and information technology have made the world a much smaller place and have created a significantly more intense competitive business environment. Many companies, such as Maytag, are struggling in today's global market. To better understand their competition and benchmark costs, Maytag buys competitor brands and ships them to Jackson, Tennessee, where engineers disassemble them and examine every part to determine what they would cost to produce in the United States or abroad. For example, Maytag learned that the only way to match prices for a G.E. side-by-side refrigerator made in Mexico was to assemble it in Mexico. Although Maytag wants to avoid moving its assembly oper-ations out of the United States, it might have to do so to keep costs competitive and remain profitable.

As the second episode illustrates, blue-collar jobs are not the only ones moving off U.S. shores. Information-intensive work can be performed anywhere. Intel Chairman Andrew Grove has raised new questions about "the law of comparative advantage as the cost of communicating across continents shrinks to zero."[4] The hollowing out of U.S. manufacturing jobs that occurred during the 1980s is now happening in services. For example, AOL Time Warner Inc. employs 1,500 workers at its call center in Bangalore, India.[5] AOL has turned its focus from growth to cutting costs. Gartner, Inc. market researchers estimate it costs 40 to 50 percent less to operate the call center in India than in the United States. EarthLink Inc. and Yahoo Inc. have also opened call center and software development offices in India. Such "offshoring" has prompted a backlash in the United States. Some state legislatures are supporting bills that would require state contractors to use U.S.-based employees. Some stockholders of major corporations have placed nonoutsourcing amendments on the ballots at annual stockholders meetings.

However, some firms, such as Allen-Edmonds Shoe Corporation, described in the third episode, resist the strategy of moving offshore. "The commitment to quality is my life. It's the way we live; it's the way I was raised. I surround myself with people who have the same philosophy," Stollenwerk concluded. He is willing to sacrifice short-term gains for the long-term good of his company and its 700 people as they serve this high-quality niche market.

These episodes point to the trade-offs between key operations issues of cost, quality, and customer service that most firms must wrestle with. Although cost is often the predominant issue, customer service is also used to justify offshoring decisions: "... the reality is we are in a global company and have customers around the world," said a Lucent Technologies manager. "We have to shift work close to our customers for fast delivery and customization, and remain competitive." For others, like Allen-Edmonds, the issue is quality.

Today's managers face difficult decisions in balancing these objectives to create value for their customers and stakeholders. The creation of value depends on an effective system of linked facilities and processes that involves everyone in the organization—not simply those in operations—such as marketing, finance/accounting, information systems, and human resource personnel. This system characterizes the concept of a *value chain,* which we will soon define and which is a dominant theme of this book. Therefore, it is important for every business student to understand how operations management influences the design and management of value chains, which is our focus in this chapter. In addition, today's operations managers increasingly deliver goods and services to multiple markets and operate in a shrinking global business environment. As one chief financial officer wrote in a *CFO Magazine* survey, "You cannot compete globally unless you use global resources."[6] Thus, we emphasize the importance of understanding the global business environment, local culture, and their impact on value chain design and operations.

VALUE AND SUPPLY CHAINS

Today's consumers demand innovative products, high quality, quick response, impeccable service, and low prices; in short, they want *value* in every purchase or experience. One of the most important points that we can emphasize in this book is

The underlying purpose of every organization is to provide value to its customers and stakeholders.

Value *is the perception of the benefits associated with a good, service, or bundle of goods and services (that is, the customer benefit package) in relation to what buyers are willing to pay for them.* The decision to purchase a good or service or a customer benefit package is based on an assessment by the customer of the perceived benefits in relation to its price. The customer's cumulative judgment of the perceived benefits leads to either satisfaction or dissatisfaction. One of the simplest functional forms of value is

> Value = Perceived benefits/Price (cost) to the customer

If the value ratio is high, customers perceive the good or service favorably, and the organization providing it is more likely to be successful.

To increase value, an organization must

a. increase perceived benefits while holding price or cost constant,
b. increase perceived benefits while reducing price or cost, or
c. decrease price or cost while holding perceived benefits constant.

In addition, proportional increases or decreases in perceived benefits as well as price results in no net change in value. Management must determine how to maximize value by designing processes and systems that create and deliver the appropriate goods and services customers want to use, pay for, and experience.

A *competitively dominant customer experience is often called a* **value proposition**.[7] Companies such as Wal-Mart, Dell, and Royal Bank of Canada know that superior value propositions produce sustained returns over the long run much better than fad products or strong geographic presence. They retain and grow their most profitable customers and acquire more of them, and organize and execute their operations to support their value propositions. A winning value proposition is one that meets the full set of customer needs, including price.

The focus on value has forced many traditional goods-producing companies to add services to their customer benefit packages. If the quality or features of goods cannot be improved at a reasonable cost and prices cannot be lowered, then enhanced or additional services may provide better total value to customers. Frequently, the profits (or gross margins) made from services are higher than for goods. For example, the Instrument Systems Division of Hewlett-Packard (HP) faced a problem when a key competitor announced a price decrease for voltmeters. Should HP do nothing and risk losing sales, or should it lower its price to retain volume

Learning Objective
To define value and three ways to increase it, to describe a value chain using input-output or pre- and postservice paradigms, and to distinguish between a value chain and supply chain.

Value *is the perception of the benefits associated with a good, service, or bundle of goods and services (that is, the customer benefit package) in relation to what buyers are willing to pay for them.*

A competitively dominant customer experience is often called a **value proposition**.

and lose revenue? A third alternative was chosen instead: to hold the price steady, but increase the warranty from one to three years. The warranty on the voltmeter is a form of insurance to reduce customer risks of purchase. The product's reliability was quite high, so the additional cost for the extra warranty would be much less than the potential revenue loss. Also, rather than having customers wait for a failing voltmeter to be repaired, HP improved its warranty policy to include shipment of a new unit within 24 hours. Here, services such as the warranty and quick shipping capability added value to the goods and services bundle. The perceived benefits of those additional services actually increased HP market share and profitability in this target market.

The integration of services in manufacturing was recognized some time ago. "In the same way that service businesses were managed and organized around manufacturing models during the industrial economy, we can expect that manufacturing businesses will be managed and organized around service models in this new economy."[8] A goods-producing company can no longer be viewed as simply a factory that churns out physical goods, because customer perceptions of goods are influenced highly by such facilitating services as financing and leasing, shipping and installation, maintenance and repair, and technical support and consulting. Coordinating the operational capability to design and deliver an integrated customer benefit package of goods and services is the essence of operations management and leads to the concept of a value chain.

Value Chains

*A **value chain** is a network of facilities and processes that describes the flow of goods, services, information, and financial transactions from suppliers through the facilities and processes that create goods and services and deliver them to customers.*

A **value chain** is a network of facilities and processes that describes the flow of goods, services, information, and financial transactions from suppliers through the facilities and processes that create goods and services and deliver them to customers. As shown in Exhibit 2.1, a value chain is a "cradle-to-grave" model of the operations function. The value chain begins with suppliers who provide inputs to a goods-producing or service-providing process or network of processes. Suppliers might be retail stores, distributors, employment agencies, dealers, financing and leasing agents, information and Internet companies, field maintenance and repair services, architectural and engineering design firms, and contractors, as well as manufacturers of materials and components. The inputs they provide might be physical goods such as automobile engines or microprocessors provided to an assembly plant;

Exhibit 2.1
The Value Chain

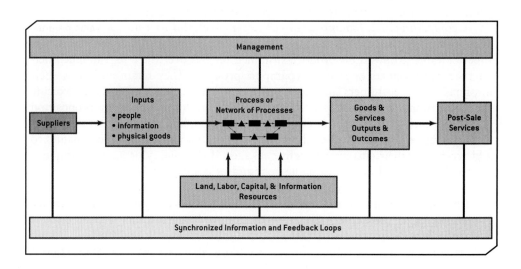

meat, fish, and vegetables provided to a restaurant; trained employees provided to organizations by universities and technical schools; or information such as computer specifications or medical diagnoses. Inputs are transformed into value-added goods and services through processes or networks of work activities, which are supported by such resources as land, labor, money, and information. The value chain outputs—goods and services—are delivered or provided to customers and targeted market segments.

The success of the entire value chain depends on the design and management of all aspects of the value chain (suppliers, inputs, processes, outputs or outcomes), including both short- and longer-term decisions. Some examples of value chains are shown in Exhibit 2.2. Note that what is being transformed can be almost anything; for instance, people as in a hospital, a physical good as in an oil refinery, information and entertainment as in the e-publishing business, or a mixture of people, physical goods, and information as in many government services.

Exhibit 2.3 shows an alternate view of the value chain from pre- and postproduction service perspectives. **Pre- and postproduction services** complete the ownership cycle for the good or service. Preproduction services include customized and team-oriented product design, consulting services, contract negotiations, product and service guarantees, customer financing to help purchase the product, training customers to use and maintain the product, purchasing and supplier services, and other types of front-end services. The focus here is "gaining a customer." These front-end value-added services often are key differentiators in the marketplace. This premise is especially true when good or service features and competitor prices are about the same (that is, product quality and price parity).

Postproduction services include on-site installation or application, maintenance and repair in the field, servicing loans and financing, warranty and claim services, warehouse and inventory management for the company and sometimes for the customers, training, telephone service centers, transportation delivery services, postsale visits to the customer's facility by knowledgeable sales and technical-support people, recycling and remanufacturing initiatives, and other back-end services. The focus here is on "keeping the customer." Postproduction services add value to the good or service and provide feedback to the manufacturing process and preproduction services. This feedback is the source of product redesign, continuous improvement, reengineering, and new products.

This view of the value chain emphasizes the notion that service is a critical component of traditional manufacturing processes. For example, Ford Motor Company found that the total value of owning a Ford vehicle averaged across all market segments for service and the vehicle was allocated as follows: The vehicle (that is, product features and performance) itself accounted for 52 percent of total value, the sales process for 21 percent, and the maintenance and repair service processes for 27 percent. These statistics are based on average customer perceptions for all cars and vary by type of vehicle and market segment.[9] Ford's research indicated that when vehicle features and quality, performance, and price per target market segment were roughly the same as competitors', presale and postproduction services were the factors that enticed customers for all target market segments. Service has become a key differentiating factor in the eyes of customers for many manufacturing firms. Ford Motor Company is continuing to develop a competitive strategy where "service is the centerpiece of their global strategy." A good example of a value chain that integrates pre- and postproduction services is described in the next section.

Pre- and postproduction services also represent huge opportunities to increase revenue and provide new sources of income. For example, Nestlé once defined its business from a physical good viewpoint as "selling coffee machines." Using service management thinking, it redefined its business from a service perspective in

Exhibit 2.2 Examples of Goods-Producing and Service-Providing Value Chains

Organization	Suppliers	Inputs	Transformation Process	Outputs	Customers and Market Segments
Auto assembly plant	Engine plant Tires Frame Axles Paint Seats	Labor Energy Auto parts Specifications	Welding Machining Assembly Painting	Automobiles Trucks	Economy Luxury Rental Trucking Ambulance Police
Airline	Food manufacturers Fuel and oil Pilot training Security	Planes Labor Baggage Energy Repair parts Knowledge	Plane repair Pilot and plane schedules Baggage service Cabin service Security system	Safe & on-time flight	Economy Luxury Private jet Business classes Cargo Mail
Oil refinery	Oil suppliers Utility companies Pipelines	Crude oil Energy Labor Equipment Specifications	Chemical reaction Separation Distribution	Gasoline Motor oil Fuel oil	Automobile gasoline stations and grades of fuel Retail stores Airplane fuel Home heating oil
Hospital	Pharmaceutical companies Equipment suppliers Food suppliers Organ donors Medical supplies	Patients Beds Staff Drugs Diagnostic equipment Knowledge	Admissions Lab testing Doctor diagnosis Food service Surgery schedules Drug administration Rehabilitation	Healthy people Lab results Accurate bills Community health education	Heart clinics Pediatrics Emergency and trauma services Ambulatory services Medical specialties and hospital wards
Pizza restaurant	Food wholesaler Equipment suppliers High school students	Food raw materials Orders Energy Labor Equipment	Order taking Home delivery In-store service Bill payment Food production	Good pizza Happy customers Quick service	Premium pizza Home delivery In-store seating Discount market Catering and group sales
State government	Highway and building contractors Employment agencies Food suppliers Equipment suppliers Other governments	Labor Energy Information Trash Crimes Disputes Sick people Low-income people	Health care benefits Food stamps Legal services Prisons Trash removal Park services License services Police services Tax services	Good use of taxpayers monies Safety net Security Reallocate taxes Clean, safe, and fun parks	Disabled people Low-income people Criminals and prisons Corporate taxes Boat licenses Building inspections Weekend vacationers Child custody services Legal court services
e-Publishers	Authors Software vendors Research articles Electronic books and readers	Labor Knowledge Software Computer servers Scanners Printers Energy	Internet network Editing text, audio, and video Publisher screening of authors' work (i.e., quality control) Promotion Payment Security	e-books downloaded to PCs and e-book readers Bytes of information and knowledge	Entertainment books Journals and magazines Time-sensitive books such as stock market information Knowledge-based textbooks Reference books Libraries

Exhibit 2.3 Pre- and Postservice View of the Value Chain

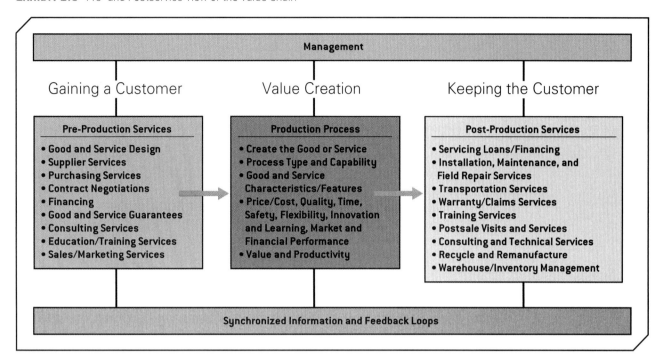

which the coffee machine became more of a peripheral good. Nestlé decided to lease coffee machines and provide daily replenishment of the coffee and maintenance of the machine for a contracted service fee. This "primary leasing service" was offered to organizations that sold more than 50 cups of coffee per day. The results were greatly increased coffee sales, new revenue opportunities, and much stronger profits. Of course, Nestlé's service vision of its business required a completely new service and logistical value chain. Moreover, the difficulty of providing this service to thousands of organizations (sites) in a geographical region is a barrier to entry for competitors and a challenge for Nestlé.

An Example of a Value Chain: Buhrke Industries, Inc.

Buhrke Industries, Inc., located in Arlington Heights, Illinois, provides stamped metal parts to many industries, including automotive, appliance, computer, electronics, hardware, housewares, power tools, medical, and telecommunications. Decades ago, as a tool and die shop, the company revolutionized the container-manufacturing industry by developing the first die to blank, form, and curl an aluminum foil tray in one stroke. Then, as the beverage industry converted to easy-open ends (pull tabs), Buhrke supplied the manufacturers with complete systems—including dies and special machinery—to fulfill their needs.

Buhrke's objective is to be a customer's best total-value producer with on-time delivery, fewer rejects, and high-quality stampings. However, the company goes beyond manufacturing goods; it prides itself in providing the best service available as part of its customer value chain. Service is more than delivering a product on time—it's also partnering with customers by providing

- personalized service for fast, accurate response,
- customized engineering designs to meet customer needs,
- preventive maintenance systems to ensure high machine uptime,

- experienced, highly trained, long-term employees, and
- troubleshooting by a knowledgeable sales staff

Many customers have strict quality and documentation requirements. Buhrke helps them meet those requirements by providing a variety of reporting services and material certifications, such as Statistical Process Control (SPC), capability reports, and many others. Buhrke meets the strict quality and documentation requirements of the International Standards Organization (ISO) and the Big Three automakers—General Motors, Ford, and DaimlerChrysler. Many manufacturing systems and much of the maintenance equipment were custom-designed by Buhrke engineers and tailored to customers' specific needs. Maintenance engineers created a Computerized Preventive Maintenance System, a control console that centralizes and monitors the maintenance schedules of all presses, increasing quality and productivity, and virtually eliminating costly equipment breakdowns.

Exhibit 2.4 illustrates the components of Buhrke's value chain. The process begins with a customer request for a quotation. The estimating department processes such job parameters as specifications, metals, finishing or packaging services, the presses that it may run on, and customer deadlines in developing a quote. Next, a sales engineer is assigned to monitor each stamping job from start to finish, so the customer may have the convenience of a single point of contact. Sales engineers work closely with engineering staff to convey customer needs. Engineers then design the best tooling for the job, using computer-assisted design processes to ensure precise designs and timely completion. After a tool is designed and built, it is main-

Exhibit 2.4 The Value Chain at Buhrke Industries (*Source:* Buhrke Industries company web site)

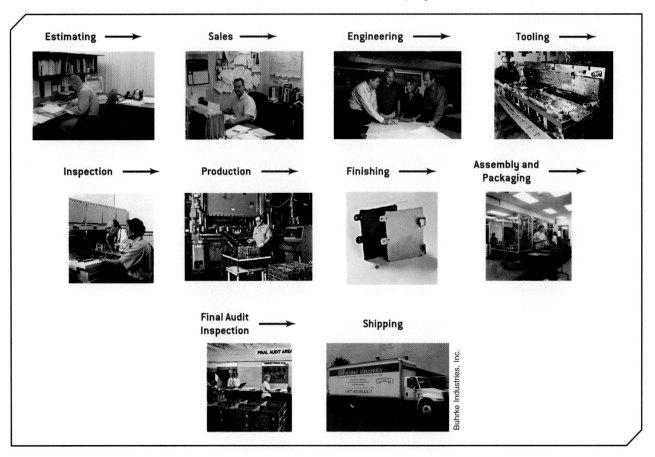

tained in an on-site tool room. Burhke's toolmakers have decades of experience constructing tools for metal stamping, and they are put on a strict maintenance regimen to assure long life and consistent stampings.

Parts are stamped on a full range of presses, from 15 tons to 200 tons, with speeds of up to 1,500 parts per minute. Inspection of raw materials, work-in-process, and finished products help ensure zero defects. The company provides a full range of secondary and finishing operations from heat-treating to powder coating to tapping to add value to customers. Customers need not ship stampings elsewhere or arrange for another service provider to finish the job.

If customers want, Buhrke will assemble the stampings with other components to deliver a complete subassembly. It will even procure parts for assembly, such as plastics that the company does not manufacture. Buhrke is also able to package finished stampings or subassemblies. Before stampings are boxed up and shipped—even after the incoming inspection and in-process audits—they go through a final audit inspection. Finally, Buhrke offers the convenience of shipping finished product where and when customers want. For further information and video tours of the plant, visit www.buhrke.com.

Supply Chains

A **supply chain** *is the portion of the value chain that focuses primarily on the physical movement of goods and materials, and supporting flows of information and financial transactions, through the supply, production, and distribution processes.* Supply chains have become a critical focus for almost every company today. For example, Exhibit 2.5 shows a conceptual model of a supply chain developed by Procter & Gamble, which began working on supply chain design issues and strategies in 1995. P&G's "Ultimate Supply System" seeks to understand the impact of tightly coupling supply chain partners to integrate information, physical material and product flow, and financial activities to increase sales, reduce costs, increase cash flow, and provide the right product at the right time at the right price to customers.[10]

A **supply chain** *is the portion of the value chain that focuses primarily on the physical movement of goods and materials, and supporting flows of information and financial transactions, through the supply, production, and distribution processes.*

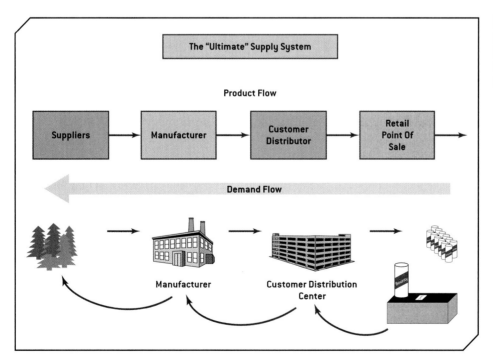

Exhibit 2.5
Procter & Gamble's Conceptual Model of a Supply Chain for Paper Products (*Source:* See Endnote 10)

Many organizations use the terms *value chain* and *supply chain* interchangeably; however, we differentiate the two in this book. A value chain is broader in scope than a supply chain and encompasses all pre- and postproduction services to create and deliver the entire customer benefit package. A value chain views an organization from the customer's perspective—the integration of goods and services to create value—whereas a supply chain is more internally focused on the creation of physical goods. The concept of value chain also encourages broader thinking about the role of goods and services in creating customer value than does the concept of a supply chain, which typically focuses on material flow and manufacturing. In addition, the broader concept of the value chain is easy to apply to service-providing organizations as well as to goods-producing firms.

VALUE CHAIN DESIGN AND MANAGEMENT

*The **operational structure** of a value chain is the configuration of resources such as suppliers, factories, warehouses, distributors, technical support centers, engineering design and sales offices, and communication links.*

Organizations face numerous decisions in designing and configuring their value chains. Looking back at Exhibits 2.1 and 2.3, we see that these must include the number, type, and location of manufacturing plants, distribution centers, retail stores, repair centers, and customer service or technical support centers; the choice of technology and processes to make goods and deliver services; ways of managing information flow throughout the value chain; the selection of suppliers and partners; and the integration of all the pieces into an effective and efficient system.

*The **operational structure** of a value chain is the configuration of resources such as suppliers, factories, warehouses, distributors, technical support centers, engineering design and sales offices, and communication links.* Different management skills are required for different operational structures. For example, Wal-Mart's value chain, though very large, is focused on purchasing and distribution and is controlled from a centralized location in Bentonville, Arkansas. In contrast, General Electric's value chain, which encompasses such diverse businesses as medical imaging, jet engines, appliances, and electrical power generation, are all quite different. Each business is a profit center with its own unique market and operating conditions. Consequently the operational structure is decentralized.

Technology enables processes and value chains to lower the cost of goods and services, speed delivery, and provide customization where required (see the OM Spotlight: Upgrading Bar Codes for Global Supply Chains). Examples include rental car transponders to speed checkout and check-in, computer-driven machines to produce manufactured parts, bar codes, geographic and wireless information systems to locate vehicles and inventory, and electronic patient medical records. The role of technology in OM is introduced in Chapter 5, and many other applications are described throughout this book. All of these technologies play a role in improving global supply chain efficiency and effectiveness.

The flow of information is an important aspect of value chain design. Information must move as fast or faster than the physical goods. For example, global buyers and sellers depend on a "letter of credit" to settle their payments. Used for about four centuries, the paper-based process requires banks to coordinate with one another and exchange documents, often across oceans, and has numerous drawbacks:

- The cost of processing trade documentation is more than 5 percent of the total annual value of world trade.
- Banks reject half of all "letters of credit" transactions because of incorrect information from the buyer or seller.
- The cost of processing a simple global transaction is about $400.
- Each transaction requires up to 24 forms to be accurately completed.[11]

Internet-based platforms are leading to vast improvements. TradeCard Inc., for example, allows the buyer to connect the flow of physical goods and the flow of

OM SPOTLIGHT

Upgrading Bar Codes for Global Supply Chains[12]

Since 1974, when a Marsh Supermarket clerk in Troy, Ohio, scanned a pack of Wrigley's gum containing the first label with lines, most bar codes in North America contained 12 lines. Yet, to do business in the world economy U.S. and Canadian manufacturers are switching to a 13-line bar code used everyplace else in the world. "What this change does is fixes the North American supply chain. It makes our system compatible with global supply chains," stated John Wilson, product manager for NCR Corporation's Retail Solutions Division.

The one-digit bar code change is just another indication that the world has become one big marketplace. Historically, it cost North American manufacturers using the 12-line bar code a few cents per inventory item to relabel their items to the 13-line bar code, not to mention the impact on supply chain shipment delays, opportunities for errors, and regulatory confusion. Most big companies now have equipment that can read both the 12- and 13-line bar codes, but smaller firms cannot afford the costly new hardware and software.

The 12- to 13-line bar code change is an example of the move toward global standardization of supply chain terminology, technology, and systems. Another change in the works is reducing the size of the bar code labels to about one-fourth their current size. Such a change would make the bar code label small enough to put on individual packages of items such as consumer products and drugs.

electronic funds and trade documents. For example, Hi-Tec Sports USA, a California-based hiking shoe company, had to issue a purchase order to one of its global suppliers in China and then open a letter of credit with its bank. The bank would then send the letter of credit and supporting documents by courier to the manufacturer's bank in China and wait for the China bank to approve the transaction, a process that could take as much as two weeks. Today, Hi-Tec uses TradeCard's system and the entire electronic process seldom takes more than one day. Moreover, Hi-Tec figures it saves 20 cents per shoe by doing an electronic letter of credit. United Parcel Service (UPS) is also pushing this type of financial service through its UPS Capital subsidiary.

Outsourcing and Vertical Integration

One of the most important decisions a firm can make about its value chain is whether to vertically integrate or outsource key business processes and functions. **Vertical integration** *refers to the process of acquiring and consolidating elements of a value chain to achieve more control.* For example, some firms might consolidate all processes for a specific product or product line in a single facility—for example, Henry Ford's early factories did everything from steel making to final assembly. Although such a strategy provides more control, it adds more complexity to managing the value chain. In contrast, a complex network of suppliers characterizes today's automobile production. Decentralizing value chain activities lessens the control that a firm has over cost, quality, and other important business metrics and often leads to higher levels of risk. These decisions depend on the economics associated with consolidation and outsourcing, the technological capabilities of the firm and external suppliers, and oftentimes, the impact on the firm's human resources. Vertical integration decisions often focus on acquiring suppliers and technological capability within the walls of the firm.

Outsourcing *is the process of having suppliers provide goods and services that were previously provided internally.* Outsourcing is the opposite of vertical integration in the sense that the organization is shedding (not acquiring) a part of itself. The organization that outsources does not have ownership of the outsourced

Vertical integration *refers to the process of acquiring and consolidating elements of a value chain to achieve more control.*

Outsourcing *is the process of having suppliers provide goods and services that were previously provided internally.*

process or function. Some large U.S. banks and airlines, for example, have outsourced their telephone call service centers to third-party suppliers within or outside the United States. Outsourcing is generally independent of location (see OM Spotlight: American Racing Wheels).

The United States has experienced three waves of outsourcing:

- The first wave involved the exodus of *goods-producing jobs* from the United States in many industries several decades ago. Companies relied on foreign factories for the production of computer components, electronics, and many other goods. Gibson Guitars, for example, produces its Epiphone line in Korea.
- The second wave involved *simple service work,* such as standard credit card processing, billing, keying information into computers, and writing simple software programs. Accenture, for example, has information technology and bookkeeping operations in Costa Rica.
- The third, and current wave, involves *skilled knowledge work,* such as that performed by engineering designers, graphic artists, architects, call center customer service representatives, and computer chip designers. For example, Massachusetts General Hospital uses radiologists located in Bangalore, India, to interpret CT scans. Procter & Gamble Co. uses employees in Manila to help prepare P&G's tax returns. Fluor Corporation of Aliso Viejo, California uses engineers and draftsmen in the Philippines, Poland, and India to develop detailed blueprints and specs for industrial construction and improvement projects.[14]

Backward integration *refers to acquiring capabilities at the front end of the supply chain (for instance, suppliers), whereas* **forward integration** *refers to acquiring capabilities toward the back end of the supply chain (for instance, distribution or even customers).*

Companies must decide whether to integrate backward (acquiring suppliers) or forward (acquiring distributors), or both. **Backward integration** *refers to acquiring capabilities at the front end of the supply chain (for instance, suppliers), whereas* **forward integration** *refers to acquiring capabilities toward the back end of the supply chain (for instance, distribution or even customers).* Large companies such as

OM SPOTLIGHT

American Racing Wheels[13]

American Racing is the largest manufacturer of custom wheels for cars, trucks, and other vehicles in the United States. In the past five years, China has built more than 30 factories to manufacture wheels. As a result, global prices for wheels have fallen anywhere from 20 to 50 percent, depending on the type of wheel. Many global wheel manufacturers outsourced their wheel production to these Chinese factories.

American Racing chose a different strategy to try to survive its Chinese competitors. It outsourced its lower-end wheels to Chinese factories, shifted some production to Mexico, and kept its highest-priced customized wheels in U.S. factories. Time will tell whether its global strategy will allow American Racing to remain globally competitive.

Source: http://www.americanracing.com/wheels/wheels.asp?section=A, October 19, 2004.

Motorola, Siemens, and Sony have the resources to build facilities in foreign lands and develop a high level of vertical integration. Their objective is to own or control most, if not all, of the supply chain. Many large chemical manufacturers—for example, DuPont, British Petroleum, Haimen Jiangbin, and GFS Chemicals—are buying raw materials suppliers and integrating backward. At the same time, chemical manufacturers in industrial countries are focusing on more profitable specialty chemicals and advanced materials. Developing these specialty chemicals by acquiring smaller specialty manufacturers and distributors is a form of forward integration.

An interesting example of the advantages of vertically integrating occurred when the director of apparel for Nike Golf watched Tiger Woods win the Masters golf tournament in 2002. He noticed that the collar on Mr. Woods Nike golf shirt had crumpled up from the heat and perspiration. The next day he called Esquel Apparel Inc. in Hong Kong and told them he wanted to change its polo-shirt collars to a shorter one that would not crumple and buckle up. Chemists and Esquel shirt designers in China began to work on a new collar fabric. Within weeks, the Chinese company flew six prototype shirts to Florida for testing, and by October, the new shirts were rolling off the assembly line in Hong Kong. The reason Esquel Apparel Inc. could do this is because it owned or controlled every supplier in the value chain—from the cotton grown in the field to the spinning mills that make the yarn to the final assembly at the factory.[15]

Break-Even Analysis for Simple Outsourcing Decisions

Clearly, strategic decisions about outsourcing in multinational organizations involve many factors that are not easily quantified or assessed, making such decisions difficult to analyze. However, outsourcing is not just an issue for large multinationals. Small manufacturers face simple outsourcing decisions all the time; a common example is whether to produce a part in-house or to outsource it to a supplier. This decision is usually based on economics, and break-even analysis, which we introduced in Chapter 1, can be used to provide insight into the best decision.

If a company decides to make a part, it typically incurs fixed costs associated with purchasing equipment or setting up a production line. Fixed costs do not vary with volume and often include the costs of constructing or buying a building, buying or leasing equipment, and administrative costs. However, the variable cost per unit will be less than if the work is outsourced to some external supplier. Variable costs are a function of the quantity produced and might include labor, transportation, and materials costs:

$$VC_1 = \text{Variable cost/unit if produced}$$
$$VC_2 = \text{Variable cost/unit if outsourced}$$
$$FC = \text{fixed costs associated with producing the part}$$
$$Q = \text{quantity produced (volume)}$$

Then,

$$\text{Total cost of production} = (VC_1)Q + FC$$
$$\text{Total cost of outsourcing} = (VC_2)Q$$

If we set these costs equal to each other, we obtain:

$$(VC_2)Q = (VC_1)Q + FC$$
$$(VC_2)Q - (VC_1)Q = FC$$
$$(VC_2 - VC_1)Q = FC$$

The break-even quantity is found by solving for Q:

$$Q^* = \frac{FC}{VC_2 - VC_1} \qquad \textbf{(2.1)}$$

Whenever the anticipated volume is greater than Q^*, the firm should produce the part in-house; otherwise, it is best to outsource. We provide a numerical example of the decision to produce in-house or outsource as a solved problem at the end of this chapter.

Value and Supply Chain Integration

Value chain integration *is the process of managing information, physical goods, and services to ensure their availability at the right place, at the right time, at the right cost, at the right quantity, and with the highest attention to quality.*

For complex value chains that incorporate numerous suppliers, facilities, and outsourced processes, firms need an approach to coordinate and manage information, physical goods, and services among all the players in the value chain. **Value chain integration** *is the process of managing information, physical goods, and services to ensure their availability at the right place, at the right time, at the right cost, at the right quantity, and with the highest attention to quality.* (A focus solely on coordinating the physical flow of materials to ensure that the right parts are available at various stages of the supply chain, such as manufacturing and assembly plants, is commonly called *supply chain integration.*) For goods-producing firms, value chain integration requires consolidating information systems among suppliers, factories, distributors, and customers; managing the supply chain and scheduling factories; and studying new ways to use technology. Major companies such as General Motors and Ford pay considerable attention to this. The key enabler that allows one to pull the pieces of the goods-producing supply chain together into a seamless and effective system is, of course, information technology.

Some firms, like Wal-Mart, manage value chain integration themselves. Others make use of third-party "system integrators" to manage the process. One example of a system integrator is Visteon. Visteon has a global delivery system of 106 factories, 11 Visteon assembly plants for major subassemblies, 41 engineering offices, and 25 customer service centers. Its clients include the 19 largest vehicle manufacturers in the world. Visteon's mission statement is

To increase shareholder value by delivering system solutions that help our customers exceed their goals, are safe and environmentally responsible, and distinguish Visteon as the supplier, employer, and community citizen of choice.[16]

Visteon coordinated the delivery of over 50 component parts for the 2002 Ford Thunderbird by managing a supply chain network of over 100 suppliers and 15 manufacturing plants in 5 countries. This strategy allowed Ford to concentrate on its strengths—managing the performance, style, and design that have drawn attention to the Thunderbird—while Visteon managed the logistics of providing global support for Ford. See the OM Spotlight on Exel for another example.

Value chain integration includes improving internal processes for the client as well as external processes that tie together suppliers, manufacturers, distributors, and customers. Other benefits are lower total value chain costs to the client, reduced inventory obsolescence, better global communication among all parties, access to new technologies, and better customer service.

Value chain integration in services—where value is in the form of low prices, convenience, and access to special time-sensitive deals and travel packages—takes many forms. For example, third-party integrators for the leisure and travel industry value chains include Orbitz, Expedia, Priceline, and Travelocity. They manage information to make these value chains more efficient and create value for their customers. Many financial services use information networks provided by third-party information technology integrators such as AT&T, Sprint, IBM, and Verizon to coordinate their value chains. Hospitals also use third-party integrators for both their information and physical goods, such as managing patient billing and hospital inventories.

OM SPOTLIGHT

Exel—A Supply Chain Integrator[17]

Exel (www.exel.com), based in the United Kingdom, is a global leader in supply chain management, providing customer-focused solutions to a wide range of manufacturing, retail, and consumer industries, and employing over 109,000 people in 2,050 locations in more than 120 countries worldwide. Exel's customers include over 70 percent of the world's largest, nonfinancial companies in industries such as health care, chemical, retail, and automotive.

Courtesy of Exel

Exel manages supply chain activities across industries and geographic regions to reduce costs, accelerate product movement, and allow manufacturers and retailers to focus on their core business. Exel is able to deliver services and solutions such as consulting, e-commerce, transport, global freight, warehousing, home delivery, labeling, and co-packing on a local, regional or global basis. With global resources and a complete spectrum of integrated services and capabilities tailored to the needs of the customer, Exel can assume the role of a global lead logistics provider to open new markets and simplify supply chain management.

VALUE CHAINS IN A GLOBAL BUSINESS ENVIRONMENT

Learning Objective
To describe the nature of a multinational enterprise and value chains in a global environment, to explain the advantages and disadvantages of offshoring decisions, to identify difficulties associated with managing global value chains, and to recognize the role of local culture in managing nondomestic operations.

Although not every organization operates in the global business environment, modern technology and distribution have made it feasible and attractive for both large and small companies to develop value chains that span international boundaries. For example, consider the situation of the household appliance market in China in the early 1990s. Siemens, Matsushita, Whirlpool, and General Electric all wanted to be the home appliance leader in the Chinese market. However, a small company in China began to sell cheap, reliable refrigerators that were designed to meet basic customer needs. The large multinational firms ignored this competition. Today, this small Chinese company has grown to a much larger multinational corporation called Haier Group (www.haieramerica.com), with sales of almost $9 billion. Haier Group manufactures over 250 models of refrigerators, air conditioners, dishwashers, and ovens. It now has 50 percent of the U.S. market for the minirefrigerators and 60 percent of the U.S. market for wine coolers, and dominates the Chinese home appliance market. In 2000, the Haier Group established a design center in Los Angeles and a factory in Camden, South Carolina, to expand its U.S. sales and bypass U.S appliance tariffs. Because global value chains are a critical issue in today's business environment, we devote a considerable amount of discussion to issues of designing and managing value chains in a global environment.

A multinational enterprise is an organization that sources, markets, and produces its goods and services in several countries to minimize costs and to maximize profit, customer satisfaction, and social welfare. Examples of multinational enterprises include British Petroleum, General Electric, United Parcel Service of America, Siemens, Procter & Gamble, Toyota, Lufthansa, and the International Red Cross. Their value chains provide the capability to source, market, create, and deliver their goods and services to customers worldwide.

Source: www.haieramerica.com

*A **multinational enterprise** is an organization that sources, markets, and produces its goods and services in several countries to minimize costs and to maximize profit, customer satisfaction, and social welfare.*

The complex value chains of multinational enterprises are a challenge to operations managers. Some issues that operations managers must confront in a global business environment include (1) how to design a value chain to meet the slower growth of industrialized countries and more rapid growth of emerging economies, (2) where to locate manufacturing and distribution facilities around the globe to capitalize on value chain efficiencies and improve customer value, (3) what performance metrics to use in making critical value chain decisions, and (4) whether partnerships should be developed with competitors to share engineering, manufacturing, or distribution technology and knowledge.

Toyota, for example, has a goal of controlling 15 percent of the world's auto market. Recognizing the huge potential in China—1.3 billion potential customers—Toyota recently began producing cars in Tianjin, the closest seaport to Beijing. Over 100 automobile companies are seeking to enter this market. However, Toyota automobiles are relatively expensive and beyond the salary of most Chinese. A Toyota Corolla sells for about $34,000 while locally made Chinese cars sell for one-half of that price. However, Toyota plans to build a new car in China for a much lower price and also plans to bundle the car with reliable maintenance and repair service. The President of Tianjin Toyota Motor Co. said, "We're going to win customers' trust through our reliable maintenance service that comes after the purchase."

To accomplish the goal of providing Chinese customers with a more complete customer benefit package, Toyota adopted several initiatives. First, it brought to Tianjin several key suppliers who make engines, seats, and so on. Second, auto maintenance and repair in China is a rag-tag set of shops and dealers with historically poor performance. Hence, the reliability of even new cars diminishes quickly. Toyota thinks its "service strategy" will differentiate its customer benefit package from its competitors. To accomplish this broader goods and services benefit package, Toyota is adding a postproduction service, which demands operations and logistical skills for both goods and services.[18]

As the race to gain market share in China's automobile market speeds up, all global automakers are pouring billions into China. For example, General Motors plans to invest $3 billion and VW $7.4 billion more. Honda, Peugeot, Nissan, and DaimlerChrysler have all made similar China-related investment announcements.[19]

To gain a better understanding of value chains in a global context, we present a case study of Rocky Shoes & Boots next.

An Example of a Global Value Chain: Rocky Shoes & Boots Company[20]

Rocky Shoes & Boots (RS&B, www.rockyboots.com) headquartered in Nelsonville, Ohio, manufactures rugged leather shoes for hiking and camping. (Timberland, Wolverine, and Rocky are popular brand names for this shoe market segment.) RS&B began making boots in 1932 as the William Brooks Shoe Company, with an average wage rate of 28 cents per hour. In the 1960s, Rocky Shoes & Boots were 100 percent "Made in America" as were more than 95 percent of all shoes sold in America.

The shoe industry depends on manual labor to bend, sew, and craft shoes. Leather and shoe-making materials are pliable, and therefore, manufacturing a shoe is very difficult for automated equipment. Stitching angles, curves, and leather thickness and textures are different from shoe to shoe, even within the same size range. In the early days, shoemakers were expert at learning how to arrange patterns close together and

Source: www.rockyboots.com

precisely slice them so that they never wasted an inch of the leather. One ill-defined pattern or inaccurate cut and thousands of dollars of leather were wasted.

Eventually, the children of the founder took over the company and suggested RS&B needed to find cheaper labor, possibly in the Dominican Republic. The response of the elderly founder was "Not in my lifetime. If we can't be in Nelsonville, we are not going to make shoes." The company went public in 1993 and stockholders and investors quickly wanted growth, lower cost, and more profit. The founder of RS&B died in 1996.

After 70 years in Nelsonville, the main factory closed in 2002. At that time local labor costs were about $11 per hour plus benefits, while in Puerto Rico the hourly rate was $6; in the Dominican Republic, $1.25; and in China, 40 cents. Today, RS&B headquarters remains in Nelsonville along with a warehouse, but all manufacturing is now done overseas, at such locations as Moca, Puerto Rico, and La Vega, Dominican Republic. RS&B's global value chain is shown in Exhibit 2.6. A pair of premium Rocky hiking boots may reflect components and labor from as many as five countries before landing on a store shelf. The principal characteristics of this global value chain are as follows:

1. Leather is produced in Australia and then shipped to the Dominican Republic.
2. Outsoles are purchased in China and shipped to Puerto Rico.
3. Gor-Tex fabric waterproofing material is made in the United States.
4. Shoe uppers are cut and stitched in the Dominican Republic and then shipped to Puerto Rico.
5. Final shoe assembly is done at the Puerto Rico factory.
6. The finished boots are packed and shipped to the warehouse in Nelsonville, Ohio.
7. Customer orders are filled and shipped to individual stores and contract customers from Nelsonville.

The challenges continue for RS&B, who must compete for sales against larger companies. RS&B remains price-competitive because of its global network and initiatives. Meanwhile, the price of boots continues to decline from roughly $95 a pair to $85 and is heading toward $75. The grandson of the founder of RS&B said, "We've got to get there, or we're not going to be able to compete."

Offshoring

As we saw in the opening chapter episodes, offshoring represents one of the most controversial topics in business today. **Offshoring** *is the building, acquiring, or moving*

of

Offshoring *is the building, acquiring, or moving of process capabilities from a domestic location to another country location while maintaining ownership and control.*

Exhibit 2.6 Rocky Shoes & Boots Value Chain

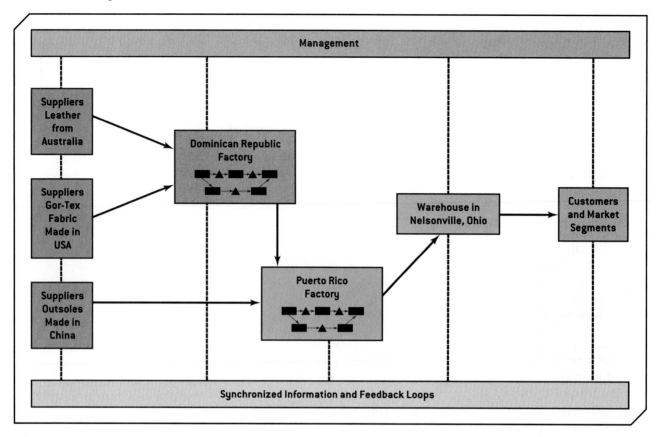

of process capabilities from a domestic location to another country location while maintaining ownership and control. According to one framework, foreign factories can be classified into one of six categories:[21]

Offshore factories *are established to gain access to low wages and other ways to reduce costs such as avoiding trade tariffs.*

Outpost factories *are established primarily to gain access to local employee skills and knowledge.*

Server factories *are established to supply specific national or regional markets.*

Source factories, *like offshore factories, are established to gain access to low-cost production but also have the expertise to design and produce a component part for the company's global value chain.*

1. **Offshore factories** *are established to gain access to low wages and other ways to reduce costs such as avoiding trade tariffs.* Such a factory is not expected to be innovative and its people follow the standard process procedures dictated by the corporation. Offshore factories usually include some primary manufacturing and secondary support processes. An offshore factory is the way most multinational firms begin their venture into global markets and value chains.

2. **Outpost factories** *are established primarily to gain access to local employee skills and knowledge.* Such skills and knowledge might include software programming, machining, sales, or call center service management. AOL's call center in India is an example of an outpost facility.

3. **Server factories** *are established to supply specific national or regional markets.* Coca-Cola bottling factories receive concentrated Coke syrup and follow specific procedures to make the final products. Because of high transportation costs, these bottling plants service local and regional markets.

4. **Source factories**, *like offshore factories, are established to gain access to low-cost production but also have the expertise to design and produce a component part for the company's global value chain.* Sony, for example, built a factory in Wales in the early 1970s and defined its strategy to produce television sets and replacement component parts for its European markets. It customized its design for the European markets.

5. **Contributor factories** *are established to serve a local market and conduct activities like product design and customization.* NCR's factory in Scotland started in the 1960s and played the role of a server factory producing cash registers and computers. By the 1980s, the factory was best described as a contributor factory and today is a lead factory designing and manufacturing automatic teller machines. Primary manufacturing, accounting, engineering design, and marketing and sales processes often reside at contributor factories.

6. **Lead factories** *are established to innovate and create new processes, products, and technologies.* Hewlett-Packard, for example, established an offshore factory in 1970 in Singapore. A decade later it had evolved into a source factory for calculators and keyboards. By the 1990s, the Singapore factory was a lead factory in keyboard and inkjet printer design and manufacturing. Lead factories must have the skills and knowledge to design and manufacturer "the next generation of products."

Offshore, outpost, and server factories are most often the first to be established and are usually the easiest. Some multinational firms keep many of these factories for strategic purposes. Other firms upgrade their offshore, outpost, and server factories to the next level—either a source or contributor factory. Not all multinational firms locate across the globe. Lego, the Danish toy maker, made a strategic decision long ago to locate its factories only in Europe and the United States. While all other toy manufacturers moved production to low-cost countries, Lego wanted to stay in countries with expertise in injection molding and mold design. It also wanted to have immediate access to the latest innovations in plastic materials. Lego justified its strategic decisions more on noneconomic reasons.

From a purely economic standpoint, offshoring can make a lot of sense because it generally lowers unit costs. Countries such as China, India, and Russia have many educated people who are eager to work at low wage rates. Many U.S. companies have made the strategic decisions necessary to locate certain functions overseas to remain globally competitive. For example, in the early 1990s, Boeing Co. began hiring Russian aerospace engineers for as little as $5,400 per year.[22] Boeing opened its Moscow Design Center in 1998 over the complaints of Seattle's 22,000 engineers represented by the Society of Professional Engineering Employees in Aerospace (SPEEA). "The underlying fear is that we're giving away our technology and our competitive advantage, and we're losing jobs," says Dave Landress, a test engineer and union representative. Although Boeing has reduced its work force at the Moscow Design Center, one of its goals is to develop an integrated 24-hour global work force. "We have achieved substantial cost reductions on every airplane we deliver with the help of our Moscow team," said Hank Queen, a Boeing vice president for engineering. Boeing also hopes a presence in Russia will help it win Russian orders for new planes.

Regulatory constraints have changed as globalization has taken root. Previously, it would have been impossible for a U.S. firm to buy a company in China because of regulatory constraints. However, Anheuser-Busch Co. bought China's Harbin Brewery Group in 2004. (China, incidentally, is the world's largest beer market.[23]) India slashed or abolished a range of taxes on consumer goods such as cell phones, computers, appliances, pharmaceuticals, and domestic airline flights. For example, the import duty on machinery was reduced to 10 percent from 25 percent. Excise duty fees on computers were cut to 8 percent from 16 percent. Import fees on electric power transmission and distribution equipment were cut to 10 percent from 25 percent. The objective is to provide greater opportunities for both domestic and foreign companies.[24]

Offshoring decisions involve determining what primary, support, and/or management processes should move to other countries (see Exhibit 2.7). Some global trade experts recommend keeping some primary processes or key parts of a manufacturing process out of foreign lands to protect the firm's core competency. Exhibit 2.7 outlines four possible scenarios. In the first scenario, all key processes remain in

Contributor factories *are established to serve a local market and conduct activities like product design and customization.*

Lead factories *are established to innovate and create new processes, products, and technologies.*

Exhibit 2.7
Four Degrees of Offshoring
Scenarios

Company Home Country Responsibility	Offshore Partner Responsibility	Example(s)	Degree of Offshoring
Primary Processes Support Processes Management Processes		Firms such as Harley-Davidson, Maytag, German Metro AG, Priceline.com, and Health Choice Network	None
Primary Processes Support Processes Management Processes		Service call centers and sales offices for firms such as Texaco Chevron, Microsoft, and American Express	Low
Primary Processes Support Processes Management Processes		Multinational firms such as Boeing, Coca-Cola, FedEx, Cisco, and Dell Computer	Moderate
Primary Processes Support Processes Management Processes		Multinational firms such as Procter & Gamble, Seimens, Airbus, General Electric, Honda, and UPS	High

the home country, even though the firm sells its products overseas. The second scenario represents a low degree of offshoring in which some noncritical support processes are moved overseas. A more common scenario is to offshore many primary as well as support processes while keeping management processes consolidated at the corporate headquarters. Finally, true global multinational firms locate all of their key processes across the globe for more effective coordination and local management. The global alignments, of course, may change over time.

The decision to offshore or outsource involves a variety of economic and noneconomic issues. China, India, and other nations now offer many new market opportunities along with large numbers of talented employees (see the OM Spotlight: Chevron Texaco in the Phillippines). Exhibit 2.8 summarizes a few key statistics on U.S., China, and India work forces.

Exhibit 2.8
Comparison of Work Forces in the United States, India, and China

Characteristic	United States	India	China
Total population	0.29 billion	1.07 billion	1.30 billion
Civilian work force	147 million	470 million	744 million
Population under age 25	35%	53%	41%
No. college graduates per year	1.3 million	3.1 million	2.8 million
No. computer science graduates per year	53,000	75,000	50,000
Percent of country with electricity	100%	60%	98%
Illiteracy rate	5%	35%	15%

Source: O'Sullivan, K., and Durfee, D., "Offshoring by the Numbers," *CFO Magazine*, June 2004, p. 54.

OM SPOTLIGHT

Chevron Texaco in the Philippines[25]

It's 3 A.M. in the morning and 750 men and women are jammed into a Chevron Texaco Corporation call center in Manila, Philippines. They're busy handling credit card queries from Chevron customers, mainly in the United States. They drink cappuccinos and eat junk food to stay up all night. Most of the call center employees are very well educated, such as one employee who graduated from the University of Philippines in 1998 with degrees in German and Italian. The co-worker next to him is a young woman who has a degree in communications. They make about $13,000 per year, which is well above the average worker in the Philippine economy.

The employee turnover rate for this type of work is only 10 percent per year in the Philippines in contrast to 70 percent in the United States. The Philippine employees speak English perfectly and are committed to training programs and doing the job well. The only problem one call center manager noted was that "the Filipino employees are too polite, leading to longer, costly phone chats. We have to teach them to be more rude."

Because global companies are able to hire the best talent in the Philippines, Procter & Gamble, Eastman Kodak, American Express, Intel, and Microsoft have also set up customer service centers there. They handle increasingly complicated calls such as how to operate and take the best picture using Kodak cameras, how to fix software problems, and how to plan a trip overseas.

Exhibit 2.9 summarizes the key issues in these decisions. For example, Dell moved a customer call center to Bangalore, India, to lower costs. Later, Dell closed the call center servicing high-end Optiplex desktop and Latitude notebooks because of what Dell said was dissatisfaction with the level of technical support customers were receiving. The work is now done in Texas, Idaho, and Tennessee. Dell justified the call center's India location on costs, an economic reason, and later moved the call center back to the United States for noneconomic reasons.

Moving skilled service work offshore, however, incurs some risk—see Exhibit 2.10. From an operations perspective, work that can be easily measured and monitored, such as detecting keystroke errors in transaction processing, are good candidates for moving offshore. Activities in the moderate and high-risk categories have

Exhibit 2.9
Example Issues to Consider When Making Offshore Decisions

Economic reasons
Low labor costs
Lower import duties and fees
Lower capital costs
Grow global market share
Avoid national currency fluctuations
Preempt competitors from entering global market(s)
Hire worldwide skills and knowledge workers
Build robust value chain networks for global markets
Build relationships with government officials
The negative impact and media attention on remaining employees
Potential loss of intellectual property
Lose control of key processes
Develop secure sources of supply and reduce risks
Build relationships with suppliers
Possible political instability in offshore country
Lack of communication and/or technical skills
Learn foreign markets and cultures

Noneconomic reasons

Exhibit 2.10
Offshore Candidates for Service and Information Work Activity

LOW RISK	MODERATE RISK	HIGH RISK
Transaction processing	Underwriting insurance	Equity research
Telemarketing	Management information systems	Cash flow forecasting
Benefits administration	Customer service	Asset accounting
	Loan-asset management	Investment analysis
	Accounts receivable/payable	Customer data analytics
	Technical support	Pricing
		Working capital management
		Executive decision support

Source: Harris, R., "Offshoring by the Numbers," *CFO Magazine*, June 2004, p. 58.

"carry-forward" implications when errors and service upsets happen. For example, an error in technical support can result in hours or days of lost time. Mistakes in a cash flow forecast may drive a business to increase debt when it is not necessary.

Firms that partner with foreign companies must also evaluate the risk associated with protecting their intellectual property. For example, weak laws and regulations to protect intellectual property rights violations make partnering in China a risky business venture. Take the situation of Schwinn Bicycle Company. It entered into a contract manufacturing agreement with a manufacturing company in Taiwan. Within a decade, the Taiwan Company became Giant Manufacturing (www.giant-bicycles.com) and broke its supplier relationship with Schwinn. Giant started producing its own bicycle brand name and has opened up a U.S. subsidiary in the United States.[26] However, many firms decide to take such risks because of the significant market potential, low production costs, and high rate of economic growth.[27]

Many types of Giant Manufacturing bikes are sold in the United States

AP/PRNewswire GIANT BICYCLE INC.

Offshoring and outsourcing decisions can also have detrimental impacts on people and their jobs, resulting in negative publicity and political backlash. Some U.S. labor unions see global offshoring and outsourcing as a short- and long-term problem. Indiana Governor Joe Kernan, for example, barred a software firm from India from bidding on a $15.2 million project the state had just awarded two weeks earlier to an American firm. The India firm had the lowest bid by some $8 million, according to the Indianapolis Star newspaper, and Indiana taxpayers will pay more for this software project.[28] Exhibit 2.11 summarizes the major advantages and disadvantages of global offshoring and outsourcing.

Some companies resist offshoring.[29] Toyota, for example, produces Corollas in Silicon Valley, California, one of the costliest places on earth. Toyota says, "The best supply chain is short." Moving manufactured goods 500 feet in 24 hours is better than shipping them 5,000 miles in 25 days across political and logistical boundaries. The consulting firm McKinsey & Company notes that companies that offshore often overrate the value of wage savings and underestimate the impact of inventory, obsolescence, currency risk, and speed of service. For instance, long overseas shipment times can translate into price declines of 2 to 6 percent, not to mention currency risks and swings. Staying close to the market and customers has advantages. One Los Angeles manufacturer of casual wear can fill orders of up to 160,000 units in 24 hours. The entire supply chain is located in downtown L.A.— design, weaving, dyeing, sewing, packaging, and shipment. The supply chain is short, all in one location, and serves a niche market.

McKinsey & Company recommend considering the following three issues in deciding whether to offshore or not:

- Clearly define the main competitive advantages in key markets (Chapter 4). Understand and specify the operating metrics such as customer response time,

Exhibit 2.11

Example Advantages and
Disadvantages of Global
Offshoring and Outsourcing

Advantages of Global Offshoring and Outsourcing	Disadvantages of Global Offshoring and Outsourcing
Lower total cost of goods and services	Higher local unemployment; costs of unemployment benefits; lack of health care
Organizational survival in the face of global competition	High retraining costs
New business from markets where jobs reside	More uncertainty and less job security in the future
Opportunities for more interesting work by moving mundane jobs	Difficulty of coordinating a global work force and meeting project/customer deadlines
Lower global inflation	Less control of core outsourced capabilities
24/7 customer care and services	Reverse brain drain and transfer of knowledge to other firms
Tapping expertise of workers around the world	Political fallout and restrictive laws

Source: Harris, R., "Offshoring by The Numbers," *CFO Magazine*, June 2004, p. 58.

manufacturing cost, and inventory (Chapter 3). The firm should also evaluate its tolerance for risks like supply chain interruptions, cost variances stemming from currency swings, and compromised process or intellectual property.

- If labor costs are 40 percent or more of a product's cost, seeking low wages is imperative. But operations strategies and methods such as using automation (Chapter 5) and/or lean production (Chapter 17) are alternatives to offshoring.
- Focus on designing manufactured goods to minimize production costs (Chapter 6), carefully source raw materials and parts from suppliers (Chapters 9 and 12), and work for much greater efficiencies of overhead processes (Chapter 6).

We added to these recommendations references to subsequent chapters that address these issues to clearly show that a broad understanding of operations management is necessary to evaluate such decisions. After considering these issues plus many others, most manufacturers will still decide to move some processes offshore. But offshoring is not a panacea. Short, direct supply chains scaled to match local market sizes are an alternative operations strategy and supply chain structure to offshoring.

James Womack, the co-author of *The Machine That Changed the World*, states that "outsourcing production, in whole or part, makes the most sense if a manufactured product is stable, requires lots of labor, and doesn't need lots of technical support." He recommends a product-by-product analysis to determine what production is appropriate to move where, instead of the argument that if everyone else is going to China we should go.[30] The issue for operations managers is that the decisions to vertically integrate, offshore processes and jobs, and/or outsource processes and jobs are very difficult decisions that help define the organization's value and supply chains and competitive capabilities. These types of decisions help establish the operational structure.

Management Issues in Global Value Chains

Complex, global value chains are more difficult to manage than small, domestic value chains. Some of the many issues include the following:

- Global supply chains face higher levels of risk and uncertainty, requiring more inventory and day-to-day monitoring to prevent product shortages. Work force

disruptions such as labor strikes and government turmoil in foreign countries can create inventory shortages and disrupting surges in orders. Extra finished goods inventory may be carried close to the customer's location if the supply chain includes overseas suppliers. Ensuring that foreign factories have a reliable supply of raw materials and component parts may also involve carrying higher levels of inventory.

- Transportation is more complex in global value chains. For example, tracing global shipments normally involves more than one mode of transportation and foreign company. One Chinese company is becoming the worldwide leader in shipping containers—a basic piece of equipment for global transportation firms and supply chains. The company set up six factories in the 1990s along the coast of China to manufacture shipping containers. Quickly learning how to manufacture refrigerated containers, it soon became the leader in the design and manufacture of containers for air, sea, road, and rail transportation services. Today, China International Marine Containers (CIMC, www.cimc.com) is a $1 billion firm with almost 50 percent of the global standard freight and refrigerated container markets.

- The transportation infrastructure may vary considerably in foreign countries. The coast of China, for example, enjoys much better transportation, distribution, and retail infrastructures than the vast interior of the country. Moving goods to the interior of the country can be slow, expensive, and sometimes impossible. Each country has its own unique transportation characteristics, including the threat of terrorism, political and border disruptions, and changes in import/export laws, tariffs, and regulations.

- Global purchasing can be a difficult process to manage when sources of supply, regional economies, and even governments change. Daily changes in international currencies necessitate careful planning and, in the case of commodities, consideration of futures contracts. New sources of supply frequently enter the global mix, requiring purchasing managers to reevaluate their decisions. These decisions can have far-reaching implications for operations, particularly when quality and delivery performance are considered.

- International purchasing can lead to disputes and legal challenges relating to such things as price fixing and quality defects. A legal case on global price-fixing of vitamins is now on the docket of the U.S. Supreme Court. International quality, cost, and delivery disputes have few legal options, and therefore, it is imperative that global supplier relationships be well established.

- Privatizing companies and property is another major change in global trade and regulatory issues. India is an example of how many countries are redefining their approach to business with a wave of privatization. The Indian government, for example, recently sold Bharat Aluminum Co. to a private investor. This was one of over 250 companies owned by the central government that it plans to sell. India has already sold its state-owned telephone companies and biggest auto manufacturer to private investors.[31] East Europe, China, Brazil, and Russia are also initiating private ownership of assets such as land, equipment, and businesses. This privatization movement also helps improve the efficiency and effectiveness of global supply chains.

Value Chains and Local Culture

Global organizations must balance the risk of designing and managing global value chains against the potential benefits of emerging markets. Each country has certain skills and resources, and marketplace potential. The example countries listed in Exhibit 2.12 are actively involved in global supply chains and their restructuring.

To build an effective global supply chain, organizations must not only know their own processes, resources, and capabilities but also those of the countries where the firm's resources are located. To extend the firm's value chain to other nations

Argentina	China	Ireland	Philippines	South Africa
Brazil	Costa Rica	Israel	Poland	Thailand
Bulgaria	Czech Republic	Malaysia	Romania	Ukraine
Chile	Hungary	Mexico	Russia	Vietnam
	India	New Zealand	Singapore	

Exhibit 2.12

Example Countries Participating in Global Supply Chain Development

Source: Datz, T., "Outsourcing World Tour," *CIO Magazine*, July 15, 2004, pp. 42–56. Reprinted through the courtesy of CIO. Copyright © 2005 CXO Media Inc. All rights reserved.

requires an understanding of national cultures and practices. **Culture** *is the sum of beliefs, rules, rituals, practices, institutions, language, and behaviors that characterize societies or organizations.* Culture defines the unique lifestyle for a nation or region. Since businesses locate their factories, call centers, warehouses, and offices around the world, operations managers need to be sensitive and understand the local culture. Notions of authority, time, color, value, respect, humor, work ethic, manners, and social status may be quite different from one's own norms. Exhibit 2.13 documents a few cultural differences that impact business operations.

Culture *is the sum of beliefs, rules, rituals, practices, institutions, language, and behaviors that characterize societies or organizations.*

Cultural differences have been studied in detail, so there is much opportunity to learn about these issues. For example, because Chinese words are pictures, the Chinese think more in terms of holistic thoughts and process information emphasizing the big picture over details. This cultural difference is called "zhengti guannian," or holistic thinking. Americans think sequentially, individualistically, and focus on details. They break complex situations into a series of smaller issues such as delivery dates, price, and quantity. Chinese tend to talk about all issues at once, skipping among them, and from the American point of view, never seem to settle anything. Obviously, this one cultural difference can have a major impact on designing, implementing, and managing any operations initiative.[32]

U.S. growth per capita, a common measure of the standard of living, increased at twice the rate of Europe's largest economies in the 1990s. The U.S. unemployment

The promise of overtime wages is not attractive in some countries.
The status distinction between blue- and white-collar workers may not exist.
The top floor of a retail store is reserved for the "bargain basement goods."
Nodding in agreement may mean "Yes, I hear you," not "Yes, I agree."
Black or white packaging is the color of mourning in some cultures.
Deadlines may not be "exact" but interpreted as "within the next few days."
To do business effectively, one must speak the local language.
Something "tried and true" is preferred to something "new and innovative."
The numbers 13 and 4 represent bad luck in some cultures.
Some factories must be stopped several times a day for prayer.
Some cultures do not allow women to work in a factory.
Working less hours and making less money may be viewed as more important than making more.

Exhibit 2.13

Example Cultural Differences that Impact Business

OM SPOTLIGHT

Europe's Work Force Working Less[33]

In an era of globalization, many European countries are trying an unusual experiment—trying to be globally competitive while working less. For example, Uwe Lang, a 34-year-old German supervisor at Eberspaecher AG, which makes car-heating systems, leaves work each day at 3 P.M. in the course of a 35-hour workweek. His two three-week vacations allow him time to relax and visit family and friends. He worked just 12 days in May because of four national holidays. Other European countries also have reduced their workweek and have extended vacation time.

At an economic summit in Lisbon, Spain, in 2000, the European Union government leaders set a goal of becoming the most competitive economy in the world by the end of the decade. Nevertheless, France extended its three-year old law reducing the workweek from 39 to 35 hours. Parents in Sweden now get an extra 30 days of parental leave at 80 percent of their salary. Six weeks vacation per year is the norm across Europe. The average German worker puts in about 1,400 hours a year, a 17 percent decrease from 1980, according to the Organization for Economic Cooperation and Development. In contrast, Americans are working about the same hours as they were in 1980, about 1,800 per year. European labor unions argue that reduced work hours would spur job growth by spreading the same amount of work among more people.

rate is lower and its productivity rate is higher than any European country. Global competition is forcing European countries to change their work hour laws and practices (see OM Spotlight: Europe's Work Force Working Less). Given the economic results of the past 15 years, European governments are beginning to promote part-time and other flexible work schemes. The French government, for example, is now allowing overtime. The German government is scaling back jobless benefits to push the unemployed into the work force. Italy wants to remove a law passed in the 1970s that makes it hard for large firms to fire employees.

The complexity of designing and managing in a global environment requires interacting with people from many different backgrounds and cultures, reevaluating global product mix changes, overcoming global regulatory barriers, and redesigning the operational and logistical structures. The Internet is also driving the restructuring of value chain and operational structures. In Part II of this book we will study many topics related to the structure of operations and value chains, the types of decisions that need to be made, and approaches to making these decisions.

SOLVED PROBLEMS

SOLVED PROBLEM #1

Suppose that a manufacturer needs to produce a custom aluminum housing for a special customer order. Because it currently does not have the equipment necessary to make the housing, it would have to acquire machines and tooling at a fixed cost (net of salvage value after the project is completed) of $250,000. The variable cost of production is estimated to be $20 per unit. The company can outsource the housing to a metal fabricator at a cost of $35 per unit. The customer order is for 12,000 units. What should the manufacturer do?

Solution:

VC_1 = Variable cost/unit if produced = $20
VC_2 = Variable cost/unit if outsourced = $35
FC = Fixed costs associated with producing the part = $250,000
Q = Quantity produced

Using Equation 2.1, we obtain

$$Q = \frac{\$250,000}{\$35 - \$20} = 16,667 \text{ units}$$

In this case, because the customer order is for only 12,000 units, which is less than the break-even point, the least-cost decision is to outsource the component.

KEY TERMS AND CONCEPTS

Backward integration
Culture
Culture differences
Economic and noneconomic decision criteria
Forward integration
Global challenges
Global labor rates
Global value chain decision areas
Global value (supply) chains
Global work force characteristics
Impact of technology on global value chains
Inventory role in global value chains
Multinational enterprise

Offshoring
Operational structure
Outsourcing
Pre- and postproduction services
Six categories of offshore factories
Supply chains
Trade and regulatory issues
Value
Value chain integration
Value chains
Value proposition
Vertical integration

QUESTIONS FOR REVIEW AND DISCUSSION

1. Explain the notion of *value*, and what organizations can do to provide value to customers.

2. Provide an example comparing a good or service by its value and its perceived benefits and price. How did your assessment of value lead to a purchase (or nonpurchase) decision?

3. What is a *value proposition*? How does this relate to the concept of a customer benefit package that we discussed in Chapter 1?

4. What is a *value chain*? Why is it important for every manager to understand this concept?

5. Think of some bundle of goods and services that you have recently purchased. Provide two examples of pre- and/or postproduction services that created value.

6. Contrast the two views of a value chain. What are the advantages of each?

7. What is a supply chain? How does it differ from a value chain?

8. How does the operational structure of a value chain influence the operations management decisions that need to be made in managing the value chain?

9. Explain how technology can improve value chain effectiveness. Provide some examples.

10. What is *vertical integration*? What issues must managers consider when deciding the level of vertical integration?

11. Contrast the difference between backward integration and forward integration. What are the pros and cons of each strategy?

12. What is *outsourcing*? How does it differ from vertical integration? What implications have the three waves of outsourcing had for the national and global economy?

13. When should primary processes and core competencies be outsourced to other countries?

14. What is *value chain integration*? Explain the role of third-party integrators.

15. What is a multinational enterprise? What challenges does it present to operations managers?

16. What are the advantages and disadvantages of Rocky Shoe & Boot Company moving all production and assembly off U.S. shores? What should be the policy for federal and state governments for Rocky Shoe & Boot Company employees who are laid off? What type of resource support should government provide, or should government not interfere—whatever the consequences?

17. What is *offshoring*? For what reasons do firms choose this strategy?

18. What do you think of the idea of locating call centers in small U.S. towns instead of locating offshore? What are the advantages and disadvantages of these two options?

19. Explain the six categories of foreign factories and how they impact operations management. Under what circumstances would you develop a lead factory in a foreign country? Explain.

20. Summarize the key issues that managers face with global value chains in comparison with simple, domestic value chains.

21. Explain why it is important for operations managers to understand the local culture and practices of the countries in which a firm does business. What are some of the potential consequences if they don't?

22. One study that focused on the impact of China trade on the U.S. textile industry noted that 19 U.S. textile factories were closed and 26,000 jobs lost in 2004 and 2005. If these factories had not closed, it would have cost U.S. consumers $6 billion more in higher textile prices. Assuming these facts are true, offer an argument for or against off-shoring U.S. jobs.

PROBLEMS AND ACTIVITIES

1. Describe a value chain based upon your work experience, summer job, or experience as a customer. Sketch a picture of it (as best you can). List suppliers, inputs, resources, outputs, customers, and target markets (similar to Exhibits 2.1 or 2.2).

2. Document the global supply chain for a business of interest to you, and sketch out a picture similar to the Procter & Gamble diagram. Why did the organization use global resources to accomplish its goals? Explain.

3. Read the *Harvard Business Review* article by J. L. Graham and N. M. Lam, "The Chinese Negotiation," October 2003, pp. 19–28. Summarize its lessons in one page or less.

4. Research current articles relating to offshoring and outsourcing, focusing on business, operations, and political issues. Summarize your findings in a paper of three to five pages.

5. A firm is evaluating the alternative of manufacturing a part that is currently being outsourced from a supplier. The relevant information is

For in-house manufacturing:
Annual fixed cost = $45,000
Variable cost per part = $130

For purchasing from supplier:
Purchase price per part = $160

   a. Using this information, determine the break-even quantity for which the firm would be indifferent between manufacturing the part in-house or outsourcing it.

   b. If demand is forecast to be greater than 1,500 parts, should the firm make the part in-house or purchase it from a supplier?

   c. The marketing department forecasts that the upcoming year's demand will be 1,200 units. A new supplier offers to make the parts for $140 each. Should the company accept the offer?

   d. What is the maximum price per part the manufacturer should be willing to pay to the supplier if the forecast is 800 parts?

CASES

TUNEMAN[34]

The 1998 Digital Millennium Copyright Act requires Internet providers to provide upon subpoena the names of people suspected of operating pirate web sites. However, the U.S. Supreme Court decided not to become involved in a dispute over illegal downloading of music files. The Court refused to give the recording industry broad power to force Verizon Communications and other Internet service providers to identify subscribers who share copyrighted songs online. The Court said it was up to the United States Congress, not courts, to expand the 1998 law to cover popular file-sharing networks.

Music downloading has become a very controversial subject. The Recording Industry Association of America (RIAA) argues that 2.6 billion music files are illegally downloaded each month and this law is needed to identify downloading culprits. On September 8, 2003, RIAA filed lawsuits against 261 people for allegedly downloading thousands of copyrighted songs via popular Internet file-sharing networks. These people copied an average of 1,000 songs into their files for free.

Lester Tune, the founder of TuneMan, one of the more popular downloading sites, debated the issue with a corporate regulator on a recent talk show. He brought the audience to their feet after exclaiming, "Well, people listen to music on the radio for free, so what's the big deal?" In response, the corporate regulator was vehement, "We want people to stop engaging in the theft of music so that people can go on making it. We need to figure out where customer ownership begins in the value chain. We are about to destroy the long history of professional songwriters and performers in America. Who's going to pay the royalties?"

Many music-downloading providers now require customers to pay a fee, while some sites provide free and legal downloads. RealNetworks, for example, sold 3 million songs at 49 cents each during a three-week promotion and then returned to its regular rate of 99 cents per song. iTunes, Napster, Universal Music Group, and others are all struggling to define a value chain structure that is fair to all parties—the creators of the song, the distributors, the web sites, and the customers. Clearly, the value chain in the music industry is changing dramatically.

Questions for Discussion

1. Draw the "bricks and mortar" value chain by which records, tapes, and CDs are created, distributed, and sold in retail stores. Use formats similar to Exhibits 2.1 to 2.5, and write a one-page description of how this value chain works and how each player makes money.

2. Develop an alternative value chain structure for this industry, and justify your recommendations. Use formats similar to Exhibits 2.1 to 2.5, and write a one-page description of how this value chain works and how everyone makes money.

3. Explain and compare the role of operations in the two value chain structures you developed in questions 1 and 2.

THE RISKY OUTSOURCING DECISION

Mike Dunn, the Chief Operating Officer of a major designer of video games is considering outsourcing some of its software development activities to firms in other countries. Many factors support this decision. For example, many other countries have a highly-educated workforce with considerable experience in software development applications; and costs and tax incentives provided by local governments are very favorable. However, Tom Matthews, the firm's legal counsel, was more skeptical, particularly with the sensitivity of launching innovative new titles and the short product life of video games. He had heard of situations in which proprietary product information was leaked to competitors by employees of outsourcing contractors, even in spite of contractual agreements that required vendors to abide by all U.S. regulatory requirements and Federal Trade Commission data protection and security requirements. In meeting with Mike, Tom pointed out six key risks associated with outsourcing:

1. **Country Risk:** political, socio-economic, or other factors may amplify any of the traditional outsourcing risks, including those listed below.

2. **Operations/Transaction Risk:** weak controls may affect customer privacy.

3. **Compliance Risk:** offshore vendors may not have adequate privacy regulations.

4. **Strategic Risk:** different country laws may not protect "trade secrets."

5. **Credit Risk:** a vendor may not be able to fulfill its contract due to financial losses.

6. **Intellectual Property Risk:** a vendor may learn how to do the business better than the outsourcers.

Mike replied, "I tend to agree, but we need to do something to cut our costs. I'd like you to come back to me with some ideas for mitigating these risks so we can move confidently into some type of outsourcing agreement."

Questions for Discussion

1. What ideas can you develop for avoiding or reducing the risks that Tom brought up?

2. Should design and development processes be outsourced, or only transaction processing, basic coding, and software maintenance? Explain your reasoning.

3. What "best practices" can companies develop for outsourcing software projects? You might wish to conduct a Web search for help on this topic.

ENDNOTES

[1] Aeppel, T., "Three Countries, One Dishwasher," *Wall Street Journal*, October 6, 2003, p. B1.

[2] Niquette, M., "Going, going, gone," *The Columbus Dispatch*, Columbus, Ohio, November 9, 2003, p. F1.

[3] "It's All About the Shoes," *Fast Company*, New York, NY, September 2004, p. 85, http://pf.fastcompany.com/magazine/86/stollenwerk.html.

[4] "Review & Outlook—Creative Jobs Destruction," *Wall Street Journal*, January 6, 2004, p. A16.

[5] Angwin, J., "AOL's Tech Center in India Is Money-Saver," *Wall Street Journal*, August 7, 2003, p. B4.

[6] O'Sullivan, K., and Durfee, D., "Offshoring by the Numbers," *CFO Magazine*, June 2004, p. 53.

[7] Selden, Larry, and Colvin, Geoffrey, "What Customers Want," *Fortune*, July 3, 2003, pp. 122–128.

[8] Davis, S., *Future Perfect*, New York: Addison-Wesley, 1987, p. 108.

[9] Ford Motor Company, Owner Loyalty and Customer Satisfaction Survey Results, 1994, p. 4.

[10] Wegryn, Glenn W., and Siprelle, Andrew J., "Combined Use of Optimization and Simulation Technologies to Design an Optimal Logistics Network," http://www.simulationdynamics.com/PDFs/Papers/CLM%20P&G%20Opt&Sim.pdf.

[11] Kahn, G., "Financing Goes Just-in-Time," *Wall Street Journal*, June 4, 2004, p. A10.

[12] Keefe, B., "Glitches possible during massive bar-code upgrade," *The Columbus Dispatch*, Columbus, Ohio, December 12, 2004, p. F10.

[13] Ansberry, C., and Aeppel, T., "U.S. Companies Customize, Rethink Strategies to Compete With Products from Abroad," *Wall Street Journal*, October 6, 2004, p. B6.

[14] "Is Your Job Next?" *Business Week*, February 3, 2003, pp. 50–60.

[15] Kahn, G., "Tiger's New Threads," *Wall Street Journal*, March 26, 2004, p. B1.

[16] "Delivering Integration Management," *Featured Stories*, June 24, 2002, www.visteon.com.

[17] http://www.exel.com, October 14, 2004.

[18] Kageyama, Y., "Great expectations," *The Columbus Dispatch*, Columbus, Ohio, April 27, 2002, p. E1.

[19] Kurtenback, E., "GM to invest $3 billion in Chinese ventures," *The Columbus Dispatch*, Columbus, Ohio, June 8, 2004, pp. C1–C2.

[20] Price, R., "Rocky clocks out," *The Columbus Dispatch*, Columbus, Ohio, April 28, 2002, pp. A1, A8–A9 and April 29, 2002, pp. A1, A4–A5.

[21] Ferdows, K., "Making the Most of Foreign Factories," *Harvard Business Review*, March–April, 1997, pp. 73–88.

[22] "The New Cold War at Boeing," *Business Week*, February 3, 2003, pp. 58–59.

[23] Baglole, J., and Bilefsky, D., "Anheuser-Busch Wins China Brewer," *Wall Street Journal*, June 4, 2004, p. A3.

[24] Solomon, Sharma S., and Ramakrishnan, V., "India Unveils Broad Tax Cuts," *Wall Street Journal*, January 9, 2004, p. A6.

[25] "The Way, Way Back Office," *Business Week*, February 3, 2003, p. 60.

[26] Bartmess, A. D., "The Plant Location Puzzle," *Harvard Business Review*, March–April, 1994, p. 12.

[27] Zeng, M. and Williamson, P. J., "The Hidden Dragons," *Harvard Business Review*, October, 2003, pp. 31–39.

[28] "Review & Outlook—Creative Jobs Destruction," *Wall Street Journal*, January 6, 2004, p. A16.

[29] Sternfels, R., and Ritter, R., "When Offshoring Doesn't Make Sense," *Wall Street Journal*, October 19, 2004, p. B8.

[30] Ansberry, C., and Aeppel, T., "U.S. Companies Customize, Rethink Strategies to Compete With Products from Abroad," *Wall Street Journal*, October 6, 2004, p. B1.

[31] Solomon, J., and Slater, J., "India's Economy Gets a New Jolt From Mr. Shourie," *Wall Street Journal*, January 9, 2004, p. A1.

[32] Graham, J. L., and Lam, N. M., "The Chinese Negotiation," *Harvard Business Review*, October, 2003, pp. 19–28.

[33] Rhoads, C., "Short Work Hours Undercut Europe In Economic Drive," *Wall Street Journal*, August 8, 2002, p. A1.

[34] Facts in this case are based on Holland, G., "Supreme Court rejects appeal in music downloading battle," *The Northwest Herald*, October 19, 2004, http://www.nwherald.com/print/281665778400853.php. However, TuneMan is fictitious, so students, please don't try to search for it!

Chapter Outline

CHAPTER 3

Measuring Performance in Operations

Learning Objectives

1. To understand the principal types of performance measures used in organizations and by operations managers and to be able to identify important measures and indicators to manage and improve business performance.

2. To understand the importance of evaluating relationships and cause-and-effect linkages among performance measures and approaches that companies use to understand such relationships.

3. To understand the characteristics of a good measurement system and how to select appropriate measures to support operations.

4. To understand how measurement systems are integrated into comprehensive models of business performance as a basis for better design and improvement of operations.

ROLAND WEIHRAUCH/DPA/Landov

- Imagine entering the cockpit of a modern jet airplane and seeing only a single instrument there.[1] How would you feel about boarding the plane after the following conversation with the pilot?

  Passenger: I'm surprised to see you operating the plane with only a single instrument. What does it measure?

  Pilot: Airspeed. I'm really working on airspeed this flight.

  Passenger: That's good. Airspeed certainly seems important. But what about altitude? Wouldn't an altimeter be helpful?

  Pilot: I worked on altitude for the last few flights and I've gotten pretty good on it. Now I have to concentrate on proper airspeed.

  Passenger: But I notice you don't even have a fuel gauge. Wouldn't that be useful?

  Pilot: You're right; fuel is significant, but I can't concentrate on doing too many things well at the same time. So on this flight I'm focusing on airspeed. Once I get to be excellent at airspeed, as well as altitude, I intend to concentrate on fuel consumption on the next set of flights.

© Getty Images/PhotoDisc

- Waiting in my car in a bank drive-through teller line is not my idea of fun. The automobile air conditioner was rattling and not doing a very good job keeping me cool on this hot summer day. I noted the time I arrived in line, and when I drove up to the teller window I placed my deposit in the window and exchanged greetings with the bank teller. As she finished my transaction and gave me my deposit slip she said, "Mr. Worthington, your account balance is printed on the back of the deposit slip and I also credited this account for $5 because you had to wait over 5 minutes in line." Stunned, I responded by saying, "Wow! How did you know I waited 7 minutes in line?" "We are trained, Mr. Worthington, to do this in support of our bank's service guarantee, so I continuously keep my eye on the clock and the last car in line," noted the bank teller with a smile. As I drove off, I thought to myself, "What a great bank!"

- "OK people, listen up! We just got a memo from the Vice-President of Manufacturing and the Director of Human Resources. They've been told that we're taking too long to develop and get our new products and designs out to the market. From now on, your incentive bonus will be tied to how quickly you can roll out new products. Right now we're averaging about 18 months. Our objective is to get it down to 3 months or the stock options will dry up!"

  One year later . . . "OK people, listen up! Great job on reducing the new product development time! In the past year, you've managed to reduce the average cycle time down to 4 months. Great job! Our bonus will be up about 50 percent this year! Keep up the good work and let's meet that 3-month goal.

  Another year later . . . "OK people, listen up! I just got a memo directly from the CEO. For the past year and a half, the company's stock price has steadily declined and the shareholders are ready to revolt. Marketing did a comprehensive survey and found out that the customers absolutely hate the designs we've been sending to them. We've taken a big hit in revenue and are losing customers left and right. What's going on?"

Discussion Questions: What measures do you use to evaluate a company's goods or services? How do the measures that your professors use to evaluate you influence your school activities and priorities?

Managers make many important decisions that affect how an organization provides value to its customers. To know whether their decisions are effective and to guide the organization on a daily basis, they need a means of understanding performance at all levels of the organization as well as in operations. In the value chain model (Chapter 2), we saw the importance of synchronized information and feedback loops as the foundation for integrating and managing all the elements of the value chain. Information provides the basis for evaluating suppliers and letting them know how well they are performing; for determining the quality of inputs, process performance, outputs, and outcomes; for evaluating customer's postsale experiences to determine their satisfaction; and to provide a basis for further improvements in goods and services and the processes that produce and deliver them. In addition, good information is vital to coordinating the flow of materials and information within the value chain and managing all aspects of its operations. We will have more to say about measurement and the value chain later in this chapter.

Good decisions are facilitated through *measurement*, which is the common theme of those anecdotes that opened the chapter. In the first one, you would probably be more than a bit uneasy about flying with this pilot. However, the analogy to business is not that far-fetched. Many companies still manage their organizations by concentrating primarily on financial measures and pay little attention to operational and other measures that are important to the business and its customers. On the other hand, what a surprise the bank customer received in the second episode as a result of the trained and empowered bank teller who measured waiting time and delivered excellent customer service. Can you figure out the underlying issue in the third episode? (We will learn the answer in the next section.)

Measurement provides an objective basis for making decisions. Jeff Bezos, CEO of Amazon.com, explained the importance of making fact-based decisions this way: "For every leader in the company, not just for me, there are decisions that can be made by analysis. These are the best kind of decisions! They're fact-based decisions. The great thing about fact-based decisions is that they overrule the hierarchy. The most junior person in the company can win an argument with the most senior person with a fact-based decision. Unfortunately, there's this whole other set of decisions that you can't ultimately boil down to a math problem."[2] This also means that operations managers must rely on good judgment as well as data-driven analysis.

We can pose several questions related to measurement in operations.

- How should we measure the performance of goods and services?
- How should we measure the performance of processes throughout the value chain?
- How should we measure overall organizational performance, and how does it relate to internal operations?

In this chapter we examine the topic of performance measurement in operations, processes, and at the organizational level. In later chapters, we will examine other detailed measures of performance that relate to specific operations management decisions, such as inventory performance, service waiting times, and manufacturing efficiency. Effective measurements help mangers to understand current performance, predict future performance, and better communicate with all levels of management and the work force.

Learning Objective
To understand the principal types of performance measures used in organizations and by operations managers and to be able to identify important measures and indicators to manage and improve business performance.

Measurement *is the act of quantifying the performance criteria (metrics) of organizational units, goods and services, processes, people, and other business activities.*

THE SCOPE OF PERFORMANCE MEASUREMENT

Information is derived from the analysis of data. Data, in turn, come from measurement. **Measurement** *is the act of quantifying the performance criteria (metrics) of organizational units, goods and services, processes, people, and other business activities.* For example, the ground-operations area of American Airlines is concerned primarily with the service passengers receive at airports.[3] It routinely measures several factors that customers have told it are important, such as ticket-counter waiting time, cabin-door opening time after gate arrival, bag-delivery time, and cabin cleanliness. The data are collected by monthly self-audits at each airport and by a field support team of trained observers who visit airports to check those performance characteristics as well as other factors such as safety. Various managers, including the executive vice president of operations, review results. They analyze trends and, if warranted, put corrective measures in place. As another example, a restaurant manager might measure food quality and service quality, cost, productivity, order accuracy, order speed, on-time delivery performance from suppliers, and a host of other performance measures. These measures might be compared with customer satisfaction data to help understand how satisfaction can be maintained or improved. The OM Spotlight on eBay provides another example of the scope and importance of measurement in today's competitive organizations.

Good performance measures enable managers to control processes and make decisions on the basis of facts, not opinions. Moreover, they provide a "scorecard" of performance, help identify performance gaps, and make accomplishments visible to the work force, the stock market, and other stakeholders. Knowing that one is doing a good job—or a better job than before—is a powerful motivator for most workers. However, the wrong kind of performance metric can be dangerous. The popular phrase "How you are measured is how you perform" can destroy good intentions. Can you now determine what went wrong in the third episode at the

OM SPOTLIGHT

Measurement at eBay[4]

A saying around eBay's headquarters is, "If it moves, measure it." Meg Whitman, eBay's CEO, personally monitors a host of measurements and indicators, including such standard ones for Internet companies as how many people visit the web site, how many register to become users, how long each user remains per visit, how long pages take to load, and so on. She also monitors eBay's "take rate"—the ratio of revenues to the value of goods traded on the site, and what days are the busiest to determine when to offer free listings in order to stimulate the supply of auction items (Mondays in June are slow; Fridays in November rock). She even monitors the "noise" on eBay's discussion boards, online forums where users discuss, among other things, their opinion of eBay's management (Level 1 means "silent," and 10 means "hot" or "the community is ready to kill you." Normal for eBay is about 3).

To Whitman, measurements are a sign of a system that is process-oriented. The more stats, the more early warnings and the more levers to pull to make things work. Yet she is aware of the danger of "paralysis by analysis." As she noted, "You have to be careful because you could measure too much."

beginning of this chapter? The engineers were able to get products developed much faster by designing trivial products that customers did not want! After all, this is how they were evaluated and rewarded.

Many businesses manage operations using a limited set of performance data. For example, they may only look at such financial measures as costs or revenues, or productivity measures as labor efficiency or equipment utilization. A limited performance measurement system is myopic—it cannot see the complexity of the entire organization. On the other hand, too many performance measures can be as bad as not having enough. When Ford studied Mazda's management approaches, former CEO Donald Peterson observed, "Perhaps, most important, Mazda had been able to identify the types of information and records that were truly useful. It didn't bother with any other data. [At Ford] we were burdened with mountains of useless data and stifled by far too many levels of control over them."[5] Thus, selecting the right measures—not too many and not too few—is a very important decision all managers must make.

At the operational level, firms tend to acquire volumes of data. Although such data may be useful and necessary for running daily operations, they generally are not appropriate for senior executive review. Organizations need a process for transforming data, usually in some integrated fashion, into information that higher levels of management can understand and work with. For instance, some companies develop an aggregate customer satisfaction index (CSI) by weighting satisfaction results, market share, and gains or losses of customers. As one example, Federal Express aggregates ten key performance measures into their Service Quality Indicator, which is reviewed daily by senior management (see the OM Spotlight later in this chapter).

World-class organizations normally use between three to ten performance measures per process, depending on a host of issues such as the complexity of goods and services, number of market segments, competitive pressures, and opportunities for failure. Stock analysts and traders typically place no more than eight performance measures on one computer screen, because the simultaneous evaluation of more than eight performance measures seems to be the upper limit for the human mind. However, by using smart technology, such as statistical analyses and other quantitative decision support systems, managers can gain meaningful insights from a much larger number of performance variables.

Performance measures can be classified into several key categories:

- financial,
- customer and market,
- safety,
- quality,
- time,
- flexibility,
- innovation and learning,
- productivity.

Within each of these categories are organizational-level measures that are of interest primarily to senior managers, as well as more specific measures that are used by operations managers. Some of them are summarized in Exhibit 3.1. We will provide an overview of these categories to help you better understand the scope of performance measurement.

Financial Measures

Financial measures often take top priority in for-profit organizations. Cost and price are obvious indicators of performance. For example, the banking industry monitors closely the costs associated with checking account transactions. Internet banking is being promoted because it has a distinct cost advantage: The estimated transaction costs typically are 1 percent of branch bank transaction costs. Businesses track prices

Exhibit 3.1

The Scope of Business and Operations Performance Measurement

Performance Measurement Category	Typical Organizational-Level Performance Measures	Typical Operational-Level Performance Measures
Financial	Revenue and profit Return on assets Earnings per share	Labor and material costs Cost of quality Budget variance
Customer and market	Customer satisfaction Customer retention Market share	Customer claims and complaints Type of warranty failure/upset Sales forecast accuracy
Safety	Number of accidents/injuries Lost workdays	Safety audit score Workplace safety violations
Quality	Goods quality Service quality Environmental quality	Defects/unit Call center courtesy Toxic waste discharge rate
Time	Speed Reliability	Flow (processing or cycle) time Percent of time meeting promise (due) date
Flexibility	Design flexibility Volume flexibility	Number of engineering changes Assembly line changeover time
Innovation and learning	New product development rates Employee satisfaction Employee turnover	Number of patent applications Number of improvement suggestions implemented Percent of workers trained on statistical process control
Productivity	Sales/square foot Production cost/payroll dollar	Shipment dollars/labor-hour Units produced/labor-hour Transactions/labor-hour

charged by suppliers as part of their process to evaluate suppliers and to predict the effects on the company's financial stability.

Traditional financial measures that companies use include revenue, return on investment, operating profit, pretax profit margin, asset utilization, growth, revenue from new goods and services, earnings per share, and other liquidity measures. Key financial measures at Boeing Airlift and Tanker Programs, which produces large military transports in a capital-intensive industry, are return on sales, return on net assets, and net asset turnover. The Ritz-Carlton Hotel Company, on the other hand, monitors earnings before taxes, depreciation, and amortization, administrative costs, and gross profit among its key financial indicators. One financial performance measure that many organizations do *not* use is the *cost of quality*, which is a measure of what poor quality is costing an organization. Managers should use this information to prioritize and gauge the effectiveness of improvement initiatives. This is discussed thoroughly in Chapter 15.

Nonprofit organizations, such as the Red Cross, churches, and government agencies, focus more on minimizing costs and maximizing value to their target markets, customers, and society. Monitoring cost and adherence to budgets is an important factor in their operational success.

Customer and Market Measures

You have probably completed customer satisfaction surveys at a restaurant or after an Internet purchase, or perhaps have lodged a complaint. Through customer and market feedback, an organization learns how satisfied its customers and stakeholders are with its goods and services and performance. Measures of customer satisfaction reveal areas that need improvement and show whether changes actually result in improvement. *An effective customer-satisfaction measurement system provides a company with customer ratings of specific goods and service features and indicates the relationship between those ratings and the customer's likely future buying behavior.* It tracks trends and reveals patterns of customer behavior from which the company can predict future customer needs and wants. It also tracks and analyzes complaints and other measures of dissatisfaction.

At a basic level, customer satisfaction should be measured in three areas:

1. goods quality,
2. service quality, and
3. response time.

Satisfaction attributes related to goods quality might be customers' perceptions of the clarity of the music from a DVD player or the cleanliness of a hotel room; service quality attributes might include the effectiveness of technical support or the behavior of service workers; and time-related performance might include satisfaction with waiting times or promptness in resolving a complaint. For example, 3M's automotive trades business has as its direct customers automotive distributors, while end users are the secondary group. Service quality and response times are key satisfaction measures for distributors, and product quality is the principal satisfaction indicator for end users.[6] At Federal Express, customers are asked to rate everything from billing to the performance of couriers, package condition, tracking and tracing capabilities, complaint handling, and helpfulness of employees. A restaurant might rate food appearance, taste, temperature, and portions, as well as cleanliness, staff friendliness, attentiveness, and perception of value.

Other customer-focused performance measures include customer retention, gains and losses of customers and customer accounts, customer complaints, warranty claims, measures of perceived value, loyalty, positive referral, and customer

An effective customer-satisfaction measurement system provides a company with customer ratings of specific goods and service features and indicates the relationship between those ratings and the customer's likely future buying behavior.

relationship building. In addition, measures and indicators of product and service performance that have strong correlation with customer satisfaction are appropriate to monitor. STMicroelectronics, for example, tracks the number of nonconforming production lots, which play a significant role in complaints received by their customers.

Customer satisfaction data should include comparisons with key competitors, but that is not possible if a company surveys only its own customers. Consequently, companies often rely on third parties to conduct blind surveys to determine who key competitors are and how their goods and services compare. Such information may reveal key customer benefit package features that are being overlooked. An effective customer-satisfaction measurement system provides a company with customer ratings of specific goods and service features and indicates the relationship between those ratings and the customer's likely future buying behavior. It tracks trends and reveals patterns of customer behavior from which the company can predict future customer needs and wants. Each market segment can have different demographic and behavioral characteristics, goods and services preferences, relative weights of key performance measures, and price (cost) sensitivity.

Marketplace performance indicators could include market share, measures of business growth, new product and geographic markets entered, and percentage of new product sales as appropriate. In a commodity market (the egg further-processing industry—making liquid egg products from raw eggs) in which Sunny Fresh Foods competes, its performance drivers include the U.S. share of market and total pounds of egg products sold. In the highly competitive semiconductor industry, STMicroelectronics looks not only at sales growth but also at differentiated product sales.

Safety

Safety is such a basic attribute that it is hardly noticed. However, when a safety issue arises, it captures the attention of everyone. Measuring safety is vital to all organizations, as the well-being of its employees and customers should be an organization's principal concern. Moreover, safety enhances employee productivity and morale, as described by the OM Spotlight on Dana Corporation. Federal and state agencies require organizations to track and report safety. Examples of safety-related performance measures include accident rates, the parts per million of arsenic in a public water supply, or the security in a hotel room.

Quality

Quality *measures the degree to which the output of a process meets customer requirements.*

Goods quality *relates to the physical performance and characteristics of a good.*

Everyone expects quality. **Quality** *measures the degree to which the output of a process meets customer requirements.* Quality applies to both goods and services. **Goods quality** *relates to the physical performance and characteristics of a good.* For example, the J. D. Power automotive surveys publish the average number of problems reported per vehicle in the first 90 days of ownership, a popular measure of quality from the consumer's perspective. David A. Garvin describes many dimensions of quality by which consumers evaluate goods:[8]

1. *Performance: a good's primary operating characteristics.* Using an automobile as an example, these would include such things as acceleration, braking distance, steering, and handling.
2. *Features: the "bells and whistles" of a good.* A car may have power options, a tape or CD deck, antilock brakes, and reclining seats.
3. *Reliability: the probability of a good's surviving over a specified period of time under stated conditions of use.* A car's ability to start on cold days and frequency of failures are reliability factors.

OM SPOTLIGHT

Dana Corporation[7]

Safety awareness may not be the sole reason for the success of Dana Corporation's Hopkinsville, Kentucky, plant but it certainly has been a major contributor. The plant is recognized as a world-class factory. Awards are many, and include winning Industry Week's Ten Best Plants Award twice, Saturn's Quality Award four times, and the State of Kentucky's Governor's Gold Award twice. Dana Hopkinsville, which employs 670 teammates in a 400,000-sq.-ft. facility, manufactures full structural frames for automobiles for companies such as General Motors, Isuzu, Toyota, and Mercedes. The plant has produced more than 6 million frame assemblies. In a typical year, the plant handles about 160,000,000 pounds of steel. All teammates are salaried employees and there are no time cards or clocks in the plant. All of the plant's 98 teams are cross-trained on other team jobs. Training is intense with an average of 72 hours pre–employment training and many post–training programs.

A high degree of attention to safety is critical in a plant where heavy machinery and welding are used. Safety is closely integrated with Dana Hopkinsville plant's continuous quality improvement initiatives. Since 1990, 185,506 employee ideas and suggestions for improvement have been submitted and 84 percent of those have been implemented. This works out to about 30 improvement suggestions per employee per year! As rare as accidents are at the plant, when they do happen the entire facility is shut down. "This, of course, sends a very strong message that we care," says Pat Pilleri, the plant manager. "Everyone is taken off the plant floor. The accident is documented and all plant supervisors explain who is hurt and what happened to all teammates." To encourage safety awareness, a 5-minute safety talk is given to all employees at the beginning of every shift. Supervisors also have a 2-hour safety meeting each week. There are many formal safety programs that provide training, support, awareness, and rewards to Dana teammates. The results attest to the success of the plant's approaches: the plant's Lost Time Accident (LTA) rate from 1997 to 2000 was 39 times lower (better) than comparable companies in their S.I.C. code safety category, and the absenteeism rate is less than 1 percent.

4. *Conformance: the degree to which physical and performance characteristics of a good match preestablished standards.* A car's fit and finish and freedom from noises and squeaks can reflect this.
5. *Durability: the amount of use one gets from a good before it physically deteriorates or until replacement is preferable.* For a car this might include corrosion resistance and the long wear of upholstery fabric.
6. *Serviceability: the speed, courtesy, and competence of repair work.* An automobile owner might be concerned with access to spare parts, the number of miles between major maintenance services, and the expense of service.
7. *Aesthetics: how a good looks, feels, sounds, tastes, or smells.* A car's color, instrument panel design, control placement, and "feel of the road," for example, may make it aesthetically pleasing.

Goods quality is generally measured using instruments, technology, and data collection processes. For example, the dimensions and weight of a good such as a laptop computer, its storage capacity, battery life, and actual speed are easy to measure.

A common measure of goods quality is the number of **nonconformities per unit,** *or* **defects per unit,** *which is computed by dividing the total number of defects found by the number of items examined.* Because of the negative connotation of "defect" and its potential implications in liability suits, many organizations use the term *nonconformity*; however, quite a few still use the term *defect.* Nonconformities per unit are often reported as rates per thousand or million, and the measure **dpmo— defects per million opportunities**—is often used.

A common measure of goods quality is the number of **nonconformities per unit,** *or* **defects per unit,** *which is computed by dividing the total number of defects found by the number of items examined.*

Companies often classify defects into three categories:[9]

1. *Critical defect—one that judgment and experience indicate will surely result in hazardous or unsafe conditions for individuals using or experiencing the good or service.* For a restaurant, this might be meat that is not cooked properly. For a manufacturer, it might be a tire sidewall that is not strong enough. For an airline, it might be a landing gear that fails to lock prior to landing. Every effort should be made to identify and prevent critical defects.
2. *Major defect—one that is not critical but is likely to materially reduce the usability of the good or service for its intended purpose.* For a restaurant, this might be delivering the wrong meal to the wrong customer. For a manufacturer, it might be a zoom lens on a digital camera that does not work. For an airline, it might be not having a seat available for the passenger due to overbooking the flight. Obviously, such defects should be avoided whenever possible.
3. *Minor defect—one that is not likely to materially reduce the usability of the good or service for its intended purpose.* An example at a restaurant might be a pizza that is poorly sliced. For a DVD manufacturer, it might be a misprint in the user's manual that causes customer confusion as to how to use the DVD. For an airline, it might be the passenger cabin is too cold for some customers. Minor defects may draw negative responses from customers and hurt long-term customer loyalty.

Service quality *is consistently meeting or exceeding customer expectations (external focus) and service delivery system performance (internal focus) for all service encounters.* Many companies, including Amazon, Federal Express, and Nordstrom's, have worked hard to provide superior service quality to their customers. Measuring service quality is paramount in such organizations (see the OM Spotlight on Federal Express). Service quality examples include the knowledge and human interaction skills of the service provider when interacting with the customer, such as fielding questions at a telephone contact center or accurate preparation of a tax return.

Service quality measures are based primarily on human perceptions of service collected from customer surveys, focus groups, and interviews. Research has shown that customers use five key dimensions to assess service quality:[10]

1. *Tangibles*: physical facilities, uniforms, equipment, vehicles, and appearance of employees (that is, the physical evidence);
2. *Reliability*: ability to perform the promised service dependably and accurately;
3. *Responsiveness*: willingness to help customers and provide prompt recovery to service upsets;
4. *Assurance*: knowledge and courtesy of the service providers and their ability to inspire trust and confidence in customers;
5. *Empathy*: caring attitude and individualized attention provided to customers.

These five dimensions help form the basis for quality measurement in service organizations. Note that all but the first pertain to behavioral characteristics at the service encounter level, which are more difficult to measure than physical and technical characteristics. For example, American Express Travel Related Services managers monitor telephone representatives' conversations with the customer for politeness, tone of voice, empathy toward resolving the customer's query or problem, accuracy of the transaction, and so on. They also compare the judgments of the in-house reviewers to the judgments of customers in post–transaction interviews to assess the relevance of their internal measurements.

Every service encounter provides an opportunity for error. *Errors in service creation and delivery are sometimes called* **service upsets** *or* **service failures**. In services, a measure of quality analogous to defects per unit is errors per million opportunities (epmo). Service measures should be linked closely to customer satisfaction so that they form the basis for improvement efforts. For example, a restaurant manager might keep track of the number and type of incorrect orders or measure the

Service quality is consistently meeting or exceeding customer expectations (external focus) and service delivery system performance (internal focus) for all service encounters.

Errors in service creation and delivery are sometimes called **service upsets** *or* **service failures**.

OM SPOTLIGHT

Federal Express

Federal Express developed a composite measure of its service performance called the Service Quality Indicator (SQI), which is a weighted sum of ten factors reflecting customers' expectations of company performance. These are as follows:

Error Type	Description	Weight
1. Complaints reopened—customer complaints (on traces, invoices, missed pickups, etc.) reopened after an unsatisfactory resolution		3
2. *Damaged packages*—packages with visible or concealed damage or spoilage due to weather or water damage, missed pickup, or late delivery		10
3. *International*—a composite score of performance measures of international operations		
4. *Invoice adjustments*—customer requests for credit or refunds for real or perceived failures		1
5. *Late pickup stops*—packages that were picked up later than the stated pickup time		3
6. *Lost packages*—claims for missing packages or with contents missing		10
7. *Missed proof of delivery*—invoices that lack written proof of delivery information		1
8. *Right date late*—delivery past promised time on the right day		1
9. *Traces*—package status and proof of delivery requests not in the COSMOS IIB computer system (the FedEx "real time" tracking system)		3
10. *Wrong day late*—delivery on the wrong day		5

Source: Service Quality Indicators at FedEx (internal company document).

The weights reflect the relative importance of each failure. Losing a package, for instance, is more serious than delivering it a few minutes late. The index is reported weekly and summarized on a monthly basis. Continuous improvement goals for the SQI are set each year. SQI is really a measure of process effectiveness. Meeting SQI performance goals also can account for as much as 40 percent of a manager's performance evaluation!

time from customer order to delivery. A hotel might have determined that there are 100 opportunities for error during the hotel check-in process. If the hotel had 200 check-ins in one day, the total opportunities for error were 20,000. A total of 40 service upsets were recorded by well-trained hotel check-in staff, for an error rate of 40/20,000 or 2 per thousand, which is equivalent to 2,000 epmo.

In addition to goods and service quality, environmental quality has captured the attention of many operations managers in recent years. **Environmental quality** *focuses on designing and controlling work processes to improve the environment.* For example, Texas Nameplate, Inc. uses toxic chemicals in its etching process; thus, it monitors the pH level and amount of suspended metals in water discharge to meet local regulations. Instead of wire mesh and nets that trap and kill fish, American Electric Power uses watertight speakers to play music to fish to keep them out of power plant intake valves. Honda of America requires reusable containers and packaging for most automobile parts and no longer needs to use or recycle cardboard and other packaging materials. Measuring environmental quality provides a means for organizations to meet their public and social responsibilities.

Environmental quality *focuses on designing and controlling work processes to improve the environment.*

Time

Time relates to two types of performance measures—the *speed* of doing something (such as the time to process a customer's mortgage application) and the *reliability*

Processing Time—*the time it takes to perform some task.*

Queue Time *is a fancy word for* **wait time**—*the time spent waiting.*

Cycle Time (flow time) *refers to the time it takes to accomplish one cycle of a process that performs work.*

of doing something (such as meeting promised delivery dates for electronic component parts). Speed can lead to a significant competitive advantage. Progressive Insurance, for example, boasts that it settles auto insurance claims before competitors know there has been an accident![11] Speed is usually measured in clock time, whereas reliability is usually measured by quantifying the variance around average performance or targets. A simple metric is **processing time**—*the time it takes to perform some task.* For example, to make a pizza, a worker needs to roll out the dough, spread the sauce, and add the toppings, which might take 3 minutes. **Queue time** *is a fancy word for* **wait time**—*the time spent waiting.*

Many companies use cycle time or flow time as a key organizational metric to measure speed. **Cycle time (flow time)** *refers to the time it takes to accomplish one cycle of a process that performs work.* Examples would be the time from when a customer orders a product to the time that it is delivered, the time to prepare an insurance policy, or the time to develop and introduce a new product. For example, think of ordering a pizza for pickup. The tasks involved and the time to accomplish each task are

1. placing the order (1 minute),
2. assembling the pizza (3 minutes),
3. baking the pizza (15 minutes),
4. cutting and packaging (1 minute).

Because each task must take place sequentially, the total cycle time is $1 + 3 + 15 + 1 = 20$ minutes per pizza. However, if a pizza is to be delivered, then the cycle time might include waiting for a batch of pizzas to be completed along with the transportation time, making cycle time variable. In such cases, one would be concerned with the average cycle time.

Manufacturing Lead Time *represents the time between the release of an order to production and shipment to the customer, and typically includes setup, processing, transportation, and waiting between operations.*

Purchasing Lead Time *is the time required to obtain the purchased item, including order preparation, supplier lead time, transportation, and receiving and storage.*

Another common measure used in operations to monitor time is lead time. Lead time is used in various ways, depending on the context. For example, **manufacturing lead time** *represents the time between the release of an order to production and shipment to the customer, and typically includes setup, processing, transportation, and waiting between operations;* **purchasing lead time** *is the time required to obtain the purchased item, including order preparation, supplier lead time, transportation, and receiving and storage.*

An important aspect of measuring time is the variance around the average time, as unanticipated variability is what often leads to an unhappy customer experience. Variability is usually measured by statistics such as the standard deviation or mean absolute deviation. For example, suppose that one company takes 10 days to process a new life insurance application plus or minus 1 day, while another takes 10 days plus or minus 5 days. Which life insurance process will give the best service to its customers? Which firm would you rather do business with?

Flexibility

Flexibility *is the ability to adapt quickly and effectively to changing requirements.*

Goods and Service Design Flexibility *is the ability to develop a wide range of customized goods or services to meet different or changing customer needs.*

Flexibility *is the ability to adapt quickly and effectively to changing requirements.* Flexibility can relate either to adapting to changing customer needs or to volume of demand (see the OM Spotlight on Nissan). **Goods and service design flexibility** *is the ability to develop a wide range of customized goods or services to meet different or changing customer needs.* Examples of design flexibility include Dell's ability to provide a wide range of customized computer hardware to accommodate home users, small businesses, and large companies' server needs, or a health club's ability to customize an individual client's workout or provide cardio rehabilitation classes for heart patients. Such flexibility requires a highly adaptable operations capability. In the past, increased flexibility generally cost more money and demanded premium prices, making it difficult to compete on low cost. Today, however, technology and software solutions provide the capability of simultaneously achieving low costs and high design flexibility. Design flexibility is often evaluated by such

OM SPOTLIGHT

Nissan Flexibility[12]

Nissan Motor Company's new Canton, Mississippi assembly plant is far more flexible in adjusting to market changes than most other automobile facilities. Its Smyrna, Tennessee plant also exhibits similar flexibility. The Canton plant was designed with the same flexibility, shop floor smarts, and management-dominated work rules that made Nissan's older plant in Smyrna the most productive factory in North America year after year, according to Harbour & Associates. The Smyrna plant builds a car in just under 16 labor hours—6 fewer than the average Honda or Toyota plant, 8 fewer than GM, and 10 fewer than Ford.

Canton can send a minivan, pickup truck, and sport-utility vehicle down the same assembly line, one after another, without interruption. The company plans to build five different models in this one plant alone. In the body shop, Nissan can weld bodies for different cars and trucks using the same machines. Computer-controlled robots quickly change weld points to adjust. Highly automated paint processes can paint all kinds of vehicles one after another, with no downtime for reconfiguration. Another reason for its high level of flexibility is the use of modular assemblies that can be outsourced to other suppliers.

measures as the rate of new product development or the percent of a firm's product mix that has been developed over the past 3 years.

Volume flexibility *is the ability to respond quickly to changes in the volume and type of demand.* This might mean rapid changeover from one product to another as the demand for certain goods increases or decreases or the ability to produce a wide range of volumes as demand fluctuates. The Nissan Spotlight shows how volume flexibility can be accomplished. A hospital may have intensive-care nurses on standby in case of a dramatic increase in patient demand because of an accident or be able to borrow specialized diagnostic equipment from other hospitals when needed. Measures of volume flexibility would include the time required to change machine setups or the time required to "ramp up" to an increased production volume in response to surges in sales.

Volume flexibility *is the ability to respond quickly to changes in the volume and type of demand.*

Innovation and Learning

Innovation and learning depend on the way an organization uses its knowledge assets; that is, how it manages its people, their creativity, and their capabilities. **Innovation** *refers to the ability to create new and unique goods and services that delight customers and create competitive advantage.* Many goods and services are innovative when they first appear—think of the iPod and Palm Pilot. However, competitors quickly catch up; thus, innovation needs to be a constant process for many companies and must be measured and assessed. **Learning** *refers to creating, acquiring, and transferring knowledge and modifying the behavior of employees in response to internal and external change.* For instance, when something goes wrong in one office or division, can the organization ensure that the mistake is not repeated and does not occur in other offices or divisions? The importance of innovation and learning was well stated when Bill Gates said, "Microsoft is always two years away from failure."

Innovation *refers to the ability to create new and unique goods and services that delight customers and create competitive advantage.*

Learning *refers to creating, acquiring, and transferring knowledge and modifying the behavior of employees in response to internal and external change.*

Measures of innovation and learning focus on an organization's people and infrastructure. Key measures might include intellectual asset growth, patent applications, the number of "best practices" implemented within the organization, and the percentage of new products developed over the past few years in the product portfolio. Of particular importance are measures associated with an organization's human resource capabilities. These can relate to employee training and skills development, well-being, satisfaction, and work system performance and effectiveness. Examples include health, absenteeism, turnover, employee satisfaction, training hours per employee, training effectiveness, and measures of improvement in job effectiveness. For instance, The Ritz-Carlton Hotel Company tracks percent turnover very closely, as this measure is a key indicator of employee satisfaction and the effectiveness of the selection and training processes.

Productivity

One of the most important measures for an operations manager is productivity. **Productivity** *is the ratio of output of a process to the input:*

$$\text{Productivity} = \text{Quantity of output} / \text{Quantity of input}$$

As output increases for a constant level of input, or as the amount of input decreases for a constant level of output, productivity increases. Thus, a productivity measure describes how well the resources of an organization are being used to produce output.

Productivity is often confused with efficiency or effectiveness. **Efficiency** *is the degree to which a process generates outputs with the minimal consumption of inputs or generates a maximum amount of outputs for a given amount of inputs.* **Effectiveness** *is achieving the organization's objective, mission, or goal through the eyes of the customer; that is, doing the right things efficiently.* When all of your customers are consistently happy and willing to repurchase your good or service, then you are being effective. People now realize that doing unnecessary or non-value-added work efficiently is not productive. Hence, productivity is more closely related to effectiveness than efficiency.

Productivity is similar to the notion of value that we defined in Chapter 1: the ratio of perceived benefits (an output) to price (an input). However, productivity differs from value in that productivity is a measure internal to the firm, whereas value is an external measure from the customer's viewpoint. The denominator in the productivity ratio is often expressed as cost. However, price may or may not reflect the actual cost to make the good or create the service, since prices are often set based on "what the market will bear" and have little direct relationship with costs.

Outputs are easier to measure for goods than for services. Goods output can be stated in physical units such as parts, tons, or finished units. Service outputs are often based on customer perceptions of service, and, therefore, are less tangible and more difficult to include in productivity measures. The ways in which output and input are measured can provide very different measures of productivity. Outputs include such goods and services as the number of pizzas produced, customer satisfaction scores per employee contact-hour, the number of new life insurance policies issued, or the number of lines of computer code written. However, high productivity is useless if the output being produced is defective or does not meet customers' expectations. Because quality should be included in productivity measurement or a fixed quality level assumed, more appropriate definitions of outputs might be the number of pizzas or life insurance policies that meet customer requirements or the number of error-free lines of code written. Thus, a more appropriate definition of productivity is

$$\text{Productivity} = \text{Quantity of acceptable output} / \text{Quantity of input}$$

Productivity is usually expressed in one of three forms: as total productivity, multifactor productivity, or partial factor productivity. **Total productivity** *is the ratio of total output to total input:*

$$\text{Total productivity} = \text{Total output} / \text{Total input}$$

Total input consists of all resources used in the creation and delivery of goods and services; for example, total input includes labor, capital (buildings, equipment), raw

---

Productivity *is the ratio of output of a process to the input.*

Efficiency *is the degree to which a process generates outputs with the minimal consumption of inputs or generates a maximum amount of outputs for a given amount of inputs.*

Effectiveness *is achieving the organization's objective, mission, or goal through the eyes of the customer; that is, doing the right things efficiently.*

Total productivity *is the ratio of total output to total input.*

materials, information, and energy. Those resources are often converted to currency units of measures, such as dollars or euros, so that a single figure can be used as an aggregate measure of total input. Examples of total productivity ratios are tons of steel produced per dollar of input, total dollar value of life insurance policies written per dollar of input, and total revenue of software sold per dollar of input. The total output and total input need not be in the same units. For example, total output could be expressed as the number of units produced (tons of steel) and total inputs could be expressed in dollars ($).

Total productivity ratios reflect simultaneous changes in inputs and outputs. As such, they provide the most inclusive type of index for measuring productivity. However, total productivity ratios do not show the interaction between each input and output separately and thus are too broad to be used as a tool for improving specific areas of operations. **Multifactor productivity** *is the ratio of total output to a subset of inputs:*

$$\text{Multifactor productivity} = \text{Total output} / \text{Subset of inputs}$$

For example, a subset of inputs might consist of only labor and materials, or only labor and capital. The use of a multifactor measure as an index of productivity, however, may ignore important inputs and thus may not accurately reflect overall productivity.

Finally, **partial-factor productivity** *is the ratio of total output to a single input:*

$$\text{Partial-factor productivity} = \text{Total output} / \text{Single input}$$

The U.S. Bureau of Labor Statistics uses "total economic output per total worker-hours expended" as a measure of national productivity; in doing so, the bureau is computing a partial-factor productivity measure.

Operations managers generally utilize partial productivity measures—particularly labor-based measures—because the data are readily available. In addition, since total or multifactor measures provide an aggregate view, partial-factor productivity measures are easier to relate to specific processes. However, labor-based measures do not include equipment and automation in the input; thus, when equipment replaces labor, misinterpretation may occur.

Exhibit 3.2 shows several generic examples of commonly used partial productivity measures for both goods-producing and service-providing organizations. For example, "units of output per labor-hour" might represent the number of radios produced per labor-hour in a factory, number of transactions per teller-hour in a bank, lines of computer code per hour, or restaurant meals served per employee-day.

To illustrate how partial-productivity measures can be used to track trends and better understand business performance, we will consider a division of Miller Chemicals that produces water purification crystals for swimming pools. The major inputs

Multifactor productivity *is the ratio of total output to a subset of inputs.*

partial-factor productivity *is the ratio of total output to a single input.*

Labor Productivity	Capital Productivity
Units of output per labor-hour	Units of output per dollar input
Value added per labor-hour	Dollar output per dollar input
Dollar output per labor-hour	Inventory turnover ratio (dollar sales per
Shipments per labor-dollar	dollar inventory)
Machine Productivity	**Energy Productivity**
Units of output per machine-hour	Units of output per kilowatt-hour
Tons of output per machine-hour	Units of output per energy-dollar
	Production value per barrel of fuel

Exhibit 3.2
Examples of Partial Productivity Measures

used in the production process are labor, raw materials, and energy. The spreadsheet in Exhibit 3.3 shows the amount of output produced and input used for 2005 and 2006. By dividing the pounds of crystals produced by each input individually, we obtain the partial productivity measures shown in the last three columns.

An example of a multifactor productivity measure is output per non-labor-dollar. For 2005 we have

$$\frac{100,000}{\$5,000 + \$30,000} = 2.857 \text{ lb / non-labor-dollar}$$

For 2006 we have

$$\frac{150,000}{\$6,000 + \$40,000} = 3.261 \text{ lb / non-labor-dollar}$$

Thus we see that the output per non-labor-dollar was higher in 2006. A total productivity measure can be computed by dividing the total output by the total cost. For 2005 we have

$$\text{Total productivity} = \frac{100,000}{\$180,000 + \$5,000 + \$30,000} = 0.465 \text{ lb / dollar}$$

For 2006 we have

$$\text{Total productivity} = \frac{150,000}{\$350,000 + \$6,000 + \$40,000} = 0.379 \text{ lb / dollar}$$

These measures provide a basis for tracking trends, setting performance targets, designing bonus compensation plans, and looking for improvement opportunities. In doing so, it is often beneficial to compare similar operations within a firm, or to compare the firm's performance against industrywide data or world-class benchmarks. For example, a quick-service restaurant might compare the productivity data of different franchised outlets to determine relative rates of performance or compare them to competitor benchmarks.

Productivity is an important macroeconomic measure. *Fortune* magazine noted that "Stronger productivity is a key reason this recession [during 2001–2002] has been one of the mildest on record. It's why real disposable income, which typically declines during a downturn, has kept growing. . . . It means we can grow faster without igniting inflation. . . . It's also important because faster growth has a way of turning federal budget deficits into surpluses."[13] Labor productivity, in particular, is a powerful indicator of an economy's strength. Because productivity is a relative measure, it must be compared to something to be meaningful. It can be compared to values for similar businesses or to the firm's own productivity data. This allows measurement of the impact of certain decisions, such as the introduction of new processes, equipment, worker motivation techniques, and so forth.

Exhibit 3.3
Productivity Calculations for Miller Chemicals

	2005	2006		2005	2006
Outputs					
Pounds of crystals	100,000	150,000			
Inputs			*Productivity measure*		
Direct labor-hours	20,000	28,000	Output/direct labor-hour	5.000	5.357
Direct labor cost	$180,000	$350,000	Output/direct labor-dollar	0.556	0.429
Energy used (kWh)	350,000	400,000	Output/kilowatt-hour	0.286	0.375
Energy cost	$ 5,000	$ 6,000	Output/energy-dollar	20.000	25.000
Raw materials used (lb)	120,000	185,000	Output/lb. of raw material	0.833	0.811
Raw material cost	$ 30,000	$ 40,000	Output/raw material dollar	3.333	3.750

A **productivity index** *is the ratio of productivity measured in some time period to the productivity in a base period.* For instance, if the base-period productivity is computed to be 1.25 and the next period's productivity is 1.18, the ratio 1.18/1.25 = 0.944 indicates that productivity has decreased to 94.4 percent of the base-period value. By tracking such indexes over time, managers can evaluate the success (or lack of success) of various projects and decisions.

Consider the Miller Chemicals Company example we have discussed. If we use 2005 as a base period, we can compute a productivity index for 2006 by dividing each productivity measure for 2006 by its 2005 value. For example, the 2006 productivity index for output/direct labor-hour is 5.357 ÷ 5.000 = 1.071, which indicates that productivity has increased by 7.1 percent. The last column of Exhibit 3.4 summarizes the productivity indexes (the remainder of the table is identical to Exhibit 3.3). How would you interpret the indexes?

Total or multifactor productivity measures are generally preferable to partial measures. The reason is that focusing on productivity improvement in a narrow portion of an organization may actually decrease overall productivity. A simple example illustrates this point. Suppose productivity is measured by

$$\frac{\text{Total units produced}}{\text{Total labor cost} + \text{Total equipment cost}}$$

Assume 10,000 units are being produced currently, with annual labor and equipment costs of $50,000 and $25,000, respectively. Thus, the measure of productivity is

$$\frac{10,000}{\$50,000 + \$25,000} = .133 \text{ units of output per dollar input}$$

Labor productivity, however, is measured for this example as

$$\frac{10,000}{\$50,000} = .20 \text{ units of output per labor-dollar}$$

Suppose a $10,000 reduction in labor can be achieved by investing in a more advanced machine. Labor productivity will increase to

$$\frac{10,000}{\$40,000} = .25 \text{ units of output per labor-dollar}$$

Thus, from a partial-productivity perspective, this investment appears to be attractive. If the annual cost with the new equipment increases to $40,000, however, productivity would be

$$\frac{10,000}{\$40,000 + \$40,000} = .125 \text{ units of output per dollar input}$$

Exhibit 3.4
Computing Productivity Indexes for Miller Chemicals

	2005	2006		2005	2006	2006 Index
Outputs						
Pounds of crystals	100,000	150,000				
Inputs			*Productivity measure*			
Direct labor-hours	20,000	28,000	Output/direct labor-hour	5.000	5.357	1.071
Direct labor cost	$180,000	$350,000	Output/direct labor-dollar	0.556	0.429	0.771
Energy used (kWh)	350,000	400,000	Output/kilowatt-hour	0.286	0.375	1.313
Energy cost	$ 5,000	$ 6,000	Output/energy-dollar	20.000	25.000	1.250
Raw materials used (lb)	120,000	185,000	Output/lb. of raw material	0.833	0.811	0.973
Raw material cost	$ 30,000	$ 40,000	Output/raw material dollar	3.333	3.750	1.125

and hence overall productivity would actually decrease. It is therefore necessary to examine the simultaneous effects of all changes on productivity.

Selecting the right productivity measures is not always an easy task. For example, a common definition of nursing productivity in the health care field is "hours per patient day." This measure ignores indirect nursing care, ancillary costs, and overhead. A better way of defining nursing productivity is the ratio of the total revenues generated by patients admitted to the unit to all resources consumed in treating the patient. Using the wrong measures (unintentionally or intentionally) can provide misleading information to managers and result in poor decisions. Consider, for example, an employee earning $18,000 per year who produces 1,000 units of output per year. A trainee of lesser skill is hired at $10,000 to assist this employee, and together they produce 1,700 units per year. A partial measure of labor productivity is

$$\frac{\text{Number of units produced per year}}{\text{Labor-years}} = \frac{1,700}{2}$$

$$= 850 \text{ units of output per labor-year}$$

Because the current (one-person) system has a labor productivity value of 1,000, we conclude that productivity has decreased in terms of average output per worker. However, suppose labor productivity is measured as number of units produced per dollar input. For the one-person system, the labor productivity is equal to

$$\frac{\text{Number of units}}{\text{Dollar input}} = \frac{1,000}{\$18,000} = 0.056 \text{ units per labor-dollar}$$

Computing the same measure with the trainee, we find that the labor productivity is $1,700 \div \$28,000 = 0.061$. On that basis, hiring the trainee resulted in about a 9 percent improvement in productivity. In such situations, it is better to use the units per dollar input productivity measure since it takes into account the *relative* value of the inputs; that is, the difference in wages implies a difference in skill level. The first measure, on the other hand, implicitly assumes that each labor-year is equivalent. The point of these illustrations is that we must be very careful when using partial-productivity measures.

Learning Objective
To understand the importance of evaluating relationships and cause-and-effect linkages among performance measures and approaches that companies use to understand such relationships.

LINKING INTERNAL AND EXTERNAL PERFORMANCE MEASURES

We have previously noted that performance data need to be aggregated into useful measures that top managers can understand and apply in strategic planning and decision-making and discussed how Federal Express aggregates different quality components into a single index as an example. However, simple aggregation of data is not enough. Managers must also understand the cause-and-effect linkages between key measures of performance. These relationships often explain the impact of (internal) operational performance on external results, such as profitability, market share, or customer satisfaction. For example, how do goods- and service-quality improvement impact revenue growth? How do improvements in complaint handling affect customer retention? How do increases or decreases in employee satisfaction affect customer satisfaction? How do changes in customer satisfaction affect costs and revenues? Knowing these relationships helps operations managers make more effective decisions that will eventually impact the bottom-line results of the organization.

The quantitative modeling of cause-and-effect relationships between external and internal performance criteria is called
interlinking.

The quantitative modeling of cause-and-effect relationships between external and internal performance criteria is called **interlinking.**[14] Interlinking tries to quantify the performance relationships between all parts of the value chain—the processes ("how"), goods and services outputs ("what"), and customer experiences and outcomes ("why"). With interlinking models, managers can objectively make internal

OM SPOTLIGHT

Florida Power and Light[15]

In studying the telephone operation of its customer-service centers, Florida Power and Light (FP&L) sampled customers to rate their level of satisfaction with waiting times on the telephone. Satisfaction was clearly related to time and began to fall significantly at about 2 minutes (see Exhibit 3.5). FP&L also found that customer satisfaction is directly related to how callers perceive the quality of the phone representatives. To improve customer satisfaction, FP&L developed a system to notify customers of the anticipated wait and give them a choice of holding or deferring the call to a later time. Customers were actually willing to wait longer without being dissatisfied if they knew the length of wait ahead of time; thus, customer satisfaction was improved even when call traffic was heavy.

decisions that impact external outcomes, for example, determining the effects of adding resources or changing the operating system to reduce waiting time. This is management by fact, not management by opinion. The OM Spotlight shows how Florida Power and Light has used interlinking to improve its operations and increase customer satisfaction.

The ability to develop interlinking models generally requires strong analytical capability, understanding of statistical methods, and computer technology. The capabilities of today's spreadsheet and database software, such as Microsoft Excel and Access, make this relatively simple to do. For example, Sears provided a consulting group with 13 financial measures, hundreds of thousands of employee satisfaction data points, and millions of data points on customer satisfaction. Using advanced statistical modeling, the analysts discovered that employee attitudes about the job and the company are key factors that predict their behavior with customers, which, in turn, predicts the likelihood of customer retention and recommendations that, in turn, predict financial performance. Sears was able to predict that if a store increased its employee satisfaction score by 5 units, customer satisfaction scores would go up by 2 units, and revenue growth would beat the stores' national average

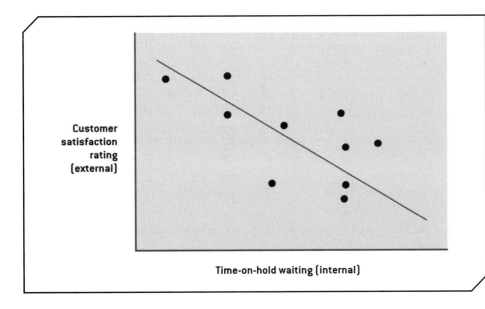

Exhibit 3.5
Interlinking Internal and External Performance Measures

by 0.5 percent.[16] However, not all interlinking models need to be based on sophisticated statistical and computer models. Ames Rubber Corporation, for example, has shown that analyzing simple trend graphs can provide important insights about the relationships among measures that impact business decisions and strategy. For example, it has found that the quality of the production process outputs (yield rate) increase as employee turnover decreases and that lost-time accidents decrease with increasing training hours, leading to new initiatives for training and HR policies.

Another example of an interlinking model is the financial **value of a loyal customer (VLC)**, *which quantifies the total revenue or profit each target market customer generates over some time frame.* The VLC also provides an understanding of how customer satisfaction and loyalty affects the bottom line. Many organizations lose customers because of poor goods quality or service performance. This is often the result of operations managers failing to consider the economic impact of lost customers when they cut service staff or downgrade product designs. Likewise, many organizations do not understand the economic value of potential new customers when evaluating proposed goods or service improvements on a strict economic basis. Understanding the effects of operational decisions on revenue and retention can help organizations more appropriately use their resources. When one considers the fact that it costs 3 to 5 times more to acquire a new customer than keep an existing customer, it is clear why customer retention is often the focus of top-management improvement initiatives and strategies.

We will walk through an example of computing the average value of a loyal customer. Suppose that a computer manufacturer estimates that its annual customer retention rate is 80 percent, which means that 20 percent of customers who purchase a computer will not buy from the manufacturer again (we call this the **customer defection rate** = 1 − *customer retention rate*). Assume that fixed costs are 35 percent and the manufacturer makes a before-tax profit margin of 10 percent. Therefore, the incremental contribution to profit and overhead is 45 percent. We also assume that customers buy a new computer every 2 years at an average cost of $1,000.

On an annual basis, the average contribution to profit and overhead of a new customer is $1,000 × 0.45 × 0.5 = $225 (the multiplier of 0.5 takes into account that customers purchase a new machine every 2 years). If 20 percent of customers do not return each year, then, on average, the buying life of a customer is 5 years (1/0.2 = 5). Therefore, the average value of a loyal customer over their average buying life is $225 per year × 5 years = $1,125.

Now suppose that the customer defection rate can be reduced to 10 percent by improving the quality of the goods and services the company provides. In this case, the average buying life doubles and the average value of a loyal customer increases to $225 per year × 10 years = $2,250. If goods and service improvements can also lead to a market share increase of 100,000 customers, the total contribution to profit and overhead would be $225,000,000 ($1,000 × 0.45 × 0.5 × 10 × 100,000).

We can summarize the logic of these calculations with the following equation:

$$VLC = P \times CM \times RF \times BLC \qquad \textbf{[3.1]}$$

where P = the revenue per unit.

> CM = contribution margin to profit and overhead expressed as a fraction (that is, 0.45, 0.5, and so on).
>
> RF = repurchase frequency = 1/(years or fraction of years between purchases); that is, 1/0.5 = 2 if repurchased every 6 months, 1/2 if every 2 years, and so on.
>
> BLC = buyer's life cycle, computed as 1/defection rate, expressed as a fraction (1/0.2 = 5 years, 1/0.1 = 10 years, and so on).

By multiplying the VLC times the absolute number of customers gained or lost, the total market value can be found.

---

*The **value of a loyal customer (VLC)**, quantifies the total revenue or profit each target market customer generates over some time frame.*

Customer defection rate = 1 − customer retention rate.

One study found that it cost an average of $51 to recruit a new credit card customer and that new customers are slow to use the card. In the first year, the credit card company recovers only an average of $30, but during the second year they add $42 of revenue. In subsequent years, the revenue per loyal customer increases sharply, and as credit card purchases increase, operating costs decline. The lesson is that the longer the organization keeps the customer, the more profitable is the relationship. In one automobile service company, the profit from a fourth-year customer is more than triple the profit that the same customer generates in the first year. The co-owner of five Domino's Pizza stores in Maryland calculated that regular loyal customers were worth more than $5,000 over the life of a 10-year buying cycle. This works out to a loyal pizza customer in this local market spending about $42 per month on Domino's Pizza.[17]

DESIGNING PERFORMANCE MEASUREMENT SYSTEMS FOR OPERATIONS

Learning Objective
To understand the characteristics of a good measurement system and how to select appropriate measures to support operations.

What makes a good performance measurement system for operations? Many organizations define specific criteria for selecting and deleting performance measures from the organization's information system. IBM Rochester, for example, asks the following questions:

- Does the measurement support our mission?
- Will the measurement be used to manage change?
- Is it important to our customers?
- Is it effective in measuring performance?
- Is it effective in forecasting results?
- Is it easy to understand/simple?
- Are the data easy/cost-efficient to collect?
- Does the measurement have validity, integrity, and timeliness?
- Does the measure have an owner?

Good performance measures are actionable. **Actionable measures** *provide the basis for decisions at the level at which they are applied*—the value chain, organization, process, department, workstation, job, and service encounter. They should be meaningful to the user, timely, and reflect how the organization generates value to customers. Performance measures should support, not conflict with, customer requirements. For example, customers expect timely response when calling a customer support number. A common operational measure is the number of rings until the call is picked up. If a company performs well on this measure but puts the customer on hold or in a never-ending menu, then a conflict clearly exists.

Actionable measures *provide the basis for decisions at the level at which they are applied.*

Another characteristic of a good performance measurement system is the ability to accurately aggregate performance from the lowest level of the organization to the highest levels to support senior management reviews. This is a challenge for operations managers who typically manage the daily execution of the organization's plans and mission. Operations managers—indeed, all middle managers—need to be able to translate the language of "things" into the language of dollars—what senior management understands and uses. This requires a broad range of interdisciplinary skills such as understanding how standard costs are calculated or how to justify the purchase of new equipment using financial measures such as internal rate of return and net present value.

To generate useful operational performance measures a systematic process is required.[18]

1. *Identify all customers of the value chain and determine their requirements and expectations.* Organizations need answers to key questions: Who are my

customers? What do they expect? This might entail using customer surveys, focus groups, and user panels.

2. *Define the work process that provides the good or service.* Key questions include: What do I do that impacts customer needs? What is my process?

3. *Define the value-adding activities and outputs that compose the process.* This step—identifying each part in the system in which value is added and an intermediate output is produced—weeds out activities that do not add value to the process and that contribute to waste and inefficiency. Analysis performed in this step identifies the internal customers within the process along with their needs and expectations.

4. *Develop specific performance measures.* Each key activity identified in step 3 represents a critical point where value is added to the output for the next (internal) customer until the final output is produced. At these checkpoints, performance can be measured. Key questions include: What factors determine how well the process is producing according to customer requirements? What deviations can occur? What sources of variability can occur?

5. *Evaluate the performance measures to ensure their usefulness.* Questions to consider include: Are measurements taken at critical points where value-adding activities occur? Are measurements controllable? Is it feasible to obtain the data needed for each measure? Have operational definitions for each measurement been established? **Operational definitions** *are precise definitions of measurements that have no ambiguities.* For example, when measuring "invoice errors," a precise definition of what is an error and what is not is needed. Does an error include an omission of information, wrong information, or misspelling? Operational definitions provide a common understanding and enhance communication throughout the organization.

Operational definitions *are precise definitions of measurements that have no ambiguities.*

To illustrate this approach, consider the process of placing, cooking, and delivering a pizza order. A pizza business is a bundle of goods and services (that is, the customer benefit package)—order taking, pizza, and delivery. Customer expectations for such a process might be a good-tasting pizza prepared with the toppings requested, a quick delivery, and a fair price. The process that provides this customer benefit package is shown in Exhibit 3.6. The order taker is an internal service provider whose internal customer is the cook, who relies on accurate and timely information from the order taker. The cook's internal customer is the driver who serves the external customer.

Some possible performance measures are

- Number of pizzas, by type per hour. If the number is consistently high during certain times of the day or days of the week (that is, peak demand periods), then more delivery drivers or new ovens are needed to meet delivery-time standards or perhaps cooking and preparation time could be reduced by better workplace design or faster cooking ovens.
- Number of pizzas rejected per number prepared and delivered. A high number can indicate inaccurate order taking (service content) or a lack of proper training of cooks that results in poor-quality pizza (goods content). Also, pizza delivery drivers can deliver pizzas that are too cold or have slid to one side of the box (goods content).
- Order entry to customer delivery time. A long time might indicate a problem with order taking, cooking procedures and expertise, driver capacity or training, oven capacity, and so on. Time is a very important performance measure for a pizza delivery service.
- Number of errors in payments and collections. Numerous errors can result in lost revenue to the drivers and the company and eventually in lost profits. Higher prices are one solution but this decision may make the pizza store noncompetitive.
- Raw materials (dough, toppings, and so on) or finished pizzas inventory in average units and dollars per day. A high inventory might result in spoilage and

Exhibit 3.6 Example of a Pizza Ordering and Delivery Process

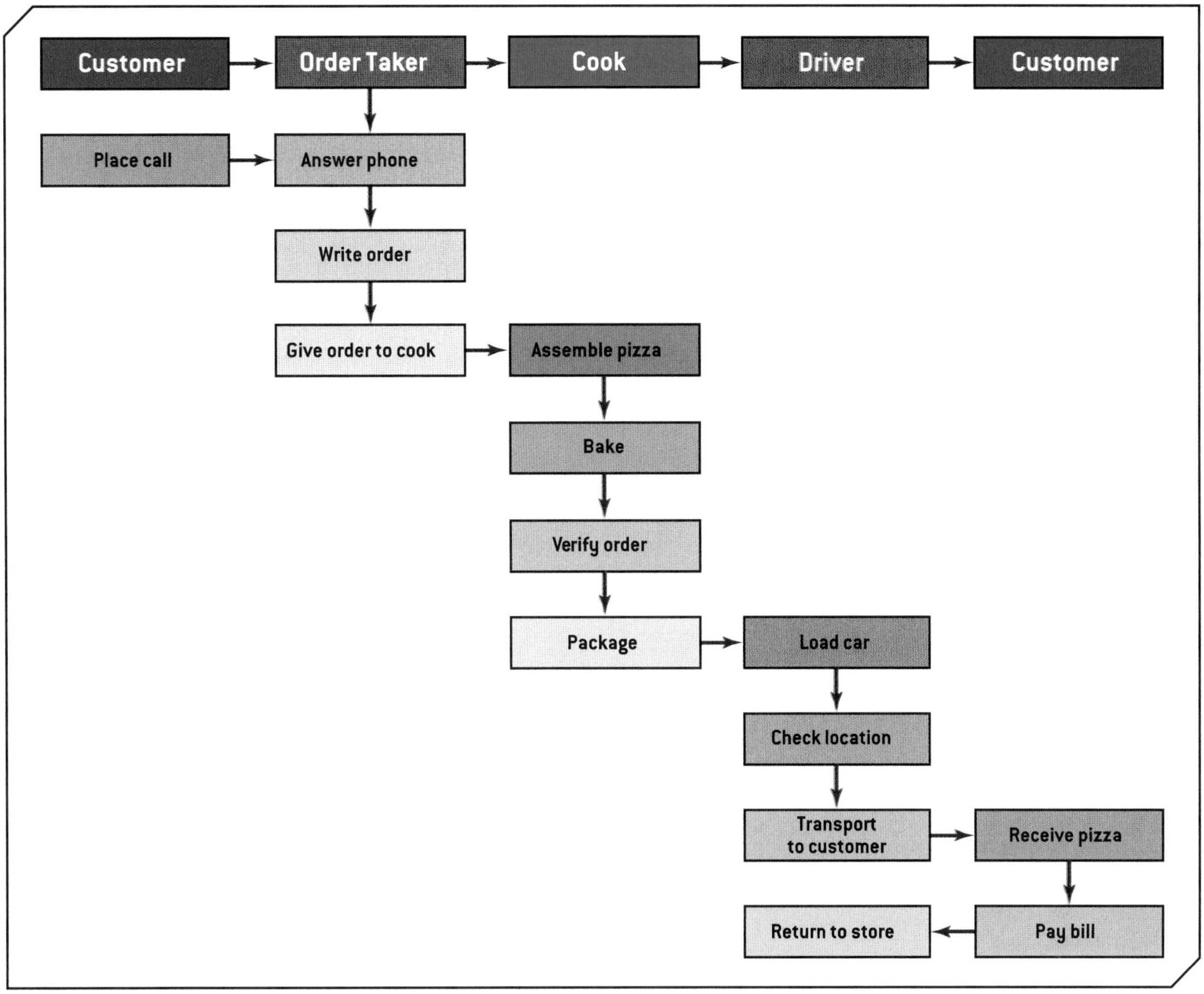

excess operating costs. Low inventory might result in stockouts, lost orders, or excessive customer delivery time.

Notice that these performance measures are related to the customer's expectations of goods (pizza) and service (order taking, delivery) performance prior to actually receiving the outputs. Can you think of any other useful performance measures for a pizza business?

Information Reliability and Accessibility

The familiar computer cliché "Garbage in, garbage out" applies equally well to any kind of data. Any measurement is subject to error. **Information reliability** *means how well a measuring instrument, such as a dimensional gauge, an automated scanner, or a questionnaire, consistently measures the "true value" of the performance characteristic being measured.* Properly calibrating and periodically checking measuring instruments and methods assure information reliability in goods-producing industries. In services, a useful approach to ensuring information reliability is periodic auditing of the data collection processes by internal cross-functional teams or external auditors. Standardized forms, clear instructions, and adequate training help to ensure that data collection is performed correctly and consistently.

Information reliability *means how well a measuring instrument, such as a dimensional gauge, an automated scanner, or a questionnaire, consistently measures the "true value" of the performance characteristic being measured.*

Of course, if reliable and accurate data are the lifeblood of superior performance, then late and inaccurate data are the Achilles' heel of value chain performance. Decisions based on bad data are usually bad decisions. One study found that a well-regarded retail chain had 16% of its inventory reported as stockouts (called "phantom" stockouts) when in fact the items were available but had been misplaced on the store floor or storage area. Phantom stockouts reduced this company's profit by a whopping 25%! Accounting practices in another company gave credit for items shipped in error from the manufacturer but not from the company's own distribution centers. Therefore, the managers of company stores were not motivated to carefully check the accuracy of deliveries from the distribution centers but they checked them closely for manufacturers. The result was lost and misplaced inventory that was not accurately recorded in the company's information system.[19]

It also makes no sense to collect data if they are not available to the right employees when they need them. Thus good information management depends on *information accessibility* as much as reliability. In most companies, data are accessible to top managers and others on a need-to-know basis. In progressive companies, performance data are accessible to everyone. At Milliken, a major textile company, all databases, including product specifications, process data, supplier data, customer requirements, and environmental data, are immediately available to every associate throughout the computer network. A customer service representative need not tell a customer to wait for a call-back while needed information is obtained. Electronic charts showing key performance measures and trends are displayed throughout the plant and in business-support departments. Such data accessibility empowers employees and helps them participate in improvement efforts. The Ritz-Carlton Hotel Company has a similar information system that supports service encounter execution.

Learning Objective
To understand how measurement systems are integrated into comprehensive models of business performance as a basis for better design and improvement of operations.

MODELS OF ORGANIZATIONAL PERFORMANCE

Four models of organizational performance—the Malcolm Baldrige National Quality Award Framework, the Balanced Scorecard, the Value Chain Model, and the Service-Profit Model—provide popular frameworks for thinking about designing, monitoring, and evaluating performance. The first two models provide more of a "big picture" of organizational performance, and the last two provide more detailed frameworks for operations managers. Although OM focuses on execution and delivery of goods and services to customers, it is important to understand these "big picture" models of organizational performance because operations managers must communicate with all functional areas. In addition, understanding these models helps you to better appreciate the interdisciplinary nature of an organization's performance system, the role that operations plays, and why operations managers need interdisciplinary skills.

Malcolm Baldrige National Quality Award Framework

The Malcolm Baldrige National Quality Award (MBNQA)—now known as the Baldrige National Quality Program—has been one of the most powerful catalysts for improving organizational performance in the United States, and indeed, throughout the world, in all sectors of the economy, including manufacturing, service, small business, health care, and education. The award was created to help stimulate American organizations to improve quality, productivity, and overall competitiveness and to encourage the development of high-performance management practices through innovation, learning, and sharing of best practices. Considerable evidence exists that it is working. An annual study conducted by the National Institute of Standards and Technology finds that publicly traded Baldrige winners have

Baldrige National Quality Program

generally outperformed the S&P 500 stock market index.[20] For a profile of a recent winner, see the OM Spotlight on Clarke American.

Organizations can receive Baldrige awards in each of the original categories of manufacturing, small business, and service, and since 1999, in nonprofit education and health care. Other nonprofit awards are scheduled to begin in 2007. The program's web site at www.baldrige.org provides a wealth of current information about the award, the performance criteria, award winners, and other aspects of the program. Although the award itself receives the most attention, the primary purpose of the program is to provide a framework for performance excellence through self-assessment to understand an organization's strengths and weaknesses, thereby setting priorities for improvement. This framework, shown in Exhibit 3.7, defines the *Criteria for Performance Excellence*. The criteria are designed to encourage companies to enhance their competitiveness through an aligned approach to organizational performance management that results in

1. delivery of ever-improving value to customers, resulting in improved market-place success;
2. improvement of overall company performance and capabilities; and
3. organizational and personal learning.

OM SPOTLIGHT

Clarke American[21]

Headquartered in San Antonio, Texas, Clarke American supplies personalized checks, checking-account and bill-paying accessories, financial forms, and a growing portfolio of services to more than 4,000 financial institutions in the United States. In addition to filling more than 50 million personalized check and deposit orders every year, Clarke American provides 24-hour service and handles more than 11 million calls annually. Since 1996, Clarke American's market share has increased by 50 percent. Revenues were over $460 million in 2001.

The company is organized into a customer-focused matrix of three divisions and 11 processes. It is in a nearly continual state of organizational redesign, reflecting ever more refined segmentation of its partners and efforts to better align with these customers' requirements and future needs.

In the early 1990s, when an excess manufacturing capacity in check printing triggered aggressive price competition, Clarke American elected to distinguish itself through service. Company leaders made an all-out commitment to ramp up the firm's "First in Service®" (FIS) approach to business excellence. Comprehensive in scope, systematic in execution, the FIS approach defines how Clarke American conducts business and how all company associates are expected to act to fulfill the company's commitment to superior service and quality performance.

In 2000, associates averaged 76 hours of training, more than the "best in class" companies tracked by the American Society for Training and Development. In 2001, more than 20,000 process improvement ideas saved the company an estimated $10 million. Since the program started in 1995, implementation rates for employee ideas have increased from below 20 percent to 70 percent in 2001. At the same time, financial rewards flowed back to associates, who averaged nearly $5,000 in bonus and profit-sharing payouts.

Since 1995, Clarke American has invested substantially in new technology, using it to reduce cycle time, errors, hazardous materials, and waste, and has dramatically improved quality. Annual growth in company revenues has increased from a rate of 4.2 percent in 1996 to 16 percent in 2000, compared to the industry's average annual growth rate of less than 1 percent over the 5-year period.

Baldrige National Quality Program

Exhibit 3.7
Malcolm Baldrige National
Quality Award Model of
Organizational Performance

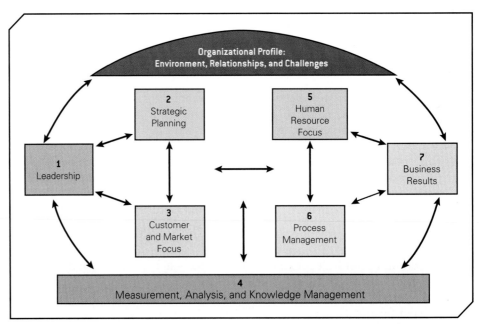

Source: 2006 Malcolm Baldrige National Quality Award Criteria, U.S. Dept. of Commerce.

The criteria consist of a hierarchical set of *categories*, *items*, and *areas to address.* The seven categories are

1. *Leadership:* This category focuses on how senior leaders address values, directions, and performance expectations, and also focuses on customers and other stakeholders, empowerment, innovation, and learning. Also included is the organization's governance and how it addresses its public and community responsibilities.
2. *Strategic Planning:* This category focuses on how the organization develops strategic objectives and action plans, how the chosen strategic objectives and action plans are implemented, and how progress is measured.
3. *Customer and Market Focus:* In this category, the focus is on how the organization determines requirements, expectations, and preferences of customers and markets, and how the organization builds relationships with customers and determines the key factors that lead to customer acquisition, satisfaction, loyalty, and retention and to business expansion.
4. *Measurement, Analysis, and Knowledge Management:* This category focuses on how an organization selects, gathers, analyzes, manages, and improves its data, information, and knowledge assets.
5. *Human Resource Focus:* This category addresses how an organization's work systems and employee learning and motivation enable employees to develop and utilize their full potential in alignment with the organization's overall objectives and action plans. Also included are the organization's efforts to build and maintain a work environment and an employee support climate conducive to performance excellence and to personal and organizational growth.
6. *Process Management:* This category examines the key aspects of process management, including product, service, and business processes for creating customer and organizational value, as well as key support processes.
7. *Business Results:* This category looks at the organization's performance and improvement, in key business areas—customer satisfaction, product and service performance, financial and marketplace performance, human resource performance, operational performance, and government and social responsibility.

The criteria are designed to help organizations focus on results and understand the impact that management practices and decisions have on these results. In essence, the criteria framework represents a macro-level interlinking model that relates management practices to business results. For example, if senior managers understand their customers and lead the planning process effectively (categories 1, 2, and 3), and then translate plans into actions through people and processes (categories 4 and 5), then positive business results should follow. Category 4—Information and Analysis— provides the foundation for assessment of results and continual improvements.

Although the criteria provide an overall business management framework and address many things that top-level managers must be concerned with, many aspects of the criteria are particularly relevant to operations managers, most notably, categories 4, 5, and 6.[22] Exhibit 3.8 summarizes the key questions addressed in the criteria in these categories.

In examining these questions, we see that most of them address critical issues with which operations managers must be concerned. For example, to deliver customized goods and services to customers, employees need information at the right place and time. This requires a *process* for collecting the data, turning it into useful information, ensuring that it is accurate and valid, and making that information available to the right people. This is the focus of category 4. The criteria force an organization to think about how this process is designed and implemented. For example, The Ritz-Carlton Hotel Company's information system allows employees to obtain information about individual guest requirements, such as what wines they have ordered for dinner in the past at any Ritz-Carlton hotel, whether they prefer turn-down service in the evening, and at what time they would like it. This information system capability helps hotel employees "anticipate customer wants and needs at the service encounter level" before they happen. In this case, the hotel employees can make sure they have the guest's favorite wines in stock and notify housekeeping about evening turn-down service *before* he or she arrives.

Category 4 is closely tied to category 7, Business Results, which asks organizations to provide data showing levels and trends for key performance measures across a balanced set of metrics, including customer-focused results, financial and market results, human resource results, organizational effectiveness results, and governance and social responsibility results. Results provide the feedback to operations managers for managing processes on a daily basis as well as to senior-level management for setting long-term directions. These certainly are vital issues that operations managers must consider in their role as leaders in building and sustaining a productive work environment.

In a similar fashion, categories 5 and 6 deal with issues that operations managers face on a daily basis—managing people and processes—the means by which work gets accomplished in any organization. The remaining categories of the Baldrige criteria are more strategic in nature and are critical to issues faced by senior leaders in the organization. By answering such questions, an organization can better understand how it accomplishes work and identify gaps in its management approaches and opportunities to improve them. In this fashion, the Baldrige criteria become a useful tool for self-assessment and improvement of operational capabilities and a model of organizational performance.

The Balanced Scorecard Model

Robert Kaplan and David Norton of the Harvard Business School, in response to the limitations of traditional accounting measures, popularized the notion of the *balanced scorecard*, which was first developed at Analog Devices. Its purpose is "to translate strategy into measures that uniquely communicate your vision to the organization." Their version of the balanced scorecard, as shown in Exhibit 3.9, consists of four performance perspectives:

- *Financial Perspective:* Measures the ultimate value that the business provides to its shareholders. This includes profitability, revenue growth, stock price, cash flows, return on investment, economic value added (EVA), and shareholder value.

Exhibit 3.8 Example OM-Related Questions in Baldrige Categories 4, 5, and 6

Category 4—Measurement, Analysis, and Knowledge Management	Category 5—Human Resource Focus	Category 6—Process Management
• How do you select, collect, align, and integrate data and information for tracking daily operations and for tracking overall organizational performance? • How do you select and ensure the effective use of key comparative data and information to support operational and strategic decision making and innovation? • What analyses do you perform to support your senior leaders' organizational performance review? • How do you communicate the results of organizational-level analyses to work groups and functional-level operations to enable effective support for their decision making? • How do you make needed data and information available? How do you make them accessible to employees, suppliers/partners, and customers, as appropriate? • How do you ensure that hardware and software are reliable, secure, and user-friendly?	• How do you organize and manage work and jobs to promote cooperation, initiative/innovation, your organizational culture, and the flexibility to keep current with business needs? How do you achieve effective communication and knowledge/skill sharing across work units, jobs, and locations, as appropriate? • How do you motivate employees to develop and utilize their full potential? Include formal and/or informal mechanisms you use to help employees attain job- and career-related development/learning objectives and the role of managers and supervisors in helping employees attain these objectives. • How does your employee performance management system, including feedback to employees, support high performance and a customer and business focus? How do your compensation, recognition, and related reward/incentive practices reinforce these objectives? • How do you identify characteristics and skills needed by potential employees? How do you recruit, hire, and retain new employees? • How do you improve workplace health, safety, and ergonomics? How do employees take part in improving them? Include performance measures and/or targets for each key environmental factor. • How do you determine the key factors that affect employee well-being, satisfaction, and motivation?	• What are your design processes for goods and services and their related operations/delivery systems and processes? • How do you incorporate changing customer/market requirements into goods and service designs and operation/delivery systems and processes? • How do you incorporate new technology, including e-technology, into goods and services and into operations/delivery systems and processes, as appropriate? • How do your design processes address design quality and cycle time, transfer of learning from past projects and other parts of the organization, cost control, new design technology, productivity, and other efficiency/effectiveness factors? • How do you design your operation/delivery systems and processes to meet all key operational performance requirements? • How do you coordinate and test your design and operation/delivery systems and processes? Include how you prevent defects/rework and facilitate trouble-free and timely introduction of products/services. • How does your day-to-day operation of key operation/delivery processes ensure meeting key performance requirements? • What are your key performance measures used for the control and improvement of these processes? Include how in-process measures and real-time customer and supplier/partner input are used in managing your goods and service processes, as appropriate. • How do you perform inspections, tests, and process/performance audits to minimize warranty and/or rework costs, as appropriate? Include your prevention-based processes for controlling inspection and test costs, as appropriate. • How do you improve your operating systems and processes to achieve better process performance and improvements to goods and services, as appropriate? How are improvements shared with other organizational units and processes and your suppliers/partners, as appropriate?

- *Customer Perspective:* Focuses on customer wants and needs and satisfaction as well as market share and growth in market share. This includes safety, service levels, satisfaction ratings, delivery reliability, number of cooperative customer-company design initiatives, value of a loyal customer, customer retention, percent of sales from new goods and services, and frequency of repeat business.

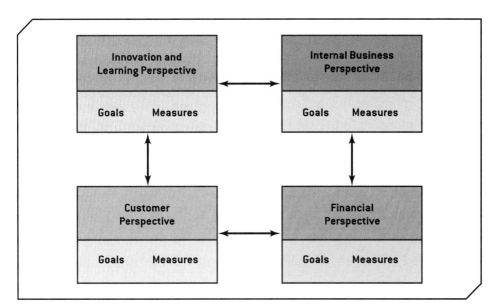

Exhibit 3.9
The Balanced Scorecard Performance Categories and Linkages

Source: Kaplan, R. S., and Norton, D. P., "The Balanced Scorecard—Measures That Drive Performance," *Harvard Business Review*, January–February 1992, p. 72.

- *Innovation and Learning Perspective:* Directs attention to the basis of a future success—the organization's people and infrastructure. Key measures might include intellectual and research assets, time to develop new goods and services, number of improvement suggestions per employee, employee satisfaction, market innovation, training hours per employee, hiring process effectiveness, revenue per employee, and skills development.
- *Internal Perspective:* Focuses attention on the performance of the key internal processes that drive the business. This includes such measures as goods and service quality levels, productivity, flow time, design and demand flexibility, asset utilization, safety, environmental quality, rework, and cost.

The internal perspective is most meaningful to operations managers, as they deal with the day-to-day decisions that revolve around creating and delivering goods and services. As noted in Chapter 1, the internal perspective includes all types of processes: value creation processes, support processes, and general management or business processes.

The balanced scorecard is designed to be linked to an organization's strategy. The linkages between corporate and operations strategy and associated performance measures (called *competitive priorities*) are discussed in Chapter 4. Top management's job is to guide the organization, make trade-offs among these four performance categories, and set future directions. For example, companies with most of their goods and services in mature businesses such as refrigerators and furniture emphasize maximizing cash flow and harvesting profits. Their customer's idea of value may focus on delivery and low cost. Operations play a vital role in creating customer value by being highly efficient. Firms with many new goods and services, especially in new industries such as computer chips and the Internet, emphasize growth and a rapid succession of new and improved goods and services. Their customer's idea of value is a steady stream of innovative goods and services. Here, operations must have the capability to change quickly. The performance measures that each firm selects must support the achievement of the firm's strategy and their customers' notion of value.

A good balanced scorecard contains both leading and lagging performance measures. *Lagging measures* (outcomes) tell what has happened; *leading measures* (performance drivers) predict what will happen. For example, customer survey results about recent transactions might be a leading indicator for customer retention whereas customer retention is a lagging indicator, employee satisfaction might be a leading indicator for employee turnover, and so on. These leading and lagging performance measures help establish interlinking models and quantify cause-and-effect relationships. For example, many companies have discovered that improving internal capabilities such as people skills and goods and service quality leads to improved customer satisfaction and loyalty, which in turn leads to improved financial and market share performance. Understanding such relationships is important in using data and information for strategic and operational decisions. It is essential that leading performance measures be driven by characteristics that are important to customers. Also, when significant differences are found between leading and lagging measures of performance—for example, when leading measures are improving but lagging measures are not—the company may be measuring the wrong things. For

OM SPOTLIGHT

Pearl River School District[23]

Pearl River School District

Located 20 miles north of New York City in Rockland County, New York, the Pearl River School District (PRSD) provides education for 2,500 children, kindergarten through 12th grade. In addition, more than 1,000 adults participate in the district's continuing education program. PRSD's 203 teachers are distributed among three elementary schools (kindergarten through grade 4), one middle school (grades 5 through 7), and one high school (grades 8 through 12).

Over the past 8 years, spending for instruction has grown by 43 percent, an increase largely achieved through savings from operational efficiencies. Property taxes account for 82 percent of the district's annual budget, which must be approved by local voters. In 1992, school administrators initiated a process to continuously improve student performance and deliver value for the entire community, including teachers, families, taxpayers, and businesses. PRSD has been both strongly focused on its core mission—"every child can and will learn"—and persistent in its pursuit of the district's three strategic goals: improving academic performance, improving public perception of the district by incorporating quality principles and values, and maintaining fiscal stability and improving cost effectiveness.

PRSD's "balanced scorecard"—a scannable composite of leading and lagging indicators of progress toward meeting goals and underpinning strategic objectives—provides continuous, up-to-date tracking of district performance. Related tracking measures are employed on successively finer scales: school, grade, classroom, teacher, and student. Regardless of focus, all PRSD goals must be specific, measurable, achievable, relevant, and timely. Measures also focus on community and employee satisfaction, and local voters typically approve the district's annual budget by a two-to-one majority or better.

PRSD also has created a team structure that makes the success of students a shared responsibility that transcends grade levels and schools. It eliminated department chairs and four curriculum directors. Now, all instructional staff are organized under one K–12 curriculum director; elementary teachers work in grade-level teams, middle school teachers work in cross-discipline teams, and high school teachers work in subject-area departments. Principals have day-to-day responsibility for managing faculty and staff, but the job of designing and delivering instructional programs belongs primarily to teachers. The percentage of students graduating with a Regents diploma, a key PRSD objective, has increased from 60 percent in 1996 to 86 percent in 2001, only 4 percentage points below the state's top performer. Many other external and internal performance measures have greatly improved since 1996.

an example of using the balanced scorecard, see the OM Spotlight on Pearl River School District, a 2001 Baldrige winner and one of the first education recipients.

The Value Chain Model

A third way of viewing performance measurement is through the value chain concept itself. Of the four models of organizational performance presented in this chapter, the value chain model is probably the dominant model, especially for operations managers. Recall from Chapter 1 that a value chain is a synchronized network of processes that includes suppliers and inputs, processes and associated resources, goods and service outputs and outcomes, customers and their market segments, synchronized information and feedback loops, and management of the value chain. Exhibit 3.10 shows the value chain structure and suggests some typical measures that managers might use to evaluate performance at each point in the value chain. These measures are used by middle managers, first-line supervisors, and employees to monitor and control their processes. However, senior managers generally are not interested in all the details that these individuals need on a daily basis; thus, their measures must be aggregated into broader business performance measures that are useful to top management in assessing and improving overall value chain performance (as suggested by the dashed lines in the figure). These include aggregate financial, market,

Exhibit 3.10 Examples of Value Chain Performance Measurements

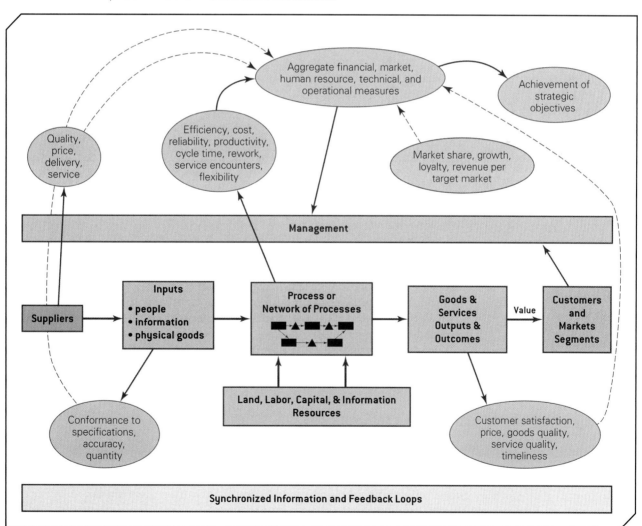

human resource, and operational measures as well as the innovation and learning measures of the balanced scorecard. These provide measures of achievement of strategic objectives. Often, operational performance measures are translated into dollars—the language that senior managers and stakeholders clearly understand. Next, we discuss some of the measurement issues associated with the value chain.

Suppliers provide goods and services inputs to the value chain that are used in the creation and delivery of value chain outputs. Measuring supplier performance is critical to managing a value chain. If the quality of purchased goods and services is poor, the quality of the customer benefit package will probably also be poor. If suppliers cannot provide accurate and timely delivery, it is difficult for their customers to meet their schedules. Therefore, an organization needs to obtain goods and service-related performance data on its suppliers, as well as time-based data. Typical supplier performance measures include quality of the inputs provided, price, delivery reliability, and service measures such as rates of problem resolution. Good supplier-based performance data are also the basis for cooperative partnerships between suppliers and their customers.

Operations managers have the primary responsibility to design and manage the processes and associated resources that create value for customers. Process data can reflect defect and error rates of intermediate operations and also efficiency measures such as cost, flow time, delivery variability, productivity, schedule performance, equipment downtime, preventive maintenance activity, rates of problem resolution, energy and equipment efficiency, and raw material usage. For example, Motorola measures nearly every process in the company, including engineering design, order entry, manufacturing, human resources, purchasing, accounting, and marketing, for improvements in error rates and flow times. One of its key business objectives is to reduce total organizational flow time—the time from the point a customer expresses a need until the customer pays the company for the good or service.

Measuring goods and service outputs and outcomes tells a company whether its processes are providing the levels of quality and service that customers expect. In goods-producing organizations, outputs are often tested for functional performance and defects prior to shipping, which provides information about how well the manufacturing process has done its job. Service operations are often audited to determine if the proper customer-focused procedures were followed, such as the tone of voice and empathy the telephone customer service representative shows in solving the customer's problem. Organizations measure outputs and outcomes using metrics such as unit cost, defects per million opportunities, and lead time. Through customer and market information, an organization learns how satisfied its customers and stakeholders are with its goods and services and performance and how best to configure the goods and services (that is, customer benefit packages). Measures of customer satisfaction and retention reveal areas that need improvement and show whether changes actually result in improvement.

Synchronized information and feedback loops provide the means of coordinating the value chain's physical and information flows and for assessing whether the organization is achieving its strategic objectives. This is similar to the role of Information and Analysis in the Malcolm Baldrige framework. One objective of timely information sharing is to reduce or replace assets (employees, inventory, trucks, buildings, and so on) with smart and timely performance information. Linking the diverse information within a value chain together in a timely fashion helps to create superior value chain performance, such as that exhibited by organizations like General Electric and Wal-Mart, who use information and performance measurement systems better than their competitors. For example, the sales of G.E. light bulbs in Wal-Mart stores are recorded immediately at G.E. factories and production is scheduled to real-time sales data. Fewer resources are needed to achieve performance goals when "information replaces assets." That is, inventories are reduced, flow times are shorter, quality is better, and costs are lower.

The coordination of information within the value chain makes it a powerful model for viewing organizational performance. Some of the key interlinking relationships that organizations should consider are

- How is supplier delivery reliability related to process performance?
- How does supplier quality relate to final goods output quality?
- How is equipment downtime related to process efficiency?
- How is process throughput related to process output quality?
- How is the order fulfillment rate related to customer satisfaction?
- How is unit cost related to market share?
- How is inventory accuracy related to revenue per square foot of retail space?
- How is process efficiency related to profitability?
- How is the speed of information sharing related to customer satisfaction?

The challenge is to model these performance relationships throughout the value chain so the drivers of customer value and value chain efficiencies are well understood.

Professional and trade associations, such as the American Hospital Association (see OM Spotlight on this topic), Institute for Electrical and Electronics Engineers, Society of Automotive Engineers, American Institute of Certified Public Accountants, and American Hotel and Lodging Association, frequently collect and monitor the overall performance of their industry. These data can provide individual organizations with benchmarks and comparisons useful in evaluating their own performance and setting priorities for improvement.

OM SPOTLIGHT

Hospital Performance Consortium[24]

A consortium of 96 U.S. companies plans to evaluate hospitals on the basis of better patient care, not cheaper care. The theory is that better care will reduce total health care costs in the long run. The focus is on clinical quality in the health care value chain where hospitals are the major contributor. Companies such as Boeing, IBM, United Parcel Service, and General Electric are in the consortium and call themselves the *Leapfrog Group*. The group spends over $52 billion on health care annually for 28 million people.

Leapfrog was formed in 2000 partly because of a government study that found that medical mistakes in hospitals result in between 44,000 and 98,000 deaths a year and produce more than $20 billion in added costs. Leapfrog says 60,000 lives would be saved annually if the 2,800 urban acute-care hospitals adopted three basic practices. The practices are whether hospitals computerize doctor's orders and mistake-proof associated processes, use specialized doctors in intensive-care units, and have extensive experience in certain procedures (that is, focused expertise, analogous to a focused factory in manufacturing).

The plan calls for patients to choose quality hospitals and is a departure from traditional managed care where workers were shepherded into health care networks with the lowest rates. Of course, to accomplish these objectives hospitals must redesign their processes and practices to ensure superior quality, and define performance measures that reflect these three clinical quality goals. The next step is to define the performance relationships among these measures (that is, interlinking). Leapfrog plans to collect and report hospital performance data and act as an education source if hospitals need help in redoing processes and performance metrics.

The Service-Profit Chain Model

The **service-profit chain** was first proposed in a 1994 *Harvard Business Review* article and is most applicable to service environments.[25] Exhibit 3.11 is one representation of the SPC, and many variations of this model have been proposed in academic and practitioner articles. Many companies, such as Citibank, General Electric, Intuit, Southwest Airlines, Taco Bell, Marlow Industries, and Xerox, have used this model of organizational performance. The theory of the service-profit chain is that employees, through the service delivery system, create customer value and drive profitability. As J. W. Marriott, the founder of Marriott Hotels said long ago, "Happy employees create happy customers."

The model is based on a set of cause-and-effect linkages between internal and external performance, and in this fashion, defines the key performance measurements on which service-based firms should focus. Because much of the value created in service processes is at the service encounter level, the service-profit chain focuses on employees or service providers (see the OM Spotlight: ServiceMaster's Professional Service Provider). The differences between goods-producing and service-providing organizations described in Chapter 1 also help make clear why employees are so important in services. Healthy, motivated, well-trained, and loyal employees demonstrate higher levels of satisfaction that result in higher retention and productivity. This leads to higher levels of external service value to customers. External service value is created by service providers mainly at the service encounter level. Buyers of services focus on outcomes, results, and experiences. Ultimately, good value creates higher customer satisfaction and loyalty, which in turn leads to higher revenue growth and profitability.

Internal service quality is influenced by the way an organization designs and manages jobs, the workplace, and the working environment. This includes employee training and development, recognition and rewards, employee empowerment, attention to health and safety, benefits, and corporate culture. We will discuss these issues further in Chapter 17. In Exhibit 3.11, the internal service delivery system is analogous to categories 5 (Human Resource Focus) and 6 (Process Management) in the Malcolm Baldrige framework as well as the internal perspective of the balanced scorecard. Thus, the measurements associated with these perspectives are equally applicable to the SPC model. These measures might include performance of

Exhibit 3.11 The Service-Profit Chain Model

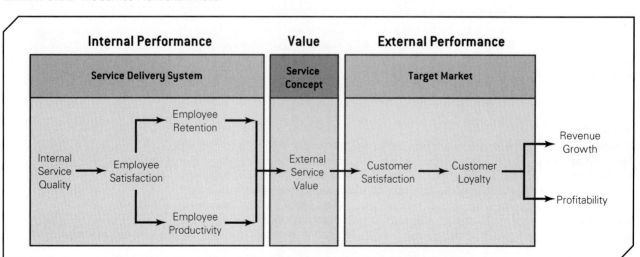

Adapted from J. L. Heskett, T. O. Jones, G. W. Loveman, W. E. Sasser, Jr., and L. A. Schlesinger, "Putting the Service-Profit Chain to Work," *Harvard Business Review*, March–April 1994, pp. 164–174.

OM SPOTLIGHT

ServiceMaster[26]

A brochure from ServiceMaster states: "Thanks for choosing Tru-Green ChemLawn, one of the ServiceMaster companies, for your lawn care service. We appreciate your business, and because you are our customer, we're offering you a FREE membership in the *ServiceMaster Home Service Center*, normally a $79 value. As a member, you'll be able to schedule all kinds of home services, at any time, day or night, by Internet or phone. So, whether you need pest control (Terminix), heating and air (American Residential Services), maid service (Merry Maids), plumbing (Rescue Rooter), home warranty plans (American Home Shield), on-site furniture repair (Furniture Medic), home inspections (AmeriSpec), carpet cleaning (ServiceMaster Clean), or other home services (Service-Master Home Service Center), we have it. So join today, it's FREE and you can get special savings as shown in the brochure. Count on convenience, quality, protection, and savings!"

ServiceMaster uses a wide variety of internal and external performance measures. Within the organization it has adopted a performance measurement system that focuses on best practices and plans to replicate those practices in its 5,400 service centers. Its internal measurement system emphasizes metrics that are "close to the customer," such as the percent of time ServiceMaster meets its scheduled appointment times, and data-driven audits by team captains on the quality of service provided, such as cleaning a home. Employee satisfaction surveys are closely monitored. Financial performance measures, of course, are the primary external performance indicators, but customer satisfaction surveys are also very important at ServiceMaster. (See the Service-Profit Chain in Exhibit 3.11.)

One objective of ServiceMaster is to develop a sense of professionalism among all of its service providers. It does this by extensive training programs and stressing "the importance of the mundane" such as cleaning a floor or unclogging a drain. For each individual service, the process and possible service encounters are studied, best practices adopted, and everyone is trained on the process. Its video training library is an integral part of its internal service quality initiative focused on the employee. Possible questions customers may ask the service provider are studied and recommended service-provider responses (script dialogues) are built into the training programs. Since the service provider is normally in or around customers' most treasured possession—their home—every effort is made to mistake-proof the service experience. The service provider must have service management skills that include technical expertise, the ability to cross-sell other ServiceMaster services, and good human interaction behaviors. That is why the service profit-chain focuses on the service provider and highlights the importance of service encounters.

hiring and recruitment processes, safety and accident rates, employee satisfaction, absenteeism, turnover, productivity, service quality, timeliness, employee improvement suggestions, customer satisfaction, complaints, and compliments. Specific training measures, for example, might include training hours per employee and training effectiveness based on posttraining survey results or job performance assessments. For instance, General Electric tries to hire the best people and complement this hiring strategy by having one of the highest training hours per employee rates of any organization in the world. Measures of service value include service quality outcomes and perceptions. The customer and financial measures that we discussed earlier in this chapter can be used to evaluate the external perspectives in this model.

The causal nature of this model suggests numerous interlinking questions. Some of these might be: How does employee satisfaction relate to employee retention? and How does customers' satisfaction relate to repeat purchases? Considerable research supports the SPC model. IBM's AS/400 Division in Rochester, Minnesota, for example, conducted a study using 10 years' of data and found strong correlations among key measures of employee satisfaction, customer satisfaction, and market share. The strongest correlations are summarized in Exhibit 3.12, and the interlinking model that resulted is shown in Exhibit 3.13. IBM's model is quite similar to the service profit chain.

Exhibit 3.12 IBM AS/400 Division Performance Measure Correlations (1984–1994 Data)

	Market Share	Customer Satisfaction	Productivity	Cost of Quality	Employee Satisfaction	Job Satisfaction	Satisfaction with Manager	Right Skills
Market Share	1.00	0.71	0.97	−0.86	0.84	0.84	—	0.97
Customer Satisfaction	0.71	1.00	—	−0.79	0.70	—	—	0.72
Productivity	0.97	—	1.00	—	0.93	0.92	0.86	0.98
Cost of Quality	−0.86	−0.79	—	1.00	—	—	—	—
Employee Satisfaction	0.84	0.70	0.93	—	1.00	0.92	0.92	0.86
Job Satisfaction	0.84	—	0.92	—	0.92	1.00	0.70	0.84
Satisfaction with Manager	—	—	0.86	—	0.92	0.70	1.00	0.92
Right Skills	0.97	0.72	0.98	—	0.86	0.84	0.92	1.00

Source: Steven H. Hoisington and Tse-Hsi Huang, "Customer Satisfaction and Market Share: An Empirical Case Study of IBM's AS/400 Division," in *Customer-Centered Six Sigma*, Earl Naumann and Steven H. Hoisington (Milwaukee, WI: ASQ Quality Press, 2001).

Exhibit 3.13 IBM AS/400 Division Interlinking Model

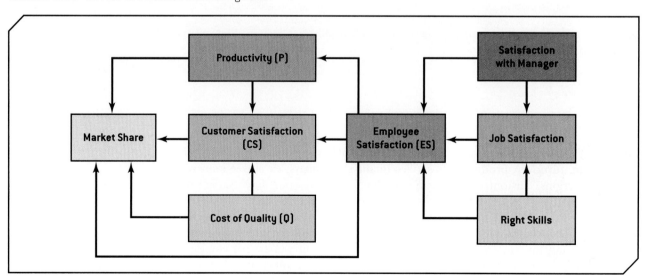

Source: Steven H. Hoisington and Tse-Hsi Huang, "Customer Satisfaction and Market Share: An Empirical Case Study of IBM's AS/400 Division," in *Customer-Centered Six Sigma*, Earl Naumann and Steven H. Hoisington (Milwaukee, WI: ASQ Quality Press, 2001).

SOLVED PROBLEMS

SOLVED PROBLEM #1

Costs, revenue, and other relevant information for two nursing units that admit and treat similar patients during a 6-month period are shown in Exhibit 3.14. Compute the total dollar value of inputs for each unit, total productivity, and the partial-productivity measure of direct nursing labor productivity. How do the units compare?

Solution:

Total inputs in dollars are calculated by multiplying total patient days by the number of nursing hours per patient day and the total direct nursing care cost per hour, and adding the remaining costs per patient day multiplied by the number of patient days to the fixed overhead cost. Thus, for Unit A, the total dollar value of inputs are

$$(5,000)(4.7)(\$15.75) + (\$35.50)(5,000) + (\$267.00)(5,000) + (\$31.50)(5,000) + \$102,311.00 = \$2,142,436.00$$

Thus, Unit A's total productivity is computed as the total revenues generated (output) divided by the total dollar value of inputs used, or $2,394,500/$2,142,436 = 1.12. Similar calculations are used for Unit B.

Total direct nursing costs for Unit A are computed as (5,000)(4.7)($15.75) = $370,125. Dividing total revenues by this value provides the partial-productivity measure for direct nursing labor productivity.

We see that Unit A is more productive than Unit B by (1.12 − 0.95)/0.95 = 17.9%. Moreover, Unit A is also more productive based on a labor (partial) productivity measure of 6.47 versus 5.75 for Unit B. These productivity ratios assume that quality is the same in both nursing units. The ratios might be adjusted by measuring the degree to which each nursing unit complies with accrediting standards or by infectious disease rates per thousand patients.

Nursing Unit Productivity Measures	Unit A	Unit B
Total patient days	5,000	6,120
Direct nursing hours/patient day	4.70	4.60
Total direct nursing care cost/hour	$ 15.75	$ 17.85
Total indirect nursing care cost/patient day	$ 35.50	$ 42.25
Average room and bed cost/patient day	$ 267.00	$ 325.00
Variable overhead cost/patient day	$ 31.50	$ 28.80
Fixed overhead cost/nursing unit	$ 102,311.00	$ 110,425.00
Revenues generated per unit	$2,394,500.00	$2,887,000.00
Total inputs	$2,142,436.00	$3,036,764.20
Total productivity	1.12	0.95
Total direct nursing cost	$ 370,125.00	$ 502,513.20
Total direct (partial) labor productivity	6.47	5.75

Exhibit 3.14
Nursing Unit Productivity Analysis

SOLVED PROBLEM #2

A factory department consists of three types of employees: laborers earning $10 per hour, machine operators earning $15 per hour, and machinists earning $30 per hour. For a certain job, over two periods, the performance shown here was collected:

Type of Employee	Labor Hours per Period	
	Period 1	Period 2
Laborer	20	16
Machine operator	12	16
Machinist	6	11

Output increased by 20 percent in period 2. How has productivity changed?

Solution:

Because labor costs are given, we will use a total labor-cost productivity measure. With no knowledge of actual output figures, we index output for period 1 as 100 and for period 2 as 120 (or 1.0 and 1.2, for example). Then we divide the output index for each period by the sum of the input costs to obtain the productivity measure.

The total labor costs for each period are shown next.

	Period 1	Period 2
Laborer	$200	$160
Machine operator	$180	$240
Machinist	$180	$330
Total	$560	$730

The productivity index for period 1 is 100/560 = 0.1786; for period 2 it is 120/730 = 0.1644. The relative change in productivity in period 2 is (0.1644 − 0.1786)/0.1786 = −0.0795, or a decline of −7.95 percent. Management should identify possible reasons factory productivity decreased in period 2 and work to fix or improve the problem or situation.

SOLVED PROBLEM #3

A steel company produces long, thin sheets of steel called coils that each weigh 10 to 15 tons. The slitting operation involves cutting the coils into smaller widths. An average of 5,000 tons per month is sold. The scrap rate from this operation is 3 percent. Material costs are $600 per ton. It takes 0.75 hours of labor at a rate of $20 per hour to produce 1 ton sold.

a. How many tons per month must be produced to meet the sales demand?

b. What annual savings would result from decreasing the scrap rate from 3 percent to 2 percent?

Solution:

a. The required production to make 5,000 tons of good steel with a 3 percent scrap rate is 5,000/(1 − 0.03) = 5,155 tons (not 5,000 times 1.03!).

b. The required production to make 5,000 tons of good steel with a 2 percent scrap rate is 5,000/0.98 = 5,102 tons. If the scrap rate is 3 percent, the additional 155 tons per month requires $93,000 ($600/ton)(155 tons) in material and (0.75)(20)(155) = $2,325 in labor, for a total of $95,325. If the scrap rate is 2 percent, the additional 102 tons costs $61,200 in material and $1,530 in labor, for a total of $62,730. The difference incurred by reducing the scrap rate from 3 to 2 percent is $32,595 per month, or $391,140 annually. Even a small improvement in internal failure costs can result in big savings!

SOLVED PROBLEM #4

What is the value of a loyal customer (VLC) in the small contractor target market segment who buys an electric drill on average for $100 every 4 years, when the gross margin on the drill averages 50 percent and the customer retention rate is 60 percent? What if the customer retention rate increases to 80 percent? What is a 1 percent change in market share worth to the manufacturer if it represents 100,000 customers? What do you conclude?

Solution:

If customer retention rate is 60 percent, the average customer defection rate = (1 − Customer retention rate). Thus, the customer defection rate is 40 percent, or 0.4. The average buyers life cycle is 1/0.4 = 2.5 years. The repurchase frequency is every 4 years, or (1/4) 0.25. Therefore,

$$VLC = P \times RF \times CM \times BLC =$$
$$(\$100)(0.25)(0.50)(1/0.4) = \$31.25$$

The value of a 1 percent change in market share = (100,000 customers)($31.25/customer) = $3,125,000.

If the customer retention rate is 80 percent, the average customer defection rate is 0.2, and the average buyers life cycle is 1/0.2 = 5 years. Then,

$$VLC = P \times RF \times CM \times BLC =$$
$$(\$100)(0.25)(0.50)(1/.2) = \$62.50$$

The $31.25 and $62.50 are the value of a loyal customer over their buying life given the assumptions, respectively. Thus, the value of a 1 percent change in market share = (100,000 customers) ($62.50/customer) = $6,250,000.

KEY TERMS AND CONCEPTS

Actionable measures
Balanced scorecard
Baldrige Award
Buyer's life cycle
Critical defect
Customer and market
Customer retention (defection) rate
Customer-satisfaction measurement system
Defects (errors) per million opportunities (dpmo)
Effectiveness
Efficiency
Environmental quality
Errors per million opportunities (epmo)
Financial
Flexibility
  Design flexibility
  Volume flexibility
Goods quality dimensions
  Conformance
  Durability
  Features
  Performance
  Reliability
  Serviceability
Information reliability
Innovation and learning
Interlinking
Major defect
Measurement
  Category
  Defined
  Number

Minor defect
Multifactor productivity
Nonconformities (defects) per unit
Operational definitions
Partial-factor productivity
Productivity
Productivity index
Quality
  Goods
  Service
Repurchase frequency
Safety
Service profit-chain
Service quality dimensions
  Assurance
  Empathy
  Reliability
  Responsiveness
  Tangibles
Service upsets
Time
  Manufacturing lead time
  Processing (cycle or flow) time
  Purchasing lead time
  Queue time
Total productivity
Value chain model
Value of loyal customer (VLC)

QUESTIONS FOR REVIEW AND DISCUSSION

1. For the bank teller customer episode at the beginning of the chapter, define good service from the customer's viewpoint. How would you measure the performance of the bank teller? What actions must you take to ensure superior service encounters between the customer and bank teller? Explain.

2. For the bank teller customer episode at the beginning of the chapter, how do the seven differences between goods versus services presented in Chapter 1 impact this service encounter situation? Explain.

3. What are the uses and benefits of good performance measurement?

4. Why is safety important in organizations? Is it a prerequisite to other performance measures such as quality and productivity? Explain.

5. Why is the term *nonconformity* often used instead of *defect* or *error*?

6. Describe the five key dimensions of service quality.

7. Of what value are customer-satisfaction measures to managers?

8. What is interlinking? What benefits do interlinking models provide organizations?

9. Identify specific *internal* performance measures that would be useful in each of the following operations: (a) hotel, (b) post office, (c) department store, (d) bus system, and (e) emergency room.

10. Identify specific *external* performance measures that would be useful in each of the following operations: (a) hotel, (b) post office, (c) department store, (d) bus system, and (e) emergency room.

11. Identify and discuss two example performance relationships you would like to find between the internal and external performance measures you identified in Questions 9 and 10?

12. Explain the differences between total, multifactor, and partial-factor productivity measurements. Why are total or multifactor measures preferable to partial-productivity measures?

13. How does productivity measurement differ in manufacturing and service organizations?

14. Identify a customer benefit package you buy and use, and explain three reasons why customers defect. What do you recommend for stopping these customer defections?

15. Identify and briefly describe a buying situation that was good and enhanced your customer loyalty toward the good or service.

16. Estimate the value of a loyal customer over the 40-year buying life of a loyal Volvo automobile owner. (You need to make assumptions about the frequency of purchase over 40 years, average car value/price and type, buy or lease.)

17. When the value of a loyal customer (VLC) market segment is high, should these customers be given premium goods and services for premium prices? If the VLC is low, should they be given less service? Explain.

18. What do we mean by information reliability? Why is it important? How should data be managed?

19. Why is information accessibility important? How does information technology help?

20. How can measurement help in the daily operations of your college or university?

21. Discuss what performance measures can be used in a fraternity or student organization to evaluate efficiency and effectiveness. What cause-and-effect (interlinking) performance relationships would be of interest to the organization?

22. Interview managers at a local company to identify the key business measures (financial, market, supplier, employee, process, information, innovation, and so on) for that company. What quality indicators does that company measure? What cause-and-effect (interlinking) performance relationships would be of interest to the organization?

23. Many restaurants and hotels use "tabletop" customer-satisfaction surveys. Find several of them at local businesses and evaluate the types of questions and items included in the surveys. What internal performance measures might be appropriate to link to these external measures?

24. Design a customer-satisfaction survey for some organization or process in which you are involved. Explain how you derived the questions in your survey. How might you use the results of the survey for improvement?

25. Explain how productivity measures can be misleading if quality is not taken into account or assumed to be equal.

26. In the making of cheese, companies test milk for somatic cell count to ensure prevention of diseases and test it for bacteria to determine how clean it is. They also perform a freezing-point test to see that the milk has not been diluted with water (if diluted, it will freeze at a lower temperature and increase production costs, since all excess water must be extracted). Final cheese products are subjected to tests for weight, foreign elements, chemicals, and taste and smell. What customer-related measures might interlink with those internal measures?

27. Define and explain any one of the four models of organizational performance. How might the model be applied to an organization that you are familiar with, such as fast-food, quick-service automobile oil and lube service, bookstores, retail stores, and so on? (Provide example measures of all performance categories in the model you select.)

PROBLEMS AND ACTIVITIES

1. A major airline is attempting to evaluate the effect of recent changes it has made in scheduling flights between New York City and Los Angeles. The data available are

	Number of Flights	Number of Passengers
Month prior to schedule change	20	8,335
Month after schedule change	24	10,608

   a. Using passengers per flight as a productivity indicator, comment on the apparent effect of the schedule change.

   b. Suggest another measure of productivity that the airline may want to consider.

2. A hamburger factory produces 50,000 hamburgers each week. The equipment used costs $5,000 and will remain productive for 3 years. The labor cost per year is $8,000.

   a. What is the productivity measure of "units of output per dollar of input" averaged over the 3-year period?

   b. We have the option of $10,000 equipment, with an operating life of 5 years. It would reduce labor costs to $4,000 per year. Should we consider purchasing this equipment (using productivity arguments alone)?

3. For the Miller Chemicals example, suppose that for 2006 output was only 140,000 lb while direct labor hours and costs are 10% higher. How do the productivity measures and indexes change?

4. Productivity measures for a manufacturing plant over a 6-month period follow:

Month	Jan.	Feb.	Mar.	Apr.	May	June
Productivity	1.46	1.42	1.49	1.50	1.30	1.25

Using January as the base period, compute a productivity index for February to June, and comment on what those productivity indexes tell about the productivity trend.

5. The data shown apply to the first two quarters of the current year. Using total-dollar measures of input and output, compare the total profit and productivity achieved for the two quarters. How does second-quarter productivity compare with the first-quarter productivity? Use partial-factor productivity to identify what might be done to improve productivity and profitability during the third quarter.

	First Quarter	Second Quarter
Unit selling price	$20.00	$21.00
Total units sold	10,000	8,500
Labor hours	9,000	7,750
Labor cost/hour	$10.00	$10.00
Material usage (lb)	5,000	4,500
Material cost/pound	$15.00	$15.50
Other costs	$20,000	$18,000

6. A manufacturing firm uses two measures of productivity:

   a. Total sales/Total inputs

   b. Total sales/Total labor inputs

Given the following data for the last 3 years, calculate the productivity ratios. How would you interpret the results? All figures are in dollars.

	Year 1	Year 2	Year 3
Sales	$110	$129	$124
Materials	62	73	71
Labor	28	33	28
Overhead	8	12	10

7. A fast-food restaurant has a drive-through window and during peak lunch times can handle a maximum of 80 cars per hour with one person taking orders, assembling them, and acting as cashier. The average sale per order is $5.00. A proposal has been made to add two workers and divide the tasks among the three. One will take orders, the second will assemble them, and the third will act as cashier. With this system it is estimated that 120 cars per hour can be serviced. All workers earn the minimum wage. Use productivity arguments to recommend whether or not to change the current system.

8. A computer software firm provides a 20' × 30' office for its six systems analysts and plans to hire two additional analysts. To maintain a 100-square-foot working space per analyst, the firm's owner-manager is considering expansion. The cost of expansion is $40 per square foot with annual maintenance costs of $4 per square foot. The useful life of floor space is 20 years. By how much should employee productivity increase to justify the additional expenditure? The current salary of the systems analysts is $25,000.

9. What is the average value of a loyal customer (VLC) in a target market segment if the average purchase price is $70 per visit, the frequency of repurchase is

every month, the contribution margin is 20 percent, and the average customer defection rate is 25 percent? If a continuous improvement goal is set of a 20 percent defection rate next year and 15 percent 2 years from now, what are the revised *VLCs* over their average buying life?

10. What is the average defection rate for grocery store shoppers in a local area of a large city if they spend $50 per visit, shop 52 weeks per year, the grocery store has a 16 percent gross margin, and the value of a loyal customer is estimated at $2,000 per year?

11. Interview some managers at one or more local companies about their approach to performance measurement. Do they use a balanced scorecard? What types of measures are used in daily operations activities? How are operational measures captured at lower levels of the organization elevated to senior managers?

12. Go to the Baldrige web site, www.baldrige.org, and find the links to award winners. Review some of their application summaries and summarize the types of performance measures that these companies use.

13. The balanced scorecard was originally developed by Arthur M. Schneiderman at Analog Devices. Visit his web site, www.schneiderman.com, and read the articles to answer the following questions:

    a. How was the first balanced scorecard developed?
    b. What steps should an organization follow to build a good balanced scorecard?
    c. Why do balanced scorecards fail?

CASES

GREYHOUND INSURANCE COMPANY

"Ray, our check processing system is in trouble! Keying errors, missed postings, and delayed work are creating an avalanche of customer complaints. And this department is averaging a 36 percent turnover rate over the last 3 months for our most stressful job. The research unit is upset because they must resolve the customer problems caused by our errors." These were the agitated comments of Tom Harlan, the vice president of check processing for Greyhound Insurance Company. Ray Shuman, the manager of check processing, slumped in his chair as he faced his boss, Harlan.

Slowly Shuman responded, "Well, Tom, we are placing too much emphasis on productivity and cost reduction numbers. We need a better performance measurement system. Our people are unmotivated. They won't do what they are supposed to do! There is nothing to sustain the improvement efforts."

Two weeks later Shuman left the company and took another job. Now Harlan was searching for a new manager who could get this process in shape quickly. Where should he look for a new manager? What personal characteristics and skills should he look for in hiring a replacement manager? And, most importantly, how can this new manager quickly improve the performance of check processing?

The Greyhound Insurance Company receives payments from a wide variety of individual customers, corporations, trust accounts, associations, and so on. The first major process step (check preparation) occurs when incoming customer envelopes are opened, sorted by work type, and prepped for high-speed capture on automated equipment. Mail that is all the same size, bar coded, and with the insurance payment coupon facing the front of the envelope is called regular mail and processed first. The check processing center works two shifts with about 30 employees.

The second major step (check processing) is where the automated processing of the physical documents as well as transferring key information to computer records and images is performed. The physical documents are printed on the first pass with a sequence number for audit purposes. Also, the payment coupon and check are separated, and images are taken of both. This imaging process is called the temporary digital image. Additional information is then keyed from these images rather than the physical documents, such as the dollar payment amount. A second pass is required through the automated equipment to encode the dollar amount onto the checks.

Customer correspondent information that accompanies these checks is also collected. Customers often send complaint letters and other correspondence with their checks although they should send it to a separate address. The checks are then bundled and sorted by bank and geographical area and then distributed. The computerized account information is held in a computer master file for use in customer account status reporting.

The problems in the check processing area illustrate the fact that isolated areas and processes sometimes drift and get into a poor performance cycle. The issue is how to turn things around and improve performance quickly. This backroom process is having a negative effect on internal performance and external customer satisfaction. As one manager noted, "There are no backroom processes anymore, all processes have front room implications."

The following incidents and insights help us understand the nature of the information-intensive process at the time of the case.

1. Employee opinion surveys show that teamwork was fair within work units but broke down across work units and departments.

2. Human behavior was a major factor in payment patterns, and therefore, workload levels. It was difficult to predict customer demand (payment workload), and payment due dates were not a good predictor of actual customer payment patterns. Therefore, staffing levels traditionally were held constant while workload varied greatly. Employees were bored on Monday evenings with little to do but on Friday they often had to work overtime to finish all the work. Before and after holidays were also peak demand periods.

3. Electronic (checkless) banking using the Internet was beginning to level off the growth in paper checks but forecasting the eventual decline in paper check processing was difficult at the present time. It was difficult to forecast human behavior.

4. The failure of the key operator to refer to the amount written in words (that is, the legal line) when unsure about the numerical amount on the check was the number-one cause of "controllable" errors. The second most frequent cause of errors was mistakes in encoding where trailing zeros were omitted. The trailing-zero problem was associated with a few individual keyers who were temporary employees.

5. The management of the check process was organized on a two-shift basis. One shift supervisor complained that "there is too much conflict among shift supervisors. No one owns the total process!"

Harlan wondered how he should address the questions posed at the beginning of the case. He was a senior manager—he couldn't quit! He had to fix the check process and turn performance around or he would be looking for a job too! He was responsible!

He had collected performance data, a sample of which is shown in Exhibit 3.15, and he wondered what these data might tell him. How could he use these data to establish a baseline performance level upon which to measure the success or failure of the new manager's initiatives? Were any of these performance measures related (interlinked) in Exhibit 3.15? How could he break this cycle of failure? What are the characteristics of an "ideal" performance system for Greyhound's check processing?

Month	Volume (000)	Unit Cost ($)	Operator Turnover Rate (%)	Productivity (Vol/Std. Hr.)
1	1,994	2.356	16.0	174.86
2	1,882	2.601	18.0	161.47
3	1,974	1.894	18.0	155.34
4	1,954	1.799	30.0	163.17
5	1,759	2.346	18.0	144.16
6	2,234	1.779	10.0	187.92
7	1,722	2.806	18.0	152.82
8	1,928	2.246	26.0	166.54
Average	1,931	2.228	19.3	163.29
Std. Dev.	158	0.378	6.1	13.59
Max	2,234	2.806	30.0	187.92
Min	1,722	1.779	10.0	144.16

Exhibit 3.15
Sample of Check Processing Performance Data

Notes:
Volume—activity levels (in thousands) defined by whatever is contained in a customer's envelope.
Unit Cost—cost per transaction unit processed.
Productivity—the volume processed per standard employee hour.
Employee Turnover Rate (%)—only for the most stressful check-keying job.

THE EXCELSIOR INN

The Excelsior Inn, a 450-room hotel, has gathered a considerable amount of data and is trying to estimate its "return on quality." The hotel manager is interested in determining what return on investment could be achieved if she invested in additional service. She conducted an experiment with hotel guests regarding the cleanliness of the hotel (rooms, lobby, lobby restrooms, restaurant, hotel uniforms, elevators, signs, and so on). The following data are taken from a pilot study where various amounts of additional labor and training, above the present standard, were applied to hotel cleanliness. These measurements have been expressed in annual dollar amounts, based on wages, fringe benefits, and training of current employees. Customers were then surveyed to determine their levels of satisfaction/dissatisfaction. Percentages of dissatisfied customers have been matched with annual dollars of improvement efforts from the study.

a. Use regression analysis to determine the best equation that can be used to estimate the reduction in customer dissatisfaction based on the "Super Clean Hotel Strategy." What would be the appropriate level of effort to apply, based on your calculations and judgment? How would you describe your analysis in terms of interlinking?

b. Suppose that each point of market share increase brings in approximately $600,000 of additional

profit per year, and the cost per year is your suggested investment in improvement (from part a). What would be the "return on quality improvement" based on a 3-year discounted cash flow at 10 percent of the investment costs, if the hotel manager estimated that she could realize a 2.5 percent increase in market share? (*Hint:* Return on quality = Annual profit increase/Discounted present value of investment.)

Service Improvement Investment [$1,000]	Percent of Customers Dissatisfied
0	0.200
50	0.150
150	0.100
260	0.076
290	0.067
300	0.059
450	0.052
600	0.045
750	0.040
900	0.035
1,050	0.031
1,200	0.027
1,350	0.024
1,500	0.021
1,650	0.017
1,800	0.014
1,950	0.010
2,100	0.007

BankUSA: CREDIT CARD DIVISION

BankUSA operates in 20 states and provides a full range of financial services for individuals and business. The Credit Card Division is a profit center and has experienced a 20 percent annual growth rate over the last 5 years. The Credit Card Division processes two types of credit (bank) cards. One type is for traditional card issuers such as savings and loan banks, credit unions, small banks without credit card processing capability, selected private-label firms such as a retail chain, and BankUSA's own credit cards. This "individual customer" market segment involves about 15,000,000 cardholders. These credit card services include producing and mailing the plastic credit cards to customers, preparing and mailing monthly statements to customers, handling all customer requests such as stop payments and customer complaints, and preparation and distribution of summary reports to all internal and external customers.

The second major category of credit card customers includes major brokers and corporations such as IBM, Dean Witter, State Farm Insurance, and Merrill Lynch. These corporate customers use all the services of tradi-

tional card issuers but also usually have electronic access to their account files and desired a cash management type service. Although there are less than 3,000,000 cards issued, the dollar volume of transactions processed is about equal to the traditional individual card issuers.

"Our internal operational measures seem to be good," Juanita Sutherland, the president of BankUSA's Credit Card Division, stated, "but the customer perceives our performance as poor based on marketing's recent customer survey. So, what's going on here? Can anyone at this meeting explain to me this mismatch between these two different sources of information? Is it an important problem or not?"

H.C. Morris, the vice president of operations, quickly responded, "Juanita, one reason there's a mismatch is that operations doesn't have a say in the customer survey's design or performance criteria. We don't ask the same questions or use the same criteria!"

"Wait a minute H.C.! We often ask you operations folks for input into our customer survey design but the job usually gets shuttled to your newest MBA who doesn't have enough company knowledge to truly help us out," stated Bill Barlow, the corporate vice president of marketing, as he leaned forward on the conference room table.

"O.K.," Sutherland interjected, "I want you two to work on this issue and tell me in one week: (1) What are the major problems? (2) What steps are required to develop a good internal and external performance and information system? (3) How should internal and external performance data be related? (4) What is the real service level? What operations measures internally or what marketing measures externally are needed? I've got another appointment so I must leave now but you two have got to work together and figure this thing out. I'm worried that we are losing customers!"

At a subsequent meeting between Morris and Barlow and their respective operations and marketing staffs, the following comments were made:

- "Reports are routed to over 1,200 institutions (that is, card issuers), some on a daily and weekly basis but most on a monthly and quarterly basis. We don't have total control over providing accurate and timely report distribution because we must depend on other banks for certain detailed information such as debt notices and various transportation modes such as airborne courier service."

- "The trends in the marketing customer survey are helpful to everyone but the performance criteria simply do not match up well between marketing and operations."

- "Who cares about averages? If a client bank or corporate customer gets a quarterly performance report from us and it says we are meeting 99.2 percent of our service requirements but they are getting bad service, then they wonder how important a customer they are to us."

- "Plastic card turnaround performance is very good based on the marketing survey data, but the wording of the customer survey questions on plastic card turnaround time is vague."

- "Operations people think they know what constitutes excellent service but how can they be sure?"

- "You'll never get marketing to let us help them design 'their' customer survey," said an angry operations supervisor. "Their marketing questions and what really happens are two different things."

- "We need a consistent numerical basis for knowing how well process performance matches up with external performance. My sample of data (see Exhibit 3.16) is a place to start."

- "Multiple sites and too many services complicate the analysis of what our basic problem is."

- "If your backroom operational performance measures really do the job, who cares about matching marketing and operations performance information. The backroom is a cost center, not a profit center!"

The meeting ended with a lot of arguing but not much progress. Both functional areas were protecting their "turf." How would you address Sutherland's questions?

Exhibit 3.16
Sample Internal and External Credit Card Division Performance Data

Month	Customer Satisfaction Percent (%)	New Applicant Processing Time (Days)	Plastic Production Turnaround Time (Days)
1	92.4	2.2	0.9
2	94	1.4	0.7
3	93.8	2	0.8
4	96.2	2.5	0.6
5	95.7	2.3	0.7
6	93.9	2.1	0.7
7	96.5	1.7	0.5
8	97.1	1.9	0.8
9	96.9	2.4	0.6
10	98.1	1.5	0.7
11	96.8	1.9	0.7
12	97.7	1.6	0.8
13	98	1.3	0.5
14	98.6	1.4	0.7
15	97.3	1.3	0.6

ENDNOTES

[1] Kaplan, Robert S., and Norton, David P., *The Balanced Scorecard*, Boston, MA: Harvard Business School Press, 1996, p. 1.

[2] Deutschman, Alan, "Inside the Mind of Jeff Bezos," *Fast Company*, August 2004, pp. 52–58.

[3] Private communication from Stephen D. Webb, manager of quality control, ground operations, American Airlines.

[4] Lashinsky, Adam, "Meg and the Machine," *Fortune*, September 1, 2003, pp. 68–78.

[5] Godfrey, Blan, "Future Trends: Expansion of Quality Management Concepts, Methods, and Tools to All Industries," *Quality Observer* 6, no. 9, (September 1997), pp. 40–43, 46.

[6] Geanuracos, John, and Meiklejohn, Ian, *Performance Measurement: The New Agenda; Using Non-Financial Indicators to Improve Profitability*, London: Business Intelligence, 1993.

[7] American's Best Plants—Dana Corp.," *Industry Week*, October 19, 1998, and presentation by Mr. Harland Sarbacker, Plant Manager, Dana Corporation, Center for Excellence in Manufacturing Management, Fisher College of Business, Ohio State University, Columbus, Ohio, November 30, 2001.

[8] Garvin, David A., "What Does Product Quality Really Mean?" *Sloan Management Review* 26, no. 1, (1984), pp. 25–43.

[9] Hayes, Glenn E., and Romig, Harry G., *Modern Quality Control*, Encino, CA: Benziger, Bruce & Glencoe, Inc., 1977.

[10] Parasuraman, A., Zeithaml, V. A., and Berry, L. L., "SERVQUAL: A Multiple-Item Scale for Measuring Consumer Perceptions of Service Quality," *Journal of Retailing* 64, no. 1 (Spring 1988), pp. 12–40.

[11] "Are You Built for Speed?" *Fast Company*, June 2003, p. 85.

[12] Welch, David, "How Nissan Laps Detroit," *BusinessWeek*, December 22, 2003, pp. 58–60.

[13] Bernasek, Anna, "The Productivity Miracle is for Real," *Fortune*, March 18, 2002, p. 84.

[14] Collier, David A., *The Service/Quality Solution*, Milwaukee, WI: ASQC Quality Press, and Burr Ridge, IL: Richard D. Irwin, 1994, pp. 235–260. Also, see, for example, Collier, D. A., "A Service Quality Process Map for Credit Card Processing," *Decision Sciences* 22, no. 2, 1991, pp. 406–20 or Wilson, D. D., and Collier, D. A., "The Role of Automation and Labor in Determining Customer Satisfaction in a Telephone Repair Service," *Decision Sciences* 28, no. 3, 1997, pp. 1–21.

[15] Graessel, Bob, and Zeidler, Pete, "Using Quality Function Deployment to Improve Customer Service," *Quality Progress* 26, no. 11 (November 1993), pp. 59–63.

[16] "Bringing Sears Into the New World," *Fortune*, October 13, 1997, pp. 183–184.

[17] Reichheld, F. F., and Sasser, W. E., "Zero Defections: Quality Comes to Services," *Harvard Business Review* 68, no. 5, 1990, pp. 105–111.

[18] U.S. Office of Management and Budget, "How to Develop Quality Measures That Are Useful in Day-to-Day Measurement," U.S. Department of Commerce, National Technical Information Service (January 1989).

[19] Raman, A., DeHoratius, N., and Ton, Z., "The Achilles' Heel of Supply Chain Management," *Harvard Business Review*, May 2001, Reprint # F015C.

[20] "Baldrige Award Winners Beat the S&P 500 for Eight Years," National Institute of Standards and Technology, www.nist.gov/public_affairs/releases/go2-11.htm.

[21] *Source:* http://www.nist.gov/public_affairs/clarke.htm.

[22] 2002 Baldrige Criteria, http://www.baldrige.org/Business_Criteria.htm.

[23] *Source:* http://www.nist.gov/public_affairs/pearlriver.htm.

[24] Adapted from "Employers Group to Unveil Plan to Reduce Medical Errors," *Wall Street Journal*, January 17, 2002, p. B2. Reprinted by permission of Dow Jones, Inc. via Copyright Clearance Center, Inc.

[25] Heskett, J. L., Jones, T. O., et al., "Putting the service-profit chain to work," *Harvard Business Review* 72, no. 2, 1994, pp. 164–174.

[26] www.Join.WeServeHomes.com.

Chapter Outline

CHAPTER 4

Operations Strategy

Learning Objectives

1. To understand how customer wants and needs drive strategic thinking in a firm and their consequences for designing and managing operations within the value chain.

2. To learn the five major competitive priorities important to business success and what they mean for operations.

3. To understand the process of strategic planning at the organizational level and its relationship to operations strategy.

4. To understand how operations strategy can support and drive the achievement of organizational objectives, and to learn the key elements of an operations strategy.

5. To understand the operations design choices and infrastructure decisions from the perspective of defining an operations strategy and trade-offs that need to be made in developing a viable operations strategy.

6. To be able to identify and understand the seven decision areas in Hill's operations strategy framework.

7. To be able to analyze a real organization's operations strategy and apply the strategy development framework.

- Rival golf club equipment manufacturers TaylorMade and Callaway are both based in Carlsbad, California. That's about where the similarity ends. Callaway made clubs for average golfers, while TaylorMade took the clubs pro golfers were using and adjusted them to suit amateurs. Callaway focused on management and production efficiency while sticking to core product designs, much the way Ford built cars around a basic chassis. TaylorMade, however, was constantly reinventing its product lines, and in an industry that expected product cycles to last 18 months or longer, began releasing new drivers and irons in rapid-fire succession. Even new product launches show the difference between these companies: Callaway typically launched products with lengthy PowerPoint presentations, while TaylorMade turned them into huge pep rallies. TaylorMade's strategy seems to have paid off; late in 2003 it overtook Callaway in market share for metalwoods.[1]

Getty Images

- George Huber addressed his management team at New Mexico National Bank and Trust, "The results of our first customer survey are in, and there are a few surprises. We knew they wanted competitive rates on savings and checking accounts, but more importantly, the survey indicates that friendly service and convenience are actually *more* important. We've been devoting all our resources to keeping costs low, but this throws a new twist into the mix." "What this means for us," interjected Paul Westel,

VP of operations, "is that we need to take a hard look at our current strategy. We've been focusing on the wrong priorities. This also means that we need to better analyze where we locate our ATMs and branch operations, and whether we should partner with a grocery store or maybe even a fast-food chain to establish a presence in their stores." "And," noted Deb Hamilton, VP of human resources, "we need to revamp our hiring and training programs; we've been getting a lot of complaints lately about 'uncaring' tellers." CFO Sarah Reimer observed, "This can affect nearly everything we do!" "That's right," said George. "I want each of you to think about what these results mean for your area of the business and report back to me next week. I'll suggest a new statement of our mission and vision. We need to start at the top."

Getty Images/PhotoDisc

- "Dad, don't you have a big account at Global Financial Services?" Jessie Parker asked. "Sure," her father replied. "They provide excellent service; whenever I call to talk to a broker, I get routed to a 'preferred client' advisor. They get me off the phone quickly with all my questions answered." "That's what I thought," said Jessie. "I opened an account with them when I started my job after graduating last year, but I've noticed that I have to wait quite a long time for an advisor to answer. While I'm waiting, a recording is urging me to visit their web site for frequently asked questions or to use their automated phone system. I'm much more comfortable speaking to a live person. I wonder how big an account I need to be a 'preferred client'?"

Discussion Questions: What differences would the different strategies chosen by Callaway and TaylorMade—sticking to core product designs versus continual innovation—have for key operations management decisions (consider the decision areas discussed in Chapter 2 for designing value chains)? Should organizations create strategies in response to customer wants and needs, or should they create strategies and then try to influence customer behavior to meet the strategic goals?

Every organization has a myriad of choices in deciding where to focus its efforts—for example, on low cost, high quality, quick response, or flexibility and customization—and in designing their operations to support their chosen strategy. The differences between Callaway and TaylorMade clearly show the significantly different strategies that competitors in the same industry can choose. As the second episode suggests, these choices should be driven by the most important customer requirements and expectations. In particular, what happens in operations—on the front lines and on the factory floor—must support the strategic direction the firm has chosen. In recent years, to respond to a significant financial crisis since the 9/11 terrorist attacks, several major U.S. airlines have closed or plan to close hubs in the long-standing hub-and-spoke system, adding instead more direct city-to-city flights.

In a strategy to become more efficient and cut costs, airlines are making major changes in their operating and value chain structure, which will undoubtedly have implications for customers. However, an industry consultant noted that "hubs are essential . . . but the hub model is changing in how it is operated." One change by Delta in its Atlanta hub is abandoning the concept of having groups of flights scheduled closely together to allow passengers to connect easily. This decision was made to obtain cost savings and efficiencies that are expected to outweigh any revenue effects.[2]

Any change in a firm's customer benefit package or strategic direction typically has significant consequences for the entire value chain and for operations. Although it may be difficult to change the *structure* of the value chain, operations managers have considerable freedom in determining what components of the value chain to emphasize, selecting technology and processes, making human resource policy choices, and in making other relevant decisions to support the firm's strategic emphasis. Fidelity Investments (the basis for the third episode), for instance, discovered that when a customer does limited business and calls a service representative too frequently, costs can outweigh profits.[3] So when such customers called, Fidelity's reps began teaching them how to use its automated phone lines and web site, which were designed to be friendlier and easier to use. These customers could talk to a service representative, but the phone system routed them into longer queues so the most profitable customers could be served more quickly. If these lower-account-balance customers switched to lower-cost channels such as the web site, Fidelity became more profitable. If they did not like the experience and left, the company became more profitable without them. However, 96 percent of them stayed and most switched to lower-cost channels, and customer satisfaction actually increased as these customers learned to get faster service. This operations strategy helped the firm to lower costs and focus on the most profitable customers. In essence, Fidelity influences customer behavior within its value chain to create better operational efficiency.

Competitive advantage *denotes a firm's ability to achieve market and financial superiority over its competitors.* In the long run, a sustainable competitive advantage provides above-average performance and is essential to survival of the business. Creating a competitive advantage requires a fundamental understanding of two things. First, management must understand customer wants and needs—and how the value chain can best meet these needs through the design and delivery of customer benefit packages that are attractive to customers. Second, management must build and leverage operational capabilities to support desired competitive priorities. **Competitive priorities** *represent the strategic emphasis that a firm places on certain performance measures and operational capabilities within a value chain.* In other words, operations must be aligned strategically with customer needs to create value. Understanding competitive priorities and their relationships to customer benefit packages provides a basis for designing the processes that create and deliver goods and services. These issues will be addressed in detail in Chapters 6 and 7. For now, we will focus on understanding how managers think about customer wants and needs and competitive priorities, and then discuss how managers develop an operations strategy, build capability, and achieve competitive advantage.

Competitive advantage
denotes a firm's ability to achieve market and financial superiority over its competitors.

Competitive priorities
represent the strategic emphasis that a firm places on certain performance measures and operational capabilities within a value chain.

Learning Objective
To understand how customer wants and needs drive strategic thinking in a firm and their consequences for designing and managing operations within the value chain.

UNDERSTANDING CUSTOMER WANTS AND NEEDS

Because the fundamental purpose of an organization is to provide goods and services of value to customers, it is important to first understand customer needs and requirements and also to understand how customers evaluate goods and services. However, a company usually cannot satisfy all customers with the same goods and services. Often, customers must be segmented into several natural groups, each with unique wants and needs. These segments might be based on buying behavior, geography, demographics, sales volume, profitability, or expected levels of service. By understanding differences among such segments, a company can design the most appropriate customer benefit packages, competitive strategies, and processes to create the goods and services to meet the unique needs of each segment.

To correctly identify what customers expect requires being "close to the customer." There are many ways to do this, such as having employees visit and talk to customers, having managers talk to customers, and doing formal marketing research. Marriott Corporation, for example, requires their top managers to annually work a full day or more in the hotels as bellhops, waiters, bartenders, front-desk service providers, and so on to gain a true understanding of customers' wants and needs and the types of issues that their hotel service providers must face in serving the customer. Good marketing research includes such techniques as focus groups, salesperson and employee feedback, complaint analysis, on-the-spot interviews with customers, videotaped service encounters, mystery shoppers, telephone hotlines, Internet monitoring, and customer surveys.

Identifying and defining the true wants and needs of customers are not easy, as customers may not always know what they want. Traditional market research may not always provide accurate information on latent needs and may even backfire. For example, Ford listened to a sample of customers and asked if they wanted a fourth door on the Windstar minivan. Only about a third thought it was a great idea, so Ford scrapped the idea. Chrysler, on the other hand, spent a lot more time living with owners of vans and observing their behavior, watching them wrestle to get things in and out, noting all the occasions where a fourth door would really be convenient, and was very successful after introducing a fourth door.[4] Thus, a company must make special effort to identify these goods and service features.

Sony and Seiko, for instance, go beyond traditional market research and produce dozens, even hundreds, of audio products and wristwatches with a variety of features to help them understand what excites and delights the customer. Those models that do not sell are simply dropped from the product lines. Of course, the cost per unit of these items is relatively low. To practice this strategy effectively, marketing efforts must be supported by highly flexible manufacturing systems that permit rapid setup and quick response to changing volumes and product features.

Creating breakthrough goods or services sometimes requires that companies ignore customer feedback and take risks. As Steve Jobs of Apple Computer noted about the iMac, "That doesn't mean we don't listen to customers, but it's hard for them to tell you what they want when they've never seen anything remotely like it. Take desktop video editing. I never got one request from someone who wanted to edit movies on his computer. Yet now that people see it, they say, 'Oh my God, that's great!' "[5]

Dissatisfiers, Satisfiers, and Exciters/Delighters

Japanese professor Noriaki Kano suggested three classes of customer requirements:

1. **Dissatisfiers**: *requirements that are expected in a good or service*. In an automobile, a radio and driver-side air bag are expected by the customer, who generally do not state so but assume them as given. For a hotel, the customer assumes the hotel room is safe and clean. If these features are not present, the customer is dissatisfied, sometimes very dissatisfied.

2. **Satisfiers**: *requirements that customers say they want*. Many car buyers want a sunroof, power windows, or antilock brakes. Likewise, a hotel guest may want an

Dissatisfiers: *requirements that are expected in a good or service.*

Satisfiers: *requirements that customers say they want.*

exercise room, hot tub, or a restaurant in the hotel. Providing these goods and service features creates customer satisfaction by fulfilling customer's wants and needs.

Exciters/delighters: *new or innovative good or service features that customers do not expect.*

3. **Exciters/delighters:** *new or innovative good or service features that customers do not expect.* The presence of unexpected features leads to surprise and excitement and enhances the customer's perceptions of value. Collision avoidance systems or an automobile navigation system, for example, can surprise and delight the customer and enhance the customer's feeling of safety. Adding exciting music and laser lights can entertain and delight customers as they shop for clothes in retail stores. Within the framework of the customer benefit package introduced in Chapter 1, these features are usually peripheral goods or services.

In the Kano classification system, dissatisfiers and satisfiers are relatively easy to determine through routine marketing research. For example, the hot-selling Ford F-150 pickup truck relied on extensive consumer research at the beginning of the redesign process. Perhaps one of the best examples of understanding customer needs and using this information to improve competitiveness is Frank Perdue's chicken business.[6] Perdue learned what customers' key purchase criteria were. These included a yellow bird, high meat-to-bone ratio, no pinfeathers, freshness, availability, and brand image. He also determined the relative importance of each criterion and how well the company and its competitors were meeting each one. By systematically improving his ability to exceed customers' expectations relative to the competition—that is, provide the exciters/delighters—Perdue gained market share even though his chickens were premium-priced. Among Perdue's innovations was using a jet engine to dry the chickens after plucking, allowing the pinfeathers to be singed off.

As customers become familiar with new goods and service features that delight them, these same features become part of the standard customer benefit package over time. Eventually, exciters/delighters become satisfiers. For instance, antilock brakes and air bags certainly were exciters/delighters when they were first introduced. Now, most car buyers expect them as a standard part of the customer benefit package associated with automobiles. Likewise, wireless computer access in hotel rooms once differentiated one hotel from another with business customers but now are an ordinary part of most hotel's customer benefit package. In fact, the absence of hotel room online computer capability is a dissatisfier today. Camera phones were a customer delighter and quickly became a satisfier in the highly competitive cell phone market. As goods and service features evolve, customer expectations continually increase, reaching new performance plateaus for that industry.

Basic customer expectations— dissatisfiers and satisfiers—are generally considered the minimum performance level required to stay in business and are often called **order qualifiers.**

Order winners *are goods and service features and performance characteristics that differentiate one customer benefit package from another and win the customer's business.*

Basic customer expectations—dissatisfiers and satisfiers—are generally considered the minimum performance level required to stay in business and are often called **order qualifiers.** The unexpected features that surprise, entertain, and delight customers by going beyond the expected often make the difference in closing a sale. **Order winners** *are goods and service features and performance characteristics that differentiate one customer benefit package from another and win the customer's business.* For example, decades ago financing the sale of an automobile was not nearly as important as financing and leasing options today. If three automobiles are roughly equal in terms of goods quality, manufacturer and dealer service quality, and price (that is, price and quality parity), then an attractive leasing package bundled with the other goods and services may very well be the order winner.

Search, Experience, and Credence Attributes

Consumers want quality in the goods and services they purchase. The concept of quality can mean several different things, from a vague notion of "excellence" to the ability of a production process to conform to engineering specifications. One of the more popular definitions is *fitness for intended use*. This characterizes how well a good or service performs its function and meets a customer's needs. For example, does an automobile have advanced safety features? Is the car fun to drive? Will it start every day in all weather conditions? Are the brakes working and safe? Is it free from rattles and squeaks? Is the cost of maintenance low? Are the controls easy to read and use? Consumers, therefore, evaluate various goods and service attributes in forming perceptions about the quality of goods and services.

Research suggests that customers use three types of attributes in evaluating the quality of goods and services: search, experience, and credence.[7] **Search attributes** *are those that a customer can determine prior to purchasing the goods and/or services.* These attributes include things like color, price, freshness, style, fit, feel, hardness, and smell. Goods such as supermarket food, furniture, clothing, automobiles, and houses are high in search attributes. **Experience attributes** *are those that can only be discerned after purchase or during consumption or use.* Examples of these attributes are friendliness, taste, wearability, safety, fun, and customer satisfaction. **Credence attributes** *are any aspects of a good or service that the customer must believe in but cannot personally evaluate even after purchase and consumption.* Examples would include the expertise of a surgeon or mechanic, the knowledge of a tax advisor, or the accuracy of tax preparation software. In these situations, the customer does not have the opportunity, expertise, or experience to evaluate the quality of the good or service, but can only have faith and trust that the good performs as it should or the service provider has done the job right. This classification has several important implications for operations. For example, the most important search and experience attributes should be evaluated during design, measured during manufacturing, and drive key operational controls to ensure that they are built into the good with high quality. Credence attributes stem from the nature of services (see Chapter 1), the design of the service system, and the training and expertise of the service providers.

These three evaluation criteria form an evaluation continuum from easy to difficult, as shown in Exhibit 4.1. This model suggests that goods are easier to evaluate than services, and that goods are high in search qualities whereas services are high in experience and credence attributes. Of course, goods and services are usually combined and configured in unique ways, making for an even more complex customer evaluation process.

In this new millennium, customers are placing more emphasis on intangible attributes than on tangible attributes. Customers purchase things that add value to how they feel (the ambience of a restaurant), how much fun they have (climbing a rock wall in a retail store while shopping), how well they are informed (knowing their exact location while driving via a global positioning system), how they are treated (the empathy the doctor and staff exhibit when a serious injury victim arrives in the hospital), and how they can share experiences (e-mailing a picture from a camera phone). Avis discovered, for example, that customers were typically anxious when returning rental cars. They were worried about making their flights and communicating with their offices. In response, Avis installed monitors showing flight departure times and status and built a communications center for people who needed to make phone calls, send faxes, or plug in laptops.[8] Thus, understanding experience and credence attributes is important for businesses to succeed.

Customers evaluate services in ways that are often different from the ways they evaluate goods. These are summarized here along with significant issues that affect operations.

- Customers seek and rely more on information from personal sources than from nonpersonal sources when evaluating services prior to purchase. Operations must ensure that accurate information is available and that experiences with prior services and service providers results in positive experiences and customer satisfaction.

Search attributes *are those that a customer can determine prior to purchasing the goods and/or services.*

Experience attributes *are those that can only be discerned after purchase or during consumption or use.*

Credence attributes *are any aspects of a good or service that the customer must believe in but cannot personally evaluate even after purchase and consumption.*

Exhibit 4.1
How Customers Evaluate Goods and Services

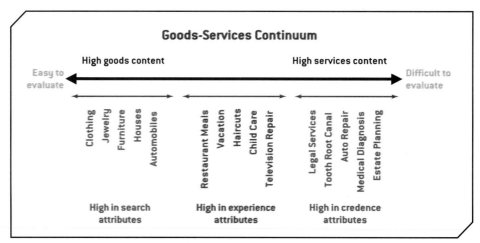

Source: Adapted from V. A. Zeithamel, "How Consumer Evaluation Processes Differ Between Goods and Services," in J. H. Donnelly and W. R. George, eds., *Marketing in Services*, published by the American Marketing Association, Chicago, 1981, pp. 186–199. Reprinted with permission from the American Marketing Association.

- Customers use a variety of perceptual features in evaluating services. The design and daily operations of service facilities must create a positive image and meet or exceed their expectations. Safety, friendliness, professionalism, and speed of service are examples that can enhance or damage the customer's perception of the value of the service.
- Customers normally adopt innovations in services more slowly than they adopt innovations in goods. Examples include new medical treatments, different curricula in secondary schools, and different banking technology such as off-site tellers accessed through video screens. Service processes must be flexible to accommodate rapid innovation.
- Customers perceive greater risks when buying services than when buying goods. Because services are intangible, customers cannot look at or touch them prior to the purchase decision. They only experience the service when they actually go through the process. This is why many are hesitant to use online banking or bill paying.
- Dissatisfaction with services is often the result of customers' inability to properly perform or coproduce their part of the service. A wrong order placed on the Internet can be the result of customer error despite all efforts on the part of the company to provide clear instructions. The design of services must be sensitive to the needs to educate customers on their role in the service process.

These insights help to explain why it is more difficult to design services and service processes than goods and manufacturing operations.

Learning Objective
To learn the five major competitive priorities important to business success and what they mean for operations.

COMPETITIVE PRIORITIES

Every organization is concerned with building and sustaining a competitive advantage in its markets. A strong competitive advantage is driven by customer needs and aligns the organization's resources with its business opportunities. A strong competitive advantage is difficult to copy, often because of a firm's culture, habits, or sunk costs. For example, why doesn't every company copy Dell's superior direct personal computer business model? Dell's approaches are hardly a secret; Michael Dell has even written a book about it. Competitors have copied its web site with stunning precision, but they face far greater difficulty copying other processes—order entry, billing, customer contact centers, purchasing, scheduling, assembly, and logistics—that Dell has built around its direct model over several decades. Competitors are burdened by longstanding relationships with suppliers and distributors and by a different culture.[9]

Competitive advantage can be achieved in different ways, such as outperforming competitors on price or quality, responding quickly to changing customer needs in designing goods and services, or providing rapid design or delivery (see the OM Spotlight on BMW). In general, organizations can compete on five key competitive priorities:

1. cost,
2. quality,
3. time,
4. flexibility, and
5. innovation.

In Chapter 3 we discussed how these can be measured to evaluate operations performance. How operations are designed and managed can have a significant impact on these performance measures. Here we want to investigate their role in defining an operations strategy.

All of these competitive priorities are vital to success. For example, no firm today can sacrifice quality simply to reduce costs or emphasize flexibility to the extent that it would make its goods and services unaffordable. However, organizations generally make trade-offs among these competitive priorities and focus their efforts along one or two key dimensions. For example, Dell Computer (1) manufactures PCs with high goods quality, (2) configures them to customer specifications, and

OM SPOTLIGHT

BMW[10]

The banner "Customers Drive our Future" greets visitors to BMW's Spartanburg, South Carolina, plant, which produces roadsters and sport utility vehicles. BMW operates one of the cleanest and quietest assembly plants in the industry, with three distinctive competencies: speed, flexibility, and quality. BMW's approach to meeting its cost challenges is to speed things up. The idea here is as you speed things up, costs decrease. The plant was launched in 23 months. The X5 SUV was developed in 35 months, and the company has an aggressive 30% reduction target for new product development cycles. The way to customize every car to meet individual customer's needs is to have "efficient flexibility." With 22 color options when the Z3 roadster was introduced, 123 center consoles, and 26 wheel options, BMW has become a master at information technology and logistics. Its demand flexibility extends to management and people; it is introducing two 10-hour shifts to accommodate the growth of the X5. Finally, its commitment to quality, as exemplified by consistent fit and finish tolerances and elimination of tolerance "stack-up" with a new door-hanging technology, is imperative to meet the needs of its demanding customer base. These attributes are a stark contrast to the traditional German style of operations, which is essentially to engineer until it can't be engineered any more.

(3) tries to deliver them quickly to customers. However, they are not always the least-expensive machines available, and customers must wait longer to get them as opposed to picking one off the shelf at a retail store. Hence, high goods quality and flexibility are top competitive priorities at Dell whereas cost and delivery time are of somewhat lesser importance.

Cost

Many firms gain competitive advantage by establishing themselves as the low-cost leader in an industry. These firms handle high volumes of goods and services and achieve their competitive advantage through low prices. Examples of firms that practice a low-cost strategy are Honda Motor Co., Marriott's Fairfield Inns, Merck-Medco On-line Pharmacy, Southwest Airlines (see the OM Spotlight), and Wal-Mart's Sam's Club.

Almost every industry has a low-price market segment. Although prices are generally set outside the realm of operations, low prices cannot be achieved without strict attention to cost and the design and management of operations (see the OM Spotlight on IBM). Costs accumulate through the value chain and include the costs of raw materials and purchased parts, direct manufacturing cost, distribution, post-sale services, and all supporting processes. Design significantly affects the costs of manufacturing, warranty and field repair, and such non-value-added costs as redesign and rework. General Electric, for example, discovered that 75 percent of its manufacturing costs are determined by design. Through good design and by chipping away at costs, operations managers help to support a firm's strategy to be a low-price leader. They emphasize achieving economies of scale and finding cost advantages from all sources in the value chain.

Low cost can result from high productivity and high capacity utilization. More importantly, improvements in quality lead to improvements in productivity, which in turn lead to lower costs. Thus, a strategy of continuous improvement is essential to achieving a low-cost competitive advantage. Lower costs also result from

OM SPOTLIGHT

Southwest Airlines[11]

The only major airline that has been profitable during 2001 and 2002 is Southwest Airlines. Other major U.S. airlines have had to collectively reduce costs by $18.6 billion or 29 percent of their total operating expenses to operate at the same level (cost per mile) as Southwest. The high-cost airlines such as United and American face enormous pressure from low-fare carriers such as Southwest Airlines. Mr. Roach, a long-time industry consultant says, "The industry really is at a point where survival is in question." For example, the cost to fly one seat one mile on US Airways is 69 percent higher than on Southwest. US Airways filed for bankruptcy in August, 2002. Northwest and Continental Airlines all have costs at least 40 percent higher than Southwest, and Northwest and Delta have recently filed for bankruptcy.

Historically, large network carriers such as United and American Airlines did not have to match Southwest's cost per seat-mile because they could command higher prices due to premium service, first-class cabins, frequent flyer loyalty, and greater network breadth and amenities. But while everyone else's passenger volume is down, Southwest's has increased. Now all carriers are forced to cut service, eliminate flights to smaller cities, use smaller, more fuel-efficient planes, and reduce the frequency of flights. American, by one study's estimate, needs to cut costs by $3.6 billion per year and so far has only been able to reduce costs by $1.1 billion. A low-cost strategy can reshape industry structure and allow the firm to survive in an economic downturn.

OM SPOTLIGHT

IBM[13]

In IBM's manufacturing strategy for a high-volume, low-cost product (summarized next), notice the planned involvement of manufacturing in the design, development of production processes, and quality-assurance systems. Note also how all the components of the business strategy relate to the ultimate objectives of high volume and low cost. For instance, automated production helps to achieve a high volume of production; customizing in distribution centers eliminates the need for great product variety in the manufacturing function itself and reduces the cost of maintaining large manufacturing inventories. The key elements of its strategy are:

- *Early manufacturing involvement* in the design of the product both for make-versus-buy decisions and for assurance that the production processes can achieve required tolerances.

- *Design for automation* by minimizing the number of parts, eliminating fasteners, providing for self-alignment with no adjustments, making parts symmetrical where possible, avoiding parts that interfere with automation, making parts rigid and stiff, providing close tolerances, and making assembly one-sided.

- *Limited models and features* to ensure stable product design, group engineering changes for the "model year," and customization of the product in distribution centers.

- *Building to plan* for finished goods owned by sales, continuous-flow manufacturing, supplier integration, zero defects, reduction of work-in-process inventory, and a multiskilled, focused team.

- *Defect-free* at shipment.

innovations in product design and process technology that reduce the costs of production and from efficiencies gained through meticulous attention to operations. Many Japanese firms have exploited this approach. Japanese companies adopted many product innovations and process technologies that were developed in the United States. They refined the designs and manufacturing processes to produce high-quality products at low costs, resulting in higher market shares.

A cost leader can achieve above-average performance if it can command prices at or near the industry average. However, it cannot do so with an inferior product. For example, the problems with focusing on costs at the expense of quality are illustrated by the case of the Schlitz Brewing Company.[12] In the early 1970s, Schlitz, the second-largest brewer in the United States, began a cost-cutting campaign. It included reducing the quality of ingredients in its beers by switching to corn syrup and hop pellets and shortening the brewing cycle by 50 percent. In the short term, it achieved higher returns on sales and assets than Anheuser-Busch (and the acclaim of Wall Street analysts). *Forbes* magazine stated, "Does it pay to build quality into a product if most customers don't notice? Schlitz seems to have a more successful answer." But customers do recognize inferior products. Soon after, market share and profits fell rapidly. By 1980, Schlitz's sales had declined 40 percent, the stock price fell from $69 to $5, and the company was eventually sold. The product must be perceived as comparable with competitors' or the firm will be forced to discount prices well below competitors' prices to gain sales. This can cancel any benefits that result from cost advantage.

Quality

The role of quality in achieving competitive advantage was demonstrated by several research studies. PIMS Associates, Inc., a subsidiary of the Strategic Planning Institute, for example, maintains a database of 1,200 manufacturing companies and studies the impact of goods quality on corporate performance.[14] PIMS researchers have found the following:

- Businesses offering premium quality goods usually have large market shares and were early entrants into their markets.
- Quality is positively and significantly related to a higher return on investment for almost all kinds of market situations. PIMS studies have shown that firms with superior goods quality can more than triple return on sales over goods perceived as having inferior quality.
- A strategy of quality improvement usually leads to increased market share but at a cost in terms of reduced short-run profitability.
- High goods quality producers can usually charge premium prices.

Exhibit 4.2 summarizes the impact of quality on profitability. The value of a good or service in the marketplace is influenced by the quality of its design. Improvements in performance, features, and reliability will differentiate the good or service from its competitors, improve a firm's quality reputation, and improve the perceived value of the customer benefit package. This allows the company to command higher prices and achieve an increased market share. This, in turn, leads to increased revenues that offset the added costs of improved design. Improved conformance in production leads to lower manufacturing and service costs through savings in rework, scrap, and warranty expenses. The net effect of improved quality of design and conformance is increased profits. In addition, the four models of organizational performance described in Chapter 3—Malcolm Baldrige National Quality Award Criteria, balanced scorecard, value chain model, and the service-profit chain—highlight many of these same performance relationships.

In many industries, strategies often led to trade-offs between quality and cost; some company strategies are willing to sacrifice quality in order to develop a low-cost advantage. Such was the case with new automobile start-ups, especially with Hyundai Motor Co. However, goods quality has evolved over the years and now is generally considered to be an order qualifier (see the OM Spotlight on Hyundai). Operations managers deal with quality issues on a daily basis; these include ensuring that goods are produced defect-free or that service is delivered flawlessly. In the long run, it is the design of goods and service processes that ultimately define the quality of outputs and outcomes.

Time

In today's society, time is perhaps the most important source of competitive advantage. Customers demand quick response, short waiting times, and consistency

Exhibit 4.2
Interlinking Quality and
Profitability Performance

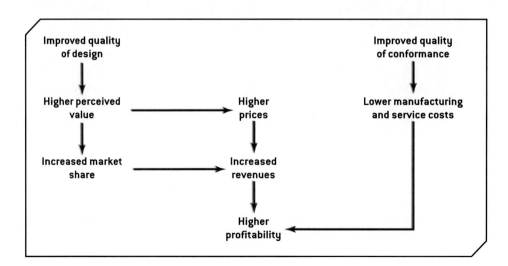

OM SPOTLIGHT

Hyundai Motor Company[15]

Hyundai Motor Company automobiles had been viewed as low-cost knockoffs of Japanese cars. When Hyundai's new CEO, Chung Mong Koo, took over in 1999, he walked on the factory floor and demanded a peek under the hood of a Sonata sedan. He didn't like what he saw: loose wires, tangled hoses, bolts painted four different colors. On the spot, he demanded that the bolts be painted black and ordered workers not to release any car unless all was orderly under the hood. The plant chief recalls Chung fuming: "The only way we can survive is to raise our quality to Toyota's level." Within months, he established quality-control units, promoted a pair of U.S. designers, and sold 10 percent of the company to Daimler-Chrysler with the aim of building a strategic alliance. He poured money into research and development to build cars that not only compete on price but also on quality. Hyundai bought several new Toyota and Honda SUVs and tore them apart to analyze them and devise features that would set their product apart. Hyundai innovations ranged from a cup holder large enough to hold a liter soft drink bottle to extra power ports for cell phones. Their strategy is to be the low-cost producer (the order winner) and maintain competitive goods quality (the order qualifier). Not long after, Hyundai rose near the top of the J.D. Powers' Initial Quality ranking.

in performance. Many firms such as Charles Schwab, Clarke American Checks, CNN, Dell, FedEx, and Wal-Mart know how to use time as a competitive weapon to create and deliver superior goods and services.

Reductions in flow time serve two purposes. First, they speed up work processes so that customer response is improved. Deliveries can be made faster and more often on time. Second, reductions in flow time can only be accomplished by streamlining and simplifying processes and value chains to eliminate non-value-added steps such as rework and waiting time. This forces improvements in quality by reducing the opportunity for mistakes and errors. By reducing non-value-added steps, costs are reduced as well. Thus, flow-time reductions often drive simultaneous improvements in quality, cost, and productivity (see the OM Spotlight on Procter & Gamble). Developing processes and using technology efficiently to improve speed and time reliability are some of the most important activities for operations managers.

OM SPOTLIGHT

Procter & Gamble

One example of flow-time reduction is Procter & Gamble's over-the-counter (OTC) clinical division, which conducts clinical studies that involve testing drugs, health care products, or treatments in humans.[16] Such testing follows rigorous design, conduct, analysis, and summary of the data collected. P&G had at least four different ways to perform a clinical study and needed to find the best way to meet its research and development needs. To do this, it focused on flow-time reduction. Its approach built on fundamental high-performance management principles: focusing on the customer, fact-based decisions, continual improvement, empowerment, the right leadership structure, and an understanding of work processes. An example is shown in Exhibit 4.3. The team found that final reports took months to prepare. Only by mapping the existing process did they fully understand the causes of long flow times and the amount of rework and recycling during review and sign-off. By restructuring the activities from sequential to parallel work and identifying critical measurements to monitor the process, they were able to reduce the time from several months to less than 4 weeks.

Exhibit 4.3 Final Report "Is" and "Should" Process Example

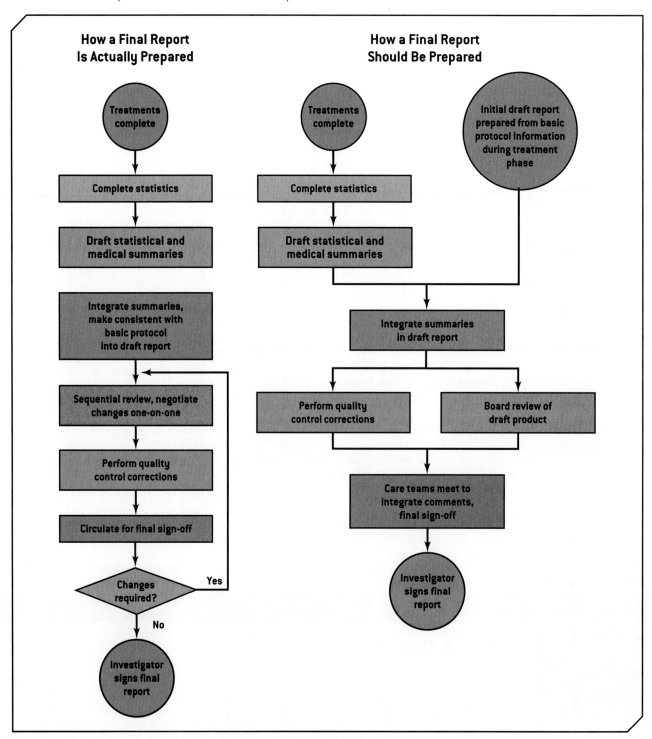

Source: David A. McCarney, Robert W. Bogs, and Linda M. Bayuk, "More, Better, Faster From Total Quality Effort," *Quality Progress*, August 1999, pp. 43–50. © 1999. American Society for Quality. Reprinted with permission.

Significant reductions in flow time cannot be achieved simply by focusing on individual subprocesses; cross-functional processes must be examined all across the organization. This forces the company to take a system's view of operations and to engage in cooperative behaviors.

Flexibility

Success in globally competitive markets requires a capacity for both design and demand flexibility. The automobile industry, for example, is constantly developing new models. Companies that can exploit flexibility by building several different vehicles on the same assembly line at one time, enabling them to switch output as demand shifts, will be able to sell profitably at lower volumes. This is one key advantage that Japanese manufacturers have over U.S. automakers. Honda's two plants that produce Acura's MDX crossover sport utility vehicle and the less-expensive Honda Pilot can produce any combination of 300,000 MDX, Pilot, and Odyssey minivans. This allows Honda to concentrate on whatever model happens to be in greatest demand.[17] In contrast, competitors like Ford, GM, and Daimler-Chrysler have as many as three factories dedicated to a single vehicle.

Enablers of design flexibility include close relationships with customers to understand their emerging wants and needs, outsourcing and make-versus-buy trade-offs, empowering employees as decision makers, effective manufacturing and information technology, and close supplier and customer relationships. For example, Harley-Davidson's annual output is relatively small (around 52,000 bikes per year). However, it offers numerous models, accessories, and customized features that make almost every bike unique. It can do so because its manufacturing operations are built around programmable robots and other forms of flexible automation.[18]

Flexibility is manifest in mass customization strategies that are becoming increasingly prevalent today. **Mass customization** *is being able to make whatever goods and services the customer wants, at any volume, at any time for anybody, and for a global organization, from any place in the world.*[19] Some examples include Sign-tic company signs that are uniquely designed for each customer from a standard base sign structure; business consulting; Levi's jeans that are cut to exact measurements; personal web pages; estate planning; Motorola pagers customized in different colors, sizes, and shapes; personal weight-training programs; and modular furniture that customers can configure to their unique needs and tastes. Customer involvement might occur at the design (as in the case of Sign-tic signs), fabrication (Levi's jeans), assembly (Motorola pagers), or postproduction (modular furniture) stages of the value chain. Mass customization requires companies to align their activities around differentiated customer segments and to design goods, services, and operations around flexibility. High levels of flexibility might require special strategies such as modular designs, interchangeable components, and postponement strategies. These allow companies to build standard components and configure them at the last possible moment to meet customers' unique needs. Flexible operations require sharing manufacturing lines and specialized training for employees. They also require attention to outsourcing decisions, agreements with key suppliers, and innovative partnering arrangements, because delayed shipments and a complex supply chain can hinder flexibility.

Mass customization *is being able to make whatever goods and services the customer wants, at any volume, at any time for anybody, and for a global organization, from any place in the world.*

Innovation

Innovation *is the discovery and practical application or commercialization of a device, method, or idea that differs from existing norms.* Innovations in all forms encapsulate human knowledge. Over the years, innovations in goods (such as telephones, automobiles, refrigerators, computers, optical fiber, satellites, and cell phones) and services (self-service, all-suite hotels, health maintenance organizations, and Internet banking) have improved the overall quality of life. Within business organizations, innovations in manufacturing equipment (computer-aided design, robotic automation, and smart tags) and management practices (customer satisfaction surveys, quantitative decision models, and the Malcolm Baldrige criteria) have allowed organizations to be more efficient and better meet customers' needs.

Innovation *is the discovery and practical application or commercialization of a device, method, or idea that differs from existing norms.*

Many firms focus on research and development for innovation as a core component of their strategy. Such firms are on the leading edge of product technology, and their ability to innovate and introduce new products is a critical success factor. Product performance, not price, is the major selling feature. When competition enters the market and profit margins fall, these companies often drop out of the market while continuing to introduce innovative new products. These companies focus on outstanding product research, design, and development; high product quality; and the ability to modify production facilities to produce new products frequently.

As global competition increases, the ability to innovate has become almost essential for remaining competitive. National Cash Register, for example, clung to outdated mechanical technologies for years while competitors developed innovative new electronic systems. The lack of innovation nearly destroyed the company. Today, leading companies do not wait for customers to change; they use innovation to create new customer needs and desires. At 3M, for example, every division is expected to derive 25 percent of its sales each year from products that did not exist 5 years earlier. This forces managers to think seriously about innovation. Such a spirit of continuous improvement not only will result in new products, but also will help operations managers to create better processes.

STRATEGIC PLANNING

Learning Objective
To understand the process of strategic planning at the organizational level and its relationship to operations strategy.

Strategy is a pattern or plan that integrates an organization's major goals, policies, and action sequences into a cohesive whole.

Core Competencies—*the strengths unique to that organization.*

Strategic planning *is the process of determining long-term goals, policies, and plans for an organization.*

The direction an organization takes and the competitive priorities it chooses are driven by its strategy. The concept of strategy has different meanings for different people. **Strategy** *is a pattern or plan that integrates an organization's major goals, policies, and action sequences into a cohesive whole.*[20] Basically, a strategy is the approach by which an organization seeks to develop the capabilities required for achieving its competitive advantage. Effective strategies develop around a few key competitive priorities—such as low cost or fast service time—which provide a focus for the entire organization and exploit an organization's **core competencies**—*the strengths unique to that organization.* Such strengths might be a particularly skilled or creative work force, good customer relationship management, clever bundling of goods and services, strong supply chain networks, extraordinary service, marketing expertise, or the ability to rapidly develop new products or change production-output rates.

Strategic planning *is the process of determining long-term goals, policies, and plans for an organization.* The objective of strategic planning is to build a position that is so strong in selected ways that the organization can achieve its goals despite unforeseeable external forces that may arise. Strategy is the result of a series of hierarchical decisions about goals, directions, and resources; thus, most large organizations have three levels of strategy: corporate, business, and functional. At the top level, *corporate strategy* is necessary to define the businesses in which the corporation will participate and develop plans for the acquisition and allocation of resources among those businesses. *The businesses in which the firm will participate are often called* **strategic business units (SBUs)** *and are usually defined as families of goods or services having similar characteristics or methods of creation.* For small organizations, the corporate and business strategies frequently are the same.

The businesses in which the firm will participate are often called **strategic business units (SBUs)** *and are usually defined as families of goods or services having similar characteristics or methods of creation.*

SBUs might be organized by process or customer benefit packages such as home, life, automobile, and medical insurance, or Medicare versus private insurance customer benefit packages, or by physical goods such as the steel, glass, and plastics divisions. Or in some organizations by target market segments such as food for babies, adults, and the elderly or computer chips for the personal computer, server, cell phone, and handheld digital assistant target market segments.

For example, at one point during Jack Welch's tenure as CEO of General Electric, he formulated a strategy in which each business was to be either number 1 or number 2 in its market. Those that could not meet this corporate objective were sold. A corporate strategy requires consideration of such factors as current market share, internal strengths and weaknesses, and competitors' strengths and weaknesses. Corporate strategic planning addresses such questions as: What are our objectives? What are our greatest challenges? What must we do particularly well? How will we measure success?

The second level of strategy is generally called *business strategy*, and defines the focus for SBUs. The major decisions involve which markets to pursue and how best to compete in those markets, that is, what competitive priorities the firm should pursue. Strategic plans generally differ among SBUs but must be consistent with the overall corporate strategy. For example, an appliance division of a large goods-producing firm might decide to produce standard dishwashers and compete on low costs, while an electronics division might focus on customized products and compete on innovation and design flexibility.

Finally, the third level of strategy is *functional strategies*, the means by which business strategies are accomplished. *A functional strategy is the set of decisions that each functional area—marketing, finance, operations, research and development, engineering, and so on—develops to support its particular business strategy.*

Our particular focus will be on operations strategy—*how an organization's processes are designed and organized to produce the type of goods and services to support the corporate and business strategies.* Business strategy has historically emphasized marketing and financial considerations, and operations strategy has received the least amount of high-level management attention. In some organizations, operations is not considered a factor of the corporate strategy. Consequently, operations managers have often been placed in the position of having to react to strategic plans that were developed from primarily financial and marketing perspectives, often with disastrous results. For example, a marketing-driven strategy might require a wide line of goods with required short delivery times; these would necessitate short production runs and fast changeover that a firm's facilities might not be designed for.

Today, managers have recognized that the value chain can be leveraged to provide a distinct competitive advantage and that operations is a core competency for the organization. Whoever has superior operational capability over the long term is the odds-on favorite to win the industry shakeout. Before we address operations strategy in detail, we discuss the typical strategic planning process that most organizations use.

The Strategic Planning Process

The strategic planning process consists of two main parts: *development* and *implementation*. Strategy development *refers to a company's approach, formal or informal, for making key long-term business decisions.* The process typically takes into account customer and market requirements, the competitive environment, industry structure and nonindustry competitors, financial and societal risks, human resource capabilities and needs, technological capabilities, and supplier capabilities. This strategy development process might include environmental scanning, global and local business intelligence, market or sales forecasts, target market characteristics and analysis, quantitative models or simulations, evaluating alternative "what-if" scenarios, and other tools to develop strategies to bridge the gap between where the organization is now and where it wants to be in 2, 4, or 10 years. Strategies might involve developing new goods or services, expanding existing or entering new markets, growing revenue, adding new peripheral services, reducing cost, controlling the value chain, providing great service, or establishing global alliances. Strategies

A functional strategy is the set of decisions that each functional area—marketing, finance, operations, research and development, engineering, and so on—develops to support its particular business strategy.

Operations strategy—*how an organization's processes are designed and organized to produce the type of goods and services to support the corporate and business strategies.*

Strategy development *refers to a company's approach, formal or informal, for making key long-term business decisions.*

Strategy implementation *refers to the development of specific action plans derived from strategy that clearly describe the things that need to be done, human resource plans and support, performance measures and indicators, and resource deployment to ensure that plans and strategies are successfully executed.*

The **strategic mission** *of a firm defines its reason for existence.*

might also be directed toward making the company a preferred supplier, a low-cost producer, a technology leader, or a market innovator.

Strategy implementation *refers to the development of specific action plans derived from strategy that clearly describe the things that need to be done, human resource plans and support, performance measures and indicators, and resource deployment to ensure that plans and strategies are successfully executed.* The alignment of corporate strategy with functional strategies is a key task of senior management. Usually, both of these steps are integrated into one strategic planning process, especially in smaller organizations.

In most organizations, the organization's mission and values drive strategy. *The* **strategic mission** *of a firm defines its reason for existence.* For example, the strategic mission of Pal's Sudden Service (see Chapter 1 for an introduction to this company) is "To deliver excellence in food service while providing a menu focused on exceptional quality." *The* **strategic vision** *describes where the organization is headed and what it intends to be.* Pal's strategic vision is shown at the left.

Values *are attitudes and policies for all employees to follow that direct the journey to achieving the organization's vision.* Values are reinforced through conscious and subconscious behavior at all levels of the organization. Over time, customers recognize a strong organizational value system through repetitive service encounters, and this interaction and experience builds customer loyalty, and eventually profits. The service-profit chain introduced in Chapter 3 is one way strong organizational values and clear corporate objectives lead to increasing market share, customer satisfaction, and profits. Pal's Values and Code of Ethics statement is shown on the left.

A firm's strategic mission and values guides the development of strategies by establishing the context within which daily operating decisions are made and how resources are allocated and setting limits on available strategic options. In addition, they help to make trade-offs among the various performance measures and between short- and long-term goals. The approaches that Pal's listed in its Vision Statement essentially define the basic strategy needed to achieve its vision of being the preferred quick-service restaurant. However, the business environment can easily change, and strategies need to respond dynamically to such changes. For instance, a small company like Pal's might find itself in a tight labor market and would need to develop strategies to address this threat. This is done through some type of a systematic "what-if" strategic planning process.

The Pal's strategic planning process, which is performed annually, focuses on a 2-year planning horizon. The major steps are as follows:

Step 1—Gather and Analyze Strategic Performance Data (strengths, weaknesses, opportunities, and threats): In addition to collecting data from all levels of the organization, Pal's gathers data from our primary stakeholders (i.e., customers/market, employees, community, competitors, banks, regulatory,

---

Pal's Vision Statement

To be the preferred quick service restaurant in our market achieving the largest market share by providing:

- The quickest, friendliest, most accurate service available
- A focused menu that delights customers
- Daily excellence in our product, service, and systems execution
- Clean, organized, sanitary facilities
- Exceptional value
- A fun, positive and profitable experience for all stakeholders

Source: Pal's Sudden Service

Pal's Values and Code of Ethics

Positive Energy
We will always nurture a positive, enthusiastic atmosphere, which will foster mutual trust and respect among employees, customers, and suppliers. Further, we will always operate with open agendas, positive interactions and genuine motives.

Honesty and Truthfulness
We will always be honest and truthful in all relationships, respecting and relying on each other.

Employee Well Being
We will always provide a safe, healthy, and desirable workplace.

Citizenship
We will always provide community involvement through personal and company contributions of time, efort, and resources. Through our best effort and consideration, we will always protect public health, safety, and the environment.

Golden Rule
We will always do unto others as we would have them do unto us.

Source: Pal's Sudden Service

suppliers/partners, and food industry). The leadership team analyzes all data using a SWOT (Strengths, Weaknesses, Opportunities, and Threats) analysis and risk review.

Step 2—Review/Analyze Existing Strategic Directions/Documents: Analyzed data from step 1 are used to evaluate the appropriateness of the existing strategic documents/outputs (Mission, Values/Code of Ethics, and Key Business Drivers).

Step 3—Revise/Develop Strategy: Results of the SWOT analysis and risk data from step 1 are used to perform various functions (e.g., visioning, forecasting, projections, options development, brainstorming, scenarios). Strategic documents and outputs from step 2 are used as references to ensure consistency is maintained during the establishment of short-term and longer-term strategic objectives and action plans. Strategic data analyses and interpretations are carefully evaluated against their own operational requirements, capabilities, and available capital before strategic objectives and plans are chosen.

Step 4—Deploy Objectives and Action Plans: Deploying objectives and action plans to all levels of the Pal's organization and to all stakeholders involves developing item-specific action (implementation) plans, which are analyzed and integrated into a single, coordinated, large-scale action plan designed to accomplish the overall objective.

Step 5—Review Progress and Results: The Leadership Team reviews progress and results using Pal's Management Review Process.

Step 6—Continually Evaluate and Improve Strategic Planning Process: The Leadership Team devotes part of its annual planning agenda to evaluating and improving strategic objective selection, action planning, deployment, our capabilities for tracking and achieving performance relative to plans, improvement planning, benchmarking, innovation, problem solving, and performance.

Pal's strategic planning process demonstrates how one company approaches the challenges of strategic planning. Each organization has its own unique ways of doing strategy development and implementation. The next step is to translate business strategy into operations.

*The **strategic vision** describes where the organization is headed and what it intends to be.*

***Values** are attitudes and policies for all employees to follow that direct the journey to achieving the organization's vision.*

OPERATIONS STRATEGY

*An **operations strategy** defines how an organization will execute its chosen business strategies.* Developing an operations strategy involves translating competitive priorities into operational capabilities by making a variety of choices and trade-offs for design and operating decisions. That is, operating decisions must be aligned with achieving the desired competitive priorities. For example, if corporate objectives are to be the low-cost and mass-market producer of a good, then adopting an assembly line type of process is how operations can help achieve this corporate objective.

What kind of an operations strategy might a company like Pal's Sudden Service have? Consider the implications for operations management of the basic strategy stated in its vision:

1. *The quickest, friendliest, most accurate service available.* To achieve quick and accurate service, Pal's needs highly standardized processes. The staff at each Pal's facility is organized into process teams along the order-taking, processing, packaging, and order-completion line. The process layout is designed so that raw materials enter through a delivery door and are worked forward through the store with one process serving the next. Employees must have clearly defined roles and responsibilities, understanding of all operating and service procedures

Learning Objective
To understand how operations strategy can support and drive the achievement of organizational objectives, and to learn the key elements of an operations strategy.

*An **operations strategy** defines how an organization will execute its chosen business strategies.*

and quality standards, and job flexibility through cross-training to be able to respond to volume cycles and unplanned reassignments of work activities. To ensure friendly service, Pal's uses specific performance criteria to evaluate and select employees who demonstrate the aptitude, talents, and characteristics to meet performance standards, invests heavily in training, and pays close attention to employee satisfaction.

2. *A focused menu that delights customers.* They must understand their customers' likes and dislikes of their products and services as well as their competitors'. Although this would fall within the realm of marketing, such a marketing strategy must be coordinated with operations to ensure that planned response times can be achieved and that any menu changes can be quickly adapted to its operations. Such questions as these are addressed during the design stage: Are our customer needs data and market trend data objective, valid, and credible? What new capabilities will we need? What similar or related things are our competitors doing? Do our suppliers have the capacity to support this new offering? Is the appropriate technology available? Does Pal's have the capability to fully support this new offering? Pal's new product design process begins with customer-defined quality, focuses on maintaining or improving critical cycle times for speed, tests new technologies, and assesses overall feasibility and capability of new designs.

3. *Daily excellence in product, service, and systems execution.* Successful day-to-day operations requires employees to effectively apply Pal's On-Line Quality Control process, consisting of four simple steps: standardize the method or process, use the method, study the results, and take control. With Pal's high-speed work, processes are running so rapidly that visual operational standards must be mentally ingrained to achieve compliance to standards. Visual standardization is a critical element of training and development. Each employee is thoroughly trained and coached on precise work procedures and process standards, focusing on developing a visual reference to verify product quality. Performance is also maintained through various process automation and measurement components to minimize variation and ensure accuracy. Employees are also trained to analyze results against process standards and measures and are given the authority to recognize problems and take appropriate action.

4. *Clean, organized, sanitary facilities.* Pal's focuses on prevention—eliminating all possible causes of accidents—first, then finding and eliminating causes of actual incidents. In-house health and safety inspections are conducted monthly using the FDA Food Service Sanitation Ordinance. Results are compiled and distributed to all stores within 24 hours with any identified improvements applied in each store.

5. *Exceptional value.* Value is created by continually improving the goods and services that customers receive while maintaining low costs. Through methods of listening and learning from customers and studies of industry standards and best practices, Pal's has designed the following into its operations: convenient locations with easy ingress and egress, long hours of operation (6:00 A.M. to 10:00 P.M.), easy-to-read 3-D menus, direct fact-to-face access to order taker and cashier/order deliverer, fresh food (cooked hot dogs are discarded after 10 minutes if not purchased), a 20-second delivery target, and a web site for contacting the corporate office and stores. Pal's selects suppliers carefully to ensure not only product quality and on-time delivery but also the best price for the volume level purchased. Overall supply chain costs are minimized by maintaining only a few, long-term core suppliers.

From this discussion of Pal's Sudden Service, it is clear that how operations are designed and implemented can have a dramatic effect on business performance and achievement of the strategy. Therefore, operations require close coordination with functional strategies in other areas of the firm, such as marketing and finance. For example, decisions to discount goods to increase demand might put such a strain on operations that it would be impossible to satisfy the resulting volume of demand and, hence, dissatisfy many customers. Financial decisions to reduce costs might adversely impact quality by reducing technology or training investments. Similarly, operations decisions such as updating facilities or technology might temporarily reduce production and impact marketing efforts. It is important that managers understand the relationships between operations and other areas of the firm and take a systems view when making key decisions.

In some companies, the operations strategy *is* their business strategy. Wal-Mart, for example, focuses its competitive strategy on controlling the entire value chain to create a competitive advantage that few competitors can copy easily (see the OM Spotlight). Wal-Mart places huge order quantities with its suppliers and demands substantial price discounts, frequent delivery of the best-selling goods, and supplier management of the inventory in the 2,600 U.S. Wal-Mart stores. The company established optical laboratories next to airport cargo hubs to supply their 1,500 optical operations within Wal-Mart stores. Information system capability allows Wal-Mart to make and execute these order requirements better than other retailers. The dominant player within the value chain is not suppliers, wholesalers, manufacturers, distributors, or transportation firms, but the retail store toward the end of the value chain—Wal-Mart!

OM SPOTLIGHT

Wal-Mart[21]

Wal-Mart has more than 3,000 stores across the United States and about 1,000 stores internationally. The Retail Divisions include Wal-Mart Stores, Sam's Club, Supercenters, Neighborhood Markets, International, and Walmart.com. Specialty Divisions include Tire & Lube Express, Pharmacy, Vacations, Used Fixture Auctions, and Optical. Wal-Mart employees more than 962,000 associates in the United States and 282,000 internationally. Sam Walton's strategy was simple: "Give people high value, low prices, and a warm welcome."

Sam Walton built Wal-Mart on the revolutionary philosophies of excellence in the workplace, customer service, and always having the lowest prices. The company was founded on the Three Basic Beliefs Mr. Sam established in 1962 and which are continually stressed by senior executives:

1. *Respect for the Individual*—"We are a group of dedicated, hardworking, ordinary people who have teamed together to accomplish extraordinary things. We have very different backgrounds, different colors and different beliefs, but we do believe that every individual deserves to be treated with respect and dignity." Don Soderquist, senior vice chairman of Wal-Mart Stores, Inc. (retired).
2. *Service to Our Customers*—"Wal-Mart's culture has always stressed the importance of Customer Service. Our Associate base across the country is as diverse as the communities in which we have Wal-Mart stores. This al-

lows us to provide the Customer Service expected from each individual customer that walks into our stores." Tom Coughlin, president and chief executive officer, Wal-Mart Stores division.
3. *Strive for Excellence*—"Sam was never satisfied that prices were as low as they needed to be or that our products' quality was as high as they deserved—he believed in the concept of striving for excellence before it became a fashionable concept." Lee Scott, president and chief executive officer of Wal-Mart Stores, Inc.

John Zich/Bloomberg News/Landov

This approach leads to low cost, fast and reliable delivery, a broad selection of goods, and volume and product flexibility—all the things that create value for its customers. Wal-Mart also uses service to enhance the shopping and buying experience by having greeters to direct and help customers as they enter the huge stores, which often include banking, optical, shoe and leather, pharmacy, gasoline, and automobile repair services. In an annual survey by WSL Strategic Retail, a consulting firm, 25 percent of Americans say Wal-Mart is their favorite store, and 58 percent of children age 8 to 18 declared Wal-Mart their favorite place to shop. Wal-Mart is also credited with a substantial impact on productivity in the U.S. economy in the 1990s. As Bradford C. Johnson wrote in an article in the *McKinsey Quarterly*, "More than half of the U.S. productivity acceleration in the retailing of general merchandise can be explained by only two syllables: Wal-Mart."[22]

A Framework for Operations Strategy

Operations design choices *are the decisions management must make as to what type of process structure is best suited to produce goods or create services.*

Infrastructure *focuses on the nonprocess features and capabilities of the organization and includes the work force, operating plans and control systems, quality control, organizational structure, compensation systems, learning and innovation systems, and support services.*

A useful framework for strategy development that ties corporate and marketing strategy to operations strategy was proposed by Professor Terry Hill at Templeton College, Oxford University and is shown in Exhibit 4.4.[23] It was originally designed for goods-producing organizations, but it can also be applied to service-providing firms. This framework defines the essential elements of an effective operations strategy in the last two columns—*operations design choices* and *building the right infrastructure*.

Operations design choices *are the decisions management must make as to what type of process structure is best suited to produce goods or create services.* It typically addresses six key areas—types of processes, value chain integration and outsourcing, technology, capacity and facilities, inventory and service capacity, and trade-offs among these decisions. **Infrastructure** *focuses on the nonprocess features and capabilities of the organization and includes the work force, operating plans and control systems, quality control, organizational structure, compensation systems, learning and innovation systems, and support services.* The infrastructure must support process choice and provide managers with accurate and timely information to make

Exhibit 4.4 Hill's Strategy Development Framework

Corporate Objectives	Marketing Strategy	How Do Goods and Services Qualify and Win Orders in the Marketplace? (Competitive Priorities)	Operations Strategy	
			Operations Design Choices	Infrastructure
• Growth • Survival • Profit • Return on investment • Other market and financial measures • Social welfare	• Goods and services markets and segments • Range • Mix • Volumes • Standardization versus customization • Level of innovation • Leader versus follower alternatives	• Safety • Price (cost) • Range • Flexibility • Demand • Goods and service design • Quality • Service • Goods • Environment • Brand image • Delivery • Speed • Variability • Technical support • Pre- and postservice support	• Type of processes and alternative designs • Supply chain integration and outsourcing • Technology • Capacity and facilities (size, timing, location) • Inventory • Trade-off analysis	• Work force • Operating plans and control system(s) • Quality control • Organizational structure • Compensation system • Learning and innovation systems • Support services

Source: T. Hill, *Manufacturing Strategy: Text and Cases*, 3rd ed., Burr Ridge, IL: McGraw-Hill, 2000, p. 32 and T. Hill, "Operations Management: Strategic Context and Managerial Analysis," 2nd ed. Prigrame MacMillan, 2005, p. 50. Reprinted with permission from McGraw-Hill Companies.

good decisions. These decisions lie at the core of organizational effectiveness and suggest that the integrative nature of operations management is one of the most important aspects of success.

A key feature of this framework is the link between operations and corporate and marketing strategies. Clearly, it is counterproductive to design a customer benefit package and an operations system to produce and deliver it, and then discover that these plans will not achieve corporate and marketing objectives. This linkage is described by the four major decision loops illustrated in Exhibit 4.5. Decision loop #1 ties together corporate strategy—which establishes the organization's direction and boundaries—and marketing strategy—which evaluates customer wants and needs and target market segments. By focusing on the desired set of competitive priorities and target markets, the organization can develop a set of relative priorities for each target market segment.

The output of loop #1 is the input for loop #2. Decision loop #2 describes how operations evaluates the implications of competitive priorities in terms of process choice and infrastructure. The key decisions are: Do we have the process capability to achieve the corporate and marketing objectives per target market segment? Are our processes capable of consistently achieving order winner performance in each market segment? What drives loop #2 is a rank ordering of competitive priorities for each market segment as determined by the corporate and marketing managers. For example, if a 2-day financial loan approval flow time (processing time) is desired by the corporate and marketing strategies (loop #1) but the current process is not capable of doing this work in less than 10 days (loop #2), then the corporate, marketing, and operations areas need to revise their strategies and plans. By using the latest information technology at a cost of $10 million the loan approval process can be upgraded to achieve the 2-day target flow time.

Decision loop #3 lies within the operations function of the organization and involves determining if process choice decisions and capabilities are consistent with infrastructure decisions and capabilities. Much of this book is devoted to these issues. The fourth decision loop (loop #4) represents operations' input into the corporate and marketing strategy. Corporate decision makers ultimately decide how to allocate resources to achieve corporate objectives.

The management decisions represented by these four loops are iterative and highly integrated. The more integration and communication about "what is desired" and "what is possible," the better the organization is at achieving its objectives. We will now examine the specific elements of operations strategy in this strategy development framework.

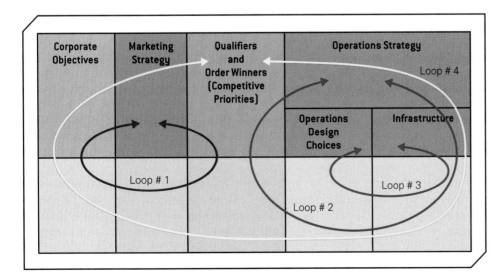

Exhibit 4.5
Four Key Decision Loops in Terry Hill's Generic Strategy Framework

OPERATIONS DESIGN CHOICE AND INFRASTRUCTURE DECISIONS

A key aspect of configuring an operations strategy is selecting and designing the key value creation processes for manufacturing and service delivery systems. Although we will examine advantages and disadvantages of process decisions and their impact on competitive priorities in Chapter 7, our focus here is on how process choice is related to strategy from a "big-picture," strategic-level perspective.

Types of Processes

In Chapter 1, we classified processes by their *purpose*:

1. *value creation processes* that focus on primary goods and service creation and delivery,
2. *support processes* that provide the infrastructure for value creation processes, and
3. *general management processes* that coordinate the value creation and support processes.

In each of these categories, operations managers have choices in selecting technology and designing processes. For example, the process of providing information to prospective students in a campus visit could be designed in several ways. Students and their parents might be herded in large groups from one function, such as admissions, financial aid, and college departments, to another in a fixed sequence. An alternative is to take smaller groups through the different functions in different sequences so that college representatives can provide more personalized attention. Virtual campus tours could also be used to reinforce actual student visits. Similar choices exist in manufacturing and other types of service processes. One of the key issues in selecting processes is to appropriately match the process to the type of good or service being produced to support competitive priorities. Other process choice issues and ways to think about processes are the subjects of Chapters 7 and 8.

Supply Chain Integration and Outsourcing

The second element of operations design choices noted in Exhibit 4.4 addresses the role of suppliers in the value chain. We introduced many of these issues in Chapter 2. Key strategic questions to consider are: Should we make components in our facilities or purchase them from external suppliers? Should we outsource support functions such as software integration or benefits administration? Should we acquire suppliers or distributors or merge with them? Should we use one or several suppliers? Should we enter into alliances with suppliers, intermediaries, or customers? Should we enter new global or local markets and does our supply chain have the capability to support this decision? What are the implications of these decisions on the information systems we need to successfully implement our strategies and plans?

Issues of cost, quality, time, and flexibility enter into such decisions. Supply chain integration might include strategic partnerships that enhance collaboration among firms that have different core competencies, joint ventures, or licensing agreements. Increased integration of suppliers, or partnership strategies, requires more complex control by operations managers. For instance, both Palm and Microsoft license their handheld operating system to many manufacturers of personal digital assistants (PDAs), and electronics firms outsource assembly operations to contract manufacturers. Many firms outsource support services like human resources or call center operations. Hewlett-Packard, for example, successfully bid on Procter &

Gamble's outsourcing of its entire information technology operation. These issues will be explored further in Chapter 9.

Technology

The technology choices impact cost, flexibility, quality, time, and innovativeness. In a fast-food restaurant, for example, should sandwiches be made to customers' orders or made to one or more specifications and stored? (See the OM Spotlight on McDonald's.) Likewise, a grocery store must decide whether or not to use scanners as opposed to manual keying in of prices. A custom product strategy requires on-time delivery, quality, and the capability to design and manufacture different products. On the other hand, companies that manufacture high-volume types of products usually benefit most from standardization in design, low manufacturing cost, and high availability of the product through inventories and distribution channels.

Technology decisions directly influence cost, flexibility, quality, and speed. A process-oriented system employing general-purpose equipment allows for flexibility in manufacturing different products. A product-oriented system, with special-purpose equipment dedicated to the production of one or a few products, provides high volume and low unit costs. In designing service delivery, questions often focus on what level of technology, mechanization, and automation should be used. Many service processes are moving toward increased levels of self-service, often computer-based, to replace traditional human interaction. For example, a bank customer has the choice of using automatic tellers or human tellers or the Internet. Issues of technology will be addressed further in Chapter 5.

Capacity and Facilities

Capacity *measures the amount of output that can be produced over a period of time.* A firm must make many strategic decisions about capacity, such as the amount of

Capacity *measures the amount of output that can be produced over a period of time.*

OM SPOTLIGHT

McDonald's[24]

PR Newswire California Milk Processor Board/AP

McDonald's used to make food to stock, storing sandwiches in a large tray used to fulfill customer orders. Although the company has about 25,000 restaurants, it had lost some of its competitive edge. Sales went flat in the mid-1990s and independent market testing showed a widening gap with competition in food quality. Worse, the customers of fast food like variety, and when they switch foods they switch restaurants. The make-to-stock system was not meeting these new demands. After 5 years of lab and market testing, McDonald's rolled out the new "Just for You" system, which began in March 1998, to create a make-to-order environment. This required a massive change in computer technology with computers coordinating orders; food production equipment using "rapid toasters" and temperature-controlled "launching zones" to replace the old heat lamps and holding bins; new food preparation tables; and retraining efforts for the entire domestic food production organization of over 600,000 crew members.

However, this system has apparently backfired. Sales did not improve as expected and customers complained about slow service. The new system increased the average service time from 2 to 3 minutes per order, and 15-minute waits were not uncommon. McDonald's stock price decreased, and rivals such as Wendy's captured additional market share.

capacity to have, the timing of capacity changes, and the type of capacity. Consequences of capacity decisions normally influence cost, flexibility, time, and quality. For example, what is the economic effect of expanding a facility versus building a new one, or of having one large facility versus several small ones? An airline might consider changing from large jets (which provide economies of scale) to smaller jets and more frequent flights (which provide a greater degree of customer service). Too high a capacity or too many facilities requires a high fixed-cost structure, while too low a capacity or not enough facilities close to the customers can result in inadequate service quality, resulting in the loss of (dissatisfied) customers. Capacity will be discussed more in Chapters 10 and 11.

Facilities decisions can have significant influence on costs and customer service. For instance, oil companies often locate processing plants near supplies of crude oil to achieve economies of scale. Individual distribution outlets are located much closer to customers. Decisions on how to structure product groups within plants, what types of processes to develop, and what volume to produce and when are important, especially in rapidly changing industries. For instance, in the semiconductor industry, small, low-volume plants are built for new products with considerable risk, whereas high-volume plants are used for stable and mature products. Facility location and capacity decisions in services require many service facilities located close to customers. A manufacturer may have five factories and ten distribution warehouses; many service firms have thousands of stores and locations and hundreds of warehouses. McDonald's and Wal-Mart, for example, have, respectively, over 30,000 and 4,000 stores worldwide. This dramatically complicates the management of facilities and is called "multisite management," which is explained in more detail in Chapter 8.

Inventory

In goods-producing firms, the role of inventory—goods stored for future use—is an important operations management decision because it provides capacity to meet demand and respond to demand variation at various stages within the supply chain. Operations managers need to consider where to position inventory within the supply chain and how much inventory to have at each stage. Managing inventories is the subject of Chapters 12 and 13.

In service organizations, as discussed in Chapter 1, physical inventory does not exist; however, adequate service capacity must be designed into the system to buffer against peak demand and variations in demand. In a service organization, service capacity substitutes for physical inventory. Key service capacity decisions include the amount of staff to schedule by day of the week and by department, the amount of additional safety needed, such as nurses and trucks, and the pricing of perishable service capacity (for instance, airline seats and hotel rooms). Inventory and service capacity decisions have a major impact on process structure, choice, efficiency, and effectiveness. Chapters 10 and 11 address service capacity in more detail.

Trade-Off Analysis

The sixth decision area for process choice in Exhibit 4.4 is trade-off analysis. The trade-offs between process choice decisions are many and often complex. Operations managers must make trade-offs between capacity and service; manual and automated equipment; alternative process designs; inventory, cost, and service; quality and costs; and the number and location of service facilities. Such decisions may be based on economics or other performance measures such as quality, time, and volume. Chapters 1 and 3 provided some basic methods for examining trade-offs, such as computing break-even quantities for make-or-buy decisions, the value of a loyal customer, and the productivity of employees.

BUILDING THE RIGHT INFRASTRUCTURE

The second component of Hill's operations strategy approach depicted in Exhibit 4.4 is infrastructure. Infrastructure represents the "behind-the-scenes" processes in a value chain, that is, the key supporting and general management processes. How these are designed and executed can easily mean the difference between success and failure in achieving organizational objectives.

Learning Objective
To be able to identify and understand the seven decisions areas in Hill's operations strategy framework.

Work Force

The management of the work force has important long-term implications for operations strategy. How work and jobs are designed to promote empowerment, innovation, and problem solving; the amount of training provided to employees; recognition and rewards; incentive and compensation systems; and sustaining a positive and motivating work environment are key operations management challenges. Because of varying levels in demand, many service organizations like Pal's Sudden Service are forced to use part-time employees and staff that are cross-trained in a variety of skills. Employees with more customer contact must understand customer interactions and have better "people skills" than task-oriented personnel who work behind the scenes. The focus on human resources was highlighted in Chapter 3 by Category 5 (Human Resource Focus) of the Baldrige criteria, two of the four performance areas (Innovation and Learning, Internal Performance) in the balanced scorecard, and the focus on the employee and internal performance in the service-profit chain. Some aspects of work design are addressed in Chapter 8.

Operating Plans and Control Systems

How operations are planned and controlled affects cost, quality, and dependability. Actual decisions are more of a tactical and operational nature, but the policies used for making such decisions have long-term effects. Scheduling, material control, capacity allocation, waiting lines, and day-to-day quality control are just some of the issues we will address throughout this book. Operating decisions such as short-term staffing and scheduling have profound effects on costs, customer satisfaction, and efficiency. For instance, many managers of grocery and discount department stores are able to shift employees from such ancillary activities as stocking shelves to staffing checkout lines as demand increases, and therefore reallocate staff capacity to improve customer service. These issues are addressed further in Chapter 14.

Quality Control

All goods and services are not designed or produced in the same fashion; for example, Cadillac automobiles, although part of General Motors, use more sophisticated technology and manufacturing processes that provide a higher level of quality (along with associated higher prices) than other GM brands. To illustrate this point, David Garvin describes the differences between Steinway & Sons and Yamaha, two of the leading manufacturers of pianos.[25] Steinway & Sons has been the industry leader because of the even voicing, sweetness of register, duration of tone, long lives, and fine cabinetwork of its pianos, each of which is handcrafted and unique in sound and style. Yamaha, in contrast, has developed a reputation for manufacturing quality pianos in a very short time. Yamaha did that by emphasizing reliability and conformance (low on Steinway's list of priorities), rather than artistry and uniqueness. Unlike Steinway & Sons, Yamaha produces its more standardized pianos on an assembly line. Whatever dimensions of quality a company chooses to emphasize should reflect customer needs and expectations. Yamaha and Steinway have successfully fulfilled two different sets of such needs and expectations, both valid.

Management has many decisions to make regarding quality control. These include what quality characteristics to monitor and measure, where in the manufacturing or service delivery process to measure them, how often to take measures and analyze the data, and what actions to take when quality problems are discovered. Quality management and control issues are discussed further in Chapters 15 and 16.

Organization Structure

Organizational structure greatly influences the ability of a firm to satisfy its customers. Traditionally, the functional structure, as represented by the typical organization chart, divides the organization into such functions as marketing, finance, operations, and so on, providing a clear chain of command and allowing specialization in work. However, it separates employees from customers, both external and internal, can inhibit agility and process improvement, and requires many hand-offs between functions. A pure process-based organization, on the other hand, is designed around teams dedicated to specific processes or projects, which are often self-managed, and promotes speed, flexibility, and internal cooperation (see Exhibit 1.7 in Chapter 1).

The Baldrige criteria, described in Chapter 3, support the notion of "organizing by process." Each process should be driven by the customer—from identifying customer wants and needs to ending with postsale services and follow-up. By assigning each process to a "process owner" or manager, responsibility and authority are clearly defined. A matrix organization blends elements of both of these organizational structures by configuring process or project teams from different functions, while maintaining functional control over individuals and technologies.

Compensation Systems

Building the human infrastructure is probably the most difficult of all management tasks. Work-force management involves many complex decisions, such as recognition and reward, advancement opportunities, training and continued education, benefits, team building and communication, empowerment, negotiation, work environment, and job shift and displacement policies. For example, compensation systems can focus on individual or team performance or some combination of them. A team-based compensation system requires a supporting organizational culture and training on team communication and brainstorming skills. An individual-based compensation system encourages independence, empowerment, and rewards the higher-performing employees. Each approach has advantages and disadvantages; however, the approach that is selected becomes a part of the operations strategy and therefore should support the achievement of a company's strategic goals and objectives.

Learning and Innovation Systems

Learning is the basis for continuous improvement and technological change. How do we record and disseminate job, process, market, and organizational knowledge accurately and quickly throughout the organization? How can we leverage past experiences in the future? What training and information support does each job need? How do we manage legacy knowledge systems while new knowledge is acquired? How do we ensure we do not have to reinvent internal and external knowledge over and over again? How can we institutionalize learning within the organization? These are the kinds of questions operations managers must help answer if the organization is to survive. Mass customization is very much dependent on learning systems. Information technology provides the capability to store organizational knowledge and use it at key points in the process to increase quality, productivity, and speed while lowering costs.

Innovation within the organization is coupled with good learning systems. The successful introduction of new goods and services and the processes that create them continuingly adds value to the firm's customer benefit packages. Rapid introduction of goods and services, a high percent of total sales from new goods and services, and research and development expense as a percent of total sales dollars are just a few of the metrics that help managers evaluate innovation.

Support Services

Support services often represent 30 to 70 percent of the cost of being in business. Each support service has at least one process. Support service processes provide services to internal (employee benefit packages) or external (customer benefit packages) customers and in doing so, create the infrastructure for an organization's primary processes. Exhibit 4.6 shows a typical list of support services to help you appreciate the amount of resources committed to support processes and why they are vital to a company's success.

Support service processes cost money, influence customer satisfaction, and consume time. Despite their importance, they often are not documented, measured, evaluated, well managed, or continuously improved. Such lack of management attention occurs both in goods-producing and service-providing organizations. In most cases, support services offer a significant opportunity for improvement in organizational effectiveness that translates to bottom-line savings.

Exhibit 4.6
Examples of Support Process

Union grievance procedures	Financial systems	Regulatory procedures
Travel services	Benefits administration	Customer-contact
Training programs	Strategic planning	procedures
Computer software	Customer complaint	Health systems and
services	processes	procedures
CBP warranty processes	Waste management	Research and development
Advertising programs	Company communication	Recognition and reward
Sales programs	systems	programs
Supplier programs	Employee counseling	Refund and recall
Claims processing	Security and safety	procedures
Environmental programs	systems	Legal and tax procedures
Franchise systems	Marketing research	Conference/meeting
Repair services	Accounting systems	administration

APPLYING THE STRATEGY DEVELOPMENT FRAMEWORK: A CASE STUDY OF MCDONALD'S

McDonald's Corporation is the world's leading food-service retailer with more than 30,000 restaurants in 121 countries serving 46 million customers each day. Because almost everyone on the planet is familiar with McDonald's goods and service delivery system, we will use it to illustrate Hill's strategy development framework.[26] Despite the operational problems that the company has encountered in recent years (as discussed in an earlier OM Spotlight), the company's vision provides the basis for its strategy:

McDonald's vision is to be the world's best quick service restaurant experience. Being the best means providing outstanding quality, service, cleanliness and value, so that we make every customer in every restaurant smile. To achieve our vision, we focus on three worldwide strategies:

(1) **Be The Best Employer**
Be the best employer for our people in each community around the world.

(2) **Deliver Operational Excellence**
Deliver operational excellence to our customers in each of our restaurants.

(3) **Achieve Enduring Profitable Growth**
Achieve enduring profitable growth by expanding the brand and leveraging the strengths of the McDonald's system through innovation and technology.

Exhibit 4.7
McDonald's Customer Benefit Package

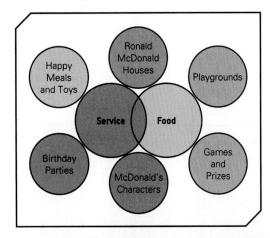

What is the customer benefit package (CBP) that McDonald's offers? Exhibit 4.7 shows the CBP, in which goods and service content (food and fast service) are equally important and the primary mission and are supported by peripheral goods and services. To support this CBP, operations must design facilities, processes, equipment, and jobs that can create and deliver the primary and peripheral goods and services to meet corporate and competitive priority goals.

Exhibit 4.8 illustrates how Hill's strategy framework can be applied to McDonald's. One corporate objective is profitable growth. Global research suggests that time pressures are causing people to eat out more than ever. The more people eat out, the more variety they want. That is why McDonald's bought such restaurant chains as Boston Market, and Chipotle (Mexican). Not only did McDonald's gain thousands of prime locations with these acquisitions, but it also broadened its food variety and portfolio. The long-term strategy is that "one brand can't be all things to all people," and these acquisitions allow it to follow the strategy of variety. This provides McDonald's with many attractive strategies, such as combo restaurants with several of these brands under one roof or a mix of these restaurants in a high traffic area. Designing the value chain to support such clusters of restaurants would represent a challenge to operations yet provide McDonald's with economies of scale and even lower costs.

The marketing strategy to support profitable growth consists of adding both company-owned and franchised McDonald's and Partner Brand restaurants. McDonald's is committed to franchising as a key strategy to grow and leverage value chain capabilities. Approximately 70 percent of McDonald's restaurants worldwide are owned and operated by independent business people—the franchisee.

The core competency to profitable growth is maintaining low cost and fast service. To support this strategy, McDonald's has many operational decisions to make such as: Adopt an assembly line approach to process design? Standardize store design to make process flow, training, and performance evaluation consistent among stores? Standardize equipment and job design work activities? The french fryer equipment and procedure is a good example of standardizing equipment design. There is "only one way to make french fries" in 30,000 stores worldwide and this contributes to the consistent quality of goods, fast service, and a standardized training program. Likewise, ordering by the numbers and digital printouts of customer orders in the drivethrough improves order accuracy and speed of service. Of course,

Exhibit 4.8 Applying the Hill's Strategy Development Framework to McDonald's

Corporate Objective Examples	Marketing Strategy Examples	How Do Goods and Services Qualify and Win Orders in the Marketplace? (Competitive Priorities)	Operations Strategy	
			Operating Design Choice Examples	Infrastructure Examples
Profitable Growth	Add worldwide 1,300 McDonald's restaurants and 150 new Partner Brand restaurants using company-owned and franchised stores	Competitive priorities tie the corporate and marketing strategies to the operational strategy ⟷	• Flow shop process design • Standardized store design • Equipment design • Job design • Order-taking process • Capacity and facility size, location, and clusters	• Hiring process and criteria • First job training • Recognition and rewards • Training for the unexpected • Keeping it simple • Manager trainee program • Coaching and counseling • Teamwork • e-mail capabilities
Operational Excellence	Ideal store location, best training and employee well-being programs	• #1 Low prices • #2 Quick service (delivery speed) • #3 High service quality	• Global value chain coordination • Suppliers • Resource scheduling • Inventory placement and control • Distribution centers • Standardized operational and job procedures	• Operating plans and control system(s) • Shift management • Supplier relations and negotiation • Equipment maintenance • Online network capability • Distribution centers
Leverage Strengths Through Innovation and Technology	Develop new food items, store and food mix Tie demand analysis to promotions	⟷ • #4 High goods quality	• Store equipment technology • Value chain information systems to tie stores, distribution centers, and suppliers together • New food products	• Quality control • Laboratory testing • Organizational structure • Compensation systems
Diversity	Long-standing commitment to a diverse work force	• #5 Demand flexibility	• Training and franchising • Process performance • Career paths	• Learning and innovation systems • Hamburger University
Social Responsibility	Being a good neighbor and partner with the local community	• #6 Brand image ⟷	• Trade-off analysis • Recycling processes • Package redesign, shipping, warehousing	• Support services • Ronald McDonald House • Mobile health centers • Youth camps

the entire human resource function is built around the needs of McDonald's value chain and operating systems. Examples of supportive infrastructure include good hiring criteria, recognition and reward programs, training, and promotion criteria.

A second corporate objective is *operational excellence*. The ultimate objective of operational excellence is satisfied customers. Operational excellence includes value chain, process, equipment, and job efficiencies, as well as superior people-related performance, all focused to support the service encounter. McDonald's strategy is to deliver exceptional customer experiences through a combination of great-tasting food, outstanding service, a good place to work, profitable growth, and consistent value. To put sparkle in McDonald's service, initiatives include training for the unexpected and keeping it simple.

To accomplish operational excellence requires answers to some of the previous questions plus answers to questions such as: How do we measure operational performance? How do we train front- and back-office employees to achieve corporate objectives? What are alternative career progression paths? What equipment and technology reduce the opportunities for errors and service upsets? What supply chain structure best services our global network of stores? Where should we locate our distribution centers? What should be the capacity of each distribution center? How many employees should work in the store on each day of the week (that is, What is the staff schedule?)?

A third corporate objective is leveraging innovation and technology capabilities. In the United States, 40 distribution centers support more than 12,000 restaurants and about 350 suppliers. Information technology is used to coordinate the activities of McDonald's value chain. In Russia, McDonald's also operates a $45-million state-of-the-art food processing and distribution center. It employees 450 people and supplies all McDonald's restaurants in Russia and 17 other countries. Every hour, the distribution center (called McComplex) produces about 15,500 buns, 13,500 pies, 15,000 kilograms of beef patties, and 2,900 liters of milk. McComplex has eight flow shop assembly lines that include meat, pie, dairy, fry, liquid, cheese, and garnish lines. All food items from over 100 suppliers are monitored through laboratory testing for conformance to quality standards. Video training, online ordering, automated french fry machines, debt cards, and daily performance reporting by store, district, region, and country are just a few of the uses of technology that support corporate strategy and objectives.

Another corporate objective is developing and maintaining a diverse work force. Diversity at McDonald's is understanding, recognizing, and valuing the differences that make each person unique. It has won many awards over the years for its diversity practices, including *Fortune* magazine's Top Places for Minorities to Work, Best Employer for Asians, and Top 50 Places for Hispanic Women to Work. In the United States, minorities and women currently represent over 34 percent of McDonald's franchisees. Hamburger University, located in Oak Brook, Illinois, has trained over 65,000 mangers in 22 different languages and also manages ten international training centers in places like Australia, England, Japan, and Germany. McDonald's takes pride in the fact that it is the "first job" for many young people throughout the world. These first-job employees learn about McDonald's values, behavior and dress standards, customer relationships, schedules, efficient operation of the delivery system, performance systems, and so on. Many of these ideas and practices are carried throughout life for thousands of people worldwide.

McDonald's supports its social responsibility objective with over 200 Ronald McDonald House charities. Social responsibility activities also include funding immunization programs for 1 million African children, Olympic youth camps, disaster relief, and sponsored mobile health centers in underserved areas.

Other corporate objectives not shown in Exhibit 4.7 include a high return on investment, exploring nontraditional locations for stores, and commitment to the environment. To support a high return on investment and exploring nontraditional store locations, McDonald's is partnering with other firms such as Amoco, Chevron, airports, and hospitals. In support of its environment-friendly corporate objective, it has purchased over $4 billion of recycled goods and redesigned its packaging to reduce total annual weight by over 400 million pounds. The success of each of these corporate initiatives requires good operations skills such as project management, inventory management, logistics, capacity analysis, scheduling, quality control, and facility location analysis. For each of these corporate initiatives to be successful requires someone in McDonald's to excel in process design and management.

RONALD MCDONALD
HOUSE CHARITIES

PR Newswire McDonald's

Competitive priorities are derived from McDonald's vision statement and strategy. The ranking in Exhibit 4.8 reflects their importance. The competitive priorities tie the corporate and marketing strategies to the operations strategy. The competitive priorities provide direction on key operations strategy issues listed in the last two columns of Exhibit 4.8. One job of senior McDonald's managers is to check all four decision loops in Exhibit 4.5 for inconsistencies or conflicts in their logic. Operations managers spend the majority of their time evaluating loops #2 and #3, but they must also communicate any potential conflicts or inconsistencies back to corporate and marketing managers through loop #4. The development of a world-class strategy for an organization is an immense challenge with many opportunities for strategic mismatches, failures, and inconsistencies.

SOLVED PROBLEMS

SOLVED PROBLEM #1

Define the customer benefit package for a health club or recreation center or gymnasium you frequent (check out the web site of your favorite club, center, or gym for more information), and use this to describe the organization's strategic mission, strategy, competitive priorities, and how it wins customers. What are the order qualifiers and winners for this organization? Second, make a list of example processes that create and deliver each good or service in the CBP you selected, and briefly describe process procedures and issues.

Solution:

One example is depicted here. Of course, health clubs and recreation centers often have unique features to differentiate them from their competition.

Mission: The mission of our health club is to offer many pathways to a healthy living style and body.

Strategy: We strive to provide our customers with superior:
- customer convenience (location, food, communication, schedules, etc.);
- clean facilities, equipment, uniforms, parking lot, and the like;

- friendly professional staff that care about you;
- ways to improve and maintain your body and mind's health and well-being.

Competitive Priorities: #1 Priority—many pathways to healthy living and a healthy body (design flexibility), #2—friendly professional staff and service encounters (service quality), #3—everything is super clean (goods and environmental quality), #4—customer convenience in all respects (time), #5—price (cost).

How to win customers? Providing a full-service health club with superior service, staff, and facilities. (Although you would not see this in company literature, this health club provides premium service at premium prices.)

Key Processes
- The food ordering and supply, preparation, delivery, and cleanup processes define the *food-service value chain*. Key procedures and issues include how the food service in the health club ensures accurate and timely ordering of all raw materials necessary to make the food served to customers; how they make the chicken salad or the six kinds of pasta served daily; whether they throw away all food at the end of the day to ensure fresh food the next day; the type of goods and service quality standards used; how the club trains all kitchen staff; and how it manages kitchen, silver and dinnerware, food, and uniform inventories.
- The *childcare process* includes rigorous procedures for checking children in and out of the childcare area. Issues include whether the childcare staff is mature, trained, and CPR certified;

what offerings are available, such as fitness classes for kids, a library and study area, educational videos, and a computer lab; the check-in and check-out process to ensure children's security; whether medicines may be administered; activities planned throughout the day; and the qualifications of the caregivers.

- The *swimming lesson process* includes a sign-up phase, potential participant medical examination phase, and a series of classes taught by certified swimming instructors who are trained in emergency services such as CPR. Issues include how the swimming class age groups (target markets) should be segmented; whether a swimming aerobics class is offered to senior citizens; how the health club keeps people safe yet teaches them to swim and have fun; lesson plans for each day; and how to schedule the 20 different swimming classes going on in May.

- The *personal trainer process* requires high design flexibility since each exercise and training program is customized to the individual. Key issues include how customers and professional trainers are assigned and scheduled; what procedures are in place when customers want to change personal trainers; how customized training programs are developed for all ages and sizes of people; what training is required of all personal trainers; whether enough personal trainer staff capacity is available; and whether the trainer keeps records of workouts and medical histories.

SOLVED PROBLEM #2

California Aggregates, a supplier of construction materials such as ready-mix concrete, sand, gravel, and other products, conducted a survey of its customers to understand their most important wants and needs. The survey revealed the following:

- Responsive to special needs
- Easy to place orders
- Consistent product quality
- On-time delivery
- Accurate invoices
- Lowest prices
- Attractive credit terms
- Salespeople's skills
- Helpful dispatchers
- Courteous drivers
- Fair and quick problem resolution

a. Draw an example customer benefit package, and define the company's strategic mission.

b. What elements of operations design choices and infrastructure in Hill's strategy framework would an operations strategy have to address to meet these customer requirements?

Solution:

Strategic mission: California Aggregates provides aggregate materials to meet or exceed customer requirements at the right price at the right time and in a friendly and helpful manner.

- Responsive to special needs—organizational structure, learning and innovation systems, skilled work force
- Easy to place orders—type of process, technology, supply chain integration
- Consistent product quality—type of process, supply chain integration and outsourcing, operating plans and control systems, quality control
- On-time delivery—type of process, technology, capacity and facilities, inventory, operating plans and control systems
- Accurate invoices—technology, support services
- Lowest prices—type of process, supply chain integration and outsourcing, trade-off analysis, inventory
- Attractive credit terms—supply chain integration and outsourcing, support services
- Salespeople's skills—work force, compensation systems, learning systems
- Helpful dispatchers—work force, compensation systems, learning systems
- Courteous drivers—work force, compensation systems, learning systems
- Fair and quick problem resolution—work force, organizational structure, learning systems, operating plans and control systems

KEY TERMS AND CONCEPTS

Capacity
Competitive advantage
Competitive priorities
Core competencies
Corporate, business, and functional levels of strategy
Cost
Customer wants and needs analysis
Dissatisfiers, satisfiers, and exciters/delighters
Flexibility
Functional strategy
Infrastructure
Innovation
Mass customization
Operations design choices

Operations strategy
Order qualifiers and winners
Quality
Search, experience, and credence attributes
Strategic business units (SBUs)
Strategic mission and vision
Strategic planning
Strategic values
Strategy
Strategy development
Strategy development framework
Strategy implementation
Time

QUESTIONS FOR REVIEW AND DISCUSSION

1. Discuss the role of operations management in overall business strategy. Why is OM critical to a successful strategy?

2. What do we mean by the term *competitive advantage*? What might the competitive advantage be for each of the following companies:

   a. Home Depot
   b. Southwest Airlines
   c. Dell Computer
   d. Toyota
   e. Avis

3. Describe some approaches that companies use to understand their customers' wants and needs. What are the advantages and disadvantages of these approaches?

4. Contrast dissatisfiers, satisfiers, and exciters/delighters. Why is this classification important for companies to understand, particularly from a strategic point of view?

5. Select a business you are familiar with and identify and explain example dissatisfiers, satisfiers, and exciters/delighters. You might look up the business on the Internet or visit the library.

6. Explain the difference between an order qualifier and an order winner. Provide some examples.

7. Give some examples of search, experience, and credence attributes for an automobile, an automobile repair service center, and cable television.

8. Select businesses you are familiar with and identify and provide examples of customers using search, experience, and credence quality to evaluate the good or service. You might also look up the businesses on the Internet or visit the library.

9. Explain the interlinking model of quality and profitability (Exhibit 4.2). How does it connect to business and operations strategy?

10. What are competitive priorities? Provide some examples of how OM influences the five major types of competitive priorities.

11. Is it possible for a world-class organization to achieve superiority in all five major competitive priorities—price (cost), quality, time, flexibility, and innovation? Explain. Justify. Provide examples pro or con.

12. Select a business you are familiar with and identify and rank order its competitive priorities as best you can, then identify the order qualifiers and winners. Justify your reasoning.

13. Explain the concept of mass customization and the role of customer participation in the process.

14. What is the difference between corporate, business, and functional strategy?

15. Select a business you are familiar with and identify its three levels of strategy—corporate, business, and functional.

16. What do we mean by *core competencies*?

17. Describe the components of the strategic planning process. What makes a good strategic planning process?

18. Why is it important to understand and communicate a firm's mission, vision, and values? How do these help direct strategy?

19. How is strategy development and implementation alike and unalike in huge conglomerate organizations such as General Electric versus small organizations such as Pal's Sudden Service? Explain.

20. What is *operations strategy*? How does it relate to corporate strategy?

21. Explain Hill's strategy development framework. What are the key elements of operations strategy within this framework?

22. Based on firsthand knowledge or research, what is the length of the useful life cycle for a good or service and its implications for any three of the following: automobiles, a cruise ship, a cruise vacation, PC operating system software, refrigerator, electric coffee maker, space shuttle, college textbooks, a night's stay in a hotel room, downloading music online, online auctions, and a beer. How does the good or service life cycle affect strategy?

PROBLEMS AND ACTIVITIES

1. Define the customer benefit package in (a) the "old days" when the automobile (that is, the physical good) itself was enough to make the sale, and (b) then do the same thing with services that complement the sale today. Define the automobile manufacturer or dealer's strategic vision, strategy, competitive priorities, and ways of winning customer orders in both situations. What are the order qualifiers and winners? What would operations have to be good at to make this a successful business or organization? Make a list of the processes you will need to implement this strategy. You can check out the web site of your favorite organization for more information.

2. A hotel has determined that its customers' most important wants and needs are
   - having correct reservation information,
   - honoring the reservation (ensuring that a room is available for a confirmed reservation),
   - fulfilling any special room type or location requests,
   - check-in speed,
   - cleanliness and servicing of the room,
   - check-out speed,
   - staff efficiency in responding to requests,
   - staff attitude and behavior,
   - having all items in the room in working order.

   a. Draw the CBP for this hotel as best you can.

   b. What elements of operations design choices and infrastructure in Hill's strategy framework would an operations strategy have to address to meet these customer requirements?

3. Define and draw the customer benefit package (see Chapter 1 for additional discussion) for any organization you are familiar with, such as
   - sporting goods store,
   - haircut salon,
   - a personal computer manufacturer,
   - college bar or restaurant,
   - the university, college, or technical school you attend,
   - pizza business,
   - a sports team,
   - library,
   - wireless telephone service,
   - an Internet business,
   - used-book exchange or bookstore.

   You can check out the web site of your favorite organization for more information. Usually you can find the organization's mission and value statements on the web.

   a. Define the firm's strategic vision, strategy, and competitive priorities. What are the order qualifiers and winners? What would operations have to be good at to make this a successful business or organization?

   b. Make a list of the key processes you will need to implement this customer benefit package and strategy. How important is operations in the success of this organization? Explain/justify. (See Solved Problem #1 for an example format.)

   c. Apply Professor Hill's framework to the organization you select.

4. Find a customer survey or satisfaction questionnaire from a local restaurant.

   a. Does each of the customer attributes surveyed address dissatisfiers, satisfiers, or exciters/delighters?

   b. What elements of process choice and infrastructure in Hill's strategy framework would an operations strategy have to address to meet these customer requirements?

5. Using the information about Pal's Sudden Service provided in this chapter, apply Hill's generic strategy framework in a fashion similar to the McDonald's example. How do the strategies of Pal's and McDonald's appear to differ? What differences exist in their operations strategies and decisions?

6. Apply Hill's generic strategy framework to one of the organizations in Questions 1, 2, 3, or 4. This will require some research to identify corporate objectives and competitive priorities. See the McDonald's example in the chapter for guidance.

7. Explore the web sites for several companies on the Fortune 500 list. Based on the information you find, on which competitive priorities do these firms appear to focus? What can you say about their operations strategy (either explicit or implied)?

CASES

THE LAWN CARE COMPANY

"Chris, we make the highest quality grass seed and fertilizer in the world. Our brands are known everywhere!" stated Caroline Ebelhar, the vice president of manufacturing for The Lawn Care Company. "Yah! But the customer doesn't have a Ph.D. in organic chemistry to know the difference between our grass seed and fertilizer compared to our competitors'! We need to be in the lawn care application service business, not just be the manufacturer of super perfect products," responded Chris Kilbourne, the vice president of marketing, as he walked out of Ebelhar's office. This on-going debate among Lawn Care's senior management team had not been resolved but the chief executive officer, Steven Marion, had been listening very closely. A major strategic decision would soon have to be made.

The Lawn Care Company, a fertilizer and grass seed manufacturer, with sales of almost $1 billion, sold some of its products directly to parks and golf courses. Customer service in this goods-producing company was historically very narrowly defined as providing "the right product to the right customer at the right time." Once these goods were delivered to the customer's premises and the customer signed the shipping documents, Lawn Care's job was done. For many park and golf course customers, a local subcontractor or the customers themselves applied the fertilizer and seed. These application personnel often did the job incorrectly using inappropriate equipment and methods. The relationship between these non-Lawn Care application service personnel, The Lawn Care Company, and the customer was also not always ideal. When the customer made claims because of damaged lawns, the question then became one of who was at fault? Did the quality of the physical product or the way it was applied cause the damage? Either way, the customers' lawns were in poor shape, and in some cases, the golf courses lost substantial revenue if a green or hole was severely damaged or not playable.

One of Lawn Care's competitors began an application service for parks and golf courses that routinely applied the fertilizer and grass seed for its primary customers. This competitor bundled the application service to the primary goods, fertilizer and grass seed, and charged a higher price for this service. The competitor learned the application business in the parks and golf course target market segment and was beginning to explore expanding into the residential lawn care application service target market. The Lawn Care Company sold the "highest quality physical products" in the industry. Its competitor sold the customer "a beautiful lawn with a promise of no hassles." To the competitor, this included an application service bundled to grass seed and fertilizer.

Questions

a. Define and draw the current customer benefit package for the firm and its competitors.

b. Define the organization's strategic mission, strategy, competitive priorities, and how it wins customers. What are the order qualifiers and winners?

c. Make a list of example processes that create and deliver each good or service in the CBP you selected, and briefly describe process procedures and issues.

d. What pre- and postservices could Lawn Care possibly offer its customers to complement the sale of the grass seed and fertilizer?

e. What problems, if any, do you see with its current strategy, vision, customer benefit package design, and pre- and postservices?

f. Should the company offer lawn care application services to the professional market? If not, why? If so, justify. What do you have to be good at to offer outstanding lawn care application services at multiple sites?

g. What are your final recommendations regarding a revised business strategy, vision, customer benefit package, the role of pre- and postservices, and so on?

THE GREATER CINCINNATI CHAMBER OF COMMERCE

Founded in 1839 to facilitate the growth and ease of commerce, the Greater Cincinnati Chamber of Commerce is a membership organization of approximately 6,700 businesses and organizations in the region that surrounds Cincinnati, Ohio. The chamber's stated purpose is to serve its members, and its mission is simple: to present Cincinnati as one of the world's favorite American business centers. The chamber delivers a diverse range of products and services, including

- new business attraction,
- business retention,
- government advocacy,
- education and training services,
- networking events,
- festivals and events,
- "Business Connections" membership directory,
- ChamberVision newsletter.

Although technically a not-for-profit organization, many chamber services are expected to generate an excess of revenues over expenses, which is required to support a variety of non-revenue-producing chamber programs. The chamber serves the region from its headquarters office located in downtown Cincinnati.

In 1996, the management group, with active involvement of a number of key board members, established the vision to guide the chamber's efforts supporting the region into the future. The vision was to "run with the gazelles," focusing on becoming as effective as other chamber benchmark cities (the "gazelles") in terms of business development and job creation. The chamber detailed its mission to guide that service as follows:

To strengthen the economic vitality and quality of life in the Greater Cincinnati region by
- generating job growth through local, national, and international economic development,
- influencing government regulations and legislation that affect business, and
- providing services that help local businesses prosper and grow.

In early 2000, the management group recognized that the vision, "run with the gazelles," while providing the region with its overall goal, did not adequately support the other key aspect of the chamber's role, helping each individual member meet the challenges of growth and success. The management group defined a new vision for the organization itself:

Be the first place that businesses in the region go for solutions to the competitive challenges of growth

Packaged with the still valid and important regional vision of running with the gazelles and the existing mission, the management group created "Beyond 2000," the chamber's revised strategic plan, combining the two complementary visions with the day-to-day foundation of the mission to fully focus the chamber for the future.

The chamber is organized in a series of product-focused departments, as shown in the table. These five departments interact directly with customer segments to develop and deliver chamber products and services.

Department	Key Services
Business Development	Educational services, networking events and activities
Downtown Council	Downtown street festivals and events
Economic Development	Business attraction—national and international, retention and expansion assistance
Government Affairs	Information, advocacy activities
Member Benefits	Benefits products to improve members' bottom line

Support groups assist these line departments in product and service delivery functions that include information services, administration, human resources, marketing/communications, and finance. In addition, the Chamber's Membership/Member Relations department serves chamber staff and members in providing information and access to chamber products and services, including membership.

The chamber has ongoing relationships with affiliate organizations housed within the chamber's downtown Cincinnati office. Those affiliates include the Cincinnati Minority Supplier Development Council, the Cincinnati Minority Enterprise Business Mentoring Program, and The Japan-America Society. The chamber participates in the Tri-State Chamber Collaborative, an organization of ten chamber senior executives, eight representing geographic segments of the region and two that represent the local Hispanic and African-American chambers. The Chamber Collaborative focuses on projects of regional importance where common goals exist and cooperation is critical to regional success. The chamber supports the Metropolitan Growth Alliance (MGA), an organization of local business leaders focused on generating regional economic growth. In 1998, the MGA sponsored a study to identify areas for action to ensure long-term regional health and vitality. The chamber had a lead role in facilitating the process of that study toward its release of results in May 1999.

In 1998, the chamber began the process of forming the Partnership for Greater Cincinnati, a broad-based initiative to unify the region's marketing efforts and economic development efforts and infrastructure. The Regional Marketing Partners (RMP) lead this marketing effort. Membership in the RMP includes five economic development leaders representing seven counties and the City of Cincinnati in the three-state area, as well as key leaders representing local chambers, industry, and the Greater Cincinnati-Northern Kentucky International Airport. More than 180 business and government entities are aligned with this effort designed to bring the vision to "run with the gazelles" to reality. More than 1,500 chamber members invested in the Partnership in 2000 through a voluntary option presented on their annual chamber dues invoice. The chamber maintains an active role in addressing issues of regional and community development and redevelopment. The chamber's reputation and credibility positions it as the organization that brings others to the table and facilitates solutions to community challenges.

In 1996, the chamber initiated efforts internally to create a team-based environment. The management group attended training in basics of team development and facilitation skills. Through this leadership initiative, the chamber has fostered the development of a culture of employee involvement. In 1998, the management group participated in a chamber-sponsored organizational development process, the Center for Excellence. This process trained the management group in the basics of Total Quality and Continuous Improvement and resulted in an implementation plan to improve performance throughout the organization. In 1999, the chamber expanded this plan through the development of the "Measurement Report Card," emphasizing measurement as the tool to drive effectiveness. This Measurement Report Card links the Strategic Plan, Program of Work, and departmental and work group measures into one unified system and incorporates a broadened set of measures, coupling financial goals with penetration and satisfaction data through the quarterly operations report.

Discussion Questions

1. Characterize the customer benefit package that the chamber offers. What other peripheral goods might the chamber provide to complement its services? How might this affect its strategy?
2. What sources of competitive advantage do you feel the chamber has? Who does it compete with?
3. Critique its mission and strategy. At what operational processes must it excel to accomplish its mission and vision?
4. In many areas, a chamber of commerce is primarily in the travel and tourism business. How does the Greater Cincinnati Chamber of Commerce appear to differentiate itself from these types of organizations?
5. Visit the chamber's web site at www.gccc.com. Has its focus changed since the time on which this case is based?

ENDNOTES

1 Rynecki, Davie, "One Town, Two Rivals," *Fortune*, July 26, 2004, pp. 110–119.
2 Pilcher, James, "Airlines Changing Hub Plans," *Cincinnati Enquirer*, September 12, 2004, pp. F1, F4.
3 Selden, Larry, and Colvin, Geoffrey, "Will this Customer Sink Your Stock?" *Fortune*, September 30, 2002, pp. 127–132.
4 "Getting an Edge," *Across the Board*, February 2000, pp. 43–48.
5 "Apple's One-Dollar-a-Year Man," *Fortune*, January 24, 2000, pp. 71–76.
6 Buzzell, Robert D., and Gale, Bradley T., *The PIMS Principles: Linking Strategy to Performance*, New York: The Free Press, 1987.

[7] Zeithaml, V. A., "How Consumer Evaluation Processes Differ Between Goods and Services," in J. H. Donnelly and W. R. George, eds., *Marketing in Services*, Chicago: American Marketing Association, 1981, pp. 186–199.

[8] Caudron, Shari, "All Shopped Out," *Across the Board*, September/October 2002, pp. 31–34.

[9] Selden, Larry, and Colvin, Geoffrey, "Will Your E-Business Leave You Quick or Dead?", *Fortune*, May 28, 2001, pp. 112–124.

[10] Ettlie, John E., "BMW: Believing the Banner," *Automotive Manufacturing and Production*, April 2001, p. 38.

[11] "Southwest Sets Standards on Costs," *Wall Street Journal*, October 9, 2002, p. A2. Reprinted by permission of Dow Jones, Inc. via Copyright Clearance Center.

[12] Gale, Bradley T., "Quality Comes First When Hatching Power Brands," *Planning Review*, July/August 1992, pp. 4–9, 48.

[13] Hales, H. Lee, "Time Has Come for Long-Range Planning of Facilities Strategies in Electronic Industries," *Industrial Engineering*, April 1985.

[14] *The PIMS Letter on Business Strategy*, Cambridge, MA: The Strategic Planning Institute, no. 4, 1986.

[15] *Business Week*, December 17, 2001, p. 84.

[16] McCamey, David A., Bogs, Robert W., and Bayuk, Linda M., "More, Better, Faster from Total Quality Effort," *Quality Progress*, August 1999, pp. 43–50.

[17] "Attack of the Killer Crossovers," *Business Week*, January 28, 2002, pp. 98–100.

[18] Grant, Robert M., Krishnan, R., Shani, Abraham B., and Baer, Ron, "Appropriate Manufacturing Technology: A Strategic Approach," *Sloan Management Review* 33, no. 1 (Fall 1991), pp. 43–54.

[19] Lafamore, G. Berton, "The Burden of Choice," *APICS—The Performance Advantage*, January 2001, pp. 40–43.

[20] Quinn, James Brian, *Strategies for Change: Logical Incrementalism*, Homewood, IL: Richard D. Irwin, 1980.

[21] Portions adapted from www.walmartstores.com, July 27, 2002.

[22] "Credit Wal-Mart for 1990's Productivity Boom," *The Columbus Dispatch*, Columbus, Ohio, March 3, 2002, p. C2.

[23] Hill, T., *Manufacturing Strategy: Text and Cases*, 3rd ed., Burr Ridge, IL: McGraw-Hill, 2000.

[24] Ettlie, John E., "What the Auto Industry Can Learn from McDonald's," *Automotive Manufacturing & Production*, October 1999, p. 42; Stires, David, "Fallen Arches," *Fortune*, April 29, 2002, pp. 74–76.

[25] Garvin, David A., *Managing Quality: The Strategic and Competitive Edge*, New York: The Free Press, 1988.

[26] www.mcdonalds.com/corporate/info/vision/index.html. This example is the book author's interpretation of McDonald's public information with the objective of illustrating Professor Terry Hill's generic strategy development framework. It may or may not be perfectly accurate and it is only partially complete due to space limitations.

Part 2

Designing Operating Systems

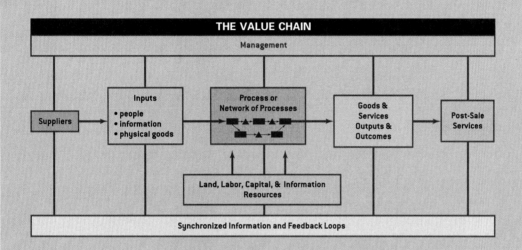

THE VALUE CHAIN

Management

Suppliers

Inputs
- people
- information
- physical goods

Process or
Network of Processes

Goods &
Services
Outputs &
Outcomes

Post-Sale
Services

Land, Labor, Capital, & Information
Resources

Synchronized Information and Feedback Loops

In this section of the book we delve into details of designing the key components of value chains. You will undoubtedly be involved in many of these issues in your future business career, no matter what your major. You will learn about:

- Technology in manufacturing, service operations, and value chains; and several important integrated operating systems that are prevalent in today's businesses.
- Designing goods, services, manufacturing processes, service delivery systems and service encounters, and how they support the strategic mission of an organization.
- Process choice and selection for both manufacturing and services; and tools and approaches used for process design, analysis, and improvement.
- Issues associated with facility layout, assembling line balancing, and work design.
- Key issues of supply chain design, including performance measurement, strategic choice, location decisions, and operational management issues.

Chapter Outline

CHAPTER 5

Technology and Operations Management

Learning Objectives

1. To gain a basic understanding of different types of technology and their role in manufacturing and service operations.

2. To understand how manufacturing and service technology is changing the role of business relationships and strengthening the value chain.

3. To understand the nature of an integrated operating system (IOS) and examine some common examples of such systems that play significant roles in operations management.

4. To understand the advantages that technology offers in operations and its impact on productivity, as well as the challenges that organizations and operations managers face in implementing and using technology.

5. To understand the processes of technology development and adoption and the role of operations in these processes.

6. To understand how scalability affects technology decisions and to be able to apply simple scoring and decision models to technology decisions.

• "A man had his head blown off," said John Brodbeck, who was 5 years old in 1930 when the steam engine blew up at his farm in Michigan. In the early 1900s—the height of steam-powered tractor use—explosions were common, averaging two a day in the United States in 1911, according to Diotima Booraem of the Smithsonian Institution in Washington D.C. The new technology of the 1910s was not safe and few people knew how to truly operate steam engines. The first agricultural steam engines arrived in the 1850s and were pulled by horses. By the 1890s, a steam-engine tractor could plow up to 75 acres per day, more than 20 times the productivity of pulling a plow using horses. By the 1920s, production of steam engines dwindled and none were sold by the end of the decade, replaced by gas-powered engines and tractors.[1]

• "I don't care about the digital revolution, you lost my pictures!" groaned Irene Edwards at the store's photo laboratory assistant. "Ma'am, we did not lose your pictures. There are no digital pictures on your memory stick," replied the young photo assistant. "You must have erased them accidentally in your digital camera or while you were trying to transfer them to your computer." "Those were pictures of my granddaughter's last high school soccer match. I'm going to sue you guys!" snarled Edwards.

158

- Recently, the U.S. Defense Department told its 43,000 suppliers that they will be required to use radio frequency ID (RFID) tags—the successor to popular bar codes. RFID tags are tiny computer chips that transmit radio signals and can be mounted on packages or shipping containers to help organizations identify product locations and movement. As such, they can assist in improving inventory management and enhancing customer service because of the ability to trace products throughout the supply chain.[2] "What are RFID tags? How does the government expect a small firm like us to use them?" said Ham Gifford, chief operating officer for Peterson Manufacturing, which makes gloves for the U.S. Army. "This is going to make a lot of problems for us," lamented Gifford.

> **Discussion Questions:** In what ways has technology benefited your life and work as a student? Describe problems that you have personally encountered in using modern technology. What operations management issues must organizations deal with when new technology is introduced?

Technology—both physical and information—has dramatically changed how work is accomplished in every industry—from mining to manufacturing to education to health care. Technology is the enabler that makes today's service and manufacturing systems operate productively and meet customer needs better than ever. Most of you probably cannot imagine living in a world without personal computers, the Internet, or wireless communications. We are sure that people in the early 1900s felt the same way about the steam engine, as did your parents and grandparents about the automobile and radios. The steam engine lasted only about 50 years before a new technology—the gasoline internal combustion engine—replaced the old technology. Although the gasoline-powered engine has prevailed for about 100 years, we are beginning to see electric, hybrid, and other potential replacements. Large mainframe computers have shrunk down to handhelds, and wireless now dominates the technological landscape.

Understanding technology in operations is critical for several reasons. First, virtually everything that is done in a business depends on some type of technology, and neither managers nor employees can do their jobs successfully without it. Second, technology is evolving at an extremely rapid pace. In your future career you will undoubtedly encounter more than one "technology revolution" that will drastically change how you work and require you to learn new skills. Finally, from an organizational perspective, technological innovation in goods, services, manufacturing, and service delivery is a competitive necessity. Jack Welch, retired CEO of GE, for example, pushed GE to become a leader among traditional old-economy companies in embracing the Internet after noticing his wife Christmas shopping on the web. "I realized that if I didn't watch it, I would retire as a Neanderthal," he was reported as saying, "So I just started reading everything I could about it." He began by pairing 1,000 web-savvy mentors with senior people to get his top teams up to Internet speed quickly.[3]

Although technology can be a blessing, it is not without problems. The risks that users of steam engines encountered in the first episode have been replaced by the frustrations of the digital age, as the second episode illustrates. Such problems are increasingly prevalent because technology often shifts the burden of production and service onto consumers, as we see in the second episode. Self-service activities, such as printing digital photos, require that customers do things right and accurately follow instructions. Minimizing the potential for such errors can be the result of effective operations management in product design and development of processes and user interfaces. For example, manufacturers might improve written instructions or the store's photo lab might offer training for customers on digital photo technology. Even when the technology itself is "bulletproof," users can easily make mistakes if it is new and unfamiliar.

To improve such critical performance measures as time, productivity, flexibility, cost, and quality, new technologies must be developed and integrated into existing goods, services, and operations. Innovations in technology will continue to develop at an increasingly faster pace. As suggested in the third episode, breakthrough technologies such as RFID tags that enhance the ability to electronically track goods through the supply chain require learning and new ways of managing. Therefore, the role of operations management in business must continually adapt to such technologies in order to improve business process effectiveness, lower cost, and provide greater customer value.

Today, the "Age of Integration" challenges managers to decide how best to combine goods, services, and technology. In this chapter, we examine different types of technology and their role in the value chain and operations management.

UNDERSTANDING TECHNOLOGY IN OPERATIONS

Learning Objective
To gain a basic understanding of different types of technology and their role in manufacturing and service operations.

We may categorize technology into two basic groups. **Hard technology** *refers to equipment and devices that perform a variety of tasks in the creation and delivery of goods and services.* Some examples of hard technology are computers, computer chips and microprocessors, optical switches and communication lines, satellites, sensors, robots, automated machines, and bar-code scanners. **Soft technology** *refers to the application of the Internet, computer software, and information systems to provide data, information, and analysis and to facilitate the accomplishment of creating and delivering goods and services.* Some examples are database systems, artificial intelligence programs, and voice-recognition software. Both types are essential to modern organizations.

Before the Industrial Revolution, manufacturing tasks such as weaving cloth or forging and bending metal were highly labor-intensive. As the Industrial Revolution progressed, basic machines such as lathes and drill presses provided more of the power for manufacturing, but workers retained much of the control of the process. The development of microprocessors paved the way for automated systems, which are continually becoming increasingly sophisticated and complex and now provide both the power and control to perform highly complex tasks with extreme precision. For instance, BMW's Dingolfing plant, 100 kilometers east of Munich, is the company's biggest production facility, employing 21,000 people who can produce up to 280,000 vehicles per year.[4] In gearing up for production of the new 7 Series in 2001, BMW invested around $2 billion in capital equipment. Among its features are a $40 million vacuum transfer press that can make a complex side panel from one single piece of sheet steel, the world's first in-line measuring equipment that can check 100% of the dimensions during the production process, and an innovative rotational dipping system to pretreat the steel and aluminum body

Hard technology refers to equipment and devices that perform a variety of tasks in the creation and delivery of goods and services.

Soft technology refers to the application of the Internet, computer software, and information systems to provide data, information, and analysis and to facilitate the accomplishment of creating and delivering goods and services.

that allows the body cavities to be flooded and emptied much better than prior technology.

Information technology also provides the ability to integrate all parts of the value chain through better management of data and information, leading to more effective strategic and operational decisions to design better customer benefit packages that support customers' wants and needs, achieve competitive priorities, and improve the design and operation of all processes in the value chain. For example, many companies have replaced paper instructions on the shop floor with computers that enable production workers to retrieve assembly instructions, current drawings, and other information whenever necessary. At Hewlett-Packard's personal computer business, virtually every computer is customized to the buyer's specifications. Computers are only partially assembled when they arrive at HP's Roseville, California, distribution center. Employees on the final assembly line, who cannot possibly be trained to assemble the myriad of combinations of modems, CPUs, and other components, use bar-code scanners as each computer comes down the assembly line. Scanning brings up detailed directions and diagrams for assembling the particular unit on a video screen in front of the worker. Procter & Gamble is leveraging the Internet to focus on consumers, suppliers, customers, and employees. Customers are using the corporate web site, www.pg.com, extensively; in one month alone in 2003 1.87 million hits were logged. Suppliers now automate their ordering processes, and employees access all of their benefit and job-related information on their internal web site.

As another example, Invensys Software Systems developed an approach called dynamic performance measures (DPM) that warns when machines are losing money for the company.[5] DPM comes with an airplanelike dashboard with dials on which yellow arrows, moving among green, gray, and red zones, indicate whether consumption of a chemical or another ingredient is within limits, borderline, or excessive. Using software linked to manufacturing process sensors that measure process flows, fluid levels, temperatures, pressures, and other variables, beeps and flashing lights alert an operator when a batch of chemicals is mixed in an improper proportion or too much energy is used in a process. The operator is able to control the economics of production in real time, making adjustments as needed. This technique was first applied in the 1990s and is catching on fast in process industries such as petroleum refining, pulp and paper, glassmaking, and pharmaceuticals. Dynegy Midstream Services reduced operating expenses by $58 million and maintenance costs by $7 million in the first year.

Both goods-producing and service-providing organizations use a combination of hard and soft technology in their operating systems to create value for customers. The ways in which people can use hard and soft technologies are limited only by one's imagination. The OM Spotlight on the Cincinnati Water Works is a good example of how both hard and soft technology are integrated throughout the value chain. Another lesson from the Cincinnati Water Works is that even a basic utility service is now a high-tech business. In the following sections, we provide an overview of the scope of technology in modern manufacturing and service systems.

Manufacturing Technology Tours

Although high-tech, automated, manufacturing processes receive a lot of media attention, much of the technology used in small- and medium-sized manufacturing enterprises around the world is still quite basic. To gain a better understanding of how technology is used and integrated into manufacturing operations, we will contrast the technology used in making two different types of products: jigsaw puzzles and machined motorcycle gears in a "plant tour" atmosphere. This will also

OM SPOTLIGHT

Cincinnati Water Works

The Cincinnati Water Works (CWW) serves approximately 1 million customers. CWW enhances its value chain through a variety of technology applications. Its billing system allows customer service representatives (CSRs) to retrieve information from customer accounts quickly using almost any piece of data such as customer name, address, phone number, Social Security number, and so on. Besides a customer's account history, the system contains everything that was said in a call, including documentation of past problems and their resolution. An integrated voice-response system provides automated phone support for bill paying and account balances, tells customers of the approximate wait time to speak to a CSR, and allows the customers to leave a message for a CSR to return a call. An information board in the department shows the number of customers waiting, average length of time waiting, and the number of CSRs that are busy and doing post–call work.

A pop-up screen provides CSRs with customer data before the phone rings so that the CSR will have the customer's information before even saying hello. Work orders taken by CSRs, such as a broken water main or leaking meter, are routed automatically to a field service supervisor for immediate attention. This system is also used internally to allocate maintenance workers when a problem arises at a pumping station or treatment facility. A geographic information system is used for mapping the locations of water mains and fire hydrants and provides field service employees, meter readers, and contractors exact information to accomplish their work. Handheld meter readers are used to locate meters and download data into computers. Touch-pad devices provide exterior connections to inside meters, eliminating the necessity to enter a house or building. CWW is also investigating automated meter readers and radio frequency devices that simply require a company van to drive by the building to automatically obtain readings.

help you to better understand key issues in manufacturing process design, which we discuss in Chapter 7.

MAKING JIGSAW PUZZLES

Drescher Paper Box in Buffalo, New York, formed in 1867, manufactures high-quality laminated cardboard jigsaw puzzles and board games and assembles them for retail stores. Drescher also produces cotton-filled jewelry boxes, candy boxes, business card boxes, and custom-made industrial boxes. Manufacturing jigsaw puzzles consists of three major steps: making the puzzle pieces, making the puzzle boxes, and final assembly. A printed picture is cut to size and laminated on a thick puzzleboard backing. Large presses are used to cut the puzzle into pieces, which are then bagged. The box-making process begins with blank cardboard. Boxes are scored and cut, then laminated with printed graphics. In the final assembly process, the puzzles are boxed and shrink-wrapped for shipment. Exhibit 5.1 illustrates the process.

From an operations perspective, it is interesting to note that Drescher decided to make its own boxes when this process might have been outsourced. Also, it is clearly economical to produce a particular puzzle in a batch to avoid expensive changeover and setup costs between different puzzle types. Can you explain how break-even analysis might be used in this decision?

MANUFACTURING MOTORCYCLE TRANSMISSION GEARS

Andrews Products is in the 26th year of making aftermarket transmission gears for Harley-Davidson motorcycles and was the original manufacturer of close-ratio gears

Exhibit 5.1 Production Process for Jigsaw Puzzle Making

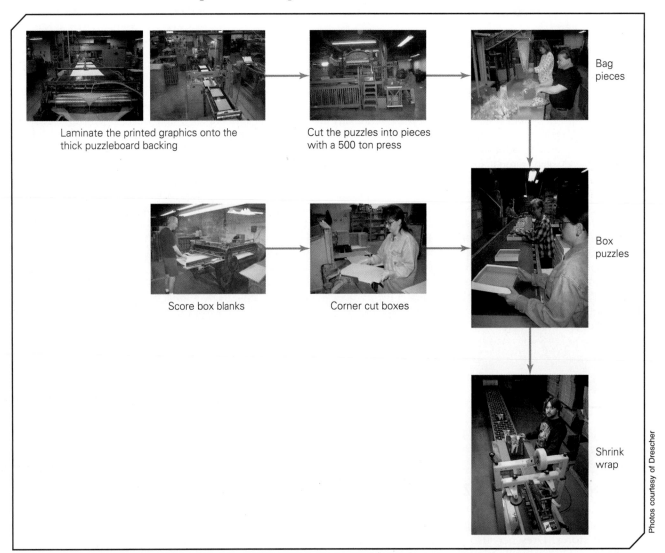

Laminate the printed graphics onto the thick puzzleboard backing

Cut the puzzles into pieces with a 500 ton press

Bag pieces

Score box blanks

Corner cut boxes

Box puzzles

Shrink wrap

Photos courtesy of Drescher

for big, twin, four-speed gearboxes in 1972. Exhibit 5.2 shows some of the technology used in the manufacturing operations. The first step for manufacturing some of their gears and cams is to cut steel slugs on a Mazak Multiplex twin-spindle machining center. These cut steel slugs are loaded using an automatic pallet changer and are machined complete in one setup. Finished parts are then automatically unloaded. This machine can operate unattended for hours at a time.

After parts have been machined on lathes, secondary operations such as keyways, drive slots, and lugs are cut with CNC vertical machining centers using such technology as a Matsuura automatic pallet changer. Final operations on these machines include a self-contained computerized inspection of slots and lugs. Pallet changes take 5 seconds. Additional steps in gear manufacture require cutting teeth on a Mitsubishi GS15 CNC gear shaper. A number of other computer-controlled gear machines are also used by Andrews Products to produce gearteeth for a variety of transmission gears.

Grinding is one of the last steps in gear or cam manufacture. A Toyoda GC32 CNC angle-head grinder is used to grind a Sportster cam gear thrust face and bearing

Exhibit 5.2 Examples of Machining Technology

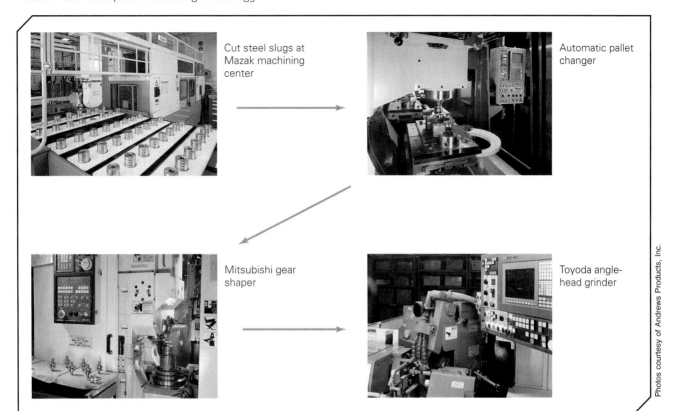

Cut steel slugs at Mazak machining center

Automatic pallet changer

Mitsubishi gear shaper

Toyoda angle-head grinder

Photos courtesy of Andrews Products, Inc.

diameter. CNC angle-head machines can grind multiple diameters in one setup and hold tolerances of 0.0003 inches (0.0076 mm) on a diameter.

Clearly, there are worlds of differences in the technology used for making puzzles and gears. Many manufacturing industries also use specialized technology. For example, to make printed circuit boards, companies use exotic-sounding processes such as vacuum lamination to bond multiple circuit boards together and surface mount technology to assemble and solder components to boards. However, from an operations management standpoint, all organizations face common issues regarding technology:

- The right technology must be selected for the goods that are produced.
- Process resources such as machines and employees must be set up and configured in a logical fashion to support production efficiency.
- Labor must be trained to operate the equipment.
- Process performance must be continually improved.
- Work must be scheduled to meet shipping commitments/customer promise dates.
- Quality must be ensured.

We will address all of these issues in subsequent chapters.

Service Technology

As we noted in Chapter 1, the vast majority of jobs in the U.S. economy are in service industries. Moreover, about 73 percent of the U.S. Gross Domestic Product is derived from services and 45 percent of an average U.S. family's budget buys services.[6] Therefore, you can easily see the profit potential of applying technology to services and have undoubtedly encountered quite a bit of service technology in your own daily lives. For instance, you have probably used an automatic teller machine (ATM) or placed an order on the Internet. Other service technologies are used behind the scenes to facilitate your experience as a customer of hotels, airlines, hospitals, and retail stores. To speed order entry for pizza delivery, for instance, many firms use a touch-sensitive computer screen that is linked to a customer database. When a repeat customer calls, the employee need only ask for the customer's phone number to bring up the customer's name, address, and delivery directions (for a new customer, the information need only be entered once). The employee would be able to address the customer immediately by name, enhancing the perception of service quality, and then enter the specific combination of toppings quickly on the touch-sensitive screen to print the order for pizza preparation, eliminating errors due to misreading of handwritten orders.

Airlines have automated many parts of the customer service experience using such technology as self-service kiosks, online check-in and boarding-pass printouts, and expanded monitors at the gates. Northwest Airlines, for example, has installed 755 kiosks at 188 airport locations since 1997. Almost two-thirds of its customers use them today, and on average, one kiosk has the capacity to replace 2.5 airline counter employees.[7] These enhancements are designed not only to improve service but to reduce costs of direct labor for a struggling industry. Pier 1 Imports uses software to ensure that no matter how a customer contacts the company—by phone, web, e-mail, or in person—it has easy access to any information about that customer. As *Fortune* magazine notes, the goal is "no surprises, no disappointments, and a customer for life."[8]

Robots, which have typically been associated with manufacturing, have found application in many areas of services, including courier and mail delivery, surgery, delivery of medical records within hospitals, fire fighting, floor cleaning, gasoline pumping, and entertainment.[9] Examples of hard and soft technology in a variety of service industries are listed in Exhibit 5.3.

E-service refers to using the Internet and technology to provide services that create and deliver time, place, information, entertainment, and exchange value to customers and/or support the sale of goods.

E-service *refers to using the Internet and technology to provide services that create and deliver time, place, information, entertainment, and exchange value to customers and/or support the sale of goods.* Companies like GE Plastics and Sotheby's use online e-service auctions to facilitate the sale of their physical goods. Many individuals use airline, hotel, and rental car web sites or "one-stop" e-services like Microsoft Expedia in planning a vacation. Other e-services such as language translation and weather information e-services provide added value. A web site or personal computer is not necessary to participate in e-services, because many other technologies—handheld PDAs, cell phones, and global positioning devices—allow customers to interact with web-based services almost anywhere and at any time. E-services might also have a temporary existence, for example, one that is focused on a specific crisis or event, such as a concert or flood disaster relief program.

Sometimes the impact of technology is unexpected. For example, nearly two-thirds of people who need psychological therapy never go to a therapist because of financial, personal, or logistical reasons.[11] One type of e-service, "e-therapy," provides anonymity as well as convenience. "You pound out an e-mail at 2 A.M. and get a reply from your therapist the next day," said Mr. John Grohol, a Boston psychologist and researcher.

Service Technology Tours

We continue with the "tour" format to introduce you to some service technology examples. The first service tour is an example of technology at work in the banking

Service Industry	Examples
Financial Services	Electronic funds transfer and e-bills Automatic teller machines Online stock trading and mortgage services Automated check-processing sorter
Utility/Government Services	Automated one-person garbage trucks Online real estate valuation and tax information Online libraries Optical mail scanners
Retail/Wholesale Services	Virtual tours of real estate offerings Supermarket's automated self-checkout and smart carts Automatic car washing system Web video cameras (webcams) in automobile dealer service bays Auto-call distribution systems
Health Care	CAT scanners Wireless web medical doctor systems Fetal monitors e-therapy medical services Digital imaging technology from remote sites Pacemakers
Education Services	Online degree-granting universities (and courses) e-books, CD-books, and e-learning Online motorist traffic schools Sports-based web games and leagues
Transportation	Vehicle global positioning services Wireless handheld inventory tracking devices RFID tags for location and inventory control Autopilot for aircraft and the Space Shuttle E-ZPass transponders and systems for highway toll booths

Exhibit 5.3
Examples of Service Technology[10]

industry. Next we discuss applications of information technology in health care. Finally, we examine the impact of technology on the transportation industry by taking a tour of United Parcel Service (UPS). Here, the software and hardware support service management skills.

TECHNOLOGY IN FINANCIAL SERVICES

Technology has been used extensively in financial services to facilitate the large number of transactions and processing activities that must occur each day. For example, massive paper-check sorting machines have been used for a long time to process approximately 70 billion paper checks written per year in the United States. The life cycle cost of printing, handling, and collecting paper checks ranges from $0.75 to $3.00 per check because of such variables as researching returned checks, sorting, printer supplies, postage, and stop payments.

Today, the ubiquitous paper checks are being replaced by electronic versions. **Electronic checks, or eChecks,** *are electronic versions of a paper check, including date, payee name, dollar amount, electronic signature, memo line, and endorsements.* An eCheckBook is like a credit or debit card except it contains a vast amount of information plus encryption tools, utilities to lock and unlock software, blank forms in electronic formats, and so on. To "sign" an eCheck, the payer enters a PIN number to unlock an encrypted and secure electronic "signature." Digital signatures are not digitized versions of a handwritten signature. Rather,

Electronic checks, or eChecks, are electronic versions of a paper check, including date, payee name, dollar amount, electronic signature, memo line, and endorsements.

Courtesy of eCheck Initiative www.echeck.org

they are mathematical calculations that provide a unique ability to identify the creator of the signature and the specific document that was signed. Exhibit 5.4 summarizes the electronic check process.

Digital technology drives the processing of eChecks. Every step in the traditional paper-based check system has a digital equivalent. The payer writes an eCheck by creating an electronic document with the required information and cryptographically signs it. The payee receives the eCheck via e-mail, verifies the payer's electronic signature, endorses the eCheck, writes out an electronic deposit slip, and signs the deposit. The payee's bank verifies the payer and payee's signatures, credits the payee's account, and forwards the check for clearing and settlement. The payer's bank verifies the payer's signature and debits the payer's account.

Electronic check systems significantly reduce operating costs; the life cycle cost of an eCheck transaction is expected to be only a few cents. In addition, the extensive security system reduces fraud losses, and the huge space requirements for the machines that sort paper checks are no longer necessary.

Digital technology is also used by JP Morgan Chase Bank investment group, which provides portfolio management, market research, and trading execution. The Cash Movement (CM) operating unit is responsible for transferring money for investment group customers. For example, a customer will sell stock and request that cash funds are sent to another institution such as a mutual fund, credit union, or another bank. Cash Movement processes billions of dollars daily through wires, checks, and Automated Clearing House (ACH) transactions. The cash movement process is an intense information-processing factory. The basic process workflow

Exhibit 5.4 The Electronic Check Process

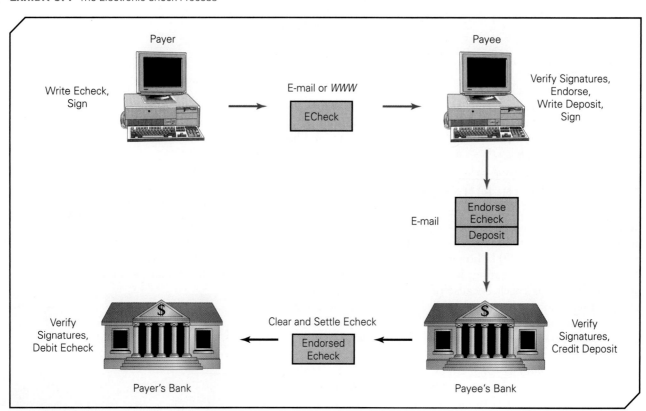

Source: M. M. Anderson, "The Electronic Check Architecture," Financial Services Technology Consortium, 1998 (http://www.echeck.org/library/wp/index.html).

is documented in Exhibit 5.5. In fact, there are about 50 more detailed process steps and checks, most of which are automated. All requested transactions are logged in the computer system and then batched for accounting and quality control purposes. Specific computer checks are made for missing and inconsistent data, and if everything is correct, the transaction is released for electronic processing. If not, the transaction is kicked out of the system for employee review and if approved, is released for electronic processing. Once the transaction is completed, it is verified, accounts are balanced, and daily reports generated.

INFORMATION TECHNOLOGY IN HEALTH CARE

To ensure quality yet dramatically reduce costs, hospitals and health care clinics are adopting electronic medical record (EMR) systems. EMR systems record all the information generated by the health care facility and its patients in electronic form. Instead of a paper-based medical chart for each patient, the doctor uses a wireless PDA or tablet PC. Some wireless EMR tablets allow the doctor to write on the tablet; others restrict the doctor to checking boxes. The EMR tablet allows both. EMR information also is easily integrated with other health care facility information systems such as billing, patient scheduling, and accounting.

The benefits of an EMR system include cost reduction, revenue enhancement, improved administrative and support process efficiency, and improved clinical efficiency and patient care. Let us examine how EMR systems accomplish these objectives.

- *Cost Reduction* The cost to photocopy medical documents requested by attorneys, insurance companies, patients, and doctors is high. Retrieval and filing of the paper-based patient charts is also a very labor-intensive task. Moreover, if a nurse or doctor has the patient's chart, then the administrative staff cannot. Electronic transmission of these documents translates directly into labor savings and reduced copying costs. With good information technology, file cabinets and associated storage space are no longer required and the patient's information is instantly available to all who need it. Medical transcriptionists spend more time transcribing and less time searching for, assembling, reassembling, and filing medical charts. At one medical clinic, transcription costs were reduced by 33 percent and transcription turnaround time went from 7 to 1 day. EMR systems also reduce the opportunities for errors and therefore improve clinical and administrative error rates. Pharmacy errors and costs are also reduced. These improvements tend to reduce malpractice insurance rates by about 5 percent.
- *Revenue Enhancement* EMR systems remind doctors, nurses, pharmacists, and patients to renew medication, schedule office visits, and so on. One Health

Exhibit 5.5 JP Morgan Chase Bank's Cash Movement Process

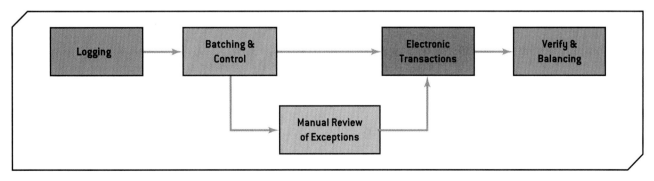

Maintenance Organization (HMO) contacted over 600 patients using the Internet that were overdue for mammograms, resulting in services that generated $670,000 in additional revenue. The benefit of an EMR system is also measured by the number of patients doctors see per day. One clinic reports the doctors see 10 to 15 percent more patients per day when using EMR.

- *Improved Administrative and Support Process Efficiency* In one medical clinic, one full-time employee filed 600 to 700 patient charts per week. With the installation of EMR, these same medical records could be downloaded in 10 minutes. Universal access to medical charts and speed of service are two other benefits of EMR. One hospital reports that when state medical auditors visited, they sat down in front of a personal computer and did their work. EMR systems are more likely to pass medical audits. Billing, pharmacy, and other support services report fewer telephone callbacks due to EMR information.

- *Improved Clinical Efficiency and Patient Care* An EMR system helps to standardize chart quality across the clinic or hospital and therefore minimize the problems that result from poor handwriting and other inconsistencies in paper-based systems. Another benefit is that EMR diagnosis-specific templates can help guide the medical staff and make sure they follow all medical protocols and tests. Graphical representations of trends in blood chemistry or pressure can also be shown to the patient during the medical service encounters. Drug and allergy interactions are also checked by redundant software in the EMR system. Drug recalls are easily communicated to everyone, and doctors can quickly query the database with their tablet PCs.

TECHNOLOGY AT UNITED PARCEL SERVICE[12]

United Parcel Service (UPS) has been in business since 1907. The company has embraced technology to achieve its mission, beginning with its first Model-T Ford in 1913, to consolidate packages for deliveries. In 1924, UPS debuted another of the technological innovations that would shape its future: the first conveyor belt system for handling packages.

In 1929, UPS became the first package delivery company to provide air service via privately operated airlines, which, however, was suspended because of economic problems resulting from the Great Depression. Air operations were resumed in 1953. In 1988, UPS received authorization from the Federal Aviation Administration (FAA) to operate its own aircraft, thereby officially becoming an airline. Recruiting the best people available, UPS merged a number of cultures and procedures into a seamless operation called UPS Airlines.

UPS Airlines was the fastest-growing airline in FAA history, formed in little more than 1 year with all the necessary technology and support systems. Today, UPS Airlines is one of the ten largest airlines in the United States. UPS Airlines features some of the most advanced information systems in the world, like the Computerized Operations Monitoring, Planning and Scheduling System (COMPASS), which provides information for flight planning, scheduling, and load handling. The system, which can be used to plan optimum flight schedules up to 6 years in advance, is unique in the industry.

By 1993, UPS was delivering 11.5 million packages and documents a day for more than 1 million regular customers. With such a huge volume, UPS had to develop new technology to maintain efficiency, keep prices competitive, and provide new customer services. Technology at UPS spans an incredible range, from small handheld devices, to specially designed package delivery vehicles, to global computer and communications systems.

The handheld Delivery Information Acquisition Device (DIAD), carried by every UPS driver, was developed to immediately record and upload delivery information to the UPS network. The DIAD information even includes digital pictures of a recipient's signature, thus giving customers real-time information about their shipments. This proprietary device also allows drivers to stay in constant contact with their headquarters, keeping abreast of changing pickup schedules, traffic patterns, and other important messages.

At the other end of the spectrum, UPSnet is a global electronic data communications network that provides an information-processing pipeline for international package processing and delivery. UPSnet uses more than 500,000 miles of communications lines and a dedicated satellite to link more than 1,300 UPS distribution sites in 46 countries. The system tracks 821,000 packages daily. Between 1986 and 1991, UPS spent U.S.$1.5 billion on technology improvements and plans to spend an additional U.S.$3.2 billion over the next 5 years. These improvements are aimed at increasing efficiency and expanding customer service.

In 1992, UPS began tracking all ground packages. In 1994, UPS.com went live, and consumer demand for information about packages in transit soared. The following year, UPS added functionality to its web site that allowed customers to track packages in transport. The resulting popularity of online package tracking exceeded all expectations. Today, UPS.com receives millions of online tracking requests daily.

By the late 1990s, UPS was in the midst of another transition. Although the core of the business remained the distribution of goods and the information that accompanies them, UPS had begun to branch out and focus on a new channel, services. As UPS management saw it, the company's expertise in shipping and tracking positioned it to become an enabler of global commerce and a facilitator of the three flows that make up commerce: goods, information, and capital. To fulfill this vision of new service offerings, UPS began strategically acquiring existing companies and creating new kinds of companies that did not previously exist. Over the course of its history, UPS has become an expert in global distribution. At UPS, global distribution involves managing not only the movement of goods but also the flow of information and finance that moves with the goods.

UPS customers have increasingly tapped into this expertise, which ultimately led to the formation of UPS Supply Chain Solutions. UPS Supply Chain Solutions is a streamlined organization that provides logistics, global freight, financial services, mail services, and consulting to enhance customers' business performance and improve their global supply chains. UPS Supply Chain Solutions are delivered by UPS Capital, UPS Logistics Group, UPS Freight Services, UPS Mail Innovations, and UPS Consulting.

Both manufacturing and service technology affect all the key competitive priorities we have discussed—cost, time, quality, flexibility, and innovation. Of course, implementing any modern technology requires good analysis and the abolishment of many traditional modes of operation, which can lead to organizational problems and resistance. Thus, operations managers need to be sensitive to the human and organizational issues that accompany technological change.

TECHNOLOGY IN VALUE CHAINS

Learning Objective
To understand how manufacturing and service technology is changing the role of business relationships and strengthening the value chain.

Although technology is vital to individual manufacturing and service operations, it is playing an increasingly important role across the entire value chain. In Chapter 2 we described two views of the value chain: the input/output model in Exhibit 2.1, and the pre- and postservice model in Exhibit 2.3. These characterizations of the value chain are found among the three major types of business relationships:

1. **B2B**—*business to business,*
2. **B2C**—*business to customer,* and
3. **C2C**—*customer to customer.*

Technology, especially the Internet and e-communications, is changing the operation, speed, and efficiency of the value chain and presents many new challenges to operations managers. In many situations, electronic transaction capability allows all parts of the value chain to immediately know and react to changes in demand and supply. This requires tighter integration of many of the components of the value chain. In some cases, technology provides the capability to eliminate parts of the traditional value chain structure and streamline operations.

Historically, value chains required numerous intermediaries such as suppliers, claims offices, warehouses, call centers, distributors, billers, and transportation firms to accomplish the objectives of providing quality and timely goods and services to customers. They facilitated the transactions between sellers and buyers in the value chain and performed tasks like order taking, order fulfillment, information and consulting exchange, financing, packaging, gift wrapping, shipping and delivery, billing, customer profile analysis, claims processing, auctions, and customer contact centers. These intermediaries most often represented brick-and-mortar resources such as buildings, people, equipment, and vehicles. Without an effective way to link these value chain players together, inventories of goods and delivery times were unpredictable and erratic. As each value chain player operated independently, the system suffered. Information sharing was virtually nonexistent, communication was slow, errors were frequent, and paper-based costs were high, requiring multiple handoffs and interfaces along the value chain. Although cost, time, flexibility, and quality trade-offs were always present, value chain managers typically focused on one performance criteria at the expense of the others.

In the mid-1990s, the Internet provided a means to better share information and enhance communication in ways unheard of previously. Electronic communications promise speed, convenience, instantaneous response-oriented services, and boundaryless global markets. Players throughout the value chain now command the virtual world of e-business, e-integration, e-procurement, e-service, e-engineering, e-marketing, and e-commerce. Along with a host of other types of technology solutions—for example, RFID chips and wireless—a new perspective and capability for the value chain has emerged—the *e-commerce view of the value chain*, shown in Exhibit 5.6. Here, buyers and sellers are connected by bricks-and-mortar intermediaries such as logistic and transportation services and/or by electronic means such as the Internet to share information directly. *An* intermediary *is any entity—real or virtual—that coordinates and shares information between buyers and sellers.* Some firms such as General Electric, Wal-Mart and Procter & Gamble use

An intermediary is any entity—real or virtual—that coordinates and shares information between buyers and sellers.

Exhibit 5.6
E-Commerce View of the Value Chain

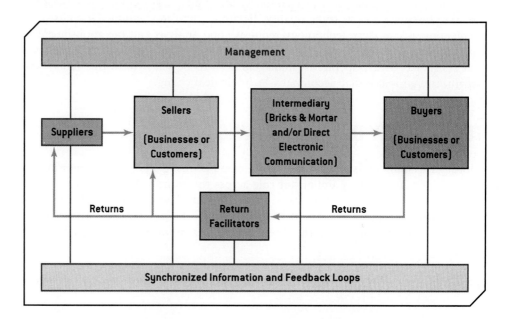

e-commerce to communicate directly with suppliers and retail stores, and thereby skip traditional bricks-and-mortar intermediaries. **Return facilitators** *specialize in handling all aspects of customers' returning a manufactured good or delivered service and requesting their money back, repairing the manufactured good and returning it to the customer, and/or invoking the service guarantee.*

Examples of e-commerce players are shown in Exhibit 5.7. If you examine a few of these web sites, you can better understand how Internet capabilities have changed the way work is accomplished, how e-services complement the sale of goods, and vice versa, and how e-commerce is restructuring entire industries and creating new ones.

Some examples of how information technology has enabled companies to build and sustain competitive advantage in a B2B, B2C, or C2C context follow.

- GE Plastics (www.geplastics.com) used the Internet to completely change how plastics are designed, ordered, researched, and delivered for B2B customers. The entire GE Plastics web site represents a value-added, information-intensive set of services—e-services—that facilitate the sale of goods—chemicals, plastics, resins, polymers, and the like. The web site has been the portal for companies to buy materials for Motorola and Nokia's cell phones, Volkswagen's instrument panels and fenders, Gillette's razors, 3Com's Palm handheld devices, Iomega ZIP drives, and Xerox copiers. GE Polymerland (www.gepolymerland.com) allows other companies to buy, design, interact, research, and participate in a global auction service for many types of chemicals and plastics. The "buy" button reveals many value-added services, such as how to place an order, order status, shipment tracking, pricing, and inventory availability. A number of Order Wizards are available to help customers evaluate chemical compatibility, color specifications, and buy options. And if all else fails, the web site gives the customer the option to talk to a live engineer about the specifics of the application.
- FedEx (www.fedex.com) is testing wireless technologies to enable couriers to send and retrieve real-time package information from handheld devices without having to run back and forth to delivery trucks. "Our focus is on developing an interactive intelligent device that moves shipping information to the courier when they're right in front of the customer," says Ken Pasley, head of wireless systems development for Federal Express.[13] "We're moving the edge of our network from the delivery van to our customer's front door!" The FedEx B2C value chain is all about saving time. Every day, over 5 million messages are sent to 40,000 FedEx delivery trucks via public cellular networks or aging FedEx proprietary satellite and repeater systems in major cities. The former communication channel is expensive and breaks down frequently, and the latter requires the driver to call an 800 telephone number or go back to the van to download the information in his or her "SuperTracker" device before uploading it to the operations center in Memphis, Tennessee. The driver frequently returns to the van only to be notified of another pickup in the building, and therefore must go back into the building, making many trips between the van and building. The current FedEx information system does not allow for up-to-date wireless

Return facilitators specialize in handling all aspects of customers, returning a manufactured good or delivered service and requesting their money back, repairing the manufactured good and returning it to the customer, and/or invoking the service guarantee.

Exhibit 5.7
Example e-Commerce Value Chain Players

Bricks-and-Mortar and Electronic-Based Integrators (Intermediary)	Business-to-Business (B2B) Sellers and Buyers	Business-to-Customer (B2C) Sellers and Buyers	Customer-to-Customer (C2C) Sellers and Buyers
ups.com	gepolymerland.com	dell.com	ebay.com
Solectron.com	transora.com	travelocity.com	sothebys.com
Fedex.com	procurenet.com	walmart.com	stamps.com
automation.rockwell.com	fansteel.com	priceline.com	ubid.com
npi.com	resellerratings.com	staples.com	Sportsline.com
bookmasters.com	olin.com	amazon.com	CDNow.com

communication with customers, and therefore results in telephone callbacks and repetitive and duplicate trips that decrease courier productivity. Wireless technology can improve the quality of the interaction (service encounters) between the driver and customer, cross-selling of services, and driver and fleet productivity (pickups/day/courier or pickups/day/van or revenue/pickup/courier).

- eBay (www.ebay.com) started out as a C2C value chain but quickly incorporated B2C and B2B transactions. The eBay business is built on the values of open communication and honesty, and the vast majority of buyers and sellers at eBay are reliable. eBay fights fraud using customer feedback that keeps track of the trustworthiness of its sellers using a point system and posts this information for all site members to see, as well as its own security monitoring processes. In the event a customer pays for an item and never receives it, eBay will reimburse buyers up to a dollar limit, minus processing costs. eBay Motors also provides additional insurance on the purchase of passenger vehicles. The eBay Store also allows the sellers to build their reputation and expertise by creating an About Me page and defining a Store Policies page. Customers can also cross-sell items with bricks-and-mortar stores. eBay provides a variety of services such as on-line seminars and interactive tutorials to help customers learn how to buy and sell on the web site, how to search for goods or services on eBay, how to add photos of your goods or services, design store fronts and marketing, and so on.

E-commerce is not simply a web-based system on the Internet, a common misunderstanding of the public and the media. The Internet is an enabler of e-commerce, but to be successful e-commerce requires a host of other resources and knowledge, such as good process and system design, quality and control checkpoints, and good day-to-day execution. In short, e-commerce requires effective operations management decisions and skills.

Business Intelligence Systems in Value Chains

The timely analysis of data is vital to the operation of today's value chains and to achieving competitive advantage. Significant improvements in information technology helps organizations collect massive amounts of data and then analyze them to better understand their customers, market segments, suppliers, third-party integrators, and operations and make decisions that reduce costs, speed time-to-market, and increase revenue.

However, much of the data that companies have are scattered about in databases in different legacy business systems. Systems are needed to help companies access, analyze, and use data they collect. **Business intelligence systems (BIS)** *consolidate data from across the organization and allow companies to integrate information into a common database for easy access and analysis* (see the OM Spotlight on Schneider National).[14] For example, the global communications company Sprint needed to be able to gather all the data about customers in its multiple data sources and analyze them to support sales and marketing efforts. Its BIS allowed it to track the effectiveness of campaigns to both attract and retain customers. Briggs & Stratton Corporation uses BIS to manage its manufacturing process without allowing the system to choke on the massive amounts of operational data it generates.

A **data warehouse** *is a large, specially designed database that allows employees to quickly conduct both historical and forward-looking analyses of business patterns.* Data warehouses consolidate information from different business processes such as accounting and marketing. A BIS also has the capability to extract key operational data and then "clean" them (called *data scrubbing*) to remove redundancies, fill in blank and missing data fields, and organize the data into consistent formats. All these data are then loaded into a relational database that analysts can dig into to identify and understand key performance relationships.

Business intelligence systems (BIS) consolidate data from across the organization and allow companies to integrate information into a common database for easy access and analysis.

A data warehouse is a large, specially designed database that allows employees to quickly conduct both historical and forward-looking analyses of business patterns.

OM SPOTLIGHT

Schneider National[15]

Schneider National is the biggest transportation and logistics company in North America, with such customers as Wal-Mart, BASF, and General Motors. Logistics and transportation are highly data-intensive; Schneider collects all kinds of documents—invoices, tracking paperwork, late-payment notices, delivery information, and accounting data every minute of every day across eight different databases. Sorting through the data to answer such questions as "why does it cost 20 cents per pound to deliver to a Ford dealership in Texas but only 17 cents to most other locations" was a painstaking process that involved special programming efforts and might take as long as a week, if the right information was found at all. Usually, the person who knew how to get the data and the person who used it were two different people. As a result, Schneider turned to BIS software for a solution. Using a software package called PowerPlay from Cognos, which takes records from the company's databases and arranges them into special information arrays called cubes (think of stacks of spreadsheets), a business analyst can drill down to find the answer to the Ford delivery question in about 10 minutes. Using the system, Schneider was able to track down reimbursements owed that had fallen through the cracks and had been impossible to collect in the past. This one application essentially paid for the system.

Many business intelligence systems incorporate **data mining**—*sophisticated statistical analysis tools and automated search algorithms such as neural networks to sift through large amounts of data to identify meaningful relationships.* U.S. West, for example, designed a data mining program to correlate data about home locations, U.S. West's trunk lines, switch capacity, and other variables to identify prospective customers. Other applications include identifying profitable customers and their demographic characteristics, prioritizing credit risk, and forecasting demand for better inventory management.

Data mining requires massive amounts of data storage space—several terabytes. A *terabyte* is 1 followed by 12 zeros. You need that to express the number of square inches in Rhode Island (4,872,996,000,000)! The capacity of data warehouse storage is beginning to increase from terabytes to petabytes—a 1 followed by 15 zeros. You need that number to express the size of Mexico in square inches (3,057,065,000,000,000)! Petabytes of data storage are needed to evaluate vast amounts of visual data, especially data from videocams located on the store, warehouse, or factory floor. For example, imagine cameras trained on the sales floor, recording the minute-by-minute flow of customer traffic and behaviors and feeding the data to a business intelligence system that analyzes the relative sales effectiveness of a given product placement or customer flow pattern or salesperson. This would allow a company to schedule and reallocate staff in real time to maximize revenue and customer service.

Proponents of business intelligence systems point to the following benefits:

- increased revenues by identifying customer interests and target market buying patterns to support cross- and up-selling,
- improved customer satisfaction by real-time tracking of customer orders and accounts,
- monitoring customer and employee store behavior and patterns to improve sales training, employee store assignments, product placement, and service encounters,
- reduced value chain costs by real-time tracking of operational and logistical metrics, and
- support for strategic decision-making by monitoring financial metrics and analyzing data to test new opportunities.

> **Data mining**—*sophisticated statistical analysis tools and automated search algorithms such as neural networks to sift through large amounts of data to identify meaningful relationships.*

In addition, business intelligence systems support the ability to understand critical relationships between internal and external performance measures that we described in Chapter 3.

INTEGRATED OPERATING SYSTEMS

An organization's processes cannot provide good customer service or efficient value chain performance without operating systems that integrate key processes and systems within the organization and share timely information with other players in the value chain. An integrated operating system (IOS) has four major characteristics:

1. *An IOS focus is on the main problem structure and processes of a specific industry, such as home insurance, airlines, family practice medical doctors, or automobile manufacturers.* For example, revenue management systems (RMS) for airlines and hotels focus on how to price perishable service capacity.
2. *An IOS addresses key decisions that need to be made to serve the customer in the best possible way.* For example, customer relationship management (CRM) systems focus on building long-term relationships with loyal customers to increase satisfaction and profits.
3. *An IOS involves the collection, storage, analysis, and dissemination of data and information via information technology to improve decision-making within the organization.* Data warehouses and data mining typically are integral parts of an IOS.
4. *An IOS is capable of making key decisions in a synchronous and timely way anywhere along the value chain.*

In the past, implementing an integrated operating system was a strategic option that senior managers debated and often slowly implemented in pieces. Today, implementing an integrated operating system is a strategic priority and the key to competitive advantage and long-term survival (see the OM Spotlight: Accounting at MetLife). IOSs are changing the world of global business by providing faster, better, and more customized goods and services at lower prices. In this section we briefly review five major types of integrated operating systems—supply chain management (SCM) systems, computer integrated manufacturing systems (CIMS), enterprise resource planning (ERP) systems, customer relationship management (CRM) systems, and revenue management systems (RMS), all of which rely heavily on technology to create and deliver goods and services. Nearly every manager will rely on at least one of these in their daily work.

Many of you will encounter IOSs in your jobs. For example, if you work in the marketing area, you will probably work extensively with customer relationship and revenue management systems. If you work in manufacturing, you will likely encounter CIMS. Nearly every business person will have some involvement in SCM and ERP. You may even be asked to select and help implement an IOS. Thus, having a strong knowledge of them along with the principles of OM to help manage and use them will certainly be valuable.

Supply Chain Management (SCM) Systems

Perhaps the most talked-about type of IOS in business today is the supply chain. As we noted in Chapter 2, supply chains differ from value chains in that a supply chain focuses mainly on material flows from suppliers through the production process, whereas a value chain encompasses all stages of manufacturing and services that are involved either directly or indirectly in satisfying customer expectations. Managing the material and information flows between and among the various

OM SPOTLIGHT

Accounting at MetLife[16]

MetLife was saddled with a plethora of disparate processes, systems, and legacy systems in the mid-1990s. The $32.5 billion financial services conglomerate served over 9 million customers and 64,000 institutions and other companies. In 1998, a new CEO, Robert H. Benmosche, challenged the company to become the "GE of the insurance industry" by integrating its processes and systems with the goal of creating a "single customer view." That is, when the customer contacts the company in any way, the MetLife service provider can see a customer's retirement accounts; health, auto, and home insurance policies; and any other services MetLife provides the customer on one computer screen anywhere in the organization and its geographically dispersed offices.

To do this, MetLife reengineered all of its processes starting with accounting processes such as the general ledger accounts. "There would be painful meetings where we would do account mapping," said Peggy Fechtmann, senior vice president and CIO of corporate systems. "So we went account by account and figured out how we were going to do it. We really had to reengineer the business processes. We were really trying to define a new model of how to do business," said Fechtmann.

MetLife looked at many system integrators such as Oracle, SAP, and PeopleSoft. Once it selected an integrator, the Information Technology Steering Committee allowed no more than a 5 percent customization of software code. Part of its ongoing system integration initiative has a 2-year payback with the goal of consolidating like systems onto common platforms and eliminating redundant processes, speeding up all processes, and greatly reducing operating cost. The MetLife corporate objective is to be completely integrated by 2007 and to become the "GE of the insurance industry."

stages in the supply chain to maximize total profitability is the objective of supply chain management. Stated simply, SCM focuses on producing the right product, in the right quantity, at the right time, in the right location, to the right customer, at the right price.

Many companies, such as Dell, have achieved phenomenal success with SCM (see the OM Spotlight on Dell). Adaptec reduced its lead time between ordering computer boards from its headquarters in Milpitas, California, and receiving them from its Singapore assembly plant from 105 to 55 days and cut its work-in-process inventory in half by better supply chain design and management. Lexmark can build customized printers, down to an order of one, with no loss of production time. Service companies also benefit. Florida Power and Light has partnered with Ryder Integrated Logistics to manage supplying electrical components like wire and transformers to rapidly restore service after natural disasters like hurricanes.

Just imagine the complexity of coordinating materials for a global organization like Ford Motor Company. Engines might be made in Mexico and Cleveland, transmissions in Germany, electronics in Thailand, interior trim and instrumentation in Canada and England, audio systems in Brazil, and brake systems in France and the United States. Effective coordination of physical and information flows requires a seamless integration of both hard and soft technology. This includes material handling systems for storing and retrieving materials quickly when they are needed in production and transportation vehicles and systems for moving materials within and between stages of the production process; information systems for order management, purchasing, production planning and control, and inventory management; and financial systems for billing customers and paying suppliers. Effective information technology, for example, allows suppliers to determine how many items their customers have on hand and how many they will need in the future, allowing them to better plan production and distribution.

IBM recently announced a strategic shift in its business plan by focusing even more on supply chain consulting and computer services.[17] In fact, it plans to shift

OM SPOTLIGHT

Supply Chain Management at Dell[18]

Dell has gone from having less than 1 percent market share in 1990 to 14 percent today. Dell has always competed on goods and service quality and design and demand flexibility. In the U.S. economic slowdown of the early 2000s, Michael Dell, the founder of Dell stated, "We've said it before and you're seeing it now—in a tough economic environment, the low-cost model is even more likely to win. Our direct model is what differentiates us and provides a structural competitive advantage, whether we're selling servers, storage products, personal computers, services, or, now, network switches. We understand better and react more quickly to customer needs, introducing new technology and passing along component cost declines almost immediately (to our customers). Talking daily with customers and having only five days' inventory is a huge advantage when inventory stifles innovation and profitability. Why don't others copy our model? That's a good question for our competitors, but the primary reason is that they're beholden to doing business through intermediaries. . . . More than ever, we're focused on customer benefit and delivering value to our customers, one element of which is price for performance. An advantage of how we do business is our operating costs are roughly half that of our competitors, yet we continue to earn the majority of industry profitability. . . . On-line tools are one area where we are simultaneously realizing efficiencies and increase in customer loyalty—approximately half our revenue is generated from the Web. We work continually to become even more efficient in how we manufacture our products. We partner with suppliers to help improve their inventory management, manufacturing processes, and overall supply chain."

Mr. Dick Hunter, Dell's vice president of supply chain management, reinforces Mr. Dell's strategy when he notes, "Material costs account for about 74 percent of our revenues. We spent about $21 billion on materials last year. Shaving 0.1 percent off can have a bigger impact than, say, improving manufacturing productivity by 10 percent. We carry about five days' worth of inventory. Our competitors carry 30, 45, or even 90 days' worth. We schedule every assembly line in every factory around the world every two hours. We typically run a factory with about five or six hours' worth of inventory on hand. This has decreased cycle time and reduced warehouse space—which we've replaced with more manufacturing lines. Our top 30 suppliers represent about 75 percent of our total costs. Throw in the next 20, and that comes to about 95 percent. We deal with all of those top 50 suppliers daily, many of them many times a day. We can alter price and product mixes in real time via Dell.com. Our competitors that are building products to sell via retail channels can't do that. Folks ask if five days inventory is the best Dell can do. Heck no, we can get to two!"

$1 billion for hard technology research and development to soft technology consulting services. Consulting and computer services make up nearly one-half of IBM's revenue. It formed a new operation called On Demand Innovation Services that will employ at least 200 research scientists and analysts. They plan to focus on supply chains and apply advanced mathematical models to do tasks such as scheduling vehicles, optimizing routes, building artificial-intelligence-based decision support systems and data warehouses, determining pricing, and enhancing organization communication. This strategic shift continues IBM's journey to reinvent itself in the global knowledge economy and marketplace. We will study supply management in more detail in Chapter 9.

Computer-Integrated Manufacturing Systems (CIMS)

Computer-integrated manufacturing systems (CIMS) *represent the union of hardware, software, database management, and communications to automate and control production activities from planning and design to manufacturing and distribution.* CIMS include many hard and soft technologies with a wide variety of acronyms, vendors, and applications and are essential to productivity and efficiency in modern manufacturing.

The roots of CIMS began with **numerical control (NC)** *machine tools, which enable the machinist's skills to be duplicated by a programmable device (originally punched paper tape) that controls the movements of a tool used to make complex*

Computer-integrated manufacturing systems (CIMS) *represent the union of hardware, software, database management, and communications to automate and control production activities from planning and design to manufacturing and distribution.*

Numerical control (NC) *machine tools enable the machinist's skills to be duplicated by a programmable device (originally punched paper tape) that controls the movements of a tool used to make complex shapes.*

shapes. For example, a part might require several holes of various sizes to be drilled. A NC drill press with an automatic tool changer would automatically position the part so that each hole is drilled in the proper order. While the part is being repositioned the tool is automatically changed when necessary. Upon completion, an operator removes the part and the machine sets up to begin a new part. The sequence of drilling is programmed so that a minimum time is required to perform all operations. The operator has only to load and unload parts and push a button to begin processing and thus can tend several NC machines at one work center. For **computer numerical control (CNC)** *machines, the operations are driven by a computer.*

Getty Images/PhotoDisc

Industrial robots were the next major advance in manufacturing automation. *A* **robot** *is a programmable machine designed to handle materials or tools in the performance of a variety of tasks.* Robots can be "taught" a large number of sequences of motions and operations and even to make certain logical decisions. Industrial robots were first introduced in 1954. In 1969, General Motors installed the first robot for spot-welding automobiles; robots now perform over 90 percent of the welds. Other typical applications are spray painting, machining, inspection, and material handling. Robots are especially useful for working with hazardous materials or heavy objects; for instance, in nuclear power plants robots are used to do work in highly radioactive areas. In services, robots help doctors complete tedious brain surgery by drilling very precise holes into the skull.

As computers and video capabilities improved, machine vision systems were developed to automatically receive and interpret an image of a real scene for purposes of obtaining information and/or controlling machines or processes. They are used for such tasks as sorting parts, assemblies, fruit, and packages by quantity, size, shape, color, or other characteristics; inspecting logs for knots and grain direction in the wood-products industry; locating parts for pickup or assembly from a moving conveyor; reading or verifying printed text or serial numbers, such as the date and lot code on pharmaceutical goods; finding defects in manufactured parts; and determining whether containers are properly filled.

Integrated manufacturing systems began to emerge with computer-aided design/computer-aided engineering (CAD/CAE) and computer-aided manufacturing (CAM) systems. **CAD/CAE** *enables engineers to design, analyze, test, simulate, and "manufacture" products before they physically exist, thus ensuring that a product can be manufactured to specifications when it is released to the shop floor.* Quality improves significantly, since the chances of machine operators entering the incorrect program are virtually eliminated. **CAM** *involves computer control of the manufacturing process, such as determining tool movements and cutting speeds.* CAM has advantages over conventional manufacturing approaches under many conditions, such as when

- several different parts with variable or cyclic demands are produced,
- frequent design changes are made,
- the manufacturing process is complex,
- there are multiple machining operations on one part, and
- expert operator skills and close control are required.

Each machine in a CAM system has the ability to select and manipulate a number of tools according to programmed instructions; thus, CAM provides a high degree of flexibility in performing and controlling manufacturing processes.

Flexible manufacturing systems (FMS) *consist of two or more computer-controlled machines or robots linked by automated handling devices such as transfer machines, conveyors, and transport systems. Computers direct the overall sequence of operations*

Computer numerical control (CNC) *machines are those for which operations are driven by a computer.*

A **robot** *is a programmable machine designed to handle materials or tools in the performance of a variety of tasks.*

CAD/CAE *enables engineers to design, analyze, test, simulate, and "manufacture" products before they physically exist, thus ensuring that a product can be manufactured to specifications when it is released to the shop floor.*

CAM *involves computer control of the manufacturing process, such as determining tool movements and cutting speeds.*

Flexible manufacturing systems (FMS) *consist of two or more computer-controlled machines or robots linked by automated handling devices such as transfer machines, conveyors, and transport systems.*

and route the work to the appropriate machine, select and load the proper tools, and control the operations performed by the machine. More than one item can be machined or assembled simultaneously, and many different items can be processed in random order.

Honda has been a pioneer in using FMS and robotic technology. Its competitive priorities are moving toward design and demand flexibility so it is changing operating systems and technology to support these priorities. Honda assembly plants use flexible manufacturing cells where the robots can be reprogrammed to build different models of cars. Honda invested $300 million in its automobile plants to improve assembly line efficiencies and add flexibility to build many different models in smaller numbers. "Inflexible plants locked into building only one or two models are dangerous in a world where customer trends and economic conditions can change very quickly," said John Adams, Honda senior vice president for manufacturing. Smart robots now replace many hydraulic machines and labor-intensive jobs. This means Honda can reprogram robots instead of having to replace equipment, jigs, and fixtures on the assembly line when making other models.[19]

Today, many companies have achieved complete integration of CAD/CAE, CAM, and FMS into what we now call computer-integrated manufacturing systems (CIMS). According to the National Research Council, companies with CIM experience have been able to

- decrease engineering design costs by up to 30 percent,
- increase productivity by 40 to 70 percent,
- increase equipment utilization by a factor of 2 to 3,
- reduce work-in-process and lead times by 30 to 60 percent, and
- improve quality by a factor of 3 to 4.

CIMS are also being used for high-volume, highly standardized production where mass-production technology has traditionally been employed. Since they allow for much smaller economically viable batch sizes, a firm is able to match its production efforts to a much wider range of demand and to create competitive advantage through rapid response to market changes and new products. By combining CIMS with the power of a web-enabled value chain, companies can achieve significant competitive advantage. Although the cost of developing and implementing a fully operational CIM system can be staggering, and a high degree of management commitment and effort is necessary, many companies are beginning to reap the rewards of carefully planned systems.

Enterprise Resource Planning (ERP) Systems

ERP systems integrate all aspects of a business—accounting, customer relationship management, supply chain management, manufacturing, sales, human resources—into a unified information system and provide more timely analysis and reporting of sales, customer, inventory, manufacturing, human resource, and accounting data.

ERP systems integrate all aspects of a business—accounting, customer relationship management, supply chain management, manufacturing, sales, human resources—into a unified information system and provide more timely analysis and reporting of sales, customer, inventory, manufacturing, human resource, and accounting data. ERP systems are vital for linking operations and other components of the value chain together. Two prominent vendors of ERP software are SAP (www.sap.com) and Oracle (www.oracle.com).

Traditionally, each department, such as finance, human resources, and manufacturing, has individual information systems optimized to the needs of that department. If the sales department wants to know the status of a customer's order, for example, someone would typically have to call manufacturing or shipping. ERP combines each department's information into a single, integrated system with a common database so that departments can easily share information and communicate with each other. ERP systems usually consist of different modules that can be implemented individually so that each department still has a level of autonomy, but they are combined into an integrated operating system. For example, when a customer's order is entered by sales, all information necessary to fulfill the order is built into the ERP system. The finance module would have the customer's order history and credit rating; the warehouse module would have current inventory levels; and the supply chain module would have distribution and shipping information. Not only would sales be able to provide accurate information about product availability and shipping dates but orders would get processed faster with fewer errors and delays.

SAP, for example, offers a wide variety of modules, including procurement (purchasing), finance, and sales, among others. The SAP Procurement Insight Package provides tools to monitor, check, and optimize complicated purchasing networks by providing access to key performance indicators related to current purchasing activities. The Financial Insight Package enables multidimensional analysis to spot trends in paying habits, monitor overdue payments, and determine days of sales outstanding. The Sales Insight Package allows a company to monitor sales initiatives, analyze sales-related data, and evaluate customer relationships. Exhibit 5.8 presents a SAP business map of the major functions of its ERP system.

ERP professionals are quick to point out that ERP is not about software, but about changing the way the organization and its operations are managed (see OM Spotlight: Dow Chemical's ERP System). Salespersons, for example, no longer simply input orders; they need to be able to deal with questions about availability and shipping. User resistance and complex coordination among divisions or departments in a company often make ERP implementation a difficult process. Kmart, for instance, had to write off $130 million for an ERP project that was never completed. Nestlé USA met considerable roadblocks in trying to implement a SAP system, taking 6 years and more than $200 million; however, it has saved the company $325 million.[20]

Most of the subsystems of ERP systems, such as customer ordering, inventory management, and production scheduling, are *real-time transaction processing systems*, as opposed to *batched processing systems*, in which a day's entire batch of transactions was typically processed during the night. In real-time processing, information

Exhibit 5.8 SAPs ERP Business Map

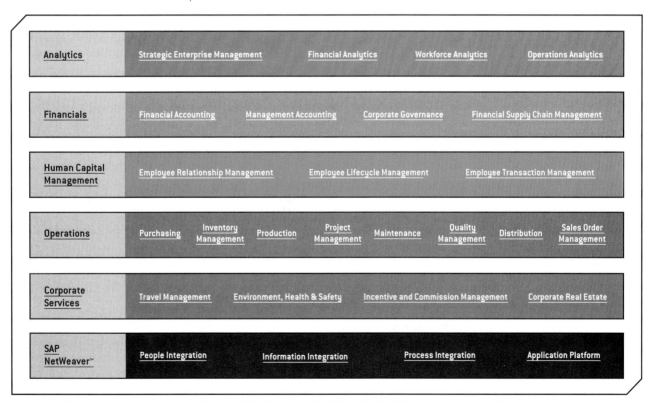

OM SPOTLIGHT

Dow Chemical's ERP System[21]

Dow Chemical is standardizing its global infrastructure with an integrated SAP r/2 ERP system that connects 50,000 employees in 170 countries. A data warehouse gives all its business units a consistent view of performance at the organization, division, process, and customer levels. Dow's ERP system also has links to many other systems such as Omnexus, a plastics industry e-marketplace, and Elemica, a B2B exchange for chemical transactions.

Dow recognized that its processes were not capable of superior customer service or an efficient supply chain without an integrated operating system. It approached this huge task with an end-to-end value chain approach, from supplier to customer, and not in a piecemeal fashion, one application or process at a time. It standardized on a global basis almost everything—hardware, software, communication platforms, accounting ledgers, customer coding, and web pages.

Dow also discovered that an integrated operating system helped it to quickly complete an $11.6 million merger with Union Carbide in 1999. Frank Luijckx, senior director of information systems said, "We achieved integration (with Union Carbide) in 12 months. What enabled this was a culture of integration." Luijckx also notes that standardizing on one ERP system led to higher productivity and better customer service. For example, if a customer wants to build a B2B link with its integrated system, Dow need only make one change. In the past, with over 20 nonintegrated systems and customer orders coming from Europe, Latin America, Asia, and Africa, Dow had to build multiple B2B links; in many cases, the links caused more problems than they solved.

is updated continuously, allowing the impacts to be reflected immediately in all other areas of the ERP system. Some business processes, however, such as the weekly payroll, monthly accounting reports, and billing, do not need real-time processing.

One problem with ERP systems is that the ERP software essentially dictates a particular way to run the business and its processes. Current processes and value chain structures may or may not conform to how the software is designed. Therefore, either the company must abandon its current practices and legacy systems and conform to the ERP system, or it must adapt the software to meet its particular needs and nuances. This transition is not easy and is filled with opportunities for failure.

Customer Relationship Management (CRM) Systems

Customer relationship management (CRM) is a business strategy designed to learn more about customers' wants, needs, and behaviors in order to build customer relationships and loyalty and ultimately enhance revenues and profits.

Satisfying customers and establishing good relationships with them is necessary for sustainable business success. Clearly, this is the ultimate purpose of a value chain. **Customer relationship management (CRM)** *is a business strategy designed to learn more about customers' wants, needs, and behaviors in order to build customer relationships and loyalty and ultimately enhance revenues and profits.* Over $11 billion was spent on CRM-related U.S. sales at the turn of the century and it is growing significantly.[22] A fourth-quarter 2001 survey by Boston-based AMR Research found that 53 percent of respondents said CRM had the biggest impact on their overall business while supply chain management (SCM) ranked second, with 14 percent of respondents claiming that it was the most important initiative.[23]

Technology, especially business intelligence systems that we described earlier in this chapter, is a key enabler of CRM. A typical CRM system includes market segmentation and analysis, customer service and relationship building, effective complaint resolution, cross-selling goods and services, and pre- and postproduction processes such as preproduction order processing and postproduction field service. Of course, the value chain must be capable of delivering what the customer wants, and that is where sound operational analysis is required.

CRM helps firms gain and maintain competitive advantage by

- segmenting markets based on demographic and behavioral characteristics,
- tracking sales trends and advertising effectiveness by customer and market segment,
- identifying which customers should be the focus of targeted marketing initiatives with predicted high customer response rates,
- forecasting customer retention (and defection) rates and providing feedback as to why customers leave the company,
- identifying which transactions are likely candidates to be fraudulent,
- studying which goods and services are purchased together, and what might be good ways to bundle them (that is, the customer benefit package),
- studying and predicting what web characteristics are most attractive to customers and how the web site might be improved, and
- linking the information above to competitive priorities by market segment and process and value chain performance.

CRM systems also provide a variety of useful operational data to managers, including the average time responding to customer questions, comments, and concerns, average order-tracking (flow) time, total revenue generated by each customer (and sometimes their family or business) from all goods and services bought by the customer—the total picture of the economic value of the customer to the firm, cost per marketing campaign, and price discrepancies.

Many companies, such as IBM, Ford, Allied Signal, and Enterprise Rent-A-Car (see the OM Spotlight on Enterprise Rent-A-Car), are adopting CRM as a way to build market share and increase profitability. Wells Fargo, for example, developed a CRM system where a key feature is the Enterprise Customer Profiling and Referrals system. This system provides customer service representatives with a real-time

OM SPOTLIGHT

Enterprise Rent-A-Car

Enterprise Rent-A-Car employs over 45,000 worldwide with sales approaching $6 billion. It provides automobile rental and leasing services to a wide range of individual and corporate customers. Their "We'll Pick You Up" service spares the customer the hassle of getting a cab or friend to drive to the rental office. It built its information technology architecture and CRM system to provide high customer satisfaction, to achieve close to zero system downtime for all 4,000 U.S rental offices, and to handle up to 2 million transactions per day and linked its service to many partnering services. For example, Geico, an insurance company, links its claims system to Enterprise's automated rental car system. By giving insurance companies like Geico access to real-time reservation information, Enterprise gets more business while the insurance companies look good to their customers by providing this extra value-added service. Everyone in the value chain benefits from this CRM system—Geico, Enterprise, and the customer. The CRM system also includes many other valuable characteristics such as an integrated accounts receivable system; a real-time car rental reservation system; links to hotels, restaurants, and city maps; and vehicle maintenance and repair records. Enterprise also owns its own satellite system so it is not at the mercy of other telecommunication systems.

The entire Enterprise CRM system supports the company's focus on customers and service. No one at a car rental site can be promoted if customer satisfaction at his or her site lags the corporate average even if the site's revenue and fleet growth is substantial. The company also ties the salaries of 20 corporate information system managers to overall corporate profits in an attempt to keep e-business designs focused on customer service. The CRM system at Enterprise duplicates many of the performance categories described by the service-profit chain model in Chapter 2.

view of the customer's total relationship with the bank. If a customer requests information about a credit card, then asks for information about paying off her mortgage, a representative does not have to log into 15 different computer screens and independent systems to answer the customer's queries—they are all available in one screen. The system prompts the representative as to what other financial services to recommend to the customer and automatically forwards those recommendations as internal sales referrals to the appropriate line of business.

Revenue Management Systems (RMS)

Many types of organizations manage perishable assets, such as a hotel room, an airline seat, a rental car, a sporting event or concert seat, a room on a cruise line, the capacity of a restaurant catering service or electric power generation, or broadcast advertising space. For such assets, which essentially represent service capacity, high utilization is the key to financial success (see Chapter 1 on the key differences between goods versus services). These assets are perishable because their revenue-generating capabilities immediately drop to zero at a certain point in time. That is, services are time-dependent and cannot be held in inventory for future sale like physical goods, for example, when a cruise leaves port with an empty cabin or an airline flight closes its doors and takes off. Once the asset is lost, its revenue is lost forever.[24]

*A **revenue management system (RMS)** consists of dynamic methods to forecast demand, allocate perishable assets across market segments, decide when to overbook and by how much, and determine what price to charge different customer (price) classes.* These four components of RMS—forecasting, allocation, overbooking, and pricing—must work in unison if the objective is to maximize the revenue generated by a perishable asset. The ideas and methods surrounding RMS are often called *yield management*. Revenue management systems integrate a wide variety of decisions and data into a decision support system used mainly by service-providing businesses.

RMS as an integrated operating system can be viewed from a strategic and tactical perspective. The strategic view involves designing customer benefit packages that cause customers to choose one service provider over the other. For example, the fixed cost of running a hotel is high, and once the hotel occupancy rate is above the break-even occupancy rate, the contribution to profit and overhead per incremental customer is high (see break-even analysis in Chapter 1). Hotel competitors use price, weekend promotions, kids-stay-free policies, senior discounts, room upgrades, and a multitude of hotel amenities in their CBPs to attract that highly profitable "extra" customer.

Tactical revenue management makes perishable assets available for sale at certain points in time and at specific prices to maximize revenues by exploiting the cost structure and economics of perishable assets over a given planning horizon. This often involves opening and closing asset availability—sometimes on an hourly basis—to maximize revenues. For example, during peak demand periods, the higher-priced market segments are left open and represent a higher percentage of total room capacity while the lowest-priced market segments are closed (that is, unavailable to customers). During off-peak demand periods, the lowest-priced market segments are made available for sale. A RMS may also use time fences to encourage booking customers in the form of advanced purchase restrictions to secure a certain and usually lower price, for example, minimum time in advance of arrival that booking must be made or staying over a Saturday night.

The earliest revenue management systems focused solely on overbooking—how many perishable assets to sell in excess of physical capacity to optimally trade off the cost of an unsold asset versus the loss of goodwill of having more arrivals than

A **revenue management system (RMS)** *consists of dynamic methods to forecast demand, allocate perishable assets across market segments, decide when to overbook and by how much, and determine what price to charge different customer (price) classes.*

assets. Most service businesses are reluctant to overbook because of the short-term negative problem of having to find a customer a room, airline seat, or concert seat. The long-term implications of overbooking perishable assets are damaged customer loyalty and therefore decreasing market share, customer retention rates, and profits. However, businesses do overbook to compensate for the no-show and cancellation probabilities. For example, certain groups and associations who book a convention at a hotel have no-show rates as high as 50 percent.

Modern RMS software simultaneously makes changes in the forecast, allocation, overbooking, and pricing decisions in a real-time operating system. Forecasts are constantly being revised. Allocation involves segmenting the perishable asset into target market categories, such as first, business, and coach classes in an airline flight. Each class is defined by its size (number of seats), price, advance purchase restrictions, and booking policies. Allocation is a real-time, ongoing method that does not end until there is no more opportunity to maximize revenue (the night or concert is over, the airplane takes off). As forecasts, bookings, and time move forward, the target market categories are redefined and prices change in an attempt to maximize revenue.

Many organizations have exploited RMS technology. For example, American Airlines increased its revenue by an estimated $1.4 billion over the 1989–1991 time frame and continues to lead the industry in the use of intelligent RMS methods.[25] As early as 1991, Marriott improved its revenues by $25–$35 million by using RMS methods. Royal Caribbean Cruise Lines obtained a revenue increase in excess of $20 million for 1 year.[26] Holiday Inn found that even small improvements in forecasting accuracy, overbooking logic, and time-dependent pricing decisions increased revenue significantly. Revenue management saved National Car Rental from liquidation in 1994. During the first year of RMS implementation, revenues at National Car Rental increased by $56 million.[27]

BENEFITS AND CHALLENGES OF TECHNOLOGY

Learning Objective
To understand the advantages that technology offers in operations and its impact on productivity, as well as the challenges that organizations and operations managers face in implementing and using technology.

A full orchestra has performed *The Marriage of Figaro* for over 200 years. Yet, the Opera Company of Brooklyn, New York, plays this Mozart classic with only 12 musicians and one computer technician overseeing the computer program that plays all other instruments. This mix of real and virtual players reduces the cost of playing a symphony by about two-thirds.[28] This high-tech and low-cost approach to playing Mozart is an example of doing more with less—a challenge that operations managers face every day.

The U.S. Labor Department reported a breathtaking annual rate of productivity growth of 8.1 percent in the third quarter of 2003. Beginning in the fourth quarter of 2001, productivity increased at an annual rate of more than 5 percent, the fastest 2-year rate in over 50 years. In comparison, productivity grew at a rate of just 1.4 percent annually between 1973 and 1995.[29] Long-term productivity growth rates usually are in the 1.5 to 3.0 percent range. The Federal Reserve Chairman, Mr. Alan Greenspan, noted that the major cause of these extraordinary increases in U.S. productivity is information technology and high-tech equipment.[30]

High productivity raises everyone's standard of living. The faster productivity grows, the faster an economy can grow without causing inflation. In the short term, the job market may be weak. But eventually firms begin hiring to keep pace with the increases in demand. One economist computes that U.S. living standards would double in 28 years with productivity growth at 2.5 percent. At 2.0 percent, it takes an additional 7 years, or 35 years, to double living standards. Here, we will describe the benefits and challenges of using technology and its impact on productivity.

Technology Benefits

Technology drives the global economy, restructures current industries, and creates new industries.[31] In 1991, for example, *Investor's Business Daily* divided the computer and semiconductor industries into 7 groups; today, that number has grown to 18 industry groups. Technology advances such as wireless communications, genetic/biomedicine, and pollution control have created new industries and many new job opportunities.

Not only does technology create new industries directly but sometimes new industries are created by the convergence of others, such as computer networking, telecommunications, and cable television. Ford and General Electric created financial services to complement the sale of their physical goods or to provide such new business opportunities as home mortgages. Wal-Mart has added pharmacy and eyeglass dispensing businesses and is using its powerful marketplace presence to launch Wal-Mart financial services and an online DVD rental business. Citigroup was the first financial services company in the United States to bring together banking (Citicorp), insurance (Travelers Life & Annuity), and investments (Salomon Smith Barney) under one umbrella. With the most diverse array of financial products and services and the greatest distribution capacity of any financial firm in the world, its 270,000 employees manage 200 million customer accounts across six continents in more than 100 countries.

Rosanne Cahn, chief economist for CS First Boston observed, "Innovation is particularly important for a high labor-cost economy such as the United States. Anything that we did yesterday someone else can do today with lower labor costs. A high labor-cost country must wake up every day and reinvent itself." Technology provides unparalleled opportunities for innovation.

Modern technology can improve productivity and quality dramatically, increase the flexibility needed to respond rapidly to changing customer demands, enhance working conditions, and improve wages because of the higher skill levels required. For example, Square D Corporation produces circuit breakers on a fully automated production line in Lincoln, Nebraska, using 37 highly trained (and high-paid) operators who replaced 250 human assemblers. The plant was designed with the full cooperation of the International Brotherhood of Electrical Workers. Although jobs for hand assemblers were reduced, more jobs for skilled machine operators, mold makers, and maintenance workers became available.[32] Technology can also free workers from onerous and dangerous jobs, such as sanding and painting automobile bodies, and enable them to engage in more creative and knowledge-intensive tasks. Thus, understanding modern technology is vital not only to individuals who manage these systems but also to others in a firm such as salespersons and customer service representatives who depend on their performance.

Other benefits of technology relate to a company's ability to improve operations and gain a competitive advantage. Technology drives simultaneous improvements in time, cost (resulting in lower prices), and quality-related performance, plus the capability to customize goods and services to smaller and smaller target market segments and ultimately to one customer at a time (see the OM Spotlight on Lands' End). Customers also enjoy the benefits of new technology. For example, shopping for the lowest-cost home mortgage via the Internet is now much easier and faster. Because of the high degree of automation in automobile assembly—robots installing automobile windshields—the unit cost per car is lowered, keeping prices affordable.

Technology Challenges

A casual reader of the e-commerce literature might conclude that the Internet is a perfect way to do business; however, the failure of hundreds of dot.coms hints at many operational problems that must be overcome if the virtual Internet world is

OM SPOTLIGHT

Lands' End Customized Online Apparel[33]

Lands' End offered an online service to customize clothes with the expectations that it would marginally add to revenue. To its surprise, customers are exceeding the goal of about 10 percent of total item sales from this customized clothing service. Now the Dodgeville, Wisconsin, firm is expanding the online program to swimsuits, men's suits and shirts, and jeans. The revised goal is 25 percent of total item sales, but what is more interesting is that this mass customization online service attracts a totally new market segment. Most of these online customers are first time Lands' End buyers. Moreover, customized jeans, for example, run about $54, $20 to $30 dollars more than regular make-to-stock jeans. Customers can input their physical dimensions and select colors, pocket styles, different fit styles, and so on.

Once the customer's order is defined, it is electronically sent directly to the factory where the order is individually cut and sewn. Customized clothes are shipped to the customer in 2 to 3 weeks from the date of the order. The factories had to switch to new machinery to quickly make the small orders. All customer body shape measurements are kept in Lands' End data warehouse and it is constantly improving the questions it asks the customer while ordering.

Lands' End, which was bought by Sears, Roebuck and Co., also benefits by having less inventory in its warehouses because more and more clothing is made-to-order. Bill Bass, senior vice president of e-commerce at Lands' End, said, "The nice thing about mass customization is that you always have what the customer wants." Bass believes one main reason for the success of this service is pure customer convenience. Returns of customized clothing average 6 percent, which is lower than that of noncustomized clothing.

to be properly integrated with the physical world. For example, the stock price of Pets.com soared to $14 in January 2000, and the company paid $2.2 million for a Super Bowl commercial. A year later, its stock price was 12 cents and it sold its URL and technology to the traditional bricks-and-mortar company PetsMart. See the OM Spotlight on WebVan for another interesting story. The perils of online shopping, using your credit card number, returning goods ordered online, and security and privacy issues are all of concern to customers.

Firms that have built their reputations on quality goods, low prices, or exceptional customer service can also have their image and reputation damaged by online shopping failures and upsets. A few of the challenges that operations managers face when trying to use the Internet to gain competitive advantage are (1) How do we integrate traditional customer orders with online orders? (2) How do we receive payment from online customers? (3) What tasks and processes should be outsourced and which ones should be kept in-house as core competencies? (4) How do we build operational and logistical process capability to complement Internet capabilities? (5) How do we handle returned goods or a customer's request to discontinue a service? and (6) How do we use the Internet to reduce total customer costs and/or value chain costs?

Consider the last question on costs—whose costs? Although the use of the Internet may reduce the cost to some of the players in the value chain, the most important player is the customer. The fact is that logistical (that is, transportation and distribution) costs are more expensive for most online businesses than for similar

OM SPOTLIGHT

The WebVan Failure[34]

One dot.com company, WebVan, focused on customers' ordering their groceries online and then picking the orders in a warehouse and delivering them to the customers' homes. The idea was to support the order-pick-pack-deliver process of acquiring groceries through an e-service at the front end of the value chain and with delivery vans at the back end of the value chain. This service made several assumptions about customer wants and needs, for example, that customers have perfect knowledge of what they want when they surf the online catalogs, that customers would be home when the delivery arrived, that what the e-catalogue shows is what the customer will get, that the customer doesn't make mistakes when selecting the items, and that time-starved customers are willing to pay a high premium for home delivery. Unfortunately, this was a very high cost process. The $30 to $40 delivery charge for complex and heterogeneous customer orders and the many opportunities for error doomed WebVan. The founders of WebVan did not clearly define their strategy and target market and properly evaluate the operational and logistical issues associated with their value chain design.

The WebVan lesson is to focus first on the business plan and operations, not the technology. If a company cannot do a good job at order accuracy, inventory management, demand forecasting, sourcing, warehousing, scheduling, capacity planning, transportation, distribution and delivery, accuracy and quality, returns, and creating good service encounters at every point of customer contact, it does not matter how good its web site might be!

---

bricks-and-mortar businesses. Compare, for example, the cost of shipping a full versus partial truckload or buying 100,000 units at discounted prices versus 10 units at regular prices. The super-efficient Wal-Mart value chain does just what it claims—it provides a wide assortment of goods and services to customers at the lowest total costs. Clothes, books, appliances, food, office supplies, furniture, and so on are frequently less expensive at a physical store than at their online counterparts when you add logistical costs such as order taking, order fulfillment, insurance, repackaging, and shipping. For pure information-intensive services such as airline e-tickets and stock trading, the Internet does lower total customer and value chain costs. However, for many other businesses it does not.

Another consistent problem that e-commerce value chains face is what to do when a business or individual customer wants to return a good or terminate the service. In the 1999 holiday season, for example, analysis revealed that 25 percent of the online purchases were returned—a value of about $1 billion.[35] Many of these stores were virtual stores with no physical place to return the good. The return process was poorly designed, and customers quickly become dissatisfied with the experience of online purchasing. Even when sellers do have a bricks-and-mortar store, they usually do not want their online merchandise and orders mixed up with their store merchandise and orders. For services, it is not uncommon for customers to switch telecommunication firms yet continue to be billed by the old service providers because the service process is not capable of quickly updating billing information and disconnecting the old service.

The cost to the seller and customer of returning a good is usually much higher online than from a bricks-and-mortar store. Also, note that the information flows are just as important as the flows of the good—somebody has to know how all this works! If the good is successfully returned, but the bill remains inaccurate and requires the customer to make multiple telephone calls to the call center to correct it, the customer may be furious and never order online from that company again. Often, the solution to the problem of returning goods is reverse logistics. **Reverse logistics** *is the use of third-party integrators and service providers that handle everything from accepting the returned good to correcting the associated bill.*

Reverse logistics *is the use of third-party integrators and service providers that handle everything from accepting the returned good to correcting the associated bill.*

Impacts of Technology on People

Technology puts more pressure on front-line employees to excel. The excuses of "I didn't know" or "I didn't have the right information" are no longer valid. For example, one major bank codes its credit card customers with colored squares on the bank's computer screens. A green square on a customer account tells the bank teller or customer service representative or loan officer that this is a very profitable customer and to grant this customer whatever he or she wants—credits for poor service, fee waivers, top priority, callbacks, upgrades, appointment times, and the "white-glove" treatment. On the other hand, a red square indicates an unprofitable customer and signals the service provider to make no special effort to help the customer. In fact, upon seeing the red square, a bank teller once told a customer, "Wow, somebody doesn't like you!" This customer episode illustrates the difficulty of getting front-line employees to do the right thing at the right time with the right customer. Customers and consumer advocacy groups do not like it when firms treat customers differently depending on what the computer screen tells the service providers.

Managers must make good decisions about introducing and using new technology. They must understand the relative advantages and disadvantages of using technologies and their impact on the work force. Although technology has proven quite useful in eliminating monotony and hazardous work and can develop new skills and talents in people, it can also rob them of empowerment and creativity. The goal of the operations manager is to provide the best synthesis of technology, people, and processes; this interaction is often called the *sociotechnical system*. Topics included here include job specialization versus enlargement, employee empowerment, training, decision support systems, teams and work groups, job design, recognition and reward, career advancement, and facility and equipment layout. These topics are covered throughout this book.

All of the models of organizational performance described in Chapter 3 have a major technology component. Many companies now have a formal management position known as the *chief information officer (CIO)* who is responsible for all of a company's information technology needs and applications. Category 4 of the Malcolm Baldrige National Quality Award that we discussed in Chapter 3 provides a glimpse of what a CIO's job entails. Typical objectives and skills of this demanding CIO job include ensuring a strategic alignment between technology and the wants and needs of customers and employees, managing vendor partnerships, designing and building the organization's information technology infrastructure, and supporting line and process managers in their assigned tasks. CIOs also need a wide variety of interdisciplinary skills, including operations and human resource management skills. A CIO is not only responsible for keeping up with information technology but is often at the center of business process reengineering and continuous improvement initiatives.

A summary of the benefits and challenges of technology is given in Exhibit 5.9. Can you think of others?

TECHNOLOGY DEVELOPMENT AND ADOPTION

Learning Objective
To understand the processes of technology development and adoption and the role of operations in these processes.

Despite its importance, many companies do not really understand technology or how to apply it effectively. The risk of a technology adoption failure is high and the survival of the firm is at stake. For example, although the VCR was invented in America and the CD player in Holland, the Japanese have dominated those industries because of their mastery of process technology. *USA Today* reported that a study by Morgan Stanley found that U.S. companies wasted $130 billion on

Exhibit 5.9

Example Benefits and
Challenges of Adopting
Technology

Benefits	Challenges
Creates new industries and job opportunities	Higher employee skill levels required, such as information technology and service management skills
Restructures old and less productive industries	Integration of old (legacy) and new technology and systems
Integrates supply and value chain players	Job shift and displacement
Increases marketplace competitiveness and maintains the survival of the firm	Less opportunity for employee creativity and empowerment
Provides the capability to focus on smaller target market segments (customize)	Protecting the employee's and customer's privacy and security
Improves/increases productivity, quality and customer satisfaction, speed, safety, and flexibility/customization—does more with less	Fewer human service providers resulting in customer ownership not being assigned, nonhuman service encounters, and inability of the customer to change decisions and return goods easily
Lowers cost	Information overload
Raises world's standard of living	Global outsourcing and impact on domestic job opportunities

ineffective technology during just 2 years at the turn of the twenty-first century.[36] For instance, Hershey Foods installed three software packages in the summer of 1999, just as retailers placed orders for Halloween. The software was incompatible with other systems, and candy piled up in warehouses because of missed or delayed deliveries. Nike installed software to let retailers order direct, but glitches led to some shoes being overstocked while more popular ones were scarce, contributing to a profit shortfall in 2000. These information technology examples are reminiscent of comparable failures of automated manufacturing technology encountered by the automobile and other industries during the 1970s. Reasons include rushing to the wrong technology, buying too much and not implementing it properly, and underestimating the time needed to make it work.

It would be wonderful if the development and adoption of technology were characterized by a steady growth rate and a smooth transition by people, organizations, and economies, but history teaches us this is not the case. An excellent explanation of how technology begins, develops through a series of ups and downs, and eventually is widely adopted in the marketplace is contained in the *2001 Intel Corporation Annual Report*.[37] Here is what Intel, who invented the first "computer on a chip" in 1971, says about the history of technology revolutions.

Historians tell us that over the last two centuries, major technological revolutions have ridden waves of boom and bust, only to rebound with periods of sustained build-out. This pattern has played out in the steel and rail industries as well as others. If history is any guide, the Internet revolution is on track for decades of growth and has yet to see its most rewarding years.

Technology development and adoption generally has three stages—birth, turbulence, and build-out:

Stage I. Birth. At the beginning of a major technological era, enabling technologies emerge and are eagerly welcomed as revolutionary. Excitement builds as technological pioneers crowd into the field and innovations flourish. In some cases, early investors make extraordinary profits, fueling speculation, chaos and investment mania, even "irrational exuberance."

Stage II. **Turbulence.** *Over investment and over capacity burst the bubble of the new technology's progress. Sometimes linked to a slowing economy, stock prices drop and even crash. Some investors lose everything; some companies fold. Investment halts as financiers retrench. Observers may declare the technology dead. But the story is by no means over.*

Stage III. **Build-out.** *Confidence returns. Real value emerges. Missing components of the technology are put in place, leading to full implementation. The technology penetrates the economy as other industries organize around it and businesses adjust to take full advantage of it. Sustained investment yields robust returns. The technology becomes the driving engine of the economy.*

Each stage in the development of technologies requires the operations area to excel at different competitive priorities. During the birth stage, design and demand flexibility are critical for gaining a competitive advantage. The best good or service design and the processes that create it are constantly changing; hence the organization must be capable of quickly changing designs and production volumes. At this stage, the cost of the new good or service is important but not as important as flexibility, speed and reliability of delivery, and the quality of the good or service.

During the turbulence stage, the objective is to consolidate resources and marketplace advantages and work on building technical and operational capability. Many industry and nonindustry competitors enter the marketplace trying to gain a competitive advantage. Cash flow, survival, and building process and value chain capabilities are the focus of organizations during these turbulent times. All firms are trying to survive the turbulent stage and be ready for the build-out stage. At one point in the 1920s, for example, there were over 6,000 firms trying to become the dominant U.S. automobile manufacturer. In the 1990s, the dot.com revolution had hundreds of firms spending most of their resources on marketing and trying to capture customers; building operational capability became a second priority. Without superior operating systems that added value to customer benefit packages, most of these dot.com firms went bankrupt.

The final stage—build-out—is where operational capability becomes the key to a winning competitive strategy. This capability can be realized with a well-synchronized value chain having coordinated physical and information flows (see the OM Spotlight: Wal-Mart's Value Chain Approach to Eyeglasses).

Examples of the Technology Adoption Process

We present two diverse examples of the process of technology development and adoption: U.S. railroads and the current global digital revolution.

The U.S. Railroad Industry. The birth to build-out story of the U.S. railroads as described by Intel occurred as follows.

Stage I. U.S. Railroad Birth. *In 1828, construction began on the first U.S. steam rail line, the Baltimore & Ohio. American innovations—more powerful locomotives and cost-effective wooden rails—soon fueled a boom. States invested heavily in rail infrastructure, and business leaders lobbied for railway links between key cities.*

Stage II. U.S. Railroad Turbulence. *Railroad speculation contributed to the depression of 1859, with many investors losing large sums. Rampant cost overruns and nationwide mania over the building of the transcontinental railroad, completed in 1869, left major rail financier Jay Cooke & Co. bankrupt by 1873.*

Stage III. U.S. Railroad Build-out. *Extended rail construction in the 1870s and 1880s facilitated the nation's industrialization and the growth of the West. Hardier steel rails replaced wood, locomotives improved, and a standard-gauge width was adopted, allowing nationwide uniformity of tracks and cars. By 1900, railroads*

OM SPOTLIGHT

Wal-Mart's Value Chain Approach to Eyeglasses[38]

Wal-Mart has optometry offices in many of its Wal-Mart and Sam's Club stores. It takes a value chain approach to competing in this business by specializing in one- to two-day production and delivery of eyeglasses to any U.S.A. store. To accomplish this time-based competition strategy, Wal-Mart built the largest eyeglass factory and technical laboratory in the United States in Obetz, Ohio. The Wal-Mart Laboratory is located in Optical Village, a cluster of eyeglass makers located next to an airport specializing in air cargo. The entire value chain except the air cargo service is owned by Wal-Mart!

Orders for eyeglasses are received electronically from all U.S. Wal-Mart and Sam's Club stores at the Obetz Optical Laboratory. "At the lab, they grind the lens to the prescrip-

tion and assemble it in the frame, and put on antiglare or other coating steps," says Kevin Clark, business development manager for Airborne-Logistics. If necessary, Wal-Mart will use the services of other optical suppliers located in Optical Village (outsourcing). When the customer's order is finished, air cargo carriers ship it overnight.

Wal-Mart opened its first optical "store-within-a-store" in 1991 and now operates stores in 1,500 of its 2,600 U.S. stores. It is the nation's third-largest retailer of eyeglasses, contact lenses, and optical services with sales of about $400 million. LensCrafters, headquartered in Cincinnati, Ohio, is the national sales leader with $1.25 billion in sales. "They (Wal-Mart) are absolutely a growing force," said Cathy Ciccolella, editor of *Vision Monthly*, an industry trade publication. "They're expanding so quickly."

owned 193,000 miles of track covering the United States, more than 10 times the mileage built in the railroad's earlier heyday in the mid-1850s, and of course, U.S. productivity soared.

The Digital Revolution. Today we find ourselves in the midst of an even more powerful technological revolution—the digital or service and information revolution. This time, however, technology can not only replace physical human and animal labor but also human knowledge and intellect. Automated factories run by a handful of people with artificial intelligence software are now a reality. Consider the following description of the ongoing digital revolution and contrast it to the railroad experience.

Stage I. Global Digital Revolution and Birth. The invention of the integrated circuit was the first of a series of defining innovations that ultimately fueled the Internet revolution. Apple and IBM personal computers entered the marketplace in the early 1980s. *Excitement over powerful microprocessors, PCs, software and the emerging Internet economy all contributed to the high-tech boom of the 1990s.* Networks are not completely developed to take full advantage of technological capabilities such as optical-fiber transmission lines and switches, quantum leaps in microprocessor power and disk storage capacity, and real or imagined barriers such as how to securely and accurately collect payments over the Internet.

Stage II. Global Digital Revolution and Turbulence. In 2000 and 2001, as hundreds of dot-coms failed to turn a profit, investor confidence slipped, triggering meltdowns throughout the technology sector. Nasdaq stocks lost more than 70% of their value, and investors lost money. Facing excess capacity, many companies cut back on their information technology expenditures, and the semiconductor industry entered its worst downturn ever. Surviving companies continue to build their operational capabilities, design and test new goods and services, and get ready for the profitable build-out stage.

Stage III. Global Digital Revolution Build-out. The world's first microprocessor was the Intel 4004 "computer on a chip" built in 1971. It was a 4-bit silicon chip packed with 2,300 transistors and had as much processing power as the old "3,000 cubic foot" ENIAC computer. In 1994, the semiconductor industry produced 176 billion computer chips and even in the economic downturn of 2001 and 2002, chips were still being manufactured at a rate close to one billion per day. The second Internet Revolution and build-out has just begun. Then, the "annual demand" for chips is expected to triple to over one trillion by 2010.[39]

For the digital build-out to occur, digital computing and communications capability must converge. The network of switches and optical transmission lines will then be indistinguishable from the servers and computers online, creating one ubiquitous global network and countless integrated value chains. IOSs will help achieve dramatic improvements in productivity. Many organizational processes will be driven or supported by all or part of this global digital network. Especially for information-intensive businesses, the operating cost per output unit will tumble to levels once thought impossible, and global productivity will soar. The successful rollout of this new wave of hard and soft technology will depend on solid operations management expertise.

MAKING TECHNOLOGY DECISIONS

A key factor that affects technology decisions is scalability. **Scalability** *is a measure of the contribution margin (revenue minus variable costs) required to deliver a good or service as the business grows and volumes increase.* Scalability is a key issue in e-commerce. **High scalability** *is the capability to serve additional customers at zero or extremely low incremental costs.* For example, Monster.com is an online job posting and placement service that is largely information-intensive. Customers can post their resumes on Monster.com's web site and print out job advertisements and opportunities on their office or home computers at their expense. This service is highly scalable because its fixed costs are approximately 80 to 85 percent of total costs. The incremental cost to serve an additional customer is very small, yet the revenue obtained from this customer remains high. If an organization establishes a business where the incremental cost (or variable cost) to serve more customers is zero, then the firm is said to be *infinitely scalable.* Online newspapers and magazines, e-banking services, and other information-intensive businesses have the potential to be infinitely scalable.

On the other hand, **low scalability** *implies that serving additional customers requires high incremental variable costs.* The previous OM Spotlight on WebVan is a good example of high order-picking and delivery costs for each additional customer with relatively low prices and little marketplace opportunity to raise prices. The complex and heterogeneous nature of individual customer grocery store orders made it difficult to recover the $30 to $40 delivery charge. The high operational and logistical variable costs per new customer doomed the dot.com company.

Many of the dot.coms that failed around the year 2000 had low scalability and unsustainable demand (volumes) created by extraordinary advertising expenses and artificially low prices. Break-even analysis can help analyze the scalability of various businesses and Internet technologies.

Quantitative Models for Technology Decisions

Some decisions involving technology can be addressed using traditional financial analyses, such as break-even analysis or calculations of net present value or internal

Learning Objective
To understand how scalability affects technology decisions and to be able to apply simple scoring and decision models to technology decisions.

Scalability *is a measure of the contribution margin (revenue minus variable costs) required to deliver a good or service as the business grows and volumes increase.*

High scalability *is the capability to serve additional customers at zero or extremely low incremental costs.*

Low scalability *implies that serving additional customers requires high incremental variable costs.*

rate of return of the investment. However, most decisions are more complex because they involve a variety of intangible factors. For example, in selecting just one piece of equipment (let alone an entirely new system or technology), managers must consider such economic factors as purchase price, installation cost, operating expenses, training costs, expected labor savings, tax implications, and other miscellaneous costs, as well as such noneconomic factors as installation time, availability of training, expected productivity improvements, supplier service and support, and flexibility.

Several techniques can be used to deal with intangible factors. One common approach is to use a scoring model. *A scoring model consists of a set of ranked attributes for each factor, often on a quantitative scale that reflects the relative importance or value of the factor.* For example, in comparing different suppliers for a similar piece of equipment, managers might rank installation time, supplier training, productivity improvement, supplier service, and flexibility of the equipment on a scale such as excellent (4), good (3), average (2), and poor (1). These rankings can be evaluated in conjunction with a financial analysis to arrive at the best choice. One might also use a different scale for each factor to "weight" them according to priority. The weighting of the factors is rather subjective and is best done after careful analysis by a group of experienced personnel.

Another formal quantitative approach to choosing among alternatives when uncertainty exists in future outcomes is decision analysis (see Supplementary Chapter E). For example, a major electric utility used a decision tree to help select between two different types of pollution-control equipment to meet new air quality standards mandated by the government. The decision was affected by a number of uncertainties, including what type of coal might be required under the law, future changes in air-quality regulations, the outcome of an ongoing plant reliability improvement program, construction costs, and electrical power requirements and costs. The company computed the annual capital and operating costs for various scenarios, estimated probabilities for uncertainties from existing data or subjective assessments, and developed a decision tree to evaluate the costs and risks associated with each technology. The decision analysis led to a selection different from the one that would have been chosen if only a traditional financial analysis had been conducted.

The Solved Problems that follow illustrate some examples of using quantitative methods and scoring models for making technology decisions.

*A **scoring model** consists of a set of ranked attributes for each factor, often on a quantitative scale that reflects the relative importance or value of the factor.*

SOLVED PROBLEMS

1. The Sterling Equipment Corporation is contemplating the purchase of an industrial robot. Equipment from four suppliers has been identified as meeting the basic technical criteria. An economic analysis resulted in the data shown in Exhibit 5.10. In addition, an evaluation of key noneconomic factors resulted in the data shown in Exhibit 5.11.

The plant manager decided to translate the noneconomic factors into numerical scores, with 4 = excellent, 3 = good, 2 = average, and 1 = poor. The results of the evaluation are shown in Exhibit 5.12. The Sterling management team needs this ro-

bot in a hurry and requires rapid service from the supplier when breakdowns occur. Therefore, the company considers these factors far more important than the others. Based on this information, what decision do you think the company should make?

Solution:

Supplier 1 clearly has significant lower economic costs. However, evaluation of the noneconomic factors leads to a different decision. If installation lead time and supplier service are the most important factors, we might consider multiplying the scores for these factors by a

Factor	Supplier 1	Supplier 2	Supplier 3	Supplier 4
Purchase cost	$50,000	$70,000	$65,000	$75,000
Installation cost	2,500	1,000	4,500	—
Operating cost	5,000	6,000	7,500	6,500
Training cost	1,000	—	1,000	1,500
Software costs	1,000	1,000	1,500	2,000
Total costs	59,500	78,000	79,500	85,000
Labor savings	30,000	40,000	30,000	45,000
Tax benefits	1,500	2,000	1,000	2,000
Total savings	31,500	42,000	31,000	47,000
Net total cost	$28,000	$36,000	$48,500	$38,000

Exhibit 5.10
Economic Analysis for Equipment Selection

Factor	Supplier 1	Supplier 2	Supplier 3	Supplier 4
Installation lead time	Good	Average	Excellent	Poor
Supplier training	Good	Poor	Good	Average
Productivity improvement	Good	Good	Good	Good
Supplier service	Good	Excellent	Excellent	Good
Flexibility	Excellent	Good	Good	Excellent

Exhibit 5.11
Noneconomic Factor Evaluation for Equipment Selection

Factor	Supplier 1	Supplier 2	Supplier 3	Supplier 4
Installation lead time	3	2	4	1
Supplier training	2	1	3	2
Productivity improvement	3	3	3	3
Supplier service	3	4	4	3
Flexibility	4	3	3	4

Exhibit 5.12
Numerical Scores for Noneconomic Factors in Equipment Selection

number greater than 1—say 3—to reflect this importance. Doing so, we have a total weighted score for each supplier:

Supplier	1	2	3	4
Total score	27	25	33	21

For example, the score for supplier 1 is calculated as $(3)(3) + 2 + 3 + (3)(3) + 4 = 27$. On the noneconomic factors, Supplier 3 is the best. This creates a dilemma—should the company spend an additional net cost of $10,500 to achieve faster installation and better service or sacrifice these attributes for a lower cost? Obviously, the ultimate decision rests with the company management, but the analysis and scoring model provides information on which to debate the issues and make a rational decision.

2. You are considering setting up an online used personal computer auction service where each customer pays $100 per year to subscribe. All PCs are shipped at the customer's expense to your repair facility located in a large city. Here, you will refurbish the PC and certify its characteristics and performance with a 1-year product and labor warranty. You then put the PCs up for sale on the auction site and ship them to the customers. Other relevant information is

Annual fixed cost = $400,000
Variable repair cost per PC = $60 per unit
Variable cost to package and ship the PC = $30

How many customers will you need to break even? Is this business venture a good idea? Explain in terms of scalability.

Solution:

The total cost is $TC = FC + VC \times D$ and the total revenue is $P \times D$, so finding D that satisfies $FC + VC \times D = P \times D$ represents the break-even quantity. Solving this equation for D, we have $D = FC/(P - VC)$, or $D = \$400,000/(100 - 90) = 40,000$ customers

The economics of this business venture do not look good. The break-even quantity is very high involving as it does complex PC refurbishing, inventory, cataloging, packaging, shipping, warehousing, and warranty processes. Variable costs are high with little ability to raise prices. The contribution margin per new customer of \$10 (\$100 − \$90) is low. Given the current logistical and operational issues and economics, this venture has low scalability and may be quite risky.

KEY TERMS AND CONCEPTS

Business intelligence systems (BIS)
Business-to-business (B2B)
Business-to-customer (B2C)
Chief information officer
Computer integrated manufacturing systems (CIMS)
Customer relationship management (CRM) systems
Customer-to-customer (C2C)
Data mining
Data scrubbing
Data warehouse
Digital technology adoption process
Electronic checks (eChecks)
Enterprise resource planning (ERP) systems
    Batch processing
    Real-time transaction processing
e-services
Global auction service
Hard technology
Infinitely scalable
Integrated operating system (IOS)
Intel's 3-stage process for technology development and adoption
    Birth
    Build-out
    Turbulence
Intermediary
Manufacturing technology

Numerical control
    Computer-aided design (CAD)
    Computer-aided engineering (CAE)
    Computer-aided manufacturing (CAM)
    Flexible manufacturing systems (FMS)
    Machine vision systems
    Robots
Perishable asset
Radio frequency tags (RFID)
Railroad technology adoption process
Return facilitators
Revenue management systems (RMS)
    Allocate
    Forecast
    Overbook
    Pricing
Reverse logistics
Scalability—high and low
Scoring model
Service technology
Sociotechnical systems
Soft technology
Supply chain management (SCM) systems
Technology and productivity
Technology in value chains
Terabytes and petabytes
Virtual store
Yield management

QUESTIONS FOR REVIEW AND DISCUSSION

1. Research RFID tags and provide examples of how they are or might be used to improve productivity.

2. Describe a situation where self-service and technology help create and deliver the customer benefit package to the customer. Provide examples of how such a system can cause a defect, mistake, or service upset.

3. Explain the difference between hard technology and soft technology.

4. Provide three examples of how technology has improved your life. Explain.

5. Provide a personal example where using new technology has resulted in some type of service upset, error, or failure. How could the process have been improved so that you would not have experienced the problem?

6. What are the major factors that have made modern technology important in today's manufacturing and service organizations?

7. In considering the four different examples of manufacturing technology we described in this chapter, explain how the technology used in making puzzles and gears are alike and different. What types of decisions do operations managers need to make in each of these situations? How are these decisions alike or different?

8. In considering the four different examples of service technology we described in this chapter, explain how the technology used in the service tours are alike and different. What types of decisions do operations managers need to make in each of these situations? How are these decisions alike or different?

9. Find at least three new applications of modern technology in business that are not discussed in this chapter. What impacts on productivity and quality do you think these applications have had?

10. For a value chain familiar to you, provide examples of "intermediaries." What do they do and how do they facilitate the buyer-seller relationship?

11. For a value chain familiar to you, provide examples of "return facilitators." What do they do and how do they facilitate the buyer-seller relationship?

12. Describe at least one application of modern technology in each of these service industries:
    a. financial services
    b. public and government services
    c. transportation services
    d. health care services
    e. educational services
    f. hotel and motel services

13. What is a business intelligence system? What benefits does a BIS provide to an organization?

14. What does Oracle (www.oracle.com) say about BIS? How does it define and view BIS?

15. Explain the role of a data warehouse and data mining in a BIS.

16. Write a short paper on data warehouses and associated inputs, outputs, and issues. What contributes to a successful data warehouse initiative?

17. How has technology impacted productivity? What role do you think it will play in the future?

18. Draw an aggregate flowchart of a B2B, B2C, or C2C value chain of interest to you, and briefly describe each major step in the value chain. How has technology been used in your value chain? Explain.

19. Explain the role of return facilitators in e-commerce. Find a specific example of one.

20. Describe an e-service, draw its place in the value chain, and discuss the impact on the employees and customers.

21. What other benefits and challenges of technology can you identify that are not contained in Exhibit 5.9? Explain.

22. What challenges do companies face when trying to implement e-commerce strategies? What can they learn from the WebVan experience?

23. Find the web site for one of the firms in Exhibit 5.7 and report on the firm's purpose, target market, role in the value chain, competitive priorities, and the role of technology. Draw the value chain and explain how these elements fit within the value chain.

24. Characterize an industry you are familiar with using Intel's three technology development stages—birth, turbulence, and build-out. What's your estimate of how long (in years) the technology development and adoption process will be?

25. How does technology impact people? What does this mean for decisions that operations managers must make?

26. Who is responsible for retraining workers displaced due to technology? Government? Business organizations? Individuals? Justify and explain.

27. What is the role of chief information officers in organizations today? What skills do they need and why?

28. What is an integrated operating system? List the major characteristics that an IOS has.

29. Write a paper on any one of the integrated operating systems introduced in the chapter—CRM, CIMS, SCM, ERP, or RMS. What role does operations play in this IOS?

30. Write a paper on a company you are familiar with that implemented any one of the integrated operating systems introduced in this chapter—CRM, CIMS, SCM, ERP, or RMS.

31. Discuss each of these statements. What might be wrong with each of them?
    a. "We've thought about computer integration of all our manufacturing functions, but when we

looked at it, we realized that the labor savings wouldn't justify the cost."

b. "We've had these computer-controlled robots on the line for several months now, and they're great! We no longer have to reconfigure the whole line to shift to a different product. I just give the robots new instructions, and they change operations. Just wait until this run is done and I'll show you."

c. "Each of my manufacturing departments is authorized to invest in whatever technologies are necessary to perform its function more effectively. As a result, we have state-of-the-art equipment throughout our factories—from CAD/CAM to automated materials handling to robots on the line. When we're ready to migrate to a CIM environment, we can just tie all these pieces together."

d. "I'm glad we finally got that CAD system," the designer said, a computer-generated blueprint in hand. "I was able to draw these plans and make modifications right on the computer screen in a fraction of the time it used to take by hand." "They tell me this new computer-aided manufacturing system will do the same for me," the manufacturing engineer replied. "I'll just punch in your specs and find out."

32. Define high and low scalability and give fresh examples of each. Justify your answer.

PROBLEMS AND ACTIVITIES

1. Research "cutting-edge" technologies that are currently being developed and comment on their possible use in operations. Some good sources are *Wired* magazine and *Scientific American* and, of course, the web.

2. Search the web sites for several of the companies listed in Exhibit 5.7 and discuss how technology supports their mission and strategy.

3. Investigate the current technology available for laptop computers. Select two or three different models and compare their features and operational characteristics, as well as manufacturer's support and service (you might wish to find some articles in magazines such as *PC World* or *PC Computing*). Explain how you might advise (a) a college student majoring in art, and (b) a salesman for a high-tech machine tool company in selecting the best computer for his or her needs.

4. Olentangy Boot Co. manufactures a specific type of boot for which the materials cost is $3.25 per pair, the variable labor cost is $4.00 per pair, and variable overhead cost is $0.80 per pair. Fixed costs are $175,000.

   a. If a pair of boots sells for a wholesale price of $14.00 per pair, how many pairs need to be produced to break even?

   b. New technology is available that molds and heat-seals the boot sole to the sides of the shoe, reducing the amount of stitching by one-half. The fixed cost is now $200,000 ($175,000 + $25,000), the revised material cost is $3.00, and the new variable labor cost is $2.20 per pair. If a pair of boots still sells for a wholesale price of $14.00 per pair, how many pairs need to be produced to break even? Would you adopt the new technology? Explain.

5. Identify a good or service and through library and web research try to define its degree of scalability. Is scalability a problem or asset for this organization? Explain. (Your answer will include many qualitative reasons but might also include fixed and variable cost analysis.)

6. A manager of Paris Manufacturing that produces computer hard drives is planning to lease a new automated inspection system. The manager believes the new system will be more accurate than the current manual inspection process. The firm has had problems with hard drive defects in the past and the automated system should help catch these defects before the drives are shipped to the final assembly manufacturer. The relevant information follows.

Current Manual Inspection System

    Annual fixed cost = $40,000
    Inspection variable cost per unit = $10 per unit

New Automated Inspection System

    Annual fixed cost = $200,000
    Inspection variable cost per unit = $0.55 per unit

   a. Suppose annual demand is 17,000 units. Should the firm lease the new inspection system?

b. Assume the cost factors given have not changed. A marketing representative of *NEW-SPEC*, a firm that specializes in providing manual inspection processes for other firms, approached Paris Manufacturing and offered to inspect parts for $11 each with no fixed cost. They assured Paris Manufacturing the accuracy and quality of their manual inspections would equal the automated inspection system. Demand for the upcoming year is forecast to be 17,000 units. Should the manufacturer accept the offer?

7. Suppose that the supplier ratings for the Sterling Equipment Corporation in Solved Problem 1 were as follows:

Factor	Supplier			
	1	2	3	4
Installation lead time	Poor	Average	Excellent	Good
Supplier training	Good	Poor	Excellent	Average
Productivity improvement	Average	Good	Excellent	Good
Supplier service	Average	Excellent	Good	Good
Flexibility	Good	Good	Excellent	Excellent

What decision would you make? Explain your reasoning.

8. Phelps Petroleum Company must decide between two methods of processing oil at a refinery. Method 1 has fixed costs of $12,000 for depreciation, maintenance, and taxes, whereas the fixed costs for Method 2 are $15,000. The variable costs depend on the chemical additives used and the heating requirements. These are $0.014 and $0.011 per bar-rel for Methods 1 and 2, respectively. Which method is more economical?

9. Maling Manufacturing needs to purchase a new piece of machining equipment. The two choices are a conventional (labor-intensive) machine and an automated (computer-controlled) machine. Profitability will depend on demand volume. The following table presents an estimate of profits over the next 3 years.

Decision	Demand Volume	
	Low	High
Conventional machine	$15,000	$21,000
Automated machine	$ 9,000	$35,000

Given the uncertainty associated with the demand volume, and no other information to work with, how would you make a decision? Explain your reasoning.

10. Martin's Service Station is considering investing in a heavy-duty snowplow this fall. Martin has analyzed the situation carefully and feels that this would be a very profitable investment if the snowfall is heavy, somewhat profitable if the snowfall is moderate, and would result in a loss if the snowfall is light. Specifically, Martin forecasts a profit of $7,000 if snowfall is heavy and $2,000 if it is moderate, and a $9,000 loss if it is light. From the Weather Bureau's long-range forecast, Martin estimates that P(heavy snowfall) = .4, P(moderate snowfall) = .3, and P(light snowfall) = .3. Use a decision tree (see Supplementary Chapter E on the Student CD-ROM) to evaluate this decision.

CASES

CONTRASTING MANUFACTURING TECHNOLOGY

Many types of manufacturing technology exist; Exhibit 5.13 defines just a few of them. Technology selection has implications for product performance, quality, operations effectiveness, and costs.

Next we describe the technology used by two different companies.

Clark Metal Products

Located in Blairsville, Pennsylvania, 40 miles east of Pittsburgh, Clark Metal Products has a modern 68,000-square-foot facility on a 7.4-acre site and incorporates a wide range of the latest in technology for metal fabri-cation and finishing. The engineering department creates Auto Cad drawings from customer specifications and offers design assistance that can produce more effective design configurations resulting in cost reductions. Clark's Flexible Manufacturing System, an Automated Punching Cell, allows the production of any number of parts at the lowest possible costs. Laser cutting tools help to reduce costs, improve performance, eliminate hard tooling, and achieve extreme accuracy. Welders apply their skills on cold-rolled steel, aluminum alloys, and stainless steel. Clark also offers powder coating as well as conventional spray finishes and screen printing services.

Exhibit 5.13 Basic Manufacturing Technology

Forming Technology	Machining Technology	Joining Technology
• Casting—forming objects by putting liquid or viscous material into a prepared mold or form. • Bending—the process by which bars, rods, wire, and sheet metal are bent into shapes in dies. • Rolling—squeezing metal between two revolving rolls. • Extrusion—forcing metal or plastics out through specially formed disks. • Forging—forming of metal by individual and intermittent applications of pressure, instead of applying continuous pressure as in rolling. • Stamping—forcing a hardened steel punch against a flat metal surface.	• Drilling—producing a hole by forcing a rotating drill against it. • Boring—enlarging a hole that has previously been drilled. • Grinding—removing metal by means of a rotating, abrasive wheel. • Milling—progressive removal of small increments of metal from the workpiece as it is fed slowly to a cutter rotating at high speed.	• Mechanical—using bolts or rivets to join two pieces. • Soldering—joining by means of a molten metal or alloy. • Welding—joining metals by concentrating heat, pressure, or both at the joint in order to coalesce the surfaces.

L A Aluminum

L A Aluminum produces lightweight aluminum castings from customers' ideas, drawings, or samples. The design and mold-making process begins with a toolmaker who creates a 3D drawing on a computer. Then he writes a computer program and sends it to an automated machining center that performs the actual cutting of a cast-iron mold. It might take several hours to actually make the mold. A first casting is made for customer evaluation, and any final design and cosmetic changes are made. After customer approval, the casting process begins. Once the mold has been prepared with the mold coat, which is used to release the casting and reduce wear to the mold, a casting is made. Next, aluminum alloy is preheated to remove any potential moisture and melted. The molten aluminum is ladled into the mold and allowed to solidify over a fixed length of time. Once this is done, the casting is removed from the mold and placed on a pallet for its journey through the rest of the process. This includes finishing, heat treating, and aging. Then the part either goes to final detailing in the finishing department or machining in the machine shop. Finish work includes deburring, sanding, grinding, plating, and coating. Other operations such as stamping part numbers, attaching labels, and packaging may also be performed. Automated machining centers are used to perform various additional operations to customer specifications. Some parts require a chemical coating to add corrosion protection and electrical conductivity in the plating department. Various quality control procedures such as hardness testing, pressure testing, and heat-treat certification are used to ensure that customer requirements are met.

Discussion Questions

1. Explain why these two companies use different manufacturing technology. For example, why does L A Aluminum use casting instead of machining to manufacture its components? How might the technologies used relate to the companies' competitive priorities?

2. How is automation used in these two companies, and what advantages do you perceive it to have for their operations?

D&C CAR WASH SERVICES

Drew Ebelhar was contemplating buying a car wash franchise as a family business. His wife Caroline and their two kids, Steve and Bonnie, and the dog, Bernie, were a close-knit family and were tired of the bureaucracy of corporate and government jobs. The dual-career family had saved about $200,000 in cash and bonds, and Drew, who was 59, could soon cash in some of his retirement accounts to free up another $200,000. These monies would be used for a down payment. One option was to buy everything outright and be the sole owner of the car wash, while another option was to buy a franchise from a national chain.

Drew and Caroline (the D&C Car Wash) needed to develop a business plan stating the strategy and mission of their business, evaluate the economics of the business, select a site and buy the property, and start up the business with an idea of providing superior customer service—a premium car washing experience. Drew had a bachelor's degree in mechanical engineering and Caroline had earned a bachelor's degree in accounting. The idea also included letting their two kids, Steve and Bonnie, work in the family-run car wash. Drew and Caroline had collected some primary information about car wash equipment and franchises and were ready to start their business plan initiative.

Car Wash Industry

In 1914, the first car assembly line was opened in Detroit, Michigan. People pushed Model-T cars through the wash stations in a circular route. A people-powered chain conveyor pulled cars through a straight (serial) assembly line by 1928. By 1932, there were 32 car washes in the United States. In the 1930s, car wash owners began to ask manufacturers if they could build automated brushes and other electromechanical car-washing devices. In 1946, the first semiautomatic car wash system was developed with an overhead sprinkler system, three sets of manually operated brushes, and a conveyer powered by an electric motor pulling cars along a straight line. By the 1950s, the automated car wash (except for vacuuming at the beginning of the process and cleaning the interior of the vehicle at the end of the process) was available from several manufacturers. Today, there are automated car wash systems in over 100 countries. It is estimated that 20 people are required to do the car-washing process manually instead of the 5 people with a robotic car wash system given the same level of quality and processing time.

Available Information Collected to Date

Investment costs are shown in Exhibit 5.14 and operating costs in Exhibit 5.15. Revenue is based on a most likely forecast of 20,000 cars per year and average revenue per vehicle of $22 for a typical modern car wash facility in an affluent suburb of a major U.S. city. The average net revenue per vehicle for detailing cars and dent repair is $100, with demand of 5 percent of total demand. The net revenue of $100 is revenue minus costs for detailing services.

The key factor in a successful car wash business is location. This includes site location, traffic density and patterns, and the demographics of the surrounding area. Drew and Caroline wondered what other characteristics make for a successful car wash service. The average car wash is open about 300 days per year with some open as little as 200 days while others are open 350 days. Some car wash conveyors are designed to process up to 155 cars per hour, but most car washes operate in the 50 cars per hour or less range. The speed of the conveyor can be changed in most car wash systems depending on demand, weather, and degree of dirt on vehicles. Some competitors use a car wash system that processes 15 to 25 cars per hour by cleaning a stationary vehicle while all equipment moves around the car. Keeping the robots operating is a struggle and all car wash owners have stories of losing a high-demand day of sales because of machine breakdowns and parts shortages.

Exhibit 5.14 D&C Car Wash Services—Investment Costs*

Type of Investment	Cost and Related Information
Site (Premium location in high-traffic intersection)	$300,000 to $600,000

Equipment
    Automated car wash system
    Initial parts inventory
    Detail equipment (professional carpet cleaning and vacuum machine, etc.) if decide to offer this service
    Other equipment (cash register, televisions for waiting area, telephone, online hookup)
	
	$300,000
	$5,000
	$7,000
	$6,000

Building
    Car wash assembly line (tunnel) building @ $50/square foot
    Detail garage @ $50/square foot (if done)
    Lobby and office complex (assume 600 sq. ft. @ $75/square foot
    Pole sign and advertising board(s)
    Licenses, inspections, building permits, incorporation fee, attorney, architect, engineer,
        environmental impact report, and utilities to property
	
	$250,000
	$50,000
	$45,000
	$8,000
	
	$50,000

Start-up—Cash on hand	$50,000 to $100,000
Property and building closing, title insurance, land survey, filing fees, appraisal, vending license and occupation fees, and environmental audits	$5,000
Total investment costs $450k + 300k + 5k + 7k + 6k + 250k + 50k + 45k + 8k + 50k + 75k + 5k =	$1,251,000

*Note that Drew and Caroline put down $400,000 of their own money to reduce total net investment costs.

Exhibit 5.15 D&C Car Wash Services—Operating Costs

Type of Operating Cost	Cost and Related Information
Chemicals and utilities	$1.50 per car
Sludge removal	$4,000 per year
Maintenance, insurance, and advertising	$1,000 per month
Accountant, attorney, and merchant fees	$500 per month
Labor (assuming an average of four full-time employees at $25,000 per year plus 20% for benefits and workers compensation insurance) including one on-duty manager @ $50,000 including benefits	$170,000
Office expense including telephone, photocopying, etc.	$500 per month
Mortgage (assuming investment cost of $1,251,000 − $400,000 down payment = $851,000 mortgage)	$6,000 per month
Car damage expense @ 0.008 of revenue ($22/car)(20,000 cars)(0.008)	$3,520

Decisions and Analysis

Drew and Caroline had many issues they wanted to address in their business plan. They also planned to visit automated conveyer car wash sites and talk to owners.

Discussion Questions

1. How might the strategy, mission, competitive priorities, and customer benefit package of this business affect their technology decisions?

2. What issues and problems should be anticipated with managing this business, particularly with respect to technology? What role does operations play in successfully handling these issues and problems?

3. What does a break-even analysis indicate about this business venture? Should Drew and Caroline go into this business?

ENDNOTES

1 "Tractors," *The Columbus Dispatch*, Columbus, Ohio, p. A2.

2 "Tiny Transmitters Likely to Replace Time-Tested Bar Codes on Products," *The Columbus Dispatch*, Columbus, Ohio, September 29, 2003, p. C1.

3 *Award, The Newsletter of Baldrigeplus*, May 7, 2000, www.baldrigeplus.com.

4 Kimberley, William, "Building the BMW 7 Series," *Automotive Design and Production*, May 2002, pp. 24–25.

5 Bylinsky, Gene, "Heroes of U.S. Manufacturing," *Fortune*, March 18, 2002, pp. 130[A]–130[L].

6 Bateson, J. E. G., and Hoffman, K. D., *Managing Service Marketing*, 4th ed., Forth Worth, TX: Harcourt College Publishers, 1999.

7 "Behind Surging Productivity: The Service Sector Delivers," *Wall Street Journal*, November 7, 2003, p. B1. Also, see http://online.wsj.com.

8 Kirkpatrick, David, "Beyond Buzz," *Fortune*, March 18, 2002, pp. 160–168.

9 McManus, Neil, "Robots at Your Service," *Wired*, January 2003, pp. 58–59.

10 Collier, D. A., "The Service Sector Revolution: The Automation of Services," *Long Range Planning*, Vol. 16, December 1983, pp. 10–20. Also, see Collier, D. A. "The Automation of the Goods-Producing Industries: Implications for Operations Managers," *Operations Management Review*, Spring 1983, pp. 7–12; and *Service Management: The Automation of Services*, Englewood Cliffs, NJ: Prentice-Hall, Inc., 1985.

11 "The Tying Cure," *Wall Street Journal*, September 16, 2002, p. R10.

12 *Source:* Company History at www.ups.com.

13 www.cooltown.hp.com/mpulse/0902-shippers.asp, September 16, 2002.

14 "Making Profit Out of Data," Special Advertising Section, *Business Week*, May 20, 2002.

15 Eryn Brown, "Slow Road to Fast Data," *Fortune*, March 18, 2002, pp. 170–172.

16 "Economies of Scale," *CIO Magazine*, August 15, 2002, p. 48. Reprinted through courtesy of *CIO*. Copyright © 2005 CXO Media, Inc.

17 "IBM is to Spend More on Services," *The Wall Street Journal*, November 20, 2002, p. B5.

18 "Ten Minutes with Michael Dell," *NASDAQ*, no. 32, September 2001, pp. 15–17.

[19] "Honda All Set to Grow," *The Columbus Dispatch*, Columbus, Ohio, September 18, 2002, pp. B1–B2.

[20] Case study reported in www.cio.com.

[21] "Strategic Alignment," *CIO Magazine*, August 15, 2002, pp. 56–64.

[22] "Behind the Numbers," *CIO Magazine*, November 2, 2000 (http://www2.cio.com/metrics/2000/metric135.html).

[23] "Customers Come First," *CIO Magazine*, February 20, 2002 (http://www2.cio.com/metrics/2002/metric325.html).

[24] Collier, David A., "New Orleans Hilton & Hilton Towers," *Service Management: Operating Decisions*, Englewood Cliffs, NJ: Prentice-Hall, Inc., 1987.

[25] Smith, Barry C., Leimkuhler, Jon F., and Darrow, Ross M., "Yield Management at American Airlines," *Interfaces* 22, no. 1, 1992, pp. 8–31.

[26] Liberman, W., "Implementing Yield Management," *ORSA/TIMS National Meeting Presentation*, San Francisco, November 1992.

[27] Geraghty, M., and Johnson, M., "Revenue Management Saves National Car Rental," *Interfaces* 12, no. 7, 1997, pp. 107–127.

[28] "Behind Surging Productivity: The Service Sector Delivers," *Wall Street Journal*, November 7, 2003. Also, see http://online.wsj.com.

[29] *Ibid.*

[30] "U.S. Producitivity Boom Continues," *The Columbus Dispatch*, Columbus, Ohio, October 24, 2002, p. B1.

[31] "Information Technology Spawns New Industries, Revitalizes Old," *Investor's Business Daily*, January 19, 1999, p. A10.

[32] Bylinsky, Gene, "America's Elite Factories," *Fortune*, August 14, 2000, p. 118.

[33] "Lands' End, Customers Reaping Rewards of Customized Apparel," *The Columbus Dispatch*, Columbus, Ohio, September 8, 2002, p. B10.

[34] "Why WebVan Went Bust," *The Wall Street Journal*, July 16, 2001, p. A22.

[35] Kimberly, A., "E-Commerce Sites Developing Return Policies," *Video Store*, January 9, 2000.

[36] Hopkins, Jim, and Kessler, Michelle, "Companies Squander Billions on Tech," *USA Today*, May 20, 2002, pp. 1A–2A.

[37] 2001 Annual Report, *Intel Corporation*, 2200 Mission College Boulevard, Santa Clara, CA (www.intel.com), pp. 3–7.

[38] "Wal-Mart Focuses on Optical Site," *The Columbus Dispatch*, Columbus, Ohio, August 24, 2001, pp. A1 and A2.

[39] 2001 Annual Report, *Applied Materials*, 3050 Bowers Avenue, Santa Clara, California, p. 19.

Chapter Outline

CHAPTER 6

Goods and Service Design

Learning Objectives

1. To understand how goods and services are designed, how OM principles can facilitate and improve the design process, and how a well-designed customer benefit package can help organizations gain competitive advantage.

2. To understand some of the fundamental design approaches and tools used for developing manufactured goods and associated manufacturing processes.

3. To understand how the elements of a service delivery system support customer benefit package design and set the stage for service encounter design and execution.

4. To understand the issues and decisions necessary to design effective service encounters.

5. To understand that primary and peripheral goods and services require well-designed manufacturing processes, service delivery systems, and service encounters through an integrative case study.

6. To understand the importance of speed of design and its implications for business strategy, and to learn some important approaches for improving design speed.

• The year was 1975. John and Michelle promised their son Michael a new bicycle for his eighth birthday. Both John and Michelle remembered their Schwinn-trademark bicycles, with their distinctive balloon tires, coaster brakes, and black and gold fenders. When they entered the Schwinn store, they felt like kids again. There on display were the same types of bikes they remembered as children. But Michael looked disappointed. After a bit of questioning, he said he wanted a faster and sleeker bike like some of his friends have. The salesperson said that they didn't have any bicycles like that, and that the bikes they sold were "classics" that everyone would love. Not to disappoint their son, John and Michelle ended up leaving and purchasing a more modern bicycle elsewhere.

PR Newswire Antonov Automotive Technologies

• In a rare partnership, Ford Motor Co. and General Motors Corp. announced plans to jointly develop a six-speed automatic transmission, with the, objective of catching up with Japanese and European automakers. The new gearbox would be 4% to 8% more fuel-efficient than today's four-speed automatic transmissions and will be used in high-volume market segments by both automakers. The collaborative effort will speed development time and lower development costs for Ford and GM. They will share basic designs, engineering and testing results to date, and work with suppliers to develop and purchase new parts but once a proven six-speed transmission is available each will assemble their own transmissions at their own plants. Ford and GM expect to save several hundred million dollars by this joint venture.[1]

Lockheed Martin/EPA/Landov

- In October 2001, *Business Week* reported that Lockheed Martin beat out Boeing for the largest defense contract in U.S. history—production of the Joint Strike Fighter jet—worth at least $400 billion. A Pentagon source noted "Compare the two designs for the Joint Strike Fighter, and you'll see the obvious: Boeing's looks like 'a flying frog with its mouth wide open.' " A senior Air Force general also observed, "the Lockheed design wins hands down." However, a Boeing spokesman retorted, "Boeing officials say looks aren't part of the design. We design our planes to go to war, not to the senior prom." *Business Week* concluded by noting that Boeing has cut some 30,000 jobs and will now likely exit the fighter-jet business.

Discussion Questions: How important is design compared to functionality in your personal purchasing decisions? Provide an example of a decision that you have made where design was an important factor in your purchase decision. Are there any risks involved in collaborating in the fashion that Ford and GM have done?

Perhaps the most important strategic decision that any firm makes involves the selection and development of new goods and services and the value chain structure and processes that make and deliver them. In fact, decisions about what goods and services to offer and how to position them in the marketplace often determine the ultimate growth, profitability, and success of the firm. The complexity of value chain design and structure is very much dependent upon the number of goods and services that an organization provides. For example, a half-century ago, the customer benefit package for an automobile consisted primarily of the vehicle itself. Today, the CBP is much more complex. Peripheral goods might include loaner cars and free snacks and drinks in the customer waiting room. Peripheral services might include leasing, home pickup and drop-off service, driver and vehicle maintenance training programs, and customer waiting rooms with access to the Internet, and babysitting. When the CBP is complex, then the network of processes necessary to create and deliver it generally is also complex, requiring a high level of coordination. Thus, organizations need to understand the implications of product decisions on process decisions and the entire value chain.

Poor product and process decisions can take a company to the brink of extinction. This, in fact, is what happened to Schwinn, the basis for the first episode.

The name Schwinn was synonymous with bicycles for most of the twentieth century.[2] Through its network of independent dealers, Schwinn sold one of every four bicycles in 1950. However, by 1975 it sold only one in ten, and by the late 1970s, Schwinn's market share had dropped below 8 percent. They were displaced by lighter, faster, sleeker, or cheaper bikes made by foreign and domestic competitors. Moreover, Schwinn's prices were high compared to those of competitors. Analysts suggest that the firm lost its competitive advantage when it resisted changing its traditionally heavier bike line to newer and lighter bicycles and mountain bikes, which made up about 80 percent of sales in the late 1990s. In other words, the company failed to respond to emerging customer wants and needs. Its customer benefit package ignored market and customer trends.

In late 1992, Schwinn (a privately held company) filed for protection under Chapter 11 of the federal bankruptcy code. Since then, the company has changed its product line to lighter, sleeker-looking bicycles, is upgrading its health and physical-fitness products line, and is employing new technologies and processes in manufacturing. But missed opportunities both in terms of (1) developing attractive new bicycles quickly that would sell in changing markets and (2) building manufacturing capability to keep quality high and costs low hurt the company. Operations management plays a major role in both situations.

The second episode highlights both the competitive and economic importance of product design and development. Ford and GM are behind Japanese and European automakers in this new technology—a six-speed fuel-efficient automobile transmission—and the only way to catch up is a joint venture. Fast product development is a critical success factor in today's environment, and even collaboration among rivals is often a necessity to compete globally. Finally, the Lockheed-Boeing episode documents the importance of fully understanding customer needs in design activities. No matter how good a product is technically, a poor design that looks like "a flying frog with its mouth wide open" will not win customers.

Economists have noted that the long-run prosperity of a nation depends on the capacity of its entrepreneurial individuals and firms to create and satisfy new customer wants.[3] In this chapter, we focus on designing goods and services to meet the wants and needs of customers and markets. We also introduce some new concepts such as customer contact and service guarantees and operations management tools such as product simplification, the Taguchi loss function, methods of evaluating system reliabilities, and a framework for integrating goods and services design. We also present an integrative case study that illustrates how goods and services are designed and bundled together in a unique way to gain competitive advantage. In the next chapter, we address process design in goods-producing and service-providing organizations.

DESIGNING GOODS AND SERVICES

In the early 1900s, Henry Ford said something to the effect of "You can have any color of car you want as long as it is black." Clearly, such a philosophy will not succeed with today's consumers. As we noted in earlier chapters, the success of a firm is driven by the customer benefit packages (CBPs) it offers and how they address both order-qualifying and order-winning criteria as perceived by consumers. For example, the automobile leasing terms and condition may be the order winner while the automobile itself is the order qualifier. However, although the design of a customer benefit package is primarily a strategic decision, marketing executives cannot make it in isolation. What products and services an organization chooses to offer depends greatly on the organization's operational capability to produce and

Learning Objective
To understand how goods and services are designed, how OM principles can facilitate and improve the design process, and how a well-designed customer benefit package can help organizations gain competitive advantage.

deliver them at the appropriate cost and level of quality. The actual design process involves many operational details and cannot be separated from the processes that create and deliver goods and services. Thus, operations managers need to be involved in design initiatives.

Designing goods and services is far more challenging today than in the past. For instance, a single state-of-the-art integrated circuit may contain millions of transistors and involve hundreds of manufacturing steps; and coordinating the disembarkation of thousands of cruise ship passengers, processing arriving passengers, cleaning and maintenance, and replenishment of food and supplies—all in a matter of hours—is clearly not a simple task. In addition, organizations cannot stand still; they must continually seek to improve designs to reduce costs and increase quality. For example, an early network interface card contained about 40 chips; five years later, the entire system board had just 19. With fewer components, there are fewer opportunities for failure and less chance of assembly error.[4]

To design and improve goods and services, most companies use some type of structured process. The typical goods and services development processes are shown in Exhibit 6.1. In general, the design of both goods and services follow a similar path. The critical differences lie in the detailed product and process design phases. We will examine each of the general steps. Later in this chapter, we will illustrate how LensCrafters uses such an approach to design its goods and services and integrate them into an effective customer benefit package.

Strategic Mission, Analysis, and Competitive Priorities

In Chapter 4 we discussed how organizations set strategic directions and competitive priorities from an understanding of their markets and of customers' wants and needs. These should be consistent with and support the firm's mission and vision. New or redesigned good and service ideas should incorporate both expressed and latent customer needs and expectations and address the competitive priorities that the firm has identified. This step of the process requires a significant amount of research and innovation involving marketing, engineering, operations, and sales functions and should involve customers, suppliers, and employees throughout the value chain. The data and information that result from this effort provide the key input for designing the final customer benefit package.

Customer Benefit Package Design and Configuration

Clearly, firms have a large variety of possible choices in configuring a customer benefit package (CBP), as we described in Chapter 1. What primary and peripheral goods and services should they include in the CBP? For example, an automobile dealer might include with a new vehicle such options as leasing, free oil changes and/or maintenance, a performance driving school, free auto washes, service pickup and delivery, loaner cars, and so on. For an interesting example, see the OM Spotlight: The "Hear Music Coffeehouse." Choosing the right combination is clearly an important decision that will affect the organization's competitive success and should not be done in an arbitrary fashion, but should rely on the data and information acquired in steps 1 and 2 of Exhibit 6.1.

Concept development *involves proposing and evaluating potential CBP ideas for feasibility.*

Concept development *involves proposing and evaluating potential CBP ideas for feasibility.* Some questions that must be addressed are: Will the CBP meet customers' requirements? What unique combination of primary and peripheral goods and services will provide a competitive advantage? Does the CBP address order-qualifying and order-winning criteria? How does it compare with competitor offerings? Do we have the operational capability to produce each good or service economically and with high quality?

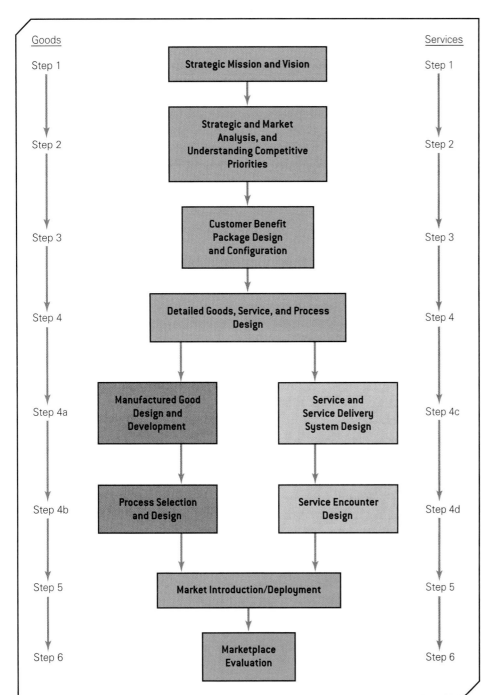

Exhibit 6.1
An Integrated Framework for
Goods and Service Design

As an example, the principal requirement of hotel guests is a clean and safe place to sleep; this represents the primary service offered by the hotel. However, customers may have other wants and needs, such as meal service, Internet access, newspapers or bottled water, and so on. The choice of such peripheral goods and services will differ by design of the concept. A budget hotel might not have a full-service restaurant and only offer a free continental breakfast; others might have a hot buffet, a standard restaurant, and/or room service. Some might have a dial-up Internet connection, and others might have high-speed access or none at all.

The "Hear Music Coffeehouse"[5]

On the trendy Third Street Promenade in Santa Monica, California, a new concept music store, known by many as the "Hear Music Coffeehouse," opened in 2004. It's a beautiful space with warm lighting and wood paneling—a place where customers can buy CDs, linger with a drink while they listen to music, and sift through thousands of songs stored in a database to create a personalized mix and burn it to a CD. What is unusual about this place is that it is a Starbucks. It is the first of several fully integrated café-music stores that Starbucks is launching with its wholly owned subsidiary, Hear Music, with plans to increase this novel customer benefit package to over 1000 stores.

Starbucks chairman Howard Schultz stumbled on Hear Music record store in Palo Alto California about five years before, and fell in love with its values of intimacy, quality and customer focus (employees can almost always suggest singers you might like if you tell them what music you already own). Hear Music was one of the first stores to introduce listening stations where shoppers can try before they buy. This is part of a long-term global strategy to leverage Starbuck's Wi-Fi capability, with hopes that record labels will develop proprietary material for the Starbucks network and possibly create the largest music store in any city in which Starbucks is located. As Schultz noted, "We've known for a long time that Starbucks is more than just a wonderful cup of coffee. It's the experience. . . . We saw that [Hear Music] were doing for music what we had done for coffee."

Essentially, CBP design and configuration choices revolve around a solid understanding of customer needs and target markets and the value that customers place on such attributes as

- **Time**—Some grocery stores now offer self-service checkout to reduce customer waiting time, and manufacturers such as Dell use the Internet to acquire customer information for more responsive product design.
- **Place**—UPS has "UPS Stores" strategically located for customer convenience that also provide packaging services; many companies offer day-care centers on site to provide convenience to their employees.
- **Information**—Bank of America provides an Internet search capability for the best home equity loan; a business dedicated to providing guitar music books and videos (www.ChordMelody.com) offers a telephone hot line to speak with a professional guitarist for advice on selecting the proper instructional and performance material. Many goods come with comprehensive user manuals.
- **Entertainment**—Dick's Sporting Goods Store provides a rock-climbing wall for children while other family members shop, a pianist serenades shoppers at Nordstrom's department stores, and some vehicles have built-in DVD players.
- **Exchange**—Retail stores such as Best Buy and Circuit City allow customers to travel to the store and buy the goods, purchase them on their web sites and have them delivered, or purchase them on the web site and have them ready to be picked up at the store.
- **Form**—For manufactured goods, form is associated with the physical characteristics of the good and addresses the important customer need of aesthetics. An interior designer might use different methods such as sketches, photographs, physical samples, or even computer-simulated renderings to show how a kitchen might be transformed.

A job-seeking service such as Monster.com provides pure information value; buying an automobile or going on a vacation involves all six attributes. One useful tool for assisting in concept development and in subsequent steps of the design process is *quality function deployment*, which will be described later in this chapter.

Detailed Goods, Services, and Process Design

If a proposal survives the concept stage—and many do not—each good or service in the CBP, as well as the process that creates them, must be designed in more detail. This is where the design of goods and services differs, as suggested by the alternate paths in Exhibit 6.1. The first three steps in Exhibit 6.1 are more strategic and conceptual in nature; step 4 focuses on detailed design and implementation.

The design of a manufactured good focuses on its physical characteristics—dimensions, materials, color, and so on. Much of this work is done by artists and engineers to translate customer requirements into physical specifications. This is the focus in step 4a in the exhibit. The process by which the good is manufactured (that is, the configuration of machines and labor) can be designed as a separate activity (step 4b), with, of course, proper communication and coordination with the designers of the good.

The design of a "service," however, cannot be done independently from the "process" by which the service is delivered. Ms. G. Lynn Shostack was one of the first to understand services and advocate a multidisciplinary approach to service design, as evidenced in the following comments made in the early 1980s:

A service is not something that is built in a factory, shipped to a store, put on a shelf, and then taken home by a consumer. A service is a dynamic, living process. A service is performed. A service is rendered. The "raw materials" of a service are time and motion; not plastic or steel. A service cannot be stored or shipped; only the means for creating it can. A service cannot be held in one's hand or physically possessed. In short, a service is not a thing.

Unfortunately, the harder service firms try to make the manufacturing model work, the more cracks appear in it. The real problem is that the functional structure itself is wrong. It reinforces piecemeal management, piecemeal knowledge and piecemeal experience, because it assumes a divisibility in services that simply does not exist.

To help service firms do formally what great service founders have done intuitively, service firms need a true service design function—one that is a permanent, ongoing part of the business.[6]

The process by which the service is created and delivered (that is, "produced") is, in essence, the service itself! For example, the steps that a desk clerk follows to check in a guest at a hotel represents the process by which the guest is served and (ideally) experiences a sense of satisfaction. Thus, service design must be addressed from two perspectives—the Service Delivery System and the Service Encounter, as noted in steps 4c and 4d in Exhibit 6.1.

Market Introduction/Deployment

In this step, the final bundle of goods and services—the customer benefit package—is advertised, marketed, and offered to customers. For manufactured goods, this includes making the item in the factory and shipping it to warehouses or wholesale and retail stores; for services, it might include hiring and training employees or staying open an extra hour in the evening. For many services, it means building sites such as branch banks or hotels or retail stores. For digital services, such as obtaining price quotes for airline flights, ordering MP3 files, or playing digital games online, this might require web page and computer server launches, upgrades, and promotions.

Marketplace Evaluation

One of the reasons that Japanese manufacturers such as Toyota and Sony dominate world markets is their relentless process of evaluating customer perceptions and satisfaction and using this intelligence to better understand customer needs and identify improvement opportunities. The marketplace is a graveyard of missed opportunities, ill-defined CBPs, and failed products resulting from ineffective operations. Ken Olsen, the president and founder of Digital Equipment Corp. stated in 1977, "There is no reason anyone would want a computer in their home."[7] Of course, you probably cannot imagine living without one! The OM Spotlight on WebVan in Chapter 5 highlights a poorly defined CBP where management did not fully understand the operations and logistical implications. Thus, the final step in designing and delivering a customer benefit package is to constantly evaluate how well the goods and services are selling and what customers' reactions to them are. The performance criteria introduced in Chapter 2 provide insights into how customers, managers, and shareholders evaluate the success or failure of the CBP and the organization's processes that produce and deliver it.

PRODUCT AND PROCESS DESIGN IN MANUFACTURING

Learning Objective
To understand some of the fundamental design approaches and tools used for developing manufactured goods and associated manufacturing processes.

In this section we focus on steps 4a and 4b in Exhibit 6.1—the detailed design process for manufactured goods. For a manufactured good, such as an automobile, computer, bank checkbook, or a textbook, the detailed design process begins by determining marketing and technical specifications. This step typically involves engineers who translate a concept into blueprints and select materials or purchased components. In addition, they must coordinate their efforts with operations managers to ensure that existing manufacturing processes can produce the design or that the right process is selected in step 4b of Exhibit 6.1.

For most manufactured goods, this phase usually includes prototype testing. **Prototype testing** *is the process by which a model (real or simulated) is constructed to test the good's physical properties or use under actual operating conditions, as well as consumer reactions to the prototypes.* For example, in developing the user interface for an automobile navigation system, BMW conducted extensive consumer tests with a keyboard, a rotating push button, and a joystick (the push button was ultimately selected).[8] Boeing's 777 jets were built using digital prototypes and simulating different operating conditions; no physical prototypes were produced.

Prototype testing *is the process by which a model (real or simulated) is constructed to test the good's physical properties or use under actual operating conditions, as well as consumer reactions to the prototypes.*

Many companies view customers as significant partners in product development. For example, Ames Rubber Corporation, a producer of rubber rollers for office machines, uses a four-step approach to product development that maintains close communication with the customer.[9] Typically, Ames initiates a new product through a series of meetings with the customer and sales/marketing or the technical services group. From these meetings, management prepares a product brief listing all technical, material, and operational requirements. The brief is forwarded to internal departments, such as engineering, quality, and manufacturing. The technical staff then selects materials, processes, and procedures and submits its selections to the customer. Upon the customer's approval, a prototype is made. Ames delivers the prototype to the customer, who evaluates and tests it and reports results to the company. Ames makes the requested modifications and returns the prototype for further testing. This process continues until the customer is completely satisfied. Next, Ames makes a limited preproduction run. Data collected during the run are analyzed and shared with the customer. Upon approval, full-scale production commences.

After the design for a manufactured good is finalized, operations managers must select the best process to make it—step 4b in Exhibit 6.1. This involves choosing the appropriate technology and equipment, as we discussed in Chapter 4, and determining the layout of the manufacturing facility. We cover process selection and design in Chapter 7 and facility layout in Chapter 8. As we noted earlier, this must be a coordinated effort with design engineers. All departments play crucial roles in the design process. The designer's objective is to design a product that achieves the desired functional requirements. The manufacturing engineer's objective is to produce it efficiently. The salesperson's goal is to sell the manufactured good, and the finance person's goal is to make a profit. Purchasing seeks parts that meet quality requirements. Packaging and distribution deliver the product to the customer in good operating condition. Clearly, all business functions have a stake in the product; therefore, all should work together. Many companies today use cross-functional product design teams that include individuals from all key functions to ensure the proper coordination (see OM Spotlight: Solar Turbines).

Robust Design and the Taguchi Loss Function

A manufactured good's performance is affected by variations that occur during production, environmental factors, and the ways in which people use it. Design should take those issues into account. A high-quality good should perform near its performance target consistently throughout its life span and under all operating conditions. Therefore, an effective design should identify the settings of product or process parameters that minimize the sensitivity of designs to sources of variation in the factory and in use. *Goods that are insensitive to external sources of variation are called* robust. An example of a robust design is the "gear effect" designed into modern golf clubs, which brings the ball back on line even if it is hit off the

Goods that are insensitive to external sources of variation are called robust.

OM SPOTLIGHT

Solar Turbines[10]

Solar Turbines, a division of Caterpillar that manufactures gas turbine products for the global market, employs a team-oriented New Product Introduction (NPI) process to meet customer needs and minimize development schedules and cost. Solar Turbines introduced the NPI process to make product development more effective and efficient. The NPI Process consists of four phases:

- Market Requirements and Concept Development,
- Product Planning,
- Development, and
- Production.

NPI teams are multifunctional groups charged with bringing a new product from concept through field operation. The teams are formed at the start of the Market Requirement and Concept phase. They include representatives from manufacturing, customer service, finance, the firm's Products Committee, project engineering, marketing, package engineering, and tur-

bine engineering, all coordinated by a team leader. Human Resources Development representatives may even support the teams during start-up to assess team effectiveness and recommend appropriate training.

In each phase of the NPI process, many activities are performed concurrently to reduce total product development time. For example, typical concurrent activities in the Product Planning phase are functional support team formation, market requirements determination, customer requirements determination, product requirement specification, competitive strategy evaluation, alternatives evaluation, risk assessment, business plan development, and products committee approval. Once the product is finalized, it is released to production. But in this case, production knows what is coming and has had a role in designing the product and selecting the process to make it. Solar has found that product development activities with the early involvement of all key stakeholders contributes to higher product quality, shorter development schedules, and lower overall product development costs.

"sweet spot" of the club. This concept can also be applied to services. For example, an automatic teller machine (ATM) provides only certain ways to process financial transactions. The customer must perform the steps in a certain fashion or sequence, or the transaction is not processed. This is not a particularly robust design.

An approach to robust design developed by Japan's Genichi Taguchi has received considerable attention. Taguchi's original premise is simple: *Instead of constantly directing effort toward controlling a process to assure consistent quality, design the manufactured good to achieve high quality despite the variations that will occur on the production line.* Taguchi's approach is based on the use of statistically designed experiments to optimize the design and manufacturing process and are being incorporated into many computer-aided design systems. ITT Corporation's implementation of Taguchi's technique cut defects by more than half, saving $60 million in the first two years.[11] AT&T also used this approach when it developed an integrated circuit for amplifying voice signals. As originally designed, the circuit had to be manufactured very precisely to avoid variations in the strength of the signal. Such a circuit would have been costly to make because of the stringent quality controls needed during the manufacturing process. But AT&T's engineers, after testing and analyzing the design, realized that if the resistance of the circuit were reduced—a minor change with no associated costs—the circuit would be much less sensitive to manufacturing variations. The result was a 40 percent improvement in quality.

Taguchi also explained the economic value of reducing variation in manufacturing. Taguchi maintained that the traditional practice of meeting design specifications is inherently flawed. For most manufactured goods, design blueprints specify a target dimension (called the *nominal*), along with a range of permissible variation (called the *tolerance*), for example, 0.500 ± 0.020 cm. The nominal dimension is 0.500 cm, but may vary anywhere in a range from 0.480 to 0.520 cm. This assumes that the customer, either the consumer or the next department in the production process, would accept any value between 0.480 to 0.520 but not be satisfied with a value outside this range. (This is sometimes called the "goal post model" of conforming to specifications.) Also, this approach assumes that costs do not depend on the actual value of the dimension as long as it falls within the specified tolerance (see Exhibit 6.2).

But what is the real difference between 0.479 and 0.481? The former would be considered as "out of specification" and either reworked or scrapped, whereas the latter would be acceptable. Actually, the impact of either value on the performance characteristic of the product would be about the same. Neither value is close to the nominal specification 0.500. The nominal specification is the ideal target value for the critical quality characteristic. Taguchi's approach assumes that the smaller the variation about the nominal specification, the better is the quality. In turn, products are more consistent, and total costs are less. The following example supports this notion.

The Japanese newspaper *Ashai* published an example comparing the cost and quality of Sony televisions at two plants in Japan and San Diego.[12] The color density of all the units produced at the San Diego plant was within specifications, whereas some of those shipped from the Japanese plant were not (see Exhibit 6.3).

Exhibit 6.2
Traditional Goal Post View of
Conforming to Specifications

However, the average loss per unit of the San Diego plant was $0.89 greater than that of the Japanese plant. This increased cost occurred because workers adjusted units that were out of specification at the San Diego plant, adding cost to the process. Furthermore, a unit adjusted to minimally meet specifications was more likely to generate customer complaints than a unit close to the original target value, therefore incurring higher field service costs. Exhibit 6.3 shows that fewer U.S.-produced sets met the target value for color density. The distribution of quality in the Japanese plant was more uniform around the target value, and though some units were out of specification, the total cost was less. Also note in Exhibit 6.3 the difference in the variance about the target value of $\sigma^2 = 8.33$ in a U.S. factory versus $\sigma^2 = 2.78$ in a Japanese factory. Which factory produces the most consistent output? Which would have the most satisfied customers?

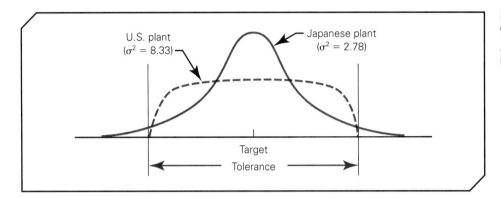

Exhibit 6.3
Variation in U.S.-Made Versus Japanese-Made Television Components

Taguchi measured quality as the variation from the target value of a design specification and then translated that variation into an economic "loss function" that expresses the cost of variation in monetary terms. Taguchi assumed that losses can be approximated by a quadratic function so that larger deviations from target cause increasingly larger losses. For the case in which a specific target value is best and quality deteriorates as the value moves away from the target on either side (called "nominal is best"), the loss function is represented by

$$L(x) = k(x - T)^2 \qquad \textbf{(6.1)}$$

where
$L(x)$ is the monetary value of the loss associated with deviating from the target, T,
x is the actual value of the dimension,
k is a constant that translates the deviation into dollars.

Exhibit 6.4 illustrates this Taguchi loss function.

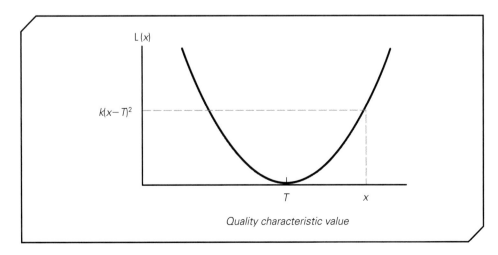

Exhibit 6.4
Nominal-Is-Best Taguchi Loss Function

The constant, k, is estimated by determining the cost of repair or replacement if a certain deviation from the target occurs, as the following example illustrates. Suppose that the specification on a part is 0.500 ± 0.020 cm. A detailed analysis of product returns and repairs has discovered that many failures occur when the actual dimension is near the extreme of the tolerance range—that is, when the dimensions are approximately 0.48 or 0.52—and costs \$50 for repair. Thus, in Equation (6.1), the deviation from the target, $x - T$ is 0.02 and $L(x) = \$50$. Substituting these values, we have

$$50 = k(0.02)^2$$

or

$$k = 50/0.0004 = 125,000$$

Therefore, the loss function is $L(x) = 125,000(x - T)^2$. This means when the deviation is 0.010, the firm can still expect an average loss per unit of

$$L(0.10) = 125,000(0.010)^2 = \$12.50$$

Knowing the Taguchi loss function helps designers to determine appropriate tolerances economically. For example, suppose that a simple adjustment can be made at the factory for only \$2 to get this dimension very close to the target. If we set $L(x) = \$2$ and solve for $x - T$, we get

$$2 = 125,000(x - T)^2$$
$$x - T = 0.004$$

Therefore, if the dimension is more than 0.004 away from the target, it is more economical to adjust it at the factory and the specifications should be set as 0.500 ± 0.004.

Quality Engineering

Quality engineering *refers to a process of designing quality into a manufactured good based on a prediction of potential quality problems prior to production.*

Quality engineering *refers to a process of designing quality into a manufactured good based on a prediction of potential quality problems prior to production.* Daimler-Chrysler, for example, began to evaluate new models for quality while they were still in the design stage. This way, parts or manufacturing processes can be changed before too much money has been spent.[13] Among the many tools of quality engineering are value engineering, value analysis, failure mode analysis, and design reviews. The object of value engineering and value analysis is to analyze the function of every component of a product, system, or service to determine how that function can be accomplished most economically, without degrading the quality of the product or service. **Value engineering** *refers to cost avoidance or cost prevention before the good or service is created.* **Value analysis** *refers to cost reduction of the manufactured good or service process.* Typical questions that are asked during value engineering/value analysis studies include

Value engineering *refers to cost avoidance or cost prevention before the good or service is created.*

Value analysis *refers to cost reduction of the manufactured good or service process.*

- What are the functions of a particular manufactured part or stage in the service process? Are they necessary? Can they be accomplished in a different way?
- What materials, if any, are used? Can a less costly material be substituted? For example, can off-the-shelf items be used in place of custom-specified components? Can plastic be used instead of steel?
- Where are the value-added steps in the process? Where are the non-valued-added steps and can they be eliminated? What are the cost implications?
- How can waste be reduced by changing the design of the good or service and its associated process?
- How can the good or service be created faster by changing the design?

One company originally made an exhaust manifold in an air compressor from cast iron, which required several machining steps. By switching to a powder metal process, it reduced four machine steps to one. The savings amounted to $50,000 per year. Another company formerly packed bottles of shampoo in plain chipboard cartons for distributors. By changing to a plastic six-pack holder similar to that used in the beverage industry, it saved more than $100,000 in the first year. Even simple ideas such as reusing packing material from incoming shipments to pack outgoing shipments have resulted in savings of more than $600,000 for many companies.[14]

Design reviews *ensure that all important design objectives are taken into account during the design process.* The purpose of a design review is to stimulate discussion and raise questions to generate new ideas and solutions to problems. Design reviews can facilitate standardization, simplification, and substitution and reduce the costs associated with frequent design changes by helping designers anticipate problems before they occur. Hence, design reviews are nothing more than good planning.

A design-review process usually includes a failure-mode-and-effects analysis. **Failure-mode-and-effects analysis (FMEA)** *is a technique in which each component of a product is listed along with the way it may fail, the cause of failure, the effect or consequence of failure, and how it can be corrected by improving the design.* For instance, one of the components of a table lamp is the socket; a typical FMEA for that component might be

Failure: cracked socket.
Causes: excessive heat, forcing the bulb too hard.
Effects: may cause shock.
Correction: use improved materials.

An FMEA can uncover serious design problems prior to manufacturing and improve the quality and reliability of a product considerably.

Even product designs that use simple components sometimes result in complex or difficult assembly operations, and inexpensive product designs sometimes result in products that are difficult or expensive to service or support. An approach to prevent such complications is design for manufacturability. **Design for manufacturability (DFM)** *is a technique for evaluating product designs to ensure they can be built efficiently using available technology.* One example of DFM in action involved a team of designers at Thermos, who were designing an electric grill with tapered legs. The manufacturing team member noted that tapered legs would have to be custom made and persuaded designers to make them straight.[15]

Product and Process Simplification

The simpler the design, the less opportunities for error, the faster the flow time, the better the chance of high process efficiency, and the more reliable the manufactured good or service process. So it comes as no surprise that some firms spend considerable resources trying to reduce product or process complexity. **Product and process simplification** *is the process of trying to simplify designs to reduce complexity and costs and thus improve productivity, quality, flexibility, and customer satisfaction.*

For example, the redesign of the Cadillac Seville rear-bumper assembly reduced the number of parts by half and cut assembly time by 57 percent, to less than 8 minutes, saving the company over $450,000 annually in labor costs.[16] Since many of the eliminated parts were squeak- and rattle-causing fasteners, nuts, bolts, and screws, the change also improved the quality of the car. Although the self-service salad bar at fast-food restaurants was popular for a while, most restaurants dropped the salad bar because of customer complaints about cleanliness, availability of certain condiments, and the interaction with other (often rude) customers. The salad bar increased the complexity of the service process, and therefore was eventually abandoned. Toyota's new engine design for a new Corolla model used 25 percent

Design reviews *ensure that all important design objectives are taken into account during the design process.*

Failure-mode-and-effects analysis (FMEA) *is a technique in which each component of a product is listed along with the way it may fail, the cause of failure, the effect or consequence of failure, and how it can be corrected by improving the design.*

Design for manufacturability (DFM) *is a technique for evaluating product designs to ensure they can be built efficiently using available technology.*

Product and process simplification *is the process of trying to simplify designs to reduce complexity and costs and thus improve productivity, quality, flexibility, and customer satisfaction.*

fewer parts than its predecessor, making it lighter, more fuel-efficient, and significantly cheaper, resulting in a $1,500 reduction in price over previous models. A simple design generally results in ease of assembly, which reduces the assembly time and requires smaller inventories. Thus, it is important that individuals who are involved in product design decisions understand the impact their decisions have on the manufacturing processes.

Product simplification encourages the use of standard parts and components that are widely available and are less expensive because vendors can produce them on a mass basis. Also, because they do not have to be designed in-house, the development time is decreased. One method of product simplification is modular design. **Modular design** *entails designing goods using modules that can be configured in many different ways, resulting in higher product variety and ease of assembly.* For example, many of the options available on automobiles can be used on a variety of models in a manufacturer's line; it is simply a matter of assembling the proper components for the customer's order. Printed circuit boards are built in modules for television sets; computing equipment is modular in the sense that different central processing units, disk drives, keyboards, and so on can be combined. Modular design enables manufacturers to accommodate varying consumer preferences and still take advantage of the low costs of mass production.

Modular design entails designing goods using modules that can be configured in many different ways, resulting in higher product variety and ease of assembly.

Design for Environmental Quality

A focus on improving the environment by better good or service design is often called green manufacturing *or* green practices.

We briefly discussed environmental quality as an important business metric in Chapter 2. Environmental concerns are placing increased pressure on goods-producing and service-providing organizations. *A focus on improving the environment by better good or service design is often called* green manufacturing *or* green practices. In Europe, for example, the European Commission has proposed a ban on materials such as lead-based solder in PCs and has imposed recycling responsibilities on manufacturers beginning in January 2004. Some mutual funds such as TIAA-CREF's Social Choice fund invest only in companies with favorable environmental practices for the company's goods, services, and processes. Hotels, cruise ships, and hospitals, for instance, must meet certain environmental standards regarding wastewater from laundries, dishwashers, sewage, and showers. Medical waste is particularly troubling given the chemical and radioactive nature of medical goods and services. Toxic chemicals are used and disposed of by manufacturers and service firms alike, such as ship builders, schools and universities, zoos, museums, airlines, remanufacturers, appliance and automobile repair shops, and utilities.

Design for Environment (DfE) is the explicit consideration of environmental concerns during the design of goods, services, and processes and includes such practices as designing for recycling and disassembly.

Pressures from environmental groups clamoring for "socially responsive" designs, states and municipalities that are running out of space for landfills, and consumers who want the most for their money have caused designers and managers to look carefully at the concept of Design-for-Environment.[17] **Design for Environment (DfE)** *is the explicit consideration of environmental concerns during the design of goods, services, and processes and includes such practices as designing for recycling and disassembly.* DfE offers the potential to create more desirable products at lower costs by reducing disposal and regulatory costs, increasing the end-of-life value of products, reducing material use, and minimizing liabilities. Food packaging for fast-food restaurants, for example, has been redesigned several times over the years and now is more recyclable and biodegradable. One aspect of designing for repairability and disassembly is that products can be taken apart for their components to be repaired and refurbished or otherwise salvaged for reuse.

General Electric's plastics division, for example, which serves the durable-goods market, uses only thermoplastics for its products.[18] Unlike many other varieties of plastics, thermoplastics can be melted down and recast into other shapes and products. GE's "refrigerator of the future" is composed of a series of plastic insulating boxes that can be taken apart quickly, with all mechanical equipment contained in a module that runs up the back of the box like a spine. That configuration makes the refrigerator not only easier to take apart but also easier to service. Modular design of equipment also speeds repair time and reduces the technical skills required to diagnose the repair problem for G.E. appliances and jet engines.

Recyclables create new challenges for designers and consumers. Designers must strive to use fewer types of materials, and the materials must have certain characteristics (such as the thermal properties of plastics) that allow them to be reused or be biodegradable. They must also refrain from using certain methods of fastening, such as glues and screws, in favor of quick-connect/disconnect bolts and the like. Obviously, these mandated changes in design have an impact on tolerances, durability, and goods quality, and thus on goods-producing processes.

In the past, Honda of America used cardboard boxes and packaging materials to ship automobile component parts and subassemblies from suppliers to their assembly plants. Today, all packaging for supplier parts and subassemblies is designed to fit on the assembly line and, when empty, the packaging and containers are sent back to the supplier to be reused on the next shipment. Pallets of used cardboard containers are a practice of the past. In addition, Honda realized that the ideal number of recycling processes is zero. Each recycling process like processing used cardboard that is eliminated reduces total operating costs. Thus product and process design can not only improve the ease of repairs in the field and disassembly and recycling but it also can lower the total cost to the company.

Many companies now subscribe to ISO 14000, a voluntary set of environmental standards that are administered by the International Organization for Standardization. The aim of the standards is to support environmental protection and prevention of pollution in balance with socioeconomic needs. These standards were developed to

- promote a common approach to environmental management,
- enhance organizations' ability to attain and measure improvements in environmental performance, and
- facilitate trade and remove trade barriers.

The ISO 14000 series of standards cover environmental management systems, environmental auditing, environmental performance evaluation, environmental labeling, life-cycle assessment, and environmental aspects in product standards. ISO 14001, a part of the series of standards, is the most well known and specifies a framework of control for an environmental management system against which an organization can be certified by a third party. By obtaining ISO 14001 certification, a company can demonstrate its commitment to the environment and develop a system for better managing environmental risks and reduce costs.

Reliability

Everyone expects the car to start each morning and the computer to work without crashing. **Reliability** *is the probability that a manufactured good, piece of equipment, or system performs its intended function for a stated period of time under specified operating conditions.* (Do not confuse this with *information reliability*, discussed in Chapter 3.) Please note that a system could be a service process where each stage (work activity or station) is analogous to a component part in a manufactured good. This definition has four important elements: *probability, time, performance, and operating conditions.*

First, reliability *is defined as a probability, that is, a value between 0 and 1.* For example, a probability of .97 indicates that, on average, 97 out of 100 times the item will perform its function for a given period of time under specified operating conditions. Often, reliability is expressed as a percentage simply to be more descriptive (97% reliable). The second element of the definition is *time.* Clearly, a

Reliability *is the probability that a manufactured good, piece of equipment, or system performs its intended function for a stated period of time under specified operating conditions.*

device having a reliability of .97 for 1,000 hours of operation is inferior to one that has the same reliability for 5,000 hours of operation, if the objective of the device is long life. **Performance** *refers to a measurable objective that describes what the good or system should do.* Some examples would be the length of time it takes to start an engine, or the speed at which an Internet connection can download a specified file size. The term *failure* is used when performance of the intended function is not met. There are two types of failures: **functional failure**—*failure that occurs in a product's life due to manufacturing or material defects such as a missing connection or a faulty component*—and **reliability failure**—*failure that occurs after some period of use.* The final component of the reliability definition is **operating conditions**, *which refers to the type and amount of use and the environment in which the good or system is used.* For example, the operating conditions of an ordinary dress watch are not the same as those of a sport watch that one might wear while swimming.

By defining a good's intended environment, performance characteristics, and lifetime, tests can be designed and conducted to measure the probability of survival (or failure). The analysis of such tests enables manufacturers to better predict reliability and to improve product and process designs accordingly. **Reliability engineering** *consists of a variety of techniques to build reliability into products and test their performance.* Reliability engineers determine failure rates of individual components to predict the reliability of complex systems. They use standardized components with proven track records and backup (redundant) components to guard against failure of main components. Life testing, that is, running devices until they fail, enables engineers to measure the failure characteristics to better understand and eliminate their causes. Other tests are designed to check products' ability to withstand environmental factors such as temperature, humidity, vibration, and shock.

Reliability management *is the total process of establishing, achieving, and maintaining reliability objectives.* It is similar in principle to total quality management in that it focuses on defining customer performance requirements and their economic impacts; selecting components, designs, and suppliers that meet reliability and cost criteria; determining reliability requirements for products, systems, and equipment; and analyzing field data as a means of improving reliability.

A **system** *is a related group of components that work together to accomplish a task.* (In addition to the common notion of a system being a group of machines in a factory, we can think of a typical manufactured good as being a system; for example, a bicycle consists of wheels, gears, suspension, and so on.) The reliability of a system is the probability that the system will perform satisfactorily over a specified period of time. Reliability can be improved by using better components or by adding redundant components. In either case, costs increase; thus, trade-offs must be made.

Many manufactured goods consist of several components that are arranged in series but are assumed to be independent of one another, as illustrated in Exhibit 6.5. If one component or process step fails, the entire system fails. If we know the individual reliability, p_j, for each component, j, we can compute the total reliability of an n-component series system, R_s. We note that the joint probability of n independent events can be computed as the product of the individual probabilities. Thus, if the individual reliabilities are denoted by $p_1, p_2, \cdots, p_n$ and the system reliability is denoted by R_s, then

$$R_s = (p_1)(p_2)(p_3) \cdots (p_n) \tag{6.2}$$

Exhibit 6.5
Structure of a Serial System

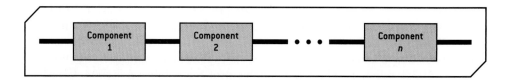

Other system designs consist of several parallel components that function independently of each other, as illustrated in Exhibit 6.6. The entire system will fail only if all components fail; this is an example of redundancy. The system reliability of an n-component parallel system is computed as

$$R_p = 1 - (1 - p_1)(1 - p_2)(1 - p_3) \cdots (1 - p_n) \qquad \textbf{(6.3)}$$

Many other systems are combinations of series and parallel components. To compute the reliability of such systems, first compute the reliability of the parallel components using Equation (6.3) and treat the result as a single series component; then use Equation 6.2 to compute the total series reliability.

Consider a new laboratory blood analysis machine consisting of three major subassemblies, A, B, and C. The manufacturer is evaluating the preliminary design of this piece of equipment. The reliabilities of each subassembly are shown in Exhibit 6.7.

To find the reliability of the proposed product design, we note that this is a series system and use Equation (6.2):

$$R_s = (.98)(.91)(.99) = .883, \text{ or } 88.3\%$$

This calculation may be used to investigate proposed design changes. For example, how much will the reliability of the equipment be improved if subassembly B is upgraded and its reliability increased to .99? Again using Equation (6.2), we compute the reliability of the new design as

$$R_s = (.98)(.99)(.99) = .961, \text{ or } 96.1\%$$

The reliability of the total product increases from 88.3% to 96.1%, or an absolute increase of 7.8%. This example demonstrates that total product reliability is only as good as the weakest link, especially when the subassemblies work in series.

Now suppose that the original subassembly B (with a reliability of .91) is duplicated, creating a parallel (backup) path as shown in Exhibit 6.8. (Assume equipment software switches to the working subassembly B.) What is the reliability of this configuration? The reliability of the parallel system for subassembly B is $R_p = 1 - (1 - .91)(1 - .91) = 1 - .0081 = .9919$. Thus, the reliability of the equipment is $R_s = (.98)(.9919)(.99) = .962$, or 96.2%. The reliability of the total product increases from 88.3% to 96.2% for an absolute increase of 7.9%. This absolute change of 7.9% is almost identical to the 7.8% computed in (b) if the reliability of subassembly B is increased from .91 to .99 and only a single subassembly is used.

Hence, with the total system reliabilities about the same (96.1% versus 96.2%), the decision comes down to the relative cost of increasing subassembly B's reliability from .91 to .99 or the cost of designing two subassemblies in parallel with the original reliability of .91. Whatever product design option is cheaper is probably the best choice in this situation.

Redundancy *is the use of backup components in a design.* For example, early designs of the space shuttle used five on-board computers each with identical software running in parallel. This system design maximizes the reliability of the on-board flight controls and system. Only the computers are precise enough to maneuver the space shuttle to the ground consistently. With humans at the controls, the variance in operating the controls is much higher than a computer-controlled landing. Five parallel on-board computers ensure crew safety and the human venture into space.

Exhibit 6.6
Structure of a Parallel System

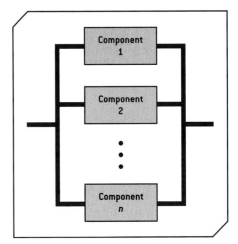

Exhibit 6.7
Subassembly Reliabilities

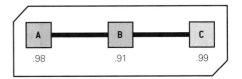

Exhibit 6.8
Modified Design

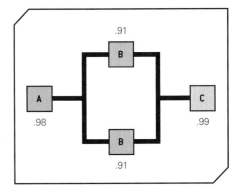

Redundancy is the use of backup components in a design.

A solved problem at the end of this chapter illustrates this analysis of an automated process with turning, milling, and grinding tasks. Reliability analysis provides an important piece of information to use along with the cost for evaluating alternative product and process designs. If we replace a manufactured component part with a work activity/work station/stage of a service process and assume independence between different process work activities, then we can apply reliability analysis to services.

SERVICE DELIVERY SYSTEM DESIGN

Learning Objective
To understand how the elements of a service delivery system support customer benefit package design and set the stage for service encounter design and execution.

Service delivery system design *includes the following:*

- *facility location and layout,*
- *the servicescape,*
- *process and job design,*
- *technology and information support systems, and*
- *organizational structure.*

Service delivery system design *includes the following:*

- *facility location and layout,*
- *the servicescape,*
- *process and job design,*
- *technology and information support systems, and*
- *organizational structure.*

Integrating all of these elements is necessary to designing a service that provides value to customers and creates a competitive advantage. A poor choice on any one of these components, such as technology or job design, can degrade service system efficiency and effectiveness. For example, a fast-food restaurant might have a good store layout and process flow but a poorly designed hiring and training program, resulting in rude or inattentive service workers who can ruin the customer's experience.

Service design is often done out in the field on a trial-and-error basis as opposed to manufactured goods, which are designed in laboratories or on a computer. This certainly makes the design of services more difficult and costly because a complete prototype must be constructed and tested with real customers. However, such experimentation is necessary in order to identify service design mistakes and correct future designs. The OM Spotlight on Wendy's discusses how this firm has implemented service delivery design.

Facility Location and Layout

Great store layout, process flow, and service encounter design are meaningless if the store is in the wrong location. A good location can partially overcome poor aspects of other service design decisions, but good job and process design can seldom overcome a poor location. Part of what the customer is buying in many services is convenience. Location affects a customer's travel time and is an important competitive priority in a service business. Health clinics, rental car firms, post offices, health clubs, branch banks, libraries, hotels, emergency service facilities, retail stores, and many other types of service facilities depend on good location decisions. Starbuck's Coffee shops, for example, are ubiquitous in many cities, airports, and shopping malls.

For services that are information-intensive, such as financial services and education, the Internet is making service facility location less important. Online banking eliminates the necessity of traveling to a banking facility. Charles Schwab, Scottrade, Fidelity, Vanguard, and other investment services do not have an extensive network of physical offices; instead, they encourage customers to use their online capabilities, which also reduces the need for call center facilities and customer service representatives. Likewise, many educational institutions now offer online degree programs that are not location dependent. We will discuss more specific issues and methods related to facility layout and location in Chapter 8.

Service Process Design at Wendy's

Wendy's bought Tim Horton's in 1995 and began experimenting with different ways to combine the two types of stores. One service design question was whether to reconfigure Wendy's and Tim Horton's service delivery systems into one common design or keep them separate. Over 20 different service facilities were built in Columbus, Ohio, the corporate headquarters, as prototype stores to study different ways to combine and integrate Tim Horton's and Wendy's service delivery systems. Experiments included building two freestanding stores—one Tim Horton's and the other Wendy's—on the same site, constructing two independent stores under one roof, and developing smaller kiosk-type stores in small lots and inside shopping malls. However, none of these alternatives combined kitchens and counter service. If a design flaw was revealed in one test store, it could be corrected in all subsequent stores.

The service system design for Wendy's included such elements as menu items, store layout and design, customer flow, training, food packaging, process and job design, and uniform design. Store layout, customer process flow in and out of the store, and where customers wait for service were so integrated that they are decided simultaneously. For example, in one Wendy's and Tim Horton's test store configuration, the condiment stand where you get napkins, forks, mustard, etc. was located too close to the service counters where customer orders were taken and food delivered. In low-to-moderate demand periods, this store layout feature did not inhibit customer flow or the service experience. But when demand was high, the queue at the service counter backed up in and around the condiment stand, causing a bottleneck. Some customers were trying to stand in line and place their orders while other customers were carrying (and

spilling) food while trying to get their napkins, condiments, etc. The crossing traffic patterns created a bottleneck with long customer queues, queues broken into pieces that disrupted the first-come-first-serve customer sequencing rule, and customer confrontations. Customer complaints were much higher and this service design destroyed the customer's "service" experience. In this store, the condiment stands were quickly moved and this service design mistake was not repeated in future store designs.

Although this design research initiative cost Wendy's about $30 million, it provided significant data to make an important strategic decision before the final prototype stores were duplicated worldwide to thousands of locations. By building these 20 different test store configurations "out in the field," Wendy's was able to assess actual staffing requirements, store efficiency, inventory, waste, customer complaint, order accuracy, waiting time, process flow, sales, and financial performance.

Wendy's International, Inc.

Servicescape

The **servicescape** *is all the physical evidence a customer might use to form an impression.*[19] The servicescape also provides the behavioral setting where service encounters take place. People around the world, for example, recognize the servicescape of McDonald's restaurants. The building design ("golden arches"), decorative schemes and colors, playground, menu board, packaging, employee uniforms, drive-through, and so on all support McDonald's competitive priorities of speed, consistency, cleanliness, and customer service. The standardization and integration of the servicescape and service processes enhances efficiency. McDonald's servicescape also helps establish its brand image. See the OM Spotlight on Kaiser Permanente as an example of the importance of designing the servicescape.

The **servicescape** *is all the physical evidence a customer might use to form an impression.*

OM SPOTLIGHT

Kaiser Permanente[21]

Kaiser Permanente is the largest health maintenance organization in the United States. As part of its long-range growth planning process, executives thought that they might have to replace existing offices and hospitals with expensive, next-generation buildings. However, with help from IDEO, an innovative design firm with offices in the United States, London, and Munich, it discovered that patients became annoyed well before seeing a doctor because checking in was a nightmare and waiting rooms were uncomfortable. Doctors and medical assistants sat too far apart, friends and relatives could not stay with the patient, and examination rooms required patients to wait alone for up to 20 minutes surrounded by threatening equipment. However, instead of overhauling its buildings, Kaiser realized that it had to overhaul its patient experience, using more comfortable waiting rooms and a lobby with clear instructions on where to go; larger exam rooms with space for several people and curtains for privacy, to make patients comfortable; and special corridors for medical staff to meet and increase their efficiency.

A servicescape has three principal dimensions:[20]

1. *Ambient conditions*—made manifest by sight, sound, smell, touch, and temperature. These are designed into a servicescape to please the five human senses. For example, a professional service organization such as a law firm might design its offices with comfortable chairs and sofas in the lobby, smooth background music, fresh flowers, and warm colors. A children's hospital might use a very different set of ambient conditions such as cheerful and upbeat background music, cartoon characters painted on walls, and stuffed animals in the waiting area.

2. *Spatial layout and functionality*—how furniture, equipment, and office spaces are arranged. This includes building footprints and facades, streets, and parking lots. A law firm would probably design various conference areas for conversations to take place in a quiet and private setting; a children's hospital would probably include safe and enclosed play areas for kids.

3. *Signs, symbols, and artifacts*—the more explicit signals that communicate an image about a firm. Examples include mission statements and diplomas on a wall, a prominently displayed company logo on company vehicles, a trophy case of awards, letterhead, and company uniforms. Luxury automobile dealers offer free food and soft drinks instead of vending machines. Kendle, Inc., a Cincinnati-based clinical research firm, displays pictures of all employees throughout the hallways of its corporate headquarters that convey something important in their lives (for example, a spouse, pet, or hobby). This conveys an impression of commitment to employees and a sense of "family" in the organization.

Some servicescapes, termed *lean servicescape environments*, are very simple. Ticketron outlets and Federal Express drop-off kiosks would qualify as lean servicescape environments, as both provide service from one simple structure. More complicated structures and service systems are termed *elaborate servicescape* environments. Examples include hospitals, airports, and universities.

The physical environment in a manufacturing facility is called the **factoryscape**.

In a similar fashion, we can call *the physical environment in a manufacturing facility the* **factoryscape**. Ambient conditions, such as noise and temperature levels, lighting conditions, odors, clean floors and equipment, and clear sightlines along factory aisles, are important design considerations. The spatial layout and functionality of the factory includes where to locate machines and materials handling equipment, how to group and organize production cells, and how factory layout supports process flow. Finally, signs, symbols, and artifacts are also important in the factory workplace. These might include documents, tools, quality storyboards posted on walls, uniforms, bulletin boards, equipment, and cafeterias. The elements of a factoryscape are as important for employees working in the facility as the elements of a servicescape are for the external customer in a service facility.

Process and Job Design

Although service design includes many factors when considered from an operations management perspective, most people think of a service as a process. **Service process design** *is the activity of developing an efficient sequence of activities to satisfy both internal and external customer requirements.* The actual process design is the specification of how the process works. The first phase is to list in detail the sequence of steps—value-adding activities and specific tasks—involved in producing a good or delivering a service, usually depicted as a flowchart. Such a graphical representation provides an excellent communication device for visualizing and understanding the process. Flowcharts can become the basis for job descriptions, employee-training programs, and performance measurement. They help managers to estimate the requirements for human resources, information systems, equipment, and facilities. As design tools, they enable management to study and analyze each job in the process prior to implementation in order to improve quality and operational performance. We discuss this in more detail in the next chapter.

Service process design is the activity of developing an efficient sequence of activities to satisfy both internal and external customer requirements.

Service process designers must concentrate on developing procedures to ensure that things are done right the first time, that interactions are simple and quick, and that human error is avoided. Fast-food restaurants, for example, have carefully designed their processes for a high degree of accuracy and fast response time.[21] New hands-free intercom systems, better microphones that reduce ambient kitchen noise, and screens that display a customer's order are all focused on these requirements. Timers at Wendy's count every segment of the order completion process to help managers identify problem areas. Kitchen workers wear headsets to hear orders as they are placed so they can begin food preparation sooner. Even the use of photos and order-by-the-number on drive-through order boards make it more likely for customers to accurately select these items; less variety means faster order fulfillment.

Technology and Information Support Systems

We discussed the importance of technology in Chapter 5 and provided examples of how it is used in services. As such, hard and soft technology is an important factor in designing services to ensure speed, accuracy, customization, and flexibility. In fact, many improvements to established services are the result of technology upgrades. Design decisions for service delivery systems focus on questions such as: What information does each service job need to accomplish its mission effectively and efficiently? What information technology best integrates all parts of the value chain? Job designs for nurses, airline flight attendants, bank tellers, police, insurance claims processors, dentists, auto mechanics and service counter personnel, engineers, hotel room maids, financial portfolio managers, purchasing buyers, and waiters are just a few examples that are highly dependent on accurate and timely information.

One example of how technology has enhanced service design is reflected in a statement by L.L. Bean: "The customer is the most important person ever in this office—in person or by mail or by phone or by the Internet." L.L. Bean implicitly recognizes the importance of alternative customer contact technologies. From L.L. Bean's customer-oriented perspective, the customer should expect and receive outstanding customer service regardless of the contact technology used. Hence, employees should be trained and service standards should be maintained for each type of contact technology.

Today, companies rely on call centers—over 60,000 in the United States and growing at 20 percent per year—as a primary means of customer contact. Call centers can be a means of competitive advantage by serving customers more efficiently and personalizing transactions to build relationships. However, they must be supported by appropriate technology, such as automating routine calls to minimize the necessity of answering the same questions over and over, and routing calls to people with appropriate skills. Inefficient processes can only lead to frustrated customers.

Not all customer contact technologies provide value to customers. Rude customer service representatives or, even worse, automated answering systems that block callers from getting through to a "real person" are among the top ten complaints to the Public Utilities Commission of Ohio and the Ohio's Consumers Council.[22] Robert Tongren, Ohio consumers' counsel, notes that while he supports the goal of telecommunication and utility competition, he said service suffers "under the continued pressure to meet the bottom-line demands of Wall Street."

Organizational Structure

The performance of a service delivery system depends on how work is organized. As we discussed in Chapter 1, "organizing by process," as opposed to organizing by function (see Exhibit 1.9), is an important aspect of a high-performing organization. A pure functional organization generally requires more handoffs between work activities, resulting in increased opportunities for errors and slower processing times. Because no one "owns" the processes, there is usually little incentive to make them efficient and to improve cooperation among business functions.

A process-based organization is vital to a good service design because services are generally interdisciplinary and cross-functional. For example, service upsets and mistakes that occur in the presence of the customer call for immediate responses by the service provider and often require extensive cooperation among various functions in a service process. A good example of service design and how all aspects of the service delivery system must be integrated is provided by Courtyard by Marriott, which we discuss next.

An Example of Service Delivery System Design: Courtyard by Marriott[23]

PR Newswire Marriott International

In the early 1980s, Marriott Corporation identified two segments of travelers who might need a new type of hotel chain: (1) business travelers who travel at least six times a year and stay in mid-level hotels or motels, and (2) pleasure travelers who travel at least twice a year and stay in hotels or motels. The challenge was to design a new hotel chain and customer benefit package that did not exist for these target markets (see steps 1 to 3 in Exhibit 6.1).

After defining the organization's mission, strategy, target markets, and relative competitive priorities (steps 1 and 2 in Exhibit 6.1), Marriott had to design the service delivery system. To design the service delivery system—step 3c in Exhibit 6.1—Marriott started with 167 possible physical features of the hotel and services to be offered, as shown in Exhibit 6.9. These features are the principal components of the CBP and associated delivery system, which were categorized into seven categories: (1) external factors, (2) rooms, (3) food-related services, (4) lounge facilities, (5) services, (6) facilities for leisure-time services, and (7) security factors. Many features in Exhibit 6.9 related to the servicescape, but others related to services such as car rental, secretarial services, and so on. Once the final set of features were determined, architects and Marriott managers designed the hotel layout, processes, job designs, and information support systems. Once a final facility design was

Exhibit 6.9 Courtyard by Marriott Service Design Options

EXTERNAL FACTORS
Building Shape
  L-shaped w/landscape
  Outdoor courtyard
Landscaping
  Minimal
  Moderate
  Elaborate
Pool type
  No pool
  Rectangular shape
  Free form shape
  Indoor/outdoor
Pool location
  In courtyard
  Not in courtyard
Corridor/View
  Outside access/restricted
    view
  Enclosed access/
    unrestricted view/
    balcony or window
Hotel size
  Small (125 rooms, 2 stories)
  Large (600 rooms, 12 stories)

ROOMS
Entertainment
  Color TV
  Color TV w/movies at $5
  Color TV w/30 channel cable
  Color TV w/HBO, movies, etc.
  Color TV w/free movies
Entertainment/Rental
  None
  Rental Cassettes/in-room Atari
  Rental Cassettes/stereo
    cassette playing in room
  Rental Movies/in-room
    BetaMax
Size
  Small (standard)
  Slightly larger (1 foot)
  Much larger (2½ feet)
  Small suite (2 rooms)
  Large suite (2 rooms)
Quality of Decor (in standard
room)
  Budget motel decor
  Old Holiday Inn decor
  New Holiday Inn decor
  New Hilton decor
  New Hyatt decor
Heating and Cooling
  Wall unit/full control
  Wall unit/soundproof/
    full control
  Central H or C (seasonal)
  Central H or C/full control
Size of Bath
  Standard bath
  Slightly larger/sink separate
  Much larger bath w/larger tub
  Very large/tub for 2

Sink location
  In bath only
  In separate area
  In bath and separate
Bathroom Features
  None
  Shower Massage
  Whirlpool (Jacuzzi)
  Steam bath
Amenities
  Small bar soap
  Large soap/shampoo/
    shoeshine
  Large soap/bath gel/
    shower cap/sewing kit
  Above items + toothpaste,
    deodorant, mouthwash

FOOD
Restaurant in hotel
  None (coffee shop next door)
  Restaurant/lounge combo,
    limited menu
  Coffee shop, full menu
  Full-service restaurant, full
    menu
  Coffee shop/full menu and
    good restaurant
Restaurant nearby
  None
  Coffee shop
  Fast food
  Fast food or coffee shop and
    moderate restaurant
  Fast food or coffee shop and
    good restaurant
Free continental
  None
  Continental included in room
    rate
Room service
  None
  Phone-in order/guest to pick up
  Room service, limited menu
  Room service, full menu
Store
  No food in store
  Snack items
  Snacks, refrigerated items,
    wine, beer, liquor
  Above items and gourmet
    food items
Vending service
  None
  Soft drink machine only
  Soft drink and snack
    machines
  Soft drink, snack, and
    sandwich machines
  Above and microwave
    available
In-room kitchen facilities
  None
  Coffee maker only
  Coffee maker and refrigerator
  Cooking facilities in room

LOUNGE
Atmosphere
  Quiet bar/lounge
  Lively, popular bar/lounge
Type of people
  Hotel guests and friends only
  Open to public—general
    appeal
  Open to public—many singles
Lounge nearby
  None
  Lounge/bar nearby
  Lounge/bar w/entertainment
    nearby

SERVICES
Reservations
  Call hotel directly
  800 reservation number
Check-in
  Standard
  Pre-credit clearance
  Machine in lobby
Check-out
  At front desk
  Bill under door/leave key
  Key to front desk/bill by mail
  Machine in lobby
Limo to airport
  None
  Yes
Bellman
  None
  Yes
Message service
  Note at front desk
  Light on phone
  Light on phone and message
    under door
  Recorded message
Cleanliness/upkeep/management
skill
  Budget motor level
  Holiday Inn level
  Nonconvention Hyatt level
  Convention Hyatt level
  Fine hotel level
Laundry/Valet
  None
  Client drop off and pick up
  Self-service
  Valet pick up and drop off
Special Services (concierge)
  None
  Information on restaurants,
    theaters, etc.
  Arrangements and
    reservations
  Travel problem resolution
Secretarial services
  None
  Xerox machine
  Xerox machine and typist
Car maintenance
  None
  Take car to service
  Gas on premises/bill to room

Car rental/Airline reservations
  None
  Car rental facility
  Airline reservations
  Car rental and airline
    reservations

LEISURE
Sauna
  None
  Yes
Whirlpool/jacuzzi
  None
  Outdoor
  Indoor
Exercise room
  None
  Basic facility w/weights
  Facility w/Nautilus equipment
Racquet ball courts
  None
  Yes
Tennis courts
  None
  Yes
Game room/Entertainment
  None
  Electric games/pinball
  Electric games/pinball/ping
    pong
  Above + movie theater,
    bowling
Children's playroom/playground
  None
  Playground only
  Playroom only
  Playground and playroom
Pool extras
  None
  Pool w/slides
  Pool w/slides and equipment
  Pool w/slides, waterfall,
    equipment

SECURITY
Security guard
  None
  11 a.m. to 7 p.m.
  7 p.m. to 7 a.m.
  24 hours
Smoke detector
  None
  In rooms and throughout hotel
Sprinkler system
  None
  Lobby and hallways only
  Lobby/hallways/rooms
24-hour video camera
  None
  Parking/hallway/public areas
Alarm button
  None
  Button in room, rings desk

Note: The 50 factors that describe hotel features and services and the associated (167) levels are categorized under seven facets. The underscored items were included in the final design of the hotel.

Source: J. Wind, P. E. Green, D. Shifflet, and M. Scarbrough, "Courtyard by Marriott: Designing a Hotel Facility with Consumer-Based Marketing Models," *Interfaces* 19, No. 1 (January–February 1989), p. 26. Reprinted with permission.

established, Marriott managers focused on locating these new hotels in the best possible locations.

A sample of potential target market customers was surveyed and various statistical techniques used to match the customer's perceptions of what an ideal hotel might look like to the 167 CBP attributes in Exhibit 6.9. The result was the final set of CBP attributes that are underlined in the exhibit. For example, under Rooms and Amenities (top of the second column of Exhibit 6.9), there were four design options: (1) small bar of soap only; (2) large bar of soap, shampoo packet and shoe shine mitt; (3) large bar of soap, bath gel, shower cap, sewing kit, shampoo packet, and special soap; and (4) large bar of soap, bath gel, shower cap, sewing kit, shampoo packet, special soap, and toothpaste. Ultimately, option #2 was chosen. Also, no secretarial services are provided on-site in this new hotel design.

This design process resulted in the Courtyard by Marriott brand. By 1991, Marriott Corporation had built over 200 Courtyard by Marriott hotels, and today has over 580. This chain contributed to Marriott's continued growth, financial health, and increasing stock values and complements their other brands, such as Fairfield and Residence Inns. It also created many thousands of new jobs, provided cross-advertising benefits and economies of scale, and enhanced the Marriott image with investors, Marriott employees, and target market customers. Courtyard by Marriott employees also knew that their hotel chain was designed based on customer perceptions of what the customer wanted in a travel-related hotel. What a splendid example of tying the organization's mission and strategy, target market analysis, customer benefit package design, and service delivery system design together.

SERVICE ENCOUNTER DESIGN

Learning Objective
To understand the issues and decisions necessary to design effective service encounters.

Service encounter design *focuses on the interaction, directly or indirectly, between the service provider(s) and the customer.*

The design of the service delivery system defines the environment where service encounters take place. Clearly, if the service delivery system design is flawed, then the service encounters will be difficult or impossible to execute well. **Service encounter design** *focuses on the interaction, directly or indirectly, between the service provider(s) and the customer.* It is during these points of contact with the customer that perceptions of the firm and its goods and services are created. Service encounter design and job design are frequently done in iterative improvement cycles.

The differences between goods and services described in Chapter 1 help us understand the importance of service encounter design. For example, the quality of the service encounter between the service provider and customer very much depends on their actions and behavior; behavior can enhance or hinder service efficiency and customer satisfaction. In contrast, a manufactured good has no human attributes. In a service, the customer frequently acts as a co-producer with the service provider. In addition, service encounters are time-dependent and cannot be stored as physical inventory. Finally, how customers evaluate goods versus services using search, experience, and credence attributes is also different, as we discussed in Chapter 3. Thus, service encounter design focuses mainly on the behavioral aspects of encounters between customers and service providers.

For example, the store layout, processes, equipment, servicescape, jobs, and service encounters at McDonald's are standardized to support the execution of service encounters. How the service provider greets a customer, takes an order, and delivers the food is clearly defined and scripted. The company uses videotapes to train employees in proper service provider behaviors and skills. One rude or poorly groomed employee can ruin the service experience for the customer. The objective of this effort is speed, efficiency, and friendly service. The challenge that a firm such as McDonald's faces is how to implement this consistently with a highly diverse work force at over 30,000 stores located around the world.

The principal issues that must be addressed in service encounter design are

- customer contact behavior and skills;
- service provider selection, development, and empowerment;
- recognition and reward; and
- service recovery and guarantees.

Customer contact *refers to the physical or virtual presence of the customer in the service delivery system during a service experience.* These elements are necessary to support excellent performance and create customer value and satisfaction. The OM Spotlight on Park Place Lexus shows how they address several of these elements.

Customer Contact Behavior and Skills

Customer contact is measured by the percentage of time the customer must be in the system relative to the total time it takes to provide the service. *Systems in which the percentage is high are called* **high-contact systems;** *those in which it is low are called* **low-contact systems.**[25,26] Examples of high-contact systems are estate planning and hotel check-in; examples of low-contact systems are construction services and package sorting and distribution.

> **Customer contact** *refers to the physical or virtual presence of the customer in the service delivery system during a service experience.*
>
> *Systems in which the percentage of time the customer must be in the system relative to the total time it takes to provide the service is high are called* **high-contact systems;** *those in which it is low are called* **low-contact systems.**

OM SPOTLIGHT

Park Place Lexus[24]

In 2005, Park Place Lexus (PPL) in Dallas, Texas, became the first automobile dealership to receive the Malcolm Baldrige National Quality Award. PPL has identified eight key value creation processes that have direct interface with Clients, including sales and valet service; significantly contribute to the delivery of service to its Clients; or provide opportunity for business growth. For all these key processes, PPL has identified process requirements as well as process measures to help them track progress on meeting these requirements. For example, for the new car sales process, PPL has identified courteous and knowledgeable sales consultants as a key requirement and measures its performance on this requirement using specific questions on the Client Satisfaction Index related to the sales experience and sales consultant. PPL has committed substantial resources to ensuring that Client relationships, once established, can be maintained in a way that contributes value to both parties. This includes the development and deployment of a Client relationship management database that tracks all aspects of the PPL-Client interaction and provides the resulting information to Members. PPL uses its Client Concern Resolution (CCR) process to address any problems that might occur in any area of the Client experience. CCR empowers the individual Member to resolve Client complaints on the spot by allowing each Member to spend up to $250 to resolve a complaint, or up to $2,000 by committee. In addition, both sales and service Clients are contacted by the Client call center after each interaction to ensure satisfaction and to proactively provide Clients with information on available products and services. PPL has instituted an extensive training program to ensure that once they have the right people in the right job, the new Member receives the right training to ensure they are successful in this job. All positions at PPL have been analyzed and specific training requirements have been identified. Each Member has a training plan that includes classroom training, on the job training, coaching and mentoring, observations, and assessments. As a result of this attention to service design and delivery, Park Place Lexus Grapevine location had a New Car Client Satisfaction Index (CSI) of 99.8 percent in 2004 making it the highest rated Lexus dealership in the nation.

The differences between high and low customer contact and their impact on operations are summarized in Exhibit 6.10. Many low-contact systems, such as processing an insurance policy, can be treated much like an assembly line, whereas service delivery systems with high customer contact are more difficult to design and control. One of the reasons for this is the variation and uncertainty that people (customers) introduce into high-contact service processes. For example, the time it takes to check a customer into a hotel can be affected by special requests (for example, a king bed

Exhibit 6.10 Operational Implications of High versus Low Customer Contact Systems

Operations Management Decision Areas	High-Contact Service Systems	Low-Contact Service Systems
Mission, strategy, and target market	Often require more personal service or premium services; focus on revenue maximization.	Focus can be directed toward convenience and efficiency; focus on cost minimization.
Customer benefit package design	High-contact services can better differentiate the CBP from competitors' offerings.	Low-contact services are more indistinguishable from competitors' offerings.
Operations planning	Planning must consider customer appointments, variable pricing, and flexibility.	Planning can focus on workload smoothing, production flow, and resource utilization.
Facility location	High-contact service facilities must locate close to the customer.	Low-contact service facilities can locate near supply, transportation, or expert labor.
Facility layout	Service facilities must accommodate customers' physical and psychological needs.	Service facilities can be designed for efficiency, speed, and low unit cost.
Job and process design	Customers participate directly in the service process, requiring more behavioral skills for service providers.	Customer does not participate in the majority of process steps; employees need more technical skills.
Servicescape	Must be elaborate, friendly, and effective; the employee is part of the servicescape.	Must be lean, functional, and efficient.
Technology and information	Requires real-time updates to support service encounter execution.	Information must be timely, but often batched to support minimum-cost transaction processing.
Organizational structure	Organized by process and must be flexible and adaptive.	Organized by process or function, and can be standardized.
Forecasting	Short-term (10- to 60-minute intervals) over small time horizons (days or weeks).	Longer-term (months or quarters) over longer-term time horizons (months or years).
Scheduling and capacity planning	Must accommodate frequent customer-driven changes and appointments; resource levels planned to meet peak demand.	Focus on back room efficiencies based on well-defined job sequences, level resource utilization, and meeting promise dates.
Quality	More intangible quality attributes such as customer perception and courtesy.	Quality standards are more easily defined and measured.
Service-provider selection, development, and empowerment	Require strong service management skills and behaviors, professional training; qualified people are hard to find.	Back room processing requires strong production skills, technical training; labor supply is more plentiful.
Recognition and reward	Rewards must be tied to behavioral skills and personal performance.	Rewards can be more easily tied to output, quality, and financial performance.
Service guarantees and recovery	Service providers must be able to respond immediately to service upsets at points of contact with customers.	Firms can handle service upsets using centralized staff in a more standard fashion and have more time to respond and correct problems.

Parts of this exhibit are based on concepts originally suggested by Richard B. Chase, "Where Does the Customer Fit in a Service Operation?" *Harvard Business Review*, November–December, 1978, pp. 137–142. Reprinted with permission.

or smoking room) and questions that customers might ask the desk clerk. Low customer contact systems are essentially free of this type of customer-induced uncertainty, and therefore capable of operating at higher levels of operating efficiency. Some hotels, for instance, have created more efficient check-in procedures for priority customers who have profiles on the hotel's computer system (that maintain customer room requests); documents and room keys are prepared in advance and simply need to be handed to the customer upon arrival. Many low-contact service systems do not interact with the customer at all; one example is a bank's check processing operation. High customer contact areas of the organization are sometimes described as the "front room" or "front office" and low customer contact areas as "back room" or "back office."

Customer-contact employees *are those people whose main responsibilities bring them into regular contact with customers—in person, by telephone, by e-mail, or through other means.* Front-line personnel who come in daily contact with customers have a significant amount of responsibility for customer satisfaction. The skills and behavior of customer-contact employees in high-contact systems—for example, ability to solve a technical problem or the tone of voice and empathy shown to customers—can either delight the customer or ruin a customer's service experience.

Customer-contact requirements *are measurable performance levels or expectations that define the quality of customer contact with representatives of an organization.* These might include such technical requirements as response time (answering the telephone within two rings), service management skills such as cross-selling other services, and/or behavioral requirements (using a customer's name whenever possible). Walt Disney Company, highly recognized for extraordinary customer service, clearly defines expected behaviors in their guidelines for guest service, which include making eye contact and smiling, greeting and welcoming every guest, seeking out guests who may need assistance, providing immediate service recovery, displaying approachable body language, focusing on the positive rather than rules and regulations, and thanking each and every guest.[27] Moreover, each customer may perceive behavior differently, which suggests that firms must pay considerable attention to selecting and training these employees.

One way to ensure consistent service and behavior from customer-contact employees is to use a script dialogue. *A* **script dialogue** *is a prescribed response to a given service situation.* A typical script dialogue states the customer query or service upset, then it defines what the service provider should say, what the customer might say, what the service provider's reply should be, and so forth. Script dialogues are often acted out in video training tapes and rehearsed in training seminars. UPS, Federal Express, Gateway Computers, Hilton Hotels, Vanguard Mutual Funds, and British Airways are just a few of the service companies that make use of script dialogues to help create more effective service encounters.

Service Provider Selection, Development, and Empowerment

Companies must carefully select customer-contact employees, train them well, and empower them to meet and exceed customer expectations. Procter & Gamble, for example, calls its consumer relations department the "voice of the company." A staff of over 250 employees handles over 3 million customer contacts each year. Their mission is stated as "We are a world-class consumer response (call) center. We provide superior service to consumers who contact Procter and Gamble, encourage product repurchase, and help build brand loyalty. We protect the Company's image and the reputation of our brands by resolving complaints before they are escalated to government agencies or the media. We capture and report consumer data to key Company functions, identify and share consumer insights, counsel product categories on consumer issues and trends, and manage consumer handling and interaction during crises." The challenge, of course, is finding, developing, and keeping really good customer-contact employees with service management skills.

Customer-contact employees *are those people whose main responsibilities bring them into regular contact with customers—in person, by telephone, by e-mail, or through other means.*

Customer-contact requirements *are measurable performance levels or expectations that define the quality of customer contact with representatives of an organization.*

PR Newswire Walt Disney World Resort

A **script dialogue** *is a prescribed response to a given service situation.*

Many companies begin with the recruiting process, selecting those employees who show the ability and desire to develop good customer relationships. Major companies such as Procter & Gamble seek people with excellent interpersonal and communication skills, strong problem-solving and analytical skills, assertiveness, stress tolerance, patience and empathy, accuracy and attention to detail, and computer literacy. Job applicants often go through rigorous screening processes that might include aptitude testing, customer service role-playing exercises, background checks, credit checks, and a medical evaluation.

Companies committed to customer relationship management ensure that customer-contact employees understand the products and services well enough to answer any question, develop good listening and human interaction skills, cross-sell and market other services of the firm, and handle service upsets and problems—service management skills. Effective training not only increases employees' knowledge but improves their self-esteem and loyalty to the organization.

One company that is a recognized leader in selection and training of its employees is The Ritz-Carlton Hotel Company. The Ritz-Carlton follows orientation training with continuous on-the-job training and, subsequently, job certification. All service providers are empowered to do whatever it takes to provide instant resolution of the customer's want, need, or problem. **Empowerment** *simply means giving people authority to make decisions based on what they feel is right, to have control over their work, to take risks and learn from mistakes, to promote change.* At The Ritz-Carlton Hotel Company, no matter what their normal duties are, employees must assist a fellow service provider who is responding to a guest's complaint or wish if such assistance is requested. Ritz-Carlton employees can spend up to $2,000 to resolve complaints with no questions asked. However, the actions of empowered employees should be guided by a common vision. That is, employees require a consistent understanding of what actions they may or should take.

Customer-contact employees also need access to the right technology and company information to do their jobs. FedEx, for example, furnishes employees with the information and technology they need to continually improve their performance. The Digitally Assisted Dispatch System (DADS) communicates to all couriers through screens in their vans, enabling quick response to pickup and delivery dispatches; it allows couriers to manage their time and routes with high efficiency. Information technology improves productivity, increases communication, and allows customer-contact employees to handle most any customer issue.

Recognition and Reward

After a firm hires, trains, and empowers good service providers, the next challenge is how to motivate and keep them. Motivation is a complex issue often studied in courses on organization behavior. Research has identified the key motivational factors to be recognition, advancement, achievement, and the nature of the work itself. Therefore, organizations that are attentive to these factors generally have more satisfied employees. A good compensation system can help to attract, retain, and motivate employees. Other forms of recognition, such as formal and informal employee and team recognition, preferred parking spots, free trips and extra vacation days, discounts and gift certificates, and a simple "thank you" from supervisors are vital to achieving a high-performance workplace.

Service Recovery and Guarantees

Despite all efforts to satisfy customers, every business experiences unhappy customers. *A* **service upset** *is any problem a customer has—real or perceived—with the service delivery system and includes terms such as service failure, error, defect, mistake, or crisis.* Service upsets can adversely affect business if not dealt with

Empowerment simply means giving people authority to make decisions based on what they feel is right, to have control over their work, to take risks and learn from mistakes, to promote change.

A **service upset** *is any problem a customer has—real or perceived—with the service delivery system and includes terms such as service failure, error, defect, mistake, or crisis.*

effectively. A company called TARP, formerly known as Technical Assistance Research Programs, Inc., conducted studies that revealed the following information:

1. The average company never hears from 96 percent of its unhappy customers. For every complaint received, the company has 26 more customers with problems, 6 of whose problems are serious.
2. Of the customers who make a complaint, more than half will again do business with that organization if their complaint is resolved. If the customer feels that the complaint was resolved quickly, the figure jumps to 95 percent.
3. The average customer who has had a problem will tell nine or ten others about it. Customers who have had complaints resolved satisfactorily will only tell about five others of the problem resolution.[28]
4. With the advent of the Internet, TARP also found that 4 percent of satisfied customers post their feelings on the web, while 15 percent of unsatisfied customers do the same.[29]

Service recovery *is the process of correcting a service upset and satisfying the customer.* Service providers need to listen carefully to determine the customer's feelings and then respond sympathetically, ensuring that the issue is understood. Then they should make every effort to resolve the problem quickly. Often this is accomplished with free meals, discount coupons, or a simple apology. Service recovery normally occurs after a service problem and when the customer is visibly upset. The key to service recovery is an "immediate response"; the longer customers wait, the angrier they might get.

Organizations have several options for managing service recovery. One approach is to collect data on the types of service failures, analyze the data, identify the most frequent or critical failures, and develop service recovery responses for each type and incorporate them in their training programs. Video or audiotapes demonstrating good and bad service incidents and how the service providers should handle them are often used for training. Script dialogues are also used for training and represent the official company response to each type of service upset, error, or mistake. Another approach is to hire good people, train them as best as possible, and empower them to respond creatively when service upsets occur. We discussed earlier how The Ritz-Carlton does this.

Many companies have well-defined processes for dealing with customer complaints. For example, at BI—a company that provides customized professional services for designing employee and customer incentives—all complaints, regardless of where they come from, are forwarded directly to the business unit manager related to the complaint.[30] The manager follows the Service Recovery Process (see Exhibit 6.11) and contacts the customer directly for clarification of the issue and additional information. Findings are then communicated to the account executive, sales manager, account manager, and all involved business unit associates via e-mail. This process enables the BI team to work in conjunction with the customer to address the failure and provide a solution that meets the customer's needs. A written follow-up of the resolution is shared with all BI team members working with the customer.

A **service guarantee** *is a promise to reward and compensate a customer if a service upset occurs during the service experience.* Unlike service recovery, which occurs after a service upset, service guarantees are offered prior to the customer experiencing the service. One objective is to encourage the customer to purchase the service. Because the customer cannot truly evaluate the service until he or she experiences it, service guarantees try to minimize the risk to the customer.[31]

There are two basic types of service guarantees. *An* **explicit service guarantee** *is a visible statement, usually in writing or communicated through the media, explaining what customers can expect in terms of service experiences and levels (the promise) and what the organization will do if it fails to deliver (the payout).* Examples of explicit service guarantees made by U.S. Bank are shown in Exhibit 6.12. Of course, the bank must have the operational capability to meet its standards of performance. *An* **implicit service**

Service recovery *is the process of correcting a service upset and satisfying the customer.*

A **service guarantee** *is a promise to reward and compensate a customer if a service upset occurs during the service experience.*

An **explicit service guarantee** *is a visible statement, usually in writing or communicated through the media, explaining what customers can expect in terms of service experiences and levels (the promise) and what the organization will do if it fails to deliver (the payout).*

An **implicit service guarantee** *is an unspoken and unwritten understanding that the organization will do whatever is necessary to satisfy customers and correct service upsets.*

Exhibit 6.11
BI Service Recovery Process

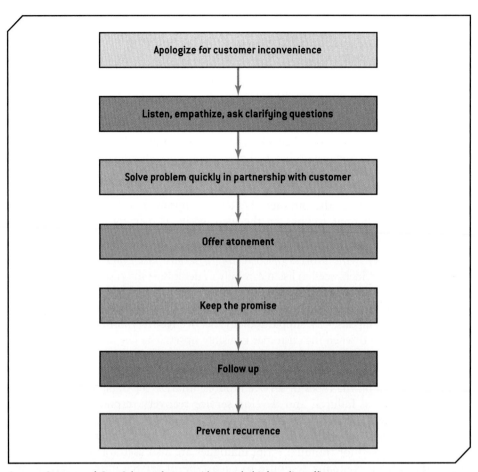

Source: Courtesy of Guy Schoenecker, president and chief quality officer.

Exhibit 6.12
U. S. Bank Service Guarantee
Examples[32]

Type of U.S. Bank Business	Example Explicit Service Guarantees
Automatic Teller Machine Service	• Provide ATM Help Desk customer service support 24 hours a day, 7 days a week. • Provide accurate monthly invoices and statements. • 100% system availability with two weeks' advance notice of any required scheduled outages. • Provide a dedicated Project Manager to every ATM installation. • If we fail to meet any of these levels of service, and you tell your banker that you did not get the service you expect and deserve, we will promptly credit your account $10.
Home Mortgage	• Provide a good-faith estimate of all loan costs to every customer at the time of application or we will pay $250 of your costs. • Knowledgeable loan officers are available 24 hours a day, 7 days a week or we pay you $25. • Acknowledge correspondence in writing within 7 business days from the receipt or we will pay you $100. • Respond to loan servicing calls received prior to 3 p.m. on the same day or we will credit your account $5.

guarantee *is an unspoken and unwritten understanding that the organization will do whatever is necessary to satisfy customers and correct service upsets.* An implicit guarantee does not specify a payout. You find this type of service guarantee most often in professional services, such as medicine and architecture, or in organizations that offer premium services, such as luxury hotels and investment firms.

AN INTEGRATIVE CASE STUDY OF LENSCRAFTERS[33]

To illustrate how goods and services are designed in an integrated fashion, we will study LensCrafters, a well-known provider of eyeglasses produced "in about an hour." We use the framework for goods and service design shown in Exhibit 6.1.

Strategic Mission, Market Analysis, and Competitive Priorities

LensCrafters (www.lenscrafters.com) is an optical chain of about 860 special service shops with on-site eyeglass production capabilities in the United States, Canada, and Puerto Rico. All resources necessary to create and deliver "one-stop shopping" and eyeglasses "in about one hour" are available in each store. If you have the opportunity to visit a store, you can see the front room retail store and back room eyeglass production laboratory, and better understand how the layout, process, job design, servicescape, and service encounters are integrated.

LensCrafters' mission statement is focused on being the best by

- "creating customers for life by delivering legendary customer service,
- developing and energizing associates and leaders in the world's best work place,
- crafting perfect-quality eyewear in about an hour, and
- delivering superior overall value to meet each customer's individual needs."[34]

This mission statement suggests that time and service quality are the most important competitive priorities and potential order winners. Customers normally make one trip to the store and complete the entire buying cycle (that is, one-stop shopping). Time, in all its forms, such as delivery speed, delivery reliability, and distance traveled to the store (convenience of location), is the key differentiator for LensCrafters. Good customer and service provider interaction, supported by friendly, caring, and professional service encounters, enhance its success. Eyeglasses, carrying cases, and other manufactured accessories represent the goods content of its CBP. Quality contact lenses and eyewear are order qualifiers and are expected by the customer. Defects in the quality of goods or poor diagnoses by store optometrists of the proper eyewear would not be tolerated by customers.

Customer Benefit Package Design and Configuration

Our perception of the LensCrafters customer benefit package is the integrated set of goods and services depicted in Exhibit 6.13. The primary good (eyewear) and the primary service (accurate eye exam and one-hour service) are of equal importance.

Getty Images/PhotoDisc

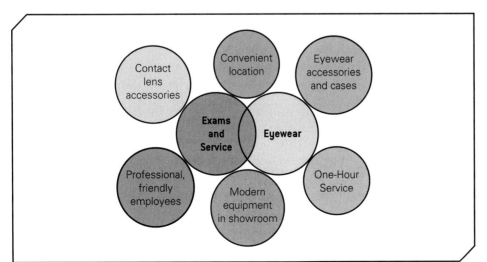

Exhibit 6.13
One Example View of LensCrafter's Customer Benefit Package

Peripheral goods and services encircle the primary ones to create "a total LensCrafters experience." Knowing the configuration of this CBP, operations managers can focus on how to create and deliver each primary and peripheral good and service and design the service delivery and service encounter systems.

Manufactured Good Design and Process Selection

Because frames and lenses are purchased from external suppliers, LensCrafters has little involvement in the actual design of the goods it sells. However, the company must address many key manufacturing process selection and design issues. The manufacturing process is integrated into the service facility to provide rapid order response, yet not sacrifice quality. In this industry, it is unusual for customers to watch their eyeglasses being made and this "service experience" is viewed as adding value. The equipment used in the labs is the most technologically advanced in the industry. The eyewear is manufactured to specifications in a clean, modern, and professionally run facility.

Other issues that LensCrafters would need to consider in designing its manufacturing processes are

- How are eyeglass lenses and frames ordered? Are these materials ordered by individual stores or consolidated by region/district? How can the high quality of eyewear be ensured? What new materials are available?
- What items should be stored at the region/district warehouse and stores? What type of purchasing and inventory control systems should be used? How should supplier performance be evaluated?
- What eyewear-making equipment should be used? What is the latest technology? Which equipment is most flexible? Should the equipment be purchased or leased? How should it be maintained and by whom?
- What is the most efficient production procedure to make the goods and meet time schedules? Where should quality be checked in the manufacturing process?

Service Delivery System Design

The service delivery system, as evidenced by the location and layout, servicescape, service processes, job designs, technology, and organizational structure, are combined into an integrated service delivery system. LensCrafters' stores are located in high traffic areas such as shopping centers and malls within five to ten miles of the target market. This provides convenient access and short travel times, enhancing the overall service experience.

A typical store layout is shown in Exhibit 6.14. The servicescape is designed to convey an impression of quality and professionalism. The store is spacious, open, clean, and carpeted, with professional merchandise display areas, modern furniture in the retail area, and modern equipment in the laboratory, technicians in white lab coats, shiny machines in the lab, and bright lights throughout. The store display cases, eye examination areas, and fitting stations are in the high-contact area where customers and service providers interact frequently. Optometry degrees, certifications, and licenses hanging on the wall provide physical evidence of employees' abilities.

A greeter directs each customer as he or she enters the store to the appropriate service area. The low-contact area of a LensCrafters store—the optical laboratory—is separated from the retail area by large glass panels. The optical laboratory becomes a "showroom" where the customer's perception of the total delivery process is established. The lab manager and technicians seldom interact with customers directly but help to create a professional impression as customers watch them make their eyeglasses.

The store is a service factory. The typical service process begins when a customer makes an appointment with an optician and continues until the eyeglasses

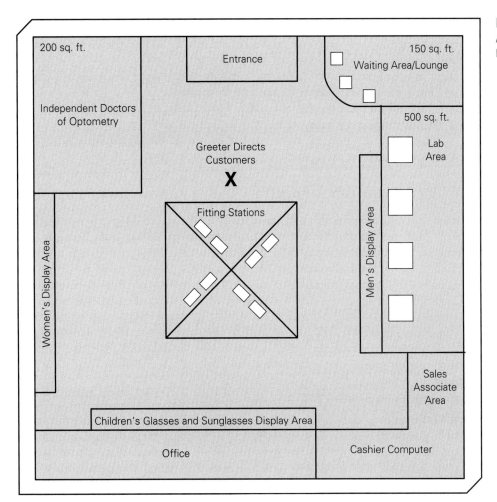

Exhibit 6.14
A Schematic of a Typical LensCrafters Store Layout

are received and paid for. Between these two events, the customer travels to the store, parks, receives a greeting from store employees, obtains an eye examination, selects frames, is measured for proper eyeglass and frame fit, watches the eyeglasses being made in the laboratory, and receives a final fitting to make sure all is well. Information flow in the forms of prescriptions, bills, and receipts complements the physical flows of people and eyewear.

Many customers stay and witness their individual pair of glasses being made. Two clocks on the wall allow customers to evaluate the total processing time of their service experience. And customers do watch those clocks! The variance around the one- to two-hour standard delivery time is low, resulting in over 90 percent of customer orders being on time, so delivery reliability is high. Other optical providers typically take from 2 to 15 days to process an order.

Each of the 11 in-store jobs, such as apprentice optician, lab manager, and assistant lab manager, requires a job description of specific responsibilities and tasks that must be performed, some of which might be performed in teams. Most of these service providers need service management skills because they are in high-contact jobs.

Some typical questions that managers would need to address for the service delivery system are

• How do we ensure that store optometrists and optical technicians have appropriate skills? Should continuing education be a paid benefit? How should professional performance be measured?

- What should happen when a customer walks into the store (for example, points of customer contact, greetings, and so on)? How should customer service, time, and service quality be measured?
- What are the best staff schedules and capacity? Equipment schedules and capacity? How should short-term demand be forecasted?
- How should the facility be maintained? How is this measured?
- What information systems are needed for patient services, billing, purchasing, customer reminder notices, and so on? How should the information systems be designed to support service delivery system efficiency and effectiveness?

Service Encounter Design

Each job at LensCrafters—sales associates, lab technicians, and doctors of optometry—requires both technical skills and service management skills. Associates are well trained, friendly, and knowledgeable about their jobs. The lab technicians are certified in all work tasks and processes. Many associates are cross-trained.

LensCrafters' service guarantee states, "If for any reason you are not completely satisfied with eyewear or service you receive from LensCrafters, we will make any adjustments you consider necessary, including replacing your lenses or frames at no additional charge." LensCrafters studies past customer complaints and claims to identify and reduce service failures and upsets. It develops standard "service recovery action plans" for each type of service failure and then makes sure all employees know what to do when a problem occurs.

At the service encounter level, key issues that managers need to consider include

- What human resource management processes and systems will ensure hiring the right people, training them properly, and motivating them to provide excellent service? What recognitions and rewards should be provided?
- How are associates trained to handle service upsets and service recovery?
- What standards should be set for grooming and appearance?
- What behavioral standards, such as tone of voice, physical mannerisms, and the words that associates use in customer interactions, should be set?
- How should employee performance be measured and evaluated?
- What can be done to make the one-hour wait a positive experience for customers?

Note that customer perceptions of service encounters are influenced by the servicescape; therefore, the design of the service delivery system and service encounters must be considered together.

Market Introduction/Deployment and Evaluation

Although the company has been around for some time, it undoubtedly faces challenges in replicating its design concept in new locations. On a continuing basis, as technology and procedures change, LensCrafters will have to develop processes to introduce changes into all existing locations to maintain operational consistency and achieve its strategic objectives. For example, how might it react as competitors such as Wal-Mart enter the optical industry? Clearly, it also needs to maintain an understanding of customer satisfaction and maintain high performance levels on a day-to-day basis at hundreds of sites. The store's information system supports these efforts by tracking customer history and eyewear preferences and sending reminders to customers to get a checkup, thereby encouraging repeat business. The system also routinely sends a sample of customers a feedback questionnaire.

As you see, LensCrafters' manufacturing and service design depends on a variety of operations management concepts, all of which are well integrated and support a rather complex customer benefit package.

DESIGN SPEED

Design speed *is the time it takes from the conception of an idea for a good, service, or customer benefit package until it is available to customers.* The importance of design speed cannot be overemphasized. To succeed in highly competitive markets, companies must churn out new goods and services quickly. Whereas automakers once took 4 to 6 years to develop new models, most are striving to do this within 24 months. In fact, Toyota's goal is just 18 months! Due to information technology, auto loans and leases are bundled to the new automobile design and can be approved in minutes in the dealer's showroom. Many multisite service businesses such as retail stores, hotels, and restaurants also want to quickly deploy new CBP and facility designs to hundreds or thousands of sites to preempt competition and gain competitive advantage.

Design speed is the time it takes from the conception of an idea for a good, service, or customer benefit package until it is available to customers.

Boeing took 54 months to design its 777 airplane, yet the company would like to reduce it to 10 months because the market changes so quickly. The product development process can be improved with various advanced technologies that we discussed in Chapter 5, such as computer-aided design (CAD), computer-aided manufacturing (CAM), flexible manufacturing systems (FMS), and computer-integrated manufacturing (CIM). These technologies automate and link design and manufacturing processes, reducing cycle times as well as removing opportunities for human error, thus improving quality. Such automation is a key factor at Toyota.[35]

Streamlining the Goods and Service Design Process

One of the most significant barriers to efficient good and service design and development is poor intraorganizational cooperation. Success demands the involvement and cooperation of many different functional groups within an organization to identify and solve design problems and to try to reduce development and market introduction times.

Unfortunately, the product development process often is performed without such cooperation. In many goods-producing firms, product development is accomplished in a serial fashion. In the early stages of development, design engineers dominate the process. Later, the prototype is transferred to manufacturing for production. Finally, marketing and sales personnel are brought into the process. This approach has several disadvantages. First, product development time is long. Second, up to 90 percent of manufacturing costs may be committed before manufacturing engineers have any input to the design. Third, the final product may not be the best one for market conditions at the time of introduction.

An approach that alleviates these problems is called concurrent engineering. **Concurrent engineering,** *or* **simultaneous engineering,** *is a process in which all major functions involved with bringing a product to market are continuously involved with product development from conception through sales.* Some major work activities are performed in parallel (simultaneously) to speed up the product development process. Such an approach not only helps achieve trouble-free introduction of products and services but also results in improved quality, lower costs, and shorter product development cycles. Typical benefits include 30 to 70 percent less development time, 65 to 90 percent fewer engineering changes, 20 to 90 percent less time to market, 200 to 600 percent improvement in quality, 20 to 110 percent improvement in white-collar productivity, and 20 to 120 percent higher return on assets.[36]

Concurrent engineering, or simultaneous engineering, is a process in which all major functions involved with bringing a product to market are continuously involved with product development from conception through sales.

Concurrent engineering involves multifunctional teams, usually consisting of 4 to 20 members and including every specialty in the company. The functions of such teams are to determine the character of the product and decide what design methods and production methods are appropriate; analyze product functions so that all design decisions can be made with full knowledge of how the item is supposed to work; perform a design for manufacturability study to determine whether the design can be improved without affecting performance; formulate an assembly sequence; and design a factory system that fully involves workers. Toyota has taken the concept a step further—by developing similar models simultaneously. Most companies develop similar models sequentially, for example, a Camry sedan followed by a Camry coupe. This ensures that problems on one model get resolved before the next one is started. By developing them simultaneously, engineering tasks overlap, allowing teams to learn from the failures and successes of different projects, saving up to 15 percent in lead time and 50 percent in engineering hours. In just 2 years, Toyota introduced 18 new or redesigned models.[37]

Information Technology in Goods and Service Design

Information technology represents another area that provides significant benefits to goods and service design. General Motors, for example, has implemented a system that allows GM employees and external auto parts suppliers to share product design information. Previously, GM had no way of coordinating its complex designs across its 14 engineering sites scattered around the world, plus the dozens of partners who design subsystems. More than 16,000 designers and other employees use the new web system designed by Electronic Data Systems Corp. to share three-dimensional designs and keep track of parts and subassemblies. The system automatically updates the master design when changes are finalized so that everyone is on the same page. As a result, GM has reduced the time to complete a full mock-up of a car from 12 weeks to 2.[38] Another example is provided in the OM Spotlight on Moen.

Sometimes information technology is a disruptive technology in that it forces an industry and its firms to radically redesign its customer benefit packages and associated processes and value chains. Most information-intensive industries are currently going through such restructuring. The book publishing and delivery industry, for instance, must deal with traditional hard-copy books, custom publishing for the college market (selected chapters from several books packaged and bound together for an individual instructor), Internet availability, e-books, and on-demand publishing where everyone can become an author. These changes not only require new approaches to the design of goods and services but also the delivery processes.

OM SPOTLIGHT

Moen Inc.[39]

Moen Inc. makes faucets for bathrooms and kitchens. In the mid-1990s, as plumbing fixtures became fashion necessities of new homes and remodeling projects, the company needed to provide a much larger set of styles in silver, platinum, and copper, instead of its current product line designed in the '60s and '70s. Moen revitalized its product design approach using the web, collaborating with suppliers in the design process. Previously, engineers would spend 6 to 8 weeks coming up with a new design, burning it onto CDs, and mailing them to suppliers in 14 countries that make the hundreds of parts that go into a faucet, who would return a CD with changes and suggestions. These needed to be reconciled with other suppliers' responses. Redesign activities and tool design and production might extend this process to up to 24 weeks.

With the web-based approach, a new faucet goes from drawing board to store shelf in 16 months, down from an average of 2 years. This time savings allowed Moen's engineers to work on three times as many projects and introduce from 5 to 15 new faucet lines each year. This helped boost sales by 17% from 1998 to 2001, higher than the industry average of 9% over the same period, and moved Moen from number 3 in market share to a tie for number 1 with rival Delta Faucet Co.

PR Newswire Moen Incorporated

Design Speed in the Global Marketplace

Globalization has important implications for goods and service development.[40] Integrated design for the global market can eliminate costly redesigns each time that the company wants to enter a new market. A "core or primary" good or service can be designed that can be tailored to meet the needs of local markets. In some cases, companies have developed specific kits for individual countries that contain preprogrammed memory chips, documentation, and special power cords. Operations plays a key role in increasing the speed of design by focusing on speeding up the value chain and its processes by eliminating bottlenecks, taking out waiting and non-value-added time, and so on. The speed of global design is a competitive advantage for firms who quickly identify an emerging target market and fulfill its customer requirements. Of course, information technology is the enabler that allows all this to happen.

The use of international design teams can turn a multinational firm's scattered operations into a competitive advantage. If the members of a design team are located throughout the world rather than at a central site, each team member can monitor local tastes, technical standards, and changing government regulations. They can also stay abreast of new technology and gain quicker access to competitors' products. Such an approach requires good global communication systems.

Quality Function Deployment

An effective approach for ensuring that customer needs are met in the design process was pioneered in Japan during the 1970s. **Quality function deployment (QFD)** *is both a philosophy and a set of planning and communication tools that focus on customer requirements in coordinating the design, manufacturing, and marketing of goods or services.* QFD can be applied to a specific manufactured good, service, or the entire CBP. QFD is a generic and integrative tool.

A major benefit of QFD is improved communication and teamwork among all constituencies in the design process—such as between marketing and product design, design and manufacturing, and purchasing and suppliers—which prevents misinterpretation of product objectives during the production process. Also, QFD helps to determine the causes of customer dissatisfaction, and it is a useful tool for competitive analysis of product quality by top managers. Most significantly, the time for new product development is reduced. QFD allows companies to simulate the effects of new design ideas and concepts, thus enabling them to gain competitive advantage by bringing new products into the market sooner.

In Chapter 3 we discussed the importance of understanding customer wants and needs from a strategic perspective. *Customer requirements, as expressed in the customer's own terms, are called the* **voice of the customer.** They represent what customers expect a product or service to have or to do. QFD focuses on turning the voice of the customer into specific technical requirements that characterize a design and provide the "blueprint" for manufacturing or service delivery. Technical requirements might include materials, size and shape of parts, strength requirements, service procedures to follow, and even employee behavior during customer interactions. The process is initiated with a matrix, which because of its structure (shown in Exhibit 6.15) is often called the **House of Quality.**

Building a House of Quality begins by identifying the voice of the customer and technical features of the design. For the voice of the customer to be effective, it is important to use the customer's own words; designers and engineers may misquote them (see the OM Spotlight on LaRosa's). The technical features, however, must be expressed in the language of the designer and engineer and form the basis for subsequent design, manufacturing, and service process activities.

The roof of the House of Quality shows the interrelationships between any pair of technical features, and these relationships help in answering questions such as "How

Quality function deployment (QFD) is both a philosophy and a set of planning and communication tools that focus on customer requirements in coordinating the design, manufacturing, and marketing of goods or services.

Customer requirements, as expressed in the customer's own terms, are called the **voice of the customer.**

Exhibit 6.15
The House of Quality

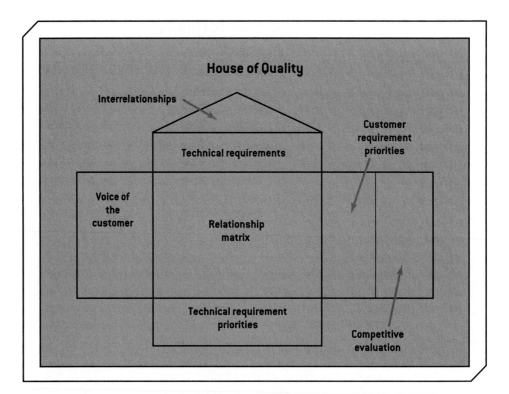

does a change in one product characteristic affect others?" and in assessing trade-offs between characteristics. Features can be examined collectively rather than individually.

Next, a relationship matrix between the customer requirements and the technical features is developed, which shows whether the final technical features adequately address the customer attributes, an assessment that may be based on expert experience, customer responses, or controlled experiments. The lack of a strong relationship between a customer attribute and any of the technical features would suggest that the final good or service will have difficulty in meeting customer needs. Similarly, if a technical feature does not affect any customer attribute, it may be redundant.

The next step is to add market evaluation and key selling points. It includes rating the importance of each customer attribute and evaluating existing products on each of the attributes to highlight the absolute strengths and weaknesses of competing products. This step links QFD to a company's strategic vision and allows priorities to be set in the design process. For example, if an attribute receives a low evaluation on all competitors' products, focusing on that attribute can help to gain a competitive advantage. Such attributes become key selling points and help in establishing promotion strategies. Next, technical features of competitive products are evaluated and targets are developed. These evaluations are compared with the competitive evaluation of customer attributes to spot any inconsistency between customer evaluations and technical evaluations. On the basis of customer-importance ratings and existing product strengths and weaknesses, targets for each technical feature are set.

The final step is to select technical features that have a strong relationship to customer needs, have poor competitive performance, or are strong selling points. Those characteristics will need to be "deployed," or translated into the language of each function in the design and process, so that proper actions and controls are taken to ensure that the voice of the customer is maintained. Characteristics that are not identified as critical do not need such rigorous attention.

The example of a House of Quality in Exhibit 6.16 is for a restaurant's attempt to develop a "signature" pizza. The voice of the customer in this case consists of four attributes. The pizza should be tasty, be healthy, be visually appealing, and should provide good value. The "technical features" that can be designed into this

OM SPOTLIGHT

LaRosa's Pizzeria

LaRosa's Pizzeria, a regional chain of informal Italian restaurants in the greater Cincinnati area, realized that customers know what they want. To gather information to help design a new restaurant configuration, it went out to current and potential customers and noncustomers in nonmarket areas to acquire the voice of the customer. However, the company found that people have a difficult time expressing their needs in ways that are meaningful to managers. This means that the company needed to effectively translate their language into actionable business terms. Here are some real examples of customers' experiences at other restaurants that LaRosa's clearly wanted to avoid:

- "So there I was, like herded cattle, standing on the hard concrete floor, cold wind blasting my ankles every time the door opened, waiting and waiting for our name to be called."
- "And then I saw a dirty rag being slopped around a dirty table."

- "This is a great place because you can just come in and plop in a booth, just like at Mom's house."
- "I swear! The salad looked like the server ran down to the river bank and picked weeds and grass—I'm never going back!"
- "The server just stood there staring at me, chomping his gum like a cow chewing its cud."
- "When they're that age, going to the bathroom is a full-contact sport—they're reaching and grabbing at everything, and you're trying to keep them from touching anything because the bathroom is so dirty."

In the last example, what the customer really was saying is "The bathroom tells me what the kitchen might be like. Do I really want to eat here?" Clean bathrooms turned out to be the most important customer requirement that the company learned from the voice of the customer process. What do you think the customers were saying in the other examples?

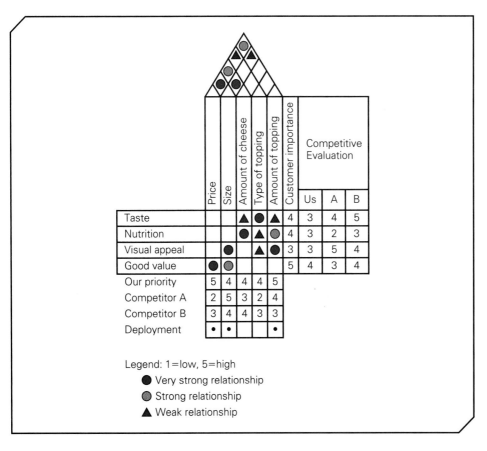

Exhibit 6.16

House of Quality Example for a Pizza

particular product are price, size, amount of cheese, type of additional toppings, and amount of additional toppings. The symbols in the matrix in Exhibit 6.16 show the relationships between each customer requirement and technical feature. For example, taste bears a moderate relationship with amount of cheese and a strong relationship with type of additional toppings. In the roof, the price and size area seem to be strongly related (as size increases, the price must increase). The competitive evaluation shows that competitors are currently weak on nutrition and value, so those attributes can become key selling points in a marketing plan if the restaurant can capitalize on them. Finally, at the bottom of the house are targets for the technical features based on an analysis of customer-importance ratings and competitive ratings. The features with asterisks are the ones to be "deployed," or emphasized, in subsequent design and production activities.

The House of Quality provides marketing with an important tool to understand customer needs and gives top management strategic direction. However, it is only the first step in the QFD process. The voice of the customer must be carried throughout the production/delivery process. Three other "houses of quality" are used to deploy the voice of the customer to (in a manufacturing setting) component parts characteristics, process plans, and quality control.

The second house is similar to the first house but applies to subsystems and components. The technical requirements from the first house are related to detailed requirements of subsystems and components (see Exhibit 6.17). At this stage, target values representing the best values for fit, function, and appearance are determined. For example, the components of a pizza (dough, toppings) would have their own unique requirements, and hence, their own House of Quality. These would be useful in communicating with external suppliers or the company commissary supplying the ingredients. In a service setting, the four houses of quality analogous to Exhibit 6.17 might be customer requirements, the service delivery system, a workstation in the process, and service encounter design.

In manufacturing, most of the QFD activities represented by the first two houses of quality are performed by the product development and engineering functions. At the next stage, the planning activities involve supervisors and production line operators. In the third house, the process plan relates the component characteristics to key process operations, the transition from planning to execution. (For the pizza example, this might involve creating a project plan for assembling and cooking.) Key process operations are the basis for a *control point*. A control point forms the basis for a quality control plan delivering those critical characteristics that are crucial to achieving customer satisfaction. This is specified in the last house of quality. At this point, for example, the pizza restaurant might determine how to measure toppings

Exhibit 6.17 The Four Houses of Quality Hierarchy

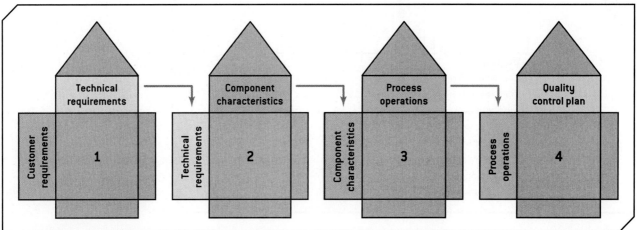

to ensure consistency, inspect the pizza before cooking, and how often to check cooking progress. Thus, the QFD process provides a thread from the voice of the customer, through design and production/delivery activities, to daily management and control.

The vast majority of applications of QFD in the United States concentrate on the first and, to a lesser extent, the second houses of quality. Lawrence Sullivan, who brought QFD to the West, suggested that the third and fourth houses of quality offer far more significant benefits, especially in the United States.[41] In Japan, managers, engineers, and workers are more naturally cross-functional and tend to promote group effort and consensus thinking. In the United States, workers and managers are more vertically oriented and tend to suboptimize for individual and/or departmental achievements. Companies in the United States tend to promote breakthrough achievements, which often inhibit cross-functional interaction. If a U.S. company can maintain the breakthrough culture with emphasis on continuous improvement through more effective cross-functional interactions as supported by QFD, it can establish a competitive advantage over foreign competitors. The third and fourth houses of quality utilize the knowledge of about 80 percent of a company's employees—supervisors and operators. If their knowledge goes unused, this potential is wasted.

SOLVED PROBLEMS

1. Fill in the House of Quality relationship matrix shown here for a screwdriver.

Legend: ● Very strong relationship
● Strong relationship
▲ Weak relationship

Solution:
There is no one universal solution to this problem. However, the relationships between the customer requirements and the technical specifications should be reasonably justified. One solution is shown here. For instance, consider the first customer requirement, "Easy to use." Clearly, price does not impact this requirement. However, designing interchangeable bits would strongly add to this requirement; a rubber grip might help some, but not as strongly. On the other hand, the rubber grip would strongly relate to the customer requirement "Comfortable" and somewhat to "Inexpensive" (because adding the rubber grip would increase the cost).

2. A quality characteristic understudy has a manufacturing specification (in cm) of 0.200 ± 0.05. Historical data indicates that if the quality characteristic takes on values larger than 0.25 cm or smaller than 0.15 cm, the product fails and a cost of \$75 is incurred. Based on these data,

   a. Determine the Taguchi Loss Function using Equation (6.1).
   b. Estimate the loss for a quality characteristic of 0.135 cm.

Solution:

a. $L(x) = \$75$
$(x - T) = 0.05$
$k = (75)/(0.05)^2$
$k = 30{,}000$

The loss function is $L(x) = 30{,}000(x - T)^2$.

b. $L(x) = 30{,}000(x - T)^2$, where $x = 0.135$ and $T = 0.200$
$L(0.135) = 30{,}000(0.135 - 0.200)^2 = \$126.75$.

This means that the firm can expect to incur a cost of $126.75 per unit when the value of the quality characteristic is 0.135 instead of the target value of 0.200.

3. An automated production system is shown in Exhibit 6.18 with three operations: turning, milling, and grinding. Individual parts are transformed from the turning center to the milling center, and then to the grinder by a robot; thus, if one machine or the robot fails, the entire production process must stop. The probability that any one component of the system will fail, however, does not depend on any other component of the system. Conceptually, we can think of the robot and machines in series, as shown in Exhibit 6.19.

a. If we assume that the reliability of the robot, turning center, milling machine, and grinder are .99, .98, .99, and .96, respectively, what is the reliability of the complete system?

b. Suppose the system is redesigned with two grinders that operate in parallel; if one grinder fails, the other grinder may still work and hence the total system will continue to function. Such a system is illustrated in Exhibit 6.20. What is the reliability of this new configuration?

Exhibit 6.18
Automated Production Center

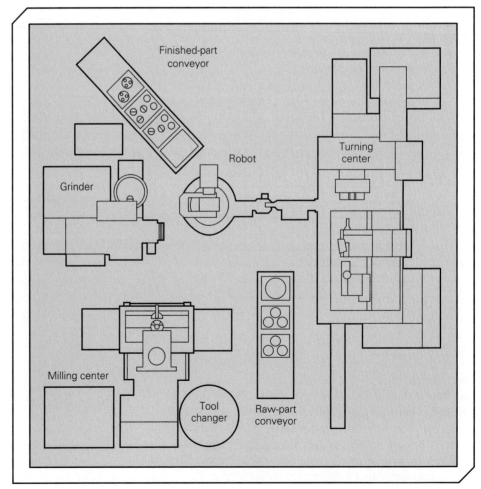

Source: John G. Holmes, "Integrating Robots into a Manufacturing System." Reprinted with permission from 1979 Fall Industrial Engineering Conference *Proceedings*. Copyright Institute of Industrial Engineers, 25 Technology Park/Atlanta, Norcross, GA 30092.

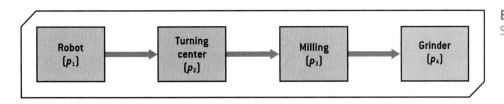

Exhibit 6.19
Series Production System

Solution:

a. Using Equation (6.2), the reliability of the system can be computed as

$$R_s = (.99)(.98)(.99)(.96) = .92, \text{ or } 92\%$$

This means there is a .92 probability that the system will be working over a specified period of time. As stated, this calculation assumes that the probability of failure of each operation in the system is independent of the others.

b. Using Equation (6.3) and letting p_{g1} denote the reliability of grinder 1 and p_{g2} denote the reliability of grinder 2, the reliability of the parallel grinders is given by

$$R_p = 1 - [(1 - p_{g1})(1 - p_{g2})]$$

Therefore, if each grinder has a reliability of .96, the reliability of both grinders together is

$$R_p = 1 - [(1 - .96)(1 - .96)] = \\ 1 - .0016 = 0.9984, \text{ or } 99.84\%$$

Notice that the total grinder reliability has increased by adding the extra machine. Now we can use Equation (6.2) to compute the total system reliability, using .9984 as the reliability of the grinders. Essentially, we have replaced the parallel grinders with one grinder whose reliability is .9984. Thus, we have

$$R_s = (.99)(.98)(.99)(.9984) = .96, \text{ or } 96\%$$

Exhibit 6.20 Series Production System with Parallel Grinders

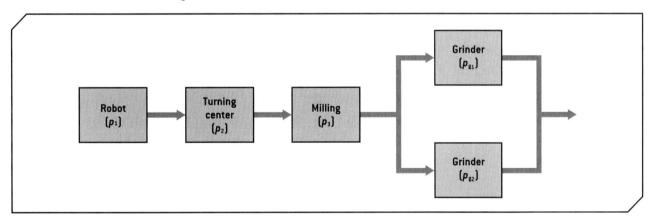

KEY TERMS AND CONCEPTS

Concept development
Concurrent engineering
Customer benefit package design and configuration
Customer contact—high and low
Customer contact requirements
Customer-contact employees
Design for manufacturability (DFM)
Design for the Environment (DfE)
Design reviews
Design speed

Elements of service delivery system design
Elements of service encounter design
Empowerment
Factoryscape
Failure-mode-and-effects-analysis (FMEA)
Functional failure
Globalization of design
Goal post model
Goods and service design framework (Exhibit 6.1)
Green manufacturing or practices

House of Quality
Impact of information technology on design speed
LensCrafters' integration of goods and services
Modular design
Operating conditions
Performance
Product and process simplification
Prototype testing
Quality engineering
Quality function deployment (QFD)
Redundancy
Reliability
Reliability engineering/management
Reliability failure
Reliability—serial and parallel
Reverse engineering
Robust design—manufactured goods
Robust design—services

Script dialogue
Service delivery system
Service design framework
    Primary or peripheral service
    Service delivery system
    Service encounter
Service encounter design
Service guarantees—explicit and implicit
Service recovery
Service upset
Servicescape—lean and elaborate
System
Taguchi loss function and model
Value analysis
Value defined from a service perspective
Value engineering
Voice of customer

QUESTIONS FOR REVIEW AND DISCUSSION

1. Explain how goods and services are designed. How is the design of manufactured goods similar to designing services? How does it differ?

2. What is concept development? What factors must organizations consider in developing concepts?

3. What is prototype testing? Why is it used?

4. What do we mean by robust design?

5. Sketch the Taguchi loss function and explain the concept behind it. How does it differ from the "goal post" model?

6. A customer service manager wishes to evaluate the loss of goodwill that results from customers waiting in line at the checkout counter. What type of Taguchi loss function should be used for this situation? How might the value of k be found?

7. What is quality engineering? How do value engineering and value analysis improve design efforts?

8. Explain the concepts of design reviews, failure-mode-and-effect-analysis, and design for manufacturability.

9. Explain how to "build in" quality into manufactured good designs. In service designs?

10. What is the rationale for product and process simplification?

11. What are the advantages of modular design? Examples?

12. Discuss the issues that manufacturers face with respect to environmental quality. What techniques and approaches can help? Answer the same questions for services.

13. Define reliability and explain the key elements of the definition.

14. What is the purpose of reliability engineering and reliability management?

15. Discuss the advantages and disadvantages of redundancy in designs.

16. Can reliability analysis be applied to a service process? If so, explain how. If not, why?

17. What are the key elements of service delivery system design? Explain how each of them contributes to a reliable service that provides customer value.

18. What is a servicescape? Choose a servicescape for a business with which you are familiar and list key physical attributes of the servicescape and their impact on customer service and value. Explain how the servicescape establishes the behavioral setting for your example.

19. Compare and contrast the servicescape and contact technology for a mass retailer store such as Target or Kmart versus a more premium retailer such as Saks Fifth Avenue or Nordstrom's. Explain.

20. Select a service system you are familiar with and define its servicescape in terms of ambient conditions, spatial layout, and signs, symbols, and artifacts.

21. Explain how the servicescape concept applies in a manufacturing facility.

22. What is service process design? How is it performed?

23. Explain the role of technology and organizational structure in service process design.

24. What is service encounter design? How do the differences between goods and services affect this activity?

25. What is customer contact? Explain the differences between high- and low-contact systems.

26. Is it easier to manage a high or low customer-contact business? Explain.

27. Characterize the following goods and services on the low–high customer-contact continuum, and justify your answer in a sentence or two.
    i. participating in a case study classroom discussion
    ii. listening and taking notes in a classroom lecture
    iii. machining an aluminum part in a factory
    iv. taking your automobile to the dealer for repair and waiting for service
    v. playing golf in a foursome of friends
    vi. driving a truck and delivering the shipment at the loading dock
    vii. handling a customer's claim on a lost shipment over the telephone
    viii. approving medical claims in an insurance company

28. What must organizations do to ensure that customer-contact employees do an effective job?

29. What is a service upset? Briefly describe a service upset you have experienced. What happened? What should have happened?

30. Explain the concept of service recovery and why it is important, and provide some examples.

31. What is a service guarantee? How do explicit and implicit service guarantees differ?

32. Find an example of a service guarantee and explain its strengths and weaknesses.

33. Identify three key characteristics or lessons about LensCrafters at each of the following three levels: (1) CBP, strategy, and competitive priorities, (2) service delivery design, and (3) service encounter design. What lessons does the Lenscrafters' case demonstrate that other organizations might learn?

34. Why is design speed important? Discuss how concurrent engineering can improve design speed.

35. Explain how various technologies described in Chapter 4 can support fast and efficient design and development.

36. How does globalization impact the design process? What unique challenges does it pose for product development managers?

37. Explain the basic principles of quality function deployment. What benefits does this methodology provide?

38. Describe the elements of the House of Quality. How is this information used in the product development effort?

39. What is the "voice of the customer"? What lessons can be learned from the LaRosa's Pizzeria spotlight?

40. How do the four Houses of Quality impact operations decisions for designing a manufacturing process? A service process?

PROBLEMS AND ACTIVITIES

1. Given the following customer requirements and technical requirements for an automobile, construct a partial House of Quality. Use your own preferences to denote relationship strengths.

Customer requirements	Technical requirements
good mileage	acceleration rate
fast response when passing	fuel economy
good handling	passing time

2. Develop a House of Quality for a manufactured good or service based on current or past work experience or something else you are familiar with. Some ideas might be a quick-service oil change, a fast-food restaurant, a DVD player, a new car, or a fitness club.

3. Exhibit 6.21 shows a partially completed House of Quality for a proposed fitness center.
    a. Examine the relationships in the roof of the House of Quality. Explain why they make sense (or if you think they do not, explain why). How would this assessment help in the design activity?
    b. Complete the matrix in the body of the House of Quality. That is, examine each pair of customer and technical requirements and determine if there is a very strong relationship, strong relationship, weak relationship, or no relationship, and fill in the appropriate symbols in the matrix.

Exhibit 6.21
House of Quality for a Fitness Center

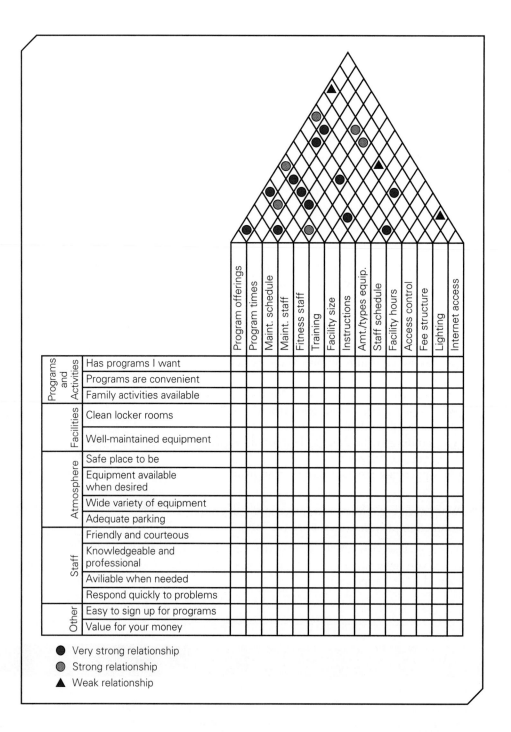

c. Suppose that the most important customer requirements identified through surveys and focus groups are "has programs I want," "family activities available," "equipment available when desired," "easy to sign up for programs," and "value for your money." "Staff available when needed" was ranked low, and the remaining requirements were ranked moderate in importance. Based on this information, identify the most important technical requirements that should be addressed in subsequent design activities.

4. Select a service at your school, such as financial aid, bookstore, curriculum advising, and so on. Propose a redesign of this service and its service delivery system. First, baseline the current service and system, and then suggest how to redesign and improve it. Make use of chapter ideas as best you can.

5. Suppose that the specifications for a part (in inches) are 6.00 ± 0.25, and that the Taguchi loss function is estimated to be $L(x) = 8,500(x - T)^2$. Determine the estimated loss if the quality characteristic under study takes on a value of 6.30 inches.

6. A quality characteristic has a specification (in inches) of 0.200 ± 0.020. If the value of the quality characteristic exceeds 0.200 by the tolerance of 0.020 on either side, the product will require a repair of $150. Develop the appropriate Taguchi loss function.

7. The manufacturing of compact discs requires four sequential steps. The reliability of each of the steps is .96, .87, .92, and .89, respectively. What is the reliability of the process?

8. The service center for a brokerage company provides three functions to callers: account status, order confirmations, and stock quotes. The reliability was measured for each of these services over 1 month with these results: 90%, 80% and 96%, respectively. What is the overall reliability of the call center?

9. The system reliability for a two-component parallel system is .99968. If the reliability of the first component is .992, determine the reliability of the second component.

10. The system reliability for a three-component series system is .893952. If the reliability of the first and third components is .96 and .97, respectively, determine the reliability of the second component.

11. Given the following diagram, determine the system reliability if the individual component reliabilities are: A = .94, B = .92, C = .97, and D = .94.

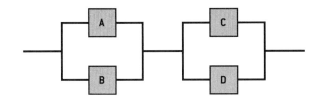

12. In a complex manufacturing process, three operations are performed in series. Because of the nature of the process, machines frequently fall out of ad-

justment and must be repaired. To keep the system going, two identical machines are used at each operation; thus, if one fails, the other can be used while the first is repaired. The reliabilities of the machines in each of the three operations are .60, .75, and .70, respectively.
   a. Analyze the system reliability, assuming only one machine at each operation.
   b. How much is the reliability improved by having two machines at each operation?

13. A school is being designed with three identical buildingwide fire alarm systems. The reliability of each fire alarm system is .995. Should the fire alarm systems be placed in series, parallel, or in a series parallel combination? Defend your recommendation using a system reliability analysis.

14. Given the following diagram, determine the overall service system reliability if the individual workstation reliabilities are: W = .98, X = .97, Y = .99, and Z = .90.

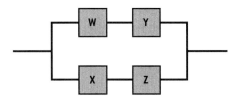

15. The reliabilities of the work activities in an insurance underwriting service process are: A = .92, B = .95, C = .93, D = .99, E = .92, F = .90, G = .97, and H = .96. The service process configuration is shown in Exhibit 6.22. What is the reliability of the total service process?

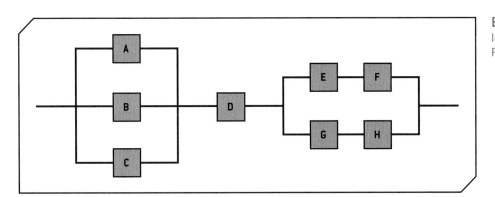

Exhibit 6.22
Insurance Underwriting Service Process Configuration

CASES

UNIVERSAL MUSIC GROUP ANNOUNCES CD PRICE CUTS[42]

Universal Music Group announced that it is reducing its prices on music CDs by 25%. Universal is lowering its wholesale price by just over $3, from $12.12 to $9.09 per CD, but it is lowering the suggested retail price by $6, from $18.98 to $12.98. With these low prices, the big box mass retailers such as Target, Wal-Mart, and Best Buy have the advantage compared to specialty music retailers. Music industry analysts think the profit margin on music CDs will drop below 10% with retail prices in the $9 to $10 range. Used CD prices are also expected to be much lower.

The result of these price reductions is that specialty music retailers and independent music stores will most likely go out of business. For example, Trans World Entertainment Corporation recently bought bankrupt Wherehouse Entertainment Inc.'s 148 music stores. "Independent record stores, too, will feel the pain. Many rely on used CDs—typically a high margin item—to boost their bottom lines," says Mike Dresse, CEO of Newbury Comics, Inc., which operates 24 music stores in the Northeast. "How are we supposed to pay our rent making 90 cents on a CD?" griped a small store owner.

a. Draw the CBP configuration for the traditional music CD available for sale in the 1980s (before the Internet). Identify primary and peripheral goods and services, and explain what the customer buys. Compare this to the CBP configuration for the music CD available via the Internet. Make assumptions as required. What is driving this change in CBP design and configuration? Explain.

b. What is the impact of these changes on service design for customers buying music CDs?

c. Why is the industry structure changing? How? How do you think customers will get their music 30 years from now?

BOURBON BANK: SERVICE GUARANTEES

"I know what we can do next, everything has been so successful so far," said Kay Ebelhar, marketing services division manager. "How about offering a *courtesy service guarantee*? We will promise to greet the customer, give them our undivided attention, and then thank them when they leave. As with our other service guarantees, if we fail to deliver superior service encounters, we'll give the customer $5.00! What do you think?" So the discussion began this Tuesday morning at the monthly meeting of the Marketing Control Task Force (MCTF). Following these words, Sarah Coleman, service guarantee manager for Bourbon Bank, pondered what the next step should be in her company's journey to become the industry leader in customer service.

Four years ago, the bank undertook an extensive study to identify the needs of its target customers and analyze the actions of its competitors. Based on the findings, the bank defined what direction to pursue for the future. Aided by extensive market research, management quickly realized that certain service features, such as convenient location, interest rates paid on customer accounts, and extended branch bank hours, had become a baseline level of performance (order qualifiers) from which nearly all competitors operated. Bourbon Bank leaders determined that in order to gain a competitive advantage, they must provide customers with superior service, in addition to the baseline features. To achieve this, the Marketing Control Task Force (MCTF) was created.

It is now October and the bank's service guarantee program has been in place for 10 months. Since January, media campaigns have announced the service guarantees to the public, and bank employees have received training about them. In this short amount of time, it has been difficult to evaluate the results of the service guarantee program. Sarah does know that the bank spent $860 for payouts during the 10 months and that there seemed to be no trend up or down in the monthly payout amounts. Sarah was the only one asking tough questions during MCTF meetings such as: Are service upsets and errors being reduced? Are employees motivated to provide exceptional service? Are the bank's processes getting better? Or, as Ms. Ebelhar suggested at the start of today's meeting, should the next step be to add one or two new service guarantees with the $5 payout? This might be just what is needed to strengthen the program and reinforce Bourbon Bank's commitment to service excellence.

The MCTF was chartered to (1) develop the service strategy for Bourbon Bank and redesign existing services to make them more competitive, (2) implement programs and activities to execute this strategy and build "process capability," and (3) help service providers consistently produce a level of service that exceeds customers' expectations. The task force was cochaired by Del Carr, president and CEO, and Kay Ebelhar, marketing services division manager. Other members of the MCTF included branch bank managers, bank advertising executives, and members with expertise in accounting, law, and finance. Bloomberg's New Service did a short television segment on the successful service guarantee program at Bourbon Bank, and Mr. Carr and the bank's board of directors were delighted about the national publicity.

MCTF developed a marketing strategy with two components. First was a focus on the bank's employees. Programs were needed to encourage employees to meet their business goals. Therefore, a four-part employee-training program was designed to help build a service culture at Bourbon Bank. The 2-day training program stressed the importance of providing superior service to customers by developing employee skills. In addition, superior service awards were created. These awards allow the bank to recognize front-line employees who consistently provide superior service to customers. Individuals who achieve the award are given a special Bourbon Bank employee pin.

Second was a focus on the bank's customers. To retain and attract customers, Bourbon Bank must provide quality service, superior to that of any other bank. This includes carefully listening to customers, anticipating their needs, and offering solutions before problems arise. As a result, the Gold Service Guarantee Program was developed with the intent of ensuring that Bourbon Bank emerges as a leader in service quality within its market. Not only was this new level of service to be a source of competitive advantage but also a fundamental component of its new corporate culture.

The initial phase of the Gold Service program consisted of a series of print, radio, and television advertising, as well as promotional campaigns geared toward customers and employees. During this "Awareness Phase," the goal was to create a general market awareness of Bourbon Bank's attention to superior service. Next came the "Action Phase." In this second phase, the bank set out to show specifically what it meant to have excellent customer service. By implementing external programs for customers, as well as internal programs for employees, it could demonstrate the bank's commitment to following through with the ideals established in the previous phase. Media campaigns played a significant role in this phase, too, and promotional videos were used internally to create service guarantee awareness and action.

Externally, the Gold Service Telephone Line was established. This telephone line would be used to answer and resolve any customer question or problem, although the average speed of answer time at the bank's customer call center was increasing, not decreasing, these past 10 months. Single-transaction express teller windows at all branch banks added friendly signs. These were aimed at satisfying those customers requiring simple transactions and quick response.

Internally, customer service training for employees was begun. An extensive 2-day training program for all 6,200 employees was developed to teach them how to live up to various attributes of the "customer service pledge." After training and signing the pledge, each employee received a paperweight inscribed with the pledge. The goal of this phase was to make "Gold Service" more meaningful and relevant to both customers and employees.

The bank initially introduced three specific guarantees. First, checking and savings account statements are guaranteed to be accurate. If there is a mistake, regardless of the reason, the customer receives $5.00. Second, customers are promised answers to their application for a home or automobile loan in the time frame specified by the customer. This guarantee is the personal commitment of the employee taking the application. If the employee does not answer within the time frame requested by the customer, Bourbon Bank will pay the customer $5.00. Finally, the Gold Service Telephone Line will be responsive to the customer in a single call. That is, the bank promises that customers will not be transferred, asked to tell their story twice, or made to search for answers themselves. If they are, the employee will award the $5.00 payout on the spot. All payouts were credited to the customers' bank accounts.

To show that all employees are involved in this program, each person was given a set of stickers labeled "Service Guaranteed." These stickers are to be applied to internal memos, reports, or any other piece of work to guarantee one's work to a co-worker or manager (that is, internal cusomters). Examples include an employee guaranteeing that a home loan application or report will be finished by a certain time, a report will be error-free, or his or her phone will never ring more than three times. These stickers were only used internally, but one idea was to also use them externally with customers.

In general, management believes that the customer will let Bourbon Bank know when it has not lived up to its guarantee. Therefore, bank employees usually do not offer the payout to the customer; rather, they allow customers to initiate the request when they judge that a service guarantee was not met. Although not strongly encouraged, an employee may invoke the guarantee in order to ensure customer satisfaction. This is left to the employee's discretion.

A five-dollar payout is associated with each guarantee and is given to the customer at the time the guarantee is invoked. In addition, a form is completed describing the incident. Either the employee or the customer can complete the form, but both must sign it to invoke the guarantee. The service-upset form is then sent to a central location for tracking. Monthly, managers receive summary reports about the guarantee infractions in their area but the reports do not identify specific individuals who might be at fault. MCTF receives a summary of this report by branch bank.

Sarah Coleman was the only member of the MCTF who had doubts about the success of the service guarantee program but she was not about to tell anyone—her job depended on the service guarantee program. Everyone else on the task force had jumped on the marketing bandwagon and hyped up the program as a solid success, even

the president and CEO, Mr. Del Carr. Privately, Sarah had many questions such as: Is the service guarantee program successful? Are these services truly redesigned? How would we know if it is successful? How should we measure the performance of our service guarantee program? What exactly are the objectives of a service guarantee program? Is a total payout of $860 over 10 months good or bad? What should the MCTF do next?

AUTOMOTIVE AIRBAG RELIABILITY[43]

Automotive air bags are designed to protect passengers from frontal or near-frontal crashes of about 12 to 14 mph. Sensors are placed on a structural member in the front of the vehicle or in the passenger compartment. The sensor sends a signal to inflate the air bag, which takes about 1/30 second. The bag then quickly deflates. Air bags have significantly improved automotive safety. The Insurance Institute for Highway Safety noted that during 1985–1992, air bags helped reduce deaths by 24 percent. By 1994 air bags were deployed approximately 200,000 times.

One important design question is the reliability of air bags. Two manufacturers set a reliability goal of at least .9999. An air bag system has three essential elements: a sensor, an actuating mechanism, and an inflating air bag. Three types of sensors—mechanical, electromechanical, and electronic—are in use. The all-mechanical sensor (AMS) is the simplest. The basic mechanism is shown in Exhibit 6.23. A steel ball in a tube or cylinder detects the deceleration of a crash. As the ball moves forward in the tube, it is resisted by a bar on a pivot. The other end of the bar is loaded by a bias spring. As the bar moves, it rotates two shafts that move off the edge of spring-loaded firing pins. The pins (called sear pins) stab dual primers, igniting a charge of boron potassium nitrate, which in turn ignites a compound of sodium azide, which then releases nitrogen gas. The gas is filtered and cooled, inflating the bag. The cover (e.g., on the steering wheel) splits open to allow the bag to inflate without damage. Exhibit 6.24 shows a block diagram of the system with reliability values of the individual components over a 10-year operating life.

Electromechanical sensor systems (EMS) also use a ball-in-tube or ball/cylinder mechanism. The ball is held in place by a magnet instead of a spring. When deceleration occurs, the ball overcomes the magnetic retention forces and travels forward until it touches two electrical contacts, closing a switch that sends current from the battery (or a large capacitor if the battery fails) to heat a bridgewire in a pyrotechnic squib, which then ignites a mixture contained in the squib cavity. The heat ignites a charge of sodium azide, producing nitrogen gas to inflate the bag. This system also has an arming sensor that prevents unwanted deployment. The electrical portion of the system is monitored by a diagnostic module to pinpoint an electrical failure if it occurs. Exhibit 6.25 shows this system and some

Exhibit 6.23 AMS Air Bag Sensor

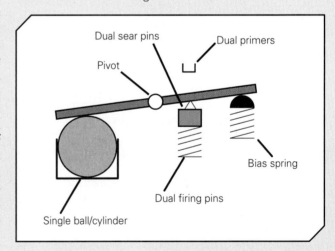

Exhibit 6.24 AMS Sensor Block Diagram

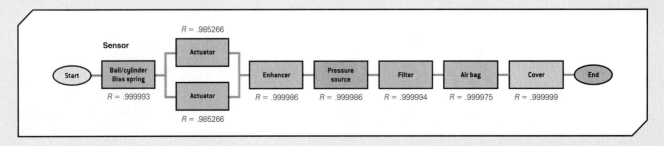

Exhibit 6.25 EMS Sensor Reliability Diagram

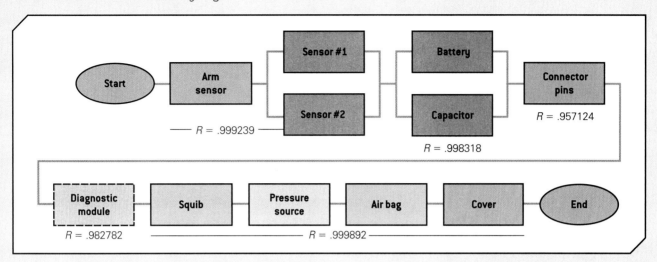

engineering estimates of the reliability of various system components.

The third type of design is an electronic sensor system (ES). Without delving into the details of its operation, which are somewhat more complex than the others, Exhibit 6.26 shows the system diagram and reliability values.

Discussion Questions

1. What is the role of the dual actuators in the mechanical air bag system? Describe the effect of having only one.

2. Compute the reliabilities of each system. What conclusions do the data suggest?

Exhibit 6.26 ES Sensor Reliability Diagram

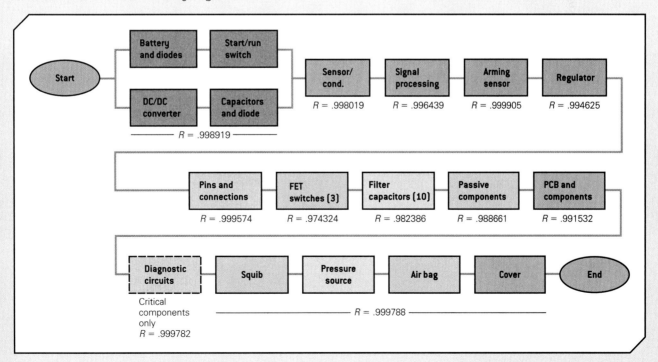

3. The following table lists some engineering calculations of system reliabilities for each type of system over time when repairability is taken into account. Plot these data on a graph. What do the data suggest?

System	Year			
	5	**10**	**15**	**17**
AMS	.999844	.999716	.999588	.999537
EMS	.999870	.999759	.999648	.999604
ES	.999190	.998494	.997799	.997521

Source: Evans/Lindsay, *Management and Control of Quality*, 5e, pp. 794–5.

ENDNOTES

[1] "Ford, GM Join Forces to Develop Six-Speed Transmission Design," *Wall Street Journal*, October 11, 2002, p. B2.

[2] Ziemba, Stanley, "A Tottering Schwinn Puts Kickstand Down," *Chicago Tribune*, October 9, 1992, pp. 1, 20; and McKinney, Jeff, "Bike Dealers Chart Decline of Schwinn," *Cincinnati Enquirer*, October 10, 1992, p. B-4.

[3] Bhide, Amar, "More, Bigger, Faster," *Across the Board*, September/October 2004, pp. 41–45.

[4] Wildstrom, Steven H., "Price Wars Power Up Quality," *Business Week*, September 18, 1995, p. 26.

[5] Overholt, Alison, "Listening to Starbucks," *Fast Company*, July 2004, pp. 48–56.

[6] Shostack, G. L. "Planning the Service Encounter" In J. A. Czepiel, M. R. Solomon, and C. F. Surprenant (eds.), *The Service Encounter*, New York: Lexington Books, p. 244.

[7] Watson, Richard T., Leyland, Pitt F., and Berthon, Pierre R., "Service: The Future of Information Technology," *DataBase* 27 (Fall), 1996, pp. 58–67.

[8] Schneider, Wolfgang, "Test Drive Into the Future," *BMW Magazine* 2, 1997, pp. 74–77.

[9] Ames Rubber Corporation, Application Summary for the 1993 Malcolm Baldrige National Quality Award.

[10] *Solar Turbines*, "New Product Introduction," BNPI/797/2.5M, 1997.

[11] "How to Make It Right the First Time," *Business Week*, June 8, 1987, p. 142.

[12] April 17, 1979; cited in Sullivan, L. P., "Reducing Variability: A New Approach to Quality," *Quality Progress* 17, no. 7 (July 1984), pp. 15–21.

[13] Taylor, Alex, III, "Can the Germans Rescue Chrysler?" *Fortune*, April 30, 2001, p. 106, 4 pages.

[14] Reuter, Vincent G., "What Good Are Value Analysis Programs?" *Business Horizons*, March–April 1986, p. 3, 7 pages.

[15] McGrath, Michael E., and Hoole, Richard W., "Manufacturing's New Economies of Scale," *Harvard Business Review*, May–June 1992, pp. 94–102.

[16] *Business Week: Quality 1991* (special issue), October 25, 1991, p. 73.

[17] Early discussions of this topic can be found in Nussbaum, Bruce, and Templeton, John, "Built to Last—Until It's Time to Take It Apart," *Business Week*, September 17, 1990, pp. 102–106. A more recent reference is Lenox, Michael, King, Andrew, and Ehrenfeld, John, "An Assessment of Design-for-Environment Practices in Leading US Electronics Firms," *Interfaces* 30, no. 3, May–June 2000, pp. 83–94.

[18] Brain Dumaine, "Payoff from the New Management," *Fortune*, December 13, 1993, pp. 103–110.

[19] Bitner, M. J., "Servicescapes: The Impact of Physical Surroundings on Customers and Employees," *Journal of Marketing* 56, no. 2, pp. 57–71; Bitner, M. J., "Managing the Evidence of Service," in Scheuing, E. E. and Christopher, W. F. (eds.), *The Service Quality Handbook*, New York: American Management Association (AMACOM), 1993, pp. 358–370.

[20] Bitner, M. J., "Servicescapes: The Impact of Physical Surroundings on Customers and Employees," *Journal of Marketing* 56, no. 2, pp. 57–71; Bitner, M. J., "Managing the Evidence of Service," in Scheuing, E. E. and Christopher, W. F. (eds.), *The Service Quality Handbook*, New York: American Management Association (AMACOM), 1993, pp. 358–370.

[21] Wright, Sarah Anne, "Putting Fast-Food To The Test," *The Cincinnati Enquirer*, July 9, 2000, pp. F1,2.

[22] Porter, Phil, "Waiting Game," *The Columbus Dispatch*, January 13, 2002, p. E1.

[23] Wind, J., Green, Shifflet, D., and Scarbrough, M., "Courtyard by Marriott: Designing a Hotel Facility with Consumer-Based Marketing Models," *Interfaces* 19, no. 1 (January–February 1989), pp. 25–47.

[24] 2005 Baldrige Award Recipient Profile, National Institute of Standards and Technology, U.S. Department of Commerce.

[25] Chase, R. B. "Where Does the Customer Fit in a Service Operation?" *Harvard Business Review*, November–December 1978, pp. 137–142.

[26] Chase, R. B. op. cit., pp. 1037–1050; "The Customer Contact Model for Organizational Design," *Management Science*, 29, no. 9, 1983, pp. 1037–1050.

[27] The Disney Institute, *Be Our Guest*, Disney Enterprises, Inc., 2001, p. 86.

[28] Albrecht, Karl, and Zemke, Ronald E., *Service America*, Homewood, IL: Dow Jones-Irwin, 1985.

[29] Goodman, John, O'Brien, Pat, and Segal, Eden, "Turning CFOs Into Quality Champions—Show Link to Enhanced Revenue and Higher Margins," *Quality Progress* 33, no. 3, March 2000, pp. 47–56.

[30] BI 1999 Malcolm Baldrige National Quality Award Application Summary.

[31] Collier, D. A., and Baker, T. K., "The Economic Payout Model for Service Guarantees," *Decision Sciences*, 36 (2) 2005, pp. 197–220. Also see Collier, D. A. "Process Moments of Trust: Analysis and Strategy," *The Service Industry Journal* 9, no. 2, April 1989, pp. 205–222.

[32] U.S. Bank Five Star Service Guaranteed, Publication #40001, 12/2001, and #40137, 3/2002. Part of US Bancorp, St Paul, Minnesota, 2002.

[33] Collier, D. A., *The Service/Quality Solution: Using Service Management to Gain Competitive Advantage*, jointly published by ASQC Quality Press, Milwaukee, Wisconsin and Irwin Professional Publishing, Burr Ridge, Illinois, 1994, pp. 121–123.

[34] www.lenscrafters.com/al_mission.html, December 2, 2002.

[35] Reitman, Valerie, and Simison, Robert L., "Japanese Car Makers Speed Up Car Making," *Wall Street Journal*, December 29, 1995, p. 17.

[36] Clausing, Don, and Simpson, Bruce H., "Quality by Design," *Quality Progress*, January 1990, pp. 41–44.

[37] Taylor, Alex, III, "How Toyota Defies Gravity," *Fortune*, December 8, 1997, pp. 100+.

[38] *Business Week* e.biz, February 18, 2002, EB15.

[39] Keenan, Faith, "Opening the Spigot," *Business Week* e.biz, June 4, 2001, EB17-20.

[40] McGrath, Michael E., and Hoole, Richard W., "Manufacturing's New Economies of Scale," *Harvard Business Review*, May–June 1992, pp. 94–102.

[41] Sullivan, L. P., "Quality Function Deployment: The Latent Potential of Phases III and IV," in A. Richard Shores (ed.), *A TQM Approach to Achieving Manufacturing Excellence*, Milwaukee, WI: ASQC Quality Press, 1990, pp. 265–279.

[42] "Universal's CD Price Cuts Will Squeeze Music retailers," *Wall Street Journal*, September 18, 2003, p. B1.

[43] Adapted from Frank, Howard, "Automotive Air Bag Reliability," Reliability Review ISSN 0277-9644, 14, no. 3, September 1994, pp. 11–22. Published for Reliability Division, American Society for Quality by Williams Enterprises.

CHAPTER 7

Process Selection, Design, and Analysis

Learning Objectives

1. To understand the major characteristics of different types of processes and why certain process choices (projects, job shops, flow shops, and continuous flow) are more appropriate for different types of goods and services (custom, option, and standard) than others.

2. To understand why product and process decisions must be made simultaneously and how the product-process matrix can guide key process choice decisions for manufacturing firms.

3. To understand the relationship between services and service delivery processes and how the service-positioning matrix can be used to help guide process choice decisions in services.

4. To understand product life cycles and how operations must respond as goods and services enter different stages of their life cycle and therefore may require different process choices.

5. To understand the objectives of process design, approaches and tools used in process design, including process mapping and value stream mapping, technology selection, and key issues of implementation planning.

6. To be able to identify opportunities for improving processes, and to understand how to use process maps to analyze and find specific areas for improvement.

7. To understand how processes can be designed to achieve high utilization of resources, to identify bottlenecks in processes, and to be able to apply Little's Law to evaluate relationships among flow time, throughput, and work in process.

- I called to make an airline flight reservation just an hour ago.[1] The telephone rang five times before a recorded voice answered. "Thank you for calling ABC Travel Services," it said. "To ensure the highest level of customer service, this call may be recorded for future analysis." Next, I was asked to select from one of the following three choices: "If the trip is related to company business, press 1. Personal business, press 2. Group travel, press 3." I pressed 1. I was then asked to select from the following four choices: "If this is a trip within the United States, press 1. International, press 2. Scheduled training, press 3. Related to a conference, press 4." Because I was going to Canada, I pressed 2.

Now two minutes into my telephone call, I was instructed to be sure that I had my customer identification card available. A few seconds passed and a very sweet voice came on, saying, "All international operators are busy, but please hold because you are a very important customer." The voice was then replaced by music. After several iterations of this, the sweet voice returned, stating, "To speed up your service, enter your 19-digit customer service number." The voice then said: "Thank you. An operator will be with you shortly. If your call is an emergency, you can call 1-800-CAL-HELP. Otherwise, please hold, as you are a very important customer." This time, in place of music, I heard a commercial about the service that the company provides.

Ten minutes passed and then a real person answered the telephone and asked, "Can I help you?" I replied, "Yes, Oh yes. Thank you!" He answered, "Please give me your 19-digit customer service number so I can verify who you are. . . . Thank you. Where do you want to go and when?" I had previously entered this number but I gave it to him again. I then explained that I wanted to go to Montreal the following Monday morning. He replied: "I only handle domestic reservations. Our international desk has a new telephone number: 1-800-1WE-GOTU. I'll transfer you." A few clicks later a message came on, saying: "All of our international operators are busy. Please hold, as your business is important to us."

- "Why do you quote a 12-month lead time for building and delivering the new Automatic Teller Machine (ATM) when it only takes 2 months to build it?" asked Thomas Andrew, the chief information officer of Bank First, during a telephone conversation to the purchasing department at Standard Equipment, Inc. "Our preproduction processes—for instance, engineering design and developing leasing—take about 6 months. It also takes 2 months to order and receive the material, and postproduction processes such as shipping, installation, and software testing take another 2 months. We also have to include billing, accounts payable, and regular ATM maintenance processes," stated David Christopher, the purchasing manager at Standard Equipment, Inc. Mr. Andrew, the customer, responded by saying, "Well, all I see is 12 months and that is too long. Maybe I should buy from someone else!"

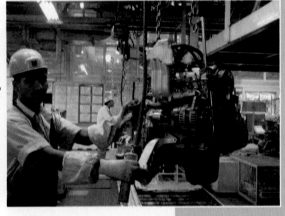

SONDEEP SHANKAR/Bloomberg News/Landov

- "Houston, we have a problem," stated Jeff Gold, the plant manager of Jackson Motor Company's engine plant, trying to inject a bit of humor into a rather tense situation. Jeff was meeting with his staff after having been called on the carpet by the VP of operations. Several years earlier Jeff had spearheaded a project to automate the entire factory with special equipment to produce eight-cylinder engines for the booming SUV market. The factory became a model of efficiency. "As you know with increasing gasoline prices, the market is shifting back to more fuel-efficient vehicles—the demand for six-cylinder engines is growing rapidly and we need to retrofit the plant to accommodate the increased demand. Tom Beller, the head of the industrial engineering department looked pale. "That's going to cost millions. . . ."

Discussion Questions: Describe a situation that you have encountered in which a process was either well designed and enhanced your customer experience, or poorly designed and resulted in dissatisfaction. How did this experience affect your perception of the organization? Why should a business consider how internal processes (which customers don't see) might affect customers' satisfaction? Do you think most businesses do this?

After goods and services are designed and tested, operations managers must determine how to configure the value chain to make goods and deliver services. In this chapter we begin to focus on the design of the value chain. As we have seen, value chains consist of networks of interrelated processes (we introduced the concept of a process in Chapter 1), which may be located within one facility or spread out across the globe. Choosing appropriate processes and designing them to interface effectively with each other is vital for an effective and efficient value chain and cannot be taken lightly. Also, people are critically important for process effectiveness. How both employees and customers are integrated into process designs will determine how well the competitive priorities discussed in Chapter 4 will be achieved. This will ultimately have a significant effect on customer satisfaction and the firm's financial performance.

Each of the introductory episodes demonstrates a key issue of process design. The first episode illustrates a process issue that every reader has most likely encountered. Many organizations face the decision of whether to use an automated answering system instead of simply having customer service representatives (CSRs) answer phone calls. A purely automated call-handling system can cost up to 100 times less than using CSRs. In this situation, however, although the automated reservation system may be justified economically, it is clearly not well designed, resulting in customer dissatisfaction. Thus, process design is an important operational decision that affects both the cost of operation and customer service. It often involves making trade-offs among cost, quality, time, and other priorities.

The second episode highlights the importance of understanding the role of processes within the value chain. In this episode, the customer sees a 12-month lead time but does not really know (or care) what processes contribute to the lead time. This is common in many manufacturing value chains, as pre- and postservices, such as product design, purchasing, warranty and claims processing, billing, and installation, often represent much of the processing time seen by the customer (revisit Exhibit 2.3), even though the primary process is producing a manufactured good. The 12-month leadtime can be shortened in many ways that do not involve the direct manufacturing processes, such as reducing the time for product design and equipment installation. Thus, operations managers need to take a broad view of process design and how it impacts the entire value chain.

Finally, process design is a complex activity. It entails selecting the right technology at a strategic level and matching the appropriate processes to the goods or services produced. The third episode, which is based on a real situation that Ford Motor Company faced long ago, shows that although processes should be designed to support the products that the firm makes to achieve high levels of efficiency, serious difficulties can occur when the product mix changes and more flexibility is needed. In Ford's case, the automated processes were so tightly wedded to the production of eight-cylinder engines that a shift to six-cylinder engines would have necessitated expensive and sweeping changes throughout the plant. Ford had to close the plant because it could not convert the specialized processes to a different set of tasks.[2]

In this chapter, we focus on fundamental concepts and methods for selecting, analyzing, designing and improving processes for goods and services. Subsequent chapters focus on many other aspects of value chain design.

PROCESS CHOICE DECISIONS

To better understand process choice decisions, we first need to understand how firms satisfy demand for goods and services. Firms generally produce either in response to customer orders and demand or in anticipation of them. This leads to three major types of goods and services: custom, option-oriented, and standard.[3] **Custom,** *or* **make-to-order, goods and services** *are generally produced and delivered as one-of-a-kind or in small quantities, and are designed to meet specific customers' specifications.* Examples include ships, weddings, certain jewelry, estate plans, buildings, and surgery. Because custom goods and services are produced on demand, the customer must wait for them, often for a long time because the good or service must be designed, created, and delivered.

Option, *or* assemble-to-order, goods and services *are configurations of standard parts, subassemblies, or services that can be selected by customers from a limited set.* Common examples are Dell computers, Subway sandwiches, machine tools, and travel agent services. Customers can configure a Dell computer by selecting among different processors, monitors, memory, storage bays, and other features. Dell does not make any of its components, but simply purchases them from suppliers and assembles the final product. Subway stocks fresh buns, onions, meats, pickles, and lettuce to all allow customers to design their preferred sandwiches. Customers planning vacations with a travel agent can choose to have the agent book hotels, airline flights, rental cars, shows, and other options or just some of them. Although the customer chooses how the good or service is configured, any unique specifications or requirements cannot generally be accommodated. In addition, the customer must wait while the product is assembled, although generally not as long as for custom products, because the parts and components are usually in stock.

Standard, *or* make-to-stock, goods and services *are made according to a fixed design, and the customer has no options from which to choose.* Appliances, shoes, sporting goods, credit cards, online web-based courses, and bus service are some examples. Standard goods are made in anticipation of customer demand and stocked in inventory and therefore are usually readily available; the customer will have to wait only if the good is out of stock or if service capacity (staff, telephone lines, equipment, and so on) is unavailable. Standard services, such as a bank's checking account service, must also anticipate future demand, but in a different way from goods-producing firms. Because services cannot inventory their output, they must forecast demand more accurately and better manage the resources needed to provide the services.

We note that manufacturing systems often use the terms *make-to-order, assemble-to-order,* and *make-to-stock* to describe the types of systems used to manufacture goods. Service businesses use these terms, although not to the same extent as goods-producing firms. The terminology is not as standardized in service industries although the concepts are similar.

Four principal types of processes are used to produce goods and services:

1. projects,
2. job shop processes,
3. flow shop processes, and
4. continuous flow processes.

Projects *are large-scale, customized initiatives that consist of many smaller tasks and activities that must be coordinated and completed to finish on time and within budget.* Some examples of projects are legal defense preparation, construction, and software development. You might anticipate that projects are often used for custom goods and services. Although this is often the case, many projects result in standardized products, such as "market homes" that are built from a standard design.

Job shop processes *are organized around particular types of general-purpose equipment that are flexible and capable of customizing work for individual customers.* Many small manufacturing companies are set up as job shops, as are hospitals and some restaurants. Job shops produce a wide variety of goods and services, often in small quantities. Thus they are often used for custom or option type products. In job shops, customer orders are generally processed in batches, and different orders may require a different sequence of processing steps and movement to different work areas. This usually requires extra time to change machine setups or process configurations between batches. The labor force must be highly skilled and able to perform a wide variety of tasks on different jobs.

Flow shop processes *are organized around a fixed sequence of activities and process steps, such as an assembly line to produce a limited variety of similar goods or services.* An assembly line is a common example of a flow shop process. Many option-oriented and standard goods and services are produced in flow shop settings. Some common examples are automobiles, appliances, insurance policies, checking account statements, and hospital laboratory work. Because the flow of work in a flow shop is usually fixed, setup and changeover times are minimal and people generally perform the same work tasks repeatedly, so skill requirements are lower than in job shops. Flow shops tend to use highly productive, specialized equipment and computer software and lend themselves to automation; however, large volumes are necessary to justify the capital expense and high degree of specialization.

Continuous flow processes *create highly standardized goods or services, usually around the clock in very high volumes.* Examples of continuous flow processes are automated car washes, paper and steel mills, paint factories, and many electronic information-intensive services such as credit card authorizations and security systems. The sequence of work tasks is very rigid and the processes use highly specialized and automated equipment that is often controlled by computers with minimal human oversight. This may require high capital investment, and the processes are designed for a very narrow range of goods or services. Exhibit 7.1 summarizes these different process types and their characteristics. The arrows in the "type of product" column indicate how these three categories (custom, option, and standard) roughly match up and overlap with the type of process.

PROCESS CHOICE IN MANUFACTURING

Once operations managers understand the type of goods that they need to create, they must select the most appropriate process. For example, computer manufacturers like Hewlett-Packard and IBM that produce standard goods for retail sales can mass-produce them on assembly lines (flow shops) very efficiently. They can exploit specialized equipment that performs highly specific manufacturing tasks. Because all goods follow the same sequence of operations, the manufacturing process is easy to control. In addition, it is easier to plan purchasing requirements, monitor inventory and material flow, and perform after-sales customer service tasks. In contrast, a firm like Dell that produces option goods to individual customers' orders needs a more complex system for purchasing, scheduling, and control of its assembly

Projects *are large-scale, customized initiatives that consist of many smaller tasks and activities that must be coordinated and completed to finish on time and within budget.*

Job shop processes *are organized around particular types of general-purpose equipment that are flexible and capable of customizing work for individual customers.*

Flow shop processes *are organized around a fixed sequence of activities and process steps, such as an assembly line to produce a limited variety of similar goods or services.*

Continuous flow processes *create highly standardized goods or services, usually around the clock in very high volumes.*

Learning Objective
To understand why product and process decisions must be made simultaneously and how the product-process matrix can guide key process choice decisions for manufacturing firms.

Exhibit 7.1 Characteristics of Different Process Types

Type of Process	Characteristics	Goods and Services Examples	Type of Product
PROJECT	One-of-a-kind	Space shuttle, cruise ships	
	Large scale, complex	Dams, bridges	
	Resources brought to the site	Skyscrapers, weddings, consulting	
	Wide variation in specifications or tasks	Custom jewelry, surgery	
JOB SHOP	Significant setup and/or changeover time	Automobile engines	**Custom or Make-to-Order**
	Low to moderate volume	Machine tools	
	Batching (small to large jobs)	Orders from small customers, mortgages	
	Many process routes with some repetitive steps	Shoes, hospital care	
	Customized design to customer's specifications	Commercial printing	
	Many different products	Heavy equipment	
	High work force skills	Legal services	
FLOW SHOP	Little or no setup or change-over time	Insurance polices	**Option or Assemble-to-Order**
	Dedicated to a small range of goods or services that are highly similar	Cafeterias	
	Similar sequence of process steps	Refrigerators, stock trades	
	Moderate to high volumes	Toys, furniture, lawn mowers	
CONTINUOUS FLOW	Very high volumes in a fixed processing sequence	Gasoline, paint, memory chips, check posting	**Standardized or Make-to-Stock**
	Not made from discrete parts	Grain, chemicals	
	High investment in equipment and facility	Steel, paper	
	Dedicated to a small range of goods or services	Automated car wash	
	Automated movement of goods or information between process steps	Credit card authorizations	
	24 hour/7 day continuous operation	Steel, electronic funds transfer	

process. The manufacturing process must have the flexibility to make many different configurations, and ensuring delivery of the right components when needed is more challenging. Such assemble-to-order systems must rely on information technology to tie together all suppliers, assembly plants, and retailers. Firms that make custom goods require investment in even more general-purpose equipment that can perform a variety of tasks. Workers also require higher levels of skills because of the high variety of work that must be accomplished.

Many goods begin as standard products and over time become more customized. Henry Ford, for example, was one of the first to standardize production of the automobile. Later, however, consumers demanded more variety of options, and the American automobile evolved into the classic option-oriented product. More recently, we have seen a trend back toward increased standardization. For instance, General Motors once installed 65 different turn-signal levers in its cars. It reduced the number of levers to 26 and then set a target of no more than 8. To further simplify its operations, General Motors embarked on a "common parts/common systems" strategy to reduce the number of basic U.S. car designs from 12 to 5. Likewise, Toyota and other Japanese manufacturers are seeking to reduce the number of different parts in their cars.[4]

Such changes in product design can have serious implications for operations. For instance, a proliferation of options results in higher inventories, increased difficulty of scheduling, and other operations management problems. This would also require a much higher level of process flexibility to accommodate all the various options. On the other hand, a move toward greater standardization would require more streamlined processes to reduce overhead and gain efficiencies for lower costs. The ability to match changes in processes and operations with product evolution can determine a company's long-run success or failure.

The Product-Process Matrix

One approach to help understand the relationships between product characteristics for manufactured goods and process choice is the product-process matrix, first proposed by Hayes and Wheelwright and shown in Exhibit 7.2.[5] The **product-process matrix** *is a model that describes the alignment of process choice with the characteristics of the manufactured good.* That is, product characteristics should drive process choices. The vertical axis classifies different process types (projects, job shops, flow shops, and continuous flow processes); the horizontal axis classifies different manufactured good characteristics in terms of volume, degree of customization, and the number and range of goods produced. This model has gained wide acceptance in describing product-process choices in goods-producing businesses.

The most appropriate match between type of product and type of process occurs along the diagonal in the product-process matrix. As one moves down the diagonal, the emphasis on both product and process structure shifts from low volume and high flexibility, to higher volumes and more standardization. This also suggests that as products evolve, particularly from entrepreneurial startups to larger and more mature companies, process changes must occur to keep pace. What often happens in many firms is that product strategies change, but managers do not make the necessary changes in the process to reflect the new product characteristics. If product and process characteristics are not well matched, the firm will be unable to achieve its competitive priorities effectively.

For example, consider a firm that manufactures only a few products with high volumes and low customization using a flow shop process structure. This process choice best matches the product characteristics. However, suppose that as time goes on and customer needs evolve, marketing and engineering functions develop more product options and add new products to the mix. This results in a larger number and variety of products to make, lower volumes, and increased customization. The firm finds itself "off-the-diagonal" and in the lower left-hand corner of the matrix (denoted by Position A in Exhibit 7.2). This results in a mismatch between product characteristics and process choice. If the firm continues to use the flow shop process, it may find itself struggling to meet delivery promises and incur unnecessary costs because of low efficiencies.

A similar situation might occur if a firm with a job shop process configuration finds that volumes of a few popular goods are increasing and that they are becoming more standardized (denoted by Position B in Exhibit 7.2). A job shop that uses general-purpose equipment to customize goods in small volumes cannot use its capability efficiently to make higher volumes of standardized goods. Such movement to the right of the diagonal makes it increasingly difficult to meet marketing requirements. Hence, the job shop capability is wasted and it may lose business to

*The **product-process matrix** is a model that describes the alignment of process choice with the characteristics of the manufactured good.*

Exhibit 7.2
Product-Process Matrix

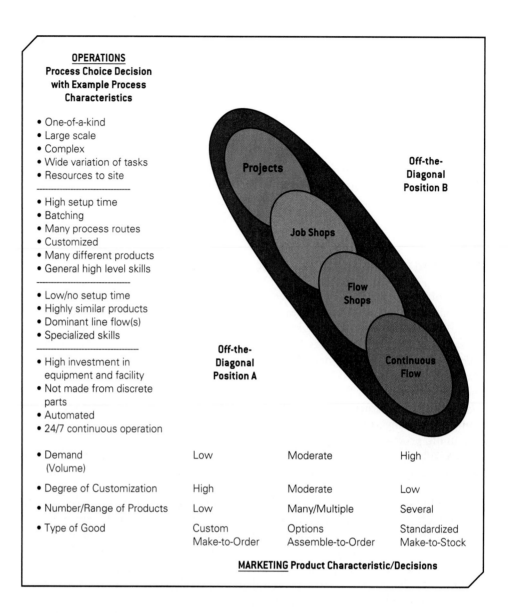

OPERATIONS
Process Choice Decision with Example Process Characteristics

- One-of-a-kind
- Large scale
- Complex
- Wide variation of tasks
- Resources to site
——————————
- High setup time
- Batching
- Many process routes
- Customized
- Many different products
- General high level skills
——————————
- Low/no setup time
- Highly similar products
- Dominant line flow(s)
- Specialized skills
——————————
- High investment in equipment and facility
- Not made from discrete parts
- Automated
- 24/7 continuous operation

Projects

Job Shops

Flow Shops

Continuous Flow

Off-the-Diagonal Position B

Off-the-Diagonal Position A

	Low	Moderate	High
• Demand (Volume)	Low	Moderate	High
• Degree of Customization	High	Moderate	Low
• Number/Range of Products	Low	Many/Multiple	Several
• Type of Good	Custom Make-to-Order	Options Assemble-to-Order	Standardized Make-to-Stock

MARKETING Product Characteristic/Decisions

more efficient flow shops that focus on only a few products and emphasize low costs and high standardization.

On the other hand, by selectively and consciously positioning a business off the diagonal of the product-process matrix, (often called a "positioning strategy"), a company can differentiate itself from its competitors (see the OM Spotlight on Becton Dickinson). However, it must be careful not to get too far off the diagonal or it must have a market where high prices absorb any operational inefficiencies. For example, Rolls-Royce produces a small line of automobiles using a process similar to a job shop rather than the traditional flow shop of other automobile manufacturers. Each car requires about 900 hours of labor. The stainless-steel radiator takes 12 hours of metal bending and hand soldering. Most automobile manufacturers assemble an entire car in that amount of time! For Rolls-Royce this strategy has worked, but their target market is willing to pay premium prices for premium quality and features.

The theory of the product-process matrix has been challenged by some who suggest that advanced manufacturing technologies may allow firms to be successful even when they position themselves off the diagonal. These new technologies

OM SPOTLIGHT

Becton Dickinson[6]

Becton Dickinson (BD) is the leading producer of needle devices for the medical industry. In 2000, President Clinton signed the Needlestick Safety and Prevention Act requiring the use of "safe sharps"—hypodermic syringes, devices used to take blood samples, and needles used in intravenous systems—that would reduce the potential of health care workers' accidently sticking themselves with a contaminated needle that might carry HIV or a fatal strain of hepatitis C. BD has been an innovator in developing new products to reduce these risks and needed to convert many of its large and older factories, which had big and inflexible manufacturing systems dedicated to low-cost production, to accommodate high-volume production of a larger variety of safe sharp products.

Spring-loaded IV catheters have 12 parts, assembled in an automated process with 48 steps carried out at incredibly fast speeds. Instead of using one long assembly line, BD's Utah plant uses a mechanized version of cell production in which parts are made or cell assemblies are produced by teams feeding a central manufacturing line. One advantage of this system is its flexibility. It is relatively easy to modify a product by altering or adding subassembly stations. BD's manufacturing process choice is somewhat off the diagonal of the product-process matrix, producing multiple products in high volumes in a more-or-less continuous flow pattern. This strategy helps the company to continue to hold and grow its market share in a highly competitive industry.

provide manufacturers with the capability to be highly flexible and produce lower volumes of products in greater varieties at lower costs. Therefore, off-diagonal positioning strategies are becoming more and more viable for many organizations and allow for "mass customization" strategies and capabilities.[7]

PROCESS CHOICE IN SERVICES

> **Learning Objective**
> To understand the relationship between services and service delivery processes and how the service-positioning matrix can be used to help guide process choice decisions in services.

In the previous section, we introduced the product-process matrix to help understand the relationships between goods and the processes used to create them and to strategically align the best process type with product characteristics and production volume requirements. However, the product-process matrix does not transfer well to service businesses and processes.[8,9] In the product-process matrix, product volume, the number of products, and the degree of standardization/customization determine the manufacturing process that should be used. This relationship between volume and process is not found in many service businesses. As some researchers concluded, ". . . in service operations, significant volume increases can be made, and frequently are made, without any change in the service process, as would be expected in manufacturing."[10] For example, to meet increased volume, service business such as retail outlets, banks, and hotels have historically added capacity in the form of new stores, branch banks, and hotels (that is, bricks and mortar) to meet demand but do not change their processes. These limitations are resolved by introducing the *service positioning matrix*. To better understand it, we first discuss the concept of a pathway in a service delivery system.

Pathways

A **pathway** *is a unique route through a service system.* Pathways can be customer or provider driven, depending on the level of control that the service firm wants to ensure. **Customer-routed services** *are those that offer customers broad freedom to*

A **pathway** *is a unique route through a service system.*

Customer-routed services *are those that offer customers broad freedom to select the pathways that are best suited for their immediate needs and wants from many possible pathways through the service delivery system.*

Provider-routed *services constrain customers to follow a very small number of possible and predefined pathways through the service system.*

select the pathways that are best suited for their immediate needs and wants from many possible pathways through the service delivery system. The customer decides what path to take through the service delivery system with only minimal guidance from management. Searching the Internet to purchase some item is one example. There are virtually an infinite number of possible pathways to select because the customer has almost complete freedom to self-design the service experience. Such a service encounter is not likely to be repeated in the future by either the same customer or by other customers, so it is clearly unique. Amusement parks, museums, and health clubs are other examples of customer-routed services with an essentially endless number of possible pathways. The OM Spotlight on Nike Town provides additional insight.

    Provider-routed *services constrain customers to follow a very small number of possible and predefined pathways through the service system.* A newspaper dispenser is an extreme example of a service system design with only one pathway, thus allowing a single service encounter activity sequence.[12] The customer must have the correct coins, put the coins in the slot, pull the handle to open the door, and take the newspaper (that is, only one predefined pathway to get a newspaper). The customer has no freedom on how to perform the task; there is no service provider there to provide help; the designer of the newspaper dispenser has predefined the sequence of tasks (that is, one pathway) to get a newspaper; and the service encounter activity sequence is highly repeatable. Another familiar example of a provider-routed service is an automobile license bureau. To renew your driver's

OM SPOTLIGHT

Nike Town[11]

"A Nike Town store is a theatrical presentation, a glittering production number starring the customer. People love to shop here. It's kind of entertainment, a social thing," said Mary Burns, store manager. At Nike Town, freedom, entertainment, color, fantasy, technical information, videos, and music are part of the customer benefit package, which are bundled with the core good—shoes. The innovative service system design encourages customers to design their own unique service experience, pathways, and sequence of service encounters. Customers set their own pace and define their pathways through the store, processing times at each stage, when they want self-service versus assistance from a sales representative, and bundle music and entertainment with buying shoes. Customers may spend 3 minutes or 3 hours in the store depending on their individual wants and needs. A 3-minute service experience would likely include relatively simple service encounter activity sequences such as checking to see if a particular shoe is in stock and either buying it or leaving if it was not. A longer service experience might include listening to music, playing basketball in five different shoes,

watching videos, and talking to store employees and other customers. The store has been so successful, Nike has opened several larger stores.

Daniel Acker/Bloomberg News/Landov

license at a state licensing office, you might follow a structured set of steps depending on the type of vehicle you want to drive, your physical capabilities such as eyesight and hearing, your age, and so on.

Some services fall in between these extremes. For example, consider placing a telephone order from a company such as L.L. Bean. The pathway is relatively constrained (that is, provider-routed) as the service representative first acquires the customer's name and address, takes the order and asks questions about colors and sizes, and then processes the credit card payment. However, while placing the order, customers have complete freedom in selecting the sequence in which items are ordered, asking questions, or obtaining additional information.

Designs for customer-routed services require a solid understanding of the features that can excite and delight customers, as well as methods to educate the customers about the variety of pathways that may exist and how to select and navigate through them. Web sites provide "site maps" and other navigation and search features (consider a site like Amazon.com). Amusement parks provide maps, entertainment schedules, information boards, and public address announcements to assist customers in their experience. In addition, how park managers staff, schedule, and train their employees can also affect customer-routed services. As noted in Chapter 6, the servicescape can have a significant impact on how effective customer-routed services are and require considerable input from the operations and process managers.

For provider-routed services, technology is often used to automate the service process. An automatic teller machine (ATM) is an example. A limited number of pathways exist—for example, getting cash, making a deposit, checking an account balance, and moving money from one account to another. A limited number of pathways are inherent in the ATM design and operation. There is almost no opportunity for the customer to change the procedure or route through the electronic network. A high degree of management control is built into the process, the service is highly repeatable, and the customer has little decision-making power in the process. Here, operations managers focus on managing the capacity of the system (telephone and optical fiber lines, servers, telephone customer contact centers and their staff, uptime, and so on), forecasting demand and scheduling resources, hiring and training people, defining and measuring customer service and quality, evaluating people and process performance, and trying to minimize costs.

The Service Positioning Matrix

The Service Positioning Matrix (SPM), shown in Exhibit 7.3, is roughly analogous to the product-process matrix for manufacturing. The SPM focuses on the service encounter level and helps management design a service system that best meets the technical and behavioral needs of customers. The position along the horizontal axis is described by the sequence of service encounters. The **service encounter activity sequence** *consists of all the process steps and associated service encounters necessary to complete a service transaction and fulfill a customer's wants and needs.* It depends on two things:

1. *The degree of customer discretion, freedom, and decision-making power in selecting the service encounter activity sequence.* Customers may want the opportunity to design their own unique service encounter activity sequence, in any order they choose.
2. *The degree of repeatability of the service encounter activity sequence.* Service encounter repeatability refers to the frequency that a specific service encounter activity sequence is used by customers. Service encounter repeatability provides

The **service encounter activity sequence** *consists of all the process steps and associated service encounters necessary to complete a service transaction and fulfill a customer's wants and needs.*

a measure analogous to product volume for goods-producing firms. Repeatability can be counted for each unique service encounter activity sequence (for example, the number of cash withdrawals at a bank's ATM). The degree of repeatability is limited by the service system design and how customers select and configure their activity sequences.

The more unique the service encounter, the less repeatable it is. A high degree of repeatability encourages standardized process and equipment design and dedicated service channels and results in lower costs and improved efficiency. A low degree of repeatability encourages more customization and more flexible equipment and process designs and typically results in higher relative cost per transaction and lower efficiency.

The position along the vertical axis of the SPM reflects the number of pathways built into the service system design by management. That is, the designers or management predefine exactly how many pathways will be possible for the customer

Exhibit 7.3 The Service Positioning Matrix

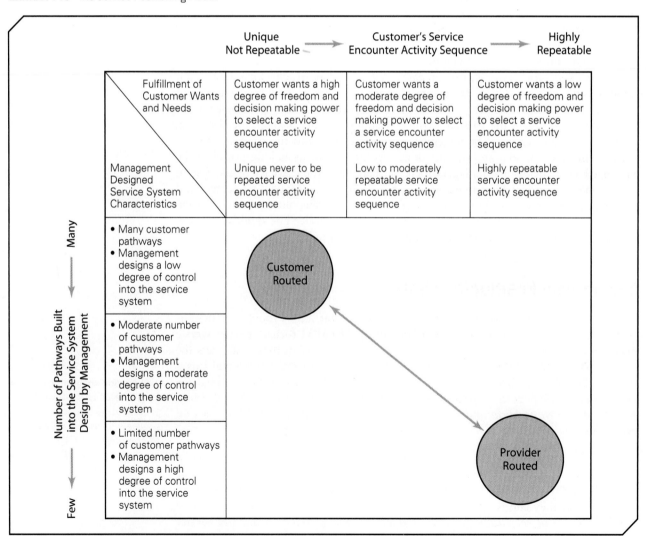

Source: Adapted from D. A. Collier and S. M. Meyer. "A Service Positioning Matrix," *International Journal of Production and Operations Management*, 18, no. 12, 1998, pp. 1123–1244. Also see D. A. Collier and S. Meyer, "An Empirical Comparison of Service Matrices." *International Journal of Operations and Production Management*, 20 (no. 5-6), 2000, pp. 705–729.

to select, ranging from one to an infinite number of pathways. This position also depends on two things:

1. *The number of unique pathways (routes) that customers can take as they move through the service system during delivery of the service.* Pathways can be visualized and counted by flowcharting the service processes. A large number of unique and predefined pathways indicate that customers have freedom to develop their own unique service experience by selecting their route through the service delivery system. A small number of unique pathways indicate that customers have little freedom to select their route. Management designs these pathway opportunities by designing the service delivery system.

2. *Management's degree of control designed into the service delivery system.* Control of the service system results from the set of decisions that management makes regarding service system design. A low degree of management control results in more customer freedom and possible pathways while a high degree of control reduces customer freedom and limits the number of pathways.

The SPM is similar to the product-process matrix in that it suggests that the nature of the customer's desired service encounter activity sequence should lead to the most appropriate service system design and that superior performance results by generally staying along the diagonal of the matrix. Like the product-process matrix, organizations that venture too far off the diagonal create a mismatch between service system characteristics and desired activity sequence characteristics. As we move down the diagonal of the SPM, the service encounter activity sequence becomes less unique and more repeatable with fewer pathways. Like the Product-Process Matrix, the midrange portion of the matrix contains a broad range of intermediate design choices.

From a strategic perspective, the Service Positioning Matrix helps managers understand the nature of the service encounter activity sequences they have created for their customers and better design the service delivery system. Using marketing research to determine the nature of the service encounter activity sequence(s) that customers want or expect, the SPM suggests the appropriate number of pathways and degree of managerial control for the service system design. It can also be used to evaluate service redesign options and features.

THE PRODUCT LIFE CYCLE AND PROCESS CHOICE DECISIONS

A product life cycle *is a characterization of product growth, maturity, and decline over time.* Two versions of the product life cycle for goods or services are shown in Exhibit 7.4. It is important to understand product life cycles because when goods and services change and mature, so must the processes and value chains that create and deliver them. Seldom does process design remain static over the entire product life cycle. It is easy to get caught in "off-the-diagonal" positions on the product-process or service positioning matrixes. To remain competitive, the challenge for operations managers is to make changes in the process and value chain design as product and market conditions change.

The traditional product life cycle (PLC) is shown in Exhibit 7.4a. It generally consists of four phases—*introduction, growth, maturity,* and *decline and turnaround.* As the life cycle illustrates, sales grow slowly immediately after a product is introduced. This is generally followed by a period of rapid growth as the product gains acceptance and markets for it develop (assuming, of course, the product survives the initial phase). The early stages of the PLC usually use project or job shop types of processes. As volume increases during the growth stage, operations managers must decide how to switch to flow shops if they are to remain cost competitive.

Exhibit 7.4
Product Life Cycles

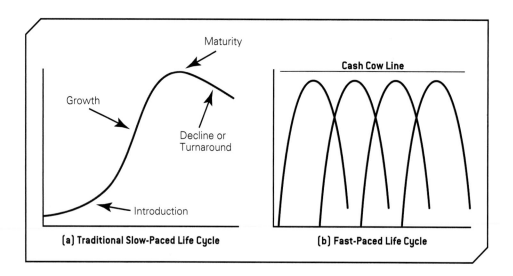

During the maturity period, in which demand levels off and no new distribution channels are available, the product design becomes standardized, which causes competitors to focus marketing strategies more on offering the best price for a similar product than on offering a significantly better product for a similar price. Finally, the product may begin to lose appeal as substitute products are introduced and become more popular. During this decline phase, the product is either discontinued or replaced by a modified or entirely new product.

For goods and services in slow-paced industries such as appliances and foods, life cycles extend over decades. In the traditional life cycle, strong positive cash flow and profits occur during the maturity stage of the life cycle. Firms work hard to extend their life cycles. For instance, Procter & Gamble develops and markets "new and improved" household cleaners, and McDonald's continually introduces games like Monopoly and other promotions. However, for many goods and services, such as cell phones and financial instruments, product life cycles might be measured in months. For others, such as e-Bay online auctions, it might be measured in minutes. In such fast-paced industries, the product life cycle is sometimes so short that the maturity phase barely exists. This results in a set of inverted U-shaped life cycles, as depicted in Exhibit 7.4b.

In fast-paced industries, the "cash cow" of a mature life cycle is generated by a relentless succession of new introductions to get profits early in the life cycle before competitors can respond. When competitors do respond or if the market does not respond favorably, the firm introduces a new good or service and tries to repeat this process frequently to build customer loyalty and grow its cash flow and profits. By doing this in many global markets simultaneously, volume is increased and costs are lowered. Here is where excellent goods and service design and development processes provide a competitive advantage. Process design flexibility is a top priority in this PLC situation.

A product's life cycle has important implications in terms of process design and choice and helps explain the product-process or service-positioning matrix. As goods and services move through different stages of their life cycle, the competitive priorities change, and, of course, the processes need to change. The best time to increase market share is in the introduction phase. Product design changes are frequent when a product is first introduced, typically to make the product more innovative. Operations managers must maintain a high degree of demand and design flexibility to be responsive to changes, and the work force must be highly skilled to adapt quickly to changing production requirements. Production runs are short and unit costs are relatively high during this phase; consequently, operations managers must cope with changing schedules and overcapacity. High capital investment in production facilities is usually not necessary. Quality is of utmost importance, and any design or manufacturing defects must be quickly identified and eliminated.

As the goods and services move into the growth stage, sales volume increases and marketing's role in the corporate strategy is enhanced. Forecasting and advertising become more critical: manufacturing must have the capacity to meet the growing demand. Operations are driven by the market, and the focus is on process innovation. Both the product and the process must achieve high reliability to eliminate "latent defects"—ones that do not appear during manufacturing but crop up after some period of product use. Production volume increases, and capacity growth and utilization become critical.

As goods and services mature, low unit costs become the top competitive priority. Manufacturing must focus on improving process efficiency and minimizing costs. Less production flexibility is needed as the product becomes more standardized, although some product innovation is possible and often desirable to maintain market share. The firm must invest in efficient and high-volume production facilities for supporting long production runs. Finally, as demand declines and a product is phased out of the marketplace, the firm must maintain control over cost. Capacity needs are reduced, and the firm might have to retool or reconfigure its plant for the next wave of products that will be produced. The lesson for operations managers is to watch and understand where an organization's goods and services are positioned on the product life cycle, because this has implications for when and how to change the process. The role of the product life cycle in choosing the best process type is one more example of the interdisciplinary nature of an operations manager's job.

PROCESS DESIGN

Learning Objective
To understand the objectives of process design, approaches and tools used in process design, including process mapping and value stream mapping, technology selection, and key issues of implementation planning.

The goal of process design is to create the right combination of equipment, work methods, and environment to produce and deliver goods and services that satisfy both internal and external customer requirements. Process design can have a significant impact on cost (and hence profitability), flexibility (the ability to produce the right types and amounts of products as customer demand or preferences change), and the quality of the output. For example, in producing a new, very small CD player, Sony had to develop entirely new manufacturing processes, because no process in existence was able to make this product as small and as accurate as the design required. FedEx developed a wireless data collection system for its value chain that employs laser scanners to manage millions of packages daily through its six main hubs, improving not only customer service but saving labor costs as well.[13]

Process design is usually accomplished using a cross-functional team of people who will be involved in the process—employees, supervisors, managers, and customers—along with the engineers and analysts who are designing the process. A senior manager often sponsors the process design initiative and team, providing both leadership and financial support. Team leaders and facilitators must be selected along with reporting formats, meeting frequencies, and milestones for deliverables.

A wide variety of issues must be addressed, many of which are listed in Exhibit 7.5. Addressing such a wide scope of issues usually requires a project management orientation (see Chapter 18) and strong project management skills.

Designing a goods-producing or service-providing process requires six major activities:

1. Define the purpose and objectives of the process.
2. Create a detailed process or value stream map that describes how the process is currently performed (sometimes called a *current state* or *baseline map*). Of course, if you are designing an entirely new process, this step is skipped.
3. Evaluate alternative process designs. That is, create process or value stream maps (sometimes called *future state maps*) that describe how the process can best achieve customer and organizational objectives.

Exhibit 7.5
Basic Process Design
Questions[14]

Why?	Why should this process exist? Why design it this way? Why are process activities/tasks in this sequence? Why automate it this way? Why organize around the process this way?
Who?	Who are the customers? Who is assigned process ownership? Who is assigned service encounter ownership? Who owns that customer?
What?	What are the customer requirements? What are the desired process outcomes/outputs? What are the process performance goals? What are the process activities and tasks? What activities/tasks add value to the customer benefit package? What activities/tasks can be combined, simplified, or eliminated? What activities/tasks can be automated? What are the barriers to successful implementation?
When?	When does the process start and end? When is each process activity performed? When should the process complete its outcome/output? When is process recovery action taken?
Where?	Where are the process boundaries and key interfaces with vendors, internal and external customers, and other processes? Where are the resource and knowledge bottlenecks? Where are processes shared or dedicated to particular consumer benefit packages and their peripheral goods or services?
How?	How is the customer benefit package created and delivered? How is process performance measured and rewarded? How are process capacities balanced? How are service upsets corrected? How can we use technology? How is feedback used as a basis for continuous improvement? How is world-class quality created and delivered at each customer contact point? How is process performance maintained and improved?

4. Identify and define appropriate performance measures for the process.
5. Select the appropriate equipment and technology.
6. Develop an implementation plan to introduce the new or revised process design. This includes developing process performance criteria and standards to monitor and control the process.

Process Design Objectives

Understanding process design objectives focuses on answering the question: What is the process intended to accomplish? An example process objective might be "to create and deliver the output to the customer in 48 hours." Another key question to consider is: What are the critical customer and organizational requirements that must be achieved? As we saw in Chapter 6, the House of Quality provides a framework to help design processes by matching customer's wants and needs to process performance criteria and characteristics.

Finally, one must also consider whether the process is to be designed for high levels of efficiency, flexibility, or fast response. Standardized processes establish consistency of output. However, standardized processes may not be able to meet the needs of different customer segments. Today, many companies use a strategy of *mass customization*—providing personalized, custom-designed products to meet individual customer preferences at prices comparable to mass-produced items. Motorola, for instance, produces one-of-a-kind pagers from more than 29 million combinations of options in a mass assembly process at a low cost. Dell Computer configures each computer system to customer specifications. Mass customization requires significantly different process designs than do traditional manufacturing processes that focus on either customized, crafted products or mass-produced, standardized products.[15]

Process and Value Stream Mapping

Process mapping is a valuable communication device to understand how processes operate and where responsibility lies, and therefore is used extensively in manufacturing and service operations design. *A process map (flowchart) describes the sequence of all process activities and tasks necessary to create and deliver a desired output or outcome.* A process map can include the flow of goods, people, information, or other entities, as well as decisions that must be made and tasks that are performed. It documents how work either is, or should be, accomplished and how the transformation process creates value. Thus, process maps are used in steps two and three of the design approach. In step two, we usually first develop a map of how the current process operates in order to understand it and identify improvements for redesign. These "baseline maps" provide a means for analyzing the process and identifying improved designs.

A process map (flowchart) describes the sequence of all process activities and tasks necessary to create and deliver a desired output or outcome.

Process maps delineate the boundaries of a process. *A process boundary is the beginning or end of a process.* The advantages of a clearly defined process boundary are that it makes it easier obtaining senior management support, assigning process ownership to individuals or teams, identifying key interfaces with internal or external customers, and identifying where performance measurements should be taken. If the scope of the process design initiative is too broad, the complexity and coordination duties become unmanageable.

A process boundary is the beginning or end of a process.

Many different types of symbols are used for process maps and vary among software packages, companies, and industries. However, the style is not as important as the content! For our purposes we will use the following symbols:

A rectangle denotes a task or work activity.

A triangle indicates waiting.

An oval denotes the "start" or "end" of the process and defines the process boundaries.

An arrow denotes movement, transfer or flow to the next task or activity.

A double-headed arrow denotes an input or arrival into a process.

A diamond denotes a decision that might result in taking alternative paths.

One example is shown in Exhibit 7.6 for an automobile repair process. Process maps clearly delineate the process boundaries.

In service applications, flowcharts generally highlight the points of contact with the customer and are often called *service blueprints* or *service maps.* Such flowcharts often show the separation between the back office and the front office with a "line of customer visibility," such as the one shown in Exhibit 7.6. This is

Exhibit 7.6
Automobile Repair Flowchart[17]

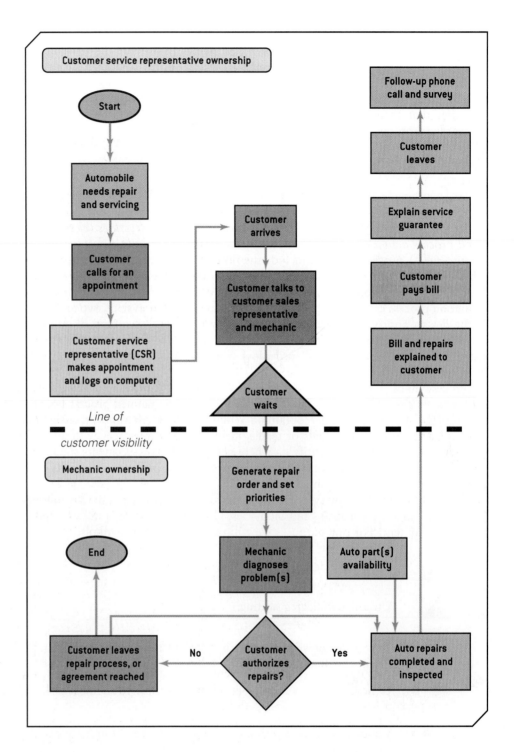

important because front office services require people with service management skills whereas back office operations rely more on production skills.

Process maps are best developed in a team atmosphere using a facilitator who can provide objectivity in resolving conflicts. The facilitator can guide the development through questions such as "What happens next?," "Who makes the decision at this point?," and "What operation is performed at this point?" Quite often, the group does not universally agree on the answers to these questions due to misconceptions about the process itself or a lack of awareness of the "big picture." Flowcharts can easily be created using Microsoft Excel using the features found on the Drawing toolbar.[16]

Process maps can be drawn at different levels of detail and aggregation, depending on the objective of the design. These levels can be described along a *hierarchy of work*:

1. Value Chain
2. Process
3. Activity
4. Task

In this hierarchy, a process is a subset of a value chain, an activity is a subset of a process, and a task is a subset of an activity. *A **task** is a specific unit of work required to create an output.* One example is drilling a hole in a steel part or completing an invoice. *An **activity** is a group of tasks needed to create and deliver an intermediate or final output.* Tasks are grouped together to form a work activity and are usually accomplished together at a **workstation**—*a location where activities are performed*—to gain job and equipment efficiencies. Workstations might be a position on an assembly line, a manufacturing cell, or an office cubicle.

As we move down the hierarchy, process maps become more detailed. For example, in Exhibit 7.6, the activity "customer calls for an appointment" might consist of several smaller tasks such as log in to the dealer's computer, ask the customer what type of repair is needed, look for open time slots that match the customer's desired appointment times, call up the customer and automobile profiles, input new information, confirm with the customer the scheduled appointment time, ask if the customer needs a loaner car, and so on. All of these tasks could have been incorporated into the flowchart, resulting in a larger and messier graphic. Such detail may not be necessary if one simply needs to understand or design the basic process flow, for instance, to reconfigure the layout of a facility. On the other hand, for instructing and training employees to perform a job, one that details the steps required at the task level would be more appropriate.

In designing processes, one often starts at an aggregate level and progressively cascades, or expands, individual elements to include increasing levels of detail. Exhibit 7.7 shows an example for the production of antacid tablets. The value chain shown in Exhibit 7.7 is a very aggregate view focused on the *goods-producing processes* (supporting services such as engineering, shipping, accounts payable, advertising, and retailing are not shown). The next level in the hierarchy of work is at the *production process* level where tablets are made. The third level focuses on the *mixing workstation* where the ingredients are unloaded into mixers. The mixer must be set up for each batch and cleaned for the next batch since many different flavors, such as peppermint, strawberry-banana, cherry, and mandarin orange, are produced using the same mixers. The fourth and final level in the work hierarchy is the *flavoring tasks*, which are defined as three tasks each with specific procedures, standard times per task, and labor requirements. These three tasks could be broken down into even more detail if required. Many flowcharting software packages provide the option to cascade up and down the hierarchy of work.

As one moves up the hierarchy, the total number of tasks that must be coordinated becomes larger. For example, at the value chain level, 3 to 30 processes need to be coordinated, encompassing thousands of associated tasks. As a result, design and management complexity increase as the scope of work content increases from the task to value chain level, as illustrated in Exhibit 7.8.

Non-value-added activities, such as transferring materials between two nonadjacent workstations, waiting for service, or requiring multiple approvals for a low-cost electronic transaction simply lengthen processing time, increase costs, and, often, increase customer frustration. Eliminating non-value-added activities in a process design is one of the most important responsibilities of operations managers. This is often accomplished using value stream mapping.

*The **value stream** refers to all value-added activities involved in designing, producing, and delivering goods and services to customers.* A value stream map (VSM)

*A **task** is a specific unit of work required to create an output.*

*An **activity** is a group of tasks needed to create and deliver an intermediate or final output.*

*A **workstation** is a location where activities are performed.*

*The **value stream** refers to all value-added activities involved in designing, producing, and delivering goods and services to customers.*

Exhibit 7.7 The Hierarchy of Work and Cascading Flowcharts for Antacid Tablets

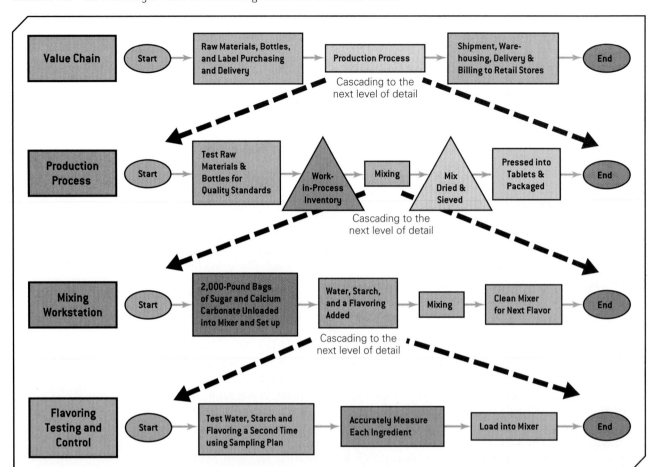

shows the process flows in a manner similar to an ordinary process map; however, the difference lies in that value stream maps highlight value-added versus non-value-added activities and include costs associated with work activities for both value- and non-value added activities.

To illustrate this, consider a process map for the order fulfillment process in a restaurant shown in Exhibit 7.9. The process starts when the restaurant waiter posts

Exhibit 7.8

Hierarchy of Work Content and Design Complexity and Coordination

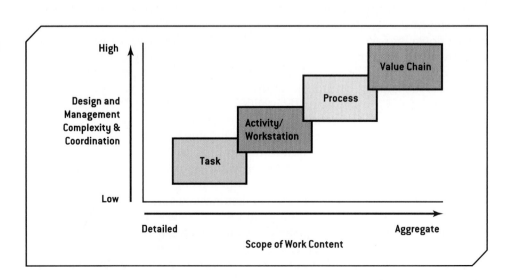

the customer's dinner order to the order board in the kitchen. Because this task takes only a couple of seconds we will assume zero time. The order waits on the kitchen's order board for an average of 5 minutes. The chef picks it up and checks the order for accuracy and understanding; this takes 1 minute. If the order is OK, the chef continues processing the order, which includes staging the raw materials; this takes about 4 minutes. If the order is not clear, the chef places the order in a special section of the order board for further waiter clarification. Next, the chef begins cooking the meal, which consists of about 12 minutes to prepare side dishes and cook meat in an oven for 10 minutes. These tasks can be done simultaneously. After the meal is cooked, the chef assembles the order; this averages 3 minutes. The order waits for the waiter to pick it up, which averages 5 minutes. If the order waits a long time at this stage of the process, the food gets cold and customer service decreases. Hence, "service standard" order posting and fulfillment time is an average of 30 minutes per order (5 + 1 + 4 + 12 + 3 + 5). The restaurant's service guarantee requires that if this order posting and fulfillment time is more than 40 minutes, the customer's order is free of charge.

The chef's time is valued at $30 per hour, oven operation at $10 per hour, precooking order waiting time at $5 per hour, and postcooking order waiting time at $60 per hour. The $60 estimate reflects the cost of poor quality for a dinner waiting too long that might be delivered to the customer late (and cold!). The $60 estimate may also include the opportunity cost of the customer not returning to the restaurant or not referring other customers to this restaurant because of this service upset. In manufacturing processes, value stream costs are more internally focused and based on actual cost accounting information. In service-providing processes, value stream costs are both internally and externally focused and based on both actual cost accounting information plus estimates of the value of loyal customers.

Exhibit 7.10 illustrates a value stream map for the order posting and fulfillment process in Exhibit 7.9. Exhibit 7.10 is one of many formats for value stream mapping. Here, non-valued-added time is 33.3 percent (10/30 minutes) of the

Exhibit 7.9 Restaurant Order Posting and Fulfillment Process

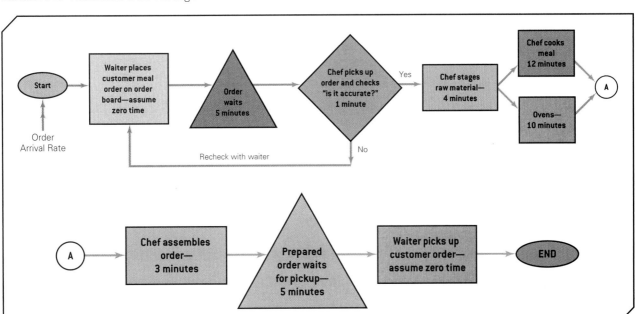

total order posting and fulfillment time, and non-value-added cost is 31.7 percent ($5.417/$17.087) of total cost. Suppose that a process improvement incorporates wireless technology to transmit food orders to the kitchen and notify the waiter when the order is ready so that the waiting time can be reduced from 10 minutes to 4 minutes on the front and back ends of the process. Hence, the total processing time is reduced from 30 to 24 minutes (a 20 percent improvement). Costs are reduced by $3.25 with a 3-minute wait time reduction on the front and back ends of the process. Therefore, cost per order goes from $17.087 to $13.837 (a 19 percent improvement). Increasing the speed of this part of the restaurant delivery process may also allow for a higher seat turnover during peak demand periods and help to increase total revenue and contribute to profit and overhead.

Exhibit 7.10

Value Stream Map for Restaurant Order Posting and Fulfillment Process

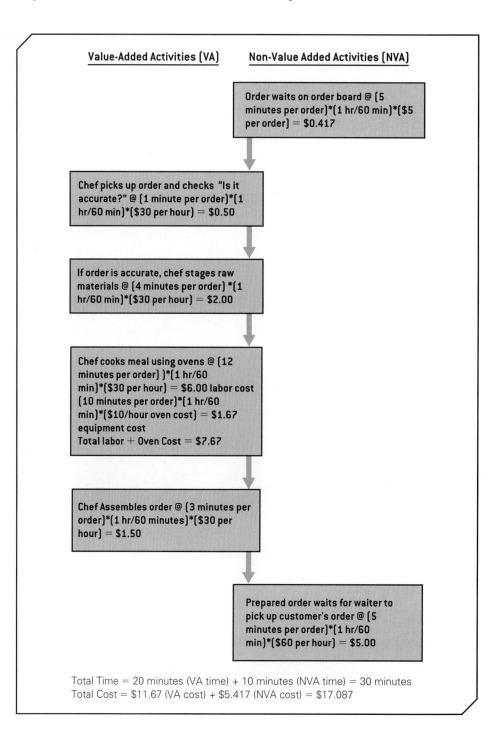

Alternative Process Designs

The next step is to evaluate alternative process designs. *A **future state map** defines a possible new process design using simple flowchart graphics and symbols depicting the sequence of all process activities and tasks necessary to create and deliver a desired output or outcome.* If the process design team thinks two or more alternative designs should be evaluated then two future state maps must be developed. For each future state map due dates should be established for each part of the process implementation along with projected costs of the new process and its implementation.

Detailed analysis of each alternative process design can include estimates of flow time, capacity and utilization, bottleneck work stations, information flows, quality and reliability improvements, waste reduction, hiring and training requirements, unit cost, product and process flexibility to customize customer's jobs, and so on. Analysis tools range from costing out the savings due to waste reduction using an electronic spreadsheet to modeling the alternative process designs using simulation as described in Supplementary Chapter D on the CD accompanying this book.

Ideally, all benefits and costs should be quantified into dollars and a formal net present value analysis done to quantify the return on investment. In practice, it often is difficult to convert, for example, process speed, reliability, and flow time into dollars. Strategic and tactical criteria must also be integrated with the economic numbers to reach a final decision. Operations managers must also understand accounting and finance if they are to collect good benefit and cost estimates, and compute the financial return of each process design alternative. Hence, the ultimate selection of alternative process design alternatives is a management decision supported by detailed process analysis.

*A **future state map** defines a possible new process design using simple flowchart graphics and symbols depicting the sequence of all process activities and tasks necessary to create and deliver a desired output or outcome.*

Process Performance Measures

Key performance measures must be identified to evaluate process performance. A good set of process performance measures helps managers to evaluate and control the process, and to base their decisions on objective information instead of opinions. We discussed many of these issues in Chapter 3. This step ensures that all participants in the process design team know what data to collect and how to compute each measure.

Each performance measure must be clearly defined, and everyone in the organization must understand the definition and how the measure is computed. For example, to measure quality, one might count the number of defects or service errors. However, what is a defect? Does it include minor cosmetic blemishes as well as non-functioning components? Creating good operational definitions of measures eliminates ambiguity and misinterpretation among users of the information. Improvement teams normally make the initial attempt to define the key process performance measures, and then disseminate them throughout the organization for feedback.

Process Equipment and Technology Selection

Although the product-process matrix and service-positioning matrix provide a structure for selecting the general type of process, operations managers must still choose specific technology and equipment to accomplish the tasks associated with turning a process design into reality. The scope of technology choices, such as programmable robots, machine vision systems, handheld wireless inventory tracking devices, computer-aided manufacturing, flexible manufacturing systems, digital imaging, and web-based applications, were discussed in Chapter 5.

Technology selection depends on a variety of economic, quantitative, and qualitative factors, much as product design does. For example, to select the best manufacturing process for fabricating an airplane wing, an engineer must have a thorough understanding of materials and their properties and the desired properties of the final product. In cutting metal, speeds depend on the type of material being cut and the cutting tool itself. Typical cutting speeds may be 600 meters per minute for aluminum and 50 meters per minute for titanium alloys; in some cases, speeds may even reach 9,000 meters per minute. The manufacturing engineer needs to know the effects of such speeds on the structural properties of the materials being cut, such as stress properties of aircraft wings. Tool life may also be substantially affected. For example, higher cutting speeds can cause cutting tools to wear out more frequently—and whenever that occurs production must be interrupted to replace them. Thus, financial considerations such as operating costs, labor, and fixed capital expenses weigh heavily in the process selection decision.

Similar decisions are made in service organizations. Hotel keys can be steel or electronic; hospital patient prescriptions can be written out or transmitted electronically; and financial transactions can be paper check or e-check. In a department store, credit verification of bankcards can be done by checking the credit card number against a printed list of local bad accounts (manual), by calling a special telephone number for authorization (mechanized), or by using automatic verification equipment at the store itself (automated). Trash collection services must decide whether to use all manual labor or automated one-person garbage trucks.

Most companies continually seek new innovations that speed up time and enhance efficiency in their value chains. The OM Spotlight on Alamo and National describes some recent innovations in the car rental industry's processes and value chain.

Implementation Planning of Final Process Design

Stakeholders include internal and external customers, suppliers, employees, managers, and many others such as regulatory agencies and communities.

Regardless of how well or poorly people and processes have performed in the past, process design requires managers to implement change. This may require changes in procedures, responsibilities, knowledge and skills, job assignments, and work habits. No process or functional area is immune to process design changes—accounting, marketing, engineering, logistics, finance, law, operations, human resource management, and so on. **Stakeholders** *include internal and external customers, suppliers, employees, managers, and many others such as regulatory agencies and communities.* Hence, management and stakeholder support and participation is the first and most important step in process design (see the OM Spotlight on AT&T Credit Corporation).

OM SPOTLIGHT

Alamo Rent-a-Car and National Car Rental[18]

Alamo Rent-a-Car and National Car Rental are testing a new technology to speed up the return process for rental cars. The device is a small transponder located in the car that records the vehicle's location, mileage, and amount of fuel in the gas tank. Customers can park their vehicle and go—all the necessary information is electronically transmitted to the rental offices. Especially for repeat customers, this technology allows the customer to avoid long lines at rental counters and parking lots. Currently, the vehicle must be within several miles of the return site to transmit car diagnostics, location, and so on. The device cannot track the vehicle away from the rental site. Preliminary tests show the electronic device is more accurate than information recorded by rental car employees, and therefore, reduces human errors. Susan Palazzese, a vice president for System Development, said that "this will shave off a significant portion of the return process and enable customers to get in and out a lot faster."

OM SPOTLIGHT

AT&T Credit Corporation[19]

In most financial companies, the back-office jobs of processing applications, claims, and customer accounts are as repetitive as assembly-line jobs. The division of labor into small tasks and the organization of work by function are characteristic of many service organizations. At AT&T Credit Corporation, which was established in 1985 to provide financing for customers who lease equipment, one department handled applications and checked the customer's credit standing, a second drew up contracts, and a third collected payments. No one person had responsibility for providing full service to a customer. Recognizing these drawbacks, the company president decided to hire his own employees and give them ownership of the process and accountability for it. Although his first concern was to increase efficiency, his approach had the additional benefit of providing more rewarding jobs.

In 1986 the company set up 11 teams of 10 to 15 newly hired workers in a high-volume division serving small businesses. The three major lease-processing functions were combined in each team. The company also divided its national staff of field agents into seven regions and assigned two or three teams to handle business from each region. The same teams always worked with the same sales staff and were able to establish personal relationships with the agents and their customers. Above all, team members took responsibility for solving customers' problems. Their slogan became, "Whoever gets the call owns the problem." Today, members make most decisions on how to deal with customers, schedule their own time off, reassign work when people are absent, and interview prospective new employees. The teams process up to 800 lease applications daily—twice as many as under the old system—and have reduced the time for final credit approval from several days to 24 to 48 hours.

Techniques of project management (see Chapter 18) can help in this task by providing guidance in breaking down the implementation requirements into manageable pieces, assigning due dates and resources, and delegating responsibility to individuals and teams. The final step is to monitor performance after implementation to ensure that the intended level of performance is actually achieved and maintained and to look for improvement opportunities. Comparing process performance to competitors or noncompeting firms through benchmarking is a useful way to monitor performance and look for improvement opportunities.

PROCESS ANALYSIS AND IMPROVEMENT

Learning Objectives
To be able to identify opportunities for improving processes, and to understand how to use process maps to analyze and find specific areas for improvement.

Few processes are designed from scratch. Many process design activities involve redesigning an existing process to improve performance. Management strategies to improve process designs usually focus on one or more of the following:

- *increasing revenue* by improving process efficiency in creating goods and services and delivery of the customer benefit package;
- *increasing agility* by improving flexibility and response to changes in demand and customer expectations;
- *increasing product and/or service quality* by reducing defects, mistakes, failures, or service upsets;
- *decreasing costs* through better technology or elimination of non-value-added activities;
- *decreasing process flow time* by reducing waiting time or speeding up movement through the process and value chain.

Some experts argue that a time-reduction strategy automatically results in lower costs, better quality, higher agility, and more opportunities to grow revenue. Hence, some organizations focus on reducing process flow times as their dominant competitive strategy.

The first step in process improvement is to measure existing performance. This provides a good basis for before-versus-after performance comparisons. In addition, consideration should be given to benchmarking performance in recognized "best practice" organizations to provide a target for improvement.

Process and value stream maps are the foundation for improvement activities. The baseline process map provides a basis for addressing the following key improvement questions:

- Are the steps in the process arranged in logical sequence?
- Do all steps add value? Can some steps be eliminated and should others be added in order to improve quality or operational performance? Can some be combined? Should some be reordered?
- Are capacities of each step in balance; that is, do bottlenecks exist for which customers will incur excessive waiting time?
- What skills, equipment, and tools are required at each step of the process? Should some steps be automated?
- At which points in the system might errors occur that would result in customer dissatisfaction, and how might these errors be corrected?
- At which point or points should performance be measured?
- Where interaction with the customer occurs, what procedures and guidelines should employees follow that will present a positive image?

Using process mapping as a basis for improvement, Motorola reduced manufacturing time for pagers from 40 days to less than 1 hour. Citibank adopted this approach and reduced internal callbacks in its Private Bank group by 80 percent and the credit process time by 50 percent, and in its Global Equipment Finance, which provides financing and leasing services to Citibank customers, lowered the credit decision cycle from 3 days to 1. Copeland Companies, subsidiaries of Travelers Life & Annuity, reduced the cycle time of processing statements from 28 days to 15 days.[20] The OM Spotlight on Boise illustrates a powerful example of process mapping.

OM SPOTLIGHT

Boise[21]

The Timber and Wood Products Division of Boise formed a team of 11 people with diverse backgrounds from manufacturing, administration, and marketing to improve a customer claims processing and tracking system that affected all areas and customers in the six regions of the division. Although external customer surveys indicated that the company was not doing badly, internal opinions of the operation were far more critical.

The first eye-opener came when the process was flowcharted and the group discovered that more than 70 steps were performed for each claim. Exhibit 7.11 shows the original flowchart from the marketing and sales department. Combined division tasks numbered in the hundreds for a single claim; the marketing and sales portion of the flowchart alone consisted of up to 20 separate tasks and 7 decisions, which sometimes took months to complete. Most of these steps added no value to the settlement outcome. The flowchart accomplished much more than just plotting Boise's time and efforts; it also helped build team members' confidence in each other and foster mutual respect. When they saw how each member was able to chart his or her part of the process and state individual concerns, everyone's reason for being on the team was validated. The group eliminated 70 percent of the steps for small claims in the original flowcharts resulting in substantial cost savings, as shown in Exhibit 7.12.

Exhibit 7.11 Original Flowchart from the Boise Marketing and Sales Department

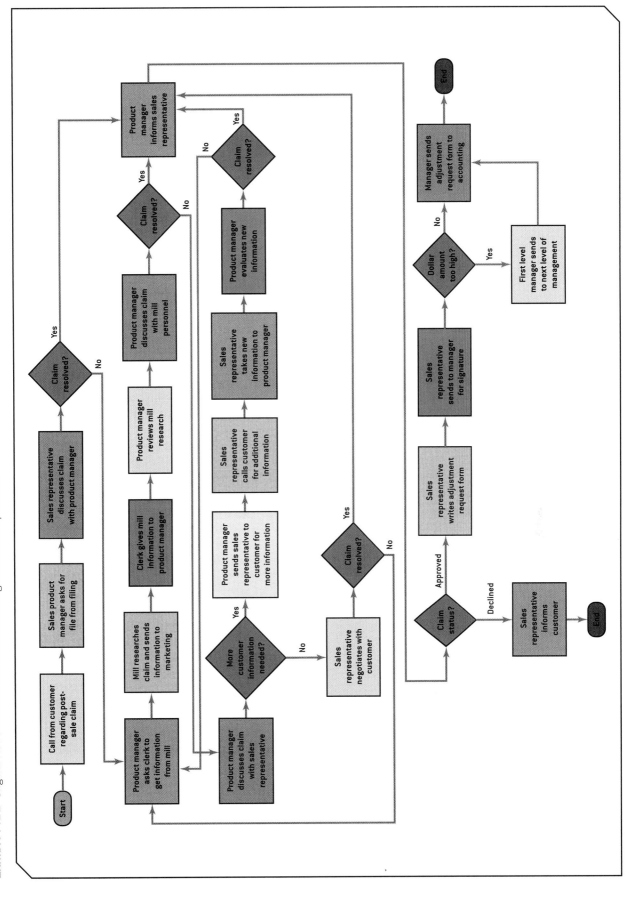

Exhibit 7.12 New Small Adjustment Request Form Process Flowchart for Boise Marketing and Sales Department

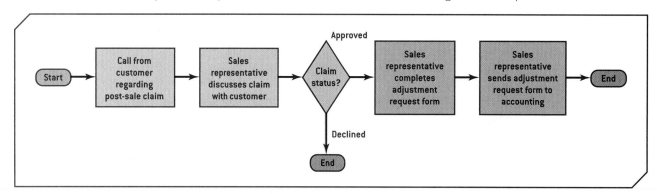

Reengineering and Creative Destruction

Reengineering has been defined as "the fundamental rethinking and radical redesign of business processes to achieve dramatic improvements in critical, contemporary measures of performance, such as cost, quality, service, and speed."

Sometimes, processes have gotten so complex that it is easier to start from a "clean sheet" rather than try to improve incrementally. Reengineering *has been defined as "the fundamental rethinking and radical redesign of business processes to achieve dramatic improvements in critical, contemporary measures of performance, such as cost, quality, service, and speed."*[22] Reengineering was spawned by the revolution in information technology and involves asking basic questions about business processes: Why do we do it? and Why is it done this way? Such questioning often uncovers obsolete, erroneous, or inappropriate assumptions. Radical redesign involves tossing out existing procedures and reinventing the process, not just incrementally improving it. The goal is to achieve quantum leaps in performance. All processes and functional areas participate in reengineering efforts, each requiring knowledge and skills in operations management.

For example, IBM Credit Corporation cut the process of financing IBM computers, software, and services from 7 days to 4 hours by rethinking the process. Originally, the process was designed to handle difficult applications and required four highly trained specialists and a series of handoffs. The actual work took only about 1.5 hours; the rest of the time was spent in transit or delay. By questioning the assumption that every application was unique and difficult to process, IBM Credit Corporation was able to replace the specialists by a single individual supported by a user-friendly computer system that provided access to all the data and tools that the specialists would use. Successful reengineering requires fundamental understanding of processes, creative thinking to break away from old traditions and assumptions, and effective use of information technology.

PepsiCo embarked on a program to reengineer all of its key business processes, such as selling and delivery, equipment service and repair, procurement, and financial reporting. In the selling and delivery of its products, for example, customer reps typically experienced stockouts of as much as 25 percent of product by the end of the day, resulting in late-day stops not getting full deliveries and the need to return to those accounts. Many other routes returned with overstock of other products, increasing handling costs. By redesigning the system to include handheld computers, customer reps can confirm and deliver that day's order and also take a future order for the next delivery to that customer.[23]

Creative destruction is the process of revamping antiquated processes over time and replacing them with new IT-enabled networks of processes.

The term creative destruction *has been coined to describe the process of revamping antiquated processes over time and replacing them with new IT-enabled networks of processes (called an IT-enabled value chain).*[24] Many examples of this new capability and restructuring were described in Chapter 5. Most experts agree that creative destruction takes about 50 years, based on studies of the steam engine and assembly line. Creative destruction focus on reengineering the organization's structure, processes, and relationships to stakeholders and entities in the value chain.

Some of the elements of creative destruction are

- **Lean organization** IT integration results in a "leaner" organization with fewer employees. However, attention to operations—such as better forecasting, scheduling, process design, purchasing, and capacity management—must be achieved for a lean organization to survive and prosper.
- **Dynamic balancing** Information developed and passed on through layers of management in the past is now available in real time to all employees in a more open situation versus a "restricted and need-to-know basis." Managers must now dynamically balance the distribution of information and decide whether to change or eliminate legacy systems.
- **Market access** With IT-enabled processes, knowledge management and intellectual assets become the central focus for gaining competitive advantage as the organization organizes by process or value chain as described in Chapter 1.
- **Customer driven** The philosophy and capability of the IT-enabled firm is now "sense and respond" versus "make and sell." Customers benefit from these new capabilities and raise their expectations of the customer benefit package.
- **Market foreclosure** Creating value to retain customers over the long term requires continuous learning and precise process and value chain coordination. If the organization fails to keep up, it is closed out of the market quickly. New structures emerge and entire industries are restructured and redesigned.
- **Global** The creative destruction cycle is complete once these transformations and remaining organizations reach global markets and use global resources.

With the rapid pace of change in business today, organizations need to think about "reinventing" themselves to maintain a competitive edge. Such changes require a significant amount of input and support from operations managers to succeed.

PROCESS DESIGN AND RESOURCE UTILIZATION

Learning Objective
To understand how processes can be designed to achieve high utilization of resources, to identify bottlenecks in processes, and to be able to apply Little's Law to evaluate relationships among flow time, throughput, and work-in-process.

Utilization *is the fraction of time a workstation or individual is busy over the long run.*

Idle machines, trucks, people, computers, warehouse space, and other resources used in a process simply drain away potential profit. **Utilization** *is the fraction of time a workstation or individual is busy over the long run.* Understanding resource utilization is an important aspect of process design and improvement. High resource utilization is critical to performance, particularly if a firm has a low-cost strategy. Even in not-for-profit organizations, wasting process resources represents poor stewardship. Today's "lean organizations" try to leverage the highest capability from all resources. However, it is difficult to achieve 100 percent utilization. For example, utilization in most job shops ranges from 65 to 90 percent. In flow shops, it might be between 80 to 95 percent, and for most continuous flow processes, above 95 percent. This should not be surprising if you think about how these processes operate. In job shops, producing a wide range of products and moving materials from one work center to another result in frequent machine changeovers and delays. In flow shops and continuous flow processes, there is less changeover and delay, resulting in higher utilization.

Service facilities have a greater range of resource utilization. Movie theaters, for example, average 5 to 20 percent utilization when seat utilization is computed over the entire week. On weekdays, many theaters have only a few customers in their theaters, whereas in the evenings and on weekends they may have a full house. Similar comments apply to hotels, airlines, and other services. For example, many airline flights during midday may be half-full or less, whereas those in the morning and evening hours are full with business travelers.

Two ways of computing resource utilization are

Utilization (U) = Resources Demanded/Resource Availability   **(7.1)**

Utilization (U) = Demand Rate/[Service Rate $\times$ Number of Servers]   **(7.2)**

In Equation (7.1), the measurement base (time, units, and so on) must be the same in the numerator and denominator. For example, if a resource is used 40 hours per week and it is available for use 50 hours per week, the resource utilization using Equation (7.1) is 80 percent. As another example, consider a multiplex movie theater with 3,000 total seats that is open 7 days a week from noon to midnight, or 12 hours per day. The total number of seats available for sale per week is 10,500 [3,000 seats/day × 7days × (12 hours/day/24 hours/day)]. If the theater sold 1,400 seats this week then, using Equation (7.1), seat utilization at this theater is Utilization (U) = Resources Demanded/Resources Available = 1,400/10,500 = 13.3 percent. Frequently, adjustments (such as accounting for lunch and break periods, meeting and training time, and overtime) are made to the numerator and denominator of Equation (7.1) to more accurately reflect the actual hours used or available.

To illustrate using Equation (7.2), assume that a telephone call center receives 30 calls per hour (the demand rate) between 7:00 to 8:00 A.M. and the call center has two service providers on duty, each of whom can handle 20 calls per hour (the service rate). Then the labor utilization would be calculated as 30/(2 × 20) = 75 percent; if three service providers are available, labor utilization is 30/(3 × 20) = 50%. However, if only one service provider is available, the labor utilization would be calculated to be 30/(1 × 20) = 150 percent! Clearly, it is impossible to use more than 100 percent of a resource, because utilization is defined as the fraction of time the worker is busy. In this situation, the calls arrive faster than the service provider is able to keep up with, so the service provider will always be busy (actual utilization is 100 percent) and many callers must wait.

For a process design to be feasible, the calculated utilization *over the long run* cannot exceed 100 percent. However, over short periods of time, it is quite possible that demand for a resource will exceed its availability. Thus, if the demand rate to the call center falls to less than 20 calls/hour (the service rate) after 8:00 A.M., one service provider will be able to catch up, although some callers might have waited a very long time.

If a manager knows any three of the four variables in Equation (7.2), then the fourth can easily be found. For example, what would be the maximum demand the call center could handle if the target utilization was 80 percent, the service rate was 20 calls per hour, and two telephone service providers were on duty between 7 and 8 A.M.? This is found by solving the equation: 80 percent = D/(2 × 30), resulting in D = 60 × 0.8 = 48 calls/hour.

These simple calculations can provide useful insight for evaluating alternative process designs. Exhibit 7.13 provides an analysis of the utilization of the restaurant order posting and fulfillment process in Exhibit 7.9. Using Equation (7.1), the resource utilization for work activity #3, assuming only one chef and two ovens, is computed as:

$$20 \text{ orders/hour}/5 \text{ orders/hour} = 400 \text{ percent}$$

Alternatively, using Equation (7.2), we have

$$20 \text{ orders/hour}/[(60 \text{ minutes/hour})/12 \text{ minutes/order}] \times (1 \text{ chef}) = 400 \text{ percent}$$

As we noted earlier, whenever the utilization is calculated to be greater than 100 percent, the work will endlessly pile up before the workstation. Therefore, this is clearly a poor process design and we need to add more resources.

A logical question to consider is how many chefs are needed to bring the utilization down below 100 percent at work activity #3? Because the chef is the highest skilled and paid employee, it would make sense to design the process so that the chef would have the highest labor utilization rate (although 100 percent would probably not be practical). This can be found by solving the equation

$$20 \text{ orders/hour}/[(5 \text{ orders/hour}) \times (X \text{ chefs})] = 1.00$$
$$(5 \text{ orders/hour}) \times 1.00 \times X = 20 \text{ orders/hour, or } X = 4.00 \text{ chefs}$$

Exhibit 7.13 Utilization Analysis of Restaurant Order Posting and Fulfillment Process

	Work Activity #1 (Chef decides if order is accurate)	Work Activity #2 (Chef stages raw materials)	Work Activity #3 (Chef prepares side dishes)	Work Activity #4 (Oven operation)	Work Activity #5 (Chef assembles order)
Order arrival rate (given)	20 orders/hr	20 orders/hr	20 orders/hr	20 orders/hr	20 orders/hr
Time per order	1 minute	4 minutes	12 minutes	10 minutes	3 minutes
Number of resources	1 chef	1 chef	1 chef	2 ovens	1 chef
Output per time period	60 orders/hr	15 orders/hr	5 orders/hr	12 orders/hr	20 orders/hr
Resource utilization with 1 chef and 2 ovens	33%	133%	400%	167%	100%

With four chefs, the resource utilizations are recomputed in Exhibit 7.14. We see that the oven is still a problem, with a calculated 167 percent utilization. To determine how many ovens to have for a 100 percent utilization, we solve the equation:

20 orders/hour/[(6 orders/hour × (Y ovens)] = 1.00
(6 orders/hour) × 1.00 × Y = 20 orders/hour, or Y = 3.33 ovens

Exhibit 7.14 Revised Utilization Analysis of Restaurant Order Posting and Fulfillment Process (4 chefs)

	Work Activity #1 (Chef decides if order is accurate)	Work Activity #2 (Chef stages raw materials)	Work Activity #3 (Chef prepares side dishes)	Work Activity #4 (Oven operation)	Work Activity #5 (Chef assembles order)
Resource utilization with 4 chefs and 2 ovens	8.33%	33%	100%	167%	25%

Rounding this up to 4, actual oven utilization would now be 83 percent (see Exhibit 7.15 for the final results).

Bottlenecks

Exhibit 7.16 shows a simplified flowchart of the order fulfillment process along with the output rates that can be achieved for each work activity. *The average number of entities completed per unit time—the output rate—from a process is called* **throughput.** Throughput might be measured as parts per day, transactions per minute, or customers per hour, depending on the context. A logical question to consider is what throughput can be achieved for the entire process. Like the weakest link of a chain, the process in Exhibit 7.16 can never produce more than 20 orders/hour—the output rate of Work Activity #3. A **bottleneck** *is the work activity that effectively limits throughput of the entire process.*

The average number of entities completed per unit time—the output rate—from a process is called **throughput.**

A **bottleneck** *is the work activity that effectively limits throughput of the entire process.*

Exhibit 7.15 Revised Utilization Analysis of Restaurant Order Posting and Fulfillment Process (4 ovens)

	Work Activity #1 (Chef decides if order is accurate)	Work Activity #2 (Chef stages raw materials)	Work Activity #3 (Chef prepares side dishes)	Work Activity #4 (Oven operation)	Work Activity #5 (Chef assembles order)
Order arrival rate (given)	20 orders/hr	20 orders/hr	20 orders/hr	20 orders/hr	20 orders/hr
Time per order	1 minute	4 minutes	12 minutes	10 minutes	3 minutes
Number of resources	4 chefs	4 chefs	4 chefs	4 ovens	4 chefs
Output per time period	240 orders/hr	60 orders/hr	20 orders/hr	24 orders/hr	80 orders/hr
Resource utilization with 4 chefs and 4 ovens	8.33%	33%	100%	83%	25%

Exhibit 7.16 Simplified Restaurant Fulfillment Process

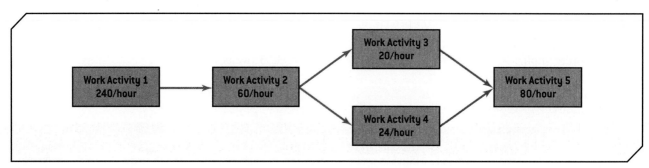

A good illustration of the concept of a bottleneck is a funnel that constricts the flow of process output, as shown in Exhibit 7.17. Downstream process work activities are "starved" and do not have enough work to keep busy. Upstream work activities whose output must sequentially go through the bottleneck work activity can only be processed at the rate of the bottleneck. If upstream work activities create more output that the downstream bottleneck work activity, the work will have to wait to be processed. The only way to improve the output rate of the process is to increase the rate of the bottleneck activity. Identifying and breaking process bottlenecks is an important part of process design and will increase the speed of the process, reduce waiting and work-in-process inventory, and use resources more efficiently (see the OM Spotlight: Tracking Hospital Patient Flow). Chapter 10 will expand on bottleneck concepts when we describe the Theory of Constraints.

Queues

A queue is a waiting line; queuing theory is the analytical study of waiting lines.

When uncertainty in demand and service rates exists in processes, queues inevitably build up. *A queue is a waiting line; queuing theory is the analytical study of waiting lines.* Waiting in line at a supermarket, post office, bank, or for a specific exercise machine at a health club are common experiences for everyone. Queues also exist in manufacturing, as work-in-process builds up at workstations.

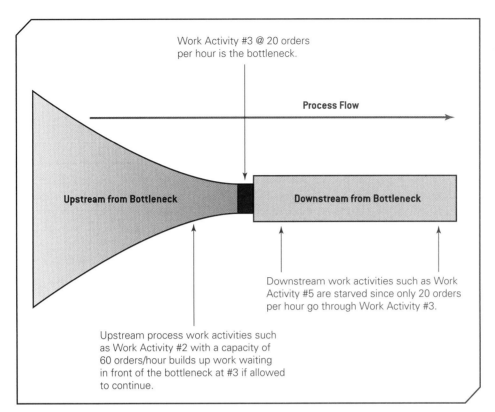

Exhibit 7.17
Funnel Analogy of Bottleneck
Work Activities

OM SPOTLIGHT

Tracking Hospital Patient Flow[25]

Hannibal Regional Hospital uses radio frequency identification technology (RFID) to track patients throughout its ambulatory care unit. Patient badges are embedded with a RFID chip that communicates via antennas throughout the hospital. The hospital unit includes a surgical suite and areas for blood transfusions, injections, and radiology. The objective was to better understand patient flow, and where and how long they wait in each process. "You cannot manage what you cannot measure," states Judy Patterson, director of preoperative services at the 91-bed hospital.

Patient tracking results found that 20 percent of outpatient treatment was being handled after official hospital hours. The solution was scheduling physicians and patients in blocks of time, identifying and breaking process bottlenecks, and tracking patient arrival times. Therefore, physicians must use their time more efficiently and be more aware of when patients arrive. Two results of these changes in scheduling and physician behavior were that patient processing time decreased and physician utilization increased.

Future uses of RFID technology include using it to track equipment such as portable X-ray machines, scopes, surgical tools, and high tech cameras. In one test situation, the technology was used to track epidural pumps in the birthing unit to solve a recurring problem. "We often had trouble finding the pumps late at night," Patterson says.

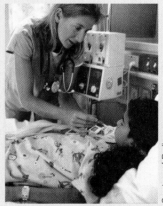

Courtesy of Radianse

All queueing systems have three elements in common:

1. *Customers* that wait for service. Customers need not be people but can be machines awaiting repair, airplanes waiting to take off, subassemblies waiting for a machine, computer programs waiting for processing, or telephone calls awaiting a customer service representative. In most queuing systems, customers arrive as individuals. In others, batches of customers are accumulated before processing. This is common in job shops and many amusement park rides.
2. *Servers* that provide the service. Again, servers need not be only people, such as clerks, customer service representatives, or repairpersons; servers may be airport runways, machine tools, repair bays, ATMs, or computers.
3. A *waiting line* or *queue*. The queue is the set of customers waiting for service. In many cases, a queue is a physical line, as you experience in a bank or grocery store. In other situations, a queue may not even be visible or even in one location, as with computer jobs waiting for processing or telephone calls waiting for an open line (see OM Spotlight: Queuing Analysis on the Web).

The customers, servers, and queues in a queuing system can be arranged in various ways. Three common queuing configurations are as follows:

1. One or more parallel servers fed by a single queue (see Exhibit 7.19a). This is the typical configuration used by many banks and airline ticket counters.
2. Several parallel servers fed by their own queues (see Exhibit 7.19b). Most supermarkets and discount retailers use this type of system.
3. A combination of several queues in series. This structure is common when multiple processing operations exist, such as in manufacturing facilities and many service systems. For instance, an assembly line is a set of workstations arranged in a serial structure—the output of one station becomes the input of another station. Another example is a drive-through at a restaurant that may have a queue of cars placing orders followed by a queue of cars at the pickup window. An example of a typical voting facility is shown in Exhibit 7.20.

OM SPOTLIGHT

Queuing Analysis on the Web

The Internet and its multitude of servers and routers must prioritize the data packets that are routed across the Internet (see Exhibit 7.18). Some data packets are assigned top priority while others wait in a cyberspace queue. Capacity bottlenecks in the Internet system can create backlogs of data packets and cause parts of the system to crash. The queuing of packets only occurs when the total number of outbound packets exceeds the capacity of the outbound communication link or application software. If a link is not congested, the router does not need to implement any queue priority rules and decisions.[26]

Message management uses queuing models to help manage, track, and predict the flow of audio, video, and text data packets through their entire life cycle.

Message management *uses queuing models to help manage, track, and predict the flow of audio, video, and text data packets through their entire life cycle.* Because each Internet application works at a certain speed and throughput rate, one cannot assume two applications can communicate in a perfectly synchronous way. Hence, queues in the Internet develop and disappear in milliseconds most of the time. Oracle, Cisco, IBM, and others work very hard to maximize the flow of data packets that move through their web-based equipment. So, the next time you log on to the Internet realize that simple and complex queuing is going on throughout the web at any moment in time.

Exhibit 7.18 Example of Queuing Messages over the Internet[27]

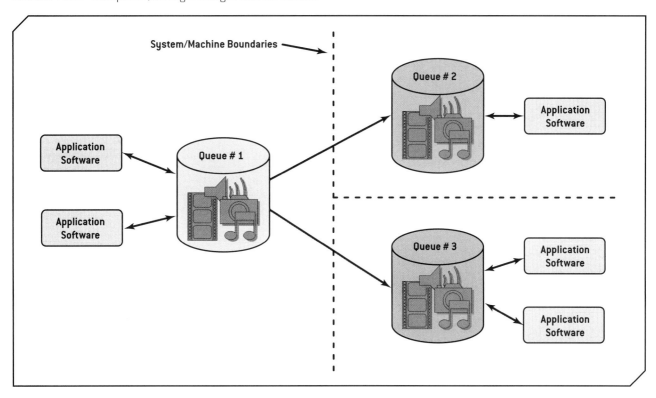

Choosing the right queuing system configuration is an important element of process design. For instance, customers become frustrated when a person enters a line next to them and receives service first. Of course, *that* customer feels a certain sense of satisfaction. People expect to be treated fairly; in queuing situations that means "first-come, first-served." In the mid-1960s, Chemical Bank was one of the

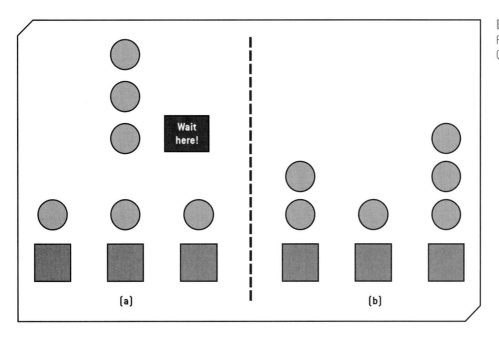

Exhibit 7.19
Parallel Servers with (a) A Single Queue and (b) Multiple Queues

Exhibit 7.20 Queues in Series in a Typical Voting Facility

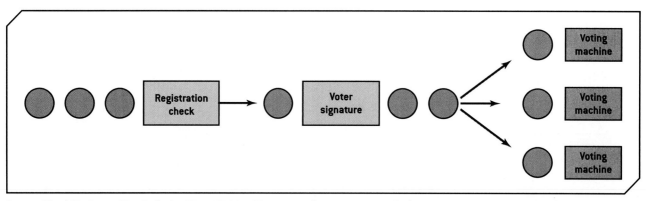

Source: Floyd H. Grant, III, "Reducing Voter Waiting Time," *Interfaces*, 10, no. 5, October 1980, pp. 19–25. Reprinted with permission.

first to switch to a serpentine line (one line feeding into several servers) from multiple parallel lines. American Airlines copied this at their airport counters and most others followed suit. Other types of services, such as the U.S. Postal Service, have migrated to single lines. Studies have shown that customers are happier when they wait in a serpentine line, rather than in parallel lines, even if that type of line increases their wait.

Fast-food franchises like Wendy's and Burger King have used single lines for many years.[28] Burger King found that multiple lines create stress and anxiety whereas using a single line allows customers to focus on what they want to order and not be distracted by which line is shorter. Other companies like McDonald's, however, have stayed with multiple lines. Some McDonald's executives feel that the multiple-line system accommodates higher volumes of customers more quickly, despite time studies that have proven a single line to be faster. But the perception of a long single line may cause customers to leave, and consumer perception is what really counts.

The principal reason to analyze queuing systems is to predict performance and help managers better allocate resources. Typical queuing performance measures include

1. percentage of time or probability that the service facilities are idle;
2. probability of a specific number of units (customers) in the system (the system includes the waiting line plus the service facility);
3. average number of units in the waiting line, L_q;
4. average number of units in the system (that is, waiting + being served), L;
5. average time a unit spends in the waiting line, W_q;
6. average time a unit spends in the system (that is, waiting + being served), W;
7. probability that an arriving unit must wait for service.

For example, if a manager can predict that a certain configuration will result in unacceptable waiting lines from the customers' perspective, then he or she might decide to add additional service facilities or staff to serve the customers. However, designing the process to avoid waiting can be costly to the service provider. Managers must weigh the benefits of shorter waiting times against these costs in process design decisions. Understanding and managing queues are vital to providing superior customer services and achieving long-run profitability.

Queuing analysis can be performed with analytical models or simulation models. Analytical models are simpler to use and can provide good estimates of the average long-run behavior of queuing systems. However, they rely on mathematical assumptions that limit their use, and they cannot address short-term dynamic behavior that occurs in queuing systems. Supplementary Chapter B provides an introduction to analytical queuing models. Simulation models are better equipped to capture the dynamic behavior over time, but are more costly and time-consuming to implement. Supplementary Chapter D addresses simulation techniques. Often, analytical and simulation models are used in combination; an analytical model is used to get the first operating system performance estimates, and then simulation provides detailed analysis, if needed.

Little's Law

At any moment of time, people, orders, jobs, documents, money, and other entities that flow through processes are in various stages of completion and may be waiting in queues. For example, in an outpatient surgical unit, some patients will be waiting in preop or postop, and some will be in surgery. **Flow time**, or **cycle time**, *is the average time it takes to complete one cycle of a process.* It makes sense that the flow time will depend not only on the actual time to perform the tasks required but also on how many other entities are in the "work-in-process" stage.

Flow time, or cycle time, is the average time it takes to complete one cycle of a process.

In 1961, Dr. J. D. C. Little developed a simple formula that explains the relationship among flow time (T), throughput (R), and work-in-process (WIP), which has come to be known as Little's Law.[29] Stated simply, Little's Law is

Work-in-process = Throughput $\times$ Flow time
or
$WIP = R \times T$ **(7.3)**

Little's Law provides a simple way of evaluating average process performance. If we know any two of the three variables, we can compute the third using Little's Law. For example, in a hospital, it would probably be difficult to physically count the number of patients at any one time because they are scattered about. However, it would be easy to measure flow time by noting when each patient enters and leaves, and to measure throughput by counting the number of patients that leave each day or hour. Little's Law can estimate the average patient load (work-in-process) that the hospital might expect. Similarly, for many high-volume factory operations, it might be difficult to measure flow time because this would require tagging the start and completion times of each individual part. However, throughput and work-in-process are normally tracked, and Little's Law can be used to estimate the average flow time.

Suppose that a voting facility similar to the one in Exhibit 7.20 processes an average of 50 people per hour and that, on average, it takes 10 minutes for each person to complete the voting process. Using Equation (7.3), we can compute the average number of voters in process:

$WIP = R \times T$
$WIP = 50$ voters/hr $\times$ (10 minutes/60 minutes per hour)
$WIP = 8.33$ voters

Therefore, on average, we would expect to find about 8 or 9 voters inside the facility.

Little's Law can be applied to many different types of manufacturing and service operations. For instance, suppose that the loan department of a bank takes an average of 6 days (0.2 months) to process an application and that an internal audit found that about 100 applications are in various stages of processing at any one time. Using Little's Law, we see that $T = 6$ and $WIP = 100$. Therefore, we can calculate the throughput of the department as

$R = WIP/T = 100$ applications/0.2 months
$= 500$ applications per month

As another example, suppose that a restaurant makes 400 pizzas per week, each of which uses one-half pound of dough, and that it typically maintains an inventory of 70 pounds of dough. In this case, $R = 200$ pounds per week of dough and $WIP = 70$ pounds. Using Little's Law, we can compute the average flow time as

$$T = WIP/R = 70/200$$
$$= 0.35 \text{ weeks, or about } 2^{1}/_2 \text{ days.}$$

This information can be used to verify the freshness of the dough.

Little's Law can also be extended to understand performance in queuing systems. We will use the notation introduced in the previous section on queuing:

L_q = average number of units in the waiting line
L = average number of units in the system (that is, waiting + being served)
W_q = average time a unit spends in the waiting line
W = average time a unit spends in the system (that is, waiting + being served)

If we also define λ = the average rate of customer arrivals to the system, then some key relationships that result from applying Little's Law are

$$L = \lambda \times W \tag{7.4}$$

and

$$L_q = \lambda \times W_q \tag{7.5}$$

Equation (7.4) states that the average number of units in the system is equal to the average arrival rate times the average time spent in the system. Equation (7.5) states a similar result for the queue itself: The average number of units in the queue is equal to the average arrival rate times the average waiting time. These formulas are useful in helping to design customer-focused service systems.

It is important to understand that Little's Law is based on simple averages for all variables. Such an analysis serves as a good baseline for understanding process performance on an aggregate basis, but it does not take into account any randomness in arrivals or service times. To evaluate the performance at a more detailed level requires the use of queuing or simulation models that we discuss in Supplementary Chapters B and D, respectively.

SOLVED PROBLEMS

SOLVED PROBLEM #1

An inspection station for assembling printers receives 40 printers/hour and has two inspectors, each of whom can inspect 30 printers per hour. What is the utilization of the inspectors? What service rate would be required to have a utilization of 85 percent?

Solution:
The labor utilization at this inspection station is calculated to be $40/(2 \times 30) = 67$ percent. If the utilization rate is 85 percent, we can calculate the target service rate (SR) by solving Equation (7.2):

$$85\% = 40/(2 \times SR)$$
$$1.7 \times SR = 40$$
$$SR = 23.5 \text{ printers/hour}$$

SOLVED PROBLEM #2

An accounts receivable manager processes 200 bills per day with an average processing time of 5 working days. What is the average number of bills in her office? What if she reduces the processing time from 5 days to 1 day using better information technology? What other advantages are there of reducing accounts receivable?

Solution:
Using Little's Law, $WIP = R \times T = (200$ invoices/day$)(5$ days$) = 1,000$ bills. If flow time is reduced from 5 days to 1 day then $WIP = R \times T = (200$ bills/day$)(1$ day$) = 200$ bills. By decreasing the flow time (T) and average outstanding accounts receivable (WIP) (notice they are directly, not inversely, related using Little's Law), more bills get out the door faster and into customers' hands. This should reduce accounts receivable while increasing cash flow and cash on hand for the company.

SOLVED PROBLEM #3

A manufacturer of personal computers operates a telephone customer contact center that provides technical assistance. Management has decided to set target labor utilization for its customer service representatives (CSRs) at 80 percent, the demand rate is 40 customer inquiries per hour, and five CSRs are on duty from 1:00 to 2:00 pm. The manager of the contact center does not have standard times and when asked about his service rate, he said, "We never had the time to develop service standards. Five CSRs seems to work well—we experiment with different staffing levels and eventually pick the one with the least customer complaints." What is the implied service rate? What is wrong with his approach to staff scheduling and customer service?

Solution:
A trial and error approach to staff scheduling in this situation means customer service is maximized probably at high costs. The objective is to maximize customer service at minimal costs, and therefore, this contact center needs a more formal approach to setting staffing levels. This can be done using Equation (7.2):

$$\text{Utilization } (U) = \text{Demand Rate/[Service Rate} \times \text{Number of Servers]}$$

$$
\begin{aligned}
\text{Service Rate} &= \text{Demand Rate/Number of Servers} \times U \\
&= 40 \text{ inquiries/hour/}(5 \text{ CSRs}) \times (0.8) \\
&= 10 \text{ inquiries/hour/CSR}
\end{aligned}
$$

SOLVED PROBLEM #4

A manufacturer of air conditioner compressors is concerned that too much money is tied up in its value chain. Average raw material and work in process inventory is $50 million. Sales are $20 million per week and finished goods inventory averages $30 million. The average outstanding accounts receivable is $60 million. Production takes, on average, 1 week to produce a compressor and the typical sales flow time is 2 weeks. Assume 50 weeks in 1 year. The value chain is:

RM & WIP Inventory → Production → Finished Goods → Sales → Accounts Receivable Processing

a. What is the flow unit in this system?

b. What is the total flow time of a throughput dollar?

c. What is the average dollar inventory in the value chain?

d. Which of the three processes—production, sales, or accounts receivable—is the best candidate for freeing up dollars for the air conditioner manufacturer?

e. What is the target level of average accounts receivable inventory if management can reduce the time a dollar spends in accounts receivable inventory (processing and collections) by one-half by improving the accounts receivable process?

f. What else does this flow-time analysis problem demonstrate?

Solution:

a. One throughput dollar ($).

b. First, review the calculations in Exhibit 7.21. If we add the flow times for each process in the value chain we obtain $.05 + .02 + .03 + .04 + .06 = .20$ years, or 10 weeks.

c. The answer using Exhibit 7.21 is: $50m + $20m + $30m + $40m + $60m = $200m.

d. Clearly, accounts receivable ties up $60m in cash and takes on average .06 years, or 3 weeks, to process and collect the money. The fact is a dollar tied up in accounts receivable is just as valuable as a dollar tied up in production or inventory.

e. $WIP = R \times T$ or $1,000m/year $\times$ .03 year = $30m instead of $60m. This improvement initiative frees up monies for other purposes or to reduce cash flow and debt needs.

f. Accounts receivable accounts for 30 percent (3/10) of the total flow time and total cash to operate the business ($60m/$200m). See Exhibit 7.21. This post-production service is a good place to start improving value chain performance. Revisit Exhibit 2.3 to see what other post-production services might be relevant. Also, look at the preproduction services, and think about their impact on total value chain flow time. This is an example of applying Little's Law to a value chain.

Exhibit 7.21 Flow Time Analysis of the Air Conditioner Compressor Value Chain

WIP = R × T	Raw Material & WIP Inventory	Production	Finished Goods Inventory	Sales Process	Accounts Receivable Inventory
Inventory (WIP)	$50m	$20m	$30m	$40m	$60m
Throughput Rate (R)	$1,000m/yr	$1,000m/yr	$1,000m/yr	$1,000m/yr	$1,000m/yr
Flow Time (T)	.05 years	.02 years	.03 years	.04 years	.06 years

*Numbers in squares are given in the problem and numbers in ovals are computed.

KEY TERMS AND CONCEPTS

Basic process design questions
Bottleneck
Cascading flowcharts
Characteristics of the four process types
Continuous flow shops
Creative destruction
Custom or make-to-order
Flow shops
Flow time analysis
  Flow time
  Throughput
  Work-in-Process Inventory
Hierarchy of work
  Activity/Workstation
  Process
  Task
  Value chain
Job shops
Little's Law
Message management
Option or assemble-to-order

Process boundary
Process choice
Process flowchart and symbols
Product life cycles
  Fast-paced
  Relationship to process type
  Traditional
Product-Process matrix
  Matrix axes
  Off-diagonal
  Positioning strategy
  Theory
Projects
Queue
Queueing system
Queuing theory
Reengineering
Resource utilization analysis
Service-Positioning matrix
  Co-routed
  Customer–routed

Degree of management control
Pathways (routes)
Provider–routed
Repeatability
Service encounter activity sequence

Stakeholders
Standard or make-to-stock
Value and non-value-added activities
Value stream mapping

QUESTIONS FOR REVIEW AND DISCUSSION

1. Explain the importance of process design in manufacturing and service operations. How does it relate to both strategic and operational management issues?

2. Define custom, option, and standard goods and services, and give a new example of each. How does the type of goods and services affect process choice?

3. Explain the characteristics of a project, job shop, flow shop, and continuous flow process.

4. What type of process—project, job shop, flow shop, and continuous flow—would most likely be used to produce the following?
   a. PDAs
   b. gasoline
   c. air conditioners
   d. customer machine tools
   e. paper
   f. many flavors of ice cream

5. Explain why it is important to make product and process decisions simultaneously.

6. Sketch the product-process matrix, and explain each axis. How do the four major types of processes fit into the product-process matrix? Explain the logic and theory of the matrix and how it helps operations managers in their decisions.

7. Develop a product-process matrix for these food services. Justify the location you specify for each.
   a. fast-food restaurant
   b. family steak house
   c. cafeteria
   d. traditional restaurant
   e. high-end French restaurant

8. How does modern technology affect the application of the product-process matrix?

9. Why is the product-process matrix not appropriate for services?

10. Define a pathway, and give an example.

11. Explain the differences between customer-routed services and provider-routed services, and give an example of each.

12. What is a service encounter activity sequence, and what factors influence it?

13. Sketch the service-positioning matrix, and explain each axis. Explain the logic and theory of the matrix.

14. How is the service-positioning matrix similar to and different from the product-process matrix?

15. What is the (traditional) product life cycle? Explain how firms make money when their goods or services follow the traditional product life cycle.

16. What is a fast-paced product life cycle? Explain how firms make money when their goods or services follow the fast-paced product life cycle.

17. What are the implications to operations managers of being in a business where traditional versus fast-paced life cycles exist? Explain.

18. Discuss the major issues that must be considered in designing processes and the key activities that must be accomplished.

19. Answer each of the process-related questions in Exhibit 7.5 in one sentence or less for a process you are familiar with.

20. What are the key objectives of process design?

21. What is a process map? How is it used in process design?

22. What are the advantages of clearly defining the process boundaries?

23. Explain the concept of the hierarchy of work. How is it useful in process design activities?

24. Draw a flowchart for a process of interest to you, such as a quick oil-change service, a factory process you might have worked in, ordering a pizza, renting a car or truck, buying products on the Internet, or applying for an automobile loan. Identify the points where something (people, information) waits for service or is held in work-in-process inventory, the estimated time to accomplish each activity in the process and the total flow time, and where in the process are the most likely tasks where defects, failures, mistakes, and service upsets might happen.

Evaluate how well the process worked and what might be done to improve it.

25. What is the value stream? How does a value stream map differ from an ordinary process map?

26. Develop a value stream map for the process you flowcharted in Question 24 to identify the value-added and non-value-added activities. How can you estimate costs and/or revenue for the process steps?

27. What types of issues must operations managers consider in making technology selection decisions?

28. What issues must managers consider in planning to implement process designs?

29. Provide some examples of strategies to improve process designs.

30. Explain how process and value stream maps can be used for improvement.

31. What is reengineering? How does it differ from other approaches to process improvement?

32. Define utilization and explain how it is computed. Why is understanding utilization important to operations managers?

33. What is a bottleneck? How can you identify the bottleneck in a process?

34. What is a queue? What elements do all queuing systems have in common?

35. What types of queuing configurations are most prevalent in manufacturing and service systems? What factors should managers consider in selecting the right configuration?

36. Describe the principal types of performance measures used in evaluating queuing systems.

37. Explain Little's Law and provide some examples of its application different from those in the text.

38. How can Little's Law be used to do a rough-cut analysis of average flow times and inventory levels in a value chain?

39. Draw a diagram similar to one in Solved Problem #4 showing the flow times for each stage in the ATM value chain episode described at the beginning of this chapter. Comment on how the customer might view the situation differently from management.

PROBLEMS AND ACTIVITIES

1. Design a process for the following activities:
   a. preparing for an exam
   b. writing a term paper
   c. planning a vacation
   d. making breakfast for your family
   e. washing your car

2. Select a service process and draw the flowchart using no more than 20 boxes, triangles, and so on, and draw the line of customer visibility. The service process can be based on your work experience, such as in accounting or human resource management, or a familiar process such as a fast service automobile oil change, buying an automobile, getting a telephone installed in your home or apartment, ordering a home delivery pizza, and using the Internet. (If a facility layout helps explain the overall service design, then include the layout.)
   a. Identify two key customer contact points in your flowchart and briefly describe how value is created at these points, possible service upsets and failures, and how management might mistake-proof these potential failure points.
   b. Describe the process in terms of value utilities, contact technologies, low and high customer contact, servicescape, and process moments of trust (maximum of one page).
   c. Are there any non-value-added steps in the process? If yes, explain. If no, justify. If not sure, explain.
   d. What process performance measures do you recommend? Define each.
   e. Give two recommendations to improve process performance.

3. A telephone call center uses three customer service representatives (CSRs) during the 8:30 A.M. to 9:00 A.M. time period. The standard service rate is 3.0 minutes per telephone call per CSR. Assuming a target labor utilization rate of 80 percent, how many calls can these three CSRs handle during this half-hour period?

4. A water resources consulting firm has three senior designers. Two of the designers have a master's degree in engineering and the other a bachelor's degree in engineering and a Ph.D. in waste management.

They travel to potential and existing water resource sites and plants to define technical projects and survey sites. Currently, the firm has 20 projects per year and each senior designer can handle 6 projects per year. What is the current labor utilization of the senior designers? What do you recommend?

5. What is the implied service rate at a bank teller window if customer demand is 18 customers per hour, two bank tellers are on duty, and their labor utilization is 90 percent?

6. How many automobile repair service counter technicians should be on duty at Greyhound's Auto Mall from 8 A.M. to noon if total demand during this time period is 28 customers, the service rate is 8 customers per hour, and the target utilization is 85 percent? How many service technicians do you recommend? Explain your answer.

7. An accounts payable manager processes 500 checks per day with an average processing time of 20 working days. What is the average number of accounts payable checks being processed in her office? What if through information technology she reduces the processing time from 20 to 5 days? What are the advantages and disadvantages of adopting this technology? Explain.

8. A manufacturer's average work-in-process inventory for Part #2934 is 1,000 parts. The workstation produces parts at the rate of 200 parts per day. What is the average time a part spends in this workstation?

9. Paris Health Clinic, located in a large city, sees patients on a walk-in basis only. On average, 10 patients per hour enter the clinic. All patients register at the registration window with a registration clerk (RC), which takes 3 minutes. After registration, but before being seen by a nurse practitioner (NP), the registration records clerk (RRC) pulls the patient's records from the records room, which takes 6 minutes. At his or her turn, each patient then sees a NP, who checks weight, temperature, and blood pressure. This work activity takes 5 minutes. The NP determines if the patient must see a doctor (MD) or can be handled by a Physician's Assistant (PA). There is one MD, one PA, one NP, one RRC, one BC, and one RC in the system at the current time.

The NP sends 40 percent of the patients to the PA and 60 percent to the MD. The PA takes on average 6 minutes per patient whereas the MD takes 15 minutes. After the patient sees the PA and/or MD, the patient pays the bill or processes insurance information with the billing clerk (BC), which takes 5 minutes per patient. Then the patient exits the process.

a. Draw a process flow diagram, label everything, and place the times and percentages given in the problem on the diagram.

b. What is the throughput in patients per hour of each stage in the process?

c. What are the labor utilization rates for the MD, NP, PA, BC, RRC, and RC? Are these values appropriate? If not, how might you redesign the process? Where is the bottleneck?

d. The PA often discovers the patient should see a MD so the patient is sent to the MD after seeing the PA 50 percent of the time. How does this change affect your answers to the preceding questions?

10. In the Paris Health Clinic situation from Problem 9, suppose that the costs of labor are MD @ $200 per hour, PA @ $50 per hour, NP @ $30 per hour, RC and BC @ $20 per hour, and RRC @ $10 per hour. The cost of a patient waiting for service is assumed to be $20 per hour.

a. What is the cost of value-adding and non-value-adding work activities in this process?

b. Draw a value stream map for this process. What do you conclude?

[*Note:* The average waiting line (queue) in front of each labor resource—MD, PA, NP, BC, RRC, and RC—can be computed using Little's Law where if WIP is greater than 1 then the difference of WIP − 1 represents the number of patients on average waiting in a queue. This assumes one employee per workstation that is always serving one patient. Also, if the average patients waiting in a queue is, say, 0.75 then this means three-quarters of a patient on average is waiting per time unit—in this case per hour.]

11. The Wilcox Student Health Center has just implemented a new computer system and service process to "improve efficiency". As pharmacy manager, you are concerned about waiting time and its potential impact on college students who "get no respect." All prescriptions (Rxs) go through the following process:

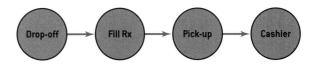

Assume that students arrive to drop-off Rxs at a steady rate of 2 Rxs per minute, with an average of one Rx per student. The average number of students in process (assume waiting and being serviced) at each station is:

Drop-off—5 students

Pick-up—3 students

Pay cashier—6 students

The fill Rx station typically has 40 Rxs in process and waiting on average. Because of this perceived long wait, 95% of the students decide to come back later for pick-up. They come back an average of 3 hours later. If the students choose to stay, their name is called as soon as the Rx is filled and they then enter the pick-up line. Assume that the system is operating at a steady state.

a. Draw a flow diagram for the entire process. Be sure to include flow paths for students (solid lines) and prescriptions (dashed lines).

b. What is the average time a student spends in the pharmacy if they stay to pick up their Rx? You may want to use the worksheet below.

c. How many minutes does the student spend in the pharmacy if they pick up 3 hours later (i.e., they go home after dropping the Rx off)?

d. What is the average time in minutes that all students spend in the pharmacy?

e. What is the average time in minutes that the Rx spends in the process? Count time from entering the drop-off line to completing payment.

WIP = R × T	Drop-off Work Station	Fill Rx Work Station	Pick-up Work Station	Cashier Work Station
Inventory (WIP)				
Throughput Rate (R)				
Flow Time (T)				

CASES

JANSON MEDICAL CLINIC

The Janson Medical Clinic recently conducted a patient satisfaction survey of 100 patients. Using a scale of 1–5, with 1 being "very dissatisfied" and 5 being "very satis-fied," the clinic compiled a check sheet for responses that were either 1 or 2, indicating dissatisfaction with the performance attributes. This is shown in Exhibit 7.22.

Exhibit 7.22
Results of Satisfaction Survey

Making an Appointment

Ease of getting through on the phone—10
Friendliness of the telephone receptionist—5
Convenience of office hours—7
Ease of getting a convenient appointment—12

Check-in/Check-out

Courtesy and helpfulness of the receptionist—7
Amount of time to register—1
Length of wait to see a physician—13
Comfort of registration waiting area—4

Care and Treatment

Respect shown by nurses/assistants—0
Responsiveness to phone calls related to care—5
How well the physician listened—3
Respect shown by the physician—2
Confidence in the physician's ability—1
Explanation of medical condition and treatment—2

Doctors have extremely busy schedules. They have surgeries to perform, and many are teaching faculty at the local medical school. Many surgeries are emergencies or take longer than expected, resulting in delays of getting back to the clinic. In the clinic, one or two telephone receptionists answer calls for three different departments, which include 20 or more doctors. Their job is basically to schedule appointments, provide directions, and transfer calls to the proper secretaries. This generally requires putting the patient on hold. Often, the receptionist must take a hand-written message and personally deliver it to the secretary because the secretary's phone line is busy. However, the receptionist can-not leave her desk without someone else to cover the phones. A student intern examined the processes for answering phone calls and registering patients. The flowcharts she developed are shown in Exhibits 7.23 and 7.24.

1. What conclusions do you reach from the satisfaction survey results? What implications would this have for a better process design?

2. Propose some process improvements to the flowcharts, and develop redesigned processes along with new flowcharts. How will your suggestions address the sources of dissatisfaction that customers cited?

Exhibit 7.23 Current Process for Answering Phone Calls

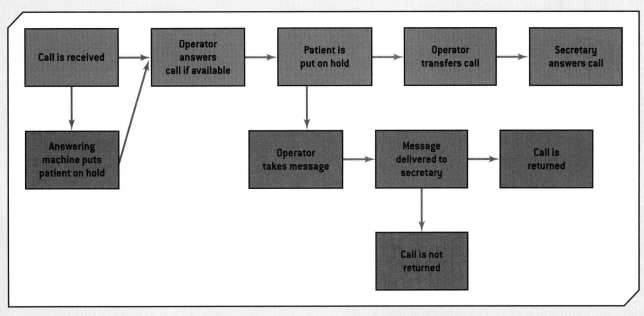

Exhibit 7.24
Current Patient Registration
Process

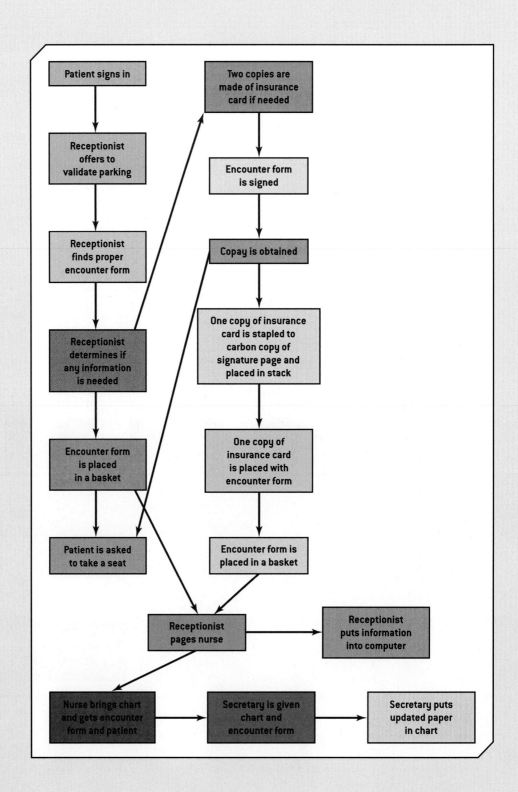

GIFFORD HOSPITAL PHARMACY

Gifford Hospital is trying to reduce costs yet improve patient and medical services. A hospital pharmacy uses two types of medications—fluids such as intravenous liquids and pharmaceuticals such as pills. The pharmacy buys drugs in bulk containers and bottles and dispenses them in smaller unit-dose amounts based on doctor's orders. The objective of the pharmacy is to "get the right drug in the right amount to the right patient at the right time." The consequences of errors in this process ranged from no visible effects on patient health to allergic reactions, or in the extreme case, to death of the patient. National studies on hospital pharmacies found error rates ranging from .01 percent (0.0001) to 15 percent (0.15).

The hospital pharmacy process at Gifford Hospital includes seven major steps:

Step 1—Receive the doctor's patient medication order via a written prescription, over the telephone, or through the hospital Internet system. This step averages 0.2 minutes per prescription and could be done by the medical technician or a legally registered pharmacist.

Step 2—Verify and validate the order through whatever means necessary. For example, if the handwriting was not legible, the doctor must be contacted to verify the medical prescription. Only a registered pharmacist could do this step, which took from 1 to 10 minutes depending on the nature of the prescription and checking out potential problems. Since only 10 percent of prescriptions required extensive verification, the weighted average time for this step is 1.9 minutes [.9 × (1 minute) + .1 × (10 minutes)].

Step 3—Determine if duplicate prescriptions exist, and check the patient's allergic reaction history and current medications. This work activity averages 1.4 minutes using the hospital pharmacy's computer system. Only a registered pharmacist can perform this step.

Step 4—Establish that the drug(s) are in stock, have not expired, and are available in the requested form and quantity. Only a registered pharmacist can perform this step and it takes 1 minute.

Step 5—Prepare the prescription including the label, and attach the proper labels to the proper bottles. Only a registered pharmacist can do this work activity and it averages 4.5 minutes.

Step 6—Store the prescription in the proper place for pickup and delivery to the patient. Only a registered pharmacist can do this step and it takes 1 minute.

Step 7—Prepare all charges, write notes or comments if needed, and close the patient's pharmacy record in the pharmacy computer system. This step takes 2 minutes and may be done by a registered pharmacist but the law does not require it.

Currently, the pharmacist(s) performs steps 2 to 7 for each patient's prescription. Two medical technicians are on duty at all times to receive the prescriptions, answer the telephone, receive supplies and stock shelves, deliver prescriptions through the service window, and interact with nurses and doctors as they visit the pharmacy service window.

You have been called in as a consultant to improve the process. Your first activity is to draw a flowchart, including processing times and capacities for each work activity. As a baseline measure, what is the labor utilization if 32 prescriptions arrive between 8 and 9 A.M. on Monday and five pharmacists are on duty? Are there other ways to organize the process and assign pharmacists to filling prescriptions in the hospital pharmacy? Clearly identify one or two alternative process designs, and discuss in one short paragraph the advantages and disadvantages of each option. What do you recommend?

THE U.S. CENSUS[30]

Every 10 years, the Census Bureau conducts a nationwide census that requires processing of more than 65 million forms from U.S. households, about 60–70 percent of which are returned by mail, the rest being picked up by Census workers and sent by FedEx to processing centers. For the 2000 Census, these forms needed to be turned into digital form—approximately 1.5 billion pages in 100 days. Tractor trailers transport the bulk mail to the processing centers and need to be unloaded. Envelopes with mailed forms must be sorted and need to be opened. To track who has filled them out, bar codes are collected and sent electronically to Census headquarters, where they are checked against a master list of 120 million addresses. Staples must be removed from the forms for scanning. Forms that are torn or dirty must be typed in manually. The scanned page images then need to be analyzed by a computer to read the answers in English or Spanish via optical character recognition. If the characters cannot be read with a high probability of accuracy, the image is sent to teams of people who decide what it says before sending it on electronically. Finally, computers must convert the images to data that are sent each night to Census Bureau headquarters. The paper forms are stored where they will be shredded and recycled.

Suppose that you have been called in as a consultant to help design the processes for handling and converting the Census forms to digital data. Considering the nature of the work that must be accomplished, develop a proposal for a process design that might be used in the processing centers. How would this situation fit in the Product-Process Matrix? What types of technology would you recommend? How might you configure the facility? How would you go about determining the number of people, machines, and computers needed? Summarize your findings and recommendations in a written report.

ENDNOTES

[1] Harrington, H. James, "Looking for a Little Service," *Quality Digest*, May 2000; www.qualitydigest.com.

[2] Gold, Bela, "CAM Sets New Rules for Production," *Harvard Business Review*, November–December 1982, p. 169.

[3] This discussion is adapted from Charles A. Horne, "Product Strategy and the Competitive Advantage," P&IM Review with *APICS News*, 7, no. 12, December 1987, pp. 38–41.

[4] Stratton, Brad, "Editorial Comment: Expanding on Deming's Fourth Point," *Quality Progress*, 27, no. 1, January 1994, p. 5.

[5] Hayes, R. H., and Wheelwright, S. C., "Linking Manufacturing Process and Product Life Cycles," *Harvard Business Review* 57, no. 1, 1979a, pp. 133–140; Hayes, R. H., and Wheelwright, S. C., "The Dynamics of Process-Product Life Cycles," *Harvard Business Review* 57, no. 2, 1979b, pp. 127–136; and Hayes, R. H., and Wheelwright, S. C., *Restoring Our Competitive Edge*, New York: John Wiley & Son, 1984.

[6] Siekman, Philip, "Becton Dickinson Takes a Plunge with Safer Needles," *Fortune*, October 1, 2001, pp. 157–168.

[7] Noori, H., *Managing the Dynamics of New Technology: Issues in Manufacturing Management*, Englewood Cliffs, NJ: Prentice-Hall, 1989.

[8] Collier, D. A., and Meyer, S. M., "A Service Positioning Matrix," *International Journal of Production and Operations Management* 18, no. 12, 1998, pp. 1123–1244.

[9] Collier, D. A., and Meyer, S., "An Empirical Comparison of Service Matrices," *International Journal of Operations and Production Management* 20, no. 5–6, 2000, pp. 705–729.

[10] Silvestro, R., Fitzgerald, L., Johnston, R., and Voss, C., "Towards a Classification of Service Processes," *International Journal of Service Industry Management* 3, no. 3, 1992, pp. 62–75.

[11] "Shoe Buyers Move to Nike Town," *The Columbus Dispatch*, Columbus, Ohio, August 1, 1991, p. 2B.

[12] Collier, D. A., "The Service Sector Revolution: The Automation of Services," *Long Range Planning* 16, December, 1983, pp. 10–20; Collier, D. A. "The Automation of the Goods-Producing Industries: Implications for Operations Managers," *Operations Management Review*, Spring, 1983, pp. 7–12.

[13] Scott, Kelly, "How Federal Express Delivers Customer Service," *APICS—The Performance Advantage*, November 1999, pp. 44–46.

[14] Collier, David A., *The Service/Quality Solution*, copublished by Irwin Professional Publishing, Burr Ridge, Illinois, and American Society of Quality, ASQ Quality Press, Milwaukee, Wisconsin, 1994, p. 115.

[15] Duray, Rebecca, and Milligan, Glenn W., "Improving Customers Satisfaction Through Mass Customization," *Quality Progress*, August 1999, pp. 60–66.

[16] See Heiser, Daniel R., and Schikora, Paul, "Flowcharting with Excel," *Quality Management Journal* 8, no. 3, 2001, pp. 26–35.

[17] Collier, David A., *The Service/Quality Solution*, copublished by Irwin Professional Publishing, Burr Ridge, Illinois, and American Society of Quality, ASQ Quality Press, Milwaukee, Wisconsin, 1994, p. 120.

[18] "Faster Way to Return Rental Cars," *Wall Street Journal*, June 12, 2003, p. D4.

[19] Adapted from Noerr, John, "Benefits for the Back Office, Too," *Business Week*, July 10, 1989, p. 59.

[20] Rucker, Rochelle, "Six Sigma at Citibank," www.insidequality.wego.net.

[21] Adapted from Kirscht, Dwight, and Tunnell, Jennifer M., "Boise Cascade Stakes a Claim on Quality," *Quality Progress* 26, no. 11, November 1993, pp. 91–96.

[22] Hammer, Michael, and Champy, James, *Reengineering the Corporation*, New York: HarperBusiness, 1993, pp. 177–178.

[23] Coleman, P. Kay, "Reengineering Pepsi's Road to the 'Right Side Up' Company," *Insights Quarterly* 5, no. 3, Winter 1993, pp. 18–35.

[24] Nolan, R. L., and Croson, D. C., *Creative Destruction: Six Stages for Transforming the Enterprise*, Boston: Harvard Business School Press, 1995.

[25] Goedert, J., "Hospital Realizes Benefits, ROI with Automated Patient Tracking," *Health Data Management*, November 2004, pp. 12, 18.

[26] http://www.cisco.com/warp/public/cc/pd/ibsw/ibdlsw/prodlit/dlsw5_rg.htm, August 8, 2004.

[27] "Oracle 8i Advanced Queuing," *Oracle*, February 1999. Exhibit SC B.1 is based on diagrams in the company paper.

[28] Gibson, Richard, "Merchants Mull the Long and the Short of Lines," *The Wall Street Journal*, September 3, 1998, p. B1.

[29] Little, J. D. C., "A Proof for the Queuing Formula: $L = \lambda W$," *Operations Research*, no. X, 1961, pp. 383–387.

[30] Adapted from information cited in "Census 2000: Turning a Pile of Paper into the USA's Digital Portrait," *USA Today*, March 20, 2000, p. 11A.

Chapter Outline

CHAPTER 8

Facility and Work Design

Learning Objectives

1. To understand different types of layout patterns, how they relate to process choice, and some of the methods of evaluating alternative layout plans.

2. To understand the key issues involved in designing product layouts and balancing assembly lines to enable efficient and economical production of goods and services.

3. To understand the major issues involved in designing process layouts, and to be able to apply simple tools to develop a good process layout design.

4. To understand the issues that operations managers must address in designing individual workstations to meet productivity, quality, and employee safety requirements.

5. To understand the importance of addressing the social and environmental aspects of work in designing jobs and team-based processes to enhance employee motivation and satisfaction.

- "You mean I have to register on the first floor, then go to the fourth floor for my X-ray, then back down to the third floor for blood and urine tests, then I get to see a doctor on the second floor! Oh! Where do I pay the bill?" remarked Bill Barlow as he held his arm that was injured. Mercy Franklin Hospital is a 100-year-old, 160-bed hospital that prides itself on great medical care and service to its community and patients. The hospital performs over 8,000 operating room procedures, handles 29,600 emergency room visits, 15,000 ambulatory procedures, and over 1 million laboratory tests, and delivers 2,200 babies and admits over 12,000 patients each year. The facility is organized into 11 medical wards and 8 support functions, but the old building was a patchwork of building additions and hallways, and the facility layout was slowing down patient flow, increasing wait times, and resulting in more and more patient complaints. It was not unusual for a patient to get totally lost in the hospital. Only the seriously injured or sick were taken around the hospital by a medical aid in a wheelchair or rolling bed. A project team was assembled by the director of hospital operations to determine how to improve facility layout, patient flow, and service. The team studied patients' flow patterns, identified repetitive patient routes through the hospital, and suggested changes in the location of several medical wards. They also moved all information-intensive offices needed by patients, such as admissions and billing, to the first floor. However, the team concluded that the hospital needed a new building to develop a facility layout that supports patient flow and hospital efficiency.

Digital Vision

- The new plant manager from a major European automaker, Stephan Junger, was meeting with his staff and engineers to discuss the design of a new plant in the United States. "This is our first venture in the U.S. Although labor rates are much higher than in Mexico or Asia, we needed closer proximity to our customers and U.S. suppliers. To compete with Japanese firms, we must lower costs. One way we can do this is to have frequent deliveries of small quantities of parts from our suppliers similar to the way Toyota does. This means that we have to make sure that we design the factory to be as efficient as possible." "Our factories are very efficient!" exclaimed Walter Denk, one of the engineers. Junger replied, "But our factories in Europe rely on storing a lot of materials and parts. I'm afraid that we might get into a real mess trying to incorporate a new process into our traditional facilities design." He suggested taking a benchmarking trip to visit similar factories in the United States and Japan. "These companies design their factories quite differently than we have in the past. We need to understand how their facility layouts support a more responsive and agile environment and improve the flow of materials and assemblies through our processes."

- Professor Frey had just taken his operations management class on a tour of Honda's automobile plant in Marysville, Ohio. During the tour, the students had a chance to see how the facility design helped to improve the efficiency of the assembly processes for the automobiles and motorcycles they manufacture. The students were also very impressed with the level of teamwork among the employees. In the following class debriefing, Steve stated that he didn't realize how important the design of the facility was in promoting teamwork and assuring quality. Arun couldn't believe that they could produce so many different models in any order on the same assembly lines. Kate observed that the entire facility shows an image of safety, efficiency, professionalism, cleanliness, quality, and excitement. "In the factory, everything has its correct place. The workers know where everything is. The facility is spotless, a lot different from my dad's machine shop." Without hesitation she said, "Wow, I think I'll buy a Honda!"

KIN CHEUNG/Reuters/Landov

Discussion Questions: Think of a facility in which you have conducted business—for instance, a restaurant, bank, or automobile dealership. How did the physical environment and layout enhance or degrade your customer experience? How important do you think that good workplace organization and cleanliness are to operations effectiveness? Do you believe that these characteristics might have a positive influence on worker morale and motivation?

This chapter addresses the next level of design decisions for value chains. Once processes are selected and designed, organizations must design the infrastructure to implement these processes. This is accomplished through the design of the physical facilities and work tasks that must be performed. Facility and work design are important elements of an organization's infrastructure and key strategic decisions that affect cost, productivity, and responsiveness. In many organizations, facility changes have been made over long periods of time without a comprehensive plan or understanding of how they support operational effectiveness or, as in the first episode, medical care and patient services.

In both goods-producing and service-providing organizations, facility layout and work design influence the ability to meet customer wants and needs and provide value. A poorly designed facility can lock management into a noncompetitive situation and be very costly to correct. For many service organizations, the physical facility is a vital part of service design, as we discussed in Chapter 6. It can also play a significant role in creating a satisfying customer experience, particularly when customer contact is high, as the first episode suggests. Washington Mutual Inc. recognized the importance of its facility layout so much that it actually patented its designs for branch banks. The patent governs such things as the kiosks where tellers stand, the circular layout of the branches, and the design and location of the "concierge" desks and children's play areas.[1]

The last two episodes suggest that the physical design of a factory needs to support operations as efficiently as possible. Mercedes-Benz located a new factory in the late 1990s in Vance, Alabama to produce its first sport-utility vehicle. One top Mercedes manager decided to adapt the best operating techniques of other companies so he hired managers from Chrysler, Ford, Mitsubishi, and Sony. But their varied backgrounds sparked lengthy debates about the facility, process, and job design. They spent many weeks hashing out a factory layout. German engineers wanted a sprawling E-shaped building with departments linked by complex conveyors. But after endless wrangling—and a break for turkey dinner—those with Japanese experience prevailed, and the group settled on a compact, rectangular factory layout.[2]

Honda of America considers its factory tours one of its best advertisements. Even though people touring the factory are not experts in facility design, process flow, and work design, they get a sense of the extraordinary efficiency and effectiveness of this world-class factory, and it suggests that high-quality products require high-quality processes.

We introduced some of the issues of good facility design in a service context in Chapter 6 in the discussion of LensCrafters and Courtyard by Marriott. Facility design is a critical factor in designing an appealing and effective servicescape. For example, many automobile dealerships have redesigned their showrooms and service departments to better accommodate the customer. Examples include adding playrooms for kids within eyesight of Mom and Dad in showrooms and service facilities that a customer can drive into and be greeted by a service representative without having to walk outside in bad weather.

In this chapter, we examine the topic of facility and work design in both goods-producing and service-providing organizations in more detail. Thus, the key objectives of facility layout are to minimize costs and maximize customer value. Key questions that organizations need to consider are: How should the facility be designed? How should materials, semifinished goods, people, and information flow through the facility? How should we group and locate service equipment, machines, departments, and offices within the facility? How do we design assembly lines for peak efficiency? How do we design jobs for individuals and teams that work well with the facility design to provide the highest levels of efficiency and quality?

Learning Objective
To understand different types of layout patterns, how they relate to process choice, and some of the methods of evaluating alternative layout plans.

Facility layout *refers to the specific arrangement of physical facilities.*

FACILITY LAYOUT

Facility layout *refers to the specific arrangement of physical facilities.* Facility layout studies are necessary whenever (1) a new facility is constructed, (2) there is a significant change in demand or throughput volume, (3) a new good or service is introduced to the customer benefit package, or (4) different processes, equipment, and/or technology are installed. The purposes of layout studies are to minimize delays in materials handling and customer movement, maintain flexibility, use labor and space effectively, promote high employee morale and customer satisfaction, provide for good housekeeping and maintenance, and enhance sales as appropriate in manufacturing and service facilities. Essentially, a good layout should support the ability of operations to accomplish its mission. If the facility layout is flawed in some way, process efficiency and effectiveness suffer. In manufacturing, facility layout is generally unique, and changes can be accomplished without much difficulty. For service firms, however, the facility layout is often duplicated in hundreds or thousands of sites. This makes it extremely important that the layout be designed properly, as changes can be extremely costly.

Layout Patterns

Four major layout patterns are commonly used in designing buildings and processes: product layout, process layout, group layout, and fixed position layout.

PRODUCT LAYOUT

*A **product layout** is an arrangement based on the sequence of operations that are performed during the manufacturing of a good or delivery of a service.* Product layouts support a smooth and logical flow where all goods or services move in a continuous path from one process stage to the next using the same sequence of work tasks and activities. Continuous-flow, mass-production, and flow shop processes are usually physically organized by product layout. One industry that uses a product-layout pattern is the winemaking industry (see Exhibit 8.1). Because all goods move in the same direction, product layouts provide an efficient flow of production and enable the use of specialized handling equipment. Other examples include credit card processing, Subway sandwich shops, paper manufacturers, insurance policy processing, and automobile assembly lines.

*A **product layout** is an arrangement based on the sequence of operations that are performed during the manufacturing of a good or delivery of a service.*

© Getty Images/PhotoDisc

Advantages of product layouts include lower work-in-process inventories, shorter processing times, less material handling, lower labor skills, and simple planning and control systems. However, several disadvantages are associated with product layouts. For instance, a breakdown of one piece of equipment can cause the entire process to shut down. In addition, since the layout is determined by the good or service, a change in product design or the introduction of new products may require major changes in the layout; thus flexibility can be limited. Therefore, product layouts are less flexible and are expensive to change. Finally, and perhaps most important, the jobs in a product-layout facility, such as those on a mass-production line, may provide little job satisfaction. This is primarily because of the high level of division of labor often required, which usually results in monotony.

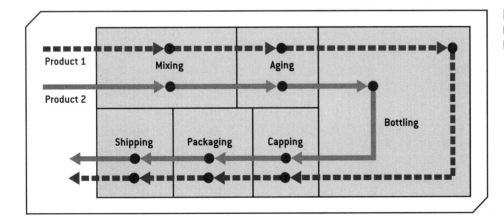

Exhibit 8.1
Product Layout for Wine Manufacturer

PROCESS LAYOUT

A **process layout** *consists of a functional grouping of equipment or activities that do similar work.*

A **process layout** *consists of a functional grouping of equipment or activities that do similar work.* For example, all drill presses or fax machines may be grouped together in one department and all milling or data entry machines in another. Depending on the processing they require, tasks may be moved in different sequences among departments (see Exhibit 8.2). Job shops are an example of firms that use process layouts to provide flexibility in the products that can be made and the utilization of equipment and labor. Legal offices, shoe manufacturing, jet engine turbine blade manufacturing, and hospitals use a process layout.

Compared to product layouts, process layouts generally require a lower investment in equipment. In addition, the equipment in a process layout is normally more general purpose whereas it is more specialized in a product layout. Also, the diversity of jobs inherent in a process layout can lead to increased worker satisfaction. Some of the limitations of process layouts are

- high movement and transportation costs, primarily because goods, paper, and people must be moved frequently between departments;
- more complicated planning and control systems, because jobs do not always flow in the same direction or require the same work tasks;
- longer total processing time, because of increased handling between departments; higher in-process inventory or waiting time, since jobs from several departments may arrive and wait at a particular department; and
- higher worker skill requirements, since workers must be able to handle the processing requirements for different orders.

CELLULAR LAYOUT

Process layouts, which dominate job shop facilities, result in a large number of setups for different jobs, as well as high handling costs and high work-in-process inventory or waiting times. Mass-production systems, on the other hand, have few setups and lower handling and work-in-process costs, since all parts go through the same sequence of work activities. In a cellular layout, the design is not according to the functional characteristics of equipment, but rather by self-contained groups of equipment (called *cells*) needed for producing a particular set of goods or services. The cellular concept was developed at the Toyota Motor Company.

An example of a manufacturing cell is shown in Exhibit 8.3. In this exhibit we see a U-shaped arrangement of machines that is typical of cellular manufacturing. The cell looks similar to a product layout, but operates differently. Within the cell, materials move clockwise or counter-clockwise from one machine to the next. The cell is designed to operate with one, two, or three employees, depending on the needed output during the day (the second figure in Exhibit 8.3 shows how two operators might be assigned to machines). Each of the machines are single-cycle automatics, so the operators unload, check the parts, load another part, and press

Exhibit 8.2

Process Layout for a Machine Shop

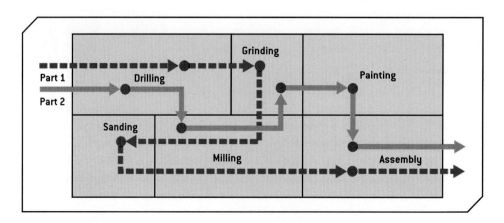

Exhibit 8.3 Cellular Manufacturing Layout

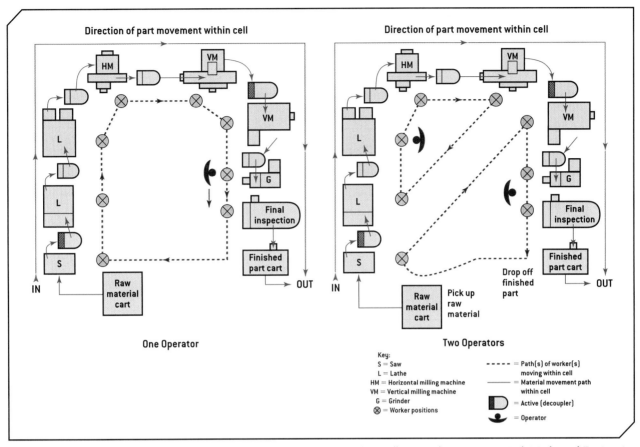

Source: J. T. Black, "Cellular Manufacturing Systems Reduce Set Up Time, Make Small-Lot Production Economical." *Industrial Engineering Magazine*, Nov. 1983. Used with permission from the author.

the start button. They pass the work along to the next worker using decoupler elements placed between the machines.

Since the workflow is standardized and centrally located in a cellular layout, materials-handling requirements are reduced, enabling workers to concentrate on production rather than on moving parts between machines. Quicker response to quality problems within cells can improve the overall level of quality. Since machines are closely linked within a cell, additional floor space becomes available for other productive uses. Because workers have greater responsibility in a cellular manufacturing system, they become more aware of their contribution to the final product; this increases their morale and satisfaction and ultimately, quality and productivity.

GROUP LAYOUT

In many situations, several different parts are very similar to each other in terms of the processing operations that are required. **Group technology** *classifies parts into families so that efficient mass-production-type layouts can be designed for the production of goods or services.* To better understand the group-technology concept, consider a facility that produces two families of parts (Exhibit 8.4). Parts in the first group are cylindrical and require operations on a lathe, a milling machine, and a drilling machine. Parts in the second group are rectangular and require shearing, milling, and drilling. The traditional process layout shown in Exhibit 8.5 places shearing machines, lathes, milling machines, and drilling machines in separate departments. As parts from each family pass through milling and drilling departments in batches, new setups on the machines must be performed. The group concept

Group technology *classifies parts into families so that efficient mass-production-type layouts can be designed for the production of goods or services.*

establishes a separate machine group consisting of milling and drilling machines for each part family (Exhibit 8.6).

Since part families have similar features, retooling is much easier; hence setup times are reduced, and the system operates in the fashion of a production line. An

Exhibit 8.4
Two Part Families

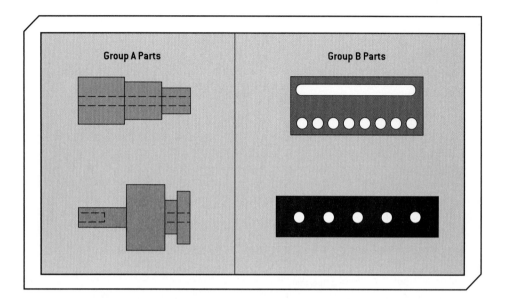

Exhibit 8.5
Process Layout Without Part Families

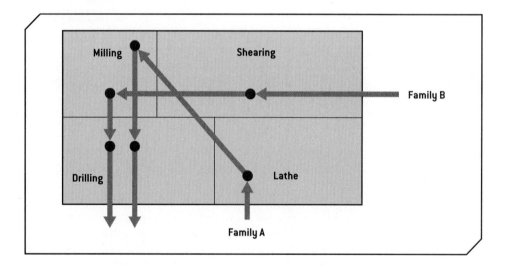

Exhibit 8.6
Group Layout Based on Part Families

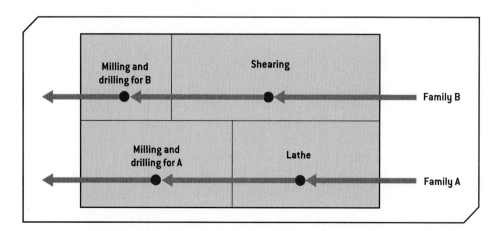

example at Rockwell's Dallas plant illustrates the improvements that can result from cellular manufacturing (see OM Spotlight on Rockwell).

Services also group work similarly to manufacturers such as legal (labor law, bankruptcy, divorce, etc.) or medical specialties (maternity, oncology, surgery, etc.). Small, mid, and large capitalization stock funds and different types of bond funds such as municipal, corporate, and federal govenent bonds are other examples of service firms grouping work by people specialty and software expertise. A family of legal, financial, or medical specialties is analogous to families of manufactured parts. In both goods-producing and service-providing firms, group layouts are used to centralize people expertise and equipment capability.

OM SPOTLIGHT

Rockwell International[3]

A group layout design at Rockwell reduced flow (processing) time by almost 90 percent. Before the new approach was implemented at Rockwell's Dallas plant, its job-shop arrangement was that pictured in Exhibit 8.7. The numbers in the squares indicate the sequence of moves throughout the shop. For example, raw stock went first to the manual mill, then to degrease, deburr, mechanical assembly, and so on. You can observe from this figure that the movement within the factory was very complex. It took a typical part 23 moves and 17.2 weeks to flow through the fabrication shop prior to assembly. This long lead time forced planners to forecast part requirements and thus created large amounts of in-process inventory. By reviewing all part designs, tooling, and fabrication methods through a group-technology part-family analysis, a cell was created that allowed parts to be made with only 9 moves in 2.2 weeks; see Exhibit 8.8. The product movement was simplified considerably. The impact on cost was substantial, but the major impact was on planning. The planner did not have to predict parts requirements; instead, it was possible to make parts in the fabrication shop fast enough that assembly could be supported without inventory buildup.

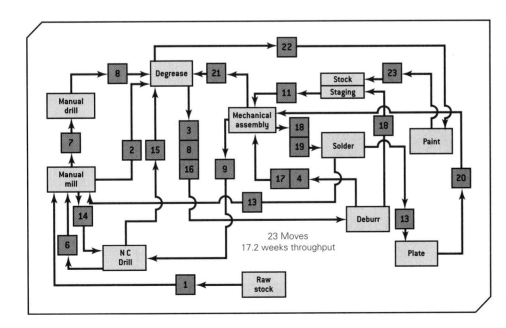

Exhibit 8.7
Process (Job Shop) Layout at Rockwell's Dallas Factory

Exhibit 8.8
Cellular Layout at Rockwell's
Dallas Factory

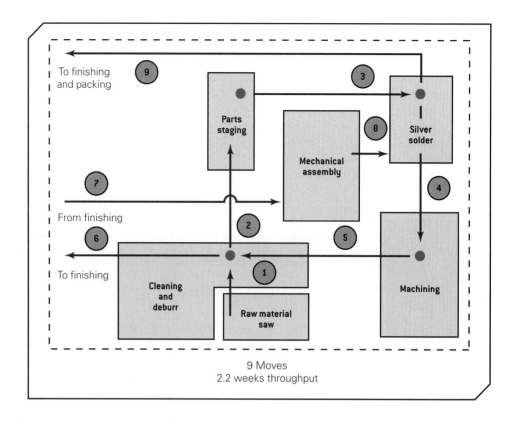

9 Moves
2.2 weeks throughput

FIXED POSITION LAYOUT

A **fixed-position layout**
consolidates the resources
necessary to manufacture a
good or deliver a service,
such as people, materials, and
equipment, in one physical
location.

A **fixed-position layout** *consolidates the resources necessary to manufacture a good or deliver a service, such as people, materials, and equipment, in one physical location.* Rather than moving work-in-process from one work center to another, it remains stationary. The production of large items such as heavy machine tools, airplanes, buildings, locomotives, and ships is usually accomplished in a fixed-position layout. This fixed-position layout is synonymous with the "project" classification of processes presented in Chapter 7. Service-providing firms also use fixed-position layouts; examples include major hardware and software installations, sporting events, and concerts.

Exhibit 8.9 summarizes the relative features of product, process, group, and fixed-position layouts. It is clear that the basic trade-off in selecting among these layout types is flexibility versus productivity. Process layouts offer high flexibility with low productivity, and product layouts have limited flexibility with high productivity. Group layouts are designed to balance the advantages of both types. Fixed-

Exhibit 8.9 Comparison of Basic Layout Patterns

Characteristic	Product Layout	Process Layout	Group Layout	Fixed-Position Layout
Demand volume	High	Low	Moderate	Very low
Equipment utilization	High	Low	Moderate	Moderate
Automation potential	High	Moderate	High	Moderate
Setup/Changover requirements	High	Moderate	Moderate	High
Flexibility	Low	High	Moderate	Moderate
Type of equipment	Highly specialized	General purpose	Moderate specialization	Moderate specialization

position layouts are most productive when all resources are on-site, and offer the flexibility to change as the situation changes.

Materials-Handling Issues

Facility layout is closely linked to materials handling, which occurs in all phases of production and ancillary activities. In the receiving department, materials must be unloaded from trucks and railroad cars and transported to storage or production. During manufacturing itself, materials must be transported between departments, to and from individual workplaces, and to assembly. Finally, the finished products must be packaged and stored for shipping. Once received by warehouses and retail stores, materials-handling procedures and equipment continue to move goods efficiently. Once one knows what needs to be moved and where it has to go, specific materials-handling equipment can be selected. Because materials-handling costs may range from 20 to 60 percent of the total production cost of a manufactured good, it is extremely important that handling be considered in the design of manufacturing systems. Common types of materials-handling systems are described next.

Industrial trucks such as forklifts are the most commonly used type of materials-handling equipment. Their primary function is maneuvering or transporting goods, and they are generally used when material is moved on an infrequent basis, movement occurs between many different locations, loads are mixed in size and weight, and most of the operations involve physical handling.

Fixed-path conveyor systems are more adaptable than industrial trucks to moving a high volume of items. The primary functions of conveyors are transportation and storage, and they are generally used when (1) the route does not vary, (2) continuous movement is required, and (3) automatic sorting, in-process inspection, or in-process storage is required.

Overhead cranes are devices fixed to supporting and guiding rails that are used to move or transfer material between points within an area. They are commonly used in operations where (1) the floor-space utilization or the product characteristics render the use of forklift trucks or conveyors undesirable, (2) travel distances and paths are reasonably restricted, and (3) the products are bulky, large, or heavy, such as engines, turbines, machine tools, and many aerospace components.

Automated storage and retrieval systems are high-technology materials-handling or storage configurations that usually involve computer control, unit loads, and digital computer interface/control. They are becoming increasingly popular because of small floor-space requirements, although the capital investment is usually significant (see OM Spotlight: Ocular Sciences Contact Lenses Distribution Center).

Tractor-trailer systems pull a train of trailers or load-carrying platforms. They offer the advantages of being able to move large volumes of bulky or heavy material over long distances and not tie up lift trucks, which are primarily used for stacking, loading, and unloading.

Automated guided vehicles (AGVs) are computer-controlled, driverless vehicles guided by wires embedded in the shop floor. Such systems are useful in transporting loads over medium to long distances and are more cost-effective than using forklift trucks with skilled operators.

OM SPOTLIGHT

Ocular Sciences Contact Lenses Distribution Center[4]

The Ocular Sciences distribution center shown in Exhibit 8.10 is designed for fast and low-cost retrieval of small manufactured items with minimal product damage. Its business requires shipment of bulk and single-unit orders of contact lenses to wholesalers, retailers, and doctor's offices. The facility design and layout approach is to fit the space around the function and process, not fit the function and process into the space. The warehouse uses a variety of automated materials-handling equipment such as fixed-path conveyor systems and automated storage and retrieval systems. The distribution system uses a sophisticated warehouse management system to provide same-day processing and shipment of orders. The distribution center is adjacent to and integrated with a contact lens factory.

Exhibit 8.10
Ocular Sciences Contact Lenses
Distribution Center[5]

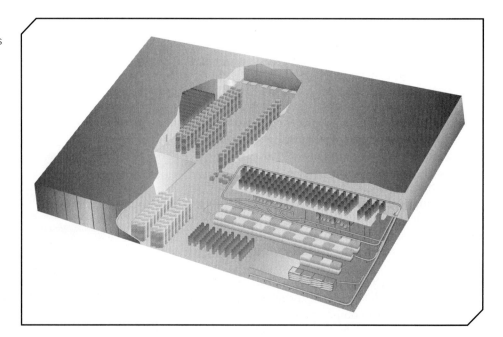

A variety of materials-handling equipment is used throughout a factory or warehouse. In the receiving and shipping activities, forklift trucks, cranes, hoists, and portable conveyors are most often used for unloading transport vehicles and moving goods to temporary storage. In storage areas and warehouses, forklift trucks are often used to store and retrieve heavy loads. In more sophisticated, high-volume operations, automated storage and retrieval systems are used. Material movement in assembly-line systems is often accomplished with conveyors. Production lines and facility layout are more effective if materials-handling considerations are integrated into the design. The key is to examine the total cost of manufacturing, not simply the costs of the equipment or parts alone.

Facility Design in Service Organizations

The design of service facilities, such as hospitals, health clubs, and amusement parks, which process customers and information rather than material goods, requires the clever integration of the servicescape, layout, and process design to support service encounters. For example, many retail stores, such as Victoria's Secret, design servicescapes to create excitement for shoppers, including background music and colorful displays. At Victoria's Secret, the layout of a typical store is defined by different zones, each with a certain type of apparel, such as women's sleepwear, intimate apparel, and personal care products. Display case placement in the store is carefully planned. A companion store, Victoria's Secret Perfume, which specializes in fragrances, color cosmetics, skincare, and personal accessories, is often placed next to and connected to a Victoria's Secret store to increase traffic and sales in both stores.

Service organizations use product, process, group, and fixed-position layouts to organize different types of work. For example, looking back at Exhibit 6.14, which shows the typical Lenscrafters facility layout, we see that the customer contact area is arranged in a process layout. In the lab area, however, where lenses are manufactured, a group layout is used.

In service organizations, the basic trade-off between product and process layouts concerns the degree of specialization versus flexibility. Services must consider the volume of demand, range of the types of services offered, degree of personalization of the service, skills of employees, and cost. Those that need the ability to provide a wide variety of services to customers with differing requirements usually use a process layout. For example, libraries place reference materials, serials, and microfilms into separate areas; hospitals group services by function also, such as maternity, oncology, surgery, and X-ray; and insurance companies have office layouts in which claims, underwriting, and filing are individual departments.

Service organizations that provide highly standardized services tend to use product layouts. For example, Exhibit 8.11 shows the layout of the kitchen at a small pizza restaurant that has both dine-in and delivery. Similarly, course registration at a college or university is probably set up in a product layout, since the registration

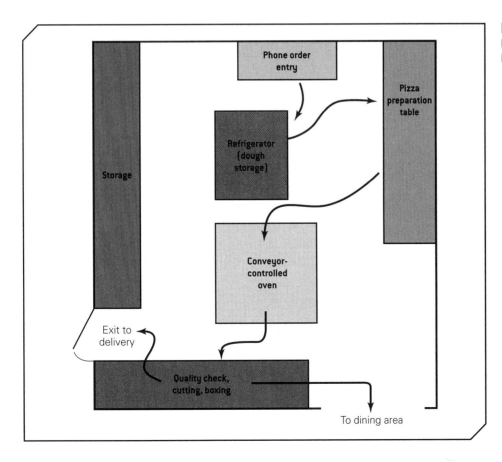

Exhibit 8.11
Product Layout for a Pizza Kitchen

registration process is similar for all students. In general, whenever little variety and personalization of services is offered and the volume of demand is high, a product layout is used.

Group layouts can also be used effectively in service operations. For example, some hospitals are challenging traditional approaches to layout and are redesigning their operations to have a higher focus on patients while also achieving higher levels of quality and efficiency.[6] Rather than shuffling patients back and forth from one functional department to another (radiology, pharmacy, physical therapy, and so on), cellular service units can be created for high-volume routine services. This "hospital-within-a-hospital" concept is supported by multifunctional teams of healthcare providers who care for patients during their entire stay, thus providing greater continuity of care as well as reducing scheduling problems and patient transportation requirements. For example, the establishment of a mini-laboratory for frequent, basic tests within a service unit can produce dramatic decreases in turnaround times.

Learning Objective
To understand the key issues involved in designing product layouts and balancing assembly lines to enable efficient and economical production of goods and services.

Flow-blocking delay *occurs when a work center completes a unit but cannot release it because the in-process storage at the next stage is full.*

Lack-of-work delay *occurs whenever one stage completes work and no units from the previous stage are awaiting processing.*

*An **assembly line** is a product layout dedicated to combining the components of a good or service that has been created previously.*

DESIGNING PRODUCT LAYOUTS

Product layouts in flow shops generally consist of a fixed sequence of workstations. Workstations are generally separated by buffers (queues of work-in-process) to store work waiting for processing and are often linked by gravity conveyors (which cause parts to simply roll to the end and stop) to allow easy transfer of work. An example is shown in Exhibit 8.12. Such product layouts, however, can suffer from two sources of delay: flow-blocking delay, and lack-of-work delay. **Flow-blocking delay** *occurs when a work center completes a unit but cannot release it because the in-process storage at the next stage is full.* The worker must remain idle until storage space becomes available. **Lack-of-work delay** *occurs whenever one stage completes work and no units from the previous stage are awaiting processing.*

These sources of delay can be minimized by attempting to "balance" the process by designing the appropriate level of capacity at each workstation. This is often done by adding additional workstations in parallel. Product layouts might have workstations in series, in parallel, or in a combination of both (Exhibit 8.13). Thus, many different configurations of workstations and buffers are possible, and it is a challenge to design the right one. Analytical techniques such as computer simulation (see Supplementary Chapter D) or waiting-line theory (see Supplementary Chapter B) are often used to support the analyses.

An important type of product layout is an assembly line. *An **assembly line** is a product layout dedicated to combining the components of a good or service that has been created previously.* Assembly lines, pioneered by Henry Ford, are vital to economic prosperity and are the backbone of many industries, such as automobiles and appliances; their efficiencies lower costs and make goods and services affordable

Exhibit 8.12
A Typical Manufacturing Workstation Layout

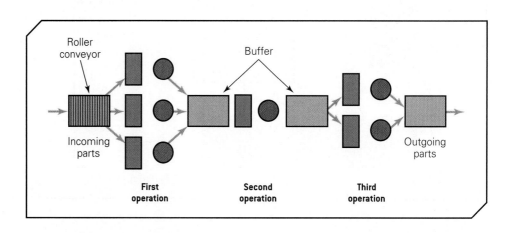

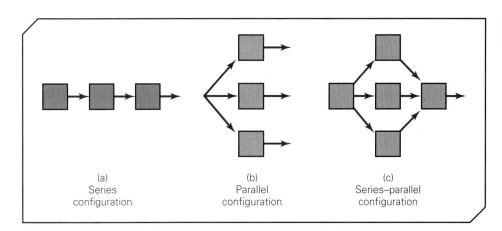

Exhibit 8.13
Product Layout Design Options

(a)
Series
configuration

(b)
Parallel
configuration

(c)
Series–parallel
configuration

to mass markets. Assembly lines are also important in many service operations, such as processing laundry, insurance policies, mail, and financial transactions.

Designing product layouts is a key strategic and tactical issue that requires constant management attention. For example, Japanese automobile manufacturers have revised their strategy to make smaller production runs economical so they can customize their cars to smaller target markets. Such a change in strategy requires a change in process design and layout and reconfiguration of assembly lines (see the OM Spotlight: Toyota and Honda). Making assembly lines efficient is the subject of assembly-line balancing, which we discuss in the next section.

OM SPOTLIGHT

Toyota and Honda[7]

Toyota and Honda are introducing new cars like Vitz, Platz, Fit, Cube, Cruze, and at a rapid pace. These small cars, which are sold mainly in Japan, represent a new era for the auto industry. As *The Wall Street Journal* reports, "The Vitz was cute, roomy, and cheap, starting at just $7,195. It was an instant hit. More important, the Vitz ushered in a new era of car-development strategy. . . . With few high-volume models, the Japanese have learned to make money on niche cars built in small numbers. Doing so requires them to slash the time they spend developing new vehicles and getting them rolling on assembly lines. The shorter lead times, in turn, allow them to pounce on new design trends and respond to ever short-lived spikes in demand."

Honda redesigned its plants so it could build almost any car in any plant. This design and demand flexibility allows it to build many models in smaller production runs than ever before. "It used to take eight months or a year to put a new model in a factory," says the silver haired Mr. Shiraishi. "Now we can make the change in two or three months," he says. However, each time a new car is built the assembly line must be rebalanced. Automotive analysts say that the Japanese firms are about twice as fast at new product development

and redoing the assembly lines as U.S. or European car makers. Japanese assembly plants are using more mixed-model assembly lines and building for small niche markets with production runs per model of only a few hundred thousand cars at a time. This design and demand flexibility allows them to quickly build cars for hot sellers and customize their cars to Japanese, European, and U.S. markets.

ISSEI KATO/Reuters/Landov

Assembly-Line Balancing

The sequence of tasks required to assemble a product is generally dictated by its physical design. Clearly, you cannot put the cap on a ballpoint pen until the ink refill has been inserted. However, for many assemblies that consist of a large number of tasks, there are a large number of ways to group tasks together into individual workstations while still ensuring the proper sequence of work. **Assembly-line balancing** *is a technique to group tasks among workstations so that each workstation has—in the ideal case—the same amount of work.* For example, if it took 90 seconds per unit to assemble an alarm clock and the work was divided evenly among three workstations, then each workstation would be assigned 30 seconds of work content per unit. Here, there is no idle time per workstation and the output of the first workstation immediately becomes the input to the next workstation. Technically, there is no bottleneck workstation and the flow of clocks through the assembly line is constant and continuous. In reality, this is seldom possible, so the objective is to minimize the imbalance among workstations while trying to achieve a desired output rate. A good balance results in achieving throughput necessary to meet sales commitments and minimize the cost of operations. Typically, one either minimizes the number of workstations for a given production rate or maximizes the production rate for a given number of workstations.

Assembly-line balancing is not just a one-time activity when a new plant or assembly line is designed. As goods and service designs change, companies must rebalance assembly lines. Rebalancing a line requires redesigning jobs and retraining workers and buying new or recalibrating old equipment and may even necessitate a new facilities configuration. Such rebalancing may be necessitated by changes in the desired output rate as customer demand changes (demand flexibility) or changes in the design to meet new customer wants and needs (design flexibility).

To begin, we need to know three types of information:

1. the set of tasks to be performed and the time required to perform each task,
2. the precedence relations among the tasks—that is, the sequence in which tasks must be performed, and
3. the desired output rate or forecast of demand for the assembly line.

The first two can be obtained from an analysis of the design specifications of a good or service. The third is primarily a management policy issue, because management must decide whether to produce exactly to the forecast, overproduce and hold inventory, subcontract, and so on. These issues will be addressed in Chapter 13.

To illustrate the issues associated with assembly line balancing, let us consider an activity consisting of three tasks as shown in Exhibit 8.14. Task A is first, takes 0.5 minute, and must be completed before task B can be performed. After task B, which takes 0.3 minute, is finished, task C can be performed; it takes 0.2 minute. Since all three tasks must be performed to complete one part, the total time required to complete one part is 0.5 + 0.3 + 0.2 = 1.0 minute.

Suppose that one worker performs all three tasks in sequence. In an 8-hour day, the worker could produce (1 part/1.0 min)(60 minutes per hour)(8 hours per day) = 480 parts/day. Hence, the capacity of the process is 480 parts/day.

> **Assembly-line balancing** *is a technique to group tasks among workstations so that each workstation has—in the ideal case—the same amount of work.*

Exhibit 8.14
A Three-Task Assembly Line

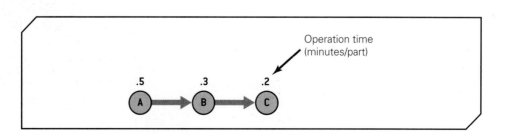

Alternatively, suppose that three workers are assigned to the line, each performing one of the three tasks. The first operator can produce 120 parts per hour, since the task time is 0.5 minute. Thus, a total of (1 part/0.5 min)(60 minutes per hour)(8 hours per day) = 960 parts/day could be sent to operator 2. Since the time operator 2 needs for the operation is only 0.3 minute, operator 2 could produce (1 part/0.3 min)(60 minutes per hour)(8 hours per day) = 1,600 parts/day. However, operator 2 cannot do so because the first operator has a lower production rate. The second operator will be idle some of the time waiting on components to arrive. Even though the third operator can produce (1 part/0.2 min)(60 minutes per hour)(8 hours per day) = 2,400 parts/day, we see that the maximum output of this three-operator assembly line is 960 parts per day. That is, workstation 1 performing task A is the bottleneck in the process.

A third alternative is to use two workstations. The first operator could perform operation A while the second performs operations B and C. Since each operator needs 0.5 minutes to perform the assigned duties, the line is in perfect balance, and 960 parts per day can be produced. We can achieve the same output rate with two operators as we can with three, thus saving labor costs. How you group work tasks and activities into workstations is important in terms of process capacity (throughput), cost, and time to do the work.

An important concept in assembly-line balancing is the cycle time. **Cycle time** *is the interval between successive outputs coming off the assembly line.* These could be manufactured goods or service-related outcomes. In the three-operation example shown in Exhibit 8.14, if we use only one workstation, the cycle time is 1 minute; that is, one completed assembly is produced every minute. If two workstations are used, as just described, the cycle time is 0.5 minute. Finally, if three workstations are used, the cycle time is still 0.5 minute, because task A is the bottleneck, or slowest operation. The line can produce only one assembly every 0.5 minute.

The cycle time (*CT*) cannot be smaller than the largest operation time, nor can it be larger than the sum of all operation times. Thus,

> Maximum operation time ≤ *CT* ≤ Sum of operation times **(8.1)**

This provides a range of feasible cycle times. In the example, *CT* must be between 0.5 and 1.0.

Cycle time is related to the output rate (*R*) by the following equation:

$$CT = A/R \qquad \textbf{(8.2)}$$

where *A* = available time to produce the output. The output rate is normally the demand forecast, adjusted for on-hand inventory if appropriate, or orders released to the factory. Both *A* and *R* must have the same time units (hour, day, week, and so on). Thus, if we specify a required output rate, we can calculate the maximum cycle time needed to achieve it. Note that if the required cycle time is smaller than the largest task time, then the work content must be redefined by splitting some tasks into smaller elements. For example, to produce at least 600 units per 8-hour shift, the cycle time must be no greater than

> (8 hours)(60 minutes/hour)/600 = 0.8 minutes

Thus, either the two- or three-station design must be used.

Alternatively, Equation 8.1 states that *R* = *A/CT*; that is, for a given cycle time, we can determine the output rate that can be achieved. For example, if we use the one-station configuration, then *R* = 480/1.0 = 480 units/shift. If we use either the two- or three-station configurations, then *R* = 480/0.5 = 960 units/shift.

For a given cycle time, we may also compute the theoretical minimum number of workstations required:

> Minimum number of workstations required = Sum of task times/Cycle time
>
> $$= \sum t/CT \qquad \textbf{(8.3)}$$

Cycle time is the interval between successive outputs coming off the assembly line.

When this number is a fraction, the theoretical minimum number of workstations should be rounded up to the next-highest integer number. For example, for a cycle time of 0.5, we would need at least $1.0/0.5 = 2$ workstations.

The following equations provide additional information about the performance of an assembly line:

Total time available = (Number of work stations)(Cycle time) = $N \times CT$ **(8.4)**

Total idle time = $N \times CT - \sum t$ **(8.5)**

Assembly-line efficiency = $\sum t/(N \times CT)$ **(8.6)**

Balance delay = $1 -$ Assembly line efficiency **(8.7)**

The total time available computed by Equation (8.4) represents the total productive capacity that management pays for. Idle time is the difference between total time available and the sum of the actual times for productive tasks, as given by Equation (8.5). Assembly-line efficiency, computed by Equation (8.6), specifies the fraction of available productive capacity that is used. One minus efficiency represents the amount of idle time that results from imbalance among workstations and is called the *balance delay*, as given by Equation (8.7).

In the example, suppose that we use three workstations with $CT = 0.5$. The total time available is $3(0.5) = 1.5$ minutes; total idle time is $1.5 - 1.0 = 0.5$ minutes; and the line efficiency is $1.0/1.5 = 0.67$. If we use two workstations as described earlier, then the line efficiency increases to 1.0, or 100 percent. One objective of assembly-line balancing is to maximize the line efficiency.

Line-Balancing Approaches

Balancing the three-task example in the previous section was quite easy to do by inspection. With a large number of tasks, the number of possible workstation configurations can be very large, making the balancing problem very complex. Decision rules, or heuristics, are used to assign tasks to workstations. Because heuristics cannot guarantee the best solution, one often applies a variety of different rules in an attempt to find a very good solution among several alternatives. For large line-balancing problems, such decision rules are incorporated into computerized algorithms and simulation models.

To illustrate a simple, yet effective, approach to balancing an assembly line, suppose that we are producing an in-line skate as shown in Exhibit 8.15. The target

Exhibit 8.15
A Typical In-Line Skate

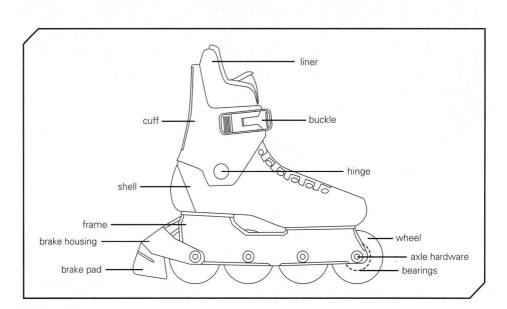

output rate is 360 units per week. The effective workday (assuming one shift) is 7.2 hours, considering breaks and lunch periods. We will assume that the facility operates 5 days per week.

Eight tasks are required to assemble the individual parts. These, along with task times, are

1. assemble wheels, bearings, and axle hardware (2.0 min),
2. assemble brake housing and pad (0.2 min),
3. complete wheel assembly (1.5 min),
4. inspect wheel assembly (0.5 min),
5. assemble boot (3.5 min),
6. join boot and wheel subassemblies (1.0 min),
7. add line and final assembly (0.2 min),
8. perform final inspection (0.5 min).

If we use only one workstation for the entire assembly and assign all tasks to it, the cycle time is 9.4 minutes. Alternatively, if each task is assigned to a unique workstation, the cycle time is 3.5 minutes, the largest task time. Thus, feasible cycle times must be between 3.5 and 9.4 minutes. Given the target output rate of 360 units per week and operating one shift per day for 5 days per week, we can use Equation (8.2) to find the appropriate cycle time:

$$CT = A/R = [(7.2 \text{ hr/shift})(60 \text{ min/hr})]/72 \text{ units/shift/day} = 6.0 \text{ min/unit}$$

The theoretical minimum number of workstations is found using Equation (8.3):

$$\sum t/CT = 9.4/6.0 = 1.57$$

or 2 rounded up.

The eight tasks need not be performed in this exact order; however, it is important to ensure that certain precedence restrictions are met. For example, you cannot perform the wheel assembly (task 3) until both tasks 1 and 2 have been completed, but it does not matter whether task 1 or task 2 is performed first because they are independent of each other. These types of relationships are usually developed through an engineering analysis of the product. We can represent them by an arrow diagram, shown in Exhibit 8.16. The arrows indicate what tasks must precede others. Thus, the arrows pointing from tasks 1 and 2 to task 3 indicate that tasks 1 and 2 must be completed before task 3 is performed; similarly, task 3 must precede task 4. The numbers next to each task represent the task times.

This precedence network helps to visually determine whether a workstation assignment is *feasible*—that is, meets the precedence restrictions. For example, in Exhibit 8.16 we might assign tasks 1, 2, 3, and 4 to one workstation, and tasks 5, 6, 7, and 8 to a second workstation, as illustrated by the shading. This is feasible

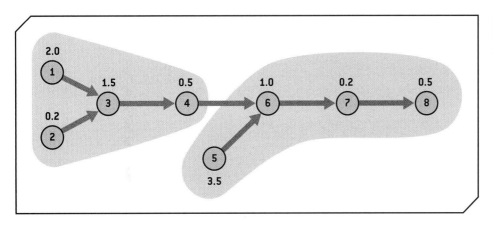

Exhibit 8.16
Precedence Network for In-Line Skate

because all tasks assigned to workstation 1 are completed before those assigned to workstation 2. However, we could not assign tasks 1, 2, 3, 4, and 6 to workstation 1 and tasks 5, 7, and 8 to workstation 2, because operation 5 must precede operation 6.

The problem is to assign the eight work activities to workstations without violating precedences or exceeding the cycle time of 6.0 minutes. One line-balancing decision rule example is to assign the task with the *largest task time first* to a workstation if the cycle time would not be exceeded. The largest-task-time-first decision rule assigns tasks with large task times first, because shorter task times are easier to fit in the line balance later in the procedure. This procedure can be formalized as follows:

1. Choose a set of "assignable tasks"—those for which all immediate predecessors have already been assigned.
2. Assign the assignable task with the *largest* task time first. Break ties by choosing the lowest task number.
3. Construct a new set of assignable candidates. If no further tasks can be assigned, move on to the next workstation. Continue in this way until all tasks have been assigned.

Let us illustrate this with the example. We will call the first workstation "A" and determine which tasks can be assigned. In this case, tasks 1, 2, and 5 are candidates, since they have no immediate predecessors. Using the decision rule—*choose the activity with the largest task time first*—we therefore assign task 5 to workstation A.

Next, we determine a new set of tasks that may be considered for assignment. At this point, we may only choose among tasks 1 and 2 (even though task 5 has been assigned, we cannot consider task 6 as a candidate because task 4 has not yet been assigned to a workstation). Note that we can assign both tasks 1 and 2 to workstation 1 without violating the cycle-time restriction.

At this point, task 3 becomes the only candidate for assignment. Since the total time for tasks 5, 1, and 2 is 5.7 minutes, we cannot assign task 3 to station 1 without violating the cycle-time restriction of 6.0 minutes. In this case, we move on to workstation B.

At workstation B, the only candidate we can assign next is task 3. Continuing, we can assign tasks 4, 6, 7, and 8 in that order and still be within the cycle-time limit. Because all tasks have been assigned to a workstation, we are finished. This assembly-line balance is summarized as follows:

Workstation	Tasks	Total Time	Idle Time
A	1, 2, 5	5.7	0.3
B	3, 4, 6, 7, 8	3.7	2.3
	Total	9.4	2.6

Using Equations (8.4) to (8.6), we may compute the following:

$$\text{Total time available} = (\text{Number of workstations})(\text{Cycle time})$$
$$= N \times CT = 2 \times 6 = 12 \text{ minutes}$$

$$\text{Total idle time} = N \times CT - \Sigma t = 2 \times 6 - 9.4 = 2.6 \text{ minutes}$$

$$\text{Assembly-line efficiency} = \Sigma t / N \times CT = 9.4/2 \times 6 = 78.3\%$$

In this example, efficiency is not very high because the precedence relationships constrained the possible line-balancing solutions. The target efficiency for most assembly lines is 80% to 90%, but this is highly dependent on things like the degree of automation, inspection stations, workforce skills, complexity of the assembly, and so on. One option is to redefine the work content for the assembly task in more detail, if this is possible, by breaking down the tasks into smaller elements with smaller task times and rebalancing the line, hoping to achieve a higher efficiency.

In the real world, assembly-line balancing is quite complicated, because of the size of practical problems as well as constraints that mechanization or tooling place on work tasks. Also, in today's manufacturing plants, there is virtually no such thing as a single-model assembly line. In the automotive industry, many model combinations and work assignments exist. Such mixed-model assembly-line-balancing problems are considerably more difficult to solve. Simulation modeling is frequently used to obtain a "best set" of assembly-line-balancing solutions and then engineers, operations managers, and suppliers evaluate and critique these solutions to find the best design.

DESIGNING PROCESS LAYOUTS

Learning Objective
To understand the major issues involved in designing process layouts, and to be able to apply simple tools to develop a good process layout design.

In designing process layouts, we are concerned with the arrangement of departments or work centers relative to each other. Costs associated with moving materials or the inconvenience that customers might experience in moving between physical locations are usually the principal design criteria for process layouts. In general, work centers with a large number of moves between them should be located close to one another. To provide a quantitative basis for layout analysis, we need to construct a load matrix. A **load matrix** *lists the number of moves from one work center to another over some time period, such as one year.*

*A **load matrix** lists the number of moves from one work center to another over some time period, such as one year.*

We will assume that cost is proportional to distance traveled. Since the distance traveled depends on the layout, we use the following approach:

1. Design a trial layout.
2. Compute the distances between work centers.
3. Multiply interdepartmental distances by the volume of flow between work centers to create a volume-distance matrix; then compute the total cost.
4. Use the volume-distance matrix created in step 3 to propose changes in the current layout. Repeat the process (from step 2) until a satisfactory layout is obtained.

An example of applying this approach follows.

Consider the situation facing Home Video Equipment, Inc. (HVE), a California company that produces video recording equipment. Increasing sales volume and new product lines have necessitated building a new plant to provide more effective distribution to the eastern United States. HVE must determine how the eight departments needed to produce the video recorders should be laid out. Estimated space needed in each department is as follows:

1. Receiving: 1,200 square feet
2. Machining: 1,800 square feet
3. Pressing: 2,400 square feet
4. Cleaning: 600 square feet
5. Plating: 1,200 square feet
6. Painting: 900 square feet
7. Assembly: 2,400 square feet
8. Shipping: 1,500 square feet

Exhibit 8.17 shows the annual number of moves (load matrix) between departments. For example, the number of moves from receiving to machining is 200; the number of moves from painting to assembly is 300; and so on. The table indicates that materials move from receiving to either machining or pressing; from machining to plating, painting, or assembly; and so on. From this information, we can draw a flowchart showing the material movement between departments. Exhibit 8.18

Exhibit 8.17 Volume (Load) Matrix for HVE, Inc.

From	Receiving	Machining	Pressing	Cleaning	Plating	Painting	Assembly	Shipping
Receiving		200	100					
Machining					350	60	20	
Pressing		150		200	100		250	
Cleaning					500		200	
Plating						50	400	
Painting							300	
Assembly								600

shows that the general direction of material flow is from receiving to machining and pressing and then to cleaning, plating, and painting, and finally to assembly and shipping. Using this information, we propose the initial layout shown in Exhibit 8.19. Each block in Exhibit 8.19 represents a 10-feet by 10-feet area. Remember that this layout is just a rough approximation of the relative shapes and sizes of departments. Detailed architectural designs must account for aisles, support pillars, office space, restrooms, and other service facilities. To compute interdepartmental distances, we shall assume that all transportation is between department centers (shown by • in Exhibit 8.19) and along the coordinate axes. That is, if departments A and B are centered at coordinates (x_A, y_A) and (x_B, y_B), respectively, the distance between them is given by Equation (8.8).

$$D_{AB} = |x_A - x_B| + |y_A - y_B| \qquad \textbf{(8.8)}$$

This is most often the case when moving items with trucks along aisles. For this layout, the distance between receiving and storage, whose center is at the point (5.5, 8), and pressing, whose center is at the point (2, 6), is

$$|5.5 - 2| + |8 - 6| = 3.5 + 2 = 5.5$$

Exhibit 8.18
Material Flow for HVE, Inc.

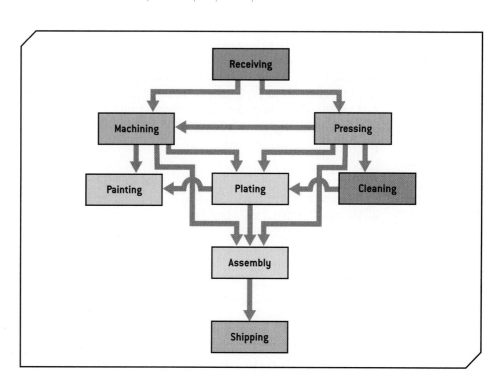

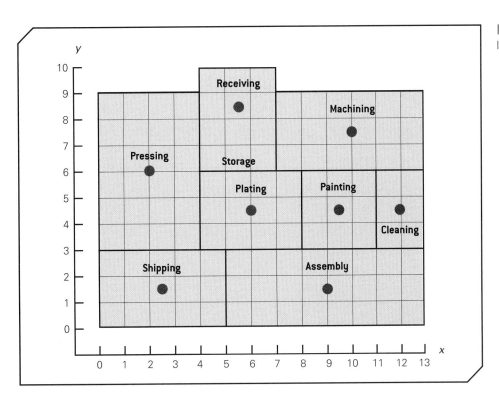

Note that the actual distance is 55 feet because of the scale used. The other interdepartmental distances are computed in a similar fashion. If those distances are multiplied by the volume (load matrix) requirements in Exhibit 8.17, we obtain the volume-distance matrix shown in Exhibit 8.20. For example, multiplying the load between receiving and pressing (100) by the distance between the departments (55) yields a volume-distance figure of 5,500, as shown in Exhibit 8.20. Since cost is assumed to be proportional to distance, the volume moved times the distance moved is a surrogate measure of cost. From this table, we see that the largest costs involve transportation between assembly and shipping, pressing and assembly, and cleaning and plating. The initial layout has other disadvantages. For instance, receiving and shipping are on opposite sides of the building. This can cause a problem if rail is used and might also cause problems in constructing access roads.

A second proposal, which places these departments on the same side of the building, is shown in Exhibit 8.21. You should verify that the total volume-distance for this layout is 214,550, which represents a 15 percent reduction over the initial

Exhibit 8.20 Volume-Distance Matrix for Initial HVE, Inc. Layout

	To							
From	**Receiving**	**Machining**	**Pressing**	**Cleaning**	**Plating**	**Painting**	**Assembly**	**Shipping**
Receiving		10,000	5,500					
Machining					24,500	1,800	1,400	
Pressing		14,250		23,000	5,500		28,750	
Cleaning					30,000		12,000	
Plating						2,000	24,000	
Painting							12,000	
Assembly								39,000

Significant potential for improvement

Total volume-distance = 251,700

Exhibit 8.21
Second Trial Layout for HVE, Inc.

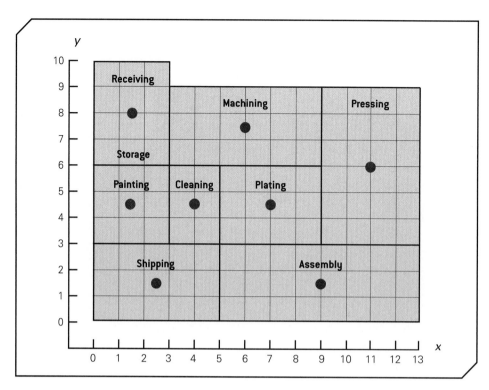

layout. This was gained by moving cleaning adjacent to plating and pressing closer to assembly. However, there is still a high cost involved in moving materials from painting to assembly and from assembly to shipping. In an effort to reduce this cost, a third alternative, shown in Exhibit 8.22, is proposed.

This layout has a total volume-distance requirement of 183,650. The basic shapes of the machining and pressing departments have been altered considerably.

Exhibit 8.22
Third Trial for HVE, Inc.

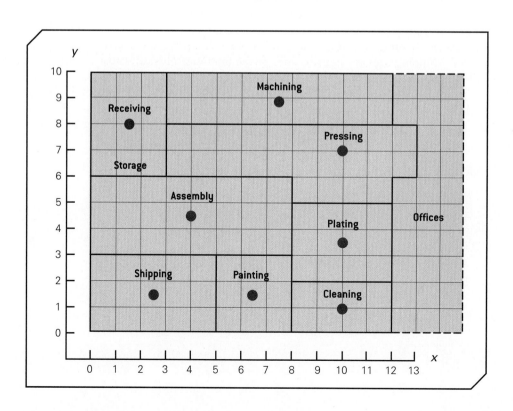

Shape requirements depend on machine sizes and processing requirements to a large extent and must be taken into account prior to a layout analysis. In addition, office space can be provided on the opposite end of the building from shipping and receiving; thus the building can maintain a rectangular shape.

A similar product layout issue is where to locate physical goods within a warehouse. Vytec Corporation, for example, makes vinyl siding and stores it in a warehouse as described in the OM Spotlight.

Process Layout Techniques and Software

The HVE example illustrates that there are a large number of alternative configurations for a process layout. In fact, there are $n!$ possible arrangements of n departments, irrespective of shape. Thus, for the Home Video Equipment example there are $8! = 40,320$ possible arrangements, which makes finding the best possible layout an extremely difficult task. Several software packages have been written expressly for facility layout; some include simulations of the entire factory layout (see OM Spotlight: DaimlerChrysler). These packages have the advantage of being able to search among a much larger number of potential layouts than could possibly be done manually. Despite the capabilities of the computer, no layout program will provide optimal solutions for large, realistic problems. Like many practical solution procedures in management science, they are heuristic; that is, they can help the user to find a very good, but not necessarily the optimal, solution.

One of the most widely used facility-layout programs is CRAFT (Computerized Relative Allocation of Facilities Technique). CRAFT attempts to minimize the total materials-handling cost in a manner similar to the approach used in the HVE example. The user must generate an initial layout and provide data on the volume between departments and the materials-handling costs. CRAFT uses the centroid of each department to compute distances and materials-handling costs for a particular layout. In an effort to improve the current solution, CRAFT exchanges two or three (in later versions, three) departments at a time and determines if the total cost has been reduced. If so, it then uses the new solution as a base for determining new

OM SPOTLIGHT

Vytec Corporation[8]

Vytec (www.vytec.com) is a leading manufacturer of vinyl siding for homes and businesses. It is a subsidiary of Owens Corning, joining them in 1997. Vytec makes 50 different product lines (called profiles) of siding, soffits, and accessories. Each profile is typically produced in 15 colors, creating 750 stock-keeping units. The finished siding is packaged in a carton that holds 20 pieces, usually 12 feet long. The cartons are stacked in steel racks (called beds). Each bed holds 30 to 60 cartons depending on the bed's location in the warehouse. Their main warehouse is more than 200,000 square feet.

Over time, demand for each siding profile changes, and some are added and discontinued. One problem the warehouse faces periodically is the need to redo the location and capacity of beds in the warehouse. Using basic layout principles, high-demand siding profiles are located closest to the shipping dock to minimize travel and order-picking time. Although management would like to find a permanent solution to this stock placement problem in the warehouse, the continuous changes in demand and product mix necessitate a new design every few years.

OM SPOTLIGHT

DaimlerChrysler[9]

DaimlerChrysler embarked on a project to digitize its end-to-end manufacturing operations in an "eight- to nine-figure investment" aimed at reducing production cycles by up to 30 percent. The "digital factory," as it is called, simulates the entire production planning process—from facility drawings to line assembly—"before one brick is put in the ground," said Susan Unger, senior vice president and chief information officer at the automaker. Designers can build virtual assembly lines and see if they fit into digitized versions of old and new Mercedes and Chrysler assembly plants. Digital humans twist and turn to perform their assembly-line duties while the software evaluates their productivity and stress—the way engineers used to do with clipboards in the past. Other benefits anticipated from the digital factory include improved quality and workflows.

potential improvements. Other programs that have been used in facilities layout are ALDEP (Automated Layout-DEsign Program) and CORELAP (COmputerized RElationship LAyout Planning). Rather than using materials-handling costs as the primary solution, the user constructs a preference table that specifies how important it is for two departments to be close to one another. These "closeness ratings" follow:

A   Absolutely necessary
B   Especially important
C   Important
D   Ordinary closeness okay
E   Unimportant
F   Undesirable

The programs attempt to optimize the total closeness rating of the layout. Computer graphics programs are providing a major advance in layout planning. They allow interactive design of layouts in real time and can eliminate some of the disadvantages, such as irregularly shaped departments, that often result from noninteractive computer packages. Graphics programs also allow more details to be incorporated in the process-layout planning effort. Aisles, obstructions, and individual machine arrangement can be considered in interactive graphics programs.

WORKPLACE DESIGN

The techniques we have described address broad layout issues in facilities. However, it is also important to pay serious attention to the design and layout of individual workstations, not only in factories but in every other facility where work is performed, such as offices, restaurants, and retail stores. Clearly, the workplace should allow for maximum efficiency and effectiveness as the work task or activity is performed, but it may also need to facilitate service management skills in high-contact, front-office environments.

Key questions that must be addressed at the workstation level include:

1. Who will use the workplace? Will the workstation be shared? How much space is required? Workplace designs must take into account different physical characteristics of individuals, such as differences in size, arm length, strength, and dexterity.

2. How will the work be performed? What tasks are required? How much time does each task take? How much time is required to set up for the workday or for a particular job? How might the tasks be grouped into work activities most effectively? This includes knowing what information, equipment, items, and procedures are required for each task, work activity, and job.

3. What technology is needed? Employees may need a computer or access to customer records and files, special equipment, intercoms, and other forms of technology.

4. What must the employee be able to see? Employees might need special fixtures for blueprints, test procedures, sorting paper, antiglare computer screens, and so on.

5. What must the employee be able to hear? Employees may need to communicate with others, wear a telephone headset all day, be able to listen for certain sounds during product and laboratory testing, or be able to hear warning sounds of equipment.

6. What environmental and safety issues need to be addressed? What protective clothing or gear should the employee wear?

To illustrate some of these issues, let us consider the design of the pizza preparation table for a pizza restaurant. The objective of a design is to maximize throughput, that is, the number of pizzas that can be made; minimize errors in fulfilling customer orders; and to minimize total flow time and customer waiting and delivery time. In slow demand periods, one or two employees may make the entire pizza. During periods of high demand, such as weekends and holidays, more employees may be needed. The workplace design would need to accommodate this.

An example of a pizza preparation workstation is shown in Exhibit 8.23. Ingredients should be put on the pizzas in the following order: sauce, vegetables (mushrooms, peppers, onions, etc.), cheese, and finally, meat. Since cheese and meat are the highest-cost items and also greatly affect taste and customer satisfaction, the manager requires that those items be weighed to ensure that the proper amounts are included. Exhibit 8.23 shows a design of the workplace for this pizza assembly process. All items are arranged in the order of assembly within easy reach of the employee and, as the front view illustrates, order tickets are hung at eye level, with the most recent orders on the left to ensure that pizzas are prepared on a first-come-first-served basis.

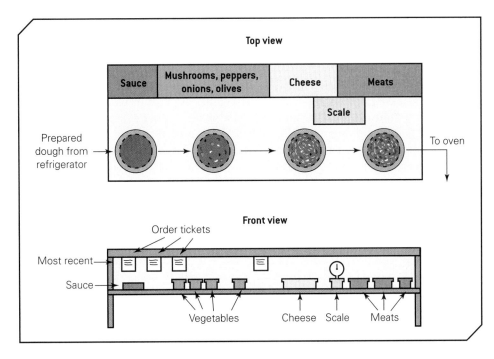

Exhibit 8.23
Pizza Preparation Workplace Design

In office cubicles, e-mails, telephone calls, cell phones, pagers, and the like interrupt office workers so much that some companies have established "information-free zones" within the office. If you work in one of these zones, all of these interruption devices are turned off or blocked from operating so employees can focus on their work. Companies think information-free zones improve employee's attention spans and productivity.

Ergonomics in Workplace Design

Ergonomics developed as a discipline during World War II, when analysts concluded that the death of many pilots was due to their not having mastered the complicated controls of their airplanes. **Ergonomics** *is concerned with improving productivity and safety by designing workplaces, equipment, instruments, computers, workstations, and so on that take into account the physical capabilities of people.* The objective of ergonomics is to reduce fatigue, the cost of training, human errors, the cost of doing the job, and energy requirements while increasing accuracy, speed, reliability, and flexibility. Although ergonomics has traditionally focused on manufacturing workers and service providers, it is also important in designing the servicescape to improve customer interaction in high-contact environments.

Ergonomics is evident in a variety of consumer products such as photocopiers and office workstations. Kodak, for example, employs some 40 ergonomists to assist in the design of cameras and copiers as well as in improving work in its own factories. The windshield-level brake light on the rear of automobiles first required in 1986 model cars resulted from ergonomic analysis that indicated such lights could reduce rear-end collisions by 50 percent.

A primary occupational hazard in industry today is musculoskeletal injury involving constriction of nerves, tendons, and ligaments and inflammation of joints, particularly in the lower back, wrists, and elbows. This injury typically is caused by mismatching human physical abilities and task-performance requirements. Jobs that require heavy lifting, repetition, or the use of improperly designed equipment are common culprits. Such injuries, known as cumulative trauma disorders (CTDs), include lower back pain, carpal tunnel syndrome, tennis elbow, and other forms of tendonitis. CTDs have become a major focus for ergonomists, particularly since the Bureau of Labor Statistics indicates that their reported incidence has more than tripled since the 1980s. Many jobs in the United States today have the potential for CTD. The result may be higher health insurance costs and liability premiums.

Ergonomic studies and proper design of the workplace can reduce or eliminate CTDs. For example, if workpieces or operators have varying heights, an adjustable workbench or floor platform can be used. At Ford Motor Company, a worker who had to assemble a steering column from the outside of the vehicle worked in an extremely bent-over-sideways position that resulted in a lot of pain and lost workdays. The solution was to create an 8-inch pit for the worker to stand in. It allowed him to do the same job at a very slight angle, effectively removing the trauma from the job. Firms such as Federal Express have instituted ergonomic initiatives that significantly reduced carpal tunnel syndrome and other stress-related injuries among its employees.

Safety in Workplace Design

Safety is one of the most important aspects of workplace design, particularly in today's society. To provide safe and healthful working conditions and reduce hazards in the work environment, the Occupational Safety and Health Act (OSHA) was passed in 1970. It requires employers to furnish to each of their employees employment and a place of employment free from recognized hazards that are causing or likely to cause death or serious physical harm. As a result of this

---

Margin note:

Ergonomics *is concerned with improving productivity and safety by designing workplaces, equipment, instruments, computers, workstations, and so on that take into account the physical capabilities of people.*

legislation, the National Institute of Occupational Safety and Health (NIOSH) was formed to enforce standards provided by OSHA. Business and industry must abide by OSHA guidelines or face potential fines and penalties.

Safety is a function of the job, the person performing the job, and the surrounding environment. The job should be designed so that it will be highly unlikely that a worker can injure himself or herself. At the same time, the worker must be educated in the proper use of equipment and the methods designed for performing the job. Finally, the surrounding environment must be conducive to safety. This might include nonslip surfaces, warning signs, or buzzers. Three key safety issues are lighting, temperature and humidity, and noise.

- *Lighting* The type and amount of illumination required depend on the nature of the job. For example, difficult inspection tasks and close assembly work require more light than operating a milling machine or loading crates in a warehouse. The quality characteristics of light vary. Glare, brightness, contrast, and uniformity may contribute to eyestrain and reduce job performance. Those factors should be considered in designing individual workstations as well as offices and factories.

- *Temperature and Humidity* Temperature and humidity affect a person's comfort and can be a very distracting influence. A temperature in the low 60s might be ideal for lifting boxes in overalls and gloves but may chill a typist's fingers. Some jobs require extreme temperatures—for example, meat-packing plants and industrial areas where considerable heat is generated by machinery. Among the alternatives for operations managers in such situations are adjusting the humidity (higher temperatures can be tolerated at lower humidity levels), increasing air circulation in high-temperature areas, limiting exposure through rest periods or job rotation, and simply providing adequate protection.

- *Noise* A third environmental factor that is often a problem is noise. Intense noise over long periods of time can result in impaired hearing. OSHA has set limits on acceptable noise levels and duration. For example, a worker cannot be subject to a 90-decibel noise level for more than 9 hours. Noise protection may require controlling the source of noise, absorbing the sound, increasing the distance from the sound, or providing ear protection. Many companies provide background music as a means of blending random noises and providing a pleasant atmosphere.

WORK AND JOB DESIGN

The physical design of a facility and the workplace can influence significantly how workers perform their jobs and their psychological well-being. Thus, operations managers who design jobs for individual workers need to understand how the physical environment can affect people. *A* **job** *is the set of tasks an individual performs.* **Job design** *involves determining the specific job tasks and responsibilities, the work environment, and the methods by which the tasks will be carried out to meet the goals of operations.*

Two broad objectives must be satisfied in job design. One is to meet the firm's competitive priorities—cost, efficiency, flexibility, quality, and so on; the other is to make the job safe, satisfying, and motivating for the worker. Resolving conflicts between the need for technical and economic efficiency and the need for employee satisfaction is the challenge that faces operations managers in designing jobs. Clearly, efficiency improvements are needed to keep a firm competitive. However,

Learning Objective
To understand the importance of addressing the social and environmental aspects of work in designing jobs and team-based processes to enhance employee motivation and satisfaction.

A **job** *is the set of tasks an individual performs.*

Job design *involves determining the specific job tasks and responsibilities, the work environment, and the methods by which the tasks will be carried out to meet the goals of operations.*

it is also clear that any organization with a large percentage of dissatisfied employees cannot be competitive. What is sought is a job design that provides for high levels of performance and at the same time a satisfying job and work environment.

The Hackman and Oldham model shown in Exhibit 8.24 attempts to explain the motivational properties of job design by tying together the technical and human components of a job. This model is an effective operationalization of formal motivation theories and research studies and has been validated in numerous organizational settings. The model contains four major parts:

1. critical psychological states,
2. core job characteristics,
3. moderating variables,
4. outcomes.

Three critical psychological states drive the model. *Experienced meaningfulness* is the psychological need of workers to feel that their work is a significant contribution to the organization and society. *Experienced responsibility* indicates the need of workers to be accountable for the quality and quantity of their work. *Knowledge of results* implies that all workers feel a need to know how their work is evaluated and what the results of the evaluation are. Affecting the critical psychological states are five core job characteristics:

1. task significance—the degree to which the job gives the participant the feeling that it has a substantial impact on the organization, or the world;
2. task identity—the degree to which the worker can perceive the task as a whole, identifiable piece of work from start to finish;
3. skill variety—the degree to which the job requires the worker to have and to use a variety of skills and talents;

Exhibit 8.24
The Hackman-Oldham Work Design Model

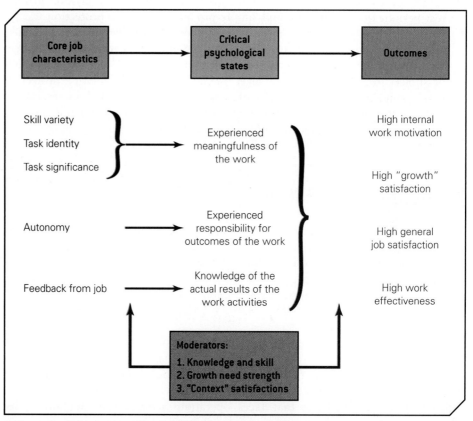

Source: J. Richard Hackman and Greg R. Oldham, *Work Redesign*, 1st edition, (figure 4.6 from p. 90). Characteristics Model © 1980. Reprinted by permission of Pearson Education, Upper Saddle River, NJ.

4. autonomy—the degree to which the task permits freedom, independence, and personal control to be exercised over the work;
5. feedback from the job—the degree to which clear, timely information about the effectiveness of individual performance is available.

For example, product layouts and assembly lines tend to diminish these job characteristics by breaking down tasks into small and repetitive elements. At a pizza restaurant, for example, a high-efficiency assembly line would result in jobs in which one individual makes dough, another puts on toppings, and another cooks the pizzas. Process layouts, on the other hand, enhance these characteristics. Thus, designing workstations whereby each person makes pizzas from start to finish would probably enhance worker satisfaction.

The relationships between the technology of operations and the social/psychological aspects of work has been understood since the 1950s and is known as the *sociotechnical approach* to job design. It provides useful ideas for operations managers. Sociotechnical approaches to work design provide opportunities for continual learning and personal growth for all employees. **Job enlargement** *is the horizontal expansion of the job to give the worker more variety—although not necessarily more responsibility.* Job enlargement might be accomplished, for example, by giving a production-line worker the task of building an entire product rather than a small subassembly, or by job rotation, such as rotating nurses among hospital wards or flight crews on different airline routes (see the OM Spotlight on Sunny Fresh Foods).

Job enrichment *is vertical expansion of job duties to give the worker more responsibility.* For instance, an assembly worker may be given the added responsibility of testing a completed assembly, so that he or she acts also as a quality inspector. A highly effective approach to job enrichment is to use teams.

A **team** *is a small number of people with complementary skills who are committed to a common purpose, set of performance goals, and approach for which they hold themselves mutually accountable.*[11] Many types of teams exist in manufacturing and service industries. Some of the more common ones are

- natural work teams, which perform entire jobs, rather than specialized, assembly-line work;
- virtual teams, in which members communicate by computer, take turns as leaders, and join and leave the team as necessary;

Job enlargement *is the horizontal expansion of the job to give the worker more variety—although not necessarily more responsibility.*

Job enrichment *is vertical expansion of job duties to give the worker more responsibility.*

A **team** *is a small number of people with complementary skills who are committed to a common purpose, set of performance goals, and approach for which they hold themselves mutually accountable.*

OM SPOTLIGHT

Sunny Fresh Foods[10]

Sunny Fresh Foods (SFF) manufactures and distributes more than 160 different types of egg-based food products to more than 1,200 U.S. food service operations such as quick-service restaurants, schools, hospitals, convenience stores, and food processors. Although production efficiency requires a product layout design in which each production department is organized into specific work or task areas, SFF has several innovative strategies to design its work systems to also provide a highly satisfying work environment for its employees. Workers are put on a "ramp-in" schedule when hired and only allowed to work for a specified number of hours initially. This not only provides better training and orientation to work tasks but also minimizes the potential for repetitive stress injuries. SFF uses a rotation system whereby workers rotate to another workstation every 20 minutes. This minimizes stress injuries, fights boredom, reinforces the concept of "internal customers," and provides a way of improving and reinforcing learning. SFF has led its industry with this approach since 1990, and OSHA standards were developed that mirror this rotation system.

- self-managed teams (SMTs), which are empowered work teams that also assume many traditional management responsibilities.

The SMT concept was developed in Britain and Sweden in the 1950s. One of the early companies to adopt SMTs was Volvo, the Swedish auto manufacturer. Procter & Gamble made pioneering efforts in SMT development in 1962, and General Motors adopted it in 1975. SMTs began to gain popularity in the United States in the late 1980s (see the OM Spotlight on AT&T Credit Corporation). SMTs

- share various management and leadership functions;
- plan, control, and improve their own work processes;
- set their own goals and inspect their own work;
- often create their own schedules and review their performance as a group;
- often prepare their own budgets and coordinate their work with other departments;
- usually order materials, keep inventories, and deal with suppliers;
- often are responsible for acquiring any new training they might need;
- often hire their own replacements or assume responsibility for disciplining their own members;
- take responsibility for the quality of their products and services.[12]

Virtual Workplaces

About two-thirds of the U.S. work force collects, organizes, analyzes, and disseminates information. Information technology is dramatically changing work

OM SPOTLIGHT

AT&T Credit Corporation[13]

In most financial companies, the jobs in the back offices consist of processing applications, claims, and customer accounts. Such jobs are similar to manufacturing assembly lines: dull and repetitive. They represent the division of labor into small tasks and the organization of work by function that is characteristic of many service organizations. At AT&T Credit Corporation, which was established in 1985 to provide financing for customers who lease equipment, one department handled applications and checked the customer's credit standing, a second drew up contracts, and a third collected payments. No one person had responsibility for providing full service to a customer.

The company president decided to hire suitable employees and give them ownership of and accountability for the process. Although his first concern was to increase efficiency, his approach provided more rewarding jobs as an additional benefit. In 1986, the company set up 11 teams of 10 to 15 newly hired workers in a high-volume division serving small business. The three major lease-processing functions were combined in each team. The company also divided its national staff of field agents into seven regions and assigned two or three teams to handle business from each region. In that way, the same teams always worked with the same sales staff, establishing a personal relationship with them and their customers. Above all, team members took responsibility for solving customers' problems. Their slogan became, "Whoever gets the call owns the problem."

Members make most decisions on how to deal with customers, schedule their own time off, reassign work when people are absent, and interview prospective new employees. The teams process up to 800 lease applications daily, more than twice the number processed under the old system, and have reduced the time for final credit approvals from several days to within 24 to 48 hours.

design, leading to "virtual worlds" that transcend time, cultural, and physical space boundaries at speeds unimagined just a few decades ago. We are witnessing the replacement of physical assets such as paper records and documentation with information-driven assets. Modern libraries now store a significant portion of archival collections electronically. Information-intensive businesses such as banking, insurance, education, law, and health care use virtual workplaces to get things done. Many firms such as AT&T and IBM are reducing office space by 25 to 67 percent.[14]

Teleworkers work in their homes, hotel rooms, airports, or other remote locations using information technology. Wireless cell phones and computers, fax machines, and virtual office vendors provide the capability to do work almost anywhere. One virtual office vendor, Officescape (www.officescape.com) states in its literature "Open a city office without really being there!" Such virtual office suppliers provide messaging and telephone answering services, schedule appointments and use of office equipment, provide physical mailing services, and other business support.

Another capability provided by information technology is the ability to assemble virtual teams of people located in different geographic locations.[15] For example, product designers and engineers in the United States can work with counterparts in Japan, transferring files at the end of each work shift to provide an almost continuous product development effort. Some of the advantages and disadvantages of virtual offices and teams are summarized in Exhibit 8.25.

The ways work gets done in virtual offices and teams is different from those in physical offices. This can affect the performance measurement issues we studied in Chapter 3 as well as the need for office space. How does an organization measure employee, team, and project performance when people only meet and work together in virtual space? Do organizations need offices at all? If so, how many? Should virtual workers share physical offices? Office space is expensive and one option to facility layout is to have no facility or one of reduced size.

Xerox, for example, required salespeople to regularly visit their office to get sales and product updates on the company's desktop computers; with remote access to the same data, this is no longer necessary. Shell Oil also found that the span of control for a manager could be increased using virtual technology. The managers spent more of their time focused on "results" of their virtual teams and employees than on how they did it.[16]

Advantages	Disadvantages
• Allows the best possible team skills and capabilities to be assembled resulting in higher-quality work.	• Team success is highly dependent on each team member doing his or her work on time.
• Allows flexible working hours.	• Lack of human socialization may hurt the productivity of the team.
• Firms become more agile and flexible with quicker response time.	• No physical offices can mean no job status.
• Allows for videoconferencing.	• Team members must be "self-starters."
• Reduces transportation costs and pollution due to commuting to work.	• Children at home don't understand the demands of a virtual home office.
• Lower total costs (pay only for what you need in expertise and time).	• Privacy and security risks.
• Reduces the cost of physical office, furniture, and parking space.	• More difficult to control the workload per team member.
• Reduces the cost of heating and air conditioning and other utilities.	• Team member calendars must be synchronized.
• Encourages cross-functional and cross-national coordination and interaction.	• Team communication may be less effective or even break down in virtual space than if all team members were in one physical location.

Exhibit 8.25
Advantages and Disadvantages of Virtual Offices and Teams

SOLVED PROBLEMS

SOLVED PROBLEM #1

The departments that process thousands of residential mortgage folders per year for safe keeping in the layout shown in Exhibit 8.26 are all the same size: 50 feet by 100 feet. Yurtle Mortgage Company is a mortgage service and warehouse with millions of original loan documents in storage. The paper folders are carried between departments on carts. Travel between departments can occur only along the coordinate axes. The number of moves per day between departments is shown in the matrix below the layout. Find the total volume-distance of the proposed layout.

Solution:

The distances between department centers with positive moves are shown in Exhibit 8.27. Multiplying the number of moves by the respective distances gives a total volume-distance of 68,500 (that is, for row A we have $50 \times 100 + 10 \times 150 + 90 \times 250 = 29,000$).

Exhibit 8.26

Yurtle Mortgage Co. Warehouse Distances and Daily Folder Volume

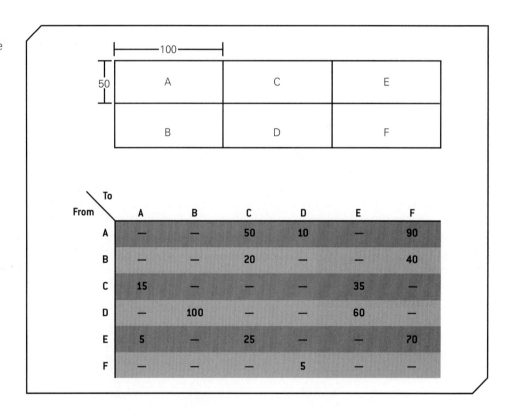

From \ To	A	B	C	D	E	F
A	—	—	50	10	—	90
B	—	—	20	—	—	40
C	15	—	—	—	35	—
D	—	100	—	—	60	—
E	5	—	25	—	—	70
F	—	—	—	5	—	—

Exhibit 8.27

Yurtle Mortgage Co. Facility Layout Distances

From \ To	A	B	C	D	E	F
A	—	—	100	150	—	250
B	—	—	150	—	—	200
C	100	—	—	—	100	—
D	—	100	—	—	150	—
E	200	—	100	—	—	50
F	—	—	—	100	—	—

SOLVED PROBLEM #2

Lou's Machine Shop departments are to be arranged in a square as shown in Exhibit 8.28. Material can be moved from any department to another; however, travel can occur only along the coordinate axes (not directly across a diagonal). Find the minimum-cost layout for the load matrix in Exhibit 8.28, assuming that the distance between adjacent departments is 1.

Solution:

As Exhibit 8.29 shows, there are only three unique arrangements for such a configuration. The total volume-distance for the best layout is calculated as $1 \times 10 + 1 \times 15 + 1 \times 25 + 2 \times 5 + 1 \times 10 + 1 \times 15 + 1 \times 20 + 2 \times 5 + 1 \times 10 = 125$.

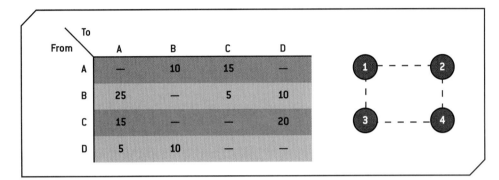

Exhibit 8.28
Lou's Machine Shop Load Matrix

Exhibit 8.29
Lou's Machine Shop Solution

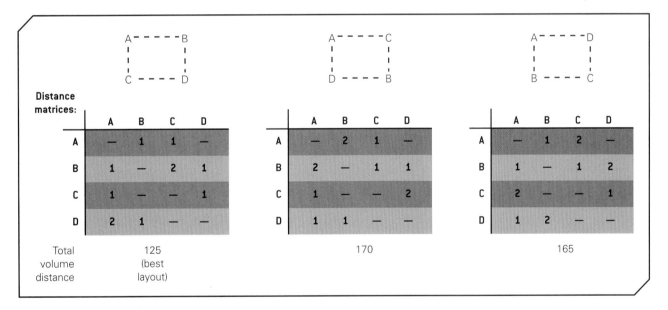

SOLVED PROBLEM #3

To make one particular model of a personal digital assistant (PDA) on an assembly line, the work content is defined by the ten tasks listed to the right.

a. Draw the precedence diagram for this assembly line.

b. What is the cycle time if you want to produce 4,500 PDAs per workday, assuming 7.5 hours per day?

c. What is the theoretical minimum number of workstations to balance this line?

Work Task	Time (seconds)	Immediate Predecessor(s)
1	3.0	None
2	2.0	None
3	1.5	1, 2
4	5.0	3
5	3.5	4
6	3.0	4
7	2.5	5, 6
8	4.0	7
9	2.0	8
10	5.5	9
	Total 32.0 seconds	

d. Using the largest-task-time-first decision rule with the shortest-task-time rule being used for breaking ties, balance this assembly line. (Make sure you do not violate precedent relationships, and the total work per workstation must be less than or equal to 6 seconds.)

e. Compute process efficiency and evaluate the resulting balance in part d.

f. Comment on the results

Solution:

a.

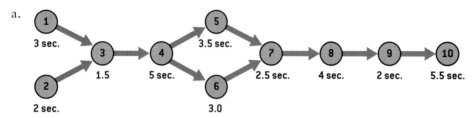

b. $CT = A/R = $ (7.5 hr/day)(60 min/hr)(60 sec/min)/(4,500 units/day)
   $= $ (27,000 sec/day)/(4,500 units/day)
   $= 6$ sec

c. $TW = $ Sum task times/$CT = 32$ sec/6 sec $= 5.33$, or rounded up to 6 workstations

d.

Workstation	Tasks	Total Time	Idle Time	Idleness %
A	1, 2	5.0	1.0	16.7%
B	3	1.5	4.5	75.0%
C	4	5.0	1.0	16.7%
D	5	3.5	2.5	41.7%
E	6, 7	5.5	0.5	8.3%
F	8, 9	6.0	0.0	0.0%
G	10	5.5	0.5	8.3%
	Total	32.0	10.0	

For this grouping of tasks into workstations, precedent relationships drive the solution. The largest-task-time first rule is only used once when making a choice on whether task 5 or 6 should be assigned to workstation D.

e. Total time available = (Number workstations)(Cycle time) = $N \times CT = 7 \times 6$ sec $= 42$ seconds

Total idle time = $N \times CT = 7 \times 6 - 32 = 10$ sec

Assembly-line efficiency $= \sum t/(N \times CT)$
$= 32/(7 \times 6) = 76.2\%$

f. The assembly-line-balance efficiency is rather low. Unit costs would also be high with this balance because we need seven workstations instead of the ideal number of six, and we are paying for 42 seconds of work content per PDA with 10 seconds of idle time per PDA. Workstation B is idle 75% of the time and workstation F is a potential bottleneck. Ideally, we would like idle time to be evenly dispersed across all workstations. We might wish to redefine the ten tasks into smaller tasks. The precedence diagram would be different, allowing for a better grouping of tasks to improve the design efficiency of this assembly line. There may be other alternative ways of grouping the work that are just as good or better than using the "largest-task-time" heuristic rule.

KEY TERMS AND CONCEPTS

Assembly line
Assembly-line balancing
Assembly-line efficiency
Computerized layout planning
CORELAP
CRAFT
Cycle time
Ergonomics
Facility layout
Flow-blocking delay
Idle time

Job
Job design
Job enlargement
Job enrichment
Lack-of-work delay
Layout patterns
    Advantages/disadvantages of each
    Fixed-position layout
    Group technology (cellular manufacturing) layout
    Process layout
    Product layout

Load matrix
Materials-handling
    Automated guided vehicles (AGVs)
    Automated storage systems
    Fixed-path conveyor
    Industrial trucks
    Overhead cranes

Tractor-trailer systems
Service organization layout issues
Team
Theoretical minimum number of workstations
Virtual workplaces
Volume-distance layout method
Workstation design

QUESTIONS FOR REVIEW AND DISCUSSION

1. What are the objectives of facility and work design? How can it help support strategic directions?

2. Under what conditions are facility-layout studies conducted?

3. Describe the major types of layout patterns. What are the advantages and disadvantages of each? Provide one example of each type of layout for goods-producing and service-providing firms.

4. Discuss the type of facility layout that would be most appropriate for
   a. printing books
   b. performing hospital laboratory tests
   c. manufacturing home furniture
   d. a hospital
   e. a photography studio
   f. a library

5. Many company cafeterias are changing from the traditional cafeteria (process) layout to a product layout in which food items are arranged into stations (salads, Italian, cold sandwiches, roast beef and ham, etc.). What types of layouts are these? Discuss the advantages and disadvantages of each type of layout.

6. What type of layout is typically used in a home kitchen? Can you suggest an alternative layout that might have some different advantages?

7. Describe the layout of a typical fast-food franchise such as McDonald's. What type of layout is it? How does it support productivity? Do different franchises (for example, Burger King or Wendy's) have different types of layouts? Why?

8. Visit a manufacturer or service organization and critique its facility design. What are the advantages and disadvantages? How does the layout affect process flows, customer service, efficiency, and cost? Describe the basic types of materials-handling systems commonly used in manufacturing.

9. Traditional guidelines for materials-handling system design are (a) the best materials handling is no materials handling; (b) the shorter the distance traveled, the better the flow; (c) straight-line materials flow paths are the best; and (d) all loads should be handled in as large a unit load as possible. Discuss why these guidelines may no longer be appropriate in today's manufacturing environment.

10. Discuss key issues in designing a layout for services.

11. What are "flow-blocking delay" and "lack-of-work delay"? What types of designs can help to reduce these two sources of delay?

12. What types of design options are typically used for product layouts?

13. What is an assembly line? Define the "assembly-line-balancing problem," and explain what information is needed to solve it.

14. Explain the process of assembly-line balancing and how to compute assembly-line-balancing performance.

15. When might you have to rebalance an assembly line? Explain.

16. How is assembly-line efficiency related to unit cost? Explain.

17. Describe the approaches used in designing process layouts. Will these approaches guarantee an "optimal" solution? Why or why not?

18. How is technology used in layout planning? Explain how CRAFT develops facility layouts.

19. What questions should be addressed in designing a workplace for an individual worker?

20. What is the role of ergonomics in job design?

21. What ergonomic issues might be appropriate to address in a home kitchen?

22. Describe the ergonomic features in the automobile that you drive most often. If it is an older model, visit a new-car showroom and contrast those features with those found in some newer models.

23. Why is safety important in any work environment? What things should manufacturing and service organizations do to ensure the safety of their employees?

24. Explain the key issues that organizations must consider in work design. How does the Hackman-Oldham model provide guidance for operations managers?

25. What is a team? How do natural work teams, virtual teams, and self-managed teams support a sociotechnical approach to work design?

26. Discuss the issues associated with virtual workplaces. What challenges do they pose for operations managers?

PROBLEMS AND ACTIVITIES

1. Given the layout of the departments in Tom's Air-Soft Gun Shop, the frequency of movements among them, and the distance between them in Exhibit 8.30, determine if less materials handling is achieved by switching departments D and F. Assume diagonal distances to be two units and horizontal/vertical distances between adjacent departments to be one unit.

2. Lou's Metal Products produces a diversified line of metal goods. An analysis of last year's production orders shows that seven groups of products account for over 95 percent of the total business volume. The production routing for these groups are as follows:

Receiving	1,500 square feet
A	2,500 square feet
B	1,500 square feet
C	2,000 square feet
D	1,000 square feet
E	500 square feet
Shipping	1,500 square feet

a. Prepare a (percent) volume travel chart using the percentages in Exhibit 8.31.

Exhibit 8.30
Tom's AirSoft Gun Shop Data

From	\multicolumn{6}{c}{Frequency of Movements To}					
	A	B	C	D	E	F
A	0	10	—	5	5	10
B	5	0	—	5	10	5
C	2	10	0	5	5	1
D	5	10	2	0	5	5
E	10	5	0	0	0	5
F	0	10	5	0	5	0

Present layout

A	B
C	D
E	F

Proposed layout

A	B
C	F
E	D

Exhibit 8.31 Data for Problem #2 Lou's Metal Products

Percent Volume		Department Operation Sequence			
Group	by Weight	1	2	3	4
1	20	A	D	E	
2	25	B	C	D	E
3	10	A	D	E	
4	15	C	B	E	
5	10	A	C		
6	8	A	B	D	E
7	8	C	B		

Exhibit 8.32 Data for CORELAP Problem #3

Function	Space Requirements (sq. ft.)
Main entry	500
Dean's office	450
Student affairs	600
Graduate lounge	400
Auditorium	3,000
Large classrooms (5)	1,000 each
Computer center	2,500
Laboratories (2)	600 each
Undergraduate lounge	600
Reading/study rooms (10)	150 each
Vending area	225

b. By trial and error on graph paper, design a good layout.

3. Using the closeness ratings of A through F described in the discussion of CORELAP, design a layout for the main floor of a new business building from the information given in Exhibits 8.32 and 8.33.

4. The DOT factory uses three types of forklift truck operating at a cost of $30, $20, and $10 per hour, respectively. The three types of equipment are housed in separate stations. The frequencies of movement to each department and the distances from each station to the four departments are given in Exhibits 8.34 and 8.35.

Exhibit 8.34
Equipment Movement Frequencies for DOT Factory Problem

Department	Type		
	I	II	III
Turning	10	15	10
Milling	25	15	15
Press shop	30	10	25
Assembly	5	15	30

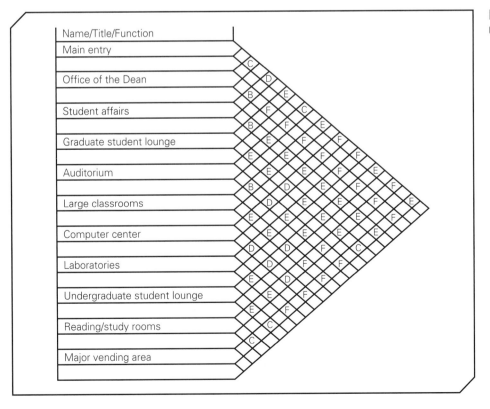

Exhibit 8.33
CORELAP Preference Table

Exhibit 8.35 Distance Data for DOT Factory Problem

From Station	To Department			
	A	**B**	**C**	**D**
1	10	10	5	5
2	5	10	5	10
3	5	5	10	10

The present layout is shown in Exhibit 8.36.

a. What is the present materials-handling requirement as measured by distance and times frequency of movement?
b. Is there any advantage in switching the assembly and milling departments?

5. Peter's Paper Clips uses a three-stage production process: cutting wire to prescribed lengths, inner bending, and outer bending. The cutting process can produce at a rate of 150 pieces per minute; inner bending, 140 pieces per minute; and outer bending, 110 pieces per minute. Determine the hourly capacity of each process stage and the number of machines needed to meet an output rate of 30,000 units per hour. How does facility layout impact your numerical analysis and process efficiency? Explain.

6. Given the following spatial requirements for the six offices of Cindy's Tax Service and the preference table in Exhibit 8.37, design a layout.

Department	1	2	3	4	5	6
Area (sq. ft.)	1,500	2,000	2,000	1,000	1,500	1,000

7. Mercy Franklin Hospital is renovating an old wing to house four departments: outpatient services, X-ray lab, physical therapy, and orthopedics. Exhibit 8.38 gives the distances in feet between each two existing rooms in the wing. That is, Rooms 1 and 2 are 40 feet apart. Exhibit 8.39 gives the average number of trips per day between each two departments.

Exhibit 8.36
DOT Factory Layout

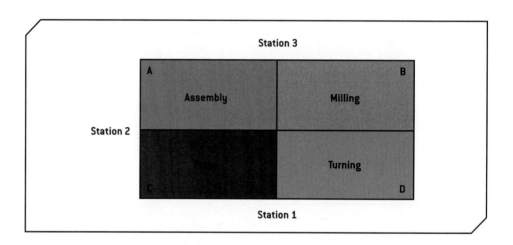

Exhibit 8.37
Cindy's Tax Service Preference Table

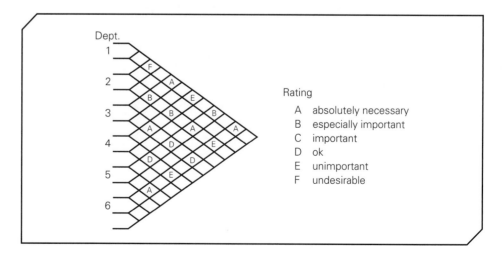

Rating
A absolutely necessary
B especially important
C important
D ok
E unimportant
F undesirable

Exhibit 8.38 Interdepartmental Distances for Mercy Hospital

Location	1	2	3	4
1	—	40	60	60
2		—	20	30
3			—	15
4				—

The hospital wants to locate each department in one of the existing four rooms so as to minimize the sum of the trips × distance. What is the best facility design? How many possible ways of locating the departments are there?

8. A company that designs and manufactures interior furnishings for fast-food chains operates a 70,000-square-foot woodworking/assembly area. This area of the plant has evolved in a rather ad hoc way over a long period of time. As new machines and processes have been adopted, they have not been well integrated into the overall process. As a result, this area of the facility is now hampered with a variety of problems and at a time of high demand for the company's products. Company managers have decided that the current layout should be studied and possibly redesigned to improve efficiency and increase production with minimum capital investment.

The 10 departments included in this area and their space requirements are

1.	Shipping and receiving	7,000 sq. ft.
2.	Raw materials storage	4,200 sq. ft.
3.	Rough cut	7,840 sq. ft.
4.	Laminate cut	3,520 sq. ft.
5.	Cabinets	4,800 sq. ft.
6.	Tables	4,200 sq. ft.
7.	Woodsleys/solid materials	2,100 sq. ft.
8.	Walls and decor	6,800 sq. ft.
9.	Hand finishing and painting	3,500 sq. ft.
10.	Final assembly and packaging	12,112 sq. ft.

Exhibit 8.40 is a from-to chart of unit flows between departments. (Material quantities are expressed in a standard "equivalent" unit.)

Exhibit 8.40 Unit Flows Between Departments

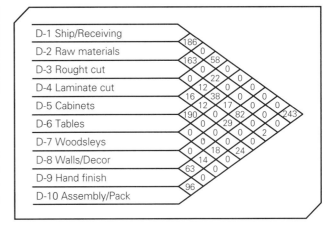

a. Develop a closeness rating for each pair of departments based on the unit flows shown here.

Unit Flow		Closeness Rating
≥50	A	Absolutely necessary
26–50	E	Especially important
16–25	I	Important
6–15	O	Ordinary
0–5	U	Unimportant

b. Design a block layout sketch for this facility. Include approximately 2,000 square feet for office, parts, and maintenance. Write a short report explaining the rationale for the final design of the facility.

9. Exhibit 8.41 is a design for a personal workstation. Discuss the ergonomic features of the design. Should any additional features be included? What criteria should be used to judge how good or bad the workstation design is?

10. An Internal Revenue Service employee responsible for the preliminary check of tax returns must determine if the return was mailed by April 15, if the return is signed, and if the necessary W2 forms are attached to the return. Thus, there are (2)(2)(2) = 8 possible outcomes corresponding to this task; for example, (return on time–signed–W2s attached),

Exhibit 8.39
Interdepartmental Trips Per Day for Mercy Hospital

Location	Outpatient Service	X-ray Lab	Physical Therapy	Orthopedics
Outpatient service	—	25	42	34
X-ray lab		—	15	55
Physical therapy			—	10
Orthopedics				—

Exhibit 8.41 Personal Computer Workstation Design

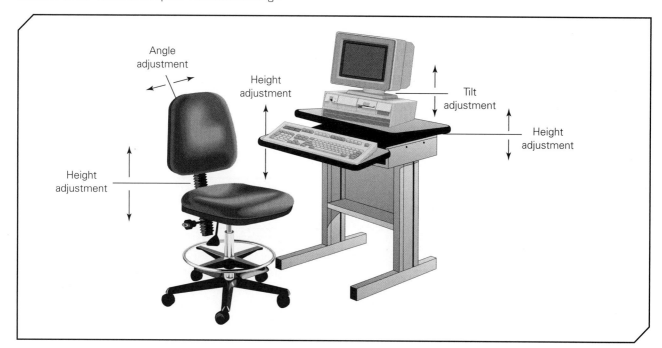

(return late–signed–W2s attached), and so on. Design a workstation for this process using both drawings and text to describe your ideas.

11. An assembly line with 30 activities is to be balanced. The total amount of time to complete all 30 activities is 42 minutes. The longest activity takes 2.4 minutes and the shortest takes 0.3 minutes. The line will operate for 450 minutes per day.
   a. What are the maximum and minimum cycle times?
   b. What output rate will be achieved by each of those cycle times?

12. In Problem 11, suppose the line is balanced using ten workstations and a finished product can be produced every 4.2 minutes.
   a. What is the production rate in units per day?
   b. What is the assembly-line efficiency?

13. A small assembly line for the assembly of power steering pumps needs to be balanced. Exhibit 8.42 is the precedence diagram. The cycle time is determined to be 1.5 minutes. How would the line be balanced using
   a. largest-processing-time-first rule?
   b. smallest-processing-time-first rule?

14. For the in-line skate assembly example in this chapter, suppose the times for the individual operations are as follows:

Task	Time (sec.)	Task	Time (sec.)
1	20	5	30
2	10	6	20
3	30	7	10
4	10	8	20

Exhibit 8.42

Precedence Diagram for Problem 13

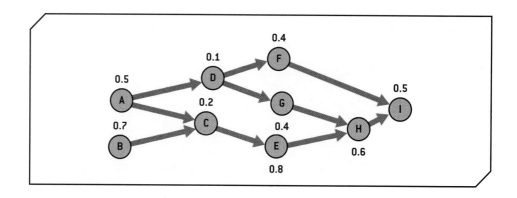

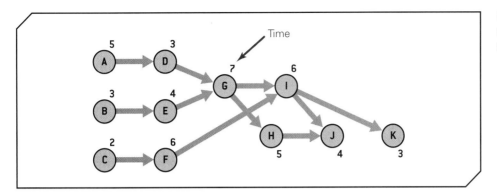

Exhibit 8.43
Precedence Diagram for
Problem 15

Assume that inspections cannot be performed by production personnel, but only by persons from quality control. Therefore, assembly operations are separated into three groups for inspection. Design production lines to achieve output rates of 120 per hour and 90 per hour.

15. Balance the assembly line in Exhibit 8.43 for (a) a shift output of 60 pieces and (b) a shift output of 40 pieces. Assume an 8-hour shift, and use the rule of choosing the assignable task with the largest processing time. Compute the line efficiency for each case.

16. Balance the assembly line in Problem 15 using the rule of choosing the assignable operation with the shortest processing time, and compare the performance of this rule with the longest-time rule.

17. For the situation in Problem 15, determine the range of feasible cycle times and the minimum and maximum output that can be achieved.

18. For the activities and precedence relations in Exhibit 8.44,
    a. draw a precedence diagram
    b. balance the assembly line for an 8-hour-shift output of 30 pieces
    c. Determine maximum and minimum cycle times

Exhibit 8.44 Data for Problem 18

Activity	Predecessors	Time per Piece (min.)
A	none	7
B	none	2
C	A	6
D	A	10
E	B	3
F	B	2
G	D, E	12
H	C	2
I	F	3
J	H, G, I	9

CASES

THE UNIVERSITY LIBRARY WORKROOM

The workroom in a university library processes about 8,000 new books each year. All new books must pass through the workroom, where they are prepared for shelving in the library's stacks. When the library was built, about 3,000 books were processed each year, and no major additions or remodeling changes have been made since then.

The process for cataloging new books is as follows:

1. Receive books from outside.

2. Move to check-in area.

3. Check if duplication of existing book.

4. Move to catalog research area.

5. Catalog—Library of Congress Classification.
   a. If no catalog number, move to storage area.
   b. Store until number available.
   c. Move to catalog research area.
   d. Catalog.

6. Move to verification area.

7. Verify.

8. Move to pocket and call number application area.

9. Install pocket and date-due slip.

10. Apply call number.

11. Store until shelving.

Exhibits 8.45 and 8.46 illustrate the current layout and workflow in the workroom. As you can see from the flow diagram, there is unnecessary movement back and forth across the workroom. In addition, the main storage shelves constitute a barrier to effective flow of materials. A new layout would result in more orderly flow, shorter distance traveled, and more book storage space.

Develop a good alternative design for the workroom. Sketch out the layout and flow diagram of your proposal similar to Exhibits 8.45 and 8.46. Explain the benefits of your proposal. What other factors should be considered?

Exhibit 8.45
Current Layout

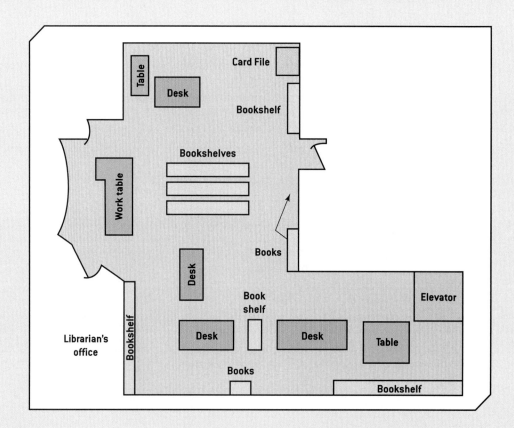

BANKUSA: CASH MOVEMENT

"Del, every wire transfer request is processed first-come-first-served. Some of these wires are for millions of dollars while others are under $100," said Betty Kelly, a 28-year-old manager of Cash Movement (CM). She continued by saying, "I'm also concerned that all wires regardless of dollar amount go through the same quality checkpoints and whether we are staffed correctly."

Betty left Del Carr's office, her boss, with many related issues on her mind. As Betty sat down in her office chair, Steve Breslin, supervisor of outgoing wires, said, "Betty, last week we processed a wire for $80,000 incorrectly to Houston Oaks Bank and now they won't give it back. What should we do?" "Steve, give me the information, and I'll call the bank now," said Betty. The rest of Betty's day was spent on recovering this money and discussing several personnel issues.

The Cash Movement (CM) operating unit is responsible for transferring money for BankUSA and any of its customers. Over 80 percent of all transaction requests were for individual customers, while the remaining requests were for commercial (business) customers. For example, a customer will sell stock and request that cash funds be sent to another institution such as a mutual fund, credit union, or another bank. The customer will request their local customer investment manager (CIM) to transfer money into or out of the account. The CIM will then request by e-mail or fax that Cash Movement process the transaction. The average demand for outgoing wires was 306 wires per day for a 7.5-hour workday. All wires must be settled on the "same day."

Cash Movement employs 20 people, with 3 managers, 10 associates in outgoing wires, 2 associates in

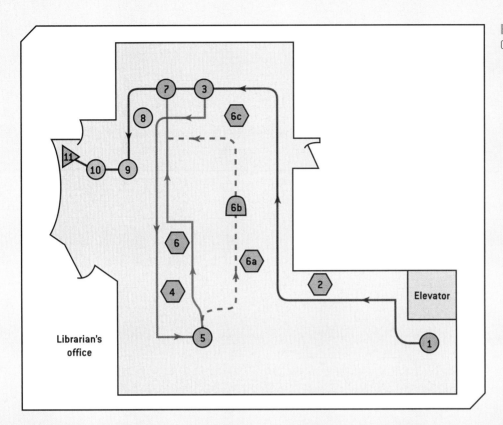

Exhibit 8.46
Current Workflow

incoming wires, 3 associates in checks, and 2 associates in other areas. The average annual salary per associate is $30,000 with an additional 30 percent for benefits and overhead costs. Overhead costs include the cost of leasing/renting the building, operation of common areas such as the cafeteria and meeting rooms, utilities, insurance, and photocopy services.

Process workflow is documented in Exhibit 8.47 with 47 detailed steps consolidated into 16 logical workgroups/activities. The first stage is external to the Cash Movement process and involves the front-room interaction between the customer (client) and the CIM. Here, an electronic transfer request can range from a few minutes to hours trying to help the customer decide what to do and may include a visit to the customer's home or office. Once the CIM e-mails or faxes a transfer request to Cash Movement, the request is logged and the outgoing wire process starts.

The logger screens each transfer request for accuracy and completeness and passes it on to the batching station. In the logger workstation, transfer requests over $50,000 are confirmed by sending an e-mail or fax to the originator of the request. Errors or incomplete information are also sent back to the originator, as shown in Exhibit 8.47 (steps 6 to 11). The outgoing wire processing time to rework a transfer request is 10 minutes per request, and approximately 3 percent of all requests must be reworked (that is, 0.3 minute/request).

The batching workstation (steps 8 to 10) organizes the work into batches of 20 to 30 transfer requests. These batches of work are then sent to the appropriate processing stations, where they are keyed into the federal wire system (steps 12 and 13). A report of all outgoing wires keyed is printed, and the dollar amount keyed is matched with the dollar amount on the adding machine tape (steps 14 to 16). If the tape and remote report do not match, the entire batch must be examined (steps 17 to 19). Once the bank's system is accessed, the authorized user enters the appropriate security code information and the appropriate funds transfer information. A second authorized person is always designated by Cash Movement to review and approve the funds transfer before the actual transfer occurs. Instructions must be submitted to the outgoing wire process for any items requiring same-day settlement no later than 4:00 P.M. EST.

As Exhibit 8.47 documents, three major quality control checkpoints must be passed before releasing the wire (steps 24 and 28). Once the wire is released, money is taken out of an internal Cash Movement account and put in the appropriate receiving institution account via the federal wire system. Cash Movement does this procedure first (steps 24 and 28). Later in the process (steps 34 to 36), it takes money out of the customer's trust account and puts it in Cash Movement's internal account (that is, an internal money transfer). Process steps 24 to

Exhibit 8.47 Outgoing Wire Process Steps and Standard Times

Process Steps (47 detailed steps aggregated into 16 steps)	Workgroup Activity Step & Number	% Work Through This Stage	Processing Times per Client Transfer Request* (minutes)
Client Requests Steps 1 to 3 (client and customer investment manager interaction, accurate collection of process input information, submit to backroom outgoing wire process for transaction execution)		100%	16 minutes (2 to 120 minutes) This front-room step is not part of the outgoing wire backroom process so ignore it.
Logging (Begin Outgoing Wire Process) Steps 4 and 5 (receive request and verify)	1	100%	0.8 minute
Steps 6, 11, and back to 4 and 5 (incorrect or missing information—rework)	2	3%	10 minutes
Step 7 (confirm if >$50,000)	3	100%	0.8 minute
Steps 8 to 10 (separate into different batches and forward)	4	100%	0.1 minute
Verify the Receipt of Fax (Wire Request) (Steps 4 to 7 above)			**First Quality Control Checkpoint**
Direct Wire Input Steps 12 and 13 (receive batches and key into system—batches are variable but a typical batch is about 30 wires, which take about 30 minutes to key into the computer)	5	100%	1 minute
Steps 14 to 16 (run remote report and tape and see if total dollar amounts match—verify)	6	100%	0.1 minute
Steps 17 to 19 (tape and remote report do not match—rework manually by checking each wire against each computer file—done by someone other than keyer)	7	3%	10 minutes
Verify the Accuracy of Wire Request (Steps 12 to 19 above with a focus on keying the wire)			**Second Quality Control Checkpoint**

*These times are based on stopwatch time studies. The weighted average time per outgoing wire is 7.05 minutes. A total of 10 people work in this process.

28 must be done by 4:00 EST, whereas steps 34 to 36 can be done later in the day. Federal regulations require by law the banks to do this transfer in these two separate procedures. The regulations do not, however, specify the sequence of these two procedures. Once steps 34 to 36 are executed, the rest of the Cash Movement process is involved in verifying the accuracy of the transaction and filing the wire information for future reference (steps 37 to 47).

A wire transfer request can "fail" in several ways, with cost consequences to the bank. For example, if the wire is processed incorrectly or not on time, the customer's transaction may fail. The effect of a failed transaction includes the customer being upset, customers leaving the bank forever, customers referring other friends and relatives to other banks, and the possible financial loss of processing the transaction the next business day at a new security price. BankUSA may have to compensate the customer for a failed transaction in terms of customer losses due to lost interest earnings on daily price changes

plus processing fees. The average processing fee is $50 per wire. Moreover, any failed transaction must be researched and reprocessed, which constitutes "internal failure costs." Research and reprocessing costs per wire are estimated at $200. CM processes about 1,500 outgoing wires per week with about one error every two weeks. Errors happen due to CM mistakes but also are caused by other BankUSA departments, other financial institutions, and customers themselves. The information flow of this electronic funds transfer system is sometimes quite complex, with BankUSA having only partial control of the value chain.

Specific types of errors include the same wire being sent out twice, not sent out at all, sent with inaccurate information on it including dollar amount, or sent to the wrong place. No dollar amount has been assigned to each type of failure. The largest risk to Cash Movement is to send the money twice or send it to the wrong institution. If CM catches the error the same day the wire is sent, the wire is requested to be returned that

Exhibit 8.47 (continued) Outgoing Wire Process Steps and Standard Times

Major Process Steps	Workgroup Number	% Work Through This Stage	Processing Times per Client Transfer Request* (minutes)
Steps 20 and 23 (receive and verify the wire's accuracy a second time in the computer—done by someone else)	8	100%	0.5 minute
Verify the Accuracy of the Keyed Wire (Steps 20 and 23 above with a focus on the wire in the computer)			**Third Quality Control Checkpoint**
Steps 24 and 28 (release the wire)	9	100%	1 minute
Steps 25 to 27 (if wire incorrect, cancel wire, and rekey—back to step 12)	10	5%	3 minutes
Step 29 (if CM needs to debit a customer's account, do steps 30 to 32 and batch and run tape)	11	70%	0.1 minute
Step 29 (if CM does not need to debit a customer's account, do step 33—wire is complete and paperwork filed)	12	30%	0.1 minute
Verify the Wire was Sent Correctly (Steps 29 to 33)			**Fourth Quality Control Checkpoint**
Steps 34 to 36 (taking money out of the customer's trust account and putting it in a Cash Management internal account)	13	100%	0.75 minute
Verify That Appropriate Funds Were Taken from the Customer's Account (Steps 34 to 36—done by someone else)			**Fifth Quality Control Checkpoint**
Step 37 (if totals on tape match totals on batch, go to steps 38 to 44)	14	97%	0.1 minute
Step 37 (if totals do not match, find the error by examining the batch of wires, then go to steps 39 to 43)	15	3%	10 minutes
Steps 45 to 47 (verify and file wire information)	16	100%	0.75 minute

*These times are based on stopwatch time studies. The weighted average time per outgoing wire is 7.05 minutes. A total of 10 people work in this process.

day. If a wire is sent in duplication, the receiving institution must receive permission from the customer to return the money to BankUSA. This results in lost interest and the possibility of long delays in returning the money or BankUSA having to take legal action to get the money back. For international transaction requests that are wired with errors, the cost of getting the money back is high. These costs are potentially so high, up to several hundred thousand dollars, that five quality control steps are built into the cash management process, as shown in Exhibit 8.47. All wires, even low dollar amounts, are checked and rechecked to ensure completeness and accuracy.

As Betty, the manager of Cash Movement, drove home, she wondered when she would ever get the time to analyze these issues. Meanwhile, she must keep her process labor utilization rates high, costs low and within budget, and process all wires accurately and on time

each and every day. She remembered taking a college course in operations management and studying the topic of assembly-line balancing (she majored in finance), but she wondered if this method would work for services.

Your task is to help Betty determine how she might use assembly-line balancing for this problem. What is the best way to group the work represented by the 16 workgroups? (Note: You do not have standard times for the 47 detailed work tasks, so ignore them and focus on the 16 workgroups/activities. Assembly-line balancing could be done with either set of information—the detailed 47 process steps or the more aggregate 16 process steps. What would be the cycle time? How many people are needed for outgoing wires using assembly-line-balancing methods versus the current staffing level of ten full-time-equivalent employees? What is the current and recommended assembly-line efficiency? What other further recommendations might you have?

ENDNOTES

[1] "Washington Mutual Patents Design of Bank Branches," www.reuters.com, July 2, 2004.

[2] "Mercedes' Maverick in Alabama," *Business Week*, September 11, 1995 (www.businessweek.com).

[3] Shunk, Dan L., "Group Technology Provides Organized Approach to Realizing Benefits of CIMS," *Industrial Engineering*, April 1985. Adapted with permission from Institute of Industrial Engineers, 25 Technology Park/Atlanta, Norcross, GA 30092.

[4] "Logistics Consultants Material Handling Projects," 2003 (www.lconsult.com/experience.html).

[5] "Logistics Consultants Material Handling Projects," 2003 (www.lconsult.com/experience.html).

[6] Lau, R. S. M., and Keenan, Ronda S., "Restructuring for Quality and Efficiency," *Journal for Quality and Participation*, July–August 1994, pp. 38–40.

[7] Zaun, Todd, "In Japan, Tiny Cars Offer a Laboratory for Very Big Ideas," *The Wall Street Journal*, August 5, 2002, pp. A1, A8.

[8] Bell, P. C., and Van Brenk, J., "Vytec Corporation: Warehouse Layout Planning," *The European Case Clearing House*, England, Case #9B03E013, (http://www.ecch.cranfield.ac.uk).

[9] "DaimlerChrysler CIO Sue Unger," *CIO Magazine*, June 15, 2003 (www.cio.com); and "DaimlerChrysler's 'Digital Factory' Gets Motoring," *Computer Weekly*, Nov. 29, 2002.

[10] Profiles of Winners, Malcolm Baldrige National Quality Award, and Sunny Fresh Foods Baldrige Application Summary, 1999, U.S. Department of Commerce, National Institute of Standards and Technology.

[11] Katzenback, Jon R., and Smith, Douglas K., "The Discipline of Teams," *Harvard Business Review*, March–April 1993, pp. 111–120.

[12] Wellins, Richard S., Byham, William C., and Wilson, Jeanne M., *Empowered Teams*, San Francisco: Jossey-Bass, 1991.

[13] Adapted from "Benefits for the Back Office, Too," *Business Week*, July 10, 1989, p. 59.

[14] Helms, M. M., and Raisszadeh, F. M. E., "Virtual Offices: Understanding and Managing What You Cannot See," *Work Study* 51, no. 5, 2002, pp. 240–247.

[15] Johnson, P., Heimann, V., and O'Neill, K., "The Wonderland of Virtual Teams," *Journal of Workplace Learning* 13, no. 1, 2001, pp. 24–29.

[16] Helms, M. M., and Raisszadeh, F. M. E., "Virtual Offices: Understanding and Managing What You Cannot See," *Work Study* 51, no. 5, 2002, pp. 240–247.

Chapter Outline

CHAPTER 9

Supply Chain Design

Learning Objectives

1. To understand the components of a supply chain, the key functions of supply chain management, and how supply chains fit into overall value chains by examining a case study of Dell.

2. To understand the common types of metrics used to evaluate supply chain performance and how they are calculated, to see how the cash-to-cash conversion cycle helps to explain supply chain performance, and to understand the "bullwhip effect."

3. To understand the scope of issues involved in designing supply chains, the differences between efficient versus responsive supply chains and pull versus push systems, the role of contract manufacturers, and design of multisite supply chains for services.

4. To understand the basic criteria and decision models used to design supply chain networks and make location decisions.

5. To be able to apply simple quantitative methods and models to help locate goods-producing or service-providing facilities.

6. To understand key design issues relating to the design of supply chain management systems, including the selection of transportation services, supplier evaluation, technology selection, and inventory management.

- "OK, I know you want to speed up your supply chain, but you don't have the information systems and supplier relationships to do it now," stated Steve Breslin, a consultant hired by a manufacturer of grass seed and fertilizer. "So Steve, how do we get started? We have little time before the company chokes on inventory—it's piling up everywhere and it's going to kill our company! We've been told in no uncertain terms that we are going to lose the Wal-Mart business if we don't get better fast!" responded Dan Saladin, the chief financial officer of the lawn care company. "Dan, we'll start by better integrating information, operations, and logistics processes. Specifically, we need to set performance target levels for inventory turnover, days' supply of inventory, accounts receivable, accounts payable, delivery times, and other key metrics. We also need to better coordinate orders with your suppliers and customers. I have no doubt that the changes I will propose will dramatically improve your supply chain's performance and have a significant impact on your bottom line!" Breslin said in a confident voice.

© Getty Images PhotoDisc

- Corning (www.corning.com) has evolved from producing glass and cookware in past decades into producing advanced technology products such as optical fiber, LCD glass for flat panel displays, precision lenses, photonic devices, and life sciences products. To help it synchronize its value chain for a diverse set of new manufactured products, Corning hired PeopleSoft, a company that specializes in supply chain, enterprise software, and consulting solutions. Doug Anderson, chief information officer for Corning's Specialty Materials, noted that "we're constantly working on yield and cycle times. We need the ability to ramp up in time to meet unexpected demand, so we put a lot of work into figuring out how much manufacturing capacity we need to have online. By having this improved information infrastructure in place, our reaction time will improve significantly."[1]

- "Well, the merger has been approved!" exclaimed Tim Rosser, the vice president of operations for Matthews Novelties, Inc., which produces a line of popular toys, many on contract from movie studios and other entertainment companies. Matthews Novelties just acquired ToyCo, a smaller company that essentially owns the market for miniature cars and trucks. "Now that we've inherited ToyCo's product line, we need to decide where to produce them. As you know, our state-of-the art die-casting factory in Malaysia operates at full capacity, and we have no room to expand the factory at the current site and no available land adjacent to it. ToyCo has two factories—one in Thailand and another in China. Labor costs in Thailand are about half of what we experience in Malaysia but their labor productivity is a lot lower. Our marketing people have also told us that the demand in China is increasing rapidly." Sharon Stein noted, "We shouldn't just make this decision on labor economics. What are building costs? What about housing and dormitory availability and education programs for employees? Do we have accurate demand forecasts? Where are the suppliers located? What regulations and restrictions do we face? How stable is their currency and political situation?" Tim readily agreed, "We have a lot of information to gather. Let's get started."[2]

Produced in China

Peter Endig/dpa/Landov

Discussion Questions: Why do you think it is important to define good metrics to monitor the performance of a supply chain? How might these measures be used in a typical company? Suppose that you wanted to locate a café on your college campus (other than in the typical student center). What factors might you consider in selecting the location?

We introduced the concept of a **supply chain** in Chapter 2, noting that a supply chain is a key subsystem of a value chain that focuses primarily on the physical movement of goods and materials along with supporting information through the supply, production, and distribution processes; whereas a value chain is broader in scope and encompasses all pre- and postproduction services to create and deliver the entire customer benefit package (see Exhibit 2.3). Financing and preventive maintenance, for example, are, respectively, pre- and postproduction services that more fully characterize the value chain.

Supply chains are all about speed and efficiency; poor supply chain performance can undermine the objectives of the firm and can easily result in loss of customers, either individual consumers or major retailers such as Wal-Mart, as seen in the first episode. This episode also suggests that companies must start with the basics, such as understanding customers and markets, designing process, and using measurements and information technology effectively, and building supplier relationships. Such basic OM skills are important in designing supply chains.

As a firm's product lines and markets change or expand, the design or redesign of supply chains becomes a critical issue. Large companies like Corning, highlighted in the second episode, have complex value chains that often require specialized software and assistance to transition to an information-enabled and integrated value chain that is flexible, fast, and price-competitive. With facilities in 34 countries, Corning's focus has been on trying to optimize its global supply chains. PeopleSoft (since bought by Oracle) began working with Corning in 1995 to improve the supply chains of 12 separate business units that execute their own sales, production, and distribution. Corning's Supply Chain Technology Strategy Group oversees these improvement initiatives and tries to minimize complexity across the whole organization. Oracle and Corning have implemented over 20 applications with very positive results. One long-term goal is to integrate Oracle's Manufacturing, Customer Fulfillment, and Supply Chain Planning systems with Corning's in-house Manufacturing Execution System to streamline and improve supply chain performance.

The third episode reflects the challenges when companies merge and must reevaluate their supply chains and locations of facilities. The location of factories, distribution centers, and service facilities establishes the infrastructure for the supply chain and has a major impact on the profitability. In today's global business environment with emerging markets and sources of supply in China and other parts of the Far East, identifying the best locations is not easy, but good location analysis can lead to major reductions in total supply chain costs and improvements in customer response.

In this chapter, we focus on understanding the role of supply chains in an organization's overall value chain, methods for designing supply chains and making associated facility decisions, and issues relating to managing the supply chain. Specifically, we will address

- choosing a supply chain structure that best supports the organization's objectives and strategy;
- determining the number, type, and location of facilities to support supply chain objectives;
- selecting the best way of distributing goods between points in the supply chain; and
- managing inventory, suppliers, and information in the broad context of a supply chain.

Learning Objective
To understand the components of a supply chain, the key functions of supply chain management, and how supply chains fit into overall value chains by examining a case study of Dell.

UNDERSTANDING SUPPLY CHAINS

Supply chains play a very critical role in organizations. The Commerce Department estimates that in the United States $1.1 trillion in inventory results in $3.2 trillion in annual retail sales. Of this, $400 billion of inventory is at retail locations, $290 billion at wholesalers or distributors, and $450 billion with manufacturers. "For a company with annual sales of $500 million and a 60 percent cost of sales, the difference between being at median in terms of supply chain performance and in the top 20 percent is $44 million of additional working capital."[3]

The basic purpose of a supply chain is to coordinate the flow of materials, services, and information among the elements of the supply chain to maximize customer value. The key functions generally include sales and order processing, transportation and distribution, operations, inventory and materials management, finance, and customer service. Supply chains must focus on exploiting demand information to better match production levels to reduce costs; tightly integrate design, development, production, delivery, and marketing; and provide more customization to meet increasingly demanding customers. As such, a supply chain is an integrated system and requires much coordination and collaboration among the various players in it.

A good example of an integrated supply chain is the dairy business.[4] Dairy cows must be milked twice a day or they get sick. Each morning, 5,000-gallon tanker trucks pick up raw milk from dairy farms and bring it to processing plants. The milk is tested for butterfat content and pumped into large holding tanks. It is then separated into cream and skim, then blended back together according to a production schedule based on actual customer orders for that day. If the dairy is short, it will buy raw milk from a competing dairy; if it has excess milk, it might convert it into cheese. The raw milk is pasteurized, tested for bacteria count, and homogenized. Next it is poured into various-sized containers, date-stamped, and transported to customers. At the end of the day, the processing line is disassembled, sterilized, and reassembled for the next day.

A goods-producing supply chain generally consists of suppliers, manufacturers, distributors, retailers, and customers, as illustrated in Exhibit 9.1. Raw materials and components are ordered from suppliers and must be transported to manufacturing facilities for production and assembly into finished goods. Finished goods

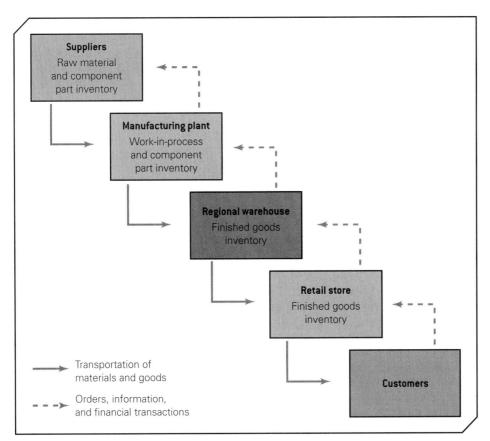

Exhibit 9.1
Typical Goods-Producing Supply Chain Structure

Distribution centers (DCs) *are warehouses that act as intermediaries between factories and customers, shipping directly to retail stores where products are made available to customers or directly to customers.*

Inventory *refers to raw materials, work-in-process, or finished goods that are maintained to support production or satisfy customer demand.*

Cross-docking *is a process by which manufactured goods are unloaded from factory shipments, staged on the docks (but not sent to storage), and quickly reloaded for shipment to individual customers.*

Supply chain management (SCM) *is the management of all activities that facilitate the fulfillment of a customer order for a manufactured good to achieve satisfied customers at reasonable cost.*

are shipped to distributors who operate distribution centers. **Distribution centers (DCs)** *are warehouses that act as intermediaries between factories and customers, shipping directly to retail stores where products are made available to customers or directly to customers.* At each factory, distribution center, and retail store, inventory generally is maintained to improve the ability to meet demand quickly. **Inventory** *refers to raw materials, work-in-process, or finished goods that are maintained to support production or satisfy customer demand.* As inventory levels diminish, orders are sent to the previous stage upstream in the process for replenishing stock. Orders are passed up the supply chain, fulfilled at each stage, and shipped to the next stage. **Cross-docking** *is a process by which manufactured goods are unloaded from factory shipments, staged on the docks (but not sent to storage), and quickly reloaded for shipment to individual customers.* Cross-docking tries to minimize unnecessary handling and costs. In some cases, the sorting is done on the truck thereby avoiding the loading and unloading at the dock.

Not all supply chains have each of the stages illustrated in Exhibit 9.1. A simple supply chain might be one that supplies fresh fish at a Boston restaurant. Being close to the suppliers (fisherman), the restaurant might purchase fish directly from them daily and cut and fillet the fish directly at the restaurant. A slightly more complex supply chain for a restaurant in the Midwest might include processing and packaging by a seafood wholesaler and air transportation and delivery to the restaurant. For consumers who want to buy fish from a grocery store, the supply chain is more complex and would include wholesale delivery and storage by the retailer.

One often hears the term **OEM**, which stands for *original equipment manufacturer*. OEMs depend on a network of suppliers and often have rather complex supply chains. One of the best examples is the automobile industry. Building a car is a very complex process and requires the coordination of a multitude of parts and components from many different suppliers. In the auto industry, the supply chain has the structure shown in Exhibit 9.2. Tier 1 suppliers are those that provide components for final assembly such as seats, dashboards, suspension systems, and so on. They in turn depend on a network of suppliers (Tier 2) for smaller components and parts.

Supply chain management (SCM) *is the management of all activities that facilitate the fulfillment of a customer order for a manufactured good to achieve satisfied customers at reasonable cost.* This includes not only the obvious functions of managing materials within the supply chain but also the flows of information and money that are necessary to coordinate the activities. The unique characteristic of SCM is that while material and logistics managers typically focus on activities within the span of their purchasing, manufacturing, and distribution processes, SCM requires a clear understanding of the interactions among all parts of the system.

The **Supply Chain Operations Reference (SCOR) model** is based on five basic functions involved in managing a supply chain and provides an excellent framework for understanding the scope of SCM.[5] These functions include:

1. *Plan*—developing a strategy that balances resources with requirements and establishes and communicates plans for the entire supply chain. This includes management policies and aligning the supply chain plan with financial plans.
2. *Source*—procuring goods and services to meet planned or actual demand. This includes identifying and selecting suppliers, scheduling deliveries, authorizing payments, and managing inventory.
3. *Make*—transforming goods and services to a finished state to meet demand. This includes production scheduling, managing work-in-process, manufacturing, testing, packaging, and product release.
4. *Deliver*—managing orders, transportation, and distribution to provide the goods and services. This entails all order management activities from processing

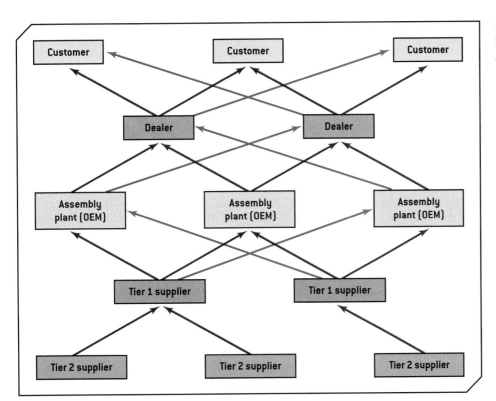

Exhibit 9.2
Supply Chain Structure in the
Automotive Industry

customer orders to routing shipments, managing goods at distribution centers, and invoicing the customer.

5. *Return*—customer returns; maintenance, repair, and overhaul; and dealing with excess goods. This includes return authorization, receiving, verification, disposition, and replacement or credit.

These functions describe the principal activities in SCM, but it is important to note that they cannot be executed effectively without understanding and segmenting customers, customizing the supply chain to each segment, listening and responding to market signals, differentiating the product as close to the customer as possible, developing strategic partnerships with suppliers, using technology wisely, and measuring performance. An interesting perspective on modern supply chain management draws upon some ancient history (see the OM Spotlight on Alexander the Great).

To better understand the role of supply chains in the context of the overall value chain, we present an overview of the value and supply chains at Dell, Inc., one of the most recognized names in the computer industry.

The Value and Supply Chain at Dell, Inc.[7]

Dell sells highly customized personal computers, servers, computer workstations, and peripherals to global corporate and consumer markets. Dell's business model is based on selling direct to customers and bypassing traditional intermediary wholesalers and distributors. Computers are assembled only in response to individual orders. Customers

OM SPOTLIGHT

Alexander the Great[6]

Alexander the Great was born in 356 B.C. and became known as one of the great military leaders and conquerors in all history, inspiring such leaders as Julius Caesar and Napoleon. Alexander's ability to consistently defeat enemy armies and expand his kingdom was a result of his proactive preparation and logical approach to warfare. Although his 35,000-man army could carry no more than a 10-day supply of food when away from sea transport, his troops marched over thousands of miles at a rate of 19.5 miles in any one day without a problem. This was due to his inclusion of logistics and supply chain management into his strategic plans. If Alexander were a CEO today, he would

- include logistics and SCM in strategic planning;
- consistently make changes in his organization that were demonstrated to provide specific benefits;

- develop a working knowledge and detailed understanding of his customers and their products, competition, industry, logistics requirements, and technologies, and utilize this knowledge, along with other assets, to develop competitive advantages, market share, and profit;
- appoint a single person to lead all logistics functions and participate in strategic planning sessions;
- develop alliances with key suppliers and service partners, accessing their infrastructure by allowing them to entrench themselves in his own company;
- use technology and other business tools only to the extent that they further the goals of profitability and competitive advantage.

And, he would probably strike fear into the hearts of his business competitors!

can place orders via the Internet, toll-free telephone lines, and at small sales outlets in some shopping malls. About half the orders are placed online; the remaining orders are placed through salespeople. Dell's value chain electronically links customers, suppliers, assembly operations, and shippers. Pre- and postproduction services are vital to Dell's value chain. Exhibit 9.3 depicts Dell's value chain, drawing upon our value chain model in Chapter 2.

PREPRODUCTION SERVICES

Preproduction services, many of which are information intensive, focus on "gaining a customer" and increasing both the efficiency and responsiveness of the supply chain. These include

- *Customer benefit package design and configuration*—Dell's primary good is, of course, the computer system. Dell offers various equipment models and configurations to meet the needs of different markets (for example, home, business, and education) and price points, all of which can be customized to individual specifications. Many peripheral goods are available, including preloaded software, printers, digital cameras, handheld PDAs, and other products. For example, Dell partnered with Lexmark International Inc. to produce Dell-labeled printers. Peripheral services include technical support and advice for configuring the right system, financing, warranty options such as next-day on-site repair, and even rapid ordering of consumable supplies. For example, customers can order new printer cartridges for Dell printers from its web site and have them delivered the next day. Dell's decision to offer printers was driven by the fact that over two-thirds of its customers said they would buy a Dell printer if they could get the same kind of service and technical support they receive with their PCs or servers. These peripheral goods and services enhance the customer benefit package. A well-designed supply chain is critical to creating and delivering the goods and services to their customers.

Exhibit 9.3 A Value Chain Model of Dell, Inc.

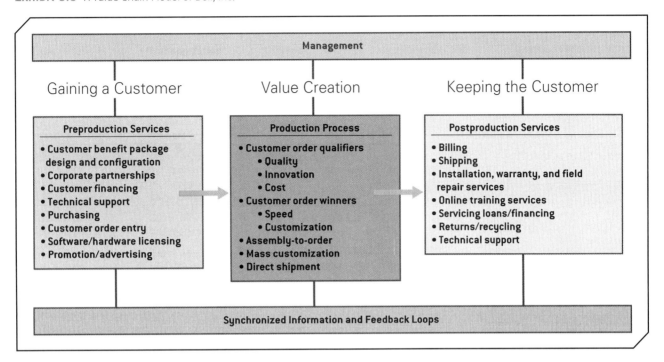

- *Corporate partnerships*—Dell has established partnerships with over 200 major corporate clients. Using secure, customized Intranet sites called Premier Pages, the clients' employees can order preauthorized Dell products online, usually at a discount. These corporate portals allow clients to create asset management reports, determine the best financing option, track leased equipment, and so on. This frees Dell's salespersons from routine sales activity and allows them to spend more time solving client problems and building long-term relationships.
- *Customer financing*—Business, education, and government customers represent a substantial portion of Dell's total revenue. Dell Financial Services (DFS) was established to help such organizations finance their purchases. Dell Preferred Account customers have special financing arrangements, such as no payments for 1 year after the date of purchase, and often have access to special rebates.
- *Technical support*—Dell's technical support call centers handle about 60,000 calls a day. Customer calls involved presale questions as well as postdelivery questions. For example, many customers have technical questions about making the correct choices for customized options or peripherals or the compatibility of various components. Therefore, technical support is both a pre- and postproduction service.
- *Purchasing*—Purchasing is a vital part of Dell's supply chain, and Dell creates strong partnerships with some 250 suppliers responsible for delivering over 3,500 parts. Supplier selection is based on cost, quality, speed of service, and flexibility, and performance is tracked using a supplier "report card." About 30 key suppliers provide 75 percent of the parts; most suppliers maintain 8 to 10 days of inventory in multivendor hubs close to Dell assembly plants. The integration of Dell and its suppliers is so close that the suppliers are treated as if they're inside Dell. As Michael Dell, the founder and CEO of Dell said, "Keep your friends close, and your suppliers closer."[8] By limiting the number of qualified suppliers, supplier negotiations are simplified. Dell's product and delivery requirements are clearly specified in all contracts. By maintaining a very

limited amount of inventory, components never become obsolete, and changing to the latest technology can be done quickly. Dell also exploits the Internet to share information and streamline purchasing.[9] For example, Dell updates its parts requirements every 2 hours. Through these approaches, Dell has reduced parts inventory from a 31-day supply in 1996 to a 4-day supply in 2003.

- *Customer order entry*—Orders start the supply chain in motion. Dell's online ordering capability gives customers the power to design and configure their customer benefit package any way they want it by selecting the specific hardware and software options, peripherals, service contracts, financing, and so on. It even provides explanations of differences in options and advice on selections. Although live customer ordering support is available via the telephone, audio prompts encourage customers to use the online capabilities.
- *Software and hardware licensing*—Dell equipment comes fully loaded with the latest software from suppliers such as Microsoft, Yahoo, and EMC Corporation (storage software). Customers expect frequent software updates with Internet and wireless network capabilities. This is an important peripheral service that is critical to equipment sales.
- *Promotion/Advertising*—Dell offers numerous special deals and promotions on its web site and the Internet within a short time after realizing it needs to shift or increase demand for its products. For example, if 40-GB hard drives are in short supply, a promotion might offer 60-GB hard drives at the same price; if demand is slow, free shipping or an instant rebate might be offered. With such short procurement and production times, the supply chain can respond quickly to new demand and supply changes and also help manage the decline and ramp up of different product life cycles.

PRODUCTION PROCESSES

The focus of the second major stage of Dell's value chain is on creating and delivering the manufactured goods. Dell operates one of the most efficient supply chains in the world. The company has been awarded over 550 patents for its business processes, from wireless factory networks to workstations that are 4 times more productive than traditional production methods and assembly lines.

The supply chain is designed to support Dell's objective of mass customization. To accomplish this objective, Dell introduced the idea of a make-to-order supply chain design to the computer industry. Dell pulls component parts into its factories based on actual customer orders and carries no finished goods inventory, relying on information technology to drive its supply chain. Suppliers' component part delivery schedules must match Dell's factory assembly schedules, which in turn must be integrated with shipping schedules. Each factory worldwide is rescheduled every 2 hours, and at the same time updates are sent to all third-party suppliers and logistics providers. For example, one Dell factory in Austin, Texas, receives parts 8 times each day for its assembly operations. Dell's production system tells all suppliers exactly what to do and when to do it. Dell might notify one of its suppliers electronically to deliver a specific quantity of parts to a specific loading dock by a certain time the next morning. This is quite different from traditional production systems that might schedule a large order quantity every 2 weeks to a regional warehouse based on forecasts of future demand.

POSTPRODUCTION SERVICES

The third stage in Dell's value chain is postproduction services, which focus on "keeping the customer." These include

- *Billing*—Dell's Premier Page customers are billed electronically. Individual customer purchases are charged to credit cards. Once the equipment is paid for, the operating system generates supplier and Dell factory production orders, shipping information, and bills.

- *Shipping*—United Parcel Service (UPS), Federal Express (FedEx), SonicAir, and Eagle Global Logistics ship Dell's products to customers. These outsourcing arrangements provide quality service as well as tracking capability during shipment. For large corporate orders, Dell might notify UPS to pick up 3,000 computers at an Austin, Texas factory and then go to a Sony factory in Mexico and pick up a matching set of 3,000 monitors. UPS matches the computers with the monitors and delivers the systems to the customer.

- *Installation, warranty, and field repair services*—Dell offers limited warranty and at-home installation and repair service on a prepaid contract basis. These options are available when the customer purchases the equipment and are executed after shipment. SonicAir handles the storage and delivery of repair parts to customers and provides 2- and 4-hour delivery service and next-day service using over 335 strategic stocking points worldwide. If a technician must be dispatched to the customer's site, the call system sends all necessary information to the technician dispatching function as well as to SonicAir. Together, Dell and SonicAir have achieved a 95 percent on-time parts delivery performance level.

- *Online training services*—Dell provides or refers customers to online training programs. Dell's online instructions are very clear, with examples and frequently asked question links. For major business and government clients, customized training software is also designed to meet specific client needs.

- *Servicing loans/financing*—Dell's Premier Pages helps key clients manage and track equipment purchases, contracts, and leasing agreements online. Customers who lease through Dell Financial Services can use these pages to obtain new lease quotes, place lease orders, and track leased assets throughout their life cycles.

- *Returns/Recycling*—With millions of obsolete computers, Dell provides the customer with a way to donate old computers to other organizations or to have them recycled and disposed of in an environmentally safe way. Once the customer receives a new Dell printer, for example, detailed instructions are provided on how to ship the old printer back to Dell's Recycling Center.

- *Technical support*—Dell's postdelivery objective is to fix problems online without having to dispatch a technician. Dell embeds diagnostic equipment and software into its equipment before it leaves the factory, making it possible to run many equipment and software checks and make fixes online. However, live technical support is also available.

In 2004, Dell was named the top company in the world (followed by Nokia and Procter & Gamble) on the basis of supply chain best practices and technologies by AMR Research. The ranking was based on key financial metrics such as return on assets and inventory turns. The importance of supply chain performance on business success was summed up by a research analyst who noted that metrics such as perfect order performance and supply chain management costs are better predictors of future profits than previous earnings.

UNDERSTANDING AND MEASURING SUPPLY CHAIN PERFORMANCE

Learning Objective
To understand the common types of metrics used to evaluate supply chain performance and how they are calculated, to see how the cash-to-cash conversion cycle helps to explain supply chain performance, and to understand the "bullwhip effect."

Supply chain managers use numerous metrics to evaluate performance and identify improvements to the design and operation of their supply chains. These basic metrics typically balance customer requirements as well as internal supply chain efficiencies and fall into several categories, as summarized in Exhibit 9.4.

Exhibit 9.4 Common Metrics Used to Measure Supply Chain Performance

Metric Category	Metric	Definition
Delivery reliability	Perfect order fulfillment	The number of perfect orders divided by the total number of orders
Responsiveness	Order fulfillment lead time	The time to fill a customer's order
	Perfect delivery fulfillment	The proportion of deliveries that were not just complete but also on time
Customer-related	Customer satisfaction	Customer perception of whether customers receive what they need when they need it, as well as such intangibles as convenient time of delivery, product and service quality, helpful manuals, and after-sales support
Supply chain efficiency	Average inventory value	The total average value of all items and materials held in inventory
	Inventory turnover	How quickly goods are moving through the supply chain
	Inventory days' supply	How many days of inventory are in the supply chain or part of the supply chain
Financial	Total supply chain costs	Total costs of order fulfillment, purchasing, maintaining inventory, distribution, technical support, and production
	Warranty/returns processing costs	The cost associated with repairs or restocking goods that have been returned
	Cash-to-cash conversion cycle	The average time to convert a dollar spent to acquire raw materials into a dollar collected for a finished good

Delivery reliability is often measured by perfect order fulfillment. A "perfect order" is defined as one that is delivered meeting all customer requirements, such as delivery date, condition of goods, accuracy of items, correct invoice, and so on. *Responsiveness* is often measured by order fulfillment lead time or by perfect delivery fulfillment. *Customer-related* measures focus on the ability of the supply chain to meet customer wants and needs. Customer satisfaction is often measured by a variety of attributes on a perception scale that might range from Extremely Dissatisfied to Extremely Satisfied. *Supply chain efficiency* measures include average inventory value and inventory turnover. Average inventory value tells managers how much of the firm's assets are tied up in inventory. Inventory turnover (IT) is computed using the following formula:

Inventory turnover (IT) = Cost of goods sold/Average inventory value   **(9.1)**

Note that inventory turnover can be computed over any time period such as months, quarters, or years. The cost of goods sold is the cost to produce the goods and services and normally does not include selling, general, administrative, research, engineering, and development expenses.

For example, if a manufacturer has a cost of goods sold of $10,600,000 and an average inventory value of $3,600,000, then inventory turnover is computed to be 2.94 times per year. "Good" values of inventory turnover depend on the industry, type of production process, and characteristics of the product, such as volume, degree of customization, and amount of technology. Supermarkets, for instance, turn their inventory over 100 times per year; customized medical testing equipment has an inventory turnover rate of only 2 or 3. Most firms turn their inventory over 5 to 10 times per year. Careful examination of Equation (9.1) suggests that to achieve such high inventory turnover rates, average inventory value must be very low, which is an important objective for many firms. This also reduces the need to finance inventories and reduces the chances of inventory obsolescence.

Inventory days' supply (IDS) is calculated by the following:

$$\text{Inventory days' supply (IDS)} = \text{Average total inventory/Cost of goods sold per day} \qquad \textbf{(9.2)}$$

The cost of goods sold per day (CGS/D) in the denominator is computed as

$$\text{Cost of goods sold per day (CGS/D)} = \text{Cost of goods sold value/Operating days per year} \qquad \textbf{(9.3)}$$

For example, if the cost of goods sold is \$10,600,000, the average inventory value is \$3,600,000, and the firm operates 250 days per year, the cost of goods sold per day is \$10,600,000/250 = \$42,400 per day. Then IDS is calculated as \$3,600,000/\$42,400 = 84.9 days supply. This suggests that perhaps too much costly inventory is being maintained. Although the time period used in these calculations is typically days, modern technology allows these metrics to be evaluated in terms of hours of inventory supply, and some supply chain managers are doing this.

Financial measures show how supply chain performance affects the bottom line. These might include total supply chain costs, costs of processing returns and warranties, and the cash-to-cash conversion cycle (described in detail in the next section).

By tracking such measures and using the results to better control and improve supply chain performance, key organizational financial measures, such as return on assets, cost of goods sold, revenue, and cash flow, can be affected. For example, a reduction in average inventory value will improve return on assets; improved supplier performance can reduce the cost of goods sold; better customer satisfaction can increase revenues; and reduced lead times can have a positive impact on cash flow. Thus, senior managers should recognize the value of good supply chain design and management and provide resources to improve it.

Cash-to-Cash Conversion Cycle

One of the more useful metrics for evaluating supply chain performance is the cash-to-cash conversion cycle, which identifies cash flows from the time costs are incurred (such as raw material inventory) to when it is paid (accounts receivable). The cycle is computed as inventory days' supply (IDS) plus accounts receivable days' supply (ARDS) minus accounts payable days' supply (APDS):

$$\text{Cash-to-cash conversion cycle} = \text{IDS} + \text{ARDS} - \text{APDS} \qquad \textbf{(9.4)}$$

where ARDS and APDS are calculated as

$$\text{ARDS} = \text{Accounts receivable value/Revenue per day} \qquad \textbf{(9.5)}$$

$$\text{APDS} = \text{Accounts payable value/Revenue per day} \qquad \textbf{(9.6)}$$

In these formulas, we compute revenue per day by

$$\text{Revenue per day (R/D)} = \text{Total revenue/Operating days per year} \qquad \textbf{(9.7)}$$

To understand the cash-to-cash conversion cycle and see how it is applied in a supply chain, we examine Dell's unique cash-to-cash conversion cycle. This also provides an interesting perspective on Dell's competitive strategy. Consider the performance data in Exhibit 9.5 for 1996 to 2003, extracted from Dell's annual reports. In 2003, for example, Dell's total revenue was \$35.4 billion with a cost of goods sold of $29.1 billion, resulting in a gross margin of $6.3 billion. Management focuses much of its attention on the gross margins per market segment with the objective of focusing on the markets it can profitability serve. Revenue per employee in 2003 was $905,371, which is 2 to 3 times more than its other competitors and has been increasing over the years.

For 2003, Dell's cost of goods sold per day was

$$\text{CGS/D} = \$29.1 \text{ billion}/365 \text{ days per year} = \$79,726,027$$

The inventory days' supply, which Dell calls "inventory velocity," was

$$\text{IDS} = \$306,000,000/\$79,726,000 = 3.8 \text{ days}$$

Dell's revenue per day was

$$\text{R/D} = \$35.4 \text{ billion}/365 \text{ days per year} = \$96,986,000$$

In addition, we find that

$$\text{ARDS} = \$2,586,000,000/\$96,986,000 = 26.8 \text{ days}$$

and

$$\text{APDS} = \$5,989,000,000/\$96,986,000 = 61.8 \text{ days}$$

Therefore, in 2003, Dell's cash-to-cash conversion cycle is

$$\text{C2C} = 3.8 \text{ days} + 26.8 \text{ days} - 61.8 \text{ days} = -31.2 \text{ days}$$

The negative value means that Dell receives customers' payments (accounts receivable) 31.2 days, on average, before Dell has to pay its suppliers (accounts payable). This means that Dell's value chain is a self-funding cash model! A negative cash-to-cash conversion cycle generates an amount of liquidity, or basically free cash flow, that funds Dell's growth and limits its need for external debt. Exhibit 9.6 illustrates this graphically.

Exhibit 9.5 Dell Computer's Cash-to-Cash Conversion Cycles 1996 to 2003

	Year							
	1996	**1997**	**1998**	**1999**	**2000**	**2001**	**2002**	**2003**
Revenue (billions $)	5.3	7.8	12.3	18.2	25.3	31.9	31.2	35.4
Cost of Goods Sold (billions $)	4.2	6.1	9.6	14.1	20.1	25.5	25.7	29.1
Gross Margin (billions $)	1.1	1.7	2.7	4.1	5.2	6.4	5.5	6.3
Number of Dell Employees	8,400	10,350	16,200	24,400	36,500	40,000	38,200	39,100
Revenue per Employee ($)	630,952	753,623	759,259	745,902	693,151	797,500	816,754	905,371
Revenue per Day (thousands $)	$14,521	$21,370	$33,699	$49,863	$69,315	$87,397	$85,479	$96,986
Cost of Goods Sold per Day (thousands $)	$11,507	$16,712	$26,301	$38,630	$55,068	$69,863	$70,411	$79,726
Total Inventory (millions $)	356.7	217.3	184.1	231.8	330.4	349.3	307.0	306.0
Inventory Days' Supply	**31.0**	**13.0**	**7.0**	**6.0**	**6.0**	**5.0**	**4.4**	**3.8**
Accounts Receivable (millions $)	609.9	790.7	1213.2	1795.1	2356.7	2796.7	2661.0	2586.0
Account Receivable Days' Supply	**42.0**	**37.0**	**36.0**	**36.0**	**34.0**	**32.0**	**31.1**	**26.8**
Accounts Payable (millions $)	479.2	1154.0	1718.6	2692.6	4020.3	5069.0	5936.0	5989.0
Accounts Payable Days' Supply	**33.0**	**54.0**	**51.0**	**54.0**	**58.0**	**58.0**	**69.4**	**61.8**
Cash Conversion Cycle (days)	**40.0**	**−4.0**	**−8.0**	**−12.0**	**−18.0**	**−21.0**	**−34.0**	**−31.2**

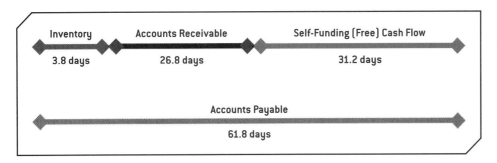

Exhibit 9.6
Dell's 2003 Negative Cash-to-Cash Conversion Cycle

Dell's extraordinary low days' supply of inventory also allows the company to take advantage of reductions in prices for chips, drives, and other computer components. Component prices generally fall dramatically after new versions are introduced, sometimes by as much as 1 percent per week. Most competitors have 20 to 60 days' supply of inventory, so they must use up their inventory before being able to take advantage of component part price reductions.

Exhibit 9.6 also illustrates the improvements that Dell has made in its supply chain. In 1996, Dell held a 31-day supply of inventory, resulting in a +40-day cash-to-cash conversion cycle. This is typical of the vast majority of businesses, which must borrow money to fund operations and improvement initiatives. In 1997, Dell achieved a dramatic reduction in inventory days' supply to 13 days. In 2003, this dropped further to 3 to 4 days, despite the difficulties of a U.S. economic recession in 2001–2002.

The Bullwhip Effect

The performance of a supply chain, in terms of both costs and service, often suffers from a phenomenon known as the **bullwhip effect**, which has been observed across most industries and increases cost and reduces service to the customer. The bullwhip effect results from order amplification in the supply chain. **Order amplification** *is a phenomenon that occurs when each member of a supply chain "orders up" to buffer its own inventory.*[10] In the case of a distributor, this might mean ordering extra finished goods; for a manufacturer, this might mean ordering extra raw materials or parts. Order amplification can be seen in Exhibit 9.7, which shows orders as compared to sales for an HP inkjet printer. The amplitude of sales over time is smaller than the variation in the order quantity. In this case, the distributor is ordering extra quantities as a hedge against the uncertainty in delivery or other factors, such as sudden surges in demand.

Order amplification increases as one moves back up the supply chain away from the retail customer. For example, small increases in demand by customers will cause distribution centers to increase their inventory. This leads to more frequent or larger orders to be placed with manufacturing. Manufacturing, in turn, will increase its purchasing of materials and components from suppliers. Because of lead times in ordering and delivery between each element of the supply chain, by the time the increased supply reaches the distribution center, customer demand may have leveled off or even dropped, resulting in an oversupply. This will trigger a reduction in orders back through the supply chain, resulting in undersupply later in time. Essentially, the time lags associated with information and material flow cause a mismatch between the actual customer demand and the supply chain's ability to satisfy that demand as each component of the supply chain seeks to manage its operations from its own perspective. This results in large oscillations of inventory in the supply chain network and characterizes the bullwhip effect.

Many firms are taking steps to counteract this phenomenon by modifying the supply chain infrastructure and operational processes. For example, instead of

Order amplification is a phenomenon that occurs when each member of a supply chain "orders up" to buffer its own inventory.

Exhibit 9.7
Order Amplification for HP
Printers

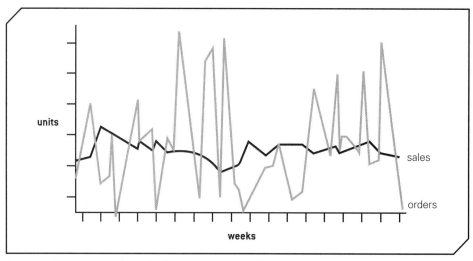

Source: Callioni, Gianpaolo, and Billington, Correy, "Effective Collaboration," *OR/MS Today*
October 2001, pp. 34–39.

ordering based on observed fluctuations in demand at the next stage of the supply
chain (which are amplified from other stages downstream), all members of the
supply chain should use the same demand data from the point of the supply chain
closest to the customer. Modern technology such as point-of-sale data collection,
electronic data interchange, and radio frequency identification chips can help to
provide such data. Other strategies include using smaller order sizes, stabilizing
price fluctuations (see the OM Spotlight on Procter & Gamble), and sharing information on sales, capacity, and inventory data among the members of the supply
chain.

DESIGNING THE SUPPLY CHAIN

Managers face numerous alternatives in designing a supply chain. For example,
most major airlines and trucking firms, for example, operate a "hub and spoke"
system, whereas others operate on a point-to-point basis. Some manufacturers use
complex networks of distribution centers, whereas others like Dell ship directly to
customers. Supply chains should support an organization's strategy, mission, and
competitive priorities. Thus, both strategic and operational perspectives must be included in supply chain design decisions.

Efficient and Responsive Supply Chains

Supply chains can be designed from two strategic perspectives—providing high efficiency and low cost or providing agile response. Efficient supply chains *are designed
for efficiency and low cost by minimizing inventory and maximizing efficiencies in
process flow.* This is especially important when low-cost, reliable, and consistent
service are key competitive priorities. A focus on efficiency works best for goods
and services with highly predictable demand, stable product lines with long life cycles that do not change frequently, and low contribution margins. In designing an
efficient supply chain, for example, an organization would seek to balance capacity and demand, resulting in low levels of inventory; might use only a few large distribution centers (as opposed to small ones) to generate economies of scale; and use
optimization models that minimize costs of routing products from factory through
distribution centers to retail stores and customers.

Learning Objective
To understand the scope of
issues involved in designing
supply chains, the differences
between efficient versus
responsive supply chains and
pull versus push systems, the
role of contract manufacturers,
and design of multisite supply
chains for services.

Efficient supply chains *are
designed for efficiency and
low cost by minimizing
inventory and maximizing
efficiencies in process flow.*

OM SPOTLIGHT

Value Pricing at Procter & Gamble[11]

"Consumers won't pay for a company's inefficiency." Thus, Edwin L. Artzt, former chairman of Procter & Gamble, one of the world's leading consumer products companies, led P&G's crusade to reduce product prices and give consumers better value. "Value pricing" was a fundamental change in long-term strategy for the company. The concept is to price products at a reasonable "everyday low price" rate, somewhere between the normal retail price and sale prices that are frequently offered. P&G learned through consumer research that up-and-down pricing policies were eroding the brands' perceived value. In other words, consumers began to think that P&G's brands were only worth their discount prices. When P&G discounted products, consumers stocked up and then substituted competitors' products when P&G's products were not on sale.

But the reasons for the switch to value pricing go deeper than consumer perceptions. Within the company, the frequent promotions sent costs spiraling. At one point, the company made 55 daily price changes on some 80 brands, which necessitated rework on every third order. Often, special packaging and handling were required. Ordering peaked during the promotions as distributors stockpiled huge quantities of goods (known as *forward buying*), which resulted in excessive overtime in the factories followed by periods of underutilization. Factories ran at 55 to 60 percent of rated efficiency with huge swings in output. These fluctuations strained the distribution system as well, loading up warehouses during slow periods and overworking the transportation systems at peak times.

With value pricing, demand rates are much smoother. Retailers automatically order products as they sell them. When 100 cases of Cheer detergent leave a retailer's warehouse, a computer orders 100 more. Both P&G and retailers save money. Plant efficiency rates have increased to over 80 percent across the company at the same time North American inventories dropped 10 percent.

Joe Higgins

The OM Spotlight on Wal-Mart highlights some of these issues. However, Wal-Mart may be facing a formidable competitor in Aldi, a German-based chain of supermarkets that some believe is more efficient than Wal-Mart. Wal-Mart's Supercenters may stock 150,000 items; Aldi has only about 700, mostly exclusive-label brands. Because it sells so few goods, it can exert strong control over quality and price and can simplify shipping and handling.[12]

On the other hand, **responsive supply chains** *focus on flexibility and responsive service and are able to react quickly to changing market demand and requirements.* A focus on flexibility and response is best when demand is unpredictable, product life cycles are short and change often because of product innovations, fast response is the main competitive priority, customers require customization, and contribution margins are high. Responsive supply chains have the ability to quickly respond to market changes and conditions faster than traditional supply chains, are supported by information technology that provides real-time, accurate information to managers across the supply chain, and use information to identify market changes and redirect resources to address these changes. From our previous discussion, it is easy to see that these characteristics apply to Dell as an example of a responsive supply chain. Sport Obermeyer, a fashion skiwear manufacturer based in Aspen, Colorado, doubled profits and grew sales by 60 percent in 2 years through improved forecasts and a more responsive supply chain.

Responsive supply chains *focus on flexibility and responsive service and are able to react quickly to changing market demand and requirements.*

OM SPOTLIGHT

Wal-Mart's Supply Chain[13]

Wal-Mart is ranked #1 in global sales of over $220 billion, surpassing global corporations such as General Motors and Exxon Mobil. Wal-Mart operates more than 3,500 discount stores and Sam's Clubs in the United States, 40 U.S. distribution centers, and over 1,200 stores in most major countries of the world. The superefficiency of Wal-Mart's supply chain is one of the major reasons it has achieved such market dominance and leadership status in the global retail industry.

A supply chain that offers a wide range of goods and services at low prices in the shortest possible time drives Wal-Mart's phenomenal growth. Due to an integrated supply chain information system, Wal-Mart replenishes its stores within 2 days while competitors take at least 5 days. Wal-Mart's shipping costs are about 3 percent of sales, whereas it is 5 percent for competitors. Wal-Mart owns and operates over 3,500 trucks and outsources the remaining shipping to third-party vendors. Wal-Mart uses cross-docking in which some finished goods are picked up at the supplier's factories, sorted out, and then directly supplied to each Wal-Mart store. These manufactured goods never see a warehouse or distribution center.

Supplier partnerships allow Wal-Mart to understand the cost structure of each good or service provided by the supplier, and they work together to drive out costs. With Wal-Mart's huge order quantities, suppliers are required to give extraordinary price discounts. Distribution centers run on a real-time information system where handheld devices, bar codes, and radio-frequency chips embedded in each good or pallet allow Wal-Mart to run a very efficient distribution center. Most supplier factories are tied directly into Wal-Mart's store information system so companies such as General Electric know exactly how many lightbulbs by type are sold in each store each day.

All of these supply chain management practices combine to create a world-class and superefficient supply chain. Some of the benefits of Wal-Mart's superefficient supply chain are faster inventory turnover, less warehouse space needed, better working capital and cash flow management, fast response to sales surges and fads, less safety stock, and prices that average 14 percent lower than competing stores.

In today's world, however, it is difficult to design a purely responsive supply chain without also focusing on efficiency. In many ways, efficiency and responsiveness go hand in hand—by streamlining operations to improve efficiency, responsiveness also naturally improves.

Push and Pull Systems

Two ways to configure and run a supply chain are as a push or pull system. A supply chain can be viewed from "left to right"—that is, materials, information, and goods are moved or pushed downstream from supplier to customer. *A push system produces goods in advance of customer demand using a forecast of sales and moves them through the supply chain to points of sale where they are stored as finished goods inventory.* Forecasting is critical, as an inaccurate sales forecast leads to either too much or too little inventory, excess capacity or capacity shortages in distribution centers, and higher stock-transfer costs. If point-of-sale forecasts are wrong, the company may be forced to move goods between distribution centers to accommodate customer demands, increasing transportation and handling costs unnecessarily. However, a push system has several advantages, such as immediate availability of goods to customers and the ability to reduce transportation costs by using full-truckload shipments to move goods to distribution centers. Push systems work best when sales patterns are consistent and when there are a small number of distribution centers and products.

In contrast, viewing the supply chain from "right to left" and transferring demand to upstream processes is sometimes referred to as a *demand chain* or *pull system*. *A pull system produces only what is needed at upstream stages in the supply chain in response to customer demand signals from downstream stages.* For example, in

A push system produces goods in advance of customer demand using a forecast of sales and moves them through supply chain to points of sale where they are stored as finished goods inventory.

A pull system produces only what is needed at upstream stages in the supply chain in response to customer demand signals from downstream stages.

a simple pull system, retailers send the order to a manufacturing facility as customer orders are placed. The manufacturing facility responds by ordering the parts needed from its suppliers. Although this results in a delay until the customer receives the finished good, it can greatly lower cost by reducing inventory requirements and ensures that the customer has the latest possible technology (or freshest goods if they are perishable). Sales forecasts are not needed, reducing uncertainty and simplifying the management of materials and purchasing functions. Dell's supply chain, which is based on an assemble-to-order process, is essentially a pull system because it holds little, if any, inventory but purchases it quickly from suppliers as needed. Pull systems are more effective when there are many production facilities, many points of distribution, and a large number of products. Pull systems are related to the concept of "just-in-time," which we discuss in Chapter 17.

Many supply chains are combinations of push and pull systems. This can be seen in the simplified version of several supply chains in Exhibit 9.8. *The point in the supply chain that separates the push system from the pull system is called the* **push-pull boundary.** For a company like Dell, the push-pull boundary is very early in the supply chain where suppliers store inventory for frequent deliveries to Dell factories. Dell also ships directly to the customer, skipping the distributors and retailers. General Motors stores finished goods closer to the customer, at dealers. GM pushes finished goods from its factories to the dealer. Dealers might install various options to customize the automobile for the customer. Customers pull the finished goods from the dealer. Thus, the push-pull boundary for General Motors is at the dealers.

The point in the supply chain that separates the push system from the pull system is called the **push-pull boundary.**

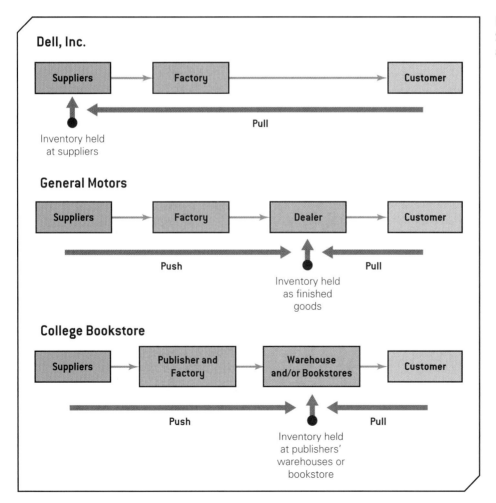

Exhibit 9.8
Supply Chain Push-Pull Systems and Boundaries

The third example in Exhibit 9.8 is the supply chain for a college textbook publisher, which begins by ordering raw materials such as paper and ink. The publisher pushes books from design through printing and stores them in warehouses. The pull system begins with instructor order forms for required textbooks and reading lists of optional or supplemental books, consolidation of these demands and estimation of the quantities needed by college bookstores, and placement of orders with publishers. The bookstore purchasing function must effectively interface with the publisher's distribution function. Publishers ship from their warehouses to bookstores or directly to bookstores from the factory.

The location of the push-pull boundary can affect how responsive a supply chain is. Many firms try to push as much of the finished product as possible close to the customer to speed up response and reduce work in process inventory requirements. **Postponement** *is the process of delaying product customization until the product is closer to the customer at the end of the supply chain.* An example is a manufacturer of dishwashers that have different door styles and colors. The manufacturer might make each type of model and send them to distribution centers, without postponement. However, this would require an extensive inventory. An alternative postponement strategy would be to manufacture the dishwasher without the door and maintain inventories of doors at the distribution centers. When orders arrive, the doors can be quickly attached and the unit can be shipped. This would reduce inventory requirements.

Postponement is the process of delaying product customization until the product is closer to the customer at the end of the supply chain.

Contract Manufacturing

One critical issue that organizations must wrestle with in designing their supply chains is the level of vertical integration. As defined in Chapter 2, vertical integration refers to the decisions of what processes are performed "in-house" and controlled by the firm and which ones are outsourced. Many supply chains use contract manufacturing as a key outsourcing strategy.

A **contract manufacturer** *is a firm that specializes in certain types of goods-producing activities, such as customized design, manufacturing, assembly, and packaging, and works under contract for end users.* Some of the major global contract manufacturers are Flextronics International Ltd., Solectron, Jabil Circuit, Hon Hai Precision Industrial, Celestica Inc., and Sanmina-SCI Corporation. These firms produce for such well-known companies as Microsoft, Motorola, and Hewlett-Packard. Outsourcing to contract manufacturers can offer significant competitive advantages, such as access to advanced manufacturing technologies, faster product time-to-market, customization of goods in regional markets, and lower total costs resulting from economies of scale.

A **contract manufacturer** *is a firm that specializes in certain types of goods-producing activities, such as customized design, manufacturing, assembly, and packaging, and works under contract for end users.*

Many contract manufacturers act more like service organizations in providing expertise in many different stages of the product development process and the supply chain. For example, Solectron, which specializes in the electronics industry, offers advanced, state-of-the-art manufacturing processes for electronic component assembly and printed circuit board manufacturing. It works closely with customers during design, prototyping, supply base planning, and production release stages. Each customer is supported by a customer focus team to ensure that customer needs are met and that any problems that arise are addressed quickly and appropriately.

Contract manufacturers often work with customers to develop supply chains that optimize cost and delivery requirements. For example, Solectron tracks supplier performance in quality, delivery, and service; if problems arise, Solectron manages the corrective action. Flextronics ships most of the cell and picture phones it makes to the United States using Federal Express; however, the much heavier phone batteries are shipped by boat, saving on airfreight. Tim Dinwiddle, Flextronics, vice president of plant operations at Doumen, China, says, "We constantly are looking for fractions of a penny cost savings."[14]

Supply Chain Design for Multisite Services

Many service organizations operate large numbers of similar facilities. For instance, McDonald's Corporation has over 30,000 stores in 121 countries, Bank of America has over 16,000 ATMs and 5,700 branch banks in the United States, and Federal Express operates over 1 million drop-off mailboxes in 215 countries. All these organizations began with a single facility. Today, entrepreneurial ventures are continually being born and developed and require effective supply chain planning as they expand and multiply to new locations. Some of these ventures might offer a stable set of goods and services and replicate themselves in new locations. Many hotel chains, fast-food operations, and retail stores fall in this category. Others might maintain a relatively small set of locations but change their bundle of goods and services frequently. Still others might do both—expand in multiple locations and add new goods and services as the venture grows.[15] **Multisite management** *is the process of managing geographically dispersed service-providing facilities.* Supply chains are vital to multisite management, and in each of these cases, it can be difficult to design a good supporting supply chain.

Multisite management *is the process of managing geographically dispersed service-providing facilities.*

In the first scenario, in which a firm has a stable customer benefit package and many identical and standardized facilities, the supply chain should focus on standard processes and performance metrics. In the early 1970s, for example, Wendy's grew its business by adding more sites while keeping its customer benefit package and facility designs relatively stable. Standardization increases control and helps lower cost. As Wendy's added sites, it continued to experiment with different food options and facility layouts and decor, but the CBP and facility design remained relatively stable. Marriott Courtyard, described in Chapter 6, is another example. In these situations, an efficient supply chain design is most appropriate.

In the second scenario, in which a firm has at most a few sites and provides a broad customer benefit package with many goods and services, the firm cannot generally compete on low cost, but rather competes on variety and service. Thus, a responsive supply chain design is best. Small firms like these have little power in the supply chain to negotiate large price breaks or leverage a small number of suppliers. Supply chains are normally restricted to the local area and may involve a diverse supplier base. Although the supply chain may be complex, having only a few sites makes it manageable.

One example is Stew Leonard's, which entrenched itself in business folklore by its passionate approach to customer service and the legendary "rules" of business: Rule #1—The Customer is Always Right and Rule #2—If the Customer is Ever Wrong, Re-Read Rule #1. The family-owned business began with a 17,000-square-foot grocery store carrying just eight items. Today, Stew Leonard's has four stores that carry only 2,000 items, chosen specifically for their freshness, quality, and value, but annual sales of nearly $300 million. Stew Leonard's was dubbed the "Disneyland of Dairy Stores" by the *New York Times*, because of its own milk-processing plant, costumed characters, scheduled entertainment, petting zoo, and animatronics throughout the stores. In 1992, Stew Leonard's earned an entry into *The Guinness Book of World Records* for having "the greatest sales per unit area of any single food store in the United States."

Finally, in the third scenario where both the customer benefit package and the number of facilities are changing simultaneously, supply chain design and management is more difficult. For example, if stores in a fast-food chain offer chicken sandwiches at some sites and only beef at the other sites, the supply chain must adjust to the additional purchasing, delivery, equipment, cooking, and inventory requirements. Likewise, if store layouts vary widely in square footage and configurations or food storage space, it is difficult to measure relative store performance and supply chain efficiency. It is also harder to manage staffing and schedules. With nonstandard facilities and changing goods and service configurations, it is virtually impossible to design an efficient or responsive supply chain. Firms that knowingly or unknowingly pursue this growth strategy often fail.

LOCATION DECISIONS IN SUPPLY CHAINS

The principal goal of a supply chain is to provide customers with accurate and quick response to their orders at the lowest possible cost. This requires a network of facilities that are located strategically in the supply chain. Thus, location decisions can have a profound effect on supply chain performance and a firm's competitive advantage (see the OM Spotlight on Toyota and Ford). For example, a manufacturing facility must be located so that materials and goods can easily be acquired from suppliers and transported to customers (which may be distributors or retail outlets). Primax, a Taiwanese producer of computer mice, operates in an industry with extremely small margins. To keep costs at a minimum, it ensures that its factories are located within a few hours of key suppliers so it can wait until the last minute to buy what it needs. Finding such clusters of networked companies is common in Asia.[16]

Facility network and location focuses on determining the best network structure and geographical locations for facilities to maximize service and revenue and to minimize costs. These decisions can become complex, especially for a global supply chain, which must consider shipping costs between all demand and supply points in the network, fixed operating costs of each distribution and/or retail facility, revenue generation per customer location, facility labor and operating costs, and construction costs.

In Chapter 2 we noted that foreign factories can be categorized into six types—offshore, outpost, server, source, contributor, and lead factories. The type of factory and its location affects the supply chain structure. For example, offshore factories

OM SPOTLIGHT

Toyota and Ford

The largest Toyota parts center in the world—843,000 square feet—was built in Northern Kentucky just west of the Greater Cincinnati/Northern Kentucky International Airport as a part of its globalization strategy.[17] The warehouse receives and stocks 42,000 repair and service parts from more than 375 North American suppliers and its assembly plants and ships parts to 20 distribution centers in North America, Europe, and Japan for Toyota dealers. Toyota has located production operations in each part of the world where it sells cars and trucks. It also has a similar distribution center in Ontario, California, to handle distribution of parts from Japan to its North American dealers. The facility has allowed Toyota to lower its inventory days of supply on some fast-moving parts down to 8 days, from a typical 30–60 days. This reduced space requirements and inventory requirements significantly.

Similarly, Ford Motor Company is planning to build a 155-acre manufacturing campus next to its Chicago assembly plant.[18] It will consist of six buildings holding nine companies who supply the assembly plant with parts. No supplier is more than one-half mile from the assembly plant. Suppliers located on the campus account for a significant amount of the value of the vehicle.

Roman Krygier, group vice president of manufacturing and quality, said, "And we know the quality's going to get better and we are going to be able to respond to customers much more quickly because we won't have to deal with suppliers 500, 600, 700 miles away." Jan Kowal, the president of Brose North America, which makes parts that are used in the car doors, said by locating next to the assembly plant it will cut its costs by as much as 20 percent. Ford plans to use the manufacturing campus concept and see if the efficiency of the value chain increases and cost decreases.

do not include product design and research functions whereas a lead factory has the expertise to design and produce the next generation of products. Each configuration of a network of facilities creates a unique cost-service trade-off. A global manufacturer, for example, might use 3 lead factories, 4 source factories, and 7 offshore factories, 10 large distribution centers (DCs), and 30 smaller district warehouses to serve retail customers worldwide. In this configuration, the firm incurs the cost of operating and maintaining inventory at the district warehouses along with the shipping costs between the DCs and the warehouses. However, being close to customers would provide quick response to orders and high reliability of delivery. An alternative might be to have only the 10 large DCs and close the 30 district warehouses. This alternative would require less inventory and operating expense but would probably result in slower average customer delivery times and less reliability or consistent service. Thus, organizations face often difficult trade-offs in balancing cost against service. An interesting example of how cost and service trade-offs were evaluated by Tesco in designing its supply chain is described in the OM Spotlight.

Larger firms have more complex location decisions; they might have to position a large number of factories and distribution centers advantageously with respect to suppliers, retail outlets, *and* each other. Rarely are these decisions made simultaneously. Typically, factories are located with respect to suppliers and a fixed set of distribution centers, or distribution centers are located with respect to a fixed set of factories and markets. A firm might also choose to locate a facility in a new geographic region not only to provide cost or service efficiencies but also to

OM SPOTLIGHT

Tesco[19]

Tesco is Britain's #1 supermarket chain and now the world's largest online grocer. Tesco accepts customer orders over the web, by fax, and by telephone. Tesco is the first grocer to make a profit delivering groceries to customers' homes. The company had to decide whether to pick grocery orders off the shelves of its stores or build separate warehouses to fill online customer orders. It decided to pick orders from its current stores and not build new warehouses for the online business. Instead of going high tech and building a separate distribution and automated warehousing system for online orders, it decided to remain simple, using about 12 people in about one-third of its stores to pull grocery products off the shelves, load them into vans, and deliver them to customers' doorsteps. In 2001, Tesco.com handled 3.7 million orders. As business grows, Tesco expects to adopt a hybrid approach with warehouses in big cities specifically designed for online customers and order picking.

Tesco's strategic plan was just the opposite of bankrupt U.S. Webvan's strategy. Webvan spent $1.2 billion building two dozen automated warehouses around the United States, each of which was to serve a 60-mile radius in major

U.S. cities like Chicago, Atlanta, and Oakland. However, because expected customer demand did not materialize, the large fixed cost of the warehousing system resulted in a loss of $5 to $30 per customer grocery order. With depreciation, marketing, and overhead costs, Webvan lost over $130 per customer order.

create cultural ties between the firm and the local community. The relationships established may attract new business and improve the firm's market position and brand image in relation to distant competitors.

Location is also critical in service value chains. A great servicescape and facility layout can seldom overcome a poor location decision, simply because customers may not have convenient access, which is one of the most important requirements for a service facility. A great location for a supermarket, fast-food restaurant, or bank can generate high customer volume even with a poorly designed facility if little competition or few alternatives are available. Service facilities such as post offices, branch banks, dentist offices, and fire stations typically need to be in close proximity to the customer. In many cases, the customer travels to the service facility, whereas in others, such as mobile X-ray and imaging centers or "on-call" computer repair services, the service travels to the customer. Criteria for locating these facilities differ, depending on the nature of the service. For example, service facilities that customers travel to, such as public libraries and urgent-care facilities, seek to minimize the maximum distance or travel time required from among the customer population. For those that travel to customer locations, such as fire stations, the location decision seeks to minimize response time to customers.

Critical Factors in Location Decisions

Location decisions in supply and value chains are based on both economic and noneconomic factors. Exhibit 9.9 is a list of some important location factors for site selection. Economic factors include facility costs, such as construction, utilities, insurance, taxes, depreciation, and maintenance; operating costs, including fuel, direct labor, and administrative personnel; and transportation costs associated with moving goods and services from their origins to the final destinations or the opportunity cost of customers coming to the facility. Many of these factors, such as construction costs, taxes, and wage rates, vary by location. Low wage rates are a major reason many companies move factories to other countries. Many states offer tax incentives to entice companies to build plants there. Transportation costs can be a large proportion of the total delivered cost of a product, however, and locating a plant far from sources of supply or customers can commit a company to significant transportation costs. Thus, the facility location decision must attempt to minimize the combined cost of producing the good or service and delivering them to customers.

Economic criteria are not always the most important factors in such decisions. Sometimes location decisions are based upon strategic objectives, such as preempting competitors from entering a geographical region. New facilities also require large amounts of capital investment and, once built, cannot easily be moved. Moreover, location decisions also affect the management of operations at lower levels of the organization. For instance, if a manufacturing facility is located far from sources of raw materials, it may take a considerable amount of time to deliver an order, and there will be more uncertainty as to the actual time of delivery. To guard against shortages, larger inventories must be carried, thus increasing costs. Likewise, if a factory or warehouse is located far from market centers, higher transportation costs are incurred in delivering finished goods to customers. The availability of labor and utilities, state and local politics, climate, and other factors all affect the productivity and quality of the operating system.

Noneconomic factors in location decisions include the availability of labor, transportation services, and utilities; climate, community environment, and quality of life; and state and local legal and political factors. There must be a sufficient supply of labor to meet planned output levels; in addition, workers must have the appropriate skills. Labor-intensive firms may want to locate where wage rates and costs of training are low. Some companies may require trucking service, and other

Exhibit 9.9 Example Location Factors for Site Selection

Labor and Demand Factors	Transportation Factors	Utilities Factors	Climate, Community Environment, and Quality of Life Factors	State and Local Legal and Political Factors
Labor supply	Closeness to sources of supply	Water supply	Climate and living conditions	Taxation climate and policies
Labor-management relations	Closeness to markets	Waste disposal	K–12 schools	Local and state tax structure
Ability to retain labor force	Adequacy of transportation modes (air, truck, train, water)	Power supply	Universities and research facilities	Opportunity for highway advertising
Availability of adequate labor skills	Costs of transportation	Fuel availability	Community attitudes	Tax incentives and abatements
Labor rates	Visibility of the facility from the highway	Communications capability	Health care facilities	Zoning laws
Location of competitors	Parking capability	Price/cost	Property costs	Health and safety laws
Volume of traffic around location	Response time for emergency services	Utility regulatory laws and practices	Cost of living	Regulatory agencies and policies

firms may require rail service. Other firms need to be close to water transportation or major airports. All production activities require such services as electricity, water, and waste removal. For example, chemical processing, paper, and nuclear power companies require large amounts of water for cooling and therefore would consider only locations near an abundant water supply. A favorable climate is good for employee well-being and morale. Taxes, the cost of living, and educational and cultural facilities are all important to employees, particularly if they are relocating. Community attitudes should also be evaluated. For example, industries that handle high-risk chemicals or radioactive substances are particularly susceptible to unfavorable public reaction and legislation and are less likely to locate in urban areas. Finally, the political attitudes of the state can be either favorable or unfavorable to locating there. Activities such as industrial development programs, revenue bond financing, state industrial loans, and tax inducements are often important factors in choosing to locate in one state instead of another.

Many location decisions, particularly for retail stores and services, are based on customer demographics. For example, a bank that needs to determine good locations for automatic teller machines (ATMs) might examine the following variables related to potential locations:

- population;
- median income, education, and age;
- number of businesses and homes with Internet service;
- number of customers using an existing ATM site;
- location of the ATM at a bank branch or not;
- number of ATM cards in a given area such as Zip code (from bank records);
- commercial or residential nature of the ATM site;
- dollar sales per retail establishment;
- traffic counts at the site (obtained from the regional planning agency);
- number of employed persons;

- number of occupied households;
- number of persons in different age groups (for example, over 60, teenagers, and so on).

This information might be analyzed with a quantitative model such as regression analysis to predict the volume of transactions in potential locations and thus determine good candidates.

Public-service facilities include fire departments, post offices, schools, police, libraries, highways, parks, government offices, road maintenance garages, and so on. Some of the typical criteria used in public-service location decisions include the average distance or time traveled by the users of the facilities and the maximum distance or travel time between the facility and its intended population. That is, "convenience" and "access" are important criteria in public-sector location decisions.

Emergency facilities such as fire stations, ambulance stations, and police substations are often located so as to minimize response time between the notification of an emergency and the delivery of service. The problem is complicated by the somewhat random and spiked nature of demand; for instance, weekend demand for ambulance and library services is often 5 to 10 times greater than average demand.

Location Decision Process

Facility location is typically conducted hierarchically and involves the following four basic decisions where appropriate:

1. global (nation) location,
2. regional location,
3. district or community location,
4. local site selection.

Many companies must cope with issues of global operations, such as time zones, foreign languages, international funds transfer, customs, tariffs and other trade restrictions, packaging, international monetary policy, and cultural practices. The global location decision involves evaluating the product portfolio, new market opportunities, changes in regulatory laws and procedures, production and delivery economics, and the cost to locate in different countries. With this information, the company needs to determine whether it should locate domestically or in another country, what countries are most amenable to setting up a facility (and what countries to avoid), and how important it is to establish a local presence in other regions of the world. Mercedes' decision to locate in Alabama was based on the fact that German labor costs were about 50 percent higher than in the southern United States; the plant also gave the company better inroads into the American market and functions as a kind of laboratory for future global manufacturing ventures.

The regional location decision involves choosing a general region of a country, such as the Northeast or South. Factors that affect the regional decision include size of the target market, the locations of major customers and sources of materials and supply; labor availability and costs; degree of unionization; land, construction, and utility costs; quality of life; and climate. The district or community location decision involves selecting a specific city or community in which to locate. In addition to the factors cited previously, a company would consider managers' preferences, community services and taxes (as well as tax incentives), available transportation systems, banking services, and environmental impacts. Mercedes settled on Vance, Alabama, after considering sites in 30 different states. Alabama pledged $250 million in tax abatements and other incentives, and the local business community came up with $11 million. The community also submitted a plan for how it would help the families of German workers adjust to life in that community. Similarly, Dell chose to locate a warehouse just north of Cincinnati because of its proximity to DHL's hub, allowing parts to be shipped overnight to most of the United States, availability of workers, and a tax incentive package. Finally, the site location decision involves the selection of a particular location within the chosen community. Site costs, proximity to transportation systems, utilities, payroll and local taxes, environmental issues, and zoning restrictions are among the factors to be considered.

QUANTITATIVE MODELS IN SUPPLY CHAIN DESIGN

As we have seen throughout this chapter, supply chain design and location decisions are quite difficult to analyze and make. Many types of quantitative models and approaches, ranging from simple to complex, can be used to facilitate these decisions. In this section, we introduce several basic approaches. Many of these are the foundation for more sophisticated models used in practice.

Location Scoring Models

The most common method for evaluating factors in a facility location study is to use a **scoring model**, *which consists of a list of major location criteria, each of which is partitioned into several levels, and an assigned score to each level that reflects its relative importance.* For example, consider these qualitative factors: climate, water availability, schools, housing, government, and labor. An illustrative scoring model is shown in the spreadsheet in Exhibit 9.10. In this exhibit, the levels for each factor range from 0, representing the least desirable, to 4, representing ideal conditions. Suppose that the Halvorsen Supply Company has identified two sites for a new facility. Using the scoring model, managers have evaluated each site as shown in columns D and E (by placing a 1 in the appropriate cells). The spreadsheet template is designed to compute the total scores for each location (and can easily be modified for additional locations). Site B appears to have an overall advantage for these criteria, but such a scoring model should only be used as a guide. Other factors such as construction, transportation, and utility costs also must be considered. The final approval, however, rests with top managers.

This model also assumes that each factor is equal in importance. This can easily be changed by multiplying the scores for a particular factor by some weight to obtain a weighted score, which might provide greater differentiation. Such a weighting of the factors is rather subjective and is best done after careful analysis by a group of experienced personnel.

Center of Gravity Method

The **center-of-gravity method** *determines the X and Y coordinates (location) for a single facility.* Although it does not explicitly address customer service objectives, it can be used to assist managers in balancing cost and service objectives. The center-of-gravity method takes into account the locations of the facility and markets, demand, and transportation costs in arriving at the best location for a single facility. It would seem reasonable to find some "central" location between the goods-producing or service-providing facility and customers at which to locate the new facility. But distance alone should not be the principal criterion, since the demand (volume, transactions, and so on) from one location to another also affects the costs. To incorporate distance and demand, the center of gravity is defined as the location that minimizes the weighted distance between the facility and its supply and demand points.

Learning Objective
To be able to apply simple quantitative methods and models to help locate goods-producing or service-providing facilities.

A **scoring model** *consists of a list of major location criteria, each of which is partitioned into several levels, and an assigned score to each level that reflects its relative importance.*

The **center-of-gravity method** *determines the X and Y coordinates (location) for a single facility.*

Exhibit 9.10
Facility Location Scoring Model

	A	B	C	D	E
1	**Facility Location Scoring Model**				
2					
3	Factor	Scoring Descriptor	Score	Site A	Site B
4	Climate	Prohibitive for manufacturing	0		
5		Susceptible to high climate variations, such as storms, f	1		
6		Moderate climate variation, possible impediments to proc	2	1	
7		Some variation to deal with, quite livable	3		
8		Ideal climate	4		1
9					
10	Water	Unavailable	0		
11		Available in small quantities, costly to import	1		
12		Available for living, limited access or purity for manufac	2	1	
13		Sufficient in quantity and purity for manufacturing	3		1
14		Virtually unlimited and pure	4		
15					
16	Schools	No schools close by	0		
17		Low quality public schools	1	1	
18		Low quality public, but good private schools	2		
19		High quality public and private schools	3		1
20		Wide variety of choices, including community colleges	4		
21					
22	Housing	No housing close by	0		
23		Little housing available and poor quality	1		
24		Good availability and reasonable costs	2		
25		Wide variety, reasonable costs	3		1
26		High quality, large variety, low cost of living	4	1	
27					
28	Government	Hostile political atmosphere	0		
29		Non cooperative local government	1		
30		Cooperative local government	2	1	1
31		Friendly and business-oriented	3		
32		Highly cooperative and pro-business	4		
33					
34	Labor	No availability of skilled or unskilled workers	0		
35		Some unskilled workers available	1		
36		Some skilled but mostly unskilled workers available	2	1	
37		Balance of skilled and unskilled workers	3		
38		Many skilled workers available	4		1
39			TOTAL	13	19

The first step in the procedure is to place the locations of existing supply and demand points on a coordinate system. The origin of the coordinate system and scale used are arbitrary, as long as the relative distances are correctly represented. Placing a grid over an ordinary map is one way to do that. The center of gravity is determined by Equations (9.8) and (9.9), and can easily be implemented on a spreadsheet.

$$C_x = \sum X_i W_i / \sum W_i \qquad \textbf{(9.8)}$$

$$C_y = \sum Y_i W_i / \sum W_i \qquad \textbf{(9.9)}$$

where

$C_x = x$ coordinate of the center of gravity
$C_y = y$ coordinate of the center of gravity
$X_i = x$ coordinate of location i
$Y_i = y$ coordinate of location i
$W_i = $ volume of goods or services moved to or from location i

The following example illustrates the application of the center-of-gravity method.

Taylor Paper Products is a producer of paper stock used in newspapers and magazines. Taylor's demand is relatively constant and thus can be forecast rather accurately. The company's two factories are located in Hamilton, Ohio, and

Kingsport, Tennessee. They distribute paper stock to four major markets: Chicago, Pittsburgh, New York, and Atlanta. The board of directors has authorized the construction of an intermediate warehouse to service those markets. Coordinates for the factories and markets are shown in Exhibit 9.11. For example, we see that location 1, Hamilton, is at the coordinate (58, 96); therefore, $X_1 = 58$ and $Y_1 = 96$. Hamilton and Kingsport produce 400 and 300 tons per month, respectively. Demand at Chicago, Pittsburgh, New York, and Atlanta is 200, 100, 300, and 100 tons per month, respectively. With that information, the center of gravity coordinates are computed as follows:

$$C_x = \frac{(58)(400) + (80)(300) + (30)(200) + (90)(100) + (127)(300) + (65)(100)}{400 + 300 + 200 + 100 + 300 + 100}$$

$$= 76.3$$

$$C_y = \frac{(96)(400) + (70)(300) + (120)(200) + (110)(100) + (130)(300) + (40)(100)}{400 + 300 + 200 + 100 + 300 + 100}$$

$$= 98.1$$

This location (76.3, 98.1) is shown by the cross on Exhibit 9.11. By overlaying a map on this figure, we see that the location is near the border of southern Ohio and West Virginia. Managers now can search that area for an appropriate site. Exhibit 9.12 is a spreadsheet (Taylor Paper Products.xls) designed to calculate the center of gravity using Equations (9.8) and (9.9).

The center-of-gravity method is often used to locate service facilities. For example, in locating a waste disposal facility, the location coordinates can be weighted by the average amount of waste generated from residential neighborhoods and industrial sites. Similarly, to locate a library, fire station, hospital, or post office, the population densities will define the appropriate weights in the model.

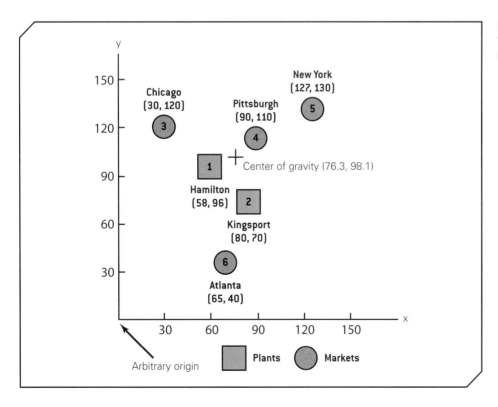

Exhibit 9.11
Taylor Paper Products Plant and Customer Locations

Exhibit 9.12
Excel Spreadsheet for Taylor
Paper Products

	A	B	C	D
1	**Taylor Paper Products**			
2				
3	**Location**	**x-coordinate**	**y-coordinate**	**Tons/month**
4	Hamilton	58	96	400
5	Kingsport	80	70	300
6	Chicago	30	120	200
7	Pittsburgh	90	110	100
8	New York	127	130	300
9	Atlanta	65	40	100
10				
11	**Center of gravity**			
12	x-coordinate	76.3		
13	y-coordinate	98.1		

Transportation Model

If facility locations are fixed, a minimum-cost location plan can be found by solving a transportation problem. This is a special type of mathematical model that arises in planning the distribution of goods and services from several supply points to several demand locations. Usually, the quantity of goods available at each supply location (origin) is limited, and a specified quantity of goods is needed at each demand location (destination). With a variety of shipping routes and differing transportation costs for the routes, the objective is to determine how many units should be shipped from each origin to each destination so that all supply capacity limits and destination demands are satisfied with a minimum total transportation cost. The problem can be modeled formally as a linear program (see Supplementary Chapter C). Supplementary Chapter C also describes how to model and solve transportation problems using Microsoft Excel Solver. In the following example, we illustrate the use of this model in finding a minimum-cost distribution plan.

Arnoff Enterprises manufactures the motherboards for a line of personal computers. They are manufactured in Seattle, Columbus, and New York and shipped to warehouses in Pittsburgh, Mobile, Denver, Los Angeles, and Washington, DC, for further distribution. Exhibit 9.13 shows a spreadsheet with the unit transportation costs, the supply at each plant, and the demand at each warehouse in rows 3 through 7. The company seeks to determine a minimum-cost distribution plan that satisfies all demands at the warehouses while ensuring that shipments from manufacturing plants do not exceed the available supplies. In addition, the company is considering closing the Denver warehouse and shifting its demand to Los Angeles. It needs to know how that would affect the total cost.

In Exhibit 9.13, the cells in the range B13:F15 represent the shipments from the plants to the warehouses. Note that the totals shipped from each plant (in cells G13:G15) do not exceed the supplies (in cells G4:G6), and that the totals shipped to each warehouse (in cells G16:F16) equal the demand (in cells B7:F7).

This model was solved using Microsoft Excel Solver described in Supplementary Chapter C. We find that the minimum total transportation cost is $150,000, which is obtained by shipping 4,000 units from Seattle to Denver, 5,000 units from Seattle to Los Angeles, 4,000 units from Columbus to Mobile, 3,000 units from New York to Pittsburgh, 1,000 units from New York to Mobile, 1,000 units from New York to Los Angeles, and 3,000 units from New York to Washington, DC.

Exhibit 9.13 Transportation Model Spreadsheet for Arnoff Enterprises (Arnoff Enterprises.xls)

	A	B	C	D	E	F	G
1	Arnoff Enterprises						
2							
3	Unit Shipping Costs	Pittsburgh	Mobile	Denver	Los Angeles	Washington	Supply (000)
4	Seattle	$ 10.00	$ 20.00	$ 5.00	$ 9.00	$ 10.00	9
5	Columbus	$ 2.00	$ 10.00	$ 8.00	$ 30.00	$ 6.00	4
6	New York	$ 1.00	$ 20.00	$ 7.00	$ 10.00	$ 4.00	8
7	Demand (000)	3	5	4	6	3	
8							
9							
10	Decision Variables and Solution						
11							
12		Pittsburgh	Mobile	Denver	Los Angeles	Washington	
13	Seattle	0	0	4	5	0	9
14	Columbus	0	4	0	0	0	4
15	New York	3	1	0	1	3	8
16		3	5	4	6	3	
17							
18	Total cost	$ 150.00					

If the Denver warehouse is closed and its demand is shifted to Los Angeles, the total cost increases by $16,000 (see Exhibit 9.14). The only difference in the solution is that Seattle now ships all 9,000 units directly to Los Angeles. Managers can now use this information to determine if the increase in transportation cost can be offset by savings from closing the Denver warehouse.

Exhibit 9.14 Optimal Distribution Plan if Denver Warehouse is Closed

	A	B	C	D	E	F	G
1	Arnoff Enterprises						
2							
3	Unit Shipping Costs	Pittsburgh	Mobile	Denver	Los Angeles	Washington	Supply (000)
4	Seattle	$ 10.00	$ 20.00	$ 5.00	$ 9.00	$ 10.00	9
5	Columbus	$ 2.00	$ 10.00	$ 8.00	$ 30.00	$ 6.00	4
6	New York	$ 1.00	$ 20.00	$ 7.00	$ 10.00	$ 4.00	8
7	Demand (000)	3	5	0	10	3	
8							
9							
10	Decision Variables and Solution						
11							
12		Pittsburgh	Mobile	Denver	Los Angeles	Washington	
13	Seattle	0	0	0	9	0	9
14	Columbus	0	4	0	0	0	4
15	New York	3	1	0	1	3	8
16		3	5	0	10	3	
17							
18	Total cost	$ 166.00					

Network Location Models

Many sites, such as emergency facilities, must be located for accessibility along public roads. Thus, the best location must take into account travel times. Consider the small township of Marymount on the outskirts of a large city. Currently, the township is serviced by the city fire department just outside the township limits. However, costs of purchasing that service have been escalating, and the township trustees have decided to organize their own fire department. The township is divided into several zones based on the geographic structure of the community. The center of each zone, the distance between zones, and the travel time in minutes along the major roads are shown in Exhibit 9.15

Where should the fire station be located? We first must define an objective to use in evaluating potential sites. Suppose the goal is to locate the station so that the maximum response time to any other zone is the shortest possible. We assume that the route taken corresponds to the shortest time between zones. For instance, suppose the station is located in zone 1. We must determine how long it would take to travel to each of the other zones in the shortest possible time. For our purposes, we do this by inspecting Exhibit 9.15 and verifying that the shortest travel times from zone 1 to all others are as follows.

To Zone	2	3	4	5	6	7	8
Shortest Time	2	6	4	4	5	7	7

For example, the shortest route from zone 1 to zone 7 is through zones 2, 5, and 6. The maximum response time from zone 1 to any other zone is 7 minutes. Next, suppose we locate in zone 2. The shortest times from zone 2 to all other zones are as follows.

To Zone	1	3	4	5	6	7	8
Shortest Time	2	4	3	2	3	5	5

The longest time is 5 minutes. Therefore, zone 2 is a better location than zone 1 according to this criterion. If we compute the shortest travel times from each zone to every other zone, we obtain the following:

	To								Longest Time
From	**1**	**2**	**3**	**4**	**5**	**6**	**7**	**8**	**(minutes)**
1	—	2	6	4	4	5	7	7	7
2	2	—	4	3	2	3	5	5	5
3	6	4	—	7	6	6	8	8	8
4	4	3	7	—	5	6	8	8	8
5	4	2	6	5	—	1	3	3	6
6	5	3	6	6	1	—	2	2	6
7	7	5	8	8	3	2	—	1	8
8	7	5	8	8	3	2	1	—	8

To minimize the longest response time, the fire station should be located in zone 2.

As computer power increases, network and transportation models are becoming more useful. Network models, for example, use the locations of facilities (called nodes) and the volume, distance, time, or cost between nodes (called arcs) to compute solutions that minimize cost, distance traveled, and response and delivery time. As Irv Lustig, an operations research analyst at ILOG Inc., said, "We're developing algorithms that are 10,000 times faster than the ones we used 15 years ago."[20]

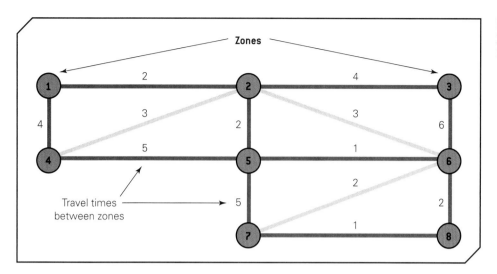

Exhibit 9.15
Zone Connections for
Marymount Township

SUPPLY CHAIN MANAGEMENT DESIGN ISSUES

Issues of supply chain structure and facility location represent broad strategic decisions in supply chain design. Managing a supply chain also requires numerous operational decisions, such as selecting transportation services, evaluating suppliers, managing inventory, and other issues.

Selecting Transportation Services

The selection of transportation services is a complex decision, since varied services are available—rail, motor carrier, air, water, and pipeline. Pipelines have limited use and accessibility and are used primarily for such products as oil and natural gas. Similarly, water transportation is generally limited to transporting large quantities of bulky items—historically, raw materials such as coal and now furniture. (See OM Spotlight: Faster Supply Chains for American Furniture Manufacturers.)

The critical factors in transportation decisions are speed, accessibility, cost, and capability. Weight restrictions and loading and unloading facilities would sometimes be included in these considerations. A comparison of three modes of transportation illustrates their differences on those factors (Exhibit 9.16). Rail transit is generally slow and is used primarily for shipping large volumes of relatively low-value items over long distances. However, rail cars often encounter long delays and are less dependable than other forms of transportation. Motor carriers have high availability and can ship nearly anywhere. Transportation costs are higher with this mode, and it is used most often for short distances and smaller shipments. Weight and size constraints limit the capability of trucks for carrying certain loads, but their scheduled service is more dependable than that of rail. Air transportation is highly dependable and very fast,

Learning Objectives
To understand key design issues relating to the design of supply chain management systems, including the selection of transportation services, supplier evaluation, technology selection, and inventory management.

Characteristic	Rail	Truck	Air
Speed	3	2	1
Accessibility	2	1	3
Cost	1	2	3
Load capability	1	2	3

Exhibit 9.16
Comparison of Transportation Modes (Note: The best ranking is 1.)

Marc Asnin/CORBIS SABA

OM SPOTLIGHT

Faster Supply Chains for American Furniture Manufacturers[21]

In the global furniture industry, quality, speed of delivery, and price are in an ongoing battle for market share. Chinese furniture manufacturers are making furniture better and are having a major impact on low- and mid-priced markets. Now they are making inroads into the upscale furniture markets by focusing on contemporary designs that are more challenging to produce because flaws are more easily seen. Certain work activities, for example, like multiple layers of finish on a smooth surface require more labor—a task tailor-made for low-wage nations like China. Furniture shipped from China normally takes 5 or 6 weeks to arrive in a U.S. seaport. In contrast, deliveries from American firms have historically taken from 6 to 12 weeks or longer—which could be a major competitive disadvantage.

In response, American manufacturers are focusing on speeding up their supply chain for custom orders. This has required major changes in their processes. Electronic submittal of orders has reduced supply chain lead time. Many assembly lines with fixed order sizes of, say, 500 pieces, have now been changed to manufacturing cells in which a small group of skilled workers makes each piece from start to finish. Another major change to reduce production time is computerized woodworking equipment that cuts furniture pieces all night and has them ready for the assemblers the next shift. Furthermore, unfinished furniture modules are stocked in inventory awaiting quick installation of the top 400 upholstery styles. Using such approaches, Lane Home Furnishings has reduced delivery time on custom upholstery pieces from 8 weeks to 30 days. Rowe's Furniture, Inc., is aiming for an industry-leading delivery target of just 10 days for customized sofas and loveseats.

although it is less accessible than the other modes. Costs are higher, but this mode of transport may be cheaper overall than surface transportation because of reduced packaging needs. Clearly, air cargo carriers cannot handle very large loads. Logistics managers are responsible for both the appropriate mode of transportation as well as the carrier that not only gives a good rate but also has proven customer-service policies for delivery, damage rates, claims handling, and so on.

Many companies are moving toward third-party logistics providers. UPS Supply Chain Solutions (SCS), a subsidiary of the giant delivery company and its fastest-growing division, is one provider that is focusing on all aspects of the supply chain, including order processing, shipping, repair of defective or damaged goods, and even staffing customer service phone centers.[22] Many companies find that hiring SCS is cheaper than staffing and running their own facilities, and small companies can exploit the advanced equipment and processes such as state-of-the-art warehouses and inventory tracking technology that they would never be able to afford on their own.

Supplier Evaluation

Many companies segment suppliers into categories based on their importance to the business and manage them accordingly. For example, at Corning, Level 1 suppliers, who provide raw materials, cases, and hardware, are deemed critical to business success and are managed by teams that include representatives from engineering, materials control, purchasing, and the supplier company. Level 2 suppliers provide specialty materials, equipment, and services and are managed by internal customers. Level 3 suppliers provide commodity items and are centrally managed by purchasing.[23]

Measurement plays an important role in supplier management. Texas Instruments measures suppliers' quality performance by parts per million defective, percentage of on-time deliveries, and cost of ownership.[24] An electronic requisitioning system permits a paperless procurement process. More than 800 suppliers are linked to Texas Instruments through an information exchange system. Integrated data systems track the incoming quality and timeliness of deliveries as materials are received. Analytical reports and online data are used to identify material defect trends. Performance reports are sent each month to key suppliers. Joint customer-supplier teams are formed to communicate and improve performance. A supplier management task force of top managers directs current and strategic approaches to improving supplier management practices.

Selecting Technology

Technology is playing an increasingly important role in supply chain design, and selecting the appropriate technology is critical for both planning and design of supply chains as well as execution. Some important needs in supply chain management include having accurate receipt information identifying goods that have been received, reducing the time spent in staging (between receipt and storage) at distribution centers, updating inventory records, routing customer orders for picking, generating bills of lading, and providing various managerial reports. SCM has benefited greatly from information technology, particularly bar coding and radio frequency identification (RFID) tags to control and manage these activities. Chapter 5 discussed the use of RFID extensively; RFID has become an important technology in supply chains.

Electronic data interchange and Internet links streamline information flow between customers and suppliers and increase the velocity of supply chains, as we illustrated with Dell. Many other firms, such as MetLife, Marriott Hotels, General Electric, Federal Express, Dow Chemical, Enterprise Rent-A-Car, and Bank of America, have exploited technology effectively in their supply chain designs. E-marketplaces offer many more options for sourcing materials and supplies and facilitate optimization of the supply chain globally.

Sophisticated mathematical models and computerized location-planning systems are used to model complex transportation configurations and conduct "what-if" analyses to evaluate alternative location strategies. Some typical uses of such a system are investigating the "what-if" effects of

1. changes in demand structure and volume;
2. changes in transportation costs;
3. transportation and labor strikes, natural disasters, and energy shortages;
4. plant-capacity expansion proposals;
5. new product lines;
6. deletion of product lines;
7. price changes and discounts;
8. emerging global or local markets;
9. transportation using public versus private carriers; and
10. facility size, type, and mix.

Geographic information systems (GIS) *are designed to store, retrieve, analyze, distribute, and map geographical data.* Coupled with a satellite-based Global Positioning System (GPS) and mobile transmitters, GIS is used extensively in location and site selection, land use planning, environmental science, transportation systems, and military planning and warfare. Procter & Gamble, for example, used GIS along with quantitative analysis tools in a decision support system for management (see OM Spotlight: Decision Support Technology at Procter & Gamble) and reduced their facilities by 20 percent, saving millions of dollars. The state of Maryland used

Geographic information systems (GIS) *are designed to store, retrieve, analyze, distribute, and map geographical data.*

GIS to identify "gaps in service" for each existing hospital location and where new hospitals might best be located. By combining data on demographics and traffic patterns, PepsiCo Inc. uses GIS to help find the best locations for new Pizza Hut and Taco Bell outlets. Federal Express also uses it to place its drop boxes and estimate the number of trucks and planes it needs during peak periods.

Trucking companies now track their trucks via GPS technology as they move across the country. In-vehicle navigational systems, vehicle location systems, emergency vehicle deployment, and traffic management are other examples of how GIS and GPS are changing all industries and their value chains.

Inventory Management

An efficient distribution system can enable a company to operate with lower inventory levels, thus reducing costs, as well as providing high levels of service that create satisfied customers. As we noted in Chapter 7, inventory is related to flow time and throughput by Little's Law. Little's Law demonstrates that we could reduce flow time by reducing inventory while holding throughput constant. This suggests that careful management of inventory is critical to supply chain time-based performance in order to respond effectively to customers. We will address inventory management techniques thoroughly in a later chapter.

Vendor-managed inventory (VMI) *is becoming a popular concept where the vendor (a consumer goods manufacturer, for example) monitors and manages inventory for the customer (a grocery store, for example).* VMI essentially outsources the inventory management function in supply chains to suppliers. VMI allows the vendor to view inventory needs from the customer's perspective and use this information to optimize its own production operations, better control inventory and capacity, and reduce total supply chain costs. VMI can also reduce the bullwhip effect discussed earlier in this chapter by allowing vendors to make production decisions using downstream customer demand data. One disadvantage of VMI is that it does not account for substitutable products from competing manufacturers and often results in higher customer inventories than necessary.

Vendor-managed inventory (VMI) *is becoming a popular concept where the vendor (a consumer goods manufacturer, for example) monitors and manages inventory for the customer (a grocery store, for example).*

OM SPOTLIGHT

Decision Support Technology at Procter & Gamble[25]

Procter & Gamble (P&G) produces and markets a variety of consumer products such as detergents, diapers, coffee, pharmaceuticals, soaps, and paper products worldwide. P&G embarked on a major strategic planning initiative called the North American Product Sourcing Study. P&G was interested in consolidating its product sources and optimizing its distribution system design throughout North America. An interactive computer-based decision support system based on a variant of the transportation model with GIS data was used to develop product sourcing and distribution options involving more than 50 product categories, 60 plants, 10 distribution centers, hundreds of suppliers, and 1,000 customer warehouses/destinations. Issues the team investigated included the impact of closing certain plants and consolidating production in others on costs and customer service. Use of the computer-based model provided rapid evaluation of a variety of strategic options. Solutions were displayed on a map of North America by means of a geographic information system. That enabled strategic planners to review immediately the impact of their decisions across North America. Annual savings amounted to approximately $200 million.

SOLVED PROBLEMS

SOLVED PROBLEM #1

Evaluate the cash-to-cash conversion cycle for a company that has sales of $3.5 million, cost of goods sold equal to $2.8 million, 250 operating days a year, total average on-hand inventory of $460,000, accounts receivable equal to $625,000, and accounts payable of $900,100. What can you conclude about the company's operating practices?

Solution:

Using Equations (9.1) to (9.7), we computed the following:

$$CGS/D = \frac{\text{Cost of goods sold value}}{\text{Operating days per year}} = \frac{\$2,800,000}{250}$$

$$= \$11,200 \text{ per day}$$

$$R/D = \frac{\text{Total revenue (sales)}}{\text{Operating days per year}} = \frac{\$3,500,000}{250}$$

$$= \$14,000 \text{ per day}$$

$$IDS = \frac{\text{Average total inventory}}{\text{Cost of goods sold per day}} = \frac{\$460,000}{\$11,200}$$

$$= 41.1 \text{ days}$$

$$IT = \frac{\text{Cost of goods sold value}}{\text{Average inventory value}} = \frac{\$2,800,000}{\$460,000}$$

$$= 6.1 \text{ turns}$$

$$ARDS = \frac{\text{Accounts receivable value}}{\text{Average inventory value}} = \frac{\$625,000}{\$14,000}$$

$$= 44.6 \text{ days}$$

$$APDS = \frac{\text{Accounts payable value}}{\text{Revenue (sales) per day}} = \frac{\$900,100}{\$14,000}$$

$$= 64.3 \text{ days}$$

Cash-to-cash conversion cycle = IDS + ARDS − APDS = 41.1 + 44.6 − 64.3 = +21.4 days. This is illustrated in the following figure:

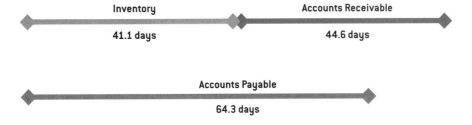

From this analysis, the firm must borrow funds to finance its inventory. Its inventory and accounts receivable cycles add up to 85.7 days, yet it must pay its bills, on average, in 64.3 days. The firm receives the customer's payments (accounts receivable), on average, 21.4 days "after" it must pay its bills to suppliers (accounts payable), so it must borrow funds to finance inventory. If by improving inventory and/or accounts receivable systems and practices the firm can shorten the 85.7 days to 64.3 days, theoretically it should not have to borrow funds to support its inventory levels. All of these numbers should be compared to industry and competitor performance standards.

SOLVED PROBLEM #2

A pizza restaurant wants to build a satellite kitchen, from which only home deliveries will be made, in a nearby suburb. The suburb is partitioned into four customer zones. The following data show population figures and travel times between the zones and three potential sites. Which site would be the best?

Customer Zone	Average Population	Travel Times (min.)		
		Site A	Site B	Site C
1	800	4	9	13
2	1,200	5	4	8
3	1,500	9	6	3
4	500	8	5	12

Solution:

Because the sites are fixed, we need only evaluate the total weighted time from each site to each customer zone. The zone population is assumed to be a good predictor of the number of customers. The total weighted times follow.

Site A:	4(800)	+ 5(1,200)	+ 9(1,500)	+ 8(500)	= 26,700
Site B:	9(800)	+ 4(1,200)	+ 6(1,500)	+ 5(500)	= 23,500
Site C:	13(800)	+ 8(1,200)	+ 3(1,500)	+ 12(500)	= 30,500

Thus, Site B appears to be the best location because it minimizes total weighted travel time.

SOLVED PROBLEM #3

An automobile dealership in a large city had four locations spread around the Standard Metropolitan Area, some as far as 60 miles apart. Each location had a dealership showroom, maintenance and repair service with a parts stockroom, and used and new vehicle lots. The coordinates in miles on an X-Y grid of each city location are shown with the number of major parts sold each month as the third coordinate. That is, Paris (20, 50, 34) is X-axis = 20 miles, Y-axis = 50 miles, and 34 parts are sold per month.

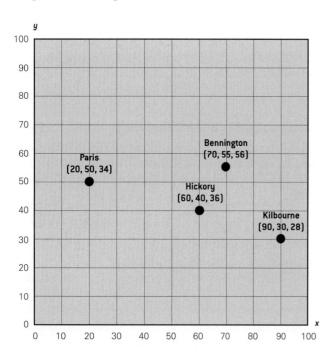

What is the best location for a central parts warehouse using the center-of-gravity method?

Solution:

Using Equations (9.8) and (9.9), we obtain:

Dealership Location	X coordinate [miles]	Y coordinate [miles]	Parts Used per Month
Paris	20	50	34
Hickory	60	40	36
Bennington	70	55	56
Kilbourne	90	30	28

$$\text{Center-of-gravity } X \text{ axis} = \frac{20(34) + 60(36) + 70(56) + 90(28)}{34 + 36 + 56 + 28}$$

$$C_x = 60.3$$

$$\text{Center-of-gravity } Y \text{ axis} = \frac{50(34) + 40(36) + 55(56) + 30(28)}{34 + 36 + 56 + 28}$$

$$C_y = 45.8$$

To minimize the weighted distance among the four user locations the center-of-gravity method gives X coordinate = 60.3 miles and Y coordinate = 45.8 miles. This location is a good place to start the search for property to locate a warehouse. In fact, these ideal coordinates (60.3, 45.8) are very close to the Hickory location (60, 40), so consideration should be given to add a central warehouse on this property if space is available.

KEY TERMS AND CONCEPTS

Accounts payable days' supply
Accounts receivable days' supply
Average inventory value
Bullwhip effect
Cash-to-cash conversion cycle
Center of gravity method

Contract manufacturing
Cross-docking
Customer satisfaction
Distribution centers
Efficient versus responsive supply chains
Geographic information system (GIS)

Inventory

Inventory days' supply

Inventory turnover

Multisite management

Order amplification

Order fulfillment lead time

Original equipment manufacturer

Perfect delivery fulfillment

Perfect order fulfillment

Postponement

Push-pull boundary

Push versus pull systems

Scoring location models

Supply chain

Supply chain management

Supply Chain Operations Reference (SCOR) model

Total supply chain costs

Transportation method

Vendor-managed inventory

Warranty/returns processing costs

QUESTIONS FOR REVIEW AND DISCUSSION

1. Explain the role of supply chains in the broader context of value chains.

2. Explain the typical structure of facilities and tiers in a supply chain.

3. What is supply chain management?

4. Search the Internet for information on one of the following companies that provide supply chain solutions: Oracle (www.oracle.com) or SAP (www.sap.com). Write a short summary of their supply chain approaches and capabilities.

5. Explain the concept of cross-docking. How does it help supply chain performance?

6. Describe the five functions of the SCOR model of supply chain management.

7. What operations and logistical skills contributed to Alexander the Great's success? How are these lessons relevant today?

8. What are the key characteristics of Dell's supply chain approach? How do they contribute to developing the company's competitive advantage?

9. What are the common metrics used to measure supply chain performance? Why are they important from both customer and internal perspectives?

10. How can a firm increase its inventory turnover rate?

11. Define the cash-to-cash conversion cycle. Why is it important and how can it be used to manage supply chains?

12. What are the implications of a negative cash-to-cash conversion cycle?

13. Explain the bullwhip effect. Why is it important for managers to understand it? What can they do to reduce it?

14. Contrast the differences between efficient and responsive supply chain designs, and give an example of each. Can a supply chain be both efficient and responsive?

15. Explain the difference between a push and a pull system. How does each affect supply chain performance?

16. Explain the concept of a push-pull boundary. Why is it important in supply chain design? Provide some examples different from those in the chapter.

17. What is contract manufacturing? Why is it important?

18. Explain multisite management and supply chain issues that are pertinent to service organizations.

19. Select a firm such as Taco Bell (www.tacobell.com), Bank of America (www.bankofamerica.com), Wal-Mart (www.walmart.com), or another service-providing organization of interest to you and write a short analysis of location and multisite management decisions that the firm faces.

20. What are some typical economic and noneconomic criteria used for making a facility location decision?

21. Interview a manager for a retail store, factory, or warehouse that was recently built in your location, and ask for an explanation of the economic and noneconomic factors that helped determine this facility's location.

22. What are the advantage and disadvantages of using scoring models for location analysis?

23. Explain the issues associated with selecting global, national, regional, and site-specific locations.

24. Define the principal criteria that might be used for locating each of the following facilities:
    - hospital
    - chemical factory
    - fire station

- elementary school
- regional warehouse

25. Explain the concept of the center-of-gravity method.

26. How are quantitative transportation and network models used to improve supply chain efficiency and effectiveness?

27. What are some of the key operational issues associated with supply chain design?

28. What are the trade-offs associated with selecting transportation services?

29. How can GIS improve the performance of supply chains in the following industries: (a) trucking, (b) farming and food distribution, (c) manufacturing, and (d) ambulance service?

30. What is vendor-managed inventory? How can it help supply chain management?

PROBLEMS AND ACTIVITIES

1. Based on the following information, how many days of supply is the firm holding (assume 250 days of operation per year)? Interpret your answer if the industry average inventory days' supply is 30 days.

Sales	$8,300,000
Cost of goods sold	$7,200,000
Gross profit	$1,100,000
Overhead costs	$600,000
Net profit	$500,000
Total inventory	$2,600,000
Fixed assets	$3,000,000
Long-term debt	$2,700,000

2. Claiken Incorporated is a supplier of axles for light trucks. It held an average axle inventory of $1.6 million last year with a cost of goods sold of $21.0 million. What is the inventory turnover for axles? A customer wants the company to increase its inventory turnover rate to 20 by implementing better inventory and operating practices. What average axle inventory level is needed to meet this 20-turn target?

3. Andrew Manufacturing held an average inventory of $1.1 million (raw materials, work-in-process, finished goods) last year. Its sales were $8.0 million and its cost of goods sold was $5.8 million. The firm operates 260 days a year. What is the inventory days' supply? What target inventory level is necessary to reach a 20- and 10-day inventory supply during the next 2 years?

4. Bragg Johnson, materials manager at Johnson & Sons, has determined that a certain product experienced 3.8 turns last year with an annual sales volume (at cost) of $975,000. What was the average inventory value for this product last year? What would be the average inventory level if inventory turns could be increased to 6.0?

5. As an operations management consultant, you have been asked to evaluate a furniture manufacturer's cash-to-cash conversion cycle under the following assumptions: sales of $23.5 million, cost of goods sold of $20.8 million, 50 operating weeks a year, total average on-hand inventory of $2,150,000, accounts receivable equal to $2,455,000, and accounts payable of $3,695,000. What do you conclude? What recommendations can you make to improve performance?

6. Look up last year's balance sheet and income statement of a company of interest to you and compute the cash-to-cash conversion cycle. Draw a diagram similar to Exhibit 9.6. What can you conclude? (Annual reports are usually available on a firm's web site.)

7. Repeat your analysis for the same firm in Problem 6 for several years prior to last, if possible. What differences do you see? What might explain any differences?

8. The following data are related to the operating costs of three possible locations for Fountains Manufacturing:

	Location 1	Location 2	Location 3
Fixed costs	$110,000	$125,000	$150,000
Direct material cost per unit	8.5	8.4	8.6
Direct labor cost per unit	4.2	3.9	3.7
Overhead per unit	1.2	1.1	1.0
Transportation costs per 1,000 units	800	1,100	950

a. Which location would minimize the total costs, given an annual production of 50,000 units?

b. For what levels of manufacture and distribution would each location be best?

9. An industrialist faced with choosing among four possible locations has developed the scoring model shown. Which location would be the best?

		Location			
Criteria	Weight	1	2	3	4
Raw material availability	0.2	G	P	OK	VG
Infrastructure	0.1	OK	OK	OK	OK
Transportation costs	0.5	VG	OK	P	OK
Labor relations	0.1	G	VG	P	OK
Quality of life	0.1	G	VG	P	OK

Points: VG = Very good: 5 points
      G = Good: 4 points
    OK = Acceptable: 3 points
     P = Poor: 1 point

10. Goslin Chemicals has decided to build a new plant in the Sunbelt to take advantage of new solar-powered heating units. Three sites have been proposed: Phoenix, Arizona; El Paso, Texas; and Mountain Home, Arkansas.
   a. Construct a scoring model using the Excel template in Exhibit 9.10 using the criteria in which the factors have the following priorities:
   (1) climate
   (2) water availability
   (3) labor and government
   (4) schools and housing
   (Factors having the same priority should be given the same weighting.)
   b. Suppose the three sites have ratings as follows. Under the system constructed in part (a) to this problem, which seems to be most preferable?

Data for Problem 10—Goslin Chemicals

			Level Assigned
Factor	Phoenix	El Paso	Mountain Home
Climate	5	4	3
Water	3	5	4
Labor	4	2	1
Government	4	5	4
Schools	5	3	2
Housing	4	2	3

11. Given the location information and volume of material movements from a supply point to several retail locations for Bourbon Hardware, find the optimal location for the supply point using the center-of-gravity method.

Retail Outlet	Location Coordinates x	y	Material Movements
1	20	5	1,200
2	18	15	2,500
3	3	16	1,600
4	3	4	1,100
5	10	20	2,000

12. Broderick's Burgers wants to determine the best location for drawing customers from three population centers. The map coordinates of the three centers follow:

Population Center 1: $X_1 = 2$ $Y_1 = 12$
Population Center 2: $X_2 = 9$ $Y_2 = 6$
Population Center 3: $X_3 = 1$ $Y_3 = 1$

   a. What location will minimize the total distance from the three centers?
   b. Population Center 1 is 4 times as large as Center 3, and Center 2 is twice as large as Center 3. The firm feels that the importance of locating near a population center is proportional to its population. Find the best location under these assumptions.

13. A large metropolitan campus needs to erect a parking garage for students, faculty, and visitors. The garage has a planned capacity of 1,000 cars. From a survey, it is estimated that 30 percent of the arrivals to campus go to the business school and adjacent buildings; 40 percent go to the engineering complex; 20 percent go to the university center area; and 10 percent go to the administrative offices (see campus map, Exhibit 9.17). Four potential sites (A, B, C, and D) are being considered. Which one would be best for the new garage?

14. The Davis national drugstore chain prefers to operate one outlet in a town that has four major market segments. The number of potential customers in each segment along with the coordinates are as follows:

Market Segment	Location Coordinates x	y	Number of Customers
1	2	18	1,000
2	15	17	600
3	2	2	1,500
4	14	2	2,400

   a. Which would be the best location by the center-of-gravity method?
   b. If after 5 years half the customers from Segment 4 are expected to move to Segment 2, where should the drugstore shift, assuming the same criteria are adopted?

Exhibit 9.17
University Campus Map

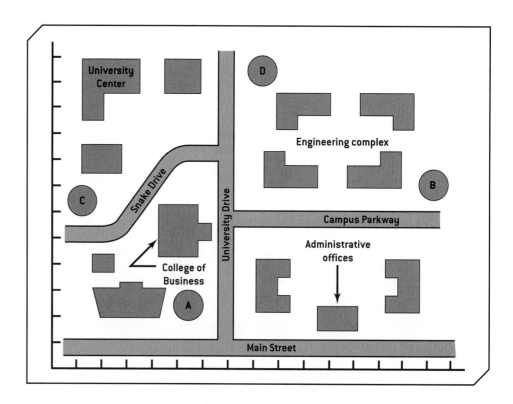

15. Microserve provides computer repair service on a contract basis to customers in five sections of the city. The five sections, the number of service contracts in each section, and the x, y coordinates of each section are as follows:

Section	No. of Contracts	Coordinates x	y
Parkview	90	8.0	10.5
Mt. Airy	220	6.7	5.9
Valley	50	12.0	5.2
Norwood	300	15.0	6.3
Southgate	170	11.7	8.3

Use the center-of-gravity method to determine an ideal location for a service center.

16. Muscle Motor Parts produces components for motorcycle engines. It has plants in Amarillo, Texas, and Charlotte, North Carolina, and supply factories in Detroit and Atlanta. Production and cost data for a major component are as follows. Formulate a transportation model to determine the best distribution plan.

Plant	Freight Costs Detroit	Atlanta	Capacity	Unit Cost
Amarillo	$12	$8	1,200	$125
Charlotte	$9	$3	3,000	$140
Demand	2,000	900		

17. Grave City is considering relocating a number of police substations to obtain better enforcement in high-crime areas. The locations being considered and the areas each could cover are listed as follows:

Potential Location for Substation	Areas Covered
A	1, 5, 7
B	1, 2, 5, 7
C	1, 3, 5
D	2, 4, 5
E	3, 4, 6
F	4, 5, 6
G	1, 5, 6, 7

Find the minimum number of locations necessary to provide coverage to all areas. Where should the police substations be located?

18. The Farmington City Council is attempting to choose one of three sites as the location for its life squad facility. The city manager has developed a matrix showing the distance (in miles) from each of the sites to the five areas that must be served.

Site	Area Served 1	2	3	4	5
A	1.2	1.4	1.4	2.6	1.5
B	1.4	2.2	1.3	2.1	0.7
C	2.7	3.2	0.8	0.9	0.7

The number of emergency runs to each of these areas over the past 3 months is: Area 1, 100; Area 2, 20; Area 3, 100; Area 4, 170; Area 5, 200.

a. If the council decides to choose the site on the basis of minimizing the longest response time, which site should be selected?

b. If the council decides to minimize the annual cost (in terms of miles traveled) of operating the facility, which site should be selected?

19. Izzy Rizzy's Trick Shop specializes in gag gifts, costumes, and novelties. Izzy owns a store on the south side of Chicago and is considering opening a second store on the north side. A sample of ten customers yielded these data.

Amount of Sale ($)	17	15	40	20	15	25	20	30	30	35
Age	20	17	32	40	35	21	18	25	36	31

Izzy believes age is the most important factor for his customers. He is considering three possible locations: one is in the high-rise, near-north side, where many singles in the 25–35 age group reside; the second is near a residential area in which the majority of the population is over 35; the third is near a college campus. From these data, where should Izzy locate?

20. The city of Binghamton is attempting to determine the best location for an ambulance facility that will serve the entire city. The network of zones within the city is shown in Exhibit 9.18. Where should Binghamton locate the service facility to minimize the maximum distance to any zone?

21. Milford Lumber Company ships construction materials from three wood-processing plants to three retail stores. The shipping cost, monthly production capacities, and monthly demand for framing lumber are shown here. Set up a spreadsheet to solve a transportation problem for finding the minimum-cost distribution plan. See Supplementary Chapter C for a discussion of how to do this and on using Excel Solver.

Plant	Store A	Store B	Store C	Capacity
1	4.5	3.1	2.0	280
2	5.1	2.6	3.8	460
3	4.1	2.9	4.0	300
Demand	250	600	150	

Exhibit 9.18
Binghamton City Data

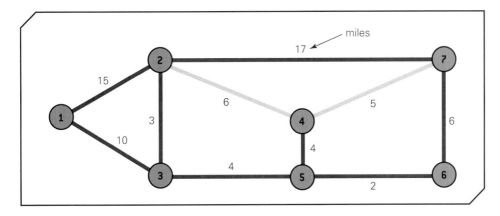

CASES

CISCO SYSTEMS CASH-TO-CASH CONVERSION CYCLE[26]

Cisco (www.cisco.com) was founded in 1984 by a small group of computer scientists from Stanford University. Since the company's inception, Cisco engineers have been leaders in the development of Internet Protocol (IP)-based networking technologies. This tradition of IP innovation continues with industry-leading products in the core areas of routing and switching, as well as advanced technologies in areas such as storage networking, network security, optical, IP telephone, and wireless networks. Cisco remains committed to creating equipment and networks that are smarter, faster, and more durable.

Cisco provides goods and services to help other firms improve the performance of their supply chains, as well as its own supply chain. Cisco provides customers with a customer benefit package characterized by

- architecture, equipment, and technology—Cisco manufactured goods provide the hardware necessary to ensure the vitality of the Internet and its availability, security, flexibility, and scalability that enables all parts of the supply chain to be connected in real time;
- software and system integrators—Cisco has developed a partner network of leading software vendors and system integrators for supply chain design that can help customize solutions and implement them;
- consulting expertise—Cisco has deployed supply chain management solutions in many firms using its goods and services.

The following data (in millions $) are provided from Cisco's 2003 annual report:

Sales	
• Manufactured Goods	$15,565
• Services	$ 3,313
• Total	$18,878
Cost of Sales	
• Manufactured Goods	$ 4,594
• Services	$ 1,051
• Total	$ 5,645
Gross Margin	
• Manufactured Goods	$10,971
• Services	$ 2,262
• Total	$13,233
Operating Expenses	
• Research and Development	$ 3,135
• Sales and Marketing	$ 4,116
• Other	$ 1,100
• Total	$ 8,351
Operating Income	$ 4,882
Inventories	$ 873
Accounts Receivable	$ 1,351
Accounts Payable	$ 594

Given that Cisco is a global company, it is assumed the business operates 365 days per year. One note in the annual report states that $873 million does not include $122 million in inventory allowances for excess and obsolete inventories determined primarily by comparing existing inventory to future demand forecasts. The note goes on to say, "Inventory management remains an area of focus as we balance the need to maintain strategic inventory levels to ensure competitive lead times versus the risk of inventory obsolescence because of rapidly changing technology and customer requirements."[27]

Managers at Cisco have watched the rapid growth of Dell Computer and have become interested in designing a better performance system for their own supply chains. One idea they want to incorporate into their supply chain's performance system is cash-to-cash conversion cycle metrics. Play the role of a consultant to evaluate their 2003 annual report data and compute inventory days' supply, accounts receivable days' supply, accounts payable days' supply, and whatever else you think might be useful in uncovering improvement opportunities. You are expected to write a preliminary management report, not to exceed three pages, on what you discovered to present in-house at a Cisco meeting in 1 week.

HOLDEN HOSPITAL BLOOD BANK

Holden Hospital has operated a Blood Donor Clinic and Transfusion Center in a downtown location for the past 30 years. However, increases in the population served and improvements in service provided have resulted in needs for additional staff and equipment. Those needs were not planned for in the original building design, and the present site has no room for expansion; consequently, center administrators are seeking to relocate. From some surveys of customers, they know that most donors travel to the center by public or private transportation. The center also delivers blood and blood products and holds mobile blood donor clinics throughout the region.

Center administrators identified the following criteria as the most important for the site-selection process:

1. access to the road network for the mobile clinics and for the blood delivery vehicles so as to increase efficiency and minimize delays, operating costs, and deterioration of blood products in transit;

2. the ability to attract a larger group of donors through better visibility or ease of access;

3. convenience to both public and private transportation;

4. little sensitivity to changes in the population distribution or in the road network;

5. ease of travel to and from work for center employees;

6. minimum internal space and lot size.

A variety of data were collected, including population data, donor data, public-transport trip data, and delivery data. However, the center administrators are unsure about what to do next.

Play the role of a consultant, and outline a plan for selecting the best location. Include a discussion of what models you might use and how you would use them, as well as any additional data that you might recommend collecting.

THE MARTIN COMPANY

The Martin Company is in the process of planning for new production facilities and developing a more efficient distribution system design. At present, it has one plant at St. Louis with a capacity of 30,000 units. Because of increased demand, management is considering four potential new plant sites: Detroit, Denver, Toledo, and Kansas City. Exhibit 9.19 summarizes the projected plant capacities, the cost per unit of shipping from each plant to each destination, and the demand forecasts over a 1-year planning horizon.

Each potential new plant has different annual fixed costs because of differences in size, taxes, wage rates, and so on. These are

Location	Annual Fixed Cost
Detroit	$175,000
Toledo	$300,000
Denver	$375,000
Kansas City	$500,000

The company wants to minimize the total annual cost. What location or combination of locations will accomplish this? Use the transportation model as a tool to help you make this decision. (See Supplementary Chapter C for a discussion of using Excel Solver to solve the transportation model.) In addition, the firm's managers want to evaluate various intangible factors in this decision, so they are not necessarily committed to the solution that has the lowest cost. Your recommendations should also include an analysis of other low-cost options that will satisfy demand. Outline your recommendations in a brief report.

Exhibit 9.19
R. K. Martin Distribution Data

Origin	Destination			Capacity
	Boston	**Atlanta**	**Houston**	
Detroit	$5/unit	$2/unit	$3/unit	30,000
Toledo	4	3	4	20,000
Denver	9	7	5	30,000
Kansas City	10	4	2	40,000
St. Louis	8	4	3	30,000
Destination Demand	30,000	20,000	20,000	

ENDNOTES

[1] "Corning," http://www.peoplesoft.com/corp/en/doc_archive/success_story/corning_ss.jsp, 2003.

[2] This scenario is based on Johnson, M. E., "Mattel, Inc: Vendor Operations in Asia," *The European Case Clearing House*, England, Case #601-038-1 (http://www.ecch.cranfield.ac.uk).

[3] PRTM Director, Mike Aghajanian.

[4] "Got Milk?", "The Performance Advantage," *APICS*, April 2001, p. 27.

[5] The Supply-Chain Council was formed in 1996–1997 as a grassroots initiative by firms including AMR Research, Bayer, Compaq Computer, Pittiglio Rabin Todd & McGrath (PRTM), Procter & Gamble, Lockheed Martin, Nortel, Rockwell Semiconductor, and Texas Instruments. See http://www.supply-chain.org/ for information on the Supply Chain council and development of the SCOR model.

[6] Van Mieghem, Timothy, "Lessons Learned from Alexander the Great," *Quality Progress*, January 1998, pp. 41–46.

[7] *Dell Fiscal 2003 Report*, www.dell.com. Also see "Dell Knows His Niche and He'll Stick with It," *USA Today*, April 5, 2004, p. 3B.

[8] Jacobs, D. G., "Anatomy of a Supply Chain," *Logistics Today* 44, no. 6, June 2003, p. 60.

[9] "Partnerships Predominate," *Modern Materials Management*, May 2001, pp. 12–13.

[10] Callioni, Gianpaolo, and Billington, Corey, "Effective Collaboration," *OR/MS Today* 28, no. 5, October 2001, pp. 34–39.

[11] Facts in this example were drawn from Gallagher, Patricia, "Value Pricing for Profits," *Cincinnati Enquirer*, 21 December 1992, pp. D-1, D-6; "Procter & Gamble Hits Back," *Business Week*, 19 July 1993, pp. 20–22, and Sapority, Bill, "Behind the Tumult at P&G," *Fortune* 7, March 1994, pp. 75–82.

[12] "The Next Wal-Mart?" *Business Week*, April 26, 2004, pp. 60–62.

[13] "Wal-Mart's Supply Chain Management Practices," *The European Case Clearing House*, Case #603-003-1, 2003, ECCH@cranfield.ac.uk.

[14] "Flextronics May Be Getting a Bum Rap," *Wall Street Journal*, April 6, 2004, p. C4.

[15] Langeard, E., and Eiglier, P., "Strategic Management of Service Development," L. L. Berry, G. L. Shostack, and G. D. Upah, *Emerging Perspectives on Services Marketing*, Chicago, IL: American Marketing Association, 1983, pp. 68–72.

[16] Kroeber, Arthur, "The Hot Zone," *Wired*, November 2002, pp. 201–205.

[17] Boyer, Mike, "The Parts Are the Whole," *Cincinnati Enquirer*, October 13, 2001, pp. C1, C2.

[18] Babwin, D., "Ford Plans Manufacturing Campus," *The Columbus Dispatch*, Columbus, Ohio, May 17, 2002, p. C8.

[19] "Tesco Bets Small—and Wins Big," *Business Week*, October 1, 2001 (www.businessweek.com).

[20] Begley, S., "Did You Hear the One About the Salesman Who Travelled Better?", *Wall Street Journal*, April 23, 2004, p. B1.

[21] "Chinese Furniture Goes Upscale," *Wall Street Journal*, November 18, 2004, p. D1.

[22] Salter, Chuck, "Surprise Package," *Fast Company*, February 2004, pp. 62–66.

[23] Kishpaugh, Larry, "Process Management and Business Results," presentation at the *1996 Regional Malcolm Baldrige Award Conference*, Boston, MA.

[24] Texas Instruments Defense Systems & Electronics Group, *Malcolm Baldrige Application Summary (1992)*.

[25] Jeffrey D. Camm, Thomas E. Chorman, Franz A. Dill, James R. Evans, Dennis J. Sweeney, and Glenn W. Wegryn, "Blending OR/MS, Judgment, and GIS: Restructuring P&G's Supply Chain," *Interfaces*, 27, 1 Jan-Feb 1997, pp. 128–142.

[26] *Cisco Systems 2003 Annual Report* (www.cisco.com).

[27] *Cisco Systems 2003 Annual Report* (www.cisco.com), p. 19.

Part 3

Managing Operations

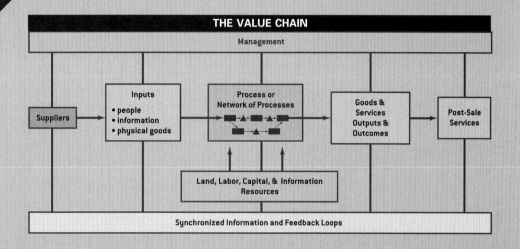

THE VALUE CHAIN

Management

Suppliers

Inputs
• people
• information
• physical goods

Process or
Network of Processes

Goods &
Services
Outputs &
Outcomes

Post-Sale
Services

Land, Labor, Capital, & Information
Resources

Synchronized Information and Feedback Loops

In this section of the book we describe a variety of issues associated with managing operations. You will learn about:

• Understanding, measuring, and making both long- and short-term capacity decisions.
• The role that forecasting plays in managing capacity and demand.
• Inventory management systems and common tools used to manage inventories.
• An overall planning framework for resource management, focusing on aggregate planning decisions and strategies, and disaggregation of aggregate plans in both manufacturing and service systems.
• Operations scheduling and sequencing, with a variety of applications in both manufacturing and services.
• Basic concepts, philosophies, and tools of quality management, including statistical process control.
• The concept of lean operating systems and the philosophy of lean thinking, tours of lean manufacturing and service organizations, and numerous tools and approaches for incorporating lean thinking into any organization.
• Project management from both an organizational and technical viewpoint, with useful tools and techniques for planning, scheduling, and controlling projects.

Chapter Outline

CHAPTER 10

Capacity Management

Learning Objectives

1. To understand the fundamental decisions that must be made in both the short and long term, how capacity influences economies and diseconomies of scale, and the impacts of capacity in managing focused and unfocused facilities.

2. To be able to identify and use different forms of capacity measurement useful to operations managers, to understand the importance

of safety capacity, and to make quantitative calculations of capacity, and use capacity measurements in operational planning decisions.

3. To understand approaches to making long-term capacity decisions and capacity expansion strategies.

4. To understand how firms deal with short-term imbalances between demand and capacity, and to learn strategies for adjusting capacity and influencing demand to achieve better resource use and efficiency.

5. To identify practical issues associated with revenue management and be able to compute simple overbooking strategies.

6. To learn the principles and logic of the Theory of Constraints, and better understand how demand, capacity, resource utilization, and process structure are related.

• McDonald's restaurants in Britain apologized to millions of unhappy customers for running out of Big Macs during a weekend 2-for-1 promotion to celebrate its 25th anniversary in Britain. The demand generated by the promotion far exceeded forecasts. The promotion caused many of the nation's 922 outlets to turn away long lines of customers.

• The Airbus A380 is the largest plane ever built with 555 seats and, with some modest redesign such as extending the length of the plane, could carry as many as 800 airline passengers. "As the most advanced aircraft, the A380 is economic, spacious and will meet the challenges of the fast-growing Chinese airline industry," Guy McLeod, president of Airbus China, told reporters during a press conference at this week's Beijing Air show. "The 2008 Olympics in Beijing and the World Expo in Shanghai will stimulate the development of China's airlines, and we believe the 555-seat A380 will be an ideal vehicle to transport tens of thousands of athletes, sports fans, businessmen and tourists to China." The pieces of the plane such as the cockpit, tail, wings, and cabin sections are so big that the factories must be reconfigured. The European Consortium that builds the Airbus must make and transport these parts, some weighting 100 tons each, among many countries, such as Spain, Britain, France, and Germany. Not only must factory capacity and scale be upsized, the elaborate transportation system to move these parts among European factories must also be changed. At a maximum speed of 15 miles per hour, the trip to the assembly factory in Toulouse, France, from the seaport of Bordeaux takes three days. The French

402

government has redone the entire 159-mile route, including 18 miles of new bypass routes around five towns, to handle the six giant truck trailers that carry these manufactured parts.[1]

© Getty Images/PhotoDisc

• "What do you mean, you have run out of refrigerated storage room?" said Charles Ebrake, chief operating officer, Pear Supreme, Inc. "I've got two refrigerated railroad cars of pears heading to your storage facility," he continued. "Sir, we got a surge in demand for our refrigerated storage and we are full. I'm really sorry but we cannot kick out our existing customers' products," said Caroline Marion, warehouse manager for Cool-It Storage. Ebrake responded, "So what am I suppose to do with millions of fresh pears headed to the northeast coast?" Marion answered, "I'd rent the refrigerated rail cars for a few more days until we can get you in our refrigerated warehouse or a public warehouse. Cool-It Storage will pay for the rail car or public storage."

Discussion Questions: Can you cite any experiences similar to the McDonald's episode where the firm's capacity has either provided you with a pleasant or unpleasant experience? What other capacity issues should airlines consider in addition to the number of seats on a plane? (Think of your own experiences.)

In a general sense, *capacity* is a measure of the capability of a manufacturing or service system to perform its intended function. In practice, it is measured by the amount of output that can be produced in a particular time period, for example, the number of hamburgers made during a weekday lunch hour or the number of patients that can be handled during an emergency room shift. Having sufficient capacity to meet customer demand and provide high levels of customer service is vital to a successful business. In the first episode, McDonald's apparently did not plan sufficient capacity in response to its promotional campaign, resulting in an overwhelming demand that it could not meet.

Capacity decisions cannot be taken lightly. The Airbus A380 highlighted in the second episode is causing quite a stir in the airline industry, as it provides a much higher capacity (as measured by the number of seats) than other aircraft. Airlines using this model would be able to increase the number of passengers served using the same number of flights on a particular route. In contrast, Airbus's rival Boeing decided to make smaller planes such as the new 200- to 300-seat 7E7 Dreamliner, which will be 20 percent more efficient than any previous airplane and is expected to start flying in 2008.[2] Clearly, more flights would be needed to achieve the same amount of passenger capacity over a fixed time period. The different capacity strategies used by Airbus and Boeing boil down to which airplane can make the most money for the company. Airbus is emphasizing big planes that fly long routes, whereas Boeing is focusing on smaller planes that allow flexibility in matching airplane route capacity to demand. The choice is highly dependent upon the forecast of demand along global air traffic routes, on the planes' efficiencies and operating costs, how customers will accept them, and the operational implications of boarding, disembarking, and baggage retrieval. Although the capacity of the airplane is of interest from a strategic perspective, such a change can also have a significant impact on operations, such as requiring redesigned maintenance facilities and baggage handling systems.

The third episode highlights the importance of accurately forecasting demand and then matching demand and capacity. Capacity shortages can be costly. Pears, for example, are perishable and cannot wait too long to be delivered to customers, and their quality is very much dependent on a controlled environment of temperature and humidity. The United States has over 3 billion gross cubic feet of refrigerated storage capacity, but it is not always in the right place at the right time. Without proper planning, companies can easily put themselves in a poor competitive position.

As these examples suggest, capacity is vital to designing and managing value chains. The resources available to the organization—facilities, equipment, and labor (technology and process selection), how they are organized (process design and facility layout), and their efficiency as determined by specific work methods and procedures (work and supply chain design) determine capacity. At every stage of the value chain, sufficient capacity must exist—and be coordinated with other stages and processes—to ensure that the flows of material, information, and customers occur smoothly and without excessive delays or inventory. ERP systems (introduced in Chapter 5), for example, must know the capacity, lead time, and capability of each key process in the value chain, such as engineering design, final assembly and shipping, purchased parts, or an advertising campaign. Thus, all the issues that we addressed in Part II of this book influence capacity.

This chapter focuses on understanding capacity and its relationship to demand and strategies for designing and managing capacity in manufacturing and service environments. Important issues to address include:

- Can the facility, process, or equipment accommodate new goods and services and adapt to changing demand for existing goods and services?
- How large should facility, process, or equipment capacity be?
- When should capacity changes take place?

UNDERSTANDING CAPACITY

Capacity *is the capability of a manufacturing or service resource such as a facility, process, workstation, or piece of equipment to accomplish its purpose over a specified time period.* Capacity can be viewed in one of two ways:

1. as the maximum rate of output per unit of time, or
2. as units of resource availability.

For example, the capacity of an automobile plant might be measured as the number of automobiles capable of being produced per week. For an electric utility, it might be measured as megawatts of electricity that can be generated per hour; and for a law firm, as billable hours per month. As a resource availability measure, capacity of a manufacturing facility is often expressed in hours of available time; for a warehouse, it might be the number of cubic feet of space available. Other examples in service organizations include the capacity of a hospital as measured by the number of beds available; for an airline, the number of seats per flight; and for a tennis club, the number of courts.

Learning Objective
To understand the fundamental decisions that must be made in both the short and long term, how capacity influences economies and diseconomies of scale, and the impacts of capacity in managing focused and unfocused facilities.

Capacity *is the capability of a manufacturing or service resource such as a facility, process, workstation, or piece of equipment to accomplish its purpose over a specified time period.*

Operations managers must decide on the appropriate levels of capacity to meet current and future demand. Thus, capacity decisions must be made for short (anywhere from a week to a year) and long (one year or longer) time horizons. Exhibit 10.1 provides examples of such capacity decisions. Short-term capacity decisions usually involve adjusting schedules or staffing levels. Longer-term decisions typically involve major capital investments.

Economies and Diseconomies of Scale

Capacity decisions are often influenced by economies and diseconomies of scale. Economies of scale *are achieved when the average unit cost of a good or service decreases as the capacity and/or volume of throughput increases.* For example, the design and construction cost per room of building a hotel decreases as the facility gets larger because the fixed cost is allocated over more rooms, resulting in a lower unit room cost. This lends support to building larger facilities with more capacity. Diseconomies of scale *occur when the average unit cost of the good or service begins to increase as the capacity and/or volume of throughput increases.* In the hotel example, as the number of rooms in a hotel continues to increase, the average cost per unit begins to increase, because of larger amounts of overhead and operating expenses. For instance, large hotels would need increasingly higher levels of amenities, such as restaurants, parking, and recreational facilities. This suggests that some optimal amount of capacity exists where costs are at a minimum.

One of the episodes at the beginning of this chapter described Airbus's new megaseat plane. In comparison to existing airplanes with less capacity, one could argue that economies of scale will reduce costs by spreading the costs of fuel and other expenses over many more passengers. However, some also argue that it is too big to be cost-effective. The A380 will only be able to land at reconfigured airport gates, may be too big for many airports to land and take off, takes too long to load and unload cargo and passengers, and is expected to be economical only on long routes. Thus, it is possible that a 555-seat airplane shows signs of diseconomies of scale, as shown in Exhibit 10.2.

Focused Factories

As a single facility adds more and more goods and/or services to its portfolio, the facility can become too large and "unfocused." At some point, diseconomies of scale arise and unit cost increases because dissimilar product lines, processes, people skills, and technology exist in the same facility. In trying to manage a large facility with too many objectives and missions, key competitive priorities such as delivery, quality, customization, and cost performance can begin to deteriorate.

Economies of scale *are achieved when the average unit cost of a good or service decreases as the capacity and/or volume of throughput increases.*

Diseconomies of scale *occur when the average unit cost of the good or service begins to increase as the capacity and/or volume of throughput increases.*

Exhibit 10.1
Examples of Short- and Long-Term Capacity Decisions

Short-Term Capacity Decisions	Long-Term Capacity Decisions
• Amount of overtime scheduled for the next week • Number of pizza delivery workers to hire on Super Bowl Sunday • Number of ER nurses on call during a downtown festival weekend • Amount of warehouse space to rent for new promotional items • Number of call center workers to staff during the holiday season	• Construction of a new manufacturing plant • Expanding the size and number of beds in a hospital • Number of branch banks to establish in a new market territory • Closing down a distribution center • Changing the cooking technology in a chain of fast-food restaurants • Adding a 20-ton stamping machine

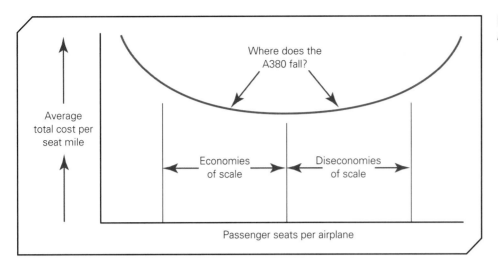

Exhibit 10.2
Airbus A380 Economies of Scale

Harvard Professor Wickham Skinner introduced the concept of a focused factory in 1974.[3] *A* **focused factory** *is a way to achieve economies of scale without extensive investments in facilities and capacity by focusing on a narrow range of goods or services, target market segments, and/or dedicated processes to maximize efficiency and effectiveness.* The focused factory argues to "divide and conquer" by adopting smaller, more focused facilities dedicated to a (1) few key products, (2) a specific technology, (3) a certain process design and capability, (4) a specific competitive priority objective such as next-day delivery, and (5) particular market segments or customers and associate volumes (see OM Spotlight: Focus Packaging, Inc.).

Two ways to execute a focused factory strategy are to (1) build separate focused facilities that are manageable and controllable, or (2) physically divide a huge facility into smaller, more focused facilities or "plants-within-plants." *A* **plant-within-a-plant** *strategy divides a facility into independent factories, each with its own core competencies.* Often this requires literally building walls to seal off one from another. Each plant-within-a-plant might have separate entrances, break areas, loading docks, and even separate food services.

CAPACITY MEASUREMENT

Capacity can be measured in a variety of ways. **Theoretical capacity** *(sometimes called design capacity) is the maximum output per unit of time the process can achieve for a short period of time under ideal operating conditions.* Theoretical capacity does not generally include adjustments for preventive maintenance or unplanned downtime and cannot be increased unless the facility or the labor force is expanded or modified (possibly through the use of overtime). Theoretical capacity may be larger or smaller than peak demand. **Effective capacity** *is the actual output per unit of time that the organization can reasonably be expected to sustain in the long run under normal operating conditions.* Effective capacity is less than theoretical capacity when losses due to scrap, worker fatigue, equipment breakdowns, and maintenance are taken into account. Effective capacity can often be increased by operational improvements such as simplified processes or equipment having lower maintenance requirements.

Setup time is an important factor in determining effective capacity. Short setup times clearly increase capacity and improve flexibility by allowing rapid changeovers to different models or products on manufacturing or assembly lines. Much work

---

A **focused factory** *is a way to achieve economies of scale without extensive investments in facilities and capacity by focusing on a narrow range of goods or services, target market segments, and/or dedicated processes to maximize efficiency and effectiveness.*

A **plant-within-a-plant** *strategy divides a facility into independent factories, each with its own core competencies.*

Learning Objectives
To be able to identify and use different forms of capacity measurement useful to operations managers, to understand the importance of safety capacity, and to make quantitative calculations of capacity and use capacity measurements in operational planning decisions.

Theoretical capacity *(sometimes called design capacity) is the maximum output per unit of time the process can achieve for a short period of time under ideal operating conditions.*

OM SPOTLIGHT

Focus Packaging, Inc.[4]

Focus Packaging, Inc. was a family-owned business in Kansas City, Missouri, that was acquired by Specialized Packaging Group in 2003. Prior to the acquisition, the firm had only one customer—Colgate-Palmolive—and made 18 different cartons for packaging a variety of items such as Irish Spring soap. The owner, Mr. Davis, stated, "I'll never have a factory with more than three customers. You're always sacrificing one for the other." Davis saw many advantages to his focused factory concept. For example, his crews did not need retraining because of changing customer requirements. They were dedicated to doing it exactly the way Colgate-Palmolive wants. Davis concluded by saying, "I am scouting for another large customer. But, a second customer will mean a second focused factory."

Effective capacity *is the actual output per unit of time that the organization can reasonably be expected to sustain in the long run under normal operating conditions.*

has gone into seeking ways to reduce setup times in manufacturing. A Japanese engineer, Shigeo Shingo, pioneered a technique called "Single Minute Exchange of Die," or SMED (a die is a fixture that attaches to a machine for forming parts). This approach has often reduced setup times from hours to minutes in many factories and increased their effective capacity. SMED often relies on simple process and layout reconfigurations that eliminate the need to retrieve a die from a tool room that might require waiting for an available forklift truck and transporting it across the factory floor. By storing dies close to the machines and using roller conveyors or similar types of equipment, machine operators can make the exchange by themselves in much less time. SMED is an important approach in "lean manufacturing," which we will discuss in Chapter 17.

Capacity provides the ability to satisfy demand. Clearly, from a practical perspective, capacity-planning decisions should be based on effective capacity rather than theoretical capacity, as ideal operating conditions are nearly impossible to sustain. To satisfy customers in the long run, effective capacity must be at least as large as the average demand. However, demand for many goods and services typically vary over time. A process may not be capable of meeting peak demand at all times, resulting in either lost sales or customers that must wait until the good or service becomes available. At other periods of time, capacity may exceed demand, resulting in idle processes or facilities or buildups in physical inventories.

For example, demand for air conditioners peaks during the summer months. For manufactured goods, available capacity, measured by the output that production is capable of providing, plus finished goods inventory produced at an earlier time can be used to help meet peak summer demand. For services, demand for a 24-complex movie theater is even more variable over time. Here, the number of theater seats available for sale measures capacity. During weekend nights with blockbuster movie premieres, peak demand approaches or exceeds theater seat capacity. Yet, on almost any weekday afternoon, less than 5 percent of a theater's capacity is being used, so capacity greatly exceeds demand by a factor of 20 or more. Exhibit 10.3 illustrates these concepts of peak demand and demand being less or more than capacity over time.

Safety Capacity

The actual utilization rates at most facilities are not planned to be 100 percent of effective capacity. Unanticipated events such as equipment breakdowns, employee

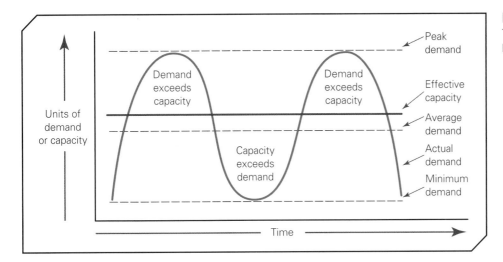

Exhibit 10.3
The Demand versus Capacity
Problem Structure

absences, or sudden short-term surges in demand will reduce the capability of planned capacity levels to meet demand and satisfy customers. This is evident in Exhibit 10.3. Therefore, some amount of **safety capacity** *(often called the* **capacity cushion***), defined as an amount of capacity reserved for unanticipated events such as demand surges, materials shortages, and equipment breakdowns,* is normally planned into a process or facility. In general, average safety capacity is defined by Equation (10.1).

Average safety capacity (%) = 100% − Average resource utilization (%)   **(10.1)**

Note that Equation (10.1) is based on average resource utilizations over some time period. For a factory, average safety capacity might be computed over a year, whereas for an individual workstation, it might be updated monthly.

The amount of planned safety capacity also depends on competitive priorities, such as cost, productivity, and customer service objectives, and the amount of variation and uncertainty associated with demand and other unanticipated events. Managers must consider the trade-offs associated with the investment in additional capacity and the risk associated with not having sufficient capacity to meet demands. Capital-intensive industries that operate continuous flow processes, such as paper mills or gasoline refineries, must maintain high utilizations to achieve high productivity and low costs. Here, the cost of idle resources is extremely high and safety capacity is generally low, for example, less than 10 percent. To do this effectively, they must ensure that equipment has high reliability and that promised delivery dates for orders do not strain the effective capacity. In job shops, we often see a high variability in setup times for different jobs, which takes away from much of the effective capacity available for producing goods. Safety capacity is generally higher to provide for this. For example, some customized job shops that manufacture replacement parts and compete on quick delivery maintain safety capacity up to 30 or 40 percent.

Similarly, for many service organizations, such as airlines and restaurants, we observe much higher variation in short-term demand. If planned utilization rates are high (that is, if safety capacity is low), then customer service problems can easily result. For most service industries, safety capacity may range from 10 to 50 percent, and therefore, according to Equation (10.1), utilization rates are in the range of 50 to 90 percent. This is typical for hospitals and hotels, for example. Although movie theaters have very low seat utilization rates, in the 5 to 20 percent range on average,

Safety capacity *(often called the* **capacity cushion***), is defined as an amount of capacity reserved for unanticipated events such as demand surges, materials shortages, and equipment breakdowns.*

or an average safety capacity of over 90 percent, they still make a profit (must be the sodas and popcorn!).

Capacity Measurement in Job Shops

Flow shops and job shops were introduced in Chapter 6 along with various ways to evaluate flow time, bottlenecks, and capacity utilization. Because the flow of work in a flow shop is usually fixed, setup and changeover time is minimal. However, in a job shop, setup time can be a substantial part of total system capacity and therefore must be included. Equation (10.2) provides a general expression for evaluating the capacity required to meet a given production volume for one work order, i.

Capacity required (C_i)
= Setup time (S_i) + Processing time (P_i) $\times$ Order size (Q_i) **(10.2)**

where C_i = capacity requirements in units of time (for instance, minutes, hours, days).

S_i = setup or changeover time for work order i as a fixed amount that does not vary with volume.

P_i = processing time for each unit of work order i (for example, hours/part, minutes/transaction, and so on).

Q_i = the size of order i in numbers of units.

If we sum the capacity requirements over all work orders, we can compute the total capacity required using Equation (10.3).

$$C = \sum C_i = \sum [S_i + P_i \times Q_i] \qquad \textbf{(10.3)}$$

To illustrate these calculations, consider Ham's Dental Office. He works a 9-hour day with 1 hour for lunch and breaks. During the first 6 months the practice is open, he does all the work, including cleaning and setting up for the next dental procedure. His administrative assistant, Ashley, answers the telephone, handles front office billing, appointments, and copayments. Setup and processing times for three procedures are shown in Exhibit 10.4. Also shown are the number of appointments and demand for each type.

On a particular day, Ashley has scheduled two first appointments for single tooth crowns, one second appointment for a single tooth crown, four appointments for tooth whitening, three first appointments for a partial denture, and two third appointments for a partial denture. Does Ham have the capacity to perform all the work? Using Equation (10.3), we see in Exhibit 10.5 that a total of 610 minutes of work are scheduled during a 480-minute workday. Therefore, there is a capacity

Exhibit 10.4

Ham's Dental Office Procedures and Times for Today

Dental Procedure	Number of Appointments	Setup or Changeover Time (minutes)	Processing Time (minutes)	Demand (No. of Patients Scheduled)
Single tooth crown	1st	15	90	2
	2nd	10	30	1
Tooth whitening	1st	5	30	4
Partial denture	1st	20	30	3
	2nd	10	20	0
	3rd	5	30	2

Exhibit 10.5 Ham's Dental Office Demand-Capacity Analysis

Dental Procedure	Appointments	Setup Times	Process Time	Number of Patients Scheduled	Total Setup Time	Total Process Time	Total Setup & Process Time
Single tooth crown	1st	15	90	2	30	180	210*
	2nd	10	30	1	10	30	40
Tooth whitening	1st	5	30	4	20	120	140
Partial denture	1st	20	30	3	60	90	150
	2nd	10	20	0	0	0	0
	3rd	5	30	2	10	60	70
					130	480	610
					21.3%	78.7%	100%

*Example computation: $C = \sum(S_i + P_i \times Q_i) = 15 \times 2 + 90 \times 2 = 210$ minutes, assuming a setup for each patient.

shortage of 130 minutes. Ham will either have to work 2 hours longer or reschedule some patients.

From this analysis, we see that 21.3% of Ham's total capacity is used to set up and change over from one dental procedure to the next. If he hires a dental assistant or technician to do this work (assuming that this can be done off-line while Ham continues to work on other patients), Ham could increase his revenue by about 20%. If he could reduce his setup times by 50 percent, the total setup time would be 65 minutes and the capacity shortage would be only 65 minutes, requiring only 1 hour of overtime.

Setup times normally represent a substantial percentage of the total capacity of most job shops. Every effort must be made to reduce setup time to the lowest possible amount so as to free up capacity for creating output.

Using Capacity Measures for Operations Planning

Capacity needs must be translated into specific requirements for equipment and labor. To illustrate this, we present a simple example. Fast Burger, Inc. is building a new restaurant near a college football stadium. The restaurant will be open 16 hours per day, 360 days per year. Managers have concluded that the restaurant should have the effective capacity to handle a peak hourly demand of 100 customers. This peak hour of demand happens 2 hours before every home football game. The average customer purchase is

　　1 burger (4-ounce hamburger or cheeseburger)
　　1 bag of french fries (4 ounces)
　　1 soft drink (12 ounces)

Consequently, management would like to determine how many grills, deep fryers, and soft-drink spouts are needed.

A 36 × 36-inch grill cooks 48 ounces of burgers every 10 minutes, and a single-basket deep fryer cooks 2 pounds of french fries in 6 minutes, or 20 pounds per hour. Finally, one soft-drink spout dispenses 20 ounces of soft drink per minute, or 1,200 ounces per hour. These effective capacity estimates are based on the equipment manufacturer's studies of actual use under normal operating conditions.

To determine the equipment needed to meet peak hourly demand, Fast Burger must translate expected demand in terms of customers per hour into needs for grills, deep fryers, and soft-drink spouts. First note that the peak hourly demand for burgers, french fries, and soft drinks are as follows:

Product	Peak Hourly Demand (ounces)
Burgers	400
French fries	400
Soft drinks	1,200

Since the capacity of a grill is (48 oz/10 min)(60 min/hr) = 288 oz/hr, the number of grills needed to satisfy a peak hourly demand of 400 ounces of burgers is

Number of grills = 400/288 = 1.39 grills

To determine the number of single-basket deep fryers needed to meet a peak hourly demand of 400 ounces of french fries, we must first compute the hourly capacity of the deep fryer.

Effective capacity of deep fryer = (20 lb/hr)(16 oz/lb) = 320 oz/hr

Hence, the number of single-basket deep fryers needed is 400/320 = 1.25.

Finally, the number of soft-drink spouts needed to satisfy peak demand of 1,200 ounces is

Number of soft drink spouts needed = 1,200/1,200 = 1.0

After reviewing this analysis, the managers decided to purchase two 36 × 36-inch grills. Grill safety capacity is 2.0 − 1.39 = 0.61 grills, or 175.7 oz/hr [(.61) × (48 oz/10 min) × (60 min/hr)], or about 44 hamburgers per hour. Management decided this excess safety capacity was justified to handle demand surges and grill breakdowns. With two grills, they reduced their risk of being unable to fill customer demand. If management installed two french fryer machines, they would have 0.8 excess machines and that was thought to be wasteful. However, they realized that if the one french fryer broke down, they would not be able to cook enough french fries so they decided to purchase two deep fryers.

Management decided to go with a two-spout soft-drink system. Although their analysis showed a need for only one soft-drink spout, the managers wanted to provide some safety capacity, primarily because they felt the peak hourly demand for soft drinks might have been underestimated and customers tend to refill their drinks in this self-service situation.

The average expected equipment utilizations for the two grills, two fryers, and two soft-drink spouts are as follows [refer to Equation (7.1) in Chapter 7]:

$$\text{Grill utilization } (U) = \text{Resources used/Resources available}$$
$$= 1.39/2.0 = 69.5\%$$

$$\text{Fryer utilization } (U) = \text{Resources used/Resources available}$$
$$= 1.2/2.0 = 60.0\%$$

$$\text{Soft-drink spout utilization } (U) = \text{Resources used/Resources available}$$
$$= 1.0/2.0 = 50.0\%$$

The managers of Fast Burger, Inc. must also staff the new restaurant for peak demand of 100 customers/hour. Assume front-counter service personnel can take and assemble orders at the service rate of 15 customers per hour and the target labor utilization rate for this job is 85%. The number of front-service counter people that should be assigned to this peak demand period can be found using Equation (7.2) in Chapter 7:

Utilization ($U\%$) = Demand rate/[Service rate × Number of servers]

or

$$0.85 = (100 \text{ customers/hour})/(15 \text{ customers/hour}) \times (\text{Number of servers})$$
$$= 12.75 \times \text{Number of servers} = 100$$
$$\text{Number of servers} = 7.8, \text{ or } 8$$

Given these capacity computations, Fast Burger management decides to assign 8 people to the front-service counter during this peak demand period. Safety capacity is included in this decision in two ways. First, the target utilization labor rate is 85% so there is a 15% safety capacity according to Equation (10.1). Second, 8 people are on duty when 7.8 are needed so there is a safety capacity of 0.2 people. The management at Fast Burger now has an equipment and labor capacity plan for this peak demand period. To make the best possible use of their capacity analysis, management must also do a good job forecasting demand—the subject of the next chapter.

LONG-TERM CAPACITY STRATEGIES

Learning Objective
To understand approaches to making long-term capacity decisions and capacity expansion strategies.

Over long time horizons, firms must anticipate growth or decline in demand and plan capital investments, which often take several months or years to complete, to provide appropriate capacity levels in the future. In developing a long-range capacity plan, a firm must make a basic economic trade-off between the cost of capacity and the opportunity cost of not having adequate capacity. Capacity costs include both the initial investment in facilities and equipment and the annual cost of operating and maintaining them. The cost of not having sufficient capacity is the opportunity loss incurred from lost sales and reduced market share. Opportunity costs, however, are very difficult to quantify. Conceptually, the level of capacity should minimize the present value of the total cost—cost of capacity plus opportunity cost—over the planning horizon.

Long-term capacity planning must be closely tied to the strategic direction of the organization—what products and services it offers. For example, many goods and services are seasonal, resulting in unused capacity during the off-season. Many firms offer **complementary goods and services**, *which are goods and services that can be produced or delivered using the same resources available to the firm, but whose seasonal demand patterns are out of phase with each other.* Complementary goods or services balance seasonal demand cycles and therefore use the excess capacity available, as illustrated in Exhibit 10.6. For instance, demand for lawn mowers peaks in the spring and summer; to balance manufacturing capacity, the producer might also produce leaf blowers and vacuums for the autumn season and snow blowers for the winter season (see the OM Spotlight on Briggs & Stratton). A sporting goods retailer in northern climates that specializes in golf equipment might sell ski equipment during the winter. Ski resorts might offer hiking and camping in the summer as a way of productively using their facilities.

A strategy for increasing long-term capacity in service organizations is to design higher levels of self-service—customer labor—into operations. Assembling furniture such as shelves or entertainment centers, cleaning up after eating in a fast-food restaurant, and completion of medical forms before medical service are some of the many processes that have incorporated self-service into their designs. With self-service, customers share in the responsibility to create and deliver their goods or services. Self-service generally reduces capacity requirements, operational costs, and training requirements for employees; it can also improve throughput time and customer convenience. However, risks to the organization exist because of the loss of

Complementary goods and services are goods and services that can be produced or delivered using the same resources available to the firm, but whose seasonal demand patterns are out of phase with each other.

Exhibit 10.6
Seasonal Demand and
Complementary Goods or
Services

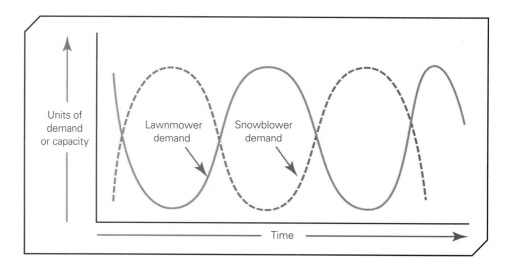

control over the process and the possibility of customer resentment, customer mistakes, and even liability.

Capacity Expansion

Capacity requirements are rarely static; changes in markets and product lines and competition will eventually require a firm to either plan to increase or reduce long-term capacity. Such strategies require determining the *amount*, *timing*, and *form* of capacity changes. To illustrate capacity expansion decisions, let us make two assumptions: (1) capacity is added in "chunks" or discrete increments, and (2) demand is steadily increasing.

Four basic strategies for expanding capacity over some fixed time horizon are shown in Exhibit 10.7 (these concepts can also be applied to capacity reduction):

1. one large capacity increase (Exhibit 10.7(a)),
2. small capacity increases that match average demand (Exhibit 10.7(b)),

OM SPOTLIGHT

Briggs & Stratton[5]

Briggs & Stratton is the world's largest producer of air-cooled gasoline engines for outdoor power equipment. The company designs, manufactures, markets, and services these products for original equipment manufacturers worldwide. These engines are primarily aluminum alloy gasoline engines ranging from 3 through 25 horsepower. Briggs & Stratton is a leading designer, manufacturer, and marketer of portable generators, lawn mowers, snow throwers, pressure washers, and related accessories. It also provides engines for manufacturers of other small-engine-driven equipment such as snowmobiles, go-karts, and jet skis.

The complementary and diverse original equipment markets for Briggs & Stratton engines allows factory managers to plan equipment and labor capacities and schedules in a much more stable operating environment. This helps minimize manufacturing costs, stabilize workforce levels, and even out volumes so that assembly lines can be used in a more efficient fashion.

3. small capacity increases that lead demand (Exhibit 10.7(c)),
4. small capacity increases that lag demand (Exhibit 10.7(d)).

The strategy in Exhibit 10.7(a) involves one large increase in capacity over a specified period. The advantage of one large capacity increase is that the fixed costs of construction and operating system setup need to be incurred only once, and thus the firm can allocate these costs over one large project. Several disadvantages are associated with this approach, however. The firm may not be able to acquire the considerable financial resources required for a major capacity expansion, and substantial risks are involved if forecasts are incorrect. Note also that if aggregate demand exhibits steady growth, the facility will be underutilized for a period of time, since the level of capacity is planned for the end of the time horizon. Other disadvantages relate to the fact that new and unforeseen products and technology, government regulations, and other factors may alter capacity requirements and process capabilities. The alternative is to view capacity expansion incrementally, as in Exhibit 10.7(b), (c), and (d).

Exhibit 10.7(b) illustrates the strategy of matching capacity additions with demand as closely as possible. This is often called a *capacity straddle strategy*. When capacity is above the demand curve, the firm has excess capacity; when it is below, there is a shortage of capacity to meet demand. In this situation, there will be short periods of over- and underutilization of resources. Exhibit 10.7(c) shows a capacity-expansion strategy with the goal of maintaining sufficient capacity to minimize the chances of not meeting demand. Here, capacity expansion leads or is ahead of demand and, hence, is called a *capacity lead strategy*. Since there is always excess capacity, safety capacity to meet unexpected demand from large orders or new customers is provided. This safety capacity also enables the firm to give good customer

Exhibit 10.7 Capacity Expansion Options

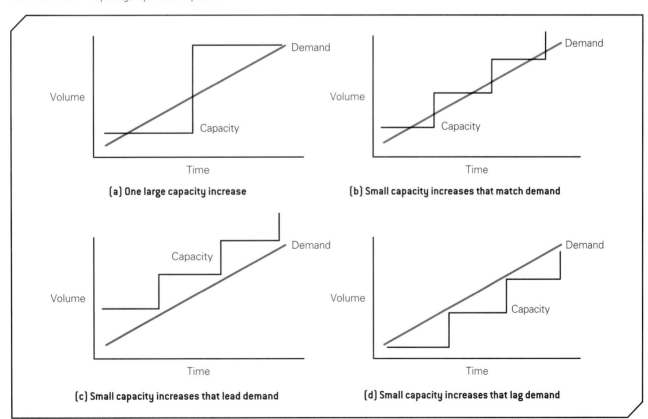

(a) One large capacity increase

(b) Small capacity increases that match demand

(c) Small capacity increases that lead demand

(d) Small capacity increases that lag demand

service, since back orders will rarely occur. Of course, this strategy is expensive. Finally, Exhibit 10.7(d) illustrates a policy of a *capacity lag strategy* that results in constant capacity shortages. Such a strategy waits until demand has increased to a point where additional capacity is necessary. It requires less investment and provides for high capacity utilization and thus a higher rate of return on investment. However, it may also reduce long-term profitability through overtime, subcontracting, and productivity losses that occur as the firm scrambles to satisfy demand. In the long run, such a policy can lead to a permanent loss of market position.

With these capacity expansion strategies, the firm has the option of making frequent small capacity increments or fewer large increments and whether to lead or lag demand. The choice should be based on careful economic analysis of the cost and risks associated with excess capacity and capacity shortages. The ability and desire of the firm to make short-term capacity adjustments must also be taken into account. For instance, some firms might subcontract out some of their demand to other firms when they are short on capacity. However, if proprietary technology is used in their operations and not available elsewhere, subcontracting would not be feasible.

Other factors should also be considered. For example, with large capacity increases, firms have potential advantages in selecting better technology and redesigning facilities to achieve more efficient process flows. It also eliminates the need for managers to continually reassess and have to decide on when to add more capacity. Of course, this also presents greater financial risk of having a large amount of unused capacity.

Applying Decision-Analysis Techniques to Capacity Decisions

As we have seen, capacity decisions are based on a mixture of both quantitative and qualitative factors. To help evaluate the quantitative factors in these decisions, formal decision-analysis techniques are often used. These methods can assist decision makers in selecting from among several capacity alternatives when future outcomes are uncertain. Decision-analysis methods are discussed in detail in Supplementary Chapter E. This section presents a simple example in which decision trees are used to help analyze a capacity-expansion decision.

Southland Corporation's decision to produce a new line of recreational products has resulted in the need to construct a new factory. The decision as to factory size depends on projections of marketplace reaction to the new product line. To conduct an analysis, marketing managers defined three levels of possible long-run demand. The following payoff table shows the projected profit in millions of dollars for the three levels of demand.

	Long-Run Demand		
Decision	**Low**	**Medium**	**High**
Small plant	$150	$200	$200
Large plant	$50	$200	$500

Assume that the best estimate of the probability of low demand is 0.20, of intermediate levels of demand is 0.15, and of high demand is 0.65. What is the recommended decision?

Exhibit 10.8 shows the decision tree for this situation. If Southland chooses to build a small plant, the expected profit is computed as

$$0.2(\$150) + 0.15(\$200) + 0.65(\$200) = \$190 \text{ million}$$

If the company chooses to build a large plant, the expected profit is

$$0.2(\$50) + 0.15(\$200) + 0.65(\$500) = \$365 \text{ million}$$

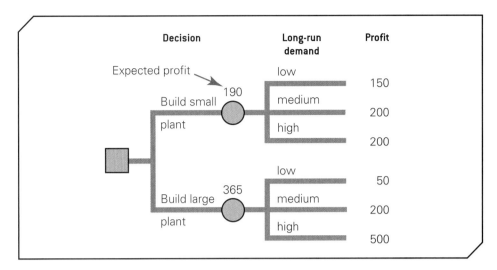

Thus, on the basis of expected value, the best decision is to build a large factory if Southland's objective is to maximize the opportunity to generate profit. Of course, the risk is that Southland may end up with excess factory capacity if demand is low.

SHORT-TERM CAPACITY MANAGEMENT

If short-term demand is stable and sufficient capacity is available, then managing operations to ensure that demand is satisfied is generally easy. However, when demand fluctuates above and below effective capacity levels, as was illustrated in Exhibit 10.3, then firms have two basic choices. First, they can adjust capacity to match the changes in demand by changing internal resources and capabilities. The second approach is to manage capacity by shifting and stimulating demand.

In many service organizations, however, it is difficult or impossible to adjust resources. Hotels, airlines, restaurants, and movie theaters have fixed capacities—for example, rooms and seats—that cannot be easily changed, and they are forced to use a level resource strategy. If demand exceeds capacity at times, these organizations incur lost sales because they cannot store inventories like manufacturing firms. To plan capacity for peak demand is a costly strategy because the average utilization will generally be low. Instead, these organizations try to alter demand patterns to better coincide with the resources that are available by influencing customer behavior. In this section we discuss these approaches.

Managing Capacity by Adjusting Short-Term Capacity Levels

When short-term demand exceeds capacity, a firm must either temporarily increase its capacity or be unable to meet all of the demand. Similarly, if demand falls well below capacity, then idle resources reduce profits. Short-term adjustments to capacity can be done in a variety of ways (see OM Spotlight: J.P. Morgan Chase's Fiduciary Operations) and are summarized next.

- *Add or share equipment*—Capacity levels that are limited by machine and equipment availability are more difficult to change in the short run because of high capital expense. However, leasing equipment as needed can accomplish this in a cost-effective manner. Another way is through innovative partnership arrangements and capacity sharing. For example, every hospital cannot afford to purchase every expensive, specialized piece of equipment. A consortium of several hospitals might be set up in which each hospital focuses on a particular specialty and shares services. Likewise, farmers often establish cooperatives to share planting and harvesting equipment.

- *Sell unused capacity*—Fixed assets that cannot be easily reduced can drain profits during periods of low demand. Some firms might sell idle capacity, such as computer storage space and computing capacity, to outside buyers and even to competitors. For example, hotels often develop partnership arrangements to accommodate their competitors' guests when they are overbooked. This cooperative approach to managing capacity tries to maximize resource utilization and customer service while keeping costs as low as possible.
- *Change labor capacity and schedules*—Labor capacity can usually be managed easily through short-term changes in work force levels and schedules. Overtime, extra shifts, temporary employees, and outsourcing are common ways of increasing capacity. Adjusting work force schedules to better coincide with demand patterns is another way. For example, hospitals and call centers create daily work schedules based on anticipated demand that varies by hour of the day and day of the week. Many quick-service restaurants employ large numbers of part-time employees with varying work schedules. A challenging task that managers face is trying to schedule them to create the necessary capacity levels to meet periods of high and low demand for different days and hours during the week. Another example is a department store that hires part-time workers during holiday shopping seasons. Manufacturing companies routinely schedule overtime or subcontract work to other firms when their capacity becomes strained. They may hire or lay off employees during longer, cyclical cycles of economic ups and downs. However, changing work force levels frequently can be very unattractive to employees and labor unions.
- *Change labor skill mix*—Hiring the right people who can learn quickly and adjust to changing job requirements and cross-training them to perform different tasks provides the flexibility to meet fluctuating demand. In supermarkets, for

OM SPOTLIGHT

J.P. Morgan Chase's Fiduciary Operations[6]

J.P. Morgan Chase's Fiduciary Operations is an area of the bank that provides operational support for individual and institutional portfolios, trust accounts, and mutual funds. One problem confronting this operations area is the different seasonal, monthly, or weekly demand patterns for its financial services. For example, summer vacations and fourth-quarter holiday activities reduce stock trading. During a typical month, demand is usually higher in the first and last weeks than in the middle. Even during a week, demand fluctuates; Mondays are usually high whereas Fridays are generally low. Overall, these result in rather complex seasonal demand patterns.

The operations manager is confronted with several staffing options. One is to use overtime and temporary contract labor to meet the highest-demand periods. A second option is to staff to peak demand throughout the year. A third option is to try to chase demand by hiring and laying off employees every month or quarter to meet these repetitive and seasonal demand patterns. A fourth option is to establish a "float pool" of highly skilled employees who are cross-trained in a wide variety of financial products and associated processes. Finally, another option is to cross-train specific employees to handle one or two other jobs with complementary seasonal cycles and share resources.

An extensive analysis of demand patterns for financial services was conducted and the processes with complementary seasonal demand patterns were identified. Cross-training was based on this analysis. The objective was to identify and match complementary demand patterns where Process A experiences peak demand periods while Process B is experiencing low demand periods. Employees were cross-trained on both types of process jobs and the performance results were substantial. These changes resulted in savings of millions of dollars.

example, it is common for employees to work as cashiers during busy periods and to assist with stocking shelves during slow periods. The challenge, of course, is to find, train, and retain these high-quality employees.

- *Shift work to slack periods*—Another strategy is to shift work to slack periods. For example, hotel clerks prepare bills and perform other paperwork at night, when check-in and check-out activity is light. This leaves them more time during the daytime hours to service customers. Manufacturers often build up inventory during slack periods and hold the goods for peak demand periods. This may increase inventory costs and space requirements but can be much less expensive than hiring, training, and reducing work force levels constantly. However, for some products that are perishable, this might not be a feasible alternative.

Managing Capacity by Shifting and Stimulating Demand

Some general approaches to influencing customers to shift demand from periods without adequate capacity to periods with excess capacity or to fill times with excess capacity, include the following:

- *Vary the price of goods or services*—Price is the most powerful way to influence demand. For example, hotels might offer last-minute specials to fill empty rooms; airlines offer better prices on off-peak days such as midweek; one restaurant cuts its meal prices in half after 9:00 P.M. to stimulate demand; and movie theaters offer cheaper matinee prices. In a similar fashion, manufacturers typically offer sales and rebates of overstocks to stimulate demand, smooth production schedules and staffing requirements, and reduce inventories. Revenue management systems, which we discuss further later in this chapter, exploit information technology to adjust prices for perishable and nonperishable goods and services based on time, resource utilization, and what is and is not selling.

- *Provide customers information*—Many call centers, for example, send notes to customers on their bills or provide an automated voice message recommending the best times to call. For example, Kohl's, a department store chain, prints on its credit card bills the following message to customers: "For personal service, Kohl's Credit Customer Care Representatives are available Sunday 9:00 A.M. to 8:00 P.M. and Monday to Saturday 7:00 A.M. to 11:00 P.M. The optimal calling time for prompt personal service is after 6:00 P.M. (CST)." Amusement parks such as Disney World use signs and literature informing customers when certain rides are normally extremely busy.

- *Advertising and promotion*—Advertising plays a vital role in influencing demand. After-holiday sales are heavily advertised in an attempt to draw customers to periods of traditionally low demand. Manufacturer or service coupons are strategically distributed to increase demand during periods of low sales or excess capacity. When such promotions occur, it is important that the operating systems are capable of performing up to promised standards. Thus, operations managers must be involved in order to plan adequate resources.

- *Add peripheral goods and/or services*—Peripheral goods and/or services can be added to the customer benefit package to increase demand during slack periods. Movie theaters offer rentals of their auditoriums for business meetings and special events at off-peak times. Shopping malls provide game arcades to attract teens after school. Fast-food chains offer birthday party planning services to fill

*A **reservation** is a promise to provide a good or service at some future time and place.*

up slow demand periods between peak meal times. Extended hours also represent a peripheral service; many supermarkets remain open 24/7 and encourage customers to shop during late night hours to reduce demand during peak times.

- *Provide reservations—A **reservation** is a promise to provide a good or service at some future time and place.* Typical examples are reservations for hotel rooms, airline seats, and scheduled surgeries and operating rooms. Reservations are a way to influence demand and match it with available capacity. Reservations also reduce the uncertainty for both the good or service provider and the customer. With advance knowledge of when customer demand will occur, operations managers can better plan their equipment and work force schedules and rely less on forecasts. Coupled with revenue management systems, reservation systems help operating managers maximize revenue and reduce forecasting errors. Made-to-order goods, such as Dell computers or custom-configured automobiles, or putting a product on lay-a-way can be thought of as forms of reservations. Commodity futures for food stocks such as wheat, orange juice, or coal are also a form of reservations in the financial markets.

REVENUE MANAGEMENT SYSTEMS

Learning Objectives
To identify practical issues associated with revenue management and be able to compute simple overbooking strategies.

Revenue management systems (RMS), also called *yield management* systems, were introduced in Chapter 5. They are dynamic, integrated operating systems that forecast demand, allocate perishable assets across market segments, decide when to overbook and by how much, and determine what price to charge different customer segments. The objective of RMS is to maximize revenue by optimizing prices and capacity utilization of each market segment. Revenue management is routinely applied to airline and concert seat planning, broadcasting station advertising time slots, cruise line and hotel rooms, public utility services, and Internet auctions. Firms such as American Airlines, Marriott, Royal Caribbean Cruise Lines, Holiday Inn, and National Car Rental have used RMS methods over the last decade with excellent financial results. Today, RMS is expanding into contract negotiating and supply chain management.

RMS approaches can have negative implications for customers. For example, customers can become quite unhappy if prices change too frequently. You may have checked an airline flight only to find that the price increases a day or two later, or have purchased a ticket and discovered that a set of previously restricted seats was made available at a lower price, and you missed it. Airline and hotel RMS systems normally update several times each day. Some firms using RMS "freeze" their prices and perishable asset (rooms, seats, and so on) allocations for a specific time. Others are trying to simplify their pricing policies for their perishable assets to reflect new and lower cost structures (see OM Spotlight: Airlines' Simplified versus Revenue Management Airfares) and are moving away from RMS methods.

Basic Economics of Managing Service Capacity Trade-offs

Services that are most amenable to RMS have one or more of the following characteristics: (1) perishability, (2) segmented markets, (3) advance sales of the service, and (4) high fixed costs relative to variable costs. As we noted in Chapter 1, service capacity (that is, seats, rooms, electricity, doctor's appointments, advertising time slots, and so on) is time-dependent and perishable. That is, once a unit of service capacity such as a theater seat or an hour of a lawyer's time goes unused, it cannot be recaptured and the revenue opportunity is lost forever. Segmented markets often lead to differential pricing, for example, business versus leisure travelers in the airline industry. Finding the right price points for different segments is crucial to revenue maximization. Advance sales are important to RMS because of the time

OM SPOTLIGHT

Airlines' Simplified versus Revenue Management Airfares[7]

American and Delta Airlines are simplifying their airfares in response to competitive pressures from lower-cost airlines such as Southwest and Jet Blue. In the continued restructuring of the U.S. airline industry, fare simplification is one competitive response to attract customers and avoid bankruptcy. American capped its top last-minute one-way coach price at $699, while Delta set a $499 price. Delta has also eliminated its requirement for a Saturday night stayover to qualify for the lowest-cost fares. Other U.S. airlines may soon match these simplified airfares while trying to reduce their labor costs and increase operating system productivity.

Investment analysts, such as Gary Chase at Lehman Bros., say simplified fares will cut total revenue for the big, high-cost airlines at a time when they are posting losses. Kevin Mitchell, chairman of the Business Travel Coalition, says, "If they did this a year ago, they would have incurred a lot more financial losses because their cost structure was worse than it is today. On the other hand, if they waited a year to get their cost structure the way it needs to be, they'd

lose even more market share to low-cost carriers." Only time will tell if these simple airfare structures and rules are better than revenue management systems in the long run.

sensitivity of price. Finally, the cost structure of the service business is characterized by high fixed costs relative to variable costs. For example, hotels, cruise ships, and airlines have fixed costs ranging from 50 to 80 percent of total costs. Once the service provider reaches the sales break-even point, contribution to profit and overhead is directly related to sales increases.

Consider a major convention hotel with two categories of customers—short-notice reservations from business travelers or longer-notice reservations from convention association groups. The data for one day is given in Exhibit 10.9. Notice that the variable cost per room night is the same for both the business and convention customers. The $20 variable cost per room night includes the labor and cleaning supplies to clean the room, the water and electricity used in the room during the customer's stay, washing and pressing sheets and towels, and incidentals such as shampoo and soap. Fixed overhead includes the monthly financial fees for the debt to build and equip the hotel, the management staff, and basic hotel services such as the health club and concierge desk regardless of how many people are staying in the hotel.

The contribution to profit and overhead can be calculated using the following formula:

$$\text{Contribution to profit and overhead (\$)} = (P_B - VC) \times D_B + (P_C - VC) \times D_C \qquad \textbf{(10.4)}$$

For the data in Exhibit 10.9, we have

$$\begin{aligned}\text{Contribution to profit and overhead (\$)} &= (\$140 - \$20) \times 300 + \\ &\quad (\$80 - \$20) \times 700 \\ &= \$36,000 + \$42,000 \\ &= \$78,000\end{aligned}$$

Exhibit 10.9

Basic Hotel Customer and Economic Information for One Day

Characteristic/Variable	Business Hotel Customers (*B*)	Convention Association Hotel Customers (*C*)
Customers for this day (*D*)	300 room nights rented (D_B)	700 room nights rented (D_C)
Average price/room night (*P*)	$140 ($P_B$)	$80 ($P_C$)
Variable cost/room night (*VC*)	$20	$20
Maximum price/room night (called the rack rate)	$180	$100
Maximum number rooms available for sale this day	350 room nights available	800 room nights available

Hotel management is evaluated on several performance metrics, but hotel management effectiveness as defined by Equation (10.5) often affects manager compensation.

Hotel management effectiveness (%)
= Actual hotel revenue/Maximum possible hotel revenue

$$= \frac{(\text{Actual prices for each room night}) \times (\text{Actual number of room nights rented})}{(\text{Maximum legal price for each room night}) \times (\text{Maximum number of room nights available in hotel})} \quad \textbf{(10.5)}$$

For this example, the hotel management effectiveness percentage is computed as follows:

$$\begin{aligned} \text{Hotel management effectiveness (\%)} &= \frac{(\$140 \times 300 \text{ rooms}) + (\$80 \times 700 \text{ rooms})}{(\$180 \times 350 \text{ rooms}) + (\$100 \times 800 \text{ rooms})} \\ &= \frac{\$42{,}000 + \$56{,}000}{\$63{,}000 + \$80{,}000} = \frac{\$98{,}000}{\$143{,}000} = 74.1\% \end{aligned}$$

Basic economics tells us that as the price increases, demand usually decreases and vice versa. Thus, this effectiveness measure is influenced by the prices that the hotel manager sets. The hotel manager must carefully assess the impact that pricing decisions have on demand and adjust prices for both market segments to best use the capacity available. From a revenue management perspective, these decisions are often made on a weekly or daily basis. In doing so, management is simultaneously considering both marketing and operations decision variables—price and capacity—which is the essence of service management.

Hotel managers can use Equations (10.4) and (10.5) in spreadsheet models as new individual business customer reservations and possible convention groups come in to decide whether to book a large convention (and lots of rooms) at a discounted room price or wait and allocate rooms to higher-priced business customers. In the preceding example, we see that room capacity utilization is 87 percent (1,000 rooms/1,150 rooms = 87%). Room price discounting is 22.2 percent for business customers ($180 − $140/$180 = 0.222) and 20.0 percent for convention customers ($100 − $80/$100 = 0.20). The hotel manager is doing a relatively good job in managing room capacity.

Overbooking Strategies and Analysis

One of the difficulties with advance reservation or appointment systems is that customers may book a reservation but not show up or cancel at the last minute, leaving the organization with unused capacity. One of the most important uses of RMS is to analyze overbooking strategies to make better capacity management decisions. **Overbooking** *is accepting more reservations than capacity available, assuming that a certain percentage of customers will not show up or cancel prior to using the service.*

Service providers can make two types of errors in determining the appropriate level of overbooking:

1. not overbooking enough, resulting in lost revenue associated with idle resources such as airline seats, hotel rooms, or idle doctors and staff;
2. overbooking too much, requiring that some customers be turned away even though they had a reservation and perhaps providing some form of compensation.

We will present a simple example that illustrates these issues.

The Zeus Rental Car Company is interested in controlling rental reservations for midsize cars for one particular day: June 1. This includes any reservation where the customer will have the car on June 1, for instance, picking the car up on May 28, driving it on June 1, and returning it on June 3. Assume that customers pay $40 per day to rent the car. Hence, if a car is unused, the lost revenue is $40. However, if a reservation is accepted but no car is available, Zeus must provide a full-size or luxury model at the same price. Because this car could be rented at a higher price, Zeus will lose the additional revenue that it could have earned by renting it or might possibly have to turn customers away if no other cars are available. Let us assume that this penalty, which includes the opportunity cost of losing future revenue from the customer, is $150.

Suppose that Zeus currently has 10 midsize cars available for June 1 and that the demand for these cars is high so that Zeus can always book more reservations than the available capacity. Clearly, it can accept up to ten reservations and guarantee a car for each customer. Zeus also knows from historical records that some customers don't show up or cancel their reservations. Therefore, Zeus might consider booking more than ten reservations. If it books more than ten (that is, overbooks), there is still a chance that all cars will be rented, but also a chance that more than ten customers will show up and request a car.

From historical records, Zeus has calculated the probability that a customer who has made a reservation will not show up is about 20 percent. Based on this, the actual numbers of customers that show up depends on the number of reservations accepted and is shown in Exhibit 10.10.* For example, if 11 reservations are accepted, the probability that all 11 customers will show up is .09; the probability that only 10 will show up is .24, and so on. For notational purposes, we will let $P(x|n)$ be the probability that x customers will show up if n reservations are booked. Thus, $P(11|11) = .09$ and $P(10|11) = .24$, and so on.

Overbooking *is accepting more reservations than capacity available, assuming that a certain percentage of customers will not show up or cancel prior to using the service.*

Exhibit 10.10 Probabilities of Zeus Customers Showing Up

	Number of Customers Showing Up								
Number of Reservations	**5**	**6**	**7**	**8**	**9**	**10**	**11**	**12**	**13**
10	0.03	0.09	0.2	0.3	0.27	0.11	0	0	0
11	0.01	0.04	0.11	0.22	0.3	0.24	0.09	0	0
12	0	0.02	0.05	0.13	0.24	0.28	0.21	0.07	0
13	0	0.01	0.02	0.07	0.15	0.25	0.27	0.18	0.05

*These probabilities are based on the binomial distribution, namely, the probability that x customers will show up from n reservations, assuming a constant probability of showing up being .80.

What remains to be done is to compute the expected profit associated with each potential overbooking decision. Suppose that Zeus decides to book only $n = 10$ reservations. Zeus will receive $40 for each customer that shows up and will incur no overbooking costs. Therefore, the expected net revenue will be

Net revenue for booking 10 reservations $= \$40 \times [5 \times P(5|10) + 6 \times P(6|10) + 7 \times P(7|10) + 8 \times P(8|10) + 9 \times P(9|10) + 10 \times P(10|10)]$

$= \$40[5 \times 0.03 + 6 \times 0.09 + 7 \times 0.2 + 8 \times 0.3 + 9 \times 0.27 + 10 \times 0.11] = \$320.80$

Now consider booking 11 reservations. If 11 customers actually show up, Zeus incurs an overbooking penalty of $150 for the 11th customer (they can't rent more than 10 cars). The net revenue is

Net revenue for booking 11 reservations $= \$40 \times [5 \times P(5|11) + 6 \times P(6|11) + 7 \times P(7|11) + 8 \times P(8|11) + 9 \times P(9|11) + 10 \times P(10|11)] - \$150 \times$ Probability that more than 10 show up

$= \$40[5 \times 0.01 + 6 \times 0.04 + 7 \times 0.11 + 8 \times 0.22 + 9 \times 0.3 + 10 \times 0.24] - \$150 \times 0.09 = \$303.30$

Similar calculations for 12 and 13 reservations are

Net revenue for booking 12 reservations $= \$40 \times [6 \times P(6|12) + 7 \times P(7|12) + 8 \times P(8|12) + 9 \times P(9|12) + 10 \times P(10|12)] - \$150 \times$ Probability that more than 10 show up

$= \$40[6 \times 0.02 + 7 \times 0.05 + 8 \times 0.13 + 9 \times 0.24 + 10 \times 0.28] - \$150 \times 0.21 - \$300 \times 0.07 = \$206.30$

Net revenue for booking 13 reservations $= \$40 \times [6 \times P(6|13) + 7 \times P(7|13) + 8 \times P(8|13) + 9 \times P(9|13) + 10 \times P(10|13)] - \$150 \times$ Probability that more than 10 show up

$= \$40[6 \times 0.01 + 7 \times 0.02 + 8 \times 0.07 + 9 \times 0.15 + 10 \times 0.25 + 11 \times 0.27 + 12 \times 0.18 + 13 \times 0.05] - \$150 \times 0.27 - \$300 \times 0.18 - \$450 \times 0.05 = \$67.40$

We see that the highest expected net revenue occurs when Zeus accepts only 10 reservations, or equivalently, does not overbook at all.

In practice, revenue management is far more complex than this example and employs more sophisticated optimization and simulation approaches and specialized software packages.[8]

THEORY OF CONSTRAINTS

The **Theory of Constraints (TOC)** *is a set of principles that focuses on increasing total process throughput, net profits, and return on investment by maximizing the utilization of all bottleneck work activities and workstations.* Dr. Eliyahu M. Goldratt introduced TOC in a fictional novel, *The Goal.*[9] The philosophy and principles of TOC are valuable in understanding demand and capacity management.

The traditional OM definition of throughput is the average number of goods or services completed per time period by a process. TOC views throughput differently: **Throughput** *is the amount of money generated per time period through actual sales.* For most business organizations, the goal is to maximize throughput, thereby maximizing cash flow. Inherent in this definition is that it makes little sense to make a good or service until it can be sold and that excess inventory is wasteful.

In TOC, *a* **constraint** *is anything in an organization that limits it from moving toward or achieving its goal.* Constraints determine the throughput of a facility, because they limit production output to their own capacity. There are two basic types of constraints: physical and nonphysical constraints.

A **physical constraint** *is associated with the capacity of a resource such as a machine, employee, or workstation.* Physical constraints result in process bottlenecks. *A* **bottleneck (BN) work activity** *is one that effectively limits the capacity of the entire process.* At a bottleneck, the input exceeds the capacity, restricting the output that is capable of being produced. *A* **nonbottleneck (NBN) work activity** *is one in which idle capacity exists.*

A **nonphysical constraint** *is environmental or organizational, such as low product demand or an inefficient management policy or procedure.* Inflexible work rules, inadequate labor skills, and poor management are all forms of constraints. Removing nonphysical constraints is not always possible.

Because the number of constraints is typically small, TOC focuses on identifying them, managing BN and NBN work activities carefully, linking them to the market to ensure an appropriate product mix, and scheduling the NBN resources to enhance throughput. These principles are summarized in Exhibit 10.11.

TOC helps managers understand the relationship between demand, capacity, and resource utilization. Consider the three process structures shown in Exhibit 10.12. In the first one described in Exhibit 10.12(a), a bottleneck workstation is feeding nonbottleneck workstations. Since NBN workstation capacity of 160 units is higher than the BN workstation with a capacity of 80 units, all output from the BN is quickly moved through the two-stage process to meet demand and is sold. No work-in-process inventory accumulates in front of the downstream NBN workstations. The resource utilization at the BN is computed using Equation (7.1) introduced in Chapter 7:

$$\text{Utilization } (U\%) = \text{Resources demand/Resource availability}$$
$$= 80 \text{ units}/80 \text{ units} = 100\%$$

Exhibit 10.11
Basic Principles of the Theory of Constraints

Nonbottleneck Management Principles	Bottleneck Management Principles
Move jobs through nonbottleneck workstations as fast as possible until the job reaches the bottleneck workstation.	Only the bottleneck workstations are critical to achieving process and factory objectives and should be scheduled first.
At nonbottleneck workstations, idle time is acceptable if there is no work to do, and therefore, resource utilizations may be low.	An hour lost at a bottleneck resource is an hour lost for the entire process or factory output.
Use smaller order (also called lot or transfer batches) sizes at nonbottleneck workstations to keep work flowing to the bottleneck resources and eventually to the marketplace to generate sales.	Work-in-process buffer inventory should be placed in front of bottlenecks to maximize resource utilization at the bottleneck.
An hour lost at a nonbottleneck resource has no effect on total process or factory output and incurs no real cost.	Use large order sizes at bottleneck workstations to minimize setup time and maximize resource utilization.
	Bottleneck workstations should work at all times to maximize throughput and resource utilization so as to generate cash from sales and achieve the company's goal.

Likewise, the utilization at the NBN, if it only makes what is needed, is 50% (80/160). Using TOC logic, it is acceptable for the NBN workstations to be idle as long as everything possible is being done to maximize throughput and utilization at the BN workstations. This is a radical change from the conventional wisdom to maximize utilization of all workstations. Operations managers have traditionally thought that everyone had to be busy all the time or something was wrong. TOC argues that by maximizing resource utilization for all NBN workstations, the system creates excess inventory that may not be sold. In addition, maximizing NBN utilization increases operating expenses and purchasing costs.

In the process structure in Exhibit 10.12(b), a NBN workstation feeds a BN workstation. The NBN workstation producing at full capacity (that is, 100% utilization) creates 160 units; however, the BN workstation can use only 80 units, so 80 units accumulate in front of the BN as work-in-process inventory. There is no need for the NBN to produce more than 80 units, so the target NBN utilization should be 50%, or perhaps a little higher to provide some safety capacity against uncertainty.

The third process structure shown in Exhibit 10.12(c) defines a BN and NBN workstation working in parallel, supplying their output to a downstream work-

Exhibit 10.12
Theory of Constraint Principles Applied to Different Process Structures

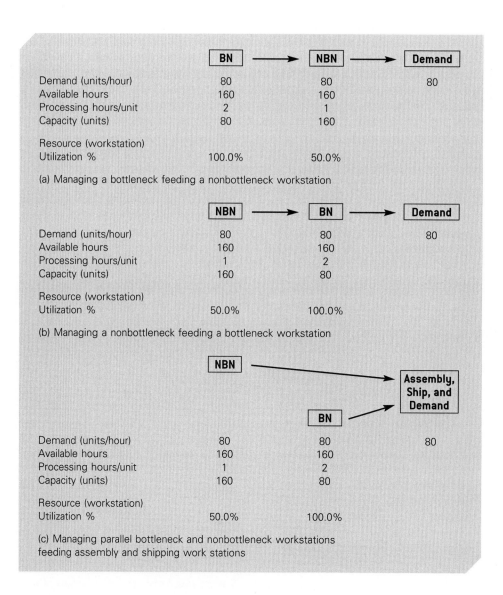

station such as an assembly or shipping workstation. Again, there is no need for the NBN workstation to produce more than 80 units, so NBN utilizations should be targeted at about 50%, as previously described.

In general, the TOC has been successful in many companies (see the OM Spotlight: Kreisler Manufacturing Corporation). As TOC evolved, it has been applied not only to manufacturing but to other areas such as distribution, marketing, and human resource management. Binney and Smith, maker of Crayola crayons, and Procter & Gamble both use TOC in their distribution efforts. Binney and Smith had high inventory levels yet poor customer service. By using TOC to better position its distribution inventories, it was able to reduce inventories and improve service. Procter & Gamble reported $600 million in savings through inventory reduction and elimination of capital improvement through TOC. A government organization that produces publications of labor statistics for the state of Pennsylvania used TOC to better match work tasks to workers to reduce idle labor and overtime requirements and to increase throughput, job stability, and profitability.[10]

Applying TOC can be challenging. In a flow shop, bottlenecks can easily be identified and do not change over time. In a job shop, however, bottlenecks may move as conditions, such as the product mix and job order quantities, change, making them more difficult to identify and manage.

OM SPOTLIGHT

Kreisler Manufacturing Corporation[11]

Kreisler Manufacturing Corporation is a small, family-run company that makes metal components for airplanes. Their clients include Pratt & Whitney, General Electric, Rolls-Royce, and Mitsubishi. The company was in its fifth straight year of losses when the company's president read *The Goal* and saw the vision for what Kreisler could do to solve its production problems.

All supervisors and managers were sent to The Goldratt Institute's TOC for Production Training. After learning about TOC, managers identified several areas of the factory, including the Internal Machine Shop and Supplier Deliveries, as bottlenecks, and began to focus on maximizing throughput at these bottlenecks. Setups were videotaped to see exactly what was happening. It was discovered that 60 percent of the time it took to complete a setup involved the worker looking for materials and tools. To remove this constraint, Kreisler assembles all the necessary materials and tools for setup into a prepackage "kit," thus cutting 60 percent off the setup time.

Kreisler also created a "visual factory" by installing red, yellow, and green lights on every machine. If a workstation is being starved or production stops, the operator turns on the red light. If there is a potential crisis or there is a risk of starving the constraint workstation, the worker turns on the yellow light. If all is running smoothly, the green light is on. Giving the machine operator control over these signals instilled a sense of ownership in the process and caught the attention and interest of everyone in the factory. In the early stages of implementing TOC, there were many red lights; today, they are green. By applying TOC, on-time deliveries increased to 97% from 65%, and 15% of the factory's "hidden capacity" was revealed and freed up. In addition, WIP inventory was reduced by 20% and another 50% reduction is expected.

SOLVED PROBLEMS

SOLVED PROBLEM #1

An automobile transmission-assembly factory normally operates two shifts per day, 5 days per week. During each shift, 400 transmissions can be completed under ideal conditions. Under normal operating conditions, 340 transmissions/shift/day are completed. Over the next 4 weeks, the factory has planned shipments according to the following schedule:

Week	1	2	3	4
Shipments	2,600	2,400	3,200	3,800

a. What is the monthly theoretical capacity?

b. What is the monthly effective capacity?

c. For this shipment schedule and assuming zero finished goods inventory at the end of the month, what is the actual utilization rate (%)?

Solution:

a. Theoretical capacity = (2 shifts/day)(5 days/week) (400 transmissions/shift) (4 weeks/month)
= 16,000 transmissions/ month

b. Effective capacity = (2 shifts/day)(5 days/week) (340 transmissions/shift) (4 weeks/month)
= 13,600 transmissions/month

c. Utilization (%) = Resources demanded or used/ Resources available
= 12,000/13,600 = 88.2%

Also, note that planned shipments are 111.8 percent (3,800/3,400) of effective capacity in week 4. So, during the last week of the month's "surge in production," the factory assembled 3,800 transmissions, very close to its ideal capacity of 4,000 per week.

SOLVED PROBLEM #2

Mary Johnson, the tax assessor for Yates County, has estimated that her office must perform 180 property reevaluations per day. Each staff member assigned to the reevaluation will work an 8-hour day with 1 hour for break and lunch. If it takes a staff member 10 minutes to do a reevaluation, and the average utilization of any staff member is 75%, how many staff members must be assigned to this project?

Solution:

Service rate = (7 effective hours/day) × (6 reevaluations/hour) = 42 reevaluations/day

Using Equation (7.2), we have

Utilization (U%)
= Demand rate/[Service rate × Number of servers]

or

$$0.75 = \frac{180 \text{ reevaluations/day}}{(42 \text{ reevaluations/day})} \times \text{(Number of servers)}$$

$31.5 \times S = 180$
$S = 5.7$, or about six staff members.

SOLVED PROBLEM #3

Mama Mia's Pizza must decide on the number of delivery employees to have for Super Bowl Sunday. Based on its volume of orders and available drivers, the store manager can estimate delivery times fairly accurately. If they have too many drivers, the extra wages cut into the store's profits. However, if the staffing level is too low, the store risks losing profits because customers might decide not to order if they perceive that the delivery time will be too long. Based on past history, the store manager knows that he will need 5, 7, or 10 drivers, depending on the volume of demand, which is un-

certain. He developed the following net profit estimates for each scenario:

Delivery Capacity	Low	Demand Medium	High
5	$1,500	$1,500	$1,500
7	$1,250	$1,800	$1,800
10	$900	$1,600	$2,500

Based on the hype and interest in this year's game, he estimates the probabilities of demand to be P(low) = .5,

$P(\text{medium}) = .3$, and $P(\text{high}) = .2$. How many drivers should he plan for?

Solution:

A decision tree for this situation is shown in Exhibit 10.13. The expected profits for each staffing level are:

5 Drivers: $.5(\$1,500) + .3(1,500) + .2(1,500)$
= $1,500

7 Drivers: $.5(\$1,250) + .3(1,800) + .2(1,800)$
= $1,525

10 Drivers: $.5(\$900) + .3(1,600) + .2(2,500)$
= $1,430

Therefore, even though the most likely level of demand is low, the store manager should plan on a capacity level of 7 drivers.

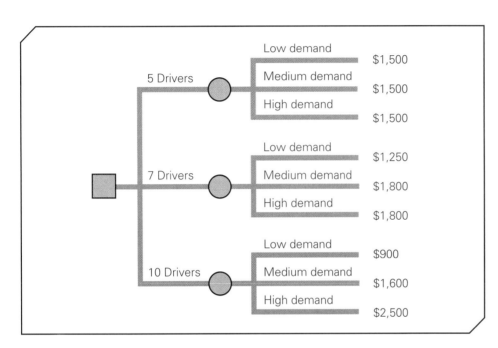

Exhibit 10.13
Decision Tree for Solved Problem #3

5 Drivers
- Low demand — $1,500
- Medium demand — $1,500
- High demand — $1,500

7 Drivers
- Low demand — $1,250
- Medium demand — $1,800
- High demand — $1,800

10 Drivers
- Low demand — $900
- Medium demand — $1,600
- High demand — $2,500

KEY TERMS AND CONCEPTS

BN and NBN resource utilization
Bottlenecks (BN)
Capacity
Capacity decision tree analysis
Capacity lag strategy
Capacity lead strategy
Capacity straddle strategy
Chase resource strategy
Complementary goods and services
Constraints—physical and nonphysical
Diseconomies of scale
Economies of scale
Effective capacity
Five ways to shift and stimulate demand
Focused factories

Four capacity expansion strategies
Job shop capacity analysis
Level resource strategy
Nonbottlenecks (NBN)
Overbooking
Peak demand
Plant-within-a-plant
Processing time
Reservations
Safety capacity
Setup time
Short- and long-term planning horizons
Theoretical capacity
Theory of constraint principles
Throughput

QUESTIONS FOR REVIEW AND DISCUSSION

1. What are three general decisions that managers need to make regarding capacity?

2. Explain the formal definition of *capacity*.

3. Provide some examples of short- and long-term capacity decisions different from Exhibit 10.1.

4. Explain the concepts of economies and diseconomies of scale and their importance to capacity decisions.

5. What is a focused factory? How can it make more efficient use of capacity?

6. Can you identify a focused factory in a service facility? Explain.

7. Can you identify a plant-within-a-plant in a service facility? Explain.

8. Explain the difference between theoretical and effective capacity.

9. Why is safety capacity important? Provide some examples of safety capacity in manufacturing and service organizations.

10. Explain how safety capacity and utilization are related.

11. Define capacity measures for a
    a. brewery
    b. airlines
    c. police precinct
    d. movie theater
    e. restaurant
    f. pizza store
    g. photocopy service
    h. software programming

12. Identify and briefly explain ways to manage short-term capacity.

13. Why are setup and changeover times important factors in determining capacity?

14. Explain the differences between short- and long-term capacity management strategies.

15. Discuss various ways for shifting and stimulating demand.

16. What are the economic issues involved in both short- and long-term capacity management strategies?

17. What are complementary goods and services, and why do firms often incorporate them into their product lines?

18. Discuss four strategies used for capacity expansion. What are the risks and benefits of each strategy?

19. Provide an example where cross-training reduces the total capacity needed and explain how.

20. How are decision-analysis techniques applied to capacity decisions? Make up a capacity planning problem using decision trees and solve it.

21. Why do service organizations use revenue management systems (RMS)? What are the advantages and possible disadvantages?

22. Under what operating conditions is RMS most appropriate?

23. Explain why Equation (10.5) captures both marketing and operations decisions.

24. What are the basic principles of the Theory of Constraints? How do these principles impact costs?

25. Compare and contrast Dr. Goldratt's definition of throughput with the more traditional definition.

26. Explain how actual resource utilization might be only 40% at a nonbottleneck workstation by applying the Theory of Constraints.

27. How would you apply the Theory of Constraints to a quick-service automobile oil change service? Explain.

28. Explain why bottlenecks move or do not move in flow shops versus job shops. How does this affect the operations manager's job?

PROBLEMS AND ACTIVITIES

1. Hickory Manufacturing Company forecasts the following demand for a product (in thousands of units) over the next 5 years:

Year	1	2	3	4	5
Forecast demand	114	129	131	134	133

Currently, the manufacturer has eight machines that operate on a 2 shift (8 hours each) basis. Twenty days per year are available for scheduled maintenance of equipment. Assume there are 250 workdays in a year. Each manufactured good takes 26 minutes to produce.

a. What is the capacity of the factory?
b. At what capacity levels (hours of work per year) will the firm be operating over the next 5 years?
c. Does the firm need to buy more machines? If so, how many? When? If not, justify.

2. The consumer loan division of a major bank wants to determine the size of the staff it would need to process up to 200 loan applications per day. It estimated that each loan officer can process a loan application in approximately 20 minutes. If the efficiency of a loan officer is 0.8 (80%) and each loan officer works 7 hours each day, how many loan officers would be needed to handle that volume of business?

3. The roller coaster at Treasure Island Amusement Park consists of 15 cars, each of which can carry up to three passengers. According to a time study, each run takes 1.5 minutes and the time to unload and load riders is 3.5 minutes. What is the maximum effective capacity of the system in number of passengers per hour?

4. The basic pizza-making process consists of (1) preparing the pizza, (2) baking it, and (3) cutting and boxing (or transferring to a platter for dine-in service). It takes 5 minutes to prepare a pizza, 8 minutes to bake it, and 1 minute to cut and box or transfer. If the restaurant has only one preparer, what is the theoretical capacity of the pizza-making operation in pizzas per hour? What if two preparers are available? Will this change the bottleneck?

5. Worthington Hills grocery store has five regular checkout lines and one express line (12 items or less). Based on a sampling study, it takes 11 minutes on average for a customer to go through the regular line and 4 minutes to go through the express line. The store is open from 9 A.M. to 9 P.M. daily.

a. What is the store's maximum capacity (customers processed per day)?

b. What is the store's capacity by day of the week if the five regular checkout lines operate according to the following schedule? (The express line is always open.)

Hours/Day	Mon.	Tue.	Wed.	Thur.	Fri.	Sat.	Sun.
9–12 A.M.	1	1	1	1	3	5	2
12–4 P.M.	2	2	2	2	3	5	4
4–6 P.M.	3*	3	3	3	5	3	2
6–9 P.M.	4	4	4	4	5	3	1

*A 3 means three regular checkout lines are open on Monday from 4 to 6 P.M.

6. The quad chairlift at Whiteface Mountain Ski Resort carries four skiers in each chair to the top of the intermediate slope in 4 minutes based on timing a large sample of skiers. The time between loading skiers on successive chairs is 15 seconds.

a. What is the effective capacity of the system in number of skiers per hour?
b. If only one skier gets on the chair being loaded approximately 10 percent of the time, will the capacity of the system be affected? Explain.
c. Frequently it is necessary to stop the chairlift temporarily to assist beginning skiers in getting on and off safely. How could the resort's operations manager assess the effect of this practice on the lift capacity?

7. Bennington Products makes four products on three machines. The production schedule for the next 6 months is as follows:

	Production schedule					
Product	Jan.	Feb.	Mar.	Apr.	May	Jun.
1	200	0	200	0	200	0
2	100	100	100	100	100	100
3	50	50	50	50	50	50
4	100	0	100	0	100	0

The number of hours (hours/product/machine) each product requires on each machine is as follows:

	Product			
Machine	1	2	3	4
1	0.25	0.15	0.15	0.25
2	0.33	0.20	0.30	0.50
3	0.20	0.30	0.25	0.10

Setup times are roughly 20 percent of the operation times. The machine hours available during the 6 months are as follows:

Machine	Jan.	Feb.	Mar.	Apr.	May	Jun.
1	120	60	60	60	60	60
2	180	60	180	60	180	60
3	120	60	120	60	120	60

Determine whether there is enough capacity to meet the product demand. Make sure you state any assumptions.

8. Given the following data for Albert's fabricating production area:

Fixed costs for one shift	= $60,000
Unit variable cost	= $7
Selling price	= $12
Number of machines	= 5
Number of working days in year	= 340
Processing time per unit	= 60 minutes

a. What is the capacity with a single 8-hour shift?
b. What is the capacity with two shifts? The additional fixed cost for a second shift is $40,000.
c. What is the break-even volume with a single-shift operation?
d. What is the maximum revenue with a single shift?
e. What is the break-even volume with a two-shift operation?
f. Draw the break-even chart.

9. The process for renewing a driver's license at the Archer County Courthouse is as follows. First, the clerk fills out the application, then the clerk takes the driver's picture, and finally the typist types and processes the new license. It takes an average of 5 minutes to fill out an application, 1 minute to take a picture, and 7 minutes to type and process the new license.

a. If there are two clerks and three typists, where will the bottleneck in the system be? How many drivers can be processed in 1 hour if the clerks and typists work at 80 percent efficiency?
b. If 40 drivers are to be processed each hour, how many clerks and typists should be hired?

10. A plant manufactures three products, A, B, and C. A drill press is required to perform one operation for each product. Machine operators work at 75 percent efficiency and the machines have 95 percent efficiency. The plant operates 8-hour shifts 20 days per month. The operation times for each product follow:

Product	A	B	C
Operation time (minutes/product)	5.0	1.85	7.0

Determine the amount of equipment and number of machine operators needed to produce 10,000 units per month.

11. Tony's Income Tax Service is determining its staffing requirements for the next income tax season. Income tax preparers work 50 hours per week from January 15 through April 15. There are two major tasks: preparation of short forms and preparation of long forms. The time normally needed to prepare a short form is 15 minutes; long forms takes 50 minutes if all customer records are in order. Fifteen percent of customers using the long form have complicated problems that require approximately 1/2 hour of additional work. The usual mix of customers requiring long versus short forms is 40 to 60 percent. Preparers work at 85% efficiency. Tony expects 1,000, 3,500 and 5,000 customers for each of the three months, respectively. How many preparers are needed each month to meet that demand?

12. A state department of transportation district is responsible for 300 miles of highway. During a winter storm, salt trucks spread an average of 400 pounds of salt per mile and travel at an average speed of 25 mph. Because of nonproductive travel time, the average efficiency of the trucks (that is, the productive time spent salting the roads) is 60 percent. How many 7-ton trucks will be needed to complete the process of salting all roads within 2 hours?

13. The Gray Corporation is considering constructing a new plant to handle a new product line of synthetic drugs. A large plant and a small plant are being considered. The decision will depend on the long-run average demand. The probability of high demand is estimated to be .65; moderate demand, .15; and low demand, .20. The payoff (in thousands of dollars per year over a 10-year horizon) is projected as follows:

	Long-run average demand		
Decision	**High**	**Medium**	**Low**
Build large	250	100	25
Build small	100	100	75

Construct a decision tree for this problem and determine the optimal strategy.

14. For the Gray Corporation in Problem 13, suppose the facility decision can be time-phased; that is, if a small plant is built, the company will consider expanding it in 3 years if initial demand is high. If the initial demand is moderate or low, then no further decisions will be considered. Revise the decision tree to account for this. (*Hint:* There will be two decision nodes.)

15. For the situation described in Problem 14, suppose the payoffs for building a small plant initially and then expanding are

Long-run average demand		
High	**Medium**	**Low**
200	90	10

Further, suppose that the probabilities of initial demand being high, moderate, and low are .60, .20, and .20, respectively. Also, if the initial demand is high, then the probabilities of long-run average demand being high, moderate, and low are .85, .10, and .05, respectively. Will Gray's decision strategy differ in this case?

16. Your first job is in hotel management and recently you were promoted to hotel manager for a large convention hotel in downtown New Orleans. Answer the following questions given the information in the table below for 1 day. What is the total contribution to profit and overhead? What is your hotel effectiveness percentage? What are the implications of these numbers to your career?

17. Using the data for Zeus Rental Car Company, do a relative cost analysis holding the cost of an idle car (currently $40) constant and varying the cost of overbooking (currently $150) from $35 to $300. What do you discover?

18. A regional airline that operates a 50-seat jet prices the ticket for one popular business flight at $250. If the airline overbooks the reservations, overbooked passengers receive a $300 travel voucher. The airline is considering overbooking by up to five seats, and the demand for the flight always exceeds the number of reservations it might accept. The probabilities of the number of passengers who will show up are given in the table at the bottom of the page. Determine the best overbooking policy that the airline should follow.

19. Industrial Testing, Inc. makes and sells electronic testing equipment in the industrial market. Two products, called Microtester and Macrotester, are assembled from two components: C1 and C2. Each Microtester is assembled from two C1s and one C2; each Macrotester is assembled from two C1s and three C2s.

   Three machines are used in the production of components C1 and C2. Component C1 requires $1^1/_2$ hours on machine 1, 2 hours on machine 2, and 1 hour on machine 3. Component C2 requires 1 hour on machine 1, $1^1/_2$ hours on machine 2, and 3 hours on machine 3.

   Industrial Testing is forecasting annual demand of 2,900 units of the Microtester and 2,100 units of the Macrotester. Planning is now underway for additional equipment. In particular, managers want to know how many of each of the machines is needed. Experience with the three machines suggests actual utilization rates of .97, .95, and .92 for machines 1, 2, and 3, respectively. The firm is planning a single-shift operation, which provides 2,000 working hours per year. How many machines of each type are required to produce parts C1 and C2?

20. A stamping press makes parts of vehicle seat belts with a setup time of 100 minutes and a processing time of 0.25 minute per part.

Table for Problem 16.

Characteristic/Variable	Business Hotel Customers (B)	Convention Association Hotel Customers (C)
Customers for this day (D)	200 room nights rented (D_B)	500 room nights rented (D_C)
Average price/room night (P)	$110 ($P_B$)	$75 ($P_C$)
Variable cost/room night (VC)	$25	$25
Maximum price/room night (called the rack rate)	$150	$100
Maximum number rooms available for sale this day	300 room nights available	700 room nights available

Table for Problem 18.

Number of reservations	**Number of passengers showing up**										
	45	**46**	**47**	**48**	**49**	**50**	**51**	**52**	**53**	**54**	**55**
50	.100	.150	.150	.200	.300	.100					
51	.080	.130	.180	.150	.250	.110	.100				
52	.060	.125	.175	.200	.250	.100	.050	.040			
53	.040	.050	.070	.200	.250	.150	.100	.080	.060		
54	.020	.040	.050	.090	.120	.210	.180	.140	.100	.050	
55	.010	.030	.040	.060	.100	.120	.200	.180	.150	.090	.020

a. If an order arrives for 800 parts, how many hours will it take to finish the job?
b. What is the average time (total work content) per part?
c. How many hours will it take to finish each job if the order sizes are 8,000 and 80,000? What is the average time (total work content) per part?
d. What do you conclude by comparing the average times for order sizes of 800, 8,000, and 80,000?

21. Kennedy's Creek Fishing Company produces a variety of fly rods with the following machining times for reel parts:

Machined part	Machine setup time	Processing time	Order size quantity	Next month's forecasts
Reel Part 3012	60 min	72 sec	500	4,000 parts
Reel Part 1022	30 min	30 sec	1,000	7,000
Reel Part 6087	45 min	48 sec	2,000	12,000

The company has two machining lathes that currently operate 20 days a month for 7.5 hours per day. Do they have enough machining capacity to meet next month's demand? Make a final set of recommendations.

CASES

APPLETON PULP AND PAPER MILL

Appleton Corporation is one of the largest forest products companies in the world, converting trees into three basic product groups: (1) building materials, such as lumber and plywood; (2) white paper products, including printing and writing grades of white paper; (3) brown paper products, such as liner board and corrugated containers. Given the highly competitive markets within the forest products industry, survival dictates that Appleton maintain its position as a low-cost producer of quality products. That requires an ambitious capital program to improve the timber base and to build modern, cost-effective timber conversion facilities.

An integrated pulp and paper mill is a facility in which wood chips and chemicals are processed to produce paper products or dried pulp. First, wood chips are cooked and bleached in the pulp mill; the resulting pulp is piped directly into storage tanks, as shown in Exhibit 10.14. From the storage tanks the pulp is sent to either the paper mill or a dryer. In the paper mill, the pulp is routed to one or more paper machines, which produce the finished paper products. Alternatively, the pulp is sent to a dryer, and the dried pulp is then sold to paper mills that do not have the capability of producing their own pulp. The total system is a large facility costing several hundred million dollars.

One of Appleton's major pulp and paper facilities consists of a pulp mill, three paper machines, and a dryer. As the facility developed, the pulp mill was found to produce more pulp than the combination of paper machines and the dryer could use. The pulp mill has a

Exhibit 10.14
Pulp and Paper Process

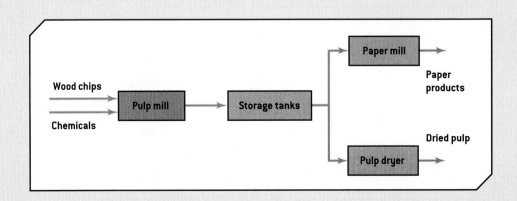

capacity of 940 tons per day (TPD), the three paper machines together average 650 TPD of pulp use, and the dryer can handle 200 TPD. One question of interest is whether it would be worthwhile to invest in improvements to increase the capacity of the dryer.

Managers realized that all of the equipment in the mill is subject to downtime and to variations in efficiency. For example, suppose that on one day the pulp mill is inoperable for more than the average length of time and the paper machines are having less than the usual downtime. In this case, very little pulp would be available for the dryer, regardless of its capacity. The lack of pulp would not "average out" on days when the opposite conditions occur, as much more pulp would be available than the pulp dryer could handle. Consequently, the pulp storage tanks would become full, and the pulp mill would have to shut down. Thus, the decision to increase the capacity of the drier cannot be made without considering pulp production.

Further studies determined the following information about the capacities of the components of the integrated pulp and paper mill.

Pulp Mill The pulp mill is assumed to have an average production rate of 1,044 TPD when operating, with an average of 10 percent downtime. The actual downtime varies. For example, one day the pulp mill might be down 2 percent of the time, the next day 20 percent, and so on.

Paper Machines The rate of pulp flow to the paper machines in a time period is a function of the type of paper being made and the amount of downtime on the paper machines. The rate of pulp flow depends on the schedule of types of paper to be made. The average is 650 TPD, but varies between 500 and 800 TPD. Each machine's downtime averages 5 percent of the total working hours.

Pulp Dryer The capacity of the dryer is assumed to be 200 TPD. Dryer downtime averages 15 percent.

Storage Tanks The connecting link between the pulp mill, the paper machines, and the dryer is the pulp storage tanks. In the model, all pulp produced by the pulp mill is added to the inventory in the tanks. All pulp drawn by the dryer and paper machines is subtracted from the inventory. If the storage tanks are empty, the model must shut down the paper machines. If the tanks are full, the pulp mill must be shut down. The actual rate at which the dryer is operated at any moment must be set by the plant manager to try to keep the storage tanks from becoming "too empty" or "too full."

Question 1: How much additional pulp could be produced and dried, given possible capacity increases to the dryer? How high can the dryer capacity be increased until no further benefits will be realized?

Question 2: Describe an approach for determining the effect on production output of increasing pulp capacity. Try to develop a spreadsheet model to help your analysis. You might consider using simulation, described in Supplementary Chapter D, and incorporating Crystal Ball into your analysis.

DAVID CHRISTOPHER, ORTHOPEDIC SURGEON

David Christopher received his medical degrees from the University of Kentucky and the University of Virginia. He did his residency and early surgeries at Duke University Medical Center. Eight years ago, he set up his own orthopedic surgery clinic in Atlanta, Georgia. Today, one other doctor has joined his clinic in addition to 12 support personnel such as X-ray technicians, nurses, accounting, and office support. The medical practice specializes in all orthopedic surgery except it does not do spinal surgery. Their clinic has grown to the point where both orthopedic surgeons are working long hours and Dr. Christopher is wondering whether he needs to hire more surgeons.

An orthopedic surgeon is trained in the preservation, investigation, and restoration of the form and function of the extremities, spine, and associated structures by medical, surgical, and physical means. He or she is involved with the care of patients whose musculoskeletal problems include congenital deformities, trauma, infections, tumors, metabolic disturbances of the musculoskeletal system, deformities, injuries, and degenerative diseases of the spine, hands, feet, knee, hip, shoulder, and elbow in children and adults. An orthopedic surgeon is also concerned with primary and secondary muscular problems and the effects of central or peripheral nervous system lesions of the musculoskeletal system. Osteoporosis, for example, results in fractures, especially fractured hips, wrists, and the spine. Treatments have been very successful in getting the fractures to heal.

Dr. Christopher collected the data in Exhibit 10.15 as an example of their typical workweek. Both surgeons work 11 hours each day with 1 hour off for lunch, or 10 effective hours. All surgeries are performed from 7:00 A.M. to 12:00 noon 4 days a week. After lunch from noon to 1:00 P.M., the surgeons see patients in the hospital and at the clinic from 1:00 P.M. to 6:00 P.M. On weekends and Fridays, the surgeons rest, attend conferences and professional meetings, and sometimes do guest lectures at a nearby medical school. The doctors want to leave a safety capacity each week of 10 percent for unexpected problems with scheduled surgeries and emergency patient arrivals.

The setup and changeover times in Exhibit 10.15 reflect time between each surgery to clean up, rest, review the next patient's medical record for any last-minute issues, and get ready for the next surgery. Dr. Christopher feels these changeover times help ensure the quality of their surgery by giving them time between operations. For example, standing on a concrete floor and bending

over a patient in a state of concentration places great stress on the surgeon's legs and back. Dr. Christopher likes to sit down for a while between surgeries to relax. Some surgeons go quickly from one patient to the next, but Dr. Christopher thinks this practice of rushing could lead to medical and surgical errors.

Dr. Christopher wants answers to the following questions: What is their current weekly workload? Should they hire more surgeons, and if so, how many? What other changes could they make to maximize patient throughput and surgeries, and therefore revenue, yet not compromise on the quality of medical care.

Exhibit 10.15
Orthopedic Surgeons One-Week Surgery Workload

Orthopedic Surgery Procedure	Surgeon Changeover Time (minutes)	Surgery Time (minutes)	Surgeon Identity	Demand (No. of Patients Scheduled Weekly)
Rotator cuff repair	15	45	B	2
Cartilage knee repair	15	30	B	1
Fracture tibia/fibula	15	60	B	1
Achilles tendon repair	20	30	B	3
ACL ligament repair	20	60	B	4
Fractured hip	20	90	A	0
Fractured wrist	20	75	A	2
Fractured ankle	20	90	A	1
Hip replacement	60	150	A	2
Knee replacement	60	120	A	3
Shoulder replacement	60	180	B	1
Big toe replacement	45	90	B	0

RECORDING FOR THE BLIND

Recording for the Blind is a national nonprofit service organization that provides recorded educational books at no charge to blind and physically and perceptually handicapped students and professionals. Because the capacity of its New York location was limited and insufficient for future expansion, the organization moved in 1983 to a new modern-design, one-level facility in Princeton, New Jersey. The move led to the design and implementation of an updated, integrated operating system (IOS) utilizing high-technology automated material handling.

A capacity-planning study was undertaken to examine present and future client needs, resources, availability of technology, labor requirements, and capital and operational costs. With demand increasing at 8 to 9 percent per year and only 16 percent of the budget coming from federal funds, cost savings was a primary goal. A second goal was to reduce the lead time for duplicating a book and processing an order.

Exhibit 10.16 shows that the demand pattern for books is seasonal, with peaks in January, June, and September. Low-demand months can be used to balance yearly capacity needs. A standby library was created to store multiple copies of preduplicated best sellers. However, only a limited inventory is possible. Five percent of the titles constitute 50 percent of the demand, whereas 95 percent are in a bracket of highly random demand pattern.

To define total capacity requirements for calculating the workstation loads and labor needs, a 3-year (Year 1 to 3) demand pattern was analyzed. A production-capacity requirement of 450 books per day was established. With a 95 percent efficiency, that yields an average of 427 books per day. The calculations were based on a demand trend of 88 percent growth per year (see Exhibit 10.17). The actual performance before the move was standing at 74 percent productivity (333 books per day in 1982) with 39 production-line em-

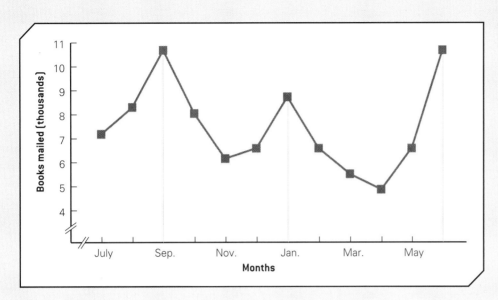

Exhibit 10.16
Five Years' Average Monthly Demand

ployees. The new system had to provide, at the same cost per book or less, an increase of 28 percent in the daily production average.

New automated equipment and system integration were the key elements in achieving the organization's objectives. For example, an automated storage and retrieval system was designed for rapid access to the 20,000 most active titles; conveyors were designed to connect all workstations; tape-duplicating machines were modified to double their speed; and automated sorting equipment with laser scanners was proposed for use in restocking returned items.

After 2 years' experience with the new system, Recording for the Blind had a 21 percent productivity improvement, enabling it to provide 27 percent more books in Year 3 than in Year 1. Unit costs were reduced

by 16 percent, and 97 percent of orders were mailed within 5 working days from receipt. These percent changes and expected trends are summarized in Exhibit 10.18.

Questions for Analysis

1. Explain how Recording for the Blind determined the required operating capacity needed.

2. Were the actions Recording for the Blind took rational from a capacity management viewpoint? Explain its decisions in the context of the topics discussed in this chapter.

3. What other possible actions might it take to manage capacity in relation to demand. Outline a plan as if you were consulting for the organization.

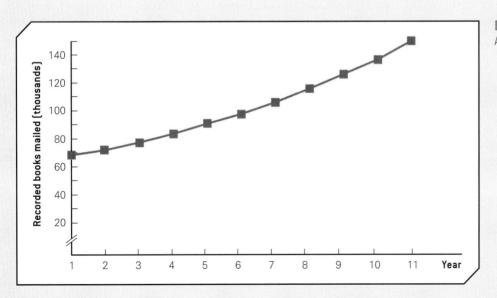

Exhibit 10.17
Annual Demand Projections

Exhibit 10.18
Books Produced and Cost per
Book Percentage Change

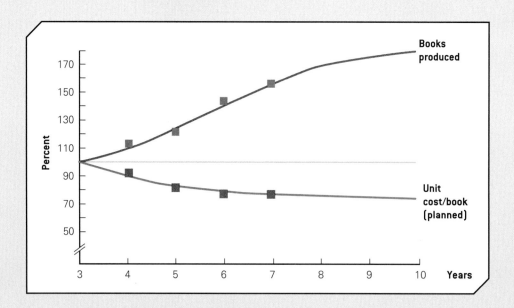

ENDNOTES

[1] "Giant New Jetliner Faces Jumbo Problem: Assembly Required," *Wall Street Journal On Line*, December 16, 2003, http://online.wsj.com/article_print/0,,SB1071533393226741900,00.html and http://www.airbus.com/airbus4u/articles_detail.asp?ae_id=1370.

[2] "Boeing's New Baby," *Wall Street Journal*, November 18, 2003, p. B1.

[3] Skinner, W., "The Focused Factory," *Harvard Business Review*, May–June, 1974, pp. 113–121.

[4] http://www.strategosinc.com/focused_factory_example.htm.

[5] http://www.briggsandstratton.com.

[6] "Bank One Workers Brace for Impact," *The Columbus Dispatch*, Columbus, Ohio, April 11, 2004, p. F1, and one of the authors' executive education clients.

[7] "American Joins Delta to Cut, Simplify Fares," *USA Today*, January 7, 2005, p. B1; "Wooing Business Travelers Viewed as Tall Order," *The Columbus Dispatch*, Columbus, Ohio, January 8, 2005, p. C2.

[8] Baker, T. K., and Collier, D. A., "The Benefit of Optimizing Prices to Manage Demand in Hotel Revenue Management Systems," *Production and Operations Management* 12, no. 4, 2003, pp. 502–518; and Baker, T. K., and Collier, D. A., "A Comparative Revenue Analysis of Hotel Yield Management Heuristics," *Decision Sciences* 30, no. 1, Winter, 1999, pp. 239–263. Ashgate Publishing Limited, Hampshire, UK, reprinted this article in the volume on *Decision Science—The International Library of Management*, July 2000.

[9] Goldratt, Eliyahu M., and Cox, Jeff, *The Goal*, Second Revised Edition, Croton-on-Hudson, N.Y.: North River Press, 1992; and Goldratt, Eliyahu M., *The Theory of Constraints*, Croton-on-Hudson, N.Y.: North River Press, 1990.

[10] Pastore, Jeremy, Sundararajan, Sekar, and Zimmers, Emory W., "Innovative Application," *APICS—The Performance Advantage* 14, no. 3, March 2004, pp. 32–35.

[11] http://www.goldratt.com/kreisler.htm.

Chapter Outline

CHAPTER 11

Forecasting and Demand Planning

Learning Objectives

1. To understand the need for forecasts and the implications of information technology for forecasting in the value chain.

2. To understand the basic elements of forecasting, namely, the choice of planning horizon, different types of data patterns, and how to calculate forecasting errors.

3. To be aware of different forecasting approaches and methods.

4. To understand basic time-series forecasting methods, be aware of more advanced methods, and use spreadsheet models to make forecasts.

5. To learn the basic ideas and method of regression analysis.

6. To understand the role of human judgment in forecasting and when judgmental forecasting is most appropriate.

7. To know that judgment and quantitative forecast methodologies can complement one another, and therefore improve overall forecast accuracy.

- Russ Newton recently joined Health Products, Inc., a company that designs and manufactures hospital equipment, such as beds and other specialized furniture. Russ had worked for the firm as a co-op while he was in business school, and his ability to develop Microsoft Excel applications impressed his supervisors. Russ's new manager had just the job for him. The company's top managers had expressed the need for better data to support their strategic planning. Their forecasts of the market potential for key products had not been very accurate in recent years. Most forecasting was done simply by gathering sales managers' opinions, and very little had been driven by data or an understanding of the key factors, such as governmental policies, population demographics, and hospital occupancy rates and capital spending, that influence demand. Russ was assigned to develop a forecasting model to predict the market growth for each of the firm's five product categories. In talking to various managers in the company, Russ was overwhelmed with the many factors that the managers thought would influence demand and the huge amount of economic and industry data that was available. He was a bit apprehensive and wondered how he could approach this important assignment.

- Mandy Alan, the national sales forecasting manager at Galaxy Communications, surveyed the managers gathered in the conference room. Galaxy Communications is a regional telecom, offering traditional residential and commercial telephone service as well as wireless plans. "We're getting a lot of customer complaints," she said. "We always seem to be running out of stock of key equipment for installation and repair, and customers complain about long waits for customer service. It seems to me that we simply can't do a good job of forecasting the demand for each type of telecommunication service so that we can accurately determine our equipment and staffing needs. We need help and we need it quickly. Any ideas?"

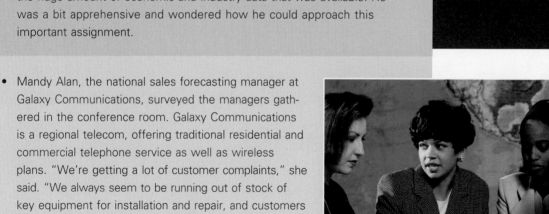

© Getty Images/PhotoDisc

- The demand for rental cars in Florida and other warm climates peaks during college spring break season. Call centers and rental offices are flooded with customers wanting to rent a vehicle. National Car Rental took a unique approach by developing a customer-identification forecasting model, by which it identifies all customers who are young and rent cars only once or twice a year. These demand analysis models allow National to call this target market segment in February, when call volumes are lower, to sign them up again. The proactive strategy is designed to both boost repeat rentals and smooth out the peaks and valleys in call center volumes.[1]

PRNewsFoto/Volkswagen of America, Inc. and Scholastic Corporation

Discussion Questions: Think of a pizza delivery franchise located near a college campus. What factors that influence demand do you think should be included in trying to forecast demand for pizzas? How might these factors differ for a franchise located in a suburban residential area?

Forecasting *is the process of projecting the values of one or more variables into the future.* Good forecasts are needed in all organizations to drive analyses and decisions related to operations. Forecasting is a key component in many types of integrated operating systems that we described in Chapter 5, such as supply chain management, customer relationship management, and revenue management systems.

> **Forecasting** *is the process of projecting the values of one or more variables into the future.*

The first episode highlights both the complexity of modern forecasting and the importance of using good analytical approaches instead of simply "going with the gut" and using salespersons' opinions. In the health care industry, for example, the demand for hospital beds and related products is driven in part by population demographics, hospital admissions and surgical procedures rates, hospital construction, interest rates, and many other factors. Identifying these factors, collecting historical data to understand trends, and building a useful forecasting model is a very challenging task. Good models can provide the type of information that top managers need to plan product development, long-term capacity decisions, and other key strategic decisions.

Forecasting is also vital for daily operations, as the second episode illustrates. Poor forecasting can result in poor inventory and staffing decisions, resulting in part shortages, inadequate customer service, and many customer complaints. In the telecommunications industry, competition is fierce; and goods and services have very short life cycles. Changing technology, frequent price wars, and incentives for customers to switch services increase the difficulty of providing accurate forecasts.

Many firms integrate forecasting with value chain and capacity management systems to make better operational decisions. National Car Rental, for example, is using data analysis and forecasting methods in its value chain to improve service and reduce costs. Instead of accepting customer demand as it is and trying to plan resources to meet the peaks and valleys, its models help to shift demand to low demand periods and better use its capacity. The proactive approach to spring break peak demand helps plan and coordinate rental office and call center staffing levels and schedules, vehicle availability, advertising campaigns, and vehicle maintenance and repair schedules. Many commercial software packages also tie forecasting modules into supply chain and operational planning systems.

Good forecasting and demand planning systems result in higher capacity utilization, reduced inventories and costs, more efficient process performance, more flexibility, improved customer service, and increased profit margins. In this chapter, we discuss the role of forecasting in OM. We begin by describing the role of forecasting in the broader context of demand planning. Then we introduce a variety of quantitative and qualitative forecasting methods and approaches.

Learning Objective
To understand the need for forecasts and the implications of information technology for forecasting in the value chain.

FORECASTING AND DEMAND PLANNING

Organizations make many different types of forecasts. Consider a consumer products company, such as Procter & Gamble, that makes many different goods in various sizes. Top managers need long-range forecasts expressed in total sales dollars for use in financial planning and for sizing and locating new facilities. At lower organizational levels, however, managers of the various product groups need aggregate forecasts of sales volume for their products in units that are more meaningful to them—for example, pounds of a certain type of soap—to establish production plans. Finally, managers of individual manufacturing facilities need forecasts by brand and size—for instance, the number of 64-ounce boxes of Tide detergent—to plan material usage and production schedules. For such a company, forecasts also need to be tied to different global markets and must be consistent across organizational levels to be effective planning aids. In addition, special forecasts—such as forecasts of material and production costs, prices, and so on—may be required for new products and promotional items. Clearly, forecasts are of many different types and in different units of measurement, depending on their purpose. Similarly, airlines need long-range forecasts of demand for air travel to plan their purchases of airplanes and short-term forecasts to develop seasonal routes and schedules; university administrators require enrollment forecasts; city planners need forecasts of population trends to plan highways and mass transit systems; and restaurants need forecasts to be able to plan for food purchases.

In many organizations, such as the airline, hospitality, and retail industries, demand is highly seasonal over a year or may vary significantly with the day of the week or the time of day. Grocery stores, banks, and similar organizations need very short-term forecasts to plan work-shift scheduling and vehicle routing and make other operating decisions to accommodate such variations in demand. Many firms that provide customized services find it easy to forecast the number of customers that will demand service in a particular time period but quite difficult to forecast the mix of services that will be required or the time it will take to provide those services. Hence, such firms need special forecasts of service mix. Operations managers would find it quite difficult to do their jobs without good forecasts.

Accurate forecasts are needed throughout the value chain, as illustrated in Exhibit 11.1, and are used by all functional areas of an organization, such as accounting, finance, marketing, operations, and distribution. One of the biggest problems with forecasting systems is they are driven by different departmental needs and incentive systems, and therefore, multiple sets of data exist for similar customers, work orders, and process performance. This leads to conflicting forecasts and organizational inefficiencies. One way to avoid these problems is by having only one integrative database that helps synchronize the value chain.

Forecasting is typically included in comprehensive value chain and demand-planning software systems. These systems integrate marketing, inventory, sales, operations planning, and financial data. For example, the SAP Demand Planning module enables companies to integrate planning information from different de-

Exhibit 11.1 The Need for Forecasts in a Value Chain

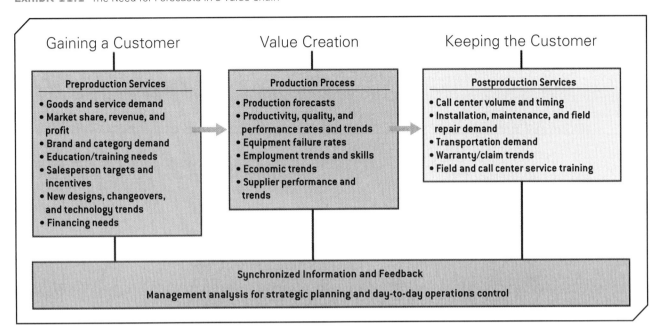

partments or organizations into a single demand plan. Some software vendors are beginning to use the words *demand planning* or *demand chain* instead of *supply chain*. This name change highlights the fact that customer's wants and needs define the customer benefit package and that customer demand pulls goods and services through the supply chain. We discuss the ideas and methods of pulling goods and services through the value chain in Chapter 9.

SAP Demand Planning offers these key capabilities:[2]

- *Multilevel planning*—SAP Demand Planning enables a firm to view, forecast, and plan products on any level and in any dimension. Planning can be based on product, geography, or time and can be initiated from the top down or from the bottom up.
- *Data analysis*—Managers can easily analyze planning data in tables and as graphics, and intuitive navigation features enable them to move through various levels of data.
- *Statistical forecasting*—SAP Demand Planning supports a full range of forecasting methods that use past sales to identify level, trend, or seasonal patterns and regression tools to predict consumer behavior by determining the impact of causal factors such as price, number of displays, number of stores, weather, and demographics.
- *Trade promotion support*—SAP Demand Planning generates promotion-driven forecasts on top of a baseline forecast. Firms can model promotional demand based on profitability goals or historical patterns. Using historical sales estimates, SAP Demand Planning can automatically detect a promotion pattern that occurred in the past.
- *Collaborative demand planning*—This capability enables planners to share demand plans among key players in the value chain. Users can pilot collaborative planning processes and deploy them widely and access graphics that enable them to view large amounts of data. Firms can also collect, forecast, and plan demand from multiple input sources. Finally, users can view planning books over the Internet, allowing easy access for suppliers and customers with limited IT capabilities.

OM SPOTLIGHT

Collaborative Demand Planning at Colgate-Palmolive[3]

Colgate-Palmolive is a global consumer products company with such products as toothpaste, laundry detergents, pet foods, and soap and operates in over 200 countries. About 80 percent of its employees are located outside the United States. The company uses an integrated operating system to give its customers and suppliers complete access to business-critical data such as order status, forecasts, production plans and schedules, and worldwide inventory status. The system provides the platform for collaboration on many supply chain decisions such as demand planning.

To reduce supply chain costs, Colgate-Palmolive implemented three supply chain strategies simultaneously. First, it established a vendor-managed inventory program (see Chapter 9) with key customers to reduce channel inventory and cycle times. Colgate also wanted to move from regional to global sourcing of raw materials, component parts, and packaging. Finally, Colgate implemented a collaborative supply chain planning process with its suppliers and customers to manage promotional demand, improve forecasts,

and synchronize activities along the supply chain. These initiatives have improved on-time order performance from 70 to 98 percent for vendor-managed inventories, reduced total inventories by 10 percent, and improved customer order fulfillment rates to 95 percent.

Victor Fisher/Bloomberg News/Landov

Information technology provides the capability to share time-sensitive information all along the value chain. This information sharing is reducing the need for forecasting in the traditional sense (see the OM Spotlight on Colgate-Palmolive). In the past, companies conducted planning based on known customer orders or forecasts of future customer orders. By sharing information across the value chain about customer order status, customer and supplier delivery schedules, backorders, and inventory status, companies in the value chain reduce their need for forecasts and also improve the accuracy of the forecasts they have to make. SAP calls this *collaborative demand planning* (see Exhibit 11.2).

Exhibit 11.2
Impact of Collaborative Demand Planning

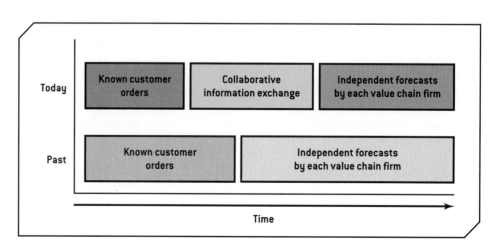

BASIC CONCEPTS IN FORECASTING

Before diving into the process of developing forecasting models, it is important to understand some basic concepts that are used in model development. These concepts are independent of the type of model and provide a foundation for users to make better use of the models in operations decisions.

Forecast Planning Horizon

Forecasts of future demand are needed at all levels of organizational decision-making. *The* **planning horizon** *is the length of time on which a forecast is based.* Long-range forecasts cover a planning horizon of 1 to 10 years and are necessary to plan for the expansion of facilities and to determine future needs for land, labor, and equipment. When and where to build new retail stores, factories, schools, libraries, distribution centers, hospitals and clinics, and emergency service facilities for the police and fire departments are dependent on long-range forecasts. Mistakes in long-term forecasts can result in firms overbuilding their infrastructure, and therefore, creating huge cost disadvantages. Likewise, long-term forecast mistakes also result in underbuilding, and therefore, missed opportunities to gain market share and generate revenue.

Intermediate-range forecasts over a 3- to 12-month period are needed to plan work-force levels, allocate budgets among divisions, schedule jobs and resources, and establish purchasing plans. For example, a purchasing department may negotiate a substantial discount by contracting to order a large amount of a particular good or service over the next year. Intermediate-range forecasts also help human resources departments plan for future hiring, employee training, and so on.

Short-range forecasts focus on the planning horizon of up to 3 months and are used by operations managers to plan production schedules and assign workers to jobs, to determine short-term capacity requirements, and to aid shipping departments in planning transportation needs and establishing delivery schedules.

The **time bucket** *is the unit of measure for the time period used in a forecast.* A time bucket might be a year, quarter, month, week, day, hour, or even a minute. For a long-term planning horizon, a firm might forecast in yearly time buckets; for a short-range planning horizon, the time bucket might be an hour or less. Customer call centers, for example, forecast customer demand in 5-, 6-, or 10-minute intervals. Selecting the right planning horizon length and time bucket size for the right situation is an important part of forecasting.

Data Patterns in Times Series

Statistical methods of forecasting are based on the analysis of historical data, called a time series. *A* **time series** *is a set of observations measured at successive points in time or over successive periods of time.* A time series provides the data for understanding how the variable that we wish to forecast has changed historically. For example, the daily ending Dow Jones stock index is one example of a time series; another is the monthly volume of sales for a product. To explain the pattern of data in a time series, it is often helpful to think in terms of five characteristics: *trend, seasonal, cyclical, random variation, and irregular (one-time) variation.* Different time series may exhibit one or more of these characteristics. Understanding these characteristics is vital to selecting the appropriate forecasting model or approach.

TRENDS

*A **trend** is the underlying pattern of growth or decline in a time series.*

*A **trend** is the underlying pattern of growth or decline in a time series.* Although data generally exhibit random fluctuations, a trend shows gradual shifts or movements to relatively higher or lower values over a longer period of time. This gradual shifting over time is usually due to such long-term factors as changes in performance, technology, productivity, population, demographic characteristics, and customer preferences.

For example, a manufacturer of industrial photographic equipment may see substantial month-to-month variability in the number of cameras sold. Reviewing the sales over the past 10 years, however, this manufacturer may find a steady increase in the annual sales volume. Exhibit 11.3 shows a straight-line, or linear, trend, that explains the steady increase in the sales data over time.

Trends can be increasing or decreasing and can be linear or nonlinear. Exhibit 11.4 shows various trend patterns. Linear increasing and decreasing trends are shown in Exhibit 11.4(a) and (b), and nonlinear trends are shown in Exhibit 11.4(c) and (d).

SEASONAL PATTERNS

***Seasonal patterns** are characterized by repeatable periods of ups and downs over short periods of time.*

***Seasonal patterns** are characterized by repeatable periods of ups and downs over short periods of time.* Seasonal patterns may occur over a year; for example, the demand for cold beverages is low during the winter, begins to rise during the spring, peaks during the summer months, and then begins to decline in the autumn. Manufacturers of coats and jackets, however, expect the opposite yearly pattern. Exhibit 11.5 shows an example of natural gas usage in a single-family home over a two-year period, which clearly exhibits a seasonal pattern.

We generally think of seasonal patterns occurring within 1 year, but similar repeatable patterns might occur over the weeks during a month, over days during a week, or hours during a day. For instance, pizza delivery peaks on the weekends, and grocery store traffic is higher during the evening hours. Likewise, customer call center volume might peak in the morning and taper off throughout the day. Different days of the week might have different seasonal patterns.

Exhibit 11.3
Linear Trend of Industrial Photographic Equipment

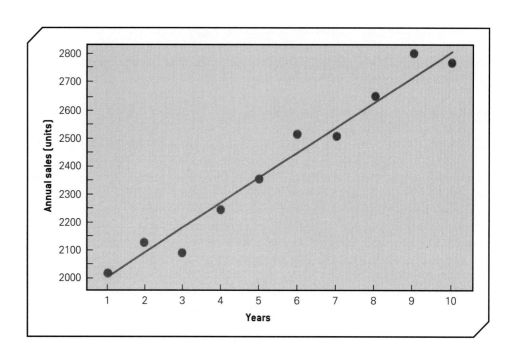

Exhibit 11.4 Example Linear and Nonlinear Trend Patterns

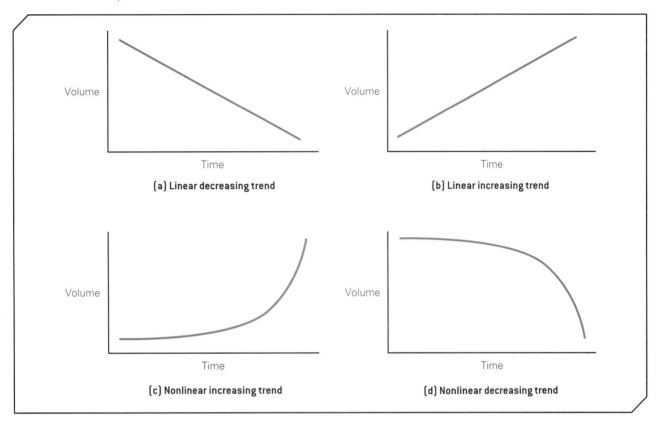

(a) Linear decreasing trend

(b) Linear increasing trend

(c) Nonlinear increasing trend

(d) Nonlinear decreasing trend

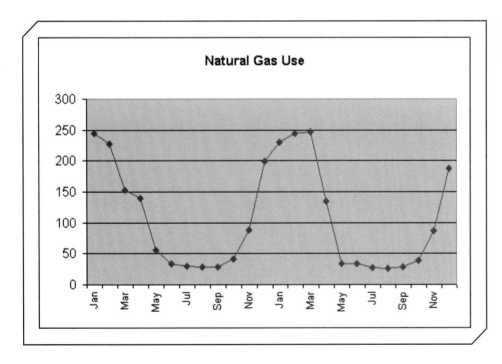

Exhibit 11.5
Seasonal Pattern of Home
Natural Gas Usage

CYCLICAL PATTERNS

Cyclical patterns *are regular patterns in a data series that take place over long periods of time.*

Cyclical patterns *are regular patterns in a data series that take place over long periods of time.* Exhibit 11.6 shows an example of multiyear cyclical movements occurring along with an increasing trend. A common example of a cyclical pattern is the movement of stock market values during "bull" and "bear" market cycles.

RANDOM VARIATION

Random variation *(sometimes called* noise*) is the unexplained deviation of a time series from a predictable pattern, such as a trend, seasonal, or cyclical pattern.*

Random variation *(sometimes called* noise*) is the unexplained deviation of a time series from a predictable pattern, such as a trend, seasonal, or cyclical pattern.* Random variation is caused by short-term, unanticipated, and nonrecurring factors and is unpredictable. Because of random variation, forecasts are never 100 percent accurate. In the ideal situation, random variation should be normally distributed about the average. That is crucial for operations managers to remember when using forecasts in decision-making. The best that can be hoped for is to identify the trend, seasonal, and/or cyclical patterns that a time series might exhibit in order to develop a useful forecast.

IRREGULAR (ONE-TIME) VARIATION

Irregular variation *is one-time variation that is explainable.*

Irregular variation *is one-time variation that is explainable.* For example, a hurricane can cause a surge in demand for building materials, food, and water. Likewise, a major snowstorm can reduce retail sales significantly. After the 9/11 terrorist attacks on the United States, many forecasts that predicted U.S. financial trends and airline passenger volumes had to be discarded due to the effects of this one-time event. One-time events result in data outliers that can normally be discarded. In some cases, such as 9/11, the irregular variation has a longer-term effect on data patterns.

An example of a time series is given in the spreadsheet in Exhibit 11.7. These data represent the call volumes over 24 quarters from a call center at a major financial institution. The data are plotted on a chart in Exhibit 11.8. We can see both an increasing trend over the entire 6 years along with seasonal patterns within each of the years. For example, during the first three quarters of each year, call volumes increase,

Exhibit 11.6
Trend and Business Cycle Characteristics (each data point is 1 year apart)

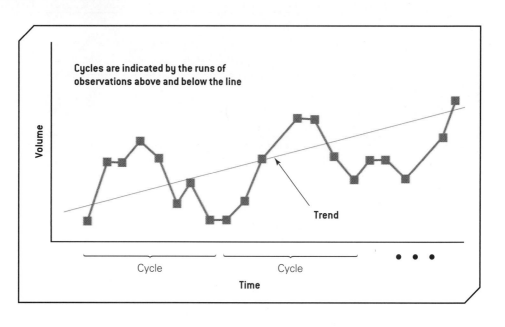

Cycles are indicated by the runs of observations above and below the line

Volume

Trend

Cycle   Cycle

Time

	A	B	C	D
1	**Period**	**Year**	**Quarter**	**Call Volume**
2	1	1	1	362
3	2	1	2	385
4	3	1	3	432
5	4	1	4	341
6	5	2	1	382
7	6	2	2	409
8	7	2	3	498
9	8	2	4	387
10	9	3	1	473
11	10	3	2	513
12	11	3	3	582
13	12	3	4	474
14	13	4	1	544
15	14	4	2	582
16	15	4	3	681
17	16	4	4	557
18	17	5	1	628
19	18	5	2	707
20	19	5	3	773
21	20	5	4	592
22	21	6	1	627
23	22	6	2	725
24	23	6	3	854
25	24	6	4	661

Exhibit 11.7
Call Center Volume

followed by a rapid decrease in the fourth quarter as customers presumably turn their attention to the holiday season. To develop a reliable forecast for the future, we would need to take into account both the long-term trend and the annual seasonal pattern. Operations managers can use this information to better plan staffing levels and schedules, vacations, and project and technology changeovers.

Forecast Errors and Accuracy

All forecasts are subject to error, and understanding the nature and size of errors is important to making good decisions. For example, the top managers of the health care products company in one of the opening episodes who need to predict the size of the hospital bed market for the next year will want to know if their forecast has a 5 percent, 10 percent, or 50 percent error.

We denote the historical values of a time series by $A_1, A_2, \ldots, A_T$. In general, A_t represents the value of the time series for period t. We will let F_t represent the forecast value for period t. When we make this forecast, we will not know the actual value of the time series in period t, A_t. However, once A_t becomes known, we can assess how well our forecast was able to predict the actual value of the time series. **Forecast error** *is the difference between the observed value of the time series and the forecast, or $A_t - F_t$.* Because of the inherent inability of any model to forecast accurately, we use quantitative measures of forecast accuracy to evaluate how well the forecasting model performs. Clearly, we want to use models that have small forecast errors.

Forecast error *is the difference between the observed value of the time series and the forecast, or $A_t - F_t$.*

Exhibit 11.8
Chart of Call Volume

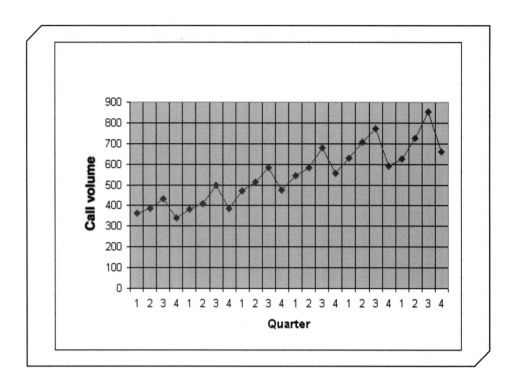

Suppose that a forecasting method provided the forecasts in column E of Exhibit 11.9 for the call volume time series we discussed earlier. The forecast errors are computed in column F. As a means of measuring forecast accuracy, we might simply add up the forecast errors. However, if the errors are random (as they should be if the forecasting method is appropriate), some errors will be positive and some will be negative, resulting in a sum near zero regardless of the size of the individual errors.

One way to avoid this problem is by squaring the individual forecast errors and then averaging the results over all T periods of data in the time series. This measure is called the mean square error, or MSE, and is calculated as

$$\text{MSE} = \frac{\sum(A_t - F_t)^2}{T} \qquad \textbf{(11.1)}$$

For the call center data, this is computed in column H of Exhibit 11.9. The sum of the squared errors is 87910.6, and therefore MSE is 87,910.6/24 = 3,662.94. MSE is probably the most commonly used measure of forecast accuracy. (Sometimes the square root of MSE is computed; this is called the *root mean square error, RMSE.*)

Another common measure of forecast accuracy is the mean absolute deviation (MAD), computed as

$$\text{MAD} = \frac{\sum|(A_t - F_t)|}{T} \qquad \textbf{(11.2)}$$

This measure is simply the average of the sum of the absolute deviations for all the forecast errors. Using the information in column J of Exhibit 11.9, we compute MAD as 1,197/24 = 49.88.

Exhibit 11.9 Forecast Error of Example Time Series Data

	A	B	C	D	E	F	G	H	I	J	K	L
1	Period	Year	Quarter	Call At Volume	Forecast Ft	Error (At - Ft)		Squared Error		Absolute Deviation		Percentage Error
2	1	1	1	362	343.8	18.20		331.24		18.2		5.03%
3	2	1	2	385	361.6	23.40		547.56		23.4		6.08%
4	3	1	3	432	379.4	52.60		2766.76		52.6		12.18%
5	4	1	4	341	397.2	-56.20		3158.44		56.2		16.48%
6	5	2	1	382	415	-33.00		1089.00		33		8.64%
7	6	2	2	409	432.8	-23.80		566.44		23.8		5.82%
8	7	2	3	498	450.6	47.40		2246.76		47.4		9.52%
9	8	2	4	387	468.4	-81.40		6625.96		81.4		21.03%
10	9	3	1	473	486.2	-13.20		174.24		13.2		2.79%
11	10	3	2	513	504	9.00		81.00		9		1.75%
12	11	3	3	582	521.8	60.20		3624.04		60.2		10.34%
13	12	3	4	474	539.6	-65.60		4303.36		65.6		13.84%
14	13	4	1	544	557.4	-13.40		179.56		13.4		2.46%
15	14	4	2	582	575.2	6.80		46.24		6.8		1.17%
16	15	4	3	681	593	88.00		7744.00		88		12.92%
17	16	4	4	557	610.8	-53.80		2894.44		53.8		9.66%
18	17	5	1	628	628.6	-0.60		0.36		0.6		0.10%
19	18	5	2	707	646.4	60.60		3672.36		60.6		8.57%
20	19	5	3	773	664.2	108.80		11837.44		108.8		14.08%
21	20	5	4	592	682	-90.00		8100.00		90		15.20%
22	21	6	1	627	699.8	-72.80		5299.84		72.8		11.61%
23	22	6	2	725	717.6	7.40		54.76		7.4		1.02%
24	23	6	3	854	735.4	118.60		14065.96		118.6		13.89%
25	24	6	4	661	753.2	-92.20		8500.84		92.2		13.95%
26						Sum		87910.60	Sum	1197	Sum	218.13%
27						**MSE**		**3662.94**	**MAD**	**49.88**	**MAPE**	**9.09%**

A third measure of forecast error is the mean absolute percentage error (MAPE):

$$\text{MAPE} = \frac{\sum |(A_t - F_t)/A_t| \times 100}{T} \qquad \textbf{(11.3)}$$

This is simply the average of the percentage error for each forecast value in the time series. These calculations are shown in column L of Exhibit 11.9, resulting in MAPE = 218.13%/24 = 9.09 percent. Using MAPE, the forecast differs from actual call volume on average by plus or minus 9.09 percent.

A major difference between MSE and MAD is that MSE is influenced much more by large forecast errors than by small errors (because the errors are squared). The values of MAD and MSE depend on the measurement scale of the time-series data. For example, forecasting profit in the range of millions of dollars would result in very large values, even for accurate forecasting models. On the other hand, a variable like market share, which is measured as a fraction, will always have small values of MAD and MSE. Thus, the measures have no meaning except in comparison with other models used to forecast the same data. MAPE is different in that the measurement scale factor is eliminated by dividing the absolute error by the time-series data value. This makes the measure easier to interpret. The selection of the best measure of forecasting accuracy is not a simple matter; indeed, forecasting experts often disagree on which measure should be used.

TYPES OF FORECASTING APPROACHES

Forecasting methods can be classified as either statistical or judgmental. **Statistical forecasting** *is based on the assumption that the future will be an extrapolation of the past.* Statistical forecasting methods use historical data to predict future values. Many different techniques exist; which technique should be used depends on the variable being forecast and the time horizon. Statistical methods can generally be categorized as *time-series methods*, which extrapolate historical time-series data, and *regression methods*, which also extrapolate historical time-series data but can also include other potentially causal factors that influence the behavior of the time series. **Judgmental forecasting** *relies upon opinions and expertise of people in developing forecasts.* For example, suppose that we are asked to forecast the length of time before a current technology becomes obsolete. Certainly past data are no help here. The forecast can only be developed in a qualitative fashion by experts who are knowledgeable about changing technology. As we will discuss later, many organizations use a combination of both types of approaches. Exhibit 11.10 summarizes some of the basic forecasting approaches that are used in business; however, many other methods exist that are not listed here. See the OM Spotlight for an interesting contrast of statistical versus judgmental forecasts.

Forecasting Software

Microsoft Excel provides a convenient platform to implement many of the forecasting techniques shown in Exhibit 11.10. It is relatively easy to design spreadsheets for simple forecasting approaches that we will discuss in this chapter. Excel also has some built-in tools for some of these techniques. In addition to Excel, many

Exhibit 11.10 Classification of Basic Forecasting Methods

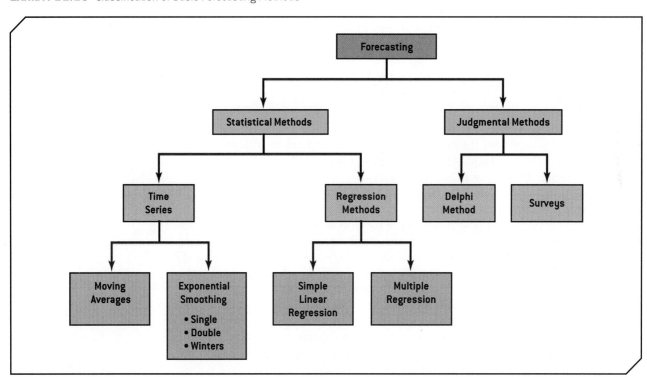

OM SPOTLIGHT

Statistical Versus Judgmental Forecasting[4]

A $2 billion consumer packaged goods company gained significant benefits from implementing a better forecasting system. At the time, the company was selling roughly 1,000 make-to-stock finished goods at 10,000 customer shipment locations, which were served through ten regional distribution centers. The company needed good weekly forecasts for each of the 1,000 finished goods by distribution center. The forecasting approach depended heavily on numbers generated by sales representatives. However, this approach had failed to work. First, the sales representatives had no particular interest in forecasting. They had no training or skill in forecasting and their judgment forecasts on an item and weekly basis were not very good. Second, forecast errors for individual items cancelled each other out when they were aggregated to the assigned distribution center.

Today, standard statistical forecasting approaches are integrated into all company forecasts. Sales representatives have more time to build customer relationships and generate revenue. The company also established a weekly consensus process to review and override the statistical forecasts at the product group level only. Modest changes in the statistical forecasts are made about half the time. However, of these override decisions, only 40 percent improved the original forecasts—60 percent of the time management overrides made the forecasts worse!

commercial software packages and general statistical analysis programs, such as SPSS, Minitab, and SAS, have forecasting features or modules. With these software packages, users must choose the forecasting model and may also have to specify the model parameters. This requires a solid understanding of the assumptions and capabilities of the various models, some in-depth knowledge of the mathematics behind the procedures, and often numerous experimental trials to identify the best forecasting model. Various other stand-alone software packages exist that automate some of these tasks. Some will find the optimal model parameters that will minimize some measure of forecast accuracy. Others will even attempt to determine the best forecasting method to use automatically.

CBPredictor is an Excel add-in that was developed by Decisioneering, Inc., and is included in *Crystal Ball* on the text CD-ROM. *CBPredictor* includes many different time-series forecasting approaches that we will discuss in this chapter. We will illustrate how *CBPredictor* works after we present these approaches. Surveys of forecasting software packages are routinely published in *ORMS Today*, a publication of the Institute for Operations Research and the Management Sciences (INFORMS).[5] See www.orms-today.com for further information.

STATISTICAL FORECASTING MODELS

A wide variety of statistical forecasting models have been developed, and we cannot discuss all of them. However, we present some of the basic and more popular approaches used in OM applications.

Learning Objective
To understand basic time-series forecasting methods, be aware of more advanced methods, and use spreadsheet models to make forecasts.

Single Moving Average

A **moving average** *(MA)*
forecast is an average of the
most recent "k" observations
in a time series.

The single moving average concept is based on the idea of averaging random fluctuations in a time series to identify the underlying direction in which the time series is changing. *A* **moving average** *(MA) forecast is an average of the most recent "k" observations in a time series.* Thus, the forecast for the next period $(t + 1)$, which we denote as F_{t+1}, for a time series with t observations is

$$F_{t+1} = \sum(\text{most recent "}k\text{" observations})/k$$
$$= (A_t + A_{t-1} + A_{t-2} + \cdots + A_{t-k+1})/k \qquad \textbf{(11.4)}$$

MA methods work best for short planning horizons when there is no major trend, seasonal, or business cycle patterns, that is, when demand is relatively stable and consistent. As the value of k increases, the forecast reacts slowly to recent changes in the time series because more older data are included in the computation. As the value of k decreases, the forecast reacts more quickly. If a significant trend exists in the time-series data, moving-average-based forecasts will lag actual demand, resulting in a bias in the forecast.

To illustrate the moving-averages method, consider the data presented in Exhibit 11.11. These data and chart show the number of gallons of milk sold each month at Gas-Mart, a local convenience store. To use moving averages to forecast the milk sales, we must first select the number of data values to be included in the moving average. As an example, let us compute forecasts based on a 3-month moving average $(k = 3)$. The moving-average calculation for the first 3 months of the milk-sales time series, and thus the forecast for month 4, is

$$F_4 = \frac{172 + 217 + 190}{3} = 193.00$$

Since the actual value observed in month 4 is 233, we see that the forecast error in month 4 is $233 - 193 = 40$. The calculation for the second 3-month moving average (F_5) is

$$F_5 = \frac{217 + 190 + 233}{3} = 213.33$$

This provides a forecast for month 5. The error associated with this forecast is $179 - 213.33 = -34.33$. A complete summary of these moving-average calculations is shown in Exhibit 11.12. The mean square error for these forecasts is 1,457.33.

The number of data values to be included in the moving average is often based on managerial insight and judgment. Thus, it should not be surprising that for a particular time series, different values of k lead to different measures of forecast accuracy. One way to find the best number is to use trial and error to identify the value of k that minimizes MSE for the historical data. Then, if we were willing to assume that the number that is best for the past will also be best for the future, we would forecast the next value in the time series using the number of data values that minimized the MSE for the historical time series. Exhibit 11.13 shows an analysis of 2-, 3-, and 4-month moving averages for the milk-sales data. We see that among these options, a 3-month moving average forecast provides the smallest value of MSE.

MICROSOFT EXCEL DATA ANALYSIS MOVING AVERAGE TOOL

Excel provides a simple tool for computing moving-average forecasts. From the *Tools* menu, select *Data Analysis*, and then *Moving Average*. (The *Data Analysis* tools are a standard Excel feature. If they do not appear under the *Tools* menu,

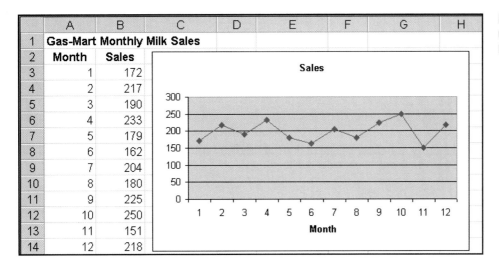

Exhibit 11.11
Gas-Mart Milk Sales Time-Series
Data

Exhibit 11.12 Summary of 3-Month Moving-Average Forecasts

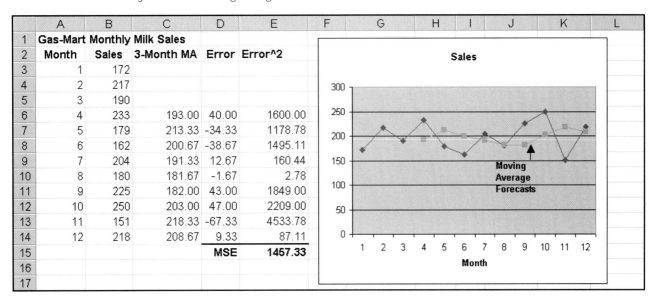

Exhibit 11.13 Milk-Sales Forecast Error Analysis

	A	B	C	D	E	F	G	H	I	J	K	L
1	Gas-Mart Monthly Milk Sales										Squared Errors	
2	Month	Sales	2-Month MA	Error	3-Month MA	Error	4-Month MA	Error		2-Month MA	3-Month MA	4-Month MA
3	1	172										
4	2	217										
5	3	190	194.50	-4.50						20.25		
6	4	233	203.50	29.50	193.00	40.00				870.25	1600.00	
7	5	179	211.50	-32.50	213.33	-34.33	203.00	-24.00		1056.25	1178.78	576.00
8	6	162	206.00	-44.00	200.67	-38.67	204.75	-42.75		1936.00	1495.11	1827.56
9	7	204	170.50	33.50	191.33	12.67	191.00	13.00		1122.25	160.44	169.00
10	8	180	183.00	-3.00	181.67	-1.67	194.50	-14.50		9.00	2.78	210.25
11	9	225	192.00	33.00	182.00	43.00	181.25	43.75		1089.00	1849.00	1914.06
12	10	250	202.50	47.50	203.00	47.00	192.75	57.25		2256.25	2209.00	3277.56
13	11	151	237.50	-86.50	218.33	-67.33	214.75	-63.75		7482.25	4533.78	4064.06
14	12	218	200.50	17.50	208.67	9.33	201.50	16.50		306.25	87.11	272.25
15										16147.75	13116.00	12310.75
16									MSE	1614.78	1457.33	1538.84

select *Add-Ins* from the *Tools* menu and select them.) In the dialog box that Excel displays, you need to enter the *Input Range* of the data, the *Interval* (the value of k), and the first cell of the *Output Range*. To align the actual data with the forecasted values in the worksheet, select the first cell of the *Output Range* to be one row below and to the right of the first time-series value. You may also obtain a chart of the data and the moving averages as well as a column of standard errors by checking the appropriate boxes. However, we do *not* recommend using the chart or error options because the forecasts are not properly aligned with the data (the forecast value aligned with a particular data point represents the forecast for the *next* month) and thus can be misleading. Rather, we recommend that you generate your own chart as we did in Exhibit 11.12. Exhibit 11.14 shows the results produced by the *Moving Average* tool (with some customization of the chart to show the months on the x axis). Note that the forecast for month 4 is aligned with the actual value for month 3 on the chart. Compare this to Exhibit 11.12 and you can see the difference.

Weighted Moving Average

In the simple moving average approach, the data are weighted equally. This may not be desirable, as we might wish to put more weight on recent observations than on older observations, particularly if the time series is changing rapidly. For example, you might assign a 60 percent weight to the most recent observation, 30 percent to the observation two periods prior, and the remaining 10 percent of the weight to the observation three periods prior. A general formula for a weighted moving-average forecast obtained by weighting the most recent k observations is

$$F_{t+1} = w_t A_t + w_{t-1} A_{t-1} + w_{t-2} A_{t-2} + \cdots + w_{t-k+1} A_{t-k+1} \qquad \textbf{(11.5)}$$

where w_t represents the weight assigned to time period t. Note that all the weights must add to 1.0. Exhibit 11.15 shows a comparison of a 60-30-10 percent weighted moving average with the original 3-month moving-average model. We see that the weighted forecasts provide a smaller MSE. An interesting problem is to determine the best set of weights. We leave this to you as a problem at the end of the chapter.

Exhibit 11.14 Results of Excel Moving Average Tool (note misalignment of forecasts with the time series)

	A	B	C
1	Gas-Mart Monthly Milk Sales		
2	Month	Sales	Forecast
3	1	172	
4	2	217	#N/A
5	3	190	#N/A
6	4	233	193
7	5	179	213.333333
8	6	162	200.666667
9	7	204	191.333333
10	8	180	181.666667
11	9	225	182
12	10	250	203
13	11	151	218.333333
14	12	218	208.666667
15			206.333333

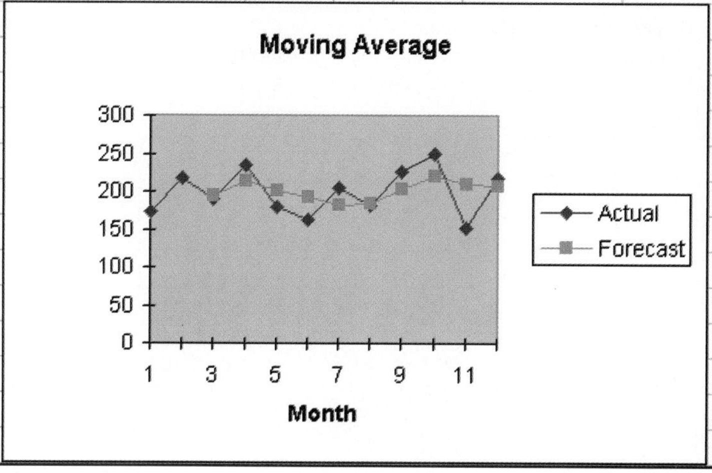

Exhibit 11.15 Comparison of 3-Month Moving Average and Weighted Moving Average Models

	A	B	C	D	E	F	G	H	I
1	Gas-Mart Monthly Milk Sales							Error Analysis	
2	Month	Sales	3-Month MA	Error	3-Month Weighted	Error		3-Month MA	3-Month Weighted
3	1	172							
4	2	217							
5	3	190							
6	4	233	193.00	40.00	187.30	45.70		1600.00	2088.49
7	5	179	213.33	-34.33	210.50	-31.50		1178.78	992.25
8	6	162	200.67	-38.67	201.80	-39.80		1495.11	1584.04
9	7	204	191.33	12.67	209.70	-5.70		160.44	32.49
10	8	180	181.67	-1.67	176.40	3.60		2.78	12.96
11	9	225	182.00	43.00	176.40	48.60		1849.00	2361.96
12	10	250	203.00	47.00	198.90	51.10		2209.00	2611.21
13	11	151	218.33	-67.33	200.50	-49.50		4533.78	2450.25
14	12	218	208.67	9.33	225.10	-7.10		87.11	50.41
15								13116.00	12184.06
16							MSE	1457.33	1353.78

Single Exponential Smoothing

Single Exponential smoothing (SES) *is a forecasting technique that uses a weighted average of past time-series values to forecast the value of the time series in the next period.* SES forecasts are based on averages using and weighting the most recent actual demand more than older demand data. SES methods do not try to include trend or seasonal effects. The basic exponential-smoothing model is

$$F_{t+1} = \alpha A_t + (1 - \alpha)F_t = F_t + \alpha(A_t - F_t) \tag{11.6}$$

Single Exponential smoothing (SES) is a forecasting technique that uses a weighted average of past time-series values to forecast the value of the time series in the next period.

where α is called the **smoothing constant** ($0 \le \alpha \le 1$). To use this model, set the forecast for period 1, F_1, equal to the actual observation for period 1, A_1. Note that F_2 will also have the same value.

Using the two preceding forms of the forecast equation, we can interpret the simple exponential smoothing model in two ways. In the first model shown in Equation 11.6, the forecast for the next period, F_{t+1}, is a weighted average of the forecast made for period t, F_t, and the actual observation in period t, A_t. The second form of the model in Equation 11.6, obtained by simply rearranging terms, states that the forecast for the next period, F_{t+1}, equals the forecast for the last period, F_t, plus a fraction, α, of the forecast error made in period t, $A_t - F_t$. Thus, to make a forecast once we have selected the smoothing constant, we need only know the previous forecast and the actual value.

To illustrate the exponential-smoothing approach to forecasting, consider the milk-sales time series presented in Exhibit 11.16 using $\alpha = 0.2$. As we have said, the exponential-smoothing forecast for period 2 is equal to the actual value of the time series in period 1. Thus, with $A_1 = 172$, we will set $F_1 = 172$ to get the computations started. Using Equation (11.6) for $t = 1$, we have

$$F_2 = 0.2A_1 + 0.8F_1 = 0.2(172) + 0.8(172) = 172.00$$

For period 3 we obtain

$$F_3 = 0.2A_2 + 0.8F_2 = 0.2(217) + 0.8(172) = 181.00$$

By continuing these calculations, we are able to determine the monthly forecast values and the corresponding forecast errors shown in Exhibit 11.16. The mean squared error is MSE = 1285.28. Note that we have not shown an exponential-smoothing forecast or the forecast error for period 1, because F_1 was set equal to A_1 to begin the smoothing computations. You could use this information to generate a forecast for month 13 as

$$F_{13} = 0.2A_{12} + 0.8F_{12} = 0.2(218) + 0.8(194.59) = 199.27$$

Exhibit 11.17 is the plot of the actual and the forecast time-series values. Note in particular how the forecasts "smooth out" the random fluctuations in the time series.

Exhibit 11.16

Summary of Single Exponential Smoothing Milk-Sales Forecasts with $\alpha = 0.2$

	A	B	C	D	E
1	Gas-Mart Monthly Milk Sales				
2		Alpha	0.2		
3	Month	Sales	Exponential Smoothing Forecast	Error	Error^2
4	1	172	172.00		
5	2	217	172.00	45.00	2025.00
6	3	190	181.00	9.00	81.00
7	4	233	182.80	50.20	2520.04
8	5	179	192.84	-13.84	191.55
9	6	162	190.07	-28.07	788.04
10	7	204	184.46	19.54	381.91
11	8	180	188.37	-8.37	69.99
12	9	225	186.69	38.31	1467.44
13	10	250	194.35	55.65	3096.44
14	11	151	205.48	-54.48	2968.44
15	12	218	194.59	23.41	548.18
16				MSE	1285.28

Exhibit 11.17

Graph of Single Exponential Smoothing Milk-Sales Forecasts with $\alpha = 0.2$

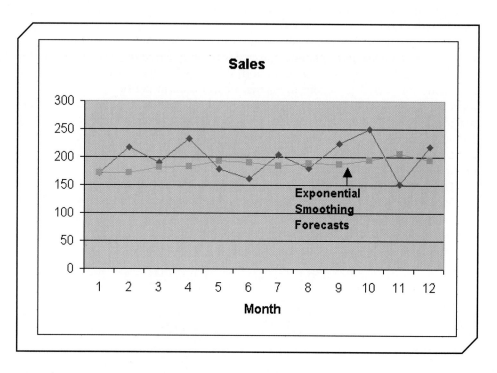

By repeated substitution for F_t in the equation, it is easy to demonstrate that F_{t+1} is a decreasingly weighted average of all past time-series data. To see this, suppose we have a time series with three observations: A_1, A_2, and A_3. Initially, $F_1 = A_1$. Thus, the forecast for period 2 is

$$F_2 = \alpha A_1 + (1 - \alpha)F_1$$
$$F_2 = \alpha A_1 + A_1 - \alpha A_1$$
$$F_2 = A_1$$

To obtain the forecast for period 3 (F_3), we substitute $F_2 = A_1$ in the expression for F_3. The result is

$$F_3 = \alpha A_2 + (1 - \alpha)F_2$$
$$F_3 = \alpha A_2 + (1 - \alpha)A_1$$

To go one step further, substituting this expression for F_3 in the expression for F_4, we obtain

$$F_4 = \alpha A_3 + (1 - \alpha)F_3$$
$$= \alpha A_3 + (1 - \alpha)[\alpha A_2 + (1 - \alpha)A_1]$$
$$= \alpha A_3 + \alpha(1 - \alpha)A_2 + (1 - \alpha)^2 A_1$$

We see that F_4 is a weighted average of the first three time-series values and that the sum of the weights is equal to 1. For instance, if $\alpha = 0.2$, then

$$F_3 = 0.2A_2 + 0.8A_1$$
$$F_4 = 0.2A_3 + (0.2)(0.8)A_2 + (1 - 0.2)^2 A_1 = 0.2A_3 + 0.16A_2 + 0.64A_1$$

As the number of data points increases, the weights associated with older data get progressively smaller. For example, we see that the weight on A_2 dropped from 0.2 to 0.16, and the weight on A_1 dropped from 0.8 to 0.64 as we added a new data point.

A similar argument can be made to show that any forecast F_{t+1} is a weighted average of *all* the previous time-series values. Thus, exponential smoothing models "never forget" past data as long as the smoothing constant is strictly between 0 and 1. In contrast, MA methods "completely forget" all the data older than k periods in the past. Typical values for α are in the range of 0.1 to 0.5. When $\alpha = 0.1$, exponential smoothing assigns about 90 percent of the weight to the last 22 periods. With $\alpha = 0.5$, exponential smoothing assigns about 90 percent of the weight to the last 4 periods. Thus, larger values of α place more emphasis on recent data. If the time series is very volatile and contains substantial random variability, a small value of the smoothing constant is preferred. The reason for this choice is that since much of the forecast error is due to random variability, we do not want to overreact and adjust the forecasts too quickly. For a fairly stable time series with relatively little random variability, larger values of the smoothing constant have the advantage of quickly adjusting the forecasts when forecasting errors occur and therefore allowing the forecast to react faster to changing conditions.

The smoothing constant is approximately related to the value of k in the moving-average model by the following relationship:

$$\alpha = 2/(k + 1) \tag{11.7}$$

Therefore, an exponential smoothing model with $\alpha = 0.5$ is roughly equivalent to a moving-average model with $k = 3$. Equation (11.7) allows one to switch between a k-period simple moving average and exponential smoothing with a smoothing constant α, with similar results. Similar to the MA model, we can experiment to find the best value for the smoothing constant to minimize the mean square error or one of the other measures of forecast accuracy. Using a spreadsheet, we could easily evaluate a range of smoothing constants to try to find the best values.

One disadvantage of exponential smoothing is that if the time series exhibits a positive trend, the forecast will lag the actual values and, similarly, will overshoot the actual values if a negative trend exists. It is good practice to analyze new data to see whether the smoothing constant should be revised to provide better forecasts. If values of α greater than 0.5 are needed to develop a good forecast, then other types of forecasting methods might be more appropriate.

CBPredictor

CBPredictor is an Excel add-in that is included with certain versions of *Crystal Ball*. The student version of *Crystal Ball* that accompanies this text includes *CBPredictor*. After *CBPredictor* has been installed, it may be accessed in Excel from the *CB Run* menu; if the menu is not present in Excel, make sure that the *Crystal Ball* box is checked in the *Tools...Add-Ins* window. When *CBPredictor* is started, the dialog box shown in Exhibit 11.18 appears. The dialog box contains four tabs that query you for information one step at a time. *Input Data* allows you to specify the data range on which to base your forecast; *Data Attributes* allows you to specify the type of data and whether or not seasonality is present; *Method Gallery* (see Exhibit 11.19) allows you to select any or all of eight time-series methods, including single moving average, single exponential smoothing, and other methods we briefly describe in the next section. *CBPredictor* will run each method you select and will recommend the one that best forecasts your data, along with the best model parameters (such as the number of periods in the moving average or the value of α in exponential smoothing). The final tab, *Results*, allows you to specify a variety of reporting options.

We will illustrate the use of *CBPredictor* for the single moving-average and single exponential methods as selected in the Methods Gallery dialog in Exhibit 11.19. After running *CBPredictor*, several new worksheets are created in the Excel workbook: *Report*, *Chart*, *Results Table*, and *Methods Table*. The *Report* worksheet contains the calculated forecasts for the best model along with forecast error analysis. Exhibit 11.20 shows a portion of the results. *CBPredictor* found that single exponential smoothing provided the best model with $\alpha = 0.178$. The forecast for month 13 is 198.21, with a 90 percent confidence interval of (136.67, 259.74).

Exhibit 11.18
CBPredictor Input Data Dialog

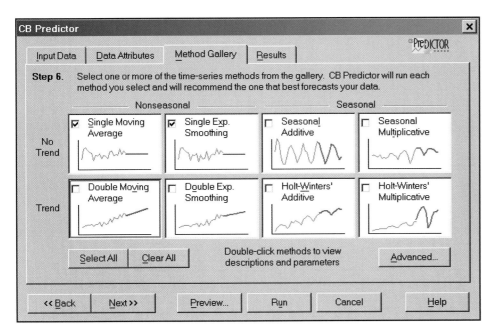

Exhibit 11.19
CBPredictor Methods Gallery Dialog

Because this confidence interval has a large range—123.07 gallons of milk—there is a significant potential for error in using the point estimate forecast of 198.21. The *Report* worksheet also shows the RMSE, MAD, and MAPE error metrics along with some advanced statistical measures. The Durbin–Watson statistic checks for autocorrelation, which measures how strongly successive values of the data may be correlated with each other, with values of 2 indicating no autocorrelation. The Ljung–Box statistic measures whether a set of autocorrelations are significantly different from a set of autocorrelations that are all zero. Large values suggest that the model used is poor. Theil's U statistic is a relative error measure that compares the results with a naïve forecast. A value less than 1 means that the forecasting technique is better than guessing; a value equal to 1 means that the technique is about as good as guessing; and a value greater than 1 means that the forecasting technique is worse than guessing. In this example, we see that the forecasting techniques provide managers with a useful decision aid. The other worksheets provide the information used in the *Report* in a bit more detail. These features make *CBPredictor* a simple yet very powerful tool for forecasting.

Advanced Forecasting Models

As we noted, MA and SES models work best for time series that do not exhibit trend or seasonality. Several other methods are often used when trend or seasonal factors exist. These are

- *Double moving average*—used for time series with a linear trend
- *Double exponential smoothing*—used for time series with a linear trend
- *Seasonal additive*—used for time series with seasonality that is relatively stable over time
- *Seasonal multiplicative*—used for time series with seasonality that is increasing or decreasing in magnitude over time
- *Holt–Winters additive*—used for time series with both a linear trend and seasonality that is relatively stable over time
- *Holt–Winters multiplicative*—used for time series with both a linear trend and seasonality that is increasing or decreasing in magnitude over time

Exhibit 11.20
Portions of *CBPredictor Report* Worksheet

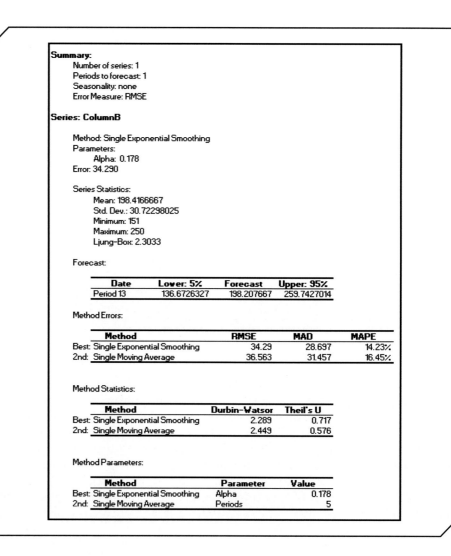

The theory and formulas for these models are quite a bit more complicated than for single moving average or single exponential smoothing, so we shall not cover them here. Instead, we will demonstrate the use of *CBPredictor* for applying some of these methods. Note that the graphs shown in the *Method Gallery* in Exhibit 11.19 suggest visually the method that is best suited for the data. Therefore, to select the proper method, you should always chart a time series first to scope out its characteristics or simply let *CBPredictor* run all models and identify the best.

To illustrate this, let us use the call center time series in Exhibit 11.7. This time series shows both a linear trend as well as seasonality. The seasonal pattern also appears to be increasing in magnitude over time, suggesting that the Holt–Winters multiplicative method is most appropriate. However, we will run all models in *CBPredictor* and see if this is true.

In the Data Attributes tab of the *CBPredictor* dialog, note that we specify that the data are in quarters with a seasonality of 4 quarters (see Exhibit 11.21). This ensures that the seasonal models will be tested. In the *Results* tab, we also specify that *CBPredictor* forecast the next four quarters. As expected, the Holt–Winters multiplicative model has the best error measures, as shown in Exhibit 11.22. You can see from the chart that the model provides a very good fit to the time series. The chart shows how well the model has forecasted the historical data along with forecasts for the next four quarters. The confidence intervals show that the fore-

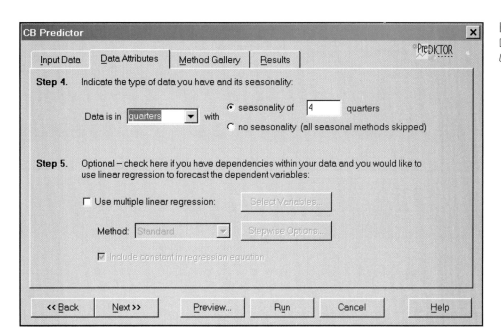

Exhibit 11.21
Data Attributes Tab of
CBPredictor Dialog

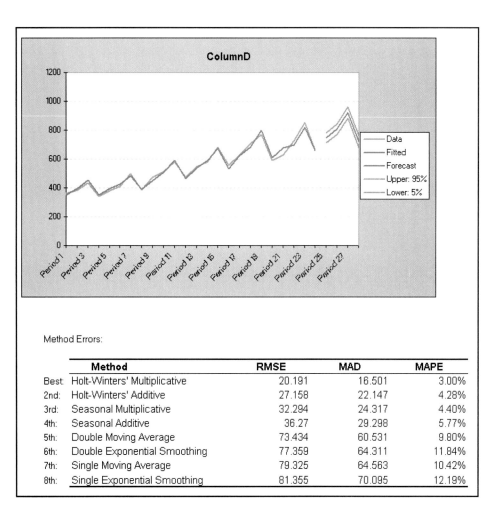

Exhibit 11.22
CBPredictor Results

Method Errors:

	Method	RMSE	MAD	MAPE
Best:	Holt-Winters' Multiplicative	20.191	16.501	3.00%
2nd:	Holt-Winters' Additive	27.158	22.147	4.28%
3rd:	Seasonal Multiplicative	32.294	24.317	4.40%
4th:	Seasonal Additive	36.27	29.298	5.77%
5th:	Double Moving Average	73.434	60.531	9.80%
6th:	Double Exponential Smoothing	77.359	64.311	11.84%
7th:	Single Moving Average	79.325	64.563	10.42%
8th:	Single Exponential Smoothing	81.355	70.095	12.19%

casts should be quite accurate. *CBPredictor* pastes the forecasts in the data worksheet as specified in the *Results* tab. These are shown in Exhibit 11.23.

Exhibit 11.23
Call Center Volume Forecasts
for Year 7

	A	B	C	D	E
1	Period	Year	Quarter	Call Volume	
2	1	1	1	362	
3	2	1	2	385	
4	3	1	3	432	
5	4	1	4	341	
6	5	2	1	382	
7	6	2	2	409	
8	7	2	3	498	
9	8	2	4	387	
10	9	3	1	473	
11	10	3	2	513	
12	11	3	3	582	
13	12	3	4	474	
14	13	4	1	544	
15	14	4	2	582	
16	15	4	3	681	
17	16	4	4	557	
18	17	5	1	628	
19	18	5	2	707	
20	19	5	3	773	
21	20	5	4	592	
22	21	6	1	627	
23	22	6	2	725	
24	23	6	3	854	
25	24	6	4	661	**Forecasts**
26	25	7	1		748.1127808
27	26	7	2		808.7917057
28	27	7	3		921.1043844
29	28	7	4		719.5947499

Learning Objective
To learn the basic ideas and
method of regression analysis.

Regression analysis *is a
method for building a
statistical model that defines a
relationship between a single
dependent variable and one
or more independent
variables, all of which are
numerical.*

REGRESSION AS A FORECASTING APPROACH

Regression analysis *is a method for building a statistical model that defines a relationship between a single dependent variable and one or more independent variables, all of which are numerical.* Regression analysis has wide applications in business; however, we will restrict our discussion to simple applications in forecasting. We will first consider only simple regression models in which the value of a time series (the dependent variable) is a function of a single independent variable, time.

Exhibit 11.24 shows total energy costs over the past 15 years at a manufacturing plant. The plant manager needs to forecast costs for the next year to prepare a budget for the VP of finance. The chart suggests that energy costs appear to be increasing in a fairly predictable linear fashion and that energy costs are related to time by a linear function

$$Y_t = a + bt \tag{11.8}$$

where Y_t represents the estimate of the energy cost in year t. If we can identify the best values for a and b, which represent the intercept and slope of the straight line

Exhibit 11.24 Factory Energy Costs

	A	B	C	D	E	F	G	H	I
1	**Factory Energy Costs**								
2	**Year**	**Energy Costs**							
3	1	$ 15,355.38							
4	2	$ 15,412.91							
5	3	$ 15,926.64							
6	4	$ 16,614.18							
7	5	$ 16,918.69							
8	6	$ 16,837.14							
9	7	$ 16,812.51							
10	8	$ 17,102.45							
11	9	$ 17,461.89							
12	10	$ 17,846.76							
13	11	$ 18,187.93							
14	12	$ 18,782.19							
15	13	$ 18,863.18							
16	14	$ 18,914.00							
17	15	$ 19,319.15							

that best fits the time series, we can forecast cost for the next year by computing $Y_{16} = a + b(16)$.

Simple linear regression finds the best values of a and b using the *method of least squares*. The method of least squares minimizes the sum of the squared deviations between the actual time-series values (A_t) and the estimated values of the dependent variable (Y_t).

EXCEL'S ADD TRENDLINE OPTION

Excel provides a very simple tool to find the best-fitting regression model for a time series. First, select the chart in the worksheet. Then select the *Add Trendline* option from the *Chart* menu. The dialog box in Exhibit 11.25 is displayed, and you may choose among a linear and a variety of nonlinear functional forms to fit the data. Selecting an appropriate nonlinear form requires some advanced knowledge of functions and mathematics, so we will restrict our discussion to the linear case. From the *Options* tab (see Exhibit 11.26), you may customize the name of the trendline, forecast forward or backward, set the intercept at a fixed value, and display the regression equation and R-squared value on the chart by checking the appropriate boxes. Once Excel displays these results, you may move the equation and R-squared value for better readability by dragging them with a mouse. For the linear trendline option only, you may simply click on the data series in the chart to select the series, and then add a trend line by clicking on the right mouse button (try it!). Exhibit 11.27 shows the result. The model is

$$\text{Energy cost} = \$15,112 + 280.66(\text{Time})$$

Thus, to forecast the cost for the next year, we compute

$$\text{Energy cost} = \$15,112 + 280.66(16) = \$19,602.56$$

We could forecast further out into the future if we wish, but realize that the uncertainty of the accuracy of the forecast will be higher. The R^2 value is a measure of how much variation in the dependent variable (energy cost) is explained by the independent variable (time). The maximum value for R^2 is 1.0; therefore, the high

Exhibit 11.25
Add Trendline Dialog

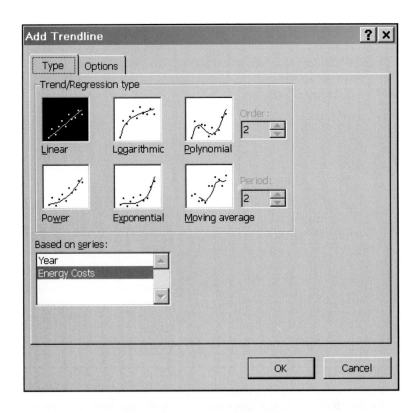

Exhibit 11.26
Add Trendline Options Tab

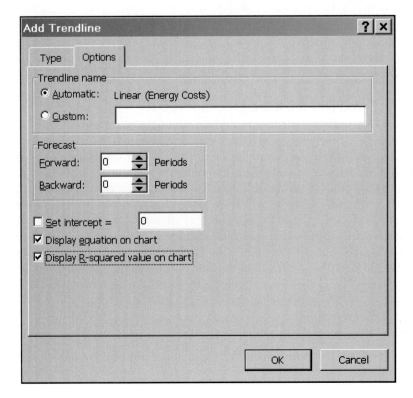

value of 0.97 suggests that the model will be a good predictor of cost. *CBPredictor* also has a regression option that can be selected in the *Data Attributes* tab. This option is useful for multiple linear regression models that involve several independent variables, which we illustrate next.

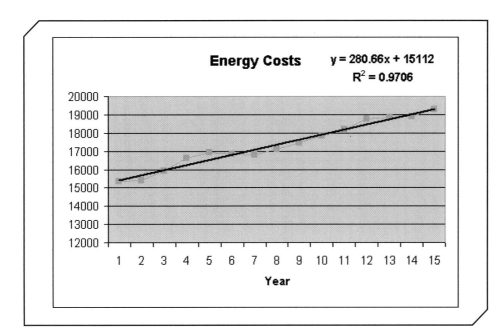

Exhibit 11.27
Least-Squares Regression Model for Energy Cost Forecasting

Causal Forecasting Models with Multiple Regression

In more advanced forecasting applications, other independent variables such as economic indexes or demographic factors that may influence the time series can be incorporated into a regression model (see OM Spotlight: California Electric Power Plant Closings). *A linear regression model with more than one independent variable is called a* multiple linear regression model.

To illustrate the use of multiple linear regression for forecasting with causal variables, suppose that we wish to forecast gasoline sales. Exhibit 11.28 shows the sales over 10 weeks during June through August along with the average price per gallon. Exhibit 11.29 shows a chart of the gasoline-sales time series with a fitted

A linear regression model with more than one independent variable is called a multiple linear regression model.

OM SPOTLIGHT

California Electric Power Plant Closings[6]

The California Independent System Operator's Board of Governors unanimously approved to close two electric power-generating plants in San Francisco by 2007. Both fossil-fuel power plants are well documented for polluting the environment. Community leaders are asking for a guaranteed date to close the two power plants down but PG&E Corporation and the board of governors cannot specify a date. Former Mayor Willie Brown promised to shut down these two plants in 1998. A PG&E spokesperson said, "If the electrical load grows unexpectedly fast, we are going to have to redo our action plan." Whether the plants can be closed is based on a demand forecast that is subject to much controversy. Area demographics, weather patterns, and economic growth patterns are all part of a demand forecast based on regression analysis.

Exhibit 11.28
Gasoline Sales Data

	A	B	C
1			
2	Gasoline Sales	Week	Price Per Gallon
3	10420	1	$ 1.95
4	7388	2	$ 2.20
5	7529	3	$ 2.12
6	11932	4	$ 1.98
7	10125	5	$ 2.01
8	15240	6	$ 1.92
9	12246	7	$ 2.03
10	11852	8	$ 1.98
11	16967	9	$ 1.82
12	19782	10	$ 1.90
13		11	$ 1.80

regression line. During the summer months, it is not unusual to see an increase in sales as more people go on vacations. The chart shows that the sales appear to increase over time with a linear trend, making linear regression an appropriate forecasting technique.

The fitted regression line is

$$Sales = 6,382 + 1,084.7 \times Week$$

The R^2 value of 0.6842 means that that about 68 percent of the variation in the data is explained by time. Using the model, we would predict sales for week 11 as

$$Sales = 6,382 + 1,084.7 \times 11 = 18,313.7$$

However, we also see that the average price per gallon changes each week, and this may influence consumer sales. Therefore, the sales trend might not simply be a factor of steadily increasing demand, but might also be influenced by the average price. Multiple regression provides a technique for building forecasting models that not only incorporate time, in this case, but other potential causal variables.

Exhibit 11.29
Chart of Sales Versus Time

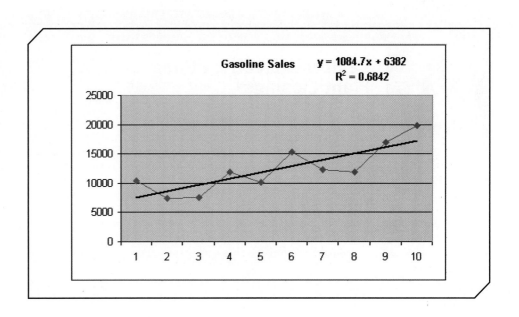

Thus, to forecast gasoline sales (that is, the dependent variable) we propose a model using two independent variables (weeks and price):

$$\text{Sales} = \beta_0 + \beta_1 \times \text{Week} + \beta_2 \times \text{Price}$$

Using the Excel Data Analysis tool for Regression, we obtain the results shown in Exhibit 11.30. The regression model is

$$\text{Sales} = 47,747.81 + 640.71 \times \text{Week} - 19,550.6 \times \text{Price}$$

This makes sense because as price increases, sales should decrease. Notice that the R^2 value is higher when both variables are included, explaining almost 86 percent of the variation in the data. The p-values for both variables are small, indicating that they are statistically significant variables in predicting sales.

Based on trends in crude oil prices, the company estimates that the average price for the next week will drop to $1.80. Then, using this model we would forecast the sales for week 11 as

$$\text{Sales} = 47,747.81 + 640.71 \times 11 - 19,550.6 \times \$1.80 = \$19,604.54$$

Notice that this is higher than the pure time-series forecast because the price per gallon is estimated to fall in week 11 and result in a somewhat higher level of sales. The multiple regression model provides a more realistic and accurate forecast than simply extrapolating the historical time series. The theory of regression analysis is much more complex than presented here, so we caution you to consult more advanced books on the subject for a more complete treatment.

JUDGMENTAL FORECASTING

Learning Objective
To understand the role of human judgment in forecasting and when judgmental forecasting is most appropriate.

When no historical data are available, only judgmental forecasting is possible. But even when historical data are available and appropriate, they cannot be the sole basis for prediction. The demand for goods and services is affected by a variety of factors, such as global markets and cultures, interest rates, disposable income,

Exhibit 11.30 Multiple Regression Results

	A	B	C	D	E	F	G
1	SUMMARY OUTPUT						
2							
3	*Regression Statistics*						
4	Multiple R	0.92577504					
5	R Square	0.857059425					
6	Adjusted R Square	0.81621926					
7	Standard Error	1702.092291					
8	Observations	10					
9							
10	ANOVA						
11		*df*	*SS*	*MS*	*F*	*Significance F*	
12	Regression	2	121596103.7	60798051.87	20.98569971	0.001104191	
13	Residual	7	20279827.17	2897118.167			
14	Total	9	141875930.9				
15							
16		*Coefficients*	*Standard Error*	*t Stat*	*P-value*	*Lower 95%*	*Upper 95%*
17	Intercept	47747.81095	14266.13592	3.346933691	0.012302289	14013.78411	81481.8378
18	Week	640.7098599	241.6857585	2.651003782	0.032893732	69.21426278	1212.205457
19	Price Per Gallon	-19550.5999	6720.128757	-2.909259719	0.022684465	-35441.16797	-3660.031835

inflation, and technology. Competitors' actions and government regulations also have an impact. Thus, some element of judgmental forecasting is always necessary. One interesting example of the role of judgmental forecasting occurred during a national recession. All economic indicators pointed toward a future period of low demand for manufacturers of machine tools. However, the forecasters of one such company recognized that recent government regulations for automobile pollution control would require the auto industry to update its current technology by purchasing new tools. As a result, this machine tool company was prepared for the new business.

One approach that is commonly used in judgmental forecasts is the Delphi method. *The* **Delphi method** *consists of forecasting by expert opinion by gathering judgments and opinions of key personnel based on their experience and knowledge of the situation.* In the Delphi method, a group of experts, possibly from both inside and outside the organization, are asked to make a prediction, such as industry sales for the next year. The experts are not consulted as a group so as not to bias their predictions—for example, because of dominant personalities in the group—but make their predictions and justifications independently. The responses and supporting arguments of each individual are summarized by an outside party and returned to the experts along with further questions. Experts whose opinions fall in the midrange of estimates as well as those whose predictions are extremely high or low (that is, outliers) might be asked to explain their predictions. The process iterates until a consensus is reached by the group, which usually takes only a few rounds.

The Delphi method can be used to predict qualitative as well as numerical outcomes. For instance, a company might be interested in predicting when a new law or regulation might pass the legislature. In a Delphi exercise, experts would be asked to select a date and justify it or select responses along some continuum, such as "highly certain" to "highly uncertain," or "strongly agree" to "strongly disagree."

Delphi results based on a few individuals are more risky than for larger groups and can be very inaccurate. However, some interesting research has observed that although any one individual might not develop accurate predictions, group consensus is often quite good.

Another common approach to gathering data for judgmental forecasts is a survey using a questionnaire, telephone contact, or personal interview. For example, telecommunication executives might be surveyed and ask to predict the cost of specific telephone services during the next 5 years. These data can be summarized and analyzed using basic statistical tools to help develop a reliable forecast. Sample sizes are usually much larger than with the Delphi method and expert opinion; however, the cost of such surveys can be high because of the labor involved, postage, low response rates, and postsurvey processing. Electronic surveys using the Internet have reduced these costs and increased the speed of obtaining results. Companies most often rely on managers' opinions for short-range forecasts and on group opinions for longer-range forecasts.

The major reasons given for using judgmental methods rather than quantitative methods are (1) greater accuracy, (2) ability to incorporate unusual or one-time events, and (3) the difficulty of obtaining the data necessary for quantitative techniques. Also, judgmental methods seem to create a feeling of "ownership" and add a commonsense dimension.

The **Delphi method** *consists of forecasting by expert opinion by gathering judgments and opinions of key personnel based on their experience and knowledge of the situation.*

FORECASTING IN PRACTICE

In practice, managers use a variety of judgmental and quantitative forecasting techniques. Statistical methods alone cannot account for such factors as sales promotions, competitive strategies, unusual economic or environmental disturbances, new product introductions, large one-time orders, labor union strikes, and so on. Many managers

Learning Objective
To know that judgment and quantitative forecast methodologies can complement one another, and therefore improve overall forecast accuracy.

begin with a statistical forecast and adjust it to account for such factors. Others may develop independent judgmental and statistical forecasts and then combine them, either objectively by averaging or in a subjective manner. It is impossible to provide universal guidance as to which approaches are best, for they depend on a variety of factors, including the presence or absence of trends and seasonality, the number of data points available, length of the forecast time horizon, and the experience and knowledge of the forecaster. Often, quantitative approaches will miss significant changes in the data, such as reversal of trends, while qualitative forecasts may catch them, particularly when using indicators as discussed earlier in this chapter. The events of 9/11, for example, made it difficult to use trends based on historical data. Quantitative forecasts often are adjusted judgmentally as managers incorporate environmental knowledge that is not captured in quantitative models.

The first step in developing a practical forecast is to understand the purpose of the forecast. For instance, if financial personnel need a sales forecast to determine capital investment strategies, a long (2- to 5-year) time horizon is necessary. For such forecasts, using aggregate groups of items is usually more accurate than using individual-item forecasts added together. These forecasts would probably be measured in dollars. In contrast, production personnel may need short-term forecasts for individual items as a basis for procurement of materials and scheduling. In this case, dollar values would not be appropriate; rather, forecasts should be made in terms of units of production. The level of aggregation often dictates the appropriate method. Forecasting the total amount of soap to produce over the next planning period is certainly different from forecasting the amount of each individual product to produce. Aggregate forecasts are generally much easier to develop, whereas detailed forecasts require more time and resources.

The choice of a forecasting method depends on other criteria as well. Among them are the time span for which the forecast is being made, the needed frequency of forecast updating, data requirements, the level of accuracy desired (see the OM Spotlight on Holland Hitch), and the quantitative skills needed. The time span is one of the most critical criteria. Different techniques are applicable for long-range,

OM SPOTLIGHT

Holland Hitch Company—Forecast Cost Versus Accuracy[7]

The Holland Hitch Company, part of the Holland Group, manufactures the coupling device used to hitch the tractor to the trailers. In the midst of a business process reengineering initiative, executives at Holland Hitch Company realized that they needed better forecast accuracy. To evaluate different forecasting software vendors, Holland Hitch had each vendor develop a forecast for this year based on the actual sales data from last year. Many other criteria were used in evaluating each vendor such as the ease of integrating with other demand planning and supply chain modules, scalability, reasonable software and training costs, and forecast accuracy. The software vendor who was hired developed forecasts across Holland's major product lines with an average of 98 percent accuracy. Other benefits of the new forecasting system were much better customer service and an increase in inventory turnover rates from the 2–3 range to the 9–10 range. These operational benefits far exceeded the cost to implement and maintain the forecasting system.

intermediate-range, and short-range forecasts. Also important is the frequency of updating that will be necessary. For example, the Delphi method takes considerable time to implement and thus would not be appropriate for forecasts that must be updated frequently.

Forecasters should also monitor a forecast to determine when it might be advantageous to change or update the model. A *tracking signal* provides a method for doing this by quantifying **bias** – *the tendency of forecasts to consistently be larger or smaller than the actual values of the time series.* The tracking method used most often is to compute the cumulative forecast error divided by the value of MAD at that point in time; that is,

$$\text{Tracking signal} = \Sigma(A_t - F_t)/\text{MAD} \qquad \textbf{(11.9)}$$

Bias is the tendency of forecasts to consistently be larger or smaller than the actual values of the time series.

Typically, tracking signals between plus or minus 4 indicate that the forecast is performing adequately. Values outside this range indicate that you should reevaluate the model used.

SOLVED PROBLEMS

SOLVED PROBLEM #1

A retail store records customer demand during each sales period. Use the following demand data to develop three-period and four-period moving-average forecasts and single exponential smoothing forecasts with $\alpha = 0.5$. Compute the MAD, MAPE, and MSE for each. Which method provides the better forecast?

Based on these error metrics, the 3-month moving average is the best method among these three. The chart showing these forecasts is shown next.

Period	Demand	Period	Demand
1	86	7	91
2	93	8	93
3	88	9	96
4	89	10	97
5	92	11	93
6	94	12	95

Solution:

	A	B	C	D	E
1	Solved Problem 1				Exponential
2	Period	Demand	3-Month MA	4-Month MA	Smoothing
3	1	86			86
4	2	93			86
5	3	88			89.5
6	4	89	89.00		88.75
7	5	92	90.00	89.00	88.88
8	6	94	89.67	90.50	90.44
9	7	91	91.67	90.75	92.22
10	8	93	92.33	91.50	91.61
11	9	96	92.67	92.50	92.30
12	10	97	93.33	93.50	94.15
13	11	93	95.33	94.25	95.58
14	12	95	95.33	94.75	94.29
15		MAD	1.93	2.09	2.53
16		MSE	5.96	6.21	9.65
17		MAPE	2.04%	2.22%	2.71%

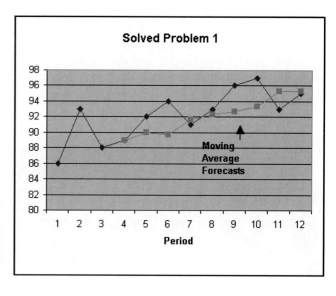

SOLVED PROBLEM #2

Average attendance figures at a major university's home football games have generally been increasing as the team's performance and popularity has been improving:

Year	Attendance
1	26,000
2	30,000
3	31,500
4	40,000
5	33,000
6	32,200
7	35,000

Solution:

A chart of these data and a fitted trend line are shown next. The forecast for the next year (Year 8) would be

$$\text{Attendance} = 1,175(8) + 27,829 = 37,229$$

However, Year 4 appears to be an unusual value, or "outlier." Outliers can significantly change the results. If we delete this value, we obtain the model $Y = 1,175x + 26,583$ with $R^2 = 0.82$. The forecast would be

$1,175(8) + 26,583 = 35,983$. Checking for outliers is an important preliminary step before doing regression. However, you should only delete outliers for logical reasons. Here, if the large attendance was because of a cross-state rivalry that was a one-time event, then it should not be included in the model.

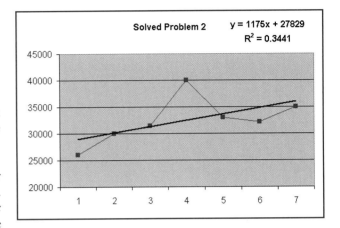

SOLVED PROBLEM #3

The data shown in Exhibit 11.31 represent the number of orders received by a supplier for a particular item from business customers. What is the best forecasting model that the firm should use? Before reading on, what method do you think *CBPredictor* will choose based on the form of the time series in Exhibit 11.31?

Solution:

Using *CBPredictor*, be sure to note that the data are in days with no seasonality in the *Data Attributes* tab. All methods were selected, and the Double Moving Average method with 8 periods was found to be the best, as shown in the following figure.

Methods	Table Items ▼ Rank	RMSE	MAD	MAPE	Durbin-Watson	Theil's U	Periods	Alpha	Beta
Double Exponential Smoothing	4	21.039	16.658	15.063	1.937	1.171		0.612	0.446
Double Moving Average	**1**	**13.292**	**10.474**	**8.277**	**1.663**	**0.885**	**8**		
Single Exponential Smoothing	3	16.783	12.33	11.834	1.888	0.763		0.357	
Single Moving Average	2	13.725	10.694	8.464	1.127	1.009	10		

If you examine the *CBPredictor Method Gallery*, you should have guessed that either a double exponential smoothing or double moving-average model would be the best because the time series show random fluctuation around a linear trend.

The chart at the right shows the fitted model against the time series. Because double exponential smoothing "smooths out" single exponential smoothing forecasts, it requires twice the number of periods before actually generating a forecast. Thus, the fitted line does not begin until period 16.

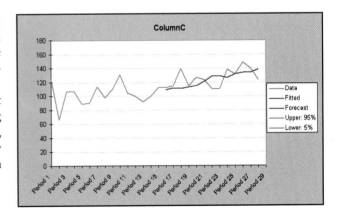

Exhibit 11.31 Data for Solved Problem #3

	A	B	C	D	E	F	G	H	I	J	K
1	Solved Problem 3										
2											
3	Week	Day	Orders								
4	1	Monday	124								
5	1	Tuesday	67								
6	1	Wednesday	107								
7	1	Thursday	107								
8	1	Friday	89								
9	1	Saturday	91								
10	1	Sunday	114								
11	2	Monday	98								
12	2	Tuesday	110								
13	2	Wednesday	131								
14	2	Thursday	105								
15	2	Friday	100								
16	2	Saturday	92								
17	2	Sunday	100								
18	3	Monday	112								
19	3	Tuesday	112								
20	3	Wednesday	115								
21	3	Thursday	140								
22	3	Friday	115								
23	3	Saturday	127								
24	3	Sunday	124								
25	4	Monday	111								
26	4	Tuesday	110								
27	4	Wednesday	139								
28	4	Thursday	132								
29	4	Friday	149								
30	4	Saturday	140								
31	4	Sunday	124								

KEY TERMS AND CONCEPTS

Bias
CBPredictor
Data patterns
  Business cycle
  Irregular variation
  Random variation (noise)
  Seasonal
  Time series
  Trend—linear and nonlinear
Forecast errors and accuracy
  Mean absolute deviation (MAD)
  Mean absolute percentage error (MAPE)
  Mean squared deviation (MSD)
Forecasting
Judgmental forecasting methods
  Delphi

Market surveys
Moving averages
Multiple linear regression model
Planning horizon
  Intermediate-range
  Long-range
  Short-range
Regression analysis
Simple regression as a forecasting tool
Single exponential smoothing (SES)
Smoothing constant
Statistical forecasting methods
Time bucket size
Tracking signal
Weighted averages

QUESTIONS FOR REVIEW AND DISCUSSION

1. What is forecasting? Why is it important at all levels of an organization and in operations in particular?

2. Discuss some forecasting issues that you encounter in your daily life. How do you make your forecasts?

3. How are forecasts used throughout the value chain?

4. What is the role of forecasting in demand planning processes?

5. Explain the importance of selecting the proper planning horizon in forecasting.

6. What is a time series, and what characteristics might it have?

7. Explain why time series might exhibit trend, cyclical, and seasonal patterns.

8. Summarize the different types of forecasting methods that are used in business.

9. What is the difference between statistical and judgmental forecasting methods?

10. Define *forecast error*. Explain how to calculate the three common measures of forecast accuracy.

11. What capabilities does *CBPredictor* have that make it superior to simply using Excel and the Data Analysis tools?

12. Explain how to compute single moving-average forecasts.

13. What is the difference between single moving average and weighted moving average? When might you choose one over the other?

14. Explain the process of single exponential smoothing.

15. How does exponential smoothing incorporate all historical data into a forecast?

16. Summarize the advanced types of forecasting models available in *CBPredictor*. To what types of time series are they most applicable?

17. How does regression differ from time-series methods?

18. What is the value of using judgmental forecasting techniques? How might one choose between statistical and judgmental methods?

19. Explain how judgmental forecasting might be used to predict the timing of market saturation of a new high-tech product.

20. Discuss some practical ways to design a forecasting system for an organization.

21. Interview a previous employer about how it makes forecasts. Document in one page what you discovered, and describe it using the ideas discussed in this chapter.

22. What is bias in forecasting? Explain the importance of using tracking signals to monitor forecasts.

PROBLEMS AND ACTIVITIES

1. Forecasts and actual sales of MP3 players at *Just Say Music* are as follows:

Month	Forecast	Actual Sales
March	150	170
April	220	229
May	205	192
June	256	271
July	250	238
August	260	255
September	270	290
October	280	279
November	296	301

a. Plot the data and provide insights about the time series.
b. What is the forecast for December, using a three-period moving average?
c. What is the forecast for December, using a four-period moving average?
d. Compute the MAD, MAPE, and MSE for parts b and c and compare your results.
e. Might double exponential smoothing work better? Why or why not? Use *CBPredictor* to answer this question.

2. For the data in Problem 1, find the best single exponential smoothing model by evaluating the MSE for α from 0.1 to 0.9, in increments of 0.1.

3. The monthly sales of a new business software package at a local discount software store were as follows:

Week	1	2	3	4	5	6
Sales	360	415	432	460	488	512

a. Plot the data and provide insights about the time series.
b. Find the best number of weeks to use in a moving-average forecast based on MSE.
c. Find the best single exponential smoothing model to forecast these data.

4. The president of a small manufacturing firm is concerned about the continual growth in manufacturing costs in the past several years. The data series of the cost per unit for the firm's leading product over the past 8 years are given as follows:

Year	Cost/Unit ($)	Year	Cost/Unit ($)
1	20.00	5	26.60
2	24.50	6	30.00
3	28.20	7	31.00
4	27.50	8	36.00

a. Construct a chart for this time series. Does a linear trend appear to exist?
b. Develop a simple linear regression model for these data. What average cost increase has the firm been realizing per year?

5. Canton Supplies, Inc. is a service firm that employs approximately 100 people. Because of the necessity of meeting monthly cash obligations, the chief financial officer wants to develop a forecast of monthly cash requirements. Because of a recent change in equipment and operating policy, only the past 7 months of data are considered relevant

Month	Cash Required ($1,000)	Month	Cash Required ($1,000)
1	205	5	230
2	212	6	240
3	218	7	246
4	224		

a. Plot the data.
b. What forecasting method do you recommend and why?
c. Use your recommendation to obtain a forecast for Month 8.

6. The Costello Music Company has been in business 5 years. During that time its sales of electric organs have grown from 12 units to 76 units per year. Fred Costello, the firm's owner, wants to forecast next year's organ sales. The historical data follow:

Year	1	2	3	4	5
Sales	12	28	34	50	76

a. Construct a chart for this time series.
b. What forecasting method do you recommend and why?
c. Use your recommendation to obtain a forecast for Years 6 and 7.

7. Consider the quarterly sales data for Kilbourne Health Club shown here:

		Quarter			Total
Year	1	2	3	4	Sales
1	4	2	1	5	12
2	6	4	4	14	28
3	10	3	5	16	34
4	12	9	7	22	50
5	18	10	13	35	76

a. Develop a 4-period moving average model and compute MAD, MAPE, and MSE for your forecasts.
b. Find a good value of α for a single exponential smoothing model and compare your results to part (a).
c. Apply CBPredictor to find the best model to forecast sales for the next four quarters.

8. The number of component parts used in a production process each of the last 10 weeks is as follows:

Week	Parts	Week	Parts
1	200	6	210
2	350	7	280
3	250	8	350
4	360	9	290
5	250	10	320

a. Developing moving average models with 2, 3, and 4 periods. Compare them using MAD, MAPE, and MSE to determine which is best.
b. Use CBPredictor to find the best forecast for the next week.

9. The manufacturer of gas outdoor grills provides sales data for the last 3 years as follows:

		Quarter Number		
Year	1	2	3	4
1	20,000	40,000	50,000	20,000
2	30,000	60,000	60,000	50,000
3	40,000	50,000	70,000	50,000

a. Develop single exponential smoothing models with $\alpha = 0.2, 0.4$, and 0.6. Compare these models using MAD, MAPE, and MSE metrics to identify the best one.
b. Use CBPredictor to find the best forecasting model. What are your forecasts for the next four quarters?

10. The historical demand for the Panasonic Model 304 Pencil Sharpener is: January, 80; February, 100; March, 60; April, 80; and May, 90 units.
a. Using a 4-month moving average, what is the forecast for June? If June experienced a demand of 100, what is the forecast for July?
b. Using single exponential smoothing with $\alpha = 0.2$, if the forecast for January had been 70, compute what the exponential forecast would have been for the remaining months through June.

c. Develop a linear regression model, and compute a forecast for June, July, and August.

d. Using a weighted moving average with weights of 0.30, 0.25, 0.20, 0.15, and 0.10, what is June's forecast?

11. Two experienced managers are resisting the introduction of a computerized exponential smoothing system, claiming that their judgmental forecasts are much better than any computer could do. Their past record of predictions is as follows:

Week	Actual Demand	Manager's Forecast
1	4,000	4,500
2	4,200	5,000
3	4,200	4,000
4	3,000	3,800
5	3,800	3,600
6	5,000	4,000
7	5,600	5,000
8	4,400	4,800
9	5,000	4,000
10	4,800	5,000

Based on whatever calculations you think appropriate, are the manager's judgmental forecasts performing satisfactorily?

12. A chain of grocery stores had the following weekly demand (cases) for a particular brand of laundry soap:

Week	1	2	3	4	5	6	7	8	9	10
Demand	31	22	33	26	21	29	25	22	20	26

a. Develop three- and four-period moving average forecasts, and compute MSE for each. Which provides the better forecast? What would be your forecast for week 11?

b. Develop an exponential smoothing forecast with smoothing constants of $\alpha = 0.1$ and 0.3. What would be your forecast for week 11?

c. Compute the tracking signal for each of your forecasts in parts (a) and (b). Is there any evidence of bias?

d. Might a different model provide better results?

13. Sales of surfboards for the last 5 years are shown here in millions of dollars.

Year, Quarter	Time (X)	Sales (Y)
1, Q1	1	2
1, Q2	2	4
1, Q3	3	5
1, Q4	4	4
2, Q1	5	3
2, Q2	6	5
2, Q3	7	7
2, Q4	8	5
3, Q1	9	4
3, Q2	10	8
3, Q3	11	9
3, Q4	12	6
4, Q1	13	5
4, Q2	14	8
4, Q3	15	10
4, Q4	16	6
5, Q1	17	6
5, Q2	18	7
5, Q3	19	9
5, Q4	20	7

a. Forecast the four quarters of Year 6 using *CBPredictor*.

b. If annual sales in Year 6 were forecast to be $40 million, what is the forecast of sales by quarter?

CASES

BANKUSA: FORECASTING HELP DESK DEMAND BY DAY (A)

"Hello, is this the Investment Management Help Desk?" said a tired voice on the other end of the telephone line at 7:42 A.M. "Yes you have the right place, how can I help you?" said Thomas Bourbon, the customer service representative (CSR) who received this inquiry. "Well, I've got a problem. My best customer, with assets of over $10 million in our bank, received his monthly trust account statement. He says we inaccurately computed the market value of one of his stocks by using an inaccurate share price. He says this error makes his statement $42,000 too low. I assured him we would research the problem and get back to him by the end of the day. Also, do you realize that I

waited over 4 minutes before you answered my telephone call!" said the trust administrator, Chris Eddins. "Mr. Eddins, give me the customers' account number and the stock in question, and I'll get back to you within the hour. Let's solve the customer's problem first. I apologize for the long wait," said Bourbon in a positive and reassuring voice.

The Help Desk supports fiduciary operations activities worldwide by answering questions and inquiries from company employees, such as portfolio managers, stock traders, backroom company process managers, branch bank managers, accountants, and trust account administrators. These internal customers originate over

98 percent of the volume of Help Desk inquiries. Over 50 different internal processes and organizational units call the Help Desk. Some external customers such as large estate and trust administrators are directly tied via the Internet to their accounts and occasionally call the Help Desk directly.

The Help Desk is a unit of the bank's fiduciary operations group. The Help Desk services internal and external customers through the identification, resolution, and reduction of future investment services inquiries. Fiduciary Operations is an area of the bank that supports many of the products and services of the BankUSA Investment Management Division. The Investment Management Division manages over $300 billion in assets for individual and institutional portfolios and mutual funds. Fiduciary Operations employs over 1,000 people with a wide range of skills, such as information and financial officers, process managers, and human resource management employees.

The Help Desk is the primary customer contact unit within Fiduciary Operations. The Help Desk employs 14 full time customer service representative (CSRs), 3 CSR support employees, and 3 managers, for a total of 20 people. The 3 CSR support employees do research on a full-time basis in support of the CSRs answering the telephone.

The skill of the Help Desk's customer service representative is critical in providing good, friendly, and competent service to both internal and external customers. The bank and its geographically dispersed businesses call the Help Desk but seldom if ever visit the call (contact) center. Although Fiduciary Operations supports many activities of the bank, such as executing billions of dollars of financial transactions daily, the interaction with the Help Desk is where company employees and managers form their impression of Fiduciary Operations. Most often these inquiries are because someone is having a problem or needs a correct and quick answer to an external customer's question.

The Help Desk handles about 2,000 calls a week. Although the Help Desk was the primary gateway and contact center for Fiduciary Operations, the pressure to reduce unit cost was ongoing. Forecast accuracy was a key input to better staffing decisions that minimize costs and maximize service. The data in Exhibit 11.32 is the number of calls per week (Call Volume), day of the week (DOW), and day of week ID (DOW ID). The data set of 16 daily observations is contained on the textbook's CD.

The senior manager of the Help Desk, Dot Gifford, established a team to try to evaluate short-term forecasting at the Help Desk. The "Help Desk Staffing Team" consisted of Gifford, Bourbon, Chris Paris, and a new employee of the bank, David Hamlet, with an undergraduate major in operations management at a leading business school. This four-person team was charged with developing a long-term forecasting procedure for the Help Desk. Gifford asked the team to make an informal presentation of their analysis in 10 days. The primary job of analysis fell on Samantha Jenkins, the newly hired operations analyst. It would be her chance to make a good first impression on her boss and colleagues.

Question for Part A of the Case: Using the information in Exhibit 11.32, what should Jenkins do to determine the best method or methods to forecast these data?

Exhibit 11.32
Example Call Volume Data by Day for BankUSA (see the file BankUSA Forecasting Case Data.xls on the student CD-ROM)

Day	CALL VOLUME	DOW	DOW ID
1	413	Fri	5
2	536	Mon	1
3	495	Tue	2
4	451	Wed	3
5	480	Thu	4
6	400	Fri	5
7	525	Mon	1
8	490	Tues	2
9	492	Wed	3
10	519	Thu	4
11	402	Fri	5
12	616	Mon	1
13	485	Tues	2
14	527	Wed	3
15	461	Thu	4
16	370	Fri	5

BANKUSA: FORECASTING HELP DESK DEMAND BY HOUR OF THE DAY (B)

Review the background on BankUSA in part A of the preceding case.

Question for Part B of the Case: The team's objectives are stated as: (1) What forecasting methods should we adopt? (2) What is the forecast for each day of next week (that is, days 11 to 15)? (3) How might these forecasts be used to drive staff planning and scheduling? Using the data in Exhibit 11.33, help Jenkins meet these objectives.

Exhibit 11.33 Help Desk Inquiry Volumes by Hour of Day (B)

Time of Day	Monday Day 1	Tuesday Day 2	Wednesday Day 3	Thursday Day 4	Friday Day 5	Weekly Total	Monday Day 6	Tuesday Day 7	Wednesday Day 8	Thursday Day 9	Friday Day 10	Weekly Total
7:00–7:30 A.M.	2	0	0	0	0	2	0	0	1	1	1	3
7:30–8:00 A.M.	2	2	4	0	3	11	3	4	3	0	2	12
8:00–8:30 A.M.	6	4	5	5	7	27	15	4	5	3	7	34
8:30–9:00 A.M.	16	26	10	7	16	75	12	11	5	9	9	46
9:00–9:30 A.M.	17	20	18	14	23	92	22	11	21	18	16	88
9:30–10:00 A.M.	22	19	29	23	23	116	25	18	25	29	20	117
10:00–10:30 A.M.	31	24	24	33	18	130	31	30	31	35	15	142
10:30–11:00 A.M.	29	40	29	31	21	150	26	30	24	33	27	140
11:00–11:30 A.M.	21	37	28	28	23	137	18	24	25	34	28	129
11:30–12:00 P.M.	19	24	28	23	22	116	32	32	27	23	22	136
12:00–12:30 P.M.	33	28	18	17	20	116	24	18	26	27	19	114
12:30–1:00 P.M.	18	18	16	15	18	85	17	32	20	23	18	110
1:00–1:30 P.M.	18	15	20	16	15	84	23	16	25	16	22	102
1:30–2:00 P.M.	23	24	15	25	15	102	15	18	16	19	13	81
2:00–2:30 P.M.	28	13	23	26	18	100	17	22	20	26	26	111
2:30–3:00 P.M.	20	23	16	26	25	117	26	27	16	20	18	107
3:00–3:30 P.M.	17	28	31	21	21	103	23	20	25	28	22	118
3:30–4:00 P.M.	30	22	22	18	23	124	21	22	19	32	18	112
4:00–4:30 P.M.	25	27	17	17	24	115	25	22	12	30	13	102
4:30–5:00 P.M.	14	16	7	8	20	75	26	20	18	18	12	94
5:00–5:30 P.M.	17	14	5	5	8	51	13	15	13	13	9	63
5:30–6:00 P.M.	5	12	3	2	10	34	5	5	6	6	5	27
6:00–6:30 P.M.	4	5	3	1	0	13	4	3	1	1	3	12
6:30–7:00 P.M.	1	3	1	0	0	5	1	0	0	1	0	2
Total	**418**	**444**	**384**	**361**	**373**	**1,980**	**424**	**404**	**384**	**445**	**345**	**2,002**

ENDNOTES

[1] "Holding Patterns," *CIO Magazine*, www.cio.com/archive May 15, 1999.

[2] http://www.sap.com/solutions/scm/demand/.

[3] "Colgate Supports Its Worldwide Brands with mySAP Supply Chain Management," http://www.sap.com/solutions/business-suite/scm/customersuccess/index.aspx, December 6, 2004.

[4] Gilliland, M., "Is Forecasting a Waste of Time?" *Supply Chain Management Review*, www.manufacturing.net/scm, July/August 2002.

[5] See, for example, Yurkiewicz, Jack, "Forecasting Software Survey," *ORMS Today* 30, no. 1, February 2003, pp. 44–51.

[6] "Cal ISO Okays Plan to Shut 2 San Francisco Power Plants," The Wall Street Journal Online, November 10, 2004, http://online.wsj.com/article.

[7] http://www.i2.com/web505/media/F8875AFA-990B-484B-A91F87436BB8B8AB.pdf.

Chapter Outline

CHAPTER 12

Managing Inventories

Learning Objectives

1. To understand the different types of inventory that firms use and their role in the value chain and to become familiar with a taxonomy of inventory concepts to support the development of useful quantitative models for inventory management.

2. To learn methods for prioritizing the importance of inventory items, maintaining accurate inventory information, and using technology for inventory management.

3. To understand a class of inventory management systems for monitoring and controlling independent demand using fixed order quantities for replenishing inventory levels.

4. To understand how inventory management systems for monitoring and controlling independent demand operate using fixed time intervals between order placements.

5. To learn special inventory models that consider back orders, price breaks, one-time ordering opportunities, and simulation as methods for inventory analysis.

- "Mr. Gales, we can't pick you up before 4 P.M. today in Orlando. The plane assigned to you needs a replacement part and it is out of stock. We are sending a different plane from San Diego to pick you up, but it can't get to Orlando until 4:00 P.M. You will be in Chicago by 6:30 P.M. You might be a little late to the golf tournament kickoff dinner," said Betty Kelly, the customer service representative for Scott Gales, a professional golfer. Gales had purchased a fractional ownership of a privately owned business jet, costing $3 million plus a monthly fee of $3,000. Fractional ownership, similar to vacation timesharing, allows the customer a specific number of flying hours in a certain type of airplane. Moreover, the company promises its customers that with 4 hours notice (called a service window), it can pick them up anywhere in the continental United States. As Betty hung up the telephone, she realized the cost to fly the plane from San Diego to Orlando to pick up Gales far exceeded the cost of the replacement part that was out of stock. The company would lose considerable money on this flight but cannot afford to lose Gales— and possibly many of his colleagues—as a customer.

- Banana Republic is a unit of San Francisco's Gap, Inc., and accounts for about 13 percent of Gap's $15.9 billion in sales. As Gap shifted its product line to basics such as cropped pants, jeans, and khakis, Banana Republic had to move away from such staples and toward trends, trying to build a name in fashion circles. But fashion items, which have a much shorter product life cycle and are riskier because their demand is more variable and uncertain, bring up a host of operations management issues. In one recent holiday season, the company had bet that blue would be the top-selling color in stretch merino wool sweaters. They were wrong. Marka Hansen, company president, noted, "The No. 1 seller was moss green. We didn't have enough."[1]

- "Where is my house mortgage? You mean you lost all of the paperwork?" H. C. Morris shouted as he talked to his banker on the telephone. "Sir, we packaged and sold the original loan to a custodian loan servicing company and they cannot find your mortgage at their warehouse. The secure and fireproof warehouse holds over 25 million home mortgage folders! Home mortgages are bought and sold many times. Do you have copies of the original loan documents?" responded the banker. "Yes, but they are photocopies and probably are incomplete," noted Morris. "Mr. Morris, we will have to re-create the entire loan package and that will take at least 2 months," said the banker. "I can't wait that long—I have to close the deal for the house in 10 days. I may lose the deal," Morris shouted again. "Sir, we will work as fast as we can but with no original mortgage documents you have no choice but to wait," sighed the banker.

© Getty Images/PhotoDisc

Discussion Questions: Can you cite any experiences in which the lack of appropriate inventory at a retail store has caused you as the customer to be dissatisfied? Consider the off-season sale racks of clothing that you have seen at a department store. Typically, most of the items are odd sizes—for instance, S or XXL. What does this suggest about the store's inventory management decisions?

Inventory *is any asset held for future use or sale.* These assets may be physical goods used in operations and include raw materials, parts, subassemblies, supplies, tools, equipment, or maintenance and repair items. For example, a small pizza business must maintain inventories of dough, toppings, sauce, and cheese, as well as supplies such as boxes, napkins, and so on. Hospitals maintain inventories of blood and other consumables, and railroads have inventories of rail cars and maintenance parts. Retail stores such as Best Buy maintain inventories of finished goods—televisions, appliances, DVDs—for sale to customers. In some service organizations, inventories are not physical goods that customers take with them, but provide capacity available for serving customers. Some common examples are airline seats, concert seats, hotel rooms, and call center phone lines. Inventories can also be intangible; for example, many organizations maintain "inventories" of intellectual assets and best-practice knowledge bases. Thus, the concept of inventory should be interpreted broadly, although many examples in this chapter deal with physical goods.

The expenses associated with financing and maintaining inventories are a substantial part of the cost of doing business (that is, cost of goods sold). Managers

Inventory *is any asset held for future use or sale.*

Inventory management
*involves planning,
coordinating, and controlling
the acquisition, storage,
handling, movement,
distribution, and possible sale
of raw materials, component
parts and subassemblies,
supplies and tools,
replacement parts, and other
assets that are needed to meet
customer wants and needs.*

are faced with the dual challenges of maintaining sufficient inventories to meet demand while at the same time incurring the lowest possible cost. **Inventory management** *involves planning, coordinating, and controlling the acquisition, storage, handling, movement, distribution, and possible sale of raw materials, component parts and subassemblies, supplies and tools, replacement parts, and other assets that are needed to meet customer wants and needs.* If the "right" inventory is carried and delivered at the "right" time, profits are increased through additional sales revenues, and customer service is enhanced. However, it is important to realize that having the wrong inventory or having it at the wrong time can seriously hurt a firm's performance. For example, ordering too many computers can easily lead to obsolescence and lower profits (or even losses) as new technology rapidly evolves.

Managing inventories is one of the most important functions of operations management in both manufacturing and service organizations. In the first episode, we see how the lack of the proper aircraft replacement parts can result in both unnecessary and excessive costs as well as dissatisfaction of the customer, with possible loss of future business. For this type of premium service, the airline needs to carry additional capacity in the form of extra planes to provide the service required by their high-income clients. Nearly every organization faces such problems; it is not uncommon for a restaurant to run out of certain entrees or desserts, particularly if they are "specials," and enough food was not ordered.

On the other hand, simply maintaining large stocks of inventory is costly and wasteful. The old concept of keeping warehouses and stockrooms filled to capacity with inventory has been replaced with the idea of producing finished goods as late as possible prior to shipment to the customer. Better information technology and applications of quantitative tools and techniques for inventory management have allowed dramatic reductions in inventory. For example, U.S. businesses reduced total inventory as a percentage of gross domestic product (GDP) from 8.3 to 3.8 percent from 1981 to 2000. This increases net working capital and reduces cash flow requirements to run the business, resulting in improved operational and financial efficiency. Inventory reduction is a vital part of becoming a "lean organization."

One-time, seasonal merchandise, such as that suggested in the Banana Republic episode, presents a different situation. Such firms must order far in advance of the actual selling season with little information on which to base their inventory decisions. The wrong choices can easily lead to a mismatch between customer demand and availability, resulting in either lost opportunities for sales or overstocks that might have to be sold at a loss or at least a minimal profit. Such decisions must take into account the trade-offs between ordering too much or too little, as well as other factors such as quantity discount price breaks.

The third episode illustrates the complexity of many inventory management systems and the need for modern technology. In a home mortgage warehouse, each original mortgage file folder contains up to ten legal documents per mortgage folder. A typical mortgage warehouse has to store, retrieve, copy, update, and ship 25 million individual mortgages and thus account for over 250 million documents. This includes record keeping, tracking document movement, and organizing loan portfolios. The mortgage business is slowly moving toward more modern methods for managing its inventory, such as scanning new mortgage documents and storing them in electronic form. However, converting existing paper documents into electronic form is cost-prohibitive and complicated by such legal issues revolving around original signatures versus electronic signatures.

One of the difficulties of inventory management is that every department in an organization generally views inventory objectives differently. The marketing department prefers high inventory levels to provide the best possible customer service.

Purchasing agents tend to buy in large quantities to take advantage of quantity discounts and lower freight rates. Similarly, operations managers want high inventories to prevent delays and buffer demand between workstations and processes. Financial personnel seek to minimize inventory investment, warehousing costs, and cash flow and thus would prefer small inventories. Top management needs to understand the effect that inventories have on a company's financial performance, operational efficiency, and customer satisfaction and strike the proper balance in meeting strategic objectives.

In this chapter, we examine the role of inventories in manufacturing and service organizations, along with many techniques and approaches for effectively managing them.

BASIC INVENTORY CONCEPTS

Many different types of inventories are maintained throughout the value chain—before, during, and after production—to support operations and meet customer demands (see Exhibit 12.1). Raw materials, component parts, subassemblies, and supplies *are inputs to manufacturing and service-delivery processes.* Examples include coal for steelmaking; automobile engines for final assembly; buns, burgers, and condiments at a quick-service restaurant; soap and shampoo at a hotel; and printer cartridges and envelopes at an office. Work-in-process (WIP) inventory *consists of partially finished products in various stages of completion that are awaiting further processing.* For example, a pizza restaurant might prepare a batch of pizzas with only cheese and sauce and add other toppings when orders are placed. This can improve service time during busy lunch periods. WIP inventory also acts as a buffer between workstations in flow shops or departments in job shops to enable the operating process to continue when equipment might fail at one stage or supplier shipments are late. Finished goods inventory *are completed products ready for distribution or sale to customers.* Finished goods might be stored in a warehouse or at the point of sale in retail stores. Finished goods inventories are necessary to satisfy customers' demands quickly without having to wait for a product to be made or ordered from the supplier.

Despite their obvious value in meeting customer demand and providing operational efficiencies, WIP and finished goods inventories have some limitations. High levels of WIP inventories, for example, can make it more difficult to change product lines, since they must be phased out when products change, thus limiting flexibility to meet changing customers' needs. In addition, large WIP inventories can hide such problems as unreliable machines, late supplier shipments, or defective parts. High levels of finished goods inventory can quickly become obsolete when technology changes or new products are introduced. The financial investment tied up in inventory that might be used more productively in the firm is clearly a concern to top management. These factors make inventory management an important activity.

Many goods move continually through the supply chain, for example, being transported by truck, train, or barge from a supplier to a factory, or from a factory to a distribution center. *Inventory that has been ordered but not yet received and is in transit is called* pipeline inventory. For example, if a computer manufacturer orders an average of 10,000 CD/DVD disk drives each week and it takes 4 weeks to ship from a factory in Asia to the United States, then the pipeline inventory is 40,000. Although pipeline inventory is not physically available to the user or customer, it must be accounted for to plan production and future replenishment orders.

Learning Objective
To understand the different types of inventory that firms use and their role in the value chain and to become familiar with a taxonomy of inventory concepts to support the development of useful quantitative models for inventory management.

Raw materials, component parts, subassemblies, and supplies *are inputs to manufacturing and service-delivery processes.*

Work-in-process (WIP) inventory *consists of partially finished products in various stages of completion that are awaiting further processing.*

Finished goods inventory *are completed products ready for distribution or sale to customers.*

Inventory that has been ordered but not yet received and is in transit is called **pipeline inventory.**

Exhibit 12.1 Role of Inventory in the Value Chain

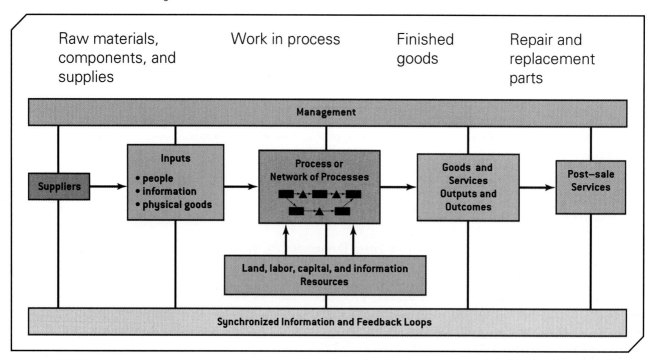

Anticipation inventory *is built up during the off-season to meet future estimated demand.*

Many goods have seasonal demand cycles and the firm might not have capacity to produce enough on a regular basis, as we discussed in Chapter 10. For example, it might be impossible to produce enough lawn mowers during a short summer selling season because of limited production capacity. **Anticipation inventory** *is built up during the off-season to meet future estimated demand.* With perishable items, however, this cannot be done and firms must resort to other means to increase capacity.

Manufacturers order raw materials or produce components on a regular basis to maintain a steady flow of inputs to support production. Similarly, wholesalers or retailers order finished goods on a regular basis to replenish their stock as customers purchase goods. For example, a retail store might have ten units of a certain type of high-definition TV in stock. It is probably not economical to order another each time one is purchased because of the high cost of shipping a single item and other administrative expenses that would be involved. Instead, the store might use some type of decision rule, such as "order seven units whenever the stock level drops to three." **Cycle inventory** *(also called* **order** *or* **lot size inventory**) *is inventory that results from purchasing or producing in larger lots than are needed for immediate consumption or sale.* The term "cycle inventory" stems from the repetitive nature of the ordering or production process. As inventory is depleted and replenished, the inventory level cycles in an up-and-down pattern. Cycle inventory may take advantage of economies of scale from quantity discounts, volume shipments, or the allocation of manufacturing setup costs over many units.

Cycle inventory *(also called* **order** *or* **lot size inventory***) is inventory that results from purchasing or producing in larger lots than are needed for immediate consumption or sale.*

Customer demand is most often highly variable and uncertain. This makes it difficult for firms to plan on appropriate inventory levels. Lack of sufficient inventory can cause production lines to shut down or customers to become dissatisfied and purchase goods and services elsewhere. To reduce the risk associated with not having enough inventory, firms often maintain additional stock beyond their normal estimates. **Safety stock inventory** *is an additional amount that is kept over and above the average amount required to meet demand.*

Safety stock inventory *is an additional amount that is kept over and above the average amount required to meet demand.*

Inventory Management Decisions and Costs

Inventory managers deal with two fundamental decisions:

1. When to order items from a supplier or when to initiate production runs, if the firm makes its own items, and
2. How much to order or produce each time a supplier or production order is placed

Practical inventory management is all about making trade-offs among the costs associated with these decisions.

Inventory costs can be classified into four major categories:

1. ordering or setup costs
2. inventory-holding costs
3. shortage costs
4. unit cost of the stock-keeping units or SKUs

Ordering costs *or* **setup costs** *are incurred as a result of the work involved in placing purchase orders with suppliers or configuring tools, equipment, and machines within a factory to produce an item.* For purchased items, these costs stem from such activities as searching and selecting a supplier, order processing, processing receiving documents, and inspecting, unpacking and storing items that have been received. If an order (sometimes called a *shop order*) is placed within the factory, setup costs include paperwork, equipment setup and calibration, startup scrap, and the opportunity cost of producing no output while the setup is done. Order and setup costs do not depend on the number of items purchased or manufactured, but rather on the number of orders that are placed.

Inventory-holding *or* **inventory-carrying costs** *are the expenses associated with carrying inventory.* Holding costs are typically defined as a percentage of the dollar value of inventory per unit of time (generally 1 year). They include costs associated with maintaining storage facilities, such as gas and electricity, taxes, insurance, and labor and equipment necessary to handle, move, and retrieve an SKU. Rent or leasing costs of warehouses, spoilage, and obsolescence might also be allocated to inventory-holding costs. However, from an accounting perspective, it is very difficult to precisely allocate such costs to an individual SKU. Essentially, holding costs reflect the opportunity cost associated with using the funds invested in inventory for alternative uses and investments. Thus, the cost of capital invested in inventory, which is the product of the value of a unit of inventory, the length of time held, and an interest rate associated with a dollar tied up in inventory, normally accounts for the largest component of inventory-holding costs. Because of the difficulty in arriving at a precise value, inventory-holding costs are often based on a combination of cost estimates derived from the accounting systems and managers' judgment. They usually range between 10 and 35 percent of the dollar value of the items.

Note that large orders require that more inventory be carried, on average. As a result, holding costs are high but fewer orders are placed, so ordering costs are low. On the other hand, if frequent small orders are placed, ordering costs are high, but holding costs are low. These costs must be balanced to achieve a minimum-cost inventory policy.

Shortage *or* **stockout costs** *are costs associated with a SKU being unavailable when needed to meet demand.* These costs can reflect backorders, lost sales, or service interruptions for external customers or costs associated with interruptions to manufacturing and assembly lines for internal customers. Some examples of shortage costs are overnight shipping for emergency orders or compensation for overbooking on an airline or at a hotel. However, like holding costs, shortage costs

Ordering costs or setup costs are incurred as a result of the work involved in placing purchase orders with suppliers or configuring tools, equipment, and machines within a factory to produce an item.

Inventory-holding or inventory-carrying costs are the expenses associated with carrying inventory.

Shortage or stockout costs are costs associated with a SKU being unavailable when needed to meet demand.

are generally difficult to quantify precisely from an accounting perspective and often represent a judgmental "penalty cost" reflective of management policies and attitudes toward allowing shortages. Shortage costs are particularly important in stochastic demand models because uncertainty and variability often lead to shortages.

The unit cost is the price paid for purchased goods or the internal cost of producing them. In most situations, the unit cost is a "sunk cost" because the total purchase cost is not affected by the order quantity. However, the unit cost of SKUs is an important purchasing consideration when quantity discounts are offered; it may be more economical to purchase large quantities at a lower unit cost to reduce the other cost categories and thus minimize total costs. When items are produced internally, the firm must allocate costs using some accounting system to arrive at the "standard unit cost" or "cost of goods sold." Activity-based costing methods help organizations measure such costs accurately. The main challenge for operations managers is to use for all SKUs item costs that are based on consistent accounting principles and procedures.

The unit cost is the price paid for purchased goods or the internal cost of producing them.

© Getty Images/PhotoDisc

Characteristics of Inventory Management Systems

A large variety of inventory situations are possible.[2] For instance, a self-serve gasoline station maintains an inventory of only a few grades of gasoline, whereas a large appliance store may carry several hundred different items. Demand for gasoline is relatively constant; the demand for air conditioners is highly seasonal and variable. If a gasoline station runs out of gas, a customer will go elsewhere. However, if an appliance store does not have a particular item in stock, the customer may be willing to order the item and wait for delivery or could go to another appliance store. Since the demand and inventory characteristics of the gasoline station and appliance store differ significantly, the proper control of inventories requires different approaches.

One of the first steps in analyzing an inventory problem should be to describe the essential characteristics of the environment and inventory system. This will be very useful when we develop quantitative models for making good inventory decisions. Although it is impossible to consider all characteristics here, we address the more important ones.

NUMBER OF ITEMS

Most firms maintain inventories for a large number of items, often at multiple locations. To manage and control these inventories, each item is often assigned a unique identifier, called a stock-keeping unit, or SKU. *A stock-keeping unit (SKU) is a single item or asset stored at a particular location.* For example, each color and size of a man's dress shirt at a department store and each type of milk (whole, 2 percent, skim) at a grocery story would be a different SKU. This helps the organization know exactly what is available at each location and facilitates ordering and accounting.

© Getty Images/PhotoDisc

A stock-keeping unit (SKU) is a single item or asset stored at a particular location.

Many inventory control models determine the inventory policy for only one SKU at a time. For organizations with hundreds or thousands of distinct SKUs, applying such models might prove difficult because many variables such as demand forecasts, cost factors, and shipping times must be updated frequently. Maintaining data integrity on thousands or hundreds of thousands of SKUs can be difficult, and decisions that inventory models recommend are only as good as the quality of the input data. In such cases, SKUs are often aggregated, or partitioned, into groups with similar characteristics or dollar value. It is easier to design effective inventory systems for controlling a smaller number of groups of items.

With multiple items, there may be various constraints such as warehouse or budget limitations that affect inventory policy. Other interactions among products also must be considered. For example, certain groups of products tend to be demanded together, such as motor oil and oil filters.

NATURE OF DEMAND

Demand can be classified as independent or dependent, deterministic or stochastic, and dynamic or static. **Independent demand** *is demand for a SKU that is unrelated to the demand for other SKUs and needs to be forecast.* This type of demand is directly related to customer (market) demand. Inventories of finished goods such as toothpaste and electric fans have independent demand characteristics.

SKUs are said to have **dependent demand** *if their demand is directly related to the demand of other SKUs and can be calculated without needing to be forecast.* For example, a chandelier may consist of a frame and six lightbulb sockets. The demand for chandeliers is independent demand and would be forecast, while the demand for sockets is dependent on the demand for chandeliers. That is, for a forecast of chandeliers we can calculate the number of sockets required.

Demand is **deterministic** *when uncertainty is not included in its characterization.* In other words, we assume that demand is known in the future and not subject to random fluctuations. In many cases, demand is highly stable and this assumption is reasonable; in others, we might simply assume deterministic demand to make our models easier to solve and analyze, perhaps by using historical averages or statistical point estimates of forecasts. **Stochastic demand** *incorporates uncertainty by using probability distributions to characterize the nature of demand.* For example, suppose that the daily demand for milk is determined to be normally distributed with a mean of 100 and a standard deviation of 10. If we develop an inventory model assuming that the daily demand is fixed at 100 and ignore the variability of demand to simplify the analysis, we have a case of deterministic demand. If a model incorporates the actual probability distribution, then it is a stochastic demand model.

Demand, whether deterministic or stochastic, may also fluctuate or be stable over time. *Stable demand is usually called* **static demand**, *and demand that varies over time is referred to as* **dynamic demand**. For example, the demand for milk might range from 90 to 110 gallons per day, every day of the year. This is an example of static demand because the parameters of the probability distribution do not change over time. However, the demand for airline flights to Orlando, Florida will probably have different means and variances throughout the year, reaching peaks around Thanksgiving, Christmas, spring break, and in the summer, with lower demands at other times. This is an example of dynamic demand.

NUMBER AND SIZE OF TIME PERIODS

In some cases, the selling season is relatively short, and any leftover items cannot be physically or economically stored until the next season. For example, Christmas trees that have been cut cannot be stored until the following year; similarly, other items, such as seasonal fashions, are sold at a loss simply because there is no storage space or it is uneconomical to keep them for the next year. In other situations, firms are concerned with planning inventory requirements over an extended number of time periods, for example, monthly over a year, in which inventory is held from one time period to the next. The type of approach used to analyze "single-period" inventory problems is different from the approach needed for the "multiple-period" inventory situation.

Independent demand *is demand for a SKU that is unrelated to the demand for other SKUs and needs to be forecast.*

SKUs are said to have **dependent demand** *if their demand is directly related to the demand of other SKUs and can be calculated without needing to be forecast.*

Demand is **deterministic** *when uncertainty is not included in its characterization.*

Stochastic demand *incorporates uncertainty by using probability distributions to characterize the nature of demand.*

Stable demand is usually called **static demand**, *and demand that varies over time is referred to as* **dynamic demand**.

For multiple-period problems, we must also consider the size of the time period for planning purposes. For a manufacturer, this might be a month; for a grocery store, it might be a week. The size of the time period will affect the responsiveness of the inventory system in providing accurate and timely information to make decisions. An inventory system that updates information quarterly is clearly not as timely as one that does so daily.

LEAD TIME

*The **lead time** is the time between placement of an order and its receipt.* Lead time is affected by transportation carriers, buyer order frequency and size, and supplier's production schedules and may be deterministic or stochastic (in which case it may be described by some probability distribution). For example, rail, truck, and air transportation have different characteristics. The lead time for products shipped by air may be less variable than that for products shipped by rail. Also included in lead time is the time the supplier needs to process the order or to produce it if it is not readily available.

STOCKOUTS

*A **stockout** is the inability to satisfy the demand for an item.* When stockouts occur, the item is either back-ordered or a sale is lost. *A **back order** occurs when a customer is willing to wait for the item; a **lost sale** occurs when the customer is unwilling to wait and purchases the item elsewhere.* Back orders result in additional costs for transportation, expediting, or perhaps buying from another supplier at a higher price. A lost sale has an associated opportunity cost, which may include loss of goodwill and potential future revenue.

From a customer service viewpoint, firms never want to incur a stockout; indeed, in situations such as with blood inventories, stockouts can be tragic. In other situations, the economic consequences can be significant. For instance, the Grocery Manufacturers of America estimates that almost 40 percent of consumers would postpone a purchase or buy elsewhere when encountering a stockout, resulting in the loss of almost $200,000 in annual sales per average supermarket. More damaging is the fact that more than 3 percent of shoppers are frustrated enough to terminate the entire shopping trip and go to another store.[3] However, in many situations, back orders may be economically justified. For instance, high-value goods such as commercial jet planes or cruise ships are always made to order; no inventory is carried and a back-order state always exists. Back orders may also be planned to smooth demand on the work force because of limited capacity. When unplanned back orders occur, one of several reasons can usually be identified, including forecast inaccuracies on usage or lead time, unreliable supplier delivery, clerical errors, quality problems, insufficient safety stock, and transportation accidents. To guard against stockouts, safety stock inventory is often maintained.

PERISHABILITY

Many SKUs are perishable in that they either deteriorate or become obsolete after a certain period of time. Fruit, milk, cheese, medicines, and other consumables have a limited shelf life. Budweiser recognized the importance of freshness of beer, which remains fresh for 8 to 10 weeks, and printed a "Born On" date on every bottle. Service capacity is analogous to physical inventory in a service system. Basketball and concert tickets have no value after the game or performance, and hotel rooms cannot generate revenue if they are not rented. Other examples of perishable items are shown in Exhibit 12.2. Inventories of perishable goods must be handled differently from nonperishable goods. In many service businesses, this involves managing service capacity and is called "yield management" (see Chapter 13, "Resource Planning").

---

*The **lead time** is the time between placement of an order and its receipt.*

*A **stockout** is the inability to satisfy the demand for an item.*

*A **back order** occurs when a customer is willing to wait for the item; a **lost sale** occurs when the customer is unwilling to wait and purchases the item elsewhere.*

Stock-Keeping Unit (SKU)	Typical Useful Shelf Life
Milk	3 to 10 days
Newspapers	a few days
Blood	up to one year
Software	3 to 36 months due to obsolescence
Computer virus protection software	days or weeks
Human organs for transplantation	hours
Airline seat, hotel room, concert seats, sporting event seats, and so on	Time of availability until time of event

Exhibit 12.2
Examples of Perishable SKUs

INVENTORY MANAGEMENT INFRASTRUCTURE

Learning Objective
To learn methods for prioritizing the importance of inventory items, maintaining accurate inventory information, and using technology for inventory management.

Inventory management systems define the operating practices that allow for the timely ordering and delivery of the correct materials to support production or customer service objectives. The principal decisions that inventory managers must make involve how much to order and when to place orders. When purchasing from a supplier, we usually call the quantity purchased the *order quantity*. When manufacturing components within a factory, we use the term *lot size*. Later in this chapter, we will describe the logic of the two basic types of inventory management systems—a fixed quantity system (FQS), in which an order for a fixed amount is placed as necessary, and a fixed period system (FPS), in which orders are placed at fixed intervals of time. Each is useful in different inventory management situations, and various quantitative models are used to help define the best operating policies. We will also examine some special inventory management situations.

No matter what type of system or model is used, operations managers must develop a supportive infrastructure for managing inventory. Operations managers face three key issues:

1. *Setting priorities for managing SKUs*—Not all SKUs need to be managed in the same fashion. ABC analysis provides a convenient approach for prioritizing inventory items.
2. *Ensuring that inventory-related data are accurate and reliable*—Cycle counting is a popular approach for doing this.
3. *Integrating technology to support inventory management.*

ABC Inventory Analysis

One useful method for defining inventory value is ABC analysis. It is an application of the *Pareto principle*, named after an Italian economist who studied the distribution of wealth in Milan during the 1800s. He found that a "vital few" controlled a high percentage of the wealth. ABC analysis consists of categorizing inventory items or SKUs into three groups according to their total annual dollar usage:

1. "A" items account for a large dollar value but a relatively small percentage of total items.
2. "C" items account for a small dollar value but a large percentage of total items.
3. "B" items are between A and C.

Typically, A items comprise 60 to 80 percent of the total dollar usage but only 10 to 30 percent of the items, whereas C items account for 5 to 15 percent of the total dollar value and about 50 percent of the items. There is no specific rule on where to make the division between A, B, and C items; the percentages used here simply serve as a guideline. Total dollar usage or value is computed by multiplying item usage (volume) times the item's dollar value (unit cost). Therefore, an A item could have a low volume but high unit cost, or a high volume and low unit cost.

An example of using ABC analysis follows. Consider the data for 20 inventoried items of a small company shown in the spreadsheet in Exhibit 12.3. The projected annual dollar usage column is found by multiplying the annual projected usage based on forecasts (in units) by the unit cost. We can sort these data easily in Microsoft Excel, where we have listed the cumulative percentage of items, cumulative dollar usage, and cumulative percent of total dollar usage. Analysis of Exhibit 12.4 indicates that about 70 percent of the total dollar usage is accounted for by the first five items, that is, only 25 percent of the items. In addition, the lowest 50 percent of the items account for only about 5 percent of the total dollar usage. Exhibit 12.5 shows a simple histogram of the ABC analysis classification scheme for this set of data.

ABC analysis gives managers useful information to identify the best methods to control each category of inventory. Class A items represent a substantial inventory investment and typically have limited availability. In many cases, they are single-sourced and thus need close control to reduce uncertainties in supply. This involves complete, accurate record keeping, continuous monitoring of inventory

Exhibit 12.3
Usage-Cost Data for 20
Inventoried Items

	A	B	C	D
1	ABC Inventory Analysis			
2				
3		Projected		Projected
4	Item	Annual		Annual
5	Number	Usage	Unit Cost	Dollar Usage
6	1	15,000	$5.00	$75,000
7	2	6,450	$20.00	$129,000
8	3	5,000	$45.00	$225,000
9	4	200	$12.50	$2,500
10	5	20,000	$35.00	$700,000
11	6	84	$250.00	$21,000
12	7	800	$80.00	$64,000
13	8	300	$5.00	$1,500
14	9	10,000	$35.00	$350,000
15	10	2,000	$65.00	$130,000
16	11	5,000	$25.00	$125,000
17	12	3,250	$125.00	$406,250
18	13	9,000	$0.50	$4,500
19	14	2,900	$10.00	$29,000
20	15	800	$15.00	$12,000
21	16	675	$200.00	$135,000
22	17	1,470	$100.00	$147,000
23	18	8,200	$15.00	$123,000
24	19	1,250	$0.16	$200
25	20	2,500	$0.20	$500

Exhibit 12.4 ABC Analysis Calculations

	A	B	C	D	E	F	G	H
28			Projected		Projected	Cumulative	Cumulative	Cumulative
29		Number	Usage	Unit Cost	Dollar Usage	Dollar	Percent	Percent
30	Rank	Item	Annual		Annual	Usage	of Total	of Items
31	1	5	20,000	$35.00	$700,000	$700,000	26.12%	5%
32	2	12	3,250	$125.00	$406,250	$1,106,250	41.27%	10%
33	3	9	10,000	$35.00	$350,000	$1,456,250	54.33%	15%
34	4	3	5,000	$45.00	$225,000	$1,681,250	62.72%	20%
35	5	17	1,470	$100.00	$147,000	$1,828,250	68.21%	25%
36	6	16	675	$200.00	$135,000	$1,963,250	73.24%	30%
37	7	10	2,000	$65.00	$130,000	$2,093,250	78.09%	35%
38	8	2	6,450	$20.00	$129,000	$2,222,250	82.91%	40%
39	9	11	5,000	$25.00	$125,000	$2,347,250	87.57%	45%
40	10	18	8,200	$15.00	$123,000	$2,470,250	92.16%	50%
41	11	1	15,000	$5.00	$75,000	$2,545,250	94.96%	55%
42	12	7	800	$80.00	$64,000	$2,609,250	97.34%	60%
43	13	14	2,900	$10.00	$29,000	$2,638,250	98.43%	65%
44	14	6	84	$250.00	$21,000	$2,659,250	99.21%	70%
45	15	15	800	$15.00	$12,000	$2,671,250	99.66%	75%
46	16	13	9,000	$0.50	$4,500	$2,675,750	99.82%	80%
47	17	4	200	$12.50	$2,500	$2,678,250	99.92%	85%
48	18	8	300	$5.00	$1,500	$2,679,750	99.97%	90%
49	19	20	2,500	$0.20	$500	$2,680,250	99.99%	95%
50	20	19	1,250	$0.16	$200	$2,680,450	100.00%	100%

levels, frequent accuracy counts, and maximum attention to order sizes and frequency of ordering. Because of these items' large cost, small lot sizes and frequent deliveries from suppliers are common and result in very short lead times, which require close cooperation between the buyer and supplier and a high level of quality. A items require close control by operations managers.

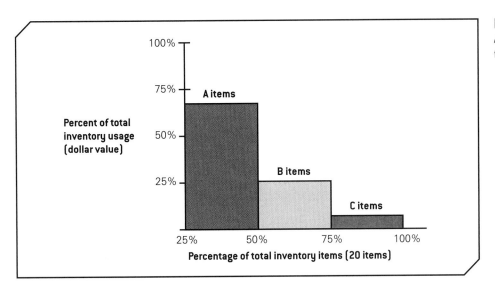

Exhibit 12.5
ABC Histogram for the Results from Exhibit 12.4

Class C items need not be as closely controlled and can be managed using automated computer systems. Large quantities of these items might be ordered to take advantage of quantity or transportation discounts, and inventory levels might simply be checked periodically without maintaining any formal records. Easy to procure from multiple suppliers, they have short lead times.

Class B items are in the middle. In many cases, these items are ordered very infrequently and consist mainly of service parts for older products still in use. Their availability may be limited, and thus long lead times can be expected. Orders are usually handled individually, which necessitates more control than is needed for C items, but they are not as critical as those for A items.

ABC analysis can be used in service organizations but may require some modifications. For example, hospitals use ABC analysis but may use more than three inventory categories. A hospital might use five categories (A, B, C, D, and E), with categories A to D defined by total dollar value. Category E, however, might be defined as a "critical SKU category" that is vital to patients' health. The SKUs might be a simple plastic clip or a tracheotomy surgical kit. Critical SKUs need very careful control to ensure their availability. Services such as a home mortgage warehouse would use ABC analysis to help control inventory and structure mortgage portfolios.

Cycle Counting

A sophisticated, computerized inventory system is worthless if it is inaccurate. Inventory systems tend to accumulate errors over time because of errors in counting and recording the amount of goods received, misidentification of the goods, theft, and so on. These errors arise from poor design of forms, untrained personnel, carelessness, or poor control. Therefore, some method of checking the actual physical inventory is necessary. One approach is to shut down the plant or warehouse periodically and count the inventory. The disadvantages of this method are that productive time is lost, and overtime premiums are usually required to accomplish the task during off-hours.

Cycle counting is a system for repetitive physical counting of inventory throughout the year.

An alternative to closing for inventory is cycle counting. **Cycle counting** *is a system for repetitive physical counting of inventory throughout the year.* It allows scheduling of physical counts to ensure that all parts are counted and that higher-value parts (A items) are counted more frequently than lower-value parts (B and C items). With cycle counting, inventory is counted when orders are placed and received, when the inventory record shows a zero or negative (obviously an error) balance, when the last item is removed from stock, or on a periodic basis.

There are several benefits to cycle counting. Errors can be detected on a more timely basis, and causes can be investigated and corrected. Annual physical inventory counts are eliminated, and the loss of productive time is minimized. A high level of inventory accuracy can be achieved on a continuous basis, and the firm can have a correct statement of assets throughout the year. Also, the specialized teams of cycle counters that are usually established for this become efficient in obtaining good counts, reconciling differences, and finding solutions to system errors.

The ABC classification is usually used to determine the frequency of cycle counting. Clearly, errors are more critical for A items, since their values are higher. FMC Corporation uses cycle counting this way.

Technology and Inventory Management

Modern technology has revolutionized inventory control and management and has been a major part of supply chain design activities. As described in previous chapters, Internet-based integrated operating systems connect customers and suppliers

OM SPOTLIGHT

FMC Corporation[4]

Cycle counting at FMC Corporation is based on ABC analysis, which resulted in the following breakdown.

Class	Number of Items/Percent		Value/Percent	
A	2,973	8%	$41,704,252	87%
B	4,155	12%	$4,292,290	9%
C	28,687	80%	$1,853,364	4%

The A items were subdivided into two classes: regular A items and super A items. Super A items have unit costs of $1,000 or greater. Management policy stated that super A items be counted every month, regular A items every 2 months, B items every 4 months, and C items once a year. The following schedule was established.

Class	Number of Items	Counts per Year	Work Days Between Counts	Days Available	Daily Counts
Super A	1,173	12	20	15	*
A	1,800	6	40	30	60
B	4,155	3	80	60	70
C	28,687	1	240	180	160

*See explanation.

Super A items are each counted once per month, resulting in (1,173)(12) = 14,076 counts per year. Average daily counts for the other classes of items are computed by dividing the number of items by the days available for counting (based on a 20-day work month). This all amounts to a total of 66,276 annual counts, or an average of 5,500 per month. The FMC warehouse in Bowling Green, Kentucky, where this approach is used, has achieved an inventory accuracy of 99 percent due to the cycle counting program.

on a real-time basis. Customer demand at point-of-sale terminals is communicated rapidly through the value chain to distribution facilities and factories, allowing for faster customer response and replenishment of inventory. Newer technologies such as wireless communication systems and radio frequency identification (RFID) chips are improving the efficiency and effectiveness of inventory management in supply chains.

Howmet Castings in Darien, Connecticut, for example, produces metal casting for aircraft engines and parts for wings, serving customers such as Boeing, General Electric, and Rolls-Royce. In the mid-1990s, inventories and processing times doubled as the company carried as much as $10 million of safety stock inventory to guard against late deliveries from suppliers. Today, Howmet Castings uses a software system that communicates both with original equipment manufacturers such as Boeing as well as all of its suppliers in its supply chain. The system can extract purchase order and part-type information and automatically route it to suppliers. Better communication allows the company to schedule its production and supplier orders more efficiently, thus maintaining fewer numbers of parts. Howmet estimates it gets about 80 percent of the system benefits while their suppliers realize the remaining 20 percent. The director of operations noted, ". . . excess inventory is waste. Now, I have reduced safety stock inventory to $6 million."[5] To effectively implement such a system, data formats, terminology, and databases must be standardized and maintained on master data files for access by appropriate players in the supply chain. Such systems improve contract negotiations, bulk buying, engineering design, and information sharing for daily operating decisions.

Telematic diagnostic and monitoring systems *are two-way wireless communication capabilities between equipment and its external environment.* Small computer chips and software are embedded in the equipment, report the equipment's location and usage, and try to recognize when something is about to go wrong. Such information is transmitted back to a company's computer and steps can be taken to perform preventive maintenance on the equipment. For example, service alerts can be sent, maintenance can be scheduled, and replacement parts can be ordered. Automobiles, jet engines, appliances, computers, and power plant equipment are just a few examples of where telematic systems are being developed.

Bar codes were one of the earliest forms of technology that dramatically improved the management and control of inventory (see, for example, OM Spotlight: Information Technology at Nissan). More recently, tiny radio frequency identification (RFID) chips embedded in packaging or products allow scanners to track SKUs as they move throughout the store.[6] RFID chips help companies locate items in stockrooms and identify where they should be placed in the store. Inventory on the shelves can easily be tracked to trigger replenishment orders. Recalled or expired products can be identified and pulled from the store before a customer can buy them, and returned items can be identified by original purchase location and date, and whether they were stolen.

Many major firms, such as Procter and Gamble and Gillette, support this technology. German retailer Metro AG will use radio frequency identification technology (RFID) to replace bar codes in its 250 stores and 10 central warehouses.[7] Metro Ag suppliers will attach RFID tags to pallets and cases, and these items will be detected by wireless readers as they move in the warehouses and stores. Metro

Telematic diagnostic and monitoring systems *are two-way wireless communication capabilities between equipment and its external environment.*

OM SPOTLIGHT

Information Technology at Nissan[8]

Nissan's plant in Sunderland, England produces more than 300,000 vehicles each year. When Nissan wanted to produce a third vehicle model, it was not able to add any capacity in the plant. Its current inventory system tracked inventory manually. Truck drivers were responsible for making a physical check of inventory before leaving the supplier. The system worked well and production downtime due to lack of inventory, extremely expensive for an automobile company, was never a problem. When Nissan decided to add the third line, however, the number of parts was doubled, and with the lack of capacity, Nissan knew it had to reduce its inventory. The manual system was no longer feasible; the solution was to implement a mobile data-gathering and communication system to track inventory in real time using bar code technology. This system ensures that accurate and timely parts information is available on demand and enables operations management to easily monitor job progress and cost efficiencies. When drivers check their loads at the suppliers, they scan the bar code labels of all parts. If there are any discrepancies, drivers can address the problem with the suppliers immediately. When they return to the bar code terminal at the plant, inventory information is updated immediately to a central database. All parts can be pinpointed within seconds. One benefit that this system provided to Nissan was the virtual elimination of inventory variances—the difference between what Nissan expects to get and what it actually receives—because it eliminated human error associated with the manual process.

says the system will reduce inventory by 20 percent and cut down on lost, stolen, or destroyed products. If this pilot program works, the next step is instantaneous checkout where wireless readers can read dozens of RFID tags as customers leave the store and automatically charge their credit cards or store accounts. Intel, SAP, and IBM are helping Metro AG with this initiative to work out the bugs in the wireless inventory tracking system.

One interesting application has been developed by CVS, a Rhode Island-based pharmacy chain, which is testing RFID technology to inform them when a customer has not picked up a prescription medicine. By merging RFID technology with Internet capabilities and other planning and inventory management software, managers will be able to better manage the entire value chain. Although current technology limits the range that RFID chips can transmit information, one can imagine a future scenario in which SKUs can be tracked throughout the entire value chain. Research is being conducted on home scanners that will alert customers when orange juice cartons are low and medicine is about to expire. However, this also brings up many legal and privacy issues; a watchdog organization called the Electronic Privacy Information Center advocates that retailers be required by law to disable the chips as customers leave the store.

FIXED QUANTITY SYSTEMS

In a **fixed quantity system (FQS)**, *the order quantity or lot size is fixed; that is, the same amount, Q, is ordered every time.* The order quantity might be chosen for convenience—a truck load, pallet load, or a prepackaged box of bolts. It might also be chosen based on the economics of ordering and holding inventory; we will develop some quantitative models later in this chapter. A very simple version of a FQS that is often used for small parts and in retail stores is called the *two-bin system.* Consider a supply of small parts kept in a bin with a second (full) bin in reserve. When the first bin is empty, a resupply order for another full bin is placed and the second bin is used. The second bin usually contains more than enough material to last until the new order is received. This system is easily implemented by placing a card at the bottom of the bin, which is turned in when the last item is taken. A variation of this system is often used in hardware stores or bookstores. You often see reorder forms in the form of small cards hanging on hooks for screws, bolts, and so on or inserted among the last few books on the shelf. When the card is reached, it is an indication to replenish the stock.

FQSs are used extensively in the retail industry. For example, most department stores have cash registers that are tied into a computer system. When the clerk enters the SKU number, the computer recognizes that the item is sold, recalculates the inventory position, and determines whether a purchase order should be initiated to replenish the stock. If computers are not used in such systems, some form of manual system is necessary for monitoring daily usage. This requires substantial clerical effort and commitment by the users to fill out the proper forms when items are used and is often a source of errors, so it is not recommended.

To better understand the issues associated with managing inventory using fixed quantity systems, examine the historical sales data for a product shown in Exhibit 12.6. The demand is relatively stable; approximately 10 units per day with a daily average range of 9.57 to 10.71 units. How might a manager apply a FQS system to make replenishment decisions?

Let us suppose that a fixed quantity of 70 units (about 1 week's demand) is ordered each time and that the first order arrives at the beginning of Monday on the first week. We can simulate the operation of this system on a day-to-day basis by monitoring the inventory level at the start and end of each day. We will assume

Exhibit 12.6 Historical Sales Data with Stable Demand Rate

	Week 1	Week 2	Week 3	Week 4	Week 5	Week 6	Week 7	Week 8	Week 9	Week 10
Monday	10	13	9	11	11	10	9	9	11	9
Tuesday	11	9	9	10	11	10	10	11	11	8
Wednesday	13	9	9	9	9	11	10	9	11	10
Thursday	10	10	11	10	10	11	10	8	12	10
Friday	9	10	9	10	11	9	10	9	11	10
Saturday	9	9	10	11	10	11	11	11	11	10
Sunday	9	10	11	10	8	10	9	11	8	10
Weekly Total	71	70	68	71	70	72	69	68	75	67
Daily Average	10.14	10.00	9.71	10.14	10.00	10.29	9.86	9.71	10.71	9.57
Overall Average	10.014									

that any orders are placed at the end of a day and that any receipts arrive at the beginning of a day. The first 7 days are shown in Exhibit 12.7. Because of the slight variability in the demand, we would be one unit short at the end of the week, but suppose this can be tolerated. However, if an order is not received by the next day, the firm would continue to run short, which would probably be undesirable. Therefore, the manager must plan to receive a new shipment of 70 units on the next day (Monday of Week 2).

This brings up the question of when to place the order. Unless the manager can call a supplier across town on Sunday afternoon and ensure delivery by the next morning, the manager must plan ahead and consider the lead time required to make the delivery. Suppose that the lead time is 2 days. To ensure arrival by the beginning of Day 8, the manager must order by the end of Day 5. Note that when the demand rate is essentially constant (deterministic) as it is here, managing this system is easy and its performance is highly predictable. With a stable demand of about 70 units per week, the manager can order every Friday, have delivery on Monday morning, and ensure that nearly all demand can be met.

Exhibit 12.8 shows a chart of the daily ending inventory levels over the 10-week period, obtained by extending the previous analysis (which you can easily do on a spreadsheet). You can see that when the inventory is replenished, the ending inventory on the previous day is always close to zero because of the relatively stable demand pattern.

Impact of Demand Variability

Now let us examine what happens when demand is highly variable, as shown in Exhibit 12.9. Although the average daily demand is still about 10, the variability within and between weeks is much higher than in the first example. In this example,

Exhibit 12.7

Simulation of One Order Cycle for a FQS with $Q = 70$

Day	Order Receipt	Beginning Inventory	Demand	Ending Inventory
1	70	70	10	60
2		60	11	49
3		49	13	36
4		36	10	26
5		26	9	17
6		17	9	8
7		8	9	−1

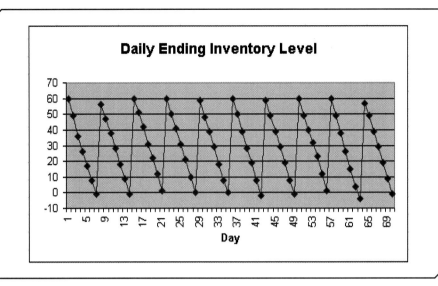

Exhibit 12.8
Simulation Chart of Ending Inventory Levels with $Q = 70$

the daily average demand ranges from 6.86 to 12.00 units. Ideally, it would be nice to plan the order so it arrives just when the inventory will reach zero, but this generally cannot be done when demand is highly variable. To see this, consider applying the same ordering policy of 70 units to arrive every Monday. Exhibit 12.10 shows the inventory pattern over the first 6 weeks, and Exhibit 12.11 shows a chart of the ending inventory over the full 10 weeks. We see that high levels of shortages occur during many weeks such as -6 on Day 6 and -11 on Day 14. This chart suggests that the inventory manager must order differently if shortages are to be avoided.

As this example shows, when demand is variable, orders cannot be placed at fixed intervals based only on average demand rates. A more appropriate way to manage a FQS is to continuously monitor the inventory level and place orders when the level reaches some "critical" value. The process of triggering an order is based on the inventory position. **Inventory position (IP)** *is defined as the on-hand quantity (OH) plus any orders placed but that have not arrived (called scheduled receipts, SR), minus any backorders (BO), or*

$$IP = OH + SR - BO \qquad \textbf{(12.1)}$$

When the inventory position falls at or below a certain value, *r*, called the *reorder point*, a new order is placed.

Inventory position (IP) *is defined as the on-hand quantity (OH) plus any orders placed but that have not arrived (called scheduled receipts, SR), minus any backorders (BO).*

Exhibit 12.9 Historical Sales Data with Variable Demand

	Week 1	Week 2	Week 3	Week 4	Week 5	Week 6	Week 7	Week 8	Week 9	Week 10
Monday	10	8	8	0	8	2	11	12	11	5
Tuesday	8	5	5	10	10	6	16	2	13	12
Wednesday	20	8	17	7	11	11	13	17	19	17
Thursday	16	16	14	10	12	3	13	15	11	7
Friday	8	7	3	4	5	15	9	14	13	15
Saturday	14	8	9	13	11	12	9	6	8	10
Sunday	6	17	7	4	7	13	13	17	5	0
Weekly Total	82	69	63	48	64	62	84	83	80	66
Daily Average	11.71	9.86	9.00	6.86	9.14	8.86	12.00	11.86	11.43	9.43
Overall Average	10.01									

Exhibit 12.10 Simulation Over 6 Weeks with $Q = 70$

Day	Order Receipt	Beginning Inventory	Demand	Ending Inventory	Day	Order Receipt	Beginning Inventory	Demand	Ending Inventory
1	70	70	10	60	22	70	66	0	61
2		60	8	52	23		61	10	49
3		52	20	32	24		49	7	32
4		32	16	16	25		32	10	25
5		16	8	8	26		25	4	10
6		8	14	−6	27		10	13	0
7		−6	6	−12	28		0	4	0
8	70	58	8	50	29	70	70	8	62
9		50	5	45	30		62	10	52
10		45	8	37	31		52	11	41
11		37	16	21	32		41	12	29
12		21	7	14	33		29	5	24
13		14	8	6	34		24	11	13
14		6	17	−11	35		13	7	6
15	70	59	8	51	36	70	76	2	74
16		51	5	46	37		74	6	68
17		46	17	29	38		68	11	57
18		29	14	15	39		57	3	54
19		15	3	12	40		54	15	39
20		12	9	3	41		39	12	27
21		3	7	−4	42		27	13	14

Why not base the reordering decision on the physical inventory level, that is, just the on-hand quantity, instead of a more complex calculation? The answer is simple. When an order is placed but has not been received, the physical stock level will continue to fall below the reorder point before the order arrives. If the ordering process is automated, the computer logic will continue to place many unnecessary orders simply because it will see the stock level being less than r, even though the original order will soon arrive and replenish the stock. By including scheduled receipts, the inventory position will be larger than the reorder point, thus preventing duplicate orders. Once the order arrives and no scheduled receipts are outstanding, then the inventory position is the same as the physical inventory. Back

Exhibit 12.11

Simulation Chart of Ending Inventory Levels for Variable Demand Case with $Q = 70$

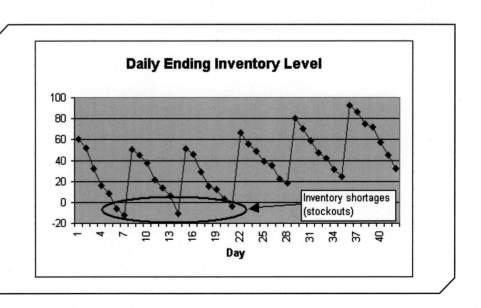

orders are included in the inventory position calculation because these items have already been sold and are reserved for customers as soon as the order arrives.

Choosing the Reorder Point

The choice of the reorder point depends on the lead time and the nature of demand. One approach to choosing the reorder point is to use the *average demand during the lead time* (μ_L). If d is the average demand per unit of time (day, week, and so on), and L is the lead time expressed in the same units of time, then the average demand during the lead time is calculated as follows:

$$r = \mu_L = d \times L \qquad \textbf{(12.2)}$$

(From a practical perspective, it is easier to work with daily data rather than annual data, particularly if a firm does not operate 7 days per week.)

For example, in the data in Exhibit 12.9, we see that the average daily demand is about 10. Therefore, if the lead time is 2 days, the average lead time demand is $\mu_L = (10)(2) = 20$. However, if we order whenever the inventory position falls to 20 or less, we run a substantial risk of running out of stock before the next shipment arrives because of the high variability in the demand. In such cases, we need to order more and carry additional safety stock inventory; this will be addressed later in the chapter. (A more complicated situation occurs when the lead time also varies; for example, if the supplier is out of stock or a shipping delay occurs, then the customer might run out of stock. However, for simplicity, we will assume that lead times are constant.)

We can increase the level of safety stock inventory by increasing the reorder point. Suppose that instead of using the average lead time demand of 20, we increase the reorder point arbitrarily to 50 units. Exhibit 12.12 shows a portion (19 days) of a simulation of our example; that is, whenever the ending inventory is 50 or less, a fixed order for 70 units is placed to arrive after a 2-day lead time. Carefully observe how the inventory position is calculated. For instance, on Day 3, the ending inventory is 32, which is below the reorder point of 50. An order is placed, so the inventory position is

$$IP = OH + SR - BO = 32 + 70 - 0 = 102$$

Day	Order Receipt	Beginning Inventory	Demand	Ending Inventory	Order Placed?	Inventory Position
1	0	70	10	60		60
2	0	60	8	52		52
3	0	52	20	32	Yes	102
4	0	32	16	16		86
5	0	16	8	8		78
6	70	78	14	64		64
7	0	64	6	58		58
8	0	58	8	50	Yes	120
9	0	50	5	45		115
10	0	45	8	37		107
11	70	107	16	91		91
12	0	91	7	84		84
13	0	84	8	76		76
14	0	76	17	59		59
15	0	59	8	51		51
16	0	51	5	46	Yes	116
17	0	46	17	29		99
18	0	29	14	15		85
19	70	85	3	82		82

Exhibit 12.12
Simulation of a Fixed Quantity System with $Q = 70$ and $r = 50$

Notice also that the time between order placement varies. This did not happen in the first example because the daily demand was relatively constant. If we continue this simulation for the full 70-day period (instead of the 19 days in Exhibit 12.12), we obtain the results shown in Exhibit 12.13 for this ordering policy. We see that by using a larger reorder point than the average lead-time demand results in only one week where a stockout occurs. However, this occurs at the expense of carrying a higher average ending inventory.

How does the order quantity affect inventory performance? Look back at the simulation of the example in Exhibit 12.12 using a 70-unit order quantity. The average ending inventory over this first week is $(60 + 52 + 32 + 16 + 8 + 64 + 58)/7 = 41.43$, or about 41 units. Suppose we order 100 units instead of 70. We would only have to order every 10 days instead of every 7, but the average ending inventory over the first week increases to about 66 units. This is shown in Exhibit 12.14. We have reduced the frequency of orders at the expense of increasing the average inventory. Similarly, a smaller order quantity will increase the frequency of ordering but decrease the average inventory (construct a similar table for $Q = 30$). Holding inventory costs money, but so does ordering and shipping. Thus, inventory managers face a critical challenge in trying to balance these costs. Quantitative models, which we introduce shortly, can help in these decisions.

Summary of Fixed Quantity Systems

A summary of fixed quantity systems is given in Exhibit 12.15. Exhibits 12.16 and 12.17 contrast the performance of FQS when demand is relatively stable and highly variable. The dark lines in these exhibits track the actual inventory levels. In Exhibit 12.16, we see that the time between orders (TBO) is also constant in the deterministic case, and therefore, the ordering cycle repeats itself exactly. Here, the TBO is constant because there is no uncertainty and average demand is assumed to be constant and continuous. Recall from our previous discussion that the reorder point should be based on the inventory position (the light line), not the physical inventory level.

Exhibit 12.13
Daily Ending Inventory for
$Q = 70$ and $r = 50$

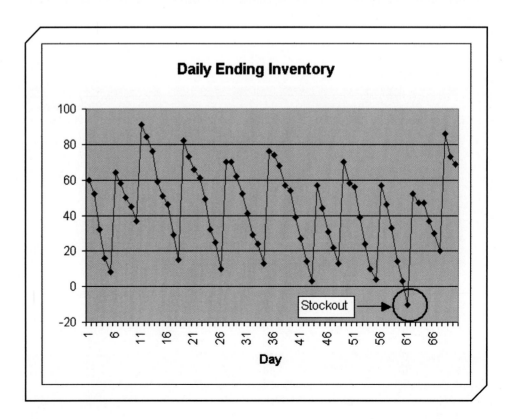

Day	Order Receipt	Beginning Inventory	Demand	Ending Inventory
1	100	100	10	90
2		90	11	79
3		79	13	66
4		66	10	56
5		56	9	47
6		47	9	38
7		38	9	29
8		29	13	16
9		16	9	7
10		7	9	−2
11	100	98	10	88
12		88	10	78
13		78	9	69
14		69	10	59

Exhibit 12.14
Simulation of a Fixed Quantity System with $Q = 100$

Managerial Decisions	Order Quantity (Q) and Reorder Point (r)
Ordering decision rule	A new order is triggered whenever the inventory position for the item drops to or past the reorder point. The size of each order is Q units.
Key characteristics	The order quantity Q is always fixed.
	The time between orders (TBO) is constant when the demand rate is stable.
	The time between orders (TBO) can vary when demand is variable.

Exhibit 12.15
Summary of Fixed Quantity System (FQS)

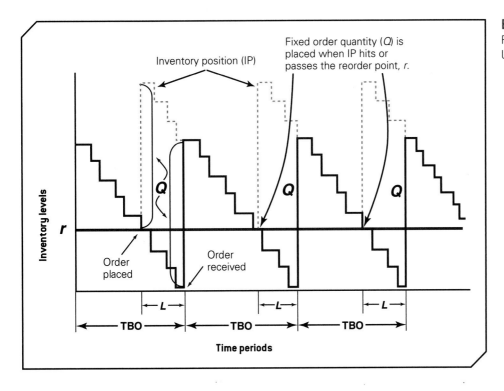

Exhibit 12.16
Fixed Quantity System (FQS) Under Stable Demand

In Exhibit 12.16 you can see that the inventory position jumps by Q when the order is placed. With the highly variable demand rate, the TBO varies while Q is constant.

Exhibit 12.17
Fixed Quantity System (FQS)
with Highly Variable Demand

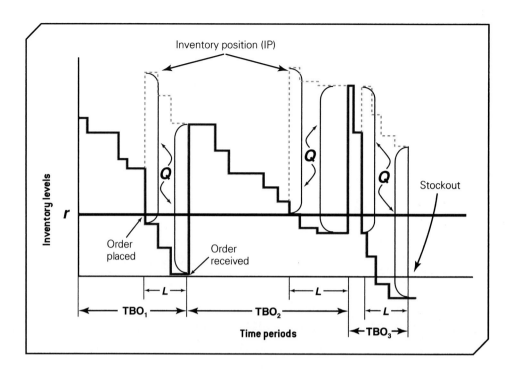

Optimal FQS Policies for Deterministic Demand: The EOQ Model

In this section, we will develop a quantitative model to find the best order quantity when demand is deterministic. Before doing so, let us gain a better understanding of the various costs that must be considered in such a model.

From this discussion of inventory costs, you may wonder how inventory models can ever be used effectively, since the important inventory costs are somewhat difficult to measure. Fortunately, inventory models are generally quite robust. That is, even if the costs used are merely good approximations, there is generally little variation in the resulting solution recommended by the inventory model. Consequently, even the simplest models have been used successfully in reducing inventory costs in many companies.

The **Economic Order Quantity (EOQ)** *model is a classic economic model developed in the early 1900s that minimizes the total cost, which is the sum of the inventory-holding cost and the ordering cost.* Several key assumptions underlie the quantitative model we will develop:

The **Economic Order Quantity (EOQ)** *model is a classic economic model developed in the early 1900s that minimizes the total cost, which is the sum of the inventory-holding cost and the ordering cost.*

- Only a single item (SKU) is considered.
- The entire order quantity (Q) arrives in the inventory at one time. No physical limits are placed on the size of the order quantity, such as shipment capacity or storage availability.
- Only two types of costs are relevant—order/setup and inventory-holding costs.
- No stockouts are allowed.
- The demand for the item is deterministic and continuous over time. This means that units are withdrawn from inventory at a constant rate proportional to time. For example, an annual demand of 365 units implies a weekly demand of 365/52 and a daily demand of 1 unit.
- Lead time is constant.

Despite these limitations—particularly the assumption of deterministic demand, which is generally not true in practice—the EOQ model provides important insights into the economics of inventory management systems and is the basis for more advanced and realistic models.

Under the assumptions of the model, the cycle inventory pattern, similar to those shown earlier in Exhibits 12.8 and 12.11, is greatly simplified. This is shown in Exhibit 12.18. Suppose that we begin with Q units in inventory. Because units are assumed to be withdrawn at a constant rate, the inventory level falls in a linear fashion until it hits zero. Because no stockouts are allowed, a new order can be planned to arrive when the inventory falls to zero; at this point, the inventory is replenished back up to Q. This cycle keep repeating. This regular pattern allows us to compute the total cost as a function of the order quantity, Q.

CYCLE INVENTORY

From the constant demand assumption, the average cycle inventory can be easily computed as the average of the maximum and minimum inventory levels:

$$\text{Average cycle inventory} = (\text{Maximum inventory} + \text{Minimum inventory})/2 = Q/2 \qquad \textbf{(12.3)}$$

If the average inventory during each cycle is $Q/2$, then the average inventory level over any number of cycles is also $Q/2$.

TOTAL COST MODEL

The inventory-holding cost can be calculated by multiplying the average inventory by the cost of holding one item in inventory for the stated period. The period of time selected for the model is up to the user; it can be a day, week, month, or year. However, because the inventory-holding costs for many industries and businesses are expressed as an annual percentage or rate, most inventory models are developed on an annual cost basis. Let

I = annual inventory-holding charge expressed as a percent of unit cost

C = unit cost of the inventory item or SKU

The cost of storing one unit in inventory for the year, denoted by C_h, is given by $C_h = I \times C$. Thus, the general equation for annual inventory-holding cost is

$$\begin{pmatrix}\text{Annual inventory-} \\ \text{holding cost}\end{pmatrix} = \begin{pmatrix}\text{Average} \\ \text{inventory}\end{pmatrix}\begin{pmatrix}\text{Annual holding} \\ \text{cost} \\ \text{per unit}\end{pmatrix} = \frac{1}{2}QC_h \qquad \textbf{(12.4)}$$

The second component of the total cost is the ordering cost. Because the inventory-holding cost is expressed on an annual basis, we need to express ordering costs as an annual cost also. Letting D denote the annual demand for the

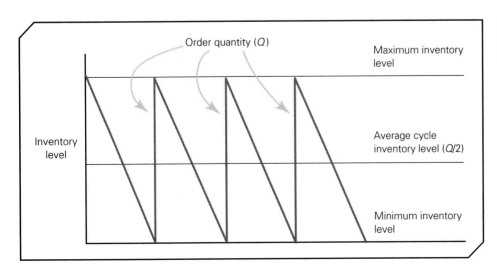

Exhibit 12.18
Cycle Inventory Pattern for the EOQ Model

product, we know that by ordering Q items each time we order, we have to place D/Q orders per year. If C_o is the cost of placing one order, the general expression for the annual ordering cost is shown in Equation (12.5).

$$\begin{array}{c}\text{Annual}\\\text{ordering}\\\text{cost}\end{array} = \left(\begin{array}{c}\text{Number of}\\\text{orders}\\\text{per year}\end{array}\right)\left(\begin{array}{c}\text{Cost}\\\text{per}\\\text{year}\end{array}\right) = \left(\frac{D}{Q}\right)C_o \qquad \textbf{(12.5)}$$

Thus the total annual cost—inventory-holding cost given by Equation (12.6) plus order or setup cost given by Equation (10.3)—can be expressed as

$$TC = \frac{1}{2}QC_h + \frac{D}{Q}C_o \qquad \textbf{(12.6)}$$

OPTIMAL ORDER QUANTITY

The next step is to find the order quantity Q that minimizes the total cost expressed in Equation (12.6). By using differential calculus, we can show that the quantity that minimizes the total cost, denoted by Q^*, is given by Equation (12.7). Q^* is referred to as the *economic order quantity*, or *EOQ*.

$$Q^* = \sqrt{\frac{2DC_o}{C_h}} \qquad \textbf{(12.7)}$$

REORDER POINT

As we noted earlier for any FQS, the reorder point is simply the average demand during the lead time as given by Equation (12.2). For the EOQ model, the only difference is that the demand per unit of time is assumed to be constant and continuous. Thus, Equation (12.2) applies here, with d being a constant, rather than an average, value. In this case, operation of the FQS under the EOQ assumptions is simplified, as shown in Exhibit 12.19.

Exhibit 12.19
Relationship Between Reorder
Point and Lead Time

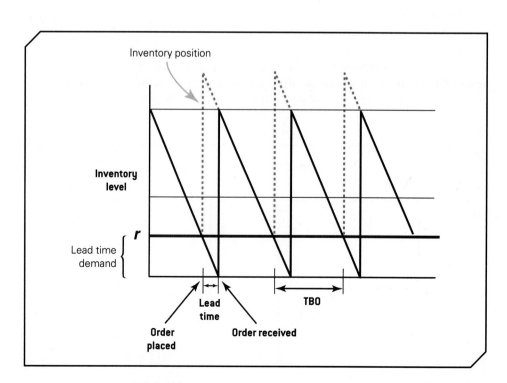

APPLYING THE EOQ MODEL

To illustrate the use of the EOQ model, let us consider the situation faced by the Merkle Pharmacies, a chain of stores in the Midwest United States. The company operates a central distribution center and ships goods purchased from manufacturers to individual stores. As its product line has grown, Merkle's managers have expressed concern about high inventory costs. As a result, Merkle's inventory manager has been asked to make a detailed cost analysis of selected items to see if a better inventory policy can be established. The inventory manager has selected one product, a popular mouthwash, for an initial study. The sales over the past 6 months have been:

Month	Demand (cases)
1	2,025
2	1,950
3	2,100
4	2,050
5	1,975
6	1,900
Total cases	12,000
Average cases per month	2,000

The inventory manager has been using the average number of cases per month as the basis for the ordering policy for this product.

Although the monthly sales data do not show a perfectly constant demand rate, the variability from month to month is low; therefore, a constant rate of 2,000 cases per month appears to be acceptable. Currently, Merkle's cost is $12.00 per case. The company estimates its cost of capital to be 12 percent. Insurance, taxes, breakage, handling, and pilferage are estimated to be approximately 6 percent of item cost. Thus the annual inventory-holding costs are estimated to be 18 percent of item cost. Since the cost of one case is $12.00, the cost of holding one case in inventory for one year is $C_h = IC = 0.18(\$12.00) = \$2.16$ per case per year.

The next step in the inventory analysis is to determine the cost of placing an order. The cost includes the salaries of the purchasing agents and clerical support staff, transportation costs, and miscellaneous costs such as paper, postage, and telephone costs, which are estimated to be $38.00 per order regardless of the quantity requested in the order. Note that the fixed cost of the purchasing department is not included in order cost. From this information, we have

$$D = 24,000 \text{ cases per year}$$
$$C_o = \$38 \text{ per order}$$
$$I = 18 \text{ percent}$$
$$C = \$12.00 \text{ per case}$$
$$C_h = IC = \$2.16$$

Thus, the minimum-cost economic order quantity (EOQ) as given by Equation (12.7) is

$$\text{EOQ} = \sqrt{\frac{2(24,000)(38)}{2.16}} = 919 \text{ cases (rounded to a whole number)}$$

For the data used in this problem, the total-cost model based on Equation (12.6) is

$$TC = \frac{1}{2}Q(\$2.16) + \frac{24,000}{Q}(\$38.00)$$

$$= 1.08Q + \frac{912,000}{Q}$$

For the EOQ of 919, the total cost is calculated to be

$$1.08 \times 919 + (24,000/919) \times (\$38.00) = \$1,984.90.$$

We can compare this total cost using EOQ with the current purchasing policy of $Q = 2,000$. The total annual cost of the current order policy is

$$TC = \$1.08(2,000) + \$912,000/2,000 = \$2,616.00$$

Thus, the EOQ analysis has resulted in a $\$2,616.00 - \$1,984.90 = \$631.10$, or 24.1 percent, cost reduction. Notice also that the total ordering costs (\$992) are equal to the total inventory holding costs (\$992). In general, this will always be true for the EOQ model.

To find the reorder point, let us suppose that the lead time to order a case of mouthwash from the manufacturer is 3 days. Considering weekends and holidays, Merkle operates 250 days per year. So, on a daily basis, the annual demand of 24,000 cases corresponds to a demand of $24,000/250 = 96$ cases. Thus we anticipate 288 cases to be sold during the 3-day lead time using Equation (12.2). Therefore, Merkle should order a new shipment from the manufacturer when the inventory level reaches 288 cases, using Equation (12.7). Also note that the company will place $24,000/919 = 26.12$, or approximately 26, orders per year. With 250 working days per year, an order would be placed every $250/26 = 9.6$ days. This represents the average time between orders (TBO) of 9.6 days in Exhibit 12.19.

As this example illustrates, the EOQ model can identify potential savings by improving ordering policies. Using spreadsheets or other computer technology, it would be easy to compute optimal policies for all SKUs or a major subgroup of SKUs.

SENSITIVITY ANALYSIS OF THE EOQ MODEL

Studying how model results change as inputs to the model change is called **sensitivity analysis.**

Because the inventory-holding charge and ordering cost are at best estimates, we may want to conduct an analysis on how the ordering policy might change as these estimates change. *Studying how model results change as inputs to the model change is called* **sensitivity analysis.** This is easy to do on a spreadsheet as shown in Exhibit 12.20. The spreadsheet also provides a variety of information from the EOQ model.

In the lower portion of the spreadsheet, we vary both the carrying charge and the order cost to understand how the optimal order quantity and total cost would change. As you can see, the value of Q^* appears relatively stable, even with some variations in the cost estimates. Based on these results, it appears that the best order quantity is somewhere around 850 to 1,000 cases and definitely not near the current order quantity of 2,000 cases. We also see that the total cost would not change very much even if the cost estimates are in error. Thus, there is very little risk associated with implementing the calculated order quantity of 919 cases. EOQ models in general are insensitive to small variations or errors in the cost estimates. Notice that the total cost curve in Exhibit 12.21 is relatively flat (shallow) around the minimum total cost solution.

Sensitivity analysis can also be used to evaluate the impact of other changes in model parameters, such as the annual demand (which generally is uncertain) or the unit cost of the item. We can also determine, for instance, that a 50 percent reduction in the order cost would result in a 41 percent reduction in the total cost. In an in-house manufacturing context, this would suggest that companies should try to reduce setup costs associated with making parts and components.

EOQ Models for Stochastic Demand

Stockouts occur whenever the lead time demand exceeds the reorder point in a deterministic situation. When demand is stochastic, then using the EOQ based only on the average demand will result in a high probability of a stockout. One way to

Exhibit 12.20 Spreadsheet for EOQ Model Calculations and Sensitivity Analysis (Economic Order Quantity Model.xls)

	A	B	C	D	E
1	**Economic Order Quantity Model**				
2					
3	**Model Inputs**			**Model Outputs**	
4					
5	Annual Demand, D	24,000		Optimal Order Quantity	918.94
6	Ordering Cost, Co	$38.00		Annual Holding Cost	$ 992.45
7	Unit Cost, C	$12.00		Annual Ordering Cost	$ 992.45
8	Carrying Charge, I	18%		Total Annual Cost	$ 1,984.90
9	Operating Days/Year	250		Maximum Inventory Level	918.94
10				Average Inventory Level	459.47
11				Number of Orders/Year	26.12
12				Cycle Time (Days)	9.57
13					
14					
15	**Sensitivity Analysis**				
16					
17			Optimal Order	Projected Total Cost	
18	Carrying Charge	Order Cost	Quantity	Using Optimal EOQ	Using Q = 919
19	16%	$ 36	948.68	$ 1,821.47	$ 1,822.39
20	16%	$ 40	1000.00	$ 1,920.00	$ 1,926.85
21	20%	$ 36	848.53	$ 2,036.47	$ 2,042.95
22	20%	$ 40	894.43	$ 2,146.63	$ 2,147.41

Exhibit 12.21 Chart of Holding, Ordering, and Total Costs

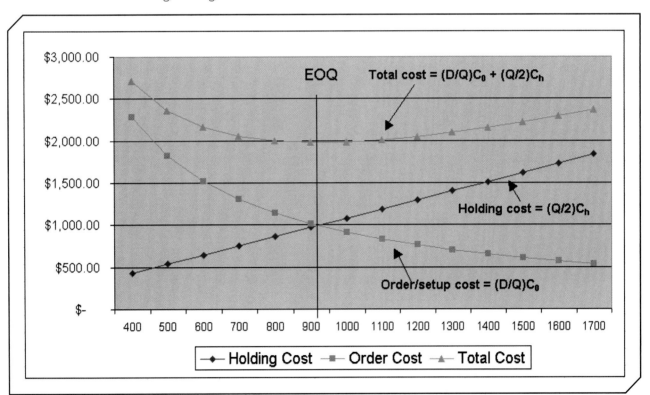

reduce this risk is to increase the reorder point to provide some safety stock if higher-than-average demands occur during the lead time. To determine the appropriate reorder point, we first need to know the probability distribution of the lead-time demand. Usually, the lead-time demand is assumed to be normally distributed. This can be verified by collecting historical data on actual demands during the lead-time period.

The appropriate reorder point depends on the risk that management wants to take of incurring a stockout. This is policy decision and there is no "optimal" solution. *A* **service level** *is the desired probability of not having a stockout during a lead-time period.* For example, a 95 percent service level means that the probability of a stockout during the lead time is .05. In other words, there is a .05 probability that the firm *will* incur a stockout. If demand for an SKU is stochastic, a manager who says he or she will never tolerate a stockout is being somewhat unrealistic, because attempting to avoid stockouts completely requires very high reorder points, which lead to high average inventory levels and high associated inventory-holding costs.

When a normal probability distribution provides a good approximation of lead-time demand, the general expression for reorder point is

$$r = \mu_L + z\sigma_L \qquad \textbf{(12.8)}$$

where μ_L = average demand during the lead time
σ_L = standard deviation of demand during the lead time
z = the number of standard deviations necessary to achieve the acceptable service level

The term "$z\sigma_L$" represents the additional inventory that is held to achieve the service level, that is, the safety stock.

It is important to understand how the mean and standard deviation of lead-time demand are computed. Based on data analysis, we would typically know the probability distribution of demand for some time interval t (for example, days or weeks), characterized by its mean μ_t and standard deviation σ_t. We assume that the lead time L is defined in the same time units. If the distributions of demand for all time intervals are identical to and independent of each other, we can appeal to some basic statistical results to find μ_L and σ_L based on μ_t and σ_t. Specifically, during the lead time L, the mean demand is proportional to L, and the standard deviation of demand is proportional to the square root of L, as given by the following formulas:

$$\mu_L = \mu_t L \qquad \textbf{(12.9)}$$

and

$$\sigma_L = \sigma_t \sqrt{L} \qquad \textbf{(12.10)}$$

APPLYING THE MODEL

To illustrate a situation with stochastic demand, we will consider the case of Southern Office Supplies, Inc., which distributes a wide variety of office supplies and equipment to customers in the Southeast. One SKU is laser printer paper, which is purchased in reams from a firm in Appleton, Wisconsin. Ordering costs are $45.00 per order, one ream of paper costs $3.80, and Southern uses a 20 percent annual inventory-holding cost rate for its inventory. The inventory-holding cost is $C_h = IC = 0.20(\$3.80) = \$0.76$ per ream per year. Although historical sales data indicate that the average annual demand is 15,000 reams, the actual distribution of demand shows considerable variability that cannot be predicted. Analysts have determined that the distribution during any week is approximately normal with a mean of $(15,000)/52 = 288.46$ and a standard deviation of approximately 71.

If we apply the EOQ model using the average annual demand, we find that the optimal order quantity would be

A **service level** *is the desired probability of not having a stockout during a lead-time period.*

$$Q^* = \sqrt{\frac{2DC_o}{C_h}} = \sqrt{\frac{2(15,000)(45)}{0.76}} = 1,333 \text{ reams}$$

Using this order quantity, Southern can anticipate placing approximately 11 orders per year (D/Q = 15,000/1,333), slightly more than a month apart.

Data indicate that it usually takes two weeks (L = 2 weeks) for Southern to receive a new supply of paper from the manufacturer. Using Equation (12.9), we calculate the average 2-week demand as (288.46 reams)(2 weeks) = 577 reams. The standard deviation during the lead time is calculated using Equation (12.10) as $71\sqrt{2}$ = 100 reams. The distribution of demand during the lead time is shown in Exhibit 12.22. This might at first suggest a 577-unit reorder point. However, if the demand during the lead time is symmetrically distributed about 577, then demand will be greater than 577 reams roughly 50 percent of the time. This means Southern would incur a stockout during half of its ordering cycles! Most managers would find this unacceptable.

Suppose Southern's managers desire a service level of .95, that is, a 5 percent probability of a stockout during a given lead-time period. With 11 orders anticipated per year, the 5 percent level of stockouts means Southern should have a stockout for this SKU roughly once every 2 years, which is deemed acceptable.

Exhibit 12.23 shows how the reorder point is calculated. From the normal distribution tables in Appendix A, we find that a 5 percent upper tail area corresponds to a standard normal z-value of 1.645. That is, the reorder point using Equation (12.8), r, is 1.645 standard deviations above the mean, or

$$r = \mu_L + z\sigma_L = 577 + 1.645(100) = 742 \text{ reams}$$

This suggests that a policy of ordering 1,333 reams whenever the inventory position reaches the reorder point of 742 will minimize inventory costs and risk at most a 5 percent probability of stockout during a lead-time period. The anticipated total annual cost for order, inventory holding cost, and safety stock inventory holding costs is computed as follows:

Ordering cost	$\left(\dfrac{D}{Q}\right)C_o = \left(\dfrac{15,000}{1,333}\right)45$	= \$506.46
Holding cost, normal inventory	$\left(\dfrac{Q}{2}\right)C_h = \left(\dfrac{1,333}{2}\right)(.76)$	= \$506.46
Holding cost, safety stock	$(165)C_h = (165)(.76)$	= \$125.40
Total cost		\$1138.32

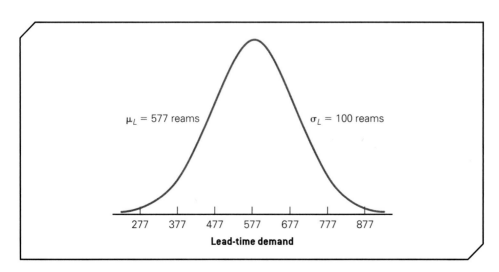

Exhibit 12.22
Lead-Time Demand for Southern Office Supplies

μ_L = 577 reams σ_L = 100 reams

277 377 477 577 677 777 877

Lead-time demand

Exhibit 12.23
Reorder point allowing a 5
percent chance of a stockout

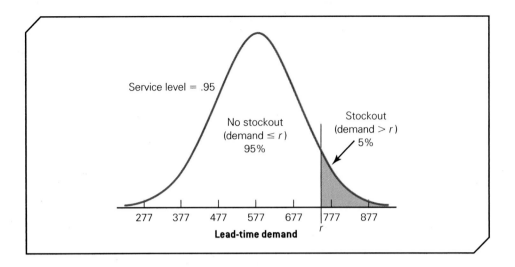

If the demand rate were constant at 15,000 reams per year as in the basic EOQ model, then the optimal policy would be $Q^* = 1,333$, $r = 577$, resulting in a total annual cost of approximately $1,013. If demand is stochastic with the previous assumptions, then $Q^* = 1,333$, $r = 742$, and total order, cycle inventory, and safety stock inventory cost is $1,138. Notice that the additional safety stock required to meet the 5 percent risk of a stockout, 165 units, incurs an additional cost of $125 per year.

Exhibit 12.24 Spreadsheet for Safety Stock Analysis (Southern Office Supplies.xls)

	A	B	C	D	E	F
1	**Southern Office Supplies**					
2						
3	**Model Inputs**			**EOQ Model Results**		
4						
5	Annual Demand	15,000		Optimal Order Quantity	1332.78	
6	Ordering Cost	$ 45.00		Annual Holding Cost	$ 506.46	
7	Unit Cost	$ 3.80		Annual Ordering Cost	$ 506.46	
8	Carrying Charge	20%		Total Annual Cost	$1,012.92	
9						
10	Lead Time Demand					
11	Mean (μL)	577		.		
12	Standard dev. (σL)	100				
13						
14						
15	**Safety Stock Analysis**					
16						Additional
17	Service	Probability	Normal probability	Reorder	Safety	Safety
18	Level	of Stockout	z-value	Point	Stock	Stock Cost
19	0.99	0.01	2.326	810	233	$ 176.80
20	0.95	0.05	1.645	741	164	$ 125.01
21	0.90	0.10	1.282	705	128	$ 97.40
22	0.85	0.15	1.036	681	104	$ 78.77
23	0.80	0.20	0.842	661	84	$ 63.96

Exhibit 12.24 is a spreadsheet for computing the costs associated with normal inventory levels using the EOQ model as well as additional costs incurred for various safety stock levels. (The z-values are found by using the Microsoft Excel function NORMINV.) We see that decreasing the service level permits a lower safety stock, although it increases the probability of a stockout. Thus, the manager must make a trade-off between inventory costs and customer service.

Safety Stock in Complex Supply Chains

Many organizations stock inventory at multiple locations in their supply chain. For example, large distributors and retail chains might have many warehouses located throughout a region, country, or around the world. Individual retail stores each represent an inventory stocking point. Such a strategy provides close proximity to the customer and improves customer response and service.

When demand is divided evenly among the multiple locations and they can transfer inventory to one another as necessary, then for a fixed service level it is possible to show that the average total inventory in the system varies with the square root of the number of inventory locations. That is, using an EOQ policy with safety stock to provide a particular service level, doubling the number of locations increases the average inventory by a factor of $\sqrt{2}$. For example, the EOQ for Southern Office Supplies was 1,333 reams, and to provide a 95 percent service level a safety stock of 164 reams was required. Thus, total average inventory is $Q/2$ + Safety stock, or $1,333/2 + 164 = 830.5$ reams. If Southern Office Supplies expands to 4 stores, then total average inventory needed to provide the same service level will increase to $\sqrt{4} \times 830.5$, or 1,661 reams. For 16 stores, it would be $\sqrt{16} \times 830.5 = 3,322$ reams. Because of the assumption that inventory can be transferred among locations, each location does not need to stock the full amount calculated by the service-level analysis.

FIXED PERIOD SYSTEMS

An alternative to a fixed order quantity system is a **fixed period system (FPS)**— *sometimes called a periodic review system—in which the inventory position is checked only at fixed intervals of time, T, rather than on a continuous basis.* At the time of review, an order is placed for sufficient stock to bring the inventory position up to a predetermined maximum inventory level, M, sometimes called the *replenishment level,* or *"order-up-to"* level. The OM Spotlight on Hewlett-Packard describes the use of a FPS at that company.

In our discussion of the sales data with a stable demand rate (Exhibit 12.6), you might have observed that using a fixed order quantity also resulted in a constant time interval between orders. Suppose that we use a FPS system with a time interval between orders of $T = 7$ days, and as before, assume a 2-day lead time. To have orders arrive on Mondays, we review the ending inventory level on Thursdays (beginning with day 5). The order quantity is computed as M minus the ending inventory at the time of review (Thursday). The value of M must be large enough to safely cover the expected demand until the next review period *and* during the lead time, that is, over a length of time equal to $T + L$. Therefore, we will set $M = 90$ to cover the demand during the review period (an average of 70 units) and the 2-day lead time (about 20 units). Exhibit 12.25 shows a simulation of this ordering policy for the first 3 weeks. Note that the amount ordered at any time varies because the order quantity is calculated by subtracting the inventory level at the time of review from the replenishment level. The chart in Exhibit 12.26 shows the ending daily inventory over all 10 weeks. Note that this is very similar to Exhibit 12.19 for the FQS system. In fact, when demand is stable and deterministic, both systems are essentially the same.

Learning Objective
To understand how inventory management systems for monitoring and controlling independent demand operate using fixed time intervals between order placement.

A **Fixed Period System (FPS)** *is an alternative to a fixed order quantity system.*

OM SPOTLIGHT

Hewlett-Packard[9]

The Hewlett-Packard (HP) Company has complex supply chains for its products. The Vancouver Division manufactures one of HP's popular printers and ships them to distribution centers (DCs) in the United States, Far East, and Europe. Because the printer industry is highly competitive, HP's dealers like to carry as little inventory as possible but must supply goods to end users quickly. Consequently, HP operates under a lot of pressure to provide high levels of availability at the DCs for the dealers. DCs operate as inventory stocking points with large safety stocks to meet a target off-the-shelf fill rate, where replenishment of goods comes from manufacturing.

The basic principles that planners follow are to set a target inventory level, usually expressed in weeks of supply, for each product at each DC based on the desired fill rate. This is a function of the length and variability of the lead time to replenish the stock from the factory and the level and variability of demand. Planners review the actual inventory position each week. This weekly review period corresponds to the frequency with which products are shipped from the factory to the DCs in Europe and Asia. Studies have shown that this frequency allows the plant to maximize the use of its shipping containers. The quantity needed to bring the inventory position back to the target level becomes the production requirement at the factory, which carries no inventory. Thus, the lead time is the sum of the transportation time to ship from the factory, the manufacturing flow time at the factory, and any possible delays due to material shortages or process disruptions. HP developed a quantitative model to compute cost-effective target inventory levels to meet fill rate requirements. The model helped to improve inventory investment by over 20 percent.

Exhibit 12.25

Simulation of FPS System with $M = 90$ Units and $T = 7$ Days

Day	Order Receipt	Beginning Inventory	Demand	Ending Inventory	Order Quantity
1		70	10	60	
2		60	11	49	
3		49	13	36	
4		36	10	26	
5		26	9	17	73
6		17	9	8	
7		8	9	−1	
8	73	72	13	59	
9		59	9	50	
10		50	9	41	
11		41	10	31	
12		31	10	21	69
13		21	9	12	
14		12	10	2	
15	69	71	9	62	
16		62	9	53	
17		53	9	44	
18		44	11	33	
19		33	9	24	66
20		24	10	14	
21		14	11	3	

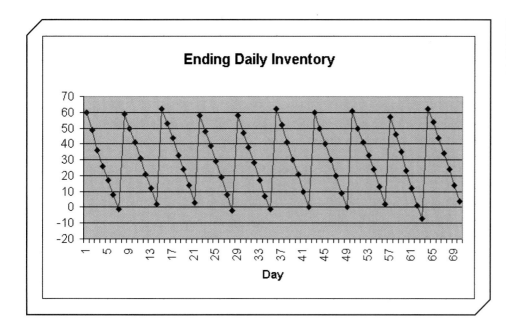

There are two principal decisions in a FPS:

1. the time interval between reviews, and
2. the replenishment level.

We can set the length of the review period judgmentally based on the importance of the item or the convenience of review. For example, management might select to review noncritical SKUs every month and more-critical SKUs every week. We can also incorporate economics using the EOQ model.

The EOQ model provides the best "economic time interval" for establishing an optimal policy for a FPS system under the model assumptions. This is given by

$$T = Q*/D = EOQ/D \qquad \textbf{(12.11)}$$

The optimal replenishment level is computed by

$$M = \mu_{T+L} = d(T + L) \qquad \textbf{(12.12)}$$

where T is the time interval between orders or review period based on the EOQ, d = demand per time period (days, weeks, months, and so on), L is the lead time in the same time units, and μ_{T+L} is the demand during the lead time plus review period.

Periodic review systems usually involve stock clerks making the rounds and physically checking the inventory levels. Notice that if the lead time is always shorter than the time between reviews, any order placed will be received before the next review time. In this case, the inventory position at the time of review will be the same as the actual physical inventory, and therefore, the ordering decision can be made by checking the physical inventory (rather than having to compute the inventory position). This makes implementation easier. The replenishment level M for each item can be identified by a tag on the shelf, and the stock clerk needs only to compare it to the number of items remaining. The advantage of a periodic review system is that inventory need not be monitored continuously, which would be difficult to do unless the system were automated.

Periodic review systems are useful when a large number of items is ordered from the same supplier, because several orders can be placed at the same time. Shipments can be consolidated, resulting in lower freight rates. Periodic review systems can simplify administrative requirements for managing inventory. For example, inventory analysts can be assigned to review groups of SKUs at fixed intervals, for instance Group A every Monday, Group B on Tuesday, and so on. In practice, the review period also depends on the capacity of the staff to perform the work.

Periodic review systems are often used to control "C" items in an ABC classification, and "A" items are usually controlled using continuous review systems. The greater the control placed on monitoring inventory levels, the higher the cost of monitoring work and information processing, but better control may result in fewer stockouts and improved customer service.

Fixed Period Systems with Stochastic Demand

Things change when demand is highly variable. If a one-week economic time interval ordering policy is applied to the data in Exhibit 12.9, we find a high risk of a shortage, as the chart in Exhibit 12.27 shows. As with the FQS system, we see a substantial risk of a stockout, even though the average daily demand is the same over the 10-week period. Therefore, we must carry safety stock to protect against shortages.

We will assume that demand during some time interval t is described by a probability distribution having mean μ_t and standard deviation σ_t. The optimal time between review periods (T) is computed by Equation (12.11). The replenishment level M under stochastic conditions is computed using the following formula:

$$M = \mu_{T+L} + z \times \sigma_{T+L} \qquad \textbf{(12.13)}$$

where μ_{T+L} = expected demand during the time interval $T + L$
$\qquad z$ = the number of standard deviations necessary to achieve the acceptable service level
$\qquad \sigma_{T+L}$ = standard deviation of demand during the time interval $T + L$.

Note that this calculation is similar to Equation (12.12) in that the first term, μ_{T+L}, represents the expected demand during the review period and lead time, and $z \times \sigma_{T+L}$ represents the safety stock required.

We can use the same statistical principles as in the stochastic demand model for the FQS to calculate μ_{T+L} and σ_{T+L}. If we know the mean μ_t and standard deviation σ_t for demand over a time interval t, then

$$\mu_{T+L} = \mu_t(T + L) \qquad \textbf{(12.14)}$$

Exhibit 12.27
Daily Ending Inventory for High Variability Sales Data

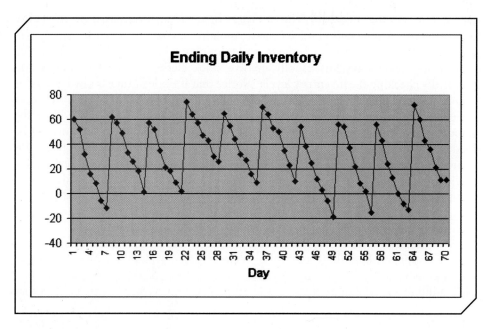

We may compute σ_{T+L} using the following formula:

$$\sigma_{T+L} = \sigma_t \sqrt{(T + L)} \qquad \textbf{(12.15)}$$

APPLYING THE MODEL

We will return to the Southern Office Supplies example where we previously computed $Q^* = 1,333$ reams and $r = 742$ reams, assuming a 95% service level and a 2-week lead time. We use the same assumptions that weekly demand is normal with a mean of 288.46 and a standard deviation of approximately 71.

Using Equation (12.11), we compute the review period as

$$T = Q^*/D = 1,333/15,000 = .0889 \text{ years}$$

If we assume 260 working days/year, this is approximately 5 weeks. From Equations (12.14) and (12.15), we obtain

$$\mu_{T+L} = \mu_t(T + L) = 288.46(5 + 2) = 2,019.22 \text{ units}$$

and

$$\sigma_{T+L} = \sigma_t\sqrt{T + L} = 71\sqrt{5 + 2} = 187.85 \text{ units}$$

Using Equation (12.13) and assuming a 5 percent risk of a stockout,

$$M = \mu_{T+L} + z\sigma_{T+L} = 2,019.22 + 1.645(187.85) = 2,328.23 \text{ units}$$

Therefore, we review the inventory position every 5 weeks and place an order to replenish the inventory up to a level of 2,328 units. Exhibit 12.28 shows a simulation of the operation of this system for Southern Office Supplies. The vertical double-headed arrows show the order quantities at each review period. Note that the safety stock maintains an adequate level of inventory to reduce the risk of stockouts.

Summary of Fixed Period Systems

A summary of fixed period systems is given in Exhibit 12.29. Exhibit 12.30 shows the system operation graphically. In Exhibit 12.29, at the time of the first review, a rather large amount of inventory (IP_1) is in stock, so the order quantity (Q_1) is

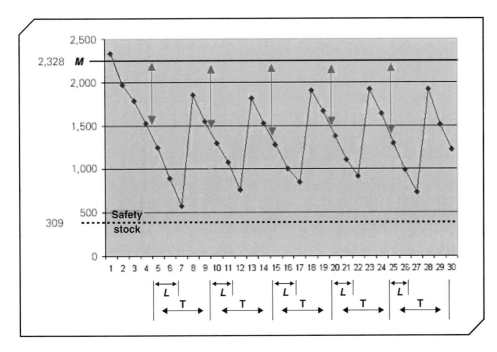

Exhibit 12.28
Simulation of Southern Office Supplies' Periodic Review Model

relatively small. Demand during the lead time was small, and when the order arrived, a large amount of inventory was still available. At the third review cycle, the stock level is much closer to zero since the demand rate has increased (steeper slope). Thus, the order quantity (Q_3) is much larger, and during the lead time, demand was high and some stockouts occurred. Note that when an order is placed at time T, it does not arrive until time $T + L$. Thus, in using a FPS, managers must cover the risk of a stockout over the time period $T + L$ and, therefore, must carry more inventory.

Exhibit 12.29
Summary of Fixed Period
Inventory Systems

Managerial Decisions	Review Period (*T*) and Replenishment Level (*M*)
Ordering decision rule	Place a new order every T periods, where the order quantity at time t is $Q_t = M - IP_t$. IP_t is the inventory position at the time of review, t.
Key characteristics	The review period, T, is constant and placing an order is time triggered.
	The order quantity Q_t varies at each review period.
	M is chosen to include the demand during the review period and lead time, plus any safety stock.
	Stockouts can occur when demand is stochastic and can be addressed by adding safety stock to the expected demand during time $T + L$ (see Equation (12.13)).

Exhibit 12.30
Operation of a Fixed Period
System (FPS)

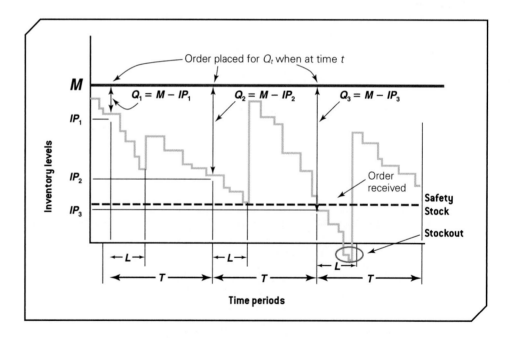

CHOOSING BETWEEN FIXED ORDER QUANTITY AND FIXED PERIOD SYSTEMS

The choice of which system—FQS or FPS—to use is not an easy decision—it is part science and part human judgment. It depends on a variety of factors, such as how many total SKUs the firm must monitor, whether computer or manual systems are used, availability of technology and human resources, the ABC profile, and the strategic focus of the organization, such as customer service or cost minimization.

FQSs maintain tighter control of inventories, because orders can be placed to ensure that stockout risks are minimized. Nevertheless, FQSs are somewhat more complex because they require continual monitoring and updating of the inventory position. This requires that accurate records of inventory positions be maintained. With today's computer systems, however, this is usually easy to do.

FPS systems are easier to manage because the inventory levels need only be checked periodically. Inventory analysts can be assigned groups of SKUs to review at fixed intervals, for instance, Group A every Monday, Group B on Tuesday, and so on. Also, in situations in which manual records must be updated, FPS systems might be more economical than FQS. FPSs are useful when a large number of items is ordered from the same supplier, because many individual orders can be placed at the same time. Thus, shipments can be consolidated into single purchase orders and trucks, resulting in lower freight rates.

An item's classification in an ABC scheme often influences the choice of inventory control system. A items require closer control and therefore benefit from more frequent reveiw periods in an FPS system or perhaps consideration of using an FQS system. C items would require less control and therefore FPS systems with longer review periods are more useful. Managers should consider the advantages and disadvantages of each type of system and the relative economics in making a decision.

SPECIAL MODELS FOR INVENTORY MANAGEMENT

Learning Objective
To learn special inventory models that consider back orders, price breaks, one-time ordering opportunities, and simulation as methods for inventory analysis.

Many other models have been developed for special inventory situations. It is impossible to describe all of them in this chapter. We will describe a few of the more common models that relate to some important types of inventory decisions.

EOQ Model with Back Orders

There are cases in which it may be desirable—from an economic point of view—to plan for and allow shortages. This situation is most common when the value per unit of the inventory is very high, and hence the inventory-holding cost is high. An example is a new-car dealer's inventory. Most customers do not find the specific car they want in stock but are willing to back-order it. Allowing back orders reduces the total cost for the customer because inventory-holding costs would typically be incorporated into the sales price, but it requires the customer to wait for the product. We present an extension to the EOQ model that allows for back orders. If we let S indicate the number of back orders that have accumulated when an order of size Q is received, the inventory system has these characteristics:

- With S back orders existing when a new shipment of size Q arrives, the S back orders will be shipped to the appropriate customers immediately, and the remaining $(Q - S)$ units will be placed in inventory.
- $Q - S$ will be the maximum inventory level.
- The inventory cycle of T days will be divided into two distinct phases: t_1 days when inventory is on hand and orders are filled as they occur and t_2 days when there is a stockout and all orders are placed on back order.

The inventory pattern for this model, where negative inventory represents the number of back orders, is shown in Exhibit 12.31.

Back-ordering costs usually involve labor and special-delivery costs directly associated with the handling of back orders. Another portion of the back-order cost can be expressed as a loss of goodwill with customers due to their having to wait for their orders. Since the goodwill cost depends on how long the customer has to wait, it is customary to adopt the convention of expressing all back-order costs in terms of how much it costs to have a unit on back order for a stated period of

Exhibit 12.31
Inventory Pattern for Back-Order Situation

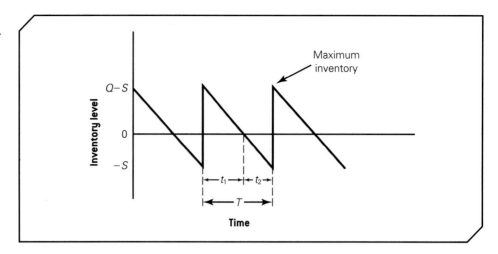

time. This method of computing cost is similar to the method we used to compute the inventory-holding cost.

Admittedly, the back-order cost rate (especially the customer goodwill cost) is difficult to determine in practice. However, noting that EOQ models are rather insensitive to the cost estimates, we should feel confident that reasonable estimates of the back-order cost will lead to a good approximation of the overall minimum-cost inventory decision. Letting C_b be the cost to maintain one item on back order for one year, the three sources of cost in this planned-shortage inventory model can be expressed as in the following equations:

$$\text{Inventory-holding cost} = \frac{(Q - S)^2}{2Q} C_h$$

$$\text{Ordering cost} = \frac{D}{Q} C_o$$

$$\text{Back-ordering cost} = \frac{S^2}{2Q} C_b$$

Thus our total-annual-cost back-order model expression (TC) becomes

$$TC = \frac{(Q - S)^2}{2Q} C_h + \frac{D}{Q} C_o + \frac{S^2}{2Q} C_b \qquad \textbf{(12.16)}$$

The minimum-cost values for Q and S can be found using calculus and are

$$Q^* = \sqrt{\frac{2DC_o}{C_h}\left(\frac{C_h + C_b}{C_b}\right)} \qquad \textbf{(12.17)}$$

and

$$S^* = Q^*\left(\frac{C_h}{C_h + C_b}\right) \qquad \textbf{(12.18)}$$

APPLYING THE MODEL

To illustrate the use of this model, consider an electronics company that is concerned about an expensive part used in television repair. The cost of the part is $125, and the inventory-holding rate is 20 percent. The cost to place an order is estimated to be $40. The annual demand, which occurs at a constant rate throughout the year, is 800 parts. Currently, the inventory policy is based on the EOQ model, with

$$Q^* = \sqrt{\frac{2DC_o}{C_h}} = \sqrt{\frac{2(800)(40)}{0.20(125)}} = 51 \text{ parts}$$

The total annual cost of inventory-holding and ordering has been

$$TC = \frac{1}{2}QC_h + \frac{D}{Q}C_o = \frac{1}{2}(51)(0.20)(125) + \left(\frac{800}{51}\right)(40)$$

$$= \$637.50 + 627.50 = \$1,265.$$

Because of the relatively high inventory investment, back-ordering is being considered.

On an annual basis, an item back-order cost of \$60 was assigned. Using Equations (12.17) and (12.18), the optimal order quantity, Q^*, and the optimal number of back orders, S^*, become

$$Q^* = \sqrt{\frac{2(800)(40)}{0.20(125)}\left(\frac{0.20(125) + 60}{60}\right)} = 60 \text{ parts}$$

and

$$S^* = 60\left(\frac{0.20(125)}{0.20(125) + 60}\right) = 18 \text{ parts}$$

Both Q^* and S^* have been rounded to whole numbers to simplify the remaining calculations. We find the following total costs associated with the inventory policy by using Equation (12.16) as follows:

$$\text{Inventory-holding cost} = \frac{(Q - S)^2}{2Q}C_h$$

$$= \frac{(60 - 18)^2}{2(60)}(0.20)(\$125) = \$367.50$$

$$\text{Ordering cost} = \frac{D}{Q}C_o = \frac{800}{600}(\$40) = \$533.33$$

$$\text{Back-ordering cost} = \frac{S^2}{2Q}C_h = \frac{(18)^2}{2(60)}(\$60) = \$162.00$$

The total cost is \$1,062.83, and hence the back-ordering policy provides a \$1,265 − \$1,062.83 = \$202.17, or 16 percent, cost reduction when compared to the EOQ model. Note that the daily demand for the part is (800 parts)/(250 days) = 3.2 parts per day. Since the maximum number of back orders is 18, we see that the length of the back-order period will be 18/3.2 = 5.6 days.

Quantity Discount Model

Many suppliers offer discounts for purchasing larger quantities of goods. This often occurs because of economies of scale of shipping larger loads, from not having to break apart boxes of items, or simply as an incentive to increase total revenue. You might have noticed such incentives at stores like Amazon.com, where CDs or DVDs are often advertised in discounted bundles—for example, two CDs by the same artist for a lower price than buying them individually.

To incorporate quantity discounts in the basic EOQ model requires us to include the purchase cost of the item in the total cost equation. We did not include the purchase cost of the item in the EOQ model because it does not affect the optimal order quantity. Because the annual demand is constant, the total annual purchase cost remains the same no matter what the individual order quantities are. However, when the unit price varies by order quantity, as would be the case with price breaks for quantity discounts, we need to incorporate that into the model. For example, a company might offer several discount categories. As an example, suppose that for every item ordered up to 1,000, a base unit price applies; if the order is for 1,001 to 2,000 items, a discounted unit price (of, perhaps, 2 percent) applies; for every additional item ordered beyond 2,000, a larger discount (say, 4 percent) applies. We cannot use the EOQ formula, because different purchase costs result in different holding-cost rates, and a calculated EOQ may not even fall within the appropriate discount category.

To compute the optimal order quantity, a three-step procedure is used.

Step 1. Compute Q^* using the EOQ formula for the unit cost associated with each discount category.

Step 2. For Q^*s that are too small to qualify for the assumed discount price, adjust the order quantity upward to the nearest order quantity that will allow the product to be purchased at the assumed price. If a calculated Q^* for a given price is larger than the highest order quantity that provides the particular discount price, that discount price need not be considered further, since it cannot lead to an optimal solution.

Step 3. For each of the order quantities resulting from steps 1 and 2, compute the total annual cost using the unit price from the appropriate discount category. The total annual cost can be found by adding the purchase cost (annual demand, D, times the unit cost, C) to Equation (12.6):

$$TC = \frac{Q}{2}C_h + \frac{D}{Q}C_o + DC \qquad \textbf{(12.19)}$$

The order quantity yielding the minimum total annual cost is the optimal order quantity.

APPLYING THE PROCEDURE

We illustrate this procedure using the example illustrated for the EOQ model. Suppose that the manufacturer of mouthwash offers this quantity-discount schedule:

Discount Category	Order Size	Discount	Unit Cost
1	0 to 3,999	0	$12.00
2	4,000 to 11,999	3%	11.64
3	12,000 and over	5%	11.40

The 5 percent discount looks attractive; however, the 12,000-case order quantity is substantially more than the EOQ recommendation of 919 cases. The purchase discount might be outweighed by the larger holding costs that would have to be incurred if this quantity was ordered.

The Excel spreadsheet in Exhibit 12.32 performs the necessary calculations. In column F we place the larger of the EOQ and the minimum order size for each discount category. For example, the EOQ for discount category 2 is

$$Q_2^* = \sqrt{2DC_o/C_h} = \sqrt{\frac{2(24,000)(38)}{(0.18)(11.64)}} = 933$$

However, since this is below the minimum required order size, we adjust the order quantity up to 4,000. Similarly, the EOQ for discount category 3 is 943, so we set the order quantity to 12,000. The cost calculations appear in columns G through J.

As you can see, a decision to order 4,000 units at the 3 percent discount rate yields the minimum-cost solution. Note that the sum of the inventory and ordering

Exhibit 12.32 Spreadsheet for Quantity-Discount Model Calculations (Quantity Discount Model.xls)

	A	B	C	D	E	F	G	H	I	J
1	**Quantity Discount Inventory Model**									
2										
3	Annual demand		24,000							
4	Cost per unit		$ 12.00							
5	Carrying charge		18%							
6	Order cost		$ 38.00							
7										
8		Min.			Unit		Annual		Annual	Annual	Total
9	Discount	Order		Unit	Holding	Order	Holding		Ordering	Purchase	Annual
10	Category	Size	Discount	Cost	Cost	Quantity	Cost		Cost	Cost	Cost
11	1	EOQ	0%	$12.00	$ 2.16	919	$ 992		$ 992	$288,000	$289,985
12	2	4,000	3%	$11.64	$ 2.10	4000	$ 4,190		$ 228	$279,360	$283,778
13	3	12,000	5%	$11.40	$ 2.05	12000	$ 12,312		$ 76	$273,600	$285,988

costs with $Q^* = 4,000$ is $4,190.40 + 228.00 = $4,418.40. This portion of the total cost is substantially more than the $1,984.90 cost associated with the 919-unit order size. In effect, the quantity-discount savings of 3 percent per unit is so great that we are willing to operate the inventory system with a substantially higher inventory level and substantially higher inventory-holding cost. Provided space is available to handle larger inventories, purchasing in larger quantities to obtain discounts is economically sound. Exhibit 12.33 shows a graph of the total cost that clearly shows the effect of the price breaks on the total cost and the optimal order quantity.

Exhibit 12.33 Graph of Total Cost for Quantity Discount Example

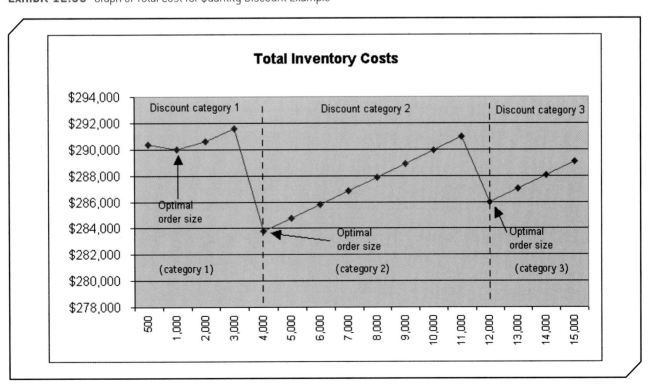

Single-Period Inventory Model

The single-period inventory model applies to inventory situations in which one order is placed for a good in anticipation of a future selling season where demand is uncertain. At the end of the period the product has either sold out or there is a surplus of unsold items to sell for a salvage value. Single-period models are used in situations involving seasonal or perishable items that cannot be carried in inventory and sold in future periods. One example is the situation faced by Banana Republic in one of the opening episodes; others would be ordering dough for a pizza restaurant, which stays fresh for only 3 days, and purchasing daily newspapers and seasonal holiday items such as Christmas trees. In such a single-period inventory situation, the only inventory decision is how much of the product to order at the start of the period. Because newspaper sales are a typical example of the single-period situation, the single-period inventory problem is sometimes referred to as the *newsvendor problem.*

The newsvendor problem can be solved using a technique called *marginal economic analysis*, which compares the cost or loss of ordering one additional item with the cost or loss of not ordering one additional item. The costs involved are defined as

c_s = the cost per item of overestimating demand (salvage cost); this cost represents the loss of ordering one additional item and finding that it cannot be sold.

c_u = the cost per item of underestimating demand (shortage cost); this cost represents the opportunity loss of not ordering one additional item and finding that it could have been sold.

The optimal order quantity is the value of Q^* that satisfies Equation (12.20):

$$P(\text{demand} \leq Q^*) = \frac{c_u}{c_u + c_s}$$ **(12.20)**

To illustrate this model, let us consider a buyer for a department store who is ordering fashion swimwear. The purchase must be made in the winter, and the store plans to hold an August clearance sale to sell any surplus goods by July 31. Each piece costs $40 per pair and sells for $60 per pair. At the sale price of $30 per pair, it is expected that any remaining stock can be sold during the August sale. We will assume that a uniform probability distribution ranging from 350 to 650 items, shown in Exhibit 12.34, describes the demand. The expected demand is 500.

The retailer will incur the cost of overestimating demand whenever it orders too much and has to sell the extra items available after July. Thus, the cost per item of overestimating demand is equal to the purchase cost per item minus the August sale price per item; that is, $c_s = \$40 - \$30 = \$10$. In other words, the retailer will lose $10 for each item that it orders over the quantity demanded. The cost of underestimating demand is the lost profit (opportunity loss) due to the fact that it could

Exhibit 12.34
Probability Distribution for Single Period Model

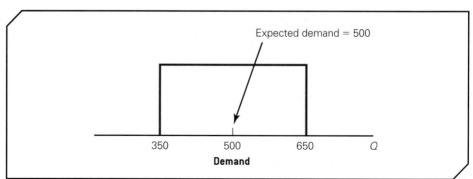

have been sold but was not available in inventory. Thus the per-item cost of under-estimating demand is the difference between the regular selling price per item and the purchase cost per item; that is, $c_u = \$60 - \$40 = \$20$. The optimal order size must satisfy this condition:

$$P(\text{demand} \leq Q^*) = \frac{c_u}{c_u + c_s} = \frac{20}{20 + 10} = \frac{20}{30} = \frac{2}{3}$$

Because the demand distribution is uniform, the value of Q^* is two-thirds of the way from 350 to 650. Thus, $Q^* = 550$ swimwear SKUs. Note that whenever $c_u < c_s$, the formula leads to the choice of an order quantity more likely to be less than demand; hence a higher risk of a stockout is present. However, when $c_u > c_s$, as in the example, the optimal order quantity leads to a higher risk of a surplus.

If the demand distribution were other than uniform, then the same process applies. To illustrate, suppose demand is normal with a mean of 500 and a standard deviation of 100. With $c_u = \$20$ and $c_s = \$10$ as previously computed, the optimal order quantity, Q^*, must still satisfy the requirement that $P(\text{demand} \leq Q^*) = 2/3$. We simply use the table of areas under the normal curve (Appendix A) to find the Q^* where this condition is satisfied. This is shown in Exhibit 12.35.

In Exhibit 12.35, the area to the left of Q^* is $P(\text{demand} \leq Q^*) = .667$. Therefore, the area between the mean, 500, and Q^* is .1667. This fact allows us to use Appendix A and determine that Q^* is $z = 0.43$ standard deviations above the mean. Therefore,

$$Q^* = \mu + 0.43\sigma = 500 + .43(100) = 543$$

Simulation Models for Inventory Analysis

In this chapter, we have concentrated on simple analytical inventory-decision models. But what should you do when the characteristics of an inventory system do not appear to agree with the assumptions of any inventory decision model? In this case, there are two alternatives: (1) attempt to develop and use a specially designed decision model that correctly reflects the characteristics of the system, or (2) develop and experiment with a computer simulation model that will indicate the impact of various decision alternatives on the cost of operating the system. Computer simulation is a powerful tool because it does not rely on restrictive assumptions the way that many analytical models do. Simulation has the flexibility to model unique features such as actual probability distributions that are difficult to represent in purely mathematical terms (see the OM Spotlight: Risk-Based Inventory Modeling

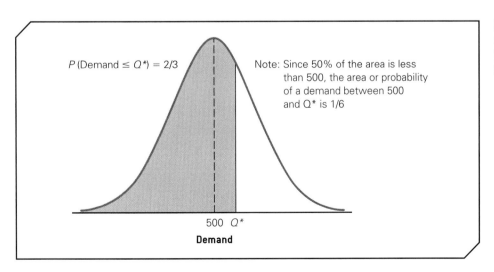

Exhibit 12.35
Optimal Order Quantity for Normally Distributed Demand Case

at Weyerhaeuser). However, building and using a simulation model can be expensive and usually requires more effort and time than analytical models. Supplementary Chapter D provides a general introduction to computer simulation in OM and includes an application to inventory analysis.

OM SPOTLIGHT

Risk-Based Inventory Simulation Modeling at Weyerhaeuser[10]

PR NewsWire
WEYERHAEUSER COMPANY

In the pulp and paper industry, pulp mills use large outside storage facilities that store inventories of wood chips. These serve as buffers against differences between mill supply and demand to reduce stockout risk and also act as a hedge against changes in wood prices and allow timely buying when prices are low. However, aging of wood during storage can affect its properties, resulting in color deterioration, decreased pulp yield, lower quality, and higher processing costs. Weyerhaeuser developed a computer model called the Springfield Inventory Target model (SPRINT) to assist inventory managers in dealing with risk in inventory-level decisions. The model projects chip inflows, outflows, and inventory levels by time period for any length of time in the future and helps managers to answer such questions as How reliable are inventory projections? What is the stockout risk in each time period? What are the total inventory costs in each period? Given future projections, what is the optimal inventory level?

The model uses probability distributions for each chip supply or usage volume and uses simulation to project expected chip deliveries, usages, and ending inventories over time, allowing the manager to assess the probability of a stockout and to translate this risk into a dollar cost. By repeatedly running the simulation model for different scenarios, the model helps managers to identify the inventory level that results in the minimum total inventory cost, balancing carrying costs with stockout costs. SPRINT has taken a lot of the guesswork out of making inventory decisions by providing objective assessments of costs and risks. Its principal benefit has been to allow managers to reduce inventories and stay within acceptable risk levels, lowering annual inventory costs by at least $2 million.

SOLVED PROBLEMS

SOLVED PROBLEM #1

Perform an ABC analysis for the items in Exhibit 12.36.

Solution:
Sorting the items in the descending order of total value we get the data in Exhibit 12.37.

The first four items account for 53 percent of dollar value and 16.6 percent of the items carried, while the last three items account for about 10 percent of the dollar value. Thus, the following classification would be

reasonable. There is no correct breakdown into A, B, and C categories, so the decision is part science (ABC analysis) and part management judgment.

Inventory Classification	Item Number
A	4, 3, 5, 12
B	11, 7, 6, 10, 8
C	9, 1, 2

Exhibit 12.36
ABC Data for Solved Problem #1

Item No.	Annual Item Usage	Item Value $	Item No.	Annual Item Usage	Item Value $
1	8,800	$68.12	7	112,000	$ 7.59
2	9,800	58.25	8	198,000	3.19
3	23,600	75.25	9	210,000	2.98
4	40,000	53.14	10	168,000	4.27
5	60,000	26.33	11	100,000	9.00
6	165,000	4.52	12	7,000	13.57

Exhibit 12.36
ABC Data for Solved Problem #1

Exhibit 12.37 Data for Solved Problem 1 Solution

Item No.	Annual Usage	Item Value $	Total $ Value	Cumulative No. Items	Cumulative Percent of Items	Cumulative Dollars $	Cumulative Percent of Value
4	40,000	53.14	2,125,600	40,000	3.43%	2,125,600	17.61%
3	23,600	75.25	1,775,900	63,600	5.46	3,901,500	32.32
5	60,000	26.33	1,579,800	123,600	10.61	5,481,300	45.40
12	70,000	13.57	949,900	193,600	16.62	6,431,200	53.27
11	100,000	9.00	900,000	293,600	25.20	7,331,200	60.73
7	112,000	7.59	850,080	405,600	34.81	8,181,280	67.77
6	165,000	4.52	745,800	570,600	48.97	8,927,080	73.95
10	168,000	4.27	717,360	738,600	63.39	9,644,440	79.89
8	198,000	3.19	631,620	936,600	80.38	10,276,060	85.12
9	210,000	2.98	625,800	1,146,600	98.40	10,901,860	90.31
1	8,800	68.12	599,456	1,155,400	99.16	11,501,316	95.27
2	9,800	58.25	570,850	1,165,200	100	12,072,166	100.00

SOLVED PROBLEM #2

A wholesaler of consumer electronics operates 52 weeks per year. The following information is for one of the video cassette recorders that it stocks and sells.

Demand = 4,500 units/year
Standard deviation of weekly demand = 12 units
Ordering costs = $40/order
Holding costs (C_h) = $3/unit/year
Cycle-service level = 90% (z-value = 1.28)
Lead time = 2 weeks
Number of weeks per year = 52 weeks

1. Using the fixed order quantity system to control inventory, compute the EOQ.

2. Compute the reorder point and state the order decision rule.

3. Compute the total order and inventory-holding costs.

The firm decided to change to a fixed period system to control the item's inventory.

4. Compute the replenishment level.

5. Suppose it is time to review the inventory position, and the current inventory = 300 units (no sched-

uled receipts or back orders). Compute the number of units, if any, that need to be ordered using a fixed period system.

6. Compare safety stock between the fixed order quantity and fixed period models. Why the difference?

Solution:

1. $EOQ = \sqrt{\dfrac{2DC_o}{C_h}} = \sqrt{\dfrac{2(4,500)40}{3}}$

   $= 346.4 \rightarrow 346$ units

2. $R = dL + z\sigma_L = (4,500/52)2 + 1.28(12\sqrt{2})$
   $= 173.08 + 21.72 = 194.8 \rightarrow 195$ units

   Order decision rule: Place a new order for 346 units when the inventory position drops to or past the reorder point of 195 units.

3. $TC = \dfrac{1}{2}QC_h + \dfrac{D}{Q}C_o$

   $= (346/2) \times \$3 + (4,500/346) \times \$40$
   $= \$519 + \$519 = \$1,038$

4. $T = \dfrac{EOQ}{D}(52 \text{ weeks/year}) = \dfrac{346}{4,500}(52)$

$= 4.00$ weeks

$M = d(T + L) + z\sigma_{T+L}$

$= \dfrac{4,500}{52}(4 + 2) + 1.28(12)\sqrt{(4 + 2)}$

$= 519.23 + 37.62 = 556.85 = 557$

5. Order quantity $(Q_1) = M - IP_1 = 557 - 300 = 257$ units

6. Safety stock for the fixed order quantity model is 21.7 units versus 37.8 units for the fixed period model. This is due to the fact that the Q and R model must protect against stockouts over the lead time (L), while the T and M model must protect against stockouts over a longer time period, $T + L$. By reducing lead times and review periods, safety stock can be reduced. It cost $48.3 more to carry the safety stock for the T and M system than the Q and R system (that is, $37.8 - 21.7$ units times $3/unit/year = \$48.3$) to maintain the same service level of 90 percent.

SOLVED PROBLEM #3

Assume the quantity-discount schedule in Exhibit 12.38 is appropriate.

Exhibit 12.38 Data for Solved Problem 3

Order Size	Discount	Unit Cost
0 to 49	0%	$30.00
50 to 99	5	28.50
100 or more	10	27.00

If annual demand is 150 units, ordering cost is $20 per order, and annual inventory-carrying cost is 25 percent, what order quantity would you recommend?

Solution:
Following the quantity discount procedure, we compute:

$Q_1 = \sqrt{2(150)(20)/[0.25(30)]} = 28.28;$
use $Q_1 = 28$

$Q_2 = \sqrt{2(150)(20)/[0.25(28.5)]} = 29.02;$
use $Q_2 = 50$ for a 5% discount

$Q_3 = \sqrt{2(150)(20)/[0.25(27)]} = 29.81;$
use $Q_3 = 100$ for a 10% discount

Category	Unit Cost	Order Quantity	Inventory Cost	Order Cost	Purchase Cost	Total Cost
1	$30.00	28	$105.00	$107	$4,500	$4,712.00
2	28.50	50	178.13	60	4,275	4,335.00
3	27.00	100	337.50	30	4,050	4,417.50

$Q = 50$ to obtain the lowest total cost. The 5 percent discount is worthwhile.

SOLVED PROBLEM #4

Juanita Sutherland, the manager of Houston Oaks Aquarium Store, wants to set up a fixed period inventory control model to order the store's fish food. Cichlid Pellets in the 8-ounce jar is a top-selling SKU, so Juanita wants to demonstrate the advantages of formal inventory control methods to her district manager. Currently, she reviews this SKU and places an order every 2 months for 8,700 jars (that is, 52,000/6, or about 8,700) but has been experiencing stockouts of the item. This was the order policy in place at the store when she became the new store manager. She collected the following information:

Demand = 52,000 jars/year
Standard deviation of weekly demand = 110 jars
Ordering costs = $45/order
Holding costs $(C_h) = \$0.50$/jar/year
Cycle-service level = 98% (z-value = 2.05)
Lead time = 2 weeks
Number of weeks per year = 52 weeks

1. Define a fixed period model based on the economics of the store.

2. At the most recent review a store employee found 1,500 jars on hand with no scheduled receipts or back orders. How many jars should now be ordered?

3. If she changed to a fixed order quantity system, define this model.

4. Compare the total order and inventory-holding cost of the fixed order quantity system with their current order policy of $Q = 8,700$ jars.

Solution:

1. $EOQ = \sqrt{\dfrac{2DS}{H}} = \sqrt{\dfrac{2(52,000)45}{0.50}} = 3,060$ jars

$T = \dfrac{EOQ}{D}(52 \text{ weeks/year}) = \dfrac{3,060}{52,000}(52)$

$\quad = 3.06 \text{ weeks} \cong 3.0 \text{ weeks}$

$M = d(T + L) + z\sigma_{T+L}$

$\quad = \dfrac{52,000}{52}(3 + 2) + 2.05(110)\sqrt{(3 + 2)}$

$\quad = 5,000 + 504.2 = 5,504$ jars

Order decision rule: Place an order every 3 weeks where the order quantity equals $Q_t = 5,504 - IP_t$.

The current ordering policy of $T = 2$ months and a fixed $Q = 8,700$ jars is neither a fixed order quantity nor fixed period model but a combination of both (that is, both T and Q are fixed). One re-

sult of the current ordering policy is to create erratic average inventory levels with the fixed Q, so there are periods with excess inventory and then periods where stockouts occur.

2. $Q_1 = 5,504 - IP_1 = 5,504 - 1,500 = 4,004$ jars

3. First, we know from our previous calculations that the EOQ = 3,060 jars.

$R = dL + z\sigma_L = (52,000/52)(2) + 2.05(110)\sqrt{2}$

$\quad = 2,000 + 318.9 = 2,319$ jars

Order decision rule: Place a new order for 3,060 jars when the inventory position drops to or past the reorder point of 2,319 jars.

4. <u>Current Order Policy</u>

$TC = \dfrac{1}{2}QC_h + \dfrac{D}{Q}C_o$

$\quad = (8,700/2) \times 0.50 + (52,000/8,700) \times 45$

$\quad = \$2,175 + \$270 = \$2,445$

<u>Fixed Order Quantity Policy</u>

$TC = \dfrac{1}{2}QC_h + \dfrac{D}{Q}C_o$

$\quad = (3,060/2) \times 0.50 + (52,000/3,060) \times 45$

$\quad = \$765 + \$765 = \$1,530$

The total annual savings for this one SKU is substantial at \$915 (\$2,445 − \$1,530) and should help justify more formal inventory systems at the Houston Oaks Aquarium Store.

SOLVED PROBLEM #5

Grateful Fred sells souvenir T-shirts at rock concerts. The shirts are specially ordered with the city and date of the concert, so he cannot take them to another city after the concert. He buys the shirts for \$15 each and sells them for \$35 before and during the concert. He sells any remaining shirts outside the concert grounds for \$10 after the concert ends and can usually dispose of all of them. For a typical concert, demand is normally distributed, with a mean of 2,500 and standard deviation of 200. How many shirts should Fred order?

Solution:

$C_o = \$15 - \$10 = \$5$

$C_u = \$35 - 15 = \$20$

$P(\text{demand} \leq Q^*) = \dfrac{C_u}{C_u + C_o} = \dfrac{20}{20 + 5} = .80$

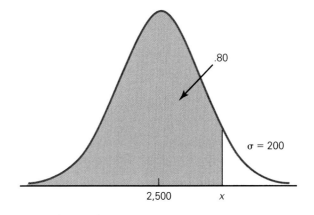

From Appendix A, $z = .84$. Thus,

$Q^* = \mu + .84\sigma = 2,500 + .84(200)$

$\quad = 2,668$ shirts

KEY TERMS AND CONCEPTS

ABC analysis
Anticipation inventory
Average total inventory at multiple stocking points
Back order
Back-order model
Chance of stockout and service levels
Cycle (order or lot size) inventory
Cycle counting
Dependent demand
Deterministic demand
Dynamic demand
Economic Order Quantity (EOQ)
Finished goods inventory
Fixed period system (FPS)
Fixed quantity system (FQS)
Independent demand
Inventory
Inventory costs
    Inventory holding (carrying) cost
    Order (setup) cost
    Shortage (stockout) costs
    Unit (item) cost
Inventory management
Inventory position (IP)
Lead time
Lost sale
Marginal economic analysis
Newsvendor problem

Number of SKUs
Operating, surplus, excess, obsolete, and new-product inventory
Perishable inventory
Pipeline inventory
Price breaks
Radio frequency identification (RFID) tags
Raw materials, component parts, subassemblies, and supplies
Reorder point
Safety stock inventory
Sensitivity analysis of EOQ
Service level
Single and two-bin system
Single-period model and decision rule
Static demand
Stochastic demand
Stock-keeping unit (SKU)
Stockout
Telematic diagnostic and monitoring systems
Time between orders (TBO)
Time period size
Total costs
    Inventory
    Order
    Safety Stock
Work-in-process (WIP) inventory

QUESTIONS FOR REVIEW AND DISCUSSION

1. Define inventory and provide some examples.

2. What is inventory management? Why is it an important function in OM?

3. How does inventory affect a firm's financial performance?

4. Explain the different types of inventories maintained in a typical value chain and state their purpose.

5. Discuss some of the issues that a small pizza restaurant might face in inventory management, forecasting, purchasing, and supplier partnerships.

6. Summarize the taxonomy for inventory management systems.

7. What is a SKU? Provide some examples in both goods and services.

8. Explain the difference between independent and dependent demand, deterministic and stochastic demand, and static and dynamic demand. Provide an example of an inventory item for each combination of these demand types (for example, independent, stochastic, and static, and so on).

9. Define *lead time*. What factors affect lead time?

10. Describe the two different types of stockouts that firms often face. What must be done to prevent them?

11. Define perishable inventory and provide some examples. How does fresh fruit differ from a concert seat even though both are perishable?

12. Explain the ABC classification for inventory. Of what value is ABC analysis?

13. What is cycle counting? How can it best be implemented?

14. Explain how modern technology such as bar coding and radio frequency identification help in inventory management.

15. What is a fixed quantity inventory system and how does it operate? What impact does demand variability have on the performance of a FQS?

16. Define inventory position. Why is inventory position used to trigger orders in a FQS rather than the actual stock level?

17. Explain how to determine the reorder point in a FQS.

18. Define and explain the different types of inventory costs that managers must consider in making replenishment decisions. How can these costs be determined in practice?

19. How does order cost differ from setup cost?

20. What is the EOQ model? What assumptions are necessary to apply it? How do these assumptions change the nature of the cycle inventory pattern graphically?

21. Explain how the total annual inventory cost is expressed in the EOQ model.

22. Discuss the sensitivity of the EOQ model's optimal solution to changes in the model parameters. Why is this important?

23. How must the EOQ model be changed to apply it in a stochastic demand situation?

24. Define service level. Why is it not necessarily desirable to attempt to attain a 100 percent service level?

25. Describe the structure and operation of a fixed period inventory system. Clearly explain how it differs from a FQS.

26. Would a pizza restaurant use a fixed order quantity or period system for fresh dough (purchased from a bakery on contract)? What would be the advantages and disadvantages of each in this situation?

27. Why does the fixed period model have to cover the time period of $T + L$ whereas the fixed order quantity model must cover only the time period L? Why is this important?

28. Explain the difference between the EOQ model and the extension to handle back orders.

29. Why are quantity discounts often given by suppliers? How do these affect the customer's inventory decisions?

30. Provide some situations where the single-period inventory model is applicable.

31. When is simulation useful in analyzing inventory systems?

32. List some products in your personal or family "inventory." How do you manage them? (For instance, do you constantly run to the store for milk? Do you throw out a lot of milk because of spoilage?) How might the ideas in this chapter change your way of managing these SKUs?

33. Interview a manager at a local business about its inventory and materials-management system, and prepare a report summarizing its approaches. Does it use any formal models? Why or why not? How does it determine inventory-related costs?

PROBLEMS AND ACTIVITIES

1. The Welsh Corporation uses 10 key components in one of its manufacturing plants. Perform an ABC analysis from the data in Exhibit 12.39. Explain your decisions and logic.

2. Develop an ABC histogram for the data in Exhibit 12.40.

3. MamaMia's Pizza purchases its pizza delivery boxes from a printing supplier. MamaMia's delivers on average 200 pizzas each month. Boxes cost 20 cents each, and each order costs $10 to process. Because of limited storage space, the manager wants to charge inventory holding at 30 percent of the cost. The lead time is 1 week, and the restaurant is open

Exhibit 12.39 ABC Data for Problem 1

SKU	Item Cost $	Annual Demand
WC219	$ 0.10	12,000
WC008	1.20	22,500
WC916	3.20	700
WC887	0.41	6,200
WC397	5.00	17,300
WC654	2.10	350
WC007	0.90	225
WC419	0.45	8,500
WC971	7.50	2,950
WC713	10.50	1,000

Exhibit 12.40
ABC Data for Problem 2

Item Number	Annual Usage	Unit Cost	Item Number	Annual Usage	Unit Cost
1	2,400	$19.51	11	500	$ 40.50
2	6,200	32.60	12	2,000	15.40
3	8,500	10.20	13	2,400	14.60
4	3,200	6.80	14	6,300	35.80
5	6,000	4.50	15	4,750	17.30
6	750	55.70	16	2,700	51.75
7	8,200	3.60	17	1,600	42.90
8	9,000	44.90	18	1,350	25.30
9	5,800	35.62	19	5,000	67.00
10	820	82.60	20	1,000	125.00

360 days per year. Determine the economic order quantity, reorder point, number of orders per year, and total annual cost. If the supplier raises the cost of each box to 25 cents, how would these results change?

4. Refer to the situation in Problem 3. Suppose the manager of MamaMia's wants to order 200 boxes each month. How much more than the optimal cost will be necessary to implement this policy?

5. A&M Industrial Products purchases a variety of parts used in small industrial tools. Inventory has not been tightly controlled, and managers think that costs can be substantially reduced. The items in Exhibit 12.41 comprise the inventory of one product line. Perform an ABC analysis of this inventory situation.

6. Given the weekly demand data in Exhibit 12.42, illustrate the operation of a continuous-review inventory system with a reorder point of 75, an order quantity of 100, and a beginning inventory of 125. Lead time is 1 week. All orders are placed at the end of the week. What is the average inventory and number of stockouts?

7. Crew Soccer Shoes Company is considering a change of its current inventory control system for soccer shoes. The information regarding the shoes is as follows:

Demand = 100 pairs/week
Lead time = 3 weeks
Order cost = $35/order
Holding cost = $2.00/pair/yr
Cycle service level = 95%
Standard deviation of weekly demand = 50
Number of weeks per year = 52

a. The company decides to use a fixed order quantity system. What would be the reorder point and the economic order quantity?

b. In this system, at the beginning of the current week, the materials manager, Emily Eddins, checked the inventory level of shoes and found 300 pairs. There were no scheduled receipts and no back orders. Should she place an order? Explain your answer.

c. If the company changes to a periodic review system and reviews the inventory every two weeks ($P = 2$), how much safety stock is required?

Exhibit 12.41
Data for Problem 5

Part Number	Annual Demand	Item Cost $	Part Number	Annual Demand	Item Cost $
A367	700	$ 0.04	P157	13	$ 3.10
A490	3,850	0.70	P232	600	0.12
B710	400	0.29	R825	15,200	0.12
C615	600	0.24	S324	20	30.15
C712	7,200	2.60	S404	400	0.12
D008	680	51.00	S692	75	12.10
G140	45	100.00	T001	20,000	0.005
G147	68,000	0.0002	X007	225	0.15
K619	2,800	5.25	Y345	8,000	0.16
L312	500	1.45	Z958	455	2.56
M582	8,000	0.002	Z960	2,000	0.001
M813	2,800	0.0012			

Exhibit 12.42 Data for Problem 6

Week	Demand	Week	Demand
1	25	7	50
2	30	8	35
3	20	9	30
4	40	10	40
5	40	11	20
6	25	12	25

Exhibit 12.43 Data for Problem 8

Day	Demand	Day	Demand
1	6	14	0
2	8	15	2
3	5	16	4
4	4	17	7
5	5	18	3
6	6	19	5
7	1	20	9
8	1	21	3
9	3	22	6
10	8	23	1
11	8	24	9
12	6	25	1
13	7		

8. Exhibit 12.43 gives the daily demand of a certain oil filter at an auto supply store. Illustrate the operation of a fixed order quantity inventory system by graphing the inventory level versus time if $Q = 40$, $R = 15$, and the lead time is 3 days. Assume that orders are placed at the end of the day and that they arrive at the beginning of the day. Thus, if an order is placed at the end of Day 5, it will arrive at the beginning of Day 9. Assume that 30 items are on hand at the start of Day 1.

9. For the data given in Problem 8, illustrate the operation of a fixed period inventory system with a reorder level of 40, a reorder point of 15, and a review period of 5 days.

10. Wildcat Tools is a distributor of hardware and electronics equipment. Its socket wrench inventory needs better management. The information regarding the wrenches is as follows:

Demand = 50 wrenches per month
Lead time = 1 month
Order cost = $20/order
Holding cost = $2.40/wrench/yr
Back-order cost = $15/back order
Cycle-service level = 90%
Standard deviation of monthly demand = 20 wrenches
Current on-hand inventory is 65 wrenches, with no scheduled receipts and no backorders.

a. The company decides to use a continuous review system. What are the recommended reorder point, safety stock, and economic order quantity?

b. Based on the information calculated in part a, should an order be placed? If yes, how much should be ordered?

c. The company wants to investigate the fixed period system with a twice per month review ($P = 2$ weeks). How much safety stock is required?

11. Tune Football Helmets Company is considering changing the current inventory control system for football helmets. The information regarding the helmets is as follows:

Demand = 200 units/week
Lead time = 2 weeks
Order cost = $60/order
Holding cost = $1.50/unit/yr
Cycle-service level = 95%
Standard deviation of weekly demand = 60
Number of weeks per year = 52

a. The firm decides to use a fixed period system to control the inventory and to review the inventory every 2 weeks. At the beginning of the current week, D. J. Jones, the materials manager, checked the inventory level of helmets and found 450 units. There were no scheduled receipts and no back orders. How many units should be ordered?

b. If the firm changes to a fixed quantity system, what would be the reorder point and the economic order quantity?

12. The reorder point is defined as the demand during the lead time for the item. In cases of long lead times, the lead-time demand and thus the reorder point may exceed the economic order quantity, Q^*. In such cases, the inventory position will not equal the inventory on hand when an order is placed, and the reorder point may be expressed in terms of either inventory position or inventory on hand. Consider the EOQ model with $D = 5,000$, $C_o = \$32$, $C_h = \$2$, and 250 working days per year. Identify the reorder point in terms of inventory position and in terms of inventory on hand for each of these lead times.

a. 5 days
b. 15 days
c. 25 days
d. 45 days

13. The XYZ Company purchases a component used in the manufacture of automobile generators directly

from the supplier. XYZ's generator production, which is operated at a constant rate, will require 1,200 components per month throughout the year. Assume ordering costs are $25 per order, item cost is $2.00 per component, and annual inventory-holding costs are charged at 20 percent. The company operates 250 days per year, and the lead time is 5 days.

a. Compute the EOQ, total annual inventory-holding and -ordering costs, and the reorder point.

b. Suppose XYZ's managers like the operational efficiency of ordering in quantities of 1,200 items and ordering once each month. How much more expensive would this policy be than your EOQ recommendation? Would you recommend in favor of the 1,200-item order quantity? Explain. What would the reorder point be if the 1,200-item quantity were acceptable?

14. The maternity ward of a hospital sends one baby blanket home with each newborn baby. The following information is available for the baby blankets:

Demand = 80 blankets/week
Standard deviation in weekly demand = 7 blankets
Desired cycle-service level = 96%
Delivery lead time = 2 weeks (delivery of the blankets, not the babies!)
Annual holding cost = $2.00
Ordering cost = $8.00/order
Cost of one blanket = $6.00
The hospital is open 52 weeks each year.

a. As the new maternity ward manager, you decide to improve the current ordering methods used for items that are stocked in the maternity ward. Calculate the economic order quantity for baby blankets.

b. Baby blankets are currently ordered in quantities of 200. How much would the maternity ward save in total annual relevant costs by changing to the EOQ?

c. You decide that a fixed order quantity system will be used for ordering the blankets. Name and calculate what must be known for implementing such a system.

15. Tele-Reco is a new specialty store that sells television sets, videotape recorders, video games, and other television-related products. A new Japanese-manufactured videotape recorder costs Tele-Reco $600 per item. Tele-Reco's inventory-carrying cost is figured at an annual rate of 22 percent. Ordering costs are estimated to be $70 per order.

a. If demand for the new videotape recorder is expected to be constant at a rate of 20 items per month, what is the recommended order quantity for the videotape recorder?

b. What are the estimated annual inventory-holding and -ordering costs associated with this product?

c. How many orders will be placed per year?

d. With 250 working days per year, what is the cycle time for this product?

16. Nation-Wide Bus Lines is proud of the 6-week driver-training program it conducts for all new Nation-Wide drivers. The program costs Nation-Wide $22,000 for instructors, equipment, and so on and is independent of the number of new drivers in the class as long as the class size remains less than or equal to 35. The program must provide the company with approximately five new fully trained drivers per month. After completing the training program, new drivers are paid $1,800 per month but do not work until a full-time driver position is open. Nation-Wide views the $1,800 as a holding cost necessary to maintain a supply of newly trained drivers available for immediate service. Viewing new drivers as inventory SKUs, how large should the training classes be in order to minimize Nation-Wide's total annual training and new-driver idle-time costs? How many training classes should the company hold each year? What is the total annual cost of your recommendation?

17. Brauch's Pharmacy has an expected annual demand for a leading pain reliever of 800 boxes, which sell for $6.50 each. Each order costs $6.00, and the inventory-carrying charge is 20 cents. The expected demand during the lead time is normal, with a mean of 25 and a standard deviation of 3. Assuming 52 weeks per year, what reorder point provides a 95 percent service level? How much safety stock will be carried? If the carrying charge were 25 cents instead, what would be the total annual inventory-related cost?

18. A product with an annual demand of 1,000 SKUs has C_o = $30 and C_h = $8. The demand exhibits some variability such that the lead-time demand follows a normal distribution, with a mean of 25 and a standard deviation of 5.

a. What is the recommended order quantity?

b. What are the reorder point and safety-stock level if the firm desires at most a 2 percent probability of a stockout on any given order cycle?

c. If the manager sets the reorder point at 30, what is the probability of a stockout on any given order cycle? How many times would you expect to stock out during the year if this reorder point were used?

19. The B&S Novelty and Craft Shop in Bennington, Vermont sells a variety of quality handmade items to tourists. It will sell 300 hand-carved miniature replicas of a colonial soldier each year, but the demand pattern during the year is uncertain. The replicas sell for $20 each, and B&S uses a 15 percent annual inventory-holding cost rate. Ordering costs are $5 per order, and demand during the lead time follows a normal distribution, with a mean of 15 and a standard deviation of 6.
    a. What is the recommended order quantity?
    b. If B&S is willing to accept a stockout roughly twice a year, what reorder point would you recommend? What is the probability that B&S will have a stockout in any one order cycle?
    c. What is the safety-stock level and annual safety-stock cost for this product?

20. The manager of an inventory system believes that inventory models are important decision-making aids. Although the manager often uses an EOQ policy, he has never considered a back-order model because of his assumption that back orders are "bad" and should be avoided. However, with top level management pressure for cost reduction, you have been asked to analyze the economics of a back-ordering policy for some products. For a specific product with $D = 800$ units per year, $C_o = \$150$, $C_h = \$3$, and $C_b = \$20$, what is the economic difference in the EOQ and the back-order model? If the manager adds constraints that no more than 25 percent of the units may be back-ordered and that no customer will have to wait more than 15 days for an order, should the back-order inventory policy be adopted? Assume 250 working days per year. If the lead time for new orders is 25 days for the inventory system, find the reorder point for both the EOQ and the back-order models.

21. Marilyn's Interiors sells silk floral arrangements in addition to other home furnishings. Because space is limited and she does not want to tie up a lot of money in inventory, Marilyn uses a back-order policy for most items. A popular silk arrangement costs her $40 to assemble and Marilyn sells an average of 15 per month. Ordering costs are $30, and she values her inventory holding cost at 25 percent. Marilyn figures the back-order cost to be $40 annually. What is the optimal order quantity and planned back-order level? What if customer cancellations and other loss of goodwill increase the back-order cost to $100 annually?

22. Apply the EOQ model to the quantity-discount situation shown in the following data:

Discount Category	Order Size	Discount	Unit Cost
1	0 to 99	0 percent	$10.00
2	100 or more	3 percent	$ 9.70

Assume that $D = 500$ units per year, $C_o = \$40$, and the annual inventory-holding cost is 20 percent. What order quantity do you recommend?

23. Allen's Shoe Stores carries a basic black dress shoe for men that sells at an approximate constant rate of 500 pairs of shoes every three months. Allen's current buying policy is to order 500 pairs each time an order is placed. It costs $30 to place an order, and inventory-carrying costs have an annual rate of 20 percent. With the order quantity of 500, Allen's obtains the shoes at the lowest possible unit cost of $28 per pair. Other quantity discounts offered by the manufacturer are listed below:

Order Quantity	Price per Pair
0-99	$36
100-199	32
200-299	30
300 or more	28

What is the minimum-cost order quantity for the shoes? What are the annual savings of your inventory policy over the policy currently being used?

24. The J&B Card Shop sells calendars featuring a different Colonial picture for each month. The once-a-year order for each year's calendar arrives in September. From past experience the September-to-July demand for the calendars can be approximated by a normal distribution with $\mu = 500$ and $\sigma = 120$. The calendars cost $3.50 each, and J&B sells them for $7 each.
    a. If J&B throws out all unsold calendars at the end of July (that is, salvage value is zero), how many calendars should be ordered?
    b. If J&B reduces the calendar price to $1 at the end of July and can sell all surplus calendars at this price, how many calendars should be ordered?

25. The Gilbert Air-Conditioning Company is considering the purchase of a special shipment of portable air-conditioners manufactured in Mexico. Each unit will cost Gilbert $80 and it will be sold for $125. Gilbert does not want to carry surplus air-conditioners over until the following year. Thus all supplies will be sold to a wholesaler, who has agreed to take all surplus units for $50 per unit. Assume that the air-conditioner demand has a normal distribution with $\mu = 20$ and $\sigma = 6$.
    a. What is the recommended order quantity?
    b. What is the probability that Gilbert will sell all units it orders?

CASES

MARGATE HOSPITAL

Cost-containment activities have become particularly important to hospital operations managers, stimulated by major revisions in health care reimbursement policies and significant growth in marketing activities by private-sector health care organizations. Recognizing that poor inventory control policies reflect ineffective use of organizational assets, many hospital managers have sought to institute more systematic approaches to the control of supply inventories.

At Margate Hospital, analysts collected data on 47 disposable SKUs in a pulmonary therapy unit. These data are shown in Exhibit 12.44 (the file Margate ABC Data.xls is available on the Student CD-ROM). Four of the SKUs are designated as critical to patient care. The hospital administrator wants to develop better inventory management policies for these items. Using the data, propose a breakdown for an ABC analysis, and clearly outline how each category of items might be managed by the hospital.

Exhibit 12.44
Hospital Data for ABC Analysis

SKU	Total Annual Usage	Average Unit Cost		SKU	Total Annual Usage	Average Unit Cost	
1	212	$ 24.00		25	8	$ 58.00	
2	210	$ 5.00		26	7	$ 65.00	
3	172	$ 27.00		27	5	$ 86.00	
4	117	$ 50.00		28	5	$ 30.00	
5	100	$ 28.00		29	4	$ 84.00	
6	94	$ 31.00		30	4	$ 78.00	
7	60	$ 58.00		31	4	$ 56.00	
8	50	$ 21.00		32	4	$ 53.00	
9	48	$ 55.00		33	4	$ 49.00	
10	48	$ 15.00		34	4	$ 41.00	
11	33	$ 73.00		35	4	$ 20.00	
12	27	$210.00	Critical	36	3	$ 72.00	Critical
13	27	$ 7.00		37	3	$ 61.00	
14	19	$ 24.00		38	3	$ 8.00	
15	18	$ 45.00	Critical	39	2	$134.00	
16	15	$160.00	Critical	40	2	$ 67.00	
17	12	$ 87.00		41	2	$ 60.00	
18	12	$ 71.00		42	2	$ 52.00	
19	12	$ 50.00		43	2	$ 38.00	
20	12	$ 47.00		44	2	$ 29.00	
21	12	$ 33.00		45	1	$ 48.00	
22	10	$ 37.00		46	1	$ 34.00	
23	10	$ 34.00		47	1	$ 29.00	
24	8	$110.00					

COLORADO TECHNICAL COLLEGE[11]

At Colorado Technical College, demand patterns in the copy-center environment had been highly seasonal, following a similar pattern during each school year, and had exhibited an increasing trend from year to year. Requests for low-demand items (odd colors of paper, for example) were very erratic, while use of high-demand items (such as $8^1/2 \times 11$, white, three-hole paper) was predictably seasonal. Unacceptably high stock levels of low-demand items were being maintained, and emergency orders on high-demand items were frequent. Data records were sparse and had been kept with little consistency, often being just monthly orders with no record of beginning or ending inventories or increased inventory with no ordering. Several of the 75 stock-keeping items (SKUs) were obtained via discount cost schedules, and one source had a $150 minimum-order requirement. Lead times generally had minor variances, with means of 1 to 10 working days.

Storage space was insufficient to accommodate a 1-week supply during peak demand and was partitioned into product families. Stockout penalties were very high, and managers placed orders at the verbal request of the workers.

The workers were well seasoned, experienced, and highly proficient in the intuitive management of the copy center. Daily work schedules were highly erratic; hence, time available to maintain an inventory control system would be very irregular. Polite political tensions existed between managers and workers, resulting from a history of poor communication, lack of resources available to assist in controlling the inventory, lack of accountability for inventory decisions, and a previous failure to implement a manual inventory control system. The workers were resistant to management control, and managers were not satisfied with the way inventory was being managed. It was evident that an inventory system was needed to achieve a balance between the workers' need for flexibility to adapt to uncertain and highly varying demand and managers' desire that the inventory be managed efficiently.

The problem solution therefore required that the workers operate an inventory control system yet be unable to manipulate the system into practical ineffectiveness. The operators would have to be given sufficient historical demand data to allow for intelligent deviation from a suggested ordering pattern and the freedom to fine-tune the ordering patterns when those patterns began to violate the constraints of limited inventory space and high stockout penalties. System integrity would have to be beyond compromise, and any deviations from a suggested order pattern would be flagged to prevent accidental, duplicate, or oversized orders.

Questions for Discussion

1. How do the behavioral and political concerns affect the design of the inventory management system?
2. Develop a thorough set of recommendations, taking into account the unique characteristics of demand and other information that would affect inventory management decisions. Present your findings in a report to the copy center manager.

KINGSTON UNIVERSITY HOSPITAL

Bonnie Ebelhar, Kingston University's director of materials management, glanced again at the papers spread across her desk. She wondered where the week had gone. On Monday, the director of university operations, Drew Paris, had asked Ebelhar to look into the purchasing and supplies systems for the hospital. Paris specifically wanted Ebelhar to evaluate the current materials management system, identify ways to reduce costs, and recommend a final plan of action. Paris explained that the university was under pressure to cut expenses, and hospital inventory did not seem to be under control. Not knowing quite what to look for, Ebelhar had spent a good part of the week collecting information—information she had organized on the papers that now covered her desk.

As Ebelhar reviewed her notes, she was struck by the variations in order sizes and order frequencies for any given hospital stock-keeping item. In some cases, items stocked out before new orders came in, whereas for other items, excessively high stock levels were being carried at (too) many hospital stocking points. She wondered whether there might be a more efficient and economical way of managing the hospital and university's inventories. Ebelhar had been exposed to inventory control techniques during her undergraduate college days.

Hospital and university supply orders were classified as either regular stock or special order. The hospital was the originator of almost all special orders. Regular stock items were characterized by their long-standing and fre-

quent use throughout the university and hospital as well as by a low risk of obsolescence. When a hospital unit (department) needed a regular stock item, that unit generally requisitioned the item. If the item were in stock, it would be delivered by the unit's next delivery date. Last year, 19,000 requisitions had been submitted to university purchasing from the hospital units.

The process of adding an item to the regular university stock list took several months. To begin the process, one of the hospital's units had to submit a purchase request (not a purchase order) to university purchasing. After receiving such a request, university purchasing would determine whether or not to carry the item. When the university did not carry an item, individual hospital units could carry the item on a special-order basis. Special-order items were supposed to be those of an experimental nature or critical to patient health care. Hospital units requiring these special items bypassed the university purchasing system. Once a special order was placed, the hospital unit informed university purchasing so that it could eventually authorize payment on the vendor's invoice. Hospital unit coordinators or head nurses were responsible for preparing and/or authorizing special orders. In total, these special orders required a significant amount of work that took unit coordinators and head nurses away from their duties. This past year, the hospital's 31 units had issued 16,000 special orders. These were in addition to the hospital's 19,000 regular requisitions, mentioned previously.

A large number of these special orders were actually placed for supplies with widespread use throughout the hospital. In many of these cases, none of the hospital's units involved had ever requested university purchasing to include the item on the regular stock list. One unit's head nurse explained that many units were afraid of stocking out of these items if they were under university control. University purchasing didn't understand the importance and technical nature of hospital inventory. The nurse cited the months-long period university purchasing needed to place new items on the regular stock list and the long lead times sometimes involved in receiving orders requisitioned from the list.

A small but significant number of special orders were placed for or by doctors with specific brand preferences. They were unwilling to use particular items that purchasing ordered and stocked. Typically, the preferred brands were more expensive than the regular SKUs carried. These orders were most common where purchases could be broken up so that state bidding procedures did not have to be followed.

Record keeping varied by order type. University purchasing maintained ongoing records only on regular stock items. Once regular stock materials were delivered to a hospital unit, university inventory clerks input this information into the university computer. University purchasing record-keeping responsibilities ended once SKUs were delivered to a hospital unit. For special orders, the hospital was responsible for recording inventory on hand and disbursements. University purchasing kept no records on the hospital's special-order inventories or for the 215 secondary hospital stocking points.

Technically, the individual hospital units were responsible for keeping inventory records and controlling materials once they were in the unit. In practice, however, few of the hospital units had any formal methods of record keeping or inventory control. Unit coordinators or head nurses arranged the ordering of materials when supplies seemed low or when hospital doctors requested a specific item. For several years, there had not been any hospitalwide physical inventory audit in the 31 hospital units. The only recent inventory audit was by the Surgical Intensive Care Unit, which discovered large amounts of obsolete and overstocked inventory items.

Since the university was a state institution, strict bidding and purchasing procedures had to be followed for both regular stock and special orders. For example, three written bids were required for an individual order of $1,000 or more. The processing of these bids often took up to 2 months. For orders between $500 and $999, three telephone bids were necessary. In these situations, purchases could be made only from the lowest bidder. Orders under $500, or items on the state contract list, could be ordered over the phone, without any bids. State contract list items were those for which statewide needs had been combined and one contract let to cover all of them.

In emergency situations, university purchasing would authorize individual hospital departments to place both regular and special orders without following the state guidelines. Ebelhar had found evidence that some hospital units were abusing this procedure, by using emergency orders to circumvent bidding requirements on big-ticket items, when the preferred vendor was unlikely to be the lowest-priced supplier.

Vendors delivered the hospital's regular stock supplies to the university warehouse. After orders were checked in, notification was sent to the hospital storeroom, and then some or all of the regular order was transferred to the hospital storeroom. Since the hospital storeroom's capacity was limited, backup regular stock was retained at the university warehouse in some cases. Special orders were shipped directly to the hospital storeroom. Once the supplies reached the hospital storeroom, the clerks placed the items in numbered bins. In addition to receiving shipments, the hospital storeroom clerks prepared and made scheduled deliveries to the hospital units, conducted visual inventory checks of the bins, ordered replenishment stock, and filled any walk-up orders.

Each week, hospital storeroom clerks made one delivery to each of the hospital's 31 units; deliveries took place daily between 7:00 A.M. and 9:00 A.M. Once supplies were delivered to the unit, a unit assistant was responsible for stocking the unit's central supply area and resupplying any ancillary stocking locations. There were no dollar limits on the amount of supplies that a hospital unit could carry at any one time. As a result, most departments carried as many supplies as was physically possible. The stock levels of the central supply area in each of individual hospital units could vary dramatically from week to week. Stock levels in the ancillary locations, however, tended to remain constant. For example, a hospital cart would have a specific list of what items to carry and how many of each. Unit personnel would then be responsible for replenishing the cart, as needed, on a daily basis.

Ebelhar had gathered information on the costs of purchasing and storing hospital supplies. She estimated that, on average, the purchasing, payables, and receiving personnel spent 6 to 7 hours processing a single purchase order. Individual purchase orders typically included three supply items (SKUs). The average hospital storeroom's wage was $15 an hour; with employee benefits and associated overhead, the cost of one worker-hour came to $18.

Ebelhar realized that a significant amount of time was spent by hospital personnel in preparing requisitions and issuing special orders. However, she was unsure how to quantify this time. After all, anywhere from 1 to 15 hospital units might requisition a particular regular stock item before the university needed to issue another order. And, in the case of special orders, processing times could

Exhibit 12.45
Kingston University Hospital SKU Data*

		Case Size		Cost Per Case	Order Lead Time
Fetal Monitoring Kits		20 kits		$844.00	5 weeks
Strike Disinfectant		4 gallons		$ 64.20	2 weeks
Fetal Monitoring Kits+					
Beginning Balance	80	Week	1		
Receipts	125	Week	3		
Ending Balance	74	Week	16		
Strike Disinfectant++					
Beginning Balance	96	Week	1		
Receipts	200	Week	7		
Ending Balance	110	Week	16		

*These inventory balances are for the central hospital storeroom only. The receipts are reasonable estimates of their current order quantities (Q).
+Number of individual kits, not cases.
++In gallons, not cases.

range from a half-hour to half a day, depending on the item. Between the hospital storeroom and the university warehouse, the university allocated 26,750 square feet of storage space to hospital uses. As mentioned earlier, the university stored an average of $2.15 million in hospital supplies in this space. Records indicated that the average annual variable and semivariable cost for storage space this year would be $2.60 per square foot. Five warehouse workers and storeroom clerks were required to handle the hospital's supplies. These individuals each earned $24,000 a year; benefits and overhead rates for these employees were the same as for other personnel, about 20 percent. Other warehouse costs, including obsolescence and taxes, were expected to reach $100,000 this year.

Ebelhar wondered how to determine an inventory-carrying cost; she was not sure what to include in the computation. In her previous jobs, Ebelhar had normally included interest or other opportunity costs when determining carrying cost. In this situation, she was unsure as to what cost components to include in the inventory-carrying cost. After all, the state allocated funds for fairly specific purposes, and the university could draw down these funds whenever necessary. The state generated these funds through tax revenues and bond issues. Recently, the state had floated a bond issue at 8.9 percent.

After reviewing her notes on the hospital's materials management situation, Ebelhar decided to take a closer look at some individual regular stock items. She sorted through the papers on her desk and found two items of interest: Fetal Monitoring Kits and Strike Disinfectant. Both SKUs were considered critical to the hospital's operations. Data on these two SKUs are shown in Exhibits 12.45 to 12.48.

Ebelhar wondered whether inventory control techniques would improve inventory ordering policies and save the state and university money. As a starting point, she decided to use the information she had collected on

Exhibit 12.46
Kingston University Hospital Aggregate Weekly Demand as Measured by Hospital Requisitions

Week	Fetal Kits*	Strike+
1	12	31
2	14	27
3	0	1
4	1	12
5	5	11
6	9	8
7	8	4
8	7	15
9	26	15
10	11	16
11	6	10
12	10	9
13	2	8
14	8	5
15	7	10
16	5	4
Total	131	186
Mean	8.19	11.63
Standard deviation	6.12	8.02
Cycle-service level	97%	90%

*Fetal Monitoring Kit demand is quoted for individual kits, not cases.
+Strike Disinfectant demand is quoted in gallons.

the Fetal Monitoring Kits and the Strike Disinfectant to evaluate and compare various inventory management systems and decision rules. A few of the questions of interest to Ebelhar are as follows:

1. What are good estimates of order cost and inventory-holding cost?

2. Define and graph a fixed order quantity (Q and r) inventory system for the two example SKUs.

Exhibit 12.47
Kingston University Hospital Fetal Monitoring Kits—Special One-Time Audit Results

	Hospital Unit	On-Hand Supply*
1.	Thomas Wing	12
2.	David Wing—Obstetrics	14
3.	Burn Center	6
4.	Coronary	6
5.	Davis Wing	10
6.	Delivery Room	16
7.	Pediatric Intensive Care	8
8.	Emergency Room	16
9.	Surgical Intensive Care	18
	Total Average Stock	106

3. Compute the total order and inventory-holding costs for the Q and r system, and compare to their current order Qs.

4. Define and graph a fixed period (T and M) inventory system for the two example SKUs.

5. Evaluate the relative size of carrying inventory at one hospital main storeroom site, 31 hospital departments and wards, and 215 stocking points in rooms, carts, and so on. What are the implications? How many stocking points do you recommend and why? Justify.

6. What should Ebelhar recommend to improve inventory-related performance? Explain. Justify.

Given the hospital's climate, current practices, and the materials management situation, Ebelhar wondered whether inventory management could really make a difference at this hospital.

Exhibit 12.48
Kingston University Hospital Strike Disinfectant—Special One-Time Audit Results

	Hospital Unit	On-Hand Supply*
1.	Thomas Wing	2
2.	Blood Bank	8
3.	Burn Center	4
4.	Coronary	3
5.	Cardiac Cath Laboratory	5
6.	Andrew Wing	2
7.	Delivery Room	2
8.	Dentistry	1
9.	Emergency Room	2
10.	Family Practice	1
11.	Hematology	12
12.	Internal Medicine	2
13.	Medical Intensive Care	2
14.	Medical Technology	4
15.	Chris Wing	3
16.	David Wing—Obstetrics	6
17.	Operating Room	8
18.	Oral Surgery	5
19.	Otolaryngology	4
20.	Pediatric Intensive Care	2
21.	Radiology	2
22.	Renal Division	3
23.	Respiratory Therapy	6
24.	Surgical Intensive Care	14
	Total Average Stock	103

*On-hand supply of gallons of Strike Disinfectant found last week during the special audit. This count was taken on Thursday for all hospital units and their respective secondary stocking points.

ENDNOTES

[1] Lee, Louise, "Yes, We Have a New Banana," *BusinessWeek*, May 31, 2004, pp. 70–72.
[2] A more complete technical classification and survey of inventory problems is given in Silver, E. A., "Operations Research in Inventory Management," *Operations Research* 29 (1981), pp. 628–645.
[3] Grocery Manufacturers of America, "Full-Shelf Satisfaction—Reducing Out-of-Stocks in the Grocery Channel, 2002 Report. www.gmabrtands.com/publications
[4] Cantwell, Jim, "The How and Why of Cycle Counting: The ABC Method," *Production and Inventory Management* 26, no. 2, 1985, pp. 50–54.
[5] "Hot Potato," *Chief Information Officer (CIO) Magazine*, January 15, 2003, p. 72.
[6] "Chips Soon May Replace Bar Codes," *The Sun News*, Myrtle Beach, S.C., July 9, 2003, pp. 1D and 3D.
[7] Delany, K. J., "Inventory Tool to Launch in Germany," *The Wall Street Journal*, January 12, 2004, p. B5.
[8] "Accurate Inventory Fuels Nissan Plant's Drive to Add Third Production Line," *Frontline Solutions*, August 2000, pp. 25, 30.
[9] Hau, L. Lee, Billington, Corey, and Carter, Brent, "Hewlett-Packard Gains Control of Inventory and Service Through Design for Localization," *Interfaces* 23, no. 4, July–August, 1993, pp. 1–11.
[10] Finke, Gary, "Determining Target Inventories of Wood Chips Using Risk Analysis," *Interfaces* 14, no. 5, September–October 1984, pp. 53–58.
[11] This case was inspired by Hayes, Timothy R., "An Inventory Control System for The Colorado School of Mines Quick Copy Center," *Production and Inventory Management Journal* 35, no. 4, Fourth Quarter 1994, pp. 50–53.

Chapter Outline

CHAPTER 13

Resource Management

Learning Objectives

1. To understand aggregate planning and disaggregation in a high-level resource planning framework for both goods-producing and service-providing organizations.

2. To learn aggregate planning strategies, problem structure, and decision options for addressing fluctuating demand in goods-producing and service-providing organizations.

3. To learn how goods-producing organizations develop executable detailed plans and schedules by disaggregating aggregate plans.

4. To learn how service-providing organizations develop executable plans and schedules by disaggregating aggregate plans.

- "I had to idle all but 6 of my 18 employees because of a shortage of concrete," said Matthew Cunningham, president of a construction firm in West Palm Beach, Florida. "The last few months we averaged between 500 and 900 tons of poured concrete for sidewalks, but this month we will not pour more than 90 tons. They tell me China is to blame. The concrete industry should have done more planning and better forecasting of global demand!" continued Cunningham.[1]

- "Ever since we've expanded our product line, we've had difficulty in managing all the purchased parts and subassemblies we need to get the final products out," lamented Mark DeWitt, the plant manager at Reimer Enterprises. "You think?" smirked Sharon in a very cynical tone of voice. "Every time your department decides to schedule a different product, I'm forced to deal with a basketful of orders for each of the component parts. The bean counters are on my back to lower costs and the foremen keep telling me that we're either short on certain parts or that I ordered too much and they don't have room to store it. I'm ready for an extended vacation!" "I hear you loud and clear, Sharon," replied DeWitt. "I know I dropped the ball on this one. We certainly have to investigate better resource planning systems. We've grown so fast that I didn't realize how antiquated our manual documentation and production systems have gotten. The reason I called this meeting is to invite you to meet with some software vendors I have scheduled this afternoon."

- "The corporate office just doesn't get it! They set a budget and staffing level that doesn't fit this location. I can't do the work and ensure accuracy of the patient's prescriptions when the corporate office gives me an annual budget for only two pharmacists and two pharmacy technicians," exclaimed Bill Carr, the manager of a retail pharmacy in a high-growth suburban location. The store was part of a national pharmaceutical chain with over 1,000 locations in the United States. The pharmacy was open 16 hours a day on Monday through Saturday and 10 hours on Sunday. Carr established two shifts for these professionals but they were now exhausted. The most senior pharmacists had already threatened to quit if something wasn't done to correct the problem soon. Carr also had considered reducing the time the store was open, but that hurt store revenue.

> **Discussion Questions:** Can you cite any recent examples of poor resource management by businesses that you might have read about in the newspaper or business magazines? Think about planning a party or some student-related function. What resources do you need to pull it off, and how might you plan to ensure that you have everything at the right time?

Resource management *deals with the planning, execution, and control of all the resources that are used to produce goods or provide services in a value chain.* Resources include materials, equipment, facilities, information, technical knowledge and skills, and of course, people. Typical objectives of resource management are to (1) maximize profits and customer satisfaction, (2) minimize costs, or (3) for not-for-profit organizations such as government and churches, maximize benefits to their stakeholders.

Poor resource planning and management can have detrimental effects throughout the value chain as the first episode illustrates. In recent years, the United States consumed over 100 million metric tons of cement, the essential ingredient for concrete for building roads, dams, homes, and commercial buildings. Of that total, 19 million tons were imported. Industry experts say that growth and expansion in China along with poor aggregate planning by the industry is leading to worldwide shortages in the global concrete industry. One U.S. congressional leader, Mark Foley, a Republican from Florida, asked the Commerce Department to investigate what can be done to alleviate the cement shortages. "If left unaddressed, a slowdown in the construction industry could have a cascading effect on other sectors of the economy," Representative Foley said in the letter.[2]

In complex manufacturing environments, trying to manage inventories of purchased parts, subassemblies, and other components is a complex task, as the second episode suggests. It is quite different from managing inventories of end items that are driven by customer demand, as manufacturing inventories directly depend on the forecasts for finished goods and must be carefully managed in the portion of the supply chain culminating with final assembly. Fortunately, some good techniques have been developed and have evolved into sophisticated software packages that allow operations managers to have current, complete, and accurate information to manage these inventories.

The third episode highlights the difficulty service managers face when corporate budgets constrain their ability to grow and build market share. Here, a high-growth suburb with many new homeowners has created a situation where demand exceeds capacity. The pharmacy is constrained by too few pharmacists and technicians and therefore is confronted with options such as overtime, reduced store hours, and higher chance of errors. Clearly, resources must be matched better to the needs of customers and the level of demand.

In this chapter we focus on approaches to resource planning, beginning with an aggregate view of what resources a firm needs to meet its anticipated demand, and how such resource plans are translated into day-to-day operational decisions. The next chapter focuses on the details of executing plans, that is, creating resource and customer schedules, such as job sequences and staffing assignments.

Resource management deals with the planning, execution, and control of all the resources that are used to produce goods or provide services in a value chain.

Learning Objective
To understand aggregate planning and disaggregation in a high-level resource planning framework for both goods-producing and service-providing organizations.

Aggregate planning is the development of a long-term output and resource plan in aggregate units of measure.

RESOURCE PLANNING FRAMEWORK FOR GOODS AND SERVICES

A generic framework for resource planning is shown in Exhibit 13.1. This framework is broken down into three basic levels. Level 1 represents aggregate planning. **Aggregate planning** *is the development of a long-term output and resource plan in aggregate units of measure.* Aggregate plans define output levels over a planning horizon of 1 to 2 years, usually in monthly or quarterly time buckets. They normally focus on product families or total capacity requirements rather than individual products or specific capacity allocations. Aggregate plans also help to define budget allocations and associated resource requirements. Aggregate planning is driven by longer-term forecasts and demand estimation techniques that we discussed in Chapter 11. See the OM Spotlight on Candy Manufacturing for an example.

Aggregate planning is driven by demand forecasts. As discussed in Chapter 11, high-level forecasts are often developed for aggregate groups of items. For instance, a consumer-products company like Procter and Gamble might produce laundry soap in a variety of sizes. However, it might forecast the total demand for the soap in dollars over some future time horizon, regardless of product size. Aggregate planning would then translate these forecasts into monthly or quarterly production plans. This is often done by cross-functional teams of manufacturing, marketing, and financial managers, who must consider the plant's ability to meet forecasts, taking into account such capacity limitations as supply availability, equipment, and

OM SPOTLIGHT

Aggregate Planning for Candy Manufacturing

Aggregate plans at a company that was acquired by Nestle are focused on quality, personnel, capital, and customer-service objectives.[3] The company exported confectionery and grocery products (for example, candy bars, boxed chocolates, cookies, and peanut butter) to over 120 countries. The Canadian factory in Toronto manufactured 16 major brand items that generated 75 distinct product lines.

One of the major brand items that had a highly seasonal demand was boxed chocolates. Boxed chocolates were produced in three types, with a total of nine distinct end items: Black Magic, in 2-lb, 1 1/2-lb, 1-lb, and 1/2-lb boxes; Rendezvous, in 14-oz boxes; and Dairy Box, in the same four sizes as Black Magic.

Forecasting was accomplished by dividing the year into 13 periods of 4 weeks each. Sales planning provided an end-item forecast, by period, for the full 13 periods. This estimate was updated every 4 weeks, reflecting the latest information on available inventories and estimated sales for the next 13 periods.

Aggregate planning was performed by first converting all end items to a poundage figure. The planning task was focused on calculating levels of production that will best meet the quality, personnel, capital, and customer service restrictions. These restrictions were:

1. *Quality*—An important quality consideration was the age of the product when it reaches the consumer. It is essential that products reach the consumer within well-defined, acceptable time periods to ensure freshness.
2. *Personnel*—It was stated company policy and practice to maintain a stable work force. Short-term capacity can be increased with overtime and/or with part-time employees.
3. *Capital restrictions*—The amount of inventory investment had become a major concern, and inventory levels must be kept low to meet restrictions on capital investment.
4. *Customer service levels*—The nature of the industry made it necessary to strive for 100 percent customer service. The desire to minimize inventory investment often conflicted with this goal.

Exhibit 13.1 Framework for Resource Management Planning for Goods and Services

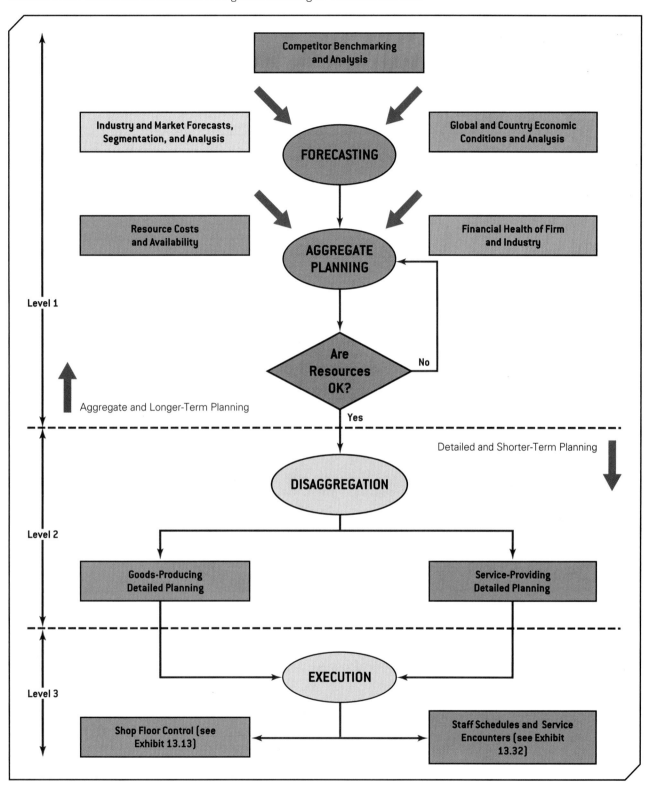

labor. If the forecast exceeds the total factory or supplier capacity, managers might have to consider some strategic resource changes, or shorter-term alternatives such as overtime or subcontracting, or simply decide not to meet the forecasted demand.

It is important to ensure that aggregate plans are feasible; that is, sufficient resources are available to meet planned output levels. A rough-cut capacity check as shown in Exhibit 13.1 is an important step to ensure that such plans are within the capabilities of organization and value chain resources. Aggregate planning and disaggregation methods in goods-producing industries are complex because of the necessity to coordinate purchasing, production, and material transfers throughout the production system. As we shall see, goods-producing firms typically have more levels of disaggregation planning than do service-providing firms.

In Exhibit 13.1, Level 2 planning is called disaggregation. **Disaggregation** *is the process of translating aggregate plans into short-term operational plans that provide the basis for weekly and daily schedules and detailed resource requirements.* To disaggregate means to break up or separate into more detailed pieces. Disaggregation specifies more-detailed plans for the creation of individual goods and services or the allocation of capacity to specific time periods. For goods-producing firms, disaggregation takes Level 1 aggregate planning decisions and breaks them down into such details as order sizes and schedules for individual subassemblies and resources by week and day.

To illustrate aggregate planning and disaggregation, a producer of ice cream might use long-term forecasts to determine the total number of gallons of ice cream

Disaggregation *is the process of translating aggregate plans into short-term operational plans that provide the basis for weekly and daily schedules and detailed resource requirements.*

DAVID DYSON/BLOOMBERG NEWS/Landov

to produce each quarter over the next 2 years. This projection provides the basis for determining how many employees and other resources such as delivery trucks would be needed throughout the year to support this plan. Disaggregation of the plan would involve developing targets for the number of gallons of each flavor to produce (which would sum to the aggregate planned number for each quarter); purchasing requirements for cream, chocolate, and other ingredients; work schedules and overtime plans; and so on. As another example, an airline might use long-term passenger forecasts to develop monthly aggregate plans based on the number of passenger miles each month. This aggregate plan would also specify the resource requirements in terms of total airline capacity, flight crews, and so on. Disaggregation would then create detailed point-to-point flight schedules, crew work assignments, food purchase plans, aircraft maintenance schedules, and other resource requirements.

Level 3 focuses on executing the detailed plans made at Level 2, creating detailed resource schedules and job sequences. **Execution** *refers to moving work from one workstation to another, assigning people to tasks, setting priorities for jobs, scheduling equipment, and controlling processes.* Level 3 planning and execution in manufacturing is sometimes called *shop floor control* and is addressed further in the next chapter.

Execution *refers to moving work from one workstation to another, assigning people to tasks, setting priorities for jobs, scheduling equipment, and controlling processes.*

Resource management for most service-providing organizations generally does not require as many intermediate levels of planning as it does for manufacturing. Service firms frequently take their aggregate plans and disaggregate them down to the execution level as detailed front-line staff and resource schedules, job sequences, and service encounter execution. There are several reasons for this:

- Most manufactured goods are discrete and are "built up" from many levels of raw materials, component parts, and subassemblies. Even nondiscrete manufactured goods such as gasoline or paint have intermediate production stages where additional ingredients and batch processing are required. Food preparation, cooking, packaging, and delivery have fairly discrete levels of building the meal. However, many services are instantaneous or continuous and nondiscrete, such as credit card authorizations or a telephone call or seeing a movie or arriving for service at a bank teller window. Hence, there is no need for multiple levels of planning for some services.

- Services do not have the advantage of physical inventory to buffer demand and supply uncertainty, so they must have sufficient service capacity on duty at the right time in the right place to provide good service to customers, and this puts a premium on excellent short-term demand forecasting and resource scheduling. Remember from Chapter 1 that service capacity is a surrogate for physical inventory. Coupled with the fact that demand for services is very time-dependent, especially over the short term, many services are created and delivered on short notice. This "immediacy of service creation and delivery" does not allow slow, methodical intermediate levels of planning and storage of many services.

Some services, however, use the three levels of planning similar to manufacturing firms. For example, many service facilities, such as fast-food restaurants, need to be in close proximity to the customer, requiring them to be scattered within a geographical area. In these cases, the firm creates aggregate plans at the corporate level and then disaggregates them by region or district (geographically). This is similar to Level 2 intermediate planning in manufacturing. Regional and district offices further disaggregate these plans and budgets given the intermediate-level budgets and resource constraints. Level 3 resource planning and execution occurs at the store level, where local forecasts, food and other supply orders, staff work shifts and schedules, and service encounters are created.

AGGREGATE PLANNING DECISIONS AND STRATEGIES

Learning Objective
To learn aggregate planning strategies, problem structure, and decision options for addressing fluctuating demand in goods-producing and service-providing organizations.

Aggregate planning is most challenging when demand fluctuates over time, because it may be difficult or costly to match demand changes or impractical not to. For example, demand for many types of products, such as air conditioners, skis, cruise packages, and airline flights, are seasonal, and it is not always possible to have sufficient manufacturing or service capacity to meet all demand when it occurs. As a result, companies might have to manufacture and stock goods in the off-season or reposition cruise ships or airplanes at different times of the year. In general, managers have a variety of options in developing aggregate plans in the face of fluctuating demand: demand management, production-rate changes, work-force changes, and inventory smoothing. These are summarized in Exhibit 13.2. The choice of strategy depends on corporate policies, practical limitations, and cost factors.

Demand Management

Marketing strategies, such as those described in Chapter 10, can be used to influence demand and to help create more feasible aggregate plans. For example, pricing and promotions can increase or decrease demand or shift it to other time periods. This is a useful strategy for manufacturers when it is costly to increase production to meet surges in demand. It also demonstrates the importance of understanding the entire production system and supply chain and of cooperation between functions such as marketing and manufacturing.

Exhibit 13.2
Example Aggregate Planning
Variables and Revenue/Cost
Implications

Aggregate Planning Decision Options	Revenue/Cost Implications
Demand Management • Pricing strategies • Promotions and advertising	• Increased revenue and lower unit costs • Economies of scale
Production rate • Overtime • Undertime • Subcontracting	• Higher labor costs and premiums • Idle time/lost opportunity costs • Overhead costs and some loss of control
Work force • Hiring • Layoffs • Full- and part-time labor mix	• Acquisition and training costs • Separation costs • Labor cost and productivity changes
Inventory • Anticipation (build) inventories • Allow stockouts • Plan for back orders	• Inventory carrying costs • Lost sales (revenue) and customer loyalty costs • Back-order costs and customer waiting costs
Facilities, Equipment, and Transportation • Open/closed facilities and hours • Resource utilization • Mode (truck, rail, ship, air) • Capacity and resource utilization	• Variable and fixed costs • Speed and reliability of service and delivery • Low to high utilization impact on unit costs • Inbound and outbound costs per mode • Number of full or partial loads

In services, recall that demand is time-dependent and there is no option to store the service. A hotel manager, for example, may advertise a low weekend rate to the local market in an attempt to increase short-term revenue and contribution to profit and overhead. Thus, demand management strategies are crucial for good aggregate planning and capacity utilization.

Production-Rate Changes

One means of increasing the output rate without changing existing resources is through planned overtime. Generally, this requires wage premiums to be paid. Alternatively, hours can be reduced during slow periods through planned undertime. However, reduced overtime pay or sitting idle can seriously affect employee morale. Subcontracting during periods of peak demand may also alter the output rate. This would probably not be a feasible alternative for some companies, but it is effective in industries that manufacture a large portion of their own parts, such as the machine-tool industry. When business is brisk, components can be subcontracted; when business is slow, the firm may act as a subcontractor to other industries that may be working at their capacity limit. In that way, a stable work force is maintained.

Work-Force Changes

Changing the size of the work force is usually accomplished through hiring and layoffs. Both have disadvantages. Hiring additional labor usually results in higher costs for the personnel department and for training. Layoffs result in severance pay and additional unemployment insurance costs, as well as low employee morale. Also, seniority "bumping" practices can change the skills mix of the work force and result in inefficient production. A stable work force may be obtained by staffing for peak demand levels, but then many employees may be idle during low-demand periods. The candy manufacturing company cited in the previous OM Spotlight used both work-force and production-rate changes to meet fluctuating demand.

In many industries, changing work-force levels is not a feasible alternative. In firms that consist primarily of jobs with low skill requirements, however, it may be cost-effective. The toy industry is a good example. Accurate forecasts for the winter holiday season cannot be made until wholesale buyers have placed orders, usually around midyear. Toy companies maintain a minimal number of employees until production is increased for the holidays. Then they hire a large number of part-time workers in order to operate at maximum capacity. As another example, the U.S. Postal Service hires extra mail carriers during the holiday season to increase its capacity. In general, service facilities must meet demand through work-force changes, because other alternatives are simply not feasible.

Inventory Changes

In Chapter 12 we discussed the function of inventories. In planning for fluctuating demand, inventory is often built up during slack periods and held for peak periods. However, this increases carrying costs and may necessitate more warehouse space. For some products, such as perishable commodities, this alternative cannot be considered. A related strategy is to carry back orders or to tolerate lost sales during peak demand periods. But this may be unacceptable if profit margins are low and competition is high. Stockouts for a manufactured good, for example, reduce revenue and may have a long-term effect on customer loyalty and retention.

Facilities, Equipment, and Transportation

Facilities, equipment, and transportation generally represent long-term capital investments. For example, whether a factory has two or three plastic injection molding machines affects the cost per part depending on how fixed and variable costs are allocated. Short-term changes in facilities and equipment are seldom used in traditional aggregate planning methods because of the capital costs involved. However, in some cases, it might be possible to rent additional equipment such as industrial forklifts, small machines, trucks, or warehouse space to accommodate periods of high demand. Aggregate planning of inbound and outbound goods, supply chain structures, and alternative modes of transportation are used for many multisite service firms and goods-producing supply chains.

Aggregate Planning Strategies

To illustrate some of the major issues involved with aggregate planning, consider the situation faced by Golden Beverages, a producer of two major products—Old Fashioned and Foamy Delite root beers. The spreadsheet in Exhibit 13.3 shows a monthly aggregate demand forecast for the next year. Notice that demand is in barrels per month—an aggregate unit of measure for both products. Golden Beverages operates as a continuous flow factory and must plan future production for a demand forecast that fluctuates quite a bit over the year, with seasonal peaks in the summer and winter holiday season.

How should Golden Beverages plan its overall production for the next 12 months in the face of such fluctuating demand? Suppose that the company has a normal production capacity of 2,200 barrels per month and a current inventory of 1,000 barrels. If it produces at normal capacity each month, we have the aggregate plan

Exhibit 13.3

Level Aggregate Production
Plan for Golden Beverages
(Golden Beverages.xls)

	A	B	C	D	E	F	G
1	**Golden Beverages Production Plan**						
2	**Level Production Strategy - 2200 barrels/month**						
3							
4	Production cost ($/bbl)			$ 70.00			
5	Inventory holding cost ($/bbl)			$ 1.40			
6	Lost sales cost ($/bbl)			$ 90.00			
7	Overtime cost ($/bbl)			$ 6.50			
8	Undertime cost ($/bbl)			$ 3.00			
9	Rate change cost ($/bbl)			$ 5.00			
10	Normal production rate			2,200			
11							
12					Cumulative		
13			Cumulative		Product	Ending	Lost
14	Month	Demand	Demand	Production	Availability	Inventory	Sales
15						1,000	
16	January	1,500	1,500	2,200	3,200	1,700	0
17	February	1,000	2,500	2,200	5,400	2,900	0
18	March	1,900	4,400	2,200	7,600	3,200	0
19	April	2,600	7,000	2,200	9,800	2,800	0
20	May	2,800	9,800	2,200	12,000	2,200	0
21	June	3,100	12,900	2,200	14,200	1,300	0
22	July	3,200	16,100	2,200	16,400	300	0
23	August	3,000	19,100	2,200	18,600	0	500
24	September	2,000	21,100	2,200	21,300	200	0
25	October	1,000	22,100	2,200	23,500	1,400	0
26	November	1,800	23,900	2,200	25,700	1,800	0
27	December	2,200	26,100	2,200	27,900	1,800	0
28						3,200	
29		Production	Inventory	Lost Sales	Overtime	Undertime	Rate Change
30	Month	Cost	Cost	Cost	Cost	Cost	Cost
31							
32	January	$ 154,000	$ 2,380	$ -	$ -	$ -	$ -
33	February	$ 154,000	$ 4,060	$ -	$ -	$ -	$ -
34	March	$ 154,000	$ 4,480	$ -	$ -	$ -	$ -
35	April	$ 154,000	$ 3,920	$ -	$ -	$ -	$ -
36	May	$ 154,000	$ 3,080	$ -	$ -	$ -	$ -
37	June	$ 154,000	$ 1,820	$ -	$ -	$ -	$ -
38	July	$ 154,000	$ 420	$ -	$ -	$ -	$ -
39	August	$ 154,000	$ -	$ 45,000	$ -	$ -	$ -
40	September	$ 154,000	$ 280	$ -	$ -	$ -	$ -
41	October	$ 154,000	$ 1,960	$ -	$ -	$ -	$ -
42	November	$ 154,000	$ 2,520	$ -	$ -	$ -	$ -
43	December	$ 154,000	$ 2,520	$ -	$ -	$ -	$ -
44		$ 1,848,000	$ 27,440	$ 45,000	$ -	$ -	$ -
45							
46	Total cost	$ 1,920,440					

shown in Exhibit 13.3. To calculate the ending inventory for each month, we use using Equation (13.1).

$$\text{Beginning inventory} + \text{Production} - \text{Demand} = \text{Ending inventory} \qquad \textbf{(13.1)}$$

For example, January is $1,000 + 2,200 - 1,500 = 1,700$ and February is $1,700 + 2,200 - 1,000 = 2,900$.

A **level production strategy** *plans for the same production rate in each time period.*

A **level production strategy** *plans for the same production rate in each time period.* The aggregate plan for Golden Beverages shown in Exhibit 13.3 is an example of a level production strategy with a constant production rate of 2,200 barrels per month. The lower portion of the spreadsheet translates the aggregate plan into dollars for production, inventory, lost sales, overtime, and undertime. This provides information to managers for budgeting and financing.

A level strategy avoids changes in the production rate, working within normal capacity restrictions. Labor and equipment schedules are stable and repetitive, making it easier to execute the plan. However, inventory builds up to a peak of 3,200 barrels in March and lost sales are 500 barrels in August due to inventory shortages. This level production strategy is illustrated graphically in Exhibit 13.4. Notice that the cumulative inventory exceeds cumulative demand by 7,600 − 4,400 = 3,200 barrels in March and cumulative demand exceeds cumulative inventory by 18,600 − 19,100 = −500 barrels in August.

An alternative to a level production strategy is to match production to demand every month. *A* **chase demand strategy** *sets the production rate equal to the demand in each time period.* While inventories will be reduced and lost sales will be eliminated, many production-rate changes will dramatically change resource levels (that is, the number of employees, machines, and so on). A chase demand strategy for Golden Beverages is shown in Exhibit 13.5 with a total cost of $1,835,050. As compared with the level production strategy documented in Exhibit 13.2, the cost of the chase demand strategy is $1,920,440 − 1,835,050 = $85,390 less. Notice that no inventory carrying or lost sales costs are incurred, but substantial overtime, undertime, and rate-change costs are required. This might be difficult to execute, as the work force may object to such frequent hiring, layoffs, and rate changes, or it might be contrary to management policy. The chase demand strategy is shown graphically in Exhibit 13.6. In this case, of course, the cumulative demand and product availability lines are identical.

Given the large number of aggregate planning decision variables with an infinite number of possible levels and combinations, countless alternative aggregate plans could be developed. With a spreadsheet model, "what-if?" analyses can easily evaluate alternative strategies. A recommended heuristic approach is to begin with a level production strategy meeting whatever inventory targets and other objectives are required. Then, by trail and error, seek to improve the baseline solution. Graphs

A **chase demand strategy** *sets the production rate equal to the demand in each time period.*

Exhibit 13.4 Graph of 2,200 Barrels/Month Level Production Strategy

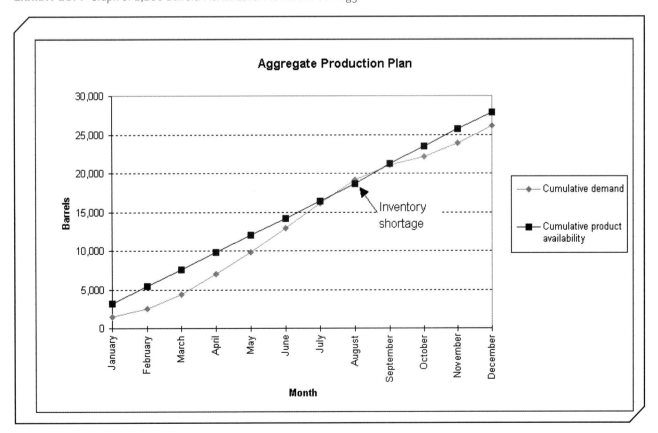

Exhibit 13.5

Chase Demand Strategy for
Golden Beverages

	A	B	C	D	E	F	G
1	Golden Beverages Production Plan						
2	Chase Demand Strategy						
3							
4	Production cost ($/bbl)			$ 70.00			
5	Inventory holding cost ($/bbl)			$ 1.40			
6	Lost sales cost ($/bbl)			$ 90.00			
7	Overtime cost ($/bbl)			$ 6.50			
8	Undertime cost ($/bbl)			$ 3.00			
9	Rate change cost ($/bbl)			$ 5.00			
10	Normal production rate			2,200			
11							
12					Cumulative		
13			Cumulative		Product	Ending	Lost
14	Month	Demand	Demand	Production	Availability	Inventory	Sales
15						1,000	
16	January	1,500	1,500	500	1,500	0	0
17	February	1,000	2,500	1,000	2,500	0	0
18	March	1,900	4,400	1,900	4,400	0	0
19	April	2,600	7,000	2,600	7,000	0	0
20	May	2,800	9,800	2,800	9,800	0	0
21	June	3,100	12,900	3,100	12,900	0	0
22	July	3,200	16,100	3,200	16,100	0	0
23	August	3,000	19,100	3,000	19,100	0	0
24	September	2,000	21,100	2,000	21,100	0	0
25	October	1,000	22,100	1,000	22,100	0	0
26	November	1,800	23,900	1,800	23,900	0	0
27	December	2,200	26,100	2,200	26,100	0	0
28		2,175				1,000	
29		Production	Inventory	Lost Sales	Overtime	Undertime	Rate Change
30	Month	Cost	Cost	Cost	Cost	Cost	Cost
31							
32	January	$ 35,000	$ -	$ -	$ -	$ 5,100	$ 8,500
33	February	$ 70,000	$ -	$ -	$ -	$ 3,600	$ 2,500
34	March	$ 133,000	$ -	$ -	$ -	$ 900	$ 4,500
35	April	$ 182,000	$ -	$ -	$ 2,600	$ -	$ 3,500
36	May	$ 196,000	$ -	$ -	$ 3,900	$ -	$ 1,000
37	June	$ 217,000	$ -	$ -	$ 5,850	$ -	$ 1,500
38	July	$ 224,000	$ -	$ -	$ 6,500	$ -	$ 500
39	August	$ 210,000	$ -	$ -	$ 5,200	$ -	$ 1,000
40	September	$ 140,000	$ -	$ -	$ -	$ 600	$ 5,000
41	October	$ 70,000	$ -	$ -	$ -	$ 3,600	$ 5,000
42	November	$ 126,000	$ -	$ -	$ -	$ 1,200	$ 4,000
43	December	$ 154,000	$ -	$ -	$ -	$ -	$ 2,000
44		$ 1,757,000	$ -	$ -	$ 24,050	$ 15,000	$ 39,000
45							
46	Total cost	$ 1,835,050					

of the cumulative demand and product availability often assist in identifying improved solutions. Also, examining individual cost categories can highlight areas where costs can be reduced. Good solutions using spreadsheets can be found by trial-and-error approaches.

Linear Programming Approaches to Aggregate Planning

Although a trial-and-error spreadsheet approach will find a relatively low-cost aggregate planning solution, it is not likely to find a minimum cost solution. Linear programming (LP) is one technique for finding the minimum cost solution, and many firms use it for aggregate planning purposes. Supplementary Chapter C describes linear programming models and solution techniques, and we develop a linear programming model for Golden Beverages in that supplement. Using linear programming with a beginning and ending inventory of 1,000 barrels, the minimum total cost for Golden Beverages is $1,822,455, shown in Exhibits 13.7 and 13.8. The solution is similar to the chase demand strategy and is only $12,595 less.

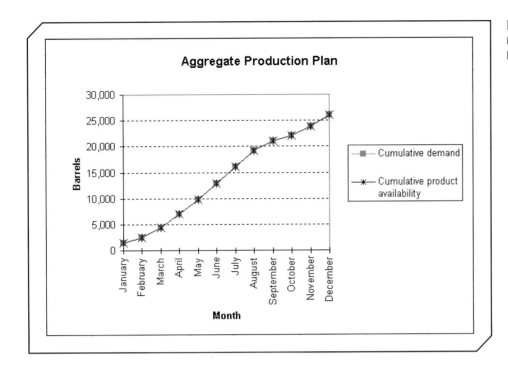

Exhibit 13.6
Graph of Aggregate Chase Demand Strategy

However, it may not be practical because it requires many production-rate changes and much overtime and undertime.

Aggregate Planning for Services

Services face many of the same issues in planning and managing resources as do manufacturing firms. To illustrate how the concepts we developed can be applied in a service organization, consider Golden Resort, a 145-acre oceanfront resort located in Myrtle Beach, South Carolina that is owned and operated by a major corporation. The resort includes two major hotels, three conference centers, a health club, fishing lakes and woods, four condominium towers, a kid's water park, and a tennis club and courts and is located next to the longest pier on the east coast of the United States. The resort is well landscaped with the natural beauty of the lakes, woods, ocean, gardens, and wildlife, such as black swans and colorful mallard ducks. The entire resort and its inherent experiences and food services define the consumer benefit package.

The tennis club and four courts are located next to the Sport & Health Club. All courts are lighted for night play, and there is no more room to build additional tennis courts. The demand for tennis courts is highly seasonal, with peak demand in June, July, and August. In the summer months when resort rooms are 98 percent to 100 percent occupied, requests for court time far exceed capacity, and owner and hotel guest complaints were increasing dramatically.

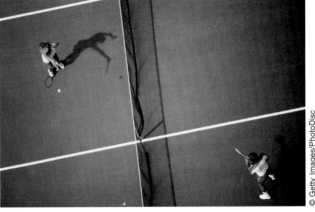

Exhibit 13.7

Linear Programming Aggregate Planning Solution for Golden Beverages

	A	B	C	D	E	F	G
1	**Golden Beverages Production Plan**						
2	**Linear Programming Solution**						
3							
4	Production cost ($/bbl)			$ 70.00			
5	Inventory holding cost ($/bbl)			$ 1.40			
6	Lost sales cost ($/bbl)			$ 90.00			
7	Overtime cost ($/bbl)			$ 6.50			
8	Undertime cost ($/bbl)			$ 3.00			
9	Rate change cost ($/bbl)			$ 5.00			
10	Normal production rate			2,200			
11							
12					Cumulative		
13			Cumulative		Product	Ending	Lost
14	Month	Demand	Demand	Production	Availability	Inventory	Sales
15						1,000	
16	January	1,500	1,500	750	1,750	250	0
17	February	1,000	2,500	750	2,500	0	0
18	March	1,900	4,400	2,249	4,749	349	0
19	April	2,600	7,000	2,251	7,000	0	0
20	May	2,800	9,800	2,800	9,800	0	0
21	June	3,100	12,900	3,150	12,950	50	0
22	July	3,200	16,100	3,150	16,100	0	0
23	August	3,000	19,100	3,000	19,100	0	0
24	September	2,000	21,100	2,000	21,100	0	0
25	October	1,000	22,100	1,667	22,767	667	0
26	November	1,800	23,900	1,667	24,433	533	0
27	December	2,200	26,100	1,667	26,100	0	0
28		2,175				1,000	
29		Production	Inventory	Lost Sales	Overtime	Undertime	Rate Change
30	Month	Cost	Cost	Cost	Cost	Cost	Cost
31							
32	January	$ 52,500	$ 350	$ -	$ -	$ 4,350	$ 7,250
33	February	$ 52,500	$ 0	$ -	$ -	$ 4,350	$ 0
34	March	$ 157,425	$ 489	$ -	$ 318	$ -	$ 7,495
35	April	$ 157,575	$ 0	$ -	$ 332	$ -	$ 11
36	May	$ 196,000	$ 0	$ -	$ 3,900	$ -	$ 2,745
37	June	$ 220,500	$ 70	$ -	$ 6,175	$ -	$ 1,750
38	July	$ 220,500	$ -	$ -	$ 6,175	$ -	$ 0
39	August	$ 210,000	$ -	$ -	$ 5,200	$ -	$ 750
40	September	$ 140,000	$ -	$ -	$ -	$ 600	$ 5,000
41	October	$ 116,667	$ 933	$ -	$ -	$ 1,600	$ 1,667
42	November	$ 116,666	$ 747	$ -	$ -	$ 1,600	$ 0
43	December	$ 116,667	$ (0)	$ -	$ -	$ 1,600	$ 0
44		$ 1,757,000	$ 2,589	$ -	$ 22,100	$ 14,100	$ 26,667
45							
46	Total cost	$ 1,822,455					

Management at Golden Resort developed the aggregate plan shown in Exhibit 13.9. Currently, it employs four full-time tennis staff under a level resource strategy, with a capacity of 933 hours per month. Demand for tennis courts varies from 180 hours in December to a peak of 1,580 hours in July. The parameters of the situation are shown in Exhibit 13.9—$15 per hour court fee, the assumption of the courts being open 12 hours, and full-time staff works an 8-hour shift. Exhibit 13.10 computes the total tennis revenue generated as $137,850 per year while costs are $236,089, resulting in a net loss of $98,239.

Because the tennis club is a peripheral service in the customer benefit package, the corporate target for the tennis club is to break even or make a small profit. Other peripheral services such as food service (hotel restaurants, pool bars, and so on) also have profit targets near or around their break-even points. Some peripheral services, such as the children's water park, generate no additional revenue, are expensive to maintain, and lose money, but they are very much appreciated by families and are important in drawing them to the resort. The corporation makes its major profit and supports the peripheral services through such primary services as hotel room rentals and condominium owner's homeowner association monthly fees.

Exhibit 13.8 Graph of Linear Programming Aggregate Plan

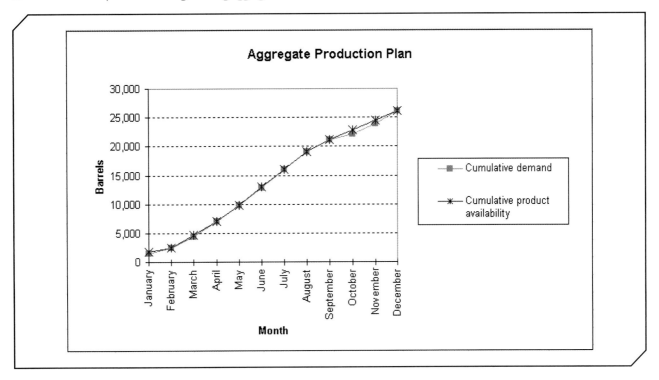

The manager of the health club considers a chase resource strategy with a base full-time tennis staff of two people and the use of part-time staff for much of the year. This aggregate plan is shown in Exhibit 13.11. Two full-time staff result in 467 hours of capacity per month, and the addition of 10 part-time staff in July and August increases staff capacity to 1,633 work hours. It is important to understand the parameter estimates and assumptions of each alternative aggregate plan. The costs and assumptions are identical for the level and chase strategies in Exhibits 13.9 to 13.12, except that for July and August available court hours are increased to match staff hours (that is, 1,633 staff and court hours). Exhibit 13.12 computes the total revenue generated as $142,875 per year while costs are $130,200, resulting in a net profit of $12,675.

As with Golden Beverages, there are many different "what-if?" scenarios one could quickly evaluate with these aggregate-planning models. For example, due to process improvements or better technology, the production rate at Golden Beverages could increase, production costs could change, and so on. For Golden Resort, management may want to investigate increasing the court fee to, for example, $20 per hour, or expanding the hours of operation per court per day from 12 to, say, 16. Aggregate planning at Golden Beverages and Golden Resort are more alike than different, but each organization and industry has its own unique characteristics.

DISAGGREGATION IN MANUFACTURING

Learning Objective
To learn how goods-producing organizations develop executable detailed plans and schedules by disaggregating aggregate plans.

Disaggregation at Level 2 provides the link between aggregate plans developed at Level 1 and detailed execution at Level 3. For example, although Golden Beverages created aggregate plans in terms of total root beer production, it must determine how many barrels of individual products—Old Fashioned and Foamy Delight—to

Exhibit 13.9 Golden Resort Level and Full-Time Staff Aggregate Plan

Golden Resort Tennis Court Resource Planning	Level and Full-Time Staff Plan
Court fee per hour ($/hour)	$15.00
Full-time tennis staff average labor and benefit cost ($/hour)	$16.50
Part-time tennis staff average labor and no benefit cost ($/hour)	$10.00
Overtime cost per full-time employee ($/hour) @50% premium	$24.75
Overtime cost per part-time employee ($/hour) @50% premium	$15.00
Undertime cost is loss of court fee ($/hour)—perishable asset	$15.00
Hiring cost of part-time staff	$600
Layoff cost of part-time staff	$300
Lost sale and goodwill cost ($/hour)—no court time—poor service	$100.00
Hours of operation per court per day	12
Days of operation per court per year	350
Number of tennis courts	4
Hours of operation per court per month	350
Total hours of operation all courts per month	1,400
Full- and part-time tennis staff days per month	25
Full-time tennis staff workday (hours)	8.0
Part-time tennis staff workday (hours)	4.0

Month	Number of Full-Time Staff Equivalent	Number of Part-Time Staff Equivalent	Total FTE & PTE Hours	Court Hours Demand	Cumulative Court Hours Demand	Court Hours Available	Cumulative Court Capacity	Excess (+) Shortage (−) Court Hours	Lost Sales & Goodwill Court Hours (Poor Service)
January	4	0	933	320	320	1,400	1,400	1,080	0
February	4	0	933	430	750	1,400	2,800	970	0
March	4	0	933	670	1,420	1,400	4,200	730	0
April	4	0	933	700	2,120	1,400	5,600	700	0
May	4	0	933	790	2,910	1,400	7,000	610	0
June	4	0	933	1,410	4,320	1,400	8,400	−10	10
July	4	0	933	1,580	5,900	1,400	9,800	−180	180
August	4	0	933	1,555	7,455	1,400	11,200	−155	155
September	4	0	933	870	8,325	1,400	12,600	530	0
October	4	0	933	520	8,845	1,400	14,000	880	0
November	4	0	933	510	9,355	1,400	15,400	890	0
December	4	0	933	180	9,535	1,400	16,800	1,220	0

Exhibit 13.10 Golden Resort Level and Full-Time Staff Aggregate Plan Costs

Golden Resort Tennis Court Resource Planning

Level and Full-Time Staff Plan

Month	Revenue Generated	Monthly Full-Time Labor Cost	Monthly Part-Time Labor Cost	Hire & Rate-Change Cost	Layoff & Rate-Change Cost	Full-Time Overtime Cost	Lost Sales Cost (no court time) Poor Service	Loss Revenue Opportunity or Cost of Undertime
January	$ 4,800	$ 13,200	$ 0	$ —	$ —	$ 0	$ —	$ 16,200
February	$ 6,450	$ 13,200	$ 0	—	—	0	—	$ 14,550
March	$ 10,050	$ 13,200	$ 0	—	—	0	—	$ 10,950
April	$ 10,500	$ 13,200	$ 0	—	—	0	—	$ 10,500
May	$ 11,850	$ 13,200	$ 0	—	—	0	—	$ 9,150
June	$ 21,000	$ 13,200	$ 0	—	—	$11,798	$ 1,000	$ —
July	$ 21,000	$ 13,200	$ 0	—	—	$16,005	$18,000	$ —
August	$ 21,000	$ 13,200	$ 0	—	—	$15,386	$15,500	$ —
September	$ 13,050	$ 13,200	$ 0	—	—	0	—	7,950
October	$ 7,800	$ 13,200	$ 0	—	—	0	—	13,200
November	$ 7,650	$ 13,200	$ 0	—	—	0	—	13,350
December	$ 2,700	$ 13,200	$ 0	—	—	0	—	18,300
Totals	$137,850	$158,400	$ —	$ —	$ —	$43,189	$34,500	$114,150
Total cost	$236,089							
Profit	$ (98,239)							

Exhibit 13.11 Golden Resort Chase and Full- and Part-Time Staff Aggregate Plan Costs

Golden Resort Tennis Court Resource Planning	Part-Time Chase Staff Plan
Court fee per hour ($/hour)	$15.00
Full-time tennis staff average labor and benefit cost ($/hour)	$16.50
Part-time tennis staff average labor and no benefit cost ($/hour)	$10.00
Overtime cost per full-time employee ($/hour) @50% premium	$24.75
Overtime cost per part-time employee ($/hour) @50% premium	$15.00
Undertime cost is loss of court fee ($/hour)—perishable asset	$15.00
Hiring cost of part-time staff	$600
Layoff cost of part-time staff	$300
Lost sale & goodwill cost ($/hour)—no court time—poor service	$100.00
Hours of operation per court per day	12
Days of operation per court per year	350
Number of tennis courts	4
Hours of operation per court per month	350
Total hours of operation all courts per month	1,400
Full- and part-time tennis staff days per month	25
Full-time tennis staff workday (hours)	8.0
Part-time tennis staff workday (hours)	4.0

Month	Number of Full-Time Staff Equivalent	Number of Part-Time Staff Equivalent	Total FTE & PTE Hours	Court Hours Demand	Cumulative Court Hours Demand	Court Hours Available	Cumulative Court Capacity	Excess (+) Shortage (−) Court Hours	Lost Sales & Goodwill Court Hours (Poor Service)
January	2	0	467	320	320	1,400	1,400	1,080	0
February	2	0	467	430	750	1,400	2,800	970	0
March	2	2	700	670	1,420	1,400	4,200	730	0
April	2	2	700	700	2,120	1,400	5,600	700	0
May	2	3	817	790	2,910	1,400	7,000	610	0
June	2	8	1,400	1,410	4,320	1,400	8,400	−10	10
July	2	10	1,633	1,580	5,900	1,633	10,033	53	0
August	2	10	1,633	1,555	7,455	1,633	11,666	78	0
September	2	4	933	870	8,325	1,400	13,066	530	0
October	2	1	583	520	8,845	1,400	14,466	880	0
November	2	1	583	510	9,355	1,400	15,866	890	0
December	2	0	467	180	9,535	1,400	17,266	1,220	0

Chapter 13: Resource Management

Exhibit 13.12 Golden Resort Chase and Full- and Part-Time Staff Aggregate Plan Costs

Golden Resort Tennis Court Resource Planning / **Part-Time Chase Staff Plan**

Month	Revenue Generated	Monthly Full-Time Labor Cost	Monthly Part-Time Labor Cost	Hire & Rate-Change Cost	Layoff & Rate-Change Cost	Full-Time Overtime Cost	Lost Sales Cost (no court time) Poor Service	Loss Revenue Opportunity or Cost of Undertime
January	$ 4,800	$ 6,600	$ 0	$ —	$ —	$ 0	$ —	$ 16,200
February	$ 6,450	$ 6,600	$ 0	$1,200	$ —	$ 0	$ —	$ 14,550
March	$ 10,050	$ 6,600	$ 2,000	$ —	$ —	$ 0	$ —	$ 10,950
April	$ 10,500	$ 6,600	$ 2,000	$ 600	$ —	$ 0	$ —	$ 10,500
May	$ 11,850	$ 6,600	$ 3,000	$3,000	$ —	$ 0	$ —	$ 9,150
June	$ 21,000	$ 6,600	$ 8,000	$1,200	$ —	$ 0	$1,000	$ —
July	$ 23,700	$ 6,600	$10,000	$ —	$ —	$ 0	$ —	$ 795
August	$ 23,325	$ 6,600	$10,000	$ —	$1,800	$ 0	$ —	$ 1,170
September	$ 13,050	$ 6,600	$ 4,000	$ —	$ 900	$ 0	$ —	$ 7,950
October	$ 7,800	$ 6,600	$ 1,000	$ —	$ —	$ 0	$ —	$ 13,200
November	$ 7,650	$ 6,600	$ 1,000	$ —	$ 300	$ 0	$ —	$ 13,350
December	$ 2,700	$ 6,600	$ 0	$ —	$ —	$ 0	$ —	$ 18,300
Totals	$142,875	$79,200	$41,000	$6,000	$3,000	$ —	$1,000	$116,115
Total cost	$130,200							
Profit	$ 12,675							

produce each month. This provides the basis for detailed purchasing and production schedules for all raw materials and components that comprise the finished good or support service delivery.

For manufacturing firms, Exhibit 13.13 shows a typical system for disaggregating aggregate plans into executable operations plans. Three important techniques in this process are master production scheduling (MPS), materials requirements planning (MRP), and capacity requirements planning (CRP).

Exhibit 13.13 Disaggregation Framework for Manufacturing Plans and Schedules

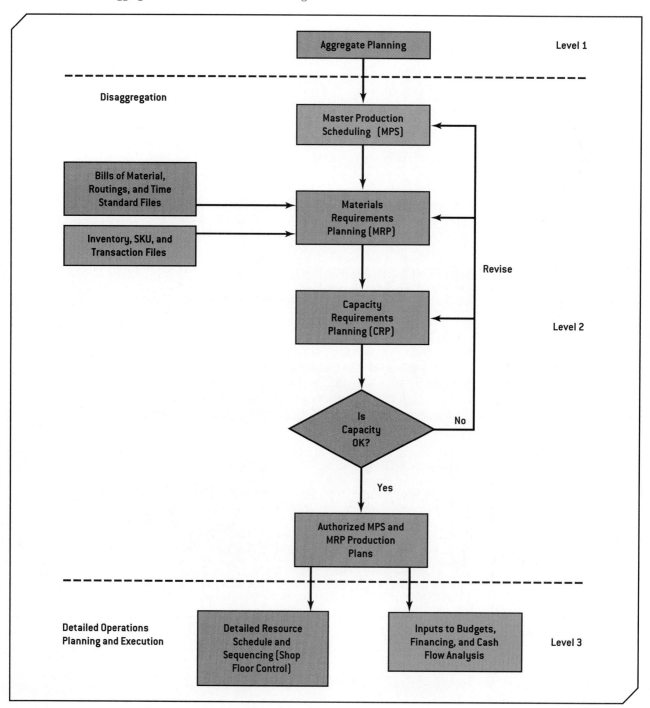

Master Production Scheduling

A **master production schedule (MPS)** *is a statement of how many finished items are to be produced and when they are to be produced.* An example of a portion of an MPS with an 8-week planning horizon is shown in Exhibit 13.14. Typically, the master schedule is developed for weekly time periods over a 6- to 12-month horizon. The purpose of the master schedule is to translate the aggregate plan into a separate plan for individual finished goods. It also provides a means for evaluating alternative schedules in terms of capacity requirements, provides input to the MRP system, and helps managers generate priorities for scheduling by setting due dates for the production of individual items.

Developing the MPS can be a very complicated task, especially for products with a large number of operations. For example, Dow Corning used 12 master schedulers who were responsible for scheduling 4,000 packaged products over a 26-week time horizon. In process industries with only a few different operations, master production scheduling is somewhat easier.

The MPS is developed differently depending on the type of industry (make-to-stock versus make-to-order) and the number of items produced (few or many). For make-to-stock industries, a net demand forecast (that is, after on-hand inventory is subtracted) is used. If only a few final products are produced, the MPS is a statement of the individual product requirements. If many items are produced—for instance, more than 100—it is impractical to develop an MPS on an individual-product basis. In such cases, individual products are usually grouped into product families, and some method of proportionately decomposing the plan into a schedule for individual items is employed. A common approach is to use historical product sales mix percentages to disaggregate product groups to individual products.

For make-to-order industries, order backlogs provide the needed customer-demand information; thus the known customer orders (called *firm orders*) determine the MPS. In some industries where a few basic subassemblies and components are assembled in many different combinations to produce a large variety of end products, the MPS is usually developed for the basic subassemblies and not for the ultimate finished goods. Therefore, a different plan and schedule is needed to assemble the final finished good. *A **final assembly schedule (FAS)** defines the quantity and timing for assembling subassemblies and component parts into a final finished good.* Major subassemblies such as automobile engines, transmissions, dashboards, and so forth are built based on a MPS of the manufacturer or supplier. Honda, for example, uses a FAS for Honda Accords and Civics at its Marysville, Ohio assembly

A **master production schedule (MPS)** *is a statement of how many finished items are to be produced and when they are to be produced.*

A **final assembly schedule (FAS)** *defines the quantity and timing for assembling subassemblies and component parts into a final finished good.*

Exhibit 13.14 Eight-Week Master Production Schedule Example

		Week								
		1	2	3	4	5	6	7	8	
	Model A		200		200		350			MPS
	Model B	150	100		190			120		Planned Quantities
	•	•	•	•	•	•	•	•	•	
	•	•	•	•	•	•	•	•	•	
	•	•	•	•	•	•	•	•	•	
Totals		X			75		75	75		60	
Aggregate production plans (units)			500	800	350	600	280	750	420	300	

factory. Honda's Engine Factory in Anna, Ohio uses a MPS to plan production of its engines.

Materials Requirements Planning

To produce a finished product, many individual parts or subassemblies must be manufactured or purchased and then assembled together. Fixed order quantity and fixed-period inventory systems (see Chapter 12) were used long ago for planning materials in manufacturing environments. However, these systems did not capture the dependent relationships between the demand for finished goods and their raw materials, components, and subassemblies. This insight led to the development of materials requirements planning.

Materials requirements planning (MRP) is a forward-looking, demand-based approach for planning the production of manufactured goods and ordering materials and components to minimize unnecessary inventories and reduce costs. MRP projects the requirements for the individual parts or subassemblies based on the demand for the finished goods as specified by the MPS. The primary output of an MRP system is a time-phased report that gives (1) the purchasing department a schedule for obtaining raw materials and purchased parts, (2) the production managers a detailed schedule for manufacturing the product and controlling manufacturing inventories, and (3) accounting and financial functions production information that drives cash flow, budgets, and financial needs.

MRP depends on understanding three basic concepts—(1) the concept of dependent demand, (2) the concept of time-phasing, and (3) lot sizing to gain economies of scale.

DEPENDENT DEMAND IN MRP SYSTEMS

Recall from Chapter 12 that *independent* demand is directly related to customer (market) demand and needs to be forecast. Inventories of finished goods have independent demand characteristics. In contrast, the demand for materials and components used to produce finished goods is dependent on the number of finished goods planned. *Dependent demand is demand that is directly related to the demand of other SKUs and can be calculated without needing to be forecasted.* After a master production schedule is created for finished goods, the demand for all materials and components can be calculated. Note that dependent demand for subassemblies, components, and raw materials is deterministic because no uncertainty needs to be considered.

The concept of dependent demand is best understood by examining the bill of materials. *A bill of materials (BOM) defines the hierarchical relationships between all items that comprise a finished good, such as subassemblies, purchased parts, and manufactured in-house parts.* Some firms call the BOM the *product structure*. A BOM may also define standard times and alternative routings for each item.

Exhibit 13.15 shows the structure of a typical BOM. *End-items are finished goods scheduled in the MPS or FAS that must be forecast.* These are the items at level 0 of the BOM. For example, item A in Exhibit 13.15 is an end-item. *A parent item is manufactured from one or more components.* Items A, B, D, F, and H are parents in Exhibit 13.15. End-items are composed of components and subassemblies. *Components are any item (raw materials, manufactured parts, purchased parts) other than an end-item that goes into a higher-level parent item(s).* Items B, C, D, E, F, G, H, and I are all components in the BOM in Exhibit 13.15. *A subassembly always has at least one immediate parent and also has at least one immediate component.* Subassemblies (sometimes called *intermediate items*) reside in the middle of the BOM; items B, D, F, and H in Exhibit 13.15 are examples. BOMs for simple assemblies might be flat, having only 2 or 3 levels, while more complex BOMs may have up to 15 levels.

Materials requirements planning (MRP) *is a forward-looking, demand-based approach for planning the production of manufactured goods and ordering materials and components to minimize unnecessary inventories and reduce costs.*

Dependent demand *is demand that is directly related to the demand of other SKUs and can be calculated without needing to be forecasted.*

A bill of materials (BOM) *defines the hierarchical relationships between all items that comprise a finished good, such as subassemblies, purchased parts, and manufactured in-house parts.*

End-items *are finished goods scheduled in the MPS or FAS that must be forecast.*

A parent item *is manufactured from one or more components.*

Components *are any item (raw materials, manufactured parts, purchased parts) other than an end-item that goes into a higher-level parent item(s).*

A subassembly *always has at least one immediate parent and also has at least one immediate component.*

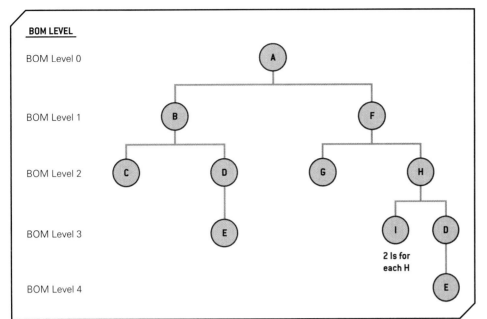

Exhibit 13.15
Example of a Bill of Material and Dependent Demand

Component part commonality *refers to components that have more than one parent.*[4] Note that item D in the BOM in Exhibit 13.15 has two different parents—items B and H. Component part commonality focuses on the standardization of parts across product lines. As described in Chapter 5, product simplification and modular design initiatives try to use common parts to increase volumes and reduce costs. For example, if the manufacturer increases the degree of component part commonality from no common components to using item D twice for end-item A as shown in Exhibit 13.15, the demand for items D and E increases. Therefore, production volumes increase and fixed costs are spread over more units, further reducing unit costs. In addition, component part commonality leads to higher volumes of parts and allows the manufacturer to negotiate price breaks for purchased parts and raw materials (see OM Spotlight: Gillette). Component part standardization also can help reduce engineering design costs and repair service cost. The globalization of markets is also pushing firms to customize the end-items that the customer sees but standardize what they customer does not see, such as component parts and raw materials across global product lines.

Component part commonality *refers to components that have more than one parent.*

OM SPOTLIGHT

Gillette[5]

When the new CEO of Boston-based Gillette Co. took over in 2001, high costs relative to competitors ranked #1 on his hit list of improvement initiatives. Product and part standardization forms a big piece of Gillette's strategic cost improvement initiative. Plastic resins, steel blades, and packaging materials, for example, had proliferated to the point where similar products used very different component parts. "We're looking for opportunities to take 100 part numbers down to 50, which will allow us to offer more attractive volumes to global suppliers," commented Mike Cowhig, senior VP of Gillette's global supply chain. Gillette saved $90 million the first year of the standardization program. Such initiatives helped to make Gillette an attractive acquisition. In 2005, Procter & Gamble announced that it negotiated a deal to acquire the company.

To understand the nature of dependent demand, assume that we wish to produce 100 units of end-item A in Exhibit 13.15. Exhibit 13.16 shows the calculations for each of the items in the BOM, taking into account on-hand inventory. For each unit of A, we need one unit of items B and F. We have 33 units on hand for subassembly B, so we need to make only 100 − 33, or 67, units of B. Similarly, we have 20 units of F available and therefore require an additional 100 − 20 = 80 units. Next, at Level 2 of the BOM, for each unit of B, we need one unit of components C and D; and for each F, we need one unit of components G and H. Because we only need to produce an additional 67 units of B, and we have 12 units of component C on hand, we need to produce an additional 67 − 12 = 55 units of C.

You should check the remaining calculations in Exhibit 13.16. Note that item D is a common subassembly that is used in both subassemblies B and H. Thus, we must include the requirements of item B (67 units) and item H (50 units) in computing the number of Ds to produce: 67 + 50 − 47 = 70 units.

Time-Phasing and Lot Sizing in MRP

Although the dependent demand calculations as described in the previous section provide the number of components or subassemblies needed in the BOM, they do not specify when orders should be placed or how much should be ordered. Because of the hierarchy of the BOM, there is no reason to order something until it is required to produce a parent item. Thus, all dependent demand requirements do not need to be ordered at the same time, but rather are *time-phased* as necessary. In addition, orders might be consolidated to take advantage of ordering economies of scale—this is called *lot sizing*. **MRP explosion** *is the process of using the logic of dependent demand to calculate the quantity and timing of orders for all subassemblies and components that go into and support the production of the end-item(s).* In this section we will illustrate the process of time phasing and demonstrate three simple lot-sizing rules.

Time buckets *are the time period size used in the MRP explosion process and usually are 1 week in length.* Although small buckets such as 1 day are good for scheduling production over a short time horizon, they may be too precise for longer-range planning. Thus, larger buckets such as months are often used as the planning horizon gets longer. In this chapter, we assume that all time buckets are 1 week in length. Many MRP and ERP software packages also offer the option of "bucket-less" MRP that do their planning by date.

To include time phasing and lot sizing into the MRP explosion process we need to define some new terms and the concept of an MRP record. An MRP record consists of the following:

- **Gross requirements (GR)** *are the total demand for an item derived from all of its parents.* This is the quantity of the component needed to support production at

MRP explosion *is the process of using the logic of dependent demand to calculate the quantity and timing of orders for all subassemblies and components that go into and support the production of the end-item(s).*

Time buckets *are the time period size used in the MRP explosion process and usually are 1 week in length.*

Gross requirements (GR) *are the total demand for an item derived from all of its parents.*

Exhibit 13.16
Dependent Demand Calculations

Item	On-Hand Inventory	Dependent Demand Calculations
A	0	100 − 0 = 100
B	33	100 − 33 = 67
C	12	67 − 12 = 55
D	47	67 + 50 − 47 = 70
E	10	70 − 10 = 60
F	20	100 − 20 = 80
G	15	80 − 15 = 65
H	30	80 − 30 = 50
I	7	50 × 2 − 7 = 93

the next-higher level of assembly. Gross requirements can also include maintenance, repair, and spare-part components that are added to the dependent demand requirements.

- **Scheduled or planned receipts (S/PR)** *are orders that are due or planned to be delivered.* A scheduled receipt was released to the vendor or shop in a previous time period and now shows up as a scheduled receipt. (In some of our examples we assume, for simplicity, that all scheduled receipts are zero.) A planned order receipt is defined later. If the order is for an outside vendor, it is a *purchase order.* If the order is produced in-house, it is a *shop or manufactured order.*
- **Planned order receipt (PORec)** *specifies the quantity and time an order is to be received.* When the order arrives it is recorded, checked into inventory, and available for use. It is assumed to be available for use at the beginning of the period.
- **Planned order release (PORel)** *specifies the planned quantity and time an order is to be released to the factory or a supplier.* It is a planned order receipt offset by the item's lead time. Planned order releases generate the gross requirements for all components in the MRP logic.
- **Projected on-hand inventory (POH)** *is the expected amount of inventory on hand at the beginning of the time period considering on-hand inventory from the previous period plus scheduled receipts or planned order receipts minus the gross requirements.* The formula for computing the projected on-hand inventory is defined by Equation (13.2) as follows:

Projected on-hand = On-hand inventory + Scheduled or planned receipts − Gross requirements
in period t (POH$_t$)   in period $t-1$ (OH$_{t-1}$)   in period t (S/PR$_t$)   in period t (GR$_t$)

or

$$POH_t = OH_{t-1} + S/PR_t - GR_t \qquad \textbf{(13.2)}$$

We can organize the calculations shown and the time-phasing information into a table called an *MRP record.* An MRP record typically has five rows of information for each week or time period:

Gross requirements
Scheduled receipts
Projected on-hand inventory
Planned order receipts
Planned order releases

Some software packages use from three to six rows. For example, the four-row MRP format uses the gross requirements, schedules receipt, projected on-hand inventory, and the planned order release rows.

Lot sizing is the process of determining the appropriate amount and timing of ordering to reduce costs. It can be uneconomical to set up a new production run or place a purchase order for the demand in each time bucket. Instead, it is usually better to aggregate orders and achieve economies of scale. Many different lot-sizing rules have been proposed. Some are simple heuristic rules, whereas others seek to find the best economic trade-off between the setup costs associated with production and the holding costs of carrying inventory. We discuss three common lot-sizing methods for MRP—lot-for-lot (LFL), fixed order quantity (FOQ), and periodic order quantity (POQ).

To illustrate these, we will consider the production of a simple product (A) whose bill of materials and inventory records are given in Exhibits 13.17 and 13.18. Note that item B is a common component for both items A and C; therefore, we cannot compute the gross requirements for item B until the planned order releases for items A and C have been determined.

Scheduled or planned receipts (S/PR) *are orders that are due or planned to be delivered.*

Planned order receipt (PORec) *specifies the quantity and time an order is to be received.*

Planned order release (PORel) *specifies the planned quantity and time an order is to be released to the factory or a supplier.*

Projected on-hand inventory (POH) *is the expected amount of inventory on hand at the beginning of the time period considering on-hand inventory from the previous period plus scheduled receipts or planned order receipts minus the gross requirements.*

Lot sizing *is the process of determining the appropriate amount and timing of ordering to reduce costs.*

Exhibit 13.17
Bill of Material

Exhibit 13.17
Bill of Material

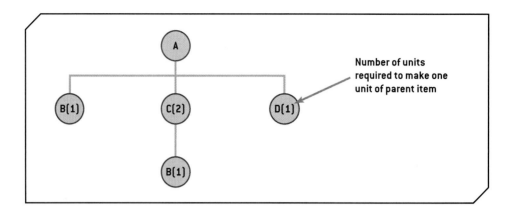

Exhibit 13.18
Item Inventory File

Data category	Item B	Item C	Item D
Lead time (weeks)	1	2	1
Beginning (on-hand) inventory	100	10	40
Scheduled receipts	none	200 (week 2)	50 (week 3)

Suppose that the MPS calls for 150 units of product A to be completed in week 4, 300 units in week 5, 50 units in week 6, and 200 units in week 7. We assume that the lead time is 1 week. The MPS in Exhibit 13.19 shows the demand for product A. The planned order releases are offset by 1 week to account for the lead time.

First consider item C. The MRP explosion is given in Exhibit 13.20. Notice from the BOM in Exhibit 13.17 that two units of item C are needed to produce one unit of end-item A. Therefore, the gross requirements for item C in Exhibit 13.20 are directly derived from the planned order releases in the MPS in Exhibit 13.19 (that is, $150 \times 2 = 300$ units in period 3, $300 \times 2 = 600$ units in period 4, and so on).

An ordering schedule that covers the gross requirements for each week is called lot-for-lot (LFL). In other words, we simply place orders each week to ensure that enough inventory is available to prevent shortages. If LFL is used for all dependent items, it clearly shows the true nature of dependent demand. Notice that LFL requires four planned orders and the average inventory during this planning horizon is $10 + 210 + 0 + 0 + 0 + 0 + 0 = 220/7 = 31.4$ units/week. The LFL rule minimizes the amount of inventory that needs be carried; however, it ignores the costs associated with purchase orders or production setups. Thus, this rule is best applied when inventory carrying costs are high and setup/order costs are low.

The projected on-hand quantity assumes the receipt of the planned order or scheduled receipt (S/PR_t) and is computed using Equation (13.2). LFL always tries to drive inventory levels to zero. We must compute the planned order release for item C before we can do the same for item B.

An ordering schedule that covers the gross requirements for each week is called lot-for-lot (LFL).

Exhibit 13.19
Example MPS

MPS	Lead time = 1 week for assembly						
Week	1	2	3	4	5	6	7
Product A—end-item	0	0	0	150	300	50	200
Planned order release	0	0	150	300	50	200	0

Item C (two units of C are needed for one unit of A) Description		Lot size: LFL Lead time: 2 weeks						
Week		1	2	3	4	5	6	7
Gross requirements		0	0	300	600	100	400	0
Scheduled receipts			200					
Projected OH inventory	10	10	210	0	0	0	0	0
Planned order receipts		0	0	90	600	100	400	0
Planned order releases		90	600	100	400			

Exhibit 13.20
MRP Record for Item C Using
the Lot-for-Lot (LFL) Rule

For example, using Equation (13.2) we compute the following:

$$POH_1 = OH_0 + S/PR_1 - GR_1 = 10 + 0 - 0 = 10$$
$$POH_2 = OH_1 + S/PR_2 - GR_2 = 10 + 200 - 0 = 210$$
$$POH_3 = OH_2 + S/PR_3 - GR_3 = 210 + 90 - 300 = 0$$
$$POH_4 = OH_3 + S/PR_4 - GR_4 = 0 + 600 - 600 = 0$$
$$POH_5 = OH_4 + S/PR_5 - GR_5 = 0 + 100 - 100 = 0$$
$$POH_6 = OH_5 + S/PR_6 - GR_6 = 0 + 400 - 400 = 0$$
$$POH_7 = OH_6 + S/PR_7 - GR_7 = 0 + 0 - 0 = 0$$

The planned order releases in Exhibit 13.20 are planned but have not yet been released. *The action bucket is the current time period*. When a planned order release reaches the action bucket, analysts evaluate the situation and release the order to the appropriate provider—supplier or in-house work center. In Exhibit 13.20, for example, only the planned order of 90 units of item C is in the action bucket or current time period of week 1. Therefore, the planned order needs to be released in week 1 and will show up the next week in the scheduled receipts row. Clearly, the total number of MRP calculations is enormous in multiproduct situations with many components, making a computer essential. Action notices are usually computer-generated and provide a variety of information to help inventory planners make decisions about order releases delaying scheduled receipts, and expediting when necessary.

A second approach to lot sizing is to use a large lot size for every purchase order or production run. Typically, this lot size is a fixed quantity. *The fixed order quantity (FOQ) rule uses a fixed order size for every order or production run*. This is similar to the fixed order quantity approach for independent demand items. The FOQ can be a standard-size container or pallet load or determined economically using the economic order quantity formula in Chapter 12. In the rare case where the FOQ does not cover the gross requirements, the order size is increased to equal the larger quantity, and FOQ defaults to LFL.

The rationale for the FOQ approach is that large lot sizes result in fewer orders and setups and therefore reduce the costs associated with ordering and setup. This allows the firm to take advantage of price breaks by suppliers, avoid less-than-truckload shipments (which are usually more expensive than full truck loads), and production economies of scale. However, this creates larger average inventory levels that must be held at a cost, and it can distort the true dependent demand gross requirements for lower-level components. Thus, the FOQ model is best applied when inventory carrying costs are low and setup/order costs are high.

We will illustrate this rule for item B in Exhibit 13.17. Exhibit 13.21 shows the MRP explosion. Note that component part commonality increases the dependent demand requirements as shown in the gross requirements row. For example, the 700-unit gross requirement in period 4 is due to the planned order release in the

*The **action bucket** is the current time period.*

*The **fixed order quantity (FOQ)** rule uses a fixed order size for every order or production run.*

Exhibit 13.21

Item B Fixed Order Quantity (FOQ) Lot Sizing and MRP Record

Item B Description		Week	1	2	3	4	5	6	7

Lot size: 800 units
Lead time: 1 week

Item B Description				Lot size: 800 units Lead time: 1 week					
Week		1	2	3	4	5	6	7	
Gross requirements		90	600	250	700	50	200	0	
Scheduled receipts									
Projected OH inventory	100	10	210	760	60	10	610	610	
Planned order receipts		0	800	800	0	0	800	0	
Planned order releases		800	800			800			

MPS for 300 units of item A in week 4 plus the planned order release for parent item C of 400 units.

Suppose that the FOQ is chosen using the EOQ as $\sqrt{2 \times 10{,}000 \text{ units} \times \$64/\$1} = \sqrt{640{,}000} = 800$ units. Using Equation (13.2), we compute the following projected on-hand inventories for each period:

$$POH_1 = OH_0 + S/PR_1 - GR_1 = 100 + 0 - 90 = 10$$
$$POH_2 = OH_1 + S/PR_2 - GR_2 = 10 + 800 - 600 = 210$$
$$POH_3 = OH_2 + S/PR_3 - GR_3 = 210 + 800 - 250 = 760$$
$$POH_4 = OH_3 + S/PR_4 - GR_4 = 760 + 0 - 700 = 60$$
$$POH_5 = OH_4 + S/PR_5 - GR_5 = 60 + 0 - 50 = 10$$
$$POH_6 = OH_5 + S/PR_6 - GR_6 = 10 + 800 - 200 = 610$$
$$POH_7 = OH_6 + S/PR_7 - GR_7 = 610 + 0 - 0 = 610$$

Notice that FOQ results in three planned orders and an average inventory is 10 + 210 + 760 + 60 + 10 + 610 + 610 = 2,270/7 = 324.3 units/week. To understand the difference with LFL, we encourage you to compare these results to the LFL approach.

The final rule we discuss is periodic order quantity. *The* **periodic order quantity POQ)** *orders a quantity equal to the gross requirement quantity in one or more predetermined time periods minus the projected on-hand quantity of the previous time period.* For example a POQ of 2 weeks orders exactly enough to cover demand during a 2-week period, and therefore may result in a different quantity every order cycle. The POQ might be selected judgmentally—for example, "order every 10 days"—or be determined using an economic time interval, which is the EOQ divided by annual demand (D). For example, if EOQ/D = 0.1 of a year, and assuming 250 working days per year, then POQ = 25 days, or about every 5 weeks. A POQ for a 1-week time period is equivalent to LFL. Using this rule, the projected on-hand inventory will equal zero at the end of the POQ time interval.

We illustrate this rule for item D using a POQ = 2 weeks. The result is shown in Exhibit 13.22. Using Equation (13.2), we compute the following:

$$POH_1 = OH_0 + S/PR_1 - GR_1 = 40 + 0 - 0 = 40$$
$$POH_2 = OH_1 + S/PR_2 - GR_2 = 40 + 0 - 0 = 40$$
$$POH_3 = OH_2 + S/PR_3 - GR_3 = 40 + 50 + 360 - 150 = 300$$
$$POH_4 = OH_3 + S/PR_4 - GR_4 = 300 + 0 - 300 = 0$$
$$POH_5 = OH_4 + S/PR_5 - GR_5 = 0 + 250 - 50 = 200$$
$$POH_6 = OH_5 + S/PR_6 - GR_6 = 200 + 0 - 200 = 0$$
$$POH_7 = OH_6 + S/PR_7 - GR_7 = 0 + 0 - 0 = 0$$

The **periodic order quantity POQ)** *orders a quantity equal to the gross requirement quantity in one or more predetermined time periods minus the projected on-hand quantity of the previous time period.*

Item D Description

Lot size: POQ = 2 weeks
Lead time: 1 week

Week		1	2	3	4	5	6	7
Gross requirements				150	300	50	200	
Scheduled receipts				50				
Projected OH inventory	**40**	40	40	300	0	200	0	0
Planned order receipts		0	0	360	0	250	0	0
Planned order releases			**360**		**250**			

Exhibit 13.22
Item D Fixed Period Quantity (POQ) Lot Sizing and MRP Record

The first time that POH becomes negative "without" a planned order receipt is in week 3 (40 + 50 − 150 = −60). Therefore, if we order 60 units to cover week 3 requirements plus 300 units to cover week 4 requirements, we have an order quantity of 360 units. The next time the POH is negative "without" a planned order receipt is week 5 (0 + 0 − 50 = −50). This requires us to order 50 units to cover week 5 requirements plus 200 units to cover week 6 requirements. For this example, POQ results in two planned orders of 360 and 250 units. The average inventory is 40 + 40 + 300 + 0 + 200 + 0 + 0 = 580/7 = 82.9 units/week.

The POQ approach results in moderate average inventory levels compared to FOQ because it matches order quantities to time buckets. Furthermore, it is easy to implement because inventory levels can be reviewed according to a fixed schedule. However, POQ creates high average inventory levels if the POQ becomes too long, and it can distort true dependent demand gross requirements for lower-level components. An economic-based POQ model is best applied when inventory carrying costs and setup/order costs are moderate.

As you see, lot-sizing rules affect not only the planned order releases for the particular item under consideration but also the gross requirements of all lower-level component items. Some MRP users only use the simple LFL rule; others apply other approaches to take advantage of economies of scale and reduce costs. Exhibit 13.23 summarizes the MRP explosion for the BOM in Exhibit 13.17.

MRP II and Capacity Requirements Planning

In the mid-1970s, **manufacturing resource planning**, known as **MRP-II**, began to replace the first-generation MRP systems. MRP-II systems made it possible to integrate material, production, and capacity constraints into the calculation of overall production capabilities. Supported by new shop-floor reporting capabilities, firms could now more efficiently schedule and monitor the execution of production plans. MRP-II systems also became more integrated with the firm's accounting, financial, engineering, and sales functions.

MUNSHI AHMED/BLOOMBERG NEWS/Landov

Although these systems were quite efficient, they were often inflexible when it came to producing variable quantities of more custom products on short order. As more attention began to be paid to the customer in the value chain, firms recognized the need to create or adapt new products and services on a timely basis to meet customers' specific needs.

One main difference between MRP and MRP-II is that MRP develops its subassembly, component part, and raw materials plans without considering capacity limitations. It simply determined what materials and components were required in order to meet the MPS and often resulted in an infeasible plan. A significant enhancement to MRP incorporated capacity requirements planning (CRP) into the planning and scheduling process (see Exhibit 13.13). **Capacity requirements planning**

Exhibit 13.23
Summary of MRP Explosion for
Bill of Material in Exhibit 13.17

MPS   **Lead time = 1 week for assembly**

Week	1	2	3	4	5	6	7
Product A—end-item	0	0	0	150	300	50	200
Planned order releases	0	0	150	300	50	200	0

Item C (two units of C are needed for one unit of A)   Lot size: LFL
Description   Lead time: 2 weeks

Week		1	2	3	4	5	6	7
Gross requirements		0	0	300	600	100	400	0
Scheduled receipts			200					
Projected OH inventory	10	10	210	0	0	0	0	0
Planned order receipts		0	0	90	600	100	400	0
Planned order releases		90	600	100	400			

Item B   Lot size: 800 units
Description   Lead time: 1 week

Week		1	2	3	4	5	6	7
Gross requirements		90	600	250	700	50	200	0
Scheduled receipts								
Projected OH inventory	100	10	210	760	60	10	610	610
Planned order receipts		0	800	800	0	0	800	0
Planned order releases		800	800			800		

Item D   Lot size: POQ = 2 weeks
Description   Lead time: 1 week

Week		1	2	3	4	5	6	7
Gross requirements				150	300	50	200	
Scheduled receipts				50				
Projected OH inventory	40	40	40	300	0	200	0	0
Planned order receipts		0	0	360	0	250	0	0
Planned order releases			360		250			

Capacity requirements planning (CRP) *is the process of determining the amount of labor and machine resources required to accomplish the tasks of production on a more detailed level, taking into account all component parts and end-items in the materials plan.*

(CRP) is the process of determining the amount of labor and machine resources required to accomplish the tasks of production on a more detailed level, taking into account all component parts and end-items in the materials plan. For example, in anticipation of a big demand for pizzas on Super Bowl Sunday, one would have to ensure that sufficient capacity for dough making, pizza preparation, and delivery is available to handle the forecasted demand. MRP-II uses CRP to develop its detailed plans, usually in an iterative procedure, and also ties its production plans to budget and cash flow systems of the firm.

Capacity requirements are computed by multiplying the number of units scheduled for production at a work center by the unit resource requirements and then adding in the setup time. These requirements are then summarized by time period and work center. To illustrate CRP calculations, suppose the planned order releases for a component are as follows:

Time period	1	2	3	4
Planned order release	30	20	40	40

Assume the component requires 1.10 hours of labor per unit in Work Center D and 1.5 hours of setup time. We can use Equation (10.2) from Chapter 10 to compute the total hours required (called *work center load*) on Work Center D:

Capacity required (C_i) = Setup time (S_i) + Processing time (P_i) × Order size (Q_i)

The capacity requirement in period 1 is 1.5 hours + (1.10 hours/unit)(30 units) = 34.5 hours. Similarly, in period 2 we have 1.5 hours + (1.10 hours/unit)(20 units) = 23.5 hours, and in periods 3 and 4 we have 1.5 hours + (1.10 hours/unit)(40 units) = 45.5 hours. The total load on Work Center D is 149 hours during these 4 weeks, or 37.25 hours per week if averaged.

Such information is usually provided in a **work center load report**, as illustrated in Exhibit 13.24. If sufficient capacity is not available, decisions must be made about overtime, transfer of personnel between departments, subcontracting, and so on. The master production schedule may also have to be revised to meet available capacity by shifting certain end-items to different time periods or changing the order quantities. For example, the workload in Exhibit 13.24 in periods 3 and 4 could be scheduled to period 2 to fill the idle time and avoid overtime in periods 3 and 4. However, additional inventory carrying costs would be incurred. So, as you see, leveling out work center load involves many cost trade-offs. This closed-loop, iterative process provides a realistic deployment of the master schedule to the shop floor.

MRP System Data Accuracy and Safety Stock

The key inputs to an MRP system were shown in Exhibit 13.13 and include the MPS, bill of materials for each physical good that is manufactured, and inventory, SKU and transaction files. MRP systems require a lot of information that must be

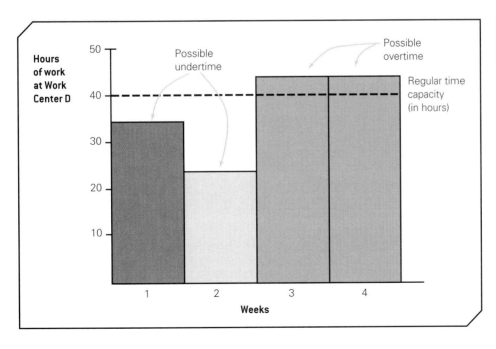

Exhibit 13.24
Work Center D Example Load Report

stored and managed in databases. For example, the *route file* contains the routing information for each customer's order, including part numbers, operations performed, standards, and so on; the *work-center file* includes capacity information; and the *customer-order file* contains the data on each customer's order. These files involve a lot of data collection and processing, and accuracy is vitally important. Automatic identification systems such as bar coding or RFID tags are often used to help improve data accuracy.

Another issue is whether to use safety stock in an MRP system to guard against uncertainty. Uncertainty can take the form of *quantity uncertainty*, such as scrap and output rates, and/or *timing uncertainty*, such as the delivery date of a scheduled receipt. Safety stock increases inventory levels and therefore costs. Some MRP experts argue that safety stock should not be used in an MRP system because it distorts the true dependent demands between parent and component items. Others argue it should only be used at the end-item and purchased-item levels of the bills of material (that is, the top and bottom of the bills of material). Still others believe that safety stock should only be used for items in the BOM with high uncertainty in the demand, supply, or production of the component.

Learning Objective
To learn how service-providing organizations develop executable plans and schedules by disaggregating aggregate plans.

DISAGGREGATING SERVICE PLANS

As we noted earlier, disaggregating aggregate plans for most service organizations does not require as many intermediate levels of planning, such as master production scheduling and materials requirements planning, as in manufacturing. The aggregate plans developed in the Golden Resorts example (see Exhibits 13.9 to 13.12) essentially combine both Level 1 and Level 2 planning by specifying the number of full- and part-time employees needed each month. For instance, the chase demand plan uses two full-time employees from January to December and zero part-time employees in December to ten part-time employees in July and August. Exhibit 13.25 illustrates the nature of aggregate planning and disaggregation in services.

Once Golden Resort management decides on implementing either the chase or level aggregate plans, Level 3 planning and execution for Golden Resorts consists of taking these full- and part-time staff levels and monthly schedules and developing a daily staff schedule for each month, implementing employee training, recognition and reward, and customer feedback systems, and creating appropriate service encounters between the staff and tennis customers.

Dependent demand also occurs in service businesses, but few managers recognize it. Many service organizations such as restaurants and retail stores offer repeatable and highly structured services and have high goods content of 50 percent or more. Therefore, the logic of dependent demand can be used to plan the goods-content portion of the customer benefit package. For example, meals in a restaurant can be thought of as end-items. The service required to assemble an order can be defined in terms of the bill of material (BOM) and lead times. Solved problem #2 is an example of using dependent demand in a gift-wrapping shop. The Park Plaza Hospital case at the end of this chapter shows how dependent demand concepts and methods are applied for hospital surgery.

*A **bill of labor (BOL)** is a hierarchical record analogous to a BOM that defines labor inputs necessary to create a good or service.*

For labor-intensive services, the analogy to the BOMs in Exhibits 13.15 and 13.17 is a bill of labor (BOL). *A **bill of labor (BOL)** is a hierarchical record analogous to a BOM that defines labor inputs necessary to create a good or service.* For example, a BOL for surgery includes the doctors and supporting surgery technicians and nurses. A broader concept is a *bill of resources (BOR)* where the labor, information (like X-rays, blood tests, and so on), equipment, instruments, and parts are all defined in a BOM format to support each specific type of surgery.

Exhibit 13.25 Two Levels of Disaggregation for Many Service Organizations

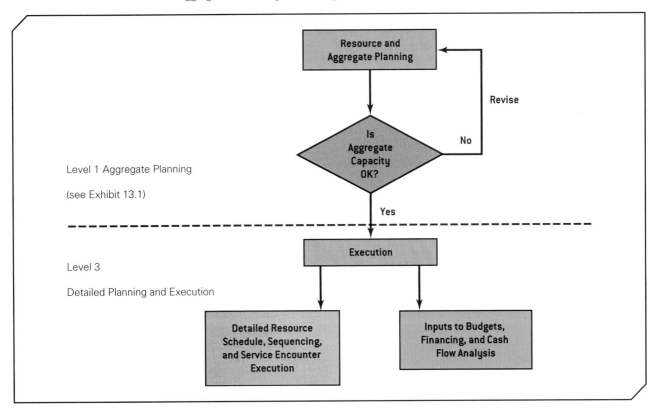

SOLVED PROBLEMS

SOLVED PROBLEM #1

Given the demand pattern shown at the bottom of the page, compute the cost of a level production strategy if the unit production cost is $1.20, overtime cost is $1.30 per unit, undertime cost is $1.40 per unit, and inventory-holding cost is 20 cents per unit per month.

Assume a desired ending inventory of 24,000. The beginning inventory is 20,000 units. The capacity for regular production is 24,000 units, and overtime capacity is 4,000 units.

Solution:
Total demand is 283,000; thus, average production level is 23,917. (See table, next page.)

Month	1	2	3	4	5	6	7	8	9	10	11	12
Demand (1000s)	24	22	26	20	20	20	22	23	24	26	28	28

Month	Demand	Production	Inventory	Production Costs	Inventory Costs	Shortage Costs	Overtime Costs	Total Costs
1	24,000	23,917	19,917	$ 28,700	$ 3,983	$ —	$ —	$ 32,683
2	22,000	23,917	21,834	$ 28,700	$ 4,367	$ —	$ —	$ 33,067
3	26,000	23,917	19,751	$ 28,700	$ 3,950	$ —	$ —	$ 32,650
4	20,000	23,917	23,668	$ 28,700	$ 4,734	$ —	$ —	$ 33,434
5	20,000	23,917	27,585	$ 28,700	$ 5,517	$ —	$ —	$ 34,217
6	20,000	23,917	31,502	$ 28,700	$ 6,300	$ —	$ —	$ 35,000
7	22,000	23,917	33,419	$ 28,700	$ 6,684	$ —	$ —	$ 35,384
8	23,000	23,917	34,336	$ 28,700	$ 6,867	$ —	$ —	$ 35,567
9	24,000	23,917	34,253	$ 28,700	$ 6,851	$ —	$ —	$ 35,551
10	26,000	23,917	32,170	$ 28,700	$ 6,434	$ —	$ —	$ 35,134
11	28,000	23,917	28,087	$ 28,700	$ 5,617	$ —	$ —	$ 34,317
12	28,000	23,917	24,004	$ 28,700	$ 4,800	$ —	$ —	$ 33,500
	283,000	287,004	330,526	$344,400	$66,104	$ —	$ —	$410,504

SOLVED PROBLEM #2

Caroline graduated from a small college and decided to open a gift-wrap shop in a major shopping mall in Myrtle Beach, South Carolina. She realized the demand for boxes, tape, bows, and wrapping paper was dependent upon the demand for her four wrapping options: basic and deluxe wrap, and small or large box. She thought that MRP logic and the LFL lot-sizing rule could be used because it would reduce her inventory requirements. About 50 percent of her business was contract wrapping for holiday gifts for businesses. The remainder of her business was related to sales at the mall and is forecast. Caroline defined the following four bills of materials:

Small Box Basic Wrap

Small box—1
Regular paper—2 feet
Tape—6 inches
Basic bow—1
To/From name tag—1

Large Box Basic Wrap

Large box—1
Regular paper—4 feet
Tape—10 inches
Basic bow—1
To/From name tag—1

Small Box Deluxe Wrap

Small box—1
Deluxe paper—2 feet
Tape—6 inches
Deluxe bow—1
Deluxe card—1

Large Box Deluxe Wrap

Large box—1
Deluxe paper—4 feet
Tape—10 inches
Deluxe bow—1
Deluxe card—1

The historical gift wrap mix is 15 percent small box/basic wrap, 20 percent large box/basic wrap, 35 percent small box/deluxe wrap, and 30 percent large box/deluxe wrap.

a. If 100 packages are forecast each nonholiday and weekday, how much tape is required? How much tape is required for 200 such days?

b. How much deluxe paper is required?

c. If the cost of boxes, deluxe bows, tape, and so on, are known, could Caroline compute the cost of all wrapping supplies each day and week?

Solution:

a. Tape—small boxes = (15 + 35 boxes) × (6 inches)
= 300 inches

Tape—large boxes = (20 + 30 boxes) × (10 inches)
= 500 inches

Total tape per day = 800 inches

Tape for 200 nonholidays and weekdays = (800 inches/day) × (200 days/year) = 160,000 inches, or 13,333 feet, or 4,444 yards

b. Deluxe paper—small boxes = (35 boxes) × (2 feet)
= 70 feet

Deluxe paper—large boxes = (30 boxes) × (4 feet)
= 120 feet

Total deluxe paper per day = 190 feet

c. Yes. By using the concepts of dependent demand she could forecast demand for the four end-items (forecast orders) and add contract demand (firm orders) and establish the master production schedule. Then she could calculate the dependent demand for all raw materials (box, paper, tape, tags) and component parts (bows, cards) by time period over the planning horizon. Component cost could then be multiplied times the dependent demand quantities to compute a total cost.

SOLVED PROBLEM #3

Exhibits 13.26 and 13.27 are the bills of material and inventory records for two products, A and B, and their components. The MPS for product A calls for completion of 100 units in period 2, 125 units in period 4, and 150 units in period 6. The MPS for product B calls for completion of 75 units in week 3, 75 units in week 4, 125 units in week 5, and 100 units in week 7. The manufacturing lead time for products A and B is 1 week. The numbers in parentheses are the number of parts needed to make the parent item. Compute a full MRP explosion and apply the appropriate lot sizing rules to determine a schedule of planned order releases.

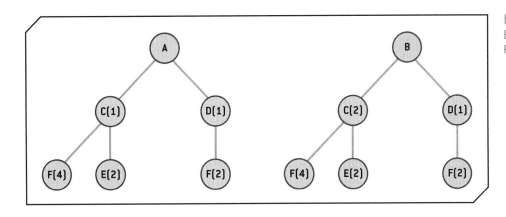

Exhibit 13.26
Bill of Material for Solved Problem #1

Exhibit 13.27 Component Part Information for Solved Problem #3

	Part C	Part D	Part E	Part F
Lot size rule	FOQ = 250	LFL	FOQ = 1000	POQ = 2 weeks
Lead time (wks)	2	1	1	2
Scheduled receipts	300 week 1	none	none	1,000 week 2
Beginning inventory	0	125	750	2,500
Spare-parts orders	none	100 each in weeks 3 and 6	none	none
Source of item	Manufactured in-house	Manufactured in-house	Manufactured in-house	Purchased item from supplier

Solution:

Week	1	2	3	4	5	6	7
Customer req. A		100		125		150	
Customer req. B			75	75	125		100
MPS start A	**100**		**125**		**150**		
MPS start B		**75**	**75**	**125**		**100**	

(continued on the next page)

Item C

Lot-size rule: FOQ = 250 units
Lead time: 2

Week		1	2	3	4	5	6
Gross requirements		100	150	275	250	150	200
Scheduled receipts		200					
Projected on-hand inventory	0	200	50	25	25	125	175
Planned receipts				250	250	250	250
Planned order releases		250	250	250	250		

For MRP Item C in week 2, two units of C are needed to make end-item B, so $2 \times 75 = 150$ units. In week 3, $2 \times 75 = 150$ units for end-item B + 125 units for end-item A = 275 units.

$$POH_1 = OH_0 + S/PR_1 - GR_1 = 0 + \blacksquare - 100 = 200$$
$$POH_2 = OH_1 + S/PR_2 - GR_2 = 200 + 0 - 150 = 50$$
$$POH_3 = OH_2 + S/PR_3 - GR_3 = 50 + 250 - 275 = 25$$
$$POH_4 = OH_3 + S/PR_4 - GR_4 = 25 + 250 - 250 = 25$$
$$POH_5 = OH_4 + S/PR_5 - GR_5 = 25 + 250 - 150 = 125$$
$$POH_6 = OH_5 + S/PR_6 - GR_6 = 125 + 250 - 200 = 175$$

Item D

Lot-size rule: LFL
Lead time: 1

Week		1	2	3	4	5	6
Gross requirements		100	75	300	125	150	200
Scheduled receipts							
Projected on-hand inventory	125	25	0	0	0	0	0
Planned receipts			50	300	125	150	200
Planned order releases		50	300	125	150	200	

For Item D in week 3, 125 units are from end-item A, 75 from end-item B, and 100 are spare parts, for a total of 300 units. In week 6, 100 units are from end-item B and 100 units are spare parts, for a total of 200 units.

$$POH_1 = OH_0 + S/PR_1 - GR_1 = 125 + 0 - 100 = 25$$
$$POH_2 = OH_1 + S/PR_2 - GR_2 = 25 + 50 - 75 = 0$$
$$POH_3 = OH_2 + S/PR_3 - GR_3 = 0 + 300 - 300 = 0$$
$$POH_4 = OH_3 + S/PR_4 - GR_4 = 0 + 125 - 125 = 0$$
$$POH_5 = OH_4 + S/PR_5 - GR_5 = 0 + 150 - 150 = 0$$
$$POH_6 = OH_5 + S/PR_6 - GR_6 = 0 + 200 - 200 = 0$$

Item E		Week	1	2	3	4	5	6	Lot-size rule: FOQ = 1,000 Lead time: 1

Item E — **Lot-size rule: FOQ = 1,000** / **Lead time: 1**

Week		1	2	3	4	5	6
Gross requirements		500	500	500	500		
Scheduled receipts							
Projected on-hand inventory	**750**	250	750	250	750	750	750
Planned receipts			1,000		1,000		
Planned order releases		1,000		1,000			

For item E, two units are needed for each parent item C that are made, and therefore, $2 \times 250 = 500$ units.

$$POH_1 = OH_0 + S/PR_1 - GR_1 = 750 + 0 - 500 = 250$$
$$POH_2 = OH_1 + S/PR_2 - GR_2 = 250 + 1{,}000 - 500 = 750$$
$$POH_3 = OH_2 + S/PR_3 - GR_3 = 750 + 0 - 500 = 250$$
$$POH_4 = OH_3 + S/PR_4 - GR_4 = 250 + 1{,}000 - 500 = 750$$
$$POH_5 = OH_4 + S/PR_5 - GR_5 = 750 + 0 - 0 = 750$$
$$POH_6 = OH_5 + S/PR_6 - GR_6 = 750 + 0 - 0 = 750$$

Item F — **Lot-size rule: POQ = 2 weeks** / **Lead time: 2**

Week		1	2	3	4	5	6
Gross requirements		1,100	1,600	1,250	1,300	400	
Scheduled receipts							
Projected on-hand inventory	**2,500**	1,400	800	1,300 (1st POQ Cycle)	0	0 (2nd POQ Cycle)	0
Planned receipts				1,750		400	
Planned order releases		1,750		400			

Item F has two parents—C and D—and four units of F are required for each unit of C and two units of F for each unit of D. For example, in week 1 the item C planned order release is for $250 \times 4 = 1{,}000$ units plus a planned order release for item D of $50 \times 2 = 100$ units, so the total dependent requirements for item F are 1,100.

$$POH_1 = OH_0 + S/PR_1 - GR_1 = 2{,}500 + 0 - 1{,}100 = 1{,}400$$
$$POH_2 = OH_1 + S/PR_2 - GR_2 = 1{,}400 + 1{,}000 - 1{,}600 = 800$$
$$POH_3 = OH_2 + S/PR_3 - GR_3 = 800 + 1{,}750 - 1{,}250 = 1{,}300$$
$$POH_4 = OH_3 + S/PR_4 - GR_4 = 1{,}300 + 0 - 1{,}300 = 0$$
$$POH_5 = OH_4 + S/PR_5 - GR_5 = 0 + 400 - 400 = 0$$
$$POH_6 = OH_5 + S/PR_6 - GR_6 = 0 + 0 - 0 = 0$$

The first time the POH is negative is in week 3, where $800 + 0 - 1{,}250 = -450$ units short. Since the POQ = 2 weeks, we order exactly enough to cover weeks 3 and 4 requirements, or $450 + 1{,}300 = 1{,}750$ units. At the end of week 4, the POH is zero. In week 5, the POH again goes negative, where $0 + 0 - 400 = -400$. In the second POQ order cycle, we order exactly enough to cover weeks 5 and 6 requirements, or $400 + 0 = 400$ units.

KEY TERMS AND CONCEPTS

Action bucket
Aggregate planning
Aggregate planning decision variables
Bill of labor (BOL)
Bill of material (BOM)
Capacity requirements planning (CRP)
Chase demand strategy
Component part commonality
Components
Dependent demand
Dependent demand in services
Disaggregation
End-items
Execution or shop floor control
Final assembly schedule (FAS)
Fixed order quantity (FOQ)
Gross requirements (GR)
Level production strategy
Levels of the BOM
Lot-for-lot (LFL)
Lot sizing

Manufacturing resource planning (MRP-II)
Master production scheduling (MPS)
Materials requirements planning (MRP)
MRP explosion
Net requirements
On-hand inventory
Parent item
Periodic order quantity (POQ)
Planned order receipt (PORec)
Planned order release (PORel)
Projected on-hand quantity (POH)
Purchased and raw material items
Resource management
Scheduled receipts (S/PR)
Service disaggregation and levels
Subassembly
Three levels of planning
Time buckets
Time-phased requirements and lead times
Work center load report

QUESTIONS FOR REVIEW AND DISCUSSION

1. Define resource management, and explain its objectives and the effects of poor resource management in the value chain.

2. What is aggregate planning? Why is it used?

3. Explain the concept of disaggregation and how it relates to aggregate planning.

4. Describe and explain the three levels of resource planning for goods-producing firms.

5. What is the purpose of rough-cut capacity planning?

6. How does aggregate planning and disaggregation differ between manufacturing and service organizations?

7. Describe the major decision options that can be considered for aggregate planning.

8. Explain the difference between a level production strategy and a chase demand strategy. How does the choice of strategy affect costs?

9. Interview a production manager at a nearby goods-producing company to determine how the company plans its production for fluctuating demand. What approaches does it use?

10. What is a master production schedule? How does it differ from a final assembly schedule? Explain how one is constructed.

11. What is materials requirements planning? Of what value is it to organizations?

12. Explain the concept of dependent demand.

13. What is a bill of materials? Sketch a small example. What is the analogy of the BOM in services?

14. What is component part commonality? How does it affect MRP calculations?

15. Explain the concepts of time-phasing and MRP explosion.

16. How can the MRP concept be applied in a service organization? Provide some examples.

17. Construct a bill of materials for your college curriculum, thinking of core courses, electives, and so

on as components of the end-item. How might MRP concepts apply?

18. Explain the pros and cons for the LFL, FOQ, and POQ lot-sizing methods.

19. Draw a simple bill of materials (BOM) for an automobile given the following requirements: (a) clearly label the end-item and each component; (b) BOM must contain no more than ten items; (c) BOM must contain at least three levels (you may count the end-item Level 0).

20. What weaknesses of MRP led to the development of MRP-II? Explain the purpose and objectives of MRP-II.

PROBLEMS AND ACTIVITIES

1. The forecast demand for fudge for the next 4 months is 120, 160, 20, and 70 pounds.

   a. What is the recommended production rate if a level strategy is adopted with no back orders or stockouts? What is the ending inventory for month #4 under this plan?

   b. What is the level production rate with no ending inventory in month #4?

2. Kings Appliance Manufacturers makes toasters and wants to evaluate a level strategy against a chase strategy. The quarterly demand forecasts are: Q1—11,000, Q2—15,000, Q3—18,000, and Q4—31,000. The beginning finished goods inventory level is 3,000 units. No back orders are allowed. The average cost per unit is $200 and the output rate is 100 units/employee/quarter.

   a. If a level production strategy is followed, what quarterly production rate is required to meet demand and yield zero finished goods inventory at the end of quarter 4? How many employees are needed each quarter?

   b. If a chase production strategy is followed, what quarterly production rate is required to meet demand and yield zero finished goods inventory at the end of quarter 4? How many employees are needed each quarter?

3. The Westerbeck Company manufactures several models of automatic washers and dryers. The projected requirements over the next year for their washers is shown in the chart at the bottom of this page.

   Current inventory is 100 units. Current capacity is 960 units per month. The average salary of production workers is $1,300 per month. Overtime is paid at time-and-a-half up to 20 percent additional time. Each production worker accounts for 30 units per month. Additional labor can be hired for a training cost of $250, and current workers can be laid off at a cost of $500. Any increase or decrease in the production rate costs $5,000 for tooling, setup, and line changes. This does not apply, however, to overtime. Inventory-holding costs are $25 per unit per month. Lost sales are valued at $75 per unit. Determine at least two different production plans, trying to minimize the cost of meeting the next year's requirements.

4. Recreation Inc. assembles jet skis and snowmobiles from subassemblies and component part suppliers. Both end-items use the same small engines and many common parts. The following information in the first column, page 578, is available to plan production for next year:

Month	Jan	Feb	Mar	Apr	May	June	Jul	Aug	Sep	Oct	Nov	Dec
Requirement	800	1,030	810	900	950	1,340	1,100	1,210	600	580	890	1,000

Production Costs

Regular time—$15 per unit
Overtime—$22.50 per unit
Subcontract—$30 per unit
Hiring cost—$300 per full-time employee
Layoff cost—$1,500 per full-time employee
Back-order cost—$24 per unit per quarter
(based on back orders at end of quarter)
Inventory carrying costs—$3 per unit per quarter
based on average inventory during each quarter
Beginning inventory—600 jet skis and 400
snowmobiles

Production Rates

Regular time—500 units per full-time employee
per quarter of either end-item
Maximum overtime—200 units per full-time
employee per quarter of either end-item
Initial work-force size—44 full-time employees
beginning in quarter 1
Assume 100 percent utilization of employees on
regular time, and therefore, each employee
produces 500 units. If overtime is used, another
200 units can be produced per employee.
No part-time employees are used due to the high
skill levels of these jobs.

Demand Forecasts

Quarter	Jet Skis	Snowmobiles
1	10,000	9,000
2	15,000	7,000
3	16,000	19,000
4	3,000	10,000

Develop an aggregate plan that uses a level production strategy each quarter using full-time employees only. Ending inventory and back orders for quarter 4 must be equal to zero. Summarize the plan, its costs, and consequences.

5. The Silver Star Bicycle Company will be manufacturing men's and women's models of its Easy-Pedal ten-speed bicycle during the next 2 months, and the company would like a production schedule indicating how many bicycles of each model should be produced in each month. Current demand forecasts call for 150 men's and 125 women's models to be shipped during

the first month and 200 men's and 150 women's models to be shipped during the second month. Additional data are shown in Table 1 at the bottom of the page.

Last month Silver Star used a total of 4,000 hours of labor. Its labor relations policy will not allow the combined total hours of labor (manufacturing plus assembly) to increase or decrease by more than 500 hours from month to month. In addition, the company charges monthly inventory at the rate of 2 percent of the production cost based on the inventory levels at the end of the month. Silver Star would like to have at least 25 units of each model in inventory at the end of the 2 months.

a. Establish a production schedule that minimizes production and inventory costs and satisfies the labor-smoothing, demand, and inventory requirements. What inventories will be maintained, and what are the monthly labor requirements?

b. If the company changed the constraints so that monthly labor increases and decreases could not exceed 250 hours, what would happen to the production schedule? How much would the cost increase? What would you recommend?

6. Given the bill of material for the printer cartridge (A) shown here, a gross requirement to build 200 units of A, an on-hand inventory level for end-item A of 80 units, and assuming zero lead times for all items A, B, C, D, and E, compute the net requirements for each item.

Item	On-Hand Inventory	Net Req.
A	30	?
B	50	?
C	90	?
D	70	?
E	15	?

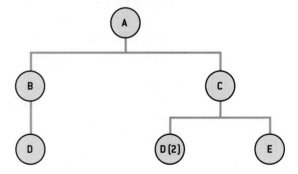

Table 1.

Model	Production Costs	Labor Required for Manufacturing (hours)	Labor Required for Assembly (hours)	Current Inventory
Men's	$40	10	3	20
Women's	$30	8	2	30

7. Given the following information, complete the MRP record and explain what it tells the inventory analyst to do.

Lot-size rule: Fixed Q = 100 units Lead time = 3 weeks			Safety stock: 0 units Current on-hand quantity = 80 units						
Weeks		1	2	3	4	5	6	7	8
Gross requirement		20	0	60	0	100	80	0	60
Scheduled receipts			100						
Projected on hand	80								
Planned receipts									
Planned order releases									

8. Each bank teller workstation is forecast to process 400 transactions (the end-item) on Friday. The bank is open from 9:00 A.M. to 7:00 P.M. on Friday with 90 minutes for lunch and breaks. Three teller windows are open on Friday. A work-study analysis reveals that the breakdown of the transaction mix is 40 percent deposits, 45 percent withdrawals, and 15 percent transfers between accounts. A different form is used for each type of transaction, so there is one deposit slip per deposit, one withdrawal slip per withdrawal, and two transfer slips per transfer.

a. How many transfer slips are needed on Friday?
b. How many withdrawal slips are needed on Friday?
c. Deposit slips are delivered every second day. If the on-hand balance of deposit slips is 50 at this bank, how many deposit slips should be ordered?
d. What is the end-item and component part in this bank example?
e. What are the implications of having too many or too few deposit, withdrawal, and transfer slips? Explain.

9. Irene's Kitchen & Catering Service sells three kinds of cakes—single, double, and triple layers. The product mix is 30 percent single layer, 50 percent double layer, and 20 percent triple layer. The bills of

material are shown in the table at the bottom of the page.

a. Irene's forecast for cakes for the next 3 months is 40 cakes a day or 2,880 cakes (40 cakes/day × 24 workdays/month × 3 months). How much cake mix does she need?
b. How much butter is needed?
c. How many eggs are needed?

10. The MPS for product A calls for 100 units to be completed in week 4 and 200 units in week 7 (the lead time is 1 week). Spare part demand for Item B is 10 units per week. The bill of materials and inventory records for product A are below and in the first column on page 580.

Bill of Material

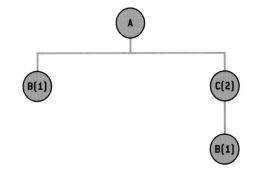

Single-Layer Cake	Double-Layer Cake	Triple-Layer Cake
Cake mix—1.16 lb	Cake mix—1.75 lb	Cake mix—3.65 lb
Butter—0.5 cups	Butter—0.75 cups	Butter—1 cup
Eggs—3	Eggs—4	Eggs—5

	Item	**Item**
Data category	B	C
Lot-sizing rule	FOQ = 500	LFL
Lead time (weeks)	2	3
Beginning (on-hand) inventory	100	10
Scheduled receipts	none	200 (week 2)

   a. Develop a material requirement plan for the next 7 weeks for items B and C.
   b. Will any action notices be generated? If so, what are they and explain why they must be generated.

11. David Christopher is an orthopedic surgeon who specializes in three types of surgery—hip, knee, and ankle replacements. The surgery mix is 40 percent hip replacement, 50 percent knee replacement, and 10 percent ankle replacement. Partial bills of materials for each type of surgery are shown in Table 2.

   a. Given that Dr. Christopher is scheduled to do five hip replacements, three knee replacements, and one ankle replacement next week, how many surgical kits and part packages of each type should the hospital have available next week?
   b. How many total pints of blood are needed next week?
   c. Design a "mistake-proof" system to ensure each patient gets the correct blood type.
   d. What are the implications of a shortage (stockout) of a surgical kit or part package discovered several hours before the operation? What if a part package has a missing part that is not discovered until surgery begins?

12. Consider the master production schedule, bills of material, and inventory data shown below and on page 581. Complete the MPS and MRP explosion, and identify what actions, if any, you would take given this requirements plan.

Table 2.

Hip Replacement	**Knee Replacement**	**Ankle Replacement**
Surgical kits #203 & #428	Surgical kit #203	Surgical kit #108
Hip part package #A	Knee part package #V	Ankle part package #P
Patient's blood type—6 pints	Patient's blood type—4 pints	Patient's blood type—3 pints

Master Production Schedule

	Weeks							
	1	2	3	4	5	6	7	8
Customer req. "A"		5		8			10	
Customer req. "B"						5		10

Lead time for Product "A" is 1 week.
Lead time for Product "B" is 2 weeks.

Bills of Material

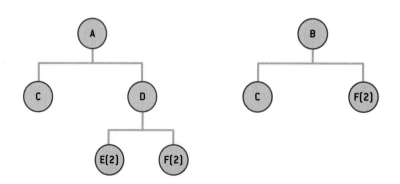

Item File

	Item			
	C	D	E	F
Lot-sizing rule	LFL	LFL	FOQ (25)	POQ (P = 2)
Lead time (weeks)	3	1	3	1
Beginning (on-hand) inventory	5	8	19	3
Scheduled receipts	8 in week 1	None	25 in week 3	20 in week 1

13. The BOM for product A is shown next and data from the inventory records are shown in the table. In the master production schedule for Product A, the MPS quantity row (showing completion dates) calls for 250 units in week 8. The lead time for production of A is 2 weeks. Develop the materials requirements plan for the next 8 weeks for Items B, C, and D.

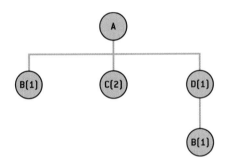

Data Category	B	C	D
Lot-sizing rule	P = 2	FOQ = 1,000	LFL
Lead time	2 weeks	1 week	2 weeks
Scheduled receipts	100 (week 1)	0	0
Beginning (on-hand) inventory	0	100	0

14. Garden Manufacturing is a small, family-owned garden tool manufacturer located in Florence, South Carolina. The bill of materials for models A and B of a popular garden tool are shown in Exhibit 13.28 and other information in Exhibit 13.29. There is considerable component part commonality between these two models, as shown by the BOM.

The MPS calls for 100 units of Tool A to be completed in week 5 and 200 units of Tool A to be completed in week 7. End-item A has a 2-week lead time. The MPS calls for 300 units of Tool B to be completed in week 7. End-item B has a 1-week lead time. Do an MRP explosion for all items required to make these two garden tools. What actions, if any, should be taken immediately and what other potential problems do you see?

Exhibit 13.28
BOM for Two Garden Manufacturing End-Item Tools

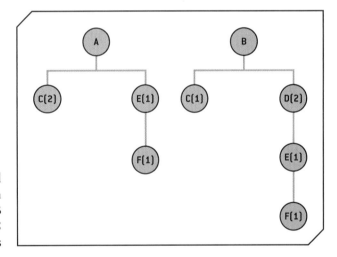

Exhibit 13.29
Component part information

Data Category	Item			
	C	D	E	F
Lot-sizing rule	FOQ = 400	LFL	POQ = 4	LFL
Lead time	1 week	2 weeks	2 weeks	1 week
Scheduled receipts	450 (week 1)	50 (week 1)	None	None
Beginning inventory	100	70	50	900

CASES

IN-LINE INDUSTRIES (A)

In-Line Industries (ILI) produces recreational in-line skates (see Exhibit 13.30). Demand is seasonal, peaking in the summer months, with a smaller peak demand during December. For one of its more popular models that is being introduced with some cosmetic upgrades, ILI has forecasted the following demand in pairs of skates for the next year:

Month	Demand (pairs)
January	300
February	550
March	900
April	1,500
May	2,500
June	3,000
July	1,400
August	1,000
September	600
October	400
November	700
December	1,800

The manufacturing cost is $80 for each pair of skates, including materials and direct labor. Inventory-holding cost is charged at 20 percent of the manufacturing cost per month. Because this is an "on-demand" good, customers will most likely buy another model if it is not available, thus the lost sales cost is the marginal profit, which is the manufacturer markup of 100 percent, or $80. The normal production rate is 1,000 pairs per month. However, changing the production rate requires administrative costs and is computed to be $1 per unit. Overtime can be scheduled at a cost computed to be $10 per pair. Because ILI produces a variety of other products, labor can be shifted to other work, so undertime cost is not relevant. ILI would like to evaluate the level and chase demand strategies. Your report should address not only financial impacts but potential operational and managerial impacts of the different strategies.

Optional Assignment: ILI would like to know the minimum cost aggregate plan. (Some hints: One approach is to try different scenarios using the spreadsheets you just developed and seek to minimize the total cost. Another option is to model this aggregate planning situation using linear programming—see Supplementary Chapter C.)

Exhibit 13.30
In-Line Skate

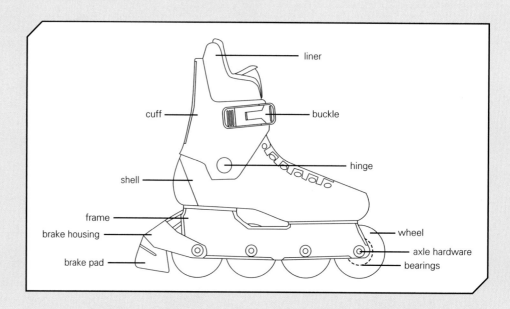

IN-LINE INDUSTRIES (B)

The BOM, current inventory, and lead time (in months) for the in-line skates in ILI Case (A) is shown in Exhibit 13.31. Using the chase demand strategy you developed in ILI Case (A), develop a complete MRP week-by-week schedule using lot-for-lot (LFL) to meet production requirements for the first quarter of the year

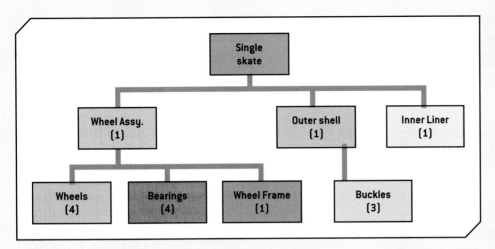

Exhibit 13.31
In-Line Skate Bill of Material
and Related Information

Item	Inventory	Lead Time
Pair skates	50	1 weeks
Wheel assembly	100	2
Outer shell	25 pairs	3
Inner liner	0 pairs	3
Wheels	1,500	1
Bearings	3,000	1
Wheel frame	600	2
Buckles	5,000	1

(January to March). Assume for simplicity that there are 4 weeks per month.

The following assignment questions may help focus your attention on a few key issues. In answering these, do not redo the MRP explosion but simply discuss the pertinent issues.

a. When must the process of ordering and producing in-line skates to meet demand for these 3 months begin?

b. What are the cost and capacity implications from the planned schedule of order releases?

c. What would be the effect on part planned order releases if a level aggregate plan was used instead of a chase strategy?

d. What would be the pros and cons of reducing part lead times by one-half?

e. Do you see any opportunities to use lot sizing to batch order quantities? Select one part and explain/justify.

f. What other insights do you have? Is this a good planned order release schedule?

PARK PLAZA HOSPITAL[6]

Park Plaza Hospital is a privately owned, 374-bed facility with a surgical suite of nine operating rooms in Houston, Texas. These operating rooms are reserved at least a week in advance by physicians with surgery privileges at the hospital. Thus, at any time, the schedule of planned operations for the next 7 days is known with some certainty. Anything beyond that horizon is far less certain. After an operation has been entered on the surgical schedule, it must be confirmed on two other occasions: 72 hours before and 48 hours before the operation. This scheduling process allows the assignment of staff (nurses, orderlies, and so on) and the preparation of the necessary supplies and equipment for the specific procedure. The patient is generally admitted to the hospital about 12 hours before the operation.

Most surgery is performed during normal working hours (7 A.M. to 5 P.M.), Monday through Friday and some Saturdays. The operations themselves average about 45 minutes. Obviously, however, different operations take different amounts of time; there is no set time for any procedure, and they differ from case to case and physician to physician. This lack of predictability is further complicated by evidence that physicians perceive that they work more quickly than they actually do. As a result, the surgical schedule for any given operating room on any given day (and hence, for the 7-day planning horizon) is not entirely fixed. The schedule includes such information as: date, operating room number, scheduled time, patient name, patient room number, operation, physician, estimated time, and planned anesthesia.

Supplies for any operation fit into three general categories:

1. Disposable items that can be used only once.
2. Reusable instruments that are recycled and used again; that is, they are cleaned, sterilized, and placed back into inventory (for example, pickups, clamps, and so on).
3. A limited number of high-technology instruments— the limitation is due to their high costs (for example, a CAT scan, heart-lung machine, and so on).

In addition, the stock required for any operation depends on the particular procedure and physician—each having his or her preference as to the instruments and disposable supplies needed for a given procedure. Supplies and instruments are drawn from inventory according to a Physician's Preference Sheet that lists these requirements by procedure and by physician. The goal of the MRP system for Park Plaza is to ensure that these required supplies arrive at the proper place (the correct operating room) at the proper time, correctly assigned by surgical procedure and physician, and that appropriate and accurate inventory levels are maintained.

The first component of the resource planning system is a 7-day surgical schedule. In this case, however, each product is defined as a specific physician performing a specific procedure. This definition is necessary, as has been explained, because the physicians have different preferences. Thus, if we have k physicians, each performing n procedures, we can identify as many as k times n separate products. The surgical requirements file contains the materials and supplies needed for the various procedures. Each unique procedure can be viewed as an end-item at Level 0. Lower-level components are the supplies required for a particular surgical procedure in accordance with physician preference. Thus, the items on the Physician's Preference Sheet are defined as Level 1 components that must be ready for use (sterilized if appropriate) in the procedure.

All items that require sterilization are considered Level 2 subassemblies with lead times equal to their required sterilization time (which ranges from 5 minutes to 16 hours) and recycling. Although this means that inventory records must be kept on two levels, such a scheme provides an effective method for handling items that must be sterilized. Sterilization units can be viewed as machine centers with limited capacity. Outputs of the system are a projected load for sterilization and a schedule for release of sterilized items to projected inventory.

The procedure for systems operation is shown in Exhibit 13.32. The system operation begins with an inquiry to the surgical schedule. If capacity is available in the surgical schedule, the procedure is to update the schedule by inserting the surgery in the appropriate spot. The schedule is then exploded through the surgical requirements file to generate gross requirements for all necessary materials and supplies. Note that a specific identified product (a particular physician performing a specific procedure) is traceable to a single Physician's Preference Sheet. The gross requirements thus generated are netted against the projected on-hand inventory for all items required. A sample record for a reusable component is shown in Exhibit 13.33.

The key database elements of the system are the Surgical Schedule File, Inventory Item File, and Surgical Requirements File. The *Surgical Schedule File* should contain all posted surgeries for a specific day and their anticipated needed times for each operating room. It includes such data as

- operation number,
- scheduled date and time,
- operating room number,
- patient room number,
- patient name,
- surgical procedure(s),
- anesthesia,
- physician name.

The *Inventory Item File* is a time-phased inventory record of surgical supplies and instruments required by one or more procedures. Particular care must be taken in this file to distinguish between disposable and reusable items. Data in this file include

- unique item number,
- description of the item,
- level,
- gross requirements,
- quantity on hand (current, allocated, projected available),
- scheduled receipts,
- planned order releases,
- standard inventory ordering data (lot size, order point, lead time, vendor information),
- recycling time (if applicable).

The *Surgical Requirements File* identifies quantities of each item needed for each procedure as well as the specific size and/or brand of the item. The file is divided

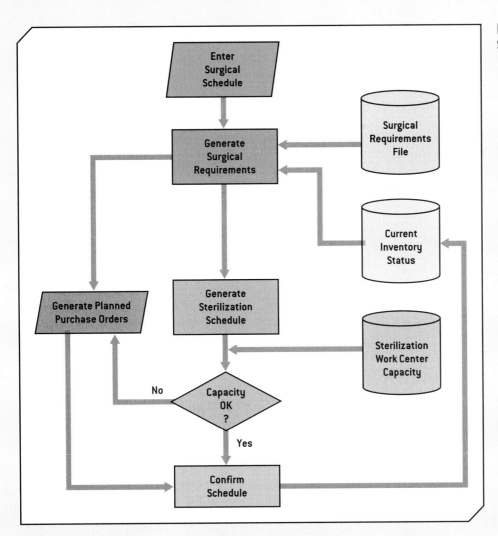

ITEM: Blade, #10	Sterilization lead time: 2 periods; Procurement lead time: 1 period											

	Period											
	0	1	2	3	4	5	6	7	8	9	10	11	12
Gross requirements		5	5	10	10	10	15			5	10		
Scheduled receipts													
Projected sterilized				5	5	10	10	10	10	5		5	10
Projected on-hand	15	10	5	0	0	0	0	10	20	20	10	15	25
Net requirements					5		5						
Planned order receipts					5		5						
Planned order releases				5		5							

into two parts: common items and preference items. The common items are those materials used by all physicians when performing the procedure; the preference items reflect physician differences in surgical material requirements. Collectively, these items establish the inventory requirements for each procedure in this manner:

- level 0 element number (procedure identifier),
- lower-level element numbers of common items,
- lower-level element numbers of preference items (for each physician associated with Level 0 element number).

Exhibit 13.34 illustrates the surgical requirements file for a bronchoscopy. Observe that the upper portion lists the inventory items used by all physicians; the lower portion lists the additional inventory items requested by specific physicians. In the environment for which the system was developed, the chief nurse of the surgical suite functions as the medical analogue to the materials manager. He or she is in charge of all surgical-scheduling and equipment-sterilization activities and is responsible for inventory management of all required medical supplies for the surgical suite—all tools, instruments, and equipment (not medications) required for all procedures.

The storeroom, sterilization facilities, and operating rooms themselves are located in one contiguous area under the chief surgical nurse's control. In this area, an inventory of the more than 2,000 items used in the various surgical procedures is maintained. Inventory balances are updated by an on-line, transaction-driven system that provides a complete inventory status report for all items each week. In addition, personnel have easy access to the current level of inventory on hand for each item.

The entire system is designed to be operated by nursing personnel. Its success and acceptance stem from two factors:

1. Reliability of operation. It generates reliable schedules and ensures adequate supplies. The reduction of problems in this area has led to greater physician satisfaction and a more harmonious relationship with nursing personnel.

2. Simplicity of operation. Its outputs include a daily schedule of surgical procedures, a list of items to be drawn from the storeroom, a list of items to be purchased, and a sterilization schedule.

Exhibit 13.34 Surgical Requirements for a Bronchoscopy

Common items
    Bronchoscopy set, rigid
    Suction tubing
    Telescope, right angle
    Telescope, forward oblique
    Glass slides
    Fixative
    Specimen trap
    Table cover
    Towels
Preference items
    Dr. *****
        Flexible bronchoscope
        Gloves, size 6 1/2 brown
    Dr. *****
        Gloves, size 7 1/2
        Local set

Questions for Discussion

1. Define the customer benefit package (CBP) for this hospital surgery. How does it differ from the CBP for manufacturers? Explain.

2. Explain the analogies between the elements of this resource planning system and a traditional manufacturing resource planning system. For example, what is the analogue to a BOM in this situation? An MPS?

3. What person in the surgical suite is the analogue to the materials manager in a traditional manufacturing environment? Briefly describe this person's duties.

4. A pure MRP system and lot-for-lot logic tries to drive inventory to zero in manufacturing. Do you want to drive inventory to zero in this situation? Why or why not?

5. What are the primary factors that determine the success and acceptance of MRP in the surgical suite?

ENDNOTES

[1] Carlton, J., "Cement Shortages Bedevil Builders," *The Wall Street Journal*, May 20, 2004, p. A2.

[2] Ibid.

[3] Adapted from Visagie, Martin S., "Production Control on a Flow Production Plant" *APICS 1975 Conference Proceedings*, pp. 161–166.

[4] Collier, D. A., "The Measurement and Operating Benefits of Component Part Commonality," *Decision Sciences* 12, no. 1, 1981, pp. 85–96.

[5] "Gillette Chief Uses Standardization to Save," *Purchasing Magazine Online*, November 6, 2002, http://www.manufacturing.net/pur/index.asp?layout=articlePrint&articleID=CA257494.

[6] Steinberg, E., Khumawala, B., and Scamell, R., "Requirements Planning Systems in the Healthcare Environment," *Journal of Operations Management* 2, no. 4, 1982, pp. 251–259.

Chapter Outline

CHAPTER 14

Operations Scheduling and Sequencing

Learning Objectives

1. To identify characteristics of scheduling at different organizational planning levels, and describe the application of computers to scheduling problems.

2. To become acquainted with different types of scheduling approaches in MRP systems, staff assignments, and appointment systems.

3. To apply basic sequencing rules to develop schedules that meet important operations performance criteria.

4. To learn and apply specific sequencing methods to specific problem structures such as the single- and two-resource sequencing problem, batch production of multiple products using a common resource, and the simulation of alternative dispatching rules.

5. To explain the need for monitoring and controlling schedules using a Gantt chart, and list reasons why planned schedules do not always achieve their intended results.

- Jean Rowecamp, clinical coordinator of nursing services, was faced with a deluge of complaints by her nursing staff about their work schedules and complaints by floor supervisors about inadequate staffing. The nurses complained they were having too many shift changes each month. Supervisors said they had too many nurses during the days and not enough at night and on the weekends. It seems that nothing she did would satisfy everyone. The nurses were unionized, so she couldn't schedule them more than 7 consecutive working days and required at least 16 hours between shift changes. Nurses were constantly asking her for "special requests" for personal time off, despite the negotiated procedures for bidding for shifts and vacation times. Jean lamented that she became an administrator and longed for the days when she was just a simple caregiver.

- "It used to be easy running this shop in the early days," exclaimed Andy Thomas, the foreman for the sheet metal stamping machine shop. Thomas was meeting with the company president and founder, Chris Kelton. "With only a handful of jobs at one time, I always knew the status of each, and determining when to start each job to meet the customer's due date wasn't a problem. Today, we have hundreds of jobs, and the salespeople keep putting pressure on us by promising delivery dates that we can't always meet. I'm spending hours each day trying to get a schedule that works, and then new jobs and material delays usually set me back to square one the next day. Chris, I really need some help here."

- "I count four employees stocking shelves, one person mopping the supermarket floor, and three employees talking over by the customer service desk," stated Tom McCord as he glanced at his wristwatch to a women standing in line at the checkout aisle. "Yes," the women responded, "they have low prices but I always have to wait for service. Wouldn't it be great if they could do both?" By the time McCord got his turn at the checkout cashier, 9 minutes had passed. "Those three employees over there have been talking for 10 minutes—Why don't they help?" McCord said to the exhausted checkout person. "Sir, as soon as I saw the line build up, I turned my flashing red light on but my supervisor is one of those three people talking by the service desk, and she hasn't seen my flashing light yet," said the beleaguered cashier.

Discussion Questions: Why is it difficult to schedule staff in a hospital or airline? Can you think of any situations in which an organization's scheduling has provided you with either a positive or negative experience? As a student, how do you schedule your homework, school projects, and study activities? What criteria do you use?

Scheduling *refers to the assignment of start and completion times to particular jobs, people, or equipment.* Scheduling is prevalent in nearly every organization. For example, fast-food restaurants, hospitals, and call centers need to schedule employees for work shifts; doctors, dentists, and stockbrokers need to schedule patients and customers; airlines must schedule crews and flight attendants; sports organizations must schedule teams and officials; court systems must schedule hearings and trials; factory managers need to schedule jobs on machines and preventive maintenance work; and salespersons need to schedule customer deliveries and visits to potential customers. Many schedules are repeatable over the long term, such as those for retail store staff and assembly-line employees. Others might change on a monthly, weekly, or even daily basis, as might be the case with call center employees, nurses, or salespeople.

A concept related to scheduling is sequencing. **Sequencing** *refers to determining the order in which jobs or tasks are processed.* For example, triage nurses must decide on the order in which emergency patients are treated; housekeepers in hotels must sequence the order of rooms to clean; operations managers who run an automobile assembly line must determine the sequence by which different models are produced; and airport managers must sequence outgoing flights on runways. Note that in all these situations, processing takes place using a common resource with limited capacity. Thus, the sequence will ultimately determine how well the resource is used to achieve some objective, such as meeting demand or customer due dates. Generally, a sequence specifies a schedule, and we will see this in various examples later in this chapter.

Creating schedules is not easy. The first two episodes highlight the complexity of scheduling. In the first episode, service capacity must be well matched with demand to maximize service and minimize costs. Union work-force rules and special requests further complicate the process. In the second, the sheer volume of variety of jobs can make scheduling a nightmare in even small manufacturing shops. For large plants, good scheduling can only be done using sophisticated computer-based systems. Many organizations, such as fast-food restaurants, call centers, and professional sports teams, face similar scheduling issues.

The third episode illustrates that good scheduling approaches may not work if managers and supervisors are not diligent in executing them. This episode highlights the importance of front-line management and real-world execution. No doubt,

Scheduling refers to the assignment of start and completion times to particular jobs, people, or equipment.

Sequencing refers to determining the order in which jobs or tasks are processed.

you too have experienced similar situations and thought "there must be a better way." Fortunately, many simple and effective approaches can assist operations managers in their scheduling efforts.

Good scheduling and sequencing techniques are vital to effective operation of value and supply chains. This chapter addresses key issues and methods for scheduling and sequencing in manufacturing and service organizations. Some of the methods generate optimal solutions to minimize or maximize some scheduling criterion; other methods create good approximate solutions. Although many optimization approaches are based on linear or integer programming (see Supplementary Chapter C) models, they can be difficult to formulate, difficult to collect accurate data for, and difficult to solve. In this chapter, we illustrate simple tools for several types of scheduling problems.

Learning Objective
To identify characteristics of scheduling at different organizational planning levels, and describe the application of computers to scheduling problems.

THE SCOPE OF SCHEDULING AND SEQUENCING

Scheduling and sequencing are some of the more common activities that operations managers perform every day in every business. They are fundamental to all three levels of aggregation and disaggregation planning as we described in the previous chapter. Good schedules and sequences lead to efficient execution of manufacturing and service plans. Exhibit 14.1 summarizes how scheduling and sequencing fit into these three levels. Our focus here is on Level 3—namely, detailed scheduling, sequencing, and day-to-day execution.

Exhibit 14.1 Scheduling in the Three Levels of Aggregate and Disaggregate Planning

Planning Level	Characteristics	Goods-Producing Examples	Service-Providing Examples
Level 1	• Long-range scheduling to meet future aggregate demand (see Exhibit 13.1) • Level, chase, and optimization-based aggregate planning strategies • Focus on planning by sales dollars, product line or group, year, quarter, and month	• Scheduling work shifts using full- and part-time labor • Planning new hires • Assigning overtime and undertime • Scheduling subcontracting • Scheduling production or output rates	• As discussed in Chapter 13, aggregate planning in services is similar to goods-producing industries (see Exhibit 13.1)
Level 2	• Medium-range scheduling to meet demand by month, week, or day (see Exhibit 13.13) • Focus on planning • Disaggregation into planned orders for end-items, sub-assemblies, parts, and raw materials	• Creating a master production schedule • Scheduling MRP-generated order releases for sub-assemblies, component parts, and raw materials	• Matching resources to demand • Staff scheduling • Equipment scheduling such as delivery trucks, airplanes, computers, automatic teller machine maintenance, etc.
Level 3	• Short-range scheduling and sequencing by hour and minute of the day • Resource constrained • Focus on real-time execution • Prioritize jobs and customers • Daily and hourly decisions and trade-offs between revenue, quality, service, and costs	• Prioritize and sequence jobs, products, and parts processing through one or more resources • Dispatching parts, labor, and equipment to achieve the production of goods • Focus on execution and shop floor control	• Prioritize back-office (low-contact) jobs and front-office (high-contact) customers • Dispatching field service, flight attendant, and installation crews and equipment • Focus on service encounter execution

Scheduling systems require much of the data and information that we discussed in Chapter 13, such as aggregate planning decisions and outputs, bills of material, routing information for customer orders, work tasks and process sequences, standard times, and so on. They also require accurate data and information about the types of jobs that can be processed by different resources; processing, setup, and changeover times; customer due dates or shipping dates; resource availability; number of shifts required; and process and equipment downtime and planned maintenance. Level 3 outputs typically include detailed schedules and sequences and resource load and order-status reports.

Scheduling and sequencing in back-office or low-contact service processes is similar to that for goods-producing processes (see Exhibit 5.10 to review issues related to high and low customer contact). Low-contact service processes often deal with information such as hospital patient admissions, credit card transactions, and U.S. government Social Security benefits. The information is processed in paper or electronic form and is used in many functional areas of the organization, such as human resource management and accounting. Therefore, the same scheduling and sequencing concepts and methods used in manufacturing are beneficial in low-contact service processes (see the OM Spotlight: Telling Umpires Where to Go).

OM SPOTLIGHT

Telling Umpires Where to Go

One of the authors developed annual schedules for umpires in the American Baseball League for many years before this activity was merged with the National League. Some of the critical factors in developing these schedules were to ensure that umpire crews were not assigned to consecutive series with the same team if possible, that the number of times a crew was assigned to a team was balanced over the course of the season, that travel sequences be rational and realistic, and that a variety of constraints be met. For instance, it makes more sense to schedule a crew to several consecutive series out on the East Coast or West Coast and move them to nearby cities rather than shuttle them back and forth across the country.

Various constraints limited the scheduling possibilities. For example, one could not schedule a crew for a day game in another city after working a night game on the previous day. In addition, crews need time to rest and travel between game assignments. When traveling from the West Coast to Chicago or further east, for example, crews needed a day off to account for time changes and flight schedules. Flights into and out of Canada required more time because of customs. Crews were given time off every 7 weeks, and the number of off-days needed to be balanced across all crews during the season.

All these factors needed to be considered in the context of the game schedule, which was created well in advance.

The complexity of these quantitative and qualitative factors precluded a purely automated process and relied heavily on the experience and judgment of the human scheduler, with computer-based assistance to provide important information to make good scheduling decisions.

Exhibits 14.2 and 14.3 show a portion of the schedule developed one year along with a portion of a typical crew schedule. Microsoft Excel® was used to facilitate the scheduling process and evaluate scheduling statistics.

SHAUN BEST/Reuters/Landov

Exhibit 14.2 Portion of American League Umpire Schedule

#	Date	SEA	OAK	ANA	TEX	KC	MIN	CWS	DET	CLE	TOR	TB	BAL	NYY	BOS
2	4/5	CWS N 6	NYY N 5		DET D 8	BOS D 4							TB D 3		
3	4/6	CWS N 6	NYY N 5	CLE N 2	DET N 8		TOR N 7								
4	4/7	CWS N 6	NYY D 5	CLE N 2	DET N 8	BOS N 4	TOR N 7						TB N 3		
5	4/8			CLE N 2		BOS N 4	TOR N 7						TB N 3		
6	4/9	OAK N 2			ANA N 5		CLE N 6	KC D 3				BOS N 8	TOR N 4	DET D 7	
7	4/10	OAK N 2			ANA N 5		CLE N 6	KC D 3				BOS N 8	TOR D 4	DET D 7	
8	4/11	OAK D 2			ANA D 5		CLE D 6	KC D 3				BOS D 8	TOR D 4	DET D 7	
9	4/12	OAK N 1			ANA D 5				MIN D 4	KC D 7	TB N 6				
10	4/13	TEX N 1	ANA N 3								TB N 6		BAL N 8		CWS D 5
11	4/14	TEX N 1	ANA N 3						MIN N 4	KC N 7	TB N 6		BAL N 8		
12	4/15	TEX D 1	ANA D 3						MIN N 4	KC N 7	TB N 6		BAL N 8		CWS N 5
13	4/16		TEX N 1	SEA N 4		CWS N 3				NYY N 6	MIN N 8	BAL N 5	TB N 7		
14	4/17		TEX D 1	SEA N 4		CWS D 3				NYY D 6	MIN D 8	BAL D 5	TB D 7		
15	4/18		TEX D 1	SEA D 4		CWS D 3				NYY D 6	MIN D 8	BAL D 5	TB D 7		

Exhibit 14.3

A Portion of a Typical Umpire Crew Schedule (Crew 6 in Exhibit 14.2. "H" denotes an assignment with the team at home; the visiting team is denoted by "X".)

#	Date	SEA	OAK	ANA	TEX	KC	MIN	CWS	DET	CLE	TOR	TB	BAL	NYY	BOS
2	4/5	H						X							
3	4/6	H						X							
4	4/7	H						X							
5	4/8														
6	4/9						H			X					
7	4/10						H			X					
8	4/11						H			X					
9	4/12										H	X			
10	4/13										H	X			
11	4/14										H	X			
12	4/15										H	X			
13	4/16									H				X	
14	4/17									H				X	
15	4/18									H				X	

In front-office or high-contact service processes, such as hotel check-in and check-out, live banking transactions, medical exams, and legal consultation, customer participation in the processes result in a higher degree of uncertainty. As a result, customer routings and standard processing times are more uncertain than in back-office and manufacturing environments. Frequently, the standard deviation of standard processing times is much larger for these processes. Therefore, service managers do not have complete control over scheduling and sequencing for high-contact service processes.

Computer-Based Scheduling

It is not uncommon for a manufacturing facility to have hundreds of workstations or machine centers and to process thousands of different parts. Managers of such facilities also need daily or even hourly updates on the status of production to meet the information needs of supply chain managers, sales and marketing personnel, and customers. Similarly, service managers often manage dozens of part-time workers with varying work-availability times (think of a fast-food restaurant manager near a college campus), or ever-changing workloads and demands (think of a hospital nurse administrator). The complexity of these situations dictates that effective scheduling systems be computerized, not only for generating schedules but also for retrieving information so that a salesperson can check the status of a customer's order or project a delivery date. Thus, implementing scheduling systems requires good information technology support.

Computer-based scheduling systems can perform three major tasks: schedule generation, schedule evaluation, and automated scheduling.[1] **Schedule generation** *is the creation of a schedule.* This is usually done using some type of algorithm or set of rules. However, computer-generated schedules often cannot incorporate many factors that are important to operations managers, such as special customer requests. As a result, they need to be reviewed by operations managers for practicality and feasibility, and the human scheduler uses his or her judgment and experience to improve the schedule.

Some computer-based systems incorporate such "intelligence" and evaluate schedules. **Schedule evaluation** *is the process of assessing schedules to determine feasibility and to estimate future performance measures.* Finally, the most sophisticated systems can perform all these tasks automatically. **Automated scheduling** *is the process of generating a schedule, evaluating it, usually through simulation of work area operations, identifying potential problems, and creating a revised schedule.* Many benefits can accrue from choosing the right scheduling system, as Tibor Machine Products, a small company in the Chicago area, discovered in the OM Spotlight.

Schedule generation *is the creation of a schedule.*

Schedule evaluation *is the process of assessing schedules to determine feasibility and to estimate future performance measures.*

Automated scheduling *is the process of generating a schedule, evaluating it, usually through simulation of work area operations, identifying potential problems, and creating a revised schedule.*

Scheduling in Supply Chains

In Chapter 9, we described the decisions necessary to design a supply chain. The network of processes in a supply chain all need to be synchronized. Thus, scheduling and information exchange are at the heart of managing an efficient and responsive supply chain. Supply chain facilities, processes, and logistics must be well scheduled if the supply chain is to be effective.

Consider, for example, UPS, the world's largest package delivery company and a global leader in supply chain services. UPS offers an extensive range of options

OM SPOTLIGHT

Tibor Machine Products[2]

As Tibor Machine Products changed its marketing strategy to develop new customers and new markets, it discovered some difficult challenges in its manufacturing scheduling process. The unique requirements of new customers resulted in longer and more complex product routings and more variation in ordering patterns. Tibor was using a basic MRP system that assumed infinite factory capacity to generate its schedules. In its new environment, it needed to generate schedules quickly in an easy-to-understand format, make what-if analyses, and quickly regenerate a schedule. A new software package that considered capacity constraints helped the company schedule jobs and provided many other long-term benefits, including a large reduction in lot sizes, identification of production bottlenecks, better overtime planning, and even better equipment acquisition.

for synchronizing the flow of goods, information, and funds. In 2004, UPS agreed to acquire Menlo Worldwide Forwarding, Inc., a subsidiary of CNF, which is a global freight forwarder that provides a full suite of heavy airfreight forwarding services, ocean services, and international trade management, including customs brokerage.[3] Freight forwarders keep the supply chain operating efficiently by moving goods where they are needed on time and at the lowest possible cost. Menlo Worldwide operates in more than 175 countries and territories in the world. The acquisition reinforces UPS's strategy of providing broad supply chain solutions to enable global commerce. As a result of the acquisition, UPS will expand its global capabilities and add guaranteed heavy airfreight services around the world, enabling customers to reach the global marketplace faster. This also means UPS will introduce new time-definite products such as overnight, two-day, and deferred heavy airfreight. Each of these time-dependent services requires different resource schedules and priority sequences for operations activities, such as loading and unloading goods, airplane flight schedules, customer delivery sequences, package and freight handling systems and procedures, and so on.

Given that many supply chains are based on just-in-time operating systems, it should come as no surprise that the timing and speed of the supply chain are of paramount importance. Important supply chain decisions are the amount of information to share among suppliers and customers and the means by which this can be accomplished. Computer-generated schedules and the sharing of production, purchasing, inventory, delivery, and customer information among suppliers and buyers in the supply chain enables faster service at lower cost. The web provides a communication infrastructure by which the status and updated schedules can be provided quickly to all parties in the supply chain. Enterprise resource planning (ERP) systems link together all parties in goods-producing supply chains. Customer relationship management (CRM) and revenue management systems (RMS) are also linking together parties in service-providing supply chains.

Learning Objectives
To become acquainted with different types of scheduling approaches in MRP systems, staff assignments, and appointment systems.

SCHEDULING APPLICATIONS AND APPROACHES

Scheduling applies to all aspects of the value chain, from planning and releasing orders in a factory, determining work shifts for employees, and making deliveries to customers. Many problems, such as staff scheduling, are similar across different organizations. Quite often, however (as with the baseball umpiring situation or scheduling classrooms and teachers at a university), unique situational factors require a unique solution approach. In this section we present a few common applications of scheduling that are prevalent in operations management.

Scheduling in MRP Systems

What may not have been apparent in Chapter 13 is that scheduling is the principal basis for materials requirements planning (MRP). The master production schedule (MPS) drives the dependent demand requirements for all components. MRP is a Level 2 scheduling process and paves the way for Level 3 sequencing decisions where detailed decisions about specific job schedules and sequences are made, which we will describe in more detail later in this chapter. Planned order releases create an important "forward-looking" schedule for all subassemblies, component parts, and raw materials. Exhibit 14.4 shows a MRP record for a steel spring with three planned order releases for 40 units in periods 1, 3, and 4. This schedule information is used by capacity requirements planning (CRP) to determine workloads for key work centers and also plays a critical role in purchasing materials and scheduling employees and work shifts.

Part: Steel Spring		Lead time = 1 week		Fixed Order Quantity = 40 springs			
Period		1	2	3	4	5	6
Gross requirements (GR)		20	20	30	30	20	10
Scheduled receipts (S/PR)		30					
Projected on-hand inventory (POH)	5	15	35	5	15	35	25
Planned order releases (POR)		40		40	40		

Exhibit 14.4
Example MRP Record

Staff Scheduling

Staff scheduling problems are prevalent in service organizations because of high variability in customer demand. Examples include scheduling call center representatives, hotel housekeepers, tollbooth operators, nurses, airline reservation clerks, police officers, fast-food restaurant employees, and many others. In a typical fast-food restaurant, for example, employee requirements vary dramatically as sales volume fluctuates over each day and even by hour of the day, resulting in a very complex scheduling problem. For instance, whereas only two employees may be required in the grill and counter areas during slow periods, ten or more may be needed during peak periods. Shifts might vary from 3 to 8 hours, and employees might differ in their availability for work each day of the week because of school or family schedules. Full- and part-time employees also have very different costs associated with their employment, such as health benefit and retirement plans. Finally, the skills and performance levels required for the various workstations and areas differ. A typical fast-food operation might have five different types of work areas, 150 employees, and 30 work shifts. This represents more than 100,000 possible scheduling assignments! Staff scheduling is also only as good as the forecast of demand that can vary greatly by month, week, day, and hour of the day.

Staff scheduling attempts to match available personnel with the needs of the organization by

1. accurately forecasting demand and translating it into the quantity and timing of work to be done,
2. determining the staffing required to perform the work by time period,
3. determining the personnel available and the full- and part-time mix,
4. matching capacity to demand requirements, and developing a work schedule that maximizes service and minimizes costs.

The first step requires converting demand to a capacity measure, that is, the number of staff required. For instance, we might determine that for every $400 dollars of sales forecast, we need one additional full-time employee. The second step determines the quantity and timing of the work to be done in detail, usually by hour of the day, and sometimes in 5- to 10-minute time intervals. Determining the staffing required must take into account worker-productivity factors, personal allowances, sickness, vacations, no-shows, and so on. Personnel availability, the third step, is a function of the employee labor pool and of the use of part-time and temporary employees and other sources of labor.

Step 4 focuses on the matching of capacity to demand requirements; this is the essence of scheduling. Different approaches are required for different situations because of the nature of constraints. If service demands are relatively level over time, as in the case of hotel housekeepers, it is usually easy to schedule personnel on standard weekly work shifts. If the workload varies greatly within a shift, as is the case for telephone customer service representatives, the problem becomes one of scheduling shifts to meet the varying demand. Staff scheduling is challenging because of the unique characteristics of services we described in Chapter 1. Let us examine a relatively simple problem of scheduling personnel with consecutive days off in the face of fluctuating requirements.[4]

T. R. Accounting Service is developing a work-force schedule for 3 weeks from now and has forecast demand and translated it into the following minimum personnel requirements for the week:

Day	Mon.	Tue.	Wed.	Thur.	Fri.	Sat.	Sun.
Minimum Personnel	8	6	6	6	9	5	3

The staff requirements are for full-time accountants who do accounting work such as end-of-month financial statements, tax record organization, and federal, state, and local tax payments. T.R., the owner of the accounting service, wants to schedule the employees so that each employee has two *consecutive* days off and all demand requirements are met.

The staffing procedure is as follows. First, we locate the *set of at least two consecutive days with the smallest requirements*. That is, we find the day with the smallest staff requirements, the next-smallest, and so on, until there are at least two consecutive days. Sunday and Saturday, for example, have requirements of 3 and 5, respectively, while all others are greater than 5. We then circle the requirements for those two consecutive days. Thus we have the following, for employee 1:

Day	Mon.	Tue.	Wed.	Thur.	Fri.	Sat.	Sun.
Requirements	8	6	6	6	9	(5)	(3)

We assign accountant 1 to work on all days that are not circled, that is, Monday through Friday. Then we subtract 1 from the requirement for each day that accountant will work. This gives us the following requirements that remain:

Day	Mon.	Tue.	Wed.	Thur.	Fri.	Sat.	Sun.
Requirements	7	5	5	5	8	5	3

The procedure is repeated with this new set of requirements for accountant 2.

Day	Mon.	Tue.	Wed.	Thur.	Fri.	Sat.	Sun.
Requirements	7	(5)	(5)	(5)	8	(5)	(3)

When there are several alternatives, as in this case, we do one of two things. First, we try to choose a pair of days with the lowest total requirement. If there are still ties, we are to choose the first available pair that makes the most sense to the scheduler. Hence, we again use Saturday and Sunday as days off for accountant 2, since this pair has the smallest total requirement of 8. We subtract 1 from each working day's requirement, yielding the following:

Day	Mon.	Tue.	Wed.	Thur.	Fri.	Sat.	Sun.
Requirements	6	4	4	4	7	5	3

Circling the smallest requirements until we obtain at least two consecutive days again yields the following for employee 3.

Day	Mon.	Tue.	Wed.	Thur.	Fri.	Sat.	Sun.
Requirements	6	④	④	④	7	5	③

Notice that Sunday is not adjacent to Tuesday, Wednesday, or Thursday, so we cannot use Sunday in the schedule. Remember we are looking for consecutive pairs of days. Let's choose the Tuesday-Wednesday. The remaining requirements are:

Day	Mon.	Tue.	Wed.	Thur.	Fri.	Sat.	Sun.
Requirements	5	4	4	3	6	4	2

Continuing with this procedure, we obtain the sequence of requirements shown in Exhibit 14.5 (with circled numbers representing the lowest-requirement pair selected). The final accountant schedule is shown in Exhibit 14.6. Even though some requirements are exceeded, such as Thursday with a demand for 6 accountants yet we schedule 8, the solution minimizes the number of employees required. A more difficult problem that we do not address is that of determining a schedule of rotating shifts so that employees do not always have the same two days off. Over a predetermined longer cycle such as a quarter, all employees rotate thru all possible

Exhibit 14.5
Scheduling Procedure for T.R. Accounting Service

Employee Number	Mon.	Tue.	Wed.	Thur.	Fri.	Sat.	Sun.
4	5	4	4	3	6	④	②
5	4	3	③	②	5	4	2
6	3	2	3	2	4	③	①
7	②	①	2	1	3	3	1
8	2	1	①	⓪	2	2	0
9	①	⓪	1	0	1	1	0
10	1	⓪	⓪	0	0	0	0

Exhibit 14.6
Final Accountant Schedule

Employee Number	Mon.	Tue.	Wed.	Thur.	Fri.	Sat.	Sun.
1	X	X	X	X	X		
2	X	X	X	X	X		
3	X			X	X	X	X
4	X	X	X	X	X		
5	X	X			X	X	X
6	X	X	X	X	X		
7		X		X	X	X	X
8	X	X			X	X	X
9			X	X	X	X	X
10	X			X	X	X	X
Total	8	6	6	8	10	6	6

days off. This makes for a fair and more equitable staff schedule, but it is complicated and beyond the scope of this book.

Many software packages are available to help with staff scheduling (see the OM Spotlight: Software to Schedule Anywhere). However, scheduling is so integrated with the practices and culture of the organization that these standardized software packages normally need to be modified to work well in specific operating environments. Accurate input data and the user's understanding of how the software techniques develop the schedules are other challenges when adopting off-the-shelf scheduling software.

Appointment Systems

Everyone is familiar with appointments. From an operations' perspective, appointments can be viewed as a reservation of service time and capacity, such as a medical doctor's time. Using appointments provides a means to maximize the use of time-dependent service capacity and reduce the risk of no-shows. Appointment systems are used in many businesses, such as consulting, tax preparation, music instruction, and medical, dental, and veterinarian practices. Indirectly, appointments reduce the cost of providing the service because the service provider is idle less each workday. Without appointments and more service-provider idle time, non-revenue-generating time periods, prices would increase.

Unlike a manufactured part, people's unique needs and behavior can affect the efficiency of appointment systems. For example, a high no-show rate can disrupt a well-designed appointment system leading to more overbooking, and possibly longer

OM SPOTLIGHT

Software to Schedule Anywhere[5]

One provider of small business software offers an online employee scheduling system called Schedule-Anywhere (ScheduleAnywhere.com). This service allows managers to schedule employees from any computer with Internet access, whether at work, at home, or on the road. "With over 60,000 users, we get a lot of feedback on what people really need in an employee scheduling system," said Jon Forknell, vice president and general manager of Atlas Business Solutions. "Many of our customers told us they needed an online solution that was affordable and easy to use." ScheduleAnywhere gives users the power to

- schedule employees from any computer with Internet access
- create schedules by position, department, location, etc.
- view schedule information in a 1-day, 7-day, 14-day, or 28-day format
- enter staffing requirements and view shift coverage
- see who's scheduled and who's available
- automatically rotate or copy employee schedules
- preschedule time-off requests

- avoid scheduling conflicts
- give employees read/write or read-only access to schedules

waiting times. Much of what we learned in previous chapters, such as designing the servicescape, service encounters, and facility layout, affects processing people using an appointment system. If a children's hospital, for instance, has brightly colored and clean waiting rooms with interesting toys and books and friendly staff, the kids and parents may perceive their waiting times as short or at least reasonable. The appointment system must try and accommodate customers and forecast their behavior, such as the no-show rate or a difficult customer who demands more processing time.

Four decisions to make regarding designing an appointment system are the following:

1. *Determine the appointment time interval* such as 1 hour or 15 minutes. Some professional services such as dentists and physicians use smaller appointment intervals and then take multiples of it, depending on the type of procedure thought to be required by the patient. A dentist, for example, might select 6-minute intervals and then for each type of dental procedure (teeth cleaning, tooth filing, cap tooth, root canal, and so on) use multiples of this baseline interval, such as 36 minutes for a tooth filling. These appointment intervals usually do not include time for breaks, fatigue, and paperwork tasks. If service providers want a scheduled break, they would simply tell the appointment scheduling person to block out time from 10:00 A.M. to 10:30 A.M. and 2:30 P.M. to 3:00 P.M. each day.

2. Based on an analysis of each day's customer mix, *determine the length of each workday and the time off-duty.* Typical questions to answer include: Should we book customers 10 hours a day for 4 days and free up Friday for rest and relaxation and other duties? Should we book customers for 8 hours on Monday, Wednesday, and Friday and for 10 hours on Tuesday and Thursday so people do not have to miss work? Should we take the last week of December, March, June, and September off every year? Once the on- and off-duty days for the year (annual capacity) are determined and assuming a certain customer mix and overbooking rate (see Step 3), the service provider can forecast expected total revenues for the year.

3. *Decide how to handle overbooking* for each day of the week. Often, customers do not show up as scheduled. If the no-show percentage is low, say 2 percent, then there may be no need to overbook. However, once the no-show percentage reaches 10 percent or more, overbooking is usually necessary to maximize revenue and make effective use of perishable and expensive time. Determining overbooking policies is facilitated by revenue management approaches that we discussed in Chapter 10.

4. *Develop customer appointment rules* that maximize customer satisfaction. For example, some service providers leave one appointment interval open at the end of each workday. Others schedule a 60-minute lunch interval but can squeeze in a customer during lunch if necessary. These planned idle-time intervals can be thought of as safety capacity. This allows the service provider some flexibility in accommodating special customer situations and special customers. If the last appointment interval is not used, the service provider uses it to catch up on other duties or goes home early. Telephone and electronic appointment reminders are another way to help maximize service-provider utilization. Other examples of customer appointment rules include the following: (1) Business customers have priority over residential customers. (2) Residential customers asking for reschedules are assigned the lowest priority. (3) New customer installations are higher priority than existing customer maintenance and repair jobs.

Consider the appointment schedule for part of a dentist's day. Suppose that the dental office has tried to contact a particular patient but received no response.

Should they hold the appointment time for this patient or book another patient at this time? Given the perishable nature of professional service-provider's time and the loss of revenue, most service providers overbook or have procedures to place customers on waiting lists that they can call at a few hours' notice. If the dentist overbooks and everyone shows up, not only will the dentist's workday likely be extended but customers will be unhappy due to extended waiting times. Such trade-offs between generating revenue, perishable service-provider capacity, and customer behavior are made daily in professional service-provider offices. In addition, some doctors, lawyers, consultants, and dentists schedule their appointments for 10 hours from Monday to Thursday and use Friday to Sunday for professional meetings, 3-day weekends of rest and relaxation, and catching up on professional reading and paperwork.

Learning Objective
To apply basic sequencing rules to develop schedules that meet important operations performance criteria.

SEQUENCING

Sequencing is necessary when several activities (manufacturing goods, servicing customers, delivering packages, and so on) use a common resource. The resource might be a machine, a customer service representative, or a delivery truck. Sequencing can be planned, in which case it creates a schedule. For example, if a student plans to begin homework at 7:00 P.M. and estimates that it will take 60 minutes to complete an OM assignment, 45 minutes to read a psychology chapter, and 40 minutes to do statistics homework, then sequencing the work from most favorite to least favorite—OM, Psychology, and Statistics—creates the schedule:

Assignment	Start Time	End Time
OM	7:00	8:00
Psychology	8:00	8:45
Statistics	8:45	9:25

In many services, the servicescape often creates physical and subliminal cues for sequencing people. Ropes and signs create paths for checking into a hotel or going to a movie. Rental car agencies have dedicated lines for frequent customers. Airports use a series of lights, numbers, lines, and control tower protocols to help organize waiting lines and sequencing of airplane takeoffs and landings.

Sequencing Performance Criteria

In selecting a specific scheduling or sequencing rule, a manager must first consider the criteria on which to evaluate schedules. These criteria are often classified into three categories:

1. process-focused performance criteria,
2. customer-focused due-date criteria, and
3. cost-based criteria.

The applicability of the various criteria depends on the availability of data. Later we will show how these performance measures are applied to various sequencing rules.

Process-focused performance criteria pertain only to information about the start and end times of jobs and focus on shop performance such as equipment utilization and WIP inventory. Two common measures are flow time and makespan. **Flow time** *is the amount of time a job spent in the shop or factory.* Low flow times reduce WIP inventory. Flow time is computed using Equation (14.1).

Flow time *is the amount of time a job spent in the shop or factory.*

$$F_i = \sum p_{ij} + \sum w_{ij} = C_i - R_i \qquad \textbf{(14.1)}$$

where

F_i = flow time of job i
$\sum p_{ij}$ = sum of all processing times of job i at workstation or area j
   (run + setup times)
$\sum w_{ij}$ = sum of all waiting times of job i at workstation or area j
C_i = completion time of job i
R_i = ready time for job i where all materials, specifications, and so on are available

Makespan *is the time needed to process a given set of jobs.* A short makespan aims to achieve high equipment utilization and resources by getting all jobs out of the shop quickly. Makespan is computed using Equation (14.2).

$$M = C - S \qquad \textbf{(14.2)}$$

where

M = makespan of a group of jobs
C = completion time of *last* job in the group
S = start time of *first* job in the group

Due-date criteria pertain to customers' required due dates, or internally determined shipping dates. Common performance measures are lateness and tardiness, or the number of jobs tardy or late. **Lateness** *is the difference between the completion time and the due date (either positive or negative).* **Tardiness** *is the amount of time by which the completion time exceeds the due date.* (Tardiness is defined as zero if the job is completed before the due date, and therefore no credit is given for completing a job early.) In contrast to process-focused performance criteria, these measures focus externally on customer satisfaction and service. They are calculated using Equations (14.3) and (14.4).

$$L_i = C_i - D_i \qquad \textbf{(14.3)}$$
$$T_i = \text{Max}\,(0, L_i) \qquad \textbf{(14.4)}$$

where

L_i = lateness of job i
T_i = tardiness of job i
D_i = due date of job i

A third type of performance criteria is cost-based. Typical cost includes inventory, changeover or setup, processing or run, and material-handling costs. This cost-based category might seem to be the most obvious criteria, but it is often difficult to identify the relevant cost categories, obtain accurate estimates of their values, and allocate costs to manufactured parts or services correctly. In most cases, costs are considered implicitly in process performance and due-date criteria.

Sequencing Rules

Two of the most popular sequencing rules for prioritizing jobs are

- shortest processing time (SPT)
- earliest due date (EDD)

In using one of these rules, a manager would compute the measure for all competing jobs and select them in the sequence according to the criterion. For example, suppose that the student we discussed earlier sequenced the homework according to SPT. The sequence would be statistics, psychology, and OM. These rules are often applied when a fixed set of jobs needs to be sequenced at one point in time.

Makespan is the time needed to process a given set of jobs.

Lateness is the difference between the completion time and the due date (either positive or negative).

Tardiness is the amount of time by which the completion time exceeds the due date.

In other situations, new jobs arrive in an intermittent fashion, resulting in a constantly changing mix of jobs needing to be sequenced. In this case, we assign priorities to whatever jobs are available at a specific time and then update the priorities when new jobs arrive. Some examples of these priority rules are

- first-come-first-serve (FCFS)
- fewest number of operations remaining (FNO)
- least work remaining (LWR)—sum of all processing times for operations not yet performed
- least amount of work at the next process queue (LWNQ)—amount of work awaiting the next process in a job's sequence

A useful sequencing rule that incorporates due dates is called the critical ratio rule. *The critical ratio is defined as the time remaining until the due date divided by the number of days required to complete the job.*

*The **critical ratio** is defined as the time remaining until the due date divided by the number of days required to complete the job.*

$$\text{Critical ratio (CR)} = \frac{\text{Due date} - \text{Current date}}{\text{Total processing time remaining}} \qquad \textbf{(14.5)}$$

The total processing time remaining includes run, changeover/setup, transport, and waiting times. CR uses two criteria—the customer's due date, an external performance measure, and the total processing time remaining, an internal measure. One could think of the numerator as a marketing-driven performance metric and the denominator as an operation-focused metric.

The critical ratio provides immediate information on the status of jobs relative to their due dates. For instance, if it takes 8 days to complete an order and it is needed in 10 days, the critical ratio is $10/8 = 1.25$. If the CR is greater than 1, the job is ahead of schedule; if it is equal to 1, the job is on time; and if it is less than 1, the job is behind schedule. The use of this index enables managers to see easily the status of all jobs and to place priorities accordingly. The critical ratio sequencing rule is to schedule the job with the smallest critical ratio first.

To illustrate the critical ratio rule, consider the job information shown in Exhibit 14.7 from Value Medical Practice Evaluation (VMPE), Inc. Lucy C. Springs, president and founder of VMPE, Inc., conducts medical practice evaluations throughout the United States. An evaluation requires VMPE, Inc. to visit the medical practice sites, analyze the financial and accounting records, and meet with many different people such as health care payers, doctors, attorneys, and hospitals administrators. The deliverable output is a consultant report placing an economic value on the medical practice under different scenarios. Many client due dates are based on court schedules and must be met. Clients include a variety of physician practices, long-term care companies, home health companies, university and community hospitals, medical device companies, medical service providers, pharmaceutical and biotech companies, and managed care insurance payers.

Exhibit 14.7 shows the current mix of work. To set priorities on which job to do next, Springs decided to prioritize her work using the critical ratio sequencing rule. The current calendar day is 130.

The critical ratio analysis summarized in Exhibit 14.7 indicates that the jobs should be sequenced as follows: A (CR = 1.2), F (1.7), D (2.6), B (3.0), E (3.6), C (4.1), and G (6.1). Springs updates all of her client jobs every Saturday to make sure she and her professional staff meet all deadlines. For a professional consulting service, this is one way of trying to achieve excellent customer service.

The SPT and EDD rules generally work well in the short term, but in most situations, new orders and jobs arrive intermittently and the schedule must accommodate them. If SPT were used in a dynamic environment, a job with a large processing time might never get processed. In this case, some time-based exception rule (such as "if a job waits more than 40 hours, schedule it next") must be used to avoid this problem.

Audit Job	Promised Due Date (Day #1 to 365)	Due Date − Current Date (Time remaining until due date)	Total Processing Time Remaining	Critical Ratio Using Equation (14.5)
A	136	6 days	5 days	1.2
B	220	90 days	30 days	3.0
C	192	62 days	15 days	4.1
D	196	66 days	25 days	2.6
E	202	72 days	20 days	3.6
F	147	17 days	10 days	1.7
G	191	61 days	10 days	6.1

Exhibit 14.7
Valuation Client Information for VMPE, Inc.

Different rules lead to different results and performance. The SPT rule tends to minimize average flow time and work-in-process inventory and maximize resource utilization. The EDD rule minimizes the maximum of jobs past due but doesn't perform well on average flow time, WIP inventory, or resource utilization. The FCFS rule is used in many service delivery systems and does not consider any job or customer criterion. FCFS only focuses on the time of arrival for the customer or job. The FNO rule does not consider the length of time for each operation; for example, a job may have many small operations and be scheduled last. Generally, this is not a very good rule. The LWNQ rule tries to keep downstream workstations and associated resources busy.

APPLICATIONS OF SEQUENCING RULES

Learning Objectives
To learn and apply specific sequencing methods to specific problem structures such as the single- and two-resource sequencing problem, batch production of multiple products using a common resource, and the simulation of alternative dispatching rules.

Sequencing in a job shop, in which several different goods or services are processed, each of which may have a unique routing among process stages, is generally very complex, but some special cases lend themselves to simple solutions. These special cases provide understanding and insight into more complicated scheduling problems. The special cases considered in this chapter are (1) scheduling on a single workstation or processor and (2) scheduling on two workstations or processors. Then we will discuss dispatching and simulation-based sequencing.

Single-Resource Sequencing Problem

The simplest sequencing problem is that of processing a set of jobs on a single processor. This situation occurs in many firms. For example, in a serial manufacturing process, a bottleneck workstation controls the output of the entire process. Thus, it is critical to schedule the bottleneck equipment efficiently. In other cases, such as in a chemical plant, the entire plant may be viewed as a single processor. Single processors for service situations include processing people for a driver's license eye exam, patients through an X-ray or CAT scanning machine, trucks through a loading/unloading dock, or financial transactions through a control workstation. For the single-processor sequencing problem, a very simple rule—shortest processing time—finds a minimal average flow time sequence. An example of its use follows.

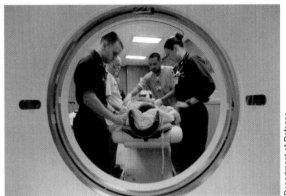

Department of Defense

Consider a workstation that has one maintenance mechanic to repair failed machines. We can think of the mechanic as the processor (scarce resource) and the machines awaiting repair as the jobs. Let us assume that six machines are down, with estimated repair times given here, and that no new jobs arrive.

Job (Fix Machine #)	1	2	3	4	5	6
Processing Time (hours)	10	3	7	2	9	6

No matter which sequence is chosen, the makespan is the same, since the time to process all the jobs is the sum of the processing times, or in this example, 37 hours. Therefore, we use average flow time as the criterion to minimize the average time a job spends in the workstation. The idea here is to get the most jobs done as soon as possible. Applying the SPT rule, we use the job sequence 4-2-6-3-5-1. We assume that all jobs are ready for processing at time zero (that is, $R_i = 0$ for all jobs i). Then the flow times (F_i) for the jobs are computed as follows:

Job Sequence	Flow Time
4	2 hours
2	2 + 3 = 5 hours
6	5 + 6 = 11 hours
3	11 + 7 = 18 hours
5	18 + 9 = 27 hours
1	27 + 10 = 37 hours

The average flow time for these six jobs is $(2 + 5 + 11 + 18 + 27 + 37)/6 = 100/6 = 16.67$ hours. This means that the average time a machine will be out of service is 16.7 hours. The SPT sequencing rule maximizes workstation utilization and minimizes average job flow time and work-in-process inventory. For example, if you switch jobs 4 and 6 so the job sequence is 6-2-4-3-5-1, note that the average flow time increases to 18 hours. We encourage you to work through the calculations to show this. As long as no additional jobs enter the mix, all will eventually be processed. Of course, the job with the longest processing time will wait the longest (and this customer might not be very happy), but on average, SPT will reduce the average flow time.

When processing times are relatively equal, then most operating systems default to the first-come-first-serve (FCFS) sequencing rule. There are, of course, exceptions to this rule. For example, a job for a firm's most important customer might be pushed to the front of the sequence, or the maître'd at a restaurant might seat a celebrity or VIP before other patrons.

In many situations, jobs have due dates that have been promised to customers. Although SPT provides the smallest average flow time and smallest average lateness of all scheduling rules that might be chosen, in a dynamic environment, jobs with long processing times are continually pushed back and may remain in the shop a long time. Thus it is advantageous to consider sequencing rules that take into account the due dates of jobs.

A popular and effective rule for scheduling on a single processor (resource) is the earliest-due-date rule (EDD), which dictates sequencing jobs in order of earliest due date first. This rule minimizes the maximum job tardiness and job lateness. It does not minimize the average flow time or average lateness, as SPT does, however. An example of how the earliest due-date rule is used follows.

Suppose an insurance underwriting work area (that is, the single processor) has five commercial insurance jobs to quote that have these processing times and due dates.

Job	Processing Time (p_{ij})	Due Date (D_i)
1	4	15
2	7	16
3	2	8
4	6	21
5	3	9

If the jobs are sequenced by-the-numbers in the order 1-2-3-4-5, then the flow time, tardiness, and lateness for each job are calculated using Equations (14.1), (14.3), and (14.4) as follows:

Job	Flow Time (F_i)	Due Date	Lateness $(L_i = C_i - D_i)$	Tardiness (Max $(0, L_i)$)
1	4	15	−11	0
2	4 + 7 = 11	16	−5	0
3	11 + 2 = 13	8	5	5
4	13 + 6 = 19	21	−2	0
5	19 + 3 = 22	9	13	13
Average	69/5 =13.8		0	3.6

Using Equation (14.3), the makespan is $M_t = C_t - S_t = 22 - 0 = 22$. If we use the SPT rule to schedule the jobs, we obtain the sequence 3-5-1-4-2. The flow time, tardiness, and lateness are then given as follows:

Job	Flow Time (F_i)	Due Date (D_i)	Lateness $(L_i = C_i - D_i)$	Tardiness (Max $(0, L_i)$)
3	2	8	−6	0
5	2 + 3 = 5	9	−4	0
1	5 + 4 = 9	15	−6	0
4	9 + 6 = 15	21	−6	0
2	15 + 7 = 22	16	6	6
Average	10.6		−3.2	1.2

Note that the makespan is 22 and that the maximum tardiness and the maximum lateness are both 6. Using the earliest-due-date rule (EDD), we obtain the sequence 3-5-1-2-4. The flow time, tardiness, and lateness for this sequence are given in the following table:

Job	Flow Time (F_i)	Due Date (D_i)	Lateness $(L_i = C_i - D_i)$	Tardiness (Max $(0, L_i)$)
3	2	8	−6	0
5	2 + 3 = 5	9	−4	0
1	5 + 4 = 9	15	−6	0
2	9 + 7 = 16	16	0	0
4	16 + 6 = 22	21	1	1
Average	10.8		−3.0	0.2

The results of applying three different sequencing rules to the five jobs are shown in Exhibit 14.8. Note that the SPT rule minimizes the average flow time and number of jobs in the system. The EDD rule minimizes the maximum lateness and tardiness. As previously noted, the SPT rule is internally focused whereas the EDD rule is focused on external customers. Using a by-the-numbers sequencing rule, as in 1-2-3-4-5, results in very poor relative performance. This result helps illustrate that random or commonsense sequencing rules seldom give better results than the SPT or EDD rules for sequencing jobs over a single processor.

Exhibit 14.8 Comparison of Three Ways to Sequence the Five Jobs

Performance Criteria	Sequence 1-2-3-4-5	Sequence 3-5-1-4-2 (SPT)	Sequence 3-5-1-2-4 (EDD)
Average Flow Time	13.8	10.6	10.8
Average Lateness	0	−3.2	−3.0
Maximum Lateness	13	6	1
Average Tardiness	3.6	1.2	0.2
Maximum Tardiness	13	6	1

Two-Resource Sequencing Problem

As explained in Chapter 7, a flow shop is a job shop in which all jobs have the same routing. In this section, we consider a flow shop with only two resources or workstations. We assume that each job must be processed first on Resource #1 and then on Resource #2. Processing times for each job on each resource are known. In contrast to sequencing jobs on a single resource, the makespan can vary for each different sequence. Therefore, for the two-resource sequencing problem, it makes sense to try to find a sequence with the smallest makespan.

S. M. Johnson developed the following algorithm in 1954 for finding a minimum makespan schedule.[6] The following algorithm (procedure) defines Johnson's sequencing rule for the two-resource problem structure.

1. List the jobs and their processing times on Resources #1 and #2.
2. Find the job with the shortest processing time (on either resource).
3. If this time corresponds to Resource #1, sequence the job first; if it corresponds to Resource #2, sequence the job last.
4. Repeat steps 2 and 3, using the next-shortest processing time and working inward from both ends of the sequence until all jobs have been scheduled.

Consider the two-resource sequencing problem posed by Hirsch Products. It manufactures certain custom parts that first require a shearing operation (Resource #1) and then a punch-press operation (Resource #2). Hirsch currently has orders for five jobs, which have processing times (days) estimated as follows:

Job	Shear	Punch
1	4 days	5 days
2	4	1
3	10	4
4	6	10
5	2	3

The jobs can be sequenced in any order but they must be sheared first. Therefore, we have a flow shop situation where each job must first be sequenced on the shear operation and then on the punch operation.

Suppose the jobs are sequenced by-the-numbers in the order 1-2-3-4-5. This schedule can be represented by a simple Gantt chart showing the schedule of each job on each machine along a horizontal time axis (see Exhibit 14.9). This shows, for instance, that Job 1 is scheduled on the shear for the first 4 days, Job 2 for the next 4 days, and so on. We construct a Gantt chart for a given sequence by scheduling the first job as early as possible on the first machine (shear). Then, as soon as the job is completed, it can be scheduled on the punch press, provided that no other job is currently in progress. First, note that all jobs follow each other on the shearing machine. Because of variations in processing times, however, the punch press, the second operation, is often idle while awaiting the next job. The makespan is 37 days, and the flow times in days for the jobs follow:

Job	1	2	3	4	5
Flow Time (days)	9	10	22	34	37

Thus the average flow time as shown in Exhibit 14.9 is (9 + 10 + 22 + 34 + 37)/5 = 22.4 days. Also, note with this job sequence the idle time for the punch press in days 0 to 4, 10 to 18, and 22 to 24, for a total of 14 days idle. The resource utilization of the punch press (Resource #2) is 23/37 or 62.2 percent, which is not so good. The expensive punch-press resource is idle, producing no output 37.8 percent of the time! The point here is that job sequencing affects resource utilization too!

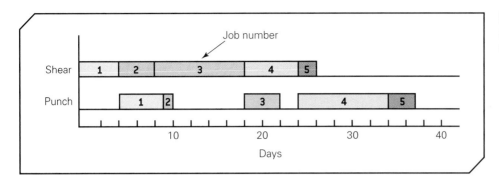

Exhibit 14.9
Gantt Job Sequence Chart
for Hirsch Product Sequence
1-2-3-4-5

Applying Johnson's rule, we find that the shortest processing time is for Job 2 on the punch press.

Job	Shear	Punch
1	4 days	5 days
2	4	1
3	10	4
4	6	10
5	2	3

Since the minimum time on either machine is on the second machine, Job 2, with a 1-day processing time, is scheduled last.

___   ___   ___   ___   __2__

Next, we find the second-shortest processing time. It is 2 days, for Job 5 on machine 1. Therefore, Job 5 is scheduled first.

__5__   ___   ___   ___   __2__

In the next step, we have a tie of 4 days between Job 1 on the shear and Job 3 on the punch press. When a tie occurs, either job can be chosen. If we pick Job 1, we have the following sequence:

__5__   __1__   ___   ___   __2__

Continuing with Johnson's rule, the last two steps yield the complete sequence.

__5__   __1__   ___   __3__   __2__
__5__   __1__   __4__   __3__   __2__

The Gantt chart for this sequence is shown in Exhibit 14.10. The makespan is reduced from 37 to 27 days, and the average flow time is also improved from 22.4 to 18.2 days. As noted, the total idle time on the punch press is now only 4 days, resulting in a punch-press resource utilization of 23/27 or 85.2 percent and we gain 10 days to schedule other jobs. If the sequencing problem structure fits the assumptions of Johnson's rule, it is a powerful algorithm.

Dispatching and Simulation-Based Sequencing

Real-life sequencing problems in job shops are often too large and complex to find optimal solutions, except for some special cases like the single- or two-resource problems that we described in the previous sections. In the most general job shop situation, we must sequence n jobs on m machines, and each job may have a unique

Exhibit 14.10
Gantt Job Sequence Chart
for Hirsch Product Sequence
5-1-4-3-2

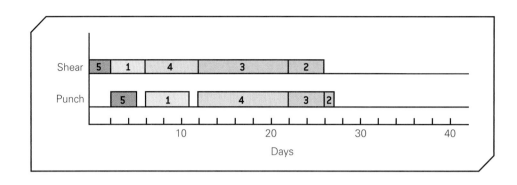

routing. If so, there are up to $(n!)^m$ possible schedules. For example, when $n = 5$ and $m = 4$, there are more than 200 million sequences! These problems are too difficult to solve optimally, and heuristic methods are used.

Another problem with optimization-based approaches is they assume that all jobs are available at the same time and no new jobs are created during processing. In real manufacturing environments, scheduling is dynamic—jobs are continually being created, eliminated, and changed and unforeseen events such as machine breakdowns occur that invalidate previously developed schedules. Hence, sequencing decisions must be made over time. **Dispatching** *is the process of selecting jobs for processing and authorizing the work to be done.* A good example is a taxicab dispatcher. When a taxi driver drops off a customer, the dispatcher tells the driver what customer to pick up next based on the requests currently waiting (see OM Spotlight: Dispatching of Tank Trucks for Mobil Oil Corporation). Dispatching is a Level 3 activity where plans are executed. In goods-producing businesses, dispatching is part of "shop floor control." In service-providing businesses, dispatching can be done in the front or back offices. An example of dispatching in the front office might be giving one customer priority over another. An example in the back office would be rerouting delivery trucks to new destinations based on updates on customer needs and current delivery performance.

Because of the randomness in job arrivals and processing times in realistic operating environments, it is not easy to identify which sequencing rule is the best. Simulation-based approaches apply one or more dispatching rules to rank the order of jobs waiting to be processed at a machine in order to use available capacity effectively. Simulation modeling enables a manager to experiment with a model of the production system to choose the best dispatching rule for a particular set of criteria and shop conditions (see Supplementary Chapter D on simulation). Simulations of dispatching rules are normally conducted over sufficiently long periods of time and for reasonably realistic shop configurations. Extensive studies have been conducted to analyze dispatching rules.[7] There is no single best rule to use for job-shop scheduling, since these rules are very dependent on the shop configuration and the sequence of job arrivals. However, the simulation studies have shown that the shortest-processing-time (SPT) rule, though very simplistic, is one of the best rules. We will illustrate the general approach using a simple example.

Lynwood Manufacturing is a small job shop with a lathe, drill press, milling machine, and grinder. Jobs arrive as customers place orders. For simulation purposes, the job arrivals must be specified. This is usually done through analysis of historical data. Let us assume that four jobs will arrive in the near future. Their characteristics are given in Exhibit 14.11.

We also need a method of depicting the status of the shop at any point in time. We can do this with the type of illustration shown in Exhibit 14.12. In this illustration, a box represents each machine; circles in and above the box denote jobs being processed and waiting. Beneath each box is listed the completion time of any job that is being processed by that machine.

Dispatching *is the process of selecting jobs for processing and authorizing the work to be done.*

OM SPOTLIGHT

Dispatching of Tank Trucks for Mobil Oil Corporation[8]

Mobil Oil Corporation runs a nation-wide system for dispatching and processing customer orders for gasoline and distillates. It is an integrated operating system that controls the flow of billions in annual sales from initial order entry to final delivery, confirmation, and billing. Although the entire dispatching process is overseen by a handful of people in a small office, it operates more efficiently than the old manual system in all respects: It provides better customer service; greatly improved credit, inventory, and operating cost control; and significantly reduced distribution costs. Central to this new system is computer-assisted dispatch (called CAD at Mobil), designed to assist human dispatchers in real time as they determine the means by which ordered product will be safely and efficiently delivered to customers.

The objectives of the dispatching process are to minimize the cost of delivered product, to balance the workload among the company trucks, and to load the maximum weight on a truck while adhering to all laws and proper loading rules. These conflicting objectives must be met within the constraints of maintaining customer service levels.

Under the best of conditions, dispatching is hard work. The dispatcher must attend to myriad details of customer, vehicle fleet, and product status. Dispatching petroleum tank trucks involves following intricate rules governing safe and efficient operation. The costs of distribution are very sensitive to dispatching decisions, and even small errors in judgment can severely disrupt daily operations. For example, one must account for several factors, such as each terminal having different products available and a product having a different cost at each terminal. Although over 20 products may be distributed, three grades of motor gasoline constitute most of the volume. The trucks available include Mobil's own trucks and hired trucks. The trucks have different capacities,

different numbers and sizes of separate bulk cargo compartments, and different cost structures. Assigning orders to trucks may require adjusting the ordered quantities of products so that they will fit into the truck compartments. Further, equipment compatibility must be considered, and the routes must reflect the various weight jurisdictions through which the trucks pass, as well as the cost of road and bridge tolls.

Dispatching decisions pertain to (1) assigning orders to terminals, (2) assigning orders to delivery trucks, (3) adjusting order quantities to fit truck compartments, (4) loading trucks to their maximum legal weight, and (5) routing trucks and sequencing deliveries. The CAD system developed to automate the dispatching process makes major business decisions involving (1) owned versus hired transportation, (2) sourcing, (3) vehicle loading, and (4) routing. CAD cannot completely replace the human dispatcher, because many crucial aspects of the dispatching process are not quantifiable. Annual net cost savings is in the millions of dollars from smarter dispatching.

Job	Arrival Time	Processing Sequence (Processing Time)
1	0	$L(10), D(20), G(35)$
2	0	$D(25), L(20), G(30), M(15)$
3	20	$D(10), M(10)$
4	30	$L(15), G(10), M(20)$

Exhibit 14.11
Job Data for Lynwood Manufacturing

Exhibit 14.13 is a flowchart of the simulation process. In simulating the behavior of the Lynwood Manufacturing job shop over time, we increment time by five units, because the processing times (in Exhibit 14.11) are in multiples of 5. Further, we assume that the time needed to move jobs between machines is negligible.

Exhibit 14.12

Status of Lynwood Job Shop
at Any Point in Time

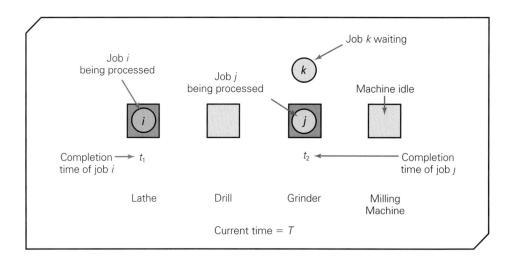

Exhibit 14.13

Flowchart for Simulating
Lynwood Manufacturing
Job Shop

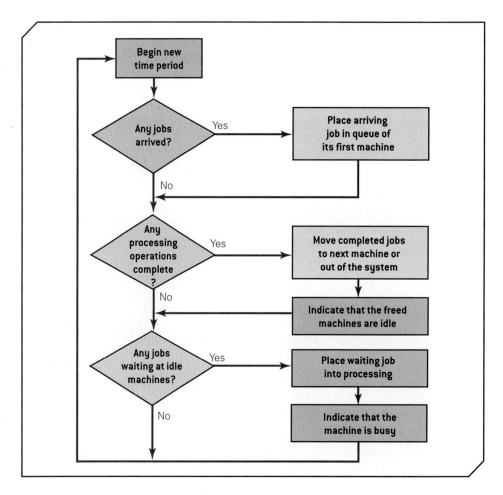

We begin the simulation at time $T = 0$ and use the least-work-remaining rule
to schedule jobs. At time 0, Jobs 1 and 2 arrive. Job 1 is immediately scheduled on
the lathe, and Job 2 is assigned to the drill press. The status of the shop at time 0
is as shown in Exhibit 14.14.

Within a particular time interval only two possible events can occur: either a new
job arrives or the processing of some job is completed. If nothing occurs during a time
interval, we simply move on to the next interval. In this example, nothing occurs at
time 5, but Job 1 is finished on the lathe at time 10. Since Job 2 is still on the drill

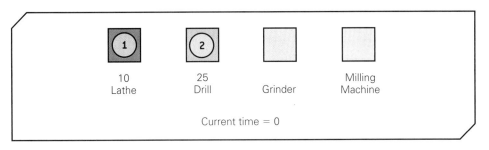

Exhibit 14.14
Status of Lynwood Job Shop at Time 0

press at time 10, Job 1 must wait. The status of the shop then is as shown in Exhibit 14.15.

Nothing happens at time 15. At time 20, Job 3 arrives and joins the queue at the drill press, as shown in Exhibit 14.16.

At time 25, Job 2 is completed on the drill press. A decision must be made whether to schedule Job 1 or Job 3 next. The work remaining for Job 1 is 20 + 35 = 55, and for Job 3 the total remaining processing time is 10 + 10 = 20. Thus, Job 3 is scheduled next, and Job 2 moves to the lathe, as shown in Exhibit 14.17. Continuing in this way, we trace the status of the shop over time, as shown in Exhibit 14.18, until all four jobs are completed.

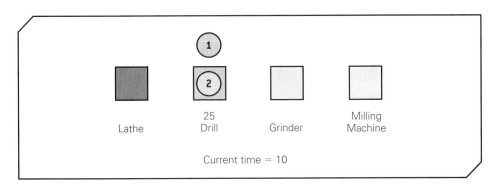

Exhibit 14.15
Status of Lynwood Job Shop at Time 10

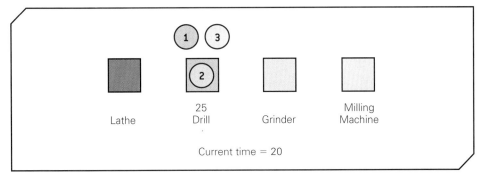

Exhibit 14.16
Status of Lynwood Job Shop at Time 20

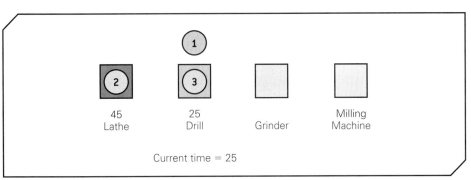

Exhibit 14.17
Status of Lynwood Job Shop at Time 25

Exhibit 14.18
Simulation of Lynwood Job
Shop over Time

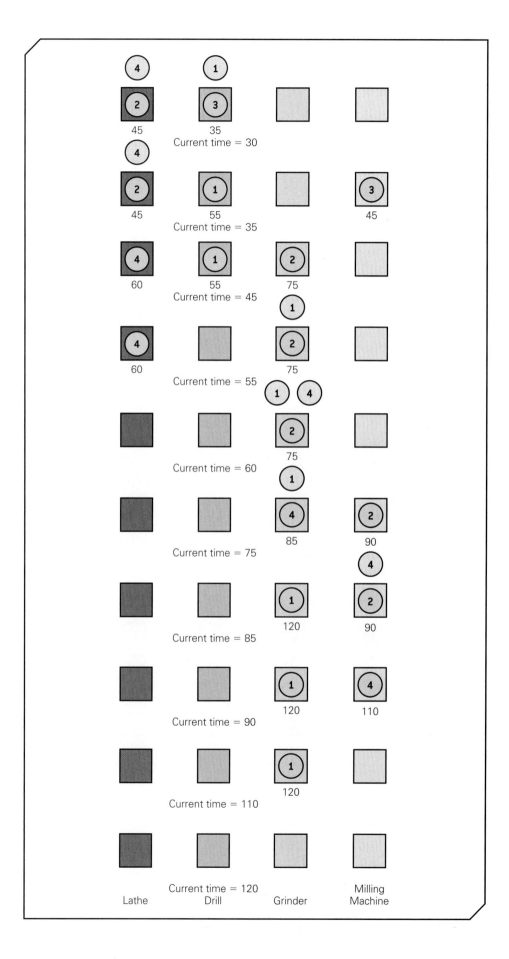

Exhibit 14.19 Gantt Chart for Lynwood Job Shop Using Least-Remaining-Work Rule

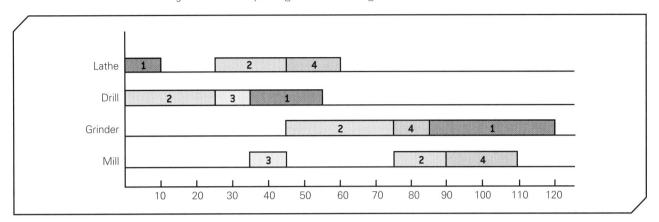

We can construct a bar chart of the result of this scheduling process, as shown in Exhibit 14.19. Statistics on machine utilization and job-waiting times and completion times can now be computed easily and used as measures for comparing various dispatching rules. A summary is provided in Exhibit 14.20. Simulations such as these also give the manager an idea of where bottlenecks might occur or where more capacity is needed.

Batch Production Sequencing and Scheduling

Many organizations face unique sequencing and scheduling issues, and customized solution approaches are often developed and used. Clearly, it is impossible to describe the full spectrum of applications. However, in this section we illustrate one particular problem structure that many manufacturing firms face: that of sequencing different manufactured goods on common facilities (see OM Spotlight: Scotts Company). For example, a soft-drink manufacturer may produce several flavors at one facility, a soap company may package several sizes on the same packaging lines, or an ice-cream maker uses the same equipment to produce different flavors. In these situations, products are generally produced in batches. The decisions faced by managers of such production systems are how much to produce in each batch and the sequence, or order, in which the batches are to be produced.

The batch quantity (which can be equivalently characterized as the length of time for a production run) and the frequency of production affect inventory levels and setup costs. A setup cost is incurred each time a changeover for a new product is required. With longer production runs, more inventory is carried and fewer setups are incurred. When several products share common facilities, however, batch sizes must be modified, because product sequencing also affects cost. For instance, setup costs may vary with the sequence of product changeovers, as in changing a packaging line from small to medium size versus small to large size, or going from cola to lemon-lime versus cola to diet cola.

Discussion in this section is limited to inventory considerations. A technique that is often used in batch-processing situations is *scheduling by run out time*. This technique can be illustrated with an example.

Job	Waiting Time	Completion Time	Machine	Idle Time*
1	55	120	Lathe	75
2	0	90	Drill	65
3	25	45	Grinder	45
4	65	110	Mill	75

Exhibit 14.20
Simulation Results for Lynwood Job Shop Using Least-Work-Remaining Rule

*Makespan minus processing time

OM SPOTLIGHT

Scotts Miracle-Gro Company[9]

The year 1928 was the first year of the Academy Awards, penicillin was invented, the first televisions were sold, and a small company in Marysville, Ohio, O.M. Scotts & Sons, introduced Turf Builder, the world's first fertilizer for home lawns. The Scotts Company knew it was onto something with Turf Builder. After all, consumers loved the product, and in 1940 sales of Scotts Turf Builder had reached an all-time high. During the 1960s, the company introduced a line of Turf Builder products to control weeds, crabgrass, insects, and lawn diseases. And lawns in the South received a boost when Scotts unleashed a new product, a weed and feed product that is safe for St. Augustine grass. During the 1990s, the company developed Patchmaster®, a product that combines grass seed, starter fertilizer, and mulch for repairing bare spots in lawns. Later, GrubEx®, a product designed to control lawn-destroying grubs, was developed.

When Scotts produced only one product, scheduling was quite easy. Today, however, production must schedule a broad variety of Turf Builder related products in its processing factories. Scotts tries to minimize changeovers and setups yet gain economies of scale by long production runs while maintaining inventory and customer service levels. The run out method of batch scheduling was used at one time to schedule Scott's factories. Today, more sophisticated methods such as linear programming and simulation are used to schedule the multiple batches of product for their factories.

Suppose a consumer-products company produces five sizes of a laundry soap at one plant. Lot sizes and demand data are given in Exhibit 14.21. The first question to ask is whether capacity is sufficient to meet the demand for all product sizes. To produce the weekly demand for the small size requires 150/833 = 0.18 week. The medium size requires 250/1,000 = 0.25 week; the large size, 150/750 = 0.20 week; the jumbo size, 100/900 = 0.11 week; and the giant size, 100/600 = 0.17 week. Thus, meeting the total weekly demand requires 0.18 + 0.25 + 0.20 + 0.11 + 0.17 = 0.91 week of production time. This leaves machinery idle 9 percent of the time. The idle time can be used for setup and maintenance. When capacity is not sufficient, shortages will occur. This means that the aggregate plan is inconsistent with the capacity available.

Suppose the company adopts a "cyclic" schedule of producing the economic lot size for each product size in rotation. From Exhibit 14.21 we see that it would take a total of 1.2 + 0.8 + 2.0 + 2.0 + 1.0 = 7 weeks to produce the economic lot sizes of all products. Let us see what would happen during that time. For the small size, we begin with an inventory of 800 units. If we produce 1,000 units, we will have a total of 1,800 units available to satisfy the demand during the 7 weeks until we produce the small size again. Since 7 weeks' demand is 7(150) = 1,050 units, we see that we will be able to cover the demand and have some inventory remaining when the next production cycle begins.

Product Size	Economic Lot Size	Production Time (weeks)	Production Rate (units/week)	Demand (units/week)	Current Inventory
Small	1,000	1.2	833	150	800
Medium	800	0.8	1,000	250	600
Large	1,500	2.0	750	150	2,000
Jumbo	1,800	2.0	900	100	2,500
Giant	600	1.0	600	100	525

Exhibit 14.21
Lot Size and Demand Data for Five Manufactured Product Sizes

Now consider the medium size. With an initial inventory of 600, producing 800 units will make 1,400 units available for satisfying the 7 weeks' demand. However, 7 weeks' demand is 7(250) = 1,750 units; the cyclic economic-lot-size schedule will lead to shortages. An alternative is to use run out time as a scheduling rule. The run out time (R) for a product is defined by Equation (14.6) as

$$R = \text{Inventory level/Demand rate} \qquad \textbf{(14.6)}$$

That is, the run out time is the length of time inventory will be available to satisfy demand.

If run out times are calculated for each product size, we can schedule the product with the smallest run out time first. The run out times in weeks for each product size are calculated as shown in Exhibit 14.22. Thus, we would schedule the medium size first. From Exhibit 14.21, we see that the lot size of 800 will take 0.8 week to produce. At the end of 0.8 week, the updated inventory levels are found by subtracting 0.8 week's demand from the current levels, as shown in Exhibit 14.23. Next, we use these updated inventory levels to compute new run out times, as shown in Exhibit 14.24, and then we select the next product size to run, which would be the giant size.

Size	Run Out Time
Small	800/150 = 5.33
Medium	600/250 = 2.40
Large	2,000/150 = 13.33
Jumbo	2,500/100 = 25.00
Giant	525/100 = 5.25

Exhibit 14.22
Run Out Times for Five Manufactured Product Sizes

Size	Inventory
Small	800 − 150(0.8) = 680
Medium	600 − 250(0.8) + 800 = 1,200
Large	2,000 − 150(0.8) = 1,880
Jumbo	2,500 − 100(0.8) = 2,420
Giant	525 − 100(0.8) = 445

Exhibit 14.23
Updated Inventory for Five Manufactured Product Sizes

Size	Run Out Time
Small	680/150 = 4.53
Medium	1,200/250 = 4.80
Large	1,880/150 = 12.53
Jumbo	2,420/100 = 24.20
Giant	445/100 = 4.45

Exhibit 14.24
New Run Out Times Based on Updated Inventory

Notice that in using the smallest run out time, we are not scheduling all products in a rotating sequence. Instead, we schedule them one at a time in response to current inventory levels and anticipated demand. This is, then, a dynamic approach. It does not consider inventory-holding costs, stockout costs, or setup costs. Even with this rule, shortages may occur. (More sophisticated mathematical models exist, but they are beyond the scope of this book.) Managers should carefully examine projected inventory levels for all products to see if they are being depleted too fast or building up to unnecessarily high levels. Production schedules can be adjusted, if necessary, by aggregate planning approaches, such as overtime, undertime, or other capacity-change strategies.

SCHEDULE MONITORING AND CONTROL

Murphy's law states that if something can go wrong it will, and this is especially true with schedules. Thus, it is important that progress be monitored on a continuing basis. For example, in manufacturing, the master scheduler must know the status of orders that are ahead of schedule or behind schedule due to shortages of material, workstations that are backlogged, changes in inventory, labor turnover, and sales commitments. Schedules must be changed when these things occur. Therefore, reschedules are a normal part of scheduling.

Short-term capacity fluctuations also necessitate changes in schedules. Factors affecting short-term capacity include absenteeism, labor performance, equipment failures, tooling problems, labor turnover, and material shortages. They are inevitable and unavoidable. Some alternatives available to operations managers for coping with capacity shortages are overtime, short-term subcontracting, alternate process routing, and reallocations of the work force, as described in the previous chapter.

Gantt (bar) charts are useful tools for monitoring schedules, and an example is shown in Exhibit 14.25. The red shaded areas indicate completed work. This chart shows, for example, that Job 4 has not yet started on machine 2, Job 1 is currently behind schedule on machine 3, and Jobs 2 and 5 are ahead of schedule. Perhaps needed material has not been delivered for Job 4, or perhaps machine 3 has had a breakdown. In any event, it is up to production-control personnel to revise the schedule or to expedite jobs that are behind schedule. Many other types of graphical aids are useful and commercially available.

Exhibit 14.25
Gantt Chart Example for Monitoring Schedule Progress

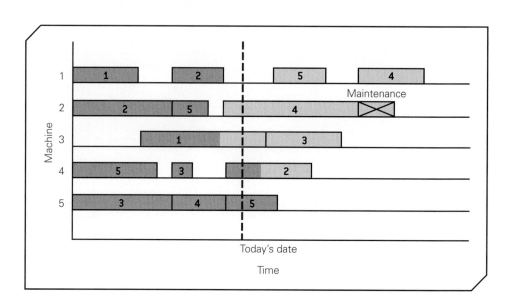

SOLVED PROBLEMS

SOLVED PROBLEM #1

Five tax analysis jobs are waiting to be processed by Martha at T. R. Accounting Service. Use the shortest-processing-time (SPT) and earliest-due-date (EDD) sequencing rules to sequence the jobs. Compute the flow time, tardiness, and lateness for each job, and the average flow time, average tardiness, and average lateness for all jobs. Which rule do you recommend? Why?

Job	Processing Time (days)	Due Date
1	7	11
2	3	10
3	5	8
4	2	5
5	6	17

Solution:

The SPT sequence is 4-2-3-5-1.

Job	Flow Time (F_i)	Due Date (D_i)	Lateness ($L_i = C_i - D_i$)	Tardiness (Max (0, L_i))
4	2	5	−3	0
2	2 + 3 = 5	10	−5	0
3	5 + 5 = 10	8	2	2
5	10 + 6 = 16	17	−1	0
1	16 + 7 = 23	11	12	12
Average	11.2		+1.0	2.8

The EDD sequence is 4-3-2-1-5.

Job	Flow Time (F_i)	Due Date (D_i)	Lateness ($L_i = C_i - D_i$)	Tardiness (Max (0, L_i))
4	2	5	−3	0
3	2 + 5 = 7	8	−1	0
2	7 + 3 = 10	10	0	0
1	10 + 7 = 17	11	6	6
5	17 + 6 = 23	17	6	6
Average	11.8		−1.6	2.4

Given the nature of the data this is not an easy decision. The SPT rule minimizes average flow time and average lateness but Job 5 is extremely late by 12 days. The EDD rule minimizes the maximum job tardiness and lateness. Jobs 1 and 5 are tardy by 6 days. If Job 5 is a big client with significant revenue potential, then the EDD rule is probably best.

SOLVED PROBLEM #2

A manufacturing process involving machined components consists of two operations done on two different machines. The status of the queue at the beginning of a particular week is as follows:

Job Number	Number of Components	Scheduled Time on Machine 1 (min. per piece)	Scheduled Time on Machine 2 (min. per piece)
101	200	2.5	2.5
176	150	1.5	0.5
184	250	1.0	2.0
185	125	2.5	1.0
201	100	1.2	2.4
213	100	1.2	2.2

The processing on machine 2 must follow processing on machine 1. Schedule these jobs to minimize the makespan. Illustrate the schedule you arrive at with a bar chart.

Solution:

Because this is a two-machine flow shop problem, Johnson's rule is applicable. Total time in minutes on each machine is the product of the number of components and the unit times, as shown here.

Job	Machine 1	Machine 2	Job	Machine 1	Machine 2
101	500	500	185	312.5	125
176	225	75	201	120	240
184	250	500	213	120	220

The sequence specified by Johnson's rule is 201-213-184-101-185-176. The schedules are shown in two different versions of Gantt charts below.

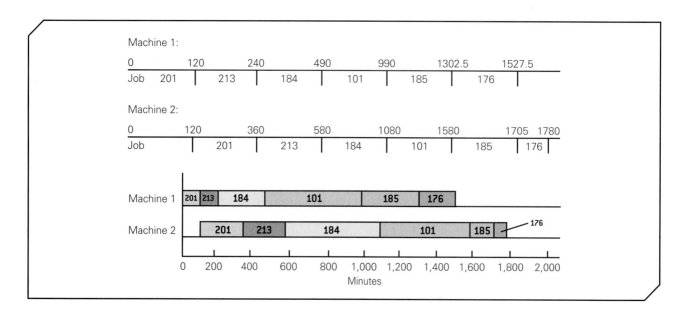

SOLVED PROBLEM #3

A detergent manufacturer uses a single facility for filling and packaging all four of its products. The inventory at the beginning of a particular week, the average demand, the production rate, and lot size are given in Exhibit 14.26 (in ounces). If the run out time method is used for scheduling this activity, how would the activity be scheduled during the first 2 weeks?

Solution:
The initial solution is as follows:

Product	Inventory	Demand	Run Out Time
1	10,000	5,000	2.0 Schedule first
2	12,000	4,000	3.0
3	15,000	3,000	5.0
4	6,000	1,000	6.0

Since the economic lot size for Item 1 (Brand A, Size A) is 10,000, that is, half of 1 week's run, the next decision

arises after one-half week. Thus, at time = 0.5 week, we have:

Product	Inventory	Demand	Run Out Time
1	17,500	5,000	3.5
2	10,000	4,000	2.5
3	13,500	3,000	4.5
4	5,500	1,000	5.5

Schedule Product 2, which takes 1 week. Note that the inventory for Product 1, 17,500, is computed as 10,000 − 0.5(5,000) + 10,000. Schedule the next product at time = 1.5 weeks.

Product	Inventory	Demand	Run Out Time
1	12,500	5,000	2.5
2	11,000	4,000	2.75
3	10,500	3,000	3.5
4	4,500	1,000	4.5

Exhibit 14.26
Data for Detergent Manufacturer

Product	Weekly Inventory	Demand	Production Rate/Week	Lot Size
Brand A, Size A	10,000	5,000	20,000	10,000
Brand A, Size B	12,000	4,000	5,000	5,000
Brand B, Size A	15,000	3,000	12,000	6,000
Brand C, Size A	6,000	1,000	2,000	1,000

Schedule Product 1, which takes 0.5 week. This takes us through the first 2 weeks.

SOLVED PROBLEM #4

During your first job as an assistant fast-food manager you were asked to forecast demand and develop a staffing schedule for the last week of the month. Your demand forecasts converted into the minimal full-time equivalent employee (FTE) requirements for cash register and service counter employees are shown in Table 1.

Each employee should have two consecutive days off. How many employees are required and what is a feasible schedule?

Solution:

One of several alternative staff schedule solutions is shown in Table 2. Notice that after scheduling four FTE we did a demand-staff capacity check to see where we stand. Four FTEs does a good job of covering the demand forecasts.

The final employee work schedule requires four people as follows:

Employee	Work Schedule
1	Mon., Thur., Fri., Sat., Sun.
2	Wed., Thur., Fri., Sat., Sun.
3	Mon., Tue., Fri., Sat., Sun.
4	Tue., Wed., Thur., Fri., Sat.

This ensures that all four employees are assigned a full week of work. On days when excess labor is on duty, employees can work on other tasks such as cleaning equipment and so on. Part-time employees could help out on Saturday or the fast-food manager(s) could help out or service would simply not be so great on Saturday.

Table 1.

Day	Mon.	Tue.	Wed.	Thur.	Fri.	Sat.	Sun.
Minimum Personnel	2	1	1	3	4	5	2

Table 2.

Step #	Mon.	Tue.	Wed.	Thur.	Fri.	Sat.	Sun.
1	2	(1)	(1)	3	4	5	2
2	(1)	(1)	1	2	3	4	1
3	1	1	(0)	(1)	2	3	0
4	(0)	0	0	1	1	2	(0)
# On Duty	2	2	2	3	4	4	3
Minimum Personnel	2	1	1	3	4	5	2
Over/Under Check	0	+1	+1	0	0	−1	+1

KEY TERMS AND CONCEPTS

Appointments
Automated scheduling
Critical ratio rule
Dispatching
Earliest-due-date (EDD) rule
Flow time

Gantt charts
Johnson's two-resource sequencing rule
Lateness
Makespan
Multiple-criteria rules
Run out method

Schedule evaluation
Schedule generation
Scheduling
Sequencing
Shortest-processing-time (SPT) rule

Simulation
Single-criterion rules
Staff scheduling method
Tardiness

QUESTIONS FOR REVIEW AND DISCUSSION

1. Define scheduling and sequencing. How do these concepts differ? How are they similar?

2. Explain how scheduling affects customer service and costs. Provide an example.

3. Explain how scheduling supports the three levels of aggregate and disaggregate planning.

4. Interview an operations manager at a nearby manufacturing or service company to find out about scheduling problems the company faces and how they are addressed.

5. Are MRP planned order releases considered sequencing? Yes or no? Explain.

6. Explain how computer-based scheduling systems incorporate schedule generation, schedule evaluation, and automated scheduling.

7. Discuss how you decide to schedule your school assignments. Do your informal scheduling rules correspond to any of those in this chapter?

8. Explain the role of scheduling and sequencing in supply and value chains.

9. Discuss scheduling and sequencing issues in municipal services such as garbage collection, school bus routing, or snowplowing. What types of criteria and approaches might be used?

10. Provide some examples of staff scheduling in service organizations.

11. Why are appointment systems used? What decisions are necessary to design an appointment system?

12. Evaluate a good or bad experience you might have had with an appointment from both the customer (you) and organization's perspective. What factors do you think led to this experience?

13. Explain the difference between flow time and makespan. Why are these criteria important from the perspective of operations performance?

14. Explain the difference between lateness and tardiness. Why might an organization use one over the other? Provide an example that supports your opinion.

15. What are the advantages and disadvantages of the SPT and EDD sequencing rules?

16. Explain why any sequence chosen in a single-machine scheduling problem will not affect makespan.

17. Distinguish between static and dynamic job arrival patterns. Why does this make a difference?

18. Summarize the procedure used for the two-resource sequencing problem (Johnson's sequencing rule).

19. Make up a numerical example using critical ratios. How does CR differ from SPT and EDD?

20. Why is dispatching used? How is simulation used to evaluate its performance?

21. Explain how the run out method works for batch sequencing and scheduling.

22. How can organizations monitor schedules? Why is it important to do so?

PROBLEMS AND ACTIVITIES

1. A hospital emergency room needs the following numbers of nurses:

Day	M	T	W	T	F	S	S
Min. Number	4	3	2	5	7	8	3

Each nurse should have two consecutive days off. How many full-time nurses are required and what is a good nurse schedule?

2. A supermarket has the following minimum personnel requirements during the week. Each employee is required to have two consecutive days off. How many regular employees are required and what is a good schedule?

Day	Mon.	Tue.	Wed.	Thur.	Fri.	Sat.	Sun.
Min. Personnel	4	4	5	6	6	5	4

3. An insurance claims work area has five claims waiting for processing as follows:

Job	Processing Time	Due Date
A	15	26
B	25	32
C	20	35
D	10	30
E	12	20

Compute the average flow time, tardiness, and lateness for the following sequences:
   a. SPT sequence
   b. earliest-due-date sequence
   c. B-A-E-C-D

What sequencing rule do you recommend and why?

4. Mike Reynolds has four assignments due in class tomorrow, and his class times are as follows:

Class	Time
Finance 216	8 A.M.
OM 385	10 A.M.
Marketing 304	12 noon
Psychology 200	4 P.M.

Each class lasts 1 hour, and Mike has no other classes. It is now midnight, and Mike estimates that the finance, OM, marketing, and psychology assignments will take him 4, 5, 3, and 6 hours, respectively. How should he schedule the work? Can he complete all of it?

5. A small consulting group of a computer systems department has seven projects to complete. How should the projects be scheduled? The time in days and project deadlines are as follows:

	Project						
	1	2	3	4	5	6	7
Time	4	9	12	16	9	15	8
Deadline	12	24	60	28	24	36	48

6. Susie Davis owns Balloons Aloha and must fill balloons with helium and assemble them into certain configurations today for parties. Her six customer jobs all need to use the same helium tank (that is, the single processor), and she was wondering what might be the best way to sequence these jobs. Her processing time estimates are as follows:

Job	1	2	3	4	5	6
Processing Time (min.)	240	130	210	90	170	165

   a. Her assistant store manager thinks the jobs should be processed in numerical order. Compute the average flow time, lateness, and tardiness for this group of jobs.
   b. In what order would the jobs be processed using the SPT rule? Compute the average flow time, lateness, and tardiness for this group of jobs. Compare this answer with your answer to part a.
   c. Why would the SPT rule be preferable to any other approach?

7. Tony's Income Tax Service personnel can estimate the time required to complete customers' tax returns by using the following time standards assuming all information is available:

IRS Form	Standard Time (min.)
1040 short	10
1040 long	15
Schedule A	15
Schedule B	5
Schedule G	10
Schedule C	15
Schedule SE	5
Form 2106	10

One morning, five customers are waiting, needing the following forms filled out. They arrived in the order A-B-C-D-E.

Customer	Forms
A	1040 long, schedules A and B
B	1040 long, schedules A, B, SE, and 2106
C	1040 short
D	1040 long, schedules A, B, and G
E	1040 long, schedules A, B, C, and 2106

   a. If these customers are processed on a first-come, first-served (FCFS) basis, what is the flow time, lateness, and tardiness for each and the averages?
   b. If SPT is used, how will these performance metrics differ?

8. An attorney's office operates with a single copier. At the beginning of a particular day, the following

jobs are waiting for processing. All jobs must be distributed to clients or in court by 9:00 A.M. and it is now 7:30 A.M.

Job	Job Content
1	500 regular size paper 250 legal size paper
2	100 regular size paper 400 legal size paper
3	1,000 regular size paper
4	1,500 legal size paper
5	1,200 regular size paper 300 legal size paper

Regular size paper takes an average of 1.0 second per page to complete; the legal size paper takes 1.2 seconds per page. These times include allowances for stapling, bundling, moving, and changeover time. If processing is always by job, calculate the average flow time, lateness, and tardiness for this group of jobs using the following sequencing rules:

a. First-come, first-served rule (by-the-numbers of 1-2-3-4-5).
b. SPT rule.
c. What is the makespan in both cases?
d. Will all jobs be completed by 9:00 A.M.?

9. Monday morning Baxter Industries has the following jobs waiting for processing in two departments, milling and drilling, in that order:

Time Required (hours)

Job	Mill	Drill
216	8	4
327	6	10
462	10	5
519	5	6
258	3	8
617	6	2

Develop a minimum makespan schedule using Johnson's rule. Graph the results on a bar chart.

10. Assuming an 8-hour workday, suppose the following two new jobs arrive Wednesday morning for the situation in Problem 7:

Job	Mill	Drill
842	4	7
843	10	8

How should the schedule be changed for these eight jobs?

11. Dan's Auto Detailing business performs two major activities: exterior cleanup and interior detailing. Based on the size of car and condition, time estimates for six cars on Monday morning are as shown in the accompanying table:

Car Number

	1	2	3	4	5	6
Exterior	60	75	90	45	65	80
Interior	30	40	20	30	15	45

Sequence the cars so that all exterior detailing is done first and total completion time is minimized. Draw a Gantt chart of your solution. Evaluate the idle time, if any, for these two resources—exterior and interior cleaning capability.

12. Compute the number of possible schedules for a general job shop with n jobs and m machines for each of these cases:

a. $n = 3$, $m = 2$
b. $n = 2$, $m = 3$
c. $n = 3$, $m = 3$
d. $n = 4$, $m = 4$

What do you conclude from these computational results? Explain.

13. Burt's Machine Shop has seven jobs with different due dates arriving at his two-machine flow shop in the following sequence.

			Processing Time (days)	
Job	Arrival Date	Due Date	Machine 1	Machine 2
1	0	6	1	3
2	1	6	4	1
3	2	12	5	4
4	4	8	3	1
5	6	15	1	3
6	8	16	4	2
7	10	20	1	5

a. Compute the critical ratio of all waiting jobs at the time that a new job arrives, and use this to select the sequence by which to process the jobs.
b. Construct a bar chart for the schedule. How much idle time is there for each machine? What is the lateness of all jobs?

14. Burt's Machine Shop has six jobs with different due dates and processing times and their current status is summarized as follows. Compute the critical ratio for these jobs and the recommended job sequence.

Job Number	Due Date – Current Date (time remaining until due date)	Total Processing Time Remaining
11	5 days	3 days
12	2 days	7 days
13	4 days	5 days
14	3 days	6 days
15	8 days	7 days
16	6 days	9 days

15. Referring to the example of batch scheduling laundry soap product sizes in the chapter, suppose that the demands for the five products are 250, 300, 500, 800, and 300 units per week, respectively. Show that

a. demand greatly exceeds available capacity,
b. using the run out time method will eventually result in shortages.

16. A soft-drink manufacturer bottles six flavors on a single machine. Relevant data are given as follows:

Flavor	Economic Lot Size (gallons)	Bottling Time (hours)	Demand (gallons/day)	Current Inventory
Cola	7,500	32	3,000	5,000
Orange	4,000	17	1,000	3,000
Diet cola	5,000	21	2,000	4,500
Lemon-lime	2,000	8	800	1,500
Ginger ale	3,000	13	700	2,000
Club soda	3,500	15	1,200	2,100

Using the smallest run out time method, which flavor should be produced first? What inventory levels will result? Assume three shifts per day and 8 hours per shift.

CASES

HICKORY BANK (A)

Chris Thomas, president of Hickory Bank, was disturbed about the bank's recent financial performance. A small commercial bank in a Southern city of 120,000 people, Hickory Bank had recorded a net loss of $2.043 million last year on total assets of $439.33 million, the first annual loss in Hickory Bank's history. Local shareholders would give him one more year to turn bank operations around. The big banks might buy out Hickory Bank at a bargain price if current management failed in its turnaround initiatives.

Teller staffing and personnel expenses were one of the few major bank expenses over which Thomas had direct control, and he needed to use every available means to get expenses back in line. Hickory Bank believed in providing superior service, but it seemed to Thomas that many times the tellers were not busy. What complicated the analysis even more was that some branches had no growth in deposits and customers while other branches were growing. Given the bank's financial condition, he wanted to make sure the tellers were being properly utilized. He needed to develop a consistent methodology to determine teller capacity and scheduling that could be applied to all branches.

Hickory Bank began operations in May 1927. Throughout the uncertain years of the 1930s, the bank continued to be a friendly source of funds for many borrowers and a safe place for savings. The bank was operating six separate branches in this small city. The bank's 132 full- and part-time employees considered Hickory Bank an excellent place to work, which was reflected in the low turnover rate. Many of the employees started as tellers and worked their way up. Further, Hickory Bank had a reputation for paying its employees more than the other local financial institutions.

Banking hours were 9:00 A.M. to 4:30 P.M. Monday through Thursday and 9:00 A.M. to 7:00 P.M. on Friday. The full-time tellers earned an average of $9.45 per hour, worked 40 hours a week, and worked 50 weeks per year. A head teller's responsibilities required that he or she be out of the teller window for about 2 hours each full workday. The part-time tellers worked no more than 1,000 hours per year and earned an average of $7.60 per hour. The Personnel Department estimated that benefits cost the bank an additional 33 percent of a full-time employee's base wage rate. Part-time employees did not receive the benefits package.

Tellers were entitled to a paid 15-minute break and an unpaid 1-hour lunch break each day. On Fridays, an additional 30-minute supper break was given. The minimum shift for a part-time employee was 4 hours. If the shift was 5 hours or longer, the teller received a 1-hour lunch break. If the shift was less than 5 hours, a half-hour break was given.

Teller staff levels were currently determined based on the perceived need by the branch manager and the head of personnel. Most branches were staffed with full-time employees to meet perceived peak customer demand based on past experience. To determine customer arrival patterns, a sample was taken by studying the Paris branch from July 2nd through July 16th. The actual customer arrivals per 1-hour time period for the drive-in and lobby were recorded. Since tellers could quickly switch between the lobby and drive-in stations, only the total current transaction volume (lobby and drive-in) for the Paris branch is shown in Exhibit 14.27.

Paris was a growing community of 5,800 people located 5 miles west of the city. Paris was primarily a bedroom community with several of the county's largest employers located on the town's outskirts. The Paris branch ranked third of Hickory Bank's branches, with $38.4 million in total deposits and 4,662 deposit accounts. The branch ranked second in loan dollar volume.

In addition to Sarah Coleman, the assistant vice president and manager, the branch was staffed with a loan interviewer, five full-time tellers including the head teller, and no part-time tellers. Coleman had 28 years with Hickory Bank and had held a variety of positions before becoming branch manager. She had a high school education, had attended a few classes at Ball State University, and had graduated from the National Installment Loan School at the University of Oklahoma. She was energetic and enthusiastic about all aspects of her job and was involved in many Paris community activities. She had the ability to get customers and employees

excited about Hickory Bank. To break the ice on her first day at the branch, she wore her old Paris High School cheerleader outfit. Coleman spent a large proportion of her time out of the branch drumming up business. Consequently, she spent less time with branch operations than some of the other branch managers. Coleman expected deposits, accounts, loan volume, and the number of customers from current levels to double in the next 2 years. The Paris branch was the fastest-growing branch within the Hickory Bank system.

The average customer service rates were 2.00 minutes for the lobby and 1.50 minutes for the drive-in. The lobby at the Paris branch had four teller windows. A drive-in facility, operated by two tellers at all times (except during lunches and breaks), served a total of three lanes. Customer demand was higher for the drive-in windows than the lobby. The drive-in teller stations were conveniently located a few feet from the lobby teller stations. Tellers were scheduled to work 8:30 A.M. to 4:45 P.M. Monday through Thursday and 8:30 A.M. to 7:15 P.M. on Friday. It took the tellers about 5 minutes to set up their teller stations each morning.

Chris Thomas thought the answer to his high expense problems might be buried in the data collected from the Paris branch, but he was not quite sure how to uncover it. He needed to get a handle on the existing service levels, staff capacity, and teller schedules now and in 2 years if he was going to be able to improve the bank's performance. In many ways, the Paris branch was the most difficult to analyze because it was growing. Whatever solution was worked out, he wanted it to be documented, step-by-step, in the bank's operating manuals and applied later at all six branches.

Exhibit 14.27 Hickory Bank Actual Number of Customer Arrivals for Paris Branch Bank

Time Period	Fri* 7/2	Tue 7/6	Wed 7/7	Thu 7/8	Fri 7/9	Mon 7/12	Tue 7/13	Wed 7/14	Thu 7/15	Fri 7/16	Total	% of Day
9:00–10:00	36	36	16	26	31	22	14	15	27	43	266	10.9%
10:00–11:00	35	29	12	32	35	29	34	16	35	22	279	11.4
11:00–12:00	31	23	31	36	40	26	20	16	29	28	280	11.4
12:00–1:00	39	12	32	37	32	18	29	20	45	30	294	12.1
1:00–2:00	34	11	18	27	29	15	16	12	25	32	219	9
2:00–3:00	38	13	16	30	26	27	12	17	27	24	230	9.4
3:00–4:00	59	12	33	41	48	25	19	27	38	37	339	13.9
4:00–4:30	23	10	14	11	31	16	20	18	20	27	190	7.8
4:30–5:30	63	*	*	*	42	*	*	*	*	36	141	5.8
5:30–6:30	42	*	*	*	32	*	*	*	*	38	112	4.6
6:30–7:30	34	*	*	*	28	*	*	*	*	24	86	3.7
Total	434	146	172	240	374	178	164	141	246	341	2,436	100%
% of Week	N/A	16%	18%	26%	40%	17%	15%	13%	23%	32%		

N/A—Not Available

*The bank was closed on Monday, July 5, in observance of July 4. The bank closes at 4:30 P.M. Monday through Thursday.

STEPHENS INDUSTRIES[10]

Stephens Industries operates a small factory that manufactures and assembles one product for the automotive industry. Demand for the product is essentially unlimited because of the size of the factory, as is the raw material supply. The assembly is made from four different parts, each of which requires three to five manufacturing operations on three common machining centers (see Exhibit 14.28). Each part requires a 60-minute setup for each operation. From an accounting perspective, each part has an inventory value of $100 the moment it is started at the first operation. Assembly and shipment occur instantaneously when a matched set of parts is available. At the start, no WIP inventory exists in the system, and the three machines (A, B, and C) are not set up.

Stephens' objective is to produce as much as possible. The best schedule is the one that generates the most throughput without violating any of these constraints:

1. The schedules must be realistic (for instance, you cannot run two parts on the same machine simultaneously).

2. Inventory must never exceed $50,000 (500 parts).

3. At least 140 assemblies must be shipped each week.

4. At least 680 assemblies must have been shipped by the end of the first 4 weeks.

5. Only 40 days (8 weeks) of production time are available, and the plant can work 24 hours a day.

You have been hired to develop a schedule that meets these constraints. Show the results with a bar chart. (This case would make a good competitive team project to see who can develop the best schedule.)

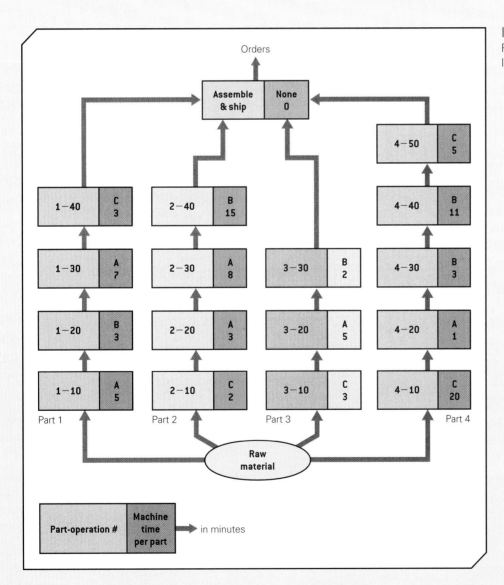

Exhibit 14.28
Product Routing, Stephens Industries Case

ENDNOTES

[1] Pritsker, A. Alan B., and Snyder, Kent, "Simulation for Planning and Scheduling," *APICS—The Performance Advantage* no. 8, August 1994, pp. 36–41.

[2] Corso, Joseph, "Challenging Old Assumptions with Finite Capacity Scheduling," *APICS—The Performance Advantage* no. 11, November 1993, pp. 50–53.

[3] UPS to Acquire Menlo Worldwide Forwarding, October 5, 2004, Press Release, http://ups.com/pressroom/us/press_releases/press_release/0,1088,4466,00.html.

[4] This approach is suggested in Tibrewala, R., Phillippe, D., and Browne, J., "Optimal Scheduling of Two Consecutive Idle Periods," *Management Science* 19, no. 1, September 1972, pp. 71–75.

[5] http://www.abs-usa.com/news/scheduleanywhere.epl, September 10, 2004.

[6] Johnson, S. M., "Optimal Two- and Three-Stage Production Schedules with Setup Times Included," Naval Research Logistics Quarterly 1, no. 1, March 1954, pp. 61–68.

[7] A survey of results can be found in Blackstone, J. H., Phillips, D. T., and Hogg, G. L., "A State-of-the-Art Survey of Dispatching Rules for Manufacturing Job Shop Operations," *International Journal of Production Research* 20, 1982, pp. 27–45.

[8] Brown, Gerald G., Ellis, Carol J., Graves, Glenn W., and Ronen, David, "Real-Time, Wide-Area Dispatch of Mobil Tank Trucks," *Interfaces* 17, no. 1, 1987, pp. 107–120.

[9] http://lawncare.scotts.com, September 10, 2004.

[10] Adapted from "The OPT Quiz," Creative Output Inc.

Chapter Outline

CHAPTER 15

Quality Management

Learning Objectives

1. To learn how quality management has evolved and changed focus over the years and why organizations need to continue to place a significant amount of emphasis on quality.

2. To understand what quality means in manufacturing and service operations, how organizations should address customer expectations and perceptions, and how quality is integrated into operations through customer focus, continuous improvement, and employee involvement.

3. To understand the quality philosophies and principles of Deming, Juran, and Crosby and how these individuals influenced the quality management practices of today's organizations.

4. To become acquainted with the International Organization for Standardization's ISO 9000:2000 requirements, documentation, and certification for meeting a family of quality standards used in many international markets.

5. To understand the principal activities that organizations must incorporate into an effective quality management system to support operations.

6. To understand the basic philosophy and methods of Six Sigma and how it is applied in organizations to improve quality and operations performance.

7. To learn about the features of elementary quality analysis and improvement tools and be able to apply them to practical business problems.

• "Wow!" exclaimed Lauren when she saw the ski runs at Deer Valley Resort in Park City, Utah. "Thanks for taking me! This sure beats the little ski hill we have in the Midwest." "You bet. Too bad Mom doesn't ski; look at what she's missing. Just take it slow and make sure I can keep up with you!" replied her dad. He knew that Deer Valley has been called "The Ritz-Carlton" of ski resorts, and this was his first trip to Utah also. He was expecting exceptional services and a superior ski vacation experience after all he had read in ski magazines.

He wasn't disappointed. When he drove up to the slopes, a curbside ski valet took their equipment from his car, parking lot attendants directed him to the closest available parking, and a shuttle transported them from the lot to Snow Park Lodge. From the shuttle, he and his daughter walked to the slopes on heated pavers that prevent freezing and assist in snow removal. At the end of the day, they were able to store their skis without charge at the lodge and easily retrieve them the next morning. "I really can't believe how short the lift lines are!" Lauren observed. "Neither can I," replied

her dad, "I especially like the complimentary mountain tours so we can get to know this place a little better." In one ski magazine, he had read about how the resort offers tours for both expert and intermediate skiers and limits the number of skiers on the mountain to reduce lines and congestion. Everyone is committed to ensuring that each guest has a wonderful experience, from "mountain hosts" stationed at the top of the lifts who answer questions and provide directions, to the friendly workers at the cafeterias and restaurants, whose food is consistently rated number one by ski-enthusiast magazines. "Lauren, what do you say we take a break for lunch? I heard the turkey chili is fantastic!"

- Haller Breweries' CEO Ray White gathered his management team. "Ladies and gentlemen, we are facing a crisis. Sales have fallen 40 percent over the past year, and just in case you hadn't noticed, our stock price slipped from $70 a few years ago to less than $10." George Green, the company's chief financial officer, replied, "I can't understand it. After our cost reduction program a few years ago, we dramatically increased the return on sales and asset utilization." Operations Manager Stephanie Scarlet jumped in, "Yes, we switched to corn syrup and hop pellets in our brewing formula and shortened the brewing time by 50 percent. *Business News* magazine even confirmed our strategy in that article—what was it? Oh, yeah. 'Does it Pay to Build Quality if Customers Don't Notice?'" "Well," replied Mr. White, "maybe they did."

DOUG KANTER/BLOOMBERG NEWS/Landov

- Although Hyundai Motor Co. dominated the Korean car market, it had a poor reputation for quality overseas, with doors that didn't fit properly, frames that rattled, and engines that delivered poor acceleration. In addition, the company was losing money. When Chung Mong Koo became CEO in 1999, he visited Hyundai's plant at Ulsan. To the shock of his employees, who hardly ever see a CEO, Chung walked onto the factory floor and looked under the hood of a Sonata sedan. He didn't like what he saw: loose wires, tangled hoses, bolts painted four different colors—the kind of sloppiness that would never be seen in a Japanese car. On the spot, he instructed the plant chief to paint all bolts and screws black and ordered workers not to release a car unless all was orderly under the hood. "You've got to get back to basics. The only way we can survive is to raise our quality to Toyota's level" he fumed.[2] The next year, U.S. sales rose by 42 percent, and in 2004, Hyundai tied with Honda as the second-best carmaker on the J.D. Powers Initial Quality ranking.

The concept of quality is fundamental to business operations. In 1887, William Cooper Procter, grandson of the founder of Procter & Gamble, told his employees, "The first job we have is to turn out quality merchandise that consumers will buy and keep on buying. If we produce it efficiently and economically, we will earn a profit, in which you will share." Procter's statement addresses three issues that are critical to operations managers: *productivity*, *cost*, and *quality*. Of these, the most significant factor in determining the long-run success or failure of any organization is quality. High quality of goods and services can provide an organization with a competitive edge; reduces costs due to returns, rework, scrap, and service upsets; increases productivity, profits, and other measures of success; and most importantly, generates satisfied customers, who reward the organization with continued patronage and favorable word-of-mouth advertising. The Deer Valley episode is a good example of this.

However, as the second example—which was based on the actual experience of Schlitz Brewing Co., once the second-largest brewer in the United States that eventually met its demise[3]—suggests, quality cannot be sacrificed simply for cost reduction or the hope of increased profits. The long-term sustainability of any organization depends on meeting customers' quality expectations.

The third example shows the importance of leadership, persistence, and an almost fanatical obsession with quality. One of the keys to Hyundai's success, in addition to investing heavily in research and development and employee training, was creating a quality control czar, who studied quality manuals of U.S. and Japanese automakers and developed their own, making it clear who is responsible for each manufacturing step, what outcome is required, and who checks and confirms performance levels. When customers reported faulty warning lights and hard-to-start engines, Chung set up a $30 million computer center where 71 engineers simulate harsh conditions to test electronics, reducing problems in these areas from 23.4 to 9.6 per 100 vehicles.[4]

Today, the high quality of goods and services is simply expected by consumers and business customers and is essential to survival and competitive success. To understand this better, just consider Ford Motor Company. During the 1980s, Ford fought its way from the bottom of Detroit's Big Three automakers to the top of the pack by a concerted effort to improve quality and better meet customer needs and expectations. It quickly became a highly profitable business. However, on January 12, 2002, a newspaper headline read "Ford to cut 35,000 jobs, close 5 plants." CEO William Ford is cited as stating, "We strayed from what got us to the top of the mountain, and it cost us greatly.... We may have underestimated the growing strength of our competitors. There were some strategies that were poorly conceived, and we just didn't execute on the basics of our business." The article goes on to observe that Ford "has been dogged by quality problems that forced the recall of several new models, including the Explorer, one of the top money-makers."[5] One of the key elements of Ford's 2002 Revitalization Plan was to "Continue Quality Improvements." In fact, the *top two* "vital few priorities" set by Ford's president for North America were "Improve quality."

Quality must be addressed throughout the value chain, beginning with suppliers and extending through operations and postsale services. **Quality management** *refers to systematic policies, methods, and procedures used to ensure that goods and services are produced with appropriate levels of quality to meet the needs of customers.* From the perspective of operations, quality management deals with key issues relating to how goods and services are designed, created, and delivered to meet customer expectations. We discussed the strategic role of quality and important design issues for goods and services earlier in this book. Our focus in this chapter is how operations should be managed to ensure that outputs meet the requirements established in design activities; that is, what must managers do on a daily basis to ensure quality? This chapter and the next focus on the philosophy and tools of modern quality management.

> **Quality management** *refers to systematic policies, methods, and procedures used to ensure that goods and services are produced with appropriate levels of quality to meet the needs of customers.*

A BRIEF HISTORY OF QUALITY MANAGEMENT

> **Learning Objective**
> To learn how quality management has evolved and changed focus over the years and why organizations need to continue to place a significant amount of emphasis on quality.

Why so much emphasis on quality today? It helps to review a bit of history. Quality assurance, usually associated with some form of measurement and inspection activity—two important aspects of quality management—has been an important aspect of production operations throughout history.[6] Egyptian wall paintings from around 1450 B.C. show evidence of measurement and inspection. Stones for the pyramids were cut so precisely that even today it is impossible to put a knife blade between the blocks. The Egyptians' success was due to the consistent use of well-developed methods and procedures and precise measuring devices.

During the Industrial Revolution, the use of interchangeable parts and the separation of work into small tasks necessitated careful control of quality, leading to the dependence on inspection to identify and remove defects. Eventually, production organizations created separate quality departments. This artificial separation of production workers from responsibility for quality assurance led to indifference to quality among both workers and their managers. During World War II, many quality specialists were trained to use statistical tools, and statistical quality control became widely known and gradually adopted throughout manufacturing industries. However, because upper managers had delegated so much responsibility for quality to others, they gained little knowledge about quality, and when the quality crisis hit years later, they were ill-prepared to deal with it. Concluding that quality was the responsibility of the quality department, many upper managers turned their attention to output quantity and efficiency because of the shortage of civilian goods.

During this time, two U.S. consultants, Dr. Joseph Juran and Dr. W. Edwards Deming, introduced statistical quality control techniques to the Japanese to aid them in their rebuilding efforts. A significant part of their educational activity was focused on upper management, rather than quality specialists alone. With the support of top managers, the Japanese integrated quality throughout their organizations and developed a culture of continuous improvement.

Improvements in Japanese quality were slow and steady; some 20 years passed before the quality of Japanese products exceeded that of Western manufacturers. By the 1970s, primarily due to the higher quality levels of their products, Japanese companies had made significant penetration into Western markets. Most major U.S. companies answered the wake-up call by instituting extensive quality improvement campaigns, focused not only on conformance but also on improving design quality. A Westinghouse (now CBS) vice president of corporate productivity and quality summed up the situation by quoting Dr. Samuel Johnson's remark: "Nothing concentrates a man's mind so wonderfully as the prospect of being hanged in the morning."

One of the most influential individuals in the quality revolution was W. Edwards Deming. In 1980, NBC televised a special program entitled *If Japan Can . . . Why Can't We?* The widely viewed program revealed Deming's key role in the development of Japanese quality, and his name was soon a household word among corporate executives. Although Deming had helped to transform Japanese industry three decades earlier, it was only then that U.S. companies asked for his help. From 1980 until his death in 1993, his leadership and expertise helped many U.S. companies to revolutionize their approach to quality.

As organizations began to integrate quality principles into their management systems, the notion of total quality management, or TQM, became popular. TQM represented a focus on quality throughout the value chain, rather than simply during production operations, and the involvement of every individual and function in the organization. Quality took on a new meaning of organization-wide performance excellence rather than an engineering-based technical discipline. Unfortunately, with all the hype and rhetoric (and the unfortunate three-letter acronym, TQM, that turns some individuals off), many companies that scrambled to institute quality programs failed in their haste. As a result, TQM met some harsh criticism. However, those organizations that succeeded in building and sustaining quality have reaped the rewards associated with higher customer loyalty, employee satisfaction, and business performance. Despite the demise of TQM as a quality "program," its basic principles took root in many organizations and have remained important management practices. Today, most people simply use the term *total quality* to refer to the original notion of TQM.

In recent years, a new interest in quality has emerged in corporate boardrooms under the concept of *Six Sigma*, a customer-focused and results-oriented approach to business improvement. Six Sigma integrates many quality tools and techniques that have been tested and validated over the years, with a bottom-line orientation that has high appeal to senior managers. We discuss Six Sigma in more detail later in this chapter. Health care is one industry that is adopting fundamental quality principles and methods, including Six Sigma initiatives (see the OM Spotlight below).

OM SPOTLIGHT

Poor Quality Costs in U.S. Health Care[7]

"Poor quality in health care costs the typical employer an estimated $1,700 to $2,000 for each covered employee each year," said Jim Mortimer, president of the Midwest Business Group on Health. That is about a third of the $4,900 spent on each employee on health care last year. IBM, General Motors, and Xerox are among the firms that offer lower monthly premiums to employees who choose health plans with the best quality results. Diane Bechel, a health care expert at Ford Motor Company, estimated that the company saved more than $5,000 on care for each of 500 employees, retirees, and family members who used hospitals that met certain quality standards, including a lot of experience with certain surgical procedures and good communication with patients. Verizon, IBM, Xerox, and Empire Blue Cross recently started to pay a 4 percent bonus for employee care to a handful of hospitals that met quality and patient safety goals for prescription drug orders and intensive care units. Eight hospitals so far have received the bonuses. Incentives like these from Fortune 500 companies are driving Six Sigma and other quality management initiatives in U.S. health care.

One U.S. government study for Medicare and Medicaid Services projects national spending on health care to soar to $2.82 trillion in 2011, almost double 2001's $1.42 trillion. If current trends continue, "the cost of poor-quality care will likely exceed $1 trillion by 2011," the study said.

UNDERSTANDING QUALITY

Learning Objective
To understand what quality means in manufacturing and service operations, how organizations should address customer expectations and perceptions, and how quality is integrated into operations through customer focus, continuous improvement, and employee involvement.

In Chapter 3, we discussed performance measurement. Recall that quality (of goods and services, as well as environmental quality) was one of the major types of performance measures that drive operations. Quality can be a confusing concept, partly because people view quality in relation to differing criteria based on their individual roles in the value chain. In addition, the meaning of quality has evolved as the quality profession has grown and matured. Neither consultants nor business professionals agree on a universal definition. A study that asked managers of 86 firms in the eastern United States to define quality produced several dozen different responses, including

1. perfection
2. consistency
3. eliminating waste
4. speed of delivery
5. compliance with policies and procedures
6. providing a good, usable product
7. doing it right the first time
8. delighting or pleasing customers
9. total customer service and satisfaction[8]

Many of these perspectives relate to a good or service's **fitness for use**—*the ability of a good or service to meet customer needs.* Understanding fitness-for-use criteria is important in the design process, as we discussed in Chapter 6. It is also important to understand that "fit for use" can mean different things to different people and that customer perceptions of quality are as important to understand as any measurable characteristics that a firm can quantify. Many people view quality by comparing features and characteristics of goods and services to a set of expectations, which may be promulgated by marketing efforts aimed at developing quality as an image variable in their minds. A framework for evaluating quality of both goods and services and identifying where to focus design and improvement efforts is the GAP model, which we discuss next.

Fitness for Use *is the ability of a good or service to meet customer needs.*

The GAP Model[9]

The GAP model recognizes that there are several ways to misspecify and mismanage the creation and delivery of high levels of quality. These "gaps" are shown in the model in Exhibit 15.1 and explained in the following list. The model clearly shows the complexity and interdisciplinary nature of service management and that there are many opportunities to make mistakes.

- **Gap 1** *is the discrepancy between customer expectations and management perceptions of those expectations.* Managers may think they understand why customers buy a good or service, but if their perception is wrong, then all subsequent design and delivery activities may be misdirected.
- **Gap 2** *is the discrepancy between management perceptions of what features constitute a target level of quality and the task of translating these perceptions into executable specifications.* This represents a mismatch between requirements and design activities that we discussed in Chapter 6.
- **Gap 3** *is the discrepancy between quality specifications documented in operating and training manuals and plans and their implementation.* Gap 3 recognizes that the manufacturing and service delivery systems must execute quality specifications well.

Exhibit 15.1 Gap Model of Quality

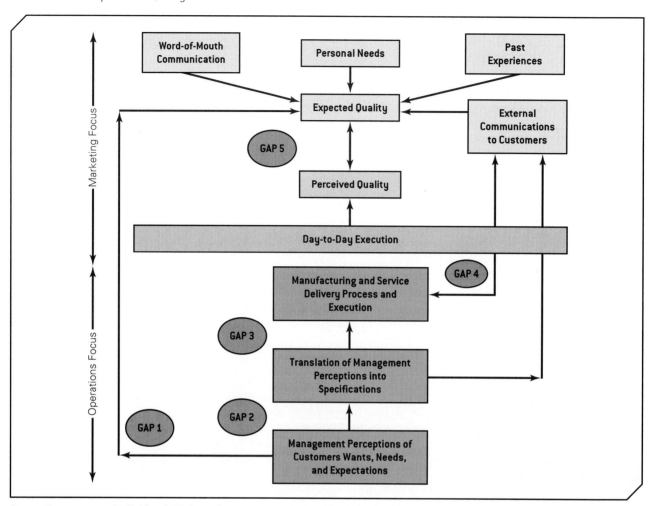

Source: Parasuraman, A., Zeithaml, V. A., and Berry, L. L., "A Conceptual Model of Service Quality and Its Implications for Future Research," *Journal of Marketing*, Fall 1985, Vol. 49, pp. 41–50. Reprinted with permission from the American Marketing Association.

- **Gap 4** *is the discrepancy between actual manufacturing and service system performance and external communications to the customers.* The customer should not be promised a certain type and level of quality unless the delivery system can achieve or exceed that level.
- **Gap 5** *is the difference between the customer's expectations and perceptions.* The fifth gap depends on the other four. This is where the customer judges quality and makes future purchase decisions.

Managers can use this model to analyze goods and services and the processes that make and deliver them to identify and close the largest gaps and improve performance. Failure to understand and minimize these gaps can seriously degrade the quality of a service and risk losing customer loyalty.

Quality in Operations

From an operations perspective, however, the most useful definition is how well the output of a manufacturing or service process conforms to the design specifications.

Quality of conformance *is the extent to which a process is able to deliver output that conforms to the design specifications.* Specifications *are targets and tolerances determined by designers of goods and services.* Targets are the ideal values for which production is to strive; tolerances are the permissible variation. We briefly discussed design specifications in Chapter 5 in the context of goods and service design. If a part is produced within the defined tolerance, for example, 0.236 ± 0.003 cm, then it conforms to the specifications. Specifications are meaningless, however, if they do not reflect attributes that are deemed important to the consumer. Ensuring quality of conformance is a major responsibility of operations managers. This is accomplished through quality control—*the means of ensuring consistency in processes to achieve conformance.* The next chapter addresses this topic in more depth.

Service quality *is consistently meeting or exceeding customer expectations (external focus) and service delivery system performance criteria (internal focus) during all service encounters.* Excellent service quality is achieved by the consistent delivery to the customer of a clearly defined customer benefit package, and associated process and service encounters, defined by many internal and external standards of performance. Performance standards are analogous to manufacturing specifications. For example, "on-time arrival" for an airplane might be specified as within 15 minutes of the scheduled arrival time. The target is the scheduled time, and the tolerance is specified to be 15 minutes.

Quality is more than simply ensuring that goods and services consistently conform to specifications. Achieving high-quality goods and services depends on the commitment and involvement of everyone in the entire value chain. The principles of total quality are simple:

1. a focus on customers and stakeholders,
2. a process focus supported by continuous improvement and learning, and
3. participation and teamwork by everyone in the organization.

First, the customer is the principal judge of quality. Thus, a quality-focused company's efforts need to extend well beyond merely meeting specifications, reducing defects and errors, or resolving complaints. They must include knowing what the customer wants, how the customer uses its goods or services, and anticipating needs that the customer may not even be able to express; designing new goods and services that truly delight the customer; responding rapidly to changing consumer and market demands; and continually developing new ways of enhancing customer relationships.

The importance of a process, as well as a customer, focus can be described by what W. Edwards Deming told Japanese managers in 1950. While presenting to a group of Japanese industrialists (collectively representing about 80 percent of the nation's capital), he drew the diagram shown in Exhibit 15.2. This diagram depicts not only the relationships among inputs, processes, and outputs but also the roles of consumers and suppliers, the interdependency of organizational processes, the usefulness of consumer research, and the importance of continuous improvement of all elements of the production system. Deming told the Japanese that understanding customers and suppliers was crucial to planning for quality. He advised them that continuous improvement of both products and production processes through better understanding of customer requirements is the key to capturing world markets. Deming predicted that within 5 years Japanese manufacturers would be making products of the highest quality in the world and would have gained a large share of the world market. He was wrong. By applying these ideas, the Japanese penetrated several global markets in less than 4 years!

The third principle is perhaps the most important. When managers give employees the tools to make good decisions and the freedom and encouragement to make contributions, they virtually guarantee that better-quality goods and services will result. Employees who are allowed to participate—both individually and in

Quality of conformance *is the extent to which a process is able to deliver output that conforms to the design specifications.*

Specifications *are targets and tolerances determined by designers of goods and services.*

Quality Control *is the means of ensuring consistency in processes to achieve conformance.*

Service quality *is consistently meeting or exceeding customer expectations (external focus) and service delivery system performance criteria (internal focus) during all service encounters.*

Exhibit 15.2
Deming's View of a Production
System

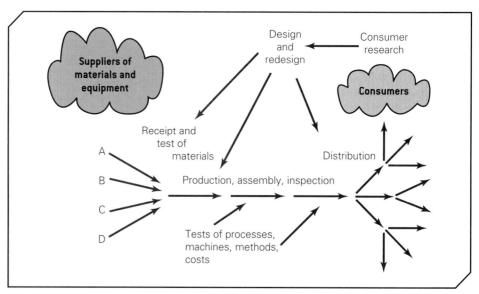

Source: Reprinted from *Out of the Crisis*, p. 5, by W. Edwards Deming, by permission of MIT and the W. Edwards Deming Institute. Published by MIT Center for Advanced Educational Services, Cambridge, MA 02139. © 1986 by The W. Edwards Deming Institute.

teams—in decisions that affect their jobs and the customer can make substantial contributions to quality. Empowering employees to make decisions that satisfy customers without constraining them with bureaucratic rules shows the highest level of trust. Another important element of total quality is teamwork, which focuses attention on both internal and external customer-supplier relationships and encourages the involvement of everyone in attacking systemic problems, particularly those that cross functional boundaries.

Every business function plays an important role in achieving quality. For example,

- Marketing and sales personnel are responsible for determining the needs and expectations of consumers.
- Product design and engineering functions develop technical specifications for products and production processes to meet the requirements determined by the marketing function.
- The purchasing department must select quality-conscious suppliers and ensure that purchase orders clearly define the quality requirements specified by product design and engineering.
- Production control must ensure that the correct materials, tools, and equipment are available at the proper time and in the proper places in order to maintain a smooth flow of production.
- Finance must authorize sufficient budgeting for equipment, training, and other means of assuring quality.
- A firm's legal department ensures that the firm complies with laws and regulations regarding such things as product labeling, packaging, safety, and transportation and has proper procedures and documentation in place in the event of liability claims against it.

Quality and Business Results

There is considerable evidence that investment in quality—not only in goods, services, and processes but in the quality of management itself—yields numerous benefits. A survey of almost 1,000 executives conducted by Zenger-Miller Achieve noted significant benefits from quality initiatives, including increased employee participation, improved product and service quality, improved customer satisfaction, improved productivity, and improved employee skills.[10] The Malcolm Baldrige National Quality Award (MBNQA) criteria and the model depicted in Exhibit 3.3 champion this notion. Baldrige Award recipients provide compelling evidence that a focus on quality leads to exceptional business results.

One of the most celebrated studies was published by Kevin Hendricks and Vinod Singhal in 1997.[11] Based on objective data and rigorous statistical analysis, the study showed that when implemented effectively, total quality management approaches improve financial performance dramatically. Using a sample of about 600 publicly traded companies that have won quality awards either from their customers (such as automotive manufacturers) or through Baldrige and state and local quality award programs, Hendricks and Singhal examined performance results from 6 years before to 4 years after winning the first quality award. The primary performance measure tracked was the percent change in operating income and a variety of measures that might affect operating income: percent change in sales, total assets, number of employees, return on sales, and return on assets. These results were compared to a set of control firms that were similar in size to the award winners and in the same industry. The analysis revealed significant differences between the sample and the control group. Specifically, the growth in operating income of winners averaged 91 percent versus 43 percent for the control group. Winners also experienced a 69 percent jump in sales (compared to 32 percent for the control group), a 79 percent increase in total assets (compared to 37 percent), a 23 percent increase in the number of employees (compared to 7 percent), an 8 percent improvement on return on sales (compared to 0 percent), and a 9 percent improvement on return on assets (compared to 6 percent). Small companies actually outperformed large companies, and over a 5-year period, the portfolio of winners beat the S&P 500 index by 34 percent.

A sample of specific operational and financial results that companies taking a total quality path have achieved include

- Among associates at Clarke American, overall satisfaction has improved from 72 percent to 84 percent over a 5-year period. Rising associate satisfaction correlated with an 84 percent increase in revenue earned per associate. Annual growth in company revenues also increased from a rate of 4.2 percent to 16 percent, compared to the industry's average annual growth rate of less than 1 percent over a 5-year period.
- Dana Corporation–Spicer Driveshaft Division lowered internal defect rates by more than 75 percent. Employee turnover is below 1 percent, and economic value added increased from $15 million to $35 million in 2 years.
- Texas Nameplate Company increased its national market share from less than 3 percent to 5 per cent over 3 years, reduced its defects from 3.65 percent to about 1 percent of billings, and increased on-time delivery from 95 to 98 percent.
- Pal's Sudden Service, a privately owned quick-service restaurant chain in eastern Tennessee, had customer quality scores averaging 95.8 percent, compared with 84.1 percent for its best competition, and improved order delivery speed by over 30 percent.
- KARLEE, a contract manufacturer of precision sheet metal and machined components, reduced waste from 1.5 percent of sales to less than 0.5 percent of sales while nearly doubling productivity over a 5-year period.
- SSM Health Care's share of the St. Louis market has increased substantially while three of its five competitors have lost market share. It has achieved a AA credit rating from Standard and Poor's for 4 consecutive years, a rating attained by fewer than 1 percent of U.S. hospitals.

Learning Objective
To understand the quality philosophies and principles of Deming, Juran, and Crosby and how these individuals influenced the quality management practices of today's organizations.

INFLUENTIAL LEADERS IN MODERN QUALITY MANAGEMENT

Many individuals have made substantial contributions to quality management thought and applications. However, three people—W. Edwards Deming, Joseph M. Juran, and Philip B. Crosby—are regarded as "management gurus" in the quality revolution. Their insights on measuring, managing, and improving quality have had profound impacts on countless managers and entire corporations around the world and laid the foundation for today's quality management practices.

W. Edwards Deming

Dr. W. Edwards Deming worked for Western Electric during its pioneering era of statistical quality control in the 1920s and 1930s. Deming recognized the importance of viewing management processes statistically. During World War II, he taught quality control courses as part of the U.S. national defense effort, but he realized that teaching statistics only to engineers and factory workers would never solve the fundamental quality problems that manufacturing needed to address. Despite numerous efforts, his attempts to convey the message of quality to upper-level managers in the United States were ignored.

Unlike other management gurus and consultants, Deming never defined or described quality precisely. In his last book, he stated, "A product or a service possesses quality if it helps somebody and enjoys a good and sustainable market."[12] The Deming philosophy focuses on bringing about improvements in product and service quality by reducing variability in goods and services design and associated processes. Deming professed that higher quality leads to higher productivity and lower costs, which in turn leads to improved market share and long-term competitive strength. The Deming "Chain Reaction" theory (see Exhibit 15.3) summarizes this view. Deming stressed that top management has the overriding responsibility for quality improvement.

In his early work in the United States, Deming preached his 14 Points. Although management practices today are vastly different than when Deming first began to preach his philosophy, the 14 Points still convey important insights for operations managers as well as every other manager in an organization. We briefly summarize the key issues.

Point 1: *Create a Vision and Demonstrate Commitment* An organization's basic purpose is to serve its customers and employees. It must define its values, mission, and vision of the future to provide long-term direction for its management and employees. This responsibility lies with top management, who must show commitment to quality and long-term success.

Point 2: *Learn the Philosophy* Companies cannot survive if goods and services of poor quality leave their customers dissatisfied. Thus, companies must take a customer-driven approach with a never-ending cycle of improvement, and engage all employees—from the boardroom to the stockroom—in learning the principles of quality and performance excellence. Although many of these principles are indeed ingrained in managers and front-line employees through training and reinforcement of organizational values, managers need to continually renew themselves to learn new approaches and relearn many older ones.

Point 3: *Understand Inspection* Traditionally, inspection had been the principal means for quality control—let the "quality control" department find and remove

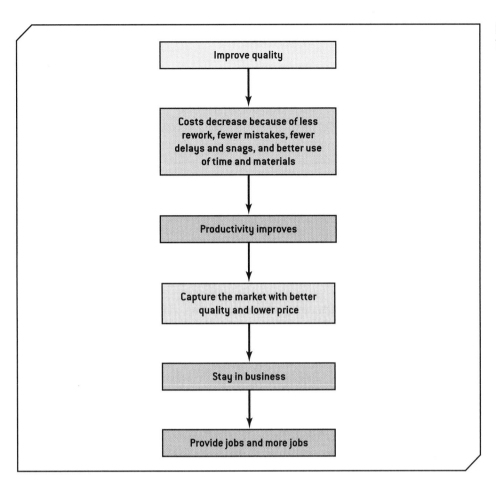

Exhibit 15.3
The Deming Chain Reaction

defective goods. This adds little value to the product, decreases productivity, and increases costs, and as we discussed earlier in this book, cannot even be done in service industries. Deming encouraged organizations to use inspection as an information-gathering tool for improvement and give this responsibility to the workers who do the work. Through better understanding of variation and statistical principles, managers can eliminate many sources of unnecessary inspection, thus reducing non-value-added costs associated with operations.

Point 4: *Stop Making Decisions Purely on the Basis of Cost* In 1931, Walter Shewhart noted that price has no meaning without quality.[13] Nevertheless, many managers will sacrifice quality for cost. Deming recognized that the direct costs associated with inferior materials that arise from scrap and rework during production or customer returns, as well as the loss of customer goodwill, can far exceed the cost "savings" achieved by using them. Today's emphasis on the value chain takes a system's view with the objective of minimizing total costs and developing stronger partnerships with customers and suppliers.

Point 5: *Improve Constantly and Forever* When quality improves, productivity improves and costs decrease, as the Deming Chain Reaction suggests. Traditionally, continuous improvement was not a common business practice; today, it is recognized as a necessary means for survival in a highly competitive and global business environment. The tools for improvement are constantly evolving, and organizations need to ensure that their employees understand and apply them effectively. This requires training, the focus of the next point.

Point 6: *Institute Training* Effective training results in improvements in quality and productivity, and also adds to worker morale. Training must transcend basic job skills like running a machine or following the script when talking to customers. For example, at Honda of America in Marysville, Ohio, all employees start out on the production floor, regardless of their job classification. Today, many companies have excellent training programs for technology related to direct production but still fail to enrich the ancillary skills of their work force. This is where some of the most lucrative opportunities exist to impact key business results.

Point 7: *Institute Leadership* Leadership goes far beyond the executive suite. For operations managers, it involves providing guidance to help employees do their jobs better with less effort, eliminating fear, encouraging innovation and risk taking, and facilitating teamwork. Leadership was, is, and will continue to be a challenging issue in every organization, particularly as new generations of managers replace those who have learned to lead.

Point 8: *Drive Out Fear* No system can work without the mutual respect of managers and workers. Fear is manifested in many ways: fear of reprisal, fear of failure, fear of the unknown, fear of relinquishing control, and fear of change. Creating a culture without fear is a slow process that can be destroyed in an instant with a transition of leadership and a change in corporate policies. Therefore, today's managers need to continue to be sensitive to the impact that fear can have on their organizations.

Point 9: *Optimize the Efforts of Teams* Teamwork helps to break down barriers between departments and individuals and helps them see how elements of the value chain are interrelated. The lack of cooperation often leads to poor quality because other departments cannot understand what their internal customers want and do not get what they need from their internal suppliers.

Point 10: *Eliminate Exhortations* Many early attempts to improve quality focused solely on behavioral change and involved posters, slogans, and motivational programs. However, the major source of many problems is the system itself. Improvement occurs by understanding the nature of processes and making decisions based on data and information.

Point 11: *Eliminate Numerical Quotas* Many organizations manage front-line workers by numbers and often compensate and reward individuals based on quantity not quality, for example, setting standards on the number of calls that a call center operator must process each hour, rather than focusing on the quality of the customer interaction. Workers may shortcut quality to reach the goal. Once a standard is reached, little incentive remains for workers to continue production or to improve quality.

Point 12: *Remove Barriers to Pride in Work* Front-line workers are often treated as, in Deming's words, "a commodity." They are given monotonous tasks, provided with inferior machines, tools, or materials, told to run defective items to meet sales pressures, and report to supervisors who know nothing about the job. Organizations must develop a work environment that is enriching, motivating, and enjoyable.

Point 13: *Encourage Education and Self-Improvement* The difference between this point and Point 6 is subtle. Point 6 refers to training in specific job skills; Point 13 refers to continuing, broad education for self-development. Organizations must invest in their people at all levels to ensure success in the long term. Today, many companies understand that elevating the general knowledge base of their work force—outside of specific job skills—has many benefits. However, others still view this as a cost that can be easily cut when financial trade-offs must be made.

Point 14: *Take Action* Any cultural change begins with top management and includes everyone. Changing an organizational culture generally meets with skepticism and resistance that many firms find difficult to deal with, particularly when many of the traditional management practices Deming felt must be eliminated are deeply ingrained in the organization's culture.

The 14 Points have become the basis for many organization's quality approaches (see the OM Spotlight on Hillerich & Bradsby Co.).

Joseph Juran

Joseph Juran also worked at Western Electric in the 1920s as it pioneered in the development of statistical methods for quality. He spent much of his time as a corporate industrial engineer and published the *Quality Control Handbook* in 1951, one of the most comprehensive quality manuals ever written. Like Deming, Juran taught quality principles to the Japanese in the 1950s and was a principal force in their quality reorganization. Juran proposed a simple definition of quality: "fitness for use."

Unlike Deming, however, Juran did not propose a major cultural change in the organization, but rather sought to improve quality by working within the system familiar to managers. He argued that employees at different levels of an organization

OM SPOTLIGHT

Hillerich & Bradsby[14]

Hillerich & Bradsby Co. (H&B) has been making the Louisville Slugger brand of baseball bat for more than 115 years. In the mid-1980s, the company faced significant challenges from market changes and competition. CEO Jack Hillerich attended a 4-day Deming seminar, which provided the basis for the company's current quality efforts. Returning from the seminar, Hillerich decided to see what changes that Deming advocated were possible in an old company with an old union and a history of labor-management problems. Hillerich persuaded union officials to attend another Deming seminar with five senior managers. Following the seminar, a core group of union and management people developed a strategy to change the company. They talked about building trust and changing the system "to make it something you want to work in."

Employees were interested, but skeptical. To demonstrate their commitment, managers examined Deming's 14 Points and picked several they believed they could make progress on through actions that would demonstrate a serious intention to change. One of the first changes was the elimination of work quotas that were tied to hourly salaries and a schedule of warnings and penalties for failures to meet quotas. Instead, a team-based approach was initiated. While a few workers took advantage of the change, overall productivity actually improved as rework decreased because workers were taking pride in their work to produce things the right way first. H&B also eliminated performance appraisals and commission-based pay in sales. The company has also focused its efforts on training and education, resulting in an openness for change and capacity for teamwork. Today, the Deming philosophy is still the core of H&B's guiding principles.

JOHN SOMMERS/Reuters/Landov

speak in their own "languages." (Deming, on the other hand, believed statistics should be the common language.) Juran stated that top management speaks in the language of dollars; workers speak in the language of things; and middle management must be able to speak both languages and translate between dollars and things. Thus, to get top management's attention, quality issues must be cast in the language they understand—dollars. Hence, Juran advocated the use of quality cost measurement, discussed later in this chapter, to focus attention on quality problems. At the operational level, Juran focused on increasing conformance to specifications through elimination of defects, supported extensively by statistical tools for analysis. Thus, his philosophy fit well into existing management systems.

Like Deming, Juran advocated a never-ending spiral of activities that includes market research, product development, design, planning for manufacture, purchasing, production process control, inspection and testing, and sales, followed by customer feedback. Juran's prescriptions focus on three major quality processes, called the Quality Trilogy: (1) quality planning—the process of preparing to meet quality goals; (2) quality control—the process of meeting quality goals during operations; and (3) quality improvement—the process of breaking through to unprecedented levels of performance. At the time he proposed this structure, few companies were engaging in any significant planning or improvement activities. Thus, Juran was promoting a major cultural shift in management thinking.

Unlike Deming, however, Juran specified a detailed program for quality improvement. Such a program involves proving the need for improvement, identifying specific projects for improvement, organizing support for the projects, diagnosing the causes, providing remedies for the causes, proving that the remedies are effective under operating conditions, and providing control to maintain improvements. Juran's approach is reflected in the practices of a wide variety of organizations today.

Philip B. Crosby

Philip B. Crosby was corporate vice president for quality at International Telephone and Telegraph (ITT) for 14 years after working his way up from line inspector. After leaving ITT, he established Philip Crosby Associates in 1979 to develop and offer training programs. He also authored several popular books. His first book, *Quality Is Free*, sold about 1 million copies and was greatly responsible for bringing quality to the attention of top corporate managers in the United States. The essence of Crosby's quality philosophy is embodied in what he calls the Absolutes of Quality Management and the Basic Elements of Improvement. Crosby's Absolutes of Quality Management include the following points:

- *Quality means conformance to requirements, not elegance.* Requirements must be clearly stated so that they cannot be misunderstood. Requirements act as communication devices and allow workers to take measurements to determine conformance to those requirements. Any nonconformance is the absence of quality.
- *There is no such thing as a quality problem.* Problems are functional in nature. Thus, a firm may experience accounting problems, manufacturing problems, design problems, front-desk problems, and so on, and the burden of responsibility for such problems falls on these functional departments. The quality department should measure conformance, report results, and lead the drive to develop a positive attitude toward quality improvement. This Absolute is similar to Deming's third point.
- *There is no such thing as the economics of quality; doing the job right the first time is always cheaper.* Crosby supports the premise that "economics of quality" has no meaning. Quality is free. What costs money are all actions that involve not doing jobs right the first time. The Deming chain reaction sends a similar message.

- *The only performance measurement is the cost of quality, which is the expense of nonconformance.* Crosby calls for measuring and publicizing the cost of poor quality. Quality cost data are useful to call problems to management's attention, to select opportunities for corrective action, and to track quality improvement over time. Such data provide visible proof of improvement and recognition of achievement. Juran supported this approach.
- *The only performance standard is "Zero Defects (ZD)."* This simply represents the philosophy of preventing defects in goods and services rather than finding them after the fact and fixing them.

Crosby's Basic Elements of Improvement are *determination, education,* and *implementation.* Determination means that top management must take quality improvement seriously. Education provides the means by which everyone in an organization learns quality principles. Finally, every member of the management team must understand the implementation process.

Comparisons of Quality Philosophies

In spite of the fact that they have significantly different approaches to implementing organizational change, the philosophies of Deming, Juran, and Crosby are more alike than different. Each views quality as imperative for future competitiveness in global markets, makes top management commitment an absolute necessity; demonstrates that quality management practices will save, not cost, money; places responsibility for quality on management, not the workers; stresses the need for continuous, never-ending improvement; acknowledges the importance of the customer and strong management–worker partnerships; and recognizes the need for and difficulties associated with changing the organizational culture.

The individual nature of business firms complicates the strict application of any one specific philosophy. Although each of these philosophies can be highly effective, a firm must first understand the nature and differences of the philosophies and then develop a quality management approach that is tailored to its individual organization. Any approach should include goals and objectives, allocation of responsibilities, a measurement system and description of tools to be employed, an outline of the management style that will be used, and a strategy for implementation. After taking these steps, the management team is responsible for leading the organization through successful execution.

ISO 9000:2000

As quality became a major focus of businesses throughout the world, various organizations developed standards and guidelines. As the European Community moved toward the European free trade agreement, which went into effect at the end of 1992, quality management became a key strategic objective. To standardize quality requirements for European countries within the Common Market and those wishing to do business with those countries, a specialized agency for standardization, the International Organization for Standardization (IOS), founded in 1946 and composed of representatives from the national standards bodies of 91 nations, adopted a series of written quality standards in 1987. They were revised in 1994, and again (significantly) in 2000. The most recent version is called the ISO 9000:2000 family of standards. The standards have been adopted in the United States by the American National Standards Institute (ANSI) with the endorsement and cooperation of the American Society for Quality (ASQ) and are recognized by about 100 countries.

ISO 9000 defines *quality system standards*, based on the premise that certain generic characteristics of management practices can be standardized and that a well-designed, well-implemented, and carefully managed quality system provides confidence that the outputs will meet customer expectations and requirements. The standards were created to meet five objectives:

1. Achieve, maintain, and seek to continuously improve product quality (including services) in relationship to requirements.
2. Improve the quality of operations to continually meet customers' and stakeholders' stated and implied needs.
3. Provide confidence to internal management and other employees that quality requirements are being fulfilled and that improvement is taking place.
4. Provide confidence to customers and other stakeholders that quality requirements are being achieved in the delivered product.
5. Provide confidence that quality system requirements are fulfilled.

The standards prescribe documentation for all processes affecting quality and suggest that compliance through auditing leads to continuous improvement. The standards are intended to apply to all types of businesses, including electronics and chemicals, and to services such as health care, banking, and transportation. In some foreign markets, companies will not buy from suppliers who are not certified to the standards. For example, many products sold in Europe, such as telecommunication terminal equipment, medical devices, gas appliances, toys, and construction products, require product certifications to assure safety. Often, ISO certification is necessary to obtain product certification. Thus, meeting these standards is becoming a requirement for international competitiveness (see OM Spotlight: Rehtek Machine Co.).

The ISO 9000:2000 standards consist of three documents:

- ISO 9000—Fundamentals and vocabulary
- ISO 9001—Requirements
- ISO 9004—Guidance for performance improvement

OM SPOTLIGHT

Rehtek Machine Co.[15]

Many small companies do not have the resources to redo their processes, documentation, and quality control systems. Stephen Reh, president of Rehtek Machine Co., spent $30,000 to upgrade equipment and computerize operations at his 12-employee contract-manufacturing firm. Reh hired a consulting firm to help him become ISO certified. Rehtek Machine Co. received a U.S. federal grant designed to help small firms improve their manufacturing operations. The consultants helped train internal ISO auditors, draw process flow diagrams, and document every work activity and manufacturing step to meet ISO standards. Many operational improvements were made as this ISO documentation was developed. Reh said, "Everything is traceable from when it comes in the door to when it leaves. There is no more confusion on the shop floor. With set procedures in place, I can sleep at night, knowing everyone is making parts according to written quality specifications. One of the first things our customers ask is are we ISO certified."

Courtesy of Rehtek Machine Company

ISO 9000 provides definitions of key terms. ISO 9001 provides a set of minimum requirements for a quality management system and is intended to demonstrate compliance with recognized quality principles to customers and for third-party certification. ISO 9004 focuses on improving the quality management system beyond these minimum requirements. The ISO 9000:2000 standards structure these into four major sections: Management Responsibility; Resource Management; Product Realization; and Measurement, Analysis, and Improvement[16] and are supported by the following eight principles:

Principle 1—Customer-Focused Organization   Organizations depend on their customers and therefore should understand current and future customer needs, meet customer requirements, and strive to exceed customer expectations.

Principle 2—Leadership   Leaders establish unity of purpose and direction of the organization. They should create and maintain the internal environment in which people can become fully involved in achieving the organization's objectives.

Principle 3—Involvement of People   People at all levels are the essence of an organization and their full involvement enables their abilities to be used for the organization's benefit.

Principle 4—Process Approach   A desired result is achieved more efficiently when related resources and activities are managed as a process.

Principle 5—System Approach to Management   Identifying, understanding, and managing a system of interrelated processes for a given objective improves the organization's effectiveness and efficiency.

Principle 6—Continual Improvement   Continual improvement should be a permanent objective of the organization.

Principle 7—Factual Approach to Decision Making   Effective decisions are based on the analysis of data and information.

Principle 8—Mutually Beneficial Supplier Relationships   An organization and its suppliers are interdependent, and a mutually beneficial relationship enhances the ability of both to create value.

ISO 9000 provides a set of good basic practices for initiating a basic quality management system and is an excellent starting point for companies with no formal quality assurance program. For companies in the early stages of developing a quality program, the standards enforce the discipline of control that is necessary before they can seriously pursue continuous improvement. The requirements of periodic audits reinforce the stated quality system until it becomes ingrained in the company.

Many organizations have realized significant benefits from ISO 9000. At DuPont, for example, ISO 9000 has been credited with increasing on-time delivery from 70 to 90 percent, decreasing cycle time from 15 days to 1.5 days, increasing first-pass yields from 72 to 92 percent, and reducing the number of test procedures by one-third. Sun Microsystems' Milpitas plant was certified in 1992, and managers believe that it has helped deliver improved quality and service to customers.[17] In Canada, Toronto Plastics, Ltd. reduced defects from 150,000 per million to 15,000 per million after 1 year of ISO implementation.[18] The first home builder to achieve registration, Michigan-based Delcor Homes, reduced its rate of correctable defects from 27.4 to 1.7 percent in 2 years and improved its building experience approval rating from the mid-60s to the mid-90s on a 100-point scale.[19]

DESIGNING QUALITY MANAGEMENT AND CONTROL SYSTEMS

First and foremost, any effective quality management system must extend throughout the value chain, and all managers in the value chain need to incorporate quality management principles into their activities. The Baldrige Criteria for Performance Excellence, described in Chapter 3, provide a framework and focus on quality management at the organizational level. At the operations level, the ISO 9000 standards define the basic elements of an effective quality management system. The following sections describe the key elements of a good quality management and control system that operations managers should apply. Additional tools for control will be introduced in the next chapter.

Contract Management, Design Control, and Purchasing

Because the ultimate objective of quality assurance is to provide goods and services that meet customer needs and requirements, the quality system should provide for contract review to ensure that customer requirements are adequately defined and documented and that the company has the capability to meet these requirements. For companies that design products, the quality system should clearly delineate responsibilities for design and development activities, the organizational and technical interfaces between groups, product requirements, and any legal or regulatory requirements. For example, if the sales and marketing or engineering departments work directly with customers in establishing designs, then the process of how this is done and communicated should be defined. In addition, processes for design review and for verifying design outputs against input requirements should be defined. In some service organizations, such as retail sales, health care, or insurance, establishing a contract and providing the service occur simultaneously. This would require appropriate training to ensure that requirements are met.

The purchasing function is critical because designs often require components or materials supplied by other firms. The purchasing function should include processes for evaluating and selecting suppliers on the basis of their ability to meet requirements, appropriate methods for controlling supplier quality, and means of verifying that purchased product conforms to requirements.

Process Control

Process control is ensuring that a process performs as it should and taking corrective action when it does not. A good process control system should include documented procedures for all key processes; a clear understanding of the appropriate equipment and working environment; methods for monitoring and controlling critical quality characteristics; approval processes for equipment; criteria for workmanship, such as written standards, samples, or illustrations; and maintenance activities. For example, Cincinnati Fiberglass, a small manufacturer of fiberglass parts for trucks, has a control plan for each production process that includes the process name, tool used, standard operating procedure, tolerance, inspection frequency, sample size, person responsible, reporting document, and reaction plan. Of particular importance is the ability to trace all components of a product back to key process equipment and operators and to the original material from which it was made. Process control also includes monitoring the accuracy and variability of equipment, operator knowledge and skills, the accuracy of measurement results and data used, and environmental factors such as time and temperature. Process control should be the responsibility of every employee who "owns" a process.

Many organizations fall into the trap of trying to control every possible quality characteristic. Time and resources preclude this goal. Process control indicators should be closely related to cost or performance, be economical to measure, and should provide information for improvement. Good places to take control measurements are before relatively high-cost operations or where significant value is added to the product; before processing operations that may make detection of defectives difficult or costly, such as operations that may mask or obscure faulty attributes, as, for example, painting; and after operations that are likely to generate a high proportion of defectives.

From a strict economic standpoint, one need only inspect everything or nothing. To illustrate this, let us consider the decision between having 100 percent inspection and no inspection after an intermediate assembly operation for an electronic calculator. To make this decision, we must compare the inspection cost to the penalty cost incurred if a nonconforming item is missed. Suppose it costs an average of 25¢ per unit for the inspector's time, equipment, and overhead. If a nonconforming part is assembled at this stage of production, the calculator will not work properly during final inspection. Rejected calculators must be disassembled and repaired; the work involved averages $8 per unit. The problem is thus to establish a break-even point for the quality level. For a lot size of 100 items, for example, 100 percent inspection costs $100(0.25)$, or $25. The cost of no inspection depends on the quality level—that is, the proportion nonconforming. If the proportion nonconforming is p, then an average of $100p$ units require rework at a cost of $8 each. Thus, the average cost of no inspection is $800p$. The break-even proportion of defective items is found by setting $25 = 800p$. Thus, $p = .03125$. Hence, if the proportion nonconforming is greater than $.03125$, it is more economical to inspect each assembly.

One should also consider the result of allowing a nonconforming item to continue through production or on to the consumer. If the result might be a safety hazard, costly repairs or correction, or some other intolerable condition, the conclusion would probably be to use 100 percent inspection.

Corrective Action and Continual Improvement

Errors in production and service will occur, for example, because of confusing instructions or drawings, unclear verbal directions, inadequate training, poor designs, confusing customer specifications, or incapable equipment. As soon as nonconforming items or errors are identified, they should be brought to the attention of someone who is authorized to take action and prevent further expense. The quality system should clearly state what actions should be taken and what should be done with any nonconforming items, for example, repair, rework, or scrap. Using techniques for quality improvement such as Six Sigma to identify the root cause and develop a solution, corrective action should be taken to eliminate or minimize the recurrence of the problem. Permanent changes resulting from corrective actions should be recorded in work instructions, product specifications, or other quality-system documentation.

Controlling Inspection, Measuring, and Test Equipment

Measuring quality characteristics generally requires the use of the human senses—seeing, hearing, feeling, tasting, and smelling—and the use of some type of instrument or gauge to measure the magnitude of the characteristic. Gauges and instruments used to measure quality characteristics must provide correct information; this is done through metrology. **Metrology** *is the collection of people, equipment, facilities, methods, and procedures used to assure the correctness or adequacy of measurements.*

Metrology *is the collection of people, equipment, facilities, methods, and procedures used to assure the correctness or adequacy of measurements.*

Metrology is vital to quality control because of the emphasis on quality by government agencies, the implications of measurement error on safety and product liability, and the reliance on improved quality control methods such as statistical process control. The need for metrology stems from the fact that every measurement is subject to error. Whenever variation is observed in measurements, some portion is due to measurement system error. Some errors are systematic; others are random. The size of the errors relative to the measurement value can significantly affect the quality of the data and resulting decisions. The evaluation of data obtained from inspection and measurement is not meaningful unless the measurement instruments are accurate and precise. To understand this, consider the fact that the total observed variation in operating systems output is the sum of the true process variation (which is what we actually want to measure) plus variation due to measurement:

$$\sigma^2_{total} = \sigma^2_{process} + \sigma^2_{measurement}$$

If the measurement variation is high, the observed results will be biased, leading to inaccurate assessment of process capabilities.

Repeatability, *or* **equipment variation**, *is the variation in multiple measurements by an individual using the same instrument.* This is a measure of how precise and accurate the equipment is. **Reproducibility**, *or* **operator variation**, *is the variation in the same measuring instrument when it is used by different individuals to measure the same parts.* This indicates how robust the measuring process is to the operator and environmental conditions. Most manufacturers conduct gage repeatability and reproducibility studies to quantify these types of variation.

Records, Documentation, and Audits

All the elements required for a quality system, such as control processes, measuring and test equipment, and other resources needed to achieve the required quality of conformance, should be documented in a quality manual, which serves as a permanent reference for implementing and maintaining the system. A quality manual need not be very complex; a small company might need only a dozen pages, whereas a large organization might need manuals for all key functions. Sufficient records should be maintained to demonstrate conformance to requirements and verify that the quality system is operating effectively. Typical records that might be maintained are inspection reports, test data, audit reports, and calibration data. They should be readily retrievable for analysis to identify trends and monitor the effectiveness of corrective actions. Other documents, such as drawings, specifications, inspection procedures and instructions, work instructions, and operation sheets are vital to achieving quality and should likewise be controlled.

Because many documents and data are generated during a product's life cycle, the quality system should include a means of controlling them. This includes such things as keeping documents and data up-to-date and removing obsolete documents, unless they are needed for legal purposes. In many situations, it is appropriate to have procedures for identifying and tracing products during all stages of production, delivery, and installation, even down to individual parts or batches. This is critical, for instance, in the food or drug industries in the event of any product recalls.

Keeping the quality control system up-to-date is not always easy. This can be facilitated through **internal audits**, *which focus on identifying whether documented procedures are being followed and are effective and report the issues to management for corrective action.* Internal audits generally include a review of process records, training records, complaints, corrective actions, and previous audit reports. Managers must use audit findings as a tool for continuous improvement, not as means of placing blame on individuals.

Repeatability, *or* **equipment variation**, *is the variation in multiple measurements by an individual using the same instrument.*

Reproducibility, *or* **operator variation**, *is the variation in the same measuring instrument when it is used by different individuals to measure the same parts.*

Internal audits *focus on identifying whether documented procedures are being followed and are effective and report the issues to management for corrective action.*

A typical internal audit begins by asking those who perform a process regularly to explain how it works.[20] Their statements are compared to written procedures, and compliance and deviations are noted. Next, the trail of paperwork or other data is examined to determine whether the process is consistent with the intent of the written procedure and the worker's explanation. Internal auditors also need to analyze whether the process is meeting its intent and objectives, thus focusing on continuous improvement.

Challenges Facing Global Companies

Multinational corporations face special challenges in implementing quality management systems.[21] Six key factors have been identified:

1. Cultural limitations
2. Insufficient management preparation
3. Insufficient employee preparation
4. Employee attitudes
5. Specific legal regulations
6. Technological limitations

Cultural differences are fairly obvious. One of the reasons that many Western nations had difficulty implementing many of the approaches developed in Japan, such as problem-solving teams, was largely due to such differences. Because quality depends so heavily on management leadership, the lack of quality-consciousness in senior management makes it difficult to introduce and implement new concepts and ideas. Many companies find the greatest challenges in Africa, China, and Central and Eastern Europe. However, as many managers have attended top business schools in the United States and in Europe, this is becoming less of a factor. Companies find employees better prepared and with better attitudes in Australia and Oceania, as well as in many parts of Asia (excluding China), while the greatest challenges again lie in Africa, China, and Central and Eastern Europe. In these regions also, companies face legal challenges because of differences in regulations. However, with the exception of Africa, technological limitations do not appear to inhibit the implementation of quality management systems.

Changing attitudes and mind-sets is a difficult process that require significant investment in education and genuine understanding by managers who run operations outside of their native land.

SIX SIGMA

Six Sigma *is a business improvement approach that seeks to find and eliminate causes of defects and errors in manufacturing and service processes by focusing on outputs that are critical to customers and results in a clear financial return for the organization.* The term *Six Sigma* is based on a statistical measure that equates to at most 3.4 errors or defects per million opportunities. An ultimate "stretch" goal of all organizations that adopt a Six Sigma philosophy is to have all critical processes, regardless of functional area, at a six-sigma level of capability—a level of near zero defects. Six Sigma has garnered a significant amount of credibility over the last decade because of its acceptance at such major firms as Motorola, Allied Signal (now part of Honeywell), Texas Instruments, and General Electric. It is facilitated through use of basic and advanced quality improvement and control tools by individuals and teams whose members are trained to provide fact-based decision-making information.

Learning Objective
To understand the basic philosophy and methods of Six Sigma and how it is applied in organizations to improve quality and operations performance.

Six Sigma is a business improvement approach that seeks to find and eliminate causes of defects and errors in manufacturing and service processes by focusing on outputs that are critical to customers and results in a clear financial return for the organization.

Measuring Quality in Six Sigma

A defect is any mistake or error that is passed on to the customer.

A unit of work is the output of a process or an individual process step.

In Six Sigma terminology, *a defect is any mistake or error that is passed on to the customer* (many people also use the term *nonconformance*). *A unit of work is the output of a process or an individual process step*. We can measure output quality by defects per unit (DPU), a popular quality measure that we introduced in Chapter 3:

Defects per unit = Number of defects discovered/Number of units produced

However, an output measure such as this tends to focus on the final product, not the process that produces the product. In addition, it is difficult to use for processes of varying complexity, particularly service activities. Two different processes might have significantly different numbers of opportunities for error, making appropriate comparisons difficult. The Six Sigma concept characterizes quality performance by *defects per million opportunities (dpmo)*, computed as DPU × 1,000,000/opportunities for error (or, as is often used in services, *errors per million opportunities—epmo*). For example, suppose that an airline wishes to measure the effectiveness of its baggage handling system. A DPU measure might be lost bags per customer. However, customers may have different numbers of bags; thus the number of opportunities for error is the average number of bags per customer. If the average number of bags per customer is 1.6, and the airline recorded 3 lost bags for 8,000 passengers in one month, then

$$epmo = (3/8{,}000) \times 1{,}000{,}000/1.6 = 234.375$$

The use of dpmo and epmo allows us to define quality broadly. In the airline case, this might mean every opportunity for a failure to meet customer expectations from initial ticketing until bags are retrieved.

Six Sigma represents a quality level of at most 3.4 defects per million opportunities. The theoretical basis for Six Sigma is explained by Exhibit 15.4 in the context of manufacturing specifications. A six-sigma quality level corresponds to a process variation equal to half of the design tolerance while allowing the mean to shift as much as 1.5 standard deviations from the target. This figure was chosen by Motorola because field failure data suggested that Motorola's processes drifted by this amount on average. The allowance of a shift in the distribution is important, since no process can be maintained in perfect control. Under this assumption, the area in either tail of the shifted curves *beyond* the six-sigma range (the tolerance limit) is only 0.0000034, or 3.4 parts per million. If the process mean is held exactly on target (the shaded distribution in Exhibit 15.4), only 1 defect per billion would be expected (the area under each tail)!

In a similar fashion, we could define three-sigma quality, five-sigma quality, and so on. A 5-sigma level corresponds to 233 dpmo, 4-sigma to 6,200 dpmo, and 3-sigma to 66,803 dpmo. What may be quite surprising to realize is that a change from 3 to 4-sigma represents a 10-fold improvement; from 4 to 5 sigma, a 30-fold improvement; and from 5- to 6-sigma, a 70-fold improvement—difficult challenges for any organization. Many companies have adopted this standard to challenge their own improvement efforts.

The sigma level can easily be calculated on an Excel spreadsheet using the formula

=NORMSINV(1 − Number of Defects/Number of Opportunities) + 1.5

or equivalently,

=NORMSINV(1 − dpmo/1,000,000) + 1.5

Using the airline example discussed earlier, if we had 3 lost bags for 8,000(1.6) = 12,800 opportunities, we would find =NORMSINV(1 − 3/12800) + 1.5 = 4.99828, or about a 5-sigma level. The truth is less impressive. It was reported that 3.67 mishandled baggage reports per 1,000 passengers were filed in May 2003, which was up from 3.31 per 1,000 a year earlier.[22] This result yields a sigma level of only 4.33, assuming 1.6 bags per passenger.

Although originally developed for manufacturing in the context of tolerance-based specifications, the Six Sigma concept has been adopted to any process and has come to signify a generic quality level of at most 3.4 defects per million opportunities. It has been applied in product development, new business acquisition, customer service, accounting, and many other business functions. For example, suppose that a bank tracks the number of errors reported in customers' checking account statements. If it finds 12 errors in 1,000 statements, this is equivalent to an error rate of 12,000 per million, (somewhere between 3.5 and 4 sigma levels).

Implementing Six Sigma

Six Sigma has developed from simply a way of measuring quality to an overall strategy to accelerate improvements and achieve unprecedented performance levels within an organization by finding and eliminating causes of errors or defects in processes by focusing on characteristics that are critical to customers.[23] The core philosophy of Six Sigma is based on some key concepts:[24]

1. emphasizing dpmo as a standard metric that can be applied to all parts of an organization: manufacturing, engineering, administrative, software, and so on
2. providing extensive training followed by project team deployment to improve profitability, reduce non-value-added activities, and achieve cycle time reduction
3. focusing on corporate sponsors responsible for supporting team activities, helping to overcome resistance to change, obtain resources, and focus the teams on overall strategic objectives
4. creating highly qualified process improvement experts ("green belts," "black belts," and "master black belts") who can apply improvement tools and lead teams
5. ensuring that appropriate metrics are identified early in the process and that they focus on business results
6. setting stretch objectives for improvement

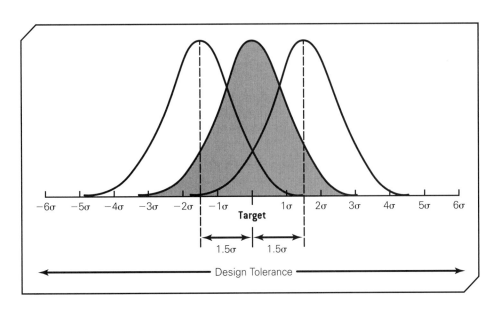

Exhibit 15.4
Six-Sigma Quality

The recognized benchmark for Six Sigma implementation is General Electric (see the OM Spotlight). GE's Six Sigma problem-solving approach (DMAIC) employs five phases:

1. *Define (D)*
   - Identify customers and their priorities.
   - Identify a project suitable for Six Sigma efforts based on business objectives as well as customer needs and feedback.
   - Identify CTQs (*critical to quality characteristics*) that the customer considers to have the most impact on quality.
2. *Measure (M)*
   - Determine how to measure the process and how is it performing.
   - Identify the key internal processes that influence CTQs and measure the defects currently generated relative to those processes.
3. *Analyze (A)*
   - Determine the most likely causes of defects.
   - Understand why defects are generated by identifying the key variables that are most likely to create process variation.
4. *Improve (I)*
   - Identify means to remove the causes of the defects.
   - Confirm the key variables and quantify their effects on the CTQs.
   - Identify the maximum acceptable ranges of the key variables and a system for measuring deviations of the variables.
   - Modify the process to stay within the acceptable range.

OM SPOTLIGHT

General Electric

The efforts by General Electric in particular, driven by former CEO Jack Welch, have brought significant media attention to the concept and have made Six Sigma a very popular approach to quality improvement. In the mid-1990s, quality emerged as a concern of many employees at GE. Jack Welch invited Larry Bossidy, then CEO of AlliedSignal, who had phenomenal success with Six Sigma, to talk about it at a corporate executive council meeting. The meeting caught the attention of GE managers and as Welch stated, "I went nuts about Six Sigma and launched it," calling it the most ambitious undertaking the company had ever taken on.[25] To ensure success, GE changed its incentive compensation plan so that 60 percent of the bonus was based on financials and 40 percent on Six Sigma and provided stock option grants to employees in Six Sigma training. In their first year, GE trained 30,000 employees at a cost of $200 million and got back about $150 million in savings. From 1996 to 1997, GE increased the number of Six Sigma projects from 3,000 to 6,000 and achieved $320 million in productivity gains and profits. By 1998, the company had generated $750 million in Six Sigma savings over and above its investment and would receive $1.5 billion in savings the next year.

GE had many early success stories. GE Capital, for example, fielded about 300,000 calls each year from mortgage customers who had to use voice mail or call back 24 percent of the time because employees were busy or unavailable. A Six Sigma team analyzed one branch that had a near perfect percentage of answered calls and applied their knowledge of their best practices to the other 41 branches, resulting in a 99.9 percent chance of customers' getting a representative on the first try. A team at GE Plastics improved the quality of a product used in CD-ROMs and audio CDs from a 3.8 sigma level to a 5.7 level and captured a significant amount of new business from Sony.[26] GE credits Six Sigma with a 10-fold increase in the life of CT scanner X-ray tubes, a 400% improvement in return on investment in its industrial diamond business, a 62 percent reduction in turnaround time at railcar repair shops, and $400 million in savings in its plastics business.[27]

5. *Control (C)*
   - Determine how to maintain the improvements.
   - Put tools in place to ensure that the key variables remain within the maximum acceptable ranges under the modified process.

Project teams are fundamental to Six Sigma. Six Sigma projects require a diversity of skills that range from technical analysis, creative solution development, and implementation (see the OM Spotlight on Ford Motor Company). Thus, Six Sigma teams not only address immediate problems but also provide an environment for individual learning, management development, and career advancement. Six Sigma teams are comprised of several types of individuals:

- *Champions*—senior-level managers who promote and lead the deployment of Six Sigma in a significant area of the business. Champions understand the philosophy and tools of Six Sigma, select projects, set objectives, allocate resources, and mentor teams. Champions own Six Sigma projects and are responsible for their completion and results; typically they also own the process that the project is focused on improving. They select teams, set strategic direction, create measurable objectives, provide resources, monitor performance, make key implementation decisions, and report results to top management. More importantly, champions work toward removing barriers—organizational, financial, personal—that might inhibit the successful implementation of a Six Sigma project.
- *Master Black Belts*—full-time Six Sigma experts who are responsible for Six Sigma strategy, training, mentoring, deployment, and results. Master Black Belts are highly trained in how to use Six Sigma tools and methods and provide advanced technical expertise. They work across the organization to develop and coach teams, conduct training, and lead change, but are typically not members of Six Sigma project teams.
- *Black Belts*—fully trained Six Sigma experts with up to 160 hours of training who perform much of the technical analyses required of Six Sigma projects, usually on a full-time basis. They have advanced knowledge of tools and DMAIC methods and can apply them either individually or as team leaders. They also mentor and develop Green Belts. Black Belts need good leadership and communication skills in addition to technical skills and process knowledge. They should be highly motivated, eager to gain new knowledge, and well respected among their peers. As such, Black Belts are often targeted by the organization as future business leaders.
- *Green Belts*—functional employees who are trained in introductory Six Sigma tools and methodology and work on projects on a part-time basis, assisting Black Belts while developing their own knowledge and expertise. Typically, one of the requirements for receiving a Green Belt designation is to successfully complete a Six Sigma project. Successful Green Belts are often promoted to Black Belts.
- *Team Members*—individuals from various functional areas who support specific projects.

Six Sigma has many benefits. For example, from 1996 to 1998, GE increased the number of Six Sigma projects from 200 to 6,000. From all these efforts, GE expected to save $7 to $10 billion over a decade. Other companies also report significant results. Between 1995 and the first quarter of 1997, Allied Signal reported cost savings exceeding $800 million from its Six Sigma initiative. Citibank groups have reduced internal callbacks by 80 percent, credit process time by 50 percent, and cycle times of processing statements from 28 days to 15 days.[28]

OM SPOTLIGHT

Ford Motor Company[29]

Ford Motor Company began developing its Six Sigma quality approach, called Consumer Driven Six Sigma, in 1999. However, the company didn't really get serious about reclaiming its motto of the 1980s, "Quality is Job 1," until 2001. That was when JD Power and Associates' Initial Quality Study ranked Ford last among the Big-Seven automakers. By 2003, the same survey ranked Ford number four and found that it was the most improved automaker of the group.

The company now has more than 200 Master Black Belts, 2,200 Black Belts, nearly 40,000 Green Belts, and 3,000 Project Champions. Ford's training of Green, Black, Master Black Belts, and Project Champions generally follows the conventional Six Sigma training process. Black Belt training is "hands-on" and "just in time." Each trainee gets 1 week of full-time training per month for 4 months. The other 3 weeks of the month require that the trainee apply the training to a live project. Ford's Six Sigma teams typically have a member of management, a Master Black Belt (MBB), a Black Belt (BB), and several Green Belts (GB) assigned to take on various roles in a project.

BBs are expected to handle two to three projects at a time. They can choose their own projects but are asked to choose them carefully to ensure that they contribute to waste elimination and/or customer satisfaction improvement. The goal is that at least half of the reduction of "Things Gone Wrong," (in "Ford-speak") will be improved through successful Six Sigma projects. Ford has implemented a unique project tracking system that has helped to promote organizational learning. The system allows member of project teams to observe what other teams are working on via an internal database.

Leaders are also expected to have hands-on involvement as Project Champions. Senior leaders are required to partner with MBBs to run performance cells. These cells are managed similarly to a manufacturing cell and benefit from the technical expertise of the MBB and the administrative experience of the manager. The process keeps new projects coming in and ensures that projects that are underway stay on track.

Overall, Ford's Six Sigma approach has contributed impressively to the bottom line. More than 6,000 projects have been completed in just 3 years, and Six Sigma has saved over $1 billion since its inception.

JEFF KOWALSKY/EPA/Landov

Six Sigma in Services and Small Organizations

Because Six Sigma was developed in the manufacturing sector, and most publicity has revolved around such companies as Motorola and GE, many people in the service sector think that Six Sigma applies only to large manufacturing companies. Nothing can be further from the truth.[30] All Six Sigma projects have three key characteristics: a problem to be solved, a process in which the problem exists, and one or more measures that quantify the gap to be closed and can be used to monitor progress. These characteristics are present in all business processes; thus, Six Sigma can easily be applied to a wide variety of transactional, administrative, and service areas in both large and small firms. Many financial services firms, like J.P. Morgan Chase & Co. and GE Capital, have used it extensively.

It is generally agreed that 50 percent or more of the total savings opportunity in an organization lies outside of manufacturing. Both manufacturing and service processes have "hidden factories," those places where the defective "product" is sent to be reworked or scrapped (revised, corrected, or discarded, in nonmanufacturing terms). Find the hidden factory and you have found one good place to look for opportunities to improve the process. Performing manual account reconciliation in accounting, revising budgets repeatedly until management will accept them, and making repeat sales calls to customers because all the information requested by the customer was not available are all examples of the hidden factory.

Because service processes are largely people-driven, measurements are often nonexistent or ill-defined, as many believe that there are no defects to measure. Therefore, one must often create good measurement systems before collecting any data. In applying Six Sigma to services, there are four key measures of the performance: *accuracy*, as measured by correct financial figures, completeness of information, or freedom from data errors; *cycle time*, which is a measure of how long it takes to do something, such as pay an invoice; *cost*, that is, the internal cost of process activities (in many cases, cost is largely determined by the accuracy and/or cycle time of the process; the longer it takes, and the more mistakes that have to be fixed, the higher the cost); and *customer satisfaction*, which is typically the primary measure of success.

Consider how a janitorial service company might use DMAIC. In the Define stage, a key question would be to define what a defect represents. One might first create a flowchart of the cleaning process, specifying what activities are performed. One example of a defect might be leaving streaks on windows, because it is a source of customer dissatisfaction—a CTQ. In the Measure stage, the firm not only would want to collect data on the frequency of defects but also information about what products and tools employees use. The Analyze stage might include evaluating differences among employees to determine why some appear better at cleaning than others. Developing a standard operating procedure might be the focus of the Improve stage. Finally, Control might entail teaching employees the correct technique and measuring improvement over time. The following OM Spotlight describes some real applications of Six Sigma in service organizations.

OM SPOTLIGHT

Six Sigma Applications in Services[31]

In one application at CNH Capital, Six Sigma tools were applied to decrease asset management cycle time in posting repossessions to a bid list and remarketing web site. Cycle time was reduced 75 percent, from 40 days to 10 days, resulting in significant ongoing dollar savings. A facility management company had a high level of "days sales outstanding." Initially, it tried to fix this by reducing the term of days in its billing cycle, which, however, upset customers. Using Six Sigma, it found that a large percentage of accounts with high days sales outstanding received invoices from the company having numerous errors. After understanding the source of the errors and making process changes, the invoice process improved and

days sales outstanding was reduced. At DuPont, a Six Sigma project was applied to improve cycle time for an employee's application for long-term disability benefits.[32] Some examples of financial applications of Six Sigma include[33]

- reducing the average and variation of days outstanding of accounts receivable
- closing the books faster
- improving the accuracy and speed of the audit process
- reducing variation in cash flow
- improving the accuracy of journal entry (most businesses have a 3–4 percent error rate)
- improving the accuracy and cycle time of standard financial reports

Six Sigma faces some challenges in small organizations. First, the culture in small organizations is usually less scientific and employees typically do not think in terms of processes, measurements, and data. Second, the processes are often invisible, complex, and not well defined or well documented. Small organizations are often confused and intimidated by the size, costs, and extensive technical training they see in large organizations that implement "formal" Six Sigma processes. Because of this, they often don't even try to adopt these approaches. Small organizations are usually lean by necessity, but not always effectively so. Their processes often operate at quality levels of 2 to 3 sigma, and they are not even aware of it. Small companies often need to bring in consultants for training or improvement initiatives in the early stages of learning. This can help to develop in-house expertise and put them on the right track.

TOOLS FOR QUALITY ANALYSIS AND IMPROVEMENT

The tools used in Six Sigma efforts have been around for a long time and may be categorized into seven general groups:

- *elementary statistical tools* (basic statistics, statistical thinking, hypothesis testing, correlation, simple regression)
- *advanced statistical tools* (design of experiments, analysis of variance, multiple regression)
- *product design and reliability* (quality function deployment, reliability analysis, failure mode and effects analysis)
- *measurement* (cost of quality, process capability, measurement systems analysis)
- *process control* (control plans, statistical process control, reducing variation)
- *process improvement* (process improvement planning, process mapping, mistake-proofing)
- *implementation and teamwork* (organizational effectiveness, team assessment, facilitation tools, team development)

You may have covered some of these tools, such as statistics and teamwork, in other courses, and some, such as quality function deployment and statistical process control, are discussed in other chapters of this book. In this section, we present some of the more important tools for quality analysis and improvement.

Cost of Quality Measurement

Quality problems expressed as the number of errors or defects—the principal metrics at the operations level—have little impact on top managers, who are generally concerned with financial and market performance, until they are translated and aggregated into financial measures. An effective way for operations managers to understand quality and how it affects what they do is to consider the costs associated with goods, services, or environmental quality. *The cost of quality refers specifically to the costs associated with avoiding poor quality or those incurred as a result of poor quality.* Cost of quality analysis can help operations managers communicate with senior-level managers, identify and justify major opportunities for process improvements, and evaluate the importance of quality and improvement in operations.

The cost of quality refers specifically to the costs associated with avoiding poor quality or those incurred as a result of poor quality.

Prevention costs are those expended to keep nonconforming goods and services from being made and reaching the customer.

QUALITY COST CLASSIFICATION

Quality costs can be organized into four major categories: prevention costs, appraisal costs, internal-failure costs, and external-failure costs. **Prevention costs** *are* *those expended to keep nonconforming goods and services from being made and reaching the customer.* They include

- *quality planning costs*—such as salaries of individuals associated with quality planning and problem-solving teams, the development of new procedures, new equipment design, and reliability studies
- *process-control costs*—which include costs spent on analyzing processes and implementing process control plans
- *information-systems costs*—which are expended to develop data requirements and measurements
- *training and general management costs*—which include internal and external training programs, clerical staff expenses, and miscellaneous supplies

Appraisal costs *are those expended on ascertaining quality levels through measurement and analysis of data to detect and correct problems.* They include

- *test and inspection costs*—those associated with incoming materials, work-in-process, and finished goods, including equipment costs and salaries
- *instrument maintenance costs*—those associated with the calibration and repair of measuring instruments
- *process-measurement and process-control costs*—which involve the time spent by workers to gather and analyze quality measurements

Internal-failure costs *are costs incurred as a result of unsatisfactory quality that is found before the delivery of a good or service to the customer.* Examples include

- *scrap and rework costs*—including material, labor, and overhead
- *costs of corrective action*—arising from time spent determining the causes of failure and correcting problems
- *downgrading costs*—such as revenue lost by selling a good or service at a lower price because it does not meet specifications
- *process failures*—such as unplanned equipment downtime or service upsets or unplanned equipment repair

External-failure costs *are incurred after poor-quality goods or services reach the customer.* They include

- *costs due to customer complaints and returns*—including rework on returned items, cancelled orders, discount coupons, and freight premiums
- *goods and services recall costs and warranty and service guarantee claims*—including the cost of repair or replacement as well as associated administrative costs
- *product-liability costs*—resulting from legal actions and settlements

An example of a prevention cost in a pizza business would be processing customer-satisfaction survey results as a basis for improved training programs. Appraisal costs might be measuring the weight of the cheese used in a pizza before pizza assembly to ensure the correct amount or the time associated with inspecting each pizza before delivery to the customer. A burned pizza that is discarded would be an internal-failure cost. Given the short shelf life of a pizza, inaccurate order taking could also cause one to throw away the finished pizza (good). The cost of pizzas sent back by customers or discounts offered because of late delivery would be examples of external-failure costs. These data can be broken down by customer benefit package, process, department, work center, time, job, service encounter type, or cost category to make data analysis more convenient and useful to managers.

Standard accounting systems are generally able to provide quality-cost data for direct labor, overhead, scrap, warranty expenses, product-liability costs, and maintenance, repair, and calibration efforts on test equipment. However, they are not

Appraisal costs *are those expended on ascertaining quality levels through measurement and analysis of data to detect and correct problems.*

Internal-failure costs *are costs incurred as a result of unsatisfactory quality that is found before the delivery of a good or service to the customer.*

External-failure costs *are incurred after poor-quality goods or services reach the customer.*

structured to capture many types of important cost-of-quality information. Costs related to service upsets, poor goods or service design, remedial engineering effort, rework, in-process inspection, and engineering-change losses must usually be estimated or collected through special efforts. Although prevention costs are the most important, it is usually easiest to determine appraisal, internal-failure, external-failure, and prevention costs, in that order.

Like productivity measures, quality costs are often reported as an index—that is, the ratio of the current value to a base-period value. Some common quality-cost indexes are quality cost per direct labor hour, quality cost per manufacturing cost dollar, quality cost per sales dollar, and quality costs per unit of production. All of those ratios and indexes, although extensively used in practice, have a fundamental problem. A change in the denominator can appear to be a change in the level of quality or productivity alone. For instance, if direct labor is decreased through managerial improvements, the direct-labor-based index will increase even if there is no change in quality. Also, the common inclusion of overhead in manufacturing cost is certain to distort results. And in services, how to allocate overhead to specific services is an ongoing problem. Nevertheless, such indexes can help in comparing quality costs over time. Generally, sales bases are the most popular, followed by cost, labor, and unit bases.[34]

Consider a printing company that produces a variety of books, brochures, reports, and other printed material for business customers. The printing manager has tracked quality-related costs over the past year. Sales were $16.2 million last year. What do the following data suggest?

Cost Element	Amount ($)
Proofreading	$ 710,000
Quality planning	10,000
Press downtime	405,000
Bindery waste paper	75,000
Checking and inspection	60,000
Customer complaints and job redo	40,000
Printing plate revisions	40,000
Quality-improvement projects	20,000
Other waste	55,000
Correction of typographic errors	300,000
Total quality-related costs	$1,715,000

The first step in the cost-of-quality analysis is to assign each quality-cost element to the appropriate category—prevention, appraisal, internal failure, or external failure:

Prevention

Quality planning	$ 10,000
Quality-improvement projects	20,000
Total	30,000

Appraisal

Proofreading	$710,000
Checking and inspection	60,000
Total	770,000

Internal failure

Press downtime	$405,000
Bindery waste paper	75,000
Printing plate revisions	40,000
Other waste	55,000
Correction of typographical errors	300,000
Total	875,000

External failure

Customer complaints and rework	$ 40,000

Internal-failure costs account for 51 percent ($875,000/$1,715,000) of the total quality-related costs, external failure 2.3 percent, prevention 1.8 percent, and appraisal costs account for 44.9 percent. Hence, although the company is spending a lot of money in appraisal (detection) activities, it still has a significant amount of internal failure. Apparently, much more effort needs to be expended on quality-improvement initiatives, particularly to reduce press downtime and typographical errors, and better practices and training for proofreading. The company is in the very early stages of continuous improvement with 95.9 percent of its quality costs in appraisal and internal-failure costs. Interestingly, external-failure costs are relatively low, meaning that it catches and corrects most errors prior to delivering the goods to customers or it doesn't do a good job of measuring customer retention and repeat business rates. Moreover, quality costs are 10.6 percent of sales, a dismal performance statistic! It is not unusual for quality costs to represent 20 percent or more of sales in manufacturing companies and over 30 percent of operating costs in service companies. Top-performing companies have quality cost as a percent of sales in the 1 percent to 5 percent range.

COMPUTING QUALITY-COST INDEXES

A company collects quality costs by cost category and product for each time period, say 1 month, as shown in the upper portion of Exhibit 15.5. It might compute a total quality-cost index as

$$\text{Quality-cost index} = \text{Total quality costs/Direct labor costs}$$

Alternatively, it might compute individual indexes by category, product, and time period, as summarized in the lower portion of Exhibit 15.5.

Such information can be used to identify areas that require improvement. Of course, it is up to managers and engineers to discover the precise nature of the improvement needed. For example, a steady rise in internal-failure costs and decline in appraisal costs might indicate a problem in assembly, maintenance of testing equipment, or control of purchased parts.

Quality costs in service organizations differ from those in manufacturing organizations. In manufacturing, they are primarily product-oriented; in services, they are process- and service-provider-dependent and usually more difficult to identify and quantify. Since quality in service organizations depends on service-provider and customer interaction, appraisal costs tend to account for a higher percentage of

Exhibit 15.5
Computing Quality-Cost Indexes

	January		February	
Cost Category	Product A	Product B	Product A	Product B
Prevention	$2,000	$4,000	$2,000	$4,000
Appraisal	$10,000	$20,000	$13,000	$21,000
Internal failure	$19,000	$106,000	$16,000	$107,000
External failure	$54,000	$146,000	$52,000	$156,000
Total	$85,000	$276,000	$83,000	$288,000
Standard direct labor costs	$35,000	$90,000	$28,000	$86,000
Quality-Cost Index				
Prevention	0.057	0.044	0.071	0.047
Appraisal	0.286	0.222	0.464	0.244
Internal failure	0.543	1.178	0.571	1.244
External failure	1.543	1.622	1.857	1.814
Total	2.429	3.067	2.964	3.349

total quality costs than they do in manufacturing. In addition, internal-failure costs tend to be lower for high-contact service organizations, because there is little opportunity to correct an error before it reaches the customer—at which point it represents an external failure. Such "service upsets" should be resolved on-the-spot by empowered and well-trained service providers. In fact, research has shown that good service recovery generally improves customer satisfaction and loyalty.

External-failure costs can become an extremely significant out-of-pocket expense to consumers of services. Consider the costs of interrupted service, such as telephone, electricity, or other utilities; delays in waiting to obtain service or excessive time in performing the service; errors made in billing, delivery, or installation; or unnecessary service. For example, a family moving from one city to another may have to pay additional costs for lodging and meals if the moving van does not arrive on the day promised; if a doctor's prescription needs to be changed because of faulty diagnosis, the patient pays for unnecessary drugs; if a computer makes a billing error, several phone calls, letters, and copies of cancelled checks may be needed to correct the mistake.

The "Seven QC Tools"

Seven simple tools—flowcharts, checksheets, histograms, Pareto diagrams, cause-and-effect diagrams, scatter diagrams, and control charts—termed the *Seven QC (quality control) Tools* by the Japanese, support quality improvement problem-solving efforts.[35] The Seven QC Tools are designed to be simple and visual so that workers at all levels can use them easily and provide a means of communication that is particularly well suited in group problem-solving efforts. We will briefly review each of these to explain their role in quality improvement.

FLOWCHARTS

To understand a process, one must first determine how it works and what it is supposed to do. Flowcharting, or process mapping, identifies the sequence of activities or the flow of materials and information in a process. Flowcharts help the people who are involved in the process understand it much better and more objectively. Understanding how a process works enables a team to pinpoint obvious problems, error-proof the process, streamline it by eliminating non-value-added steps, and reduce variation. Many types of flowcharts are used to communicate "how work gets done," and we have seen examples in previous chapters, for instance, Exhibit 1.7 for Pal's Sudden Service, Exhibit 3.3 on the time required to process reports.

Once a flowchart is constructed, it can be used to identify quality problems as well as areas for productivity improvement. Questions such as "How does this work activity or workstation affect the customer?", or "Can we improve or even eliminate this work activity?" or "Should we control a critical quality characteristic at this point?" trigger the identification of process design and improvement opportunities.

RUN CHARTS AND CONTROL CHARTS

A **run chart** is a line graph in which data are plotted over time. The vertical axis represents a measurement; the horizontal axis is the time scale. The daily newspaper usually has several examples of run charts, such as the Dow Jones Industrial Average. Run charts show the performance and the variation of a process or some quality or productivity indicator over time. They can be used to track such things as production volume, costs, and customer satisfaction indexes. Run charts summarize data in a graphical fashion that is

easy to understand and interpret, identify process changes and trends over time, and show the effects of corrective actions.

The first step in constructing a run chart is to identify the measurement or indicator to be monitored. In some situations, one might measure the quality characteristics for each individual unit of process output. For low-volume processes, such as chemical production or surgeries, this would be appropriate. However, for high-volume production processes or services with large numbers of customers or transactions, it would be impractical. Instead, samples taken on a periodic basis provide the data for computing basic statistical measures such as the mean, range or standard deviation, proportion of items that do not conform to specifications, or number of nonconformances per unit.

Constructing the chart consists of the following steps:

Step 1. *Collect the data.* If samples are chosen, compute the relevant statistic for each sample, such as the average or proportion.

Step 2. *Examine the range of the data.* Scale the chart so that all data can be plotted on the vertical axis. Provide some additional room for new data as they are collected.

Step 3. *Plot the points on the chart and connect them.* Use graph paper if the chart is constructed by hand; a spreadsheet program is preferable.

Step 4. *Compute the average of all plotted points and draw it as a horizontal line through the data.* This line denoting the average is called the center line (CL) of the chart.

If the plotted points fluctuate in a stable pattern around the center line, with no large spikes, trends, or shifts, they indicate that the process is apparently under control. If unusual patterns exist, then the cause for lack of stability should be investigated and corrective action should be taken. Thus, run charts can identify messes caused by lack of control.

A **control chart** is simply a run chart to which two horizontal lines, called *control limits*, are added: the *upper control limit (UCL)* and *lower control limit (LCL)*, as illustrated in Exhibit 15.6. Control limits are chosen statistically so that there is a high probability (generally greater than .99) that points will fall between these limits if the process is in control. Control limits make it easier to interpret patterns in a run chart and draw conclusions about the state of control. The next chapter addresses this topic in much more detail.

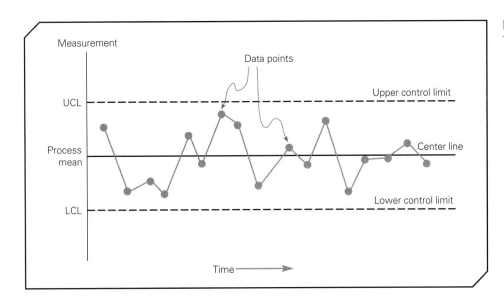

Exhibit 15.6
The Structure of a Control Chart

CHECKSHEETS

Checksheets are simple tools for data collection. Nearly any kind of form may be used to collect data. **Data sheets** are simple columnar or tabular forms used to record data. However, to generate useful information from raw data, further processing generally is necessary. Checksheets are special types of data collection forms in which the results may be interpreted on the form directly without additional processing. For example, in the checksheet in Exhibit 15.7, one can easily identify the most frequent causes of defects.

HISTOGRAMS

A histogram is a basic statistical tool that graphically shows the frequency or number of observations of a particular value or within a specified group. Histograms provide clues about the characteristics of the parent population from which a sample is taken. Patterns that would be difficult to see in an ordinary table of numbers become apparent. You are probably quite familiar with histograms from your statistics classes.

PARETO ANALYSIS

The *Pareto principle* was observed by Joseph Juran in 1950. Juran found that most effects resulted from only a few causes. For instance, in an analysis of 200 types of field failures of automotive engines, only 5 accounted for one-third of all failures; the top 25 accounted for two-thirds of the failures. He named this technique after Vilfredo Pareto (1848–1923), an Italian economist who determined that 85 percent of the wealth in Milan was owned by only 15 percent of the people. Pareto analysis separates the vital few from the trivial many and provides direction for selecting projects for improvement. For example, the checksheet in Exhibit 15.7 provides the data for a Pareto analysis. We see that the most frequent defect is Incomplete,

Exhibit 15.7
Defective Item Checksheet

Check Sheet

Product: ___ Date: ___
Factory: ___
Manufacturing stage: final insp. Section: ___
Inspector's name: ___
Type of defect: scar, incomplete, misshapen
Lot no. ___
Order no. ___
Total no. inspected: 2530

Remarks: all items inspected

Type	Check	Subtotal
Surface scars	//// //// //// //// //// //// //	32
Cracks	//// //// //// //// ///	23
Incomplete	//// //// //// //// //// //// //// //// //// ///	48
Misshapen	////	4
Others	//// ///	8
	Grand total	115
Total rejects	//// //// //// //// //// //// //// //// //// //// //// //// //// //// //// //// //// /	86

Source: Ishikawa, Kaoru, "Defective Item Checksheet," p. 33 from *Guide to Quality Control*, 1982. Asian Productivity Organization. Reprinted with permission.

followed by Surface scars and Cracks. These should be the issues that management attacks first.

Pareto diagrams can also progressively help focus in on specific problems. Exhibit 15.8 shows one example. At each step, the Pareto diagram stratifies the data to more detailed levels (or it may require additional data collection), eventually isolating the most significant issues.

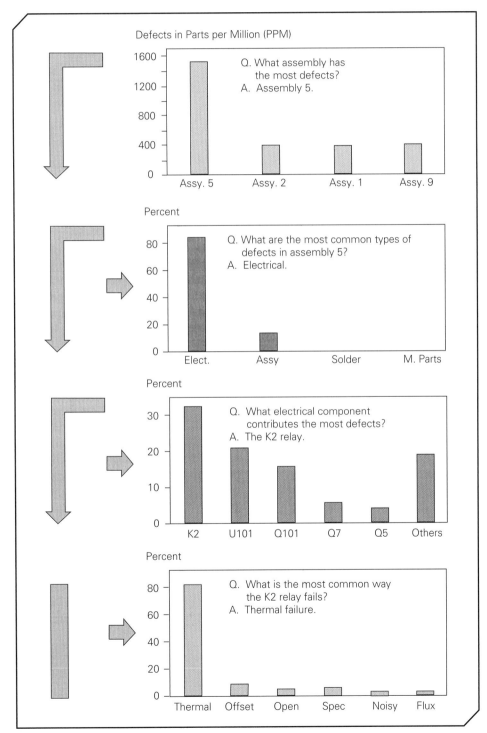

Exhibit 15.8

Use of Pareto Diagrams for Progressive Analysis

Source: *Small Business Guidebook to Quality Management*, Office of the Secretary of Defense, Quality Management Office, Washington, DC (1988).

CAUSE-AND-EFFECT DIAGRAMS

The cause-and-effect diagram is a simple, graphical method for presenting a chain of causes and effects and for sorting out causes and organizing relationships between variables. Because of its structure, it is often called a *fishbone diagram*. An example of a cause-and-effect diagram is shown in Exhibit 15.9. At the end of the horizontal line, a problem is listed. Each branch pointing into the main stem represents a possible cause. Branches pointing to the causes are contributors to those causes. The diagram identifies the most likely causes of a problem so that further data collection and analysis can be carried out.

SCATTER DIAGRAMS

Scatter diagrams are the graphical component of regression analysis. Although they do not provide rigorous statistical analysis, they often point to important relationships between variables, such as the percentage of an ingredient in an alloy and the hardness of the alloy. Typically, the variables in question represent possible causes and effects obtained from cause-and-effect diagrams. For example, if a manufacturer suspects that the percentage of an ingredient in an alloy is causing quality problems in meeting hardness specifications, an employee group might collect data from samples on the amount of ingredient and hardness and plot the data on a scatter diagram, which might indicate that lower quantities of the ingredient in the alloy are associated with increased quality problems.

Exhibit 15.9 Cause-and-Effect Diagram for Hospital Emergency Admission

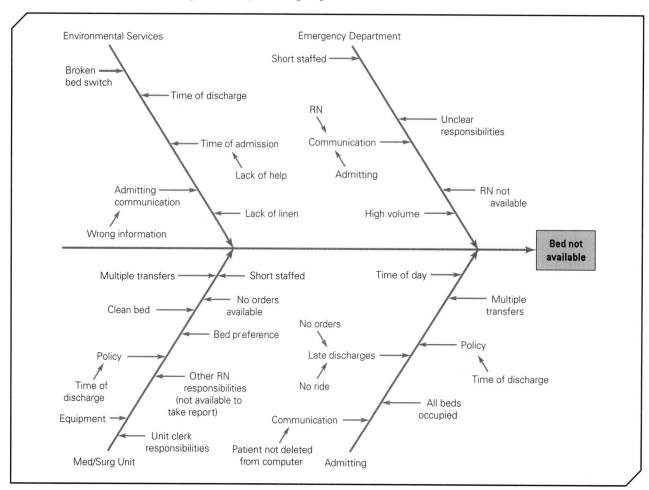

Using the Seven QC Tools for Improvement

The QC tools can be applied to the different steps of the Six Sigma DMAIC process to support the overall problem-solving and improvement effort, as shown in Exhibit 15.10.

Tool	DMAIC Application
Flowcharts	Define, Control
Checksheets	Measure, Analyze
Histograms	Measure, Analyze
Cause-and-effect diagrams	Analyze
Pareto diagrams	Analyze
Scatter diagrams	Analyze, Improve
Control charts	Control

Exhibit 15.10
Application of the Seven QC Tools in Six Sigma

Deming advocated a process similar to DMAIC to guide and motivate improvement activities, which has become known as the *Deming cycle*. The Deming cycle is composed of four stages: *plan, do, study,* and *act* (PDSA), as illustrated in Exhibit 15.11. (The third stage—study—was formerly called *check*, and the Deming cycle was known as the *PDCA cycle*.)

The Plan stage consists of studying the current situation and describing the process: its inputs, outputs, customers, and suppliers; understanding customer expectations; gathering data; identifying problems; testing theories of causes; and developing solutions and action plans. In the Do stage, the plan is implemented on a trial basis—for example, in a laboratory, pilot production process, or with a small group of customers—to evaluate a proposed solution and provide objective data. Data from the experiment are collected and documented. The Study stage determines whether the trial plan is working correctly by evaluating the results, recording the learning, and determining if any further issues or opportunities need be addressed. Often, the first solution must be modified or scrapped. New solutions are proposed and evaluated by returning to the Do stage. In the last stage, Act, the improvements become standardized and the final plan is implemented as a "current best practice" and communicated throughout the organization. This process

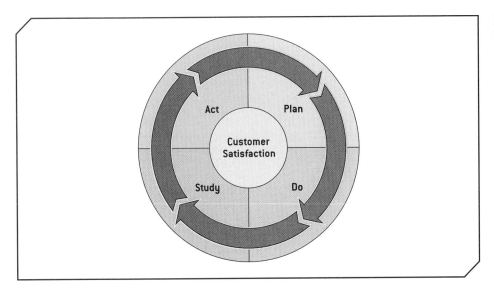

Exhibit 15.11
The Deming Cycle

then leads back to the Plan stage for identification of other improvement opportunities. Exhibit 15.12 summarizes the steps in the Deming cycle in more detail. The Seven QC tools can be used to facilitate the steps in the Deming cycle in a fashion similar to the DMAIC process as described in Exhibit 15.10.

Kaizen[36]

Kaizen *focuses on small, gradual, and frequent improvements over the long term with minimum financial investment and with participation by everyone in the organization.*

The concept of continuous improvement advocated by Deming was embraced by Japanese organizations, leading to an approach known as *kaizen*. **Kaizen** *focuses on small, gradual, and frequent improvements over the long term with minimum financial investment and with participation by everyone in the organization.* In the kaizen philosophy, improvement in all areas of business—cost, meeting delivery schedules, employee safety and skill development, supplier relations, new product development, or productivity—serve to enhance the quality of the firm. Thus, any activity directed toward improvement falls under the kaizen umbrella. At Nissan Motor Co., Ltd., for instance, management seriously considers any suggestion that saves at least 0.6 seconds in a production process. Activities to establish traditional quality control systems, install robotics and advanced technology, institute employee suggestion systems, maintain equipment, and implement just-in-time production systems all lead to improvement.

Three things are required for a successful kaizen program: operating practices, total involvement, and training.[37] First, operating practices expose new improvement opportunities. Practices such as just-in-time reveal waste and inefficiency as well as poor quality. Second, in kaizen, every employee strives for improvement. Top management, for example, views improvement as an inherent component of corporate strategy and provides support to improvement activities by allocating resources effectively and providing reward structures that are conducive to improvement. Middle management can implement top management's improvement goals by establishing, upgrading, and maintaining operating standards that reflect those

Exhibit 15.12 Detailed Steps in the Deming Cycle*

Plan
1. Define the process—its start, end, and what it does.
2. Describe the process—list the key tasks performed and the sequence of steps, people involved, equipment used, environmental conditions, work methods, and materials used.
3. Describe the players—external and internal customers and suppliers and process operators.
4. Define customer expectations—what the customer wants, when, and where, for both external and internal customers.
5. Determine what historical data are available on process performance, or what data needs to be collected to better understand the process.
6. Describe the perceived problems associated with the process, for instance, failure to meet customer expectations, excessive variation, long cycle times, and so on.
7. Identify the primary causes of the problems and their impacts on process performance.
8. Develop potential changes or solutions to the process, and evaluate how these changes or solutions will address the primary causes.
9. Select the most promising solution(s).

Do
1. Conduct a pilot study or experiment to test the impact of the potential solution(s).
2. Identify measures to understand how any changes or solutions are successful in addressing the perceived problems.

Study
1. Examine the results of the pilot study or experiment.
2. Determine whether process performance has improved.
3. Identify further experimentation that may be necessary.

Act
1. Select the best change or solution.
2. Develop an implementation plan—what needs to be done, who should be involved, and when the plan should be accomplished.
3. Standardize the solution, for example, by writing new standard operating procedures.
4. Establish a process to monitor and control process performance.

*Adapted from *Small Business Guidebook to Quality Management*, Office of the Secretary of Defense, Quality Management Office, Washington DC (1998).

goals; by improving cooperation between departments; and by making employees conscious of their responsibility for improvement and developing their problem-solving skills through training. Supervisors can direct more of their attention to improvement rather than "supervision," which, in turn, facilitates communication and offers better guidance to workers. Finally, workers can engage in improvement through suggestion systems and small group activities, self-development programs that teach practical problem-solving techniques, and enhanced job performance skills. All this requires significant training, both in the philosophy and in tools and techniques.

The kaizen philosophy has been widely adopted and is used by many firms in the United States and around the world. For example, at ENBI Corporation, a New York manufacturer of precision metal shafts and roller assemblies for the printer, copier, and fax machine markets, kaizen projects have resulted in a 48 percent increase in productivity, a 30 percent reduction in cycle time, and a 73 percent reduction in inventory.[38] Kaizen has been successfully applied in the Mercedes-Benz truck factory in Brazil, resulting in reductions of 30 percent in manufacturing space, 45 percent in inventory, 70 percent in lead time, and 70 percent in setup time over a 3-year period. Sixteen employees have full-time responsibility for kaizen activities.[39]

A **kaizen blitz** *is an intense and rapid improvement process in which a team or a department throws all its resources into an improvement project over a short time period, as opposed to traditional kaizen applications, which are performed on a part-time basis.* Blitz teams are generally comprised of employees from all areas involved in the process who understand it and can implement changes on the spot. Improvement is immediate, exciting, and satisfying for all those involved in the process (see the OM Spotlight on Magnivision).

A **kaizen blitz** *is an intense and rapid improvement process in which a team or a department throws all its resources into an improvement project over a short time period, as opposed to traditional kaizen applications, which are performed on a part-time basis.*

Poka-Yoke (Mistake-Proofing)

Human beings tend to make mistakes inadvertently. Typical process-related mistakes include omitted processing steps, processing errors, setup or changeover errors, missing information or parts, not handling service upsets properly, wrong information or parts, and adjustment errors. Errors can arise from

- forgetfulness due to lack of concentration,
- misunderstanding because of the lack of familiarity with a process or procedures,
- poor identification associated with lack of proper attention,
- lack of experience,
- absentmindedness,
- delays in judgment when a process is automated, or
- equipment malfunctions.

Poka-yoke *(POH-kah YOH-kay) is an approach for mistake-proofing processes using automatic devices or methods to avoid simple human error.* The poka-yoke concept was developed and refined in the early 1960s by the late Shigeo Shingo, a Japanese manufacturing engineer who developed the Toyota production system.[40]

Poka-yoke *(POH-kah YOH-kay) is an approach for mistake-proofing processes using automatic devices or methods to avoid simple human error.*

Poka-yoke is focused on two aspects: prediction, or recognizing that a defect is about to occur and providing a warning, and detection, or recognizing that a defect has occurred and stopping the process. Many applications of poka-yoke are deceptively simple, yet creative, and usually, they are inexpensive to implement. One of Shingo's first poka-yoke devices involved a process at the Yamada Electric plant in which workers assemble a switch having two push buttons supported by two springs.[42] Occasionally, the worker would forget to insert a spring under each button, which led to a costly and embarrassing repair at the customer's facility. In the old method, the worker would take two springs out of a large parts box and then assemble the switch. To prevent this mistake, the worker was instructed first to place two springs in a small dish in front of the parts box, and then assemble

OM SPOTLIGHT

Kaizen Blitz at Magnivision[41]

Many companies use kaizen blitz to drive improvements. Some examples of using it at Magnivision include the following:

- The molded lens department ran two shifts per day, using 13 employees, and after 40 percent rework yielded 1,300 pieces per day. The production line was unbalanced and work piled up between stations. This added to quality problems as the work-in-process was often damaged. After a 3-day blitz, the team reduced the production to one shift of 6 employees and a balanced line, reducing rework to 10 and increasing yield to 3,500 per day, saving over $179,000.

- In retail services, a blitz team investigated problems that continually plagued employees and discovered that many were related to the software system. Some of the same customer information had to be entered in multiple screens, sometimes the system took a long time to process information, and sometimes it was difficult to find specific information quickly. Neither the programmers nor the engineers were aware of these problems. By getting everyone together, some solutions were easily determined. Estimated savings were $125,000.

the switch. If a spring remains in the dish, the operator knows immediately that an error has occurred. The solution was simple, cheap, and provided immediate feedback to the employee.

Many other examples can be cited:

- Machines have limit switches connected to warning lights that tell the operator when parts are positioned improperly on the machine.
- Fast-food restaurants used automated french-frying machines that can only be operated one way and the french fries are prepackaged and the equipment automated to reduce the chance of human error.
- A device on a drill counts the number of holes drilled in a workpiece; a buzzer sounds if the workpiece is removed before the correct number of holes has been drilled.
- One production step at Motorola involves putting alphabetic characters on a keyboard, then checking to make sure each key is placed correctly. A group of workers designed a clear template with the letters positioned slightly off center. By holding the template over the keyboard, assemblers can quickly spot mistakes.
- A proxy ballot for an investment fund will not fit into the return envelope unless a small strip is detached. The strip asks the respondent to check if the ballot is signed and dated, a major source of error in returning proxy votes.
- Computer programs display a warning message if a file that has not been saved is to be closed.
- A 3.5-inch diskette is designed so that it cannot be inserted unless the disk is oriented correctly (try it!). These disks are not perfectly square, and the beveled right corner of the disk allows a stop in the disk drive to be pushed away if it is inserted correctly.

Process Simulation

Process simulation is an approach for building a logical model of a real process, and experimenting with the model to obtain insight about the behavior of the process or to evaluate the impact of changes in assumptions or potential improvements to it.

Process simulation *is an approach for building a logical model of a real process, and experimenting with the model to obtain insight about the behavior of the process* *or to evaluate the impact of changes in assumptions or potential improvements to it.* Process simulation has been used routinely in business to address complex operational problems, so it is no wonder that it is a useful tool for Six Sigma applications, especially those involving customer service improvement, cycle time reduction, and reducing variability. Process simulation should be used when the process is very complex and difficult to visualize, involves many decision points, or when the goal is to optimize the use of resources for a process.[43]

Building a process simulation model involves first describing how the process operates, normally using a process map. The process map includes all process steps, including logical decisions that route materials or information to different locations. Second, all key inputs such as how long it takes to perform each step of the process and resources needed must be identified. Typically, the activity times in a process are uncertain and described by probability distributions; this is what normally makes it difficult to evaluate process performance and identify bottlenecks without simulation. The intent is for the model to duplicate the real process so that "what-if?" questions can easily be evaluated without having to make time-consuming or costly changes to the real process. Once the model is developed, the simulation process repeatedly samples from the probability distributions of the input variables to create a distribution of potential outputs.

As an example, a common customer support process is the help desk or call center process responsible for answering and addressing customers' questions and complaints.[44] Typically, customer satisfaction ratings of the help desk are generally very low. Although this process is common, it is difficult to analyze with conventional Six Sigma tools. The measure phase usually identifies "time to resolve an issue" and "quality of the issue resolution" as the two CTQs. When these are measured, performance is generally less than a 1-sigma level, so significant improvement potential exists.

Help desks are much too complex to analyze using basic Six Sigma tools. Most help desks have two or three levels of support. When a call comes in, it often waits in a queue. When a level 1 person is available, he or she takes the call. If this person cannot resolve the issue, the call is forwarded to level 2. If the level 2 rep cannot resolve the call, it is forwarded to engineering or a similar support group. Between each of these levels, the call may end up waiting in several more queues, or the customer may be asked to wait for a callback.

By developing a process simulation model, a Black Belt can validate the model against the real process by collecting whatever data are available for model inputs, running the model, and statistically matching the results with data collected during the measure phase. Once the model is validated, analysis can begin. Most simulation packages provide operational output data for all the process steps, resource utilization data, and any additional variables tracked throughout the process. When the data are collected, it becomes a fairly straightforward task to analyze it statistically, identify bottlenecks, develop proposed solutions, and rerun the simulation to confirm the results.

To provide a simple illustration, suppose that in a phone support center, incoming calls arrive on a random basis with an average time between calls of about 5 minutes and a support representative evaluates the nature of each problem.[45] Each call takes anywhere between 30 seconds and 4 minutes, although most can be handled in about 2 minutes. The representative is able to resolve 75 percent of the calls immediately. However, 25 percent of the calls require that other support representatives do research and make a return call to the customer. The research itself combined with the return call requires an average of 20 minutes, although this time may vary quite a bit, from as little as 5 minutes to over 35 minutes. Exhibit 15.13 shows the process map for this situation, including the support representative resources.

Exhibit 15.13
Process Map for Help Desk
Simulation Model

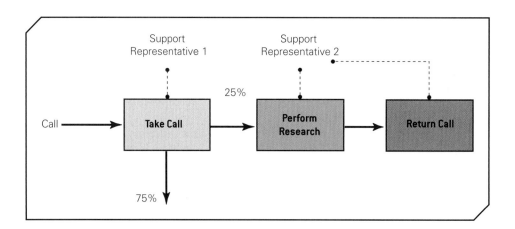

It is difficult to perform a process simulation, even for as simple a process as this, without some type of commercial simulation software. For this example, we used a package called ProcessModel,* which facilitates the simulation process by allowing you to build the model by simply "dragging and dropping" the process map symbols on the computer screen, entering the appropriate data input descriptions, and running the model. As the model runs, ProcessModel provides a visual animation of the process, allowing you to see the buildup of calls at each support stage to gain insight into the system performance.

Standard output reports, such as the one shown in Exhibit 15.14, are generated automatically. By examining these results (see the circled entries in the figure), we see that support problems waited in the *Return Call inQ* activity on average over 496 minutes and as many as 51 calls were waiting at any one time. Thus, this activity should be identified as a problem area suitable for process improvement efforts. In the RESOURCES section, we see that Support 1 was busy about half the time, while Support 2 was busy nearly 100 percent of the time. Any time human resource utilization is above 80 percent for extended periods, the system will most likely result in long waiting times and queue lengths, requiring more resources or changes in the assignment of resources. This suggests that better allocation of resources should improve performance. To reduce the customer waiting time, we

Exhibit 15.14 ProcessModel Simulation Results

Scenario = Normal Run
Replication = 1 of 1
Simulation Time = 40 hr

ACTIVITIES

Activity Name	Scheduled Hours	Capacity	Total Entries	Average Minutes Per Entry	Average Contents	Maximum Contents	Current Contents	% Util
Take Call inQ	40	999	504	1.01	0.21	5	0	0.02
Take Call	40	1	504	2.17	0.45	1	0	45.62
Perform Research inQ	40	999	114	112.50	5.34	11	4	0.53
Perform Research	40	10	110	19.92	0.91	1	1	9.13
Return Call inQ	40	999	109	496.78	22.56	51	51	2.26
Return Call	40	1	58	3.00	0.07	1	0	7.25

Source: ProcessModel Simulation Results from ProcessModel, Inc. Reprinted with permission.

Exhibit 15.14 (Continued)

ACTIVITY STATES BY PERCENTAGE (Multiple Capacity)

Activity Name	Scheduled Hours	% Empty	% Partially Occupied	% Full
Take Call inQ	40	84.85	15.15	0.00
Perform Research inQ	40	10.50	89.50	0.00
Perform Research	40	8.67	91.33	0.00
Return Call inQ	40	2.06	97.94	0.00

ACTIVITY STATES BY PERCENTAGE (Single Capacity)

Activity Name	Scheduled Hours	% Operation	% Idle	% Waiting	% Blocked
Take Call	40	45.62	54.38	0.00	0.00
Return Call	40	7.25	92.75	0.00	0.00

RESOURCES

Resource Name	Units	Scheduled Hours	Number of Times Used	Average Minutes Per Usage	% Util
Support 1	1	40	504	2.17	45.62
Support 2	1	40	168	14.08	98.58

RESOURCE STATES BY PERCENTAGE

Resource Name	Scheduled Hours	% In Use	% Idle	% Down
Support 1	40	45.62	54.38	0.00
Support 2	40	98.58	1.42	0.00

ENTITY SUMMARY (Times in Scoreboard time units)

Entity Name	Qty Processed	Average Cycle Time (Minutes)	Average VA Time (Minutes)	Average Cost
Call	390	4.19	2.18	0.43
HardCall	58	596.99	24.99	8.04

VARIABLES

Variable Name	Total Changes	Average Minutes Per Change	Minimum Value	Maximum Value	Current Value	Average Value
Avg BVA Time Entity	1	0.00	0	0	0	0
Avg BVA Time Call	391	6.10	0	0	0	0
Avg BVA Time HardCall	59	39.04	0	0	0	0

might add additional support representatives or cross-train and share the existing representatives. The simulation model can easily be modified to incorporate these changes, and the impacts on the results can be evaluated. Clearly, trying to do this in the real process would be costly and disruptive, with no guarantee that it would work.

Simulation is a rich and complex topic. Many good books exist about process simulation and we encourage you to find and explore some of them.

SOLVED PROBLEMS

1. The following cost-of-quality data were collected at the installment loan department of the Hamilton Bank. Classify these data into the appropriate cost-of-quality categories and analyze the results. What suggestions would you make to management?

Loan Processing

1.	Run credit check:	$26.13
2.	Review documents:	$3,021.62
3.	Make document corrections; gather additional information:	$1,013.65
4.	Prepare tickler file; review and follow up on titles, insurance, second meetings:	$156.75
5.	Review all output:	$2,244.14
6.	Correct rejects and incorrect output:	$425.84

7.	Reconcile incomplete collateral report:	$78.34
8.	Respond to dealer calls; address associate problems; research and communicate information:	$2,418.88
9.	Compensate for system downtime:	$519.38
10.	Conduct training:	$1,366.94

Loan Payment

1.	Receive and process payments:	$1,045.00
2.	Respond to inquiries when no coupon is presented with payments:	$783.64

Loan Payoff

1.	Receive and process payoff and release documents:	$13.92
2.	Research payoff problems:	$14.34

Solution:

		Quality Cost Categories	
Cost Elements	**Costs**	**Subtotal**	**Proportion**
APPRAISAL			
Run credit checks	$26.13		
Loan Payment and Loan Payoffs Receive and process (2 items)	$1,058.92		
Inspection Review documents	$3,021.63		
Prepare tickler file, etc.	$156.75		
Review all output	$2,244.14		
		$6,507.57	.496
PREVENTION			
Conduct training	$1,366.94		
		$1,366.94	.104
INTERNAL FAILURE COSTS			
Scrap and Rework Make document corrections	$1,013.65		
Correct rejects	$425.84		
Reconcile incomplete collateral reports	$78.34		
Compensate for system downtime	$519.38		
Loan Payment or Payoff Respond to inquiries—no coupon	$783.64		
Research payoff problems	$14.34		
		$2,820.85	.215
EXTERNAL FAILURE COSTS			
Respond to dealer calls, etc.	$2,418.88		
		$2,418.88	.185
Total costs		$13,114.24	

The external failure costs for the bank are not extremely high. However, they do represent 18.5 percent of the total quality costs. The process of working with dealers should be investigated to determine if it can be simplified, better communications established, and problems avoided in the future. The highest cost category is in appraisal costs at $6,507.57 and 49.6 percent of total quality costs. If the categories of "document review" and "review all output" can be reduced without compromising the quality of the lending procedure, these costs could be greatly improved.

2. A watch manufacturer has the option of inspecting each crystal. If a bad crystal is assembled, the cost of disassembly and replacement after the final test and inspection is $1.40. Each crystal can be tested for 8 cents. Perform a break-even analysis to determine the percent nonconforming for which 100 percent inspection is better than no inspection at all.

Solution:

$$C_1 = \$0.08$$
$$C_2 = \$1.40$$
$$C_1/C_2 = 0.057$$

Therefore, if the actual error rate is greater than 0.057, 100 percent inspection is best; otherwise, no inspection is warranted.

3. A hotel estimates that each business guest encounters 20 "moments of truth" during service encounters on a typical overnight stay. On average, the hotel has 1,000 business customers on Monday through Friday and has an average of six complaints per week. What is the epmo measure, and how close is the hotel operating to a Six Sigma level?

Solution:
The weekly number of opportunities for error is (1,000 customers/day)(20 moments of truth per customer) (5 days/week) = 100,000. Six complaints per 100,000 opportunities is equivalent to 60 complaints per million.

Using the Excel formula NORMSINV(1 − 6/100000) + 1.5, this is equivalent to a sigma level of 5.35, approaching a 6-sigma level.

4. An analysis of customer complaints at a large mail-order house revealed the following data:

Billing errors	867
Shipping errors	1,960
Unclear charges	9,650
Long delays	6,672
Delivery errors	452

Construct a Pareto diagram for these data. What conclusions can you draw?

Solution:
Total errors are 19,601. The data for each complaint category are as follows (percentages rounded to whole numbers):

Complaint	Number	Percent	Cumulative Percent
Unclear charges	9,650	49	49
Long delays	6,672	34	83
Shipping errors	1,960	10	93
Billing errors	867	4	97
Delivery errors	452	2	100

Almost half the errors are due to unclear charges, and over 80 percent are attributable to the first two categories. These are the ones to which managers should direct their attention.

KEY TERMS AND CONCEPTS

Acceptance sampling
Appraisal costs
Attribute
Black Belt
Cause-and-effect diagram
Champion
Checksheet
Common causes of variation
Control chart
Cost of quality
Critical to quality (CTQ)
Defect
Defects per unit (DPU)
Defects per million opportunities (dpmo)
Deming cycle
Deming's 14 Points
DMAIC—Define, Measure, Analyze, Improve, Control

Equipment variation
Errors per million opportunities (epmo)
External-failure costs
Fitness for use
Flowchart
GAP Model
Green Belt
Histogram
Internal audit
Internal-failure costs
ISO 9000:2000
Kaizen
Kaizen blitz
Lot
Master Black Belt
Metrology
Nonconformance

Operator variation
Pareto analysis
Pareto diagram
Poka-yoke
Prevention costs
Process simulation
Quality control
Quality management
Quality manual
Quality of conformance
Quality system standards
Repeatability
Reproducibility

Run chart
Scatter diagram
Service quality
Seven QC Tools
Six Sigma
Special causes of variation
Specifications
Stable system
Total quality
Total quality management
Unit of work
Variable data

QUESTIONS FOR REVIEW AND DISCUSSION

1. Define *quality management*. Why is it important for every manager to understand?

2. What does the history of quality management suggest to today's managers?

3. Explain the five gaps in the GAP Model. What can operations do to reduce these gaps?

4. What is the most useful definition of quality from an operations perspective? How might an operations manager use this definition in making daily decisions?

5. How do you define *service quality*? How is it similar and different from the manufacturing definition?

6. Explain the three principles of total quality.

7. Are the basic elements of total quality really any different from the practices that every manager should perform? Why do some managers find them difficult to accept?

8. How does Deming's view of a production system in Exhibit 15.2 correspond to the notion of a value chain introduced in Chapter 2?

9. Summarize the impact of quality on business results. Can you state that quality is a key "driver" of business results?

10. Summarize Deming's philosophy as expressed in the 14 Points. Explain how it differs from traditional management practices and why.

11. How might Deming's 14 Points be applied in running a college or university? How about an individual classroom?

12. Explain the Deming chain reaction.

13. What is the Deming cycle, and how does it support continuous improvement activities?

14. Explain the purpose and structure of ISO 9000:2000. How do the principles of ISO 9000 compare with the Malcolm Baldrige criteria discussed in Chapter 3?

15. Summarize the basic elements of an effective quality management system at the operations level.

16. Explain how service quality is measured. How does it differ from manufacturing, and how can such measurements be used for controlling quality in services?

17. What is Six Sigma? How is it measured?

18. Explain the key concepts used in implementing a Six Sigma quality initiative.

19. Summarize the DMAIC process for problem solving.

20. What types of individuals participate in Six Sigma projects? How do their skills differ?

21. Explain issues that service and small organizations face in implementing Six Sigma.

22. What does "cost of quality" mean? Why is it important?

23. Explain the classification of quality costs. Provide some specific examples in a fast-food operation and in the operation of your college or university.

24. How is Pareto analysis beneficial in analyzing quality costs?

25. Summarize the Seven QC Tools used for quality improvement, and provide an example of each.

26. Explain the concept of kaizen. What must an organization do to successfully operate a kaizen initiative?

27. What is a kaizen blitz? How does it differ from the original notion of kaizen?

28. What is poka-yoke? Provide some examples in your daily life.

29. How can process simulation be used in quality management activities?

PROBLEMS AND ACTIVITIES

1. Analyze the following cost data. What implications do these data suggest to managers?

| | | Product | |
	A	B	C
Total sales	$537,280	$233,600	$397,120
External failure	42%	20%	20%
Internal failure	45%	25%	45%
Appraisal	12%	52%	30%
Prevention	1%	3%	5%

Note: Figures represent percentages of quality costs by product.

2. Compute a sales-dollar index base to analyze the quality-cost information in the following table, and prepare a memo to management.

| | | Quarter | | |
	1	2	3	4
Total sales	$4,120	$4,206	$4,454	$4,106
External failure	$40.80	$42.20	$42.80	$28.60
Internal failure	$168.20	$172.40	$184.40	$66.40
Appraisal	$64.20	$67.00	$74.40	$166.20
Prevention	$28.40	$29.20	$30.20	$40.20

3. Given the cost elements in the following table, determine the total percentage in each of the four major quality-cost categories.

Cost Element	Amount ($)
Incoming test and inspection	7,500
Scrap	35,000
Quality training	0
Inspection	25,000
Test	5,000
Adjustment cost of complaints	21,250
Quality audits	2,500
Maintenance of tools and dies	9,200
Quality control administration	5,000
Laboratory testing	1,250
Design of quality assurance equipment	1,250
Material testing and inspection	1,250
Rework	70,000
Quality problem solving by product engineers	11,250
Inspection equipment calibration	2,500
Writing procedures and instructions	2,500
Laboratory services	2,500
Rework due to vendor faults	17,500
Correcting imperfections	6,250
Setup for test and inspection	10,750
Formal complaints to vendors	10,000

4. Use Pareto analysis to investigate the quality losses in a paper mill given the following data. What conclusions do you reach?

Category	Annual Loss ($)
Downtime	38,000
Testing costs	20,000
Rejected paper	560,000
Odd lot	79,000
Excess inspection	28,000
Customer complaints	125,000
High material costs	67,000

5. A manufacturer estimates that the proportion of nonconforming items in one process is 3.5 percent. The estimated cost of inspecting each item is $0.50, and the cost of replacing a nonconforming item after it leaves the production area is $25. What is the best economic inspection decision?

6. The cost to inspect a credit card statement in a bank is $0.75, and correction of a mistake later amounts to $500. What is the break-even point in errors per thousand transactions for which 100 percent inspection is no more economical than no inspection?

7. A bank has set a standard that mortgage applications be processed within 8 days of filing. If, out of a sample of 1,000 applications, 75 fail to meet this requirement, what is the epmo metric, and how does it compare with a six-sigma level?

8. Over the last year, 965 injections were administered at a clinic. Quality is measured by the proper amount of dosage as well as the correct drug. In two instances, the incorrect amount was given, and in one case, the wrong drug was given. What is the epmo metric and how does it compare with a 6-sigma level?

9. The *Wall Street Journal* reported on February 15, 2000 that about 750,000 airplane components are manufactured, machined, or assembled for Boeing Co. by workers from the Seattle Lighthouse for the Blind. A Boeing spokeswoman noted that the parts have an "exceptionally low" rejection rate of one per thousand. What is the dpmo metric, and how does it compare with a 6-sigma level?

10. A flowchart for a fast-food drive-through window is shown in Exhibit 15.15. Determine the important quality characteristics inherent in this process, and suggest possible improvements.

11. The following list gives the number of seconds customers have waited for a telephone service representative today. Construct a histogram, and discuss any conclusions you might reach.

5	7	7	15	3
21	15	22	10	8
10	6	8	18	4
14	5	7	8	10

12. The manager at a pizza franchise has logged customer complaints over the past 3 months. From the data given, construct a Pareto diagram. What should the manager do?

Type of complaint	Frequency
Wrong order	3
Late delivery	17
Not enough toppings	1
Not hot enough	8
Excessive wait in dining room	12

13. Fourteen batches of a raw material were tested for the percentage of a particular chemical (x). It is believed that the amount of this chemical influences an important quality characteristic of the final product (y). The test data follow. Construct a scatter diagram of the data, and discuss any conclusions you might reach.

x	y
3.5	7.0
3.2	8.0
4.5	8.4
1.0	7.6
3.8	10.5
5.4	9.2
5.3	11.7
6.1	10.1
6.1	11.0
6.9	10.7
7.4	9.6
7.5	8.2
8.5	9.1
8.2	11.1

14. The following list gives the number of defects found in 30 samples of 100 electronic assemblies taken on

Exhibit 15.15

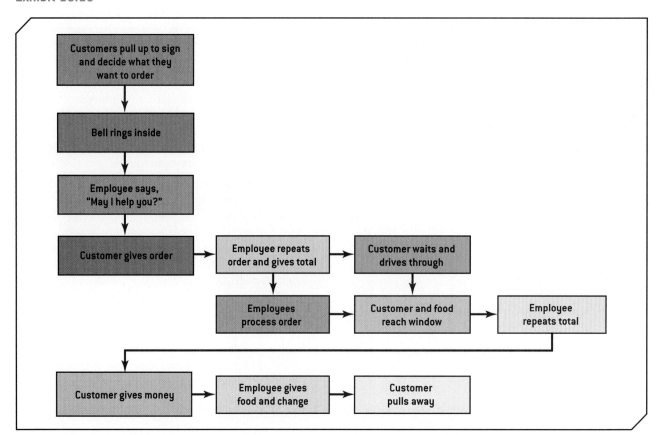

a daily basis over 1 month. Plot these data on a run chart, computing the average value (center line). How do you interpret the chart?

1	6	5	5	4	3	2	2	4	6
2	1	3	1	4	5	4	1	6	15
12	6	3	4	3	3	2	5	7	4

15. A catalog order-filling process for personalized printed products can be described as follows. Telephone orders are taken over a 12-hour period each day. Orders are collected from each order clerk at the end of the day and checked for errors by the supervisor, usually the next morning. Because of the supervisor's heavy work load, this 1-day batch of orders usually does not get to the data-processing department until after 1:00 P.M. Orders are invoiced by the data-processing department in 1-day batches and then printed and "matched back" with the original orders. (At this point, if the order is for a new customer, it is returned to the person who did the new-customer verification and set up the new account for that customer, both of which must be done before an order from a new customer can be invoiced.) The next step is order verification and proofreading. The orders, with invoices attached, are given to a person who verifies that all required information is present and correct. If there is a question, it is checked by computer or by calling the customer. Finally, the completed orders are sent to the typesetting department of the printshop.

a. Develop a flowchart for this process.
b. Discuss opportunities for improving the quality of service in this situation.

16. An independent outplacement service helps unemployed executives find jobs. One of the major activities of the service is preparing resumes. Three word processors work at the service and type resumes and cover letters. They are assigned to individual clients, currently about 120. Turnaround time for typing is expected to be 24 hours. The word-processing operation begins with clients placing work in the assigned word processor's bin. When the word processor picks up the work (in batches), it is logged in by use of a clock time stamp, and the work is typed and printed. After the batch is completed, the word processor puts the documents in the clients' bins, logs in the time delivered, and picks up new work. A supervisor tries to balance the workload for the three word processors. Lately, many of the clients have been complaining about errors in their documents—misspellings, missing lines, wrong formatting, and so on. The supervisor has told the word processors to be more careful, but the errors persist.

a. Develop a cause-and-effect diagram that might help to identify the source of errors.
b. How might the supervisor study ways to reduce the amount of errors? What tools might the supervisor use to do so, and how might they be applied?

17. Interview managers of a local company that has achieved or is pursuing ISO 9000 registration. What problems does it face or did it encounter in achieving registration?

18. List some of the common processes you perform as a student. How might you go about controlling and improving them?

19. Develop cause-and-effect diagrams for the following problems:

a. poor exam grade
b. no job offers
c. too many speeding tickets
d. late for work or school

20. Search the Internet for examples and applications of Six Sigma. Write a report on current industry practice and the benefits cited.

21. Select some process in your work or personal life (for example, something to do with a fraternity, car maintenance, or home activities), and discuss how you would apply the Six Sigma DMAIC approach to improve this process. Be specific, addressing such things as how you would collect the data, what tools you might use for analysis, and so on.

CASES

WELZ BUSINESS MACHINES

Welz Business Machines sells and services a variety of copiers, computers, and other office equipment. The company receives many calls daily for service, sales, accounting, and other departments. All calls are handled centrally through customer service representatives and routed to other individuals as appropriate. A number of customers have complained about long waits when calling for service. A market research study found that customers become irritated if the call is not answered within five rings. Scott Welz, the company president, authorized the customer service department manager, Tim, to study this problem and find a method to shorten the call-waiting time for its customers.

Tim met with the service representatives to attempt to determine the reasons for long waiting times. The following conversation ensued:

Tim: "This is a serious problem; how a customer phone inquiry is answered is the first impression the customer receives from us. As you know, this company was founded on efficient and friendly service to all our customers. It's obvious why customers have to wait: you're on the phone with another customer. Can you think of any reasons that might keep you on the phone for an unnecessarily long time?"

Robin: "I've noticed that quite often the party I need to route the call to is not present. It takes time to transfer the call and then wait to see if it is answered. If the party is not there, I end up apologizing and have to transfer the call to another extension."

Tim: "You're right, Robin. Sales personnel often are out of the office for sales calls, absent on trips to preview new products, or not at their desks for a variety of reasons. What else might cause this problem?"

Ravi: "I get irritated at some customers who spend a great deal of time complaining about a problem that I cannot do anything about except refer to someone else. Of course, I listen and sympathize with them, but this eats up a lot of time."

LaMarr: "Some customers call so often, they think we're long-lost friends and strike up a personal conversation."

Tim: "That's not always a bad thing, you realize."

LaMarr: "Sure, but it delays my answering other calls."

Nancy: "It's not always the customer's fault. During lunch times, we're not all available to answer the phone."

Ravi: "Right after we open at 9:00 A.M., we get a rush of calls. I think that many of the delays are caused by these peak periods."

Robin: "I've noticed the same thing between 4 and 5 P.M."

Tim: "I've had a few comments from department managers that they received routed calls that didn't fall in their areas of responsibility and had to be transferred again."

Mark: "But that doesn't cause delays at our end."

Nancy: "That's right, Mark, but I just realized that sometimes I simply don't understand what the customer's problem really is. I spend a lot of time trying to get him or her to explain it better. Often, I have to route it to someone because other calls are waiting."

Ravi: "Perhaps we need to have more knowledge of our products."

Tim: "Well, I think we've covered most of the major reasons as to why many customers have to wait. It seems to me that we have four major reasons: the phones are short-staffed, the receiving party is not present, the customer dominates the conversation, and you may not understand the customer's problem. We need to collect some information next about these possible causes. I will set up a data-collection sheet that you can use to track some of these things. Mark, would you help me on this?"

Over the next 2 weeks, the staff collected data on the frequency of reasons why some callers had to wait:

Reason	Total Number
A. Operators short-staffed	172
B. Receiving party not present	73
C. Customer dominates conversation	19
D. Lack of operator understanding	61
E. Other reasons	10

Discussion Questions

a. From the conversation between Tim and his staff, draw a cause-and-effect diagram.

b. Perform a Pareto analysis of the data collected.

c. What actions might the company take to improve the situation?

NATIONAL FURNITURE

National Furniture is a large retail design and furniture store. The store often orders special merchandise at the request of its customers. However, the store has recently experienced problems with the on-time delivery of these special orders. Sometimes the orders are never received, resulting in very irate customers!

The process of fulfilling a special order begins with the sales associate who records the customer information and obtains approval from a manager to process the order. The sales associate puts the form in a bin for the office manager to fax the order form to the special-order department at the regional office. When the office manager faxes the special-order forms from the bin, she files them in a notebook. If there is a problem with the order, the manager receives notification and contacts the sales associate who took the order to decide what needs to be done next. Typical problems that are often observed include sales associates not filling out the order form completely or entering a request date that is impossible to fulfill. Sometimes the sales associate does not put the form in the proper bin, so the form never gets faxed. Other times, sales associates are asked to obtain more information from the customer but fail to call the customer back or do not inform the office associate to re-fax the form after getting additional information from the customer.

At the regional office, the special-order department receives the fax from the store, reviews it, and informs the store if additional information is needed. When all the information is complete, it processes the order.

Sometimes it loses or misplaces the form after it arrives on the fax machine, orders the wrong merchandise, or fails to notify the store when additional information is needed or when the merchandise should be expected to arrive.

Discussion Questions

1. Develop a flowchart for administering special orders. What steps might you suggest to improve this process?

2. Construct a cause-and-effect diagram for identifying reasons why special orders are not received on time.

3. Discuss the relationship between the process map and the cause-and-effect diagram. How can they be used together to attack this problem?

4. How can you mistake-proof this process?

RENEWAL AUTO SERVICE

Renewal Auto Service (RAS) is a quick-service vehicle oil and lubricant change service somewhat similar to Jiffy Lube, FasLube, and Speedy Lube. The primary customer benefit package consists of providing oil, oil filters, air filters, and lubricants by polite and friendly employees who regularly interact with customers. However, RAS seeks to differentiate itself from the competition by focusing on peripheral goods and services and a customer-friendly servicescape. These include two blends of fresh coffee, tea, sodas, current magazines, and a television in the customer waiting room. Customers receive vehicle maintenance brochures and

discount coupons for their next visit. RAS also offers services that competitors do not, including cleaning the vehicle's windows outside and inside; vacuuming carpets; reviewing service history with the customer; checking tire pressure, belts, hoses, windshield wipers, coolant levels, and filters; and explaining the technical aspects of vehicle service if the customer asks or if a potential safety or mechanical problem is discovered.

The facility layout consists of three service bays with a pit below each bay for draining and changing oil and lubricants. Aboveground are all necessary tools and equipment. The customer waiting area is carpeted and

Exhibit 15.16 RAS Customer Quarterly Example Survey Results ($n = 2.6$)

Survey Question	Average Score on 1 (worst) to 5 (best) Scale
1. The total time you spent in RAS was as expected.	4.59
2. My service experience during each repeat visit is of consistent high quality.	3.94
3. Store managers monitor my vehicles maintenance and repair very well.	4.36
4. Store managers understand my individual wants and needs.	3.77
5. Standards of performance at RAS are clearly visible inside the store.	4.54
6. Standards of performance at RAS are clearly advertised in the media and help me understand what to expect during vehicle service.	4.68
7. The facility is clean and well maintained.	4.64
8. The customer waiting area is really nice and why I come here.	4.79
9. Service personnel are polite, friendly, and clearly explain technical details if I ask.	3.85
10. Store managers always go over the vehicle checksheet with me prior to paying the bill.	4.40
11. Cleaning the vehicle windows and vacuuming are extra services that I like.	4.66
12. Knowing the vehicle history makes me feel secure that I am doing the right thing in terms of vehicle maintenance and repair.	4.43
13. RAS employees are really good at what they do.	4.10
14. RAS is clearly better than competitors.	4.35

larger than competitors', with comfortable sofas and chairs. A large glass window in the waiting area allows customers to see their vehicle being serviced in any of the three bays. Employees are professionally dressed in clean blue uniforms with their first name embroidered on them. To maintain a professional appearance, employees are required to wash their arms and hands after each service job.

A comprehensive vehicle checklist is used to ensure completeness of the work and as a means of quality control. The standard time to complete a job is 16 minutes in the bay area, plus 9 minutes for customer check-in and checkout. Store managers and assistant managers are trained and empowered to approve free service if the customer is dissatisfied for any reason.

RAS surveys customers regularly as a way of understanding their perceptions of service quality. Results from 206 customer surveys over the past 3 months for nine RAS area stores are summarized in Exhibit 15.16. Samples of good and bad written customer comments are also shown in Exhibit 15.17. The vice presidents of marketing, human resource management, and operations were asked to analyze these data to determine what actions might be necessary to reward or improve performance. The V.P. of Operations, Thomas Margate, thought he would try to apply the GAP model to analyze this information. A final report to the CEO was due in 2 weeks. What recommendations would you make? (Hint: See if you can assign each survey question to a gap.)

Exhibit 15.17

Five Good and Five Bad Sample RAS Customer Written Comments

1. I come to RAS because of their outstanding vehicle technical knowledge and skills.
2. Believe it or not, I really like their coffee and enjoy reading their magazines.
3. The mechanics are very careful and conscientious when working on my car.
4. When I complained there were streaks on my windows, they redid my windows and gave me a discount coupon for my next visit—real nice people.
5. Very fast and convenient service—I'll be back.
6. Store managers are super but the employees don't like to talk to us customers.
7. I won't come back; a mechanic keeps staring at me!
8. I felt pressured to buy the air and fuel filter and I don't even know what these parts do.
9. All the mechanics seem hurried while I was there.
10. The mechanic got grease on my fender and when I asked him to please clean it off he shrugged and wiped it off with a cleaner.

ENDNOTES

[1] Harrington, H. James, "Looking for a Little Service," *Quality Digest*, May 2000; www.qualitydigest.com

[2] "Hyundai Gets Hot," *Business Week*, December 17, 2001, pp. 84–85.

[3] Gale, Bradley T., "Quality Comes First When Hatching Power Brands," *Planning Review*, July–August 1992, pp. 4–9, 48.

[4] "Hyundai: Kissing Clunkers Goodbye," *BusinessWeek*, May 17, 2004, p. 45.

[5] *The Cincinnati Enquirer*, January 12, 2002, pp. A1, A9.

[6] Early history is reported in Dague, Delmer C., "Quality—Historical Perspective," *Quality Control in Manufacturing*, Warrendale, PA: Society of Automotive Engineers, February 1981; and Provost, L. P., and Norman, C. L., "Variation through the Ages," *Quality Progress* 23, no. 12, December 1990, pp. 39–44. Modern events are discussed in Karabatsos, Nancy, "Quality in Transition, Part One: Account of the '80s," *Quality Progress* 22, no. 12, December 1989, pp. 22–26; and Juran, Joseph M., "The Upcoming Century of Quality," address to the ASQC Annual Quality Congress, Las Vegas, May 24, 1994. A comprehensive historical account may be found in Juran, J. M., *A History of Managing for Quality*, Milwaukee, WI: ASQC Quality Press, 1995.

[7] Freudenheim, M., "Study Finds Inefficiency in Health Care," *The New York Times*, 2002, http://www.nytimes.com/2002/06/11/business/11CARE.html.

[8] Tamimi, Nabil, and Sebastianelli, Rose, "How Firms Define and Measure Quality," *Production and Inventory Management Journal* 37, no. 3, Third Quarter, 1996, pp. 34–39.

[9] Parasuraman, A., Zeithaml, V. A., and Berry, L. L., "A Conceptual Model of Service Quality and Its Implications for Future research," *Journal of Marketing* 49, Fall 1985, pp. 41–50.

[10] "Progress on the Quality Road," *Incentive*, April 1995, p. 7.

[11] Hendricks, Kevin B., and Singhal, Vinod R., "Does Implementing an Effective TQM Program Actually Improve Operating Performance? Empirical Evidence from Firms That Have Won Quality Awards," *Management Science* 43, no. 9, September 1997, pp. 1258–1274. The results of this study have appeared in extensive business and trade publications such as *Business Week*, *Fortune*, and others.

[12] Deming, W. Edwards, *The New Economics for Industry, Government, Education*, Cambridge, MA: MIT Center for Advanced Engineering Study, 1993.

[13] Shewhart, Walter A., *Economic Control of Quality of a Manufactured Product*, New York: Van Nostrand, 1931.

[14] Adapted from Jacques, March Laree, "Big League Quality," *Quality Progress*, August 2001, pp. 27–34.

[15] "ISO 9000 Certification Can Be Boost for Small Companies," *The Columbus Dispatch*, Columbus, Ohio, January 22, 2002, p. C6.

[16] Source: http://www.bsi.org.uk/iso-tc176-sc2/—Document: "Transition Planning Guidance for ISO/DIS 9001:2000," ISO/TC 176/SC 2/N 474, December, 1999.

[17] "ISO 9000 Update," *Fortune*, September 30, 1996, p. 134[J].

[18] Eckstein, Astrid L. H., and Balakrishnan, Jaydeep, "The ISO 9000 Series: Quality Management Systems for the Global Economy," *Production and Inventory Management Journal* 34, no. 4, Fourth Quarter 1993, pp. 66–71.

[19] "Home Builder Constructs Quality with ISO 9000," *Quality Digest*, February 2000, p. 13.

[20] Taormina, Tom, "Conducting Successful Internal Audits," *Quality Digest*, June 1998, pp. 44–47.

[21] Karaszewski, Robert, "Quality Challenges in Global Companies," *Quality Progress*, October 2004, pp. 59–65.

[22] "Up, Up, and Away?" *Fortune*, July 21, 2003, p. 149.

[23] Snee, Ronald D., "Why Should Statisticians Pay Attention to Six Sigma?" *Quality Progress*, September 1999, pp. 100–103.

[24] Marash, Stanley A., "Six Sigma: Business Results Through Innovation," ASQ's 54th Annual Quality Congress Proceedings, pp. 627–630.

[25] Welch, Jack, *Jack: Straight from the Gut*, New York: Warner Books, 2001, pp. 329–330.

[26] Ibid., pp. 333–334.

[27] "GE Reports Record Earnings With Six Sigma," *Quality Digest*, December 1999, p. 14.

[28] Rucker, Rochelle, "Six Sigma at Citibank," *Quality Digest*, December 1999, pp. 28–32.

[29] Smith, Kennedy, "Six Sigma at Ford Revisited," *Quality Digest*, 23, no. 6, June 2003, pp. 28–32.

[30] This discussion of the applicability of Six Sigma to services is adapted from Bisgaard, Soren, Hoerl, Roger W., and Snee, Ronald D., "Improving Business Processes with Six Sigma," *Proceedings of ASQ's 56th Annual Quality Congress*, 2002, CD-ROM, and Smith, Kennedy, "Six Sigma for the Service Sector," *Quality Digest*, May 2003, pp. 23–28.

[31] Adapted from Keim, Elizabeth, Fox, LouAnn, and Mazza, Julie S., "Service Quality Six Sigma Case Studies," *Proceedings of the 54th Annual Quality Congress of the American Society for Quality*, 2000, CD-ROM.

[32] Palser, Lisa, "Cycle Time Improvement for a Human Resources Process," *ASQ's 54th Annual Quality Congress Proceedings*, 2000, CD-ROM.

[33] Hoerl, Roger, "An Inside Look at Six Sigma at GE," *Six Sigma Forum Magazine*, 1, no. 3, May 2002, pp. 35–44.

[34] Sullivan, Edward, and Owens, Debra A., "Catching A Glimpse of Quality Costs Today," *Quality Progress*, 16, no. 12, December 1983, pp. 21–24.

[35] *Reports of Statistical Application Research, Japanese Union of Scientists and Engineers*, 33, no. 2, June 1986.

[36] Imai, Masaaki, *KAIZEN—The Key to Japan's Competitive Success*, New York: McGraw-Hill, 1986.

[37] Robinson, Alan, ed., *Continuous Improvement in Operations*, Cambridge, MA: Productivity Press, 1991.

[38] Tonkin, Lea A. P., "Kaizen Blitz^SM 5: Bottleneck-Bashing comes to Rochester, NY," *Target* 12, no. 4, September/October 1996, pp. 41–43.

[39] Oakeson, Mark, "Makes Dollars & Sense for Mercedes-Benz in Brazil," *IIE Solutions*, April 1997, pp. 32–35.

[40] From *Poka-yoke: Improving Product Quality by Preventing Defects*. Edited by NKS/Factory Magazine, English translation copyright © 1988 by Productivity Press, Inc., P.O. Box 3007, Cambridge, MA 02140, 800-394-6868. Reprinted by permission.

[41] Chilson, Eleanor, "Kaizen Blitzes at Magnivision: $809,270 Cost Savings," *Quality Management Forum*, 29, no. 1, Winter 2003.

[42] Robinson, Harry, "Using Poka Yoke Techniques for Early Defect Detection," Paper presented at the Sixth International Conference on Software Testing and Analysis and Review (STAR '97).

[43] Fleming, Steve, and Manson, E. Lowry, "Six Sigma and Process Simulation," *Quality Digest*, March 2002.

[44] Ibid.

[45] This example is adapted from a tutorial for ProcessModel, a commercial simulation package. ProcessModel, Inc., 32 West Center, Suite 209, Provo, Utah 84601.

Chapter Outline

CHAPTER 16

Quality Control and SPC

Learning Objectives

1. To understand the elements of good control systems, variation in
   processes, the difference between common and special causes of
   variation, quality control metrics, and the design of quality control
   systems.

2. To understand variation in manufacturing and service processes,
   metrics for quantifying variation, and the role of control charts and

statistical process control methods in helping managers control variation.

3. To be able to construct and interpret simple control charts for both continuous and discrete data, to understand how to select the proper chart, and to understand the role of SPC in processes approaching Six Sigma capability.

4. To understand the concept of process capability and be able to analyze process capability data, compute process capability indexes, and interpret the results.

• In early June 1999, almost 100 Belgian children fell ill after drinking Coca-Cola. This incident caused the Belgian Health Ministry to require Coke to recall millions of cans of product in Belgium and to cease product distribution. Later, France and the Netherlands also halted distribution of Coke products as the contamination scare spread. It was quickly determined that contaminated carbon dioxide had been used during the carbonation process at the Antwerp bottling facility. According to the official statement from Coca-Cola, "Independent laboratory testing showed that the cause of the off-taste in the bottled products was carbon dioxide. That carbon dioxide was replaced and all bottles with off-taste have been removed from the market. The issue affects the taste of the soft drinks only. . . ."

• Marriott has become infamous for its obsessively detailed standard operating procedures (SOPs), which result in hotels that travelers either love for their consistent good quality or hate for their bland uniformity. "This is a company that has more controls, more systems, and more procedural manuals than anyone—except the government," says one industry veteran. "And they actually comply with them." Housekeepers work with a 114-point checklist. One SOP: *Server knocks three times. After knocking, the associate should immediately identify themselves in a clear voice, saying, "Room Service!" The guest's name is never mentioned outside the door.* Although people love to make fun of such procedures, they are a serious part of Marriott's business, and SOPs are designed to protect the brand. Recently, Marriott has removed some of the rigid guidelines for owners of hotels it manages, empowering them to make some of their own decisions on details.[1]

• Frank Roy, the new plant manager at a large pharmaceutical company that manufactures syringes with a self-contained, single dose of an

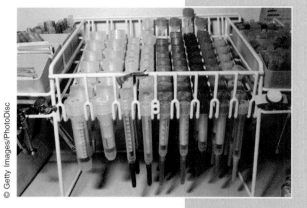

© Getty Images/PhotoDisc

injectable drug is concerned about the increased scrap that his process seems to be making. His engineering manager, Edith Berger, explained how the process works. "In the first stage, we fill sterile liquid drug into glass syringes and seal them with rubber stoppers. Next, we insert the cartridge into a plastic syringe and 'tack' the containment cap at a precisely determined length of the syringe (4.920 inches). If the tacking process results in a shorter than desired length, it leads to pressure on the cartridge stopper and a partial or complete activation of the syringe. We have to scrap these. This step seems to be producing more and more scrap and reworked syringes over the last several weeks." "What happens if the length is too long?" asked Frank. Edith replied, "If the process results in a longer than desired length, the syringe will likely be damaged in shipment and handling. However, we can rework these manually to attach the cap at a lower position. This process requires a 100 percent inspection of the tacked syringes and increases our cost." "We can't remain competitive and incur these unnecessary costs," stated Frank emphatically. "We need to get this situation under control—quickly!"

Discussion Questions: What role do you think quality control plays in creating satisfying customer experiences? What opportunities for improved quality control or use of SOPs can you think of at your college or university (e.g. bookstore, cafeteria)?

The task of quality control is to ensure that a good or service conforms to specifications and meets customer requirements by monitoring and measuring processes and making any necessary adjustments to maintain a specified level of performance.

Value chains are complex networks of internal and external processes and customer-supplier relationships. The ability to satisfy the ultimate customer—the consumer or external business customer—depends on the ability to satisfy the needs and requirements of all internal customers within the value chain. This requires a significant amount of attention to quality control at key process steps throughout the value chain. *The task of quality control is to ensure that a good or service conforms to specifications and meets customer requirements by monitoring and measuring processes and making any necessary adjustments to maintain a specified level of performance.* The consequences of a lack of good quality control systems and procedures can be serious and potentially cause large financial losses or affect a company's reputation, as the first episode illustrates. Health care is one industry that has been highly criticized for its lack of effective quality control systems. For instance, a hospital in Philadelphia promised to evaluate and redesign its laboratory procedures after state investigators confirmed that faulty lab tests led to dozens of patients receiving overdoses of a blood-thinning medication, resulting in the deaths of two patients. Retests found that 932 lab tests were improperly performed without being caught. Lawsuits on behalf of the dead patients were pending.[2]

The second episode shows the importance of quality control in ensuring consistent service experiences and creating customer satisfaction. Simple control mechanisms such as checklists and standard operating procedures provide cost-effective means of doing this. Contacting customers after a poor service experience only uncovers the damage that has already occurred, requires extraordinary measures for service recovery, and often results in lost customers. In the third episode, the pharmaceutical company has recognized the need to reduce both scrap and unnecessary inspection by instituting better controls and improving the process. Control should be performed by those who know the process best—the people who do the work. Focusing on the process, rather than the output, in a prevention-oriented strategy of control is preferable to inspecting the results and trying to deal with them.

In this chapter we focus on

- understanding quality control systems in manufacturing and service organizations;
- the foundations of statistical process control—understanding variation, selecting metrics to control, and building control charts;
- developing and using different types of control charts for manufacturing and service applications; and
- understanding the concept of process capability and how to measure it.

QUALITY CONTROL SYSTEMS

Any control system has three components:

1. a performance standard or goal,
2. a means of measuring actual performance, and
3. comparison of actual performance with the standard to form the basis for corrective action.

Learning Objective
To understand the elements of good control systems, variation in processes, the difference between common and special causes of variation, quality control metrics, and the design of quality control systems.

As one practical example, golf balls must meet five standards to conform to the Rules of Golf: minimum size, maximum weight, spherical symmetry, maximum initial velocity, and overall distance.[3] Methods for measuring such quality characteristics may be automated or performed manually. For instance, golf balls are measured for size by trying to drop them through a metal ring—a conforming ball sticks to the ring while a nonconforming ball falls through; digital scales measure weight to one-thousandth of a gram; and initial velocity is measured in a special machine by finding the time it takes a ball struck at 98 mph to break a ballistic screen at the end of a tube exactly 6.28 feet away. By comparing the measurements to the standard, golf ball manufacturers can determine whether their goods conform to the Rules of Golf. If they find some nonconformances, then some corrective action must be taken to either redesign the goods or correct the process that makes them. As another example, DaimlerChrysler manufactures the PT Cruiser at the company's Toluca Assembly Plant in Mexico. To ensure quality, the Toluca plant verifies parts, processes, fit, and finish every step of the way—from stamping and body to paint and final assembly. The quality control practices include visual management through quality alert systems, which are designed to call immediate attention to abnormal conditions. The system provides visual and audible signals for each station for tooling, production, maintenance, and material flow.[4]

Similar control measures are taken in services (we introduced service quality metrics in the previous chapter). Fast-food restaurants, for example, have carefully designed their processes for a high degree of accuracy and fast response time, using hands-free intercom systems, microphones that reduce ambient kitchen noise, and screens that display a customer's order. Timers at Wendy's count every segment of the order completion process to help managers control performance and identify problem areas.

Good control systems make economic sense. The importance of control is often explained by the *1:10:100 Rule* (see Exhibit 16.1):

If a defect or service error is identified and corrected at the design stage, it might cost $1 to fix. If it is first detected during the production process, it might cost $10 to fix. However, if the defect is not discovered until it reaches the customer, it might cost $100 to correct.

Exhibit 16.1
Economic Implications of the
1:10:100 Rule

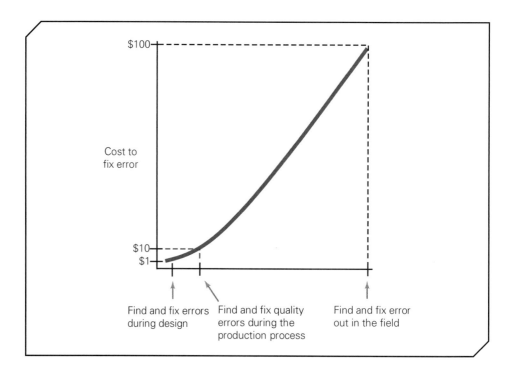

Exhibit 16.1
Economic Implications of the
1:10:100 Rule

This rule is often cited in software development. Errors in software are easy to fix early in the design and development phase. However, if a "programming bug" is not detected until the software reaches system testing, it is much more costly to fix and often results in delays in the launch date of the software. If the bugs are not found until the software is released, the cost can be very high, especially if repairs must be done at the customer's site, as is often the case with software that is embedded in industrial equipment. For commercial software, the damage to customer relationships and the long-term potential loss of future business can be staggering. It is not unusual for the ratio to be more like 1:100:1,000 or 1:1,000:10,000 in these situations.

The actual numbers are irrelevant, and the exact ratios differ among firms and industries. However, the fact is that the cost of repair or service recovery grows dramatically the further that defects and errors move along the value chain. This rule clearly supports the need for control and a focus on prevention by building quality "at the source." **Quality at the source** *means the people responsible for the work control the quality of their processes by identifying and correcting any defects or errors when they first are recognized or occur.* This requires that employees have good data collection, observation, and analysis skills, as well as the proper tools, training, and support of management.

Quality at the source *means the people responsible for the work control the quality of their processes by identifying and correcting any defects or errors when they first are recognized or occur.*

Quality Control Practices in Manufacturing

In manufacturing, control is generally applied at three key points in the supply chain: at the receiving stage from suppliers, during various production processes, and at the finished goods stage.

Incoming Control and Acceptance Sampling If incoming materials are of poor quality, then the final manufactured good will certainly be no better. The purpose of receiving control is to ensure conformance to requirements before value-adding operations begin. Historically, the quality of incoming materials has been evaluated by the receiving function through reliance on a technique known as acceptance sampling. **Acceptance sampling** *is the process of making decisions on whether to accept or reject a group of items (formally called a* lot*) purchased from some external supplier based on specified quality characteristics.* Typically, a sample is inspected and the results are compared with acceptance criteria. The acceptance criteria are determined statistically by defining a sampling plan. For example, a sampling plan might be to inspect n items from a production lot and count the number of nonconforming items in the sample. If this number is less than or equal to a statistically determined value c, the lot is accepted; otherwise, it is rejected. Acceptance sampling is relatively inexpensive and particularly well suited to destructive testing situations. It takes less time than complete inspection. It also requires less handling, which decreases the chance of damage. As with any sampling procedure, however, there is the risk of making an incorrect decision. That is, based on a sample of the items in a lot, a lot of poor quality might be accepted or a lot of good quality might be rejected. *The probability of rejecting a lot of good quality is commonly referred to as the* producer's risk*. The probability of accepting a lot of poor quality is called the* consumer's risk.

Although many companies still practice it, acceptance sampling has lost favor as an inspection practice because it is based on detection and not prevention. The burden of supplying high-quality product should rest with the suppliers themselves. Occasional inspection might be used to audit compliance, but suppliers should be expected to provide documentation and statistical evidence that they are meeting required specifications. If supplier documentation is done properly, incoming inspection can be completely eliminated. Acceptance sampling is also flawed from a statistical point of view. If a supplier maintains effective control over the process to keep variation stable over time, then the conclusion that a particular lot is unacceptable results only from statistical sampling error, not because the quality is any different from that of the other lots.

In-Process Control In-process quality control systems are needed to ensure that defective outputs do not leave the process and, more importantly, to prevent them in the first place. In designing in-process quality control systems, three key issues should be considered: *what to control, where to control,* and *how much data to gather.* Many organizations fall into the trap of trying to control every possible product or process characteristic. This can be a wasteful practice. Instead, experts suggest that the characteristics measured and controlled should be closely related to cost or key customer requirements, be easy to gather, and provide useful information to help the organization improve. The decision of where to control is fundamentally an economic one. An organization must consider trade-offs between the explicit costs of detection, repair, or replacement and the implicit costs of allowing a nonconformity to continue through the production process. These costs are sometimes difficult or even impossible to quantify. As a result, the decision is often made judgmentally. For example, a firm might choose to inspect work before relatively high-cost operations or where significant value is added to the product; before processing operations that may make detection of defectives difficult or costly, such as operations that may mask or obscure faulty attributes—for example, painting; or after operations that are likely to generate a high proportion of defectives.

The final question is whether to inspect nothing, everything, or just a sample. Unless a manufactured good requires destructive testing (in which case, sampling is necessary) or faces critical safety concerns (in which case, complete inspection is warranted or regulated by law), the best choice can be addressed economically. In fact, on a strict economic basis, the choice is to have either no inspection or complete inspection; a model for this was presented in Chapter 15.

Finished Goods Control Finished goods control is often focused on verifying that the product meets customer requirements. For many consumer products, this consists

Acceptance sampling is the process of making decisions on whether to accept or reject a group of items (formally called a lot*) purchased from some external supplier based on specified quality characteristics.*

The probability of rejecting a lot of good quality is commonly referred to as the producer's risk.

The probability of accepting a lot of poor quality is called the consumer's risk.

of functional testing. For instance, a manufacturer of televisions might do a simple test on every unit to make sure it operates properly. However, the company might not test every aspect of the television, such as picture sharpness or other characteristics. These aspects might already have been evaluated through in-process controls. Modern technology now allows for such tests to be conducted rapidly and cost-effectively. For example, imaging scanners along food packaging lines easily check for foreign particles.

Quality Control Practices in Services

Many of the same practices described in the previous section can be applied to quality control for back-office service operations such as check or medical insurance claim processing. However, one of the key differences between goods and services cited in Chapter 1 was "customers participate in many service processes, activities, and transactions." Customers introduce more uncertainty into service processes than in goods-producing processes. Therefore, front-office services that involve substantial customer contact must be controlled differently (see the OM Spotlight on The Ritz-Carlton). The day-to-day execution of thousands of service encounters is a challenge for any service-providing organization.

One way to control quality in services is to prevent sources of errors and mistakes in the first place by using the poka-yoke approaches described in Chapter 15. Another way is to hire and train service providers in service management skills as part of a prevention-based approach to quality control. The GAP model, also introduced in the previous chapter, can provide a framework for quality control by focusing on the key areas—the gaps—that service organizations must constantly strive to reduce.

Customer satisfaction measurement can provide the basis for effective control systems in services. Customer satisfaction instruments often focus on service attributes such as attitude, lead time, on-time delivery, exception handling, accountability, and technical support; image attributes such as reliability and price; and overall satisfaction measures. At FedEx, customers are asked to rate everything from billing to the performance of couriers, package condition, tracking and tracing capabilities, complaint handling, and helpfulness of employees. Xerox sends specific surveys to buyers, managers, and users. Buyers provide feedback on their perceptions of the sales processes, managers provide input on billing and other administrative processes, and users provide feedback on product performance and technical support. Customer satisfaction measurement should not be confined to external customers. Information from internal customers also contributes to the assessment of the organization's strengths and weaknesses. Often, the problems that cause employee dissatisfaction are the same issues that cause dissatisfaction in external customers. By controlling the appropriate things inside the organization, positive results can be achieved outside the organization. As J. W. Marriott once said, "Happy employees make happy customers."

The types of questions to ask in a satisfaction survey must be properly worded to achieve **actionable** results. **Actionable** *means that responses are tied directly to key business processes, so that what needs to be corrected or improved is clear and information can be translated into cost/revenue implications to support good management decisions.* One example of a simple satisfaction survey for Hilton Hotels is shown in Exhibit 16.2. The survey asks direct and detailed questions about the guest bathroom, including such potential dissatisfiers as shower water pressure and temperature and bathtub/sink drainage, and likelihood of future recommendation and also has space for open-ended comments.

Satisfaction surveys create a lot of data. Most service firms simply track trends and usually have standards for determining when low scores, such as those below 4.0 on a 5.0 ordinal scale, should be investigated and corrective action taken. In-

Actionable *means that responses are tied directly to key business processes, so that what needs to be corrected or improved is clear and information can be translated into cost/revenue implications to support good management decisions.*

Exhibit 16.2
Hilton Hotel Guest Survey

Completely fill in your response	● Correct	**GUEST**Scope

Please rate your satisfaction with the comfort level of your accommodations.

Hilton

Level of Satisfaction

	Low		Avg.		High	N/A
	1 2	3	4 5	6 7		

Accommodations look and smell clean and fresh: ☐ ☐ ☐ ☐ ☐ ☐ ☐   ☐
Clean and comfortable linens: ☐ ☐ ☐ ☐ ☐ ☐ ☐   ☐
Comfort level of pillow: ☐ ☐ ☐ ☐ ☐ ☐ ☐   ☐
Comfort level of mattress: ☐ ☐ ☐ ☐ ☐ ☐ ☐   ☐
Easily regulated room temperature: ☐ ☐ ☐ ☐ ☐ ☐ ☐   ☐
Housekeeping during stay: ☐ ☐ ☐ ☐ ☐ ☐ ☐   ☐
Overall satisfaction with this Hilton: ☐ ☐ ☐ ☐ ☐ ☐ ☐
Likelihood you would recommend Hilton: ☐ ☐ ☐ ☐ ☐ ☐ ☐
Likelihood, **if returning to the area**, you would
    return to this Hilton: ☐ ☐ ☐ ☐ ☐ ☐ ☐
Value of accommodations for price paid: ☐ ☐ ☐ ☐ ☐ ☐ ☐

Primary purpose of visit? ☐ Individual business ☐ Convention/Meeting ☐ Pleasure
How many times have you been a guest at this Hilton? ☐ 1 ☐ 2 ☐ 3 ☐ 4 ☐ 5+
Did you have a hotel product or service problem during your stay? ☐ Yes ☐ No
If yes—did you report it to the staff?   ☐ Yes ☐ No
If yes—was it resolved to your satisfaction? ☐ Yes ☐ No
If yes—what was the nature of the problem? _____

Please share any thoughts on any other aspects of your visit, including the names of
any staff members who made your stay more enjoyable: _____
_____
_____
_____

Name: _____ Daytime Phone: _____

Date of Stay: _____   Room: _____
PLEASE DO NOT WRITE BELOW THIS LINE FD2

Source: Reprinted with permission of UniFocus, LP. © 2000 UniFocus.

dividual comments are often reviewed by customer service representatives or by general management. Survey results are often used in performance reviews, so managers have incentives to ensure that customers are satisfied.

Many companies have integrated customer feedback into their continuous improvement activities and in redesigning goods and services. For example, Skilled Care Pharmacy, located in Mason, Ohio, is a $25-million, privately held, regional provider of pharmaceutical products delivered within the long-term care, assisted-living, hospice, and group home environments. Skilled Care developed a Customer Grade Card, benchmarked from Baldrige winner Wainwright Industries, to measure customer satisfaction and provide a simple control mechanism. The Grade Card uses the school-like A-B-C-D scoring system shown in Exhibit 16.3. The scores from the four questions covering Quality, Responsiveness, Delivery, and Communication are converted from letters to numbers and averaged. Any questions that were graded C or below generate an immediate phone call and/or personal visit to the facility by the Customer Care Team to investigate and resolve the issue. An example of how the feedback was used for improvement revolved around low scores received for "Delivery." Management determined there was potential risk for losing valuable customers. Upon investigation, it became evident that the issue was not timely

Exhibit 16.3
Skilled Care's Customer Grade
Card Scoring System

A = Customer Totally Satisfied		100 points
B = Customer Generally Satisfied		90 points
C = Customer Generally Dissatisfied		50 points
D = Customer Totally Dissatisfied		0 points

delivery, but the system of cutoff times for ordering medications for same-day delivery. If the customer missed the cutoff time, it did not receive the order until the next day; therefore, Skilled Care was considered to be "late." The response to this customer need was to extend pharmacy ordering hours and aggressively modify staff schedules for the order processing and pharmacy departments. In turn, it was able to offer an additional 5 hours for customers to phone or fax medication orders for receipt the same day. As a result, satisfaction scores for "Delivery" rose dramatically.

OM SPOTLIGHT

The Ritz-Carlton Hotel Company

The approach used by the Ritz-Carlton Hotel Company to control quality is proactive because of its intensive personalized service environment.[5] Systems for collecting and using quality-related measures are widely deployed and used extensively throughout the organization. For example, each hotel tracks a set of Service Quality Indicators on a daily basis. The Ritz-Carlton recognizes that many customer requirements are sensory (see the idea of a servicescape in Chapter 5) and, thus, difficult to measure. However, by selecting, training, and certifying employees in their knowledge of the Ritz-Carlton Gold Standards of service, they are able to assess their work through appropriate sensory measurements—taste, sight, smell, sound, and touch—and take appropriate actions.

The company uses three types of control processes to deliver quality:

1. Self-control of the individual employee based on their spontaneous and learned behavior.
2. Basic control mechanism, which is carried out by every member of the work force. The first person who detects a problem is empowered to break away from routine duties, investigate and correct the problem immediately, document the incident, and then return to their routine.
3. Critical success factor control for critical processes. Process teams use customer and organizational requirement measurements to determine quality, speed, and cost performance. These measurements are compared

against benchmarks and customer satisfaction data to determine corrective action and resource allocation.

In addition, the Ritz-Carlton conducts both self- and outside audits. Self-audits are carried out internally at all levels, from one individual or function to an entire hotel. Process walk-throughs occur daily in hotels; senior leaders assess field operations during formal reviews at various intervals. Outside audits are performed by independent travel and hospitality rating organizations. All audits must be documented, and any findings must be submitted to the senior leader of the unit being audited. They are responsible for action and for assessing the implementation and effectiveness of recommended corrective actions.

FOUNDATIONS OF STATISTICAL PROCESS CONTROL

Statistical process control (SPC) *is a methodology for monitoring quality of manufacturing and service delivery processes to help identify and eliminate unwanted causes of variation.* The outputs of any goods- or service-producing process have some variation. Variation occurs for many reasons, such as inconsistencies in material inputs; changes in environmental conditions (temperature, humidity); machine maintenance cycles; tool wear; and human fatigue. Some variation is obvious, such as inconsistencies in meal delivery times or food quantity at a restaurant; other variation—such as minute differences in physical dimensions of machined parts—is barely perceptible, but can be determined through some type of measurement process. Understanding variation and choosing the right metrics to monitor a process are vital prerequisites for implementing statistical process control systems.

Understanding Variation

Walter Shewhart is credited with recognizing the distinction between two principal types of variation at Bell Laboratories in the 1920s. **Common cause variation** *is the result of complex interactions of variations in materials, tools, machines, information, workers, and the environment.* Such variation is a natural part of the technology and process design and cannot be controlled; that is, we cannot influence each individual output of the process. It appears at random, and individual sources or causes cannot be identified or explained. However, their combined effect is usually stable and can be described statistically. For example, if you would measure and record the times it takes to cook and deliver a customer's meal at a restaurant on a typical Saturday night, you would observe some statistical variation, which would be due to the random mix and sequence of orders in the kitchen, variations in the preparation and cooking times, and variation in waiting for servers to pick the meals up.

Common causes of variation generally account for about 80 to 95 percent of the observed variation in a process. It can be reduced only if better technology, process design, or training is provided. This clearly is the responsibility of management. One of the goals of the Six Sigma approaches that we discussed in the previous chapter is to try to identify significant sources of common cause variation and reduce it through improvements in the design of processes and application of technology. Statistical analysis techniques, such as Design of Experiments that you might have encountered in other courses, help to isolate individual sources of variation so they can be improved.

Special (or assignable) cause variation *arises from external sources that are not inherent in the process, appear sporadically, and disrupt the random pattern of common causes.* Special cause variation occurs sporadically and can be prevented or at least explained and understood. For example, a tool might break during a process step, a worker might be distracted by a colleague, or a bus load of tourists stops at a restaurant (resulting in unusual wait times). Special cause variation tends to be easily detectable using statistical methods because they disrupt the normal pattern of measurements. When special causes are identified, short-term corrective action generally should be taken by those who own the process and are responsible for doing the work, such as machine operators, order-fulfillment workers, and so on.

A system governed only by common causes is called a **stable system.** Understanding a stable system and the differences between special and common causes of variation is essential for managing any system. If we don't understand the variation in a system, we cannot predict its future performance. For example, suppose that under normal circumstances, the lead time to produce and deliver a customer's

Learning Objective
To understand variation in manufacturing and service processes, metrics for quantifying variation, and the role of control charts and statistical process control methods in helping managers control variation.

Statistical process control (SPC) *is a methodology for monitoring quality of manufacturing and service delivery processes to help identify and eliminate unwanted causes of variation.*

Common cause variation *is the result of complex interactions of variations in materials, tools, machines, information, workers, and the environment.*

Special (or assignable) cause variation *arises from external sources that are not inherent in the process, appear sporadically, and disrupt the random pattern of common causes.*

A system governed only by common causes is called a **stable system.**

order is between 20 and 25 days. If the system is stable, salespeople can promise delivery to customers within this time frame. However, if special causes that are not controlled cause the range of the lead times to sometimes increase from 15 to 30 days, or jump to an average of 30–35 days with no predictability, salespeople will not be able to provide any assurance to their customers about delivery. This might result in disruptions of normal work schedules, unnecessary outsourcing costs, or customer complaints.

Keeping special cause variation from occurring is the essence of quality control. *If no special causes affect the output of a process, we say that the process is* **in control***; when special causes are present, the process is said to be* **out of control***.* A process that is in control does not need any changes or adjustments; an out-of-control process needs correction. However, employees often make two basic mistakes when attempting to control a process:

1. adjusting a process that is already in control, or
2. failing to correct a process that is out of control.

While it is clear that a truly out-of-control process must be corrected, many workers mistakenly believe that whenever process output is off-target, some adjustment must be made. Actually, overadjusting a process that is in control will *increase* the variation in the output. Thus, employees must know when to leave a process alone to keep variation at a minimum.

In Chapter 2 we introduced many of the basic metrics that are used to measure and evaluate quality, including nonconformities per unit, defects per million opportunities (dpmo), and service errors per million opportunities (epmo). Operations managers use such metrics as a basis for quality control. Methods for measuring such quality characteristics may be automated or performed manually by the work force. One of the most popular approaches to quality control is the use of statistical process control, which we describe later in this chapter.

Quality Control Metrics and Measurement

Controlling a process begins with understanding how a process works: what materials, equipment, information, people, and other resources are needed; what steps and activities occur during the process; who makes decisions at various stages in the process and what information is needed to make those decisions; and if things go wrong, what needs to be done to correct them.

Data for process control generally come from some type of measurement or inspection process. The true purpose of inspection is to provide information to control and improve the process effectively. Thus, inspection activities must be integrated throughout the production process, usually at the receipt of incoming materials, during the manufacturing process, and upon completion of production, to provide useful information for daily control as well as for long-term improvement.

Quality control metrics and indicators can be either discrete or continuous. *A* **discrete metric** *is one that is calculated from data that are counted.* In quality control, discrete measurements are often called *attributes data*. Visual inspection and observation is often used to gather such data. For example, we might observe whether a quality characteristic is either present or absent in the product or service under consideration. A dimension on a machined part is either within tolerance or out of tolerance, an order is either complete or incomplete, or a service experience is either good or bad. We can count the number of parts within tolerance, the number of complete orders, or the number of good service experiences. The number of acceptable outcomes is an example of a discrete metric. Usually, we divide this by the total number to obtain the fraction or percentage of parts, orders, or service experiences that are acceptable. This is a more common discrete metric used in quality control. In other cases, the entity that we are analyzing can have multiple

If no special causes affect the output of a process, we say that the process is **in control***; when special causes are present, the process is said to be* **out of control***.*

A **discrete metric** *is one that is calculated from data that are counted.*

defects or errors. For instance, an order might be missing one or more items. If we only look at whether the order is good or bad, we have no information on whether a bad order has only one missing item or many. If we count the number of defects or errors for each order and compute the average number of errors per order, we have a more relevant metric. Another common example of a discrete metric that many organizations use is the number of complaints per customer or per time period (see OM Spotlight: Bad Service Is Remembered). An obvious approach to address this is to count the frequency and type of complaints, identify those that occur the most, and take action.

A **continuous metric** *is one that is calculated from data that are measured as the degree of conformance to a specification on some continuous scale of measurement.* In quality control, continuous measurements are often called *variables data*. Examples are length, weight, and time. Thus, rather than determining whether the diameter of a shaft is just in or out of tolerance, we might measure the actual value of the diameter. Customer waiting time, order lead time, and the weight of cereal in a box are other examples. Continuous metrics are generally summarized with such statistics as averages and standard deviations.

A continuous metric is one that is calculated from data that are measured as the degree of conformance to a specification on some continuous scale of measurement.

It is important to understand that collecting discrete data is usually easier than collecting continuous data since the assessment can usually be done more quickly by a simple inspection and count, whereas continuous metrics require the use of some type of measuring instrument. In a statistical sense, however, discrete data provide less information than continuous data and require a larger sample size to obtain the same amount of statistical information about the quality of what is measured. This difference can become significant when inspection of each item is time-consuming or expensive.

Service Quality Metrics and Measurement

One of the challenges of developing effective quality management systems for services is measurement. Most quality metrics in "back office" service environments revolve around goods and information. These are well defined and relatively easy to measure. Examples in services include time (waiting time, service time, delivery time) and number of nonconformances. Insurance companies, for example, measure the time to complete different transactions such as new issues, claim payments, and cash surrenders. Hospitals measure the percentage of nosocomial infections and

OM SPOTLIGHT

Bad Service Is Remembered[6]

The American Customer Satisfaction Index rated automobile service the highest followed by gas stations, supermarkets, retail stores, hotels, motion pictures, computer stores, banking, restaurants, telecommunications, utilities, hospitals, newspapers, and airlines. As we drop down this list, we find organizations for which many customers have had bad experiences. For example, the Public Utilities Commission of Ohio found that "rude customer-service representatives" and "automated answering systems" that block callers from getting through to a real person are two of the top ten customer complaints. High prices, billing errors, missed installation and repair appointments, service outages, broken promises by service providers, waiting for service, and weather-related service upsets are the other top ten customer complaint categories. Gas, electric, telephone, and water utilities were the focus of the study. "Customers don't forgive and forget; bad service is remembered," said one Ohio consultant on customer service.

the percentage of unplanned readmissions to the emergency room, intensive care, or operating room within, say, 48 hours. Other quality characteristics are observable. These include the types of errors (wrong kind, wrong quantity, wrong delivery date, and so on). Hospitals might monitor the completeness of medical charts and the quality of radiology readings, measured by a double-reading process.

In services with high customer contact, many key quality measures are perceptual; that is, they measure customer perceptions of the quality of service. Employee courtesy, promptness, competency, behavior, treatment of the customer, ability to solve a customer's problem, and so on are some common examples. Even though human behavior can be observed, the task of describing and classifying the observations is far more difficult. Individual customers may perceive actual performance differently and be influenced by many factors unrelated to the actual performance of the service. Thus, the major obstacle is developing operational definitions of service provider and customer behavioral characteristics. The focus of this interaction is the service encounter. For example, how does one define courteous versus discourteous, empathy versus anger toward the customer or understanding versus indifferent? Defining such distinctions is best done by comparing behavior against understandable standards. For instance, a standard for "courtesy" might be to address the customer as "Mr." or "Ms." Failure to do so is an instance of an error. "Promptness" might be defined as greeting a customer within 5 seconds of entering the store or answering letters within 2 days of receipt. These behaviors can easily be recorded and counted. As described in Chapter 5 on service guarantees, "script dialogues" help to standardize service provider responses to certain service encounter situations.

Another issue with service quality metrics is whether to use customer perception-based or internal process-based measures. It is not uncommon to find that customer perceptions do not agree with actual operational measures. For example, customers might perceive their waiting time to be 4 or 5 minutes (and state their dissatisfaction) when the true waiting time might only be a minute and a half. This might result from prior expectations. The GAP model described in Chapter 15 can help uncover such discrepancies between customer expectations and perceptions after service. Nevertheless, perceived wait time is the "real" wait time, and management must identify ways to change perceptions, for example, by using advertising to set proper expectations, engaging customers in other activities to distract perceptions of long waits, and designing the facility so the entire waiting line is not apparent.

An established instrument for measuring the external customer perceptions of service quality is SERVQUAL.[7] The initial instrument identified ten dimensions of service quality performance: (1) reliability, (2) responsiveness, (3) competence, (4) access, (5) courtesy, (6) communication, (7) credibility, (8) security, (9) understanding/knowing the customer, and (10) tangibles. These were reduced to five dimensions based on further research: tangibles, reliability, responsiveness, assurance, and empathy. Assurance consolidated competence, courtesy, credibility, and security attributes, and is defined as the "knowledge and courtesy of service providers and their ability to convey trust and confidence." Empathy is defined as "caring, individual attention the firm provides its customers" and incorporates the attributes of access, communication, and understanding the customer. SERVQUAL is designed to apply to all service industries; however, measures specific to a certain industry or business or process may provide more accurate measures.

Internal measurements of service quality are commonly collected using some type of data sheet or checklist. Time is easily measured by taking two observations: starting time and finishing time. Many observed data assume only "yes" or "no" values. For example, a survey of pharmaceutical operations in a hospital might include the following questions:

- Are drug storage and preparation areas within the pharmacy under the supervision of a pharmacist?
- Are drugs requiring special storage conditions properly stored?

- Is patient, staff, and doctor interaction handled in a professional and friendly manner?
- Are drug emergency boxes inspected on a monthly basis?
- Is the drug emergency box record book filled out completely?

Simple checksheets can be designed to record the types of errors that occur.

Exhibit 16.4 shows some examples of many types of quality metrics used in service organizations.

Control Charts

SPC uses control charts—graphical tools that indicate when a process is in control or out of control—to measure quality. *A control chart is simply a run chart to which two horizontal lines, called control limits, are added: the upper control limit (UCL) and lower control limit (LCL).* The general structure is illustrated in Exhibit 16.5. Control limits are chosen statistically to provide a high probability (generally greater than .99) that points will fall between these limits if the process is in control. Control limits make it easier to interpret patterns in a run chart and draw conclusions about the state of control. If sample values fall outside the control limits or if nonrandom patterns occur in the chart, then special causes may be affecting the process; the process is not stable. Thus, a control chart provides a statistical basis for concluding when special causes occur in a process.

If evaluation and correction are done in real time, then the chance of producing nonconforming output is minimized. Thus, as a problem-solving tool, control charts allow employees to identify quality problems as they occur. Of course, control charts alone cannot determine the source of the problem. This requires knowledge and creativity on the part of the workers to diagnose the process and identify the root cause (see OM Spotlight: Dow Chemical Company).

A control chart is simply a run chart to which two horizontal lines, called control limits, are added: the upper control limit (UCL) and lower control limit (LCL).

Organization	Quality Measure
Hospital	Lab test accuracy Insurance claim accuracy On-time delivery of meals and medication Patient satisfaction
Bank	Check-processing accuracy Time to process loan requests
Insurance company	Claims-processing response time Billing accuracy
Post Office	Sorting accuracy Time of delivery Percentage of express mail delivered on time
Ambulance	Response time
Police Department	Incidence of crime in a precinct Number of traffic citations Empathy and respect toward crime victims
Hotel	Proportion of rooms satisfactorily cleaned Checkout time Number of complaints received
Transportation	Proportion of freight cars correctly routed Dollar amount of damage per claim
Auto service	Percentage of time work completed as promised Number of parts out of stock Politeness of service advisor

Exhibit 16.4

Examples of Service Quality Metrics

Exhibit 16.5
Structure of a Control Chart

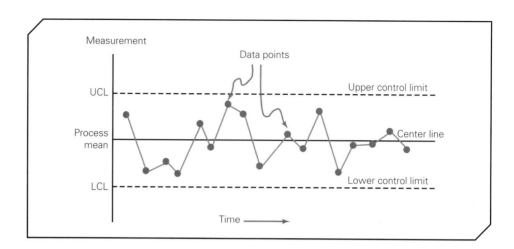

OM SPOTLIGHT

Dow Chemical Company[8]

The magnesium department of the Dow Chemical Company plant in Freeport, Texas, has produced magnesium, a silvery light metal, for nearly a century. It was the first major group in Texas Operations to train all of its technical people and managers in the use of statistical quality control (SQC) techniques, following the example set by the automobile industry.

Some of the earliest successful applications of SQC were in chemical-process areas. Exhibit 16.6 shows the improvement in the dryer analysis after SQC and retraining were implemented. In addition to the fact that the process control required significant improvement, differences between operators existed. The dark circles in Exhibit 16.6 represent one operator in question; the open circles represent the other operators. On examination, it was found that the operator had not been properly trained in the use of SQC, even though the operator had been performing the analysis for 2 years. There was immediate improvement in the consistency of the operators' analyses after retraining.

The use of control charts in the control room made the operators realize that their attempts to fine-tune the process introduced a great deal of unwanted variation. The before-and-after range charts (R-charts) show the improvement; see Exhibit 16.7.

As with many chemical and manufacturing operations, when the variability of the feedstock to one operation is reduced, it is possible to reduce the variability of the basic operation. With tighter control over the concentration of magnesium hydroxide from the filter plant, Dow was able to exert much tighter control on the subsequent neutralization operation. As seen in Exhibit 16.8, the differences are substantial. The upper control limit (UCL) on the second range chart is about where the center line is on the first. A similar situation exists on the $\bar{x}$-charts. These improve-

ments resulted without any additional instrumentation or operators.

Another application involved the casting operation. On primary magnesium, for example, Dow calculated a process-capability index—the ratio of the specified tolerance to the six-sigma natural variation—of meeting minimum magnesium content of 99.8 percent purity and found it to be over 10, based on more than 10,000 samples. Thus, there had been little incentive to use control charts in this operation because of the comfortable level of compliance. However, ingots are also graded according to their surface quality. Using control charts, Dow found that although the process was in control, the number of rejects was much higher than desired. After several months of analysis and modifications, the process was improved.

Dow has had success everywhere it has used SQC in the magnesium process. Savings of several hundred thousand dollars per year have been realized, and new applications are continually being discovered.

PR Newswire DOW CHEMICAL USA

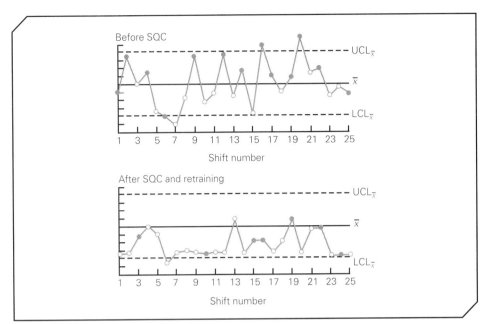

Exhibit 16.6
Before-and-After $\bar{x}$-Charts on Dryer Analysis

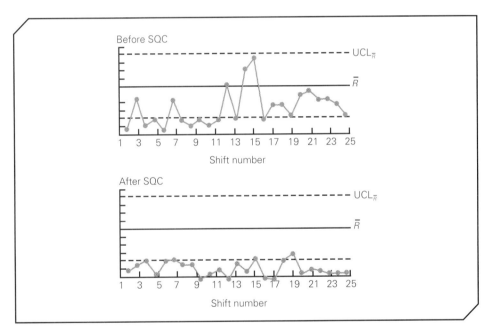

Exhibit 16.7
Before-and-After R-Charts on Dryer Analysis

The benefits of using control charts can be summarized as follows:

- Control charts are simple, effective tools for achieving statistical control. They can be maintained at the workstation by the employee who runs a machine or process, thus giving the people closest to the operation reliable information on when action should be taken and when it should not.
- When a process is in statistical control, its performance to specification is predictable. Both producer and customer can rely on consistent quality levels, and both can rely on stable costs for achieving that quality level.
- After a process is in statistical control, management can attack the systemic causes of variation in an effort to reduce it, by, for instance, improving technology or employee training.
- Control charts provide a common language for communication between the people on different shifts operating a process; between line production (operator,

Exhibit 16.8 $\bar{x}$- and R-Charts on Neutralizer Excess Alkalinity Before and After SQC

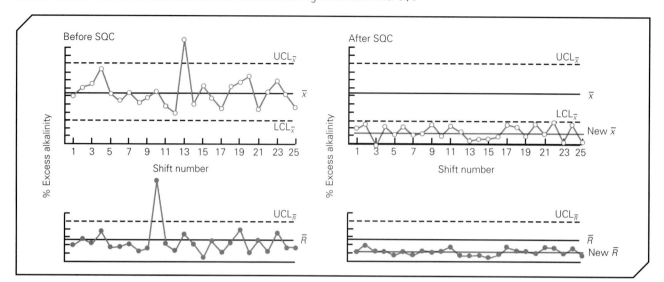

supervisor) and support activities (maintenance, material control, process engineering, quality control); between different stations in the process; between supplier and user; and between the manufacturing/assembly plant and the design-engineering activity.

By distinguishing special from common causes of variation, control charts give a good indication of whether problems are correctable locally or require management action. This minimizes the confusion, frustration, and cost of misdirected problem-solving efforts.

SPC Methodology

Control charts are relatively simple to use. The following is a summary of the steps required to develop and use control charts. Steps 1 through 4 focus on setting up an initial chart; in step 5, the charts are used for ongoing monitoring; and finally, in step 6, the data are used for process capability analysis.

1. Preparation
   a. Choose the metric to be monitored.
   b. Determine the basis, size, and frequency of sampling.
   c. Set up the control chart.
2. Data collection
   a. Record the data.
   b. Calculate relevant statistics: averages, ranges, proportions, and so on.
   c. Plot the statistics on the chart.
3. Determination of trial control limits
   a. Draw the center line (process average) on the chart.
   b. Compute the upper and lower control limits.
4. Analysis and interpretation
   a. Investigate the chart for lack of control.
   b. Eliminate out-of-control points.
   c. Recompute control limits if necessary.
5. Use as a problem-solving tool
   a. Continue data collection and plotting.
   b. Identify out-of-control situations and take corrective action.
6. Determination of process capability using the control chart data

CONSTRUCTING CONTROL CHARTS

Many different types of control charts exist. All are similar in structure, but the specific formulas used to compute control limits for them differ. Moreover, different types of charts are used for different types of metrics. Continuous data usually require $\bar{x}$-("x-bar") and R-charts. Discrete data usually require p-, c-, or u-charts.

Constructing $\bar{x}$- and R-Charts

The first step in developing $\bar{x}$- and R-charts is to gather data. Usually, about 25 to 30 samples are collected. Samples between size 3 and 10 are generally used, with 5 being the most common. The number of samples is indicated by k, and n denotes the sample size. For each sample i, the mean (denoted $\bar{x}_i$) and the range (R_i) are computed. These values are then plotted on their respective control charts. Next, the *overall mean* and *average range* calculations are made. These values specify the center lines for the $\bar{x}$- and R-charts, respectively. The overall mean (denoted $\bar{\bar{x}}$) is the average of the sample means $\bar{x}_i$:

$$\bar{\bar{x}} = \frac{\sum_{i=1}^{k} \bar{x}_i}{k} \tag{16.1}$$

The average range ($\bar{R}$) is similarly computed, using the formula

$$\bar{R} = \frac{\sum_{i=1}^{k} R_i}{k} \tag{16.2}$$

The average range and average mean are used to compute upper and lower control limits (UCL and LCL) for the R- and $\bar{x}$-charts. Control limits are easily calculated using the following formulas:

$$\begin{aligned} \text{UCL}_R &= D_4\bar{R} & \text{UCL}_{\bar{x}} &= \bar{\bar{x}} + A_2\bar{R} \\ \text{LCL}_R &= D_3\bar{R} & \text{LCL}_{\bar{x}} &= \bar{\bar{x}} - A_2\bar{R} \end{aligned} \tag{16.3}$$

where the constants D_3, D_4, and A_2 depend on the sample size (see Appendix B).

The control limits represent the range between which all points are expected to fall if the process is in statistical control. If any points fall outside the control limits or if any unusual patterns are observed, then some special cause has probably affected the process. The process should be studied to determine the cause. If special causes are present, then they are *not* representative of the true state of statistical control, and the calculations of the center line and control limits will be biased. The corresponding data points should be eliminated, and new values for $\bar{\bar{x}}$, $\bar{R}$, and the control limits should be computed.

In determining whether a process is in statistical control, the R-chart is always analyzed first. Because the control limits in the $\bar{x}$-chart depend on the average range, special causes in the R-chart may produce unusual patterns in the $\bar{x}$-chart, even when the centering of the process is in control. (An example of such distorted patterns is given later in this chapter.) Once statistical control is established for the R-chart, attention may turn to the $\bar{x}$-chart.

An Example of an $\bar{x}$-Chart and R-Chart

The Goodman Tire and Rubber Company periodically tests its tires for tread wear under simulated road conditions. To study and control its manufacturing processes, the company uses $\bar{x}$- and R-charts. Twenty samples, each containing three radial tires, were chosen from different shifts over several days of operation. Exhibit 16.9 is a spreadsheet that provides the data, sample averages and ranges, and control limits. Since $n = 3$, the control limit factors for the R-chart are $D_3 = 0$ and $D_4 = 2.57$. The control limits as computed in the spreadsheet are

$$\text{UCL} = D_4\overline{R} = 2.57(10.8) = 27.8$$
$$\text{LCL} = D_3\overline{R} = 0$$

For the $\overline{x}$-chart, $A_2 = 1.02$; thus the control limits are

$$\text{UCL} = 31.88 + 1.02(10.8) = 42.9$$
$$\text{LCL} = 31.88 - 1.02(10.8) = 20.8$$

The R- and $\overline{x}$-charts for the sample data, charted with Microsoft Excel (the Excel templates are included on the Student CD-ROM), are shown in Exhibits 16.10 and 16.11, respectively.

Interpreting Patterns in Control Charts

The location of points and the patterns of points in a control chart enable one to determine, with only a small chance of error, whether or not a process is in statistical control. A process is in control when the control chart has the following characteristics:

1. No points are outside control limits.
2. The number of points above and below the center line is about the same.
3. The points seem to fall randomly above and below the center line.
4. Most points, but not all, are near the center line, and only a few are close to the control limits.

You can see that these characteristics are evident in the R-chart in Exhibit 16.10. Therefore we would conclude that the R-chart is in control.

These characteristics stem from the assumption that the distribution of sample means, which we plot on the chart, is normal (see Exhibit 16.12). You may recall from statistics that the sampling distribution of the mean is approximately normal regardless of the original distribution. The formulas used for the upper and lower

Exhibit 16.9 Excel Template for $\overline{x}$- and R-Charts

	1	2	3	4	5	6	7	8	9	10	11	12	13	14	15	16	17	18	19	20	21	22	23	24	25	26	27	28	29	30
DATA 1	31	26	25	17	38	41	21	32	41	29	26	23	17	37	18	30	28	40	18	22	36	29	40	34	31	41	36	35	38	42
2	42	18	30	25	29	42	17	26	34	17	31	19	24	35	25	42	36	29	29	34	22	37	35	44	37	45	41	49	45	44
3	28	35	34	21	35	36	29	28	33	30	40	25	32	17	29	31	32	31	28	26	26	31	46	42	39	34	34	40	40	32
Average	33.67	26.33	29.67	21	34	39.67	22.33	28.67	36	25.33	32.33	22.33	24.33	29.67	24	34.33	32	33.33	25	27.33	28	32.33	40.33	40	35.67	40	37	41.33	41	39.33
LCLx-bar	20.83	20.83	20.83	20.83	20.83	20.83	20.83	20.83	20.83	20.83	20.83	20.83	20.83	20.83	20.83	20.83	20.83	20.83	20.83	20.83	20.83	20.83	20.83	20.83	20.83	20.83	20.83	20.83	20.83	20.83
Center	31.88	31.88	31.88	31.88	31.88	31.88	31.88	31.88	31.88	31.88	31.88	31.88	31.88	31.88	31.88	31.88	31.88	31.88	31.88	31.88	31.88	31.88	31.88	31.88	31.88	31.88	31.88	31.88	31.88	31.88
UCLx-bar	42.93	42.93	42.93	42.93	42.93	42.93	42.93	42.93	42.93	42.93	42.93	42.93	42.93	42.93	42.93	42.93	42.93	42.93	42.93	42.93	42.93	42.93	42.93	42.93	42.93	42.93	42.93	42.93	42.93	42.93
Range	14	17	9	8	9	6	12	6	8	13	14	6	15	20	11	12	8	11	11	12	14	8	11	10	8	11	7	14	7	12
LCLrange	0	0	0	0	0	0	0	0	0	0	0	0	0	0	0	0	0	0	0	0	0	0	0	0	0	0	0	0	0	0
Center	10.8	10.8	10.8	10.8	10.8	10.8	10.8	10.8	10.8	10.8	10.8	10.8	10.8	10.8	10.8	10.8	10.8	10.8	10.8	10.8	10.8	10.8	10.8	10.8	10.8	10.8	10.8	10.8	10.8	10.8
UCLrange	27.8	27.8	27.8	27.8	27.8	27.8	27.8	27.8	27.8	27.8	27.8	27.8	27.8	27.8	27.8	27.8	27.8	27.8	27.8	27.8	27.8	27.8	27.8	27.8	27.8	27.8	27.8	27.8	27.8	27.8

Spreadsheet header information:

X-bar and R-Chart

This spreadsheet is designed for up to 50 samples, each of a constant sample size from 2 to 10. Enter data ONLY in yellow-shaded cells.

Enter the number of samples in cell E6 and the sample size in cell E7. Then enter your data in the grid below.

Click on sheet tabs for a display of the control charts. Specification limits may be entered in cells N7 and N8 for process capability.

Number of samples (<= 50)	30	
Sample size (2 - 10)	3	

		A2	D3	D4	d2
Grand Average	31.877778				
Average Range	10.8	1.02	0	2.57	1.69

Process Capability Calculations		Six sigma	38.28
Upper specification	50	Cp	1.306
Lower specification	0	Cpu	0.947
		Cpl	1.666
		Cpk	0.947

Exhibit 16.10 *R-Chart for Goodman Tire Example*

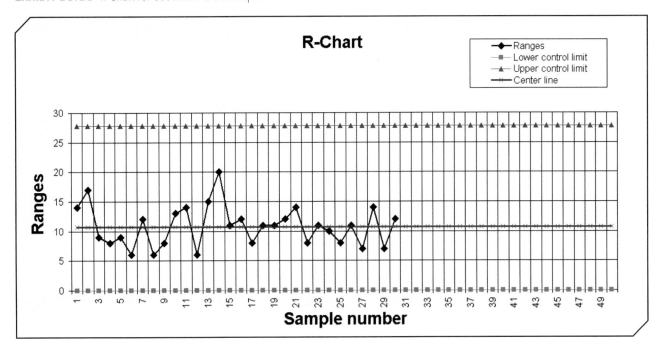

Exhibit 16.11 *x̄-Chart for Goodman Tire Example*

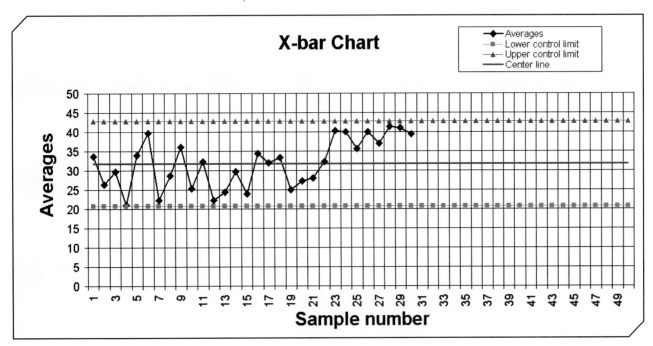

control limits set them to be 3 standard deviations from the overall mean. Thus, it will be highly unlikely that any sample mean will fall outside the control limits. Because the normal distribution is symmetric, about the same number of points should fall above as below the center line. Finally, about 68 percent of a normal distribution falls within 1 standard deviation of the mean; thus, most—but not all—points

Exhibit 16.12 Samples in a Controlled Process from a Normal Distribution

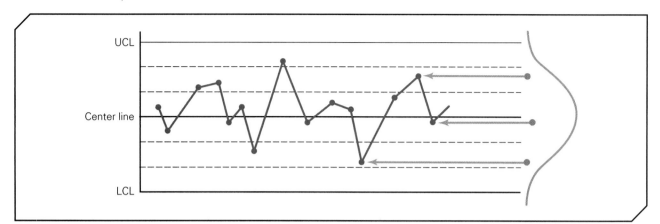

should be close to the center line. These characteristics will hold provided that the mean and variance of the original data have not changed during the time the data were collected; that is, the process is stable.

When a process is out of control, we typically see some unusual characteristics. An obvious indication that a process may be out of control is a point that falls outside the control limits. If such a point is found, you should first check for the possibility that the control limits were miscalculated or that the point was plotted incorrectly. If neither is the case, this can indicate that the process average has changed.

Another indication of an out-of-control situation is a sudden shift in the average. For example, in Exhibit 16.11, we see that the last eight points are all above the center line, suggesting that the process mean has increased. This might suggest that something is causing excessive tread wear in recent samples, perhaps a different batch of raw material or improper mixing of the chemical composition of the tires. Some typical rules that are used to identify a shift include

- 8 points in a row above or below the center line
- 10 of 11 consecutive points above or below the center line
- 12 of 14 consecutive points above or below the center line
- 2 of 3 consecutive points in the outer one-third region between the center line and one of the control limits
- 4 of 5 consecutive points in the outer two-thirds region between the center line and one of the control limits.

Some of these rules are illustrated in Exhibit 16.13. Note that if the average in the range chart shifts *down*, it indicates that the variation has decreased. This is good, and every effort should be made to understand why this occurred and to maintain the improvement.

A third thing to look for in a control chart is an increasing or decreasing trend. As tools wear down, for example, the diameter of a machined part will gradually become larger. Changes in temperature or humidity, general equipment deterioration, dirt buildup on fixtures, or operator fatigue may cause such a trend. About six or seven consecutive points that increase or decrease in value usually signify a gradual change. A wave or cycle pattern is also unusual and should be suspect. It might be a result of seasonal effects of material deliveries, temperature swings, maintenance cycles, or periodic rotation of operators. Whenever an unusual pattern in a control chart is identified, the process should be stopped until the problem has been identified and corrected.

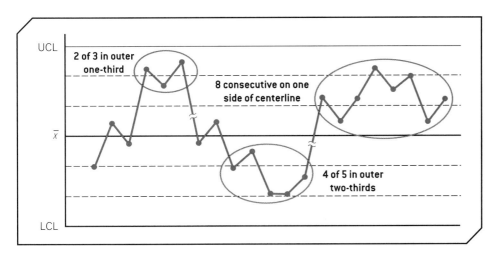

Exhibit 16.13
Illustration of Some Rules for
Identifying Out-of-Control
Conditions

All of these guidelines, which are used extensively in practice, stem from basic statistical principles and probability calculations. Analysts can also conduct formal statistical hypothesis tests, such as a number-of-runs test, to draw inferences about the state of control. More advanced books on SPC provide details of these approaches.

Constructing *p*-Charts

Recall that many quality characteristics assume only two values, such as good or bad, pass or fail, and so on. The proportion of nonconforming items can be monitored using a control chart called a *p-chart*, where *p* is the proportion of nonconforming items found in a sample. Often, it is also called a *fraction nonconforming* or *fraction defective* chart.

As with continuous data, a *p*-chart is constructed by first gathering 25 to 30 samples of the attribute being measured. The size of each sample should be large enough to have several nonconforming items. If the probability of finding a nonconforming item is small, a sample size of 100 or more items is usually necessary. Samples are chosen over time periods so that any special causes that are identified can be investigated.

Let us suppose that k samples, each of size n, are selected. If y represents the number nonconforming in a particular sample, the proportion nonconforming is y/n.

Let p_i be the fraction nonconforming in the ith sample; the average fraction nonconforming for the group of k samples, then, is

$$\bar{p} = \frac{p_1 + p_2 + \cdots + p_k}{k} \qquad \textbf{(16.4)}$$

(Note that this formula applies only when all sample sizes are the same!) This statistic reflects the average performance of the process. One would expect a high percentage of samples to have a fraction nonconforming within 3 standard deviations of $\bar{p}$. An estimate of the standard deviation is given by

$$s_{\bar{p}} = \sqrt{\frac{\bar{p}(1 - \bar{p})}{n}} \qquad \textbf{(16.5)}$$

Therefore, upper and lower control limits are given by

$$\text{UCL}_p = \bar{p} + 3s_{\bar{p}}$$
$$\text{LCL}_p = \bar{p} - 3s_{\bar{p}} \qquad \textbf{(16.6)}$$

If LCL$_p$ is less than zero, a value of zero is used.

Analysis of a p-chart is similar to that of an $\bar{x}$- or R-chart. Points outside the control limits signify an out-of-control situation. Patterns and trends should also be sought to identify special causes. However, a point on a p-chart below the lower control limit or the development of a trend below the center line indicates that the process might have improved, based on an ideal of zero defectives. Caution is advised before such conclusions are drawn, because errors may have been made in computation.

In other words, errors in calculating control limits can lead to conclusions that the process has improved when in fact it has not.

An Example of a p-Chart

The operators of automated sorting machines in a post office must read the ZIP code on letters and divert the letters to the proper carrier routes. Over a month's time, 25 samples of 100 letters were chosen, and the number of errors was recorded. Exhibit 16.14 is a spreadsheet summarizing the data and control chart calculations (available on the Student CD-ROM). The proportion of errors in each sample is simply the number of errors divided by 100. Adding the proportions defective and dividing by 25 yields

$$\bar{p} = \frac{.03 + .01 + \cdots + .01}{25} = .022$$

The standard deviation is computed as

$$s_{\bar{p}} = \sqrt{\frac{0.022(1 - 0.022)}{100}} = .01467$$

Thus UCL = .022 + 3(.01467) = .066, and LCL = .022 − 3(.01467) = −.022. Since the LCL is negative and the actual proportion nonconforming cannot be less than zero, the LCL is set equal to zero. Exhibit 16.15 shows the control chart. Although no values above the UCL or below the LCL were observed in this example, the occurrence of such values might indicate operator fatigue or the need for more experience or training.

Variable Sample Size

Often, 100 percent inspection is performed on process output during fixed sampling periods; however, the number of units produced in each sampling period may vary. In this case, the p-chart would have a variable sample size, and $\bar{p}$ must be computed differently. One way of handling this variation is to compute a standard deviation for each individual sample. Thus, if the number of observations in the ith sample is n_i, control limits are given by

$$\bar{p} \pm 3\sqrt{\frac{\bar{p}(1 - \bar{p})}{n_i}} \tag{16.7}$$

$$\text{where } \bar{p} = \frac{\sum \text{number nonconforming}}{\sum n_i}$$

The data given in Exhibit 16.16 represent 20 samples with varying sample sizes. The value of $\bar{p}$ is computed as

$$\bar{p} = \frac{18 + 20 + 14 + \cdots + 18}{137 + 158 + 92 + \cdots + 160} = \frac{271}{2,980} = .0909$$

Exhibit 16.14 Data and Calculations for *p*-Chart Example

	A	B	C	D	E	F	G	H	I	J	K	L	M
1	**Fraction Nonconforming (p) Chart**												
2	This spreadsheet is designed for up to 50 samples. Enter data ONLY in yellow-shaded cells.												
3	Click on the sheet tab to display the control chart (some rescaling may be needed).												
4													
5	**Average (p-bar)**			0.022									
6	**Avg. sample size**			100									
7										**Approximate Control Limits Using**			
8			**Sample**	**Fraction**	**Standard**					**Average Sample Size Calculations**			
9	**Sample**	**Value**	**Size**	**Nonconforming**	**Deviation**	**LCLp**	**CL**	**UCLp**		**LCLp**	**CL**	**UCLp**	
10	1	3	100	0.0300	0.0146683	0	0.022	0.066		0	0.022	0.066005	
11	2	1	100	0.0100	0.0146683	0	0.022	0.066		0	0.022	0.066005	
12	3	0	100	0.0000	0.0146683	0	0.022	0.066		0	0.022	0.066005	
13	4	0	100	0.0000	0.0146683	0	0.022	0.066		0	0.022	0.066005	
14	5	2	100	0.0200	0.0146683	0	0.022	0.066		0	0.022	0.066005	
15	6	5	100	0.0500	0.0146683	0	0.022	0.066		0	0.022	0.066005	
16	7	3	100	0.0300	0.0146683	0	0.022	0.066		0	0.022	0.066005	
17	8	6	100	0.0600	0.0146683	0	0.022	0.066		0	0.022	0.066005	
18	9	1	100	0.0100	0.0146683	0	0.022	0.066		0	0.022	0.066005	
19	10	4	100	0.0400	0.0146683	0	0.022	0.066		0	0.022	0.066005	
20	11	0	100	0.0000	0.0146683	0	0.022	0.066		0	0.022	0.066005	
21	12	2	100	0.0200	0.0146683	0	0.022	0.066		0	0.022	0.066005	
22	13	1	100	0.0100	0.0146683	0	0.022	0.066		0	0.022	0.066005	
23	14	3	100	0.0300	0.0146683	0	0.022	0.066		0	0.022	0.066005	
24	15	4	100	0.0400	0.0146683	0	0.022	0.066		0	0.022	0.066005	
25	16	1	100	0.0100	0.0146683	0	0.022	0.066		0	0.022	0.066005	
26	17	1	100	0.0100	0.0146683	0	0.022	0.066		0	0.022	0.066005	
27	18	2	100	0.0200	0.0146683	0	0.022	0.066		0	0.022	0.066005	
28	19	5	100	0.0500	0.0146683	0	0.022	0.066		0	0.022	0.066005	
29	20	2	100	0.0200	0.0146683	0	0.022	0.066		0	0.022	0.066005	
30	21	3	100	0.0300	0.0146683	0	0.022	0.066		0	0.022	0.066005	
31	22	4	100	0.0400	0.0146683	0	0.022	0.066		0	0.022	0.066005	
32	23	1	100	0.0100	0.0146683	0	0.022	0.066		0	0.022	0.066005	
33	24	0	100	0.0000	0.0146683	0	0.022	0.066		0	0.022	0.066005	
34	25	1	100	0.0100	0.0146683	0	0.022	0.066		0	0.022	0.066005	

The control limits for sample 1 are

$$LCL_p = .0909 - 3\sqrt{\frac{.0909\,(1 - .0909)}{137}} = .017$$

$$UCL_p = .0909 + 3\sqrt{\frac{.0909\,(1 - .0909)}{137}} = .165$$

Because the sample sizes vary, the control limits are different for each sample. The *p*-chart is shown in Exhibit 16.17. Note that points 13 and 15 are outside the control limits.

An alternative approach is to use the average sample size, $\bar{n}$, to compute approximate control limits. Using the average sample size, the control limits are computed as

$$UCL_p = \bar{p} + 3\sqrt{\frac{\bar{p}(1 - \bar{p})}{\bar{n}}}$$

(16.8)

$$LCL_p = \bar{p} - 3\sqrt{\frac{\bar{p}(1 - \bar{p})}{\bar{n}}}$$

Exhibit 16.15 *p*-Chart for ZIP Code Reader Example

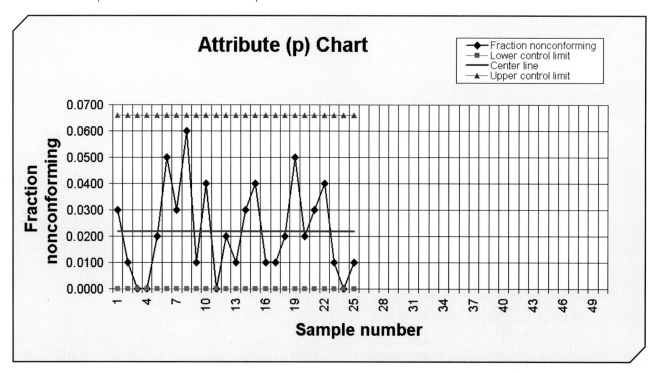

Exhibit 16.16 Data and Calculations for Variable Sample Size Example

	A	B	C	D	E	F	G	H	I	J	K	L	M
1	**Fraction Nonconforming (p) Chart**												
2	This spreadsheet is designed for up to 50 samples. Enter data ONLY in yellow-shaded cells.												
3	Click on the sheet tab to display the control chart (some rescaling may be needed).												
4													
5	**Average (p-bar)**		0.09103124										
6	**Avg. sample size**		148.85										
7										**Approximate Control Limits Using**			
8			**Sample**	**Fraction**		**Standard**				**Average Sample Size Calculations**			
9	**Sample**	**Value**	**Size**	**Nonconforming**	**Deviation**	**LCLp**	**CL**	**UCLp**		**LCLp**	**CL**	**UCLp**	
10	1	18	137	0.1314	0.0245759	0.0173	0.091	0.1648		0.020299	0.091031	0.161763	
11	2	20	158	0.1266	0.0228845	0.0224	0.091	0.1597		0.020299	0.091031	0.161763	
12	3	14	92	0.1522	0.02999	0.0011	0.091	0.181		0.020299	0.091031	0.161763	
13	4	6	122	0.0492	0.0260429	0.0129	0.091	0.1692		0.020299	0.091031	0.161763	
14	5	11	85	0.1294	0.0312004	0	0.091	0.1846		0.020299	0.091031	0.161763	
15	6	22	187	0.1176	0.0210353	0.0279	0.091	0.1541		0.020299	0.091031	0.161763	
16	7	6	156	0.0385	0.0230307	0.0219	0.091	0.1601		0.020299	0.091031	0.161763	
17	8	9	117	0.0769	0.0265936	0.0113	0.091	0.1708		0.020299	0.091031	0.161763	
18	9	14	110	0.1273	0.0274267	0.0088	0.091	0.1733		0.020299	0.091031	0.161763	
19	10	12	142	0.0845	0.0241393	0.0186	0.091	0.1634		0.020299	0.091031	0.161763	
20	11	8	140	0.0571	0.0243112	0.0181	0.091	0.164		0.020299	0.091031	0.161763	
21	12	13	179	0.0726	0.0215002	0.0265	0.091	0.1555		0.020299	0.091031	0.161763	
22	13	5	195	0.0256	0.0205993	0.0292	0.091	0.1528		0.020299	0.091031	0.161763	
23	14	15	162	0.0926	0.0226002	0.0232	0.091	0.1588		0.020299	0.091031	0.161763	
24	15	25	140	0.1786	0.0243112	0.0181	0.091	0.164		0.020299	0.091031	0.161763	
25	16	12	135	0.0889	0.0247573	0.0168	0.091	0.1653		0.020299	0.091031	0.161763	
26	17	16	186	0.0860	0.0210918	0.0278	0.091	0.1543		0.020299	0.091031	0.161763	
27	18	12	193	0.0622	0.0207058	0.0289	0.091	0.1531		0.020299	0.091031	0.161763	
28	19	15	181	0.0829	0.0213811	0.0269	0.091	0.1552		0.020299	0.091031	0.161763	
29	20	18	160	0.1125	0.022741	0.0228	0.091	0.1593		0.020299	0.091031	0.161763	

Exhibit 16.17 *p*-Chart for Variable Sample Size Example

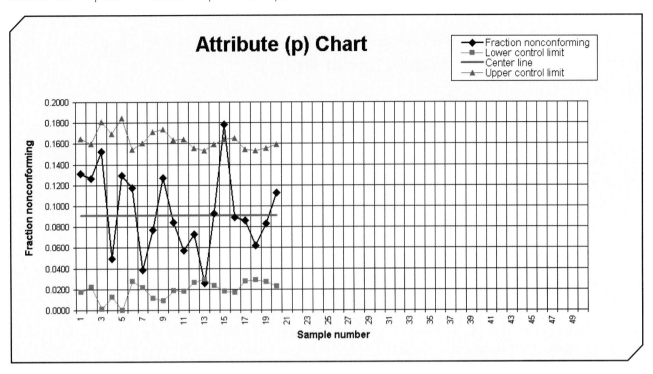

These result in an approximation to the true control limits. For the data in Exhibit 16.16, the average sample size is computed as 148.85, found by dividing the sum of the nonconformances in column B by the sum of the sample sizes used in column C. Using this value, the upper control limit is calculated to be .1618, and the lower control limit is .0203. However, this approach has several disadvantages. Because the control limits are only approximate, points that are actually out of control may not appear to be so on this chart. Second, runs or nonrandom patterns are difficult to interpret because the standard deviation differs between samples as a result of the variable sample sizes. Hence, this approach should be used with caution. Exhibit 16.18 shows the control chart for this example with approximate control limits using the average sample size. Note the difference in sample 13; this chart shows that it is in control, whereas the true control limits show that this point is out of control.

As a general guideline, use the average sample size method when the sample sizes fall within 25 percent of the average. For this example, 25 percent of 149 is 37.21. Thus, the average could be used for sample sizes between 112 and 186. This guideline would exclude samples 3, 6, 9, 11, 13, and 18, whose control limits should be computed exactly. If the calculations are performed on a computer, sample size is not an issue. However, for situations where workers need to do this manually, then using approximate limits is easier.

Constructing *c*- and *u*-Charts

A *p*-chart monitors the proportion of nonconforming items, but a nonconforming item may have more than one nonconformance. For instance, a customer's order may have several errors, such as wrong item, wrong quantity, wrong price, and so on. To monitor the number of nonconformances per unit, we use a *c*-chart or a *u*-chart. These charts are used extensively in service applications because most

Exhibit 16.18 *p*-Chart Using Average Sample Size

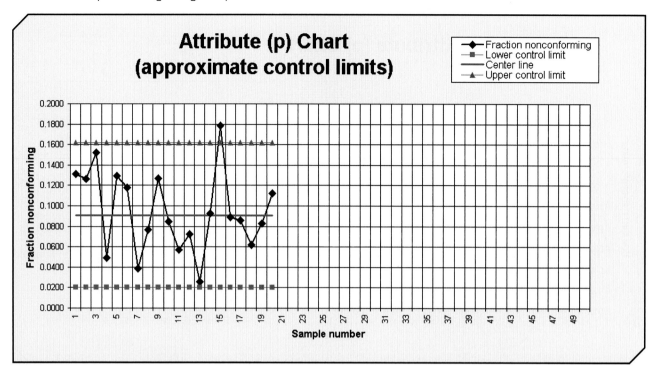

managers of service processes are interested in the number of errors or problems that occur per customer (or patient, student, order), and not just the proportion of customers that experienced problems. The *c*-chart is used to control the *total number* of nonconformances per unit when the size of the sampling unit or number of opportunities for errors is constant. If sampling unit sizes or number of opportunities for errors vary for each unit or customer, a *u*-chart is used to monitor the *average number* of nonconformances per unit.

The *c*-chart is based on the Poisson probability distribution. To construct a *c*-chart, we must first estimate the average number of nonconformances per unit, $\bar{c}$. This is done by taking at least 25 samples of equal size, counting the number of nonconformances per sample, and finding the average. Since the standard deviation of the Poisson distribution is the square root of the mean, we have

$$s_c = \sqrt{\bar{c}} \tag{16.9}$$

Thus, control limits are given by

$$UCL_c = \bar{c} + 3\sqrt{\bar{c}}$$
$$LCL_c = \bar{c} - 3\sqrt{\bar{c}} \tag{16.10}$$

An Example of a *c*-Chart

Exhibit 16.19 shows the number of machine failures over a 25-day period. The total number of failures is 45; therefore, the average number of failures per day is

$$\bar{c} = \frac{45}{25} = 1.8$$

Exhibit 16.19

Machine Failure Data for c-Chart

	A	B	C	D	E	F	G	H	I
1	**Average Number of Defects (c) Chart**								
2	This spreadsheet is designed for up to 50 samples. Enter data ONLY in yellow-shaded cells.								
3	Click on the sheet tab to display the control chart (some rescaling may be needed).								
4									
5	**Average (c-bar)**		1.8						
6	**Standard deviation**		1.341640786						
7									
8		**Number**							
9	**Sample**	**of Defects**	**LCLc**	**CL**	**UCLc**				
10	1	2	0	1.8	5.8249224				
11	2	3	0	1.8	5.8249224				
12	3	0	0	1.8	5.8249224				
13	4	1	0	1.8	5.8249224				
14	5	3	0	1.8	5.8249224				
15	6	5	0	1.8	5.8249224				
16	7	3	0	1.8	5.8249224				
17	8	1	0	1.8	5.8249224				
18	9	2	0	1.8	5.8249224				
19	10	2	0	1.8	5.8249224				
20	11	0	0	1.8	5.8249224				
21	12	1	0	1.8	5.8249224				
22	13	0	0	1.8	5.8249224				
23	14	2	0	1.8	5.8249224				
24	15	4	0	1.8	5.8249224				
25	16	1	0	1.8	5.8249224				
26	17	2	0	1.8	5.8249224				
27	18	0	0	1.8	5.8249224				
28	19	3	0	1.8	5.8249224				
29	20	2	0	1.8	5.8249224				
30	21	1	0	1.8	5.8249224				
31	22	4	0	1.8	5.8249224				
32	23	0	0	1.8	5.8249224				
33	24	0	0	1.8	5.8249224				
34	25	3	0	1.8	5.8249224				

Hence, control limits for a c-chart are given by

$$\text{UCL}_c = 1.8 + 3\sqrt{1.8} = 5.82$$
$$\text{LCL}_c = 1.8 - 3\sqrt{1.8} = -2.22, \text{ or zero}$$

The chart shown is in Exhibit 16.20 and appears to be in control. Such a chart can be used for continued control or for monitoring the effectiveness of a quality improvement program.

As long as the subgroup size is constant, a c-chart is appropriate. In many cases, however, the subgroup size is not constant or the process does not yield discrete, measurable units. For example, in the production of textiles, photographic film, or paper, there is no convenient set of items to measure. In such cases, a standard unit of measurement is used, such as nonconformances per square foot or defects per square inch. The control chart used in these situations is called a u-chart.

The variable u represents the average number of nonconformances per unit of measurement, that is, $u = \frac{c}{n}$, where n is the size of the subgroup (such as square feet). We compute the center line, $\bar{u}$, for k samples each of size n_i as follows:

$$\bar{u} = \frac{c_1 + c_2 + \cdots + c_k}{n_1 + n_2 + \cdots + n_k} \qquad \text{(16.11)}$$

The standard deviation of the ith sample is estimated by

$$s_u = \sqrt{\frac{\bar{u}}{n_i}} \qquad \text{(16.12)}$$

The control limits, based on 3 standard deviations for the ith sample, are then

$$\text{UCL}_u = \bar{u} + 3\sqrt{\frac{\bar{u}}{n_i}}$$

$$\text{LCL}_u = \bar{u} - 3\sqrt{\frac{\bar{u}}{n_i}} \qquad \text{(16.13)}$$

Note that if the size of the subgroups varies, so will the control limits.

An Example of a *u*-Chart

A catalog distributor ships a variety of orders each day. The packing slips often contain errors such as wrong purchase order numbers, wrong quantities, or incorrect sizes. Exhibit 16.21 shows the data collected during August. Since the sample size varies each day, a *u*-chart is appropriate. To construct the chart, we first compute the average number of errors per slip, u, as shown in column C of Exhibit 16.21, by dividing the total number of errors (209) by the total number of packing slips (2,785):

$$\bar{u} = \frac{209}{2,785} = 0.075$$

Exhibit 16.20 *c*-Chart for Machine Failures

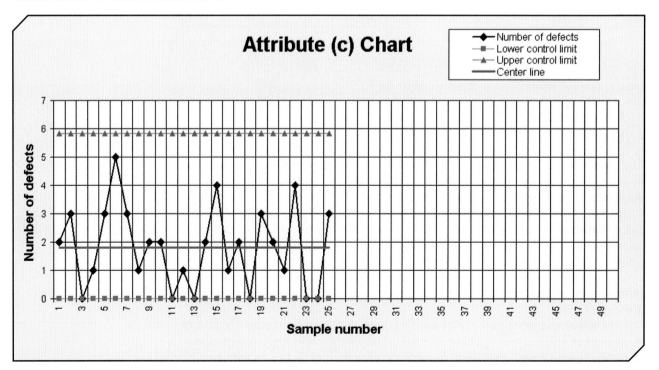

Exhibit 16.21
Data and Calculations for
u-Chart Example

	A	B	C	D	E	F	G	H
1	**Average Number of Defects Per Unit (u) Chart**							
2	This spreadsheet is designed for up to 75 samples. Enter data ONLY in yellow-shaded cells.							
3	Click on the sheet tab to display the control chart (some rescaling may be needed).							
4								
5	**Average (u-bar)**		0.075044883					
6								
7			Sample					
8		**Number**	**Unit**	**Defects**	**Standard**			
9	**Sample**	**of Defects**	**Size**	**per unit**	**Deviation**	**LCLu**	**CL**	**UCLu**
10	1	8	92	0.0870	0.028561	0	0.075	0.161
11	2	15	69	0.2174	0.032979	0	0.075	0.174
12	3	6	86	0.0698	0.02954	0	0.075	0.164
13	4	13	85	0.1529	0.029713	0	0.075	0.164
14	5	5	123	0.0407	0.024701	9E-04	0.075	0.149
15	6	5	87	0.0575	0.02937	0	0.075	0.163
16	7	3	74	0.0405	0.031845	0	0.075	0.171
17	8	8	83	0.0964	0.030069	0	0.075	0.165
18	9	4	103	0.0388	0.026992	0	0.075	0.156
19	10	6	60	0.1000	0.035366	0	0.075	0.181
20	11	7	136	0.0515	0.02349	0.005	0.075	0.146
21	12	4	80	0.0500	0.030628	0	0.075	0.167
22	13	2	70	0.0286	0.032742	0	0.075	0.173
23	14	11	73	0.1507	0.032063	0	0.075	0.171
24	15	13	89	0.1461	0.029038	0	0.075	0.162
25	16	6	129	0.0155	0.024119	0.003	0.075	0.147
26	17	6	78	0.1410	0.031018	0	0.075	0.168
27	18	3	88	0.1477	0.029202	0	0.075	0.163
28	19	8	76	0.0789	0.031423	0	0.075	0.169
29	20	9	101	0.0594	0.027258	0	0.075	0.157
30	21	8	92	0.0326	0.028561	0	0.075	0.161
31	22	2	70	0.1143	0.032742	0	0.075	0.173
32	23	9	54	0.1667	0.037279	0	0.075	0.187
33	24	5	83	0.0964	0.030069	0	0.075	0.165
34	25	13	185	0.0108	0.020141	0.015	0.075	0.135
35	26	5	137	0.0657	0.023405	0.005	0.075	0.145
36	27	8	79	0.0633	0.030821	0	0.075	0.168
37	28	6	76	0.1711	0.031423	0	0.075	0.169
38	29	7	147	0.0340	0.022594	0.007	0.075	0.143
39	30	4	80	0.1000	0.030628	0	0.075	0.167

The standard deviation for a particular sample size, n_i, is therefore

$$s_u = \sqrt{\frac{0.075}{n_i}}$$

As with a p-chart with variable sample sizes, we substitute the sample size in the formula for the standard deviation to find individual control limits. Exhibit 16.22 is the control chart generated from the spreadsheet. One point (number 2) appears to be out of control. Note that the control limits vary because of different sample sizes.

Choosing between c- and u-Charts

Since the c- and u-charts apply to situations in which the quality characteristics inspected do not necessarily come from discrete units, confusion may arise as to which chart is appropriate. The key issue to consider is whether the sampling unit is constant. For example, suppose an electronics manufacturer produces circuit boards.

Exhibit 16.22 Example of *u*-Chart

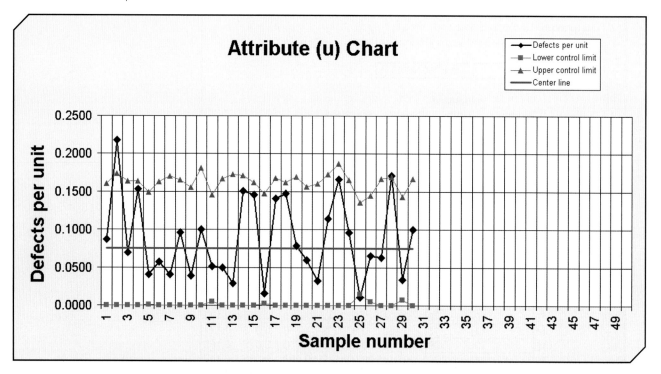

The boards may contain various defects, such as faulty components, missing connections, and so on. The sampling unit is the circuit board. If it is constant (all boards are the same), a *c*-chart is appropriate. If the process produces boards of varying sizes with different numbers of components and connections, a *u*-chart would apply.

Summary of Control Charts

Exhibit 16.23 summarizes the formulas needed for the various types of control charts we discussed in this chapter. Exhibit 16.24 provides a simple set of guidelines for choosing the proper chart. Both manufacturing and service organizations have numerous opportunities to apply all these charts throughout their value chains. The OM Spotlight on IBM shows one example of how control charts were used successfully to improve preemployment physical examinations and purchase-order processing systems.

Exhibit 16.23
Summary of Control Chart Formulas

Type of Chart	LCL	CL	UCL
$\bar{x}$ (with R)	$\bar{\bar{x}} - A_2\bar{R}$	$\bar{\bar{x}}$	$\bar{\bar{x}} + A_2\bar{R}$
R	$D_3\bar{R}$	$\bar{R}$	$D_4\bar{R}$
p	$\bar{p} - 3\sqrt{\dfrac{\bar{p}(1-\bar{p})}{n}}$	$\bar{p}$	$\bar{p} + 3\sqrt{\dfrac{\bar{p}(1-\bar{p})}{n}}$
c	$\bar{c} - 3\sqrt{\bar{c}}$	$\bar{c}$	$\bar{c} + 3\sqrt{\bar{c}}$
u	$\bar{u} - 3\sqrt{\dfrac{\bar{u}}{n}}$	$\bar{u}$	$\bar{u} + 3\sqrt{\dfrac{\bar{u}}{n}}$

Exhibit 16.24 Choosing the Right Control Chart

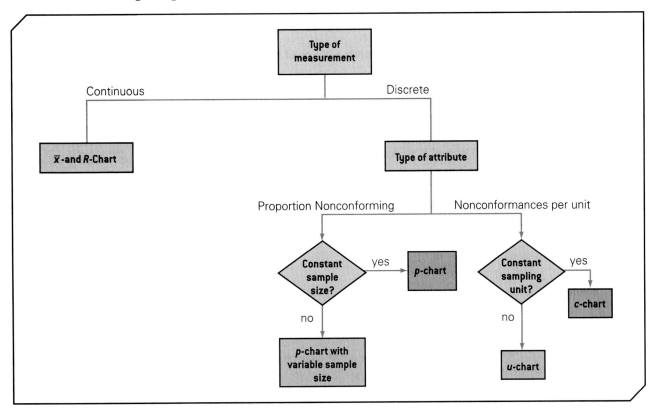

PRACTICAL ISSUES IN SPC IMPLEMENTATION

Although SPC has been around a long time, there are still many organizations that do not use it despite its value. Companies considering using it must address the same fundamental issues in organizational change as they would in implementing an ERP or CRM system. Management must be dedicated to its success. This means that training and other resources such as instrument calibration and maintenance must be committed. Management commitment will be evident at times when control charts dictate that corrective action must delay a shipment, for example. If management ignores what SPC suggests, then workers will quickly see that they are wasting their time and stop using the technique. In addition, users must understand the economics associated with SPC in designing appropriate control charts. This is discussed next.

Control Chart Design

Designing control charts involves three key issues:

1. sample size,
2. sampling frequency, and
3. tightness of control limits.

A small sample size is desirable to keep the cost associated with sampling low. The time a worker spends taking the sample measurements and plotting a control chart represents nonproductive time (in a strict accounting sense only!). On the other hand, large sample sizes provide greater degrees of statistical accuracy in

OM SPOTLIGHT

IBM[9]

© Getty Images/PhotoDisc

At one IBM branch, preemployment physical examinations took too long and taxed the medical staff assigned to conduct them. Such examinations are vital for assuring that employees can perform certain jobs without excess stress and that they pose no health threat to other employees. Therefore, the challenge IBM faced was to maintain the quality of the exam while reducing the time needed to perform it by identifying and eliminating waiting periods between the various parts of it.

Preliminary control charts revealed that the average time required for the examination was 74 minutes, but the range varied greatly. New equipment and additional training of the medical staff were suggested as means of shortening the average time. Initial charts indicated that the process was out of control, but continued monitoring and process improvements lowered the average time to 40 minutes, and both the average and range were brought into statistical control with the help of $\bar{x}$- and R-charts.

Another problem involved purchase orders. The steps in processing purchase orders are fairly routine. The person requesting an item or service fills out a requisition and forwards it to a buyer who translates it into an order. The buyer selects a vendor, usually after a number of bids. But at this IBM branch, time and money were being lost by human error in the purchase-order processing system, and both requesters and buyers were contributing to the problem. Of great concern were nonconforming documents originated by the purchasing department itself. The department started to count them. Data on weekly purchase orders and orders in error were monitored, and a p-chart was constructed that showed an average error rate of 5.9 percent. After the buyers reviewed the data, they found that the process had actually changed during the data collection period, resulting in a shift in the mean to 3.7 percent. The use of the chart also showed out-of-control conditions resulting from vacations. Substitute buyers created a high percentage of rework because of the workload and their unfamiliarity with particular aspects of the process. Preventive measures were created for peak vacation periods to provide sufficient coverage and ensure that backup personnel understood the process better.

estimating the true state of control. Large samples also allow smaller changes in process characteristics to be detected with higher probability. In practice, samples of about 5 have been found to work well in detecting process shifts of 2 standard deviations or larger. To detect smaller shifts in the process mean, larger sample sizes of 15 to 25 must be used.

For attributes data, too small a sample size can make a p-chart meaningless. Even though many guidelines such as "use at least 100 observations" have been suggested, the proper sample size should be determined statistically, particularly when the true portion of nonconformances is small. If p is small, n should be large enough to have a high probability of detecting at least one nonconformance. For example, statistical calculations can show that if $p = .01$, then the sample size must be at least 300 to have at least a 95 percent chance of finding at least one nonconformance. This has significant implications for processes approaching Six Sigma quality levels, which we discuss in the next section.

Managers must also consider the sampling frequency. Taking large samples on a frequent basis is desirable but clearly not economical. No hard-and-fast rules exist for the frequency of sampling. Samples should be close enough to provide an opportunity to detect changes in process characteristics as soon as possible and reduce the chances of producing a large amount of nonconforming output. However, they should not be so close that the cost of sampling outweighs the benefits that can be realized. This decision depends on the individual application and volume of output.

These decisions depend on the risk of drawing the wrong conclusions similar to those in statistical hypothesis testing. For example, we could say that a Type I error occurs when an incorrect conclusion is reached that a special cause is present when in fact one does not exist. This error results in the cost of trying to find a nonexistent problem. Similarly, a Type II error occurs when special causes are present but are not signaled in the control chart because points fall within the control limits by chance. Type I errors result in an unnecessary search for a special cause of variation and may be costly in terms of lost production time and testing effort. Type II errors can be more damaging, especially if an out-of-control process is not recognized and defectives are not caught.

Standard control limits, such as those in Exhibit 16.23, are based on 3 standard deviation ranges about the mean value. These essentially provide low risk of making Type I errors. However, the wider the control limits, the greater the risk of a Type II error. Thus, in some situations, for example, when the costs associated with a Type II error is large, it may be advantageous to tighten these limits so that any nonconformances can be more easily detected even though more false alarms might occur.

Exhibit 16.25 shows how costs associated with these errors and sampling and testing should influence sample size and sample frequency decisions.

Controlling Six Sigma Processes

SPC is a useful methodology for processes that operate at a low sigma level, for example 3-sigma or less. However, when the rate of defects is extremely low, standard control charts are not effective. For example, in using a p-chart for a process with a high sigma level, few defectives will be discovered even with large sample sizes. For instance, if $p = .001$, a sample size of 500 will only have an expected number of $500(.001) = 0.5$ defects. Hence, most samples will have only zero or one defect, and the chart will provide little useful information for control. Using much larger sample sizes would only delay the timeliness of information and increase the chances that the process may have changed during the sampling interval. Small sample sizes will typically result in a conclusion that any observed defect indicates an out-of-control condition, thus implying that a controlled process will have zero defects, which may be impractical. In addition, conventional SPC charts will have higher frequencies of false alarms and make it difficult to evaluate process improvements. These issues are important for Six Sigma practitioners to understand, in order not to blindly apply tools that may not be appropriate.

PROCESS CAPABILITY

Process capability *refers to the natural variation in a process that results from common causes.* Knowing process capability allows one to predict, quantitatively, how well a process will meet specifications and to specify equipment requirements and

Learning Objective
To understand the concept of process capability and be able to analyze process capability data, compute process capability indexes, and interpret the results.

Source of Cost	Sample Size	Sampling Frequency	Control Limits
Type I error	large	high	wide
Type II error	large	high	narrow
Sampling and testing	small	low	—

Exhibit 16.25
Economic-Based Decisions in Designing SPC Procedures

Process capability *refers to the natural variation in a process that results from common causes.*

A process capability study *is a carefully planned study designed to yield specific information about the performance of a process under specified operating conditions.*

the level of control necessary. *A **process capability study** is a carefully planned study designed to yield specific information about the performance of a process under specified operating conditions.* Typical questions that are asked in a process capability study are

- Where is the process centered?
- How much variability exists in the process?
- Is the performance relative to specifications acceptable?
- What proportion of output will be expected to meet specifications?

One of the properties of a normal distribution is that 99.73 percent of the observations will fall within 3 standard deviations from the mean. Thus, a process that is in control can be expected to produce a very large percentage of output between $\mu - 3\sigma$ and $\mu + 3\sigma$, where μ is the process average. Therefore, the natural variation of the process can be estimated by $\mu \pm 3\sigma$ and characterizes the capability of the process. One way of computing the standard deviation in this formula is to take a sample of data, compute the sample standard deviation, s, and use it as an estimate of σ. A second approach, often used in conjunction with an $\bar{x}$- and R-chart, is to estimate σ by dividing the average range by a constant, d_2, which can be found in Appendix B. That is,

$$\sigma = \frac{\bar{R}}{d_2}$$

(16.14)

Capability Versus Control

Process capability has no meaning if the process is not in statistical control because special causes will bias the mean or the standard deviation. Control and capability are two different concepts. As shown in Exhibit 16.26, a process may be capable or not capable, or in control or out of control, independently of each other. Clearly, we would like every process to be both capable and in control. If a process is neither capable nor in control, we must first get it in a state of control by removing special causes of variation and then attack the common causes to improve its capability. If a process is capable but not in control, we should work to get it back in control. Therefore, we should use control charts to first eliminate any special causes before computing the process capability.

Exhibit 16.26

Capability Versus Control (arrows indicate the direction of appropriate management action)

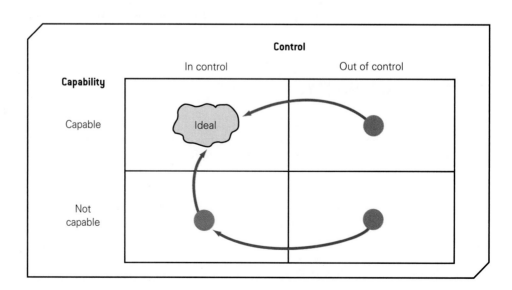

The process capability is usually compared to the design specifications to indicate the ability of the process to meet the specifications. Exhibit 16.27 illustrates four possible situations that can arise when the observed variability of a process is compared to design specifications. In part a, the range of process variation is larger than the design specification; thus it will be impossible for the process to meet specifications a large percentage of the time. Managers can either scrap or rework nonconforming parts (100 percent inspection is necessary), invest in a better process with less variation, or change the design specifications. In part b, the process is able to produce according to specification, although it will require close monitoring to ensure that it remains in that position. In part c, the observed variation is tighter than the specifications; this is the ideal situation from a quality control viewpoint, since little inspection or control is necessary. Finally, in part d, the observed variation is the same as the design specification, but the process is off-center; thus some nonconforming product can be expected.

Process Capability Index

The relationship between the natural variation and specifications is often quantified by a measure known as the **process capability index**. The process capability index, C_p, is defined as the ratio of the specification width to the natural tolerance of the process. C_p relates the natural variation of the process with the design specifications in a single, quantitative measure. In numerical terms, the formula is

$$C_p = \frac{\text{UTL} - \text{LTL}}{6\sigma} \qquad\qquad (16.15)$$

where

UTL = upper tolerance limit
LTL = lower tolerance limit
  σ = standard deviation of the process (or an estimate based on the sample standard deviation, s)

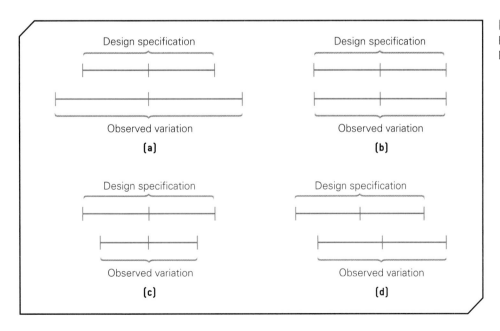

Exhibit 16.27
Process Capability Versus Design Specifications

Note that when $C_p = 1$, the natural variation is the same as the design tolerance (as in Exhibit 16.27(b)). Values less than 1 mean that a significant percentage of output will not conform to the specifications. Values of C_p exceeding 1 indicate good capability; in fact, many firms require C_p values of 1.66 or greater from their suppliers, which equates to a tolerance range of about 10 standard deviations. Because 6 standard deviations generally cover the normal variation of output, a 10-standard deviation range provides adequate comfort so that even if the process shifts a moderate amount and is undetected, nearly all of the output will still be conforming.

The value of C_p does not depend on the mean of the process; thus, a process may be off-center such as in Exhibit 16.27(d) and still show an acceptable value of C_p. To account for the process centering, one-sided capability indexes are often used:

$$C_{pu} = \frac{UTL - \mu}{3\sigma} \text{ (upper one-sided index)} \tag{16.16}$$

$$C_{pl} = \frac{\mu - LTL}{3\sigma} \text{ (lower one-sided index)} \tag{16.17}$$

$$C_{pk} = \min (C_{pl}, C_{pu}) \tag{16.18}$$

For example, a high value of C_{pu} indicates that the process is very capable of meeting the upper specification. C_{pk} is the "worst case" and provides an indication of whether both the lower and upper specifications can be met regardless of where the process is centered. This is the value that most managers pay attention to.

The Excel template for the $\bar{x}$- and R-chart calculates process capability information. Suppose that the specifications for tread wear for the Goodman Tire example used earlier require a maximum tread wear loss of 50 hundredths of an inch (the upper specification), with a lower specification of zero, and a target tread wear of 25. As we noted earlier, we must remove special cause variation before calculating process capability indexes. In the Goodman Tire example, we saw that the last eight samples appeared to have an unusual pattern in the control chart. These should be eliminated (in the Excel template, simply highlight the data for these samples and press the Delete key, and be sure to change the number of samples in cell E6). The result is shown in Exhibit 16.28.

The "Six Sigma" spread of 39.31 in cell R6 represents the range of plus or minus 3 standard deviations on either side of the mean (the denominator in the formula for C_p). Because the specification range is 50 (the numerator in the formula for C_p), we find that C_p is greater than 1.0 and represents good capability. Because the average tread wear is 29.16, the process is not centered on the target, and therefore the upper capability index is just barely greater than 1 while the lower capa-

Exhibit 16.28 Process Capability Calculations for Goodman Tire

	A	B	C	D	E	F	G	H	I	J	K	L	M	N	O	P	Q	R
5																		
6	Number of samples (<= 50)				22					Process Capability Calculations						Six sigma		39.31
7	Sample size (2 - 10)				3					Upper specification				50		Cp		1.272
8										Lower specification				0		Cpu		1.06
9	Grand Average		29.1666667	A2		D3		D4		d2						Cpl		1.484
10	Average Range		11.0909091	1.023		0		2.574		1.693						Cpk		1.06

bility index is much higher. In general, process capability is determined to be 29.16 ± 19.655, or 9.505 to 48.818. This means that as long as the process remains in control, the tread wear for individual tires can be expected to vary between about 19 and 49 hundredths of an inch when evaluated under the same simulated road conditions.

Process capability is important both to product designers and to process owners. If product specifications are too tight, the product will be difficult to manufacture. Employees who run the processes will be under pressure and will have to spend a lot of time adjusting the process and inspecting output. Control charts and process capability information are often integrated in unique ways within companies, as the OM Spotlight on Corning illustrates.

OM SPOTLIGHT

Corning Incorporated[10]

Corning Incorporated has adapted statistical quality control in a unique fashion at several of its electronic plants in the United States and in Europe. In its approach, called process control management (PCM), the burden of continuous checking is placed on the operators, and processes that continually produce excellent-quality products are seldom checked by personnel. Data obtained from several operations are fed into the system and tabulated to produce a picture of current operations. These data are available to production, quality control, and engineering for analysis and evaluation. Quality control may then increase its monitoring of processes that are questionable, while reducing involvement with those running with consistent excellence. Annual savings have been estimated at more than $200,000 in direct labor and $300,000 in yield improvement.

Analysis is based on past experience, historical data, process-capability studies, and other statistical methods. Each machine in a process is categorized as one of four quality levels identified by color codes. Level I denotes a problem-free, excellent machine or process and is identified by the color blue. Most of the machines of a process should enter this category. The manufacturing costs are low, and requirements for the next operation or for final release to the customer are satisfied. Under level 1, it is necessary only to verify that changes have not occurred. Full trust is given to production personnel at this level, and it is assumed that the process will continue in full control and produce excellent-quality parts under constant operator verification. Quality control personnel make only occasional random checks on these processes.

In level 2, the machine or process is classified as workable and is identified by the color green. This level requires that the process inspector be directed to the same machine more often than required by level 1. The machine chosen and the frequency of visits by quality control (QC) personnel is higher. Production personnel still exercise full control, but QC monitors the processes more closely to detect any deterioration and trend toward a level-3 classification.

Level 3 denotes borderline operations, and the identifying color is yellow. The inspectors are directed to step up the monitoring of these machines. Very tight control is required, and every effort is expended to bring the offending machines back into the relative safety of level 2.

In level 4, machines designated out of control (color red) are immediately shut down and repaired. Parts produced for evaluation after the machine is repaired are segregated into lots for special consideration by QC. Maximum support is provided by QC whenever machines reach this level.

Conventional control charts and process-capability studies are used to designate the levels. They enable operators to immediately detect changes in the process and alert QC personnel. QC support is directed from the process-control monitor console, which may be operated manually or be computer-supported or fully computerized. This support provides continuously adjusted levels of machines and processes and directs QC personnel to the next machine to be checked.

Corning has found that the system maintains and improves quality by motivating production department personnel and by charging them with the responsibility for making acceptable products without sacrificing yield. It also has improved interdepartmental communications by developing a feeling of teamwork. Each plant has its own adaptation of PCM to fit its specific needs.

SOLVED PROBLEMS

1. A production process, sampled 30 times with a sample size of 8, yielded an overall mean of 28.5 and an average range of 1.6.

   a. Construct R- and $\bar{x}$-charts for this process.
   b. At a later stage, 6 samples produced these sample means: 28.001, 28.25, 29.13, 28.72, 28.9, 28.3. Is the process in control?
   c. Does the following sequence of sample means indicate that the process is out of control: 28.3, 28.7, 28.1, 28.9, 28.01, 29.01? Why or why not?

Solution:
From Appendix B with $n = 8$, we have $A_2 = 0.37$, $D_3 = 0.14$, and $D_4 = 1.86$.

   a. For the $\bar{x}$-chart:

$$UCL = 28.5 + 0.37(1.6) = 29.092$$
$$LCL = 28.5 - 0.37(1.6) = 27.908$$

   For the R-chart:

$$UCL = 1.86(1.6) = 2.976$$
$$LCL = 0.14(1.6) = 0.224$$

   b. The sample mean of 29.13 is above the UCL, signifying an out-of-control condition.
   c. All points are within the control limits, and there do not appear to be any shifts or trends evident in the new data.

2. Over several weeks, 20 samples of 50 packages of synthetic-gut tennis strings were tested for breaking strength; 38 packages failed to conform to the manufacturer's specifications. Compute control limits for a p-chart.

Solution
$\bar{p} = 38/1,000 = 0.038$ and the standard deviation is $\sqrt{(0.038)(0.962)/50} = .027$

Control limits:

$$UCL = 0.038 + 3(0.027) = 0.119$$
$$LCL = 0.038 - 3(0.027) = -0.043,$$
$$\text{so set } LCL = 0$$

3. A controlled process shows an overall mean of 2.50 and an average range of 0.42. Samples of size 4 were used to construct the control charts. What is the process capability? If specifications are 2.60 ± 0.25, how well can this process meet them?

Solution:
From Appendix B, $d_2 = 2.059$ and $s = \bar{R}/d_2 = 0.42/2.059 = 0.20$. Thus, the process capability is $2.50 \pm 3(0.020)$, or 1.90 to 3.10. Because the specification range is 2.35 to 2.85 with a target of 2.60, we may conclude that the observed natural variation exceeds the specifications by a large amount. In addition, the process is off-center (see Exhibit 16.29).

Exhibit 16.29
Comparison of Observed Variation and Design Specifications for Solved Problem 3.

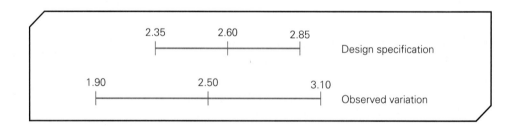

KEY TERMS AND CONCEPTS

Acceptance sampling
c- and u-charts
C_p, C_{pu}, C_{pl}, C_{pk} indexes
Common cause variation
Consumer's risk
Continuous metric

Control chart
Control chart patterns
Control limits
Discrete metric
In control
1:10:100 rule

Out of control
p-charts
Process capability
Process capability index
Process capability study
Producer's risk

Quality control
Quality at the source
Special cause variation
Stable system
Statistical process control (SPC)
$\bar{x}$- and *R*-charts

QUESTIONS FOR REVIEW AND DISCUSSION

1. What is quality control? Why is it necessary in any organization?

2. Explain the three components of any control system, and provide an example different from the one in the text.

3. What is the 1:10:100 rule? Why is it important for managers to understand?

4. What is "quality at the source"?

5. Describe the basic quality control practices used in manufacturing. In what service contexts can they be applied?

6. How does quality control in services involving customer contact differ from typical manufacturing practices?

7. How can customer satisfaction measurement provide useful information for control in services?

8. What is statistical process control?

9. What is the difference between common and special causes of variation?

10. What do we mean when we say that a process is "in control" or "out of control"?

11. Provide some examples in business or daily life in which a controlled process is erroneously adjusted and an out-of-control process is ignored.

12. Explain the difference between a discrete and a continuous metric. Provide some examples different from those in the text.

13. Explain the characteristics of service quality metrics for high-contact services. How do they differ from "back-office" services?

14. What is a control chart and what benefits can control charts provide?

15. Summarize the process used to apply SPC.

16. Describe the various types of control charts and their applications.

17. Discuss how to interpret control charts. What types of patterns indicate a lack of control?

18. What is the purpose of a process-capability study?

19. List some applications of control charts in service organizations.

20. Describe how to choose the correct control chart for a business application.

21. Develop a "personal-quality checklist" on which you tally nonconformances in your personal life (such as being late for work or school, not completing homework on time, not getting enough exercise, and so on). What type of chart would you use to monitor your performance?

22. What is the difference between capability and control?

23. What is a process capability index? Explain how process capability indexes are computed and how to interpret the results.

PROBLEMS AND ACTIVITIES

1. Thirty samples of size 3 resulted in an overall mean of 16.51 and average range of 1.30. Compute control limits for $\bar{x}$- and *R*-charts.

2. Twenty-five samples of size 5 resulted in an overall mean of 5.42 and an average range of 20. Compute control limits for $\bar{x}$- and *R*-charts, and estimate the standard deviation of the process.

3. Use the sample data in Exhibit 16.30 to construct $\bar{x}$- and R-charts. Assume that the sample size is 5.

4. Develop x- and R-charts for the data in Exhibit 16.31.

5. Thirty samples of size 3, listed in Exhibit 16.32, were taken from a machining process over a 15-hour period.

   a. Compute the mean and standard deviation of the data, and plot a histogram.
   b. Compute the mean and range of each sample, and plot them on control charts. Does the process appear to be in statistical control? Why or why not?

6. In testing the resistance of a component used in a microcomputer, the data in Exhibit 16.33 were obtained.

   Construct $\bar{x}$- and R-charts for these data. Determine if the process is in control. If it is not, eliminate any assignable causes, and compute revised limits.

7. Twenty-five samples of 100 items each were inspected, and 68 were found to be defective. Compute control limits for a p-chart.

8. At a pizza restaurant, a 20-week study of 30 pizzas per week found a total of 18 pizzas made improperly. Construct a p-chart to monitor this process.

9. The proportions nonconforming for an automotive piston are given in Exhibit 16.34 for 20 samples. Two hundred units are inspected each day. Construct a p-chart and interpret the results.

10. One hundred insurance claim forms are inspected daily for 25 working days, and the number of forms with errors are recorded as in Exhibit 16.35. Construct a p-chart. If any points are outside the control limits, assume that assignable (special) causes have been determined. Then construct a revised chart.

11. Find control limits for a c-chart with $\bar{c} = 9$.

12. Consider the following data showing the number of errors per thousand lines of code for a software development project. Construct a c-chart and interpret the results.

Sample	1	2	3	4	5	6	7	8	9	10
Number of Errors	4	15	13	20	17	22	26	17	20	22

Exhibit 16.30 Data for Problem 3

Sample	$\bar{x}$	R	Sample	$\bar{x}$	R
1	95.72	1.0	11	95.80	.6
2	95.24	.9	12	95.22	.2
3	95.18	.8	13	95.56	1.3
4	95.44	.4	14	95.22	.5
5	95.46	.5	15	95.04	.8
6	95.32	1.1	16	95.72	1.1
7	95.40	.9	17	94.82	.6
8	95.44	.3	18	95.46	.5
9	95.08	.2	19	95.60	.4
10	95.50	.6	20	95.74	.6

Exhibit 16.31 Data for Problem 4

Sample	Observations				
	1	2	3	4	5
1	3.05	3.08	3.07	3.11	3.11
2	3.13	3.07	3.05	3.10	3.10
3	3.06	3.04	3.12	3.11	3.10
4	3.09	3.08	3.09	3.09	3.07
5	3.10	3.06	3.06	3.07	3.08
6	3.08	3.10	3.13	3.03	3.06
7	3.06	3.06	3.08	3.10	3.08
8	3.11	3.08	3.07	3.07	3.07
9	3.09	3.09	3.08	3.07	3.09
10	3.06	3.11	3.07	3.09	3.07

Exhibit 16.32 Data for Problem 5

Sample	Observations		
1	3.55	3.64	4.37
2	3.61	3.42	4.07
3	3.61	3.36	4.34
4	4.13	3.50	3.61
5	4.06	3.28	3.07
6	4.48	4.32	3.71
7	3.25	3.58	3.51
8	4.25	3.38	3.00
9	4.35	3.64	3.20
10	3.62	3.61	3.43
11	3.09	3.28	3.12
12	3.38	3.15	3.09
13	2.85	3.44	4.06
14	3.59	3.61	3.34
15	3.60	2.83	2.84
16	2.69	3.57	3.28
17	3.07	3.18	3.11
18	2.86	3.69	3.05
19	3.68	3.59	3.93
20	2.90	3.41	3.37
21	3.57	3.63	2.72
22	2.82	3.55	3.56
23	3.82	2.91	3.80
24	3.14	3.83	3.80
25	3.97	3.34	3.65
26	3.77	3.60	3.81
27	4.12	3.38	3.37
28	3.92	3.60	3.54
29	3.50	4.08	4.09
30	4.23	3.62	3.00

Exhibit 16.33 Data for Problem 6

Sample	Observations		
1	414	388	402
2	408	382	406
3	396	402	392
4	390	398	362
5	398	442	436
6	400	400	414
7	444	390	410
8	430	372	362
9	376	398	382
10	342	400	402
11	400	402	384
12	408	414	388
13	382	430	400
14	402	409	400
15	399	424	413
16	460	375	445
17	404	420	437
18	375	380	410
19	391	392	414
20	394	399	380
21	396	416	400
22	370	411	403
23	418	450	451
24	398	398	415
25	428	406	390

Exhibit 16.34 Data for Problem 9

Sample	Proportion Nonconforming	Sample	Proportion Nonconforming
1	.04	11	.07
2	.05	12	.09
3	.03	13	.05
4	.02	14	.04
5	.02	15	.03
6	.04	16	.04
7	.04	17	.03
8	.06	18	.05
9	.04	19	.02
10	.08	20	.04

Exhibit 16.35 Data for Problem 10

Day	Number Nonconforming	Day	Number Nonconforming
1	2	14	2
2	1	15	1
3	2	16	3
4	3	17	4
5	0	18	0
6	2	19	0
7	0	20	1
8	2	21	0
9	7	22	2
10	1	23	8
11	3	24	2
12	0	25	1
13	0		

Exhibit 16.36 Data for Problem 14

Day	No. of Bills	No. of Errors
1	54	6
2	76	8
3	67	8
4	89	20
5	76	13
6	84	11
7	61	11
8	73	10
9	90	14
10	98	10
11	82	13
12	64	13
13	72	10
14	88	11
15	86	12

13. Find control limits for a u-chart with 9 total errors and $n = 4$; also with $n = 5$ and $n = 6$.

14. A trucking company is studying its billing process. Over a 15-day period, it obtained the results in Exhibit 16.36.

    Construct a u-chart for errors per bill. Is the process in control? Is the process satisfactory?

15. Discuss the interpretation of each of the control charts presented in Exhibit 16.37.

16. For Problem 4, estimate the natural variation in the process by first computing the sample standard deviation and then computing $\overline{R}/d_2$. Why is there a difference?

17. Suppose that a specification calls for LTL = 2.0, and UTL = 6.0. A sample of 100 parts found $\mu = 4.5$ and $\sigma = 0.5$. Compute C_p, C_{pl}, C_{pu}, and C_{pk}. Should the manager consider any action based on these results?

18. Determine the process capability for the data in Problem 6. Suppose the specifications for the resistance are 400 ± 40. Compute the capibility indexes. What would you conclude?

19. General Hydraulics, Inc., manufactures hydraulic machine tools. It has had a history of leakage trouble resulting from a certain critical fitting. Twenty-five samples of machined parts were selected, one per

Exhibit 16.37
Control Charts for Problem 15

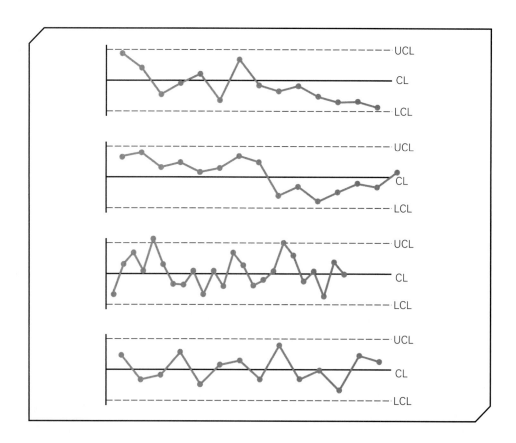

Exhibit 16.38 Data for Problem 19, Part a

	Diameter Measurement (cm) Observation			
Sample	1	2	3	4
1	10.94	10.64	10.88	10.70
2	10.66	10.66	10.68	10.68
3	10.68	10.68	10.62	10.68
4	10.03	10.42	10.48	11.06
5	10.70	10.46	10.76	10.80
6	10.38	10.74	10.62	10.54
7	10.46	10.90	10.52	10.74
8	10.66	10.04	10.58	11.04
9	10.50	10.44	10.74	10.66
10	10.58	10.64	10.60	10.26
11	10.80	10.36	10.60	10.22
12	10.42	10.36	10.72	10.68
13	10.52	10.70	10.62	10.58
14	11.04	10.58	10.42	10.36
15	10.52	10.40	10.60	10.40
16	10.38	10.02	10.60	10.60
17	10.56	10.68	10.78	10.34
18	10.58	10.50	10.48	10.60
19	10.42	10.74	10.64	10.50
20	10.48	10.44	10.32	10.70
21	10.56	10.78	10.46	10.42
22	10.82	10.64	11.00	10.01
23	10.28	10.46	10.82	10.84
24	10.64	10.56	10.92	10.54
25	10.84	10.68	10.44	10.68

shift, and the diameter of the fitting was measured. The results are given in Exhibit 16.38.

a. Construct control charts for the data in the table.
b. It was discovered that the regular machine operator was absent when samples 4, 8, 14, and 22 were taken. How will this affect the results in part a?
c. Exhibit 16.39 presents measurements taken during the next ten shifts. What information does this provide to the quality control manager?

Exhibit 16.39 Data for Problem 19, Part c

	Additional Observation			
Sample	1	2	3	4
1	10.40	10.76	10.54	10.64
2	10.60	10.28	10.74	10.86
3	10.56	10.58	10.64	10.70
4	10.70	10.60	10.74	10.52
5	11.02	10.36	10.90	11.02
6	10.68	10.38	10.22	10.32
7	10.64	10.56	10.82	10.80
8	10.28	10.62	10.40	10.70
9	10.50	10.88	10.58	10.54
10	10.36	10.44	10.40	10.66

CASES

BANKUSA: SECURITIES CONTROL

"Beverly, it takes Securities Control (SC) 15 to 30 days to identify errors originating from other groups, and then a few days more for these groups to fix the errors. During this time period, BankUSA is exposed to considerable market risk that can and *has* cost the bank a lot of money," said Craig Anderson, director of security operations, during the meeting. "Craig, our process designs and systems are not responsive enough to avoid this type of market risk," responded Beverly Thompson, the manager of SC. "Yes, that is correct," said Lori Andrew, supervisor of securities processing. "Well," said Anderson, "what are you two doing to help fix this problem? A $1 million mistake and we are all fired!"

"Craig, we are collecting data to help the process managers identify the source of errors by type. If we can send these process managers these 'error type' data along with the outage reports, they should be able to make improvements in process design and eliminate these errors (outages) and the risk associated with them," said Andrew. Also, Thompson stated, "Craig, we are trying to get the U.S. Federal Reserve to provide us with daily reconciliation reports that would allow us to identify the errors in a much more timely fashion than our current weekly reports. But to do this we also have to overcome some system changes in our internal accounting systems. Also, the national securities settlement systems are not integrated and are the source of many errors."

As Thompson and Andrew left the meeting, they discussed another problem facing Beverly and other process managers at Fiduciary Operations. "Lori, we also need to address the problem of outages that are sometimes not quickly resolved because several processes must work together to fix the cause of the outage," Thompson said. "Yes," Andrew said as someone handed her a piece of paper as they walked down the hallway, "Relogs can add 2 to 10 days to the 15- to 35-day outage research time, and therefore, expose us to more market risk and possible economic consequences. We must address this issue too!" (A "relog" occurs when an SC associate identifies the error as belonging to one department, and when that department receives the documentation and researches it, it concludes the error belongs to another department. A relog form is then filled out and SC inputs this information into the SC tracking system, and the outage is reassigned to the appropriate department.)

After Thompson returned to her office, she thought that if she did a perfect job and helped the other departments and processes "mistake-proof" their processes, her SC department would be eliminated. SC was a third-party internal control function that audits other inter-nal processes to help ensure that no errors hurt customer service or BankUSA's economic performance.

Although not a pleasant thought, Thompson's long-term goal was to eliminate her department. The costs of failure could range from an annoyed customer whose account statement was not accurate to several hundred thousand dollars due to the bank having to buy shares at higher market prices then if the trade was done on-time and accurately. Of course, SC was one operations process in a complex value chain of other non-BankUSA institutions, such as the U.S. Federal Reserve, that could cause an error. Types of errors included:

1. incorrect number of shares or trade price per share for an account,

2. incorrect account numbers and/or credit or debit in the wrong account,

3. a transaction recorded in other non-BankUSA systems that does not show up in BankUSA's systems,

4. a failed trade where Security Settlement, a process within BankUSA, booked the trade to BankUSA's system but the trade was not executed,

5. receiving or sending shares to the wrong institution.

Once these are identified, SC generates reports that go back to the process or department primarily responsible for correcting these outages. These reports go to the following six internal BankUSA processes: (1) Account Processing, (2) Security Settlement, (3) Trade Support, (4) Asset Collection, (5) Conversions, and (6) Corporate Reorganization. Any one of these internal processes, a combination of several processes, or an outside non-BankUSA institution could be the root cause of the outage.

Discussion Questions

1. Develop a statistical process control chart for the data in Exhibit 16.40. What insights, if any, are gained? How might this information be used in a continuous improvement initiative?

2. What type of information should SC be collecting? What types of reports should SC be generating to help these six processes reduce or eliminate errors and identify non-BankUSA root causes?

3. Given that SC is currently a "detection-based quality management system," develop a step-by-step action plan to move toward a "prevention-based quality management system."

4. What are your final recommendations?

Exhibit 16.40 Weekly Errors Reported by Securities Control

Month	Week No.	Total Errors	Total No. Security Assets Processed	Month	Week No.	Total Errors	Total No. Security Assets Processed
January	1	68	6,597	June	24	442	5,796
January	2	618	6,613	June	25	523	5,778
January	3	340	6,640	June	26	476	5,757
January	4	326	6,607	June	27	818	5,721
January	5	220	6,592	June	28	245	5,702
February	6	261	6,627	July	29	82	5,639
February	7	414	6,605	July	30	977	6,344
February	8	535	6,638	July	31	647	6,329
February	9	257	6,671	July	32	937	6,315
March	10	214	6,669	July	33	401	6,295
March	11	265	6,684	August	34	604	6,280
March	12	367	6,677	August	35	1054	6,322
March	13	622	6,600	August	36	977	6,342
March	14	220	6,605	August	37	324	6,300
April	15	105	6,675	August	38	68	6,354
April	16	554	6,555	September	39	261	6,325
April	17	707	6,633	September	40	602	6,305
April	18	401	6,671	September	41	923	6,293
May	19	228	6,668	September	42	672	6,281
May	20	664	6,683	September	43	109	6,248
May	21	282	6,713				
May	22	137	6,745				
May	23	249	5,807				

DEAN DOOR CORPORATION

The Dean Door Company (DDC) manufactures steel and aluminum exterior doors for commercial and residential applications. DDC landed a major contract as a supplier to Walker Homes, a builder of residential communities in several major cities throughout the southwestern United States. Because of the large volume of demand, DDC expanded its manufacturing operations to three shifts and hired additional workers.

Not long after DDC began shipping windows to Walker Homes, it received some complaints about excessive gaps between the door and frame. This was somewhat alarming to DDC, because its reputation as a high-quality manufacturer was the principal reason that it was selected as a supplier to Walker Homes. DDC placed a great deal of confidence in its manufacturing capability because of its well-trained and dedicated employees, and it never felt the need to consider formal process control approaches. In view of the recent complaints, however, Jim Dean, the company president, suspected that the expansion to a three-shift operation, the pressures to produce higher volumes, and the push to meet just-in-time delivery requests were causing a breakdown in quality.

On the recommendation of the plant manager, Dean hired a quality consultant to train the shift supervisors and selected line workers in statistical process control methods. As a trial project, the plant manager wants to evaluate the capability of a critical cutting operation that he suspects might be the source of the gap problem. The target specification for this cutting operation is 30.000 inches with a tolerance of 0.125 inch. Thus, the upper and lower specifications are LSL = 29.875 inches and USL = 30.125 inches. The consultant suggested inspecting five consecutive door panels in the middle of each shift over a 10-day period and recording the dimension of the cut. Exhibit 16.41 shows 10 days' data collected for each shift, by operator.

Discussion Questions

1. Interpret the data in Exhibit 16.41, establish a state of statistical control, and evaluate the capability of the process to meet specifications. Consider the following questions: What do the initial control charts tell you? Do any out-of-control conditions exist? If the process is not in control, what might be the likely causes, based on the information that is available?

Exhibit 16.41
DDC Production Data

Shift	Operator	Sample	Observation				
			1	**2**	**3**	**4**	**5**
1	Terry	1	30.046	29.978	30.026	29.986	29.961
2	Jordan	2	29.972	29.966	29.964	29.942	30.025
3	Dana	3	30.046	30.004	30.028	29.986	30.027
1	Terry	4	29.997	29.997	29.980	30.000	30.034
2	Jordan	5	30.018	29.922	29.992	30.008	30.053
3	Dana	6	29.973	29.990	29.985	29.991	30.004
1	Terry	7	29.989	29.952	29.941	30.012	29.984
2	Jordan	8	29.969	30.000	29.968	29.976	29.973
3	Cameron	9	29.852	29.978	29.964	29.896	29.876
1	Terry	10	30.042	29.976	30.021	29.996	30.042
2	Jordan	11	30.028	29.999	30.022	29.942	29.998
3	Dana	12	29.955	29.984	29.977	30.008	30.033
1	Terry	13	30.040	29.965	30.001	29.975	29.970
2	Jordan	14	30.007	30.024	29.987	29.951	29.994
3	Dana	15	29.979	30.007	30.000	30.042	30.000
1	Terry	16	30.073	29.998	30.027	29.986	30.011
2	Jordan	17	29.995	29.966	29.996	30.039	29.976
3	Dana	18	29.994	29.982	29.998	30.040	30.017
1	Terry	19	29.977	30.013	30.042	30.001	29.962
2	Jordan	20	30.021	30.048	30.037	29.985	30.005
3	Cameron	21	29.879	29.882	29.990	29.971	29.953
1	Terry	22	30.043	30.021	29.963	29.993	30.006
2	Jordan	23	30.065	30.012	30.021	30.024	30.037
3	Cameron	24	29.899	29.875	29.980	29.878	29.877
1	Terry	25	30.029	30.011	30.017	30.000	30.000
2	Jordan	26	30.046	30.006	30.039	29.991	29.970
3	Dana	27	29.993	29.991	29.984	30.022	30.010
1	Terry	28	30.057	30.032	29.979	30.027	30.033
2	Jordan	29	30.004	30.049	29.980	30.000	29.986
3	Dana	30	29.995	30.000	29.922	29.984	29.968

What is the process capability? What do the process capability indexes tell the company? Is DDC facing a serious problem that it needs to address? How might the company eliminate the problems found by Walker Homes?

2. The plant manager implemented the recommendations that resulted from the initial study. Because of the success in using control charts, DDC made a decision to continue using them on the cutting operation. After establishing control, additional samples were taken over the next 20 shifts, shown in the second part of the table, in Exhibit 16.42. Evaluate whether the process remains in control, and suggest any actions that should be taken. Consider the following issues: Does any evidence suggest that the process has changed relative to the established control limits? If any out-of-control patterns are suspected, what might be the cause? What should the company investigate?

Exhibit 16.42
Additional Production Data

Shift	Operator	Sample	Observation 1	2	3	4	5
1	Terry	31	29.970	30.017	29.898	29.937	29.992
2	Jordan	32	29.947	30.013	29.993	29.997	30.079
3	Dana	33	30.050	30.031	29.999	29.963	30.045
1	Terry	34	30.064	30.061	30.016	30.041	30.006
2	Jordan	35	29.948	30.009	29.962	29.990	29.979
3	Dana	36	30.016	29.989	29.939	29.981	30.017
1	Terry	37	29.946	30.057	29.992	29.973	29.955
2	Jordan	38	29.981	30.023	29.992	29.992	29.941
3	Dana	39	30.043	29.985	30.014	29.986	30.000
1	Terry	40	30.013	30.046	30.096	29.975	30.019
2	Jordan	41	30.043	30.003	30.062	30.025	30.023
3	Dana	42	29.994	30.056	30.033	30.011	29.948
1	Terry	43	29.995	30.014	30.018	29.966	30.000
2	Jordan	44	30.018	29.982	30.028	30.029	30.044
3	Dana	45	30.018	29.994	29.995	30.029	30.034
1	Terry	46	30.025	29.951	30.038	30.009	30.003
2	Jordan	47	30.048	30.046	29.995	30.053	30.043
3	Dana	48	30.030	30.054	29.997	29.993	30.010
1	Terry	49	29.991	30.001	30.041	30.036	29.992
2	Jordan	50	30.022	30.021	30.022	30.008	30.019

ENDNOTES

[1] Brown, Eryn, "Heartbreak Hotel?" *Fortune*, November 26, 2001, pp. 161–165.

[2] "Hospital to Revise Lab Procedures After Faulty Tests Kill 2," *The Columbus Dispatch*, Columbus, Ohio, August 16, 2001, p. A2.

[3] "Testing for Conformity: An Inside Job," *Golf Journal*, May 1998, pp. 20–25.

[4] "DaimlerChrysler's Quality Practices Pay Off for PT Cruiser," *News and Analysis*, Metrologyworld.com, 3/23/2000.

[5] Adapted from the Ritz-Carlton Hotel Company 1992 and 1999 Application Summaries for the Malcolm Baldrige National Quality Award.

[6] "Waiting Game," *The Columbus Dispatch*, Columbus, Ohio, January 13, 2002, pp. E1–E2.

[7] Parasuraman, A., Zeithaml, V. A., and Berry, L. L., "A Conceptual Model of Service Quality and Its Implications for Future Research," *Journal of Marketing* 49, Fall 1985, pp. 41–50.

[8] Wilson, Clifford B., "SQC + Mg: A Positive Reaction," *Quality Progress*, April 1988, pp. 475–479.

[9] McCabe, W. J., "Improving Quality and Cutting Costs in a Service Organization," *Quality Progress*, June 1985, pp. 85–89.

[10] Adapted from Basile A. Denissoff, "Process Control Management," *Quality Progress* 13, 6, June 1980, pp. 14–16.

Chapter Outline

CHAPTER 17

Lean Operating Systems

Learning Objectives

1. To learn the basic principles of lean operating systems—elimination of waste, increased speed and response, improved quality, and reduced cost—and the benefits they provide to organizations.

2. To understand the basic tools and approaches that organizations use to create a lean organization and to recognize how to apply these tools appropriately.

3. To understand how manufacturing firms apply lean tools and concepts.

4. To understand how lean tools and concepts are applied to service organizations.

5. To understand the concepts and philosophy of just-in-time operating systems and the challenges that managers face in managing JIT systems.

- "Where's our pizza?" Rachel asked. "I don't know," said her dad, "but I think I have an idea. . . ." Peering back across the next table into the kitchen, Steve saw mass confusion. The kitchen is crammed with workers running in all directions. Some workers are rushing about madly while others stand by idly, unsure of what to do. Other workers are cleaning up discarded pieces of dough and excess toppings from the floor. Several assistant managers are directing every step of the pizza-making process. Next to each workstation are piles of unfinished pizzas waiting for the addition of sauce, toppings, or cheese. Between the oven and the packaging table are piles of pizzas that have been set aside because they were made incorrectly. In one corner of the kitchen are stacked boxes of dough, meats, and cheeses from suppliers, none of which has been checked or properly stored. "Be patient, Rachel," Steve sighed, "we'll get it eventually. . . ."

- Porsche, the maker of high-end German sports cars, found sales falling to 25 percent of their 1986 peak by 1992.[1] When Wendelin Wiedeking took over as head of the company, he pushed his workers to adopt Japanese-style lean production methods. He hired two Japanese efficiency experts and personally chopped the top half off a row of shelves with a circular saw to reduce inventories. Along with more flexible, negotiated work rules, Porsche revamped its assembly process so that production of 1997 911 models would take only 60 hours, compared to 120 hours for its predecessor. The time to develop a new model was cut from 7 years to 3.

Porsche uses 300 parts suppliers, down from nearly 1,000, and a quality-control program has helped reduce the number of defective parts by a factor of 10.

- A medical laboratory had been improving the time it took from the receipt of a test sample to completion and had achieved a 30 percent reduction, primarily by using new technology. However, doctors were still asking for faster responses. The lab quality coordinator did some research and found some examples of manufacturing plants that had reduced cycle time by as much as 90 percent with little capital investment. The coordinator discovered that these improvements were not achieved simply by making each step work faster but also by identifying and reducing waste that existed between the process steps, such as movement, waiting, and inventory. By learning how these manufacturers accomplish these improvements, he was able to apply similar ideas to his laboratory service and reduce the processing time by another 20 percent.[2]

Discussion Questions: Explain the operational implications that Steve's observations of the pizza kitchen would have in creating value for customers. Can you cite any personal experiences in your work or around your school where you have observed similar inefficiencies? Why would less inventory, as suggested in the Porsche example, lead to greater efficiencies in production? Don't you think the opposite would occur?

The first scenario may be a bit difficult to imagine for a pizza business. However, it describes the classic mass-production environment typical of U.S. automobile plants a couple of decades ago: workers doing different tasks with no clear sense of teamwork and cooperation; messy factories, piles of excess inventory and raw materials awaiting inspection, and defective parts waiting disposition. The impacts on the customer were often long delivery lead times and cars having significant defects or wrong options.

Now picture a much different situation in the pizza kitchen, which is analogous to how a typical Japanese automobile plant operated several decades ago: Indirect workers, who add no value to the product, are nowhere to be seen; all workers are adding value to the pizzas. The space between production operations is small, allowing little room to store excess inventory and fostering close communication among workers. Pizzas flow smoothly from one preparation step to the next. When an incorrect order is discovered, all work stops and the team works together to uncover the reason and prevent it from occurring again. Every pizza coming out of the oven is correct and immediately boxed for delivery to the customer. There are no large supplies of dough and other ingredients; the restaurant's suppliers deliver them fresh daily. Such an organization, focused on its core capabilities and devoid of any waste, is called *lean*.

Lean enterprise *refers to approaches that focus on the elimination of waste in all forms, and smooth, efficient flow of materials and information throughout the value chain to obtain faster customer response, higher quality, and lower costs.* Manufacturing and service operations that apply the principles of lean enterprise are often called **lean operating systems.** Lean concepts were initially developed and implemented by the Toyota Motor Corporation, and lean operating systems are often

Lean enterprise *refers to approaches that focus on the elimination of waste in all forms, and smooth, efficient flow of materials and information throughout the value chain to obtain faster customer response, higher quality, and lower costs.*

benchmarked with "the Toyota production system." As one article about Toyota observed, to see the Toyota production system in action is to "behold a thing of beauty":

A Toyota assembly plant fairly hums: Every movement has a purpose, and there is no slack. Tour a typical auto plant, and you see stacks of half-finished parts, assembly lines halted for adjustment, workers standing idle. At Toyota the workers look like dancers in a choreographed production: retrieving parts, installing them, checking the quality, and doing it all in immaculate surroundings.[3]

Lean enterprise has been adopted by many companies around the world, such as Porsche, highlighted in the second episode, and has led to substantial improvements and results. More importantly, lean thinking is not just for manufacturing; the principles are simple and can easily be adapted to service organizations such as banks, hospitals, and restaurants, as the third episode illustrates. For example, banks require quick response and efficiency to operate on low margins, making many of their backroom processes, such as check sorting and mortgage processing, natural candidates for lean enterprise solutions.[4] The handling of paper checks and credit card slips, for instance, involves a physical process like an assembly line. The faster a bank moves checks and mortgages (that is, information) through its system, the sooner it can collect its funds and the better its returns on invested capital.

Why is being a lean organization important? One answer stems from the concept of value, which customers clearly expect from an organization's goods and services. As we noted earlier in this book, value is enhanced by improving the customer benefit package while simultaneously reducing the costs associated with providing it. Eliminating waste, becoming more efficient, and providing faster customer response all increase value. Secondly, cost pressures in every industry are driving companies to become more efficient, and therefore, lean operating systems are necessary for survival. Many airlines, for instance, continue to struggle to survive in the aftermath of 9/11, yet Southwest Airlines has continued to be successful because of applying lean thinking to its operations. Recent start-ups such as JetBlue, which managed to be ranked #1 in customer service and quality in 2003 while maintaining a low cost structure, are driving the major U.S. airlines to become leaner.

Lean thinking is more than a set of tools and approaches; it is a mindset that must be understood and adopted by managers and workers at all levels of the organization. Every step in the value chain affects the creation of value in some way; thus, lean principles and thinking must be applied broadly to the entire value chain. The power of information technology is helping entire industries to rethink, redefine, and restructure their value chains. Dell Computer, for example, is a recognized leader in applying lean thinking and radically changing the value chain for purchasing personal computers. Today, RFID tags are facilitating more lean thinking in organizations; we have discussed applications of RFID in Chapters 5 and 7. Six Sigma quality improvement tools are also being integrated with lean principles to simultaneously attack issues affecting quality, speed, and cost.

In this chapter we discuss the principles of lean operating systems and how they are applied in both manufacturing and service.

Learning Objective
To understand the basic objectives of lean operating systems—elimination of waste, increased speed and response, improved quality, and reduced cost—and the benefits they provide to organizations.

PRINCIPLES OF LEAN OPERATING SYSTEMS

Lean operating systems have four basic principles:

1. elimination of waste
2. increased speed and response
3. improved quality
4. reduced cost

As simple as these may seem, organizations required disciplined thinking and application of good operations management tools and approaches to achieve them.

Eliminate Waste

Lean, by the very nature of the term, implies doing only what is necessary to get the job done. Any activity, material or operation that does not add value in an organization is considered waste. Exhibit 17.1 shows a variety of specific examples. The Toyota Motor Company classified waste into seven major categories:

1. *Overproduction:* for example, making a batch of 100 when there are orders only for 50 in order to avoid an expensive setup, or making a batch of 52 instead of 50 in case there were rejects. Overproduction ties up production facilities, and the resulting excess inventory simply sits idle.
2. *Waiting time:* for instance, allowing queues to build up between operations, resulting in longer lead times and higher work-in-progress.
3. *Transportation:* the time and effort spent in moving products around the factory as a result of poor layout.
4. *Processing:* the traditional notion of waste, as exemplified by scrap that often results from poor product or process design.
5. *Inventory:* waste associated with the expense of idle stock and extra storage and handling requirements needed to maintain it.
6. *Motion:* as a result of inefficient workplace design and location of tools and materials.
7. *Production defects:* the result of not performing work correctly the first time.

Eliminating waste requires an attitude of continuous improvement and sensitivity to finding potential sources of waste and taking appropriate action. This requires the involvement and cooperation of everyone in the value chain. It also requires training and constant reinforcement by managers and supervisors. Improvement initiatives must also be implemented without disrupting current process efficiency and customer service.

Increase Speed and Response

Lean operating systems focus on quick and efficient response in designing and getting goods and services to market, producing to customer demand and delivery requirements, responding to competitor's actions, collecting payments, and addressing customer inquiries or problems. Better process design, exploiting information technology, and improved management practices, such as short cash-to-cash conversion cycles as described in Chapter 9, and Just-in-Time as described later in this chapter are some ways to meet this goal.

Exhibit 17.1 Common Examples of Waste in Organizations

Excess capacity	Overproduction	Waiting time
Inaccurate information	Produce too early	Accidents
Excess inventory	Long distance traveled	Too much space
Long changeover and setup times	Retraining and relearning time and	Unnecessary movement of materials,
Spoilage	expense	people and information
Clutter	Scrap	Equipment breakdowns
Planned product obsolescence	Rework and repair	Knowledge bottlenecks
Excessive material handling	Long unproductive meetings	Non-valued-added process steps
	Poor communication	Misrouting jobs

Perhaps the most effective way of increasing speed and response is to *synchronize the entire value chain*. By this we mean that not only are all elements of the value chain focused on a common goal but that the transfer of all physical materials and information are coordinated to achieve a high level of efficiency. This coordination might be driven by the master production schedule in an automobile assembly plant, for example, or daily sales information from all the stores in a large retail chain. Information technology has vastly improved the ability to synchronize value chains, as we have discussed in several chapters throughout this book. In addition, partnerships with suppliers and customers ensure high quality and responsive delivery.

Improve Quality

Lean operating systems cannot function if raw materials are bad, processing operations are not consistent, or machines break down. Poor quality disrupts work schedules and reduces yields, requiring extra inventory, processing time, and space for scrap and parts waiting for rework. All these are forms of waste and increase costs to the customer.

Eliminating the sources of defects and errors in all processes in the value chain greatly improves speed and agility and supports the notion of continuous flow. Using mistake-proofing approaches discussed in Chapter 15 in designing processes, improving training, or even eliminating certain work activities can help to achieve this objective. In addition, reducing process variability improves customer service, quality, and speed, while reducing costs and required capacity. This is one of the primary goals of Six Sigma quality initiatives described in Chapter 15. Many firms are now adopting the idea of "*Lean Six Sigma*," and combining lean and Six Sigma tools, concepts, and approaches.

Reduce Cost

Certainly, reducing cost is an important objective of lean enterprise. Anything that is done to reduce waste and improve quality often reduces cost at the same time. More efficient equipment, better preventive maintenance, and smaller inventories reduce costs in manufacturing firms. Simplifying processes, such as using customer labor via self-service in a fast-food restaurant, depositing a check using an automatic teller machine, and completing medical forms online before medical service are ways for service businesses to become leaner and reduce costs. Outsourcing processes for which an organization does not have sufficient expertise is another way.

Benefits of Lean Operating Systems

Proponents of lean operating systems cite many benefits, including reductions in cycle (processing) times, improvements in space utilization, increases in process throughput, smooth workloads, reductions in work-in-process and finished goods inventories, improvements in communication and information sharing in the value chain, improvements in quality and customer service, and reductions in cash flow and working capital required to run the business (see the OM Spotlight on TI Automotive).

Becoming lean requires a focus on details, discipline, persistence, and hard work to achieve results. Surveys have noted that mid-sized and large companies are likely to be familiar with lean principles and have systems in place; however, small firms have much less familiarity with the principles. Thus, considerable opportunity exists for adopting lean practices in small businesses.

OM SPOTLIGHT

TI Automotive[5]

TI Automotive (www.tiautomotive .com) is a global supplier of fully integrated vehicle fuel storage, braking, power train, and air-conditioning systems. Company sales were $2.3 billion with 130 facilities in 29 countries, 20,000 employees, and 31 manufacturing plants located in North America. In 2004, it was awarded new supply contracts worth more than $100 million from three auto manufacturers—PSA Peugeot Citröen, Toyota, and Volkswagen.

TI Automotive has implemented lean practices throughout its value chain, improving purchasing, engineering change order processing, and shipment to customers. For example, it switched from a "push-batch-queue processing" to a "pull and extended enterprise" system, achieving many of the benefits cited in the text. For example, inventory turns steadily improved from 12.7 to 22. This improvement resulted in $41 million in additional free cash flow and contributed significantly to the company's bottom line. Product quality improved from over 500 defects per million to less than 50 defects per million. Almost all TI facilities are ISO 9000 certified.

TI Automotive calls its lean practices "Common Sense Manufacturing." Much effort is spent trying to diffuse these practices to all facilities and employees as quickly as possible. According to TI Automotive, some of the keys to quickly diffusing lean practices include: (1) properly characterize and identify target innovators and early adopter groups, (2) support and invest in early innovators, (3) recognize the importance of communication channels and use them, (4) create slack resources to support successful change, (5) make early innovators' activity visible throughout the organization, and (6) require managers to lead by example, that is, "if the leader doesn't eat sauerkraut, don't expect others to do so."

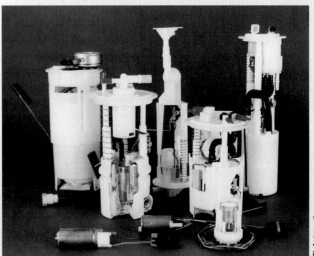

LEAN TOOLS AND APPROACHES

Meeting the objectives of lean enterprise requires disciplined approaches for designing and improving processes. Many of the tools that we have discussed in previous chapters, such as quality function deployment, value stream mapping, and the seven basic quality management tools, are important in lean thinking. In addition to these, organizations use several other tools and approaches to create a lean organization. These are summarized in this section.

Learning Objective
To understand the basic tools and approaches that organizations use to create a lean organization and to recognize how to apply these tools appropriately.

Value Stream Mapping

Value stream mapping was introduced in Chapter 7. Recall that a value stream map shows the process flows in a manner similar to an ordinary process map. However, the difference is that value stream maps highlight value-added versus non-value-added activities and include times that activities take. This makes them well suited for lean enterprise analyses. They allow one to measure the impact of value-added and non-value-added activities on the total lead time of the process and compare this to the takt time—*the ratio of the available work time to the required production volume necessary to meet customer demand*. If the value stream is faster than

Takt time is the ratio of the available work time to the required production volume necessary to meet customer demand.

the takt time, it generally means that waste in the form of overproduction is occurring; when it is less, the firm cannot meet customer demand. Value stream maps might also include other information such as machine uptime and reliability, process capacity, and size of batches moving through the process. Developing value stream maps is usually one of the first steps in applying lean principles.

Small Batch and Single-Piece Flow

Batching—*the process of producing large quantities of items as a group before being transferred to the next operation.*

One of the practices that inhibits increasing speed and response in manufacturing or service processing of discrete parts such as a manufactured part, invoices, medical claims, or home loan mortgage approvals is batching—*the process of producing large quantities of items as a group before being transferred to the next operation.* Batching results in buildup of inventories and often leads to delays in delivery as customers wait for their order to be scheduled. The alternative to batching is continuous flow (which we introduced in Chapter 7), which is typically used to produce goods such as chemicals and gasoline. Continuous flow processes, by their very nature, are highly efficient because materials move through operations without stopping. Lean operating systems seek to apply the principles of continuous flow to the production of discrete parts by reducing batch sizes, ideally to a size of one—that is, using *single-piece flow.* Many companies justify batching on the basis that pallet loads or other full containers can be moved more easily between operations. However, simple changes in plant layout and material handling systems often can support one-piece flow. Single-piece flow allows companies to better match production to customer demand (particularly if processing times are large), avoid large and expensive inventory buildups, and ensure uninterrupted movement of work-in-process through the production system.

To understand this, consider the following comparison of batch processing versus single-piece flow in Exhibit 17.2. Assume that the batch size is 100 items and that each item must be processed sequentially on three workstations. Remember, in a batch process the entire lot size is produced at workstation A before it is moved to workstation B, and so on. Therefore, it takes 3,500 seconds to process a batch of 100 items through the three workstations, as depicted in Exhibit 17.3a.

Now consider single-piece flow, as shown in Exhibit 17.3b, where the first item is processed in 5 seconds then immediately moves on to the second workstation (we assume zero delay time in moving from one workstation to another). The first item completes processing at workstation B in a total of 25 seconds, and then moves on to workstation C, finishing in a total of 35 seconds. Note that B is the bottleneck workstation; items arrive for processing at B faster than B is capable of processing them, and therefore cannot be completed faster than 20 seconds apart. So, items 2 through 100 will all be completed by workstation B in 99(20 seconds) = 1,980 seconds after item #1. Thus, the last item leaves B at time 25 + 1,980 = 2,005 seconds from the start of production. Because workstation C is not the bottleneck,

Exhibit 17.2
Batch versus Single-Piece Flow Processing

Workstation	Batch Size (Q)	Processing Time per Item	Total Time per Batch (seconds)
A	100	5 seconds	500
B*	100	20 seconds	2,000
C	100	10 seconds	1,000
		Total	3,500

*Bottleneck workstation

Source: Adapted from Jeffrey K. Pinto and Om P. Kharbanda, "How to Fail in Project Management (Without Really Trying)" Business Horizons, July/August 1996, pp. 45–53. © 1996, with permission from Elsevier.

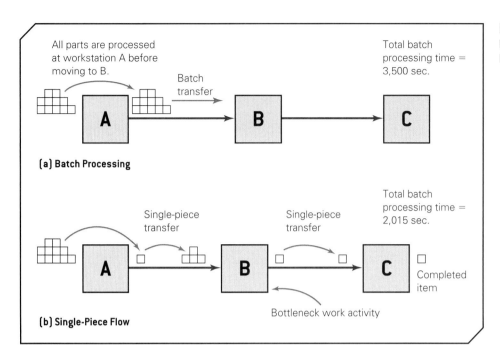

Exhibit 17.3
Batch versus Single Piece
Flow Processing

every item that arrives from B can immediately be processed, so the 100th item is completed by time $2,005 + 10 = 2,015$ seconds. This reduces the time from the batch process by $(3,500 - 2,015)/3,500$, or about 42 percent.

Batching is often necessary when producing a broad goods or service mix with diverse requirements on common equipment. When making different goods, manufacturers often need to change dies, tools, and fixtures on equipment, resulting in expensive and time-consuming setups and teardowns. For services, preprinted forms or software may have to be changed or modified. By running large batches, setups and teardowns are reduced, providing economies of scale. However, this often builds up inventory that might not match market demand, particularly in highly dynamic markets. A better strategy would be to use small batches or single-piece flow. However, to do this economically requires the ability to change between products quickly and inexpensively. Many companies have made remarkable improvements in reducing product setup times, making small-batch or single-piece flow a reality in job shop environments (see the OM Spotlight on Harley-Davidson). For example, Yammar Diesel reduced a machining-line tool setting from 9.3 hours to 9 minutes; a U.S. chain-saw manufacturer reduced setup time on a punch press from more than 2 hours to 3 minutes; and a midwestern manufacturer was able to cut equipment setup time on a 60-ton press from 45 minutes to 1 minute. This was accomplished through process improvements such as storing the required tools next to the machine, using conveyors to move the tools in and out of the machine, and improving the labeling and identification. Previously, the setup tools were poorly identified, poorly organized, and stored far from the machine, requiring a forklift to transport them. The machine operator can perform the new changeovers or setups with no indirect assistance.

Another way to improve performance when batching is necessary is to move a *portion* of a completed batch before the entire batch is finished. This is called a transfer batch. *A **transfer batch** is part of the original batch (lot) size that is completed at one workstation and moved to the next downstream workstation.* For example, in Exhibit 17.3a if the batch size is 100 items, a transfer batch of 20 items would allow downstream workstations to get the original batch out sooner.

*A **transfer batch** is part of the original batch (lot) size that is completed at one workstation and moved to the next downstream workstation.*

OM SPOTLIGHT

Harley-Davidson[6]

After Harley-Davidson's market share fell from a near monopoly to less than 30 percent in the early 1980s, the company embarked on an aggressive strategy for improving quality and manufacturing efficiency. Lean production was an important part of that effort. Simple design changes, in both products and processes, helped it achieve dramatic reductions in setup time. For example, using "C"-shaped spacing washers instead of "O" types enabled operators to loosen nuts and slide in the "C" washers from the side to reposition a machine instead of taking the nuts off and lifting the machine to replace the "O" washers. Another change involved two crankpins that were similar except for a hole drilled at a 45-degree angle in one and at a 48-degree angle in the other. It took 2 hours to reposition the machine for the new operation. Engineers designed a common hole angle in the two parts, and changeovers could be made by simply inserting or removing a set of spacers on the fixture that held the crankpin for drilling. Setup time was reduced to 3 minutes.

Feature Photo Service HARLEY-DAVIDSON CO.

The 5Ss

Workers cannot be efficient if their workplaces are messy and disorganized. Much time can be wasted looking for the right tool or moving around piles of materials that may be scattered about. Efficient manufacturing plants are clean and well organized. Firms use the "5S" principles to create this work environment. *The 5Ss are derived from Japanese terms: seiri (sort), seiton (set in order), seiso (shine), seiketsu (standardize), and shitsuke (sustain).*

The 5S Principles are seiri *(sort),* seiton *(set in order),* seiso *(shine),* seiketsu *(standardize), and* shitsuke *(sustain).*

- *Sort* refers to ensuring that each item in a workplace is in its proper place or identified as unnecessary and removed.
- *Set in order* means to arrange materials and equipment so that they are easy to find and use.
- *Shine* refers to a clean work area. Not only is this important for safety, but as a work area is cleaned, maintenance problems such as oil leaks can be identified before they cause problems.
- *Standardize* means to formalize procedures and practices to create consistency and ensure that all steps are performed correctly.
- Finally, *sustain* means to keep the process going through training, communication, and organizational structures.

These principles define a system for workplace organization and standardization. By applying these, workers develop a mindset for lean thinking that carries over into all aspects of their work.

Visual Controls

Visual controls *are indicators for operating activities that are placed in plain sight of all employees so that everyone can quickly and easily understand the status and performance of the work system.* Visual signaling systems are known as *andon*, drawing from the Japanese term where the concept first originated. For example, if a machine fails or a part is defective or manufactured incorrectly, a light might turn on or a buzzer might sound, indicating that immediate action should be taken. Many firms have cords that operators can pull that tell supervisors and other workers that a problem has occurred. Some firms, such as Honda (on the manufacturing floor) and J.P. Morgan Chase (at its call centers), use electronic "scoreboards" to keep track of daily performance. These scoreboards are located where everyone can see them and report key metrics such as volume, quality levels, speed of service, and so on.

Visual controls *are indicators for operating activities that are placed in plain sight of all employees so that everyone can quickly and easily understand the status and performance of the work system.*

Efficient Layout and Standardized Operations

The layout of offices, equipment, and processes is designed according to the best operational sequence, by physically linking and arranging work activities and process steps most efficiently, often in a linear or cellular arrangement (see Chapters 7 and 8 and the OM Spotlight: Omark). Standardizing the individual tasks by clearly specifying the proper methods and procedures to do the work reduces wasted human movement and energy.

Technology

Although most of the tools and approaches for lean enterprise that we describe are quite simple, technology is becoming increasingly important in creating lean operating systems. Chapter 5 provides many examples on how technology improves performance, so we will not repeat them here. Here, we provide some additional examples to help you understand how organizations use technology to become leaner.

New forms of automated reasoning, learning, and control are now being used in selected factory operating systems.[8] These include *expert systems* that use a set of "intelligent rules" to make logical decisions to solve a specific problem or control an operation or machine, advanced search algorithms to solve complex optimization problems, and "intelligent agents" that perform tasks such as machine scheduling,

OM SPOTLIGHT

Omark[7]

The benefits of improved layout can be seen at Omark's Guelph, Ontario, factory, which makes chain saws. Originally, the distance the product had to travel within the plant was 2,620 feet and flow time was 21 days. Within 2 years, the distance was reduced to 173 feet and the time to 3 days by moving metal-forming machines together and eliminating much of the work-in-process (WIP) inventory. Omark's ultimate strategy is to fill orders from the factory and eliminate finished-goods warehouses altogether.

material transfer, and web auction bidding. For example, Sandia National Laboratories developed an expert system that monitors and controls a factory's brazing oven, which is used to solder ceramic parts to metal parts at high temperatures. Expert systems are being developed to continually analyze a production line to improve flexibility and trim changeover times. Advanced search algorithms are being applied to operating the shop floor in new-generation ERP packages sold by Oracle, SAP, i2 Technologies, Peoplesoft, and other vendors. Intelligent agents have been used to predict when injection-molding machines are about to turn out defective products by sifting through reams of data in real time, looking for patterns that are good predictors of defective parts. When problems are identified, the operator is notified and the machine is recalibrated. If the problem threatens delivery to a key customer, the sales and plant manager might get an automatic pager alert. These technologies can eliminate the limitations and errors associated with human judgment and clearly support the four objectives of lean enterprise.

Despite the fact that most customers do not like automated telephone answering systems, such systems streamline operations and lead to dramatic reductions in costs. For example, it costs a call center about $7 on average to handle a telephone call using a real person, $2.25 per call to handle an Internet transaction with human intervention at some point in the encounter, and only 20 to 50 cents for handling a telephone call using automated technology with no human intervention. In medical practices, technology enables a reduction of the office staff to physician ratio by one-half while speeding up the examination, order fulfillment, and payment processes.

Supplier Relationship Management

Lean operating systems will not work with suppliers who miss delivery dates or provide poor-quality goods or services. The fulfillment process requires collaborative partnerships between suppliers and their customers where communication is often on a real-time basis. This includes suppliers of information, energy, transportation, warehousing, packaging, and manufactured goods (see OM Spotlight: Saturn Corporation).

In a lean environment, shipments are received in reusable, standardized containers, each containing fixed quantities, so that there is no reason to unpack and count all incoming goods. In fact, shipping containers usually are designed to go directly to the assembly line and are designed to fit in a predesigned space. This practice also eliminates the potential for damage through handling and saves space.

OM SPOTLIGHT

Saturn Corporation[9]

Saturn's automobile plant in Spring Hill, Tennessee, manages its suppliers so well that in 4 years it had to stop its production line just once and for only 18 minutes because the right part was not delivered at the right time. Saturn maintains virtually no inventory. A central computer directs trucks to deliver preinspected and presorted parts at precise times to the factory's 56 receiving docks, 21 hours a day, 6 days a week. Of Saturn's more than 300 suppliers, most are not even located near the plant, but are in 39 states and an average of 550 miles away from Spring Hill. Ryder System, the Miami transportation services company, manages the Saturn network. Tractors pulling trailers that are 90 percent full on average arrive daily at a site 2 miles from Saturn's factory. The drivers uncouple the trailers, which contain bar-coded, reusable plastic containers full of parts, and shuttle tractors deliver them to the plant. Saturn is linked electronically with all its suppliers and reorders parts each time a car comes off the assembly line, an example of a pull production system in action.

Single Minute Exchange of Dies (SMED)

Long setup times waste manufacturing resources. Short setup times, on the other hand, enable a manufacturer to have frequent changeovers and move toward single-piece flow, thus achieving high flexibility and product variety. Reducing setup time also frees up capacity for other productive uses. **Single Minute Exchange of Dies (SMED)** *refers to quick setup or changeover of tooling and fixtures in processes so that multiple products in smaller batches can be run on the same equipment.* SMED was pioneered by Toyota and other Japanese manufacturers and has been adopted by companies around the world. Some remarkable examples are Yammar Diesel's reduction of a machining-line tool setup from 9.3 hours to 9 minutes, a U.S. chainsaw manufacturer's reduction of setup time on a punch press from more than 2 hours to 3 minutes, and a midwestern manufacturer's reduction of setup time on a 60-ton press from 45 minutes to 1 minute. This was accomplished through simple process improvements such as storing the required tools next to the machine, using conveyors to move the tools in and out of the machine, and improving the labeling and identification. Although SMED originated in a factory setting, the same principles of reducing non-value-added setup and changeover time apply for any good-producing or service-providing process (see OM Spotlight: Sunset Manufacturing).

Single Minute Exchange of Dies (SMED) refers to quick setup or changeover of tooling and fixtures in processes so that multiple products in smaller batches can be run on the same equipment.

Stable Production Schedules

Lean operating systems require uniform and stable production plans and schedules. This is accomplished by using small lot sizes, freezing the production schedule, and using a pull operating system. Such stabilizing practices level out the workloads at workstations. The ideas and methods of Chapter 11 on forecasting and Chapter 13 on aggregate planning, master production scheduling, and resource planning are used to develop stable and repetitive schedules.

OM SPOTLIGHT

Sunset Manufacturing[10]

An example of how even a small business can adopt lean production principles in order to realize significant improvements is found at Sunset Manufacturing, Inc. of Tualatin, OR, a 35-person, family-owned machine shop. Because of competitive pressures and a business downturn, Sunset began to look for ways to simplify operations and cut costs. At a Kaizen event, it determined that SMED and the 5S approach could yield benefits. Several actions were taken, including: (1) standardizing parts across milling machines, (2) reorganizing the tool room, (3) incorporating the SMED approach in machine setups, and (4) implementing what was termed "dance cards" that gave operators the specific steps required for SMED of various machines and products. The results were impressive and gratifying. Tool preparation time dropped from an average of 30 minutes to less than 10 minutes, isolation and identification of worn tools was improved, safety and appearance in the tool room due to 5S application was apparent, machine setup time was reduced from an average of 216 minutes to 36 minutes (an 86 percent improvement), and the entire Kaizen event resulted in an estimated savings of $33,000 per year, with a cost to implement of less than half of that amount. The net impact was to allow smaller lots to be run, a 75 percent reduction in setup scrap, a more competitive organization to emerge, and a morale boost for team members.

Quality at the Source

Quality at the source requires doing it right the first time, and therefore, eliminates the opportunities for waste. It reduces cost as implied by the 1:10:100 Rule we discussed in Chapter 16. Employees inspect, analyze, and control their own work to guarantee that the good or service passed on to the next process stage conforms to specifications. Of course, this requires a flexible and well-educated work force to learn the concepts and methods of lean operating systems and quality management. By inspecting your own work, inspection stations and jobs along the process can be eliminated, resulting in a leaner operating system.

Continuous Improvement and Six Sigma

In order to make lean principles work, one must get to the root cause of problems and permanently remove them. Continuous improvement initiatives that we discussed in Chapter 15 are vital in lean environments, as is teamwork among all managers and employees.

Six Sigma, in particular, has emerged to be a useful and complementary approach to lean production and has led to a new concept know as *Lean Six Sigma*. For example, lean systems assume high-quality output so as to maintain an uninterrupted process flow, so a processing time reduction project might involve aspects of both lean concepts and Six Sigma. A firm might apply lean tools to streamline an order entry process and discover that significant rework is occurring because of incorrect addresses, customer numbers, or shipping charges that results in high variation of processing time. Six Sigma tools might then be used to drill down to the root cause of the problems and identify a solution.

However, major differences exist between lean enterprise and Six Sigma, such as:

- Lean enterprise addresses more visible problems in processes, for example, inventory, material flow, and safety, while Six Sigma is more concerned with less visible problems, for example, process variation.
- Lean tools are more intuitive, simpler, and easier to apply in the workplace, while some Six Sigma tools are more advanced, such as statistical analysis of variance, design of experiments, and simulations.
- Lean tools generally require less training, whereas Six Sigma tools require advanced training and expertise in statistics, control charts, and Black Belt or Master Black Belt specialists. For example, the lean tool of the 5Ss is easier to grasp than statistical methods used with control charts.

Despite these differences, they both aim to eliminate waste from the value chain and improve the design and operation of goods, services, and processes. Both are driven by customer requirements and market strategies, focus on real dollar savings, and have the ability to make significant financial impacts on the organization, and both can be used in nonmanufacturing environments, require senior leadership commitment, and use a systematic methodology for implementation. Because of these similarities, many industry training programs and consultants have begun to focus on Lean Six Sigma, drawing upon the best practices of both approaches.

Total Productive Maintenance

Lean operating systems require that all equipment and processes operate reliably. Unplanned downtime is far worse than planned downtime and scheduled maintenance. For example, a $38 roller bearing on a manufacturer's plastics extruder machine failed, resulting in misalignment of the shaft and destroying the gears, the pinion shaft, three other bearings, and an oil seal. The actual cost of materials loss and equipment repair was $13,000 plus 3 days of lost production, which was valued at over $25,000. A routine inspection by an experienced maintenance mechanic or machine operator could have prevented almost all of this loss.[11]

Therefore, maintenance should be addressed proactively, rather than reactively by fixing failures and breakdowns. **Total productive maintenance (TPM)** *is focused on ensuring that operating systems will perform their intended function reliably.* The goal of TPM is to prevent equipment failures and downtime; ideally, to have "zero accidents, zero defects, and zero failures" in the entire life cycle of the operating system.[12] TPM has been described as the health care system for the operating system. TPM seeks to

Total productive maintenance (TPM) is focused on ensuring that operating systems will perform their intended function reliably.

- maximize overall equipment effectiveness and eliminate unplanned downtime
- create worker "ownership" of the equipment by involving them in maintenance activities
- foster continuous efforts to improve equipment operation through employee involvement activities

Better equipment maintenance can increase production yields, productivity, and capacity and reduce energy losses, rework and defects, and production line shutdowns. Maintenance is the responsibility of all employees. TPM promotes practices by which employees preserve and protect their own equipment and are responsible for routine maintenance such as cleaning or tightening (see the OM Spotlight on Eastman Chemical). Equipment maintenance staff and engineers are responsible for diagnosis of problems, major repair, and inspections.

In services, reliability of computers, software, and information networks is of paramount importance. Many banks, for example, go so far as to set up a second almost duplicate operations center in case the primary operations center is out of service for some reason.

Equipment performance deteriorates over time. When equipment performance reaches a point of failure, it can idle part or all of a process or factory, which is very expensive. Thus, TPM tries to predict equipment failure rates and perform maintenance before a problem arises, as illustrated in Exhibit 17.4. With TPM, the time before deterioration in equipment performance is increased substantially. Two key TPM questions to answer are (1) How can the start of deterioration in performance be detected? (2) When should action be taken? Statistical process control charts (Chapter 15) can help in answering these questions.

OM SPOTLIGHT

Eastman Chemical Company[13]

Within 5 years of starting TPM at Eastman Chemical Company, more than 120 teams were functioning, comprising over 85 percent of the facility. In its implementation, maintenance personnel work with operators in work zones within the plant with a focus on continuous improvement of processes through improved equipment reliability and maintainability. More than 3,000 tasks have been identified as TPM tasks, 80 percent of which are being performed by the equipment operators themselves.

These include repairing equipment, changing filters, lubricating, and adjusting.

Prior to TPM, a mixer stoppage would last approximately 1 hour while maintenance personnel came and reset a tripped motor starter. Subsequently, an operator can restore production in 15 minutes or less. In one instance, after a power plant failure, a team restored production approximately 3 days sooner than would have been possible under the traditional maintenance organization, saving the company several million dollars.

Exhibit 17.4 TPM Equipment Issues and Benefits

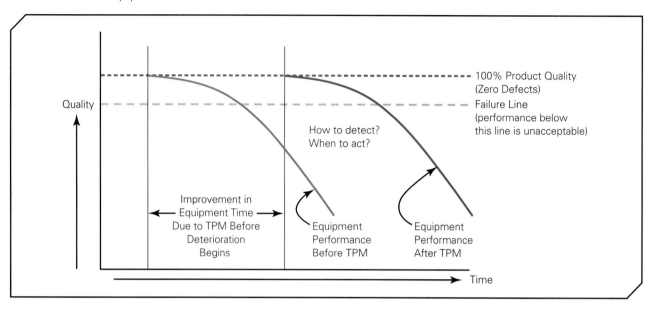

Because of its importance in lean thinking, TPM has recently been called "lean maintenance." Lean maintenance is more than preventing failures of equipment and processes; it now includes maintenance and backup systems for software and electronic network systems such as the Internet or wireless networks.

Manufactured Good Recovery

In an effort to reduce costs and essentially "do more with less," which is the essence of lean thinking, many companies are actively recovering and recycling parts (sometimes called *green manufacturing*). This can occur at various points of the supply chain, as shown in Exhibit 17.5. Once a manufactured good is discarded, one option is to resell the good or its various component parts. Other options include

- *Repairing* a manufactured good by replacing broken parts so it operates as required.
- *Refurbishing* the good by updating its looks and/or components; for example, cleaning, painting, or perhaps replacing parts that are near failure.
- *Remanufacturing* the good by returning it to close to its original specifications. This is usually done by disassembling it, cleaning or replacing many of the parts, and testing it to ensure it meets certain performance and quality standards. Certified remanufactured parts typically result in higher gross profit margins than the original, as high as 20 percent to 60 percent (see OM Spotlight: Remanufacturing Printer Ink Cartridges).
- *Cannibalizing* parts for use as replacement parts in other goods.
- *Recycling* goods by disassembling them and selling the parts or scrap materials to other suppliers. If the residual value of the manufactured good has been extracted or it is not economical to do so, the part ends up being incinerated or dumped in a landfill.

For example, a major automobile manufacturer became interested in remanufacturing transmissions to reduce the need to purchase a 10- to 20-year supply of transmission parts to service future customer needs. Each certified remanufactured transmission meets the original transmission performance and quality specifications.

Exhibit 17.5 Integrated Manufactured Good Recovery Value Chain[15]

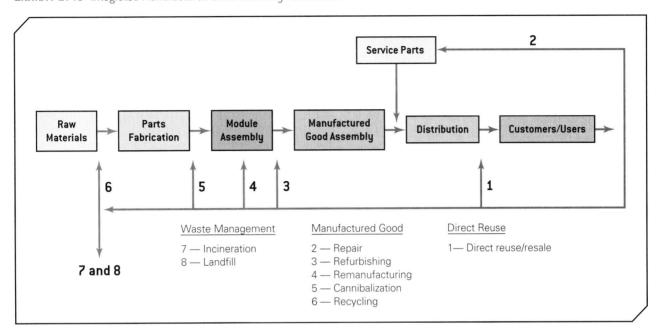

Waste Management

7 — Incineration
8 — Landfill

Manufactured Good

2 — Repair
3 — Refurbishing
4 — Remanufacturing
5 — Cannibalization
6 — Recycling

Direct Reuse

1— Direct reuse/resale

A remanufactured transmission sells for 50 percent to 75 percent of a new one. The customer wins by lowering the total cost of replacement, and the company wins by reducing its inventory carrying costs.

The next two sections take you on tours of two goods-producing and two service-providing companies. The objective is to expose you to lean thinking in a wide variety of companies using the four basic principles of lean operating systems.

OM SPOTLIGHT

Remanufacturing Printer Ink Cartridges[14]

"I paid $90 for the printer, and one ink cartridge is $36," Brian Evans said, pausing on his way out of a New York office-supply store. Companies such as Lexmark, Hewlett-Packard, Canon, and Epson have coupled low-priced inkjet and laser printers with high-priced disposable ink cartridges. But the business model has sprung a leak—remanufacturing ink cartridges.

One objective of lean operating systems is zero waste. Buying a new replacement ink cartridge reminds us that printer manufacturers create obsolete ink cartridges by design. New ink cartridges cost one-third to one-half the cost of some printers. The strategy is to almost give away the printer and make profits from the perishable items such as ink and toner cartridges. Entrepreneurs have started selling refilling kits and remanufacturing ink cartridges for less than one-half the price of a new cartridge. Printer manufacturers are resisting this infringement on their profits.

LEAN MANFACTURING TOURS

Lean manufacturing plants look significantly different from traditional plants. They are clean and organized, devoid of long and complex production lines and high levels of work-in-process, have efficient layouts and work area designs, use multiskilled workers that perform both direct and indirect work such as maintenance, and have no incoming or final inspection stations. In this section, we "tour" two manufacturing firms to examine how they focus on the four major lean objectives. In the next section, we will tour some service organizations that apply similar principles.

Gorton's of Gloucester[16]

Perhaps you have seen advertisements with the trademark "Gorton's Fisherman" highlighting the great-tasting and high-quality seafood produced by Gorton factories. Gorton, headquartered in Gloucester, Massachusetts, has been processing seafood for over 150 years. In 1998, the company embarked on a lean operating system initiative because one of its senior managers walked through the factory and noticed that raw material was brought in through the second floor freight entrance and then stored on multiple floors. The seafood was processed on the second and third floors and then shuttled back to cold storage on the first floor. Conveyers connected the processes on each floor but this senior manager challenged factory management to address the "lack of visual flow." Some of the ways in which Gorton's is applying lean principles are summarized next.

Eliminate Waste The old operating system led to many forms of waste. Miscommunication among operations on different floors created excessive handling and movement of seafood, boxes, and pallets, and the entire process often stopped or slowed down due to bottlenecks. Before lean practices were implemented, cold storage included 40,000 square feet of expensive warehouse space to keep all the raw material, work-in-process, and finished goods inventory. Today, the factory has less than 10,000 square feet of cold storage warehouse space and 50 percent less inventory, increasing working capital and reducing operating expense. The new system also freed up an entire floor of the factory for other uses, which was eventually used to produce seven new retail brand seafood lines.

Increase Speed and Response One lean systems objective was to simplify the factory by putting all seafood production on one floor. Process and value stream maps drawn for the current processes found them to be incredibly complex, with much wasted movement and lack of communication between floors. Each section of the process was isolated physically and communicating operations information was difficult. The company embarked on a two-year effort to organize the production process on one floor as a pull system. By eliminating most of the old conveyer system, all production was organized on one floor. Process flow became more continuous and stable, and the production area was much easier to clean. Employees could also see the process from beginning to end, and communication improved, resulting in fewer slowdowns and stoppages. Raw materials are now replenished only when needed. The physical changes also led to cultural changes. Employee morale increased and they could see when they needed to speed up or help out other workstations.

The new layout and improved equipment enhanced the speed and efficiency of the production process. They also reduced setup and changeover times to different products and supported continuous flow production, improving the flexibility to adapt to different production order sizes needed to meet demand. Gorton's has also applied lean practices to its new product development processes, focusing on bringing new and innovative products to market quickly and effectively.

Improve Quality Gorton's production engineers began working with their equipment suppliers to redesign the batter, breader, tempering, and cutting machines. Many of these machines were invented by Gorton's decades ago and were designed to operate in a batch production environment. The new machines were designed to reduce the variability in their output, had fewer moving parts to minimize breakdowns, simplified maintenance designs that were easy to access, and were much easier to clean.

Reduce Cost Gorton's worked with suppliers who deliver the fish, flour, batter, boxes, and so on, so that they had the information necessary to deliver goods only when necessary. What they make they sell, and consequently, food is fresher. Gorton's hosts an annual Operations Conference that includes its suppliers, large retail customers, and truckers, so everyone in the value chain can communicate with each other. At each annual conference, performance results are reported, and Gorton's gives an award called the "Gorton's Lean Corporate Challenge" to the supplier who best contributed to Gorton's lean journey.

Gorton's is also studying the use of lean practices and tools in administrative areas such as purchasing, office services, distribution, quality control, accounts receivable, and accounts payable. Its goal is to become the "Toyota of Food Processing."

Timken Company[17]

The Timken Company (www.timken.com) is a leading global manufacturer of highly engineered bearings and alloy steels and related products and services. NASA's Mars rovers use Timken precision bearings in wheel transmissions, gearboxes, rotating cameras, camera masts, and solar array panel drives. Timken employs about 18,000 employees in over 50 factories and more than 100 sales, design, and distribution centers located throughout the world.

Timken divides its business into three major groups—industrial, automotive, and steel. The industrial group accounts for about 40 percent of total sales and manufactures bearings for the aerospace, mining, agriculture, rail, heavy industry, and distribution industries. The automotive group also accounts for another 40 percent of sales and manufactures bearings and power train products, often in bundled subassemblies and modules. For both of these groups, Timken places increasing emphasis on pre- and postproduction services, such as integrated engineering solutions to customer requirements. The steel group accounts for the remaining sales and produces specialty alloy steel bars and tubes used in the other two groups.

PR Newswire THE TIMKEN COMPANY

Like most manufacturers, Timken faced intense, survival-threatening, global competition, and like many others, it placed itself on the leading edge of U.S. industrial revival. In 1989, the company launched "Vision 2000," a program of lean production initiatives that developed throughout the 1990s. A key element was increased productivity through lean-manufacturing operating principles and technologies, some of which we highlight next.

Eliminate Waste Timken's automotive business uses a "Boot Camp" in which a certain factory identifies several improvement opportunities and Timken employees and managers from other sites then try to solve these specific problems at the host factory. This is similar to a *kaizen blitz* (see Chapter 15). The problems often focus on removing non-value-added steps from processes, reducing process and equipment variation, and eliminating waste. The boot camp approach allows "fresh eyes" to evaluate improvement opportunities and present solutions to host plant management. Timken has also worked with the U.S. Department of Energy to improve the manufacture and performance of seamless tube and pipe so as to help steel producers eliminate unnecessary processing steps.

Increase Speed and Response Timken has focused on improving its product development process—a nonmanufacturing, information-intensive process—with the objective to radically reduce the total cycle time for new product development with fewer errors and to be more responsive to customer requests, competitor capabilities, and marketplace changes. Timken's objective of an integrated supply chain also focuses on agility to better meet customer wants and needs.

Timken exploited many of the technologies we described in Chapter 6, such as computer-aided design and computer-aided manufacturing (CAD/CAM), to better meet customer needs and improve design for manufacturability. It developed flexible manufacturing systems to facilitate rapid, cost-effective changeover from one product to another, combining the advantages of batch and mass production. Lean manufacturing's most distinguishing characteristic at Timken, however, was the authority and responsibility it gave to people on the shop floor. Initiatives aimed at empowering shop floor employees included more open communication, enhanced training, widespread adoption of a team approach to problem solving and decision-making, and changes in measures of performance and rewards. Teams helped to redesign machinery and reorganize equipment into flexible manufacturing cells. Timken's customers, themselves under tremendous pressure to bring new products to market, needed quicker response times. Timken research facilities led pilot production programs that enabled machine operators to have early input into the design process and resulted in significant cost savings.

Improve Quality Quality standards are determined for all manufacturing processes, and worldwide quality audits make sure that these standards are being met. Each plant is certified to ISO 9000 or other quality certifications. Timken has applied Six Sigma tools to minimize process variation. One initiative was to improve machine operator efficiency and reduce variability. Workstation processes were standardized and machine operator walking and movement time was eliminated or reduced. The result was improved quality and reduced scrap.

Total quality and continuous improvement has long been a focus for Timken. Through programs like Breakthrough and Accelerated Continuous Improvement, thousands of improvement ideas have been implemented, saving millions of dollars. In some cases, the stretch targets of 40 percent improvement in costs, quality, and service were exceeded. All manufacturing machinery must meet the company's Capability Policy for quality and consistency. Even new equipment is tested and modified to meet specifications. Sometimes these tests are conducted on the plant floor; at other times, equipment is brought to one of its research facilities for more extensive modification. As a natural evolution from traditional total quality approaches, Timken embraced Six Sigma.

Reduce Cost Timken redefined its mission statement in 1993 to be "the best-performing manufacturing company in the world as seen through the eyes of our customers and shareholders." Management made structural changes aimed at pushing its engineering culture to become more business oriented. Markets were segmented, with associates from marketing, sales, application engineering, and manufacturing forming teams, each focusing on a single market. Today, Timken factories, suppliers, and customers share information using the Internet. Purchasing, order fulfillment, manufacturing strategy implementation, Lean Six Sigma, and logistics have been brought together to create an "integrated supply chain model." The purpose of this focus is to reduce asset intensity, improve customer service and systems support, respond faster to customer needs, and better manage inventory levels.

Exhibit 17.6 Timken's DMAIC Toolkit for Lean Six Sigma

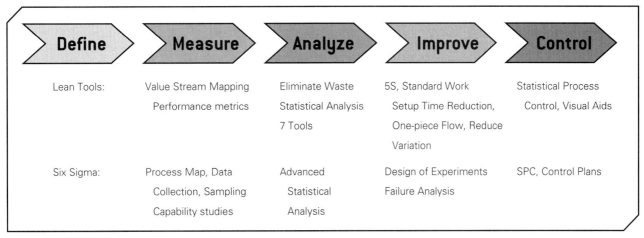

Source: Ellis, R., and Hankins, K., "The Timken Journey for Excellence," Presentation for the Center of Excellence in Manufacturing Management, Fisher College of Business, Ohio State University, Columbus, Ohio, August 22, 2003.

In the late 1990s, Timken decided to integrate its lean manufacturing practices and Six Sigma initiatives into one unified program, Lean Six Sigma. The objective of Timken's Lean Six Sigma program is "to identify and deliver value to our customers and shareholders by improving the flow of product and information through waste elimination and variation reduction." All manufacturing processes are flow-charted and the DMAIC problem-solving framework is used to generate process improvements. Exhibit 17.6 shows the wide variety of lean and Six Sigma analysis tools used throughout the company. The automotive business achieved a net documented savings of $7 million from Lean Six Sigma projects in 1 year alone.

LEAN SERVICE TOURS

Learning Objective
To understand how lean tools and concepts are applied to service organizations.

Service organizations can benefit significantly from applying lean principles. Value chains identify many preproduction services, such as financing and good/service design, and postproduction processes, such as installation/repair and consulting and technical support services (refer back to Exhibits 2.1 to 2.3). Synchronized information and feedback flows tie these different processes together.

Lean principles are not always transferable to "front-office" services that involve high customer contact and service encounters. In these situations, the service provider and firm do not have complete control over creating the service. Different customers, service encounter situations, and customer and employee behaviors cause the creation and delivery of the service to be much more variable and uncertain than producing a manufactured good in the confines of a factory. However, "back-office" service processes, such as hospital laboratory testing, check processing, and college application processing, are nearly identical to many manufacturing processes. Time, accuracy, and cost are all important to their performance, and therefore they can clearly benefit from the application of lean principles.

The following discussion shows how lean concepts have been used at SBC Communications and Southwest Airlines.

SBC Communications

SBC Communications is a major telecommunications company that provides local, long-distance, digital satellite television, and wireless and Internet access products to residential and commercial customers. One of its services is telephone installation and repair. When customers contact a call center and request telephones to be installed, removed, or repaired, the call center creates a trouble report.[18]

Eliminate Waste Excess capacity, a form of waste, is reflected in too many technicians and trucks, both of which are very expensive. By increasing technician/truck utilization by applying lean principles, excess capacity can be reduced. Unnecessary movement of technicians/trucks from job site to job site is also very wasteful and expensive. The objective of the dispatching function is to minimize the distance traveled per technician/truck. Other forms of waste in this value chain include rework, inaccurate information, missed customer appointment times, customers not being home when they said they would be, long waiting times, unnecessary rescheduling, doing non-value-added tasks, and retraining and relearning time and expense due to technician job turnover rates.

One example of how SBC addressed waste revolves around order processing. The old process batched work orders and trouble reports and processed them the evening before the next day's work. When service technicians arrived the next day, they received a printout of their work schedule and the order they should visit customer sites. This approach did not consider the changes that often occurred throughout the workday, such as customers not being home or calling to change their request. Hence, the service technicians were constantly calling in to update and revise their job assignments throughout the day. Applying lean principles to this situation, the company decided to process one trouble report at a time to each service repair technician. This is analogous to the single-piece flow idea in a lean manufacturing system. All changes to the status of trouble reports were handled in the main dispatching office. After technicians finished each job, they called the dispatcher to get their next job assignment. The dispatcher could better coordinate job assignments, taking into account technicians' locations and skills.

Increase Speed and Response Speed of service is clearly very important when a customer's telephone does not work. To respond quickly and effectively, representatives must promptly and courteously answer the customers' telephone call and quickly process the trouble report, the technician must show up when promised and perform the work professionally, and the next telephone bill must accurately reflect what was promised and done. Improving the accuracy of the standard times to perform different types of installation and repair jobs is very important to the objective of speed and response. Training also plays a role in how fast technicians can do this work. Convenience supports speed and response in a service business. For example, the appointment time must be convenient for the customer.

Improve Quality Regardless of whether the service provider is a technician or telephone customer service representative, the quality of service encounters is critical to long-term customer satisfaction. The telephone call center, a front-office, high-customer-contact function, must get accurate information as to exactly what the customer wants done. If the information at the beginning of the process is inaccurate, then rework, rescheduling, and return visits may result. Because the customer service representative is in direct contact with customers, human behavior and service management skills must be considered in meeting quality requirements. SBC identified the top ten types of service inquiries and developed standard responses (called script dialogues) to standardize service provider responses to frequently asked questions. Similar issues arise when the technician interacts with the customer and enters the home or facility. However, in such high-contact situations, lean methods and practices do not transfer as well from manufacturing.

Missed appointments, even if they arise because the customer might have forgotten, are damaging service upsets. One way of reducing this type of quality error is for the dispatching function to call customers the morning of the appointment to ensure they will be home and that the technician will have access to the facility. SBC was able to reduce the standard deviation of missed appointment times by 50 percent.

Reduce Cost Today's information and cell phone technology allows all repair technicians and job assignments in a geographical area to be coordinated more efficiently and faster than in the past. The central information processing center—the dispatching function—has more timely information than any single technician and truck. The dispatching function sets the pace of this value chain. For this service, the dispatching function is similar to a factory's master production schedule or gateway workstation. The dispatching function's objectives are to maximize customer service and technician/truck utilization and minimize costs. Therefore, smart and timely information means more can be done with fewer resources.

Southwest Airlines

Since its inception, Southwest Airlines has shown lean performance when compared to other major airlines. For example, in fiscal year 2001, the average cost to fly one available passenger seat 1 mile was 7.6¢. The next best was American West at 8.8¢, followed by TWA at 9.3¢, and all others were higher—up to 71 percent higher. One study suggested that for all other U.S. major airline carriers to get down to Southwest's cost per average seat mile, $18 billion in costs needed to be taken out of their budgets![19] What is even more significant is that Southwest has historically operated small planes and short-distance flights and therefore cannot capitalize on economies of scale available to larger airlines.

Exhibit 17.7 shows the total operating costs of the average major domestic U.S. airline. The vast majority of total airline cost focuses on operations management activities: traffic servicing (13 percent), aircraft servicing (7 percent), flight operations (47 percent), reservations and sales (10 percent), and passenger in-flight service (7 percent). Note that the first three are low-contact (back-office) operations, whereas passenger in-flight service and reservations and sales are high-contact service management functions. Therefore, taking a lean approach to all operations is vital to airline performance. Southwest is clearly a lean airline—it does more with less than any other airline competitor. Let us examine some of the reasons.

Eliminate Waste In the airline industry, idle time is the largest form of waste. Southwest locates its planes at noncongested airports to help it minimize airplane turnaround time. Fewer ancillary services reduce the opportunity for waste and inefficiencies. Southwest also enjoys a much lower employee turnover rate than its competitors, resulting in lower training costs. Its frequent-flyer program is simple: Customers receive a free flight after eight paid flights. Other major airline programs are much more complex, requiring substantial overhead to track and report frequent-flyer points earned.

All the resources at Southwest work to keep the airplanes in the air earning revenue—the primary focus of its strategy. The more time spent on the ground, the less revenue. It relies on motivated employees, a culture focused on the customer, and teamwork to accomplish this strategy. Southwest employees are cross-trained and organized into teams to accomplish all key operational activities. For example, all employees cooperate to ensure timely takeoffs and landings; it is not unusual to see pilots helping load baggage if this will get the plane off on time. This maintains smooth system schedules and reduces the need for reschedules and reticketing, both of which are a form of rework. As one example—in as fast as 15 minutes—Southwest can change the flight crew; deplane and board 137 passengers; unload

Exhibit 17.7 Total Operating Costs for Average U.S. Major Airline Carriers[20]

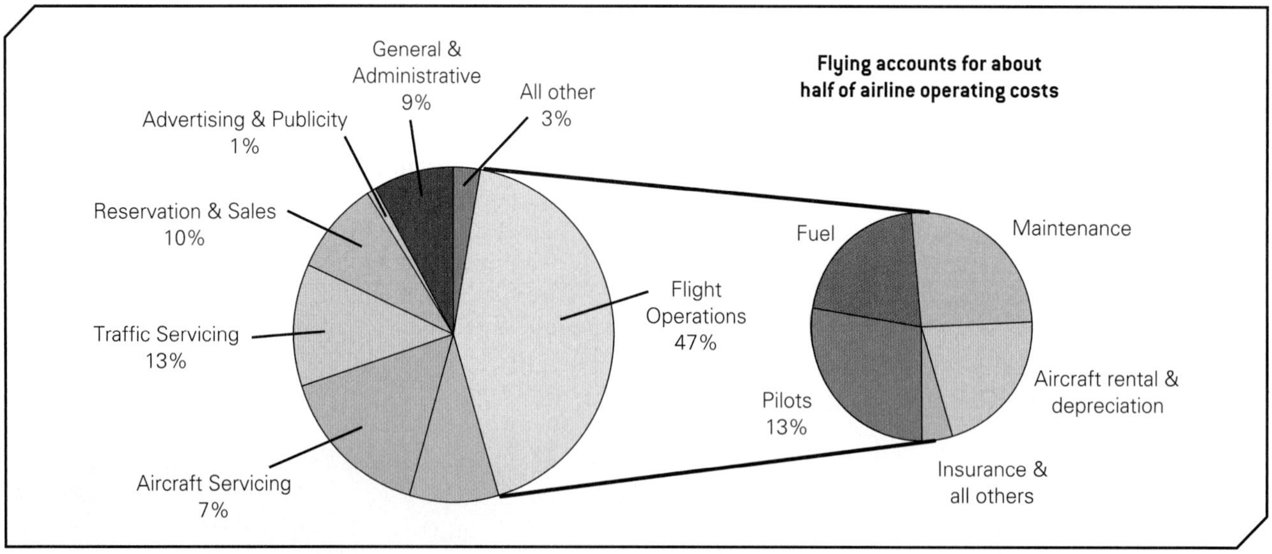

Source: "Unisys R2A Scorecard-Airline Industry Cost Management," figure 1, Unisys Corporation, Vol. 1, Issue 2, Nov. 2002. This report may be copied, in whole or in part, provided all legends, copyright, proprietary and other notices which appear herein are reproduced. © 2002 Unisys Corporation. Reprinted with permission of Unisys Corporation.

97 bags, 1,000 pounds of mail, and 25 pieces of freight; load another 123 bags and 600 pounds of mail; and pump 4,500 pounds of jet fuel into the aircraft.[21]

Increase Speed and Response Southwest uses a much simpler structure and operating system than competitors. It uses only one type of aircraft—the Boeing 737—making it easier to schedule crews, perform maintenance, and standardize such activities as boarding, baggage storage and retrieval, and cabin operations. It books direct flights from point A to B and does not rely on the hub-and-spoke system used by competitors. This makes it easier for many customers to get to their destinations, instead of, for instance, flying from Orlando to Cincinnati or Detroit and then connecting back to Nashville. A simple operating structure reduces the time it takes to make decisions and allows employees to focus on the key drivers of airline performance such as turnaround time. For example, if Southwest can turn its planes around on average in at most 1/2 hour while competitors take 1 hour, then, assuming a 90-minute flight, approximately one to two more flights per day per plane can be made. This can be a significant economic and strategic advantage.

Southwest was the first airline to introduce ticketless travel. Customers simply get a confirmation number and show up on time. A significant proportion of customers book their flights directly on Southwest.com. No in-flight full-service meals are provided either, simplifying cabin operations and eliminating the need to stock meals, which increases the time to clean up from the previous flight and prepare for the next flight. Instead, Southwest was the first airline to offer continental breakfast in the gate area, and flight attendants serve drinks and peanuts using specially designed trays. If a customer misses a flight, he or she can use the ticket for a future flight with no penalty; this reduces paperwork and processing, contributing to a leaner operation.

Improve Quality Simplified processes reduce variability in flight schedules, a major source of customer complaints, and therefore improve customers' perceptions of quality and satisfaction. Southwest encourages carry-on baggage; hence, there is less opportunity for losing, misrouting, or damaging baggage. People-oriented employees are carefully chosen and empowered to both serve and entertain passengers.

Reduce Cost Short setup and turnaround time translates into higher asset utilization and reduces the need for costly inventories of aircraft. Southwest does not have assigned seating; customers wait on a first-come, first-served basis and board in zones. This lowers costs, and only a few employees are needed to coordinate passenger boarding. In addition, rather than carry the high overhead costs of airplane maintenance and repair, Southwest outsources these tasks to third parties.

JUST-IN-TIME SYSTEMS

Just-in-Time (JIT) was introduced at Toyota during the 1950s and 1960s to address the challenge of coordinating successive production activities. An automobile, for instance, consists of thousands of parts. It is extremely difficult to coordinate the transfer of materials and components between production operations. Traditional factories use a push system, *which produces finished goods inventory in advance of customer demand using a forecast of sales.* Parts and subassemblies are "pushed" through the operating system based on a predefined schedule that is independent of actual customer demand. In a push system, a model that might not be selling well is still produced at the same predetermined production rate and held in finished goods inventory for future sale, whereas enough units of a model in high demand might not get produced.

Another problem was that traditional automobile production systems relied on massive and expensive stamping press lines to produce car panels. The dies in the presses weighed many tons and specialists needed up to a full day to switch them for a new part. To compensate for long setup times, large batch sizes were produced so that machines could be kept busy while others were being set up. This resulted in high work-in-process inventories and high levels of indirect labor and overhead.

Toyota created a system based on a simple idea: Produce the needed quantity of required parts each day. This concept characterizes a pull system, *in which employees at a given operation go to the source of required parts, such as machining or subassembly, and withdraw the units as they need them.* Then just enough new parts are manufactured or procured to replace those withdrawn. As the process from which parts were withdrawn replenishes the items it transferred out, it draws on the output of its preceding process, and so on. Finished goods are made to coincide with the actual rate of demand, resulting in minimal inventories and maximum responsiveness.

JIT systems are based on the concept of pull rather than push. In a JIT system, a key gateway workstation (such as final assembly) withdraws parts to meet demand and therefore provides real-time information to preceding workstations about how much to produce and when to produce to match the sales rate. By pulling parts from each preceding workstation, the entire manufacturing process is synchronized to the final-assembly schedule. JIT operating systems prohibit all process workstations from pushing inventory forward only to wait idle if it is not needed.

The name "just-in-time" arose from this concept of making parts from upstream processes only when needed by downstream processes. In this fashion, a JIT system can produce a steady rate of output to meet the sales rate in small, consistent batch sizes to level loads and stabilize the operating system. This dramatically reduces the inventory required between stages of the production process, thus greatly reducing costs and physical capacity requirements. Thus, JIT represents a very efficient inventory control process. An ideal JIT system would have single-piece flow if possible. Of course, to make this happen, a JIT system could not tolerate defects or long setup times; hence, continuous improvement is vital to improve quality and speed.

Learning Objective
To understand the concepts and philosophy of just-in-time operating systems and the challenges that managers face in managing JIT systems.

A push system produces finished goods inventory in advance of customer demand using a forecast of sales.

A pull system is one in which employees at a given operation go to the source of required parts, such as machining or subassembly, and withdraw the units as they need them.

Operation of a JIT System

As noted, JIT systems produce according to the rate of sales. Takt time is the production rate for one good or service based on the rate of sales. Takt time is a term used in lean operating systems and is equivalent to cycle time for assembly-line balancing as described in Chapter 8, and is computed using Equation (17.1).

$$\text{Takt time} = \frac{\text{Available time per time period}}{\text{Market demand rate per time period}} \qquad \textbf{(17.1)}$$

For example, an 8-hour workday that includes 1 hour for lunch and breaks effectively has 25,200 seconds per workday (7 hours/day × 3,600 seconds/hour). If the rate of sales is 400 units per day, then the takt time is (25,200 seconds/day)/(400 units/day) = 63 seconds/unit. If the production process pulls units through the system at the rate of 63 seconds/unit, the pace of production will match the pace of sales.

A simple generic JIT system with two process cycles—one for the customer and a second for the supply process—is shown in Exhibit 17.8. Conceptually, the customer can be an internal or external customer, and the customer-supply configuration in Exhibit 17.8 can be chained together to model a more complex sequence of production or assembly operations. In this process, the customer cycle withdraws what is needed at the time it is needed according to sales. The supply cycle creates the good to replenish only what has been withdrawn by the customer. The storage area is the interface and control point between the customer and supply cycles.

Slips, called Kanban cards (*Kanban* is a Japanese word that means "visual record" or "card"), are circulated within the system to initiate withdrawal and production items through the production process. *A **Kanban** is a flag or a piece of paper that contains all relevant information for an order: part number, description,*

*A **Kanban** is a flag or a piece of paper that contains all relevant information for an order: part number, description, process area used, time of delivery, quantity available, quantity delivered, production quantity, and so on.*

Exhibit 17.8 A Two-Card Kanban JIT Operating System

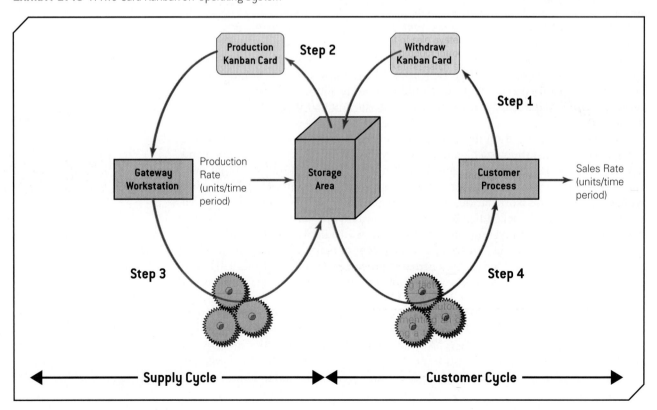

process area used, time of delivery, quantity available, quantity delivered, production quantity, and so on. Because of this, a JIT system is sometimes called a Kanban system.

The Kanban system begins when the customer buys or uses the good and an empty container is created. The withdraw Kanban (step 1) authorizes the material handler to transfer empty containers to the storage area. Withdraw Kanbans trigger the movement of parts. The material handler detaches the withdraw-ordering Kanban that was attached to the empty container and places the Kanban card in the storage area or on the Kanban receiving post, leaving the empty container(s) (step 1). A material handler for the supply cycle places a production Kanban on the empty container and this authorizes the gateway workstation to produce parts (step 2). Production Kanbans trigger the production of parts. The container holds a small lot size of parts. Without the authorization of the production Kanban, the gateway workstation and all other workstations may be idle. The gateway workstation must be scheduled to meet the sales rate and it pulls parts from all other workstations. The other workstations in the process do not need to be scheduled because they get their production orders from the production Kanban that pulls parts through the supply process. The supply process returns a full container of parts to the storage area with the production Kanban attached (step 3). The Kanban process is complete when the material handler for the customer process picks up a full container of parts and takes the production Kanban card off the container. Normally, the material handler drops off a withdrawal Kanban and empty container when picking up a full container of parts.

Note that the Kanban cards and containers are simple visual controls. Some JIT systems use the containers themselves as the signaling device and do not use Kanban cards. An empty or full container automatically tells everyone what to do and when to do it. Other types of visual controls used to pull parts through the production process include using cabinet drawers or marked-off spaces on the floor in the storage area. When the drawers or marked-off floor spaces are empty, that is the visual signal to produce another container of parts and fill the empty drawer or space.

To illustrate some examples of using Kanbans, truck drivers from component plants for a General Electric lamp division collect Kanban cards and empty containers when they unload. The card signals which components are to be delivered on the next trip. At a Hewlett-Packard plant, the signal for a subassembly shop that makes computer-system modules to send another plastic tub of parts forward is removal of the present plastic tub of parts from a sensing platform. At another Hewlett-Packard facility, an empty "Kanban square" outlined in yellow tape is the visual signal for the preceding workstation to forward another disk-drive unit.

JIT practice is to set the lot size or container size equal to about 5 percent to 20 percent of a day's demand or between 20 to 90 minutes worth of demand. The number of containers in the system determines the average inventory levels. The following equation is used to calculate the number of Kanban cards (K) required:

$$K = \frac{\text{Average daily demand during the lead time plus a safety stock}}{\text{Number of units per container}}$$

$$= \frac{d(p + w)(1 + \alpha)}{C} \qquad \textbf{(17.2)}$$

where K = the number of Kanban cards in the operating system.
   d = the average daily production rate as determined from the master production schedule.
   w = the waiting time of Kanban cards in decimal fractions of a day (that is, the waiting time of a part).

p = the processing time per part, in decimal fractions of a day.

C = the capacity of a standard container in the proper units of measure (parts, items, etc.).

α = a policy variable determined by the efficiency of the process and its workstations and the uncertainty of the workplace, and therefore, a form of safety stock usually ranging from 0 to 1. However, technically, there is no upper limit on the value of α.

For example, suppose that $d = 50$ parts/day, $w = 0.20$ day, $p = 0.15$ day, $C = 5$ parts, and $\alpha = 0.5$. Then the number of Kanban cards is calculated, using Equation (17.2), as

$$K = \frac{50(0.2 + 0.15)(1 + 0.5)}{5} = 5.25 \text{ containers} \cong 6 \text{ (rounded up to 6)}$$

The number of Kanban cards is directly proportional to the amount of work-in-process inventory. Managers and employees strive to reduce the number of cards in the system through reduced lead time (p or w), lower α values, or through other improvements. The maximum authorized inventory in the operating system is $K \times C$. In the previous example, $K \times C = 6$ Kanban sets $\times$ 5 parts per container = 30 parts.

Note that the numerator of Equation (17.2) is similar to the reorder point (r) in a FQS inventory system (see Chapter 11). Rewriting this as $d(p + w) + \alpha d(p + w)$, the first term is analogous to the demand during the lead time and the second to safety stock to buffer against inefficiencies and uncertainty. Once the system is running, supervisors can delete or add Kanban cards from or to the system as they observe that certain workstations need less or more work-in-process inventory.

WIP inventory is often viewed as an analogy to the water level in a lake, as shown in Exhibit 17.9. High levels hide critical inefficiencies such as equipment breakdowns, high scrap rates, and unreliable suppliers. By reducing inventory (and the number of Kanbans) these inefficiencies are exposed and must be solved to operate an effective JIT system.

JIT in Service Organizations

Although JIT has had its biggest impact in manufacturing, many service organizations are increasingly applying it. At the Nashua Corporation, for example, a JIT-oriented study of administrative operations reduced order-cycle time from 3 days to 1 hour, office space requirements by 40 percent, and errors by 95 percent and

Exhibit 17.9 A Water-Level Analogy of Waste

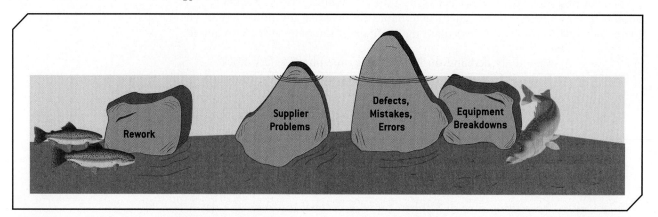

OM SPOTLIGHT

Baxter International[24]

St. Luke's Episcopal Hospital in Houston has applied JIT to its dispensing of hospital supply products. Most hospitals maintain a large inventory of supplies in a central storeroom and replenish the supplies needed in the various areas of the hospital on a regular basis. St. Luke's adopted a radical strategy; it closed its warehouse and sold its inventory to Baxter International Inc., a major hospital supplier. Baxter has become a partner with the hospital in managing, ordering, and delivering supplies. Baxter fills orders in exact, sometimes small, quantities and delivers them directly to the hospital departments, including operating rooms and nursing floors. The hospital is now saving $350,000 annually due to staff reductions and $162,500 by eliminating its inventory. Its storeroom has been converted to patient care and other productive uses.

increased productivity by 20 percent.[22] One overnight package-delivery service saw its inventory investment climb from $16 million to $34 million with conventional inventory-management techniques.[23] Implementing JIT reduced its inventory investment, but the company's major objective was to increase profits by providing a 99.9 percent level of service to its customers. Before JIT implementation, its service level—computed by dividing the number of items filled weekly by the number of items requested—was 79 percent. After JIT, the level was 99 percent, and the firm looked forward to meeting its goal. Baxter International is another service company that has experienced the benefits of a JIT system (see the OM Spotlight).

Designing Effective JIT Systems

Designing and implementing a well-run JIT system may seem simple but it is not (see OM Spotlight: The Hazards of One-Piece Flow). The entire value chain must synchronize its activities. Some of the challenging characteristics of a well-designed JIT system are summarized in Exhibit 17.10. These characteristics require knowledge and expertise in almost every topic previously covered in this book. Hence, JIT is an integrative operating system that demands the best ideas, methods, and management practices.

Exhibit 17.10 Example JIT Characteristics and Best Practices

- Setup/changeover time minimized
- Excellent preventive maintenance
- Mistake-proof job and process design
- Stable, level, repetitive master production schedule
- Phantom bill of materials with zero lead time
- Fast processing times
- Clean and uncluttered workspaces
- Very little inventory to hide problems and inefficiencies
- Use production cells with no wasted motion
- May freeze the master production schedule
- Use reusable containers
- Outstanding communication and information sharing
- Keep it simple and use visual controls
- High quality approaching zero defects
- Small repetitive order/lot sizes
- Minimize the number of parts/items
- Minimize the number of bill-of-material levels
- Facility layout that supports continuous or single-piece flow
- Minimize distance traveled and handling
- Clearly defined performance metrics
- Minimize the number of production, inventory, and accounting transactions
- Good calibration of all gauges and testing equipment
- Employees trained in quality management concepts and tools
- Excellent employee recognition and reward systems
- Employee cross-training and multiple skills
- Empowered and disciplined employees

OM SPOTLIGHT

The Hazards of One-Piece Flow[25]

An investment foundry manufactures small parts for aircraft and stationary turbine engines. The company has about 4,000 active part numbers, and they have wide variations in routings and work content. The technology is difficult, making yields and scrap rates unpredictable. Much of the equipment is large and expensive. The company had tried to apply JIT principles, but the complex product and process mix had baffled all attempts to put them into practice. For example, the product and process did not lend itself to one-piece flow. Operation times were very short, about 15–20 seconds. The parts were very small (about 1-1/2 inches). One process step, shot-blasting, required a large batch (number) of parts in order to function properly. Compounding this was the excessive distance between machines. Only after 3 years of trial and error did the firm understand the real principles of JIT and understand how to adapt it to its environment. One partial solution was to redefine the word *piece* as a JIT container of 20 castings. Small carriers were built to carry 20 castings, and queues were set up to allow accumulation of a reasonable batch quantity for shot blasting.

SOLVED PROBLEMS

SOLVED PROBLEM #1

Bracket Manufacturing uses a Kanban system for a component part. The daily demand is 800 brackets. Each container has a combined waiting and processing time of 0.34 days. The container size is 50 brackets and the safety factor (α) is 9 percent.

a. How many Kanban card sets should be authorized?

b. What is the maximum inventory of brackets in the system of brackets?

c. What are the answers to (a) and (b) if waiting and processing time is reduced by 25 percent?

d. If we assume one-half the containers are empty and one-half full at any given time, what is the average inventory in the system for the original problem?

Solution:

a. Using Equation (17.2):

$$K = \frac{d(p + w)(1 + \alpha)}{C}$$

$$= \frac{(800 \text{ units})(0.34)(1 + 0.09)}{50} = 5.93$$

$$\cong 6 \text{ (rounded up to 6)}$$

Thus, 6 containers and 6 Kanban card sets are necessary to fulfill daily demand.

b. The maximum authorized inventory is $K \times C = 6 \times 50 = 300$ brackets.

c. $$K = \frac{d(p + w)(1 + \alpha)}{C}$$

$$= \frac{(800 \text{ units})(0.255)(1 + 0.09)}{50} = 4.45$$

$$\cong 5 \text{ (rounded up to 5)}$$

Thus, 5 containers and 5 Kanban card sets are necessary to fulfill daily demand. The maximum authorized inventory is now $K \times C = 5 \times 50 = 250$ brackets.

d. The average inventory under this assumption is 300/2 = 150 brackets. Many variables in the JIT system determine whether this assumption is valid or not. For example, for a given combination of daily demand, processing and waiting times, and other process inefficiencies and uncertainties, it is possible for more or less containers to be empty (full).

SOLVED PROBLEM #2

TAC Manufacturing is implementing lean ideas and methods in its factory. It wants to compute the takt time based on its gateway assembly workstation that pulls parts from preceding workstations. The assembly workstation is available 9 hours a day; with 1 hour for lunch and breaks, it's available 8 hours per day. Daily demand is 1,000 units per day.

a. What is the takt time?

b. Show that cycle time used in balancing an assembly line is the same as takt time used by lean practitioners.

Solution:

a. Using Equation (17.1), Assembly workstation takt

$$time = \frac{(8 \times 60 \times 60)}{1,000} = \frac{28,800 \text{ seconds/day}}{1,000 \text{ parts/day}}$$
$$= 28.8 \text{ seconds/part}$$

b. From Chapter 8, cycle time is related to the output rate (R) by the following equation:

$$C = A/R \qquad \textbf{(Equation 8.2)}$$

where A = available time to produce the output and R = output rate. By definition they are the same, so cycle time = takt time = 28.8 seconds/part.

KEY TERMS AND CONCEPTS

Batching
Continuous improvement
Efficient layout and standardized work
5Ss (sort, set in order, shine, standardize, and sustain)
JIT characteristics and best practices
Just-in-time (Kanban) system
Lean enterprise
Lean operating systems
Lean Six Sigma
Manufactured Good Recovery Options
  Cannibalize
  Recycle
  Refurbish
  Remanufacture
  Repair
  Resell

Number of Kanban cards (K)
Pull operating system
Push operating system
Quality at the source
Seven types of waste
Single minute exchange of dies (SMED)
Single-piece flow
Supplier relationships
Synchronous value chain operation
Takt time
Total productive maintenance (TPM)
Transfer batch
Value stream mapping
Visual controls (andon)
Zero waste

QUESTIONS FOR REVIEW AND DISCUSSION

1. What is lean enterprise?

2. Explain the four fundamental objectives of lean operating systems.

3. What are the categories of waste as defined by Toyota? Can you cite some examples from your work experience or around your college or university?

4. Provide some examples of different types of waste in an organization with which you are familiar, such as an automobile repair shop or a fast-food restaurant.

5. What do we mean by "synchronize the entire value chain"? Why is this important to becoming lean?

6. How does quality improvement support lean enterprise?

7. What are the benefits of adopting lean operating systems?

8. Describe three lean tools and how they contribute to lean objectives.

9. What is takt time, and how does it help to assess performance of the value chain?

10. Explain the limitations of batching and how single-piece flow overcomes these limitations. Under what conditions is batching useful?

11. What are the "5Ss"? Why are they important to becoming lean?

12. What benefits do visual controls have for lean operating systems?

13. Explain the importance of short setup times in a lean environment. What approach is used to reduce setup times?

14. What types of "setups" do you perform in your work or school activities? How might you reduce the setup times?

15. What is Lean Six Sigma? Why are lean and Six Sigma concepts highly complementary?

16. Explain the role of total productive maintenance in lean operating systems.

17. Summarize the options for manufactured good recovery. How does this approach support lean objectives?

18. Would you buy a certified remanufactured automobile transmission for 60 percent of the price of a newly manufactured transmission? Why or why not?

19. Explain the role of technology in lean operating systems. Can you think of other types of technology that can support lean enterprise?

20. Explain the difference between push and pull systems. What advantages do pull systems have over push systems?

21. What is a Kanban? Explain how a Kanban system operates.

22. Explain the water-level analogy with WIP inventory.

23. Describe some of the key features of good JIT systems.

24. What is the role of suppliers in JIT systems?

25. Does a high alpha value (say $\alpha = 2$ or 3) in Equation (17.2) negate the benefits of a Kanban/JIT operating system? Explain.

26. Explain how the JIT concept can be adapted to service organizations.

27. Interview a manager at a local company that uses JIT. Report on how it is implemented and the benefits the company has realized.

28. Identify and explain one key lesson or best practice from each of the following lean operating system tours: (a) Gortons, (b) Timken, (c) SBC Communications, and (d) Southwest Airlines.

29. Compare the lean-service system of Southwest Airlines to a full-service airline such as United or British Airways on the following: (a) airplane boarding process, (b) cabin service, (c) ticket transfer to other Southwest flights, (d) frequent-flyer program, (e) baggage handling, (f) seat assignment system, and (g) service encounters.

30. Search the Internet for some manufacturing or service tours similar to the ones in this chapter. Classify their practices according to lean principles in a manner similar to the examples.

PROBLEMS AND ACTIVITIES

1. Bracket Manufacturing uses a Kanban system for a component. Daily demand is 1,000 units. Each container has a combined waiting and processing time of 0.85 days. If the container size is 70 and the alpha value (α) is 13 percent, how many Kanban card sets should be authorized? What is the maximum authorized inventory?

2. Lou's Bakery has established that JIT should be used for chocolate chips due to the high probability of the kitchen heat melting the chips. The average demand is 180 cups of chocolate chips per week. The average setup and processing time is 1/2 day. Each container holds exactly 2 cups. The current safety stock factor is 5 percent. The baker operates 6 days per week.

   a. How many Kanbans are required for the bakery?
   b. What is the maximum authorized inventory?
   c. If the average setup and processing time is reduced to 3/8ths of a day due to better training and retention of experienced employees, what are the answers to (a) and (b)?

3. An automobile transmission manufacturer is considering using a JIT approach to replenishing its stock of transmissions. Daily demand for transmission #230 is 25 transmissions per day and they are built in groups of six transmissions. Total assembly and waiting time is 3 days. The supervisor wants to use an alpha value (α) of 3, or 300%.

   a. How many Kanbans are required?
   b. What is the maximum authorized inventory?
   c. What are the pros and cons of using such a high alpha (α) value?

4. CDC Discrete Fabricators wants to produce parts in batches of 300. Each part must be processed sequentially from workstation A to B to C to D. The following information is also provided:

Workstation	Batch Size (Q)	Processing Time per Part
A	300	20 seconds
B	300	15 seconds
C	300	10 seconds
D*	300	25 seconds

*Bottleneck workstation

   a. How many seconds are required to produce the batch under the assumptions of batch processing?
   b. How many seconds are required to produce the batch under the assumptions of single-piece flow processing?
   c. Compare the two solutions in terms of time saved and any other issue(s) you think important.

CASES

COMMUNITY MEDICAL ASSOCIATES

Community Medical Associates (CMA) is a large health care system with two hospitals, 25 satellite health centers, and 56 outpatient clinics. CMA had 1.5 million outpatient visits and 60,000 inpatient admissions the previous year. Just a few years ago, CMA's health care delivery system was having significant problems with quality of care. Long patient waiting times, uncoordinated clinical and patient information, and medical errors plagued the system. Doctors, nurses, lab technicians, managers, and medical students in training were very aggravated with the labyrinth of forms, databases, and communication links. Accounting and billing were in a situation of constant confusion and correcting medical bills and insurance payments. The complexity of the CMA information and communication system overwhelmed its people.

Prior to redesigning its systems, physicians were faced with a complex array of appointments and schedules in order to see patients in the hospital, centers, and clinics. For example, an elderly patient with shoulder pain would get an X-ray at the clinic but have to set up an appointment for a CAT scan in the hospital. Furthermore, the patient's blood was sent to an off-site lab while physician notes were transcribed from tape recorders. Radiology would read and interpret the X-rays and body scans in a consultant report. Past and present medication records were kept in the hospital and off-site pharmacies. Physicians would write out on paper prescriptions for each patient. Billing and patient insurance information was maintained in a separate database. The patient's medical chart was part paper-based and part electronic. The paper medical file could be stored at the hospital, center, or clinic. Nurses handwrote their notes on each patient, but their notes were seldom input into the patient's medical records or chart.

"We must access one database for lab results, then log off and access another system for radiology, then log off and access the CMA pharmacy system to gain an integrated view of the patient's health. If I can't find the patient's records within 5 minutes or so, I have to abandon my search, and tell the patient to wait or make another appointment," said one doctor. The doctor continued, "You have to abandon the patient because you have to move on to patients you truly can diagnose and help. If you don't abandon the patient, you might make clinical decisions about the patient's health without having a complete set of information. Not having all the medical information fast has a direct impact on quality of care and patient satisfaction."

Today, CMA uses an integrated operating system that consolidates over 50 CMA databases into one. Health care providers in the CMA system now have access to these records through 7,000 computer terminals. Using many levels of security and some restricted databases, all patient information is accessible in less than 2 minutes. For example, sensitive categories of patient records, such as psychiatric and AIDS problems, were kept in super-restricted databases. It had cost CMA

$4.46 to retrieve and transport a single patient's paper-based medical chart to the proper location whereas the more complete and quickly updated electronic medical record costs $0.82 to electronically retrieve and transport once. A patient's medical records are retrieved on average 1.4 times for outpatient services and 6.8 times for inpatient admissions. In addition, CMA has spent more money on database security, although it has not been able to place a dollar value on this. Electronic security audit trails show who logs on, when, how long they view a specific file, and what information they viewed.

The same doctor who made the previous comments 2 years ago now said, "The speed of the system is what I like. I can now make informed clinical decisions for my patients. Where it used to take several days and sometimes weeks to transcribe my patient medical notes, it now takes no more than 48 hours to see them pop up on the CMA system. Often my notes are up on the system the same day. I'd say we use about one-half the paper we used with the old system. I also find myself

editing and correcting transcription errors in the database—so it is more accurate now."

The next phase in the development of CMA's integrated system was to connect it to suppliers, outside labs and pharmacies, other hospitals, and to doctor's home computers.

Case Assignment Questions

1. Explain how CMA used the four principles of lean operating systems to improve performance.

2. Draw a current and future state of the value chain for CMA's situation as best you can from case information. Give two examples of how the value chain could be synchronized to improve value chain performance.

3. Do you think applying operations management concepts and methods such as Six Sigma and lean principles can reduce U.S. health care costs? Explain. Provide examples that show how OM can help the U.S. health care industry.

BENCHMARKING JIT AT TOYOTA[26]

Richard Keever is the plant manager for a supplier of axles and other components for SUVs produced by one of the domestic automobile manufacturers. His company had been using traditional batch production methods, but as the industry has become more competitive, and customers have been demanding just-in-time deliveries, Keever realized that he must make the transition to a JIT operating environment to improve speed and response, as well as reduce cost, to help sustain the company's current competitive advantage.

Keever is well aware of Toyota's reputation for lean enterprise and decided to make a benchmarking trip to the Toyota Motor Manufacturing (TMM) plant in Long Beach, California, to learn about its JIT processes. TMM fabricates, assembles, and paints four models of truck beds for Toyota light trucks. In touring the plant and talking with the plant's managers, many of whom were there when JIT was initially implemented back in the 1970s, Keever learned much about their approaches and implementation challenges.

Kanban is used at the Toyota Long Beach plant to control the flow of material and production operations. The Kanbans in this plant are traveling paper tickets containing detailed information that provides control requirements and even satisfies accounting and Internal Revenue Service needs. This is in contrast to many Japanese plants, where Kanbans are simple (usually triangular) pieces of metal with limited information. However, the managers were quick to point out that

Kanban, by itself, is only a small piece of the total JIT planning and control system. The environment created by the Kanban attention and JIT philosophy is mostly responsible for continuous improvements in manufacturing and for reducing the WIP inventory.

Kanbans are often combined with bar coding to obtain rapid access to inventory-level information and to facilitate WIP cycle counting. Many types of Kanbans are used to trigger different operations or to order raw material. The Kanbans are placed on hooks on a board beside the entrance to each area. The hook board is the staging area for the Kanbans, which circulate between the suppliers and the warehouse, the warehouse and the press department, and so on.

TMM cycles 4,000 to 5,000 Kanbans per day, which requires an immense amount of manual sorting and placing on the proper hooks each day. The company uses a single-Kanban method of recirculation, whereby the Kanban represents both the authority to produce and also the move and identification ticket. The hook board is color-coded, as are the Kanbans, to indicate raw material or other stages of manufacturing. The motto, of course, is "no Kanban—no production."

An attempt is made to decrease the number of Kanbans each month to constantly drive down the in-process inventory and increase the inventory cycles. The objective is to reduce the lot sizes to one and the WIP inventory to zero. However, the schedule is not as rigid as in many other plants. A small safety stock is considered acceptable to allow for some flexibility in shifting the sequence of the operations or the mixture of the products. It also enables the plant to meet the schedule without exhausting the supply and interrupting the line. In the paint and stamping operations, the nature of manufacturing calls for a certain quantity per production run. In this case, a number of Kanbans accumulate before they trigger the production of the preceding operation.

The master schedule is used to calculate the number of Kanbans. The calculations are simple and mostly manual. The products are made to order, which is anticipatory due to the difficulty of coordination with Japan in terms of the precise timing and destination of the orders. Additional flexibility is built in to allow for changing priorities. Ideally, the truck should arrive in time for the bed to be assembled and then shipped to the dealers and delivered to the customers. Study teams are constantly working to coincide the orders without sacrificing the flexibility and the ability to deliver the trucks to the customers.

Visual controls are used wherever possible, using color, light boards, hook boards, charts, and graphs. The visual controls facilitate immediate identification of problems, such as shortage or excess of parts as well as any other unusual occurrence. Visual controls are also extended to testing and shipping areas. They are easy to understand and inexpensive and they allow for immediate detection. There is a control chart for each critical operation, graphing the performance of that operation versus the acceptable level. A buzzer is used to indicate a problem or a failure in a function. An unusually long buzz notifies the supervisor that the machine is out of sequence and additional help should be dispatched.

A computerized board in the assembly area contains many colored lights indicating the status of machines and orders. Another board provides information on the scheduled versus the actual production as well as the reason for the variance. It provides workers with immediate feedback and general awareness to assist them in taking corrective action when needed.

At TMM, many workers voluntarily belong to quality improvement teams, which meet weekly in paid overtime. The company initially established a team in the press area and then in the paint and the maintenance areas. The overall trend has been a rapid growth in the number of quality teams, the number of suggestions made, and the quality and complexity of suggestions. These teams were a great source of problem solving in preparation for JIT implementation.

The quality teams are particularly useful in implementing changes that workers tend to oppose. A JIT system requires many drastic changes in manufacturing.

Quality teams may be used to educate workers as to the benefits of JIT and convince them that making the necessary changes is worthwhile. Quality teams may also be used to implement and support the required changes very quickly. They usually solve a number of smaller problems while they are working on the main problem. Employee suggestions are well recognized by TMM managers and rewarded, though not necessarily financially. The company has firmly maintained the policy of retaining any worker whose job is eliminated in the productivity-improvement process by transferring his or her employment to another area.

Prior to using the JIT system at the Long Beach plant, the amount of raw material and WIP inventories and also of finished goods in the shipping area was of great concern to managers. Another concern was hidden problems in quality and material-handling procedures. A worker could produce several hours' worth of defective units before they were discovered. When JIT was first implemented, the immediate improvement was the reduction of inventories, which resulted in a major reduction in carrying and handling costs. The average WIP inventory was lowered by about 45 percent and the raw-material inventory by approximately 24 percent in 1 year. The warehousing cost of material was reduced by about 30 percent; the carrying and control costs were lowered accordingly.

As the inventory was drained, the overloaded buildings were emptied, and many hidden problems in handling and moving the material surfaced. The warehouse was reorganized, and the additional space was utilized for other productive purposes. Improvements in handling procedures resulted in shorter movement distances and fewer needs for equipment.

The material was delivered directly to the point of use. About 30 percent of the forklifts were eliminated as the average movement time and distance were reduced. In the production area, the number of presses was reduced by 30 percent. The same operations were performed with an approximately 20 percent reduction in labor, and the production volume per shift was increased by 40 percent in less than 2 years. Some of these improvements were direct results of JIT production, but many were simply due to changes made by the workers, inspired by the JIT atmosphere. The outgoing product quality was improved and warranty costs and replacement parts were reduced substantially.

The most noticeable improvements were in worker attitudes and awareness. The JIT environment offers continuous challenge in the sense that there is no reserved inventory to comfort production. As a problem arises in the sequence, the line comes to a halt immediately. Thus, the workers are constantly stimulated to discover problems and fix them. As a side benefit, absentee rates and labor turnover were substantially reduced.

During his flight back, Richard began thinking of what he needed to do to plan for implementing JIT in his plant.

Case Assignment Questions

1. What lessons did Keever learn from his benchmarking trip to Toyota?

2. What significant challenges or barriers might he face in his plant if he implemented JIT?

3. What should he tell his managers and workers tomorrow?

4. Develop a plan to implement JIT with an emphasis on what to do early in the JIT initiative.

JIT IN MAIL-ORDER PROCESSING[27]

Semantodontics is a direct marketing company that sells nationally by catalog to dentists. One of its major product lines is "personalized brochures, business cards, and patient medical handouts for dental practices." This product line was creating a larger-than-normal number of customer complaints, resulting in an increasing number of calls to the customer service department. A study of the reasons for customer service calls indicated that 64 percent of them involved two questions: What is this charge on my statement? and Where is my order?

After some investigation, both of these questions were found to be related to the long lead times required to produce personalized printed products. Customers often waited 3 or more weeks, and some statements mailed at the end of the month showed charges for orders invoiced but not yet printed. Therefore, the company began to study the process involved in meeting customer orders.

Exhibit 17.11 is a flowchart of the order-filling process. In the first step, telephone orders were taken over a 12-hour period each day. They were collected at the end of the day and checked for errors by the supervisor of the call center, usually the following morning. Depending on how busy the supervisor was, the 1-day batch of print orders would often not get to the data-processing department until after 1:00 P.M.

In the data-processing step, the telephone orders were invoiced, still in 1-day batches. Then the invoices were printed and matched back to the original orders. This step usually took most of the next day to complete. At this point in the process, if the order was for a new customer, it was sent to the person who did customer verification and set up new customer accounts on the computer. Setting up a new account would often delay an order by a day or more.

The next step was order verification and proofreading. Once invoicing was completed, the orders with invoices attached were given to a person who verified that all the required information was present and cor-

rect to permit typesetting. If there was a question at this time, the order was checked by computer or by calling the customer. It was common for this step to have a 2-day backlog of orders waiting for verification.

Finally, the completed orders were sent to the typesetting department of the print shop. Using current methods, an order for an existing customer took at least 4 days to flow from the order taker to typesetting. Often, a new customer's order took a day or two longer. In addition, there was often more than a 1-day backlog of orders at each step in the process.

Case Assignment Questions

1. Evaluate the current process from the perspective of lean operating systems and as a value stream. Outline some improvements to make this operation leaner and explain why you think your ideas will lead to improved performance.

2. It was determined that the new-customer setup procedure was the bottleneck for about 20 percent of the orders. Customer verification required looking up the customer in various directories or checking with the customer by telephone. This often took a day or more to complete. Can you think of ways to improve this?

3. Should Semantodontics set up a web site for online ordering by customers with or without human intervention? What problems do you anticipate with ordering personalized printed material online for a dental practice? Explain.

4. Define a possible future state map for this process, and explain why it should be adopted.

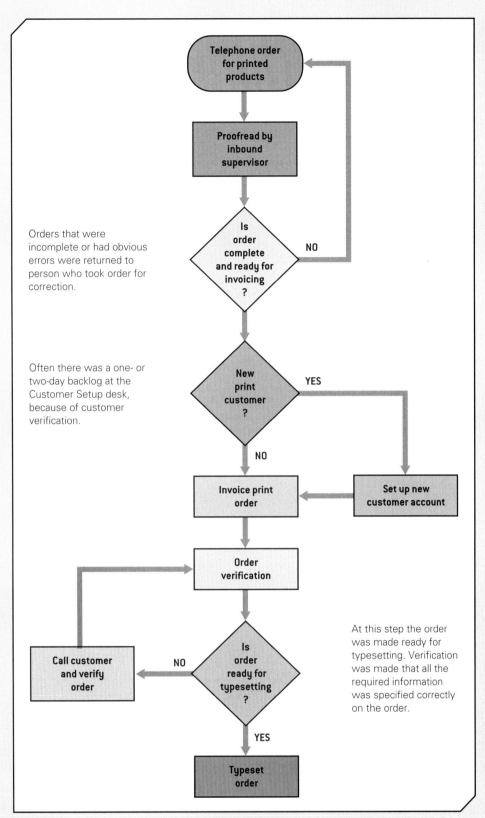

Exhibit 17.11
Flowchart of Semantodontics
Order-Filling Process

Orders that were incomplete or had obvious errors were returned to person who took order for correction.

Often there was a one- or two-day backlog at the Customer Setup desk, because of customer verification.

At this step the order was made ready for typesetting. Verification was made that all the required information was specified correctly on the order.

Source: The flowchart and background information for this case is adapted from Ronald G. Conant, "JIT in Mail-Order Operation Reduces Processing Time from Four Days to Four Hours," *Industrial Engineering* 20, no. 9 (1988), pp. 34–37. Reprinted with permission from Industrial Engineering.

ENDNOTES

[1] Woodruff, David, "Porsche is Back—and Then Some," *Business Week*, September 15, 1997, p. 57.

[2] Okes, Duke, "Organize Your Quality Toolbelt," *Quality Progress*, July 2002, pp. 25–29.

[3] Taylor, Alex, III, "How Toyota Defies Gravity," *Fortune*, December 8, 1997, pp. 100–108.

[4] Goland, Anthony R., Hall, John, and Clifford, Devereaux A., "First National Toyota," *The McKinsey Quarterly*, no. 4, 1998, pp. 58–66.

[5] Sources include the web site (http://www.tiautomotive.com) and a presentation by Eva Stewart, Lean Manufacturing Manager, TI Automotive, Center for Excellence in Manufacturing Management (CEMM), Fisher College of Business, Ohio State University, April 12, 2004.

[6] Van, Jon, "Leaks No Longer Stain Harley-Davidson Name," *Chicago Tribune*, November 4, 1991, p. 16.

[7] Schonberger, Richard J., "Just-in-Time Production Systems: Replacing Complexity with Simplicity in Manufacturing Management," *Industrial Engineering* 16, no. 10, October 1984, pp. 52–63.

[8] "Thinking Machines," *Business Week Online*, August 7, 2000. http://www.businessweek.com/archives/2000/b3693096.arc.htm.

[9] Henkoff, Ronald, "Delivering the Goods," *Fortune*, November 28, 1994, pp. 64–78.

[10] Conner, Gary, "Benefiting from Six Sigma," *Manufacturing Engineering*, February 2003, pp. 53–59.

[11] http://www.strategosinc.com/mnt.htm.

[12] Nakajima, Seiichi, "Explanation of New TPM Definition," *Plant Engineer* 16, no. 1, pp. 33–40.

[13] Maggard, Bill N., and Rhyne, David M., "Total Productive Maintenance: A Timely Integration of Production and Maintenance," *Production and Inventory Management Journal* 33, no. 4, Fourth Quarter 1992, pp. 6–10.

[14] "Ink Fight Stains Printer Companies," *The Columbus Dispatch*, Columbus, Ohio, May 6, 2002, p. E4.

[15] Thierry, M., Salomon, M., Nunen, J., and Wassenhove, L., "Strategic Issues in Product Recovery Management," *California Management Review* 37, no. 2, Winter 1995, p. 118.

[16] Whiteacre, J., "Lean Success in the Plant, the Supply Chain, and the Office," http://www.leanadvisors.com/lean/articles/gortons2004.cfm.

[17] Ellis, R., and Hankins, K., "The Timken Journey for Excellence," Presentation for the Center of Excellence in Manufacturing Management, Fisher College of Business, Ohio State University, Columbus, Ohio, August 22, 2003. Also see Timken's 2003 Annual Report and "From Missouri to Mars—A Century of Leadership in Manufacturing," http://www.timken.com.

[18] Collier, D. A., and Wilson, D. D., "The Role of Automation and Labor in Determining Customer Satisfaction in a Telephone Repair Service," *Decision Sciences* 28, no. 3, 1997, pp. 689–708; and Collier, D. A., and Wilson, D. D., "A Structural Equation Model of a Telephone Repair Service Process," *Proceedings of the Western Decision Sciences Institute*, Hawaii, March 25–29, 1997, pp. 584–586.

[19] "Unisys R2A Scorecard—Airline Industry Cost Measurement," Figure 1, *Unisys Corporation* 1, no. 2, November 2002, pp. 1–2.

[20] "Unisys R2A Scorecard—Airline Industry Cost Measurement," Figure 8, *Unisys Corporation* 1, no. 2, November 2002, p. 5.

[21] Freiberg, Kevin, and Freiberg, Jackie, *Nuts!*, Austin, TX: Bard Press, 1996, p. 59.

[22] Dickinson, Paul E., Dodge, Earl C., and Marshall, Charles S., "Administrative Functions in a Just-in-Time Setting," *Target*, Fall 1988, pp. 12–17.

[23] Inman, R., and Mehra, S., "JIT Implementation within a Service Industry: A Case Study," *International Journal of Service Industry Management* 1, no. 3, 1990, pp. 53–61.

[24] Freudenheim, Milt, "Removing the Warehouse from Cost-Conscious Hospitals," *The New York Times*, Sunday, March 3, 1991, p. F5.

[25] http://www.strategosinc.com/onepieceflow_1.htm.

[26] The information about Toyota is adapted from Sepehri, Mehran, "How Kanban System Is Used in an American Toyota Motor Facility," *Industrial Engineering* 17, no. 2, 1985.

[27] The flowchart and background information for this case is adapted from Conant, Ronald G., "JIT in a Mail-Order Operation Reduces Processing Time from Four Days to Four Hours," *Industrial Engineering* 20, no. 9, 1988, pp. 34–37.

Chapter Outline

CHAPTER 18

Project Management

Learning Objectives

1. To understand the project life cycle and identify key issues associated with project definition, planning, organizational structure, and project team management.

2. To apply the Critical Path Method (CPM) as a technique to plan, monitor, and control projects.

3. To calculate crashing schedules to reduce project completion time.

4. To incorporate uncertainty of activity time estimates into project scheduling and to calculate probabilities for project completion time.

5. To learn the capabilities and applications of contemporary project management software.

- The Olympic Games were established over 2,500 years ago in Olympia, southern Greece, to honor Zeus, following a tradition created by Hercules, who competed for the prize of an olive branch. The modern Olympic games were brought back to Athens in 1896. Athens was chosen in 1997 to host the 2004 Games, but badly underestimated the cost and overestimated its ability to meet construction and preparation schedules. Organizers were plagued with construction delays and budget overruns, forcing them to complete 7 years' work in just 4. Delays in the main stadium's glass-and-steel room pushed back delivery of the entire complex to the end of July, immediately preceding the August 13 opening ceremonies. The International Olympic Committee had even considered asking Athens organizers to cancel it.[1] Problems also occurred with other venues. Construction delays had consequences for Greece's own athletes, forcing them out of their own training centers. Even the famed Parthenon, which was to have been restored for the Games, was still shrouded with scaffolding when tourists began arriving. Despite all this, the venues were ready—although some at the last minute, and the Games were successfully completed.

- Construction of the Denver International Airport (DIA), which replaced Denver's old Stapleton Airport in 1995, was plagued by so many technical problems that its opening date was 16 months late, costing the city and airport authorities more than $1 million per day in late penalties and interest. The major problem was that the airport's state-of-the-art automated baggage handling system constantly failed, throwing luggage all around the basement of the main terminal. A representative of the firm that managed the baggage handling project noted that it simply misjudged the time expected to complete the project, trying to do a job in 4 years that should have taken 7. As the project fell further behind, human error became a more significant factor.[2] When DIA finally opened at a cost of $3 billion over budget, a storm that dumped a half-foot of snow brought it to its knees. Snow and rain leaked through the tower roof and fell on computer equipment. In 2005, United Airlines announced that it was switching back to a conventional manual system.

- After 90 years of contamination from a nearby petroleum processing facility, a major remediation project was conducted at Avila Beach, California, one of the best recreational beaches in the area. The cleanup required demolition of beachfront buildings, a section of the municipal pier, and other parts of the infrastructure before excavating and removing the contaminated soil. Prior to these activities, it was necessary to relocate sewer, water, natural gas, electric, and telephone lines to maintain uninterrupted service to portions of the nearby town. Afterwards, the streets and utilities infrastructure needed to be restored. Two historical landmarks were relocated temporarily, refurbished, and returned to their original locations. The contaminated soil was shipped off-site and the oil was collected and disposed of in a special facility. All remediation activities were completed about 5 months ahead of schedule.[3]

© Getty Images/PhotoDisc

Discussion Questions: Think of a project in which you have been involved, perhaps at work or in some student activity. Did you experience any similar types of problems that plagued the Olympic Games planners or the Denver International Airport project? If so, what factors do you think contributed to these problems? If your project went smoothly, what factors do you attribute to its success?

Many activities in designing and improving value chains require planning, scheduling, and resource allocation. Some examples that draw from previous chapters include installing new technology or integrated operating systems, reconfiguring machines and equipment to support a new facility or redesigned factory layout, and performing a Six Sigma process improvement idea. *A project is a temporary and often customized initiative that consists of many smaller tasks and activities that must be coordinated and completed to finish the entire initiative on time and within budget.* Suppose that a small business is considering expanding its facility. Some of the major tasks in planning for expansion are hiring architects, designing a new facility, hiring contractors, building the facility, purchasing and installing equipment, and hiring and training employees. Each of these major tasks consists of numerous subtasks that must be performed in a particular sequence, on time, and on budget. Taken together, these activities constitute a project.

In many firms, projects are the major value creation process, and the major activities in the value chain revolve around projects. Some examples are market research studies, construction, movie production, software development, book publishing, and wedding planning. In other firms, projects are used on an infrequent basis to implement new strategies and initiatives or for supporting value chain design and improvement activities. Some examples are preparation of annual reports, installing an automated materials handling system, or training employees to

A project is a temporary and often customized initiative that consists of many smaller tasks and activities that must be coordinated and completed to finish the entire initiative on time and within budget.

learn a new computer support system. Even U.S. courts use projects to help resolve construction claim litigations. Exhibit 18.1 lists a variety of examples of projects in many different functional areas of business.

In all project situations, projects require systematic management. **Project management** *involves all activities associated with planning, scheduling, and controlling projects.* Good project management ensures that an organization's resources are used efficiently and effectively. This is particularly important, as projects generally cut across organizational boundaries and require the coordination of many different departments and functions and sometimes companies. In addition, most projects are unique, requiring some customization and response to new challenges.

The 2004 Olympic Games provide a good example of the importance of project management and obtaining good time and cost estimates to meet the due dates. We suspect that the organizers of the first formal Olympics in 776 B.C. used basic concepts of project management. The Denver International Airport episode shows the high cost of missing project due dates. Not only must a project meet its due date but it should also produce high-quality outputs and outcomes within cost and resource constraints. The assumption of high-quality work is not always realized, since the airport roof leaked. In addition, the airport was $3 billion over budget! The third episode, however, shows how smoothly things can go with good project management. Although the remediation project required many difficult tasks, the ability to complete it ahead of schedule can only be attributed to sound planning and management.

This chapter addresses

- the scope of project management and specific approaches to project planning, scheduling, and control
- the role of leadership, team building, and skills characteristic of an effective project manager

Exhibit 18.1

Example Projects in Different Functional Areas That Impact the Value Chain

Functional Areas	Example Projects
Marketing	Point-of-sale system installation New product introduction Market research studies
Accounting and Finance	Auditing a firm's accounting and financial systems Planning a firm's initial public offering (IPO) Auditing a firm's procedures and stock trading rules for compliance with the Securities & Exchange Commission
Information Systems	Software development Software upgrades through a firm Hardware installation
Human Resource Management	Launching and coordinating training programs Annual performance and compensation review Implementing new benefits plans
Engineering	Designing new manufactured parts Implementing a new computer-aided design system Installing factory automation
Logistics	Installing an automated warehouse system Implementing an order-tracking system Building a transportation hub
Operations	Planning preventive maintenance for an oil refinery Implementing ERP software and systems Installing a revenue management system

- quantitative techniques for scheduling project activities with and without limited resources

We begin by examining the "big-picture" issues and organizational structure necessary to conduct effective projects.

THE SCOPE OF PROJECT MANAGEMENT

Learning Objective
To understand the project life cycle and identify key issues associated with project definition, planning, organizational structure, and project team management.

Most projects go through similar stages from start to completion. These stages characterize the project life cycle and form the basis for effective project management.

1. *Define:* Projects are implemented to satisfy some need; thus the first step in managing a project is to clearly define the goal of the project, responsibilities, deliverables, and when it must be accomplished. A common way to capture this information is with a specific and measurable *statement of work*. For example, the goal of an accounting audit might be to "audit the firm's accounting and financial statement and submit a report by December 1, 2005 that determines statement accuracy in accordance with generally accepted accounting principles in the United States of America. The audit fee shall not exceed $200,000." Here, the accounting audit firm sets the goal of the audit in terms of work content, delivery date, and cost.
2. *Plan:* In this stage, the steps needed to execute a project, determine who will perform them, and identify their start and completion dates are developed. Planning entails breaking down a project into smaller activities and developing a project schedule by estimating the time required for each activity and scheduling them so they meet the project due date. A company accounting and financial audit may include work activities such as the purchase order and accounts payable processes, revenue and accounts receivable processes, and electronic funds transfer and records. Different work teams may be assigned to these project activities under the accounting principle of *separation of duties*, to ensure audit objectivity.
3. *Organize:* This stage focuses on orchestrating the resources to execute the plan cost-effectively. Organizing involves such activities as forming a team, allocating resources, calculating costs, assessing risk, preparing project documentation, and ensuring good communications. It also requires identifying a project manager who provides the leadership to accomplish the project goal. A variety of resources may be required for project activities, such as the following:
   - executives, managers, and supervisors
   - professional and technical personnel
   - transportation services
   - capital equipment
   - utilities
   - materials
   - temporary offices
   - equipment and tools
   - Internet access
   - clerical services

   The project manager must determine how many of these resources are required, if they are available, and where in the organization they can be obtained. Then the manager must bring these resources together at the proper times to perform the activities of the project. Virtual teams are sometimes used to accomplish project work such as engineering and business consulting.
4. *Control:* This stage assesses how well a project meets its goals and objectives and makes adjustments as necessary. Controlling involves collecting and assessing

status reports, managing changes to baselines, and responding to circumstances that can negatively impact the project participants.

5. *Close:* Closing a project involves compiling statistics, releasing and/or reassigning people, and preparing "lessons learned."

Most firms have adopted a project life cycle model and often refer to it as their *project management methodology* (see the OM Spotlight: Xerox Global Services).

OM SPOTLIGHT

Xerox Global Services

Xerox Global Services is a consulting, integration, and outsourcing arm of Xerox Corporation with a vision "To provide the most comprehensive, most effective connections between people, knowledge and documents that the world has ever seen." To meet this challenge, they provide a portfolio of services that include I/T Managed Services such as technology deployment, asset management, and procurement; Business Innovation, including knowledge management, application integration, and systems integration; Office Services that include document assessment, asset optimization, and help desk support; and Hosted Services, which include imaging, repository, and document management services. These services are applied at the strategic, process, and infrastructure levels and address not only technology issues but also people, process, and culture issues.

Central to Xerox Global Services delivery of services is project management, which is described by their Client Engagement Process called "X5 Methodology":

1. *Discovery* There is no such thing as an off-the-shelf solution. Every client is different. Every situation requires a unique response. There may be opportunities to draw on previous solutions, but we never, never start with answers—we start with questions.
2. *Definition* Define the client's requirements. Define the scope of the project. Define the deliverables. Make everything measurable. Take a "no surprises" approach to every project.
3. *Start-up* Create a detailed project plan based on everything learned in the Discover and Definition phases. Make sure everyone understands it. Stick to it.
4. *Delivery* Implement according to plan. Follow best practices. Constantly monitor progress. Test as appropriate. Assume nothing. Cut no corners. Work fast, but work smart. If changes are necessary, make sure everyone knows what, why, when, and how. Once implemented, we provide the support and ongoing management.
5. *Evaluation* Is the solution meeting or exceeding expectations? How can it be made even better? What about ongoing evaluations management? What has changed since the solution was implemented that must be addressed?

The project manager manages a team that includes technical resource specialists, consultants, and project coordinators. The principal role of the project manager at Xerox Global Services is that of a customer advocate—to ensure that expectations are fully met. This requires careful understanding and documentation of customer expectations such as timeliness, meeting budget, system response, and security. As John Whited, Manager, Project Office, notes, "Most projects fail because user requirements are not understood." These requirements are translated into a detailed work breakdown structure with specific tasks assigned to project team members (see Exhibit 18.2). This also helps to prepare a budget and monitor progress. Finally, after each project is completed, the team conducts a review of "lessons learned"—What went right? and What went wrong? to continuously improve the company's ability to meet its customer expectations.

Our appreciation goes to John Whited of Xerox Global Services for providing this example.

Xerox Corporation

Exhibit 18.2 Example of Xerox Global Services Project Work Breakdown Structure

Activity	SA	Consultant	PM	PCS	PARC	CKM	Extended
Acme Grinding Phase II **Requirements Specification Pricing** **4/9/02**							
				Resources			
Prepare Interview Prep Questions	4						$620.00
Prepare "Service Status" Documentation	1	1					$285.00
Prepare "Applications" Documentation	1	1					$285.00
Prepare "Project Status" Documentation	1	1					$285.00
Prepare "Knowledge Management" Documentation	1	1					$285.00
Prepare "Competitor Information" Documentation	1	1					$285.00
Prepare "Address Book" Documentation	1	1					$285.00
Interview Service Team About "Service Status"	2	2	2			2	$1,310.00
Interview Application Team About "Applications"	2	2	2			2	$1,310.00
Interview Engineering Team About "Project Status"	2	2	2			2	$1,310.00
Interview Service/Application/HR Teams About "Knowledge Management"	2	2	2			2	$1,310.00
Interview Marketing/Application Teams About "Competitor Information"	2	2	2			2	$1,310.00
Interview Sales Team About "Address Book"	2	2	2			2	$1,310.00
Interview Sales Team About Contact Management Software	2	2	2			2	$1,310.00
Prepare "Contact Management Software" Documentation	1	1					$285.00
Document Users	2						$310.00
Document Goals	4						$620.00

Legend: SA = Solution Architect; PM = Project Manager; PCS = consulting firm subcontractor; PARC = Palo Alto Research Center project consultant; CKM = Certified Knowledge Manager

Roles of the Project Manager and Team Members

Project managers have significant responsibilities. It is their job to build an effective team, motivate them, provide advice and support, align the project with the firm's strategy, and direct and supervise the conduct of the project from beginning to end. Project managers are often generalists who have diverse backgrounds and experience. In addition to managing the project, they must manage the relationships among the project team, the parent organization, and the client. In this regard, the project manager's ability to facilitate is more important than his or her ability to supervise. The project manager must also have sufficient technical expertise to resolve disputes among functional specialists. In general, successful project managers have four key skills: a bias toward task completion, technical and administrative credibility, interpersonal and political sensitivity, and leadership ability.

All the planning tools in the world cannot guarantee that a project will be successful, because work still gets accomplished by people. Good project managers recognize that people issues are as important as technical issues. Several principles can help project managers be successful.[4]

- *Manage people individually and as a project team.* Project managers need to understand that people do things because they are motivated to do them, and therefore, must pay attention to individuals and their differences, and not simply to the project itself.
- *Reinforce the commitment and excitement of the project team.* The best way to obtain commitment is to allow people to volunteer to be involved and establish a sense of ownership. They should be empowered to establish goals and objectives. Increasing the visibility of the team's efforts and successes leverages the work that people perform.
- *Keep everyone informed.* Good communication is vital to a project's success. Regular feedback ensures that stakeholders deal with facts, not rumors. Project managers also need to be good listeners.
- *Build agreements and consensus among the team.* Some studies show that project managers spend half their time managing differences. Because project teams normally do not work together, differences are inevitable, and project managers must be able to manage conflicts constructively and turn them into creative opportunities.
- *Empower the project team.* What people want most from project managers is honesty, competence, direction, and inspiration; in short, credibility. On high-performing teams, managers share their power, and all team members feel that they can contribute to the project's success and are more likely to share their ideas.
- *Encourage risk-taking and creativity.* Projects often focus on difficult, unstructured problems. Effective project managers plan time for thinking and experimentation. Fostering an open exchange of ideas and promoting exposure to new ideas enhances creative effort.

Because projects are team-based, their success depends not only on strong leadership of the project manager but also on supportive behaviors of the team members. Peter Scholtes, a leading authority on teams, has suggested ten ingredients for a successful team[5]:

1. *Clarity in team goals.* As a sound basis, a team agrees on a mission, purpose, and goals.
2. *An improvement plan.* A plan guides the team in determining schedules and mileposts by helping the team decide what advice, assistance, training, materials, and other resources it may need.
3. *Clearly defined roles.* All members must understand their duties and know who is responsible for what issues and tasks.
4. *Clear communication.* Team members should speak with clarity, listen actively, and share information.
5. *Beneficial team behaviors.* Teams should encourage members to use effective skills and practices to facilitate discussions and meetings.
6. *Well-defined decision procedures.* Teams should use data as the basis for decisions and learn to reach consensus on important issues.
7. *Balanced participation.* Everyone should participate, contribute their talents, and share commitment to the team's success.
8. *Established ground rules.* The group outlines acceptable and unacceptable behaviors.
9. *Awareness of group process.* Team members exhibit sensitivity to nonverbal communication, understand group dynamics, and work on group process issues.
10. *Use of the scientific approach.* This includes gathering and analyzing appropriate information on a rational basis and not simply relying on gut instinct.

Organizational Structure

How a project fits into a firm's organizational structure impacts its effectiveness. Some organizations use a pure project organizational structure whereby team members are assigned exclusively to projects and report only to the project manager. This approach makes it easier to manage projects, because project teams can be designed for efficiency by including the right mix of skills; however, it can result in inefficiencies because of duplication of resources across the organization, for example, having a different information technology support person on each project. A pure functional organizational structure charters projects exclusively within functional departments, such as manufacturing or research and development. Although this approach allows team members to work on different projects simultaneously and provides a "home" for the project, it ignores an important reality: In a typical functional organization, a project cuts across organizational boundaries. Assigning projects exclusively to functional areas makes communication across the organization difficult and can limit the effectiveness of projects that require a systems perspective. A practical solution to this dilemma is a matrix organizational structure, which "loans" resources to projects while still maintaining control over them. Project managers coordinate the work across the functions. This minimizes duplication of resources and facilitates communication across the organization but requires that resources be negotiated. Functional managers may be reluctant to provide the resources, and employees assigned to projects might relegate a project to a lower priority than their daily, functional job, making it difficult for the project manager to control the project.

Toyota uses a type of matrix organization. In the 1990s, Toyota divided all of its new product development projects into three centers—one responsible for rear-wheel-drive platforms and vehicles, a second for front-wheel-drive platforms and vehicles, and a third for utility vehicles and vans. Each works on about five new vehicle projects simultaneously. Subsequently, Toyota created a fourth center for components and systems. This reorganization eliminated 16 different functional engineering divisions and replaced them with 6 engineering divisions; this reduced the number of coordination tasks required for each project, as well as the number of projects managed by each functional manager. This has strengthened the role of project managers and improved interproject coordination.[6]

Factors for Successful Projects

Projects are not always successful. Information technology projects have a notorious rate of failure. One study in the United States found that over 30 percent of software projects are canceled before completion and more than half cost almost double their original estimates. The consulting firm KPMG found that projects fail because of schedule overruns, use of unproven technology, poor estimates or weak definitions of objectives, and supplier problems. Many of the factors that ensure successful project performance are quite obvious and are the same ones that are needed for any organizational change. They include strong leadership and teamwork, good two-way communication and conflict resolution, and sufficient resources. Similarly, when initiatives fail, reasons are typically the usual suspects, such as unclear objectives, poor leadership and teamwork, ineffective use of tools, and unreasonable deadlines (see the OM Spotlight on Hershey). Exhibit 18.3 summarizes the principal factors that help or hinder project management.

Ensuring project success depends on having well-defined goals and objectives, clear reporting relationships and channels of communication, good procedures for estimating time and other resource requirements, cooperation and commitment among all project team members, realistic expectations, effective conflict resolution, and top-management sponsorship.

Exhibit 18.3 Contributors and Impediments to Project Success

Contributors to Project Success	Impediments to Project Success
Well-defined and agreed-upon objectives	Ill-defined project objectives
Top-management support	Lack of executive champion
Strong project manager leadership	Inability to develop and motivate people
Well-defined project definition	Poorly defined project definition
Accurate time and cost estimates	Lack of data accuracy and integrity
Teamwork and cooperation	Poor interpersonal relations and teamwork
Effective use of project management tools	Ineffective use of project management tools
Clear channels of communication	Poor communication among stakeholders
Adequate resources and reasonable deadlines	Unreasonable time pressures and lack of resources
Constructive response to conflict	Inability to resolve conflicts

OM SPOTLIGHT

Hershey's Halloween Nightmare[7]

Some years ago, Hershey Foods Corp. decided to install an enterprise resource planning system plus companion packages from two other vendors simultaneously during one of the busiest shipping seasons. What was envisioned originally as a 4-year project was squeezed down into just 30 months, with disastrous consequences. When the system went live in July of 1999, retailers began ordering large amounts of candy for back-to-school and Halloween sales. By mid-September, the company was still having trouble pushing orders through the new system, resulting in shipment delays and deliveries of incomplete orders. The new system required enormous changes in the way Hershey's workers did their jobs, which might not have been adequately addressed in the project management design. One analyst noted that most companies install ERP systems in a more staged manner, especially when applications from multiple vendors are involved.

The ERP installation project led to another complex project—fixing the new system. The company spent 2 days reviewing the new system, developing a list of changes that needed to be made to improve the view of product inventories and the way that information flowed between different applications. Testing to ensure that the fixes were done right required significant time. When Hershey announced a 19 percent drop in third-quarter profits, the CEO noted that system fixes were taking longer than expected and requiring more extensive changes. September inventories were up 29 percent from the previous year because of the order-processing problems.

Jay Mallin/Bloomberg News/Landov

Learning Objective
To apply the Critical Path Method (CPM) as a technique to plan, monitor, and control projects.

TECHNIQUES FOR PLANNING, SCHEDULING, AND CONTROLLING PROJECTS

All project management decisions involve three factors: *time*, *resources*, and *cost*. Project managers need to know how much time a project should take and when specific activities should be started and completed so that deadlines can be established and the progress of the project monitored. They must also determine the resources, such as people and equipment, available for the project and how they should be allocated among the various activities. Finally, the cost of the project must be determined and then controlled. Project managers seek ways to minimize costs without jeopardizing deadlines.

Various techniques have long been used to help plan, schedule, and control projects. The key steps involved are

1. *Project Definition:* Identifying the activities that must be completed and the sequence required to perform them
2. *Resource Planning:* For each activity, determining the resource needs: personnel, time, money, equipment, materials, and so on
3. *Project Scheduling:* Specifying a time schedule for the completion of each activity
4. *Project Control:* Establishing the proper controls for determining progress and developing alternative plans in anticipation of problems in meeting the planned schedule

Several software packages, such as Microsoft Project™, are available to help project managers plan and manage projects. Although we will not discuss such software in detail, we will introduce the underlying techniques that are used in modern project management software.

To illustrate how these steps are applied in project management, we will use a simple example. Wildcat Software Consulting Inc. helps companies implement software integration projects. Bart Drewmore has been named the project manager in charge of coordinating the design and installation of the new software system. In the following sections, we address the various tasks involved in project definition, resource planning, project scheduling, and project control that he will face in his role as project manager.

Project Definition

The first step is to define the project objectives and deliverables. Drewmore and his project team decided on the following statements:

> **Project Objective:** To develop an integrative software package within a predetermined budgeted and promised project completion date that meets all system requirements while providing adequate interfaces with legacy systems.
> **Deliverables:** (1) new software package, (2) successful implementation of the package, (3) pretraining of sales force and PC system operators.

Next, Drewmore needed to identify the specific activities required to complete the project and the sequence in which they must be performed. **Activities** *are discrete tasks that consume resources and time.* **Immediate predecessors** *are those activities that must be completed immediately before an activity may start.* Precedence relationships ensure that activities are performed in the proper sequence when they are scheduled. Precedence relationships are determined in two ways. First, there may exist a *technical reason* why one activity should precede another. For example, it is better to drill a steel part first and then heat treat it because the quality would be better and hardened steel would burn up drill bits faster. Precedence relationships may also result from *logical workflow requirements*. For instance, it is illogical to seal an envelope before stuffing it. People who define the work breakdown structure must be experienced in knowing exactly how the work is to be accomplished.

The initial list of activities and precedence relationships associated with the software integration project is summarized in Exhibit 18.4. This information is sometimes called the "work breakdown structure." For instance, activities A and B can be started anytime, since they do not depend on the completion of prior activities.

Activities *are discrete tasks that consume resources and time.*

Immediate predecessors *are those activities that must be completed immediately before an activity may start.*

Exhibit 18.4
Project Activities and
Precedence Relationships

Activity	Activity Description	Immediate Predecessors
A	Define software project objectives, budget, due date, and possible staff	none
B	Inventory new and old software interfaces and features	none
C	Assemble teams and allocate work	A, B
D	Design and develop code from old to new databases	C
E	Design and develop code for PC network	C
F	Test and debug PC network code	E
G	Design and develop code for off-site sales force	C
H	New complete system test and debug	D, G, F
I	Train PC system and database operators	D, F
J	Train off-site sales force	H
K	Two-week beta test of new system with legacy backup system	I, J

However, activity C cannot be started until both activities A and B have been completed. Drewmore and his team reviewed and discussed the list several times to be sure that no activities were omitted from the project definition.

The activities and their sequence are usually represented graphically using a project network. *A **project network** consists of a set of circles or boxes, called **nodes**, which represent activities, and a set of arrows, called **arcs**, which define the precedence relationships between activities.* This is called an *activity-on-node (AON)* network representation. The project network for the software integration project is shown in Exhibit 18.5. See if you can draw the network given the information in Exhibit 18.4.

*A **project network** consists of a set of circles or boxes, called **nodes**, which represent activities, and a set of arrows, called **arcs**, which define the precedence relationships between activities.*

Resource Planning

Resource planning includes developing time estimates for performing each activity, other resources that may be required, such as people and equipment, and a realistic budget. In many situations, activity times can be estimated quite accurately. For example, in projects such as construction maintenance, a manager may have sufficient experience or historical data to provide fairly accurate activity time estimates. In addition, the nature of these activities may have low variability, and thus times would be relatively constant. In other cases, however, activity times are uncertain and perhaps best described by a range of possible values or a probability distribution.

Cost control is a vital part of project management. This requires good budgeting, which in turn first requires estimating the costs of completing the activities. For project activities performed on a routine basis, such as in home construction, experienced cost estimators can predict costs very accurately by using historical data, supplier pricing, and so on. For other activities, costs can only be estimated

Exhibit 18.5
Project Network for the Software
Integration Project

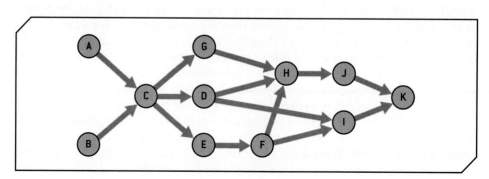

judgmentally. The components of a project that generate costs may not correspond to specific project activities, as the activities may be too detailed for conveniently controlling costs. In such cases, related activities under the control of one department or manager are often grouped together to form what are referred to as **work packages** (see OM Spotlight: Multiproject Management at AOL/Time Warner Center). Thus, project mangers must consider this when defining activities. Work packages for a construction project might include building foundations, roughing in plumbing, installing windows and doors, painting, and installing carpet. For small projects, a work package may consist of only one activity. For our example, we will assume that each activity is a work package to simplify the discussion.

Two common budgeting practices are top-down and bottom-up budgeting. **Top-down budgeting** *is a hierarchical approach that begins with senior and midlevel managers using their judgment and available data to estimate costs of major project activities.* These estimates are passed down to lower-level managers, who are responsible for breaking them down into more estimates for smaller subtasks. **Bottom-up budgeting** *starts with the lowest-level tasks, converting labor and material estimates into dollar figures and aggregating them into higher-level activities until a total project budget is developed.* This approach is typically more accurate because individuals close to the work tasks have better knowledge of costs. However, it is common for lower-level managers to pad their estimates to ensure that they will not overrun their budgets. A hybrid approach is to negotiate plans and budgets through the management hierarchy. In that way, all levels of managers participate in the process, leading to more realistic and mutually agreed-upon budgets.

Exhibit 18.6 shows the estimated times and costs for the activities in the software integration project. We'll make use of these costs later in the chapter.

Top-down budgeting *is a hierarchical approach that begins with senior and midlevel managers using their judgment and available data to estimate costs of major project activities.*

Bottom-up budgeting *starts with the lowest-level tasks, converting labor and material estimates into dollar figures and aggregating them into higher-level activities until a total project budget is developed.*

OM SPOTLIGHT

Multiproject Management at AOL/Time Warner Center[8]

Project management methods have been used to build, schedule, and allocate resources for the construction of the new AOL/Time Warner building in New York City. The $1.7 billion project is a 2.7 million square foot multiuse building that will be the future home of AOL/Time Warner's new world headquarters, Jazz at Lincoln Center, Mandarin Hotel, residential condominiums, a retail mall, office space, and a multilevel parking structure. The overall coordination of the total project and each of its subprojects, such as building the mall, hotel, and condominiums, uses project management techniques. Large multiproject management techniques must allocate resources across subprojects and perform functions such as

- scheduling and monitoring,
- creating monthly progress reports,
- coordination of multiphased occupancy scheduling for each building tenant category,

- generating milestone (Gantt chart) schedule development and status reports, and
- monitoring precedent relationships and managing resource allocations among multiple projects.

Exhibit 18.6 Wildcat Software Consulting Inc. Project Work Activities and Costs

Activity Letter	Activity Description	Immediate Predecessors	Normal Time (in weeks)	Normal Cost Estimate ($)
A	Define software project objectives, budget, due date, and possible staff	none	3	1,200
B	Inventory new and old software interfaces and features	none	5	2,500
C	Assemble teams and allocate work	A, B	2	500
D	Design and develop code from old to new databases	C	6	300
E	Design and develop code for PC network	C	5	6,000
F	Test and debug PC network code	E	3	9,000
G	Design and develop code for off-site sales force	C	4	4,400
H	New complete system test and debug	D, G, F	3	3,000
I	Train PC system and database operators	D, F	4	4,000
J	Train off-site sales force	H	2	3,200
K	Two-week beta test of new system with legacy backup system	I, J	2	1,800

Project Scheduling with the Critical Path Method

*The **critical path** is the sequence of activities that takes the longest time and defines the total project completion time.*

The **Critical Path Method (CPM)** is an approach to scheduling and controlling project activities. *The **critical path** is the sequence of activities that takes the longest time and defines the total project completion time.* Understanding the critical path is vital to managing a project because any delays of activities on the critical path will delay the entire project. CPM assumes:

- The project network defines a correct sequence of work in terms of technology and workflow.
- Activities are assumed to be independent of one another with clearly defined start and finish dates.
- The activity time estimates are accurate and stable.
- Once an activity is started it continues uninterrupted until it is completed.
- There is infinite resource capacity, at least for the initial (baseline) project analysis.

To understand CPM, we need to define several terms. We will replace the simple circled nodes in the project network with boxes that provide other useful information, as shown in Exhibit 18.7.

Exhibit 18.8 shows the software integration project network after all this information has been computed. Use this figure to help follow the discussion of how these values are found in the project scheduling process.

Exhibit 18.7
Activity-on-Node Format and Definitions

ES	N	EF
ST		ST
LS	T	LF

- Identification number (*N*) of the activity.
- Normal time (*T*) to complete the activity.
- Earliest start (*ES*) time
- Earliest finish (*EF*) time
- Latest start (*LS*) time
- Latest finish (*LF*) time
- Slack time (*ST*)—the length of time an activity can be delayed without affecting the completion date for the entire project, computed as ST = LS − ES = LF − EF.

Exhibit 18.8 Wildcat Software Consulting Activity-on-Node Project Network

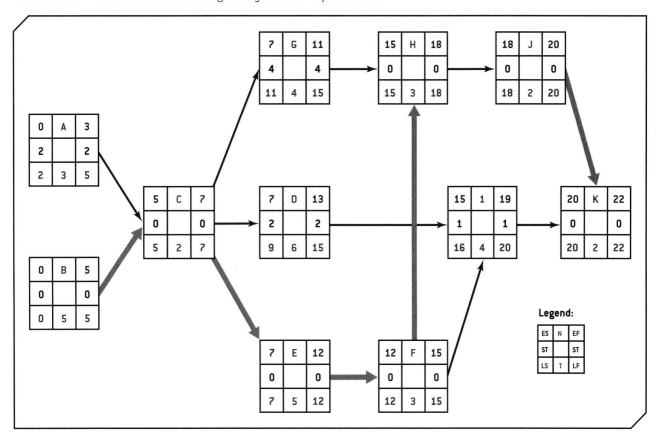

Earliest start and earliest finish times are computed by moving through the project network in a forward direction from start to finish, sometimes called the *forward pass* through the network. We begin at the start of the project by assigning all nodes without any immediate predecessors an earliest starting time of 0. Two rules are used to guide the calculations of ES and EF during this step:

Rule 1: EF = ES + T. That is, the earliest time that an activity can be completed is equal to the earliest time it can begin plus the time to perform the activity.

Rule 2: The ES time for an activity equals the largest EF time of all immediate predecessors. Therefore, whenever an activity is preceded by two or more activities, we must first compute the EF times of the preceding activities using Rule 1. Of course, if an activity has only one immediate predecessor, the ES time is simply equal to the EF time of the immediate predecessor.

To illustrate this process, note that in Exhibit 18.7, the EF time for activity A is 0 + 3 = 3 and the EF time for activity B is 0 + 5 = 5. Because both A and B are immediate predecessors to activity C, we use Rule 2 to find the EF time for activity C as the largest of 3 and 5, or 5. Then the EF time for activity C is computed using Rule 1 as EF = ES + T = 5 + 2 = 7. Activity G has only one immediate predecessor, so the EF time of activity C becomes the ES time of G. We suggest that you work through all calculations for the ES and EF times in the remainder of the network. The EF time of the last activity specifies the earliest time that the entire project can be completed. For our example, this is 22 weeks. If a project has more than one terminal activity, the earliest project completion time is the largest EF time among these activities.

Latest start and latest finish times are computed by making a *backward pass* through the network, beginning with the ending project activity or activities. First set the LF time for all terminal activities to be the project completion time. In our example, we begin with activity K, setting LF = 22, and use the following rules:

> *Rule 3:* LS = LF − T. That is, the latest start time for an activity is equal to its LF time minus the activity time.
>
> *Rule 4:* The LF time for an activity is the smallest LS time of all immediate successors. Therefore, the LS times of all successors must be computed before moving to a preceding node. If an activity has only one immediate successor, the LF time is simply equal to the LS time of that immediate successor.

To illustrate this backward pass procedure, we first compute LS = LF − T for activity K as 22 − 2 = 20. Because activity K is the only successor to activities J and I, the LF times for both J and I are set equal to 20 and their LS times are computed using Rule 3. However, consider activity F. Activity F has two successors, H and I. The ES time for H is 15 while the ES time for I is 16. Using Rule 4, we set the EF time for activity F to be the smallest of the ES times for activities H and I, or 15. We encourage you to work through the remaining calculations of this backward pass procedure to better understand how to apply these rules.

After all ES, EF, LS, and LF times of all project activities are computed, we can compute slack time (ST) for each activity. Slack time is computed as ST = LS − ES = LF − EF (note that either one can be used). For example, the slack time for activity A is 5 − 3 = 2 − 0 = 2, and the slack time for activity B is 5 − 5 = 0 − 0 = 0. Note that although the earliest start time for activity A is 3, the activity need not begin until time LS = 5 and will not delay the completion of the entire project. However, activity B must start exactly on schedule at time 0 or else the project will be delayed.

After all slack times are computed, we may find the critical path. The critical path (CP) is the longest path(s) through the project network; activities on the critical path have zero slack time (ST = 0) and if delayed will cause the total project to be delayed. The critical path for the software development project is B–C–E–F–H–J–K, and is denoted by the heavy arrows in Exhibit 18.8. If any activity along the critical path is delayed, the total project duration will be longer than 22 weeks.

There are many ways to display the information in Exhibit 18.8; a summary is given in the table in Exhibit 18.9. Using the cost information in Exhibit 18.6, the total cost to complete the project in 22 weeks is $35,900. The cost of all activities along the critical path is $26,000, or 72.4% of total project cost. If you work on an activity on the critical path, it must be completed on time; otherwise, you and your team assigned to this work activity might receive some unwanted attention. If you were a "slacker," however, where would you want to work? Probably on activity G because it has 4 weeks of slack time!

Project Control

*A **schedule** specifies when activities are to be performed.*

A **schedule** *specifies when activities are to be performed.* A schedule enables a manager to assign resources effectively and to monitor progress and take corrective action when necessary. Because of the uncertainty of task times, unavoidable delays, or other problems, projects rarely, if ever, progress on schedule. Managers must therefore monitor performance of the project and take corrective action when needed. See the OM Spotlight: Bechtel Power Corporation for an example.

Activity Name	On Critical Path	Activity Time	Earliest Start	Earliest Finish	Latest Start	Latest Finish	Slack (LS − ES)
A	No	3	0	3	2	5	2
B*	Yes	5	0	5	0	5	0
C*	Yes	2	5	7	5	7	0
D	No	6	7	13	9	15	2
E*	Yes	5	7	12	7	12	0
F*	Yes	3	12	15	12	15	0
G	No	4	7	11	11	15	4
H*	Yes	3	15	18	15	18	0
I	No	4	15	19	16	20	1
J*	Yes	2	18	20	18	20	0
K*	Yes	2	20	22	20	22	0

Exhibit 18.9
CPM Tabular Analysis for Wildcat Software Consulting Using Normal Time

Project Completion Time = 22 weeks
Total Cost of Project = $35,900 (Cost on CP = $26,000)
Number of Critical Path(s) = 1

OM SPOTLIGHT

Bechtel Power Corporation[9]

In the Bechtel Power Corporation, project-control activities begin as soon as company managers and the client define the job requirements, the scope of work, overall schedules, and the project's magnitude. Important control documents are prepared and are used to monitor the project during its planning and implementation phases. These include

- Scope of Services Manual, which establishes a baseline for identifying changes in services and a definition of engineering, home-office support, and field nonmanual services that will be performed by the company
- Division of Responsibility Document, which describes the responsibilities of the company, the client, and the major suppliers
- Project Procedures Manual, which defines the procedures involved in interface activities among the company, the client, and the major suppliers with respect to engineering, procurement, construction, preoperational services, quality assurance, quality control, project control, and communication
- Technical Scope Document, which describes the project's physical plant, establishes the design basis, and provides input to the civil/structural, architectural, plant design, mechanical, electrical, and control systems disciplines
- Project Activity Control Guide, which aids in the administration of project activities by identifying and time-phasing the development and execution of project plans, programs,

procedures, controls, and other significant activities required for effective operation of the project

After the project has been defined and the preliminary control documents prepared, the project manager and his team develop the project-control system that will be used throughout the project. The main objectives of the project-control system are to develop a plan that can be monitored and reflects expected performance of the contract work. This requires a work-control system that provides the information necessary for the team, the company managers, and the client to identify problem areas and initiate corrective action. The control system includes

- a project plan covering expected scope, schedule, and cost performance
- a continuous monitoring system that measures the performance against the project plan through the use of modular monitoring tools
- a reporting system that identifies deviations from the project plan by means of trends and forecasts
- timely actions to take advantage of beneficial trends or to correct deviations

These approaches produce the information needed by managers to evaluate the current situation and take appropriate action. Client management reports, prepared periodically, include project status, an executive summary, a production summary, and detailed reports about cost, commitments, subcontracts, and work progress.

A very useful tool for depicting a schedule graphically is a Gantt chart, named after Henry L. Gantt, a pioneer of scientific management. Gantt charts enable the project manager to know exactly what activities should be performed at a given time and, more importantly, to monitor daily progress of the project so that corrective action can be taken when necessary.

To construct a Gantt chart, we list the activities on a vertical axis and use a horizontal axis to represent time. The following symbols are commonly used in a Gantt chart:

Symbol	Description
⌐	Scheduled starting time for activity
¬	Scheduled completion time for activity
▬	Completed work for an activity
⋈	Scheduled delay or maintenance
∨	Current date for progress review

Using the information in Exhibits 18.6 and 18.8 or 18.9, we will assume that each activity will be scheduled at its early start time, as shown in Exhibit 18.10. The resulting schedule will be an "early-start" or "left-shifted" schedule. For instance, activities A and B can begin at time 0 and have durations of 3 and 5 weeks, respectively. Activity C cannot begin until A is completed; thus this activity is scheduled to begin at time 5. After activity C is completed at time 7, activities G, D, and E can then be scheduled. Activity D, for example, can start as early as week 7. Likewise, activity G can start as early as week 7. If you compare the Gantt chart in Exhibit 18.10 with the project network in Exhibit 18.8 you will see that they portray the same information, just in a different format.

Exhibit 18.10
Early Start Schedule for Wildcat Software Project

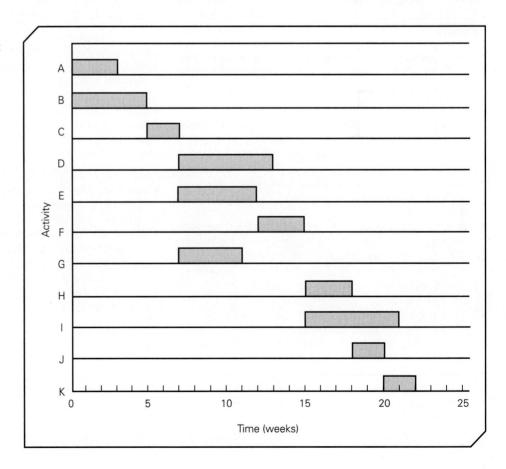

Using this early start schedule, the project is scheduled to be completed in 22 weeks. What happens if an activity on the critical path is delayed? Suppose, for example, that activity E takes 6 weeks instead of 5 weeks. Because E is a predecessor of F and the starting time of F is the same as the completion time of E, F is forced to begin 1 week later. This forces a delay in activity H that is also on the critical path, and in turn delays activities J and K. In addition, activity I is also delayed 1 week. Now it would take 23 weeks to complete the project, as shown by the Gantt chart in Exhibit 18.11.

The early-start schedule we developed in Exhibit 18.10 gives no consideration to resources. It simply assumes that sufficient resources are available for all activities scheduled at the same time. Usually, however, resources such as labor and equipment that must be shared among the activities are limited. Determining how to allocate limited resources is often a very challenging puzzle. A common objective is to minimize the project duration within the resource constraints. Project management software also creates Gantt charts assuming each activity begins at its "latest time" or a "right-shifted" schedule (Gantt charts not shown). When resources are limited, project managers with the help of the software try to level resource loads by shifting activities between these two extremes—the left- (early start dates) and right- (late start dates) shifted schedules.

Using a Gantt Chart for Progress Control

Let us return to the Wildcat Software project. Exhibit 18.12 is a Gantt progress chart for the project at week 9. We see that activities A, B, and C have already been completed, activity D is ahead of schedule, activity E has not yet begun, and activity G is right on schedule.

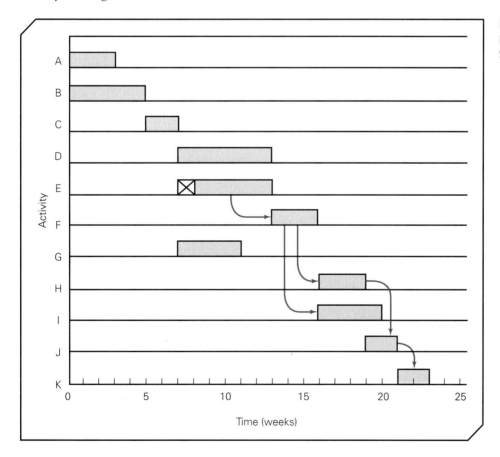

Exhibit 18.11
Example Gantt Chart of Wildcat Software with Activity E Delayed

Exhibit 18.12
Example Progress Gantt Chart
of Wildcat Software at Week 9
(dark color indicates completed
work)

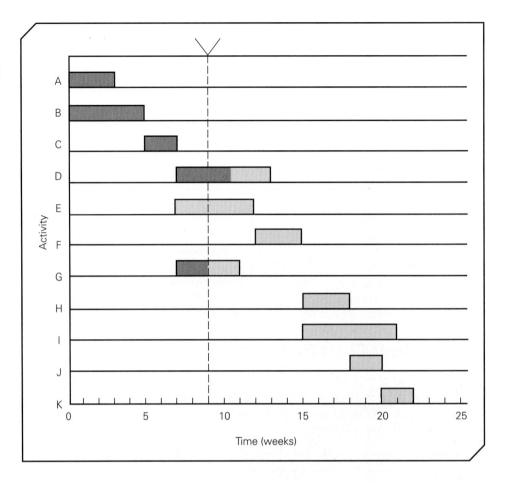

Exhibit 18.12
Example Progress Gantt Chart of Wildcat Software at Week 9 (dark color indicates completed work)

A progress chart such as this allows the manager to see the status of a project quickly. It also provides the information required to revise the schedule. For instance, since D is now a critical activity, the project will be delayed if D is late. To make sure activity D is not late, the manager may decide to add more resources to D, work overtime, and so on. These are the decisions that a project manager must make on an ongoing basis to control a project.

Budget Control

After a schedule is developed, a budget can be put together showing when costs are likely to be incurred and what they are likely to be during the project duration. Exhibit 18.13 shows the time and normal cost information for the baseline project situation at Wildcat Software assuming all activities begin at their earliest possible starting date. Compare the data in Exhibit 18.13 with Exhibit 18.6 and you will see they are identical. Notice the total project normal cost of $35,900 in Exhibits 18.9 and 18.13 are the same. We can develop a budget based on all activities being started at their earliest or latest starting times.

An effective budgetary control system monitors costs throughout the project's duration, comparing actual costs for all completed and in-process activities to the appropriate budgeted costs. It gives the project manager up-to-date information on the cost status of each activity. If actual costs exceed budgeted costs, a cost overrun has occurred. If actual costs are less than budgeted costs, we have a

Exhibit 18.13 Weekly Normal Cost Forecast for Wildcat Software Project

Activity	Week																					
	1	2	3	4	5	6	7	8	9	10	11	12	13	14	15	16	17	18	19	20	21	22
A	400	400	400																			
B	500	500	500																			
C				500	500																	
D						250	250															
E								50	50	50	50	50	50									
F								1,200	1,200	1,200	1,200	1,200										
G													3,000	3,000	3,000							
H								1,100	1,100	1,100	1,100											
I																1,000	1,000	1,000				
J																1,000	1,000	1,000	1,000			
K																			1,600	1,600	900	900
Weekly cost	900	900	900	500	500	250	250	2,350	2,350	2,350	2,350	1,250	3,050	3,000	3,000	2,000	2,000	2,000	2,600	1,600	900	900
Cumulative cost	900	1,800	2,700	3,200	3,700	3,950	4,200	6,550	8,900	11,250	13,600	14,850	17,900	20,900	23,900	25,900	27,900	29,900	32,500	34,100	35,000	35,900

cost underrun. This information enables the project manager to take corrective action when necessary.

An example of how cost overruns and underruns are detected is shown in Exhibit 18.14, which shows the cost and completion status for the Wildcat Software project as of week 10. The "% Completion" column indicates what proportion of each activity has been completed. By multiplying this percentage by the budgeted cost shown in Exhibit 18.14, we determine the budgeted cost in the next column based on the actual amount of work completed.

By subtracting the budgeted cost from the actual cost, we can determine any cost overruns or underruns. We see that activities A and G are below budget, although costs for activities C and E are exceeding their budgets. The total project is $90 over budget at the end of week 10.

Learning Objective
To calculate crashing schedules to reduce project completion time.

Crashing a project *refers to reducing the total time to complete the project to meet a revised due date.*

Crash time *is the shortest possible time the activity can realistically be completed.*

The **crash cost** *is the total additional cost associated with completing an activity in its crash time rather than in its normal time.*

TIME/COST TRADE-OFFS

One of the benefits of the Critical Path Method is the ability to consider shortening activity times by adding additional resources to selected activities and thereby reducing the overall project completion time. This is often referred to as "crashing." **Crashing a project** *refers to reducing the total time to complete the project to meet a revised due date.* However, doing so does not come without a cost. Therefore, it is necessary to evaluate the trade-offs between faster completion times and additional costs.

The first step is to determine the amount of time that each activity may be reduced and its associated cost, as shown in Exhibit 18.15. **Crash time** *is the shortest possible time the activity can realistically be completed. The* **crash cost** *is the total additional cost associated with completing an activity in its crash time rather than in its normal time.* We assume that the normal times and costs are based on normal working conditions and work practices and therefore, are accurate estimates. Some activities cannot be crashed because of the nature of the task. In Exhibit 18.15, this is evident when the normal and crash times as well as the normal and crash costs are equal. For example, activities H, I, J, and K cannot be crashed. If you examine the content of these activities, you see that activities H and K related to testing and debugging the new system software, and activities I and J related to training people to use this new software. In the judgment of the project managers, these work activities could not be expedited by adding any additional resources.

Exhibit 18.14
Activity Cost and Completion Status at End of Week 10 for Wildcat Software Project

Activity	Actual Cost	% Completion	Budgeted Cost	Difference
A	$1,050	100%	$1,200	$(150)
B	2,500	100	2,500	0
C	600	100	500	100
D	150	50	150	0
E	2,000	20	1,200	800
F	0	0	0	0
G	3,300	90	3,960	(660)
H	0	0	0	0
I	0	0	0	0
J	0	0	0	0
K	0	0	0	0
	$9,600		$9,510	$ 90

Exhibit 18.15 Wildcat Software Project Data Including Crash Times and Costs

Activity Letter	Activity Description	Immediate Predecessors	Normal Time (in weeks)	Crash Time (in weeks)	Normal Cost Estimate ($)	Crash Cost Estimate ($)
A	Define software project objectives, budget, due date, and possible staff	none	3	1	1,200	2,000
B	Inventory new and old software interfaces and features	none	5	3	2,500	3,500
C	Assemble teams and allocate work	A, B	2	1	500	750
D	Design and develop code from old to new databases	C	6	3	300	450
E	Design and develop code for PC network	C	5	3	6,000	8,400
F	Test and debug PC network code	E	3	3	9,000	9,000
G	Design and develop code for off-site sales force	C	4	3	4,400	5,500
H	New complete system test and debug	D, G, F	3	3	3,000	3,000
I	Train PC system and database operators	D, F	4	2	4,000	6,000
J	Train off-site sales force	H	2	2	3,200	3,200
K	Two-week beta test of new system with legacy backup system	I, J	2	2	1,800	1,800

For example, in the software development project, activity A can be completed in 1 week at a cost of $2,000 instead of the normal time of 3 weeks at a cost of $1,200. A key assumption with crashing is that the time can be reduced to any proportion of the crash time at a proportional increase in cost; that is, the relationship between time and cost is linear, as shown in Exhibit 18.16 for activity A. The slope of this line is the crash cost per unit of time and is computed by Equation (18.1).

$$\text{Crash cost per unit of time} = \frac{\text{Crash cost} - \text{Normal cost}}{\text{Normal time} - \text{Crash time}} \qquad \textbf{(18.1)}$$

Crashing an activity *refers to reducing its normal time possibly up to its limit—the crash time.* For example, we can crash activity A from its normal time of 3 weeks down to 1 week or anywhere in between. Because the crash cost per unit of time for activity A is ($2,000 − $1,200)/(3 − 1) = $400 per week, crashing the activity from 3 weeks to 2 weeks will result in an additional cost of $400. Likewise, crashing from 3 to 1.5 weeks will result in an additional cost of 1.5($400) = $600. Managers can crash a project and ignore the cost implications or they can search for the minimum-cost crash schedule to meet the revised due date.

> **Crashing an activity** *refers to reducing its normal time possibly up to its limit—the crash time.*

Crashing Decisions

Suppose the client asks Wildcat Software Consulting, Inc. how much it would cost to complete the project in 20 weeks instead of the current 22 weeks, and second, how much it would cost to finish the project in the fastest possible time. We can try to answer these questions by trial and error, although linear programming models can be developed that will find the optimal solutions easily (see Supplementary Chapter C).

© Getty Images/PhotoDisc

Exhibit 18.16
Normal versus Crash Activity
Analysis

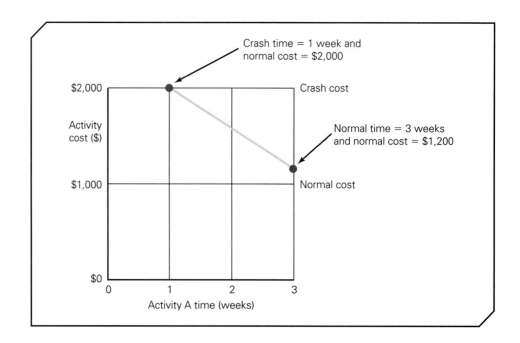

To address the first question, we need to determine the crash cost per unit of time for each activity using Equation (18.1). These are: A—$400 per week, B—$500 per week, C—$250 per week, D—$50 per week, E—$1,200 per week, G—$1,100 per week, and I—$1,000 per week. Activities F, H, J, and K cannot be crashed. Note that the only way the project completion time can be reduced is by crashing activities on the critical path. When we do this, however, another path in the network might become critical, so this must be carefully watched.

In this example, several options exist for completing the project in 20 weeks:

Crashing Option #1	**Crashing Option #2**	**Crashing Option #3**
Crash B by 1 week = $500	Crash B by 2 weeks = $1,000	Crash C by 1 week = $ 500
Crash C by 1 week = $250		Crash E by 1 week = $1,200
Additional cost = $750	Additional cost = $1,000	Additional cost = $1,700

The least-expensive option is the first. The critical path remains the same, namely, B–C–E–F–H–J–K. Exhibit 18.17 summarizes the results for this option. Notice that although activity D costs only $50 per week to crash, it is not on the critical path—crashing it would not affect the completion time.

The second question seeks to find the crash schedule that minimizes the project completion time. Again, we will address this using a trial-and-error approach. From the previous crashing solution of 20 weeks, we can identify two crashing options to shorten the project to 19 weeks:

Crashing Option #4	**Crashing Option #5**
Crash B by a 2nd week = $500	Crash E by 1 week = $1,200
Additional cost = $500	Additional cost = $1,200

The cheapest way to achieve a project completion date of 19 weeks is Option #4 by crashing B by 2 weeks and C by 1 week. The critical path for a 19-week project completion date is still B–C–E–F–H–J–K. The total project cost is now $37,150 ($35,900 + $1,000 + $250). Activities B and C have reached their crash time limits; therefore, to try to find an 18-week completion date we must examine

Activity Name	On Critical Path	Activity Time	Earliest Start	Earliest Finish	Latest Start	Latest Finish	Slack (LS − ES)
A	No	3	0	3	1	4	1
B	Yes	4	0	4	0	4	0
C	Yes	1	4	5	4	5	0
D	No	6	5	11	7	13	2
E	Yes	5	5	10	5	10	0
F	Yes	3	10	13	10	13	0
G	No	4	5	9	9	13	4
H	Yes	3	13	16	13	16	0
I	No	4	13	17	14	18	1
J	Yes	2	16	18	16	18	0
K	Yes	2	18	20	18	20	0

Exhibit 18.17
CPM Tabular Analysis for Wildcat Software Consulting for Target 20-Week Completion Time

Project completion time = 20 weeks
Total project cost = $36,650 (cost on CP = $26,750)
Number of critical paths = 1

other activities. Only one option is available because activities B, C, F, H, J, and K cannot be crashed further:

Crashing Option #6

Crash E by 1 week = $1,200
Additional cost   = $1,200

At this point, there are two critical paths: A–C–E–F–H–J–K and B–C–E–F–H–J–K. All other paths through the network are less than 18 weeks. The total project cost is now $38,350 ($35,900 + $1,000 + $250 + $1,200).

The only way to achieve a 17-week project completion time is to crash activity E a second week. The total project cost for a 17-week completion time is now $39,550 ($35,900 + $1,000 + $250 + $1,200 + $1,200), and four critical paths now exist:

CP Path 1: B–C–E–F–H–J–K
CP Path 2: A–C–E–F–H–J–K
CP Path 3: A–C–D–H–J–K
CP Path 4: B–C–D–H–J–K

All other paths are not critical. Exhibit 18.18 summarizes the results for this 17-week minimum crash cost schedule. We cannot crash any other activities to reduce the project completion time further.

UNCERTAINTY IN PROJECT MANAGEMENT

Learning Objective
To incorporate uncertainty of activity time estimates into project scheduling and to calculate probabilities for project completion time.

Another approach to project management that was developed independently of CPM is called **PERT (Project Evaluation and Review Technique)**. PERT was introduced in the late 1950s specifically for planning, scheduling, and controlling the Polaris missile project. Since many activities associated with that project had never been attempted previously, it was difficult to predict the time needed to complete the various tasks. PERT was developed as a means of handling the uncertainties in activity completion times. In contrast, CPM assumes that activity times are constant.

Exhibit 18.18 Wildcat Software Consulting 17-Week Project Schedule at Total Project Cost = $39,550

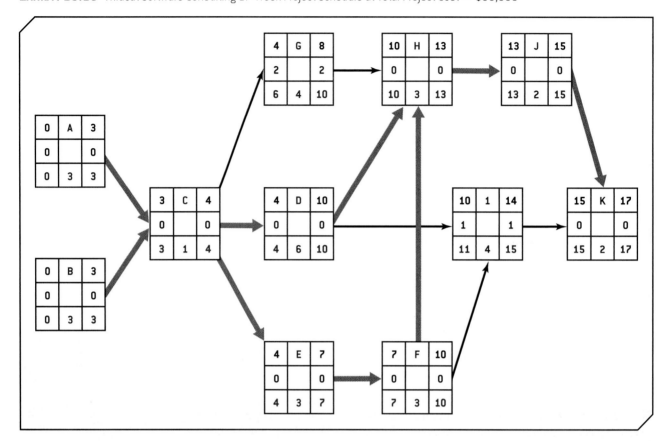

Any variation in critical-path activities can cause variation in the project-completion date. Also, if a noncritical activity is delayed long enough to expend all of its slack time, that activity will become part of a new critical path, and further delays there will extend the project-completion date. The PERT procedure uses the variance in the critical-path activities to understand the risk associated with completing the project on time.

When activity times are uncertain, they are often treated as random variables with associated probability distributions. Usually three time estimates are obtained for each activity:

1. **Optimistic time** (*a*)—the activity time if everything progresses in an ideal manner
2. **Most probable time** (*m*)—the most likely activity time under normal conditions
3. **Pessimistic time** (*b*)—the activity time if significant breakdowns and/or delays occur

Exhibit 18.19 shows an assumed probability distribution for activity B. Note that this is a positively skewed distribution, allowing for a small chance of a large activity time. Different values of *a*, *m*, and *b* provide different shapes for the probability distribution of activity times. Technically, this characterizes a *beta probability distribution*. The beta distribution is usually assumed to describe the inherent variability in these three time estimates. This approach is quite practical because managers can usually identify the best case, worst case, and most likely case for activity times, and it provides much flexibility in characterizing the distribution of times,

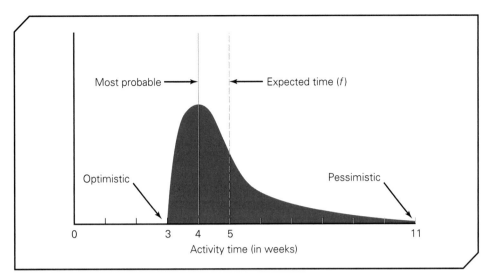

Exhibit 18.19
Activity Time Distribution for
Activity B of Wildcat Software
Project

as opposed to forcing times to a symmetric normal probability distribution. However, with today's software, any type of distribution can be used.

For the Wildcat Software integration project, we will assume that the project manager has developed estimates for these times for each activity, as shown in Exhibit 18.20. The expected time is computed using the following formula:

$$\text{Expected time} = (a + 4m + b)/6 \tag{18.2}$$

Note that the expected times correspond to the normal times we used in the CPM example. We can also show that the variance of activity times is given by the following:

$$\text{Variance} = (b - a)^2/36 \tag{18.3}$$

Both the expected times and variances are shown in Exhibit 18.20

The critical path is found using the expected times in the same fashion as in the Critical Path Method. PERT allows us to investigate the effects of uncertainty of activity times on the project completion time. In the software integration project, we found the critical path to be B–C–E–F–H–J–K with an expected completion time of 22 weeks. This is simply the sum of the expected times for the activities on the

Exhibit 18.20

Activity Time Estimates for the Wildcat Software Integration Project

Activity	Optimistic Time (a)	Most Probable Time (m)	Pessimistic Time (b)	Expected Time	Variance
A	2	3	4	3	0.11
B	3	4	11	5	1.78
C	1	2	3	2	0.11
D	4	5	12	6	1.78
E	3	5	7	5	0.44
F	2	3	4	3	0.11
G	2	3	10	4	1.78
H	2	3	4	3	0.11
I	2	3	10	4	1.78
J	1	2	3	2	0.11
K	1	2	3	2	0.11

critical path. The variance (σ^2) in project duration is given by the sum of the variances of the critical-path activities:

$$1.78 + 0.11 + 0.44 + 0.11 + 0.11 + 0.11 = 2.77$$

This formula is based on the assumption that all the activity times are independent. With this assumption, we can also assume that the distribution of the project completion time is normally distributed. The use of the normal probability distribution as an approximation is based on the central limit theorem of statistics, which states that the sum of independent activity times follows a normal distribution as the number of activities becomes large. Therefore, we can say that the project completion time for the Wildcat example is normal with a mean of 22 weeks and a standard deviation of $\sqrt{2.77} = 1.66$.

Using this information, we can compute the probability of meeting a specified completion date. For example, suppose that the project manager has allotted 25 weeks for the project. Although completion in 22 weeks is expected, the manager wants to know the probability that the 25-week deadline will be met. This probability is shown graphically as the shaded area in Exhibit 18.21. The z-value for the normal distribution at $T = 25$ is given by

$$z = (25 - 22)/1.66 = 1.81$$

Using $z = 1.81$ and the tables for the standard normal distribution (see Appendix A), we see that the probability of the project meeting the 25-week deadline is $.4649 + .5000 = .9649$. Thus, while variability in the activity time may cause the project to exceed the 22-week expected duration, there is an excellent chance that the project will be completed before the 25-week deadline.

The procedure described is only approximate, since we have assumed that the distribution of T is normal. Moreover, this method assumes that only one critical path exists; if there are two or more critical paths, this method tends to underestimate the project-completion time. Also, when several noncritical paths are close (in terms of time) to the critical path, caution must be exercised in interpreting the results, since randomness in activity times may cause one of the other paths to be critical. That is, a path with high activity time variances that is shorter than the longest critical path(s) may have a lower probability of completion than the longer critical path.

Simulation is often used to gain a clearer perspective on project-completion times and risk but requires some advanced concepts that we cannot address in this book. Another approach is to evaluate three different scenarios for a project—using only optimistic times, most likely times, and pessimistic times. This approach provides the project manager with the range of possible solutions, but no probability statements can be made using CPM and constant activity times. Finally, linear programming can be used to formulate and solve a project-management problem, as described in Supplementary Chapter D.

Exhibit 18.21

Probability of Completing the Wildcat Software Project within 25 Weeks

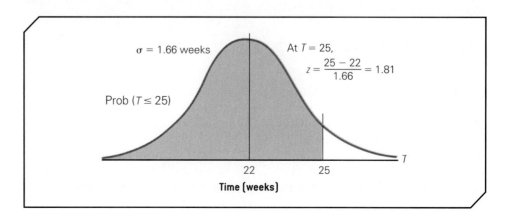

PROJECT MANAGEMENT SOFTWARE

Learning Objective
To learn the capabilities and applications of contemporary project management software.

Many different software packages exist for project management.[10] They often have an easy-to-use graphical user interface, can plan activities, schedule work to be performed, view the relationships among tasks, manage resources, and monitor project progress. Most project management software offers the following features:

- *Budgeting and cost control.* This allows users to associate cost information with each activity and project resource.
- *Calendars.* Calendars can be used to define working days and hours for each individual resource or group of resources and are used in calculating the project schedule.
- *Internet capabilities.* Many systems allow project information to be posted directly to a web site to facilitate communication among team members.
- *Graphics.* Software packages generate a variety of charts such as Gantt charts and network diagrams.
- *Importing/exporting data.* Most packages allow users to import information from other applications such as text files, spreadsheets, and databases.
- *Multiple projects and subprojects.* Software packages make it easy to manage multiple projects or to split large projects into smaller ones and coordinate the results.
- *Report generation.* Extensive reports on project time and financial performance, milestones, current progress, and resource usage are generally available.
- *Resource management.* Users can define and assign resources to activities to help manage limited resources.
- *Planning.* Most packages create a work breakdown structure to assist in defining activities and specifying activity times and precedence relationships.
- *Project monitoring and tracking.* Most packages allow the user to define a baseline plan and compare actual progress to the baseline.
- *Scheduling.* Most systems build Gantt charts and network diagrams and compute scheduled starting and ending dates.
- *Security.* Newer versions provide password-protected access to files.
- *Sorting and filtering.* This allows the user to view information in a desired order or only information that meets a certain criterion, such as tasks that are behind schedule.
- *What-if analysis.* This allows users to explore the effects of various scenarios.

Project management software is generally easy to use, accurate, and able to handle complex situations that would be difficult to compute and deal with manually. With all the features we have described, they provide powerful tools to address the complexity in large-scale business projects. The Project Management Institute (www.pmi.org) maintains a list of project management software vendors. We will illustrate some of the features of Microsoft Project in the next section.

Microsoft Project

Microsoft Project is one of the more popular project management software packages (see OM Spotlight: Project Management at the Retirement Systems of Alabama). An example output page from MS Project is shown in Exhibit 18.22. MS Project can develop schedules for any time bucket size, such as days, weeks, half-months, months, quarters, and so on. In Exhibit 18.22, the Gantt chart is by week, but all resource schedules for the Wildcat Software staff (Bob, Alice, Mary, etc.) are by hour of the day. On a computer, the Gantt chart shows the critical activities (B, C, E, F, H, J, and K) and the noncritical activities (A, D, G, and I). The baseline duration of the software integration project is 110 days or, assuming 5 days per week, 22 weeks.

Exhibit 18.22 Example MS Project Output

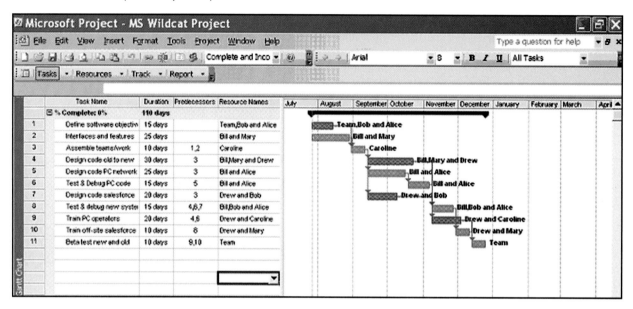

Microsoft has also integrated project management technology into the operations of an organization's accounting and financial processes, as shown in Exhibit 18.23. Project management helps in managing accounting-related projects that control costs, increase revenue, and plan audits. These capabilities allow the organization to quickly adapt to changing business conditions.

OM SPOTLIGHT

Project Management at the Retirement Systems of Alabama (RSA)[11]

The RSA of Alabama manages $25 billion in assets for about 290,000 state employees. The 250 RSA employees worked hard to manage multiple ongoing information technology projects. One project management issue was allocating resources and professional staff to multiple projects. The current resource allocation processes of phone calls, overtime and undertime, and multiple meetings just did not work. RSA had no means of knowing whether it was making the best use of individual staff member's skills. Management could not tell if a potential project was viable from a staffing perspective. For all RSA employees, accepting a new project and committing to project deadlines was a risky business. RSA needed a solid way to allocate, track, and prioritize the demands of multiple projects.

Management decided to implement Microsoft's Office Enterprise Project Management (EPM). RSA personnel were involved in an extensive 1-month training program on project management and MS Project software. Entirely new processes were created to input data, assign staff, and manage projects. Work tasks and activities were more clearly defined and processes streamlined. The number of meetings the information technology department had to attend decreased by 50 percent, freeing up the IT staff time to work on projects. At any given time about 12 projects are ongoing. Peggi Douglass, information technology services director, noted, "Exposing project data shows team members how individual tasks fit together. . . . We're not only seeing a reduction in time and effort but also enjoying reduced frustration levels. . . . EPM gives us the tools to step back and look at our whole system."

Exhibit 18.23 Microsoft's Project Management and Accounting (PMA) System[12]

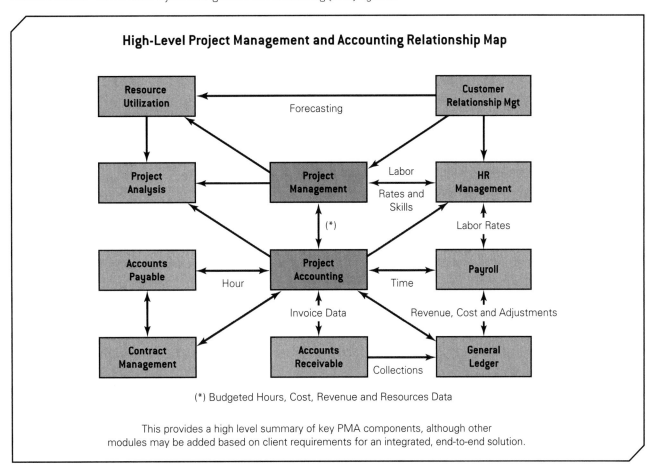

High-Level Project Management and Accounting Relationship Map

(*) Budgeted Hours, Cost, Revenue and Resources Data

This provides a high level summary of key PMA components, although other modules may be added based on client requirements for an integrated, end-to-end solution.

SOLVED PROBLEMS

SOLVED PROBLEM #1

Draw the project network for the following information. Determine the earliest completion time for the project. What is the critical path?

Activity	Immediate Predecessor	Normal Duration
A	None	6 weeks
B	A	4 weeks
C	A	4 weeks
D	B, C	7 weeks
E	C	6 weeks
F	D, E	2 weeks

(continued on the next page)

Solution:

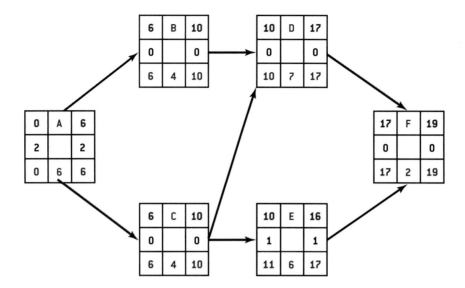

There are two critical paths—path A–B–D–F and path A–C–D–F—that take 19 weeks to complete. Only activity E has a slack time of 1 week.

SOLVED PROBLEM #2

Using the solution to Solved Problem #1 and Table 1 at the bottom of the page, crash the project by 2 weeks (1 week at a time), indicating which activities should be crashed each week and what the effect is on the total project cost.

One-Week Crash Options:
We might first look at activities common to both critical paths, namely A and D, and consider crashing each of them individually. (See charts at right.) Other options are to crash activities B and C together, activity F, and activities A and D together. The lowest-cost option is to crash activity D by 1 week, costing $200. Now all three paths through the network are critical paths with a total duration of 18 weeks.

<u>**Crashing Option #1**</u>

Crash A by 1 week = $400

<u>**Crashing Option #2**</u>

Crash D by 1 week = $200

<u>**Crashing Option #3**</u>

Crash B by 1 week = $350
Crash C by 1 week = $300
Total cost   = $650

<u>**Crashing Option #4**</u>

Crash F by 1 week = $500

<u>**Crash Option #5**</u>

Crash A by 1 week = $400
Crash D by 1 week = $200
Total cost   = $600

Table 1.

Activity	Normal Duration	Normal Cost	Crash Duration	Total Crash Cost	Crash Cost Per Week
A	6	$ 500	4	$1,300	$400
B	4	300	2	1,000	350
C	4	900	3	1,200	300
D	7	1,600	5	2,000	200
E	6	200	4	300	50
F	2	400	1	900	500

Second-Week Crash Options:

All other crash options cost more than Option #2. Therefore, we should recommend that we crash D by a second week and E by 1 week, for a total cost of $250. All three network paths take 17 weeks to complete.

The total normal costs are $3,900 plus crashing D by 2 weeks (+$400) and E by 1 week (+$50), so the total cost of a 17-week project-completion schedule is $4,350.

Crashing Option #1

Crash A by 1 week = $400

Crashing Option #2

Crash D by 1 week = $200
Crash E by 1 week = $ 50
Total cost   = $250

Crashing Option #3

Crash B by 1 week = $350
Crash C by 1 week = $300
Total cost   = $650

Crashing Option #4

Crash F by 1 week = $500

SOLVED PROBLEM #3

Consider the following simple PERT network used to remodel the kitchen at Rusty Buckets restaurant:

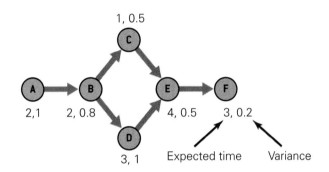

1, 0.5

2,1   2, 0.8   4, 0.5   3, 0.2

3, 1   Expected time   Variance

a. What is the expected completion time and variance for the project?

b. What is the probability that the project will meet a 12-day deadline?

Solution:

a. There are two paths—A–B–C–E–F = 12 days and A–B–D–E–F = 14 days—through the network. The critical path is A–B–D–E–F = 14 days. The variance of the project time is the sum of the activity variances on the critical path, or $1 + 0.8 + 1 + 0.5 + 0.2 = 3.5$ days.

b. $z = (12 - 14)/\sqrt{3.5} = -2/1.871 = -1.0689$. From Appendix A, the probability from 0 to $z = -1.07$ is .3577. Therefore, P(completion time = 12) = $.5000 - .3577 = .1423$. Also, note that given the high variances along the critical path, there is only a 50 percent chance of completing the project within 14 days (that is, $z = (14 - 14)/1.871 = 0$ and P(completion time = 14) = $.5000 - 0 = .5000$.

KEY TERMS AND CONCEPTS

Activities
Arcs
Bottom-up budgeting
Crash cost
Crash time
Crashing a project
Crashing an activity
Critical path (CP)
Critical Path Method (CPM)
Deliverables

Immediate predecessors
Most probable time
Nodes
Optimistic time
Pessimistic time
Project
Project Evaluation and Review Technique (PERT)
Project management
Project network
Project objective

Schedule
Statement of work

Top-down budgeting
Work packages

QUESTIONS FOR REVIEW AND DISCUSSION

1. Define a project and provide a nonmanufacturing or nonconstruction example.

2. Describe the role of the project manager. What skills should he or she possess?

3. Prepare a job profile for a newspaper advertisement for a project manager.

4. What are five ways to ensure project failure? Conversely, what should project managers do to ensure success?

5. Discuss the three key factors of the project-planning process.

6. What are the four major steps in the project-planning process?

7. What do arcs and nodes represent in a project network?

8. Define and give an example of an immediate predecessor.

9. What information do you need to collect to conduct a basic CPM model and analysis?

10. Define and explain the following terms: *normal time, crash time, earliest start time, earliest finish time, latest start time, latest finish time.*

11. Define *slack time* and how it is computed. How is it used in project scheduling and why is it important?

12. Define *critical path*. Describe, in your own words, the procedure for finding a critical path.

13. Develop a small example consisting of five activities and illustrate the ideas, rules, and mechanics of for-

ward and back passes through the project network to compute the critical path.

14. Explain the usefulness of Gantt charts to a manager.

15. How do you construct a left- or right-shifted Gantt chart?

16. Explain the concept of crashing in project management. What issues must a project manager wrestle with in making crashing decisions?

17. Discuss the importance of project control and monitoring.

18. Explain the processes for budgeting projects and controlling budgets as projects are performed.

19. Explain the concepts of optimistic time, most probable time, and pessimistic time estimates. How would you estimate these times for a specific activity?

20. Explain how to evaluate the effect of uncertainty of activity times on the total project completion time.

21. The local chapter of the Project Management Institute is planning a dinner meeting with a nationally known speaker, and you are responsible for organizing it. How could the methodology discussed in this chapter help you?

22. Find an application of project management in your own life (for example, in your home, fraternity, or business organization). List the activities and events that comprise the project, and draw the precedence network. What problems did you encounter in doing this?

PROBLEMS AND ACTIVITIES

1. The Mohawk Discount Store chain is designing a management-training program for individuals at its corporate headquarters. The company would like to design the program so that the trainees can complete it as quickly as possible. There are important precedence relationships that must be maintained

between assignments or activities in the program. For example, a trainee cannot serve as an assistant store manager until after she or he has had experience in the credit department and at least one sales department. The following data shows the activity assignments that must be completed by each trainee:

Activity	Immediate Predecessors
A	—
B	—
C	A
D	A, B
E	A, B
F	C
G	D, F
H	E, G

Construct an activity-on-node project network for this problem. Do not attempt to perform any further analysis.

2. Construct a project network for the following activities. Do not attempt to perform any further analysis.

Activity	Immediate Predecessor
A	—
B	—
C	A
D	A, B
E	C, D

(continued at the top of the next column)

Activity	Immediate Predecessor
F	C, D
G	E
H	F

3. H. C. Morris, owner of Environment Recycling, Inc., must clean up a large trash dump under a state environmental cleanup contract. The job includes separating steel and copper from the other debris. Consider the tasks, durations, and predecessor relationships in the table below.

   a. Draw the project network and fill out the table.
   b. Identify the critical path(s) and the project-completion time.
   c. What other insights, if any, are evident from your project analysis?

4. Rozales Manufacturing Co. is planning to install a new, flexible manufacturing system. The activities that must be performed, their immediate predecessors, and estimated activity times are shown in the table below. Draw the project network and find the critical path, computing early and late start days, early and late finish days, and activity slack.

Table for Problem 3.

Activity	Immediate Predecessor	Time (days)	Earliest Start	Earliest Finish	Latest Start	Latest Finish	Slack
A	—	7					
B	A	8					
C	A	12					
D	B	2					
E	C, D	8					
F	C	3					
G	F	2					
H	F	8					
I	E, G, H	8					
J	I	2					
K	G	9					

Table for Problem 4.

Activity	Description	Estimated Immediate Predecessors	Activity Time (days)
A	Analyze current performance	—	3
B	Identify goals	A	1
C	Conduct study of existing operation	A	6
D	Define new system capabilities	B	7
E	Study existing technologies	—	2
F	Determine specifications	D	9
G	Conduct equipment analyses	C, F	10
H	Identify implementation activities	C	3
I	Determine organizational impacts	H	4
J	Prepare report	E, G, I	2
K	Establish audit procedure	H	1

5. A computer-system installation project consists of eight activities. The immediate predecessors and activity times in weeks are as follows:

Activity	Immediate Predecessor	Activity Time
A	—	3
B	—	6
C	A	2
D	B, C	5
E	D	4
F	E	3
G	B, C	9
H	F, G	3

a. Draw the network for this project.
b. What are the critical-path activities?
c. What is the project-completion time?
d. Construct an early-start-date Gantt chart.
e. As a project manager, where would you focus your attention given your analysis?

6. Colonial State College is considering building a new athletic complex on campus. The complex would provide a new gymnasium for intercollegiate basketball games, expanded office space, classrooms, and intramural facilities. The activities that would have to be completed before beginning construction are listed next.

Activity	Description	Immediate Predecessors	Time (weeks)
A	Survey building site	—	6
B	Develop initial design	—	8
C	Obtain board approval	A, B	12
D	Select architect	C	4
E	Establish budget	C	6
F	Finalize design	D, E	15
G	Obtain financing	E	12
H	Hire contractor	F, G	8

a. Develop a network for this project.
b. Identify the critical path.
c. Construct an early-start-date Gantt chart.

d. Does it appear reasonable that construction could begin 1 year after the decision to begin the project? What is the project-completion time?

7. Environment Recycling, Inc. must clean up a large automobile tire dump under a state environmental cleanup contract. The tasks, durations (weeks), costs, and predecessor relationships are shown in the table below.

a. Draw the project network.
b. Identify the critical path(s).
c. What is the total project-completion time and total cost?
d. What is the total project-completion time and lowest-cost solution if the state wants to complete the project 3 weeks early?

8. Office Automation, Inc. has developed a proposal for introducing a new, computerized office system that will improve word processing and interoffice communications for a particular company. Contained in the proposal is a list of activities that must be accomplished to complete the new office-system project. Information about the activities is shown in the table on page 803.

Times are in weeks and costs are in thousands of dollars.

a. Draw the network for this project.
b. Develop a schedule for the project using normal times.
c. What is the critical path and the expected project-completion time?
d. Assume the company wants to complete the project in 26 weeks. What crashing decisions would you recommend for meeting the completion date at the least possible cost?
e. Develop an activity schedule for the crashed project using early and late start times, early and late finish times, and slack.
f. What is the added project cost to meet the 26-week completion time?

Table for Problem 7.

Activity	Predecessor(s)	Normal Time	Crash Time	Normal Cost	Crash Cost
A	—	5	4	$ 400	$ 750
B	A	12	9	1,000	2,200
C	A	7	6	800	1,100
D	C	6	5	600	1,000
E	B, D	8	6	1,200	2,200
F	D	3	2	800	1,000
G	D	3	2	500	650
H	E	4	3	400	600
I	F, G, H	6	5	900	1,300

Table for Problem 8.

Activity	Description	Immediate Predecessors	Normal Time	Crash Time	Normal Cost	Crash Cost
A	Plan needs	—	10	8	$ 30	$ 70
B	Order equipment	A	8	6	120	150
C	Install equipment	B	10	7	100	160
D	Set up training lab	A	7	6	40	50
E	Training course	D	10	8	50	75
F	Test system	C, E	3	3	60	—

9. Two international banks are integrating two financial processing software systems as a result of their merger. Preliminary analysis and interviews with all parties involved resulted in the following project information. The "systems integration team" for this project plans to define and manage this project on two levels. The following activities represent an aggregate view, and within each activity is a more detailed view with subtasks and project networks defined. All times are in weeks.

Activity	Predecessor	Normal Time	Crash Time	Normal Cost	Crash Cost
A	—	3	1	$1,000	$ 8,000
B	A	1	1	4,000	4,000
C	A	2	2	2,000	2,000
D	B,C	7	5	3,000	6,000
E	C	5	4	2,500	3,800
F	C	3	2	1,500	3,000
G	E	7	4	4,500	8,100
H	E, F	5	4	3,000	3,600
I	D, G, H	8	5	8,000	18,000

a. Draw the project network.
b. Identify the critical path.
c. What is the total project-completion time and total cost?
d. What is the total project-completion time and lowest-cost solution if the bank wants to complete the project 2 weeks early?
e. (Optional) What is the minimum-cost crash schedule? (*Hint:* Use a linear programming model to find this. See Supplementary Chapter C.)

10. A competitor of Kozar International, Inc. has begun marketing a new instant-developing film project. Kozar has had a similar product under study in its R&D department but has not yet been able to begin production. Because of the competitor's action, top managers have asked for a speedup of R&D activities so that Kozar can produce and market instant film at the earliest possible date. The predecessor information and activity time estimates in months are shown here.

Activity	Immediate Predecessors	Optimistic Time	Most Probable Time	Pessimistic Time
A	—	1	1.5	5
B	A	3	4	5
C	A	1	2	3
D	B, C	3.5	5	6.5
E	B	4	5	12
F	C, D, E	6.5	7.5	11.5
G	F	5	9	13

a. Draw the project network.
b. Develop an activity schedule for this project using early and late start and finish times, compute activity slack time, and define the critical activities.
c. What is the probability the project will be completed in time for Kozar to begin marketing the new product within 24 months?

11. Suppose the estimates of activity times (weeks) for Kozar's project are as follows:

Activity	Optimistic Time	Probable Time	Most Pessimistic Time
A	4	5	6
B	2.5	3	3.5
C	6	7	8
D	5	5.5	9
E	5	7	9
F	2	3	4
G	8	10	12
H	6	7	14

Suppose that the critical path is A-D-F-H. What is the probability that the project will be completed within

a. 20 weeks?
b. 22 weeks?
c. 24 weeks?

CASES

ST. MARY'S MEDICAL CENTER

St. Mary's Medical Center (SMMC) needs to move from its existing facility to a new and larger facility 5 miles away from its current location. Due to construction delays, however, much of the new equipment ordered for installation in the new hospital was delivered to the old hospital and put into use. As the new facility is being completed, all this equipment has to be moved from the old facility to the new one. This requires a large number of planning considerations. National Guard vehicles and private ambulances are to be contracted to move patients; local merchants would be affected by the move; police assistance would be required; and so on. The following table shows the activities and their predecessors that have been identified.

Activity		Immediate Predecessors
A	Meet with department heads	None
B	Appoint move advisory committee	None
C	Plan public relations activities	None
D	Meet with police department	None
E	Meet with city traffic engineers	A
F	Develop preliminary move plan	A
G	Develop final move plan	E, F, N
H	Establish move admissions policies	B
I	Plan dedication	C
J	Develop police assistance plan	D
K	Consult with contractor	G
L	Decide move day	K
M	Prepare final move tags	G
N	Develop patient forms	H

(continued at the top of the next column)

Activity		Immediate Predecessors
O	Publish plans	L
P	Modify plans	O
Q	Tag equipment	M
R	Implement premove admission policies	N
S	Dedication	I
T	Prepare for patient move	P, Q
U	Patient move	R, S, T
V	Secure old facility	U, J

Questions for Analysis

a. Develop a network for this project.

b. It is important to realize that the activities shown need to be broken down into more detail for actual implementation. For example, for the activity "patient move," managers have to determine which patients to move first (for example, intensive care), the equipment that would have to be in place to support each class of patient, and so on. Discuss what types of subactivities might have to be accomplished in an expanded network. You need not draw this expanded network, however.

c. Using your judgment or by discussing the nature of the activities with someone that you might consider knowledgeable in such a project, propose logical pessimistic, optimistic, and most likely times for each activity. Use this information to find the critical path and conduct a PERT analysis of the project completion time. Summarize your findings in a report to the hospital administrator.

R. A. HAMILTON COMPANY

The R. A. Hamilton Company has manufactured home workshop tools for a number of years. Recently, a member of the company's new-product research team submitted a report suggesting the company consider manufacturing a heavy-duty cordless electric drill that could be powered by a special rechargeable battery. Because no other manufacturer currently has such a product, management hopes that the product can be manufactured at a reasonable cost and that its portability will make it extremely attractive.

Hamilton's top managers have initiated a project to study the feasibility of this idea. The end result of the feasibility project will be a report recommending the action to be taken for this new product. The project manager has identified a list of activities and a range of times

necessary to complete each activity. This information is given in Exhibit 18.24.

a. Develop a complete PERT/CPM analysis for this project. Include the project network, a calculation of expected times and variances, the critical activities, and the earliest possible project-completion date. In addition, construct an early-start Gantt chart, and compute probabilities for completing the project by weeks 18, 20, 22, and 24. Discuss how this information can be used by the R. A. Hamilton project manager.

b. The costs for each activity are given in Exhibit 18.25. Develop a total-cost budget based on both an earliest-start and a latest-start schedule. Also, pre-

Exhibit 18.24
Data for R. A. Hamilton
Company Project

Activity	Description	Immediate Predecessors	Times (weeks)		
			a	*m*	*b*
A	R&D product design	—	3	7	11
B	Plan market research	—	2	2.5	6
C	Manufacturing process study	A	2	3	4
D	Build prototype model	A	6	7	14
E	Prepare market questionnaire	A	2	3	4
F	Develop cost estimates	C	2.5	3	3.5
G	Preliminary product testing	D	2.5	4	5.5
H	Market survey	B, E	4.5	5.5	9.5
I	Pricing and forecast report	H	1	2	3
J	Final report	F, G, I	1	2	3

pare an analysis for each of the three points in time shown in Exhibit 18.26. For each case, show the percentage overrun or underrun for the project to date, and indicate any corrective action that should be undertaken. Why is this information important to the project manager? (*Note:* If an activity is not listed, assume that it has not been started.)

Exhibit 18.25 Cost Data

Activity	Expected Cost (Thousands of $)
A	90
B	16
C	3
D	100
E	6
F	2
G	60
H	20
I	4
J	2

Exhibit 18.26 Project Completion Scenarios

Activity	Actual Cost (Thousands of $)	% Completion
At the end of fifth week		
A	62	80
B	6	50
At end of tenth week		
A	85	100
B	16	100
C	1	33
D	100	80
E	4	100
H	10	25
At end of fifteenth week		
A	85	
B	16	
C	3	
D	105	
E	4	100
F	3	
G	55	
H	25	
I	4	

ENDNOTES

[1] http://sportsillustrated.cnn.com/2004/olympics/2004/06/28/bc.oly.athensnotebook.ap/index.html.

[2] See Schloh, Michael, "Analysis of the Denver International Airport Baggage System," Senior Project California Polytechnic State University, 1996, http://www.csc.calpoly.edu/~dstearns/SchlohProject/csc463.html for an interesting analysis and history of the baggage-handling design and project failures.

[3] Walloch, R., Kerr, A., and Bacharach, A., "Beach Town Cleanup," *Civil Engineering*, December 2000, pp. 62–65.

[4] Randolph, W. Alan, and Posner, Barry Z., "What Every Manager Needs to Know about Project Management," *Sloan Management Review*, Summer 1988, pp. 65–73.

[5] Scholtes, Peter R., et al., *The Team Handbook: How to Use Teams to Improve Quality*, Madison, WI: Joiner Associates, Inc., 1988, pp. 6-10–6-22.

[6] Nobeoka, Kentaro, "Reorganizing for Multi-Project Management: Toyota's New Structure of Product Development Centers," Undated report, Research Institute for Economics and Business Administration, Kobe University.

[7] Stedman, Craig, "Failed ERP Gamble Haunts Hershey," *Computerworld*, November 1, 1999, http://www.computerworld.com/news/1999.

[8] Source: http://www.lovett-silverman.com/projects_a_1php, June 13, 2004.

[9] Hollenbach, F. A., "Project Control in Bechtel Power Corporation," in David I. Cleland and William R. King, eds., *Project Management Handbook*, New York: Van Nostrand Reinhold, 1983.

[10] This discussion is adapted from Appendix A in Jack Gido and James P. Clements, *Successful Project Management*, 2nd ed., Cincinnati: Thomson/South-Western, 2003.

[11] http://www.microsoft.com/resources/casestudies/CaseStudy.asp?casestudyid=15035&PF=yes, July 27, 2004.

[12] http://www.microsoft.com/Business_Solutions/document.aspx?content=/businesssolutions, July 27, 2004.

APPENDICES

Areas for the Standard Normal Distribution

Entries in the table give the area under the curve between the mean and z standard deviations above the mean. For example, for z = 1.25 the area under the curve between the mean and z is 0.3944.

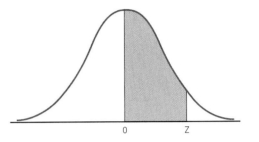

z	0.00	0.01	0.02	0.03	0.04	0.05	0.06	0.07	0.08	0.09
0.0	0.0000	0.0040	0.0080	0.0120	0.0160	0.0199	0.0239	0.0279	0.0319	0.0359
0.1	0.0398	0.0438	0.0478	0.0517	0.0557	0.0596	0.0636	0.0675	0.0714	0.0753
0.2	0.0793	0.0832	0.0871	0.0910	0.0948	0.0987	0.1026	0.1064	0.1103	0.1141
0.3	0.1179	0.1217	0.1255	0.1293	0.1331	0.1368	0.1406	0.1443	0.1480	0.1517
0.4	0.1554	0.1591	0.1628	0.1664	0.1700	0.1736	0.1772	0.1808	0.1844	0.1879
0.5	0.1915	0.1950	0.1985	0.2019	0.2054	0.2088	0.2123	0.2157	0.2190	0.2224
0.6	0.2257	0.2291	0.2324	0.2357	0.2389	0.2422	0.2454	0.2486	0.2518	0.2549
0.7	0.2580	0.2612	0.2642	0.2673	0.2704	0.2734	0.2764	0.2794	0.2823	0.2852
0.8	0.2881	0.2910	0.2939	0.2967	0.2995	0.3023	0.3051	0.3078	0.3106	0.3133
0.9	0.3159	0.3186	0.3212	0.3238	0.3264	0.3289	0.3315	0.3340	0.3365	0.3389
1.0	0.3413	0.3438	0.3461	0.3485	0.3508	0.3531	0.3554	0.3577	0.3599	0.3621
1.1	0.3643	0.3665	0.3686	0.3708	0.3729	0.3749	0.3770	0.3790	0.3810	0.3830
1.2	0.3849	0.3869	0.3888	0.3907	0.3925	0.3944	0.3962	0.3980	0.3997	0.4015
1.3	0.4032	0.4049	0.4066	0.4082	0.4099	0.4115	0.4131	0.4147	0.4162	0.4177
1.4	0.4192	0.4207	0.4222	0.4236	0.4251	0.4265	0.4279	0.4292	0.4306	0.4319
1.5	0.4332	0.4345	0.4357	0.4370	0.4382	0.4394	0.4406	0.4418	0.4429	0.4441
1.6	0.4452	0.4463	0.4474	0.4484	0.4495	0.4505	0.4515	0.4525	0.4535	0.4545
1.7	0.4554	0.4564	0.4573	0.4582	0.4591	0.4599	0.4608	0.4616	0.4625	0.4633
1.8	0.4641	0.4649	0.4656	0.4664	0.4671	0.4678	0.4686	0.4693	0.4699	0.4706
1.9	0.4713	0.4719	0.4726	0.4732	0.4738	0.4744	0.4750	0.4756	0.4761	0.4767
2.0	0.4772	0.4778	0.4783	0.4788	0.4793	0.4798	0.4803	0.4808	0.4812	0.4817
2.1	0.4821	0.4826	0.4830	0.4834	0.4838	0.4842	0.4846	0.4850	0.4854	0.4857
2.2	0.4861	0.4864	0.4868	0.4871	0.4875	0.4878	0.4881	0.4884	0.4887	0.4890
2.3	0.4893	0.4896	0.4898	0.4901	0.4904	0.4906	0.4909	0.4911	0.4913	0.4916
2.4	0.4918	0.4920	0.4922	0.4925	0.4927	0.4929	0.4931	0.4932	0.4934	0.4936
2.5	0.4938	0.4940	0.4941	0.4943	0.4945	0.4946	0.4948	0.4949	0.4951	0.4952
2.6	0.4953	0.4955	0.4956	0.4957	0.4959	0.4960	0.4961	0.4962	0.4963	0.4964
2.7	0.4965	0.4966	0.4967	0.4968	0.4969	0.4970	0.4971	0.4972	0.4973	0.4974
2.8	0.4974	0.4975	0.4976	0.4977	0.4977	0.4978	0.4979	0.4979	0.4980	0.4981
2.9	0.4981	0.4982	0.4982	0.4983	0.4984	0.4984	0.4985	0.4985	0.4986	0.4986
3.0	0.4986	0.4987	0.4987	0.4988	0.4988	0.4989	0.4989	0.4989	0.4990	0.4990

Factors for Control Charts

	x-charts				s-charts				R-charts					
n	A	A_2	A_3	c_4	B_3	B_4	B_5	B_6	d_2	d_3	D_1	D_2	D_3	D_4
2	2.121	1.880	2.659	0.7979	0	3.267	0	2.606	1.128	0.853	0	3.686	0	3.267
3	1.732	1.023	1.954	0.8862	0	2.568	0	2.276	1.693	0.888	0	4.358	0	2.574
4	1.500	0.729	1.628	0.9213	0	2.266	0	2.088	2.059	0.880	0	4.698	0	2.282
5	1.342	0.577	1.427	0.9400	0	2.089	0	1.964	2.326	0.864	0	4.918	0	2.114
6	1.225	0.483	1.287	0.9515	0.030	1.970	0.029	1.874	2.534	0.848	0	5.078	0	2.004
7	1.134	0.419	1.182	0.9594	0.118	1.882	0.113	1.806	2.704	0.833	0.204	5.204	0.076	1.924
8	1.061	0.373	1.099	0.9650	0.185	1.815	0.179	1.751	2.847	0.820	0.388	5.306	0.136	1.864
9	1.000	0.337	1.032	0.9690	0.239	1.761	0.232	1.707	2.970	0.808	0.547	5.393	0.184	1.816
10	0.949	0.308	0.975	0.9727	0.284	1.716	0.276	1.669	3.078	0.797	0.687	5.469	0.223	1.777
11	0.905	0.285	0.927	0.9754	0.321	1.679	0.313	1.637	3.173	0.787	0.811	5.535	0.256	1.744
12	0.866	0.266	0.886	0.9776	0.354	1.646	0.346	1.610	3.258	0.778	0.922	5.594	0.283	1.717
13	0.832	0.249	0.850	0.9794	0.382	1.618	0.374	1.585	3.336	0.770	1.025	5.647	0.307	1.693
14	0.802	0.235	0.817	0.9810	0.406	1.594	0.399	1.563	3.407	0.763	1.118	5.696	0.328	1.672
15	0.775	0.223	0.789	0.9823	0.428	1.572	0.421	1.544	3.472	0.756	1.203	5.741	0.347	1.653
16	0.750	0.212	0.763	0.9835	0.448	1.552	0.440	1.526	3.532	0.750	1.282	5.782	0.363	1.637
17	0.728	0.203	0.739	0.9845	0.466	1.534	0.458	1.511	3.588	0.744	1.356	5.820	0.378	1.622
18	0.707	0.194	0.718	0.9854	0.482	1.518	0.475	1.496	3.640	0.739	1.424	5.856	0.391	1.608
19	0.688	0.187	0.698	0.9862	0.497	1.503	0.490	1.483	3.689	0.734	1.487	5.891	0.403	1.597
20	0.671	0.180	0.680	0.9869	0.510	1.490	0.504	1.470	3.735	0.729	1.549	5.921	0.415	1.585
21	0.655	0.173	0.663	0.9876	0.523	1.477	0.516	1.459	3.778	0.724	1.605	5.951	0.425	1.575
22	0.640	0.167	0.647	0.9882	0.534	1.466	0.528	1.448	3.819	0.720	1.659	5.979	0.434	1.566
23	0.626	0.162	0.633	0.9887	0.545	1.455	0.539	1.438	3.858	0.716	1.710	6.006	0.443	1.557
24	0.612	0.157	0.619	0.9892	0.555	1.445	0.549	1.429	3.895	0.712	1.759	6.031	0.451	1.548
25	0.600	0.153	0.606	0.9896	0.565	1.435	0.559	1.420	3.931	0.708	1.806	6.056	0.459	1.541

Source: Adapted from Table 27 of ASTM STP 15D ASTM Manual on Presentation of Data and Control Chart Analysis. © 1976 American Society for Testing and Materials, Philadelphia, PA.

APPENDIX C

Random Digits

63271	59986	71744	51102	15141	80714	58683	93108	13554	79945
88547	09896	95436	79115	08303	01041	20030	63754	08459	28364
55957	57243	83865	09911	19761	66535	40102	26646	60147	15702
46276	87453	44790	67122	45573	84358	21625	16999	13385	22782
55363	07449	34835	15290	76616	67191	12777	21861	68689	03263
69393	92785	49902	58447	42048	30378	87618	26933	40640	16281
13186	29431	88190	04588	38733	81290	89541	70290	40113	08243
17726	28652	56836	78351	47327	18518	92222	55201	27340	10493
36520	64465	05550	30157	82242	29520	69753	72602	23756	54935
81628	36100	39254	56835	37636	02421	98063	89641	64953	99337
84649	48968	75215	75498	49539	74240	03466	49292	36401	45525
63291	11618	12613	75055	43915	26488	41116	64531	56827	30825
70502	53225	03655	05915	37140	57051	48393	91322	25653	06543
06426	24771	59935	49801	11082	66762	94477	02494	88215	27191
20711	55609	29430	70165	45406	78484	31639	52009	18873	96927
41990	70538	77191	25860	55204	73417	83920	69468	74972	38712
72452	36618	76298	26678	89334	33938	95567	29380	75906	91807
37042	40318	57099	10528	09925	89773	41335	96244	29002	46453
53766	52875	15987	46962	67342	77592	57651	95508	80033	69828
90585	58955	53122	16025	84299	53310	67380	84249	25348	04332
32001	96293	37203	64516	51530	37069	40261	61374	05815	06714
62606	64324	46354	72157	67248	20135	49804	09226	64419	29457
10078	28073	85389	50324	14500	15562	64165	06125	71353	77669
91561	46145	24177	15294	10061	98124	75732	00815	83452	97355
13091	98112	53959	79607	52244	63303	10413	63839	74762	50289
73864	83014	72457	22682	03033	61714	88173	90835	00634	85169
66668	25467	48894	51043	02365	91726	09365	63167	95264	45643
84745	41042	29493	01836	09044	51926	43630	63470	76508	14194
48068	26805	94595	47907	13357	38412	33318	26098	82782	42851
54310	96175	97594	88616	42035	38093	36745	56702	40644	83514
14877	33095	10924	58013	61439	21882	42059	24177	58739	60170
78295	23179	02771	43464	59061	71411	05697	67194	30495	21157
67524	02865	39593	54278	04237	92441	26602	63835	38032	94770
58268	57219	68124	73455	83236	08710	04284	55005	84171	42596
97158	28672	50685	01181	24262	19427	52106	34308	73685	74246
04230	16831	69085	30802	65559	09205	71829	06489	85650	38707
94879	56606	30401	02602	57658	70091	54986	41394	60437	03195
71446	15232	66715	26385	91518	70566	02888	79941	39684	54315
32886	05644	79316	09819	00813	88407	17461	73925	53037	91904
62048	33711	25290	21526	02223	75947	66466	06232	10913	75336

Source: Reprinted from page 44 of *A Million Digits With 100,000 Normal Deviates,* by the Rand Corporation. New York: The Free Press, 1955. © 1955 by The Rand Corporation. Used by permission.

INDEX

INDEX